HALSBURY'S
Laws of England

FIFTH EDITION
2016

Volume 77

This is volume 77 of the Fifth Edition of Halsbury's Laws of England, containing the titles MISTAKE, MORTGAGE, and NATIONAL CULTURAL HERITAGE.

The titles MISTAKE, MORTGAGE, and NATIONAL CULTURAL HERITAGE replace the titles MISTAKE, MORTGAGE, and NATIONAL CULTURAL HERITAGE contained in volume 77 (2010). Upon receipt of volume 77 (2016), volume 77 (2010) may be archived.

For a full list of volumes comprised in a current set of Halsbury's Laws of England please see overleaf.

Fifth Edition volumes:

1 (2008), 2 (2008), 3 (2011), 4 (2011), 5 (2013), 6 (2011), 7 (2015), 8 (2015), 9 (2012), 10 (2012), 11 (2015), 12 (2015), 12A (2015), 13 (2009), 14 (2009), 15 (2009), 16 (2011), 17 (2011), 18 (2009), 19 (2011), 20 (2014), 21 (2011), 22 (2012), 23 (2013), 24 (2010), 25 (2010), 26 (2010), 27 (2015), 28 (2015), 29 (2014), 30 (2012), 31 (2012), 32 (2012), 33 (2013), 34 (2011), 35 (2015), 36 (2015), 37 (2013), 38 (2013), 38A (2013), 39 (2014), 40 (2014), 41 (2014), 41A (2014), 42 (2011), 43 (2011), 44 (2011), 45 (2010), 46 (2010), 47 (2014), 47A (2014), 48 (2008), 48 (2015), 49 (2008), 49 (2015), 51 (2013), 52 (2014), 53 (2014), 54 (2008), 55 (2012), 56 (2011), 57 (2012), 58 (2014), 58A (2014), 59 (2014), 59A (2014), 60 (2011), 61 (2010), 62 (2012), 63 (2012), 64 (2012), 65 (2015), 66 (2015), 67 (2008), 68 (2008), 69 (2009), 70 (2012), 71 (2013), 72 (2015), 73 (2015), 74 (2011), 75 (2013), 76 (2013), 77 (2016), 78 (2010), 79 (2014), 80 (2013), 81 (2010), 82 (2010), 83 (2010), 84 (2013), 84A (2013), 85 (2012), 86 (2013), 87 (2012), 88 (2012), 88A (2013), 89 (2011), 90 (2011), 91 (2012), 92 (2015), 93 (2008), 94 (2008), 95 (2013), 96 (2012), 97 (2015), 97A (2014), 98 (2013), 99 (2012), 100 (2009), 101 (2009), 102 (2010), 103 (2010), 104 (2014)

Consolidated Index and Tables:

2015 Consolidated Index (A–E), 2015 Consolidated Index (F–O), 2015 Consolidated Index (P–Z), 2016 Consolidated Table of Statutes, 2016 Consolidated Table of Statutory Instruments, etc, 2016 Consolidated Table of Cases (A–G), 2016 Consolidated Table of Cases (H–Q), 2016 Consolidated Table of Cases (R–Z, ECJ Cases)

Updating and ancillary materials:

2015 Annual Cumulative Supplement; Monthly Current Service; Annual Abridgments 1974–2014

January 2016

HALSBURY'S
Laws of England

Volume 77

2016

Members of the LexisNexis Group worldwide

United Kingdom	RELX (UK) Ltd, trading as LexisNexis, 1–3 Strand, London WC2N 5JR and 9–10 St Andrew Square, Edinburgh EH2 2AF
Australia	Reed International Books Australia Pty Ltd trading as LexisNexis, Chatswood, New South Wales
Austria	LexisNexis Verlag ARD Orac GmbH & Co KG, Vienna
Benelux	LexisNexis Benelux, Amsterdam
Canada	LexisNexis Canada, Markham, Ontario
China	LexisNexis China, Beijing and Shanghai
France	LexisNexis SA, Paris
Germany	LexisNexis GmbH, Dusseldorf
Hong Kong	LexisNexis Hong Kong, Hong Kong
India	LexisNexis India, New Delhi
Italy	Giuffrè Editore, Milan
Japan	LexisNexis Japan, Tokyo
Malaysia	Malayan Law Journal Sdn Bhd, Kuala Lumpur
New Zealand	LexisNexis New Zealand Ltd, Wellington
Singapore	LexisNexis Singapore, Singapore
South Africa	LexisNexis, Durban
USA	LexisNexis, Dayton, Ohio

FIRST EDITION	*Published in 31 volumes between 1907 and 1917*
SECOND EDITION	*Published in 37 volumes between 1931 and 1942*
THIRD EDITION	*Published in 43 volumes between 1952 and 1964*
FOURTH EDITION	*Published in 56 volumes between 1973 and 1987, with reissues between 1988 and 2008*
FIFTH EDITION	*Published between 2008 and 2014, with reissues from 2014*

ISBN 978-1-4057-6684-5

9 781405 766845

ISBN for the set: 9781405734394
ISBN for this volume: 9781405766845
Typeset by LexisNexis
Printed and bound by CPI Group (UK) Ltd, Croydon, CR0 4YY

Visit LexisNexis at www.lexisnexis.co.uk

MISTAKE

Consultant Editor

ANDREW TETTENBORN, LLB (Cantab),
Professor of Commercial Law,
Institute of International Shipping and Trade Law,
Swansea University;
Barrister (non-practising)

MORTGAGE

Consultant Editor

THOMAS JEFFERIES, BA,
of the Middle Temple, Barrister

NATIONAL CULTURAL HERITAGE

Consultant Editor

TATIANA FLESSAS, BA (cum laude), JD, LLM (Merit), PhD,
Associate Professor, London School of Economics

The law stated in this volume is in general that in force on 1 December 2015, although subsequent changes have been included wherever possible.

Any future updating material will be found in the Current Service and annual Cumulative Supplement to Halsbury's Laws of England.

TABLE OF CONTENTS

HOW TO USE HALSBURY'S LAWS OF ENGLAND

Volumes

Each text volume of Halsbury's Laws of England contains the law on the titles contained in it as at a date stated at the front of the volume (the operative date).

Information contained in Halsbury's Laws of England may be accessed in several ways.

First, by using the tables of contents.

Each volume contains both a general Table of Contents, and a specific Table of Contents for each title contained in it. From these tables you will be directed to the relevant part of the work.

Readers should note that the current arrangement of titles can be found in the Current Service.

Secondly, by using tables of statutes, statutory instruments, cases or other materials.

If you know the name of the Act, statutory instrument or case with which your research is concerned, you should consult the Consolidated Tables of statutes, cases and so on (published as separate volumes) which will direct you to the relevant volume and paragraph.

(Each individual text volume also includes tables of those materials used as authority in that volume.)

Thirdly, by using the indexes.

If you are uncertain of the general subject area of your research, you should go to the Consolidated Index (published as separate volumes) for reference to the relevant volume(s) and paragraph(s).

(Each individual text volume also includes an index to the material contained therein.)

Updating publications

The text volumes of Halsbury's Laws should be used in conjunction with the annual Cumulative Supplement and the monthly Noter-Up.

The annual Cumulative Supplement

The Supplement gives details of all changes between the operative date of the text volume and the operative date of the Supplement. It is arranged in the same volume, title and paragraph order as the text volumes. Developments affecting particular points of law are noted to the relevant paragraph(s) of the text volumes.

For narrative treatment of material noted in the Cumulative Supplement, go to the Annual Abridgment volume for the relevant year.

Destination Tables

In certain titles in the annual *Cumulative Supplement*, reference is made to Destination Tables showing the destination of consolidated legislation. Those Destination Tables are to be found either at the end of the titles within the annual *Cumulative Supplement*, or in a separate *Destination Tables* booklet provided from time to time with the *Cumulative Supplement*.

The Noter-Up

The Noter-Up is contained in the Current Service Noter-Up booklet, issued monthly and noting changes since the publication of the annual Cumulative Supplement. Also arranged in the same volume, title and paragraph order as the text volumes, the Noter-Up follows the style of the Cumulative Supplement.

For narrative treatment of material noted in the Noter-Up, go to the relevant Monthly Review.

REFERENCES AND ABBREVIATIONS

ACT	Australian Capital Territory
A-G	Attorney General
Admin	Administrative Court
Admlty	Admiralty Court
Adv-Gen	Advocate General
affd	affirmed
affg	affirming
Alta	Alberta
App	Appendix
art	article
Aust	Australia
B	Baron
BC	British Columbia
C	Command Paper (of a series published before 1900)
c	chapter number of an Act
CA	Court of Appeal
CAC	Central Arbitration Committee
CA in Ch	Court of Appeal in Chancery
CB	Chief Baron
CCA	Court of Criminal Appeal
CCR	County Court Rules 1981 (as subsequently amended)
CCR	Court for Crown Cases Reserved
CJEU	Court of Justice of the European Union
C-MAC	Courts-Martial Appeal Court
CO	Crown Office
COD	Crown Office Digest
CPR	Civil Procedure Rules
Can	Canada
Cd	Command Paper (of the series published 1900–18)
Cf	compare
Ch	Chancery Division
ch	chapter
cl	clause
Cm	Command Paper (of the series published 1986 to date)
Cmd	Command Paper (of the series published 1919–56)
Cmnd	Command Paper (of the series published 1956–86)
Comm	Commercial Court

Comr .... Commissioner

Court Forms (2nd Edn) .... Atkin's Encyclopaedia of Court Forms in Civil
Proceedings, 2nd Edn. See note 2 post.

CrimPR .... Criminal Procedure Rules

DC............................. Divisional Court

DPP............................ Director of Public Prosecutions

EAT............................ Employment Appeal Tribunal

EC .... European Community

ECJ .... Court of Justice of the European Community
(before the Treaty of Lisbon (OJ C306,
17.12.2007, p 1) came into force on 1 December
2009); European Court of Justice (after the Treaty
of Lisbon (OJ C306, 17.12.2007, p 1) came into
force on 1 December 2009)

EComHR .... European Commission of Human Rights

ECSC.......................... European Coal and Steel Community

ECtHR Rules of Court ..... Rules of Court of the European Court of Human
Rights

EEC............................ European Economic Community

EFTA .... European Free Trade Association

EGC .... European General Court

EWCA Civ .... Official neutral citation for judgments of the Court
of Appeal (Civil Division)

EWCA Crim .... Official neutral citation for judgments of the Court
of Appeal (Criminal Division)

EWHC .... Official neutral citation for judgments of the
High Court

Edn .... Edition

Euratom...................... European Atomic Energy Community

EU .... European Union

Ex Ch .... Court of Exchequer Chamber

ex p........................... ex parte

Fam............................ Family Division

Fed............................ Federal

Forms & Precedents (5th
Edn) .... Encyclopaedia of Forms and Precedents other
than Court Forms, 5th Edn. See note 2 post

GLC .... Greater London Council

HC............................. High Court

HC............................. House of Commons

HK............................. Hong Kong

HL............................. House of Lords

IAT .... Immigration Appeal Tribunal

ILM............................ International Legal Materials

INLR .... Immigration and Nationality Law Reports

IRC	Inland Revenue Commissioners
Ind	India
Int Rels	International Relations
Ir	Ireland
J	Justice
JA	Judge of Appeal
Kan	Kansas
LA	Lord Advocate
LC	Lord Chancellor
LCC	London County Council
LCJ	Lord Chief Justice
LJ	Lord Justice of Appeal
LoN	League of Nations
MR	Master of the Rolls
Man	Manitoba
n.	note
NB	New Brunswick
NI	Northern Ireland
NS	Nova Scotia
NSW	New South Wales
NY	New York
NZ	New Zealand
OHIM	Office for Harmonisation in the Internal Market
OJ	The Official Journal of the European Union published by the Publications Office of the European Union
Ont	Ontario
P.	President
PC	Judicial Committee of the Privy Council
PEI	Prince Edward Island
Pat	Patents Court
q.	question
QB	Queen's Bench Division
QBD	Queen's Bench Division of the High Court
Qld	Queensland
Que	Quebec
r.	rule
RDC	Rural District Council
RPC	Restrictive Practices Court
RSC	Rules of the Supreme Court 1965 (as subsequently amended)
reg	regulation
Res	Resolution
revsd	reversed

Rly	Railway
s	section
SA	South Africa
S Aust	South Australia
SC	Supreme Court
SI	Statutory Instruments published by authority
SR & O	Statutory Rules and Orders published by authority
SR & O Rev 1904	Revised Edition comprising all Public and General Statutory Rules and Orders in force on 31 December 1903
SR & O Rev 1948	Revised Edition comprising all Public and General Statutory Rules and Orders and Statutory Instruments in force on 31 December 1948
SRNI	Statutory Rules of Northern Ireland
STI	Simon's Tax Intelligence (1973–1995); Simon's Weekly Tax Intelligence (1996-current)
Sask	Saskatchewan
Sch	Schedule
Sess	Session
Sing	Singapore
TCC	Technology and Construction Court
TS	Treaty Series
Tanz	Tanzania
Tas	Tasmania
UDC	Urban District Council
UKHL	Official neutral citation for judgments of the House of Lords
UKPC	Official neutral citation for judgments of the Privy Council
UN	United Nations
V-C	Vice-Chancellor
Vict	Victoria
W Aust	Western Australia
Zimb	Zimbabwe

NOTE 1. A general list of the abbreviations of law reports and other sources used in this work can be found at the beginning of the Consolidated Table of Cases.

NOTE 2. Where references are made to other publications, the volume number precedes and the page number follows the name of the publication; eg the reference '12 Forms & Precedents (5th Edn) 44' refers to volume 12 of the Encyclopaedia of Forms and Precedents, page 44.

NOTE 3. An English statute is cited by short title or, where there is no short title, by regnal year and chapter number together with the name by which it is commonly known or a description of its subject matter and date. In the case of a foreign statute, the mode of citation generally follows the style of citation in use in the country concerned with the addition, where necessary, of the name of the country in parentheses.

NOTE 4. A statutory instrument is cited by short title, if any, followed by the year and number, or, if unnumbered, the date.

TABLE OF STATUTES

TABLE
OF STATUTORY INSTRUMENTS

TABLE OF CIVIL PROCEDURE

Civil Procedure Rules 1998, SI 1998/3132 (CPR)

Practice Directions supplementing CPR

Other Practice Directions etc

TABLE OF EUROPEAN
UNION LEGISLATION

TABLE OF CONVENTIONS, ETC

TABLE OF CASES

41

C

D

E

G

H

I

K

M

N

S

Z

MISTAKE

1. INTRODUCTION TO THE LAW OF MISTAKE

1. Overview of mistake. Mistake has long been considered to have an important impact on moral responsibility[1]. It is also important in relation to questions of legal responsibility. This title deals with the consequences of mistake (whether of fact or law) as a ground for relief, or the basis of a defence, between the parties to civil proceedings. The effect of misrepresentation resulting in a mistake of one or more of the parties to civil litigation is principally dealt with elsewhere in this work[2], as are the effect of a mistake on criminal liability[3], and the effect of mistake on marriage or civil partnership[4].

1   See eg Aristotle *Nicomachean Ethics* Bk 5, viii.
2   As to the distinction between misrepresentation and mistake see MISREPRESENTATION vol 76 (2013) PARA 701 et seq.
3   See CRIMINAL LAW vol 25 (2010) PARA 15.
4   See MATRIMONIAL AND CIVIL PARTNERSHIP LAW vol 72 (2015) PARAS 46, 348.

2. Relevance of law and equity. The effect of mistake differed originally as between common law and equity[1]. The difference is still of more than historical importance, despite fusion of the two systems[2]. The legal rules still apply to claims for the recovery of money paid under a mistake[3], or of property purportedly transferred under a mistake[4], and to cases where a party to a claim on a contract or specialty[5] is entitled to the plea non est factum[6], or where the case of one of the parties to a claim founded on contract is that there was no contract between them[7]. On the other hand the rule that, in case of conflict, the rules of equity prevail[8] ensures that, where the remedy sought is equitable in origin, as when a claimant claims rectification[9], the return on equitable grounds of money[10] or property[11], and on occasion where the rights of innocent third persons are involved[12], the wider rules of the old equitable jurisdiction are applicable.

1   See EQUITABLE JURISDICTION vol 47 (2014) PARA 39.
2   See EQUITABLE JURISDICTION vol 47 (2014) PARA 1 et seq; and PARAS 3–4.
3   See PARAS 64, 65.
4   See PARAS 67, 68.
5   Ie a contract made by deed: see CONTRACT vol 22 (2012) PARAS 216–217.
6   See PARA 12.
7   See PARAS 13, 16.
8   See the Senior Courts Act 1981 s 49(1); and EQUITABLE JURISDICTION vol 47 (2014) PARA 99.
9   See PARAS 53–63.
10 See PARA 65.
11 See PARA 68.
12 See PARA 38.

2. LEGAL CONSEQUENCES AND TYPES OF MISTAKE

(1) THE LEGAL CONSEQUENCES OF MISTAKE

(i) Mistake as a Ground for Relief

3.   Mistake as a ground for relief at common law. At common law[1] mistake founds relief in four cases only, namely:

(1)   in claims to recover money paid under a mistake[2];

(2)   in claims to recover property which was prevented from passing by reason of a mistake[3];

(3)   in claims to recover damages in respect of a mistake induced by fraudulent[4] or non-fraudulent misrepresentation[5];

(4)   as a defence in claims in contract where a mistake of fact was of such a nature as to preclude the formation of any contract in law[6].

It must not be assumed that the kind of mistake that would justify one of these claims is the same as would justify the others. So cases where the claimant succeeds in restitution for mistake[7] do not establish that a contract would be avoided for mistake[8], and mistakes grounding restitutionary remedies are much wider than those which vitiate the intention to pass property[9].

1   As to the consequences of mistake at common law see PARA 7. As to mistake in equity see PARAS 4, 8.
2   See PARA 64.
3   See PARA 67.
4   As to fraudulent misrepresentations see MISREPRESENTATION vol 76 (2013) PARAS 754–760. As to the remedies available in respect of fraudulent misrepresentation see MISREPRESENTATION vol 76 (2013) PARA 780.
5   As to non-fraudulent misrepresentations see MISREPRESENTATION vol 76 (2013) PARAS 761–763. As to the remedies available in respect of non-fraudulent misrepresentation, including the statutory right to damages provided by the Misrepresentation Act 1967, see MISREPRESENTATION vol 76 (2013) PARAS 781, 800.
6   See PARAS 13, 16; and CONTRACT vol 22 (2012) PARA 207.
7   See RESTITUTION vol 88 (2012) PARA 433 et seq.
8   *Citibank NA v Brown Shipley & Co Ltd, Midland Bank plc v Brown Shipley & Co Ltd* [1991] 2 All ER 690 at 700–701, [1991] 1 Lloyd's Rep 576 at 584 per Waller J; cf *Norwich Union Fire Insurance Society Ltd v WH Price Ltd* [1934] AC 455, PC; *Shamil Bank of Bahrain EC v Beximco Pharmaceuticals Ltd* [2004] EWCA Civ 19 at [58], [2004] 4 All ER 1072, [2004] 1 WLR 1784 per Potter LJ.
9   *Barclays Bank Ltd v WJ Simms, Son & Cooke (Southern) Ltd* [1980] QB 677 at 689, [1979] 3 All ER 522 at 530 per Robert Goff J. See also RESTITUTION vol 88 (2012) PARA 428 et seq.

4.   Mistake as a ground for relief in equity. In equity mistake is said to relieve in a much wider range of cases than at common law[1]. This includes:

(1)   rectification of documents which do not accurately record the transaction concerned[2];

(2)   a defence to some suits for specific performance of contracts[3];

(3)   proceedings to recover (or regularise) money paid and other assets transferred by mistake[4];

(4)   the so-called doctrine of proprietary estoppel[5].

Formerly, it also included rescission of certain contracts or other transactions entered into where the common law would give no relief[6].

Moreover, equity often imposes a duty on a party in certain cases to speak out, and hence silence may constitute a representation justifying relief for the mistaken party[7].

The distinction between mistake at common law and in equity is also important because of its effect on the rights of third parties. Mistake may mean that at law property may not pass, and hence third parties cannot acquire title to it[8]. However, in equity the transaction may be voidable, so that property may pass, albeit provisionally[9], and third party rights may be protected provided they were acquired in good faith[10].

1   Meagher, Gummow and Lehane *Equity—Doctrines and Remedies* (5th Edn, 2015) Chs 14, 20, 27; and EQUITABLE JURISDICTION vol 47 (2014) PARAS 8, 39 et seq. As to the consequences of mistake in equity see PARA 8. As to mistake at common law see PARAS 3, 7.
2   See PARAS 53–63.
3   See PARA 47.
4   See PARAS 65, 68.
5   See PARA 31.
6   See PARAS 48–52.
7   See PARA 27; and ESTOPPEL vol 47 (2014) PARA 362.
8   See PARAS 24–26.
9   See PARA 26.
10 See PARA 38.

5.   Mistake as a ground for relief in cases other than common law or equity. Mistake may be made a ground for relief by statute, for example, in relation to the assessment of a solicitor's costs[1], or in income tax matters[2]; however, an agreement between the Inland Revenue and a taxpayer is subject to the ordinary law of rectification of contracts[3].

Mistake may also be a ground for relief where it occurs in the legal process itself, as when an appearance is entered in a claim by mistake[4], or money is paid into court by mistake[5], or money so paid is accepted on a mistaken view of the statement of claim[6], or is paid out by mistake[7]: however, whether it is a ground for relief in an agreement to compromise litigation depends on the principles applicable to ordinary contracts, taking into account elements of public policy[8].

By statutory intervention, mistake is now a ground for relief in certain cases concerning wills[9], where rectification for mistake was not previously possible[10].

Special rules relate to mistakes made in entering into contracts uberrimae fidei, that is, of the utmost good faith, such as contracts of insurance[11], contracts of salvage[12], and perhaps family compromises[13].

1   See the Solicitors Act 1974 s 57(5); *Rutter v Sheridan-Young* [1958] 2 All ER 13, [1958] 1 WLR 444, CA; and LEGAL PROFESSIONS vol 66 (2015) PARA 713.
2   See INCOME TAXATION vol 58 (2014) PARA 589; INCOME TAXATION vol 59 (2014) PARAS 2220–2223.
3   See *R v Inspector of Taxes, ex p Bass Holdings Ltd, Richart (Inspector of Taxes) v Bass Holdings Ltd* [1993] STC 122, (1992) 65 TC 495; and INCOME TAXATION vol 59 (2014) PARA 2267.
4   *Firth v John Mowlem & Co Ltd* [1978] 3 All ER 331, [1978] 1 WLR 1184, CA.
5   *Spurr v Hall* (1877) 2 QBD 615 at 623–624 per Field J.
6   *S Kaprow & Co Ltd v Maclelland & Co Ltd* [1948] 1 KB 618, [1948] 1 All ER 264, CA. See also CIVIL PROCEDURE vol 12A (2015) PARA 1604.
7   See *Slater v Slater* [1897] 1 Ch 222n; and LEGAL PROFESSIONS vol 65 (2015) PARA 552. See also *Gainsborough Mixed Concrete Ltd v Duplex Petrol Installations Ltd* [1968] 3 All ER 267 at 268, [1968] 1 WLR 1463 at 1465–1466, CA, per Lord Denning MR.
8   See *OT Africa Line Ltd v Vickers plc* [1996] 1 Lloyd's Rep 700; *Brennan v Bolt Burdon (a firm)* [2004] EWCA Civ 1017, [2005] QB 303, [2004] 3 WLR 1321; and PARA 23.
9   See the Administration of Justice Act 1982 s 20; and PARA 59.
10 Cf *Re Reynette-James, Wightman v Reynette-James* [1975] 3 All ER 1037, [1976] 1 WLR 161.
11 See the Consumer Insurance (Disclosure and Representations) Act 2012; and INSURANCE vol 60 (2011) PARA 34 et seq. Special statutory rules for non-consumer insurance contracts will also have effect from 12 August 2016 (ie the date on which the Insurance Act 2015 Pt 2 (ss 2–8) comes into force: s 23(2)): see Pt 2 (ss 2–8); and INSURANCE.

12 See SHIPPING AND MARITIME LAW vol 94 (2008) PARA 969.
13 See PARA 23; and SETTLEMENTS vol 91 (2012) PARA 903 et seq.

(ii) Classification of Mistakes

6. Sources and types of mistake. Mistakes may arise from ignorance, misconception, or forgetfulness. Generally speaking, in considering the consequences of mistake, no distinction is drawn by the law between these different sources[1].

Mistakes may be divided into:

(1)   those which prevent there being an effective consent to a particular transaction[2]; and

(2)   those which consist in a failure to express correctly in a written document the intention of the parties with regard to a particular transaction[3].

Mistakes within head (1) above may be further subdivided according to whether they are mistakes as to law, or mistakes as to fact[4]. Mistakes as to private rights historically were classed rather among instances of error in fact than among instances of error in law[5], even where there are no circumstances of circumvention or fraud[6]. This distinction is now less important[7].

Mistakes of fact may be divided into:

(a)   mistakes as to the nature of the transaction[8];

(b)   mistakes as to the identity of the other party to the transaction[9]; and

(c)   mistakes as to the subject matter or other terms of the transaction, which may be either as to the identity of, or as to some fact materially connected with, the subject matter of the transaction, or as to the terms of the transaction[10].

1 See PARA 36.
2 See PARAS 12–16.
3 See PARA 33.
4 As to mistakes of law see PARAS 9–11. As to mistakes of fact see PARA 12 et seq.
5 *Denys v Shuckburgh* (1840) 4 Y & C Ex 42; and see PARA 10.
6 *Clifton v Cockburn* (1834) 3 My & K 76 at 99 per Lord Brougham LC.
7 See PARA 9.
8 See PARA 12.
9 See PARAS 13–15.
10 See PARA 16.

(iii) Consequences of Mistake

7. Consequences of mistake at common law. At common law a mistake, if it operates at all, will generally negative consent[1]. However, it will not so operate where the mistake was not material (that is, the mistaken party would still have consented if he had known the true position)[2]. Thus where A intends to sell one thing, and B to buy another, there is no contract, even though A and B mistakenly think (or A alone thinks) that they are referring to the same thing[3]. Similarly if the mistake is over terms rather than subject matter[4]. So too if A intends to contract with B alone, and mistakenly deals with C, there is no contract[5]. The principle is not confined to contract. If A intends to give property in goods to B alone, but mistakenly delivers them to C, normally property does not pass[6]. But all these cases are subject to the doctrine of estoppel, which may operate so as to prevent a mistaken party from denying the existence of that consent which is necessary for the validity of the transaction concerned[7].

Mistakes which do not negative consent are sometimes said to 'nullify' consent in certain circumstances, and hence to render a contract void[8]. The precise meaning of this is unclear. Probably all it means is that such mistakes may be taken into account as part of the construction of the transaction, that is, in the contractual allocation of risk[9]. Thus where A sells to B something which, unknown to either, never existed[10], or has already ceased to exist[11], there is a valid contract, but either or both parties (depending on construction) may be not liable to perform in the circumstances. Only if, on the true construction of the agreement, neither party is bound (so that the contract is deprived of all practical content) does it approach accuracy to describe the contract as 'void'. The question is instead simply who (if anyone) is to take the risk[12]. Another way of putting the same point is to imply a condition precedent to the obligation to perform[13]. The same reasoning can in principle apply to a mistaken sale or letting to a person of his own property[14]. If a party pays (or otherwise performs) when he need not have done so, there will be restitutionary consequences[15]. Whether there is a category of case, going beyond the construction of the contract and the allocation of risk, where common mistake simply avoids the contract without more, is a difficult question: in principle it is doubtful, but there is some support for this view[16], although there are few reported examples[17].

1 *Norwich Union Fire Insurance Society v WH Price Ltd* [1934] AC 455 at 463, PC; *Whittaker v Campbell* [1984] QB 318 at 326–327, [1983] 3 All ER 582 at 585–586 per Robert Goff LJ; cf *Bell v Lever Bros Ltd* [1932] AC 161 at 217, HL, per Lord Atkin. There is thus no room in the common law for the civilian doctrine distinguishing mistakes as to substance and attributes of the subject matter of a contract: *Associated Japanese Bank (International) Ltd v Crédit du Nord SA* [1988] 3 All ER 902 at 912–913, [1989] 1 WLR 255 at 268 per Steyn J.

2 *Mackie v European Assurance Society* (1869) 21 LT 102; *Smith v Wheatcroft* (1878) 9 ChD 223; *Dennant v Skinner* [1948] 2 KB 164, [1948] 2 All ER 29.

3 See PARA 16 et seq.

4 See PARA 16.

5 See PARAS 13–15.

6 See PARA 25.

7 See PARA 27.

8 *Bell v Lever Bros Ltd* [1932] AC 161 at 217, HL, per Lord Atkin; and CONTRACT vol 22 (2012) PARA 467.

9 *Huddersfield Banking Co Ltd v Henry Lister & Son Ltd* [1895] 2 Ch 273, CA; *Couturier v Hastie* (1856) 5 HL Cas 673 at 681 per Lord Cranworth LC; *Clark v Lindsay* (1903) 88 LT 198 at 202 per Channell J; *William Sindall plc v Cambridgeshire County Council* [1994] 3 All ER 932 at 951–952, [1994] 1 WLR 1016 at 1034–1035, CA, per Hoffmann LJ; *Great Peace Shipping Ltd v Tsavliris Salvage (International) Ltd, The Great Peace* [2002] EWCA Civ 1407 at [77]–[82], [2003] QB 679, [2002] 4 All ER 689 per Lord Phillips of Worth Matravers MR; and see PARA 17 et seq.

10 *McRae v Commonwealth Disposals Commission* (1950) 84 CLR 377, Aust HC; cf *Associated Japanese Bank (International) Ltd v Crédit du Nord SA* [1988] 3 All ER 902, [1989] 1 WLR 255 (agreement to guarantee finance lease of non-existent goods).

11 *Couturier v Hastie* (1856) 5 HL Cas 673; *Strickland v Turner* (1852) 7 Exch 208; *Clark v Lindsay* (1903) 88 LT 198; *Solle v Butcher* [1950] 1 KB 671 at 691, [1949] 2 All ER 1107 at 1119, CA, per Denning LJ; *Frederick E Rose (London) Ltd v William H Pim Jnr & Co Ltd* [1953] 2 QB 450 at 460, [1953] 2 All ER 739 at 746–747, CA, per Denning LJ. The Sale of Goods Act 1979 s 6 (see SALE OF GOODS AND SUPPLY OF SERVICES vol 91 (2012) PARA 55) reproduces this rule in the context of sales of specific goods.

12 See PARA 19.

13 *Associated Japanese Bank (International) Ltd v Crédit du Nord SA* [1988] 3 All ER 902, [1989] 1 WLR 255; *Apvodedo Nv v Collins* [2008] EWHC 775 (Ch), [2008] All ER (D) 246 (Apr); *Graves v Graves* [2007] EWCA Civ 660, [2007] 3 FCR 26, [2008] HLR 143; *Butters v BBC Worldwide Ltd* [2009] EWHC 1954 (Ch), [2009] BPIR 1315, [2009] All ER (D) 171 (Aug) (revsd in part sub nom *Perpetual Trustee Co Ltd v BNY Corporate Trustee Services Ltd, Butters v BBC Worldwide Ltd* [2009] EWCA Civ 1160, [2010] Ch 347, [2010] 3 WLR 87).

14 See PARA 21.

15 See PARAS 29–31.
16 *Associated Japanese Bank (International) Ltd v Crédit du Nord SA* [1988] 3 All ER 902, [1989] 1 WLR 255; *Great Peace Shipping Ltd v Tsavliris Salvage (International) Ltd, The Great Peace* [2002] EWCA Civ 1407 at [84]–[94], [2003] QB 679, [2002] 4 All ER 689 per Lord Phillips of Worth Matravers MR.
17 *Scott v Coulson* [1903] 2 Ch 249 may be one such: see PARA 18.

8. Consequences of mistake in equity. If consent is negatived through mistake, and the transaction void at law, equity will not make it valid[1]. Moreover, a transaction which is valid at law will be voidable in equity only where the mistake of one party is accompanied by fraud or taking by surprise by the other[2]. A mutual mistake of both parties will not render a contract voidable in equity if the contract is valid and enforceable on ordinary principles of common law[3].

There are circumstances where the conditions for a transaction to be void are satisfied in equity, but not at law. Suppose A purports to let property to B which (unknown to both) A holds on trust for B. The letting is valid at law. However, if B had been legal (rather than equitable) owner, it would (probably) have been void at law[4]. Equity follows the law and the letting is voidable[5]. A similar result follows where A contracts to buy B's equitable interest in a trust fund on the footing that B's interest is joint with C's, and subject to survivorship. In fact C is dead, and B owns the whole. The contract will not be enforced in equity[6]. Additional consequences in equity relate to the availability of specific performance in a claim on the contract[7], and (more controversially) to the question whether property transferred under a mistake can be said to pass at all[8].

1   See *Solle v Butcher* [1950] 1 KB 671 at 694, [1949] 2 All ER 1107 at 1120, CA, per Denning LJ. This point remains true despite the disapproval of the result in *Solle v Butcher* by the Court of Appeal in *Great Peace Shipping Ltd v Tsavliris Salvage (International) Ltd, The Great Peace* [2002] EWCA Civ 1407, [2003] QB 679, [2002] 4 All ER 689 (see note 3).
2   See *Earl Beauchamp v Winn* (1873) LR 6 HL 223 at 233 per Lord Chelmsford. This appears to be an equitable form of estoppel: see PARA 27.
3   See *Great Peace Shipping Ltd v Tsavliris Salvage (International) Ltd, The Great Peace* [2002] EWCA Civ 1407 at [153]–[160], [2003] QB 679, [2002] 4 All ER 689 per Lord Phillips of Worth Matravers MR (disapproving *Solle v Butcher* [1950] 1 KB 671, [1949] 2 All ER 1107, CA); and see further PARA 49. This case disapproved the previous line of authorities which had held that a transaction that was valid at law was voidable in equity if there was a mutual mistake of both parties that effected the essence of the contract: see eg *Solle v Butcher* [1950] 1 KB 671 at 692–693, [1949] 2 All ER 1107 at 1119–1120, CA, per Denning LJ; *Grist v Bailey* [1967] Ch 532, [1966] 2 All ER 875; *Magee v Pennine Insurance Co Ltd* [1969] 2 QB 507 at 514, [1969] 2 All ER 891 at 893, CA, per Lord Denning MR; *Associated Japanese Bank (International) Ltd v Crédit du Nord SA* [1988] 3 All ER 902 at 912, [1989] 1 WLR 255 at 267–268 per Steyn J; *William Sindall plc v Cambridgeshire County Council* [1994] 3 All ER 932 at 959, [1994] 1 WLR 1016 at 1042, CA, per Evans LJ.
4   See PARA 21.
5   *Cooper v Phibbs* (1867) LR 2 HL 149; Matthews 'A Note on *Cooper v Phibbs*' (1989) 105 LQR 599; and see EQUITABLE JURISDICTION vol 47 (2014) PARA 41.
6   *Colyer v Clay* (1843) 7 Beav 188.
7   See PARA 47.
8   See PARAS 24–26.

(2) MISTAKE OF LAW

9. Relief previously not generally available. Originally, and as a general rule, relief would not be granted at common law on the ground of mistake, if the mistake was one of law as distinguished from one of fact[1]. The distinction between mistakes of law and mistakes of fact was never clearly defined by the courts[2], but the mistake of law had to be one of the general law for relief not to be granted[3], for example, the legal interpretation of a contract[4] or the construction of a statute[5].

Although relief is now available in certain contexts, for example claims to recover mistaken payments[6] and misrepresentations of law[7], the precise scope of the change in law is not entirely settled and some reference to the original position is appropriate.

In equity, the strict common law rule has never applied[8].

1   *Lowry v Bourdieu* (1780) 2 Doug KB 468; *Bilbie v Lumley* (1802) 2 East 469; *Stockley v Stockley* (1812) 1 Ves & B 23 at 30; *Cockerell v Cholmeley* (1830) 1 Russ & M 418 (affd (1832) 8 Bli NS 120); *Marshall v Collett* (1835) 1 Y & C Ex 232; *Directors etc of Midland Great Western Rly of Ireland v Johnson* (1858) 6 HL Cas 798 at 810; *Morley v Clavering* (1860) 29 Beav 84 at 87 per Sir John Romilly MR; *Eaglesfield v Marquis of Londonderry* (1876) 4 ChD 693 at 709, CA, per James LJ; *British Homophone Ltd v Kunz and Crystallate Gramophone Record Manufacturing Co Ltd* (1935) 152 LT 589; *André et Cie v Ets Michel Blanc et Fils* [1979] 2 Lloyd's Rep 427, CA; *Gee v News Group Newspapers Ltd* (1990) Times, 8 June.

2   *Daniell v Sinclair* (1881) 6 App Cas 181 at 190–191, PC; *André et Cie v Ets Michel Blanc et Fils* [1979] 2 Lloyd's Rep 427 at 430, CA, per Lord Denning MR; and see *Clifton v Cockburn* (1834) 3 My & K 76 at 99 per Lord Brougham LC; Winfield 'Mistake of Law' (1943) 59 LQR 327; Wilson 'A Note on Fact and Law' (1963) 26 MLR 609; Mureinik 'The Application of Rules: Law or Fact?' (1982) 98 LQR 587. See also RESTITUTION vol 88 (2012) PARA 432 et seq.

3   *Cooper v Phibbs* (1867) LR 2 HL 149 at 170 per Lord Westbury; *Jackson v Stopford* [1923] 2 IR 1, CA; *Lee-Parker v Izzet* [1971] 3 All ER 1099, [1971] 1 WLR 1688; *Beesly v Hallwood Estates Ltd* [1960] 2 All ER 314 at 323–324, [1960] 1 WLR 549 at 560 per Buckley J (affd [1961] Ch 105, [1961] 1 All ER 90, CA); *ITC Pension Fund Ltd v Pinto* (1975) 237 Estates Gazette 725; *Holder v Holder* [1968] Ch 353, [1968] 1 All ER 665, CA; *Re Freeston's Charity* [1979] 1 All ER 51, [1978] 1 WLR 741, CA.

4   *Directors etc of Midland Great Western Rly of Ireland v Johnson* (1858) 6 HL Cas 798 at 811 per Lord Chelmsford LC; *Powell v Smith* (1872) LR 14 Eq 85; *Hart v Hart* (1881) 18 ChD 670; *Stewart v Kennedy (No 2)* (1890) 15 App Cas 108, HL; *Wilding v Sanderson* [1897] 2 Ch 534, CA; cf *Re Butlin's Settlement Trusts, Butlin v Butlin* [1976] Ch 251, [1976] 2 All ER 483; *Re Slocock's Will Trusts* [1979] 1 All ER 358.

5   *National Pari-Mutuel Association Ltd v R* (1930) 47 TLR 110, CA. See also *Re Hatch, Hatch v Hatch* [1919] 1 Ch 351; *Ord v Ord* [1923] 2 KB 432 at 445–446 per Lush J; *Friends' Provident Life Office v Hiller Parker May & Rowden* [1997] QB 85, [1995] 4 All ER 260, CA.

6   See *Kleinwort Benson Ltd v Lincoln City Council* [1999] 2 AC 349, [1998] 4 All ER 513, HL; *Nurdin & Peacock plc v DB Ramsden & Co Ltd* [1999] 1 All ER 941, [1999] 1 WLR 1249; PARAS 11, 64.

7   *Pankhania v Hackney London Borough Council* [2002] EWHC 2441 (Ch), [2002] NPC 123, [2002] All ER (D) 22 (Aug).

8   See PARA 65.

10. Circumstances in which relief might have been granted. For the purposes of the strict common law rule, there was no mistake of general law where there was ignorance of a private right, even though the private right was the result of a matter of law[1], or depended on rules of law applied to the construction of legal documents[2]. Nor was there any mistake of general law where there was ignorance of a right which depended on questions of mixed law and fact, and a statement of fact which involved a conclusion of law is still a statement of fact and not a statement of law[3]. Mistake as to the law of a foreign country was held to be a mistake of fact[4].

However, even where the mistake was held to be in a matter of law, the court might grant relief, if there were circumstances which made it inequitable on the facts of the particular case that the act should stand[5]. But relief would not be granted where a party, having been made aware of the question of law on which his title depended, under circumstances which might have given him equitable right to relief, determined to waive it[6].

There are authorities that a representation of law founded an estoppel by representation[7], and authorities that it did not[8]. The cases are not completely consistent, but the distinction in broad terms appears to be between representations as to private rights or construction, and representations as to general law[9].

1   *Cooper v Phibbs* (1867) LR 2 HL 149 at 170 per Lord Westbury; *Earl Beauchamp v Winn* (1873) LR 6 HL 223; *Huddersfield Banking Co Ltd v Henry Lister & Son Ltd* [1895] 2 Ch 273, CA; *Anglo-Scottish Beet Sugar Corpn Ltd v Spalding UDC* [1937] 2 KB 607, [1937] 3 All ER 335; *Solle v Butcher* [1950] 1 KB 671, [1949] 2 All ER 1107, CA. See also *Clifton v Cockburn* (1834) 3 My & K 76; *Denys v Shuckburgh* (1840) 4 Y & C Ex 42.
2   *Earl Beauchamp v Winn* (1873) LR 6 HL 223; *Daniell v Sinclair* (1881) 6 App Cas 181 at 191 per Sir Robert P Collier; *Re Jones' Estate* [1914] 1 IR 188 at 193.
3   *Eaglesfield v Marquis of Londonderry* (1875) 4 ChD 693 at 702, CA, per Jessel MR.
4   *Leslie v Baillie* (1843) 2 Y & C Ch Cas 91; *Lazard Bros & Co v Midland Bank Ltd* [1933] AC 289, HL; *Richard West & Partners (Inverness) Ltd v Dick* [1969] 2 Ch 424 at 430, [1969] 1 All ER 289 at 290 per Megarry J (affd [1969] 2 Ch 424, [1969] 1 All ER 943, CA); *André et Cie v Et Michel Blanc et Fils* [1979] 2 Lloyd's Rep 427, CA; *The Amazonia* [1990] 1 Lloyd's Rep 236, CA; and see also *Shamil Bank of Bahrain EC v Beximco Pharmaceuticals Ltd* [2004] EWCA Civ 19 at [58]–[60], [2004] 4 All ER 1072, [2004] 1 WLR 1784 per Potter LJ (Sharia law).
5   *Clifton v Cockburn* (1834) 3 My & K 76 at 99 per Lord Brougham LC; *Watson v Marston* (1853) 4 De GM & G 230 at 236 per Knight Bruce LJ. See also *Stone v Godfrey* (1854) 5 De GM & G 76 at 90 per Turner LJ; *Re Saxon Life Assurance Society* (1862) 2 John & H 408 at 412 per Page Wood V-C (affd 1 De GJ & Sm 29); *Allcard v Walker* [1896] 2 Ch 369 at 381 per Stirling J; *Re Jones' Estate* [1914] 1 IR 188; *Burroughes v Abbott* [1922] 1 Ch 86 at 95 per Lawrence J; *Jervis v Howle and Talke Colliery Co Ltd* [1937] Ch 67, [1936] 3 All ER 193; *Kiriri Cotton Co Ltd v Dewani* [1960] AC 192, [1960] 1 All ER 177, PC; *Re Butlin's Settlement Trusts, Butlin v Butlin* [1976] Ch 251, [1976] 2 All ER 483; *Re Slocock's Will Trusts* [1979] 1 All ER 358; and see EQUITABLE JURISDICTION vol 47 (2014) PARA 39 et seq.
6   See *Stone v Godfrey* (1854) 5 De GM & G 76 at 90 per Turner LJ; *Rogers v Ingham* (1876) 3 ChD 351, CA.
7   *Sarat Chunder Dey v Gopal Chunder Lala* (1892) LR 19 Ind App 203; *Gresham Life Assurance Society v Crowther* [1914] 2 Ch 219, PC; *American Surety Co v Calgary Milling Co* (1919) 48 DLR 295 at 300, PC; *De Tchihatchef v Salerni Coupling Ltd* [1932] 1 Ch 330; *Re Eaves, Eaves v Eaves* [1940] Ch 109, [1939] 4 All ER 260, CA; *Singh v Jamal Pirbhai* [1951] AC 688 at 699, PC; *Moorgate Mercantile Co Ltd v Twitchings* [1976] QB 225 at 242, [1975] 3 All ER 314 at 323, CA, per Lord Denning MR (on appeal [1977] AC 890, [1976] 2 All ER 641, HL); *Lyle-Meller v A Lewis & Co (Westminster) Ltd* [1956] 1 All ER 247 at 251, [1956] 1 WLR 29 at 35–36, CA, per Denning LJ; *Taylors Fashions Ltd v Liverpool Victoria Trustees Co Ltd, Old & Campbell Ltd v Liverpool Victoria Friendly Society* [1982] QB 133n, sub nom *Taylor Fashions Ltd v Liverpool Victoria Trustees Co Ltd, Old & Campbell Ltd v Liverpool Victoria Trustees Co Ltd* [1981] 1 All ER 897; and see ESTOPPEL vol 47 (2014) PARA 381.
8   *Re the Local Government Superannuation Acts 1937 and 1939, Algar v Middlesex County Council* [1945] 2 All ER 243 at 251 per Humphreys J; *London County Territorial and Auxiliary Forces Association v Nichols, London County Territorial and Auxiliary Forces Association v Parker* [1949] 1 KB 35 at 50, [1948] 2 All ER 432 at 435, CA, per Scott LJ; *Kai Nam v Ma Kam Chan* [1956] AC 358, [1956] 2 WLR 767, PC.
9   See PARA 27; and ESTOPPEL vol 47 (2014) PARA 381.

11.   Abolition of distinction between mistake of law and mistake of fact. A claim to recover money paid by mistake[1] will no longer fail merely on the basis that the mistake is one of law[2].

However, this abolition of the distinction between mistake of law and mistake of fact[3] poses some problems, the first of which is the extent of the change. The abolition of the 'mistake of law' rule in restitutionary claims for money paid under a mistake[4] does not in itself apply to other common law claims based on mistake, that is: (1) claims to recover property alleged not to have passed by reason of mistake[5]; (2) claims based on misrepresentation[6]; and (3) claims where it is alleged that by reason of mistake there was no enforceable contract at all[7]. Nor does it in terms affect the rule against estoppel based on representation as to the general law[8]. However, the common basis of these various claims strongly suggests that the rule should be the same, and for claims falling within heads (2) and (3) this view is supported by some authority[9].

The second problem is how the change in the restitutionary rule affects future judicial changes in substantive law. The declaratory theory of judicial decision implies that, where action was taken in the past on the basis of a view of the law later shown (because of a development or change in the common law) to be erroneous, such action was taken on the basis of a mistake of law, even though, on the view held at the time, there was no mistake[10]. But the statutory postponement of the limitation period because of mistake[11] does apply to mistakes of law[12]. Consequently, whenever a higher court changes the law by judicial decision, a fresh six year limitation period will commence in which payments made, however long ago, on the basis of the old law can be recovered, on the basis that they have been made under a mistake of law[13]. This may also be the case in claims within heads (1) and (2) above, though probably not head (3) (as the claim is not for relief from the consequences of a mistake).

A different aspect of the second problem is the effect on agreements to compromise litigation where the state of the law subsequently changes. Rather than accept that such agreements may be void as made under a mistake of law, the judges have so far preferred to see the compromise of litigation as an exception which, on public policy grounds, is not to be disturbed[14].

1   See PARA 64.
2   *Kleinwort Benson Ltd v Lincoln City Council* [1999] 2 AC 349, [1998] 4 All ER 513, HL; *Nurdin & Peacock plc v DB Ramsden & Co Ltd* [1999] 1 All ER 941, [1999] 1 WLR 1249. This follows statutory and judicial reform elsewhere in the Commonwealth: see eg *Air Canada v British Columbia* (1989) 59 DLR (4th) 161 (Canada); *David Securities Pty Ltd v Commonwealth Bank of Australia* (1992) 175 CLR 353 (Australia); *Willis Faber Enthoven (Pty) Ltd v Receiver of Revenue* 1992 (4) SA 202 (South Africa); *Morgan Guaranty Trust Co of New York v Lothian Regional Council* 1995 SLT 299, Ct of Sess (Scotland).
3   For a discussion of the historical development of the law in relation to mistakes of fact and mistakes of law see RESTITUTION vol 88 (2012) PARA 432 et seq. See also PARAS 9–11.
4   See RESTITUTION vol 88 (2012) PARA 436 et seq.
5   See PARAS 67, 68.
6   See MISREPRESENTATION vol 76 (2013) PARA 710.
7   See PARAS 13–16; and CONTRACT vol 22 (2012) PARA 207.
8   See PARA 27.
9   See *Pankhania v Hackney London Borough Council* [2002] EWHC 2441 (Ch) at [58], [2002] NPC 123 per Mr Rex Tedd; *Brennan v Bolt Burdon (a firm)* [2004] EWCA Civ 1017 at [10], [12] and at [63], [2005] QB 303, [2004] 3 WLR 1321 per Maurice Kay LJ and Sedley LJ respectively; *Shamil Bank of Bahrain EC v Beximco Pharmaceuticals Ltd* [2004] EWCA Civ 19 at [58], [2004] 4 All ER 1072, [2004] 1 WLR 1784 per Potter LJ.
10   *Kleinwort Benson Ltd v Lincoln City Council* [1999] 2 AC 349 at 377–384, [1998] 4 All ER 513 at 534–540, HL, per Lord Goff of Chieveley.
11   See the Limitation Act 1980 s 32(1)(c); and LIMITATION PERIODS vol 68 (2008) PARA 1230.
12   *Kleinwort Benson Ltd v Lincoln City Council* [1999] 2 AC 349 at 377–389, [1998] 4 All ER 513 at 543–544, HL, per Lord Goff of Chieveley.
13   *Kleinwort Benson Ltd v Lincoln City Council* [1999] 2 AC 349 at 416–418, [1998] 4 All ER 513 at 568–569, HL, per Lord Hope of Craighead; *Deutsche Morgan Grenfell Group plc v IRC* [2006] UKHL 49, [2007] 1 AC 558, [2007] 1 All ER 449.
14   See *Brennan v Bolt Burdon (a firm)* [2004] EWCA Civ 1017 at [23], at [31] and at [63], [2005] QB 303, [2004] 3 WLR 1321 per Maurice Kay LJ, Bodey J and Sedley LJ respectively; *Kyle Bay Ltd v Underwriters subscribing to policy No 019057/08/01* [2007] EWCA Civ 57, [2007] Lloyd's Rep IR 460, [2007] All ER (D) 93 (Feb); and PARA 23.

(3) MISTAKE OF FACT

(i) Mistake as to Nature of Transaction

12. Mistake as to the nature, character or effect of a document or transaction. A mistake as to the nature, character or effect of a document or other transaction may entitle a party to it to raise the plea of non est factum[1]. The test is whether the document is fundamentally different in nature, character or effect from that which the party intended to sign[2]. It is a subjective test[3], but the party relying on the plea must not have been negligent[4]. It is not necessary that there should be any fraud[5].

In cases where the plea is not available, the erroneous belief of one of the contracting parties in relation to the nature of the obligations which he has undertaken is not sufficient to give him the right to rescind, unless the belief has been induced by the representation, fraudulent or otherwise, of the other party to the contract[6].

1 As to the plea of non est factum see CONTRACT vol 22 (2012) PARA 285. See also DEEDS AND OTHER INSTRUMENTS vol 32 (2012) PARAS 269–273.
2 *Saunders (Executrix of the Will of Gallie) v Anglia Building Society* [1971] AC 1004, [1970] 3 All ER 961, HL.
3 *Saunders (Executrix of the Will of Gallie) v Anglia Building Society* [1971] AC 1004 at 1035–1036, [1970] 3 All ER 961 at 980, HL; *United Dominions Trust Ltd v Western* [1976] QB 513 at 523, [1975] 3 All ER 1017 at 1023, CA.
4 *Saunders (Executrix of the Will of Gallie) v Anglia Building Society* [1971] AC 1004, [1970] 3 All ER 961, HL. For examples of negligence precluding reliance on the doctrine see *Crédit Lyonnais v PT Barnard & Associates Ltd* [1976] 1 Lloyd's Rep 557 and *Avon Finance Co Ltd v Bridger* [1985] 2 All ER 281, CA.
5 *Mills v IRC* [1973] Ch 225, [1972] 3 All ER 977, CA; revsd on other grounds sub nom *IRC v Mills* [1975] AC 38, [1974] 1 All ER 722, HL. See also *Foster v Mackinnon* (1869) LR 4 CP 704 at 711 per Byles J; *Bank of Ireland v M'Manamy* [1916] 2 IR 161. Cf *Hasham v Zenab* [1960] AC 316 at 335, PC, per Lord Tucker.
6 *Stewart v Kennedy (No 2)* (1890) 15 App Cas 108 at 121–122, HL, per Lord Watson; *Wilding v Sanderson* [1897] 2 Ch 534, CA; *Faraday v Tamworth Union* (1916) 86 LJ Ch 436, 81 JP 81; and see MISREPRESENTATION vol 76 (2013) PARA 702.

(ii) Mistake as to Identity of Party

13. Mistake by one party as to the identity of the other. Subject to the operation of the doctrine of estoppel[1], where a mistake is made by one party to a transaction as to the identity of the other[2], there is no agreement formed[3]. But where the mistake is merely as to an attribute of the other party the mistake does not vitiate the transaction at law[4], although if the error was induced by the other party's misrepresentation the contract may be voidable[5]. The misdescription of the purchaser of land does not render a conveyance inoperative or prevent the legal estate from passing where it can be ascertained who was meant by the person misdescribed[6].

1 See PARA 27.
2 It does not matter for these purposes whether the person actually exists: *Newborne v Sensolid (Great Britain) Ltd* [1954] 1 QB 45, [1953] 1 All ER 708, CA. As to persons dealing in each other's presence see PARA 14.
3 *Duff v Budd* (1822) 3 Brod & Bing 177 at 183; *Boulton v Jones* (1857) 2 H & N 564; *Hardman v Booth* (1863) 1 H & C 803; *Heugh v London and North Western Rly Co* (1870) LR 5 Exch 51 at 57–58 per Martin B; *Cundy v Lindsay* (1878) 3 App Cas 459, HL; *Ingram v Little* [1961] 1 QB 31, [1960] 3 All ER 332, CA. Similarly, where one party intends to give property to another but mistakenly deals with a third, the third party acquires no title: see PARA 24.

4   See *King's Norton Metal Co v Edridge Merrett & Co Ltd, King's Norton Metal Co v Roberts*
     (1897) 14 TLR 98, CA; and PARA 15.
5   See MISREPRESENTATION vol 76 (2013) PARA 782.
6   *Wray v Wray* [1905] 2 Ch 349, following *Maugham v Sharp* (1864) 17 CBNS 443; *Potter v
     Duffield* (1874) LR 18 Eq 4; *Lovesy v Palmer* [1916] 2 Ch 233; *Davies v Sweet* [1962] 2 QB 300,
     [1962] 1 All ER 92, CA; *F Goldsmith (Sicklesmere) Ltd v Baxter* [1970] Ch 85, [1969] 3 All ER
     733 (misdescription of vendor; vendor entitled to specific performance); and see CONVEYANCING
     vol 23 (2013) PARA 469.

14. Parties dealing in each other's presence. Where the parties are dealing in each
other's presence, there is a presumption that each party intends to deal with the
person in front of him[1]; but it is clear that this presumption may be rebutted[2], for
example if the contract itself makes it clear that no agreement is intended except
with the actual person named in it[3]. However, care must be taken to distinguish
this situation from the situation where there is a contract, because either no
mistake was made at the time of contracting[4], or because the mistake made at the
time of contracting was immaterial to the formation of the contract[5]. The position
where an agent is involved is considered later[6].

1   *Lewis v Averay* [1972] 1 QB 198, [1971] 3 All ER 907, CA; *Ingram v Little* [1961] 1 QB 31 at
     50, [1960] 3 All ER 332 at 336–337, CA, per Sellers LJ, at 57 and 341 per Pearce LJ, and at 66
     and 347 per Devlin LJ dissenting. See also *Barclays Bank Ltd v Okenarhe* [1966] 2 Lloyd's Rep
     87; *Shogun Finance Ltd v Hudson* [2003] UKHL 62 at [185]–[187], [2004] 1 AC 919, [2004]
     1 All ER 215 per Lord Walker.
2   See eg *Ingram v Little* [1961] 1 QB 31, [1960] 3 All ER 332, CA. Cf *Lake v Simmons* [1927] AC
     487, HL; *Re International Society of Auctioneers and Valuers, Baillie's Case* [1898] 1 Ch 110;
     Whittaker v Campbell [1984] QB 318 at 327, [1983] 3 All ER 582 at 586, CA, per Robert Goff LJ.
3   *Shogun Finance Ltd v Hudson* [2003] UKHL 62, [2004] 1 AC 919, [2004] 1 All ER 215 (written
     hire-purchase agreement unequivocally naming intended party).
4   *Phillips v Brooks Ltd* [1919] 2 KB 243, on the assumption that the rogue made no representation
     as to his identity until after the contract had been made. This is the explanation of the case offered
     in *Ingram v Little* [1961] 1 QB 31 at 51, [1960] 3 All ER 332 at 337, CA, per Sellers LJ and at
     60 and 343 per Pearce LJ. Of the reports of *Phillips v Brooks Ltd* above three suggest that the
     rogue said he was Sir George Butler as soon as he entered the shop (88 LJKB 953, 35 TLR 470,
     24 Com Cas 263) and two suggest that he said this a little later ([1919] 2 KB 243, 121 LT 249).
     If, in *Phillips v Brooks Ltd* above, the representation as to identity was made before the formation
     of the contract, an alternative explanation of the case may be that offered in note 5.
5   See eg *Smith v Wheatcroft* (1878) 9 ChD 223; *Dennant v Skinner and Collom* [1948] 2 KB 164,
     [1948] 2 All ER 29 (the auctioneer was prepared to knock the cars down to the rogue whatever
     his identity). Cf *Fellowes v Lord Gwydyr and Page* (1829) 1 Russ & M 83; *Raffles v Wichelhaus*
     (1864) 2 H & C 906 (two ships of the same name); *Fung Ping Shan v Tong Shun* [1918] AC 403,
     PC (conveyance signed by party in name of another).
          This may be the explanation of *Phillips v Brooks Ltd* [1919] 2 KB 243 (see note 4); it seems
     to be offered by Viscount Haldane in *Lake v Simmons* [1927] AC 487 at 501, HL. See also *Fawcett
     v Star Car Sales Ltd* [1960] NZLR 406, NZ CA.
          As to the formation of a contract in general see CONTRACT vol 22 (2012) PARA 231 et seq.
6   See PARA 15.

15. Identity and attributes. While a mistake as to the identity of one of the
parties to a transaction prevents the creation of a contract[1], a mistake which is
merely as to an attribute of the other party, for example his wealth or
creditworthiness[2], or even the name of a person there present[3], does not vitiate the
transaction at law[4]. However, as the identity of a person may be described as the
sum of his attributes, what at first sight appears to be merely a mistake as to
attributes may in fact go to identity[5].

Special consideration must be given to the situation where the rules of agency
are concerned. The general rule is that an agent is not a party to a contract made
between his principal and a third party[6]; but this rule may be displaced where the
agent purports to contract as co-principal[7], or by reason of the doctrine of
undisclosed principal[8], or if the distinction in personality between principal and

agent is immaterial for the purposes of formation of agreement[9]. Where A intends to contract as principal, but knows that the offeror[10] thinks that A is contracting as agent for P, A cannot for his own benefit accept the offer made to P[11]. Where A intends to contract as agent for P, but knows that the offeror thinks that A is contracting as principal, P will usually be able to take the benefit of the contract by reason of the doctrine of undisclosed principal[12]; but, P will not be able to do so where A knows that the identity of the offeree is material, either in the sense that the offeror positively wishes to contract with A as principal[13], or possibly that the offeror does not wish to contract with P[14].

1 See PARAS 13, 14.
2 *King's Norton Metal Co v Edridge Merrett & Co Ltd, King's Norton Metal Co v Roberts* (1897) 14 TLR 98, CA.
3 *Phillips v Brooks Ltd* [1919] 2 KB 243; *Lake v Simmons* [1927] AC 487, HL; *Lewis v Averay* [1972] 1 QB 198, [1971] 3 All ER 907, CA.
4 See, however, the criticism of this distinction between identity and attributes made by Lord Denning MR in *Lewis v Averay* [1972] 1 QB 198, [1971] 3 All ER 907, CA at 206–207 and at 911.
5 See eg *Cundy v Lindsay* (1878) 3 App Cas 459, HL; *Ingram v Little* [1961] 1 QB 31, [1960] 3 All ER 332, CA.
6 See AGENCY vol 1 (2008) PARA 121 et seq.
7 See eg the Partnership Act 1890 s 5; and PARTNERSHIP vol 79 (2014) PARA 39. As to joint promises see CONTRACT vol 22 (2012) PARA 640 et seq.
8 Under this doctrine, both the agent and the undisclosed principal may sue or be sued by the third party on the contract: see further AGENCY vol 1 (2008) PARAS 125, 156 et seq.
9 *Fawcett v Star Car Sales Ltd* [1960] NZLR 406, NZ CA.
10 As to offer and acceptance in the formation of a contract see CONTRACT vol 22 (2012) PARA 233 et seq.
11 *Hardman v Booth* (1863) 1 H & C 803; *Lake v Simmons* [1927] AC 487, HL. See also *Higgons v Burton* (1857) 26 LJ Ex 342; *Morrisson v Robertson* 1908 SC 332, Ct of Sess. Distinguish *Citibank NA v Brown Shipley & Co Ltd, Midland Bank plc v Brown Shipley & Co Ltd* [1991] 2 All ER 690, [1991] 1 Lloyd's Rep 576 (mistake as to identity of mere messenger).
12 See note 8.
13 *Greer v Downs Supply Co* [1927] 2 KB 28, CA.
14 *Said v Butt* [1920] 3 KB 497; *Archer v Stone* (1898) 78 LT 34. The matter here is uncertain; for a contrary view see *Dyster v Randall & Sons* [1926] Ch 932, [1926] All ER Rep 151. See further AGENCY vol 1 (2008) PARA 125 et seq.

(iii) Mistake as to Identity of Subject Matter or Terms of Transaction

16. Mistake as to terms or mistake as to quality. Where the parties do not in fact agree on what is the subject matter of the contract, for example because A intends to sell one thing, and B to buy another[1], then, subject to the operation of the doctrine of estoppel[2], there is no contract between them. The same result follows where the parties do not in fact agree on what are the terms of the agreement[3].

A mistake as to the terms of the offer must be carefully distinguished from a mistake as to the quality[4] of what is being offered[5]. A mistake as to the terms which are being offered raises problems of offer and acceptance[6]; but a mistake as to the quality of what is being offered usually does not. Whilst in an extreme case, a mistake as to the quality of what is being offered might negative the agreement by destroying the subject matter[7], it will not usually prevent the formation of an agreement[8] because it is well established that a mistaken motive of one party cannot prevent the formation of an agreement[9], even if realised by the other party[10].

1 *Thornton v Kempster* (1814) 5 Taunt 786; *Raffles v Wichelhaus* (1864) 2 H & C 906; *Henkel v Pape* (1870) LR 6 Exch 7; *Falck v Williams* [1900] AC 176, PC. As to the effect of false description see DEEDS AND OTHER INSTRUMENTS vol 32 (2012) PARA 428.

2　See PARA 27.

3　*Smith v Hughes* (1871) LR 6 QB 597; *Gill v McDowell* [1903] 2 Ir 463; *Branwhite v Worcester Works Finance Ltd* [1969] 1 AC 552, [1968] 3 All ER 104, HL. As to the interpretation of express contractual terms in general see CONTRACT vol 22 (2012) PARA 357 et seq. As to the admissibility of oral evidence to explain a written contract see PARAS 40–44.

4　As to mistakes as to quality see PARA 20.

5　*Smith v Hughes* (1871) LR 6 QB 597 (seller provided a sample). As to contractual terms see CONTRACT vol 22 (2012) PARA 352 et seq.

6　As to offer and acceptance in the formation of a contract see CONTRACT vol 22 (2012) PARA 233 et seq.

7　*Bell v Lever Bros Ltd* [1932] AC 161 at 227, HL, obiter per Lord Atkin.

8　*Bell v Lever Bros Ltd* [1932] AC 161, HL; *Diamond v British Columbia Thoroughbred Breeders' Society and Boyd* (1965) 52 WWR 385, 52 DLR (2d) 146 (BC).

9　*Balfour v Sea Fire Life Assurance Co* (1857) 3 CBNS 300; *Scrivener v Pask* (1866) LR 1 CP 715, Ex Ch; *Pope and Pearson v Buenos Ayres New Gas Co* (1892) 8 TLR 758, CA. Cf *Gill v M'Dowell* [1903] 2 IR 463.

10　*Smith v Hughes* (1871) LR 6 QB 597 at 603 per Cockburn CJ: 'the passive acquiescence of the seller in the self-deception of the buyer will [not] entitle the latter to avoid the contract'; *Statoil ASA v Louis Dreyfus Energy Services LP, The Harriette N* [2008] EWHC 2257 (Comm), [2009] 1 All ER (Comm) 1035, [2008] 2 Lloyd's Rep 685. See also *Turner v Green* [1895] 2 Ch 205.

(iv)　Mistake of Fact Materially Connected with Subject Matter of Transaction

17.　Common mistake as to existence of subject matter or its essential element. Where parties enter into a contract under a common mistake as to the existence of the subject matter or of some fact or facts forming an integral element of the subject matter, it is a question of construction as to whether either or both of them is or are relieved of liability to perform[1]. In most such cases, both parties are relieved of liability, because the consideration for which each party contracted has failed[2] and, deprived of any effective content, the contract has the appearance of having been void ab initio[3].

Where the contract concerned is one for the sale of specific goods, and the goods have perished by the time of the contract without the seller's knowledge, by a special statutory rule the contract is void[4].

In modern times the position has been stated thus: for common mistake to avoid a contract there must be a common assumption as to the existence of a state of affairs as to which there must be no warranty that that state exists, and nor must it be attributable to the fault of either party, but it must render performance of the contract impossible[5]. It has also been said that the mistake must render the subject matter of the contract radically different from the subject matter which the parties believed to exist[6].

1　*Couturier v Hastie* (1856) 5 HL Cas 673 at 681 per Lord Cranworth LC; *Clark v Lindsay* (1903) 88 LT 198 at 202 per Chanell J; *McRae v Commonwealth Disposals Commission* (1950) 84 CLR 377, Aust HC; *Frederick E Rose (London) Ltd v William H Pim Jnr & Co Ltd* [1953] 2 QB 450 at 460, [1953] 2 All ER 739 at 746–747, CA, per Denning LJ; *Whittaker v Campbell* [1984] QB 318, [1983] 3 All ER 582; cf *Associated Japanese Bank (International) Ltd v Crédit du Nord SA* [1988] 3 All ER 902, [1989] 1 WLR 255. As to construction of a contract see CONTRACT vol 22 (2012) PARA 357 et seq.

2　*Huddersfield Banking Co Ltd v Henry Lister & Son Ltd* [1895] 2 Ch 273 at 281 per Lindley LJ; *Hong Kong Fir Shipping Co Ltd v Kawasaki Kisen Kaisha Ltd* [1962] 2 QB 26 at 66, [1962] 1 All ER 474 at 485, CA, per Diplock LJ. As to failure of consideration see RESTITUTION vol 88 (2012) PARA 487.

3　See CONTRACT vol 22 (2012) PARA 207.

4　See the Sale of Goods Act 1979 s 6; and SALE OF GOODS AND SUPPLY OF SERVICES vol 91 (2012) PARA 55. 'Specific goods' means goods identified and agreed on at the time a contract of sale is made and includes an undivided share, specified as a fraction or percentage, of such goods: see s 61(1) (amended by the Sale of Goods (Amendment) Act 1995 s 2(d)).

5   *Great Peace Shipping Ltd v Tsavliris Salvage (International) Ltd, The Great Peace* [2002] EWCA Civ 1407 at [76], [2003] QB 679, [2002] 4 All ER 689 per Lord Phillips of Worth Matravers MR. See also *Apvodedo Nv v Collins* [2008] EWHC 775 (Ch), [2008] All ER (D) 246 (Apr). See also CONTRACT vol 22 (2012) PARA 467.

6   *Associated Japanese Bank (International) Ltd v Crédit du Nord SA* [1988] 3 All ER 902, [1989] 1 WLR 255; *Kyle Bay Ltd v Underwriters subscribing to policy No 019057/08/01* [2007] EWCA Civ 57, [2007] Lloyd's Rep IR 460, [2007] All ER (D) 93 (Feb).

18. Examples of mistake as to subject matter relieving mistaken party from liability. In the case of a contract for the sale of a cargo supposed to exist and to be capable of transfer, but which in fact had been sold and delivered to others before the contract was made, it was held that the vendor could not recover the price of the cargo[1]. Similarly, when an annuity is sold after, and in ignorance of the fact that, it has ceased to exist, the purchase money may be recovered as having been paid without consideration[2]; and it is likewise if parties to litigation over certain chattels enter into a consent order on the common but mistaken belief that the chattels concerned were never fixed to the soil and have never become fixtures[3]. The same result was held to have occurred where a contract of hire of a room to watch a procession was entered into in ignorance of the existing fact of the cancellation of the procession[4].

Where a fund is held in trust for two persons equally, if living, with benefit of survivorship between them, and one of them sells his reversionary interest, the other being dead at the time, and that fact is not known either to the vendor or to the purchaser, the contract will not be enforced[5]. Again, if a premium is paid and accepted for the renewal of a policy after the death of the insured, even though both parties are ignorant of his death, the payment does not in such circumstances revive the policy[6]. And where a contract for the sale of a policy on the life of a man who is dead is entered into by both parties, in the belief that the assured is alive, and is completed by assignment, the transaction will be set aside[7].

For the same reason, if a deed of separation is entered into between the parties in the belief that they were respectively husband and wife, whereas in fact they were not lawfully married, neither party is obliged to perform[8]. Similarly, parties who make a contract for the exploitation by A of a crop on B's land[9], or for the mining by A of clay from B's land[10], which the land could never produce are not liable to perform.

1   *Couturier v Hastie* (1856) 5 HL Cas 673 (contract contemplated that something existed to be sold, which in the event was not the case). This case was decided prior to the enactment of the Sale of Goods Act 1893 (now consolidated into the Sale of Goods Act 1979): see SALE OF GOODS AND SUPPLY OF SERVICES vol 91 (2012) PARAS 6–7.

2   *Strickland v Turner* (1852) 7 Exch 208; *Kennedy v Thomassen* [1929] 1 Ch 426. As to failure of consideration see RESTITUTION vol 88 (2012) PARA 487 et seq.

3   *Huddersfield Banking Co Ltd v Henry Lister & Son Ltd* [1895] 2 Ch 273, CA.

4   *Griffith v Brymer* (1903) 19 TLR 434 (mistake as to the state of facts went to root of the matter; contract void). See also *Clark v Lindsay* (1903) 88 LT 198.

5   *Colyer v Clay* (1843) 7 Beav 188.

6   *Pritchard v Merchants' and Tradesmen's Life Assurance Society* (1858) 3 CBNS 622.

7   *Scott v Coulson* [1903] 2 Ch 249, CA.

8   *Galloway v Galloway* (1914) 30 TLR 531, DC; *Law v Harragin* (1917) 33 TLR 381.

9   *Sheikh Bros Ltd v Ochsner* [1957] AC 136, [1957] 2 WLR 254, PC (mistake as to a matter of fact which was essential to the agreement).

10   *Lord Clifford v Watts* (1870) LR 5 CP 577 (on the construction of the deed, it was the intention of the parties that the covenant to dig the specified amount of clay should only take effect if that amount of clay existed in the land).

19. Mistake as to subject matter not relieving from liability. There are cases, however, where, on the true construction of the contract, one party or the other bore the risk that the facts would turn out differently from supposed, and that person was held liable under a contract to perform accordingly[1]. In considering the contractual allocation of risk in the absence of warranty, the maxim *caveat emptor* is relevant[2].

There are also cases where the contract has been held not void at law, but voidable in equity because of a mistake as to subject matter[3], but these must now be treated as being no longer authoritative[4].

1 See eg *Barr v Gibson* (1838) 3 M & W 390; *McRae v Commonwealth Disposals Commission* (1950) 84 CLR 377, Aust HC; *William Sindall plc v Cambridgeshire County Council* [1994] 3 All ER 932, [1994] 1 WLR 1016, CA; cf *Associated Japanese Bank (International) Ltd v Crédit du Nord SA* [1988] 3 All ER 902, [1989] 1 WLR 255 (subject matter of lease and guarantee non-existent; guarantee contained condition precedent that lease related to existing machines; contract void ab initio). See also SPECIFIC PERFORMANCE vol 95 (2013) PARA 301 et seq.
2 Literally 'buyer beware': see SALE OF GOODS AND SUPPLY OF SERVICES vol 91 (2012) PARA 78.
3 See *Solle v Butcher* [1950] 1 KB 671, [1949] 2 All ER 1107, CA; *Peters v Batchelor* (1950) 100 L Jo 718, CA; *Grist v Bailey* [1967] Ch 532, [1966] 2 All ER 875; *Magee v Pennine Insurance Co Ltd* [1969] 2 QB 507 at 514, [1969] 2 All ER 891 at 893, CA, per Lord Denning MR; *Curtin v Great London Council* (1971) 69 LGR 281 at 284, CA, per Lord Denning MR; *Laurence v Lexcourt Holdings Ltd* [1978] 2 All ER 810, [1978] 1 WLR 1128.
4 See *Great Peace Shipping Ltd v Tsavliris Salvage (International) Ltd, The Great Peace* [2002] EWCA Civ 1407 at [153]–[160], [2003] QB 679, [2002] 4 All ER 689 per Lord Phillips of Worth Matravers MR (disapproving *Solle v Butcher* [1950] 1 KB 671, [1949] 2 All ER 1107, CA); see also *William Sindall plc v Cambridgeshire County Council* [1994] 3 All ER 932 at 952, [1994] 1 WLR 1016 at 1036, CA, per Hoffmann LJ (doubting *Grist v Bailey* [1967] Ch 532, [1966] 2 All ER 875; *Laurence v Lexcourt Holdings Ltd* [1978] 2 All ER 810, [1978] 1 WLR 1128); and PARA 49. See also EQUITABLE JURISDICTION vol 47 (2014) PARA 41.

20. Mistakes as to quality. Where the parties enter a contract under a mistake as to some quality of the subject matter, the inquiry should start with the construction of the contract[1]. Where the contractual intention was that the subject matter was guaranteed by the supplier to have some quality, and it did not, then prima facie the supplier is in breach of his contract[2], and the recipient has his remedies accordingly (which may include being relieved of liability to perform)[3]. Where there is no such intention however, it is unlikely that a mistake as to quality will be construed as sufficient for either or both parties to be relieved of liability to perform[4]. Thus if goods are sold under a known trade description and they match that description[5], or if they are sold by sample and they match the sample[6], the fact that both parties mistakenly believe such goods to have a particular quality is generally irrelevant. Where a company paid a large sum to determine service contracts which (unknown to it) it might have determined for nothing, the company was still bound[7]; likewise the agreement was binding where a vessel was chartered to provide immediate short-term assistance in a salvage operation, but it was later discovered that it could not reach the stricken vessel in time to be of any use, owing to a common mistake as to its location[8].

1 As to the rules of construction see CONTRACT vol 22 (2012) PARA 357 et seq; and DEEDS AND OTHER INSTRUMENTS vol 32 (2012) PARA 364 et seq.
2 *Gompertz v Bartlett* (1853) 2 E & B 849 at 853 per Lord Campbell CJ. See also SALE OF GOODS AND SUPPLY OF SERVICES vol 91 (2012) PARA 74.
3 As to mistakes as to quality relieving from liability see PARA 21. As to remedies see PARA 34 et seq.
4 *Scott v Littledale* (1858) 8 E & B 815; *Frederick E Rose & Co (London) Ltd v William H Pim Jnr & Co Ltd* [1953] 2 QB 450 at 459, [1953] 2 All ER 739 at 745, CA, per Singleton LJ; *Oscar Chess Ltd v Williams* [1957] 1 All ER 325 at 326–327, [1957] 1 WLR 370 at 373, CA, per Denning LJ (description of car as a 1948 model was not intended to be a term of the contract). See also *R v Morris, Anderton v Burnside* [1984] AC 320, [1983] 3 All ER 288, HL, doubting *Dip Kaur v Chief Constable of Hampshire* [1981] 2 All ER 430, [1981] 1 WLR 578.
5 *Harrison & Jones Ltd v Bunten & Lancaster Ltd* [1953] 1 QB 646, [1953] 1 All ER 903; and see SALE OF GOODS AND SUPPLY OF SERVICES vol 91 (2012) PARA 75.

6   *Carter v Crick* (1859) 4 H & N 412.

7   *Bell v Lever Bros Ltd* [1932] AC 161, HL (mistake went to quality, not the subject matter, of the service contracts). See also RESTITUTION vol 88 (2012) PARA 434.

8   *Great Peace Shipping Ltd v Tsavliris Salvage (International) Ltd, The Great Peace* [2002] EWCA Civ 1407, [2003] QB 679, [2002] 4 All ER 689.

21.   Mistakes as to quality relieving from liability. There are a few cases where the parties will be relieved from performance because of their mistake as to quality[1]. The difficulty is to determine whether the mistake goes to the substance of the whole consideration[2].

In one case a purchaser agreed to buy an estate which, unknown to him, already belonged to him; as neither party was obliged to perform in those circumstances, the purchaser could recover back the price paid[3]. Again, where a finance company accepted an offer to buy a car on hire-purchase which, unknown to the parties, had by then been stolen and severely damaged, neither party was liable under the contract[4]. Finally, where a company issued bonus shares as fully paid in the belief that it had power to do so, but in fact in the circumstances it had power only to issue such shares nil paid, the whole issue was void[5].

These cases are to be contrasted with the cases in which the parties got what they bargained for[6].

1   See *Associated Japanese Bank (International) Ltd v Crédit du Nord* [1988] 3 All ER 902 at 909–911, [1989] 1 WLR 255 at 264–269 per Steyn J. As to mistakes as to quality generally see PARA 20. See also CONTRACT vol 22 (2012) PARA 467.

2   *Kennedy v Panama, New Zealand and Australia Royal Mail Co (Ltd)* (1867) LR 2 QB 580.

3   *Bingham v Bingham* (1748) 1 Ves Sen 126; *Cooper v Phibbs* (1867) LR 2 HL 149 (tenant took lease of land belonging to landlord at law, but belonging to himself in equity); Matthews 'A Note on *Cooper v Phibbs*' (1989) 105 LQR 599. See also *Bell v Lever Bros Ltd* [1932] AC 161 at 218, HL, per Lord Atkin; *Norwich Union Fire Insurance Society v WH Price Ltd* [1934] AC 455 at 463, PC; *Bligh v Martin* [1968] 1 All ER 1157 at 1162, [1968] 1 WLR 804 at 813–814 per Pennycuick J.

4   *Financings Ltd v Stimson* [1962] 3 All ER 386, [1962] 1 WLR 1184, CA.

5   *EIC Services Ltd v Phipps* [2004] EWCA Civ 1069, [2005] 1 All ER 338, [2005] 1 WLR 1377.

6   See eg the cases cited in PARA 20.

22.   Unilateral mistake as to quality. A fundamental mistake by one party[1], not as to the terms, but as to the quality of the subject matter of the agreement does not invalidate the agreement[2], or otherwise give ground for relief in equity[3], even where the other party knows of the mistake[4], unless in the circumstances he[5] or his agent[6] has misled the mistaken party, or his knowledge and failure to disabuse him amounts to equitable fraud[7], or there is a duty to speak breach of which may found an estoppel[8].

There are old cases of unilateral mistake where equity intervened because one party perceived the mistake of the other and took advantage of it[9], as where a parent took advantage of a child just come of age[10] or where persons ignorant of their rights released them to a person knowing of them[11], or where the mistaken party could properly be regarded as a 'poor and ignorant person'[12]. But these are best regarded as turning on the equitable doctrine of undue influence[13] or some rule analogous to it, rather than as impugning the general principle stated above[14].

1   See eg *Thornton v Kempster* (1814) 5 Taunt 786 (broker employed by seller and buyer to negotiate sale gave to buyer a sale note for Riga Rhine hemp instead of St Petersburgh hemp); *Scriven Bros & Co v Hindley & Co* [1913] 3 KB 564 (defendants made a bid for tow at auction under the belief it was hemp; form of catalogue prepared by auctioneer contributed to defendants' mistake).

2   *Morley v Clavering* (1860) 29 Beav 84 (restrictive covenants in a lease); *Smith v Hughes* (1871) LR 6 QB 597 (new oats bought in the belief they were old oats); *Johnson v Islington Union* (1909) 73 JP 172 (tender for goods). See also RESTITUTION vol 88 (2012) PARA 434.

3   *Riverlate Properties Ltd v Paul* [1975] Ch 133, [1974] 2 All ER 656, CA; *George Wimpey UK Ltd v VIC Construction Ltd* [2005] EWCA Civ 77, 103 ConLR 67, [2005] BLR 135, [2005] All ER

(D) 37 (Feb); *Statoil ASA v Louis Dreyfus Energy Services LP, The Harriette N* [2008] EWHC 2257 (Comm) at [105], [2009] 1 All ER (Comm) 1035, [2008] 2 Lloyd's Rep 685 per Aikens J. See also EQUITABLE JURISDICTION vol 47 (2014) PARA 40.

4 *Smith v Hughes* (1871) LR 6 QB 597 at 607 per Blackburn J; *Statoil ASA v Louis Dreyfus Energy Services LP, The Harriette N* [2008] EWHC 2257 (Comm) at [88], [2009] 1 All ER (Comm) 1035, [2008] 2 Lloyd's Rep 685 per Aikens J.

5 *Goddard v Jeffreys* (1881) 51 LJ Ch 57; *Wilding v Sanderson* [1897] 2 Ch 534, CA; *Jennings v Jennings* [1898] 1 Ch 378; *Faraday v Tamworth Union* (1916) 86 LJ Ch 436, 81 JP 81.

6 *Scriven Bros & Co v Hindley & Co* [1913] 3 KB 564 (see note 1; defendants not bound).

7 *Monaghan County Council v Vaughan* [1948] IR 306 at 315 per Dixon J; *Pateman v Pay* (1974) 232 Estates Gazette 457; *A Roberts & Co Ltd v Leicestershire County Council* [1961] Ch 555, [1961] 2 All ER 545; *Redbridge London Borough Council v Robinson Rentals Ltd* (1969) 211 Estates Gazette 1125; *Riverlate Properties Ltd v Paul* [1975] Ch 133, [1974] 2 All ER 656, CA; *Taylor v Johnson* (1983) 151 CLR 422.

8 See PARA 27.

9 *Cocking v Pratt* (1750) 1 Ves Sen 400; *M'Carthy v Decaix* (1831) 2 Russ & M 614 at 622 per Lord Brougham LC; *Sturge v Sturge* (1849) 12 Beav 229; *Coward v Hughes* (1855) 1 K & J 443 at 449 per Page Wood V-C; *Broughton v Hutt* (1858) 3 De G & J 501.

10 *Cocking v Pratt* (1750) 1 Ves Sen 400; *Re Garnett, Gandy v Macaulay* (1885) 31 ChD 1 at 10 per Brett MR and at 17 per Fry LJ.

11 *Cann v Cann* (1721) 1 P Wms 723 at 727 per Macclesfield LC; *Pusey v Desbouvrie* (1734) 3 P Wms 315; *Ramsden v Hylton* (1751) 2 Ves Sen 304; *Re Garnett, Gandy v Macaulay* (1885) 31 ChD 1, CA.

12 *Fry v Lane* (1888) 40 ChD 312; *Cresswell v Potter* [1978] 1 WLR 255n. See also EQUITABLE JURISDICTION vol 47 (2014) PARA 30.

13 As to undue influence see EQUITABLE JURISDICTION vol 47 (2014) PARA 18 et seq.

14 Cf *Riverlate Properties v Paul* [1975] Ch 133, [1974] 2 All ER 656, CA; and see EQUITABLE JURISDICTION vol 47 (2014) PARA 41.

23. Compromises and family arrangements. Agreements to compromise litigation or to avoid disputes are contracts governed by the ordinary rules of the law of contract[1]. Hence in principle they should be capable of being vitiated by common mistake of law[2]. However, it will be a question of construction whether an alleged mistake has that consequence[3]. For example, general words are unlikely to be interpreted as giving up rights of which the parties were then unaware[4]. Moreover, there are public policy considerations to be taken into account[5]. Thus, where there is a 'give-and-take' settlement of claims, a compromise will not be set aside even if subsequently it appears that the parties were mistaken on a point of law[6]. The position is even more so when there is simply doubt as to what the law is, rather than a mistaken belief[7].

Equity will also relieve a party who, in ignorance of a plain and settled principle of law is induced to give up a portion of his indisputable property to another under the name of a compromise[8]. Similarly, relief may be granted where parties, being ignorant of facts on which their rights depend or erroneously assuming that they know their rights, deal with the property accordingly and not upon the principle of compromising doubts[9]. A compromise based on a mutual mistake of account inducing the compromise will also be set aside[10]. There are also cases in which transactions with 'poor and ignorant persons' have been set aside[11].

1 *Huddersfield Banking Co Ltd v Henry Lister & Sons Ltd* [1895] 2 Ch 273, CA; *OT Africa Line Ltd v Vickers plc* [1996] 1 Lloyd's Rep 700. As to the law of contract in general see CONTRACT.

2 See PARA 9 et seq.

3 *Brennan v Bolt Burdon (a firm)* [2004] EWCA Civ 1017 at [10], [2005] QB 303, [2004] 3 WLR 1321 per Maurice Kay LJ.

4 *Bank of Credit and Commerce International SA v Ali* [2001] UKHL 8 at [9]–[10], [2002] 1 AC 251, [2001] 1 All ER 961 per Lord Bingham of Cornhill.

5 *Brennan v Bolt Burdon (a firm)* [2004] EWCA Civ 1017, [2005] QB 303, [2004] 3 WLR 1321.

6 *Huddersfield Banking Co Ltd v Henry Lister & Sons Ltd* [1895] 2 Ch 273, CA; *Holsworthy UDC v Holsworthy RDC* [1907] 2 Ch 62; *Brennan v Bolt Burdon (a firm)* [2004] EWCA Civ 1017,

[2005] QB 303, [2004] 3 WLR 1321; *Kyle Bay Ltd v Underwriters subscribing to policy No 019057/08/01* [2007] EWCA Civ 57, [2007] Lloyd's Rep IR 460, [2007] All ER (D) 93 (Feb).

7 See *Kleinwort Benson Ltd v Lincoln City Council* [1999] 2 AC 349 at 410, [1998] 4 All ER 513 at 562, HL, per Lord Hope of Craighead; and also *Butters v BBC Worldwide Ltd* [2009] EWHC 1954 (Ch), [2009] BPIR 1315, [2009] All ER (D) 171 (Aug) (revsd in part sub nom *Perpetual Trustee Co Ltd v BNY Corporate Trustee Services Ltd, Butters v BBC Worldwide Ltd* [2009] EWCA Civ 1160, [2010] Ch 347, [2010] 3 WLR 87). See further PARA 11.

8 *Naylor v Winch* (1824) 1 Sim & St 555 at 564 per Sir John Leach V-C (affd (1828) 7 LJOS Ch 6); *Re Roberts, Roberts v Roberts* [1905] 1 Ch 704, CA.

9 See SETTLEMENTS vol 91 (2012) PARAS 915, 919.

10 *Pritt v Clay* (1843) 6 Beav 503; *Stainton v Carron Co* (1861) 30 LJ Ch 713.

11 See PARA 22.

(4) OTHER CHARACTERISTICS OF MISTAKE

(i) Mistake Preventing the Passing of Property

24. Contracts affected by mistake. Where a contract is ineffective for some reason other than mistake, and chattels are transferred pursuant to it, the invalidity of the contract does not prevent ownership passing to the transferee, provided the transferor intended to transfer it[1]. The rule is the same with contracts affected by mistake, as regards real property and intangibles. As regards chattels, however, matters are different. Here the validity of the transferee's title depends on that of the underlying contract, thus a contract void for mistake passes no title at all[2]. By contrast, a contract voidable for fraud passes a title, but only a precarious voidable title, liable to be divested by notice from the transferor[3].

The point is of importance where the rights of third party purchasers claiming under the transferee are in issue. Where the original contract was void, the rule *nemo dat quod non habet*[4] means that even if he acted in complete good faith the purchaser gets no title at all, since the transferee had none to give him[5]. By contrast, if the original contract was voidable, and steps had not been taken to avoid it at the time of the resale to the purchaser, then owing to the rule that a contract may not be rescinded so as to impugn the rights of third parties acting in good faith and for value, the purchaser gets an indefeasible title[6]. If steps had previously been taken to avoid the contract, then the rule *nemo dat quod non habet* is likely to apply so as to prevent the purchaser getting good title[7].

1 *Stocks v Wilson* [1913] 2 KB 235, [1911–13] All ER Rep Ext 1512 (contract affected by minority (though now there may be a restitutionary liability under the Minors' Contracts Act 1987 s 3 (see CHILDREN AND YOUNG PERSONS vol 9 (2012) PARA 24))); *Singh v Ali* [1960] AC 167, [1960] 1 All ER 269, PC (illegal contract); *Sharma v Simposh Ltd* [2011] EWCA Civ 1383, [2013] Ch 23, [2012] 2 All ER (Comm) 288 (contract ineffective under the Law of Property (Miscellaneous Provisions) Act 1989 s 2 (see CONVEYANCING vol 23 (2013) PARA 151)). See also Swadling 'Rescission, Property, and the Common Law' (2005) 121 LQR 123.

2 *Cundy v Lindsay* (1878) 3 App Cas 459, [1874–80] All ER Rep 1149, HL; *Ingram v Little* [1961] 1 QB 31, [1960] 3 All ER 332, CA. See also *Shogun Finance Ltd v Hudson* [2003] UKHL 62, [2004] 1 AC 919, [2004] 1 All ER 215 (void hire-purchase contract could not cause car to be 'bailed . . . under a hire-purchase agreement' within the Hire-Purchase Act 1964 s 27 (see CONSUMER CREDIT vol 21 (2011) PARAS 134–135)).

3 *Phillips v Brooks Ltd* [1919] 2 KB 243, [1918–19] All ER Rep 246; *Car and Universal Finance Co Ltd v Caldwell* [1965] 1 QB 525, [1964] 1 All ER 290, CA; *Lewis v Averay* [1972] 1 QB 198, [1971] 3 All ER 907, CA; *Neo Neon Ltd v Western Alliance Ltd* [2015] EWHC 2864 (QB).

4 Ie no one can give what he does not have. This rule is contained in statute: see the Sale of Goods Act 1979 s 21; and SALE OF GOODS AND SUPPLY OF SERVICES vol 91 (2012) PARA 148.

5 See *Hardman v Booth* (1863) 1 H & C 803; *Cundy v Lindsay* (1878) 3 App Cas 459; *Ingram v Little* [1961] 1 QB 31, [1960] 3 All ER 332.

6   *Phillips v Brooks Ltd* [1919] 2 KB 243, [1918–19] All ER Rep 246; *Lewis v Averay* [1972] 1 QB
    198, [1971] 3 All ER 907. This rule is contained in the Sale of Goods Act 1979 s 23 (see SALE OF
    GOODS AND SUPPLY OF SERVICES vol 91 (2012) PARA 152.
7   *Car and Universal Finance Co Ltd v Caldwell* [1965] 1 QB 525, [1964] 1 All ER 290. See also
    Newtons of Wembley Ltd v Williams [1965] 1 QB 560, [1964] 3 All ER 532, CA. In some cases
    however the purchaser may be able to invoke the exception to nemo dat contained in the Sale of
    Goods Act 1979 s 25(1) (see SALE OF GOODS AND SUPPLY OF SERVICES vol 91 (2012) PARAS
    156, 252): see *Newtons of Wembley Ltd v Williams*.

25. Mistake as to persons or formalities preventing the passing of property.
Where A intends to pass property in money[1] or other chattels[2] by delivery to B,
but mistakenly delivers to C, property does not pass either to B or to C.

Where A intends to pass property by deed to B, but misdescribes him, the court
will give effect to it if B's identity can be ascertained[3]. If A intends B but
mistakenly names C, the court may rectify the deed[4].

If, by mistake, the wrong person is registered as proprietor of registered land,
property passes to that person[5], but the register may be rectified so as to correct
the mistake[6]. Where A intends to pass property to B, but mistakenly fails to
comply with the relevant legal formalities, property will not pass at law[7]. It may
pass in equity if B has given valuable consideration[8], or relies on the purported gift
to his prejudice[9], or is subsequently appointed A's executor[10], or perhaps
administrator[11], but otherwise equity will not perfect an imperfect gift[12].

1   *R v Middleton* (1873) LR 2 CCR 38; *Morgan v Ashcroft* [1938] 1 KB 49 at 64–66, [1937] 3 All ER
    92 at 97–98, CA, per Sir Wilfred Greene MR.
2   *Hoare v Great Western Rly* (1877) 37 LT 186 at 187 per Lord Coleridge CJ; *Lancashire and
    Yorkshire Rly Co v MacNicoll* (1918) 118 LT 596; *R v Hudson* [1943] KB 458, [1943] 1 All ER
    642, CCA; *Ingram v Little* [1961] 1 QB 31, [1960] 3 All ER 332, CA.
3   *Wray v Wray* [1905] 2 Ch 349, 74 LJ Ch 687; and see PARAS 13–15.
4   See PARA 33.
5   See the Land Registration Act 2002 s 58; and REAL PROPERTY AND REGISTRATION vol 87
    (2012) PARA 384.
6   See the Land Registration Act 2002 s 65, Sch 4; *Norwich and Peterborough Building Society
    v Steed* [1993] Ch 116, [1993] 1 All ER 330, CA (decided under corresponding provisions of the
    Land Registration Act 1925 (repealed)); and REAL PROPERTY AND REGISTRATION vol 87 (2012)
    PARA 493 et seq.
7   *Jones v Lock* (1865) 1 Ch App 25; *Richards v Delbridge* (1874) LR 18 Eq 11; *Crago v Julian*
    [1992] 1 All ER 744, [1992] 1 WLR 372, CA. As to the legal formalities see CONTRACT vol 22
    (2012) PARA 220 et seq; REAL PROPERTY AND REGISTRATION vol 87 (2012) PARA 245 et seq.
    See also DEEDS AND OTHER INSTRUMENTS vol 32 (2012) PARAS 223–224.
8   *Holroyd v Marshall* (1862) 10 HL Cas 191; *Pullan v Koe* [1913] 1 Ch 9.
9   *Dillwyn v Llewellyn* (1862) 4 De GF & J 517.
10 *Strong v Bird* (1874) LR 18 Eq 315; and see WILLS AND INTESTACY vol 103 (2010) PARA 626.
11 *Re Gonin* [1979] Ch 16, [1977] 2 All ER 720.
12 *Milroy v Lord* (1862) 4 De GF & J 264; *Pappadakis v Pappadakis* (2000) Times, 19 January; cf
    Re Rose, Rose v IRC [1952] Ch 499, [1952] 1 All ER 1217, CA. See also GIFTS vol 52 (2014)
    PARAS 267, 270.

26. Other mistakes preventing the passing of property. If A by mistake hands
over to B property different from that which he intends to hand over, it appears
that property does not pass at law[1].

If A intends to pass property to B and complies with the relevant formalities
then as a general rule, and subject to any estoppel[2], property passes at law[3]. It does
not matter if A was mistaken as to some other matter which was the motive for
the transaction, for example that B was poor, when in fact he is rich[4], or that A
owed B the sum paid, when in fact he did not[5].

There is some authority for saying that if A pays B money under a factual
mistake he retains an equitable property in it[6], but this has been doubted[7]. In
addition, the Supreme Court has confirmed that, where A gives to B under some

mistake of sufficient gravity as to render it unjust or unconscionable to leave it uncorrected, the court may set aside the gift in equity[8]. A gift by a husband to his wife, not realising that the property would fall within a covenant to settle after-acquired property in their marriage settlement[9]; a release by a father of his protected life interest in favour of his children (the remaindermen), not realising that this would cause a forfeiture and impose a discretionary trust[10]; and a transfer made for the purpose of reducing liability to inheritance tax in the mistaken belief by the transferor that he had a real chance of surviving for the requisite period[11], have all been set aside in equity on the ground of mistake[12].

1 *R v Ashwell* (1885) 16 QBD 190 at 201; cf *Ilich v R* (1987) 162 CLR 110.
2 *Lancashire and Yorkshire Rly Co v MacNicoll* (1918) 118 LT 596; and see PARA 27.
3 *Ogilvie v Littleboy* (1897) 13 TLR 399, CA; affd (1899) 15 TLR 294, HL.
4 *Wilson v Thornbury* (1875) 10 Ch App 239; *Morgan v Ashcroft* [1938] 1 KB 49 at 66, [1937] 3 All ER 92 at 98, CA, per Sir Wilfrid Greene MR.
5 *Moynes v Coopper* [1956] 1 QB 439, [1956] 1 All ER 450; *Ilich v R* (1987) 162 CLR 110.
6 *Chase Manhattan Bank NA v Israel-British Bank (London) Ltd* [1981] Ch 105, [1979] 3 All ER 1025; *R v Shadrokh-Cigari* [1988] Crim LR 465, CA. See also *IVS Enterprises Ltd v Chelsea Cloisters Management Ltd* [1994] EGCS 14, 13 TLI 111, CA.
7 *Westdeutsche Landsbank Girozentrale v Islington London Borough Council* [1996] AC 669 at 714, [1996] 2 All ER 961 at 996, HL, per Lord Browne-Wilkinson.
8 *Pitt v Holt, Futter v Futter* [2013] UKSC 26, [2013] 2 AC 108, [2013] 3 All ER 429 (elaborating on the approach taken by Lloyd LJ in the same case in the Court of Appeal ([2011] EWCA Civ 197, [2012] Ch 132, [2011] 2 All ER 450) applying *Ogilvie v Littleboy* (1897) 13 TLR 399; affd (1899) 15 TLR 294). See also *Freedman v Freedman* [2015] EWHC 1457 (Ch), [2015] WTLR 1187. Such a mistake makes the disposition voidable in equity but not void at law: *Kennedy v Kennedy* [2014] EWHC 4129 (Ch) at [41], [2015] WTLR 837 per Sir Terence Etherton C. See also GIFTS vol 52 (2014) PARA 261; and TRUSTS AND POWERS vol 98 (2013) PARA 80.
9 *Ellis v Ellis* (1909) 26 TLR 166.
10 *Gibbon v Mitchell* [1990] 3 All ER 338, [1990] 1 WLR 1304 (although the approach in that case—equity may intervene where the mistake is as to the effect of the transaction rather than as to the consequences—was doubted in *Pitt v Holt, Futter v Futter* [2013] UKSC 26, [2013] 2 AC 108, [2013] 3 All ER 429 (see text and note 8) and other cases (*Sieff v Fox* [2005] EWHC 1312 (Ch) at [106], [2005] 3 All ER 693, [2005] 1 WLR 3811 per Lloyd LJ; *Wolff v Wolff* [2004] EWHC 2110 (Ch), [2004] STC 1633, [2004] WTLR 1349) and has been not followed in others (*Ogden v Trustees of the RHS Griffiths 2003 Settlement* [2008] EWHC 118 (Ch), [2009] Ch 162, [2008] 2 All ER 654; *Fender (administrator of FG Collier & Sons Ltd) v National Westminster Bank plc* [2008] EWHC 2242 (Ch), [2008] 3 EGLR 80, [2008] 48 EG 102)). See also *Dent v Dent* [1996] 1 All ER 659 at 669, [1996] 1 WLR 683 at 693 per David Young QC; and *AMP (UK) Ltd plc v Barker* (2000) 3 ITELR 414 at [80]–[82] per Lawrence Collins J.
11 *Ogden v Trustees of the RHS Griffiths 2003 Settlement* [2008] EWHC 118 (Ch), [2009] Ch 162, [2008] 2 All ER 654. See also *Bhatt v Bhatt* [2009] EWHC 734 (Ch), [2009] STC 1540, [2009] All ER (D) 58 (Apr) (transfer of assets following erroneous tax advice set aside).
12 See also PARA 50.

(ii) Limitations on Mistake

27. Estoppel as a limitation on the principles governing the law of mistake. Where there is no genuine consensus between parties, and therefore prima facie there should be no contract, estoppel may nonetheless have effect to prevent a party from denying that a consensus with the other party exists[1]. This can apply in relation to mistake as to the parties[2], mistake as to the subject matter[3], or indeed mistake as to any other terms of a contract[4]. It is no objection that the estoppel relates to questions of private rights or construction issues[5], and it seems that there can be no estoppel as to matters of general law[6].

Estoppel may also operate in equity where a party has a duty to speak, but remains silent[7]. If A has actual knowledge that B mistakenly believes that A owes an obligation to B (or that B has a right against A) which would be to

B's disadvantage if A thereafter denied the obligation, A is under a duty to disclose the non-existence of the obligation or right in question[8].

1   See ESTOPPEL vol 47 (2014) PARA 355 et seq.
2   *Cornish v Abington* (1859) 4 H & N 549; *Spiro v Lintern* [1973] 3 All ER 319, [1973] 1 WLR 1002, CA. This may also explain *Mackie v European Assurance Society* (1869) 21 LT 102 (contractor mistaken as to other party's identity, even if not liable to suit, may nevertheless enforce the contract against that party). As to mistake as to identity of a party see PARAS 13–15.
3   *Scott v Littledale* (1858) 8 E & B 815; *Van Praagh v Everidge* [1902] 2 Ch 266 (revsd on other grounds [1903] 1 Ch 434, CA); *Robinson, Fisher and Harding v Behar* [1927] 1 KB 513. As to mistake as to identity of subject matter see PARA 16.
4   *Smith v Hughes* (1871) LR 6 QB 597 at 607 per Blackburn J; *Haymen v Gover* (1872) 25 LT 903; *Harris v Great Western Rly* (1876) 1 QBD 515 at 530 per Blackburn J; *Islington Union v Brentnall and Cleland* (1907) 71 JP 407, 5 LGR 1219; *Howatson v Webb* [1908] 1 Ch 1, CA; cf *McCutcheon v David MacBrayne Ltd* [1964] 1 All ER 430 at 436–437, [1964] 1 WLR 125 at 133–134, HL, per Lord Devlin.
5   See PARA 10.
6   See PARA 10; cf *Kleinwort Benson Ltd v Lincoln City Council* [1999] 2 AC 349, [1998] 4 All ER 513, HL; *Brennan v Bolt Burdon (a firm)* [2004] EWCA Civ 1017, [2005] QB 303, [2004] 3 WLR 1321. See also *Briggs v Gleeds (Head Office)* [2014] EWHC 1178 (Ch), [2015] Ch 212, [2015] 1 All ER 533.
7   See ESTOPPEL vol 47 (2014) PARA 362.
8   *Pickard v Sears* (1837) 6 Ad & El 469; *Ramsden v Dyson and Thornton* (1866) LR 1 HL 129; *Spiro v Lintern* [1973] 3 All ER 319, [1973] 1 WLR 1002, CA.

28. Objective view as alternative to estoppel. There is support for an alternative view that the strict principle of consensus is tempered, not by estoppel[1], but by an objective principle, that is, that one party is bound if his words or conduct are such as to induce the other party reasonably to believe that the first was assenting to the terms proposed by the second[2]. These cases are, however, also consistent with estoppel. The matter is controversial[3], but there is no doubt that estoppel is a general doctrine, not confined to contracts[4], whilst the objective principle is only applicable to contract[5].

1   See PARA 27.
2   *Taylor v Johnson* (1983) 151 CLR 422; *Centrovincial Estates plc v Merchant Investors Assurance Co Ltd* [1983] Com LR 158, CA; *Whittaker v Campbell* [1984] QB 318 at 326–327, [1983] 3 All ER 582 at 585–586, DC, per Robert Goff LJ; *Allied Marine Transport Ltd v Vale do Rio Doce Navegacao SA, The Leonidas D* [1985] 2 All ER 796, [1985] 1 WLR 925, CA; *Food Corpn of India v Antclizo Shipping Corpn, 'The Antclizo'* [1987] 2 Lloyd's Rep 130, CA (affd [1988] 2 All ER 513, [1988] 1 WLR 603); *Shogun Finance Ltd v Hudson* [2003] UKHL 62 at [65], [81] and [87], at [123] and at [183], [2004] 1 AC 919, [2004] 1 All ER 215 per Lord Millett, Lord Phillips of Worth Matravers MR and Lord Walker respectively.
3   See Atiyah 'Contracts, Promises and the Law of Obligations' (1978) 94 LQR 193; Atiyah 'The Hannah Blumenthal and Classical Contract Law' (1986) 102 LQR 363 at 364–365.
4   See eg *Pickard v Sears* (1837) 6 Ad & El 469 (trover); *Freeman v Cooke* (1848) 2 Exch 654 (trover); *Lancashire and Yorkshire Rly Co v MacNicoll* (1918) 118 LT 596 (passing of property by delivery).
5   *Taylor v Johnson* (1983) 151 CLR 422; *Centrovincial Estates plc v Merchant Investors Assurance Co Ltd* [1983] Com LR 158, CA; *Whittaker v Campbell* [1984] QB 318 at 326–327, [1983] 3 All ER 582 at 585–586, DC, per Robert Goff LJ; *Allied Marine Transport Ltd v Vale do Rio Doce Navegacao SA, The Leonidas D* [1985] 2 All ER 796, [1985] 1 WLR 925, CA; *Food Corpn of India v Antclizo Shipping Corpn, 'The Antclizo'* [1987] 2 Lloyd's Rep 130, CA.

(iii) Mistaken Payments, Improvements, Services Rendered and Goods Supplied

29. Mistaken payments. The recovery of money paid under a mistake is dealt with in detail elsewhere in this work[1].

1   See PARAS 64, 65; RESTITUTION vol 88 (2012) PARAS 428–443.

30. Services rendered and goods supplied by mistake. Historically, the courts have been less willing to grant relief to a person who rendered services to another by mistake than to a person who paid money by mistake[1]. One reason may be that services, unlike money, cannot be restored[2]. The general rule is that, where the recipient of services has neither requested them[3] nor freely accepted them[4], he has no liability to pay for them or for any benefit thereby conferred[5]. In exceptional cases, however, liability has attached, as where the services would have had to be performed by someone if not the claimant[6], or where (if this is different) the defendant's statutory duty was mistakenly performed by the claimant[7].

Where goods are supplied by mistake, the matter is complicated by the question of the passing of property. If property does not pass[8], the supplier has his proprietary remedies[9]. If property does pass, the recipient must pay for them if he requested them[10] or freely accepted them[11]; otherwise he need not[12].

1   As to recovery of money paid under a mistake see PARAS 64, 65; and RESTITUTION vol 88 (2012) PARAS 428–443.
2   See *Taylor v Laird* (1856) 25 LJ Ex 329 at 332 per Pollock CB: 'One cleans another's shoes; what can the other do but put them on?'
3   Cf *British Steel Corpn v Cleveland Bridge and Engineering Co Ltd* [1984] 1 All ER 504 at 511 per Robert Goff J.
4   *Munro v Butt* (1858) 8 E & B 738; *Leigh v Dickeson* (1884) 15 QBD 60 at 64–65, CA, per Brett MR; *Falcke v Scottish Imperial Insurance Co* (1886) 34 ChD 234 at 249, CA, per Bowen LJ; *Sumpter v Hedges* [1898] 1 QB 673, CA.
5   See RESTITUTION vol 88 (2012) PARAS 415, 527.
6   *Craven-Ellis v Canons Ltd* [1936] 2 KB 403, [1936] 2 All ER 1066, CA.
7   *County of Carleton v City of Ottawa* (1965) 52 DLR (2d) 220, Can SC.
8   See PARAS 24–26.
9   See PARAS 67, 68.
10   Cf *Rover International Ltd v Cannon Film Sales Ltd (No 3)* [1989] 3 All ER 423, [1989] 1 WLR 912, CA (a case on services, but which is still relevant to the point).
11   *Laird v Pim* (1841) 7 M & W 474; *Sumpter v Hedges* [1898] 1 QB 673, CA. See also the Sale of Goods Act 1979 s 30; and SALE OF GOODS AND SUPPLY OF SERVICES vol 91 (2012) PARA 159 et seq.
12   See eg *Boulton v Jones* (1857) 2 H & N 564.

31. Mistaken improvements to property. As with services[1], the general rule is that, in the absence of request or free acceptance[2] a person whose property is mistakenly improved by another is under no liability to pay for that improvement, and neither does the improver acquire any proprietary interest in the property concerned[3]. One general exception to this is the law of maritime salvage[4]. A second, minor exception may be where the true owner of the chattels claims to recover possession from the mistaken improver, and the court awards possession on condition that the improver's expenditure is reimbursed[5]. It seems that, if the chattel gets back into the owner's hands by another route, the improver has no freestanding claim[6].

There is also a third, more important, exception dealt with elsewhere in this work: proprietary estoppel[7].

1   See PARA 30.
2   See RESTITUTION vol 88 (2012) PARAS 415, 527.
3   See *Falcke v Scottish Imperial Insurance Co* (1886) 34 ChD 234, CA; and RESTITUTION vol 88 (2012) PARAS 414–417, 440. See also *Nutt v Read* (1999) 32 HLR 761, (1999) Times 3 December, CA.
4   See *Falcke v Scottish Imperial Insurance Co* (1886) 34 ChD 234, CA; and SHIPPING AND MARITIME LAW vol 94 (2008) PARA 925.
5   See the Torts (Interference with Goods) Act 1977 s 6(1); *Greenwood v Bennett* [1973] QB 195, [1972] 3 All ER 586, CA; and TORT vol 97 (2015) PARA 678.

6 This seems to be the reasoning of Phillimore and Cairns LJJ in *Greenwood v Bennett* [1973] QB 195, [1972] 3 All ER 586. Contra, however, Lord Denning MR in the same case: [1973] QB 195 at 202, [1972] 3 All ER 586 at 589.

7 See ESTOPPEL vol 47 (2014) PARAS 309, 392. There is some debate as to how far (if at all) the doctrine of proprietary estoppel is distinct from that of so-called 'common intention constructive trust': see TRUSTS AND POWERS vol 98 (2013) PARA 120.

(5) THIRD PARTY DETERMINATIONS

32. Binding nature of third party determinations. Where parties to a contract agree that something (whether price, value or otherwise) should be determined by an independent person acting as agent, whose determination is to be conclusive, in the absence of fraud, collusion, or manifest or material error[1], they are bound by that determination because they have so agreed[2]. In itself it is irrelevant whether the determination gives reasons or not[3]. What matters is whether it is possible to say from all the evidence properly before the court what the expert has done and why[4]. And the question then is not whether he is mistaken in the result[5], but whether he has departed from his instructions in a material way[6]. Any departure is material unless it can truly be characterised as trivial in the sense that it could make no possible difference to either party[7], or if it is such a departure as the parties would reasonably have regarded as being sufficient to invalidate the determination[8]; and if material departure can be shown, then the determination can be challenged[9]. If material departure cannot be shown, then, in the absence of manifest or material error[10], the determination is binding[11]. The same principles apply to the decision of an expert as to which other expert should be appointed to determine the substantive question[12].

In seeking, in a non-speaking valuation, to discern the expert's reasons for his decision, no encouragement will be given to any attempt to infer what is happening behind the curtain[13]. But the expert's decision-making authority does not ordinarily extend to questions of law such as the meaning of a contract or lease, and so if it is clear from the determination that the expert has decided such a question wrongly as a matter of law he must have gone outside that authority[14].

The rules of natural justice do not apply to an expert determination, whether by virtue of the Human Rights Act 1998 or otherwise[15].

1 See note 10.
2 *Campbell v Edwards* [1976] 1 All ER 785 at 788, [1976] 1 WLR 403 at 407, CA, per Geoffrey Lane LJ; *Baber v Kenwood Manufacturing Co Ltd* [1978] 1 Lloyd's Rep 175, CA; *Shell UK Ltd v Enterprise Oil plc* [1999] 2 All ER (Comm) 87, [1999] 2 Lloyd's Rep 456; *Soules CAF v Louis Dreyfus Negoce SA* [2000] 2 All ER (Comm) 154, [2000] 2 Lloyd's Rep 307; *Veba Oil Supply and Trading GmbH v Petrotrade Inc* [2001] EWCA Civ 1832, [2002] 1 All ER 703, [2002] 1 Lloyd's Rep 295, CA; *Homepace Ltd v Sita South East Ltd* [2008] EWCA Civ 1, [2008] 1 P & CR 436, [2008] All ER (D) 18 (Jan); and see BUILDING CONTRACTS vol 6 (2011) PARA 501; LANDLORD AND TENANT vol 62 (2012) PARA 457.
3 *Jones v Sherwood Computer Services plc* [1992] 2 All ER 170 at 177, [1992] 1 WLR 277 at 284, CA, per Dillon LJ. See also *Invensys plc v Automotive Sealing Systems Ltd* [2002] 1 All ER (Comm) 222 (where reasons are given, a court should consider those reasons when determining whether there was an error in the determination).
4 *Jones v Sherwood Computer Services plc* [1992] 2 All ER 170 at 177, [1992] 1 WLR 277 at 284, CA, per Dillon LJ.
5 See eg *Jones v Jones* [1971] 2 All ER 676, [1971] 1 WLR 840.
6 *Jones v Sherwood Computer Services plc* [1992] 2 All ER 170 at 179, [1992] 1 WLR 277 at 287, CA, per Dillon LJ; cf *Dean v Prince* [1954] Ch 409, [1954] 2 All ER 749, CA.
7 *Veba Oil Supply and Trading GmbH v Petrotrade Inc* [2001] EWCA Civ 1832 at [26], [2002] 1 All ER 703, [2002] 1 Lloyd's Rep 295 per Simon Brown LJ.

8   *Veba Oil Supply and Trading GmbH v Petrotrade Inc* [2001] EWCA Civ 1832 at [47], [2002] 1 All ER 703, [2002] 1 Lloyd's Rep 295 per Dyson LJ.
9   *Macro v Thompson (No 2)* [1997] 1 BCLC 626, [1996] BCC 707, CA; *Shell UK Ltd v Enterprise Oil plc* [1999] 2 All ER (Comm) 87, [1999] 2 Lloyd's Rep 456; *Veba Oil Supply and Trading GmbH v Petrotrade Inc* [2001] EWCA Civ 1832, [2002] 1 All ER 703, [2002] 1 Lloyd's Rep 295. Even if the expert holds a public office, this does not mean that the challenge must be by way of judicial review: see *Mercury Communications Ltd v Director General of Telecommunications* [1996] 1 All ER 575, [1996] 1 WLR 48, HL; and BUILDING CONTRACTS vol 6 (2011) PARA 501.
10 'Manifest or material error' may comprise 'oversights and blunders so obvious as to admit of no difference of opinion' (*Healds Foods Ltd v Hyde Dairies Ltd* (1 December 1994, unreported), QBD, per Potter J (affd on appeal 6 December 1996, unreported, CA); *Conoco (UK) Ltd v Phillips Petroleum Co (UK) Ltd* (19 August 1996, unreported) per Morison J; *Dixons Group plc v Murray-Oboynski* (1997) 86 BLR 16) or 'oversights and blunders so obvious and obviously capable of affecting the determination as to admit of no difference of opinion' (*Veba Oil Supply and Trading GmbH v Petrotrade Inc* [2001] EWCA Civ 1832 at [33], [2002] 1 All ER 703, [2002] 1 Lloyd's Rep 295 per Simon Brown LJ).
11 *Jones v Sherwood Computer Services plc* [1992] 2 All ER 170, [1992] 1 WLR 277; *Nikko Hotels (UK) Ltd v MEPC plc* [1991] 2 EGLR 103, [1991] 28 EG 86; *Pontsarn Investments v Kansallis-Osake-Pankki* [1992] 1 EGLR 148, [1992] 22 EG 103; *Dixons Group plc v Murray-Oboynski* (1997) 86 BLR 16; *Shell UK Ltd v Enterprise Oil plc* [1999] 2 All ER (Comm) 87, [1999] 2 Lloyd's Rep 456; *Veba Oil Supply and Trading GmbH v Petrotrade Inc* [2001] EWCA Civ 1832, [2002] 1 All ER 703, [2002] 1 Lloyd's Rep 295.
12 *Epoch Properties Ltd v British Home Stores (Jersey) Ltd* [2004] JLR 306, [2004] 3 EGLR 34, Jersey CA.
13 *Morgan Sindall plc v Sawstons Farms (Cambs) Ltd* [1999] 1 EGLR 90, [1999] 07 EG 135, CA; *Doughty Hanson & Co Ltd v Roe* [2007] EWHC 2212 (Ch), [2008] 1 BCLC 404, [2007] All ER (D) 56 (Oct).
14 *National Grid Co plc v M25 Group Ltd* [1999] 1 EGLR 65, [1999] 08 EG 169, CA; *Homepace Ltd v Sita South East Ltd* [2008] EWCA Civ 1, [2008] 1 P & CR 436, [2008] All ER (D) 18 (Jan); *Menolly Investments 3 Sarl v Cerep Sarl* [2009] EWHC 516 (Ch), 125 ConLR 75, [2009] All ER (D) 238 (Mar).
15 *Owen Pell Ltd v Bindi (London) Ltd* [2008] EWHC 1420 (TCC), [2008] BLR 436. As to the principles of natural justice generally see JUDICIAL REVIEW vol 61 (2010) PARAS 629–630.

(6) MISTAKE IN THE EXPRESSION OF INTENTION

33. Instrument in terms contrary to intention. Where the intention of the parties to an otherwise valid transaction is recorded in terms which do not accurately reflect that intention, the court may correct the mistake in the record in order to give effect to the intention. Where the transaction is a unilateral one (for example, a deed poll[1] or a will[2]), the intention concerned is that of the maker alone[3]. Where it is a bilateral or multilateral transaction, in order for the court to correct the document, the intention that must be inaccurately recorded is the common intention of the parties to it[4].

However, the common intention concerned is not necessarily the genuine intention of all parties; the doctrine of estoppel has a role to play[5]. Thus the court may intervene where one party mistakenly believes that the document records his intention, and the other party realises the mistake but says nothing[6]. On the other hand, if the other party does not realise the first party's mistake, the court will not assist[7]. It does not matter whether the mistake involved is one of fact or of law[8]. But it must be proved to a high standard before the court will override what is recorded[9].

The court intervenes in these cases in two main ways:
(1)   applying the rules of construction to interpret the faulty document in the intended sense[10]; and

(2)   rectifying the document so as to make it accord with the intended transaction[11].

Usually these are alternatives, in that, if the true meaning appears on construction there is nothing to rectify, even if sometimes it is unclear which is the appropriate remedy[12]. But rectification may sometimes be granted notwithstanding that the true meaning can be ascertained by construction[13].

There is nothing to prevent a party to the same claim seeking rectification of an agreement and specific performance of the agreement as rectified[14].

1   See PARA 60.
2   See PARA 59.
3   See PARA 53.
4   See PARA 53.
5   See PARA 27.
6   See eg *A Roberts & Co Ltd v Leicestershire County Council* [1961] Ch 555, [1961] 2 All ER 545 (action for rectification allowed).
7   See eg *Riverlate Properties Ltd v Paul* [1975] Ch 133, [1974] 2 All ER 656, CA (action for rescission unsuccessful); *George Wimpey UK Ltd v VIC Construction Ltd* [2005] EWCA Civ 77, [2005] BLR 135, (2005) Times, 16 Feb (action for rectification unsuccessful).
8   See PARA 57.
9   See PARA 57.
10 There are two sets of rules of construction: those relating to inter vivos documents (see CONTRACT vol 22 (2012) PARA 357 et seq) and those relating to wills (see WILLS AND INTESTACY vol 102 (2010) PARA 186 et seq).
11 See PARAS 53–63.
12 *Cowen v Truefitt* [1899] 2 Ch 309, CA.
13 *Standard Portland Cement Co Pty Ltd v Good* (1982) 47 ALR 107, PC.
14 *Craddock Bros v Hunt* [1923] 2 Ch 136, CA; *United States of America v Motor Trucks Ltd* [1924] AC 196, PC; *Dundee Farm Ltd v Bambury Holdings* [1978] 1 NZLR 647, CA. As to specific performance generally see SPECIFIC PERFORMANCE vol 95 (2013) PARA 301 et seq.

3. REMEDIES

(1) RELIEF IN CASES OF MISTAKE

(i) Kinds of Relief Available and When Available

34. Relief available in case of mistake. The relief to be granted in case of mistake may be:

(1)   application of the rules of construction of documents[1];

(2)   refusal of specific performance or of damages for breach of contract[2];

(3)   rescission[3];

(4)   rectification[4];

(5)   recovery of money paid under mistake[5];

(6)   recovery of property transferred under mistake[6]; or

(7)   reopening of settled accounts[7].

In addition to these remedies, a mistaken party may be able to plead the mistake as a defence to a claim on a contract, by showing that, as a result, there was no contract[8], or that he is relieved of liability to perform under it[9]. Such a party may also be able in an appropriate case to seek a declaration of non-liability[10].

The principles of agency have no part to play in the court's approach to the just correction of mistakes in legal transactions[11].

1   As to rules of construction relating to inter vivos documents see CONTRACT vol 22 (2012) PARA 357 et seq; and to rules of construction relating to wills see WILLS AND INTESTACY vol 102 (2010) PARA 186 et seq.

2   See PARA 47.

3   See PARAS 48–52.

4   See PARAS 53–63.

5   See PARAS 64, 65.

6   See PARAS 67, 68.

7   See PARA 66.

8   See PARAS 12–16.

9   See PARAS 18, 21.

10   *Société Maritime et Commerciale v Venus Steam Shipping Co Ltd* (1904) 9 Com Cas 289.

11   See *Secured Residential Funding plc v Douglas Goldberg Hendeles & Co* (2000) Times, 26 April, [2000] All ER (D) 578, CA. As to the principles of agency in general see AGENCY vol 1 (2008) PARA 1 et seq.

35. Proof of causative role of mistake required before relief will be granted. In order to obtain relief on the ground of mistake, the party seeking it must prove that his conduct has been determined by the mistake[1]. If the mistake played no causative part at all[2], and hence his conduct would have been the same even if he had not made the mistake, then he is not entitled to relief[3]. Whether it suffices for the mistake to be causative in this sense, or whether there is a further requirement that it be in some way fundamental, depends on the context in which the matter arises. In the case where mistake is relied on in order to recover money paid, for example, the preponderance of authority requires merely a causative mistake[4]. In order to escape from a contract, by contrast, a great deal more is needed[5].

1   *Carpmael v Powis* (1846) 10 Beav 36 at 43 per Lord Langdale MR (mistake of fact); *Stone v Godfrey* (1854) 5 De GM & G 76 (mistake of law); *Trigge v Lavallee* (1863) 15 Moo PCC 270 at 298 per Lord Langdale MR (mistake of both law and fact); *Bernard & Shaw Ltd v Shaw* [1951] 2 All ER 267; *United Overseas Bank v Jiwani* [1977] 1 All ER 733 at 737, [1976] 1 WLR 964 at 968 per Mackenna J; *North Western Gas Board v Manchester Corpn* (1963) 61 LGR 241 at 250

per Megaw J (revsd on another point [1963] 3 All ER 422, [1964] 1 WLR 64, CA). As to the abolition of the distinction between mistake of law and mistake of fact see PARA 11.

2   The better authority is that the error need merely be an effective cause, not necessarily the sole cause, of the party's action. This is certainly the case with misrepresentation (see eg *Assicurazioni Generali SpA v Arab Insurance Group* [2002] EWCA Civ 1642 at [59], [2003] 1 All ER (Comm) 140, [2003] 1 WLR 577n per Clarke LJ; *Street v Coombes* [2005] EWHC 2290 (Ch) at [93], [2005] All ER (D) 119 (Oct) per Launcelot Henderson QC)) and there is no reason not to apply this reasoning to all mistake. See also MISREPRESENTATION vol 76 (2013) PARA 770.

3   *Holt v Markham* [1923] 1 KB 504 at 515, CA, per Scrutton LJ; *Home and Colonial Insurance Co Ltd v London Guarantee and Accident Co Ltd* (1928) 45 TLR 134; *Robert A Munro & Co v Meyer* [1930] 2 KB 312; *United Overseas Bank v Jiwani* [1977] 1 All ER 733 at 737, [1976] 1 WLR 964 at 968–969 per Mackenna J; *Shamil Bank of Bahrain EC v Beximco Pharmaceuticals Ltd* [2004] EWCA Civ 19 at [60], [2004] 4 All ER 1072, [2004] 1 WLR 1784 per Potter LJ.

4   *Barclays Bank Ltd v WJ Simms, Son and Cooke (Southern) Ltd* [1980] QB 677 at 695, [1979] 3 All ER 522 at 535 per Robert Goff J; *Lloyds Bank plc v Independent Insurance Co Ltd* [2000] QB 110 at 115–116, [1999] 1 All ER (Comm) 8 at 11–12, CA, per Waller LJ. Cf *Dextra Bank & Trust Co Ltd v Bank of Jamaica* [2001] UKPC 50 at [30], [2002] 1 All ER (Comm) 193 per Lord Bingham and Lord Goff. It seems there needs to be a 'causative mistake of sufficient gravity' for a voluntary disposition to be set aside: *Pitt v Holt, Futter v Futter* [2013] UKSC 26 at [122], [2013] 2 AC 108, [2013] 3 All ER 429 per Lord Walker and more recently *Freedman v Freedman* [2015] EWHC 1457 (Ch), [2015] WTLR 1187 (disposition set aside because made under false belief that no adverse tax consequences).

5   *Bell v Lever Bros Ltd* [1932] AC 161, HL; *Great Peace Shipping Ltd v Tsavliris Salvage (International) Ltd), The Great Peace* [2002] EWCA Civ 1407, [2003] QB 679, [2002] 4 All ER 689.

36.   The extent of mistake: instances where relief will be granted. The court may grant relief whether the mistake was due to ignorance[1], misconception[2] or forgetfulness[3]. It is no necessary bar to relief that the party alleging the mistake had the means of knowing the facts[4], but in some contexts such negligence will prevent relief being given[5].

1   *Cocking v Pratt* (1750) 1 Ves Sen 400; *East India Co v Donald* (1804) 9 Ves 275; *Hore v Becher* (1842) 12 Sim 465; *Bell v Gardiner* (1842) 4 Man & G 11; *David Securities Pty Ltd v Commonwealth Bank of Australia* (1992) 175 CLR 353 at 369, 374. Pure ignorance may not suffice for some purposes however: *Pitt v Holt, Futter v Futter* [2013] UKSC 26, [2013] 2 AC 108, [2013] 3 All ER 429 per Lord Walker.

2   *Strickland v Turner* (1852) 7 Exch 208; *Colyer v Clay* (1843) 7 Beav 188; *Cochrane v Willis* (1865) 1 Ch App 58; *Scott v Coulson* [1903] 2 Ch 249, CA; *Harryman v Collins* (1854) 18 Beav 11; *Concoran v Wade* [1913] 1 IR 25. Ignorance may lead to a false belief or assumption which the law will recognise as a mistake: *Pitt v Holt, Futter v Futter* [2013] UKSC 26, [2013] 2 AC 108, [2013] 3 All ER 429 per Lord Walker.

3   *Kelly v Solari* (1841) 9 M & W 54; *Lucas v Worswick* (1833) 1 Mood & R 293; *Lady Hood of Avalon v Mackinnon* [1909] 1 Ch 476; and see *Baker v Courage & Co* [1910] 1 KB 56 at 65 per Hamilton J; cf *Barrow v Isaacs & Son* [1891] 1 QB 417, CA; *Eastern Telegraph Co Ltd v Dent* [1899] 1 QB 835, CA (where relief was refused); *Samuel Properties (Developments) Ltd v Hayek* [1972] 3 All ER 473, [1972] 1 WLR 1296, CA. Forgetfulness is not, as such, a mistake, but it can lead to a false belief or assumption which the law will recognise as a mistake: *Pitt v Holt, Futter v Futter* [2013] UKSC 26, [2013] 2 AC 108, [2013] 3 All ER 429 per Lord Walker.

4   *Kelly v Solari* (1841) 9 M & W 54; *Bell v Gardiner* (1842) 4 Man & G 11; *Brownlie v Campbell* (1880) 5 App Cas 925 at 952, HL, per Lord Hatherley; *Wilmott v Barber* (1880) 15 ChD 96; *Re Chaplin, Milne, Grenfell & Co Ltd* (1914) 31 TLR 279; cf *New Brunswick and Canada Rly and Land Co v Conybeare* (1862) 9 HL Cas 711 at 742, HL, per Lord Chelmsford; *Secretary of State for Employment v Wellworthy (No 2)* [1976] ICR 13.

5   For example, where it is sought to plead mistake to escape from a contract: *Associated Japanese Bank (International) Ltd v Crédit du Nord SA* [1988] 3 All ER 902 at 913, [1989] 1 WLR 255 at 268–269 per Steyn J.

37.   Instances where relief will not be granted. In the following cases the court will not intervene, despite the mistake:

(1)   where, although the parties are not in fact *ad idem*[1], there is a consensus by estoppel which is accurately recorded in any document[2];

(2)   where, although there is a common mistake, the parties' agreement (accurately recorded) on its true construction validly allocates the risk of mistake to one or other party[3];

(3)   where, although there is a mistake against which the court would in principle relieve by rescission or rectification[4], a third party has acquired legal or (possibly) equitable rights in the subject matter of the transaction[5], or in a case of rectification a judgment founded on a particular construction of that document has been given and satisfied[6];

(4)   where, in the case of a claim to rescind a contract, it is impossible to restore the parties substantially to their original position[7];

(5)   where an applicable limitation period has expired or (in the case of an equitable claim to relief) the claimant is guilty of laches[8];

(6)   where, in the case of a claim for relief from a contract, the claimant has acquiesced in the mistake for a long period[9] with knowledge of the relevant facts[10], or has positively affirmed the transaction, for example by taking a benefit under it[11] with knowledge of the facts and relevant law[12].

The fact that an agreement for sale or lease of land has been carried into execution by conveyance is not of itself a bar to rescission if this is otherwise justified[13]. By statute, moreover, the same is true for contracts generally, at least where misrepresentation is in issue[14].

1   Ie of the same mind.
2   See PARA 33.
3   See PARA 19.
4   As to rescission see PARAS 48–52. As to rectification see PARAS 53–63 et seq.
5   See PARA 38.
6   See PARA 46.
7   See PARA 39.
8   See PARA 45.
9   *Rogers v Ingham* (1876) 3 ChD 351 at 357, CA, per Mellish LJ; *Re Hulkes, Powell v Hulkes* (1886) 33 ChD 552 at 561 per Chitty J.
10 *Holder v Holder* [1968] Ch 353, [1968] 1 All ER 665, CA; *Re Freeston's Charity* [1979] 1 All ER 51 at 62, [1978] 1 WLR 741 at 754, CA, per Goff LJ.
11 See *Clough v London and North Western Rly Co* (1871) LR 7 Exch 26.
12 See *Peyman v Lanjani* [1985] Ch 457, [1984] 3 All ER 703, CA.
13 *Jones v Clifford* (1876) 3 ChD 779; *Debenham v Sawbridge* [1901] 2 Ch 98 at 109 per Byrne J; *Scott v Coulson* [1903] 2 Ch 249, CA; cf *Svanioso v McNamara* (1956) 96 CLR 186 at 198–199; and see CONVEYANCING vol 23 (2013) PARA 462 et seq.
14 Misrepresentation Act 1967 s 1. See also MISREPRESENTATION vol 76 (2013) PARAS 703, 816.

38. Effect of third party rights. The court will not intervene to set aside a transaction or to rectify a document on the ground of mistake as against a third party who has become a purchaser for value of a legal estate or interest without notice[1]. For this purpose, the assignee of a lease who assumes liability for the tenant's covenants and gives an indemnity to him for their due performance is a purchaser for value[2]. On the other hand a claim to rescind or to rectify for mistake is not defeated by a volunteer who acquires a legal (or equitable) interest, even without notice[3].

The authorities dealing with the case where a third party acquires an equitable interest for value without notice are unsettled. On one side there are cases referring to the right to rescind or to rectify as a 'mere equity' which is said to be defeated by even an equitable purchaser for value[4]. On the other side there are cases treating such rights as interests in the land[5], which on principle should not be defeated by the purchaser, even without notice, of merely an equitable interest[6]. But the matter is complicated by the fact that the original owner, by handing over deeds or other indicia of title to the other party (who thereafter deals as apparent owner with the third party), may nevertheless be estopped, as against the third party, from asserting his own interest[7], and, since this principle applies in equity as at law[8], such estoppels may explain the original authorities[9].

A member of a company pension scheme who has provided consideration for the benefits thereunder can be a purchaser for value, at least for some purposes[10]. Usually, however, such a person has no expectation of receiving enhanced benefits through a mistake, and gives no additional consideration for such enhancement, and hence cannot claim to be a purchaser for value preventing rectification[11].

1   *Garrard v Frankel* (1862) 30 Beav 445 at 459–460 per Sir John Romilly MR; *Smith v Jones* [1954] 2 All ER 823, [1954] 1 WLR 1089. The same applies to rescission for fraud: see eg *Phillips v Brooks Ltd* [1919] 2 KB 243; *Lewis v Averay* [1972] 1 QB 198, [1971] 3 All ER 907, CA. As to purchasers for value without notice see EQUITABLE JURISDICTION vol 47 (2014) PARAS 119 et seq, 130 et seq. See also CONVEYANCING vol 23 (2013) PARA 191.
2   *Harris v Tubb* (1889) 42 ChD 79; *Nurdin & Peacock plc v DB Ramsden & Co* [1999] 1 All ER 941, [1999] 1 WLR 1249.
3   *Load v Green* (1846) 15 M & W 216; *Scholefield v Templer* (1859) 4 De G & J 429; *Re Eastgate* [1905] 1 KB 465; *Car and Universal Finance Co Ltd v Caldwell* [1965] 1 QB 525, [1964] 1 All ER 290, CA.
4   *Phillips v Phillips* (1861) 4 De GF & J 208; *Ernest v Vivian* (1863) 33 LJCh 513; *Cave v Cave* (1880) 15 ChD 639; *Latec Investments Ltd v Hotel Terrigal Pty Ltd* (1965) 113 CLR 265.
5   *Stump v Gaby* (1852) 2 De GM & G 623; *Gresley v Mousley* (1859) 4 De G & J 78; *Dickinson v Burrell* (1866) LR 1 Eq 337; *Re Sherman, Re Walters, Trevenen v Pearce* [1954] Ch 653, [1954] 1 All ER 893; *Blacklocks v JB Developments (Godalming) Ltd* [1982] Ch 183 at 196, [1981] 3 All ER 392 at 400 per Mervyn Davies J; *Nurdin & Peacock plc v DB Ramsden & Co* [1999] 1 All ER 941, [1999] 1 WLR 1249.
6   *Eyre v Burmester* (1862) 10 HL Cas 90.
7   *Pickard v Sears* (1837) 6 Ad & El 469; *Eastern Distributors Ltd v Goldring* [1957] 2 QB 600, [1957] 2 All ER 525, CA; *Moorgate Mercantile Co Ltd v Twitchings* [1976] QB 225 at 242, [1975] 3 All ER 314 at 323, CA, per Lord Denning MR (on appeal [1977] AC 890, [1976] 2 All ER 641, HL).
8   Ashburner *Principles of Equity* (2nd Edn, 1933) p 57; *Earl Aldborough v Trye* (1840) 7 Cl & Fin 436 at 463–464, HL, per Lord Cottenham LC; *Rice v Rice* (1854) 2 Drew 73 at 83; *Rimmer v Webster* [1902] 2 Ch 163 at 173–174 per Farwell J.
9   See in particular *Phillips v Phillips* (1861) 4 De GF & J 208 at 217 per Lord Campbell LC; cf *Eyre v Burmester* (1862) 10 HL Cas 90.
10 See *Kerr v British Leyland (Staff) Trustees Ltd* [1986] CA Transcript 286, CA; *Stannard v Fisons Pensions Trust Ltd* [1992] IRLR 27 at 31, [1991] PLR 225 at 232, CA, per Dillon LJ; *Imperial Group Pension Trust Ltd v Imperial Tobacco Ltd* [1991] 2 All ER 597 at 605–606, [1991] 1 WLR 589 at 597, per Browne-Wilkinson V-C; *McDonald v Horn* [1995] 1 All ER 961 at 972–973, [1995] ICR 685 at 695, CA, per Hoffmann LJ.
11 See *AMP (UK) Ltd plc v Barker* (2000) 3 ITELR 414 at [77]–[79] per Lawrence Collins J; *Gallaher Ltd v Gallaher Pensions Ltd* [2005] EWHC 42 (Ch) at [147], [2005] All ER (D) 177 (Jan) per Etherton J.

39. Where restitutio in integrum impossible. Equity will not generally award rescission[1] of a mistaken transaction where it is impossible to restore the parties to substantially their original positions[2]. However, relief will not be denied in a proper case where it is merely difficult to do so[3]. Where substantial, but not precise, restoration is possible the court may order rescission on the basis of restoring the parties so far as practically possible to do so[4]. For this purpose ancillary relief may be granted, such as an account of profits[5], or an allowance for work done[6], or a sum paid for benefits enjoyed[7]. In Australia[8], but not in England[9], a transaction may be rescinded pro tanto, that is, to reduce it to a level free from the vitiating factor. It seems that the practicality of making restitution in these cases is to be considered as at the time of judgment[10].

1   As to rescission see PARAS 48–52.

2 *Blackburn v Smith* (1848) 2 Exch 783; *Re Saxon Life Assurance Society* (1862) 2 John & H 408 (affd 1 De GJ & Sm 29); *Bateman v Boynton* (1866) 1 Ch App 359 at 367 per Turner LJ; *Erlanger v New Sombrero Phosphate Co* (1878) 3 App Cas 1218, HL; *Thorpe v Fasey* [1949] Ch 649, [1949] 2 All ER 393, HL. Cf however *Smith New Court Securities Ltd v Citibank NA* [1997] AC 254 at 262, sub nom *Smith New Court Securities Ltd v Scrimgeour Vickers (Asset Management) Ltd* [1996] 4 All ER 769 at 774 per Lord Browne-Wilkinson. See also CONTRACT vol 22 (2012) PARA 553.
3 *Earl Beauchamp v Winn* (1873) LR 6 HL 223 at 232 per Lord Chelmsford.
4 *Newbigging v Adam* (1886) 34 ChD 582, CA (on appeal sub nom *Adam v Newbigging* (1888) 13 App Cas 308, HL); *Alati v Kruger* (1955) 94 CLR 216 at 223–224; *Vadasz v Pioneer Concrete (SA) Pty Ltd* (1995) 184 CLR 102.
5 *Erlanger v New Sombrero Phosphate Co* (1878) 3 App Cas 1218, HL.
6 *O'Sullivan v Management Agency and Music Ltd* [1985] QB 428, [1985] 3 All ER 351, CA.
7 *Hulton v Hulton* [1917] 1 KB 813 at 826, CA, per Scrutton LJ; *Midland Bank plc v Greene* [1994] 2 FLR 827, (1993) 27 HLR 350.
8 *Vadasz v Pioneer Concrete (SA) Pty Ltd* (1995) 184 CLR 102.
9 *TSB Bank plc v Camfield* [1995] 1 All ER 951, [1995] 1 WLR 430, CA; but cf *Barclays Bank plc v Caplan* [1998] 1 FLR 532, 78 P & CR 153.
10 See Meagher, Gummow and Lehane *Equity—Doctrines and Remedies* (5th Edn, 2015) para 25-100, and the cases there cited.

(ii) Evidence on which Relief will be Granted

40. Position at common law. At common law, oral evidence is not in general admissible to show that a written contract, interpreted according to the ordinary rules of construction, does not express the true and complete intention of the parties[1]. So, at common law, if an agreement is ambiguous, oral evidence as to the intention of the parties with a view to showing that some term or word has been inserted or omitted by mistake is inadmissible[2]. However, when there is a latent ambiguity in the agreement, oral evidence may be received for the purpose of explaining what the parties to an agreement meant[3]. When there is a patent ambiguity, that is, an ambiguity on the face of the instrument itself, the instrument may be void for uncertainty[4].

1 See CONTRACT vol 22 (2012) PARA 288; EQUITABLE JURISDICTION vol 47 (2014) PARA 40.
2 *Hitchin v Groom* (1848) 5 CB 515.
3 *Hitchin v Groom* (1848) 5 CB 515 at 520 per Wilde CJ. See also DEEDS AND OTHER INSTRUMENTS vol 32 (2012) PARA 409.
4 See DEEDS AND OTHER INSTRUMENTS vol 32 (2012) PARA 408.

41. Equitable rules. In equity, oral evidence is admissible to make out a case for rectification or rescission of an instrument[1], or to show that what purports to be an agreement is not in fact an agreement at all, for example, where it has been signed by mistake[2]. In such cases the evidence is admissible, not to contradict what appears on the face of the agreement (which the court will not allow), but to prove the existence of a mistake which could not otherwise be proved[3]. Similarly, where mistake cannot be established without evidence, equity will allow a defendant in a claim for specific performance to support a defence founded on mistake by evidence outside the agreement[4], the evidence being introduced not to explain nor alter the agreement, but consistently with its terms, to show circumstances of mistake or fraud which would make the specific performance of the contract as executed unjust[5].

1 *Dowager Countess of Shelburne v Earl of Inchiquin* (1784) 1 Bro CC 338 at 341 per Lord Thurlow LC (on appeal sub nom *Earl of Inchinquin v Fitzmaurice* (1875) 5 Bro Parl Cas 166); *Baker v Paine* (1750) 1 Ves Sen 456; *Stait v Fenner* [1912] 2 Ch 504 at 519 per Neville J; *Shipley UDC v Bradford Corpn* [1936] Ch 375 at 394–395 per Clauson J (on appeal [1936] Ch 399n, 154 LT 444, CA); *Joscelyne v Nissen* [1970] 2 QB 86, [1970] 1 All ER 1213, CA; *Chartbrook Ltd v*

Persimmon Homes Ltd [2009] UKHL 38 at [42], [2009] AC 1101, [2009] 4 All ER 677 per Lord Hoffmann. As to rescission see PARAS 48–52. As to rectification see PARAS 53–63.

2 *Pym v Campbell* (1856) 6 E & B 370 at 374 per Crompton J; and see *Pattle v Hornibrook* [1897] 1 Ch 25 at 30 per Stirling J.

3 *Baker v Paine* (1750) 1 Ves Sen 456 at 457 per Hardwicke LC; and see DEEDS AND OTHER INSTRUMENTS vol 32 (2012) PARAS 389–390.

4 *Marquis of Townshend v Stangroom* (1801) 6 Ves 328; *Clarke v Grant* (1807) 14 Ves 519 at 524–525; *Ramsbottom v Gosden* (1812) 1 Ves & B 165 at 168 per Sir William Grant MR; *Clowes v Higginson* (1813) 1 Ves & B 524 at 527; *Malins v Freeman* (1837) 2 Keen 25, (1837) 48 ER 537; *Manser v Back* (1848) 6 Hare 443 at 448; *Wood v Scarth* (1855) 2 K & J 33.

5 *Clowes v Higginson* (1813) 1 Ves & B 524 at 527 per Sir Thomas Plumer V-C. As to specific performance see PARA 47.

42. Effect of antecedent written agreement. If there is a previous written agreement which is unambiguous, the disputed instrument will be re-formed in accordance with it, and, if the agreement is ambiguous, oral evidence may be used to explain it according to the ordinary rules applicable in cases of ambiguity[1]. Where the original agreement is of doubtful construction and the conveyance is definite and unequivocal, it is not easy to avoid the conclusion that the conveyance may be the best evidence of the actual agreement between the parties[2]. If the previous written agreement is clear but is vitiated by the same mistake as is complained of in the instrument, that mistake may be proved by extrinsic evidence, and then the court will rectify the instrument to make it correspond with the real agreement[3]. However, where such a previous agreement is negatived by a mistake it cannot be a basis for rectification[4].

1 *Murray v Parker* (1854) 19 Beav 305 at 308 per Sir John Romilly MR. The Court of Appeal has stated that it would be inappropriate to stretch the rules of interpretation to achieve this end where rectification is the obvious remedy: *Cherry Tree Investments Ltd v Landmain Ltd* [2012] EWCA Civ 736 at [32]–[38], [2013] Ch 305, [2013] 2 WLR 481 per Lewison LJ.

2 *Humphries v Horne* (1844) 3 Hare 276 at 278.

3 *Craddock Bros v Hunt* [1923] 2 Ch 136, CA; *United States of America v Motor Trucks Ltd* [1924] AC 196 at 201–202, PC.

4 *Monaghan County Council v Vaughan* [1948] IR 306 at 315 per Dixon J. As to rectification see PARAS 53–63.

43. Limitations on relief on oral evidence only. The court is always more cautious about rectifying a document on oral evidence alone[1]. If there is nothing but the recollection of witnesses whose reliability is doubted by the court, and the defendant denies the case set up by the claimant, the claimant may be without remedy[2]. Yet a mistake may nonetheless be rectified where it is clearly proved by oral evidence, even though there is nothing in writing to which the oral evidence may attach[3]. The court may order rectification[4] or rescission[5] on the ground of mistake on the claimant's evidence alone where no further evidence can be obtained, but it requires clear and distinct evidence that there was a different intention when the document was executed[6]. The court is more willing to correct a deed by oral evidence when there is anything in writing beyond the oral evidence[7]. In nearly all cases in which the court has re-formed a settlement, there has been something beyond the oral evidence, such as the instructions for preparing the conveyance or a note by the attorney, and the mistake has been properly accounted for[8].

1 *Alexander v Crosbie* (1835) L & G temp Sugd 145 at 149 per Sir Edward Burtenshaw Sugden LC. See also *Barrow v Barrow* (1854) 18 Beav 529 (on appeal 5 De GM & G 782, CA); *Kemp v Rose* (1858) 1 Giff 258 at 266; *Meeking v Meeking* (1916) as reported in 115 LT 623.

2 *Mortimer v Shortall* (1842) 2 Dr & War 363; and see *Lord Irnham v Child* (1781) 1 Bro CC 92 at 93 per Lord Thurlow LC; *Marquis of Townshend v Stangroom* (1801) 6 Ves 328 at 334 per

Lord Eldon LC; *Fowler v Fowler* (1859) 4 De G & J 250 at 274 per Lord Chelmsford LC; *Bentley v Mackay* (1862) 4 De GF & J 279 at 287 per Turner LJ; *Bloomer v Spittle* (1872) LR 13 Eq 427 at 431 per Lord Romilly MR.

3   *Alexander v Crosbie* (1835) L & G temp Sugd 145 at 150; *Barrow v Barrow* (1854) 18 Beav 529 at 532 per Sir John Romilly MR; *M'Cormack v M'Cormack* (1877) 1 LR Ir 119, CA; *Cook v Fearn* (1878) 48 LJ Ch 63. The oral evidence must point to a continuing intention different from that which was expressed. Whether the continuing intention need be proved objectively, from the point of view of a hypothetical third party observer, or subjectively, from the point of view of the parties themselves, remains uncertain: compare *Britoil plc v Hunt Overseas Oil Inc* [1994] CLC 561, CA with *Chartbrook Ltd v Persimmon Homes Ltd* [2009] UKHL 38, [2009] AC 1101, [2009] 4 All ER 677. As to the effect on rectification of an 'entire agreement' clause see *Procter & Gamble Co v Svenska Cellulosa Aktiebolaget* [2012] EWHC 498 (Ch), [2012] All ER (D) 73 (Mar).

4   *Hanley v Pearson* (1879) 13 ChD 545; *Cook v Fearn* (1878) 48 LJ Ch 63; and see *Smith v Iliffe* (1875) LR 20 Eq 666; *Re Colebrook's Conveyances, Taylor v Taylor* [1973] 1 All ER 132, [1972] 1 WLR 1397. As to rectification see PARAS 53–63.

5   *Lady Hood of Avalon v Mackinnon* [1909] 1 Ch 476. As to rescission see PARAS 48–52.

6   *Tucker v Bennett* (1887) 38 ChD 1 at 15, CA, per Cotton LJ; *Bonhote v Henderson* [1895] 2 Ch 202, CA; *Fredensen v Rothschild* [1941] 1 All ER 430.

7   *Mortimer v Shortall* (1842) 2 Dr & War 363.

8   *Alexander v Crosbie* (1835) L & G temp Sugd 145 at 149 per Sir Edward Burtenshaw Sugden LC; and see *Mortimer v Shortall* (1842) 2 Dr & War 363 at 374 per Sir Edward Burtenshaw Sugden LC; *M'Cormack v M'Cormack* (1877) 1 LR Ir 119; *Welman v Welman* (1880) 15 ChD 570 at 576 per Malins V-C; *Johnson v Bragge* [1901] 1 Ch 28; *Re Butlin's Settlement Trusts, Butlin v Butlin* [1976] Ch 251, [1976] 2 All ER 483.

44.   Contracts required to be in writing. Oral evidence is admissible to make out a case for rectification of a contract[1] if there are no written instructions in existence[2] and notwithstanding statutory provisions requiring contracts to be in writing[3], and also notwithstanding that the party who adduces that evidence is claiming specific performance of the rectified contract[4]. The contract when rectified becomes a document sufficient to satisfy the statutory requirements[5].

1   *Barrow v Barrow* (1854) 18 Beav 529 (on appeal 5 De GM & G 782, CA); *Johnson v Bragge* [1901] 1 Ch 28. As to rectification see PARAS 53–63.

2   *Lackersteen v Lackersteen* (1860) 30 LJ Ch 5.

3   See *Thomas v Davis* (1757) 1 Dick 301 at 303 per Sir Thomas Clarke MR; *Rogers v Earl* (1757) 1 Dick 294; *Re Boulter, ex p National Provincial Bank of England* (1876) 4 ChD 241; *Johnson v Bragge* [1901] 1 Ch 28. As to such statutory provisions see CONTRACT vol 22 (2012) PARA 222 et seq.

4   *Craddock Bros v Hunt* [1923] 2 Ch 136, CA; *United States of America v Motor Trucks Ltd* [1924] AC 196 at 201, PC; *Whiting v Diver Plumbing and Heating Ltd* [1992] 1 NZLR 560. As to specific performance see PARA 47.

5   *Craddock Bros v Hunt* [1923] 2 Ch 136, CA; *United States of America v Motor Trucks Ltd* [1924] AC 196 at 201, PC; *Whiting v Diver Plumbing and Heating Ltd* [1992] 1 NZLR 560.

(iii)   Effect on Relief for Mistake of Lapse of Time and Satisfaction of Judgments

45.   When lapse of time is a bar. In relation to lapse of time, there are three matters to consider: (1) lapse of time in itself; (2) statutory limitation periods; and (3) laches.

Lapse of time may sometimes in practice be a bar to rectification[1] on account of the lack of evidence and the doubt arising from it[2], or may afford evidence of acquiescence[3], but the mere lapse of time of itself, even if a long period, will not be a bar to an equitable remedy if the mistake is clearly made out[4]. The time to be considered is the date of the notice of the error and not the date when the error was made[5].

Statutory periods of limitation in claims for relief from the consequences of mistake run from the date of discovery of the mistake or the date on which it could by the exercise of reasonable diligence have been discovered[6], unless the claim is in respect of property to which a third person has acquired rights by purchase for value without knowledge of the mistake or reason to believe it had been made[7]. In the latter case, it seems, time runs from the date on which the original cause of the claim accrued. Where the discovery of a mistake is the result of judicial interpretation of a statutory provision, the date of discovery for these purposes is the date of the decision[8]. But the limitation periods for claims founded on tort[9], claims founded on simple contract[10], claims for libel or slander[11], claims to enforce awards[12], claims on a specialty[13], claims to recover sums under statute[14] and claims to enforce judgments[15] do not apply to claims for equitable relief except in so far as they may be applied by the court by analogy, as they would have been prior to the coming into operation of the Limitation Act 1939[16]. In such cases, the statutory limitation period does not absolutely bind the courts, but they adopt it to assist their discretion[17].

Nothing in the Limitation Act 1980 affects the equitable jurisdiction to refuse relief on the ground of acquiescence, or otherwise[18]. 'Acquiescence' refers to the case where a person whose rights are being infringed stands by and takes no action, so that the infringer believes that his infringement is being sanctioned[19]. This is an equitable form of estoppel[20]. The alternative expression refers to laches, that is, negligent inactivity[21]. This will only operate where there is no statutory bar, whether express or by analogy[22]. Laches arises where the infringer's circumstances have changed so that it would be inequitable to assert rights as a result of the inactivity of the person whose rights have been infringed[23], following notice by that person of the mistake[24]. A purchaser of an estate or interest to which equitable rights (to rescission or rectification) attach is in no better position, so far as laches is concerned, than is his vendor[25].

1 *Bloomer v Spittle* (1872) LR 13 Eq 427 (questioned in *Beale v Kyte* [1907] 1 Ch 564). As to rectification see PARAS 53–63.
2 *Wolterbeek v Barrow* (1857) 23 Beav 423.
3 *Life Association of Scotland v Siddal* (1861) 3 De GF & J 58 at 72 per Turner LJ.
4 *Wolterbeek v Barrow* (1857) 23 Beav 423 at 431 per Sir John Romilly MR; *Tull v Owen* (1840) 4 Y & C Ex 192 at 203–204; *Millar v Craig* (1843) 6 Beav 433; *M'Cormack v M'Cormack* (1877) 1 LR Ir 119, CA; *Fullwood v Fullwood* (1878) 9 ChD 176; *Re Garnett, Gandy v Macaulay* (1885) 31 ChD 1, CA; *Allcard v Skinner* (1887) 36 ChD 145 at 175, CA, per Cotton LJ; *Burroughes v Abbott* [1922] 1 Ch 86; *Weld v Petre* [1929] 1 Ch 33, CA; *Eason v Brownrigg* [1998] CLY 3659. See also *Gallaher Ltd v Gallaher Pensions Ltd* [2005] EWHC 42 (Ch) at [159]–[160], [2005] All ER (D) 177 (Jan) per Etherton J (undertakings given removing all possible prejudice).
5 *Beale v Kyte* [1907] 1 Ch 564; *Corcoran v Wade* [1913] 1 IR 25.
6 See the Limitation Act 1980 s 32(1)(c) (amended by the Consumer Protection Act 1987 Sch 1 para 5); and LIMITATION PERIODS vol 68 (2008) PARA 1230.
7 See the Limitation Act 1980 s 32(3), (4); and LIMITATION PERIODS vol 68 (2008) PARA 1222.
8 *Deutsche Morgan Grenfell Group plc v IRC* [2006] UKHL 49, [2007] 1 AC 558, [2007] 1 All ER 449.
9 See the Limitation Act 1980 s 2; and LIMITATION PERIODS vol 68 (2008) PARA 979.
10 See the Limitation Act 1980 s 5; and LIMITATION PERIODS vol 68 (2008) PARA 952.
11 See the Limitation Act 1980 s 4A; and LIMITATION PERIODS vol 68 (2008) PARA 996.
12 See the Limitation Act 1980 s 7; and LIMITATION PERIODS vol 68 (2008) PARA 974.
13 See the Limitation Act 1980 s 8; and LIMITATION PERIODS vol 68 (2008) PARA 975.
14 See the Limitation Act 1980 s 9; and LIMITATION PERIODS vol 68 (2008) PARA 952.
15 See the Limitation Act 1980 s 24; and LIMITATION PERIODS vol 68 (2008) PARA 1010.
16 See the Limitation Act 1980 s 36(1) (amended by the Administration of Justice Act 1985 s 57(5); the Defamation Act 1996 s 5(1), (5), (6)); and LIMITATION PERIODS vol 68 (2008) PARA 919. The Limitation Act 1939 (which consolidated the earlier enactments concerned with the limitation

of actions and was itself consolidated into the Limitation Act 1980) came into operation on 1 July 1940 (see the Limitation Act 1939 s 34(2) (repealed)).

17 *Brooksbank v Smith* (1836) 2 Y & C Ex 58 at 60 per Alderson B; *Knox v Gye* (1872) LR 5 HL 656 at 674 per Lord Westbury.

18 Limitation Act 1980 s 36(2) (see LIMITATION PERIODS vol 68 (2008) PARA 919).

19 *Duke of Leeds v Earl of Amherst* (1846) 2 Ph 117 at 123 per Lord Cottenham LC.

20 *De Bussche v Alt* (1878) 8 ChD 286 at 314, CA, per Thesiger LJ.

21 Co Litt 380b; *Smith v Clay* (1767) 3 Bro CC 639n; *Partridge v Partridge* [1894] 1 Ch 351 at 360 per North J. As to laches generally see EQUITABLE JURISDICTION vol 47 (2014) PARA 253 et seq.

22 *Archbold v Scully* (1861) 9 HL Cas 360; *Re Pauling's Settlement Trusts, Younghusband v Coutts & Co* [1961] 3 All ER 713 at 735, [1962] 1 WLR 86 at 115 per Wilberforce J (affd [1964] Ch 303 at 353, [1963] 3 All ER 1 at 20, CA, per Upjohn LJ).

23 *Lindsay Petroleum Co v Hurd* (1874) LR 5 PC 221 at 239–240, PC; *Erlanger v New Sombrero Phosphate Co* (1878) 3 App Cas 1218 at 1279, HL, per Lord Blackburn; *Orr v Ford* (1989) 167 CLR 316 at 330–346; *Frawley v Neill* (1999) 143 Sol Jo LB 98, (1999) Times, 5 April, CA.

24 *Beale v Kyte* [1907] 1 Ch 564 at 566 per Neville J.

25 *Ernest v Vivian* (1863) 33 LJ Ch 513 at 517–518. As to rescission see PARAS 48–52. As to rectification see PARAS 53–63.

46. Effect of judgment or award. After money has been paid under a judgment of a court of competent jurisdiction founded on a particular construction of an agreement and the judgment has thereby been satisfied, it is too late to bring a claim to rectify the agreement on the ground that such a construction was contrary to the intention of all parties[1]. But where rectification is outside the terms of a submission to an arbitrator who makes an award, rectification may later be claimed in a claim to enforce that award[2].

1 *Caird v Moss* (1886) 33 ChD 22, CA; and see EQUITABLE JURISDICTION vol 47 (2014) PARA 40.

2 *Crane v Hegeman-Harris Co Inc* [1939] 1 All ER 662, [1971] 1 WLR 1390n; affd [1939] 4 All ER 68, CA.

(2) SPECIFIC PERFORMANCE

47. Mistake as a defence to a suit for specific performance. Specific performance is equitable relief, given by the court to enforce against a defendant the duty of doing what he agreed by contract to do[1]. Where a contract is void, no question of specific performance (or of damages[2]) arises. On the other hand, if a contract is valid, but the defendant was mistaken in some way (ex hypothesi insufficient to avoid the contract), the court may in its discretion refuse to award specific performance to the claimant[3], and may leave him to his remedy of damages at law[4]. But the court will only do so where a hardship amounting to injustice would have been inflicted on him by holding the defendant to his bargain[5]. Even then the court may award specific performance to some lesser extent which avoids the hardship[6], or specific performance may be granted on terms[7], or with an abatement (or increase) of the purchase price[8].

1 As to specific performance generally see SPECIFIC PERFORMANCE vol 95 (2013) PARA 301 et seq.

2 As to damages generally see DAMAGES vol 29 (2014) PARA 301 et seq.

3 *Bligh v Martin* [1968] 1 All ER 1157 at 1162, [1968] 1 WLR 804 at 814 per Pennycuick J; *Heath v Heath* [2009] EWHC 1908 (Ch) at [26], [2009] Fam Law 1044, [2009] P & CR D58 per Purle J.

4 See eg *Malins v Freeman* (1837) 2 Keen 25, (1837) 48 ER 537; *Wood v Scarth* (1855) 2 K & J 33.

5 *Tamplin v James* (1880) 15 ChD 215 at 221, CA, per James LJ; *Slee v Warke* (1949) 86 CLR 271 at 278; *Fragomeni v Fogliani* (1968) 42 ALJR 263.

6 *Preston v Luck* (1884) 27 ChD 497, CA.

7 *Baskcomb v Beckwith* (1869) LR 8 Eq 100 (plaintiff obliged to enter restrictive covenant); *Grist v Bailey* [1967] Ch 532, [1966] 2 All ER 875 (defendant to enter into fresh contract at a proper price, if required by the plaintiff).

8   *Cato v Thompson* (1882) 9 QBD 616, CA; *Re Aspinall and Powell's Contract* (1889) 5 TLR 446; *Rudd v Lascelles* [1900] 1 Ch 815; *Jacobs v Revell* [1900] 2 Ch 858; *Watson v Burton* [1956] 3 All ER 929, [1957] 1 WLR 19.

(3) RESCISSION

48.   Rescission as a remedy. The term 'rescission' bears a number of meanings in English law[1]. This is apt to cause confusion[2]. For the purposes of this title it refers to the process by which a transaction, valid at law, is set aside by a court of equity for mistake[3]. In considering rescission as a remedy, it must be remembered that before 1875 courts of equity exercised a number of different jurisdictions[4]. These included: (1) that which was concurrent with courts of common law (for example, cases of fraud); (2) that which was auxiliary to the common law (for example, bills of discovery); and (3) that which was exclusive to equity (for example, trusts)[5]. Equitable remedies, including rescission, might be available in all of these, but authorities on rescission in one of these jurisdictions are not necessarily determinative in others[6], and authorities dealing with rescission for misrepresentation[7] may not necessarily govern rescission for mistake, as rescission in the former case was the act of the innocent party[8], whereas in the latter it was the act of the court[9].

If the mistake was such as to prevent property passing, whether at law or in equity, rescission has nothing to do with the matter[10].

1   See CONTRACT vol 22 (2012) PARA 553.
2   *Mersey Steel and Iron Co v Naylor, Benzon & Co* (1882) 9 QBD 648 at 671, CA, per Lindley LJ; *Buckland v Farmer and Moody* [1978] 3 All ER 929 at 938, [1979] 1 WLR 221 at 231–232, CA, per Buckley LJ; *Johnson v Agnew* [1980] AC 367 at 396–398, [1979] 1 All ER 883 at 892–894, HL, per Lord Wilberforce; *Photo Productions Ltd v Securicor Transport Ltd* [1980] AC 827 at 844, [1980] 1 All ER 556 at 562, HL, per Lord Wilberforce.
3   See eg *Cooper v Phibbs* (1867) LR 2 HL 149.
4   The Supreme Court of Judicature Acts 1873 and 1875 brought together the administration of law and equity: see EQUITABLE JURISDICTION vol 47 (2014) PARA 1.
5   Story *Equity Jurisprudence* ss 75–76, 960, 1480; Snell *Equity* (33rd Edn, 2015) paras 1-015–1-031; 1 Holdsworth's History of English Law pp 453–469; Meagher, Gummow and Lehane *Equity—Doctrines and Remedies* (5th Edn, 2015) paras 1-090–1-110.
6   Sugden *Vendors and Purchasers* (14th Edn, 1862) pp 797–798. See also *Alati v Kruger* (1955) 94 CLR 216 at 223–224; *O'Sullivan v Management Agency and Music Ltd* [1985] 3 All ER 351 at 364–365, CA, per Dunn LJ; Meagher, Gummow and Lehane *Equity—Doctrines and Remedies* (5th Edn, 2015) paras 25-095–25-110.
7   As to rescission for misrepresentation see MISREPRESENTATION vol 76 (2013) PARA 811.
8   *Reese River Silver Mining Co v Smith Ltd* (1869) LR 4 HL 64; *Abram Steamship Co Ltd v Westville Shipping Co Ltd* [1923] AC 773, HL.
9   *Cooper v Phibbs* (1867) LR 2 HL 149.
10 See PARAS 24–26, 67, 68.

49.   Rescission for mistake. Historically it is doubtful that equity had any role in setting aside mistaken transactions, other than to follow the law[1]. It is true that from the mid-twentieth century a line of authorities evolved which suggested that it had a wider jurisdiction[2], stating that equity could not only set aside a transaction for mistake on grounds which, if they existed at law, would result in the parties being not liable to perform[3], but could do so also on grounds which would not have that effect at law. But these were discountenanced by the Court of Appeal at the start of this century, when that court decided definitively that there was in fact no jurisdiction to grant rescission of a contract on the ground of common mistake where that contract was valid and enforceable on ordinary principles of common law[4].

These authorities had also asserted a power to set aside transactions, in the exercise of discretion, on terms[5] going beyond restitutio in integrum[6] or the taking of accounts[7]. This assertion must now, however, be considered afresh: the authorities were based on precedent which would not bear their weight[8]; one has been expressly disapproved by the Court of Appeal[9]; and others have been strongly doubted[10].

There is also authority that there is no equitable jurisdiction to grant rescission of a contract where one party has made a unilateral mistake as to a fact or state of affairs which is the basis upon which the terms of the contract are agreed, but that assumption does not become a term of the contract[11].

1   *Stewart v Stewart* (1839) 6 Cl & Fin 911 at 968, HL, per Lord Cottenham LC; *Re Tyrell, Tyrell v Woodhouse* (1900) 82 LT 675; cf Story *Equity Jurisprudence* Ch V; and see Meagher, Gummow and Lehane, *Equity—Doctrines and Remedies* (5th Edn, 2015) paras 14-065–14-080.
2   See *Solle v Butcher* [1950] 1 KB 671 at 692–693, [1949] 2 All ER 1107 at 1119–1120, CA, per Denning LJ; *Magee v Pennine Insurance Co Ltd* [1969] 2 QB 507 at 514, [1969] 2 All ER 891 at 893, CA, per Lord Denning MR; *Associated Japanese Bank (International) Ltd v Crédit du Nord SA* [1988] 3 All ER 902 at 914, [1989] 1 WLR 255 at 270 per Steyn J; *William Sindall plc v Cambridgeshire County Council* [1994] 3 All ER 932 at 959, [1994] 1 WLR 1016 at 1042, CA, per Evans LJ.
3   Eg *Cooper v Phibbs* (1867) LR 2 HL 149.
4   See *Great Peace Shipping Ltd v Tsavliris Salvage (International) Ltd, The Great Peace* [2002] EWCA Civ 1407 at [157], [2003] QB 679, [2002] 4 All ER 689 per Lord Phillips of Worth Matravers MR (disapproving *Solle v Butcher* [1950] 1 KB 671, [1949] 2 All ER 1107, CA). The court held that the decision in *Solle v Butcher* above, and the cases which followed it (see the text and notes 2, 3), amounted less to an equitable mitigation of the common law rule established in *Bell v Lever Bros Ltd* [1932] AC 161, HL (that mistake will not avoid a contract unless it renders its subject matter essentially and radically different from that which the parties had believed to exist: see PARAS 7, 17–19) than to a redrawing of that rule's boundaries for which there was no equitable justification: *Great Peace Shipping Ltd v Tsavliris Salvage (International) Ltd, The Great Peace* above at [156] per Lord Phillips of Worth Matravers MR.
5   See *Solle v Butcher* [1950] 1 KB 671 at 697, [1949] 2 All ER 1107 at 1122, CA, per Denning LJ; *Grist v Bailey* [1967] Ch 532, [1966] 2 All ER 875.
6   See PARA 39.
7   See PARA 52.
8   *Cooper v Phibbs* (1867) LR 2 HL 149; Matthews 'A Note on *Cooper v Phipps*' (1989) 105 LQR 599.
9   See *Great Peace Shipping Ltd v Tsavliris Salvage (International) Ltd, The Great Peace* [2002] EWCA Civ 1407 at [153]–[160], [2003] QB 679, [2002] 4 All ER 689 per Lord Phillips of Worth Matravers MR (disapproving *Solle v Butcher* [1950] 1 KB 671, [1949] 2 All ER 1107, CA).
10 *Fawcett v Star Car Sales Ltd* [1960] NZLR 406 at 416–418, NZCA, per Gresson P; *William Sindall plc v Cambridgeshire County Council* [1994] 3 All ER 932 at 952, [1994] 1 WLR 1016 at 1035, CA, per Hoffmann LJ.
11 *Statoil ASA v Louis Dreyfus Energy Services LP, The Harriette N* [2008] EWHC 2257 (Comm), [2009] 1 All ER (Comm) 1035, [2008] 2 Lloyd's Rep 685 (disapproving statements made by Andrew Smith J in *Huyton SA v Distribuidora Internacional de Productos Agricolas SA* [2002] EWHC 2088 (Comm) at [455], [2002] All ER (D) 387 (Oct)).

50. Rescission of voluntary instruments. In a proper case the court will set aside a voluntary deed executed for the purpose of carrying out trusts declared orally, but which is wholly inconsistent with those trusts[1], or which does not carry out the full arrangement, even after the death of the grantee[2] or of both the donor and donee[3].

Similarly, an appointment will be set aside where the appointor exercises the power in forgetfulness that he has already made an appointment earlier to the same person[4], where the power is exercised in ignorance of serious breaches of duty owed by the appointee to the appointor[5] or, in the case of a disposition made with a view to minimising tax, in ignorance of a provision making it ineffective to do so[6].

It used to be the case that a deed would only be set aside if the relevant mistake was as to the effect of the deed itself rather than a mistake merely as to its consequences or the advantages to be gained by entering into it[7]. However, the Supreme Court has now made it clear that a deed may be set aside where there is a causative mistake either as to the legal character or nature of the relevant transaction or some matter of fact or law basic to the transaction, where the mistake was of sufficient gravity to make it unjust or unconscionable to leave it uncorrected[8].

There is a wide equitable jurisdiction to relieve from the consequences of mistake[9], and there is no reason in principle why this jurisdiction should be limited to voluntary settlements in the strict sense[10].

To be distinguished from the right to set aside a disposition for mistake is the rule that where a trustee exercises a discretion under the terms of a trust (eg a power of appointment), but fails to take into account considerations which he ought to have taken into account, or takes into account considerations which he ought not to have taken into account, and this would[11] or might[12] have made a material difference in exercising the discretion, such exercise is open to attack[13]. Considerations which the trustee ought to have taken into account may include the fiscal consequences of the particular exercise of discretion[14]. For such an attack to succeed, there must however be shown to be a breach of duty or default on the part of the trustee[15], hence where trustees properly rely on professional advice it is closed off, even where that advice turns out to be egregiously wrong[16]. In principle, where the exercise of discretion is successfully attacked on these grounds it should be void, and the majority of the cases so hold[17]. However, a modern view is that it is voidable only, so that the terms may be imposed to prevent injustice[18]. The court will not apply these principles so as to do something which the trustee might have done, but in fact by mistake did not do[19].

1   *Lister v Hodgson* (1867) LR 4 Eq 30.
2   *Hughes v Seanor* (1870) 18 WR 1122.
3   *Phillipson v Kerry* (1863) 32 Beav 628.
4   *Lady Hood of Avalon v Mackinnon* [1909] 1 Ch 476.
5   *Sybron Corpn v Rochem Ltd* [1984] Ch 112, [1983] 2 All ER 707, CA.
6   *Pitt v Holt, Futter v Futter* [2013] UKSC 26 at [129]–[135], [2013] 2 AC 108, [2013] 3 All ER 429 per Lord Walker.
7   *Gibbon v Mitchell* [1990] 3 All ER 338, [1990] 1 WLR 1304; *Pitt v Holt, Futter v Futter* [2011] EWCA Civ 197, [2012] Ch 132, [2011] 2 All ER 450 (revsd in part on appeal [2013] UKSC 26, [2013] 2 AC 108, [2013] 3 All ER 429). As to the difficult distinction between effect and consequences see *Wolff v Wolff* [2004] EWHC 2110 (Ch), [2004] STC 1633; *Sieff v Fox* [2005] EWHC 1312 (Ch), [2005] 3 All ER 693, [2005] 1 WLR 3811 (overruled on other grounds by *Pitt v Holt, Futter v Futter* [2011] EWCA Civ 197, [2012] Ch 132, [2011] 2 All ER 450); *Allnutt v Wilding* [2006] EWHC 1905 (Ch), 150 Sol Jo LB 1057, [2006] All ER (D) 375 (Jul) (affd [2007] EWCA Civ 412, [2007] WTLR 941, [2007] All ER (D) 41 (Apr)).
8   *Pitt v Holt* [2013] UKSC 26, [2013] 2 AC 108, [2013] 3 All ER 429. These requirements are not met in circumstances in which the donor deliberately ran the risk, or must be taken to have run the risk, of being wrong (for example in arranging a disposition in an artificial tax avoidance attempt): *Pitt v Holt* above at [113], [114], [135].
9   *Gibbon v Mitchell* [1990] 3 All ER 338 at 341, [1990] 1 WLR 1304 at 1307 per Millett J.
10 *AMP (UK) Ltd plc v Barker* (2000) 3 ITELR 414 at [82] per Lawrence Collins J. So it has been applied to an instrument mistakenly discharging a mortgage following the lender's oversight: *NRAM Plc v Evans* [2015] EWHC 1543 (Ch), [2015] BPIR 888.
11 *Re Hastings-Bass, Hastings-Bass v IRC* [1975] Ch 25, [1974] 2 All ER 193; *Mettoy Pension Trustees Ltd v Evans* [1991] 2 All ER 513 at 555, [1990] 1 WLR 1587 at 1624 per Warner J; *Abacus Trust Co (Isle of Man) Ltd v NSPCC* [2001] STC 1344; *Green v Cobham* [2002] STC 820; *Abacus Trust Co (Isle of Man) Ltd v Barr* [2003] EWHC 114 (Ch), [2003] Ch 409, sub nom *Re Barr's Settlement Trusts, Abacus Trust Co (Isle of Man) Ltd v Barr* [2003] 1 All ER 763.

12 *Kerr v British Leyland (Staff) Trustees Ltd* [1986] CA Transcript 286, CA; *Stannard v Fisons Pensions Trust Ltd* [1992] IRLR 27, [1991] PLR 225, CA; *AMP (UK) Ltd plc v Barker* (2000) 3 ITELR 414; *Hearn v Younger* [2002] EWHC 963 (Ch), [2003] OPLR 45.

13 *Re Hastings-Bass, Hastings-Bass v IRC* [1975] Ch 25 at 41, [1974] 2 All ER 193 at 203 per Buckley LJ. Cf *Smithson v Hamilton* [2007] EWHC 2900 (Ch), [2008] 1 All ER 1216, [2009] ICR 1 (action compromised: see *Smithson v Hamilton* [2008] EWCA Civ 996) (the rule in *Re Hastings-Bass* above applies to things done by trustees, not to things done by settlors in the context of private trusts or by employers in the context of pension trusts). See also TRUSTS AND POWERS vol 98 (2013) PARA 418.

14 *Green v Cobham* [2002] STC 820; *Abacus Trust Co (Isle of Man) Ltd v NSPCC* [2001] STC 1344; *Burrell v Burrell* [2005] EWHC 245 (Ch) at [19], [2005] STC 569, [2005] All ER (D) 351 (Feb) per Mann J.

15 *Abacus Trust Co (Isle of Man) Ltd v Barr* [2003] EWHC 114 (Ch), [2003] Ch 409, sub nom *Re Barr's Settlement Trusts, Abacus Trust Co (Isle of Man) Ltd v Barr* [2003] 1 All ER 763; *Pitt v Holt* [2013] UKSC 26, [2013] 2 AC 108, [2013] 3 All ER 429.

16 *Pitt v Holt* [2013] UKSC 26, [2013] 2 AC 108, [2013] 3 All ER 429.

17 *Kerr v British Leyland (Staff) Trustees Ltd* [1986] CA Transcript 286, CA; *Mettoy Pension Trustees Ltd v Evans* [1991] 2 All ER 513, [1990] 1 WLR 1587; *Stannard v Fisons Pensions Trust Ltd* [1992] IRLR 27, [1991] PLR 225, CA; *AMP (UK) Ltd plc v Barker* (2000) 3 ITELR 414; *Abacus Trust Co (Isle of Man) Ltd v NSPCC* [2001] STC 1344; *Green v Cobham* [2002] STC 820.

18 *Abacus Trust Co (Isle of Man) Ltd v Barr* [2003] EWHC 114 (Ch), [2003] Ch 409, sub nom *Re Barr's Settlement Trusts, Abacus Trust Co (Isle of Man) Ltd v Barr* [2003] 1 All ER 763; cf *Burrell v Burrell* [2005] EWHC 245 (Ch) at [24], [2005] STC 569, [2005] All ER (D) 351 (Feb) per Mann J; *Gallaher Ltd v Gallaher Pensions Ltd* [2005] EWHC 42 (Ch) at [162]–[170], [2005] All ER (D) 177 (Jan) per Etherton J.

19 *Breadner v Granville-Grossman* [2001] Ch 523, [2000] 4 All ER 705.

51. Passing of property.

If property passes as a result of fraud, the innocent party has the option to rescind the transaction, and revest title in himself[1]. For chattels this was so both at law and in equity; in such a case, the legal title revests without the assistance of the court[2], and the innocent party kept out of possession can thereafter maintain an action for unlawful interference with goods[3]. In the case of other property, such as money, rescission creates an equitable interest in favour of the innocent party, from which it follows that the latter may be able to follow that money into any proceeds[4]. In the case of land, the common law cannot act, and equity has to intervene, to order the revesting of the legal estate[5]. If, before this occurs, the innocent party retakes possession, the transferee is able to maintain an action at law[6].

However, where mistake not induced by fraud is concerned, the matter is entirely in equity. On rescission the innocent party obtains at most an equitable interest in the property concerned[7], and the legal title will not revest until either there is a retransfer, or a vesting order is made. Even though the equitable interest may revert ab initio, that will not render automatically wrong anything done by the legal owner up until then[8].

1 *Clough v London and North Western Rly Co* (1871) LR 7 Exch 26.
2 *Clough v London and North Western Rly Co* (1871) LR 7 Exch 26; *Car and Universal Finance Co Ltd v Caldwell* [1965] 1 QB 525, [1964] 1 All ER 290, CA.
3 *Car and Universal Finance Co Ltd v Caldwell* [1965] 1 QB 525, [1964] 1 All ER 290; *Neo Neon Ltd v Western Alliance Ltd* [2015] EWHC 2864 (QB). As to actions for unlawful interference with goods see TORT vol 97 (2015) PARA 602 et seq.
4 *Shalson v Russo* [2003] EWHC 1637 (Ch), [2005] Ch 281, [2005] 2 WLR 1213. See also *National Crime Agency v Robb* [2014] EWHC 4384 (Ch), [2015] 3 WLR 23.
5 *Feret v Hill* (1854) 15 CB 207.
6 *Feret v Hill* (1854) 15 CB 207.
7 *Cooper v Phibbs* (1867) LR 2 HL 149.
8 *Bristol and West Building Society v Mothew* [1998] Ch 1 at 23, [1996] 4 All ER 698 at 716–717, CA, per Millett LJ.

52. Procedure for claims for rescission. A claim for the setting aside or cancellation of an instrument in writing is assigned to the Chancery Division of the High Court[1].

Where a voluntary deed is impeached, the burden of supporting it does not necessarily rest on those who set it up[2]. Where an appointment under a settlement is set aside, the court may direct a note of the appointment and a copy of the order rescinding it to be indorsed on the settlement[3].

When a conveyance is set aside on the ground of mistake, an account of rents and profits may be directed and interest charged on purchase money[4]. Occupation rent may also be charged, and sums expended on repairs and improvements may be ordered to be repaid[5]. Other orders indemnifying the parties so that they may be restored to their original positions may also be made, but damages cannot be given[6].

Where a lease of a dwelling house was granted under a mutual misapprehension that it was not within the Rent Acts[7], the lease was set aside on terms which would enable the tenant either to stay on at the proper rent or to leave[8]. Where a contract of sale of freehold property was negotiated under the mistaken belief that it was subject to a statutory tenancy, it was set aside on the condition that the vendor should enter into a fresh contract at a proper vacant possession price if required by the purchaser[9]. However, more recent English authority holds that rescission is an 'all or nothing' remedy: if it applies, it applies to set aside the whole transaction, subject only to restitutio in integrum[10].

Where a party to a contract containing an exclusive jurisdiction clause claims rescission of the contract on the grounds of fraud or mutual mistake, that party may not be required to comply with the jurisdiction clause[11].

1 See the Senior Courts Act 1981 s 61(1), Sch 1 para 1(g); and COURTS AND TRIBUNALS vol 24 (2010) PARA 704. As to the assignment of proceedings in the High Court generally see CIVIL PROCEDURE vol 11 (2015) PARA 94 et seq. As to the consequences of commencing proceedings in the wrong division see *Apac Rowena Ltd v Norpol Packaging Ltd* [1991] 4 All ER 516. As to the rectification or setting aside of deeds generally see DEEDS AND OTHER INSTRUMENTS vol 32 (2012) PARA 267 et seq.
2 *Henry v Armstrong* (1881) 18 ChD 668; *Tucker v Bennett* (1887) 38 ChD 1 at 9, CA, per Cotton LJ.
3 *Lady Hood of Avalon v Mackinnon* [1909] 1 Ch 476 at 484 per Eve J.
4 *Neesom v Clarkson* (1842) 2 Hare 163; *Bloomer v Spittle* (1872) LR 13 Eq 427.
5 *Neesom v Clarkson* (1842) 2 Hare 163; *Bloomer v Spittle* (1872) LR 13 Eq 427; *Devald and Davald v Zigeuner and Zigeuner* (1958) 16 DLR (2d) 285. See also *Nutt v Read* (16 February 1999, unreported) (affd (1999) 32 HLR 761, (1999) Times 3 December, CA).
6 As to the distinction between an indemnity and damages see *Whittington v Seale-Hayne* (1900) 82 LT 49, 16 TLR 181; and EQUITABLE JURISDICTION vol 47 (2014) PARA 14.
7 As to the Rent Acts see LANDLORD AND TENANT vol 63 (2012) PARA 924.
8 *Solle v Butcher* [1950] 1 KB 671 at 689, 696–698, 707, [1949] 2 All ER 1107 at 1118, 1122, 1128, CA, per Denning LJ (although this decision has been disapproved by the Court of Appeal on the grounds that the equitable jurisdiction supporting it did not exist: see *Great Peace Shipping Ltd v Tsavliris Salvage (International) Ltd, The Great Peace* [2002] EWCA Civ 1407 at [153]–[160], [2003] QB 679, [2002] 4 All ER 689 per Lord Phillips of Worth Matravers MR; and PARA 49).
9 *Grist v Bailey* [1967] Ch 532, [1966] 2 All ER 875 (doubted in *William Sindall plc v Cambridgeshire County Council* [1994] 3 All ER 932 at 952, [1994] 1 WLR 1016 at 1035, CA, per Hoffmann LJ).
10 See PARA 39.
11 *Credit Suisse First Boston (Europe) Ltd v Seagate Trading Co Ltd* [1999] 1 All ER (Comm) 261, [1999] 1 Lloyd's Rep 784 (the allegation of mutual mistake impeaches the jurisdiction clause by reason of lack of consent).

(4) RECTIFICATION

53. General considerations affecting the grant of relief. Rectification is an equitable remedy by which the court will modify the terms of a written instrument so as to give effect to the intention of the parties to it[1]. That intention may be genuinely agreed on by the parties (where there is consensus ad idem), or it may be by estoppel (where it is the intention of only one of them, but the other is estopped from denying that it is his as well)[2]. It is thus the mistake in the way in which the agreement is expressed in writing that is rectified, and not a mistake in the agreement itself[3]. In the case of a deed poll or voluntary transaction, it is the intention of the maker or donor that must be considered[4].

If the parties' genuine or estoppel consensus is accurately recorded in the document, there can be no rectification[5]. However, the document can be rectified if both parties believe that the document expresses their (genuine or apparent) consensus but they are both mistaken in that on its true construction it does not carry out their common intention[6]. Thus an intention to transfer enough shares to achieve a capital gains tax saving may found rectification where, owing to a miscalculation, not enough shares have been transferred[7]. Rectification on these grounds is available not only where particular words have been added, omitted or wrongly written as a result of careless copying or the like, but also where the words of the document were purposely used but it was mistakenly considered that they bore a different meaning from their correct meaning as a matter of construction[8].

A document can also be rectified where one party sees that the other mistakenly believes that the document expresses that other's own intention, realises that this mistake may operate to that party's disadvantage, but says nothing about it and executes the instrument as it stands[9]. In such a case, there is no estoppel consensus on the terms of the document, because the knowing party is not deceived by the mistaken party's representation that he intended to be bound by those terms[10]. Instead there is an estoppel binding the knowing party, preventing him from relying on the document to show that a different agreement was made to that alleged by the mistaken party[11]. Thus, as against the mistaken party, the document does not avail the knowing party, and equity will rectify it to make it conform to the agreement the mistaken party believed to exist[12].

In the case of common mistake there are (or may be) cross representations, but they can only found estoppels preventing either party from setting up the document as the true agreement between them, and therefore preventing either party from resisting rectification[13].

Except in the circumstances described above, there can be no rectification. In particular, unilateral mistake by itself will not suffice[14]. It is not the function of the court to rectify an agreement merely because one party has been tough or successful in negotiations and the other has been unwise, missed a point or has failed to appreciate the likely consequences of the agreement[15].

For a successful claim to rectify, there is no need for an antecedent binding agreement[16]. English authorities indicate that some outward manifestation of accord of intention must be shown[17]. This may be more difficult where the document has been drafted on behalf of both parties by a third party[18].

In rectifying a document, the court acts on the principle that the parties are to be placed as far as possible in the same position as that in which they would have stood if the error to be corrected had not been made[19]. The mere fact that the sole purpose of rectification is a tax advantage is not a bar[20]. Nor is the fact that the mistake occurred through the negligence of the claimant or his adviser[21]. Where the document concerned has been drafted by a third party, there is no reason in principle why rectification should not be available both in cases where a different person is responsible for preparing the text for each party and where only one person has that responsibility for both parties, although there may be evidential difficulties in establishing either the necessary agreement or common intention (in the former case) or the 'outward expression' (in the latter case)[22].

Normally a claim for rectification must be specifically pleaded, but the court may grant relief even though it is not asked for in the statement of case[23]. The pleading by one party of alternative forms of rectification does not negate the existence of a common intention[24]. The court will not act on the footing of fraud unless fraud is pleaded with the utmost particularity[25].

1   *Crane v Hegeman-Harris Co Inc* [1939] 4 All ER 68, [1971] 1 WLR 1390n, CA; *Joscelyne v Nissen* [1970] 2 QB 86, [1970] 1 All ER 1213, CA; *Re Butlin's Settlement Trusts, Butlin v Butlin* [1976] Ch 251, [1976] 2 All ER 483; *Re Slocock's Will Trusts* [1979] 1 All ER 358; *Chartbrook Ltd v Persimmon Homes Ltd* [2009] UKHL 38, [2009] AC 1101, [2009] 4 All ER 677; and see CONTRACT vol 22 (2012) PARA 361; EQUITABLE JURISDICTION vol 47 (2014) PARA 40; and TRUSTS AND POWERS vol 98 (2013) PARA 80 et seq.
2   See PARA 27.
3   *Mackenzie v Coulson* (1869) LR 8 Eq 368 at 375 per James V-C ('courts of equity do not rectify contracts; they may and do rectify instruments purporting to have been made in pursuance of the terms of contracts'); *Mace v Rutland House Textiles Ltd (in administrative receivership)* [1999] 46 LS Gaz R 37. *Frederick E Rose (London) Ltd v Williams H Pim Jnr & Co Ltd* [1953] 2 QB 450, [1953] 2 All ER 739, CA illustrates this proposition neatly: because the written contract reflected what the parties had agreed, albeit mistakenly, there could be no rectification.
4   See PARA 60.
5   *Riverlate Properties Ltd v Paul* [1975] Ch 133, [1974] 2 All ER 656, CA.
6   *Rooke v Lord Kensington* (1856) 2 K & J 753; *Sells v Sells* (1860) 1 Drew & Sm 42; *Earl of Bradford v Earl of Romney* (1862) 30 Beav 431 at 438 per Sir John Romilly MR; *Eaton v Bennett* (1865) 34 Beav 196; *Re Walsh's Estate* (1867) 15 WR 1115 at 1117 per Brewster C; *Paget v Marshall* (1884) 28 ChD 255; *May v Platt* [1900] 1 Ch 616 at 623 per Farwell J; *Slack v Hancock* (1912) 107 LT 14; *Whiteley v Delaney* [1914] AC 132, HL; *Letts v Excess Insurance Co* (1916) 32 TLR 361; *United States of America v Motor Trucks Ltd* [1924] AC 196, PC; *Blay v Pollard* [1930] 1 KB 628 at 633, CA, per Scrutton LJ; *Wilson v Wilson* [1969] 3 All ER 945, [1969] 1 WLR 1470; *Weeds v Blaney* (1977) 247 Estates Gazette 211, CA; *Agip SpA v Navigazione Alta Italia SpA, The Nai Genova and Nai Superba* [1984] 1 Lloyd's Rep 353 at 359, CA, per Slade LJ; *London Regional Transport v Wimpey Group Services Ltd* (1986) 53 P & CR 356, [1986] 2 EGLR 41; *Hamed El Chiaty & Co (t/a Travco Nile Cruise Lines) v Thomas Cook Group Ltd, The Nile Rhapsody* [1992] 2 Lloyd's Rep 399 (affd [1994] 1 Lloyd's Rep 382, CA). The pleading by one party of alternative forms of rectification does not negate the existence of a common intention: *Swainland Builders Ltd v Freehold Properties Ltd* [2002] EWCA Civ 560, [2002] 2 EGLR 71, [2002] 23 EG 123.
7   *Prowting 1968 Trustee One Ltd v Amos-Yeo* [2015] EWHC 2480 (Ch).
8   *Jervis v Howle and Talke Colliery Co Ltd* [1937] Ch 67, [1936] 3 All ER 193; *Whiteside v Whiteside* [1950] Ch 65, [1949] 2 All ER 913, CA; *Joscelyne v Nissen* [1970] 2 QB 86, [1970] 1 All ER 1213, CA; *Re Butlin's Settlement Trusts, Butlin v Butlin* [1976] Ch 251 at 260–261, [1976] 2 All ER 483 at 487 per Brightman J; *Re Slocock's Will Trusts* [1979] 1 All ER 358; *Anfrank Nominees Pty Ltd v Connell* (1989) 1 ACSR 365 at 367–368; *Grand Metropolitan plc v William Hill Group Ltd* [1997] 1 BCLC 390; *AMP (UK) Ltd plc v Barker* (2000) 3 ITELR 414; *Ashcroft v Barnsdale* [2010] EWHC 1948 (Ch), [2010] STC 2544.
9   *A Roberts & Co Ltd v Leicestershire County Council* [1961] Ch 555, [1961] 2 All ER 545; *Riverlate Properties Ltd v Paul* [1975] Ch 133, [1974] 2 All ER 656, CA; *Weeds v Blaney* (1977) 247 Estates Gazette 211, CA; *Commission for the New Towns v Cooper (GB) Ltd* [1995] Ch 259, [1995] 2 All ER 929, CA. Cf *Board of Trustees of the National Provident Fund v Brierley Investments Ltd* [1997] 1 NZLR 1 at 6, PC (party did not knowingly take advantage of other party's mistake); *Templiss Properties Ltd v Hyams* [1999] EGCS 60; *Tri-Star Customs and Forwarding Ltd v Denning* [1999] 1 NZLR 33, NZCA; *Chartbrook Ltd v Persimmon Homes Ltd* [2009] UKHL 38, [2009] AC 1101, [2009] 4 All ER 677; *Transview Properties Ltd v City Site Properties Ltd* [2009] EWCA Civ 1255, [2009] All ER (D) 255 (Nov). See also PARA 27.
10 See eg *Hartog v Colin and Shields* [1939] 3 All ER 566.
11 *A Roberts & Co Ltd v Leicestershire County Council* [1961] Ch 555, [1961] 2 All ER 545.

12 See eg *Commission for the New Towns v Cooper (GB) Ltd* [1995] Ch 259, [1995] 2 All ER 929, CA.
13 *Joscelyne v Nissen* [1970] 2 QB 86, [1970] 1 All ER 1213, CA; cf *Thomas Bates & Sons Ltd v Wyndham's (Lingerie) Ltd* [1981] 1 All ER 1077, [1981] 1 WLR 505, CA.
14 *A Roberts & Co Ltd v Leicestershire County Council* [1961] Ch 555, [1961] 2 All ER 545; *Riverlate Properties Ltd v Paul* [1975] Ch 133, [1974] 2 All ER 656, CA; *George Wimpey UK Ltd v VIC Construction Ltd* [2005] EWCA Civ 77, [2005] BLR 135, (2005) Times, 16 Feb.
15 *Oceanic Village Ltd v Shirayama Shokusan Co Ltd* [1999] EGCS 83; and see PARA 55.
16 *Shipley UDC v Bradford Corpn* [1936] Ch 375 at 395 per Clauson J (on appeal [1936] Ch 399n, 154 LT 444, CA); *Crane v Hegeman-Harris Co Inc* [1939] 1 All ER 662, [1971] 1 WLR 1390n (affd [1939] 4 All ER 68, CA); *Slee v Warke* (1949) 86 CLR 271; *Joscelyne v Nissen* [1970] 2 QB 86, [1970] 1 All ER 1213, CA; *Maralinga Pty Ltd v Major Enterprises Pty Ltd* (1972) 128 CLR 336 at 350 per Hope J; cf *Mackenzie v Coulson* (1869) LR 8 Eq 368 at 375 per Sir WM James V-C; *Lovell & Christmas Ltd v Wall* (1911) 104 LT 85, 27 TLR 236, CA; *United States of America v Motor Trucks Ltd* [1924] AC 196 at 200–201, PC.
17 *Frederick E Rose (London) Ltd v William H Pim Jnr & Co Ltd* [1953] 2 QB 450 at 461–462, [1953] 2 All ER 739 at 747–748, CA, per Denning LJ; *Joscelyne v Nissen* [1970] 2 QB 86, [1970] 1 All ER 1213, CA; *AMP (UK) Ltd plc v Barker* (2000) 3 ITELR 414 at [60] per Lawrence Collins J; *JIS (1974) Ltd v MCE Investment Nominees Ltd* [2003] EWCA Civ 721 at [31]–[34], [2003] 24 LS Gaz R 36, [2003] All ER (D) 155 (Apr) per Carnwath LJ; *Chartbrook Ltd v Persimmon Homes Ltd* [2009] UKHL 38, [2009] AC 1101, [2009] 4 All ER 677; cf Bromley 'Rectification in Equity' (1971) 87 LQR 532. Cf also the view taken by the Australian authorities, that it is enough that the parties can be proved in some admissible way in fact to have had the intention: *Bishopsgate Insurance Australia Ltd v Commonwealth Engineering (NSW) Pty Ltd* [1981] 1 NSWLR 429; *Pukallus v Cameron* (1982) 180 CLR 447 at 552; *Elders Trustee and Executor Co Ltd v EG Reeves Pty Ltd* (1987) 78 ALR 193 at 253–254 per Gummow J; cf *Westland Savings Bank v Hancock* [1987] 2 NZLR 21 at 29–30 per Tipping J.
18 *Mace v Rutland House Textiles Ltd (in administrative receivership)* [1999] 46 LS Gaz R 37.
19 *Walker v Armstrong* (1856) 8 De GM & G 531 at 544 per Turner LJ; *KPMG LLP v Network Rail Infrastructure Ltd* [2007] EWCA Civ 363 at [16], [2008] 1 P & CR 187, [2007] All ER (D) 245 (Apr) per Carnwath LJ; and see *Barrow v Barrow* (1854) 18 Beav 529 at 532 per Sir John Romilly MR.
20 *Re Colebrook's Conveyances, Taylor v Taylor* [1973] 1 All ER 132, [1972] 1 WLR 1397; *Re Slocock's Will Trusts* [1979] 1 All ER 358 at 363 per Graham J.
21 *Templiss Properties Ltd v Hyams* [1999] EGCS 60.
22 *Mace v Rutland House Textiles Ltd (in administrative receivership)* [1999] 46 LS Gaz R 37.
23 *Butler v Mountview Estates Ltd* [1951] 2 KB 563 at 571, [1951] 1 All ER 693 at 700 per Danckwerts J.
24 See *Swainland Builders Ltd v Freehold Properties Ltd* [2002] EWCA Civ 560, [2002] 2 EGLR 71, [2002] 23 EG 123.
25 *Blay v Pollard* [1930] 1 KB 628, CA.

54. Instruments which may be rectified. In a proper case the court will rectify a court order[1], a deed of settlement[2], an appointment[3], a deed of revocation[4], a deed of variation[5], a lease[6], a bond[7], a bill of exchange[8], bought and sold notes[9], a tax computation[10], a schedule of quantities annexed to a contract to execute works for a gross sum, purporting to show how the gross sum is made up[11], an insurance policy[12], a form to withdraw funds from an insurance policy[13] and a declaration of shipment under a marine insurance policy, even after a loss has become known[14].

There are special rules relating to the rectification of wills[15], to the rectification of the land register[16], to the rectification of the register of common land or town or village greens[17], and to the rectification of contracts for the sale or other disposition of an interest in land[18].

1 *Standley v Stewkesbury* [1998] 2 FLR 610, CA; cf *Loseby v Newman* [1995] 2 FLR 754, CA (court will not rectify defective committal order unless there are exceptional circumstances).
2 *Walsh v Trevanion* (1848) 16 Sim 178 at 179 (subsequent proceedings (1850) 15 QB 733); *Ashhurst v Mill, Mill v Ashhurst* (1848) 7 Hare 502; *Torre v Torre* (1853) 1 Sm & G 518; *Smith v Iliffe* (1875) LR 20 Eq 666; *Cogan v Duffield* (1876) 2 ChD 44, CA; *Re Bird's Trusts* (1876) 3 ChD 214; *Hanley v Pearson* (1879) 13 ChD 545; *Welman v Welman* (1880) 15 ChD 570;

   Fitzgerald v Fitzgerald [1902] 1 IR 477, CA; *Banks v Ripley* [1940] Ch 719, [1940] 3 All ER 49; *Re Butlin's Settlement Trust, Butlin v Butlin* [1976] Ch 251, [1976] 2 All ER 483; *Re Slocock's Will Trusts* [1979] 1 All ER 358.

3 *Wilkinson v Nelson* (1861) 9 WR 393.

4 *Re Walton's Settlement, Walton v Peirson* [1922] 2 Ch 509, CA.

5 *Seymour v Seymour* (1989) Times, 16 February.

6 *Mortimer v Shortall* (1842) 2 Dr & War 363; *Murray v Parker* (1854) 19 Beav 305; *Paget v Marshall* (1884) 28 ChD 255; *Cowen v Truefitt Ltd* [1899] 2 Ch 309, CA; cf *Smith v Jones* [1954] 2 All ER 823, [1954] 1 WLR 1089 (tenant not entitled to rectification of tenancy agreement against bona fide purchaser for value without notice); *KPMG LLP v Network Rail Infrastructure Ltd* [2007] EWCA Civ 363, [2008] 1 P & CR 187, [2007] All ER (D) 245 (Apr) (landlord unable to establish convincing proof). As to the need for convincing proof see PARA 57.

7 *Simpson v Vaughan* (1739) 2 Atk 31; *Bishop v Church* (1751) 2 Ves Sen 371; *Thomas v Frazer* (1797) 3 Ves 399; *Burn v Burn* (1798) 3 Ves 573; *Hodgkinson v Wyatt* (1846) 9 Beav 566 at 569.

8 *Druiff v Lord Parker* (1868) LR 5 Eq 131.

9 *Caraman, Rowley and May v Aperghis* (1923) 40 TLR 124.

10 *R v Inspector of Taxes, ex p Bass Holdings Ltd, Richart (Inspector of Taxes) v Bass Holdings Ltd* [1993] STC 122.

11 *Neill v Midland Rly Co* (1869) 20 LT 864.

12 See *Henkle v Royal Exchange Assurance Co* (1749) 1 Ves Sen 317.

13 *Lobler v Revenue and Customs Comrs* [2015] UKUT 152 (TCC), [2015] STC 1893, [2015] All ER (D) 14 (Apr).

14 *Stephens v Australasian Insurance Co* (1872) LR 8 CP 18.

15 See WILLS AND INTESTACY vol 102 (2010) PARAS 187, 188.

16 See PARA 25.

17 See the Commons Act 2006 s 19; and COMMONS vol 13 (2009) PARA 534.

18 Where a contract for the sale or other disposition of an interest in land satisfies the conditions of the Law of Property (Miscellaneous Provisions) Act 1989 s 2 (see CONVEYANCING vol 23 (2013) PARA 151) by reason only of the rectification of one or more documents in pursuance of an order of a court, the contract comes into being, or is deemed to have come into being, at such time as may be specified in the order: s 2(4). See *Oun v Ahmad* [2008] EWHC 545 (Ch), [2008] 2 P & CR D7, 152 Sol Jo (no 14) 32, [2008] All ER (D) 270 (Mar) (court unable to rectify a document to include a term the parties agreed should be omitted from the written record, and hence could not produce a valid contract for the purposes of the Law of Property (Miscellaneous Provisions) Act 1989 s 2).

55. When rectification will not be granted. The court will not rectify an instrument when no relief is required as between the parties to it[1], although that does not mean that there must be an adversarial issue between them[2].

The court will not rectify a settlement to make it conform with what would have been the contract between the parties had they taken all the material facts known by them into consideration[3]; nor does the doctrine extend to cases where as regards some particular subject matter the parties had no intention at all, even if it could be shown that had it been in their minds they would have had some particular intention with regard to it[4]. Rectification will also not be granted in order retrospectively to impute an intention that was not present at the time the instrument was executed[5], nor so as to make a document do something other than that which was intended at the time of its drafting, even if that other thing would be more in keeping with the draftsman's intentions or it would in fact be impossible to do what the document attempted to do[6]. It is not the function of the court to rectify an agreement merely because one party has been tough or successful in negotiations and the other has been unwise, missed a point or has failed to appreciate the likely consequences of the agreement[7]. If the written contract accurately gives effect to the intention of the parties, frustration of that intention by a later statute is not a ground for rectification[8], nor is the fact that the court considers that the suggested rectification would be better[9].

Where the contract accurately describes the subject matter of the contract, it will not be rectified because the parties mistakenly believed it to have different features or to include other property within it[10].

The right to rectify can be lost by the acquisition of rights in the subject matter of the transaction by a purchaser for value without notice[11].

The court has no jurisdiction to rectify the articles of association of a company[12].

1   *Whiteside v Whiteside* [1950] Ch 65, [1949] 2 All ER 913, CA; *Van der Linde v Van der Linde* [1947] Ch 306. Cf *Behrers v Heilbut* (1956) 222 LT Jo 290; *Re Slocock's Will Trusts* [1979] 1 All ER 358 at 363 per Graham J.
2   *Re Colebrook's Conveyances, Taylor v Taylor* [1973] 1 All ER 132, [1972] 1 WLR 1397; *Re Slocock's Will Trusts* [1979] 1 All ER 358; *Seymour v Seymour* (1989) Times, 16 February; *Lake v Lake* [1989] STC 865.
3   See *Barrow v Barrow* (1854) 18 Beav 529 at 533, where the court did not deal with the question of rectification (on appeal 5 De GM & G 782); *Frederick E Rose (London) Ltd v Williams H Pim Jnr & Co Ltd* [1953] 2 QB 450, [1953] 2 All ER 739, CA; *Tankel v Tankel* [1999] 1 FLR 676.
4   *Harlow Development Corpn v Kingsgate (Clothing Productions) Ltd* (1973) 226 Estates Gazette 1960.
5   *Bank of Scotland v Brunswick Developments (1987) Ltd (No 2)* 1999 SLT 716, HL.
6   *Collins v Jones* (2000) Times, 3 February.
7   *Oceanic Village Ltd v Shirayama Shokusan Co Ltd* [1999] EGCS 83.
8   *Pyke v Peters* [1943] KB 242.
9   *Tankel v Tankel* [1999] 1 FLR 676.
10 *Pukallus v Cameron* (1982) 180 CLR 447.
11 See PARA 38.
12 *Scott v Frank F Scott (London) Ltd* [1940] Ch 794, [1940] 3 All ER 508, CA. See also COMPANIES vol 14 (2009) PARA 234.

56.   Relief for party who prepared the instrument. It seems that the court is less willing to rectify an instrument where the party seeking relief is the person who prepared and perfected it[1], but in a proper case the court will not, on this account, refuse to grant relief[2], although it may refuse to give him his costs[3].

1   *Ex p Wright* (1812) 19 Ves 255; *Collett v Morrison* (1851) 9 Hare 162 at 176–177 per Turner V-C.
2   *Ball v Storie* (1823) 1 Sim & St 210; *Murray v Parker* (1854) 19 Beav 305; *Fowler v Scottish Equitable Life Insurance Society* (1858) 28 LJCh 225; *Vergottis & Co v H Ford & Co Ltd* (1918) 34 TLR 233; *Weeds v Blaney* (1977) 247 Estates Gazette 211, CA; *Eason v Brownrigg* [1998] CLY 3659.
3   *Murray v Parker* (1854) 19 Beav 305; cf *Weeds v Blaney* (1977) 247 Estates Gazette 211, CA.

57.   Matters to be proved before rectification is granted. To justify the court correcting a mistake in an instrument, the evidence must be clear and unambiguous ('convincing proof'[1]) that a mistake (whether of fact or law[2]) has been made in recording the parties' intention[3], what that intention was[4] and that the alleged intention to which it is desired to make the agreement conformable continued concurrently in the parties' minds down to the time of the execution of the instrument[5]. In considering the intentions of a collective body (such as a group of trustees or a committee of a board), it is their collective intention which is relevant for these purposes, although there is no requirement to show evidence of their agreement or accord[6]. Thus the court will not add to a settlement a power which the claimant states that he intended to be added, but to his knowledge was not contained in it when he executed it[7]; nor will the court normally supply a provision which the evidence shows was intentionally omitted[8]. The party seeking to rectify must also be able to show precisely the form to which the deed ought to be altered[9].

1   *Joscelyne v Nissen* [1970] 2 QB 86 at 98, [1970] 1 All ER 1213 at 1222, CA, per Russell LJ; *Thomas Bates & Sons Ltd v Wyndham's (Lingerie) Ltd* [1981] 1 All ER 1077, [1981] 1 WLR 505, CA; *Agip SpA v Navigazione Alta Italia SpA, The Nai Genova and Nai Superba* [1984] 1 Lloyd's Rep 353 at 359, CA, per Slade LJ; *Grand Metropolitan plc v William Hill Group Ltd* [1997] 1 BCLC 390 at 394 per Arden J; *Lansing Linde Ltd v Alber* [2000] Pensions LR 15 at 44

per Rimer J; *AMP (UK) Ltd plc v Barker* (2000) 3 ITELR 414 at [59] per Lawrence Collins J; *KPMG LLP v Network Rail Infrastructure Ltd* [2007] EWCA Civ 363 at [27], [2008] 1 P & CR 187, [2007] All ER (D) 245 (Apr) per Carnwath LJ.

2   *Re Butlin's Settlement Trusts, Butlin v Butlin* [1976] Ch 251, [1976] 2 All ER 483; *Re Slocock's Will Trusts* [1979] 1 All ER 358.

3   *Beaumont v Bramley* (1822) Turn & R 41 at 50 per Lord Eldon LC; *Mortimer v Shortall* (1842) 2 Dr & War 363 at 373 per Sir Edward Burtenshaw Sugden LC; *Parsons v Bignold* (1843) 13 Sim 518 (affd (1846) 15 LJ Ch 379); *Rooke v Lord Kensington* (1856) 2 K & J 753; *Fowler v Fowler* (1859) 4 De G & J 250; *Rake v Hooper* (1900) 83 LT 669, 17 TLR 118; *Joscelyne v Nissen* [1970] 2 QB 86, [1970] 1 All ER 1213, CA; *Pukallus v Cameron* (1982) 180 CLR 447 at 457; *Hamed El Chiaty & Co (t/a Travco Nile Cruise Lines) v Thomas Cook Group Ltd, The Nile Rhapsody* [1992] 2 Lloyd's Rep 399 (affd [1994] 1 Lloyd's Rep 382, CA).

4   *Slee v Warke* (1949) 86 CLR 271; *Ernest Scragg & Sons Ltd v Perseverance Banking and Trust Co Ltd* [1973] 2 Lloyd's Rep 101, CA; *Harlow Development Corpn v Kingsgate (Clothing Productions) Ltd* (1973) 226 Estates Gazette 1960; *Crawley Borough Council v Bradford & Bingley Building Society* (23 July 1998, unreported), CA.

5   *Dowager Countess of Shelburne v Earl of Inchiquin* (1784) 1 Bro CC 338 at 341 per Lord Thurlow LC; *Marquis of Townshend v Stangroom* (1801) 6 Ves 328 at 333–334 per Lord Cottenham LC; *Marquess of Breadalbane v Marquess of Chandos* (1837) 2 My & Cr 711 at 739–740 per Lord Cottenham LC; *Marquess of Exeter v Marchioness of Exeter* (1838) 3 My & Cr 321; *Hills v Rowland* (1853) 4 De GM & G 430; *Rooke v Lord Kensington* (1856) 2 K & J 753 at 763–764; *Wright v Goff* (1856) 22 Beav 207 at 214 per Sir John Romilly MR; *Fowler v Fowler* (1859) 4 De G & J 250 at 264, 273 per Lord Chelmsford LC; *Sells v Sells* (1860) 1 Drew & Sm 42; *Bentley v Mackay* (1862) 4 De GF & J 279; *Earl of Bradford v Earl of Romney* (1862) 30 Beav 431; *Re Walsh's Estate* (1867) 15 WR 1115 at 1117 per Brewster C; *Rake v Hooper* (1900) 83 LT 669, 17 TLR 118; *Crane v Hegeman-Harris Co Inc* [1939] 1 All ER 662 at 664, [1971] 1 WLR 1390n at 1391n per Simonds J (affd [1939] 4 All ER 68, CA); *Fredensen v Rothschild* [1941] 1 All ER 430; *Gilhespie v Burdis* (1943) 169 LT 91; *Dormer v Sherman* (1966) 110 Sol Jo 171, CA; *Agip SpA v Navigazione Alta Italia SpA, The Nai Genova and Nai Superba* [1984] 1 Lloyd's Rep 353 at 359, CA, per Slade LJ; *Eason v Brownrigg* [1998] CLY 3659; *Swainland Builders Ltd v Freehold Properties Ltd* [2002] EWCA Civ 560 at [32]–[34], [2002] 2 EGLR 71 per Peter Gibson LJ; *JIS (1974) Ltd v MCE Investment Nominees Ltd* [2003] EWCA Civ 721 at [25], [2003] 24 LS Gaz R 36, [2003] All ER (D) 155 (Apr) per Carnwath LJ; *James Hay Pension Trustees Ltd v Cooper Estates Ltd* [2005] EWHC 36 (Ch) at [14], [2005] All ER (D) 144 (Jan) per Hart J; *Chartbrook Ltd v Persimmon Homes Ltd* [2009] UKHL 38, [2009] AC 1101, [2009] 4 All ER 677; *Re IBM Pension Plan, IBM United Kingdom Pensions Trust Ltd v IBM United Kingdom Holdings Ltd* [2012] EWHC 2766 (Ch), [2012] All ER (D) 118 (Oct).

6   *AMP (UK) Ltd plc v Barker* (2000) 3 ITELR 414 at [66] per Lawrence Collins J. See also *Re IBM Pension Plan; IBM United Kingdom Pensions Trust Ltd v IBM United Kingdom Holdings Ltd* [2012] EWHC 2766 (Ch), [2012] All ER (D) 118 (Oct).

7   *Harbridge v Wogan* (1846) 5 Hare 258.

8   *Rake v Hooper* (1900) 83 LT 669, 17 TLR 118; but see PARA 54. Cf *Re Butlin's Settlement Trusts, Butlin v Butlin* [1976] Ch 251, [1976] 2 All ER 483 (where a term was deliberately inserted).

9   *Fowler v Fowler* (1859) 4 De G & J 250; *Earl of Bradford v Earl of Romney* (1862) 30 Beav 431 at 439 per Lord Chelmsford MR; *Duke of Sutherland v Heathcote* [1892] 1 Ch 475 at 486, CA; *Pukallus v Cameron* (1982) 180 CLR 447; *Eason v Brownrigg* [1998] CLY 3659; *Pappadakis v Pappadakis* (2000) Times, 19 January.

58. Marriage settlements. In the case of a marriage settlement where a post-nuptial settlement differs from articles entered into before marriage, the court will apparently always set up the articles[1]. Similarly when an ante-nuptial settlement purports to be in pursuance of articles entered into before marriage and there is any variance, no evidence beyond the articles is necessary in order to have the settlement rectified[2]. There must be clear evidence of the terms of the articles and a mere recital of their terms in a post-nuptial settlement will not enable what has been recited to be set up as against the terms of the settlement itself[3]. Even when the settlement contains no reference to the articles, if it can be shown that the settlement was intended to be in conformity with the articles and there is clear and satisfactory evidence showing that the discrepancy has arisen from mistake, the court will re-form the settlement and make it conformable to the real intention of the parties[4]. Moreover, the court looks at the intention rather than the actual words of the articles, and where a post-nuptial or an ante-nuptial settlement purports to be made in pursuance of ante-nuptial articles, then even though the limitations of the settlement may agree with the words of the articles, if it does not carry out the intent, the court will reform it[5]. Where the settlement carries out the settlor's instructions there is no case for rectification[6].

Where the husband undertakes the duty of having the marriage settlement prepared as agent for the wife, and the settlement is not such as the court would sanction in the absence of agreement and does not carry out the wife's intention, the settlement may be rectified so as to accord with that intention[7].

1   *Bold v Hutchinson* (1855) 5 De GM & G 558; *Kent v Brown* (1942) 43 SR(NSW) 124. As to marriage articles see SETTLEMENTS vol 91 (2012) PARA 529 et seq.
2   *Bold v Hutchinson* (1855) 5 De GM & G 558.
3   *Mignam v Parry* (1862) 31 Beav 211.
4   *Bold v Hutchinson* (1855) 5 De GM & G 558; *King v King-Harman* (1873) 7 IR Eq 446.
5   *Cogan v Duffield* (1875) LR 20 Eq 789 (affd (1876) 2 ChD 44 at 49, CA, per James LJ); and see *Herring-Cooper v Herring-Cooper* [1905] 1 IR 465 (post-nuptial); *Smith v Iliffe* (1875) LR 20 Eq 666 (ante-nuptial).
6   *Constantinidi v Ralli* [1935] Ch 427.
7   *Corley v Lord Stafford* (1857) 1 De G & J 238; *Clark v Girdwood* (1877) 7 ChD 9, CA; *Lovesy v Smith* (1880) 15 ChD 655. As to the rectification of family settlements see *Hoblyn v Hoblyn* (1889) 41 ChD 200; *McCausland v Young* [1949] NI 49. As to family settlements generally see SETTLEMENTS vol 91 (2012) PARA 903 et seq.

59. Rectification of a will. Until 1982[1], the court's power to rectify a will was limited[2], but since 1982 the law has been liberalised and a will may now be rectified if the court is satisfied that it is so expressed as to fail to carry out the testator's intentions, in consequence of a clerical error or a failure to understand his instructions[3]. Rectification of a will is dealt with elsewhere in this work[4].

1   Ie prior to the enactment of the Administration of Justice Act 1982 (see WILLS AND INTESTACY vol 102 (2010) PARA 187).
2   See WILLS AND INTESTACY vol 102 (2010) PARA 187.
3   Administration of Justice Act 1982 s 20(1); and see WILLS AND INTESTACY vol 102 (2010) PARA 188. 'Clerical error' means an inadvertent error in the process of recording the intended words of the testator in the drafting or transcription of his will: *Wordingham v Royal Exchange Trust Co Ltd* [1992] Ch 412, [1992] 3 All ER 204 (an omission from an updated will of a clause from an earlier will held to constitute a clerical error). See also *Re Segelman* [1996] Ch 171, [1995] 3 All ER 676 (a draftsman's failure to appreciate the significance or effect of words is capable of being a clerical error). The Supreme Court has held that the term should be given a wide meaning: see *Marley v Rawlings* [2014] UKSC 2, [2015] AC 129, [2014] 1 All ER 807.
4   See WILLS AND INTESTACY vol 102 (2010) PARA 186 et seq.

60. Rectification of voluntary instruments. A voluntary deed as well as a settlement for value may be re-formed or rectified in a proper case[1]. If the grantor agrees, the court may rectify a voluntary deed by setting aside a part of it only and allowing the remainder to stand[2]; if the grantor does not agree, the instrument can only be set aside in toto, if at all[3]. The same follows where the deed fails in substance to carry out the parties' intention[4]. A grantor may make a fresh deed and, with the grantee's consent, cancel the old one, but he cannot be compelled to alter the grant, and, if the grantor contests it, the deed must stand or fall in its actual condition without alteration[5]. Even if the evidence shows that the grantor did intend otherwise than as expressed in the deed, the court will not compel him now to introduce a clause into the deed which he does not choose to introduce, for there can be no specific performance of an intention to make a voluntary deed[6]. Generally speaking there can be no rectification without the grantor's consent[7], but after his death rectification can be sought, on proof that the instrument did not carry his intention into effect[8].

If a settlement does not involve an actual bargain between the settlor and the trustees, the settlor may seek rectification on proof that it does not express his true intention or the true intention of himself and any party with whom he has bargained; he need not show failure to express the trustees' intention[9]. Where a deed is made in exercise of a power by more than one person, it is the collective intention that must be objectively manifested[10]. On the other hand the court will hesitate to rectify a voluntary settlement at the settlor's instance merely on his own evidence as to his intention, unsupported by other evidence such as written instructions[11], even though the rectification sought would bring the settlement more into harmony with recognised precedents and what the settlor might reasonably have intended at the time[12]. However, a volunteer is entitled to take proceedings to have an error in a settlement rectified[13], even though the effect would be to carry back the settled fund to the original settlor[14], but the court will only act on the clearest and most certain demonstration of error and of actual intention[15].

The court will not rectify a settlement which the settlor intended to execute, where he mistakenly believed that the fiscal consequences of making such a settlement were different from what they actually were, as the settlement correctly recorded his intentions[16].

1   *Walker v Armstrong* (1856) 8 De GM & G 531; *Bonhote v Henderson* [1895] 1 Ch 742 (affd [1895] 2 Ch 202, CA); *Behrers v Heilbut* (1956) 222 LT Jo 290; *Re Butlin's Settlement Trusts, Butlin v Butlin* [1976] Ch 251 at 260, [1976] 2 All ER 483 at 487 per Brightman J; *Re Slocock's Will Trusts* [1979] 1 All ER 358. See also TRUSTS AND POWERS vol 98 (2013) PARA 80. As to the revocation and avoidance of gifts see GIFTS vol 52 (2014) PARA 257 et seq.
2   *Turner v Collins* (1871) 7 Ch App 329 at 342 per Lord Hatherley LC.
3   *Phillipson v Kerry* (1863) 32 Beav 628 at 637–638 per Sir John Romilly MR; *Turner v Collins* (1871) 7 Ch App 329 at 342 per Lord Hatherley LC.
4   *Phillipson v Kerry* (1863) 32 Beav 628.
5   *Broun v Kennedy* (1863) 33 Beav 133 at 147 per Sir John Romilly MR (on appeal (1864) 4 De GJ & Sm 217); and see *Phillipson v Kerry* (1863) 32 Beav 628 at 637–638 per Sir John Romilly MR.
6   *Lister v Hodgson* (1867) LR 4 Eq 30 at 34, 36 per Sir John Romilly MR; *Thompson v Whitmore* (1860) 1 John & H 268 at 273 per Sir W Page Wood V-C; *M'Mechan v Warburton* [1896] 1 IR 435; cf *Weir v Van-Tromp* (1900) 16 TLR 531.
7   *Tucker v Bennett* (1887) 38 ChD 1 at 14–15, CA, per Cotton LJ; *Rake v Hooper* (1900) 83 LT 669, 17 TLR 118.
8   *Lister v Hodgson* (1867) LR 4 Eq 30, 34; *Weir v Van Tromp* (1900) 16 TLR 531 (claim for rectification dismissed); *Christie v Public Trustee* (1921) 22 SR(NSW) 148.
9   *Re Butlin's Settlement Trusts, Butlin v Butlin* [1976] Ch 251 at 262, [1976] 2 All ER 483 at 489 per Brightman J; *Tankel v Tankel* [1999] 1 FLR 676.
10 *AMP (UK) Ltd plc v Barker* (2000) 3 ITELR 414 at [64]–[67] per Lawrence Collins J; *Gallaher Ltd v Gallaher Pensions Ltd* [2005] EWHC 42 (Ch) at [117], [2005] All ER (D) 177 (Jan) per Etherton J; *Lansing Linde Ltd v Alber* [2000] Pensions LR 15 at 49–50 per Rimer J.
11 *Van der Linde v Van der Linde* [1947] Ch 306.
12 *Bonhote v Henderson* [1895] 1 Ch 742 (affd [1895] 2 Ch 202, CA); *Tankel v Tankel* [1999] 1 FLR 676.
13 *Thompson v Whitmore* (1860) 1 John & H 268 at 273 per Sir W Page Wood V-C; *Weir v Van Tromp* (1900) 16 TLR 531; *Re Slocock's Will Trusts* [1979] 1 All ER 358.
14 *Thompson v Whitmore* (1860) John & H 268.
15 *Weir v Van Tromp* (1900) 16 TLR 531; *Re Slocock's Will Trusts* [1979] 1 All ER 358.
16 *Allnutt v Wilding* [2007] EWCA Civ 412, 9 ITELR 806, [2007] All ER (D) 41 (Apr).

61.   Settlements under a court order. It is no objection to the exercise by the court of its jurisdiction that the settlement was made in pursuance of a court order[1]. Consent orders may be set aside, wholly or in part, or rectified on such grounds as would enable the court to set aside or rectify an agreement, for example, fraud or mutual mistake[2].

The fact that a provision is proper, and one usually inserted in marriage settlements directed by the court, is not a ground for refusing to rectify the settlement by striking the provision out when it is shown that its insertion defeats the intention[3].

1   *Smith v Illiffe* (1875) LR 20 Eq 666.
2   *Huddersfield Banking Co Ltd v Henry Lister & Son Ltd* [1895] 2 Ch 273, CA; *Wilding v Sanderson* [1897] 2 Ch 534, CA; *Standley v Stewkesbury* [1998] 2 FLR 610, CA.
3   *Torre v Torre* (1853) 1 Sm & G 518.

62. Effect of rectification. Rectification, if granted, relates back to the time when the instrument was executed[1], and after rectification the instrument is to be read as if it had been originally drawn up in its rectified form[2]. When rectified, a contract becomes a document sufficient to satisfy any statutory provision requiring the existence of a document in writing[3].

1   *Earl of Malmesbury v Countess of Malmesbury* (1862) 31 Beav 407 at 418 per Sir John Romilly MR.
2   *Craddock Bros v Hunt* [1923] 2 Ch 136 at 151, CA, per Lord Sterndale MR. See also *Re Slocock's Will Trusts* [1979] 1 All ER 358 at 363 per Graham J.
3   See PARA 44.

63. Procedure for claims for rectification. All causes and matters for rectification of deeds or other written instruments are assigned to the Chancery Division of the High Court[1]. However, a counterclaim for rectification may be entertained in the Queen's Bench Division[2], and rectification has been granted in judicial review proceedings in the Administrative Court[3]. Certain proceedings for rectification may also be taken in the county court subject to the limits on its equity jurisdiction[4]. Normally a claim for rectification must be specifically pleaded, but the court may grant the relief even though it is not asked for on the pleadings[5]. An instrument may be rectified even though a party to it is not joined or before the court where that party is not affected by the rectification[6]. However, so long as an instrument remains unaltered the court cannot avoid acting on it in that form[7].

Generally, in proceedings for rectification, oral evidence is required to be given; trial on affidavit evidence will not be ordered[8]. But when the issues of fact substantially depend on written evidence and no objection is made by either party, the court may decide the case on affidavit evidence[9] and proceedings to obtain rectification may then be commenced[10].

Where a conveyance is ordered to be rectified, the court order is sufficient without a further conveyance[11]. Sometimes the judge will authenticate the alteration by signing his initials against it[12], but this is not necessary[13]. The usual course is to direct the declaration made by the court to be indorsed on the instrument[14]. A conveyance is sometimes directed[15].

1   See the Senior Courts Act 1981 s 61(1), Sch 1 para 1(g); and COURTS AND TRIBUNALS vol 24 (2010) PARA 704. As to the assignment of proceedings in the High Court generally see CIVIL PROCEDURE vol 11 (2015) PARA 94 et seq. As to the consequences of commencing proceedings in the wrong division see *Apac Rowena Ltd v Norpol Packaging Ltd* [1991] 4 All ER 516. As to the rectification or setting aside of deeds generally see DEEDS AND OTHER INSTRUMENTS vol 32 (2012) PARA 267 et seq.
2   *Mostyn v West Mostyn Coal and Iron Co Ltd* (1876) 1 CPD 145; *Storey v Waddle* (1879) 4 QBD 289, CA; *Hamed El Chiaty & Co (t/a Travco Nile Cruise Lines) v Thomas Cook Group Ltd, The Nile Rhapsody* [1992] 2 Lloyd's Rep 399 (affd [1994] 1 Lloyd's Rep 382, CA).
3   *R v Inspector of Taxes, ex p Bass Holdings Ltd, Richart (Inspector of Taxes) v Bass Holdings Ltd* [1993] STC 122. As to the Administrative Court (formerly the Crown Office List) see COURTS AND TRIBUNALS vol 24 (2010) PARA 707. As to judicial review see JUDICIAL REVIEW vol 61 (2010) PARA 601 et seq.
4   See COURTS AND TRIBUNALS vol 24 (2010) PARA 776.

5   *Butler v Mountview Estates Ltd* [1951] 2 KB 563 at 571, [1951] 1 All ER 693 at 700 per
    Danckwerts J.
6   *Wilson v Wilson* [1969] 3 All ER 945 at 948, [1969] 1 WLR 1470 at 1473 per Buckley J.
7   *Re Malet* (1862) 30 Beav 407 at 408 per Sir John Romilly MR.
8   *Bonhote v Henderson* [1895] 1 Ch 742 (affd [1895] 2 Ch 202, CA); *Constantinidi v Ralli* [1935]
    Ch 427.
9   See *Bonhote v Henderson* [1895] 1 Ch 742 (affd [1895] 2 Ch 202, CA);
    Re Colebrook's Conveyances, Taylor v Taylor [1973] 1 All ER 132, [1972] 1 WLR 1397; *Seymour
    v Seymour* (1989) Times, 16 February; *Lake v Lake* [1989] STC 865.
10 As to the bringing of proceedings see CPR Pt 8; and CIVIL PROCEDURE vol 11 (2015) PARA 150
    et seq. Where the Pt 8 procedure cannot be used, the procedure set out in Pt 7 will apply: see CIVIL
    PROCEDURE vol 11 (2015) PARA 139 et seq.
11 *White v White* (1872) LR 15 Eq 247; *Beale v Kyte* [1907] 1 Ch 564; and see *Stock v Vining* (1858)
    25 Beav 235.
12 *Stock v Vining* (1858) 25 Beav 235.
13 *White v White* (1872) LR 15 Eq 247 at 249 per Sir James Bacon V-C.
14 See *Hanley v Pearson* (1879) 13 ChD 545 at 549 per Sir James Bacon V-C; *Johnson v Bragge*
    [1901] 1 Ch 28 at 37 per Cozens-Hardy J; *Lord Gifford v Lord Fitzhardinge* [1899] 2 Ch 32; *Re
    BT Property Trust* (31 March 1998, unreported), NSW SC.
15 *Earl of Malmesbury v Countess of Malmesbury, Phillipson v Turner* (1862) 31 Beav 407; *Clark
    v Malpas* (1862) 4 De GF & J 401; cf *Marquess of Exeter v Marchioness of Exeter* (1838) 3 My
    & Cr 321 at 326 per Lord Cottenham LC. See also *Wilson v Wilson* [1969] 3 All ER 945, [1969]
    1 WLR 1470.

(5) RECOVERY OF MONEY PAID UNDER A MISTAKE

64.   Recovery of money paid under a mistake at common law. The law relating
to recovery of mistaken payments has a long history, going back to the so-called
'common counts' for money had and received to the use of the plaintiff[1], and
before that to the old law of account[2]. Along with quantum meruit, quantum
valebat, and other counts, it became a part of the law known as quasi-contract[3],
which has now developed into the law of restitution[4], the central principle of
which is the reversal of unjust enrichment[5]. Under the umbrella of this principle,
other areas of both common law and equity have been united with that relating
to money paid under mistake[6].

In principle, money paid under mistake of law is to be treated in the same way
as money paid under mistake of fact[7]. The suggestion that this rule did not extend
to an overpayment of tax under a mistake of law[8] has been rejected[9]; but if
Parliament creates a statutory regime which is inconsistent with this common law
right, that right is displaced[10]. However, the rule does not apply to the recovery by
the state of overpayments of social security benefits made by mistake, in so far as
there is a comprehensive statutory regime prescribing all the incidents of the
benefits to which it applies and the circumstances in which repayments are to be
made[11].

The types of mistake that give rise to a restitutionary claim are discussed
elsewhere in this work[12].

1   *Bonnel v Fowke* (1657) 2 Sid 4; 3 Bl Com 162; Simpson *A History of the Common Law
    of Contract* (1st Edn, 1975) pp 494–495.
2   *Framson v Delamere* (1595) Cro Eliz 458; *Hewer v Bartholomew* (1598) Cro Eliz 614; 8
    Holdsworth's History of English Law p 92.
3   Baker 'The History of Quasi-Contract in English Law' in Cornish, Nolan, O'Sullivan and Virgo
    (Eds) *Restitution: Past, Present and Future* (1998) at p 37.
4   *Lipkin Gorman v Karpnale Ltd* [1991] 2 AC 548, [1992] 4 All ER 512, HL; *Woolwich Equitable
    Building Society v IRC* [1993] AC 70 at 196–197, [1992] 3 All ER 737 at 780–781, HL, per Lord
    Browne-Wilkinson; *Westdeutsche Landesbank Girozentale v Islington London Borough Council*

[1996] AC 669, [1996] 2 All ER 961, HL; cf *Orakpo v Manson Investments Ltd* [1978] AC 95, [1977] 3 All ER 1, HL. As to restitution in general see RESTITUTION.

5   Birks *An Introduction to the Law of Restitution* (1989) Ch I; Birks *Unjust Enrichment* (2nd Edn, 2005); and see RESTITUTION vol 88 (2012) PARA 401 et seq.

6   As to the development of the law relating to restitution claims based on mistake see RESTITUTION vol 88 (2012) PARA 432 et seq.

7   See RESTITUTION vol 88 (2012) PARA 436 et seq. See also PARA 11.
    Where money is paid by one party to another under a mistake of fact common to both parties, it is not necessary for the payer on discovering the mistake to make a demand for payment before making a claim against the payee to recover the money: *Baker v Courage & Co* [1910] 1 KB 56; *Anglo-Scottish Beet Sugar Corpn Ltd v Spalding UDC* [1937] 2 KB 607, [1937] 3 All ER 335. Where, however, payment was made after the payer had discovered the mistake on which the sum payable was calculated and the payer gave notice of the mistake to the payee, a demand for payment was held necessary: *Freeman v Jeffries* (1869) LR 4 Exch 189 at 200 per Kelly CB.
    As to defences to claims for repayment of money paid under mistake see RESTITUTION vol 88 (2012) PARA 438.

8   See *Kleinwort Benson Ltd v Lincoln City Council* [1999] 2 AC 349 at 381–382, [1998] 4 All ER 513 at 537–538, HL, per Lord Goff of Chieveley; *Woolwich Equitable Building Society v IRC* [1993] AC 70, [1992] 3 All ER 737, HL.

9   *Deutsche Morgan Grenfell Group plc v IRC* [2006] UKHL 49 at [18]–[19], [23], at [56], at [83] and at [132]–[135], [141], [2007] 1 AC 558, [2007] 1 All ER 449 per Lord Hoffmann, Lord Hope of Craighead, Lord Scott of Foscote and Lord Walker of Gestingthorpe respectively.

10 See RESTITUTION vol 88 (2012) PARA 459. See also *Monro v Revenue and Customs Comrs* [2008] EWCA Civ 306, [2009] Ch 69, [2008] 3 WLR 734, in which it was also held that the particular statutory restriction on the right of recovery was not an unjustified interference with the right to protection of property under the European Convention on Human Rights First Protocol art 1. As to the right to property protected under the European Convention on Human Rights First Protocol art 1 see RIGHTS AND FREEDOMS vol 88A (2013) PARA 534 et seq.

11 *Child Poverty Action Group v Secretary of State for Work and Pensions* [2010] UKSC 54, [2011] 2 AC 15, [2011] 1 All ER 729.

12 RESTITUTION vol 88 (2012) PARA 429 et seq.

65. Recovery of money paid under a mistake and regularisation in equity. In principle, wherever the common law would allow recovery of a mistaken payment, so too would equity[1]. In some respects, however, equity went further. First, it appears that, at least in the exclusive jurisdiction dealing with trusts and estates, equity would give relief in cases of mistake of law[2], although in the case of a claim to recover monies paid out of a deceased's estate in error, the real beneficiary must first exhaust his claim against the personal representative before claiming against the recipient of the payment[3]. Secondly, it may be that a payment made under mistake does not pass property in equity, so grounding an equitable proprietary claim[4]. Thirdly, a trustee who has overpaid a beneficiary, or paid the wrong beneficiary, can recoup the payment (or overpayment) out of any trust capital or income remaining in or coming into his hands to which the beneficiary[5] (or his assignee[6]) would be entitled[7]. This is an aspect of equitable accounting between trustee and beneficiary[8], and is unaffected by the limitation legislation[9]. In some cases equity will direct settled accounts to be reopened because of mistake[10].

In one respect however, equity is narrower than the common law. In relation to mistaken payments from trusts (but not from estates[11] or, probably, company liquidators[12]) equity will ordinarily require the recipient to repay monies wrongfully distributed to him (as opposed to setting off against other entitlement of the payee) only if there is some degree of fault on his part[13]. However, the authorities hitherto have variously made liability depend on the recipient's:

(1)   failing to make the inquiries which an honest and reasonable person would make[14];

(2)   knowledge of circumstances that would indicate the facts to a reasonable person[15]; or

(3)   knowledge of circumstances that would put a reasonable person on inquiry[16].

The position at the date at which this volume states the law seems to make liability depend on a reasonable person's state of knowledge being such as to make it unconscionable for him to retain the benefit of the payment[17].

1   See eg *Sybron Corpn v Rochem Ltd* [1984] Ch 112, [1983] 2 All ER 707, CA. As to recovery at common law see PARA 64.

2   *Re Musgrave, Machell v Parry* [1916] 2 Ch 417; *Ministry of Health v Simpson* [1951] AC 251, [1950] 2 All ER 1137, HL; *Gibbon v Mitchell* [1990] 3 All ER 338, [1990] 1 WLR 1304; and see TRUSTS AND POWERS vol 98 (2013) PARA 717. See also EQUITABLE JURISDICTION vol 47 (2014) PARAS 39, 238.

3   *Ministry of Health v Simpson* [1951] AC 251, [1950] 2 All ER 1137, HL.

4   See PARAS 24–26.

5   *Downes v Bullock* (1858) 25 Beav 54; *Re Musgrave, Machell v Parry* [1916] 2 Ch 417; *IVS Enterprises Ltd v Chelsea Cloisters Management Ltd* [1994] EGCS 14, 13 TLI 111; cf, however, *Re Horne, Wilson v Cox Sinclair* [1905] 1 Ch 76 at 80–81 per Warrington J (trustee also beneficiary).

6   *Re Moore, Moore v Moore* (1881) 45 LT 466.

7   See TRUSTS AND POWERS vol 98 (2013) PARA 717.

8   *Harris v Harris (No 2)* (1861) 29 Beav 110; *Re Robinson, McLaren v Public Trustee* [1911] 1 Ch 502.

9   *Re Robinson, McLaren v Public Trustee* [1911] 1 Ch 502.

10 See PARA 66.

11 *Ministry of Health v Simpson* [1951] AC 251, [1950] 2 All ER 1137, HL.

12 *Butler v Broadhead* [1975] Ch 97, [1974] 2 All ER 401.

13 *Bate v Hooper* (1855) 5 De GM & G 338; *Downes v Bullock* (1858) 25 Beav 54; *Hilliard v Fulford* (1876) 4 ChD 389; but see Nicholls 'Knowing Receipt: The Need for a New Landmark' in Cornish, Nolan, O'Sullivan and Virgo (Eds) *Restitution: Past, Present and Future* (1998) at p 231.

14 *Re Montagu's Settlement Trusts, Duke of Manchester v National Westminster Bank Ltd* [1987] Ch 264 at 285, [1987] 2 WLR 1192 at 1211 per Megarry V-C; *Jonathan v Tilley* (1995) 12 Trust Law International 36 at 39–42; *Hillsdown Holdings plc v Pensions Ombudsman* [1997] 1 All ER 862 at 900–903 per Knox J; *Bristol and West Building Society v Mothew* [1998] Ch 1 at 23, [1996] 4 All ER 698 at 716, CA, per Millett LJ.

15 *Belmont Finance Corpn Ltd v Williams Furniture Ltd (No 2)* [1980] 1 All ER 393 at 410, 412, CA, per Goff LJ; *Agip (Africa) Ltd v Jackson* [1990] Ch 265 at 292–293, [1992] 4 All ER 385 at 404–405 per Millett J (affd [1991] Ch 547, [1992] 4 All ER 451, CA).

16 *Citadel General Assurance Co Ltd v Lloyd's Bank Canada* (1997) 152 DLR (4th) 411.

17 *Bank of Credit and Commerce International (Overseas) Ltd (in liquidation) v Akindele* [2001] Ch 437 at 455, [2000] 4 All ER 221 at 235–236, CA, per Nourse LJ; *Niru Battery Manufacturing Co v Milestone Trading Ltd* [2003] EWCA Civ 1446 at [148], [2004] QB 985, [2004] 1 All ER (Comm) 193 per Clarke J; *Nabb Brothers Ltd v Lloyds Bank International (Guernsey) Ltd* [2005] EWHC 405 (Ch) at [71], [2005] All ER (D) 322 (Mar) per Lawrence Collins J; *Gray v Smith* [2013] EWHC 4136 (Comm) at [132]–[138], [2014] 2 All ER (Comm) 359 per Cooke J.

(6) REOPENING OF ACCOUNTS

66. Accounts drawn up under a mistake; inaccurate accounts. The court may reopen an account or give liberty to surcharge and falsify it[1] where it was drawn up under a mistake[2]. It is not necessary that money should have been actually paid, and the same rules also apply where the money has only been allowed in account[3].

Where accounts between two parties are shown to be erroneous to a considerable extent both in amount and in the number of items, or where there is a fiduciary relationship and a less considerable number of errors are shown, or where the fiduciary relationship exists and one or more fraudulent omissions or insertions in the accounts are shown, the court will reopen the account, and not merely surcharge and falsify[4]. It may also do so even if there is only a single error[5]. However, where there has been a long lapse of time and loss of books and documents, the court may decline to reopen the accounts altogether and give liberty to surcharge and falsify only, notwithstanding that numerous and important errors in the account are proved[6].

It is also now provided that any party who wishes to contend that an accounting party has or should be treated as having received more than the accounts show that he has received, or that the accounts are otherwise inaccurate, may give written notice of such objections to the accounting party[7].

1   As to the procedure for accounts and inquiries generally see CIVIL PROCEDURE vol 12A (2015) PARA 1250 et seq.
2   *Coleman v Mellersh* (1850) 2 Mac & G 309 at 314–315; *Re Webb, Lambert v Still* [1894] 1 Ch 73 at 83–84, CA, per Davey LJ.
3   *Skyring v Greenwood* (1825) 4 B & C 281; *Lucas v Jones* (1844) 5 QB 949 at 953; *Standish v Ross* (1849) 3 Exch 527 at 534 per Parke B; *Gingell v Purkins* (1850) 4 Exch 720 at 726 per Parke B; *Ehrensperger v Anderson* (1848) 3 Exch 148; *Ward & Co v Wallis* [1900] 1 QB 675.
4   *Williamson v Barbour* (1877) 9 ChD 529 at 533 per Jessel MR; and see *Re Webb, Lambert v Still* [1894] 1 Ch 73 at 83–84, CA, per Davey LJ; *Cheese v Keen* [1908] 1 Ch 245 at 251 per Neville J.
5   *Taylor v Haylin* (1788) 2 Bro CC 310; *Pritt v Clay* (1843) 6 Beav 503; and see *Gething v Keighley* (1878) 9 ChD 547 at 550 per Jessel MR; *Re Webb, Lambert v Still* [1894] 1 Ch 73 at 82, 85, CA, per Davey LJ.
6   *Millar v Craig* (1843) 6 Beav 433; *Brownell v Brownell* (1786) 2 Bro CC 62 at 63; *Re Webb, Lambert v Still* [1894] 1 Ch 73, CA. Cf *Allfrey v Allfrey* (1849) 1 Mac & G 87 at 93–94 per Lord Cottenham LC. As to the reopening of settled accounts see EQUITABLE JURISDICTION vol 47 (2014) PARA 53.
7   See CPR PD 40A—*Accounts, Inquiries etc* paras 3.1–3.3; and CIVIL PROCEDURE vol 12A (2015) PARA 1252. As to the overlap between this process and the common law grant of liberty to surcharge and falsify see EQUITABLE JURISDICTION vol 47 (2014) PARA 54.

(7) RECOVERY OF PROPERTY TRANSFERRED UNDER A MISTAKE

67.   Recovery of property transferred under a mistake at common law. Where mistake has prevented property from passing at law[1], the transferor remains legal owner, and has all the normal remedies for recovery of possession of the property concerned, whether realty[2] or personalty[3]. The transferor may normally follow his property into the hands of a third party[4], though in the case of money and negotiable instruments not against a purchaser for value[5], and also subject to the effect of transactions abroad[6]. Difficulties, however, may arise where the property becomes affixed to or mixed with property belonging to other persons[7].

1   See PARAS 24–26.
2   See REAL PROPERTY AND REGISTRATION vol 87 (2012) PARA 320 et seq.
3   See TORT vol 97 (2015) PARA 602 et seq.
4   *Reid v Metropolitan Police Comr* [1973] QB 551, [1973] 2 All ER 97, CA. Sale by market overt, in which tracing property into the hands of a third party was not possible, was abolished by the Sale of Goods (Amendment) Act 1994: see MARKETS vol 71 (2013) PARA 824; SALE OF GOODS AND SUPPLY OF SERVICES vol 91 (2012) PARA 6.
5   *Crouch v Crédit Foncier of England* (1873) LR 8 QB 374 at 381 per Blackburn J; *Moss v Hancock* [1899] 2 QB 111; *Banque Belge pour l'Etranger v Hambrouck* [1921] 1 KB 321 at 329, CA, per Scrutton LJ.
6   *Winkworth v Christie Manson and Woods Ltd* [1980] Ch 496, [1980] 1 All ER 1121.
7   See PARA 25.

68–100.   Recovery of property transferred under a mistake in equity. Where property has passed at law, but mistake has prevented it from passing in equity[1], or rescission has revested full equitable ownership in the transferor[2], the transferor as equitable owner may demand that the transferee recover the legal ownership to him or as he may direct[3]. The transferee is not, however, to be regarded as a trustee for the transferor until he has such notice of the true facts as would affect his conscience[4]. The transferor may trace his property into changes of form and into the hands of third parties, until it reaches the hands of a bona fide purchaser for value of a legal interest without notice[5].

1 See PARAS 24–26.
2 See PARA 51.
3 See *Wood v Rowcliffe* (1847) 2 Ph 382.
4 *Westdeutsche Landesbank Girozentrale v Islington London Borough Council* [1996] AC 669 at 705–706, [1996] 2 All ER 961 at 988, HL, per Lord Browne-Wilkinson.
5 See EQUITABLE JURISDICTION vol 47 (2014) PARA 238 et seq.

MORTGAGE

1. CLASSIFICATION OF MORTGAGES

(1) DEFINITIONS AND KEY CONCEPTS RELATING TO MORTGAGES

101. Meaning of 'mortgage'. A mortgage is a disposition of property as security for a debt. It may be effected by a demise or sub-demise of land[1], by a transfer of a chattel[2], by an assignment of a chose or thing in action[3], by a charge[4] on any interest in real or personal property[5] or by an agreement to create a charge[6], for securing money or money's worth, the security being redeemable on repayment or discharge of the debt or other obligation[7]. Generally, whenever a disposition of an estate or interest is originally intended as a security for money, whether this intention appears from the deed itself or from any other instrument or from oral evidence, it is considered as a mortgage and redeemable[8].

1 See PARA 161 et seq.
2 See PARA 205.
3 See PARA 206.
4 For the purposes of the Law of Property Act 1925, 'mortgage' includes any charge or lien on any property for securing money or money's worth: s 205(1)(xvi). As to the distinction between a mortgage or charge and a lien see PARA 113.
5 Cf the Law of Property Act 1925 s 205(1)(xx), by which 'property' includes any thing in action, and any interest in real or personal property. See also *Beswick v Beswick* [1968] AC 58, [1967] 2 All ER 1197, HL.
6 See PARA 217.
7 *Santley v Wilde* [1899] 2 Ch 474, CA, per Lindley MR; *Noakes & Co Ltd v Rice* [1902] AC 24 at 28, HL. As to the position where the property is situated abroad see CONFLICT OF LAWS vol 19 (2011) PARA 692.
8 Co Litt 205a note; *Maxwell v Lady Mountacute* (1719) Prec Ch 526; *Cripps v Jee* (1793) 4 Bro CC 472; *Sevier v Greenway* (1815) 19 Ves 413. See also PARA 108.

102. Characteristics of a mortgage. A mortgage consists of two things, namely a personal contract for payment of a debt and a disposition or charge of the mortgagor's estate or interest as security for the repayment of the debt; in equity the estate or interest so transferred is no more than a pledge or security[1]. Every mortgage implies a debt and a personal obligation by the mortgagor to pay it[2]. If there is a covenant or bond for its payment it is a specialty debt; if not, it is a simple contract debt[3]. A mortgagee has an insurable interest[4]. Covenants in a mortgage are subject to the doctrine against restraint of trade[5].

1 *Quarrell v Beckford* (1816) 1 Madd 269 at 278 per Plumer V-C.
2 *King v King* (1735) 3 P Wms 358; *Sutton v Sutton* (1882) 22 ChD 511 at 515, CA.
3 *King v King* (1735) 3 P Wms 358; *Duke of Ancaster v Mayer* (1785) 1 Bro CC 454 at 464; *Yates v Aston* (1843) 4 QB 182. As to covenants for payment see PARA 182.
4 As to property insurance see INSURANCE vol 60 (2011) PARA 586; and as to marine insurance see INSURANCE vol 60 (2011) PARA 238 et seq.
5 *Esso Petroleum Co Ltd v Harper's Garage (Stourport) Ltd* [1968] AC 269, [1967] 1 All ER 699, HL (provision of a tying covenant in a mortgage held unenforceable as being an unreasonable restraint of trade). As to restraint of trade see COMPETITION vol 18 (2009) PARA 377 et seq.

103. Validity of charge on mortgagor's whole estate. A charge created by a mortgage and extending to the whole of the mortgagor's real and personal property, whether present or future, may possibly be unenforceable as such, either on the ground that it is too vague to be enforced or on the ground that it is contrary to public policy that a person should be allowed to deprive himself of the whole of his livelihood[1]. Such a charge is, however, enforceable if it can be construed as confined to property existing at the date of the granting of the charge and ascertainable at the date when it is sought to enforce it[2]. Moreover, if the charge extends to future property but the particular types of property included in the general charge are separately specified, the charge may be treated as divisible[3] and enforced against after-acquired property which falls within a particular class so specified and is ascertainable at the date when it is sought to enforce the charge[4].

1   See *Re Clarke, Coombe v Carter* (1887) 36 ChD 348 at 352–353, 355, CA; *Re Turcan* (1888) 40 ChD 5 at 9, CA (covenant to settle after-acquired property); *Re Kelcey, Tyson v Kelcey* [1899] 2 Ch 530 at 532–534; *Syrett v Egerton* [1957] 3 All ER 331, [1957] 1 WLR 1130, DC, where the possibility was discussed.
2   *Re Kelcey, Tyson v Kelcey* [1899] 2 Ch 530 (agreement to charge all debtor's real and personal estates; charge enforceable against money becoming payable under assurance policy to which debtor was entitled at date of charge).
3   *Re Clarke, Coombe v Carter* (1887) 36 ChD 348, CA. See also *Re Turcan* (1888) 40 ChD 5, CA.
4   *Re Clarke, Coombe v Carter* (1887) 36 ChD 348, CA (money to which mortgagor might become entitled under will); *Syrett v Egerton* [1957] 3 All ER 331, [1957] 1 WLR 1130, DC (charge of all income and estate; charge divisible and enforceable against income). See also *Tailby v Official Receiver* (1888) 13 App Cas 523, HL (assignment of future book debts); *Re Turcan* (1888) 40 ChD 5, CA. As to the assignment of after-acquired property by way of security see PARA 247.

104. Legal mortgages. A legal mortgage of personal property is a conditional assignment to the mortgagee of the mortgagor's legal interest in it[1]. A legal mortgage of land or an interest in land must be by deed[2]. A legal mortgage of an estate in unregistered land is effected by a charge by deed expressed to be by way of legal mortgage or a demise or sub-demise for a term of years absolute[3]. The effect of a legal mortgage by demise is to vest the legal estate in the term of years created by it in the mortgagee, who, unless the deed expressly provides for possession by the mortgagor until default, is immediately entitled upon the execution of the deed to possession of the property[4]; but the mortgagor's legal estate in the reversion of the term of years is not transferred to the mortgagee until the right of redemption is destroyed by foreclosure or sale or otherwise[5]. A legal charge does not vest any estate in the mortgagee, but creates a legal interest which confers on the mortgagee the same protection, powers and remedies as a mortgage by demise[6]. A mortgage of registered land can be made only by a charge by deed expressed to be by way of legal mortgage or by charging the estate with the payment of money, and cannot be made by way of mortgage by demise[7].

1   In the Law of Property Act 1925, 'legal mortgage' means a mortgage by demise or sub-demise or a charge by way of legal mortgage, and 'legal mortgagee' has a corresponding meaning; 'mortgage money' means money or money's worth secured by a mortgage; 'mortgagor' includes any person from time to time deriving title under the original mortgagor or entitled to redeem a mortgage according to his estate interest or right in the mortgaged property; 'mortgagee' includes a chargee by way of legal mortgage and any person from time to time deriving title under the original mortgagee; and 'mortgagee in possession' is a mortgagee who, in right of the mortgage, has entered into and is in possession of the mortgaged property: s 205(1)(xvi). As to the meaning of 'mortgage' see PARA 101 note 4; and as to the meaning of 'property' see PARA 101 note 5. As to mortgages of personalty see PARA 205 et seq. See also FINANCIAL INSTRUMENTS AND TRANSACTIONS vol 49 (2015) PARA 457 et seq.
2   See the Law of Property Act 1925 s 52(1); and DEEDS AND OTHER INSTRUMENTS vol 32 (2012) PARA 214. In the Law of Property Act 1925, 'land' includes land of any tenure, and mines and minerals, whether or not held apart from the surface, buildings or parts of buildings (whether the division is horizontal, vertical or made in any other way) and other corporeal hereditaments; and also includes a manor, an advowson, a rent and other incorporeal hereditaments, and an easement, right, privilege or benefit in, over, or derived from land; 'mines and minerals' include any strata or seam of minerals or substances in or under any land, and powers of working and getting them; 'manor' includes a lordship and reputed manor or lordship; and 'hereditament' means any real property which on an intestacy occurring before 1926 might have devolved upon an heir: s 205(1)(ix) (amended by the Trusts of Land and Appointment of Trustees Act 1996 s 25(2), Sch 4).

3 See the Law of Property Act 1925 ss 85(1), 86(1); and PARAS 164–165. Formerly the legal mortgage of real property was, as the legal mortgage of personal property still is, a conditional assurance: see PARA 161.
4 As to the mortgagee's right to possession see PARAS 341, 404 et seq.
5 As to the equity of redemption or right to redeem see PARA 304 et seq.
6 See the Law of Property Act 1925 s 87(1); and PARA 165. See also *Regent Oil Co Ltd v JA Gregory (Hatch End) Ltd* [1966] Ch 402 at 433, [1965] 3 All ER 673 at 680, CA, per Harman LJ.
7 See the Land Registration Act 2002 s 23(1); and REAL PROPERTY AND REGISTRATION vol 87 (2012) PARAS 422–423.

105. Equitable mortgages. An equitable mortgage is a specifically enforceable contract to create a legal mortgage[1]. It creates a charge on the property but does not convey any legal estate or interest to the creditor; such a charge amounts to an equitable interest[2]. Its operation is that of an executory assurance which, as between the parties, and so far as equitable rights and remedies are concerned, is equivalent to an actual assurance, and is enforceable under the court's equitable jurisdiction[3]. An equitable mortgagee may elect to dispense with the mortgage and rely only on his charge, realisable by sale[4].

As a general rule all property, whether real or personal, which may be the subject of a legal mortgage can equally be charged in equity[5]: an equitable mortgage may be made by a mortgage of an equitable interest[6], by an agreement to create a legal mortgage[7], or by a mortgage which fails to comply with the formalities for a legal mortgage[8]. A mere deposit of title deeds is not effective to create an equitable mortgage over land[9].

1 *Swiss Bank Corpn v Lloyds Bank Ltd* [1982] AC 584, [1980] 2 All ER 419, CA; affd [1982] AC 584, [1981] 2 All ER 449, HL. As to equitable mortgages see further PARA 215 et seq.
2 In the Law of Property Act 1925, 'equitable interests' means all interests and charges in or over land other than legal estates (see REAL PROPERTY AND REGISTRATION vol 87 (2012) PARA 109 et seq); and 'legal estates' means the estates, interests and charges in or over land, subsisting or created at law, which are by that Act authorised to subsist or to be created as legal estates (see REAL PROPERTY AND REGISTRATION vol 87 (2012) PARAS 66–88): s 205(1)(x) (amended by the Trusts of Land and Appointment of Trustees Act 1996 s 25(2), Sch 4). See eg *Re Sharland, Kemp v Rozey (No 2)* (1896) 74 LT 664, CA.
3 See *Downsview Nominees Ltd v First City Corpn Ltd* [1993] AC 295 at 311, [1993] 3 All ER 626 at 633, PC. See also REAL PROPERTY AND REGISTRATION vol 87 (2012) PARAS 182–183.
4 *Kennard v Futvoye* (1860) 2 Giff 81 at 94; *Matthews v Goodday* (1861) 8 Jur NS 90. See also *Parker v Housefield* (1834) 2 My & K 419 at 422; *King v Leach* (1842) 2 Hare 57. As to orders for sale see PARA 621 et seq.
5 *Winter v Lord Anson* (1827) 3 Russ 488 at 493. As to legal mortgages see PARAS 104, 160 et seq.
6 See PARA 215.
7 See PARA 217.
8 See PARA 218.
9 See *United Bank of Kuwait plc v Sahib* [1997] Ch 107, [1996] 3 All ER 215, CA; and PARA 221.

106. Equitable charges. An equitable charge arises where a particular asset or class of assets is appropriated to the satisfaction of a debt or other obligation of the chargor or a third party, so that the chargee is entitled to look to the asset and its proceeds for the discharge of the liability[1]. This right creates a transmissible interest in the asset[2]. It is a security interest created without any transfer of title or possession to the beneficiary, which can be created by an informal transaction for value and over any kind of property[3].

An equitable charge on land is a security which does not create a legal estate, but only confers an equitable interest in the land upon the creditor[4]. It entitles the holder to have the property comprised in it sold by an order of the court[5] to raise the money charged on it, but, in the absence of any express provision to that effect, it does not amount to an agreement to give a legal mortgage[6], although it may, if duly registered[7], take priority over a legal estate[8]. It may be created expressly[9], or may arise where a mortgagor purports to mortgage a greater estate in property than that which he possesses[10].

Unlike an equitable charge of land, an equitable charge of a chose or thing in action usually takes the form of an assignment of the property[11], but trust receipts, by which the borrowers agree that goods purchased with advances should be held by them as agents for and in trust for the bank, may create an equitable charge on the goods[12], and a letter may amount to an equitable assignment by way of security and therefore a charge on book debts[13].

1   *Re Cosslett (Contractors) Ltd* [1998] Ch 495 at 507–508, [1997] 4 All ER 115 at 125, CA, per Millett LJ.
2   *Re Cosslett (Contractors) Ltd* [1998] Ch 495 at 508, [1997] 4 All ER 115 at 125, CA, per Millett LJ.
3   *Re Cosslett (Contractors) Ltd* [1998] Ch 495, [1997] 4 All ER 115, CA. See also *Swiss Bank Corpn v Lloyds Bank Ltd* [1982] AC 584, [1980] 2 All ER 419, CA (affd [1982] AC 584, [1981] 2 All ER 449, HL); *Carreras Rothmans Ltd v Freeman Mathews Treasure Ltd* [1985] Ch 207, [1985] 1 All ER 155; *Re Charge Card Services Ltd* [1987] Ch 150, [1986] 3 All ER 289 (affd [1989] Ch 497, [1988] 3 All ER 702, CA); *Re Bank of Credit and Commerce International SA (No 8)* [1998] AC 214, [1997] 4 All ER 568, HL; *Russell-Cooke Trust Co v Elliott* [2007] EWHC 1443 (Ch), [2007] 2 BCLC 637, [2007] All ER (D) 166 (Mar).
4   See PARA 105. The fact that an equitable charge is normally founded on contract distinguishes it from an equitable lien: see LIEN vol 68 (2008) PARA 814. See also REAL PROPERTY AND REGISTRATION vol 87 (2012) PARA 183.
5   The mode of enforcing an equitable charge is normally sale, not foreclosure: see PARA 574.
6   *United Bank of Kuwait plc v Sahib* [1997] Ch 107, [1995] 2 All ER 973 (affd on different grounds [1997] Ch 107, [1996] 3 All ER 215, CA); *Murray v Guinness* [1998] NPC 79. See also *Matthews v Goodday* (1861) 31 LJCh 282; and REAL PROPERTY AND REGISTRATION vol 87 (2012) PARAS 182–183.
7   As to registration of an equitable charge as a Class C land charge see the Land Charges Act 1972 s 2(1), (4)(iii); PARA 262.
8   See PARA 263.
9   As to the requirements for the creation of a valid equitable charge over land see PARA 219.
10 See PARA 168.
11 See CHOSES IN ACTION vol 13 (2009) PARA 26. See also PARAS 215–217.
12 See *Mercantile Bank of India Ltd v Chartered Bank of India, Australia and China, and Strauss & Co Ltd (No 2)* [1937] 4 All ER 651; cf *Re Nanwa Gold Mines Ltd, Ballantyne v Nanwa Gold Mines Ltd* [1955] 3 All ER 219, [1955] 1 WLR 1080, where subscribers had an equitable lien on funds paid by them and placed in a separate account. See also *Barclays Bank Ltd v Quistclose Investments Ltd* [1970] AC 567, [1968] 3 All ER 651, HL; *Re Kayford Ltd* [1975] 1 All ER 604, [1975] 1 WLR 279.
13 See *Re Kent and Sussex Sawmills Ltd* [1947] Ch 177, [1946] 2 All ER 638. See also PARA 110; and CHOSES IN ACTION vol 13 (2009) PARA 26.

107. Mortgagor's equity of redemption. Incident to every mortgage is the right of the mortgagor to redeem[1], a right which is called his equity of redemption, and which continues notwithstanding that he fails to pay the debt in accordance with the proviso for redemption[2]. This right arises from the transaction being considered as a mere loan of money secured by a pledge of the estate[3]. Any provision inserted in the mortgage to prevent redemption on payment of the debt or performance of the obligation for which the security was given is termed a clog or fetter on the equity of redemption, and is void[4]. The right to redeem is so inseparable an incident of a mortgage that it cannot be taken away by an express agreement of the parties that the mortgage is not to be redeemable or that the right is to be confined to a particular time or to a particular description of persons[5]. This is especially illustrated in the case of mortgages by building societies[6] where, although redemption is not contemplated for periods usually varying between 15 and 25 years, nevertheless the mortgage may expressly allow redemption at any time[7]. The right continues unless and until, by judgment for foreclosure[8] or, in the case of a mortgage of land where the mortgagee is in possession, by the running of time[9], the mortgagor's title is extinguished or his interest is destroyed by sale either under the process of the court[10] or of a power in the mortgage incident to the security[11].

1   In the case of a legal mortgage of land by demise (see PARAS 104, 164), the term demised to the mortgagee is subject to cesser on redemption, and thus the legal estate remains in the mortgagor on redemption freed from the term demised to the mortgagee: see PARA 164. A charge by way of legal mortgage similarly ceases on redemption. In the case of an assignment of personalty by way of mortgage, the right to redeem includes the right to obtain a reassignment. In the case of a charge which is an equitable security only, redemption ends the equitable charge. As to cesser and reconveyance see PARA 647 et seq.
2   In the Law of Property Act 1925, the term 'right of redemption' is generally used (see eg Sch 1 Pt VII para 1), but 'equity of redemption' also occurs (see s 115(1)(b); and PARA 650). The two expressions have the same meaning. As to the meaning of 'right of redemption' see also PARA 109 note 2. As to the equity of redemption see note 3; and PARA 304 et seq. See also *Kreglinger v New Patagonia Meat and Cold Storage Co Ltd* [1914] AC 25, HL.
3   *Seton v Slade, Hunter v Seton* (1802) 7 Ves 265 at 273. At common law, unless the mortgagor strictly complied as to time and place with the condition of payment, he forfeited his estate, which became the absolute property of the mortgagee: Co Litt 205a Butler's note. From early times, however, the courts of equity held that until foreclosure by order of the court the mortgagor, by applying within a reasonable time and offering to pay principal and interest and all proper costs, might redeem the estate forfeited at law: *Master and Fellows of Emanuel College, Cambridge v Evans* (1625) 1 Rep Ch 18. As the right was enforceable only in the courts of equity it was called the 'equity of redemption': see note 2.
4   See PARA 320. See also PARA 196.
5   Co Litt 205 note; *Newcomb v Bonham* (1681) 1 Vern 7; *Howard v Harris* (1683) 1 Vern 190; *Esso Petroleum Co Ltd v Harper's Garage (Stourport) Ltd* [1968] AC 269, [1967] 1 All ER 699, HL. See also PARA 320.
6   As to advances by building societies see FINANCIAL INSTITUTIONS vol 48 (2015) PARA 479 et seq.
7   As to the form of a building society mortgage see FINANCIAL INSTITUTIONS vol 48 (2015) PARA 487 et seq.
8   See PARA 571 et seq.
9   See PARA 338.
10 See PARA 621 et seq.
11 See PARA 443 et seq.

108. Importance of substance of the transaction. The court examines the substance of the transaction, and the mortgagor is entitled to redeem[1] notwithstanding that no right to redeem is expressly reserved[2], or that such a right has been omitted through fraud, mistake or some unfair advantage taken by the mortgagee[3]. Oral evidence is admissible to show that a proviso for redemption was omitted through fraud[4].

There are two routes by which the legal nature of the transaction can be ascertained: the external route is to show by extrinsic evidence that a written agreement is a sham intended to mask the true agreement[5]; the internal route is to ascertain from the terms of the agreement itself whether it amounts to a transaction of the legal nature the parties ascribe to it[6]. There is no one clear touchstone by which a charge may be identified: it is necessary to look at the agreement as a whole[7].

1   As to the right to redeem generally see PARAS 107, 304 et seq.
2   *Bell v Carter* (1853) 17 Beav 11; *Chambers v Goldwin* (1801) 5 Ves 834 (on appeal (1804) 9 Ves 254); *Wicks v Scrivens* (1860) 1 John & H 215 at 218.
3   *Douglas v Culverwell* (1862) 4 De GF & J 20; *England v Codrington* (1758) 1 Eden 169; *Williams v Owen* (1840) 5 My & Cr 303 at 306; *Re Duke of Marlborough, Davis v Whitehead* [1894] 2 Ch 133; *Barton v Bank of New South Wales* (1890) 15 App Cas 379, PC; *United Dominions Trust Ltd v Beech, Savan, Tabner and Thompson* [1972] 1 Lloyd's Rep 546. The former practice was to make a mortgage by an absolute conveyance with a defeasance or clause of redemption in a separate deed which could be lost or suppressed: see *Manlove v Bale and Bruton* (1688) 2 Vern 84; *Baker v Wind* (1748) 1 Ves Sen 160; *Whitfield v Parfitt* (1851) 4 De G & Sm 240.

4 *Lincoln v Wright* (1859) 4 De G & J 16; *Walker v Walker* (1740) 2 Atk 98; *Lord Irnham v Child* (1781) 1 Bro CC 92. See also DEEDS AND OTHER INSTRUMENTS vol 32 (2012) PARAS 385, 392.
5 *Barton v Bank of New South Wales* (1890) 15 App Cas 379, PC; *Snook v London and West Riding Investments Ltd* [1967] 2 QB 786, [1967] 1 All ER 518, CA; *Lloyds and Scottish Finance Ltd v Cyril Lord Carpets Sales Ltd* [1992] BCLC 609, HL; *Welsh Development Agency v Export Finance Co Ltd* [1992] BCLC 148, [1992] BCC 270, CA.
6 *Welsh Development Agency v Export Finance Co Ltd* [1992] BCLC 148, [1992] BCC 270, CA; *Lavin v Johnson* [2002] EWCA Civ 1138, [2002] All ER (D) 501 (Jul); *Dutton v Davis* [2006] EWCA Civ 694, [2006] 2 P & CR D51, [2006] All ER (D) 56 (May); *Brighton and Hove City Council v Audus* [2009] EWHC 340 (Ch), [2010] 1 All ER (Comm) 343, [2009] 2 EGLR 131.
7 *Welsh Development Agency v Export Finance Co Ltd* [1992] BCLC 148, [1992] BCC 270, CA.

109. Distinction between mortgage and sale. If an intended arrangement is not a lending and borrowing transaction but an absolute sale, accompanied by a contemporaneous agreement for repurchase or a stipulation that the conveyance should be void upon payment of a certain sum at a fixed time, this does not entitle the vendor to such a right to redeem as is incidental to a mortgage[1], but creates a mere right of repurchase to be exercised in accordance with the terms of the power[2]. The question is always whether the original transaction was a bona fide sale with a contract for repurchase, or a mortgage under the form of a sale[3]. In the former case the condition for repurchase is construed strictly against the vendor, and where there is a time limited for the purpose it must be precisely observed[4].

The three essential differences between a mortgage or charge and a sale are that:

(1) a vendor cannot recover the subject matter of the sale, whereas a mortgagor can do so by redeeming[5];

(2) a mortgagee who sells the subject matter of the mortgage must account to the mortgagor for any surplus, whereas a purchaser can retain any profit; and

(3) a mortgagee can recover any outstanding balance from the mortgagors after realising the mortgage property[6].

There can, however, be a sale of book debts even though the purchaser has recourse against the vendor to recover the shortfall if the debtor fails to pay in full or even though the purchaser has to make payments to the vendor after the debts have been got in from the debtor[7].

The transaction may be a composite one comprising a sale and mortgage to secure the unpaid price[8].

1 As to the right to redeem generally see PARAS 107, 304 et seq.
2 *Williams v Owen* (1840) 5 My & Cr 303 at 306 per Lord Cottenham LC. In the Law of Property Act 1925 'right of redemption' includes an option to repurchase only if the option in effect creates a right of redemption: see s 205(1)(xvi).
3 *Williams v Owen* (1840) 5 My & Cr 303 at 306 per Lord Cottenham LC; *St John v Wareham* (1636) cited in 3 Swan at 631; *Mellor v Lees* (1742) 2 Atk 494; *Goodman v Grierson* (1813) 2 Ball & B 274; *Longuet v Scawen* (1750) 1 Ves Sen 402 at 404; *Perry v Meddowcroft* (1841) 4 Beav 197 at 203; *Gavin's Trustee v Fraser* (1920) 57 Sc LR 595, Ct of Sess; *Warnborough Ltd v Garmite Ltd* [2003] EWCA Civ 1544, [2004] 1 P & CR D18, [2003] All ER (D) 52 (Nov); *Warnborough Ltd v Garmite Ltd* [2006] EWHC 10 (Ch), [2007] 1 P & CR 34, [2006] All ER (D) 22 (Jan).
4 *Barrell v Sabine* (1684) 1 Vern 268. See also *Joy v Birch* (1836) 4 Cl & Fin 57, HL; *Pegg v Wisden* (1852) 16 Beav 239 at 244.
5 A right of redemption may be implied in a purported assignment: *Coakley v Argent Credit Corpn plc* (4 June 1998, unreported).
6 *Re George Inglefield Ltd* [1933] Ch 1, CA; *Specialist Plant Services Ltd v Braithwaite Ltd* [1987] BCLC 1, 3 BCC 119, CA; *Re Curtain Dream plc* [1990] BCLC 925, [1990] BCC 341.
7 *Welsh Development Agency v Export Finance Co Ltd* [1992] BCLC 148, [1992] BCC 270, CA.
8 *Warnborough Ltd v Garmite Ltd* [2003] EWCA Civ 1544, [2004] 1 P & CR D18, [2003] All ER (D) 52 (Nov); *Warnborough Ltd v Garmite Ltd* [2006] EWHC 10 (Ch), [2007] 1 P & CR 34,

[2006] All ER (D) 22 (Jan); *Brighton and Hove City Council v Audus* [2009] EWHC 340 (Ch), [2010] 1 All ER (Comm) 343, [2009] 2 EGLR 131.

110. Distinction between charge and trust. A charge is created by the appropriation of specific property to the discharge of some debt or other obligation without there having been any change in ownership either at law or in equity[1]. It confers on the chargee the right to apply to the court for an order for sale or the appointment of a receiver, but no right to forfeiture or possession[2]. This is to be distinguished from the outright disposition of a beneficial interest in property by way of trust: the beneficiary under a trust is entitled to the trust property whereas a chargee is entitled to recourse to the subject property only to discharge the outstanding debt, and the chargor has a right to redemption[3].

1   *Carreras Rothmans Ltd v Freeman Mathews Treasure Ltd* [1985] Ch 207, [1985] 1 All ER 155. See also PARA 106.
2   *Carreras Rothmans Ltd v Freeman Mathews Treasure Ltd* [1985] Ch 207, [1985] 1 All ER 155. As to orders for sale see PARA 621 et seq. As to the appointment of a receiver by the court see PARA 565 et seq.
3   *Re Bond Worth Ltd* [1980] Ch 228 at 248, [1979] 3 All ER 919 at 939 per Slade J; *Carreras Rothmans Ltd v Freeman Mathews Treasure Ltd* [1985] Ch 207, [1985] 1 All ER 155; *Tatung (UK) Ltd v Galex Telesure Ltd* (1989) 5 BCC 325; *Modelboard Ltd v Outer Box Ltd* [1993] BCLC 623, [1992] BCC 945. See also *Compaq Computer Ltd v Abercorn Group Ltd* [1993] BCLC 602, [1991] BCC 484.

111. Distinction between mortgage and statutory charge. Statutory charges differ from mortgages in that mortgages arise out of agreement between the parties. The nature, effect and means of realisation of a statutory charge depend on the terms of the statute in question[1]. The following are instances of statutory charges: charging orders in favour of tenants or landlords of agricultural holdings in respect of compensation payable[2]; charges in favour of landlords of business premises in respect of compensation for or the cost of improvements[3]; charging orders on land by way of execution[4]; charges upon premises of frontagers in favour of local authorities for expenses incurred in making up private streets[5]; charges in favour of local authorities in respect of expense of executing works to housing and related administrative expenses[6]; charges to secure the repayment of discounts given to public sector tenants on the purchase of a house or flat in the event of early disposal[7]; charges on land in favour of landowners executing certain improvements[8]; charges on the property of mental patients[9]; orders charging a judgment debtor's share or interest in a partnership[10]; charges on property in connection with the provision of civil legal services under the Legal Aid, Sentencing and Punishment of Offenders Act 2012[11]; and orders charging solicitors' costs on property recovered through their instrumentality[12].

1   See eg the Housing Act 2004 ss 37, 50; HOUSING vol 56 (2011) PARAS 397, 405. See also the Charging Orders Act 1979 s 1(5); and CIVIL PROCEDURE vol 12A (2015) PARA 1465.
2   See the Agricultural Holdings Act 1986 ss 85–87; and AGRICULTURAL LAND vol 1 (2008) PARA 477 et seq.
3   See the Landlord and Tenant Act 1927 s 12, Sch 1; and LANDLORD AND TENANT vol 63 (2012) PARA 917.
4   As to charging orders see the Charging Orders Act 1979; PARA 293; and CIVIL PROCEDURE vol 12A (2015) PARA 1462 et seq.
5   See the Highways Act 1980 s 212; and HIGHWAYS, STREETS AND BRIDGES vol 55 (2012) PARA 162.
6   See the Housing Act 2004 ss 49, 50; and HOUSING vol 56 (2011) PARAS 404–405.
7   See the Housing Act 1985 ss 36, 156; the Housing Act 1988 s 79, Sch 11 paras 1, 2; the Housing Act 1996 ss 11, 11B; and HOUSING vol 56 (2011) PARA 165.
8   See the Agricultural Holdings Act 1986 s 86; and AGRICULTURAL LAND vol 1 (2008) PARA 477 et seq.

9   See the Mental Capacity Act 2005 s 18; and MENTAL HEALTH AND CAPACITY vol 75 (2013)
    PARA 727.
10 See the Partnership Act 1890 s 23(2), (3); and PARTNERSHIP vol 79 (2014) PARA 94 et seq.
11 See the Legal Aid, Sentencing and Punishment of Offenders Act 2012 s 25; and LEGAL AID vol 65
    (2015) PARA 150.
12 See the Solicitors Act 1974 s 73; and LEGAL PROFESSIONS vol 66 (2015) PARA 783 et seq.

112. Mortgage distinguished from pledge or pawn. A pledge is a species of
bailment whereby chattels are deposited by way of security with the pledgee, its
key characteristic being the actual or constructive delivery[1] of immediate
possession of the chattels in exchange for the loan but without transfer of
ownership[2]. The pledgor's right to possession is deferred to the repayment of the
debt; however, he retains the right to deal with the goods as title-holder subject to
the pledge[3]. It is said that the pledgor retains a general property in the goods,
while the pledgee takes a special property[4], but this terminology has been
criticised[5]. The pledgee does not acquire title to the goods[6], but has the power to
sell the goods in default of payment at the stipulated time, if any, or at a
reasonable time after demand and non-payment where no time for payment is
agreed upon[7].

A mortgage of chattels, on the other hand, is an assignment of a legal or
equitable interest[8]. It does not depend on the delivery of possession to the
mortgagee[9]. Pledge and pawn are theoretically interchangeable terms, but the
latter has particularly come to mean a small advance to a borrower on a pledge
of personal goods such as jewellery: depending on the size of the advance such an
agreement may be a regulated consumer credit agreement[10], and so governed by
statutory provisions[11]. There is an automatic statutory forfeiture to a pawnbroker
in respect of certain small unredeemed pawns[12]; otherwise, the right of foreclosure
is never available to a pledgee as it is to a mortgagee. On the sale of the pledged
property the pledgee holds any sum in excess of the debt on trust for the pledgor
and is liable in equity to pay interest on the retained proceeds[13].

A deposit of share certificates to secure a debt, or as cover, whether
accompanied[14] or unaccompanied[15] by a transfer in blank as to the name of the
transferee[16], amounts to an equitable mortgage and not a pledge[17]; a fortiori
where the legal estate in the shares is transferred to the lender the transaction is
a mortgage[18]. If a transfer is required to be by deed, a transfer in blank, although
subsequently completed, is not a complete security, but only evidence of an
agreement to transfer, giving the transferee an equitable title[19]. A security given by
the deposit of bearer securities has on the other hand been treated as a pledge[20].

1   *Martin v Reid* (1862) 11 CBNS 730. The deposit of share certificates is not regarded as a pledge,
    but as a charge: see the text to note 17.
2   *Coggs v Bernard* (1703) 2 Ld Raym 909; 1 Smith LC (13th Edn) 175; *Mills v Charlesworth* (1890)
    25 QBD 421 at 424, CA (revsd on the facts sub nom *Charlesworth v Mills* [1892] AC 231, HL);
    Re Cosslett (Contractors) Ltd [1998] Ch 495 at 508, [1997] 4 All ER 115 at 126, CA, per
    Millett LJ. As to pledges and pawns see further BAILMENT AND PLEDGE vol 4 (2011) PARA 188
    et seq.
3   *Franklin v Neate* (1844) 13 M & W 481; *Halliday v Holgate* (1868) LR 3 Exch 299 at 302, Ex
    Ch.
4   *Ryall v Rowles* (1750) 1 Ves Sen 348 per Burnet J; *Jones v Smith* (1794) 2 Ves 372; *Re Morritt,
    ex p Official Receiver* (1886) 18 QBD 222 at 232, CA, per Cotton LJ, and at 234 per Fry LJ;
    George Attenborough & Son v Solomon [1913] AC 76 at 84, HL, per Lord Haldane LC; *Fraser
    v Byas* (1895) 11 TLR 481; and see *Sir John Ratcliff v Davis* (1610) 1 Bulst 29 per Fleming CJ;
    and BAILMENT AND PLEDGE vol 4 (2011) PARA 209.
5   In *The Odessa* [1916] 1 AC 145 at 158–159, PC, Lord Mersey preferred the term 'special interest'
    on the ground that when the pawnee's right to sell is examined, the so-called 'special property'

which that right is said to create is in truth no property at all. See also *Mathew v TM Sutton Ltd* [1994] 4 All ER 793 at 800, [1994] 1 WLR 1455 at 1461 per Chadwick J; and BAILMENT AND PLEDGE vol 4 (2011) PARA 209.
6   *Carter v Wake* (1877) 4 ChD 605 at 606.
7   *Burdick v Sewell* (1883) 10 QBD 363 at 366–367; *Re Morritt, ex p Official Receiver* (1886) 18 QBD 222 at 232, CA.
8   *Re Cosslett (Contractors) Ltd* [1998] Ch 495 at 508, [1997] 4 All ER 115 at 126, CA, per Millett LJ.
9   *Re Cosslett (Contractors) Ltd* [1998] Ch 495 at 508, [1997] 4 All ER 115 at 126, CA, per Millett LJ; *Maugham v Sharpe* (1864) 17 CBNS 443.
10 See the Consumer Credit Act 1974 s 8(3); and CONSUMER CREDIT vol 21 (2011) PARA 51 et seq.
11 See the Consumer Credit Act 1974 ss 114–121; and CONSUMER CREDIT vol 21 (2011) PARA 217 et seq.
12 See the Consumer Credit Act 1974 s 120(1)(a); and CONSUMER CREDIT vol 21 (2011) PARAS 221, 224.
13 *Mathew v TM Sutton Ltd* [1994] 4 All ER 793, [1994] 1 WLR 1455.
14 *Stubbs v Slater* [1910] 1 Ch 632 at 639, CA; *London and Midland Bank v Mitchell* [1899] 2 Ch 161; *France v Clark* (1884) 26 ChD 257 at 262, CA, per Lord Selborne LC; cf *Deverges v Sandeman, Clark & Co* [1902] 1 Ch 579, CA.
15 *Harrold v Plenty* [1901] 2 Ch 314; *Re Davies, ex p Moss* (1849) 3 De G & Sm 599; *Re Shelley, ex p Stewart* (1864) 4 De G J & Sm 543; *Re Harrison and Ingram, ex p Whinney* [1905] WN 143.
16 See *Fry and Mason v Smellie and Taylor* [1912] 3 KB 282, CA; *Colonial Bank v Cady and Williams, London Chartered Bank of Australia v Cady and Williams* (1890) 15 App Cas 267, HL. See also PARA 211.
17 In some cases in which the distinction between a mortgage and a pledge was not material to the decision, the word 'pledge' has been used as applicable to a security by deposit of certificates of shares: see *Ellis & Co's Trustee v Dixon-Johnson* [1925] AC 489 at 493, HL, per Lord Sumner; *Halliday v Holgate* (1868) LR 3 Exch 299, Ex Ch; *Re Tahiti Cotton Co, ex p Sargent* (1874) LR 17 Eq 273 at 279–281 (where Jessel MR also uses the word 'mortgagee' in relation to the same transaction); *Colonial Bank v Cady and Williams, London Chartered Bank of Australia v Cady and Williams* (1890) 15 App Cas 267, HL.
18 *Deverges v Sandeman, Clark & Co* [1902] 1 Ch 579, CA; *General Credit and Discount Co v Glegg* (1883) 22 ChD 549.
19 *Powell v London and Provincial Bank* [1893] 2 Ch 555, CA; *France v Clark* (1884) 26 ChD 257, CA. See also PARA 237.
20 *Gorgier v Mieville* (1824) 3 B & C 45; *Donald v Suckling* (1866) LR 1 QB 585; *Carter v Wake* (1877) 4 ChD 605, doubted in *Harrold v Plenty* [1901] 2 Ch 314 at 316 per Cozens-Hardy J and in *Sadler v Worley* [1894] 2 Ch 170 at 175 per Kekewich J. See also *Stubbs v Slater* [1910] 1 Ch 632, CA; and PARA 573.

113. Mortgage distinguished from lien. A mortgage differs from a possessory lien at common law, for the lien is only a personal right to retain possession of another person's goods previously delivered for some other purpose until a debt is paid; the lien cannot generally be assigned and continues only so long as the possessor of the right holds the goods[1]. A possessory lien may be accompanied by a contractual power of sale without becoming a charge[2]. A mortgage differs also from the right of lien given by or under statute in the case of shipowners[3] and in other like cases, the remedy in each case being controlled by the terms of the relevant enactment. The implied right of the mortgagee under an equitable mortgage created by the deposit of title deeds to retain the deeds is not a separate legal or common law lien[4].

An unpaid vendor's lien arises in equity on exchange of contracts for the sale of land[5]. The vendor has an equitable lien on the property for the purchase money which he retains notwithstanding an outright conveyance of the legal estate, a receipt for the purchase money and delivery of the deeds if any part of the purchase price remains unpaid[6]. It is excluded where its retention would be inconsistent with the provisions of the contract for sale, or with the true nature of the transaction[7].

An equitable charge differs from an equitable lien in that the former arises from contract whereas the latter arises by operation of law[8]. However, equitable liens are similar to equitable charges in that they create a proprietary interest, are enforceable by judicial order for sale, and are registrable[9].

1 *Legg v Evans* (1840) 6 M & W 36 at 41; and see LIEN vol 68 (2008) PARA 810 et seq. As to equitable charges see PARA 106.
2 *Great Eastern Rly Co v Lord's Trustee* [1909] AC 109, HL; *Re Hamlet International plc (in administration), Trident International Ltd v Barlow* [1999] 2 BCLC 506, CA.
3 As to maritime lien see SHIPPING AND MARITIME LAW vol 94 (2008) PARA 1014 et seq; and as to statutory lien see SHIPPING AND MARITIME LAW vol 94 (2008) PARA 1023.
4 *Re Molton Finance Ltd* [1968] Ch 325, [1967] 3 All ER 843, CA; and see PARA 224. It is not possible to create an equitable mortgage by the deposit of title deeds alone: see PARA 221.
5 See *Barclays Bank plc v Estates and Commercial Ltd* [1997] 1 WLR 415, 74 P & CR 30, CA; and LIEN vol 68 (2008) PARAS 859–860.
6 See note 5.
7 See note 5.
8 See LIEN vol 68 (2008) PARA 814.
9 See LIEN vol 68 (2008) PARA 855 et seq.

114. Mortgage may be void or voidable in certain circumstances. A mortgage may be void or voidable in certain circumstances on the ground of mistake[1], non est factum[2], misrepresentation[3], duress[4] or undue influence[5], or if it does not comply with the necessary formalities[6], or because it constitutes a fraud against the mortgagor's general creditors[7] or an unconscionable bargain[8], or if it is given for an illegal consideration or is opposed to public policy[9]. Where part of the consideration is illegal, the security is only avoided to that extent[10]. Where a mortgagor gives security for the debts of another, the mortgage may be voidable even though the mortgagee has committed no wrong against the mortgagor, if the mortgagee has actual or constructive notice of a wrong committed by the borrower against the mortgagor[11]. A void or voidable mortgage may nonetheless constitute an equitable mortgage[12] or an equitable charge[13] and the mortgagee may have other remedies[14].

1 As to the effect of mistake in negativing or nullifying consent to a transaction see generally MISTAKE vol 77 (2016) PARA 1 et seq. As to the right of a person who has executed a deed or other document under a misapprehension as to its essential nature to deny the validity of the execution see DEEDS AND OTHER INSTRUMENTS vol 32 (2012) PARA 267 et seq.
2 See DEEDS AND OTHER INSTRUMENTS vol 32 (2012) PARAS 269–273.
3 For the circumstances in which misrepresentation renders a contract voidable see generally MISREPRESENTATION vol 76 (2013) PARA 782.
4 See CONTRACT vol 22 (2012) PARAS 292–293; EQUITABLE JURISDICTION vol 47 (2014) PARA 37.
5 See *Royal Bank of Scotland plc v Etridge (No 2)* [2001] UKHL 44, [2002] 2 AC 773, [2001] 4 All ER 449. See also CONTRACT vol 22 (2012) PARA 294 et seq; EQUITABLE JURISDICTION vol 47 (2014) PARA 18 et seq; MISREPRESENTATION vol 76 (2013) PARA 834 et seq.
6 As to legal mortgages see also PARAS 104, 160 et seq.
7 As to the avoidance of dispositions in fraud of creditors see generally BANKRUPTCY AND INDIVIDUAL INSOLVENCY vol 5 (2013) PARA 713 et seq. See also MISREPRESENTATION vol 76 (2013) PARA 863; COMPANY AND PARTNERSHIP INSOLVENCY vol 17 (2011) PARA 801 et seq.
8 See *Credit Lyonnais Bank Nederland NV v Burch* [1997] 1 All ER 144 at 151, [1997] 2 FCR 1 at 7–8, CA, per Nourse LJ; *Kalsep Ltd v X-Flow BV* [2001] All ER (D) 113 (Mar). See also EQUITABLE JURISDICTION vol 47 (2014) PARA 30; MISREPRESENTATION vol 76 (2013) PARA 850.
9 As to void and illegal contracts see generally CONTRACT vol 22 (2012) PARA 424 et seq. As to the avoidance of securities given in respect of illegal transactions see CONTRACT vol 22 (2012) PARAS 460–461. See also LICENSING AND GAMBLING vol 67 (2008) PARA 361 (securities given for gaming considerations).
10 *Sheehy v Sheehy* [1901] 1 IR 239. See also *Spector v Ageda* [1973] Ch 30, [1971] 3 All ER 417.
11 See PARA 119 et seq.
12 See PARA 218. See also PARA 168.

13 See PARAS 168, 219.
14 See PARA 125.

· (2) STATUTORY REGULATION OF MORTGAGES

115. Financial services legislation as it affects mortgages. The Financial Conduct Authority ('FCA') is responsible for regulating the firms and individuals that are involved in advising on, arranging or managing mortgages[1]. Such persons must be authorised by the FCA in order to operate. Entering into a regulated mortgage contract as lender, and administering a regulated mortgage contract are both specified kinds of activity for the purposes of financial services legislation[2].

A regulated mortgage contract entered into by a person who is neither authorised nor exempt is unenforceable, and the other party is entitled to recover any money or property paid or transferred by him under the agreement, and to recover compensation for any loss sustained as a result of having parted with it[3]. The court may, if it is just and equitable, allow the agreement to be enforced and money or property paid or transferred under it to be retained[4].

Regulated lenders are required to comply with rules made by the FCA[5], including the Mortgage Conduct of Business Rules[6]. No contravention of such rules makes a transaction void or unenforceable[7], other than those dealing with cost of credit and duration of credit agreements[8] or the produce intervention rules[9].

Activities concerning buy-to-let mortgage lending required to be regulated by the Mortgages Directive[10], are also regulated by the FCA[11].

Coverage of the financial services legislation is to be found elsewhere in this work[12].

1   As to the Financial Conduct Authority see FINANCIAL SERVICES REGULATION vol 50 (2016) PARA 6 et seq.
2   As to regulated mortgage contracts see the Financial Services and Markets Act 2000 (Regulated Activities) Order 2001, SI 2001/544, arts 61–63A; and FINANCIAL SERVICES REGULATION vol 50 (2016) PARA 287 et seq).
3   See the Financial Services and Markets Act 2000 s 26; and FINANCIAL SERVICES REGULATION vol 50 (2016) PARA 102.
4   See the Financial Services and Markets Act 2000 s 28; *Helden v Strathmore Ltd* [2011] EWCA Civ 542, [2011] Bus LR 1592, [2011] 2 BCLC 665; and FINANCIAL SERVICES REGULATION vol 50 (2016) PARA 104.
5   Ie under the Financial Services and Markets Act 2000 Pt 9A (ss 137A–141A): see FINANCIAL SERVICES REGULATION vol 50 (2016) PARA 59 et seq.
6   The Mortgage Conduct of Business Rules ('MCOB') (which came into force on 31 October 2004) are issued by the FCA as *Mortgages and Home Finance: Conduct of Business Sourcebook* (part of the FCA Handbook). Their function is to regulate the conduct of business between mortgage lenders and borrowers.
7   See the Financial Services and Markets Act 2000 s 138E(2) (added by the Financial Services Act 2012 s 24(1); *Thakker v Northern Rock plc* [2014] EWHC 2107 (QB); and FINANCIAL SERVICES REGULATION vol 50 (2016) PARA 78.
8   The Financial Services and Markets Act 2000 s 138E(2) does not apply to rules made by the FCA under s 137C (see FINANCIAL SERVICES REGULATION vol 50 (2016) PARA 61): see s 138E(3)(a) (as added: see note 7).
9   The Financial Services and Markets Act 2000 s 138E(2) does not apply to product intervention rules made by the FCA under s 137D (see FINANCIAL SERVICES REGULATION vol 50 (2016) PARA 62): see s 138E(3)(b) (as added: see note 7).
10   Ie Parliament and Council Directive (EU) 2014/17 of 4 February 2014 on credit agreements for consumers relating to residential immovable property (OJ L60, 28.2.2014, p 34).
11   See the Mortgage Credit Directive Order 2015, SI 2015/910 (amended by SI 2015/1557).
12   See FINANCIAL INSTITUTIONS; FINANCIAL INSTRUMENTS AND TRANSACTIONS; FINANCIAL SERVICES REGULATION.

116. Consumer credit legislation as it affects mortgages. The Consumer Credit Act 1974 establishes a code for the regulation of the provision to individuals of credit[1]. The Act provides for the making of regulations as to the form and content of regulated agreements[2] and deals with, amongst other things, the cancellation[3], termination[4] and enforcement[5] of, and withdrawal from[6], such agreements. With particular reference to mortgages, the Act contains provisions dealing with the form and content of certain securities provided in relation to a regulated agreement[7] and the enforcement of such securities[8]. In addition, the Act empowers the court to make orders as to credit agreements if it determines that the relationship between the creditor and the debtor arising out of the agreement is unfair to the debtor[9].

Consumer credit legislation is covered in more detail elsewhere in this work[10].

1 The Consumer Credit Act 1974 contains provisions as to the form and content of documentation and the enforcement of transactions in relation to regulated agreements: see CONSUMER CREDIT vol 21 (2011) PARA 51 et seq.
2 See the Consumer Credit Act 1974 s 60; and CONSUMER CREDIT vol 21 (2011) PARA 180. As to the meaning of 'regulated agreement' see CONSUMER CREDIT vol 21 (2011) PARA 51.
3 See the Consumer Credit Act 1974 ss 67–73; and CONSUMER CREDIT vol 21 (2011) PARA 195 et seq.
4 See the Consumer Credit Act 1974 Pt VII (ss 86A–104); and CONSUMER CREDIT vol 21 (2011) PARA 264 et seq.
5 See the Consumer Credit Act 1974 Pt IX (ss 127–144); and CONSUMER CREDIT vol 21 (2011) PARA 307 et seq.
6 See the Consumer Credit Act 1974 ss 57–58; and CONSUMER CREDIT vol 21 (2011) PARAS 193–194.
7 See the Consumer Credit Act 1974 s 105; and CONSUMER CREDIT vol 21 (2011) PARA 209.
8 See the Consumer Credit Act 1974 ss 126, 127; and CONSUMER CREDIT vol 21 (2011) PARAS 229, 308.
9 See the Consumer Credit Act 1974 ss 140A–140C; the Consumer Rights Act 2015 Pt 2 (ss 61–76); and CONSUMER CREDIT vol 21 (2011) PARAS 287–289.
10 See CONSUMER CREDIT.

117. Taxation legislation as it affects mortgages. Taxation provisions as they may affect mortgages are dealt with elsewhere in this work[1].

1 See CAPITAL GAINS TAXATION; INCOME TAXATION; INHERITANCE TAXATION. See also STAMP TAXES.

(3) COLLATERAL TRANSACTIONS ACCOMPANYING MORTGAGES

(i) Suretyship

118. Suretyship. Third persons may be made parties to mortgages in order to guarantee[1] the payment of principal and interest or interest alone, the performance of covenants, or the maintenance of the security. Where co-owners grant a charge to secure the debts of one of them, the other is a surety[2]. Although a surety undertakes only for the default of another, the practice in mortgage deeds is to make him contract and become bound as a principal so far as concerns the mortgagee, but to let him remain a surety so far as concerns the mortgagor. A mortgagee is entitled to the costs of all proceedings reasonably taken, including proceedings to obtain payments from a surety[3].

1 See FINANCIAL INSTRUMENTS AND TRANSACTIONS vol 49 (2015) PARA 767 et seq.

2   As to the effect of such a charge see FINANCIAL INSTRUMENTS AND TRANSACTIONS vol 49 (2015) PARA 777. As to the equity of exoneration see PARAS 634, 641–643.

3   *National Provincial Bank of England v Games* (1886) 31 ChD 582, CA. See also PARA 743 et seq.

119. Mortgagee may be affected by a wrong committed by another. A mortgagor whose suretyship was procured by the undue influence, misrepresentation or other legal wrong of the debtor can set aside the mortgage if either the debtor was acting as the mortgagee's agent[1] or the mortgagee had actual or constructive notice of the conduct of the debtor which vitiated the surety's consent[2]. The burden of proving that the mortgagee had actual or constructive notice that the surety's consent was improperly obtained is on the surety[3]. If the mortgagee knows of certain facts which put him on inquiry as to the fact that the surety's concurrence may have been procured by the misconduct of a third party, and he fails to take such steps as are reasonable to reduce the risk that the surety entered into the transaction under any misapprehension or as a result of undue influence, he will have constructive notice that the surety's concurrence was procured improperly[4]. If he does take such reasonable steps, he takes free from the rights of the surety[5].

1   Although there may be cases where, without artificiality, it can properly be held that a husband was acting as the agent of the creditor in procuring his wife to stand as surety, such cases will be very rare: *Barclays Bank plc v O'Brien* [1994] 1 AC 180 at 195, [1993] 4 All ER 417 at 428, HL, per Lord Browne-Wilkinson; *Bradford and Bingley Building Society v Chandock* (1996) 72 P & CR D28, CA; *Royal Bank of Scotland plc v Etridge (No 2)* [2001] UKHL 44, [2002] 2 AC 773, [2001] 4 All ER 449.

2   *Barclays Bank plc v O'Brien* [1994] 1 AC 180 at 195, [1993] 4 All ER 417 at 428, HL, per Lord Browne-Wilkinson; *Royal Bank of Scotland plc v Etridge (No 2)* [2001] UKHL 44 at [38]–[40], [2002] 2 AC 773, [2001] 4 All ER 449 per Lord Nicholls of Birkenhead, and at [143]–[146] per Lord Scott of Foscote.

3   *Barclays Bank plc v Boulter* [1999] 4 All ER 513, [1999] 3 FCR 529, HL.

4   *Royal Bank of Scotland plc v Etridge (No 2)* [2001] UKHL 44 at [41], [2002] 2 AC 773, [2001] 4 All ER 449 per Lord Nicholls of Birkenhead; *Barclays Bank plc v O'Brien* [1994] 1 AC 180 at 195, [1993] 4 All ER 417 at 429, HL. See also *Banco Exterior Internacional SA v Thomas* [1997] 1 All ER 46, [1997] 1 WLR 221, CA.

5   *Royal Bank of Scotland plc v Etridge (No 2)* [2001] UKHL 44, [2002] 2 AC 773, [2001] 4 All ER 449.

120. When the mortgagee is put on inquiry. A mortgagee is put on inquiry if the relationship between surety and debtor is known to the mortgagee and raises a legal presumption of undue influence[1]. A mortgagee is also put on inquiry if:

(1)   the transaction is not on its face advantageous to the surety; and

(2)   the mortgagee knows that the surety and debtor are married or cohabiting, or that the surety places trust and confidence in the debtor in relation to the management of his or her financial affairs[2].

The effect of this is that a mortgagee is on inquiry whenever he wishes to obtain a guarantee and the relationship between the surety and the debtor is 'non-commercial'[3].

Thus a mortgagee is put on inquiry where a mortgagor offers to stand surety for the debts of his or her spouse[4]. The same situation obtains in the case of unmarried couples where the bank is aware of the relationship[5]: cohabitation is not essential[6].

Where a wife stands surety for the debts of a company whose shares are held by her and her husband, the mortgagee is put on inquiry even when the wife is a director or secretary of the company, because the shareholding interests, and the identity of the directors, are not a reliable guide to the identity of the persons who actually have the conduct of the company's business[7]. However, where money is advanced to a husband and wife jointly, the mortgagee is not put on inquiry unless it is aware that the loan is being made for the purposes of one of them alone, as distinct from their joint purposes[8], or the mortgage also secures all monies due from either of them[9]. A remortgage of joint liabilities with a different lender would not normally put a lender on inquiry[10], but a lender who is on inquiry in relation to one mortgage is also on inquiry in relation to a remortgage[11].

A mortgagee is not required to inquire into the personal relationship between debtor and mortgagee or as to the personal motives of the surety for wanting to help the debtor[12].

1   *Royal Bank of Scotland plc v Etridge (No 2)* [2001] UKHL 44, [2002] 2 AC 773, [2001] 4 All ER 449. The relationship between husband and wife or co-habitees does not of itself give rise to such a presumption: *Royal Bank of Scotland v Etridge (No 2)*. For cases in which it does arise see EQUITABLE JURISDICTION vol 47 (2014) PARA 18 et seq; FINANCIAL INSTRUMENTS AND TRANSACTIONS vol 49 (2015) PARAS 670–671; MISREPRESENTATION vol 76 (2013) PARA 838 et seq.
2   *Barclays Bank plc v O'Brien* [1994] 1 AC 180, [1993] 4 All ER 417, HL; *Royal Bank of Scotland plc v Etridge (No 2)* [2001] UKHL 44 at [14], [21], [2002] 2 AC 773, [2001] 4 All ER 449 per Lord Nicholls of Birkenhead. In the same case Lord Scott of Foscote held that the existence of trust and confidence will be assumed where a husband and wife live together, and that a mortgagee will be required to adduce evidence to rebut the existence of trust and confidence in such cases: see *Royal Bank of Scotland plc v Etridge (No 2)* at [159].
3   *Royal Bank of Scotland plc v Etridge (No 2)* [2001] UKHL 44 at [87], [2002] 2 AC 773, [2001] 4 All ER 449 per Lord Nicholls of Birkenhead. Examples of a commercial relationship are where the grantor is paid a fee, or a company is guaranteeing the debts of another company in the same group: see *Royal Bank of Scotland plc v Etridge (No 2)* at [88] per Lord Nicholls of Birkenhead.
4   *Royal Bank of Scotland plc v Etridge (No 2)* [2001] UKHL 44 at [44]–[46], [2002] 2 AC 773, [2001] 4 All ER 449 per Lord Nicholls of Birkenhead, and at [110]–[111] per Lord Hobhouse of Woodborough; *Barclays Bank plc v O'Brien* [1994] 1 AC 180, [1993] 4 All ER 417, HL.
5   *Barclays Bank plc v O'Brien* [1994] 1 AC 180 at 198, [1993] 4 All ER 417 at 431, HL, per Lord Browne-Wilkinson; *Royal Bank of Scotland plc v Etridge (No 2)* [2001] UKHL 44 at [47], [2002] 2 AC 773, [2001] 4 All ER 449 per Lord Nicholls of Birkenhead.
6   *Massey v Midland Bank plc* [1995] 1 All ER 29 at 33, [1994] 2 FLR 342 at 345, CA, per Steyn J; *Royal Bank of Scotland plc v Etridge (No 2)* [2001] UKHL 44 at [47], [2002] 2 AC 773, [2001] 4 All ER 449 per Lord Nicholls of Birkenhead.
7   *Royal Bank of Scotland plc v Etridge (No 2)* [2001] UKHL 44 at [49], [2002] 2 AC 773, [2001] 4 All ER 449 per Lord Nicholls of Birkenhead.
8   *CIBC Mortgages plc v Pitt* [1994] 1 AC 200, [1993] 4 All ER 433, HL; *Britannia Building Society v Pugh* [1997] 2 FLR 7, 29 HLR 423, CA; *Royal Bank of Scotland plc v Etridge (No 2)* [2001] UKHL 44 at [48], [2002] 2 AC 773, [2001] 4 All ER 449 per Lord Nicholls of Birkenhead.
9   *Midland Bank v Greene* [1995] 1 FCR 365, [1994] 2 FLR 827. If the security was intended only to secure joint liabilities it may be treated as such: *Dunbar Bank plc v Nadeem* [1998] 3 All ER 876, [1998] 2 FLR 457, CA.
10 *Scotlife Home Loans (No 2) Ltd v Hedworth* (1996) 28 HLR 771, CA; *UCB Bank plc v Hedworth* [2003] EWCA Civ 1717, [2003] 3 FCR 739.
11 *Yorkshire Bank plc v Tinsley* [2004] EWCA Civ 816, [2004] 3 All ER 463, [2004] 1 WLR 2380.
12 *Banco Exterior Internacional SA v Thomas* [1997] 1 All ER 46, [1997] 1 WLR 221, CA.

121. When knowledge of a solicitor is imputed to the mortgagee. A solicitor often acts for the mortgagee and the mortgagor in relation to the mortgage. The solicitor's knowledge of facts which would put the mortgagee on inquiry is not to be imputed to the mortgagee bank unless the information came to his knowledge in his capacity as solicitor for the mortgagee bank as such[1]. Thus knowledge of a solicitor acquired when taking instructions from or giving advice to the surety is not to be imputed to the mortgagee[2]. The mortgagee does not have imputed knowledge of facts and matters which would have come to his knowledge if he had made inquiries relating to matters other than whether it would obtain good security, such as the credit status of a borrower[3].

1   See the Law of Property Act 1925 s 199(1)(ii)(b). An objective test is applied for the purpose of determining whether any fact learned by the mortgagee's solicitor ought to be treated as having been learned by the mortgagee: *Woolwich plc v Gomm* (1999) 79 P & CR 61, CA.

2   *Halifax Mortgage Services Ltd v Stepsky* [1996] Ch 207, [1996] 2 All ER 277, CA; *Barclays Bank v Thomson* [1997] 4 All ER 816, [1997] 1 FCR 541, CA; *National Westminster Bank v Beaton* (1997) 30 HLR 99, 74 P & CR D19, CA. See also *Royal Bank of Scotland plc v Etridge (No 2)* [2001] UKHL 44, [2002] 2 AC 773, [2001] 4 All ER 449.
3   *Abbey National plc v Tufts* [1999] 2 FLR 399, CA.

122. How the mortgagee may avoid constructive notice. A creditor mortgagee who is put on inquiry will have constructive notice of the surety's rights unless he takes reasonable steps to ensure that the surety understood the nature and effect of the proposed surety transaction[1]. Where, for example, the mortgagee knows only that a wife is to stand surety for her husband's debts, these requirements will normally have been satisfied if the mortgagee insists that the wife attend a private meeting (in the absence of the husband) with a representative of the mortgagee at which she is told of the extent of her liability as surety, warned of the risk she is running and urged to take independent legal advice[2]. Where the mortgagee does not wish to advise the surety himself, he must, in order to avoid being fixed with constructive notice, either communicate directly with the surety wife[3] (in which case he should not proceed with the transaction until he has received an appropriate response directly from the wife)[4], or, if he chooses not to explain the nature and implications of the transaction to the wife, must provide the wife's solicitor with sufficient financial information for this purpose[5].

Ordinarily it will not matter whether the solicitor advising the surety wife is also acting for the mortgagee in arranging for the completion of the security, or that he is also the husband's solicitor[6]; if, however, outside the ordinary course of events the mortgagee suspects the debtor of misrepresentation or undue influence, he must inform the wife's solicitor of the facts creating that suspicion or be fixed with constructive notice of any impropriety that does occur[7].

The essence of the duty of the surety wife's solicitor is to explain to her the nature and effect of the transaction[8], and it is accordingly necessary in all cases that, to avoid being fixed with constructive notice, the mortgagee obtains written confirmation from that solicitor that he has fully explained to the wife the nature of the documents and the practical implications they will have for her[9].

1   *Barclays Bank plc v O'Brien* [1994] 1 AC 180, [1993] 4 All ER 417, HL; *Royal Bank of Scotland plc v Etridge (No 2)* [2001] UKHL 44, [2002] 2 AC 773, [2001] 4 All ER 449.
2   *Barclays Bank plc v O'Brien* [1994] 1 AC 180 at 196–197, [1993] 4 All ER 417 at 429–430, HL, per Lord Browne-Wilkinson. See also *Royal Bank of Scotland plc v Etridge (No 2)* [2001] UKHL 44 at [54], [2002] 2 AC 773, [2001] 4 All ER 449 per Lord Nicholls of Birkenhead, at [147]–[148], [163], [165] per Lord Scott of Foscote, and cf at [111] per Lord Hobhouse of Woodborough.
3   See *Royal Bank of Scotland plc v Etridge (No 2)* [2001] UKHL 44 at [79(1)], [2002] 2 AC 773, [2001] 4 All ER 449 per Lord Nicholls of Birkenhead, who said that the mortgagee should inform the wife that for her own protection it will require written confirmation from a solicitor, acting for her, to the effect that the solicitor has fully explained to her the nature of the documents and the practical implications they will have for her; should tell her that the purpose of this requirement is that thereafter she should not be able to dispute that she is legally bound by the documents once she has signed them; should ask her to nominate a solicitor whom she is willing to instruct to advise her, separately from her husband, and act for her in giving the necessary confirmation to the mortgagee; should tell her that, if she wishes, the solicitor may be the same solicitor as is acting for her husband in the transaction; should ask her, where the solicitor is already acting for both her and her husband, whether she would prefer that a different solicitor should act for her regarding the bank's requirement for confirmation from a solicitor.
4   *Royal Bank of Scotland plc v Etridge (No 2)* [2001] UKHL 44 at [79(1)], [2002] 2 AC 773, [2001] 4 All ER 449 per Lord Nicholls of Birkenhead.
5   *Royal Bank of Scotland plc v Etridge (No 2)* [2001] UKHL 44 at [79(2)], [2002] 2 AC 773, [2001] 4 All ER 449 per Lord Nicholls of Birkenhead. Such information is confidential and the debtor's consent is usually required for disclosure, although consent may be implied from the husband's proposal that the wife stand as surety: *Royal Bank of Scotland plc v Etridge (No 2)* at [79(2)] per Lord Nicholls of Birkenhead, and at [190] per Lord Scott of Foscote. The lender does

not owe any general duty of disclosure to the surety wife (*Royal Bank of Scotland plc v Etridge (No 2)* at [114] per Lord Hobhouse of Woodborough, and at [189] per Lord Scott of Foscote), nor does it add to the general disclosure obligations owed by creditors to prospective sureties (*Royal Bank of Scotland plc v Etridge (No 2)* at [81] per Lord Nicholls of Birkenhead, at [114] per Lord Hobhouse of Woodborough, and at [183]–[188] per Lord Scott of Foscote).

6   *Royal Bank of Scotland plc v Etridge (No 2)* [2001] UKHL 44 at [174], [2002] 2 AC 773, [2001] 4 All ER 449 per Lord Scott of Foscote.

7   *Royal Bank of Scotland plc v Etridge (No 2)* [2001] UKHL 44 at [79(3)], [2002] 2 AC 773, [2001] 4 All ER 449 per Lord Nicholls of Birkenhead.

8   In *Royal Bank of Scotland plc v Etridge (No 2)* [2001] UKHL 44 at [58]–[63], [2002] 2 AC 773, [2001] 4 All ER 449 per Lord Nicholls of Birkenhead, and at [181]–[182], [374] per Lord Scott of Foscote, the House of Lords expressly disapproved the Court of Appeal's broader conception of the duty (cf also at [112] per Lord Hobhouse of Woodborough).

9   *Royal Bank of Scotland plc v Etridge (No 2)* [2001] UKHL 44 at [79(4)], [2002] 2 AC 773, [2001] 4 All ER 449 per Lord Nicholls of Birkenhead, and at [175] per Lord Scott of Foscote. The creditor mortgagee is under an independent duty to a surety to disclose contractual arrangements made between the debtor and the creditor mortgagee which make the terms of the principal contract materially different in a potentially disadvantageous respect from those which a surety might naturally expect: *Levett v Barclays Bank plc* [1995] 2 All ER 615, [1995] 1 WLR 1260. See also PARA 123; and FINANCIAL INSTRUMENTS AND TRANSACTIONS vol 49 (2015) PARA 665.

123. Effect of legal advice. On the matter of when a creditor mortgagee who is put on inquiry will have constructive notice of a surety's rights[1], case-law, which mainly involves a debtor husband and a surety wife, establishes that:

(1)   it is not, in general, enough that the mortgagee knows merely that the surety has a solicitor acting for her: that would not normally be sufficient to constitute the taking of reasonable steps to ensure that the nature of the risks to her arising out of the transaction have been made clear to her[2];

(2)   on the other hand, in the absence of special circumstances it would be sufficient if the mortgagee knew that the surety's solicitor had been instructed to give independent advice to her on the nature and effect of the transaction and had received confirmation that such advice had been given[3]; where the mortgagee has asked a solicitor to explain that transaction to the surety and there is no confirmation that the solicitor has done so, the mortgagee is not entitled to assume that he has and is on inquiry as to whether the solicitor has in fact advised the surety[4];

(3)   when giving advice to the surety, the solicitor is acting exclusively as the surety's solicitor[5]; it makes no difference whether he is unconnected with the debtor or the surety[6] or is also the debtor's solicitor[7] or that he has agreed to act in a ministerial capacity as the mortgagee's agent at completion[8]; whoever introduces the solicitor to the surety and asks him to advise the surety, and whoever is responsible for his fees, the mortgagee is entitled to expect the solicitor to regard himself as owing a duty to the surety alone when giving the surety advice[9]; if the solicitor accepts the mortgagee's instructions to advise the surety, he still acts as the surety's solicitor and not the mortgagee's solicitor when he interviews the surety[10];

(4)   the mortgagee is entitled to rely on the fact that the solicitor undertook the task of explaining the transaction to the surety as showing that he considered himself to be sufficiently independent for this purpose[11] and is not required to question the solicitor's independence, even if the mortgagee knows that he is also the debtor's solicitor[12]; and

(5)   the mortgagee is not concerned to question the sufficiency of the advice; if the solicitor fails properly to explain the security transaction, his knowledge of the failure is not to be imputed to the mortgagee, even

though the mortgagee asked the solicitor to advise the surety[13], and the mortgagee will be fixed with constructive notice only if he knows or has reason to suspect that the solicitor has failed properly to advise the surety, or knows facts from which he ought to have realised that the surety has not received the appropriate advice, and does nothing to remedy the situation[14].

Ultimately the issue is whether the surety has had brought home to her in a meaningful way the practical implications of the proposed transaction[15]. This does not wholly eliminate the risk that the transaction was procured by misrepresentation or undue influence, but it does ensure that the surety was fully aware of the basic elements of the transaction[16].

1   See PARA 122.
2   *Royal Bank of Scotland plc v Etridge (No 2)* [2001] UKHL 44, [2002] 2 AC 773, [2001] 4 All ER 449; *Lloyds TSB Bank plc v Holdgate* [2002] EWCA Civ 1543, [2003] HLR 335; *First National Bank plc v Achampong* [2003] EWCA Civ 487, [2004] 1 FCR 18.
3   *Royal Bank of Scotland plc v Etridge (No 2)* [2001] UKHL 44, [2002] 2 AC 773, [2001] 4 All ER 449; *First National Bank plc v Achampong* [2003] EWCA Civ 487, [2004] 1 FCR 18.
4   *Bank Melli Iran v Samadi-Rad* [1995] 3 FCR 735, [1995] 2 FLR 367, CA; *Cooke v National Westminster Bank* [1998] 3 FCR 643, [1998] 2 FLR 783, CA.
5   *Midland Bank v Serter* [1995] 3 FCR 711, 27 HLR 647, CA; *Barclays Bank plc v Thomson* [1997] 4 All ER 816, [1997] 1 FCR 541, CA; *Royal Bank of Scotland plc v Etridge (No 2)* [2001] UKHL 44, [2002] 2 AC 773, [2001] 4 All ER 449.
6   *Barclays Bank plc v Thomson* [1997] 4 All ER 816, [1997] 1 FCR 541, CA; *Royal Bank of Scotland plc v Etridge (No 2)* [2001] UKHL 44, [2002] 2 AC 773, [2001] 4 All ER 449.
7   *Midland Bank v Serter* [1995] 3 FCR 711, 27 HLR 647, CA; *Midland Bank plc v Massey* [1994] 2 FLR 342, [1994] NPC 44, CA; *Banco Exterior Internacional v Mann* [1995] 1 All ER 936, [1995] 1 FLR 602, CA; *Royal Bank of Scotland plc v Etridge (No 2)* [2001] UKHL 44, [2002] 2 AC 773, [2001] 4 All ER 449.
8   *Midland Bank v Serter* [1995] 3 FCR 711, 27 HLR 647, CA; *Halifax Mortgage Services Ltd v Stepsky* [1996] Ch 207, [1996] 2 All ER 277, CA; *Royal Bank of Scotland plc v Etridge (No 2)* [2001] UKHL 44, [2002] 2 AC 773, [2001] 4 All ER 449.
9   *Barclays Bank plc v Thomson* [1997] 4 All ER 816, [1997] 1 FCR 541, CA; *Royal Bank of Scotland plc v Etridge (No 2)* [2001] UKHL 44, [2002] 2 AC 773, [2001] 4 All ER 449.
10   *Barclays Bank plc v Thomson* [1997] 4 All ER 816, [1997] 1 FCR 541, CA; *Royal Bank of Scotland plc v Etridge (No 2)* [2001] UKHL 44, [2002] 2 AC 773, [2001] 4 All ER 449.
11   *Banco Exterior Internacional v Mann* [1995] 1 All ER 936, [1995] 1 FLR 602, CA; *Bank of Baroda v Rayarel* [1995] 2 FCR 631, 27 HLR 387, CA; *Royal Bank of Scotland plc v Etridge (No 2)* [2001] UKHL 44, [2002] 2 AC 773, [2001] 4 All ER 449.
12   *Midland Bank plc v Massey* [1994] 2 FLR 342, [1994] NPC 44, CA; *Bank of Baroda v Rayarel* [1995] 2 FCR 631, 27 HLR 387, CA; *Royal Bank of Scotland plc v Etridge (No 2)* [2001] UKHL 44, [2002] 2 AC 773, [2001] 4 All ER 449.
13   *Royal Bank of Scotland plc v Etridge (No 2)* [2001] UKHL 44 at [77], [2002] 2 AC 773, [2001] 4 All ER 449 per Lord Nicholls of Birkenhead.
14   *Royal Bank of Scotland plc v Etridge (No 2)* [2001] UKHL 44 at [57], [2002] 2 AC 773, [2001] 4 All ER 449 per Lord Nicholls of Birkenhead, and at [175] per Lord Scott of Foscote.
15   *Royal Bank of Scotland plc v Etridge (No 2)* [2001] UKHL 44 at [54], [2002] 2 AC 773, [2001] 4 All ER 449 per Lord Nicholls of Birkenhead.
16   *Royal Bank of Scotland plc v Etridge (No 2)* [2001] UKHL 44 at [54], [2002] 2 AC 773, [2001] 4 All ER 449 per Lord Nicholls of Birkenhead, and at [148], [226] per Lord Scott of Foscote.

124. The remedy of the mortgagor. The remedy of a mortgagor who executed the mortgage as a result of misrepresentation or undue influence is rescission of the mortgage, although a mortgagor is entitled to rescind a mortgage or other transaction only if he restores the benefits received[1]. A transaction may be set aside even though it is impossible to place the parties in precisely the position they were in before if the court can achieve practical justice between the parties[2]. If restitution cannot be made, the claim to rescission fails[3].

The court has no power to set aside the charge in part only or to impose terms[4].

1 *Dunbar Bank plc v Nadeem* [1998] 3 All ER 876, [1998] 2 FLR 457, CA.
2 *Spence v Crawford* [1939] 3 All ER 271, HL; *O'Sullivan v Management Agency and Music Ltd* [1985] QB 428, [1985] 3 All ER 351, CA; *Cheese v Thomas* [1994] 1 All ER 35, [1994] 1 WLR 129, CA; *Dunbar Bank plc v Nadeem* [1998] 3 All ER 876, [1998] 2 FLR 457, CA.
3 *Erlanger v New Sombrero Phosphate Co* (1878) 3 App Cas 1218, HL; *Dunbar Bank plc v Nadeem* [1998] 3 All ER 876, [1998] 2 FLR 457, CA.
4 *TSB Bank plc v Camfield* [1995] 1 All ER 951, [1995] 1 WLR 430, CA; *Castle Phillips Finance v Piddington* [1996] 1 FCR 269, (1994) 70 P & CR 592, CA; *UCB Bank plc v Hedworth* [2003] EWCA Civ 1717, [2003] 3 FCR 739, CA.

125. Remedies of mortgagee where legal charge is set aside. Where a mortgage is set aside, the mortgagee may have the benefit of an equitable mortgage[1], or be subrogated to the rights under an earlier mortgage[2], or be entitled to a restitutionary remedy[3]. If the mortgage is only set aside as against one co-owner, it may take effect as an equitable charge over the beneficial interest of the other co-owner[4].

1 See PARA 218. As to equitable mortgages see PARAS 105, 215 et seq.
2 See PARAS 386–387.
3 See RESTITUTION vol 88 (2012) PARA 401 et seq.
4 See PARAS 168, 219.

(ii) Bonds

126. Bonds as collateral security. A bond by way of collateral security to a mortgage was formerly given, by an instrument separate from the conveyance of the property, for the purpose of enabling the mortgagee to sue in debt[1]; but because an equally effective remedy is given by the covenant for payment in a mortgage[2], the bond has fallen into disuse[3].

1 The court will not allow the creditor to levy execution for more than the amount due when judgment is obtained: see *Darby v Wilkins* (1733) 2 Stra 957; *Masfen v Touchet* (1770) 2 Wm Bl 706; *Talbot v Hodson* (1816) 7 Taunt 251 at 256.
2 See PARA 181 et seq.
3 Occasionally, a promissory note accompanies a mortgage. The doctrine of merger (see PARA 678 et seq) will apply unless there is a declaration to the contrary.

2. PARTIES TO MORTGAGES

(1) ABSOLUTE OWNERS OF PROPERTY

(i) Owners and Co-owners

127. Power of owners to mortgage their property. An absolute owner of property who is not under any incapacity[1], in exercise of the plenary powers of alienation with which the law invests an absolute owner may mortgage the property[2]. Further, a registered[3] proprietor[4] is entitled to exercise owner's powers in relation to a registered estate or charge[5]: in relation to a registered estate these powers consist of power to make a disposition of any kind permitted by the general law in relation to an interest of that description, other than a mortgage by demise or sub-demise[6], and power to charge the estate at law with the payment of money[7]; in relation to a registered charge these powers consist of power to make a disposition of any kind permitted by the general law in relation to an interest of that description, other than a legal sub-mortgage[8], and power to charge at law with the payment of money indebtedness secured by the registered charge[9].

1   As to persons under disability see PARA 140 et seq.
2   See Co Litt 223a. As to restrictions on alienation see GIFTS vol 52 (2014) PARA 254; PERSONAL PROPERTY vol 80 (2013) PARA 869 et seq; REAL PROPERTY AND REGISTRATION vol 87 (2012) PARA 243.
3   'Registered' means entered in the register of title: see the Land Registration Act 2002 s 132(1). As to the register of title and registration therein see REAL PROPERTY AND REGISTRATION vol 87 (2012) PARA 328 et seq.
4   Or a person entitled to be registered as the proprietor: Land Registration Act 2002 s 24(b).
5   Land Registration Act 2002 s 24(a). As to this entitlement see further REAL PROPERTY AND REGISTRATION vol 87 (2012) PARA 424. 'Charge' means any mortgage, charge or lien for securing money or money's worth: s 132(1).
6   See the Land Registration Act 2002 s 23(1)(a); and REAL PROPERTY AND REGISTRATION vol 87 (2012) PARA 422.
7   Land Registration Act 2002 s 23(1)(b).
8   See the Land Registration Act 2002 s 23(2)(a); and REAL PROPERTY AND REGISTRATION vol 87 (2012) PARA 423. For these purposes, 'legal sub-mortgage' means a transfer by way of mortgage (s 23(3)(a)), a sub-mortgage by sub-demise (s 23(3)(b)), and a charge by way of legal mortgage (s 23(3)(c)). As to the meaning of 'legal mortgage' see PARA 104 note 1; definition applied by s 132(1).
9   Land Registration Act 2002 s 23(2)(b). See further PARA 253.

128. Power of co-owners to mortgage their property. Where more persons than one own land, they may be beneficially interested in the land either jointly or as tenants in common, but in either case the legal estate in the land will be held by not more than four of the co-owners as joint tenants upon trust for the co-owners as joint tenants in common[1]. The co-owners may mortgage the land under trustees' statutory powers[2]. Where, however, the same persons are both the trustees and the beneficiaries, they may mortgage as absolute owners[3].

Where a legal mortgage of land is made to several persons, the legal estate vests in the mortgagees or the first four named as joint tenants upon trust[4]. Where the mortgage is made to several mortgagees jointly or the mortgage money is expressed to belong to them on a joint account, that money is, as between the mortgagees and the mortgagor, deemed to be and remain money belonging to the mortgagees on a joint account, unless the contrary is expressed in the mortgage[5]. Persons dealing in good faith with several mortgagees may assume, unless the contrary is expressed in the instruments relating to the mortgage, that the mortgagees are entitled to the mortgage money on a joint account[6].

1   See the Law of Property Act 1925 ss 34, 36; the Settled Land Act 1925 s 36; the Trustee Act 1925 s 34; and REAL PROPERTY AND REGISTRATION vol 87 (2012) PARAS 198, 219; SETTLEMENTS vol 91 (2012) PARA 614; TRUSTS AND POWERS vol 98 (2013) PARAS 244, 262.

2   As to the statutory powers of trustees see PARAS 154–155. As to liability where there are several mortgagors see PARA 634.

3   A purported mortgage by one co-owner may operate as a mortgage of his beneficial interest: cf *Cedar Holdings Ltd v Green* [1981] Ch 129, [1979] 3 All ER 117, CA; *Ahmed v Kendrick* (1987) 56 P & CR 120, [1988] 2 FLR 22, CA. See also PARAS 168, 218–219. As to the power of absolute owners to mortgage their property see PARA 127.

4   Cf the text to note 1.

5   See the Law of Property Act 1925 s 111; and PARA 186.

6   See the Law of Property Act 1925 s 113(1)(a); and PARA 375. See also PARA 186.

(ii) Corporate and Unincorporate Bodies

129. Corporations and companies. A corporation created by royal charter has prima facie the power to do with its property all such acts as an ordinary person can do[1]. A corporation created by statute can mortgage its property only in so far as it is expressly or impliedly authorised by the statute[2]. Likewise, a company formed under a statute such as the Companies Act 2006 has the powers given by its constitution, although the power to borrow and secure such borrowing by mortgage will be implied if it is incidental to the purposes of the company[3]. The validity of a mortgage granted by a company may not be called into question on the ground of lack of capacity by reason of anything in the company's constitution[4]. In favour of a person dealing with a company in good faith, the power of the directors to bind the company, or authorise others to do so, is deemed to be free of any limitation under the company's constitution[5]; and for these purposes a person dealing with a company is not bound to inquire as to any limitation on the powers of the directors to bind the company or authorise others to do so[6]. A mortgagee is entitled to assume, in the absence of notice to the contrary, that the internal procedures of a company have been properly complied with[7].

A company is liable in respect of equitable mortgages entered into by its agents when acting within the scope of their authority provided it is within the company's powers[8]. In favour of a mortgagee in good faith who gives valuable consideration a legal mortgage is deemed to have been duly executed by a company if it purports to be signed by two authorised signatories, or by a director of the company in the presence of a witness who attests the signature[9].

The powers to mortgage benefices and to mortgage the glebe and profits of a benefice are considered elsewhere in this work[10].

1   *Baroness Wenlock v River Dee Co* (1883) 36 ChD 675n at 685n, CA; on appeal (1885) 10 App Cas 354, HL. See also CORPORATIONS vol 24 (2010) PARA 431. As to incorporation by charter see CORPORATIONS vol 24 (2010) PARA 329 et seq.

2   *Blackburn Building Society v Cunliffe, Brooks & Co* (1882) 22 ChD 61 at 70, CA; affd on appeal sub nom *Cunliffe, Brooks & Co v Blackburn Benefit Society* (1884) 9 App Cas 857, HL. See also CORPORATIONS vol 24 (2010) PARA 439.

3   *Re Badger, Mansell v Viscount Cobham* [1905] 1 Ch 568 at 574; and see COMPANIES vol 15 (2009) PARA 1256.

4   See the Companies Act 2006 s 39(1); and COMPANIES vol 14 (2009) PARA 265. This section has effect subject to s 42 in the case of companies that are charities: see s 39(2); and COMPANIES vol 14 (2009) PARA 265.

5   See the Companies Act 2006 s 40(1); and COMPANIES vol 14 (2009) PARA 263. However, this provision does not affect any right of a member of the company to bring proceedings to restrain

the doing of an action that is beyond the powers of the directors: see s 40(4); and COMPANIES vol 14 (2009) PARA 263. Notwithstanding this provision, transactions between a company and a director of the company or its holding company or with a person connected with such a director are voidable at the instance of the company: see s 41; and COMPANIES vol 14 (2009) PARA 264.

6   See the Companies Act 2006 s 40(2); and COMPANIES vol 14 (2009) PARA 263.
7   *Royal British Bank v Turquand* (1856) 25 LJQB 317; *County of Gloucester Bank v Rudry Merthyr Steam and House Coal Colliery Co* [1895] 1 Ch 629; *Duck v Tower Galvanizing Co Ltd* [1901] 2 KB 314; *Rolled Steel Products (Holdings) Ltd v British Steel Corpn* [1986] Ch 246 at 295, [1985] 3 All ER 52 at 86, CA, per Slade LJ. See also COMPANIES vol 14 (2009) PARA 267.
8   As to equitable mortgages see PARAS 105, 215 et seq.
9   See the Companies Act 2006 s 44; and COMPANIES vol 14 (2009) PARA 288.
10 See ECCLESIASTICAL LAW vol 34 (2011) PARAS 361, 923 et seq.

130.   Local authorities and other public authorities. All money borrowed by a local authority[1], together with any interest on it, is charged indifferently on all the revenues of the authority[2], and all securities created by a local authority rank equally without any priority[3]. Any other purported mortgage or charge of local authority property as security for money borrowed or otherwise owing is ultra vires and unenforceable[4]. A local authority may borrow money for any purpose relevant to its functions under any enactment[5] or for the purposes of the prudent management of its financial affairs[6], but may not borrow if so doing would result in a breach of limits determined by the authority of the Secretary of State[7]. A person lending money to a local authority is not bound to inquire whether the authority has power to borrow the money and will not be prejudiced by the absence of any such power[8].

A local authority[9] may advance money to a person for the purpose of acquiring or constructing a house, or converting a building into a house, or acquiring a building and converting it into a house[10]; and a local authority which is not a local housing authority[11] may advance money to a person for the purpose of altering, enlarging, repairing or improving a house[12]. Local authorities, including those which are not local housing authorities, may advance money for the purpose of facilitating the repayment of an amount outstanding on a previous loan made for any of the purposes for which they may advance money under these provisions[13]. The advance and the interest on it must be secured by mortgage and no such advance may be made unless the estate proposed to be mortgaged is either in fee simple absolute in possession, or is an estate for a term of years absolute for a period of not less than ten years in excess of the period fixed for repayment[14].

Under certain circumstances a secure tenant has a right to buy[15] property from a local authority on rent to mortgage terms[16]. The property is mortgaged to a lender who advances an initial payment to the authority towards the purchase price and the mortgage is repaid by instalments based on the rent formerly paid to the authority; the balance of the purchase price takes the form of an interest-free loan from the authority, secured by a charge on the property, to be repaid on a later disposal of the property; and the amount repayable to the local authority is adjusted to take account, inter alia, of any change in the overall value of the property at the time of disposal[17].

Local authorities have other powers to assist mortgagors, including the power to indemnify mortgagees against default[18], and to contribute towards the costs of a mortgagor's legal charge or proposed legal charge[19].

A local authority has the power to dispose of land held for housing purposes and leave part of the disposal price outstanding on a mortgage[20].

Statutory powers to mortgage property or to advance money on mortgage are conferred, where requisite, on other public authorities or institutions by statutes investing them with special functions[21]. Conversely, there may be a statutory prohibition on the mortgage or charging of assets[22].

1 For the purposes of the Local Government Act 2003 Pt 1 (ss 1–24), the following are local authorities: county, county borough and district councils (see LOCAL GOVERNMENT vol 69 (2009) PARA 23); the Greater London Authority (see LONDON GOVERNMENT vol 71 (2013) PARA 67 et seq); a functional body within the meaning of the Greater London Authority Act 1999 (see LONDON GOVERNMENT vol 71 (2013) PARA 148); a London borough council (see LONDON GOVERNMENT vol 71 (2013) PARA 20 et seq); the Common Council of the City of London (see LONDON GOVERNMENT vol 71 (2013) PARA 34 et seq) in its capacity as a local authority, police authority or port health authority (see ENVIRONMENTAL QUALITY AND PUBLIC HEALTH vol 45 (2010) PARA 102); the Council of the Isles of Scilly (see LOCAL GOVERNMENT vol 69 (2009) PARA 36); a waste disposal authority established under the Local Government Act 1985 s 10 (see ENVIRONMENTAL QUALITY AND PUBLIC HEALTH vol 46 (2010) PARA 620; LOCAL GOVERNMENT vol 69 (2009) PARA 17); a joint authority established by Pt 4 (ss 23–42) (fire and rescue services and transport) (see LOCAL GOVERNMENT vol 69 (2009) PARA 47 et seq); a joint planning board constituted for an area in Wales outside a National Park by an order under the Town and Country Planning Act 1990 s 2(1B) (see PLANNING vol 81 (2010) PARA 45); a fire and rescue authority constituted by a scheme under the Fire and Rescue Services Act 2004 s 2 or a scheme to which s 4 applies (see FIRE AND RESCUE SERVICES vol 51 (2013) PARAS 18–20); a police and crime commissioner; and any other body specified for these purposes by regulations: see the Local Government Act 2003 s 23(1) (amended by the Civil Contingencies Act 2004 s 32(1), Sch 2 para 10(3)(e); the Fire and Rescue Services Act 2004 s 53(1), Sch 1 paras 99, 100; SI 2005/886; the Local Government and Public Involvement in Health Act 2007 s 209(2), Sch 13 Pt 2 para 55(1), (2); the Police Reform and Social Responsibility Act 2011 s 99, Sch 16 Pt 3 paras 316, 317; and the Deregulation Act 2015 s 59, Sch 13 Pt 3 para 6(1), (32)(a)). Additional authorities are specified in the Local Authorities (Capital Finance and Accounting) (England) Regulations 2003, SI 2003/3146, reg 32 and the Local Authorities (Capital Finance and Accounting) (Wales) Regulations 2003, SI 2003/3239, reg 26: see LOCAL GOVERNMENT FINANCE vol 70 (2012) PARA 476 et seq. For the purposes of the Local Government Act 2003 ss 2(3), (4), 6 (see the text to notes 7, 8), references to a local authority include parish and community councils (see LOCAL GOVERNMENT vol 69 (2009) PARAS 27 et seq, 41 et seq) and charter trustees (see LOCAL GOVERNMENT vol 69 (2009) PARA 113): Local Government Act 2003 s 19(1).

2 See the Local Government Act 2003 s 13(3); and LOCAL GOVERNMENT FINANCE vol 70 (2012) PARA 481.

3 See the Local Government Act 2003 s 13(4); and LOCAL GOVERNMENT FINANCE vol 70 (2012) PARA 481.

4 See the Local Government Act 2003 s 13(1), (2); and LOCAL GOVERNMENT FINANCE vol 70 (2012) PARA 481.

5 Local Government Act 2003 s 1(a).

6 Local Government Act 2003 s 1(b). See also *Hazell v Hammersmith and Fulham London Borough Council* [1992] 2 AC 1, [1991] 1 All ER 545, HL.

7 See the Local Government Act 2003 ss 2–4; and LOCAL GOVERNMENT FINANCE vol 70 (2012) PARA 479 et seq.

8 See the Local Government Act 2003 s 6; and LOCAL GOVERNMENT FINANCE vol 70 (2012) PARA 482. See also the Local Government (Contracts) Act 1997; and LOCAL GOVERNMENT vol 69 (2009) PARA 411 et seq.

9 For these purposes, 'local authority' means a county, county borough, district or London borough council, the Common Council of the City of London or the Council of the Isles of Scilly: see the Housing Act 1985 s 4(1)(e) (amended by the Local Government (Wales) Act 1994 s 22(2), Sch 8 para 5(3); and renumbered by the Local Government and Public Involvement in Health Act 2007 s 209(2), Sch 13 Pt 2 para 41(1)); and HOUSING vol 56 (2011) PARA 10.

10 See the Housing Act 1985 s 435(1)(a)–(c); and HOUSING vol 56 (2011) PARA 660.

11 As to local housing authorities see the Housing Act 1985 s 1; and HOUSING vol 56 (2011) PARA 9.

12 See the Housing Act 1985 s 435(1A)(a); and HOUSING vol 56 (2011) PARA 660.

13 See the Housing Act 1985 s 435(1), (1A)(b); and HOUSING vol 56 (2011) PARA 660.

14 See the Housing Act 1985 s 436; and HOUSING vol 56 (2011) PARA 661.

15 As to the right to buy see LANDLORD AND TENANT vol 64 (2012) PARA 1911 et seq.

16 See the Housing Act 1985 s 143; and LANDLORD AND TENANT vol 64 (2012) PARA 1989.

17 See the Housing Act 1985 ss 143A–153; and LANDLORD AND TENANT vol 64 (2012) PARA 1989 et seq.

18 See the Housing Act 1985 s 442; and HOUSING vol 56 (2011) PARA 666.

19 See the Housing Act 1985 s 443; and HOUSING vol 56 (2011) PARA 667.

20 See the Housing Act 1985 ss 32, 33; and HOUSING vol 56 (2011) PARAS 311, 312.
21 Eg the National Trust may borrow on mortgage of its alienable property (see the National Trust Act 1907 s 22; and NATIONAL CULTURAL HERITAGE vol 77 (2016) PARA 991), and internal drainage boards may raise money on mortgage (see the Land Drainage Act 1991 s 55; and WATER AND WATERWAYS vol 101 (2009) PARA 640).
22 Eg in the case of NHS trusts: see the National Health Service Act 2006 Sch 5 para 3(3); and HEALTH SERVICES vol 54 (2008) PARA 515. As from a day to be appointed, NHS trusts in England are abolished: see the Health and Social Care Act 2012 s 179(2) (not yet in force).

131. Building societies, friendly societies etc. The power of building societies to make advances[1], the nature of the security which may be accepted or required, the redemption, enforcement and discharge of building society mortgages[2] and the powers of building societies to borrow money and give security[3] are considered elsewhere in this work.

Friendly societies and industrial and provident societies may borrow or lend on mortgage if so authorised by their rules. These societies, too, are considered elsewhere[4].

1 See FINANCIAL INSTITUTIONS vol 48 (2015) PARA 479 et seq.
2 See FINANCIAL INSTITUTIONS vol 48 (2015) PARA 487 et seq.
3 See FINANCIAL INSTITUTIONS vol 48 (2015) PARA 390 et seq.
4 As to friendly societies see FINANCIAL INSTITUTIONS vol 48 (2015) PARA 555 et seq. As to industrial and provident societies see FINANCIAL INSTITUTIONS vol 48 (2015) PARA 880 et seq.

132. Charity trustees. Land held on charitable, ecclesiastical or public trusts is now held on a trust of land, and charitable trustees have all the powers of an absolute owner, subject to statutory restrictions[1]. No mortgage of land held by or on trust for a charity other than an exempt charity[2] may be granted without an order of the court or of the Charity Commission[3] unless the charity trustees have obtained and considered proper advice given to them in writing before granting the mortgage[4]. Any mortgage of land held by or in trust for a charity must state that the land is held by or in trust for the charity[5]. It must also state whether the charity is an exempt charity and whether the mortgage is one for which general or special authority is expressly given[6]. If it is not an exempt charity and it is not a mortgage for which general of special authority is given, then the mortgage must state that it is one to which the statutory restrictions apply[7].

In the case of charity property other than land, the power to mortgage is governed by the instrument or instruments regulating the charity[8].

1 See the Trusts of Land and Appointment of Trustees Act 1996 ss 1, 2(6), 6(8); and TRUSTS AND POWERS vol 98 (2013) PARAS 6, 476.
2 As to exempt charities see CHARITIES vol 8 (2015) PARA 318 et seq.
3 As to the Charity Commission see CHARITIES vol 8 (2015) PARA 543 et seq.
4 See the Charities Act 2011 s 124(1), (2), (10); and CHARITIES vol 8 (2015) PARA 404. As to disposal of charity property generally see CHARITIES vol 8 (2015) PARA 401 et seq.
5 See the Charities Act 2011 s 125(1)(a); and CHARITIES vol 8 (2015) PARA 405.
6 See the Charities Act 2011 s 125(1)(b); and CHARITIES vol 8 (2015) PARA 405.
7 See the Charities Act 2011 s 125(1)(c); and CHARITIES vol 8 (2015) PARA 405.
8 See eg NATIONAL CULTURAL HERITAGE vol 77 (2016) PARA 949.

133. Clubs. The property of an unincorporated club[1] is normally vested in trustees[2] whose powers in relation to mortgages are governed by the rules of the club. The rules of an unincorporated club or the memorandum and articles of an incorporated club may authorise the issue of club debentures[3].

1 As to the various kinds of clubs see CLUBS vol 13 (2009) PARA 204 et seq.
2 See CLUBS vol 13 (2009) PARA 257. As to the powers of trustees to grant mortgages see PARA 153 et seq.
3 See CLUBS vol 13 (2009) PARAS 250–252.

(iii) Partnerships

134. Partner's power to mortgage otherwise than by deed. A partner[1] has an implied authority to pledge or mortgage, otherwise than by deed, the personal property belonging to the partnership, and probably also the real estate[2] if dealing in it is one of the objectives of the partnership, in order to raise money for the carrying on in the usual way of the partnership business, unless the partner so pledging or mortgaging has in fact no authority so to act for the firm, and the person with whom he is dealing either knows that he has no authority or does not know or believe him to be a partner[3]. A partner cannot validly mortgage partnership property, known to be such by the mortgagee, to secure his personal debt, without the knowledge and consent of the other partners[4], and the burden of proving that consent rests on the mortgagee[5]. Where the mortgagee does not know that the property mortgaged is partnership property, the mortgage is good[6].

This authority to mortgage the partnership property continues after dissolution so far as may be necessary to wind up the affairs of the partnership and to complete transactions begun but unfinished at the time of dissolution[7]; but a bankrupt partner is deprived of that authority[8].

1 A limited partner under the Limited Partnerships Act 1907 has no power to bind the firm: see s 6(1); and PARTNERSHIP vol 79 (2014) PARA 225. As to the meanings of 'limited partner' and 'general partner' see PARTNERSHIP vol 79 (2014) PARA 218.
2 Partnership land is held on trust: see PARA 135.
3 See the Partnership Act 1890 s 5; and PARTNERSHIP vol 79 (2014) PARA 39 et seq. See also *Butchart v Dresser* (1853) 4 De GM & G 542 (equitable mortgage of shares); *Re Ogden, ex p Lloyd* (1834) 1 Mont & A 494 (equitable mortgage of trade fixtures); *Re Litherland, ex p Howden* (1842) 2 Mont D & De G 574 (mortgage of a ship). However, one partner cannot mortgage the whole of the future profits of a voyage in the shape of unearned freight: *Guion v Trask* (1860) 1 De GF & J 373. For the effect of a mortgage by a partner of his own share in the partnership see PARA 138.
4 *Shirreff v Wilks* (1800) 1 East 48; *Wilkinson v Eykyn* (1866) 14 WR 470 (following *Young v Keighly* (1808) 15 Ves 557 and *Allen v Kilbre* (1819) 4 Madd 464); *Cavander v Bulteel* (1873) 9 Ch App 79. See also *Ridley v Taylor* (1810) 13 East 175 at 182 per Lord Ellenborough.
5 *Snaith v Burridge* (1812) 4 Taunt 684; *Re Wardley and Hodson, ex p Thorpe* (1836) 2 Deac 16; *Frankland v M'Gusty* (1830) 1 Knapp 274, PC; *Leverson v Lane* (1862) 13 CBNS 278.
6 *Reid v Hollinshead* (1825) 4 B & C 867 (following *Raba v Ryland* (1819) Gow 132 and *Tupper v Haythorne* (1815) Gow 135n).
7 See the Partnership Act 1890 s 38; and PARTNERSHIP vol 79 (2014) PARAS 46, 197. See also *Butchart v Dresser* (1853) 4 De GM & G 542; *Re Clough, Bradford Commercial Banking Co v Cure* (1885) 31 ChD 324; *Re Bourne, Bourne v Bourne* [1906] 2 Ch 427, CA (following *Re Langmead's Trusts* (1855) 20 Beav 20 (affd 7 De GM & G 353) and *Re Ryan* (1868) 3 IR Eq 222).
8 See the Partnership Act 1890 s 38; and PARTNERSHIP vol 79 (2014) PARA 46.

135. Partner's power to mortgage by deed. Neither during the continuance of the partnership nor after its dissolution can one partner by executing a mortgage deed of partnership property bind the other partners[1] unless special authority is given him to do so[2]. The common law requires that the authority must be contained in a deed; and it is not enough, either at law or in equity, that the agreement constituting the partnership is under seal unless it contains a particular authority to the partners to execute deeds on behalf of the firm[3]. Where a partner executes a mortgage deed on behalf of the firm, the partner may be bound even though the firm is not bound[4], unless he shows that his signature was conditional on the firm being bound[5]. If a partner executes a deed for himself and his partner in the presence and by the authority of his partner, the execution operates as an execution by both[6]; and even though a mortgage deed, executed by one partner alone, is not at law binding on the firm, it may be a good security in equity[7]. Partnership land is normally held by one or two partners as trustees[8].

1   *Harrison v Jackson* (1797) 7 Term Rep 207; *Steiglitz v Egginton* (1815) Holt NP 141. See also *Hawkshaw v Parkins* (1819) 2 Swan 539, where a distinction is suggested between a deed of release and a deed of grant; cf however *Juggeewundas Keeka Shah v Ramdas Brijbookundas* (1841) 2 Moo Ind App 487, PC.
2   *Steiglitz v Egginton* (1815) Holt NP 141.
3   *Harrison v Jackson* (1797) 7 Term Rep 207 at 210 per Lord Kenyon CJ.
4   *Elliot v Davis* (1800) 2 Bos & P 338. See also *Hawkshaw v Parkins* (1819) 2 Swan 539; *Cumberlege v Lawson* (1857) 1 CBNS 709.
5   *Cumberlege v Lawson* (1857) 1 CBNS 709. See also *Antram v Chace* (1812) 15 East 209; *Brownrigg v Rae* (1850) 5 Exch 489; *Gordon v Ellis* (1844) 7 Man & G 607; *Hawker v Hallewell* (1856) 3 Sm & G 194.
6   *Ball v Dunsterville* (1791) 4 Term Rep 313; approved in *Burn v Burn* (1798) 3 Ves 573 at 578 per Lord Loughborough LC. See also *Brutton v Burton and Mills* (1819) 1 Chit 707 at 709.
7   *Re Boyd, Re Wilson and Vause, ex p Bosanquet* (1847) De G 432.
8   As to the powers of trustees see PARA 153 et seq. As to the effect of a change in a firm after the partnership has mortgaged property see PARA 136. Partnership land is held on a trust of land: see the Trusts of Land and Appointment of Trustees Act 1996 s 1; and REAL PROPERTY AND REGISTRATION vol 87 (2012) PARA 105.

136. Effect on mortgage of change in partnership. Where a partnership mortgages property, the mortgage prima facie only secures advances made before any subsequent alteration in the partnership, whether by the retirement or the admission of a partner or partners or by both[1]. If, however, the mortgage was not made by deed[2], its scope may be enlarged or restricted, after an alteration in the partnership, by an oral agreement with the creditor, whether express or implied[3].

Although a mortgage made by deed cannot be varied by an oral agreement, such an agreement may apparently create an equitable mortgage by or to the new partnership subject to the prior legal mortgage by deed[4].

A mortgage of land can no longer[5] be created orally, and a validly created equitable mortgage of land cannot be varied orally[6].

1   *Ex p Kensington* (1813) 2 Ves & B 79 at 83 per Lord Eldon. Whether it extends to any advances made after alterations in the partnership depends on the terms of the mortgage.
2   *Re Hopkins, ex p Hooper* (1815) 2 Rose 328; *Royal Bank of Scotland v Christie* (1841) 8 Cl & Fin 214, HL.
3   *Ex p Kensington* (1813) 2 Ves & B 79; *Re Ablett, ex p Lloyd* (1824) 1 Gl & J 389; *Re Worters, ex p Oakes* (1841) 2 Mont D & De G 234; *Re Lendon, ex p Lane* (1846) De G 300. See also *Re Burkill, ex p Nettleship* (1841) 2 Mont D & De G 124.
4   *Re Borron, ex p Parr* (1835) 4 Deac & Ch 426.
5   Ie since 27 September 1989: see PARA 221.
6   See the Law of Property (Miscellaneous Provisions) Act 1989 s 2; and PARA 221.

137. Partner's power to lend on mortgage. A partner has authority to lend the firm's money on mortgage, when such a transaction is part of the ordinary business of the firm[1]; but a partner has, as a rule, no authority to take as security any property to which a liability is attached, such as partly paid shares in a company[2].

1   *Re Land Credit Co of Ireland, Weikersheim's Case* (1873) 8 Ch App 831.
2   See *Niemann v Niemann* (1889) 43 ChD 198, CA; and cf *Re Land Credit Co of Ireland, Weikersheim's Case* (1873) 8 Ch App 831.

138. Mortgage of share in partnership. If a partner mortgages his own share in a partnership[1], the mortgagee takes subject to equities subsisting between the partners[2].

An assignee of a share in a partnership is not, however, bound by a subsequent agreement between the assignor and another of the partners for the sale to that other partner of that share, even though that agreement is made in good faith[3]. A mortgage of a share in a partnership is not a mortgage of chattels but of a chose or thing in action, and need not be registered as a bill of sale[4].

A mortgagee of a partner's share is not entitled during the continuance of the partnership to interfere in the management, or to require accounts, or to inspect the books of the partnership business[5]. He is entitled to an inquiry as to the value of the share at the date when he took proceedings to realise his mortgage; but, if a dissolution of the partnership has previously taken place, the date of dissolution is that date at which the necessary account ought to be taken[6]. He may enforce his security by a claim for an account and foreclosure[7]. Where the mortgage is by deed, but not under a bill of sale[8], he has probably a power of sale[9] and a power to appoint a receiver[10].

1   As to a partner's power to mortgage the partnership property as distinct from his own share in the partnership see PARAS 134–135.
2   *Smith v Parkes* (1852) 16 Beav 115; *Kelly v Hutton* (1868) 3 Ch App 703; *Re Garwood's Trusts, Garwood v Paynter* [1903] 1 Ch 236. See also *Whetham v Davey* (1885) 30 ChD 574; the Partnership Act 1890 s 31; and PARTNERSHIP vol 79 (2014) PARA 125.
3   *Watts v Driscoll* [1901] 1 Ch 294, CA (distinguishing *Kelly v Hutton* (1868) 3 Ch App 703 and *Whetham v Davey* (1885) 30 ChD 574).
4   *Re Bainbridge, ex p Fletcher* (1878) 8 ChD 218. As to legal mortgages of choses or things in action see PARA 206. As to the registration of bills of sale see FINANCIAL INSTRUMENTS AND TRANSACTIONS vol 49 (2015) PARA 537 et seq.
5   See the Partnership Act 1890 s 31(1); and PARTNERSHIP vol 79 (2014) PARA 125.
6   *Whetham v Davey* (1885) 30 ChD 574.
7   *Whetham v Davey* (1885) 30 ChD 574; *Redmayne v Forster* (1886) LR 2 Eq 467; and see PARTNERSHIP vol 79 (2014) PARA 125. See also *Bentley v Bates* (1840) 4 Y & C Ex 182. As to a claim for an account see PARTNERSHIP vol 79 (2014) PARA 149 et seq. The mortgagee's claim for an account will not be stayed because of an arbitration clause in the partnership deed, at any rate where that clause does not embrace persons claiming through the partners: *Bonnin v Neame* [1910] 1 Ch 732. As to foreclosure see PARA 571 et seq.
8   *Calvert v Thomas* (1887) 19 QBD 204, CA (decided under the Conveyancing Act 1881 s 19 (repealed)). See also FINANCIAL INSTRUMENTS AND TRANSACTIONS vol 49 (2015) PARA 569.
9   See the Law of Property Act 1925 s 101; and PARA 446.
10   See the Law of Property Act 1925 s 101; and PARA 479.

(iv) Limited Liability Partnerships

139. Power of limited liability partnerships to mortgage. Two or more persons associated for carrying on a lawful business for profit can incorporate as a limited liability partnership ('LLP')[1]. An LLP is a body corporate with unlimited capacity and a legal personality separate from its members[2]. Like a company, an LLP can contract in its own name with third parties and has power to enter mortgages[3]. The precise extent of an LLP's power to enter mortgages may be defined in the LLP agreement[4].

1   See the Limited Liability Partnerships Act 2000 s 2; and PARTNERSHIP vol 79 (2014) PARA 234.
2   See the Limited Liability Partnerships Act 2000 s 1; and PARTNERSHIP vol 79 (2014) PARA 233 et seq.
3   See PARA 129.
4   Eg the partnership agreement may restrict the power of the LLP by limiting the amount the LLP may borrow. Execution of deeds and other documents by limited liability partnerships is governed by the Companies Act 2006 ss 43–47 (as modified by the Limited Liability Partnerships (Application of Companies Act 2006) Regulations 2009, SI 2009/1804, reg 4). See further PARTNERSHIP vol 79 (2014) PARA 243 et seq.

(v) Persons under Disability

A. MINORS

140. Law of mortgage as it applies to minors. A minor[1] cannot hold a legal estate and hence cannot create a legal mortgage of land[2]. A minor can avoid a contract to create a mortgage or charge[3] or a charge over his equitable interest until a reasonable time after attaining majority[4]. He can, however, ratify such a transaction after attaining his majority. Where a contract is unenforceable against a minor, or he repudiates it, because he was a minor when it was made, the court may require the minor to transfer any property acquired under the contract or any property representing it[5].

Where, however, a minor is beneficially entitled to any property, the court may, with a view to the application of the capital or income for the minor's maintenance, education or benefit, direct the trustees to raise money by mortgage of the property[6]. A mortgage in favour of a minor takes effect as a trust in favour of the minor, and a mortgage to a minor and another person of full age vests the legal estate in the other person upon trust for himself and the minor[7].

1 A 'minor' is a person under the age of 18: see the Family Law Reform Act 1969 s 1; and CHILDREN AND YOUNG PERSONS vol 9 (2012) PARAS 1–3.
2 See the Law of Property Act 1925 s 1(6). See also CHILDREN AND YOUNG PERSONS vol 9 (2012) PARAS 25, 30; REAL PROPERTY AND REGISTRATION vol 87 (2012) PARA 55. As to the meaning of 'legal estate' see PARA 105 note 2.
3 *Edwards v Carter* [1893] AC 360, HL.
4 *Edwards v Carter* [1893] AC 360, HL. To some degree a minor may also avoid a contract for the repayment of money lent to him during his minority, although this power is restricted in relation to contracts coming into being after 9 June 1987 (ie the date on which the Minors Contracts Act 1987 came into force, repealing the Infants Relief Act 1874 (which rendered void contracts with minors for the repayment of money other than contracts for necessaries) and providing that where a guarantee is given in respect of an obligation of a party to a contract after that date which is unenforceable against him because he is a minor, the guarantee is not for that reason alone unenforceable against the guarantor): see the Minors Contracts Act 1987 ss 1, 2; and CHILDREN AND YOUNG PERSONS vol 9 (2012) PARA 14.
5 See the Minors' Contracts Act 1987 s 3(1); and CHILDREN AND YOUNG PERSONS vol 9 (2012) PARA 24. See also *Nottingham Permanent Benefit Building Society v Thurstan* [1903] AC 6, HL.
6 See the Trustee Act 1925 s 53; and CHILDREN AND YOUNG PERSONS vol 9 (2012) PARAS 71, 74. Section 53 refers to 'infants' which term now has the same definition as 'minor' (see note 1): see the Family Law Reform Act 1969 s 1; and CHILDREN AND YOUNG PERSONS vol 9 (2012) PARAS 1–3.
7 See the Trusts of Land and Appointment of Trustees Act 1996 s 2, Sch 1 paras 1, 2; and CHILDREN AND YOUNG PERSONS vol 9 (2012) PARA 31.

B. PERSONS LACKING MENTAL CAPACITY

141. Person lacking mental capacity cannot create valid mortgage. The deed of a person suffering from such mental disorder as to render him incapable of understanding the effect of the deed is void[1]. A deed made by such a person during a lucid interval, the nature and effect of which he understood[2], is binding upon him unless a receiver has been appointed for him[3].

Provision is made for the property of mentally disordered persons to be protected by court order or direction[4]. In exceptional circumstances the court may authorise the loan of a patient's money upon mortgage[5].

1 *Price v Berrington* (1849) 7 Hare 394 at 402. See DEEDS AND OTHER INSTRUMENTS vol 32 (2012) PARA 268.
2 *Towart v Sellars* (1817) 5 Dow 231, HL.

3   See *Re Marshall, Marshall v Whateley* [1920] 1 Ch 284. As to the capacity of mentally disordered
    persons to execute deeds and to make contracts, and their powers of disposition and the effect of
    such dispositions generally, see MENTAL HEALTH AND CAPACITY vol 75 (2013) PARA 597 et seq.
4   See the Mental Capacity Act 2005 Pt 2 (ss 45–61); and MENTAL HEALTH AND CAPACITY vol 75
    (2013) PARA 720 et seq.
5   See *Re Ridgeways* (1825) 1 Hog 309.

C.   BANKRUPTS

142.   Law of mortgage as it applies to bankrupts. Dispositions of property made
by a bankrupt between the date of presentation of the bankruptcy petition and the
date when the property vests in the trustee are void unless approved or ratified by
the court[1], although this does not give a remedy against a mortgagee in respect of
any property or payment which he received before the commencement of the
bankruptcy in good faith, for value and without notice that the petition has been
presented[2]. In the case of land, a petition in bankruptcy does not bind a purchaser[3]
of a legal estate in good faith for money or money's worth unless for the time
being it is registered[4]. Where a petition has been registered, the title of the trustee
in bankruptcy is void as against a purchaser of a legal estate in good faith for
money or money's worth claiming under a conveyance made after the date of
registration, unless at the date of the conveyance either the registration of the
petition is in force or a bankruptcy order[5] on the petition is registered[6]. Where the
proprietor of a registered estate or charge[7] is adjudged bankrupt, the title of his
trustee in bankruptcy is void as against a person to whom a registrable
disposition[8] of the estate or charge is made if the disposition is made for valuable
consideration[9], the person to whom the disposition is made acts in good faith[10],
and at the time of the disposition no notice or restriction is entered[11] in relation
to the registered estate or charge[12] and the person to whom the disposition is made
has no notice of the bankruptcy petition or the adjudication[13]. When a person is
made the subject of a bankruptcy order, his estate[14] vests in the trustee
immediately on his appointment taking effect or, in the case of the official receiver,
on his becoming trustee, and therefore the bankrupt cannot mortgage it[15].
However, the title of a trustee in bankruptcy is void as against a purchaser of a
legal estate in good faith for money or money's worth unless the bankruptcy
order is for the time being registered[16].

A bankrupt mortgagor is not, however, civilly defunct, and may mortgage
whatever property is allowed by law, as an exception to the general rule, to remain
vested in him[17]. Thus a bankrupt may mortgage his expectation of a surplus after
payment in full of debts proved in and expenses incurred in relation to his
bankruptcy[18]. It is not necessary that the bankrupt should mortgage the surplus
expressly as such; if he mortgages specific property, and that specific property is
more than sufficient to satisfy creditors, the surplus of the property is validly
mortgaged[19]. A bankrupt may also mortgage property vested in him upon trust[20],
or immovables situated in a foreign country if the law of the place where the
property is situated permits him to do so[21].

1   See the Insolvency Act 1986 s 284(1); and BANKRUPTCY AND INDIVIDUAL INSOLVENCY vol 5
    (2013) PARA 209.
2   See the Insolvency Act 1986 s 284(4)(a); and BANKRUPTCY AND INDIVIDUAL INSOLVENCY
    vol 5 (2013) PARA 209.
3   A purchaser includes a mortgagee: see the Law of Property Act 1925 s 205(1)(xxi); Land Charges
    Act 1972 s 17(1); and CONVEYANCING vol 23 (2013) PARA 236.
4   See the Land Charges Act 1972 s 5(8); and REAL PROPERTY AND REGISTRATION vol 87 (2012)
    PARA 742. The bankruptcy petition should be registered as a pending action under the Land
    Charges Act 1972: see s 5(1)(b). Notice of a petition must be given to the Chief Land Registrar,
    for registration in the register of pending actions: see the Insolvency Rules 1986, SI 1986/1925,

rr 6.13, 6.43; and BANKRUPTCY AND INDIVIDUAL INSOLVENCY vol 5 (2013) PARAS 171, 196. Registration under the Land Charges Act 1972 is deemed to constitute actual notice: see the Law of Property Act 1925 s 198; and REAL PROPERTY AND REGISTRATION vol 87 (2012) PARA 708. Registration of a bankruptcy petition under the Land Charges Act 1972 also triggers registration by the Chief Land Registrar of a notice in respect of the pending action in relation to any registered estate or charge which appears affected: see the Land Registration Act 2002 s 86(2); and REAL PROPERTY AND REGISTRATION vol 87 (2012) PARAS 532, 743.

5 The Land Charges Act 1972 s 6(6) refers to a 'receiving order', which was the terminology used under the Bankruptcy Act 1914 (repealed). Such orders were replaced by bankruptcy orders under the Insolvency Act 1986.

6 See the Land Charges Act 1972 s 6(6); and REAL PROPERTY AND REGISTRATION vol 87 (2012) PARA 742.

7 'Registered charge' means a charge the title to which is entered in the register of title; and 'registered estate' means a legal estate the title to which is entered in the register of title, other than a registered charge: see the Land Registration Act 2002 s 132(1). As to the meaning of 'registered' see PARA 127 note 3; and as to the meaning of 'charge' see PARA 127 note 5. As to the meaning of 'legal estate' see PARA 105 note 2; definition applied by s 132(1).

8 'Registrable disposition' means a disposition which is required to be completed by registration under the Land Registration Act 2002 s 27 (see REAL PROPERTY AND REGISTRATION vol 87 (2012) PARAS 427–430): s 132(1).

9 Land Registration Act 2002 s 86(5)(a). 'Valuable consideration' does not include marriage consideration or a nominal consideration in money: s 132(1).

10 Land Registration Act 2002 s 86(5)(b).

11 Ie under the Land Registration Act 2002 s 86: see REAL PROPERTY AND REGISTRATION vol 87 (2012) PARA 532.

12 Land Registration Act 2002 s 86(5)(c)(i).

13 Land Registration Act 2002 s 86(5)(c)(ii). The rights of a trustee in bankruptcy are avoided pursuant to s 86(5) on a sale of land by a bankrupt to a bona fide purchaser at a time when no bankruptcy restriction appears on the register, notwithstanding that the purchaser seeks to register his title after a restriction has been entered: *Pick v Chief Land Registrar* [2011] EWHC 206 (Ch), [2012] Ch 564, [2012] 3 EGLR 17.

14 Ie all property belonging to or vested in the bankrupt at the commencement of the bankruptcy, and any property comprised in his estate or treated as belonging to or being vested in the bankrupt, subject to certain limited exceptions: see the Insolvency Act 1986 s 283(1); and BANKRUPTCY AND INDIVIDUAL INSOLVENCY vol 5 (2013) PARA 211. See also *Re Landau (a bankrupt), Pointer v Landau* [1998] Ch 223 at 231, [1997] 3 All ER 322 at 327 per Ferris J.

15 See the Insolvency Act 1986 s 306(1); and BANKRUPTCY AND INDIVIDUAL INSOLVENCY vol 5 (2013) PARA 398. See also *Re Robinson's Settlement, Gant v Hobbs* (1911) 28 TLR 121, where a mortgage made after the receiving order, in pursuance of a request made before the receiving order, was upheld (revsd on another point [1912] 1 ChD 717, CA).

16 See the Land Charges Act 1972 s 6(5); and REAL PROPERTY AND REGISTRATION vol 87 (2012) PARA 750. The official receiver is under a mandatory duty to give notice of a bankruptcy order to the Chief Land Registrar for registration under the Land Charges Act 1972: see the Insolvency Rules 1986, SI 1986/1925, rr 6.34, 6.46; and BANKRUPTCY AND INDIVIDUAL INSOLVENCY vol 5 (2013) PARA 201. Registration under the Land Charges Act 1972 is deemed to constitute actual notice: see the Law of Property Act 1925 s 198; and REAL PROPERTY AND REGISTRATION vol 87 (2012) PARA 785. As soon as practicable after the registration of a bankruptcy order under the Land Charges Act 1972, the registrar must, in relation to any registered estate or charge which appears to him to be affected by the order, enter in the register a restriction reflecting the effect of the Insolvency Act 1986: see the Land Registration Act 2002 s 86(4); and REAL PROPERTY AND REGISTRATION vol 87 (2012) PARAS 532, 751.

17 See the Insolvency Act 1986 s 283(2); and BANKRUPTCY AND INDIVIDUAL INSOLVENCY vol 5 (2013) PARA 211. See also *Bird v Philpott* [1900] 1 Ch 822 at 828 per Farwell J.

18 *Re Evelyn, ex p General Public Works and Assets Co Ltd* [1894] 2 QB 302, DC.

19 *Bird v Philpott* [1900] 1 Ch 822 (following *Troup v Ricardo* (1864) 4 De GJ & Sm 489; and distinguishing *Re Austin, ex p Sheffield* (1879) 10 ChD 434, CA, and *Re Leadbitter* (1878) 10 ChD 388, CA). See also *R v Adie, ex p Rushforth* (1901) 84 LT 508.

20 A bankrupt's property divisible among his creditors does not include property held by him on trust for another: see the Insolvency Act 1986 s 283(3)(a); and BANKRUPTCY AND INDIVIDUAL INSOLVENCY vol 5 (2013) PARA 211. See also *Re Whitehead* (1885) 14 QBD 419, CA.

21 As to the effect of an English bankruptcy order in relation to foreign immovables see BANKRUPTCY AND INDIVIDUAL INSOLVENCY vol 5 (2013) PARA 398; CONFLICT OF LAWS vol 19 (2011) PARA 775.

143. Property acquired after bankruptcy. After-acquired property does not vest automatically in the trustee in bankruptcy, who must claim it from the bankrupt by serving notice on him[1]: such property can therefore be effectively mortgaged by the bankrupt, before the intervention of the trustee in bankruptcy. On service of the trustee's notice of claim, the property vests in the trustee as part of the bankrupt's estate, and the trustee's title relates back to the date of acquisition of the property by the bankrupt[2]. However, no remedy lies against any person who acquires the property in good faith and for value, and without notice of the bankruptcy, whether before or after the service of the notice by the trustee[3].

Independently of these provisions, a mortgage by a bankrupt may be effective as against his trustee in two cases, namely where the mortgage is of an equitable chose or thing in action and the trustee has not perfected his title by notice[4], and where the trustee has stood by and allowed the mortgagee to advance his money upon the supposition that the bankrupt could dispose of the property[5].

1   See the Insolvency Act 1986 s 307(1); and BANKRUPTCY AND INDIVIDUAL INSOLVENCY vol 5 (2013) PARA 458 et seq.
2   See the Insolvency Act 1986 s 307(3); and BANKRUPTCY AND INDIVIDUAL INSOLVENCY vol 5 (2013) PARA 459.
3   See the Insolvency Act 1986 s 307(4); and BANKRUPTCY AND INDIVIDUAL INSOLVENCY vol 5 (2013) PARA 459. See also PARA 142.
4   *Stuart v Cockerell* (1869) LR 8 Eq 607; *Palmer v Locke* (1881) 18 ChD 381, CA. If, however, the trustee gives notice first, his title prevails: *Re Beall, ex p Official Receiver* [1899] 1 QB 688, following *Mercer v Vans Colina* (1897) 4 Mans 363.
5   *Troughton v Gitley* (1766) Amb 630; *Re Caughey, ex p Ford* (1876) 1 ChD 521 at 528, CA, per Jessel MR. As to the effect of a trustee in bankruptcy standing by see *Re Bourne, ex p Bourne* (1826) 2 Gl & J 137 at 141; *Engelback v Nixon* (1875) LR 10 CP 645; *Re France, ex p Tinker* (1874) 9 Ch App 716; *Re Rawbone's Trust* (1857) 3 K & J 476; *Tucker v Hernaman* (1853) 4 De GM & G 395.

144. Mortgage by trustee in bankruptcy. The trustee in bankruptcy has the power to mortgage any part of the property comprised in the bankrupt's estate with the sanction of the creditors' committee[1] or the court for the purpose of raising money for the payment of the bankrupt's debts[2]. The official receiver, while acting as interim receiver between the presentation of the petition and the making of the order or while acting as receiver before the property vests in the trustee in bankruptcy, has no such power to mortgage land[3].

1   As to the creditors' committee see BANKRUPTCY AND INDIVIDUAL INSOLVENCY vol 5 (2013) PARA 326 et seq.
2   See the Insolvency Act 1986 s 314(1), Sch 5 para 4; and BANKRUPTCY AND INDIVIDUAL INSOLVENCY vol 5 (2013) PARA 478. A mortgage by a trustee in bankruptcy should both relieve him of personal liability and provide that he is not to be bound personally to do anything in contravention of the insolvency legislation. As to a liquidator's power to mortgage a company's assets see COMPANY AND PARTNERSHIP INSOLVENCY vol 16 (2011) PARA 527.
3   See the Insolvency Act 1986 s 287(2); and BANKRUPTCY AND INDIVIDUAL INSOLVENCY vol 5 (2013) PARA 230.

(2) LIMITED OWNERS OF PROPERTY

(i) Settlements

145. No new strict settlements. No settlement created after 1 January 1997[1] is a settlement for the purposes of the Settled Land Act 1925 and no settlement is deemed to be made under that Act after that date[2]. Where a person purports by an instrument coming into operation after 1 January 1997 to grant an entailed interest in real or personal property, the instrument is not effective to grant an entailed interest[3].

1   Ie the date on which the Trusts of Land and Appointment of Trustees Act 1996 was brought into force by the Trusts of Land and Appointment of Trustees Act 1996 (Commencement) Order 1996, SI 1996/2974.
2   See the Trusts of Land and Appointment of Trustees Act 1996 s 2(1); and SETTLEMENTS vol 91 (2012) PARA 576. Strict settlements in existence on 1 January 1997 continue to exist until there is no relevant property (heirlooms, ie land and personal chattels to which the Settled Land Act 1925 s 67(1) (see SETTLEMENTS vol 91 (2012) PARA 842) applies): Trusts of Land and Appointment of Trustees Act 1996 s 2(4).
3   See the Trusts of Land and Appointment of Trustees Act 1996 s 2, Sch 1 para 5(1)(a). The instrument operates instead as a declaration that the property is held in trust absolutely for the person to whom an entailed interest in the property was purportedly granted: Sch 1 para 5(1)(b). See SETTLEMENTS vol 91 (2012) PARA 578.

(ii) Tenants for Life and Statutory Owners

146. General statutory power of tenant for life to mortgage. Every person who is a tenant for life[1] has powers of executing legal mortgages of the settled land for certain purposes[2]. Where there is no tenant for life, or during the minority of the tenant for life, the trustees of the settlement may exercise the statutory powers[3]. The tenant for life is given powers to shift incumbrances[4] and to vary the provisions of an incumbrance and to charge by way of additional security[5]. The statutory power to mortgage is not capable of restriction[6]. Notice of intention to mortgage must be given to the trustees of the settlement and to their solicitor[7]. The mortgage must be by demise or legal charge[8], and will override all the limitations, powers and provisions of the settlement[9], but will be subject to prior legal estates or interests[10]. In the exercise of his statutory powers the limited owner must have regard to the interests of, and is in the position of a trustee for, all persons entitled under the settlement[11].

1   Ie within the meaning of the Settled Land Act 1925, under which a 'tenant for life' includes a person not being a statutory owner who has the powers of a tenant for life: see ss 19, 117(1)(xxviii); and SETTLEMENTS vol 91 (2012) PARA 662. As to tenants in tail see PARA 148 et seq.
2   The purposes for which the power may be exercised include the discharging of incumbrances and the making of certain improvements to the land or the title to it, and are specified in the Settled Land Act 1925 s 71, as extended by other enactments: see SETTLEMENTS vol 91 (2012) PARA 750. As to mortgages for the payment of costs out of settled property see s 114(e); and SETTLEMENTS vol 91 (2012) PARA 725. Where a tenant for life executes a mortgage as absolute owner in favour of a mortgagee acting in good faith, the mortgage may be valid by virtue of s 110(1) (see SETTLEMENTS vol 91 (2012) PARA 786): see *Re Morgan's Lease, Jones v Norsesowicz* [1972] Ch 1, [1971] 2 All ER 235; cf *Weston v Henshaw* [1950] Ch 510.
3   See the Settled Land Act 1925 ss 23, 26, 117(1)(xxvi). See also CHILDREN AND YOUNG PERSONS vol 9 (2012) PARAS 33, 56 (minority of tenant for life); SETTLEMENTS vol 91 (2012) PARA 667 (no tenant).
4   See the Settled Land Act 1925 s 69; and SETTLEMENTS vol 91 (2012) PARA 752. Cf *Re Earl of Stafford and Maples* [1896] 1 Ch 235, CA.
5   See the Settled Land Act 1925 s 70; and SETTLEMENTS vol 91 (2012) PARA 756.
6   See the Settled Land Act 1925 ss 104(1), (2), 106; and SETTLEMENTS vol 91 (2012) PARAS 678, 683. Cf *Re Hazle's Settled Estates* (1885) 29 ChD 78, CA; *Re Atkinson, Atkinson v Bruce* (1886) 31 ChD 577, CA.
7   See the Settled Land Act 1925 s 101(1); and SETTLEMENTS vol 91 (2012) PARA 684. See also *Re Ray's Settled Estates* (1884) 25 ChD 464; *Duke of Marlborough v Sartoris* (1886) 32 ChD 616.
8   See the Settled Land Act 1925 s 72(1); and SETTLEMENTS vol 91 (2012) PARA 775.
9   See the Settled Land Act 1925 s 72(2); *Re Keck and Hart's Contract* [1898] 1 Ch 617; and SETTLEMENTS vol 91 (2012) PARA 775.
10 See the Settled Land Act 1925 s 72(2); and SETTLEMENTS vol 91 (2012) PARA 775. See also *Re Sebright's Settled Estates* (1886) 33 ChD 429 at 438; *Cardigan v Curzon-Howe* (1888) 40 ChD

338 (affd (1889) 41 ChD 375, CA); *Re Du Cane and Nettlefold's Contract* [1898] 2 Ch 96; *Re Mundy and Roper's Contract* [1899] 1 Ch 275, CA; *Re Dickin and Kelsall's Contract* [1908] 1 Ch 213; *Re Davies and Kent's Contract* [1910] 2 Ch 35, CA.

11 See the Settled Land Act 1925 s 107(1); and SETTLEMENTS vol 91 (2012) PARA 676. This provision does not affect the title of the estate mortgaged by a tenant for life, but it affects the tenant for life personally with liability as a trustee: *Re Marquis of Ailesbury's Settled Estates* [1892] 1 Ch 506 at 535–536, CA. Mortgages by tenants for life normally contain a provision restricting the personal liability of the tenant for life to repay the money borrowed: see PARA 157. As to the statutory power of limited owners to mortgage settled land see further SETTLEMENTS vol 91 (2012) PARAS 651–652. As to the mortgage by a tenant for life of his equitable life interest see PARA 163.

147. Limited owners with express powers to mortgage.

Express power to mortgage may be conferred on the trustees of a settlement, or on a limited owner under the settlement, if it is considered that the statutory powers[1] do not go far enough[2]. In order to prevent conflict between the powers of the limited owner and the trustees, it is, however, provided that any power conferred on the trustees must in general be exercisable by the limited owner as if it were an additional power conferred on him and not otherwise[3], and must be exercisable in the same manner and with the same effect as his statutory powers[4].

1 See PARA 146.
2 See the Settled Land Act 1925 s 109(1); and SETTLEMENTS vol 91 (2012) PARA 781.
3 See the Settled Land Act 1925 s 108(2); and SETTLEMENTS vol 91 (2012) PARA 782.
4 See the Settled Land Act 1925 s 109(2); and SETTLEMENTS vol 91 (2012) PARA 781.

(iii) Tenants in Tail

148. Power of tenant in tail to mortgage.

A tenant in tail can as such have only an equitable interest in the land entailed[1], but if he is tenant in tail in possession he will normally have the legal estate of freehold, or the legal term in leaseholds, vested in him as estate owner on the trusts of the settlement[2]. The tenant in tail then has the statutory power of mortgaging of a tenant for life[3]. However, the tenant in tail differs from other limited owners in that he possesses special statutory powers of disposing of the land entailed for an equitable interest in fee simple or any less interest[4] which are distinct from the general powers of disposition conferred upon limited owners[5]. If the settlement will not be continued by the subsistence of family charges[6], the tenant in tail can put an end to it by barring his estate tail[7] and then, by virtue of his legal estate, he becomes the absolute owner in equity and can mortgage as such. Unless the legal estate in the land entailed is vested in the tenant in tail, any mortgage by him can affect only the equitable interest in the land[8]. By virtue of his special statutory power of disposition he may execute by deed a mortgage in the form of a conveyance of the equitable interest in fee simple[9] or any less interest in the land[10]; but in the case of a tenant in tail who is not in possession, the mortgage, unless executed with the consent of the protector of the settlement[11], will convey to the mortgagee only an equitable interest in the nature of a base fee, which is unimpeachable during the survival of the issue of the tenant in tail, but is voidable upon the death of the survivor of that issue by any person next entitled in remainder on the estate tail[12].

1 See the Law of Property Act 1925 s 1(1), (3); and REAL PROPERTY AND REGISTRATION vol 87 (2012) PARA 101. As to entailed interests generally see REAL PROPERTY AND REGISTRATION vol 87 (2012) PARA 112 et seq.
2 See the Settled Land Act 1925 ss 4(2), 6(b), 7(1)–(4), 9(2), 20(1)(i), 117(1)(xxviii); and SETTLEMENTS vol 91 (2012) PARAS 590, 597–599, 663.

3 As to a tenant for life's statutory powers of mortgaging see PARA 146. 'Tenant for life' for this
   purpose includes any tenant in tail in possession other than certain tenants restrained from barring
   the entail: see the Settled Land Act 1925 ss 20(1)(i), (2), 117(1)(xxviii); and SETTLEMENTS vol 91
   (2012) PARA 663.
4 See the Fines and Recoveries Act 1833 s 15; and REAL PROPERTY AND REGISTRATION vol 87
   (2012) PARA 118. The Fines and Recoveries Act 1833 remains in force only in regard to dealings
   with equitable interests: see the Law of Property (Amendment) Act 1924 s 9, Sch 9 para 4.
5 Ie by the Settled Land Act 1925 Pt II (ss 38–72): see SETTLEMENTS vol 91 (2012) PARA 728 et seq.
6 As to the effect of family charges in constituting a settlement see the Settled Land Act 1925
   s 1(1)(v); and SETTLEMENTS vol 91 (2012) PARA 579. As to the power of a person beneficially
   entitled to land subject only to family charges to convey or create a legal estate subject to the
   charges see the Law of Property (Amendment) Act 1926 s 1; and SETTLEMENTS vol 91 (2012)
   PARA 604.
7 As to the general power of a tenant in tail to bar the entail see the Fines and Recoveries Act 1833
   s 15; and REAL PROPERTY AND REGISTRATION vol 87 (2012) PARA 118. For estates tail which
   cannot be barred see ss 18, 20; and REAL PROPERTY AND REGISTRATION vol 87 (2012) PARAS
   127–128. For the necessity for the consent of the protector of the settlement to enable a tenant in
   tail in remainder to create a larger estate than a base fee see s 34; and REAL PROPERTY AND
   REGISTRATION vol 87 (2012) PARA 123. As to the protector of the settlement see note 11.
8 See the Law of Property (Amendment) Act 1924 Sch 9 para 4, by which the Fines and Recoveries
   Act 1833 remains in force only as regards dealings with entailed interests as equitable interests; and
   note 4.
9 As the mortgage is of an equitable interest, the statutory provision which requires a legal mortgage
   of the legal estate in land to be by demise or legal charge (see PARA 164) will not apply.
10 See the Fines and Recoveries Act 1833 ss 15, 40; and REAL PROPERTY AND REGISTRATION
   vol 87 (2012) PARA 118 et seq. As to the cases in which the powers of disposition conferred by
   the Fines and Recoveries Act 1833 cannot be exercised see ss 18, 20; note 7; and REAL PROPERTY
   AND REGISTRATION vol 87 (2012) PARA 127. The necessity for the enrolment of dispositions
   under the Fines and Recoveries Act 1833 was abolished by the Law of Property Act 1925 s 133
   (repealed). As to the operation of the former law as to enrolment see *Re Pier's Estate, ex p Browne*
   (1863) 14 I Ch R 452; cf *Whitmore-Searle v Whitmore-Searle* [1907] 2 Ch 332.
11 As to the circumstances in which a protector of the settlement exists and the person who is
   protector see the Fines and Recoveries Act 1833 ss 22, 23, 25–28, 32; and REAL PROPERTY AND
   REGISTRATION vol 87 (2012) PARA 114.
12 See the Fines and Recoveries Act 1833 s 34; and REAL PROPERTY AND REGISTRATION vol 87
   (2012) PARA 130. As to the enlargement of an equitable base fee see ss 19, 35, 39; and REAL
   PROPERTY AND REGISTRATION vol 87 (2012) PARAS 131–132. Formerly, if a tenant in tail in
   remainder executed a mortgage which was not duly enrolled (see note 10) and therefore did not
   take effect under the Fines and Recoveries Act 1833, it created an estate which was unimpeachable
   during the life of the mortgagor but voidable by the entry of the issue in tail: *Hankey v Martin*
   (1883) 49 LT 560, following *Case of Fines* (1602) 3 Co Rep 84a. See also *Doe d Daniel v
   Woodroffe* (1849) 2 HL Cas 811; *Machil v Clerk* (1702) Holt KB 615.

149. Extent of disentailment by mortgage. Where a tenant in tail mortgages the
land entailed under his special statutory powers[1], the entail is in general wholly
barred in equity to the extent of the interest created by the mortgage, despite any
intention to the contrary expressed or implied in the mortgage deed[2]; but, if the
mortgage only creates an interest pour autre vie or a term of years or a charge
unsecured by a term of years or greater interest, the entail is barred only so far as
is necessary to give effect to the mortgage, notwithstanding any intention to the
contrary expressed or implied[3].

1 Ie under the Fines and Recoveries Act 1833 s 15: see PARA 148.
2 See the Fines and Recoveries Act 1833 s 21; and REAL PROPERTY AND REGISTRATION vol 87
   (2012) PARA 126. For the principle that the Fines and Recoveries Act 1833 now operates only in
   equity see PARA 148. In relation to mortgages by tenants in tail s 21 abrogated, subject to
   exceptions (see the text to note 3), the presumption that a mortgage is not intended to affect the
   title to the land subject to the mortgage: *Plomley v Felton* (1888) 14 App Cas 61, PC. Although
   the statutory provision applies despite any contrary intention indicated in the mortgage, the
   proviso for redemption may be so proved as to recreate the trusts of the original settlement: *Re
   Oxenden's Settled Estates, Oxenden v Chapman* (1904) 74 LJCh 234. As to entailed interests
   generally see REAL PROPERTY AND REGISTRATION vol 87 (2012) PARA 112 et seq.
3 See the Fines and Recoveries Act 1833 s 21; and REAL PROPERTY AND REGISTRATION vol 87
   (2012) PARA 126. This proviso has been used so as to create a mortgage of the estate tail of a

person of unsound mind without interfering further than was necessary with the remaindermen: see *Re Pares* (1876) 2 ChD 61. See also *Re Pares, Lillingston v Pares* (1879) 12 ChD 333.

150. Agreement to disentail. It seems that, despite certain statutory provisions which enact that a disposition by a tenant in tail resting only in contract is to be of no force and that the courts are not to give effect to defective dispositions[1], an agreement by a tenant in tail to disentail for the purpose of executing a legal mortgage may be specifically enforced against the tenant in tail himself[2], but not against the issue in tail if the tenant in tail dies before conveying[3], unless the remainderman was a party to the mortgage transaction[4].

1 See the Fines and Recoveries Act 1833 ss 40, 47; and REAL PROPERTY AND REGISTRATION vol 87 (2012) PARA 120.
2 *Bankes v Small* (1887) 36 ChD 716, CA. See also *Lewis v Duncombe* (1855) 20 Beav 398. Cf *Davis v Tollemache* (1856) 2 Jur NS 1181, where the court refused to compel a bankrupt tenant in tail who had merely covenanted in the mortgage deed for further assurance to execute a disentailing deed.
3 See *A-G v Day* (1749) 1 Ves Sen 218 at 224; *Hinton v Hinton* (1755) 2 Ves Sen 631 at 634.
4 See *Pryce v Bury* (1853) 2 Drew 41. See further REAL PROPERTY AND REGISTRATION vol 87 (2012) PARA 120. As to entailed interests generally see REAL PROPERTY AND REGISTRATION vol 87 (2012) PARA 112 et seq.

(3) FIDUCIARY OWNERS

(i) Personal Representatives

151. Power of personal representatives to mortgage. Personal representatives have always had power to mortgage the deceased's personal estate[1]. In dealing with personal estate, personal representatives have, for purposes of administration or during the minority of any beneficiary or the subsistence of any life interest or until the period of distribution arrives, the same power to raise money by mortgage or charge, whether or not by the deposit of documents, as a personal representative formerly had with respect to personal estate[2]. In respect of real estate, personal representatives have most of the functions and powers of trustees, with appropriate modifications[3]. A legal mortgage granted by a personal representative will not be invalidated only because the mortgagee may have notice that all the debts, liabilities, funeral and testamentary or administration duties and legacies of the deceased have been discharged or provided for[4].

1 See WILLS AND INTESTACY vol 103 (2010) PARA 1020.
2 See the Administration of Estates Act 1925 s 39(1)(i) (amended by the Trusts of Land and Appointment of Trustees Act 1996 s 25(1), (2), Sch 3 para 6(2)(a), Sch 4); and WILLS AND INTESTACY vol 103 (2010) PARA 1020. This applies in relation to the estate of a person who died since 1 January 1997 (ie the date on which the Trusts of Land and Appointment of Trustees Act 1996 was brought into force by the Trusts of Land and Appointment of Trustees Act 1996 (Commencement) Order 1996, SI 1996/2974); before that date personal representatives had the powers of trustees for sale, but the Trusts of Land and Appointment of Trustees Act 1996 has replaced trusts for sale of land with trusts of land (see s 1; and REAL PROPERTY AND REGISTRATION vol 87 (2012) PARA 105; SETTLEMENTS vol 91 (2012) PARA 510; TRUSTS AND POWERS vol 98 (2013) PARAS 6, 151). As to the powers of personal representatives see the Administration of Estates Act 1925 ss 2(1), 40, 48(2); and WILLS AND INTESTACY vol 103 (2010) PARA 1021. As to the powers of trustees to mortgage see PARA 153 et seq.
3 See the Administration of Estates Act 1925 s 39(1)(ii) (substituted by the Trusts of Land and Appointment of Trustees Act 1996 s 25(1), Sch 3 para 6(2)(b)). This applies in relation to the estate of a person who died since 1 January 1997: see note 2. As to the functions and powers of trustees see the Trusts of Land and Appointment of Trustees Act 1996 Pt I (ss 1–18); and REAL PROPERTY AND REGISTRATION vol 87 (2012) PARA 103 et seq. However s 10 (consents), s 11 (consultation) and s 14 (application for order) do not apply to personal representatives: see s 18(1).

4   See the Administration of Estates Act 1925 s 36(8); and WILLS AND INTESTACY vol 103 (2010)
    PARA 1025.

152. Necessity for all personal representatives to join in mortgage. If probate is
granted to one or some of two or more persons named as executors, a mortgage
of real estate[1] may be made by the proving executor or executors and is as
effectual as if all the persons named as executors had concurred therein[2], but
otherwise neither a legal nor an equitable mortgage of real estate can be made
without the concurrence of all the personal representatives or a court order[3].

1   'Real estate' for this purpose includes chattels real: see the Administration of Estates Act 1925
    s 3(1)(i).
2   See the Administration of Estates Act 1925 s 2(2); and WILLS AND INTESTACY vol 103 (2010)
    PARA 1023. See also *Fountain Forestry Ltd v Edwards* [1975] Ch 1, [1974] 2 All ER 280.
3   See the Administration of Estates Act 1925 s 2(2); and WILLS AND INTESTACY vol 103 (2010)
    PARA 1023.

(ii) Trustees

153. Trustee's power to mortgage. A trustee may not mortgage the trust
property[1] save in pursuance of a power to do so expressly or impliedly conferred
upon him by the instrument creating the trust[2], or in pursuance of a power
conferred by statute[3], or in pursuance of a court order[4]. A power to mortgage will
be implied from a power of sale if the power of sale is given for the purpose of
raising a particular charge, but not if the testator's object is to effect an absolute
conversion of his estate[5].

1   As to a trustee's equitable lien for expenditure on trust property see LIEN vol 68 (2008) PARA 803;
    TRUSTS AND POWERS vol 98 (2013) PARA 345.
2   *Re Bellinger, Durrell v Bellinger* [1898] 2 Ch 534 (implied powers); *Re
    Suenson-Taylor's Settlement, Moores v Moores* [1974] 3 All ER 397, [1974] 1 WLR 1280. As to
    charity trustees see PARA 132.
3   See PARAS 154–155.
4   For the court's power to authorise a mortgage by trustees see the Trustee Act 1925 s 57 (which
    does not extend to trustees of settled land: see s 57(4)); and TRUSTS AND POWERS vol 98 (2013)
    PARA 646. For the corresponding provision in relation to settled land see the Settled Land Act
    1925 s 64; and SETTLEMENTS vol 91 (2012) PARA 572.
5   *Stroughill v Anstey* (1852) 1 De GM & G 635 (following *Haldenby v Spofforth* (1839) 1 Beav 390;
    and explaining *Ball v Harris* (1839) 4 My & Cr 264); *Page v Cooper* (1853) 16 Beav 396;
    Devaynes v Robinson (1857) 24 Beav 86. It seems that in *Ball v Harris*, Lord Cottenham LC, and
    in *Mills v Banks* (1724) 3 P Wms 1 at 9, Lord Macclesfield LC, stated the law in terms which were
    too wide. See also *Bennett v Wyndham* (1857) 23 Beav 521, where a prohibition against raising
    a charge by sale was held to be also a prohibition against raising that charge by mortgage.

154. Trustees' statutory power to mortgage land. In general[1], trustees of land[2]
have in relation to the land subject to the trust the powers of an absolute owner[3],
which include the power to mortgage, save in so far as provision to the effect that
they do not apply is made by the disposition creating the trust[4]. Such powers may
not be exercised in contravention of any enactment or any rule of law or equity,
or any order made in pursuance of any such enactment or rule[5]. If the disposition
creating such a trust makes provision requiring any consent to be obtained to the
exercise of the trustees' power, the power may not be exercised without that
consent[6]. The trustees are required to consult the beneficiaries who are of full age
and beneficially entitled to an interest in possession in the land and, so far as
consistent with the general interest of the trust, give effect to the wishes of those
beneficiaries or the majority of them[7].

1   These provisions apply in relation to all trusts of land since 1 January 1997 (ie the date on which
    the Trusts of Land and Appointment of Trustees Act 1996 was brought into force by the Trusts

of Land and Appointment of Trustees Act 1996 (Commencement) Order 1996, SI 1996/2974), except in relation to a trust created by a will if the testator died before that date, and save in relation to the personal representatives of a person who died before then: see the Trusts of Land and Appointment of Trustees Act 1996 ss 3(2), 18(3), 25(2), (5), Sch 4. The Trusts of Land and Appointment of Trustees Act 1996 is stated not to apply to land which is settled land under the Settled Land Act 1925 (see SETTLEMENTS vol 91 (2012) PARA 576 et seq) and land to which the Universities and Colleges Estates Act 1925 (see EDUCATION vol 36 (2015) PARA 1329) applies: see the Trusts of Land and Appointment of Trustees Act 1996 s 1(3); and PARA 155.

2 'Trustees of land' means trustees of a trust of land; and a 'trust of land' means (subject to the Trusts of Land and Appointment of Trustees Act 1996 s 1(3): see note 1) any trust of property which consists of or includes land: s 1(1). The reference to a trust is a reference to any description of trust (whether express, implied, resulting or constructive), including a trust for sale and a bare trust, and includes a trust created, or arising, before 1 January 1997 (see note 1): s 1(2). These definitions apply in any Act unless the contrary intention appears: see the Interpretation Act 1978 s 5, Sch 1 (definitions added by the Trusts of Land and Appointment of Trustees Act 1996 s 25(4), Sch 3 para 16).

3 See the Trusts of Land and Appointment of Trustees Act 1996 s 6(1); and TRUSTS AND POWERS vol 98 (2013) PARA 476. As to the power of absolute owners to mortgage property see PARA 127 et seq.

4 See the Trusts of Land and Appointment of Trustees Act 1996 s 8(1); and TRUSTS AND POWERS vol 98 (2013) PARA 476. The right to exclude or restrict the powers of the trustees does not apply in the case of charitable, ecclesiastical or public trusts and is in all cases subject to any enactment which prohibits or restricts such a provision: s 8(3), (4).

5 See the Trusts of Land and Appointment of Trustees Act 1996 s 6(6); and TRUSTS AND POWERS vol 98 (2013) PARA 476.

6 See the Trusts of Land and Appointment of Trustees Act 1996 s 8(2); and TRUSTS AND POWERS vol 98 (2013) PARA 485. A provision requiring consent takes effect subject to any enactment which prohibits or restricts it: s 8(4).

7 See the Trusts of Land and Appointment of Trustees Act 1996 s 11(1); and TRUSTS AND POWERS vol 98 (2013) PARA 477. The obligation to consult can be excluded (see s 11(2)(a)) and does not apply in relation to a trust created or arising under a will made before 1 January 1997 or a trust created before then unless provision to the effect that it is to apply is made by deed (see s 11(2)(b), (3)).

155. Trustees' statutory powers to mortgage in other cases. In the case of trusts to which the Trusts of Land and Appointment of Trustees Act 1996 does not apply[1], where trustees are authorised by the instrument, if any, creating the trust, or by law, to pay or apply capital money subject to the trust for any purpose or in any manner, they have power to raise the money by mortgage of all or any part of the trust property for the time being in possession[2]. This power is available notwithstanding anything to the contrary contained in the instrument, if any, creating the trust, but does not apply to trustees of property held for charitable purposes, or to trustees of settled land, not also being the statutory owners[3].

1 As to the trusts of land to which the Trusts of Land and Appointment of Trustees Act 1996 does not apply see PARA 154 note 1.

2 See the Trustee Act 1925 s 16(1); and TRUSTS AND POWERS vol 98 (2013) PARA 521. The statutory power does not permit the mortgaging of the trust fund to raise money for the purchase of further investments: *Re Suenson-Taylor's Settlement, Moores v Moores* [1974] 3 All ER 397, [1974] 1 WLR 1280.

3 See the Trustee Act 1925 s 16(2); and TRUSTS AND POWERS vol 98 (2013) PARA 521. The power is available whether the trust was constituted or created before or after 1 January 1926 (ie the date on which the Trustee Act 1925 was brought into force by virtue of s 71(2) (repealed)): see s 69(1). Trustees of land formerly had, in relation to land, all the powers of a tenant for life (see PARA 146) and the trustees of a settlement under the Settled Land Act 1925 (see SETTLEMENTS vol 91 (2012) PARAS 803–806): see the Law of Property Act 1925 s 28(1) (repealed with savings). As to the similar power of charity trustees see PARA 132.

156. Protection of mortgagee dealing with trustees. A mortgagee advancing money on a mortgage purporting to be made under any trust or power vested in trustees is not concerned to see that the money is wanted, or that no more than is wanted is raised, or otherwise as to its application[1] or to see that the trustees have consulted the beneficiaries and given effect to the wishes of the majority of them[2].

A mortgagee of unregistered land may be similarly unconcerned as to beneficiaries' rights[3], and such a mortgage is not invalidated by any exclusion, limitation or restriction of the trustees' powers unless the mortgagee has actual notice thereof[4]; and a mortgagee of registered land is unaffected by any relevant limitations, since for the purpose of preventing the title of a disponee being questioned[5], a person's right to exercise owner's powers[6] in relation to a registered estate or charge[7] is free from any limitation[8] affecting the validity of a disposition[9]. Where a disposition creating a trust of land requires the consent of more than two persons to the grant of a mortgage, the consent of any two of them is sufficient in favour of a mortgagee, and the consent of a minor is not required in favour of a purchaser[10]. A mortgage of a legal estate for money or money's worth will overreach the interests of the beneficiaries under the trust if the mortgage is made by trustees of land and so long as any capital monies are advanced to not fewer than two trustees (except where the trustee is a trust corporation)[11] even if the beneficiary is in actual occupation of the land[12] or the claim to a beneficial interest is based on proprietary estoppel[13].

1   See the Trustee Act 1925 s 17; and TRUSTS AND POWERS vol 98 (2013) PARA 521.
2   Trusts of Land and Appointment of Trustees Act 1996 s 16(1). As to the trustees' duty to consult with beneficiaries, to have regard to their rights, and to obtain their consent, see ss 6(5), 7(3), 11(1); and REAL PROPERTY AND REGISTRATION vol 87 (2012) PARA 243; TRUSTS AND POWERS vol 98 (2013) PARAS 476–477.
3   See the Trusts of Land and Appointment of Trustees Act 1996 s 16(1). Section 16 applies to all mortgagees of unregistered land pursuant to a mortgage granted since 1 January 1997 (ie the date on which the Trusts of Land and Appointment of Trustees Act 1996 was brought into force by the Trusts of Land and Appointment of Trustees Act 1996 (Commencement) Order 1996, SI 1996/2974): see the Trusts of Land and Appointment of Trustees Act 1996 ss 16(7), 27(2).
4   See the Trusts of Land and Appointment of Trustees Act 1996 s 16(2). See also note 3. As to the exercise of the trustees' powers in this regard see ss 6(6), (8), 8; and TRUSTS AND POWERS vol 98 (2013) PARA 476.
5   The Land Registration Act 2002 s 26 (see the text to notes 6–9) is enacted only for this purpose, and accordingly does not affect the lawfulness of a disposition: s 26(3).
6   As to owner's powers see the Land Registration Act 2002 s 23; PARA 127; and REAL PROPERTY AND REGISTRATION vol 87 (2012) PARA 422.
7   As to the meanings of 'registered estate' and 'registered charge' see PARA 142 note 7.
8   Ie any limitation other than a limitation reflected by an entry in the register (Land Registration Act 2002 s 26(2)(a)) or imposed by or under the Land Registration Act 2002 (s 26(2)(b)). Such limitations include, for example, limitations on dealing protected by a caution, inhibition or restriction entered under the Land Registration Act 1925: see the Land Registration Act 2002 s 134, Sch 12 paras 1, 2; and REAL PROPERTY AND REGISTRATION vol 87 (2012) PARA 510 et seq.
9   See the Land Registration Act 2002 s 26(1); PARA 176; and REAL PROPERTY AND REGISTRATION vol 87 (2012) PARA 425. This has been the case since 13 October 2003 (ie the date on which s 26 was brought into force by the Land Registration Act 2002 (Commencement No 4) Order 2003, SI 2003/1725). Formerly, it was provided that a mortgagee of registered land was not affected with notice of a trust, whether express, implied or constructive: see the Land Registration Act 1925 s 74 (repealed).
10 See the Trusts of Land and Appointment of Trustees Act 1996 s 10; and TRUSTS AND POWERS vol 98 (2013) PARA 477.
11 See the Law of Property Act 1925 ss 2, 27(2); and REAL PROPERTY AND REGISTRATION vol 87 (2012) PARA 262. See also *City of London Building Society v Flegg* [1988] AC 54, [1987] 3 All ER 435, HL; *Birmingham Midshires Mortgage Services Ltd v Sabherwal* (1999) 80 P & CR 256, CA. It is not necessary for any advance to be made on the grant of the legal charge for overreaching to occur: *State Bank of India v Sood* [1997] Ch 276, [1997] 1 All ER 169, CA. See also the Trustee Act 1925 s 14 (see TRUSTS AND POWERS vol 98 (2013) PARA 517); and the Settled Land Act 1925 ss 16(2), 94, 95 (see SETTLEMENTS vol 91 (2012) PARAS 654, 669, 686). As to the meaning of 'trust corporation' see TRUSTS AND POWERS vol 98 (2013) PARA 238.
12 *City of London Building Society v Flegg* [1988] AC 54, [1987] 3 All ER 435, HL.
13 *Birmingham Midshires Mortgage Services Ltd v Sabherwal* (1999) 80 P & CR 256, CA. As to proprietary estoppel see ESTOPPEL vol 47 (2014) PARA 392 et seq.

157. Form of mortgage by trustees. A trustee or other fiduciary owner who mortgages the trust estate does not usually covenant to pay the money borrowed[1], and a provision expressly excluding any personal liability on his part for payment is commonly inserted in the mortgage. A covenant by a trustee to pay out of a trust fund prevents a personal liability being implied[2], and a covenant as trustee but not otherwise does not impose a personal liability[3]. A trustee is under no obligation to exclude the statutory power of sale which is an implied provision in every mortgage[4], but he may not insert a consolidation clause extending to mortgages other than those made by him as trustee[5]. Where, however, a trustee brings within the scope of the mortgage security other payments due from the trust estate, the case appears to be different[6].

1   See *Stroughill v Anstey* (1852) 1 De GM & G 635 at 642.
2   *Mathew v Blackmore* (1857) 1 H & N 762.
3   *Re Robinson's Settlement, Gant v Hobbs* [1912] 1 Ch 717 at 728, CA. A covenant 'as trustee but not so as to impose any personal liability' can, however, be enforced against the convenantor personally, if the effect of the qualification would be to negative the covenant, eg where the covenant is to pay and indemnify: *Watling v Lewis* [1911] 1 Ch 414 at 423–424 per Warrington J; and see *Furnivall v Coombes* (1843) 5 Man & G 736. See further DEEDS AND OTHER INSTRUMENTS vol 32 (2012) PARA 414; TRUSTS AND POWERS vol 98 (2013) PARA 523.
4   See the Law of Property Act 1925 s 182; and TRUSTS AND POWERS vol 98 (2013) PARA 700. The statutory power is given by s 101(1)(i): see PARA 446 et seq. Provisions corresponding to s 182 were first made by the Conveyancing Act 1881 s 66 (repealed).
5   See *Thorne v Thorne* [1893] 3 Ch 196.
6   *Cruikshank v Duffin* (1872) LR 13 Eq 555.

158. Trustees' power to invest by way of mortgage. The provision in the Trustee Act 2000 conferring on trustees, subject to the expression of a contrary intention in the trust instrument, the same power to make an investment of any kind[1] as if they were absolutely entitled to the trust assets[2] impliedly empowers trustees to lend trust money upon a mortgage of realty[3].

1   This power does not include power to make investments in land other than in loans secured on land: Trustee Act 2000 s 3(3).
2   See the Trustee Act 2000 s 3; and TRUSTS AND POWERS vol 98 (2013) PARA 453.
3   It is, however, considered unlikely that the standard investment criteria (see the Trustee Act 2000 s 4; and TRUSTS AND POWERS vol 98 (2013) PARA 454) would allow such investment on personal security. See also *Mills v Osborne* (1834) 7 Sim 30; *Forbes v Ross* (1788) 2 Bro CC 430; *Langston v Ollivant* (1807) Coop G 33; *Pickard v Anderson* (1872) LR 13 Eq 608; and TRUSTS AND POWERS vol 98 (2013) PARA 451.

159. Form of mortgage to trustees. A deed of mortgage to trustees should contain a statement that the money is advanced out of a joint account[1]. It should not, unless in exercise of an express authority, contain a provision that the mortgage is not to be called in for a period of years[2]. The statutory power of sale[3] ought not as a rule to be excluded where the mortgagees are trustees, but the exclusion of such a power is not necessarily a breach of trust[4].

1   See PARA 186. Where it was declared in a mortgage that the money was advanced by the mortgagees on a joint account, a power of sale given to the mortgagees, their heirs and assigns was exercisable by their survivor: *Hind v Poole* (1855) 1 K & J 383. The court would not go behind a joint account clause in the absence of notice that the mortgage money was trust money from some source other than the fact of the joint account: see *Re Harman and Uxbridge and Rickmansworth Rly Co* (1883) 24 ChD 720; *Re Jackson, Smith v Sibthorpe* (1887) 34 ChD 732; *Re Blaiberg and Abrahams* [1899] 2 Ch 340. See also *Re West and Hardy's Contract* [1904] 1 Ch 145; *Re Balen and Shepherd's Contract* [1924] 2 Ch 365.
2   *Mant v Leith* (1852) 15 Beav 524; *Vickery v Evans* (1863) 33 Beav 376.
3   See PARA 446 et seq.
4   *Farrar v Barraclough* (1854) 2 Sm & G 231. As to the investment powers and duties of trustees, and the consequences of an investment being made in breach of trust, see TRUSTS AND POWERS vol 98 (2013) PARA 446 et seq.

3. CREATION OF MORTGAGES AND CHARGES

(1) LEGAL MORTGAGES

(i) Creation of Legal Mortgages

160. Legal mortgages. A legal mortgage of unregistered land[1] can be created only by demise, sub-demise or legal charge[2]. A legal mortgage of registered land can be made only by a charge by deed expressed to be by way of legal mortgage or by charging the estate with the payment of money, and not by demise[3].

Since, by making a pledge or mortgage of his property, the owner does not cease to be the owner of the property any further than is necessary to give effect to the security he has thus created[4], he can mortgage the property again. The mortgagor of a legal estate in land retains his legal estate[5], and can create further mortgages by demise or charge[6]. A subsequent mortgage is, as between mortgagor and mortgagee, a complete security on the mortgagor's interest, saving only the rights of prior incumbrancers[7]; and, on redemption of the prior mortgage, no reconveyance is required, since a mortgage term ceases on payment off of the mortgage[8]. A subsequent mortgagee who pays off the first mortgagee may, however, call for a transfer of the first mortgage, and where there are successive mortgagees they may according to their priority exercise the right of paying off the first mortgage and taking a transfer[9].

A legal mortgage of personal chattels may be made either by pledge or, subject to certain exceptions, by bill of sale[10]. A legal mortgage of a debt or other legal chose or thing in action may be made by written assignment complying with the statutory provisions as to the assignment of such choses in action[11].

1   As to the meaning of 'land' in the Law of Property Act 1925 see PARA 104 note 2.
2   See the Law of Property Act 1925 s 205(1)(xvi); and PARA 104 note 1. As to creation of legal mortgages see PARA 161 et seq.
3   See the Land Registration Act 2002 ss 23(1), 25; and REAL PROPERTY AND REGISTRATION vol 87 (2012) PARA 422 et seq.
4   *Bradford Banking Co Ltd v Briggs, Son & Co Ltd* (1886) 12 App Cas 29 at 36, HL, per Lord Blackburn. See also PARA 304.
5   Formerly, a first legal mortgage of freehold land was by conveyance (see PARA 161), so that any subsequent mortgage was equitable only, being a mortgage of the mortgagor's equity of redemption. A subsequent mortgage was formerly called a 'puisne mortgage', but that term now means a legal mortgage not protected by deposit of documents: see the Land Charges Act 1972 s 2(1), (4)(i); and REAL PROPERTY AND REGISTRATION vol 87 (2012) PARAS 720–721.
6   As to the priority of mortgages see PARA 260 et seq.
7   See *Frazer v Jones* (1846) 5 Hare 475 at 481.
8   See the Law of Property Act 1925 s 116; and PARA 647.
9   See the Law of Property Act 1925 s 95(1), (2); and PARA 366.
10 See PARA 205. As to mortgage distinguished from pledge see PARA 112.
11 See the Law of Property Act 1925 s 136(1); and CHOSES IN ACTION vol 13 (2009) PARAS 72, 80–85. Section 136(1) validates only absolute assignments not purporting to be by way of charge only, but a mortgage in ordinary form which transfers the property with a proviso for redemption and reconveyance is such an absolute assignment: see s 136(1); and CHOSES IN ACTION vol 13 (2009) PARA 76.

(ii) Legal Mortgages of Land

A.   HISTORICAL BACKGROUND

161. Mortgages of freeholds. Before 1926, a legal mortgage of freehold property was made by the same form of assurance and framed on the same principles as an absolute conveyance, subject, however, to a proviso for redemption. Any purported conveyance of an estate in fee simple by way of mortgage[1] made after 1925 operates (to the extent of the estate of the mortgagor[2]) as a demise of the land[3] to the mortgagee[4] for a term of years absolute without impeachment of waste, but subject to cesser on redemption[5], so that a first or only mortgagee takes a term of 3,000 years from the date of the mortgage[6], and a second or subsequent mortgagee takes a term (commencing from the date of the mortgage) one day longer than the term vested in the first or other mortgagee whose security ranks immediately before that of the second or subsequent mortgagee[7].

1   As to the meaning of 'mortgage' see PARA 101 note 4.
2   As to the meaning of 'mortgagor' see PARA 104 note 1.
3   As to the meaning of 'land' see PARA 104 note 2.
4   As to the meaning of 'mortgagee' see PARA 104 note 1.
5   Law of Property Act 1925 s 85(2). Any such purported conveyance includes an absolute conveyance with a deed of defeasance and any other assurance which, but for s 85(2), would operate in effect to vest the fee simple in a mortgagee subject to redemption: s 85(2). Since 13 October 2003 (ie the date on which the Land Registration Act 2002 Sch 11 para 2 was brought into force by the Land Registration Act 2002 (Commencement No 4) Order 2003, SI 2003/1725), this provision has not applied to registered land, but, subject to that, it applies whether or not the land is registered land and whether or not the mortgage is expressed to be made by way of trust for sale or otherwise: see the Law of Property Act 1925 s 85(3) (amended by the Land Registration Act 2002 Sch 11 para 2(6)). As to registered land generally see REAL PROPERTY AND REGISTRATION vol 87 (2012) PARA 232 et seq. For examples of mortgages by trust for sale see *Re Alison, Johnson v Mounsey* (1879) 11 ChD 284, CA; *Locking v Parker* (1872) 8 Ch App 30. Note that trusts for sale are now referred to as trusts of land: see the Trusts of Land and Appointment of Trustees Act 1996 s 1; and REAL PROPERTY AND REGISTRATION vol 87 (2012) PARA 105.
6   Law of Property Act 1925 s 85(2)(a).
7   Law of Property Act 1925 s 85(2)(b).

162. Mortgages of leaseholds. Before 1926, a legal mortgage of leasehold property was made either by way of assignment of the whole term or by way of sub-demise. The former method was adopted only when the rent was small and the lessee's covenants were not burdensome, for the effect of an assignment was to establish a privity between the lessor and the mortgagee, so that the mortgagee could be sued for breach of covenant[1]. The alternative course was to demise the property to the mortgagee for the whole of the term, less one or more days[2]. Under this form of security the mortgagee was under no personal liability to the lessor[3]. The only objection to it was that it left the nominal reversion outstanding in the mortgagor. To obviate this it was the practice to insert in the mortgage a declaration by the mortgagor that he held the head term in trust for the mortgagee, but subject to the right of redemption. This was supplemented by a power for the mortgagee to remove the mortgagor and appoint a nominee of his own to be trustee in the place of the mortgagor and vest the head term in the new trustee[4]. A power of attorney to assign the nominal reversion was sometimes added.

Any purported assignment of a term of years absolute[5] by way of mortgage[6] made after 1925 operates (to the extent of the mortgagor's[7] estate) as a sub-demise of the leasehold land[8] to the mortgagee[9] for a term of years absolute, but subject to cesser on redemption[10], so that the term taken by the first or only mortgagee is ten days less than the term expressed to be assigned[11]; and the term taken by a second or subsequent mortgagee is one day longer than the term vested in the first or other mortgagee whose security ranks immediately before that of the second or subsequent mortgagee if the length of the last-mentioned term permits, and in any case a term less by one day at least than the term expressed to be assigned[12].

1   *Williams v Bosanquet* (1819) 1 Brod & Bing 238. Cf *Purchase v Lichfield Brewery Co* [1915] 1 KB 184.
2   It was held that a second mortgage by demise for a term concurrent with the first mortgage by demise created a legal term, not a mere equitable charge (*Re Moore and Hulm's Contract* [1912] 2 Ch 105); and this is so under the present system (see the Law of Property Act 1925 s 149(5)).
3   A lessor had no equity to compel a person between whom and himself there was no privity to take an assignment of the term or make himself liable on the covenants, even though such person had taken possession: *Moores v Choat* (1839) 8 Sim 508; *Moore v Greg* (1848) 2 Ph 717.
4   See *London and County Banking Co v Goddard* [1897] 1 Ch 642. A declaration of trust in favour of the mortgagee did not render him liable to the lessor for the rent and covenants of the lease: *Walters v Northern Coal Mining Co* (1855) 5 De GM & G 629. Nor did a declaration of trust prevent the trustee in bankruptcy of the mortgagor from disclaiming the nominal reversion: *Re Maughan, ex p Monkhouse* (1885) 14 QBD 956.
5   In the Law of Property Act 1925, 'term of years absolute' means a term of years (taking effect either in possession or in reversion whether or not at a rent) with or without impeachment for waste, subject or not to another legal estate, and either certain or liable to determination by notice, re-entry, operation of law or by a provision for cesser on redemption, or in any other event (other than the dropping of a life, or the determination of a determinable life interest), but it does not include any term of years determinable with life or lives or with the cesser of a determinable life interest, nor, if created after 1 January 1926, a term of years which is not expressed to take effect in possession within 21 years after its creation where required by the Law of Property Act 1925 to take effect within that period; and 'term of years' includes a term for less than a year, or for a year or years and a fraction of a year or from year to year: s 205(1)(xxvii). As to the meaning of 'legal estate' see PARA 105 note 2.
6   As to the meaning of 'mortgage' see PARA 101 note 4.
7   As to the meaning of 'mortgagor' see PARA 104 note 1.
8   As to the meaning of 'land' see PARA 104 note 2.
9   As to the meaning of 'mortgagee' see PARA 104 note 1.
10   Law of Property Act 1925 s 86(2). See also *Grangeside Properties Ltd v Collingwoods Securities Ltd* [1964] 1 All ER 143, [1964] 1 WLR 139, CA. Any such purported assignment includes an absolute assignment with a deed of defeasance and any other assurance which, but for the Law of Property Act 1925 s 86(2), would operate in effect to vest the mortgagor's term in a mortgagee subject to redemption: s 86(2). Since 13 October 2003 (ie the date on which the Land Registration Act 2002 Sch 11 para 2 was brought into force by the Land Registration Act 2002 (Commencement No 4) Order 2003, SI 2003/1725), this provision has not applied to registered land, but, subject to that, it applies whether or not the land is registered land and whether or not the mortgage is made by way of sub-mortgage of a term of years absolute, or is expressed to be by way of trust for sale or otherwise: see the Law of Property Act 1925 s 86(3) (amended by the Land Registration Act 2002 Sch 11 para 2(7)). As to registered land generally see REAL PROPERTY AND REGISTRATION vol 87 (2012) PARA 232 et seq. Note that trusts for sale are now referred to as trusts of land: see the Trusts of Land and Appointment of Trustees Act 1996 s 1; and REAL PROPERTY AND REGISTRATION vol 87 (2012) PARA 105.
11   Law of Property Act 1925 s 86(2)(a).
12   Law of Property Act 1925 s 86(2)(b).

163. Mortgages of limited interests. Formerly life estates and reversions and remainders, whether vested or contingent, could exist at law in land and might be the subject of a legal mortgage[1], but now they can exist only as equitable interests[2], and a mortgage of a life interest or reversionary interest now takes the form of an equitable mortgage effected by conveyance subject to redemption or merely by charge[3].

1   Formerly mortgages of life estates in land were sometimes made by a demise of the land for 99 years if the mortgagor should so long live. The Law of Property Act 1925 s 149(6), which converts terms determinable with life or lives into terms of 90 years determinable on notice after the dropping of a life, does not apply to a term taking effect in equity under a settlement or created out of an equitable interest under a settlement for mortgage, indemnity or other like purposes: see s 149(6) proviso (a); and LANDLORD AND TENANT vol 62 (2012) PARA 240.
2   See the Law of Property Act 1925 s 1(1), (3).

3 As to equitable mortgages see generally PARAS 105, 215 et seq. As to the statutory power of a tenant for life under a settlement to mortgage the settled land (as distinct from his own equitable life interest in it) see PARA 146. As to the court's power to grant relief in the case of unconscionable bargains made with persons having reversionary interests in property see MISREPRESENTATION vol 76 (2013) PARA 850 et seq.

B.   TYPES OF LEGAL MORTGAGE OF LAND

164. Mortgages by demise. A mortgage[1] of an estate in fee simple can be effected at law by a demise for a term of years absolute[2], subject to a provision for cesser on redemption[3]. Likewise, a mortgage of a term of years absolute is capable of being made at law by a sub-demise for a term of years absolute, less by one day at least than the term vested in the mortgagor[4] and subject to a provision for cesser on redemption[5]. As there may be concurrent demises, whether for the same or for different terms, a succession of legal mortgages by demise is possible[6].

These provisions do not apply to registered land[7].

1 As to the meaning of 'mortgage' see PARA 101 note 4.
2 As to the meaning of 'term of years absolute' see PARA 162 note 5.
3 See the Law of Property Act 1925 s 85(1). Powers to mortgage and to lend money on mortgage of an estate in fee simple are to be construed as powers to mortgage the estate for a term of years absolute, without impeachment for waste, or by a charge by way of legal mortgage or to lend on such security: s 85(4). As to the meaning of 'legal mortgage' see PARA 104 note 1. As to charges by way of legal mortgage see PARA 165.
4 As to the meaning of 'mortgagor' see PARA 104 note 1.
5 See the Law of Property Act 1925 s 86(1). Where a licence to sub-demise by way of mortgage is required, the licence must not be unreasonably refused: s 86(1). This provision applies whether or not the mortgage is made by way of sub-mortgage for a term of years absolute, or is expressed to be by way of trust for sale or otherwise: see s 86(3) (amended by the Land Registration Act 2002 s 133, Sch 11 para 2(1), (7)). Note that trusts for sale of land are now referred to as trusts of land: see the Trusts of Land and Appointment of Trustees Act 1996 s 1; and REAL PROPERTY AND REGISTRATION vol 87 (2012) PARA 105.

   Powers to mortgage or to lend money on mortgage of a term of years absolute by way of assignment are to be construed as a power to mortgage the term by sub-demise for a term of years absolute or by a charge by way of legal mortgage, or to lend on such security: see the Law of Property Act 1925 s 86(4).
6 See the Law of Property Act 1925 s 149(5).
7 See the Land Registration Act 2002 s 23(1)(a); PARA 127; and REAL PROPERTY AND REGISTRATION vol 87 (2012) PARA 422.

165. Mortgage as a legal charge. A charge by way of legal mortgage can be created on freehold and leasehold property[1]. The charge is created by deed expressed to be by way of legal mortgage[2]. It ranks as a legal estate[3], although no term of years is actually created[4], and it gives the chargee the same protection, powers and remedies as if a mortgage term for 3,000 years without impeachment of waste in the case of freeholds[5], or a mortgage sub-term less one day than the term vested in the mortgagor in the case of leaseholds[6], had been created in the chargee's favour[7]. A chargee by way of legal mortgage may take proceedings to obtain possession from the occupiers and persons in receipt of rents and profits or any of them[8], and may protect his charge by applying for relief against forfeiture, in the case of a mortgage of leasehold land[9].

1 See the Law of Property Act 1925 ss 85(1), 86(1).
2 See the Law of Property Act 1925 ss 85(1), 86(1). It is submitted that the fact that the charge is by way of legal mortgage must be expressed somewhere in the deed if it is to take effect as such: cf *Sopher v Mercer* [1967] CLY 2543 (county court).
3 See the Law of Property Act 1925 ss 1(2)(c), (4), 205(1)(x); and REAL PROPERTY AND REGISTRATION vol 87 (2012) PARA 63. See further *Caunce v Caunce* [1969] 1 All ER 722, [1969] 1 WLR 286.
4 *Weg Motors Ltd v Hales* [1962] Ch 49 at 73–74, [1961] 3 All ER 181 at 190, CA, per Lord Evershed MR, and at 77 and 192 per Donovan LJ; *Cumberland Court (Brighton) Ltd v Taylor*

[1964] Ch 29, [1963] 2 All ER 536; *Thompson (Inspector of Taxes) v Salah* [1972] 1 All ER 530. See also *Edwards v Marshall-Lee* (1975) 235 Estates Gazette 901, 119 Sol Jo 506. In *Ushers Brewery Ltd v PS King & Co (Finance) Ltd* [1972] Ch 148, [1971] 2 All ER 468, the legal charge was assumed to create a notional term.

5   Law of Property Act 1925 s 87(1)(a).
6   Law of Property Act 1925 s 87(1)(b).
7   Law of Property Act 1925 s 87(1). Section 87(1) is not affected by the Land Registration Act 2002 s 23(1)(a) (which provides that owner's powers in relation to a registered estate do not include power to mortgage by demise or sub-demises: see PARA 127): Law of Property Act 1925 s 87(4) (added by the Land Registration Act 2002 s 133, Sch 11 para 2(1), (8)). See also *Grand Junction Co Ltd v Bates* [1954] 2 QB 160 at 168, [1954] 2 All ER 385 at 388 per Upjohn J; *Belgravia Insurance Co Ltd v Meah* [1964] 1 QB 436 at 443, [1963] 3 All ER 828 at 831, CA, per Lord Denning MR; *Regent Oil Co Ltd v JA Gregory (Hatch End) Ltd* [1966] Ch 402 at 431, [1965] 3 All ER 673 at 679, CA, per Harman LJ.
8   See the Law of Property Act 1925 s 87(1).
9   See the Law of Property Act 1925 s 146(4); PARA 403; and LANDLORD AND TENANT vol 63 (2012) PARA 775.

166. Statutory mortgages. A mortgage of freehold or leasehold land may be made by a deed expressed to be by way of statutory mortgage in a prescribed form with such modifications as circumstances may require[1]. This is a special form of charge by way of legal mortgage, and is deemed to include covenants for payment of principal and interest and a proviso for discharge of the mortgaged property or transfer of the benefit as the mortgagor may direct[2].

1   See the Law of Property Act 1925 s 117(1), Sch 4 Forms 1, 4.
2   See the Law of Property Act 1925 s 117(2).

167. Mortgage by estoppel. A grantor cannot dispute the validity or effect of his own grant, and accordingly a mortgagor who has no legal estate at all[1] is estopped at common law from denying that he had a legal title[2]. The estoppel binds the mortgagor and all persons claiming under him whether for value or not, other than a bona fide purchaser for value from the mortgagor without notice of the earlier transaction[3]. The title of the mortgagee does not prevail over the title of the true owner and the persons claiming under him; if, however, the mortgagor subsequently acquires the legal title from the true owner, the estoppel is fed and the mortgagee's title becomes good against all except a bona fide purchaser for value from the mortgagor without notice of the earlier transaction[4].

Where the grant also contains an express recital or other clear and unequivocal representation of the mortgagor's title, he is estopped from denying that he had the particular title which he had asserted; the estoppel is not excluded by his ownership of some other and lesser estate[5]. In such a case, the estoppel binds the mortgagor and all persons claiming under him, whether for value or not and with or without notice; so that if the mortgagor afterwards acquires the legal estate which he had represented that he owned, the mortgagee obtains a title which is good against the whole world[6].

If a mortgagor with a defective title purports and intends to demise property for value, any interest subsequently acquired by him in that property is available to make the conveyance effectual even though the defect in title is apparent on the face of the conveyance[7]; and if the mortgagor's title is defeated, but he afterwards acquires the same land under another title, the mortgage attaches to the new title[8].

A mortgage by estoppel cannot be registered as a legal charge unless and until the estoppel is fed by the acquisition of the legal estate by the mortgagor[9].

1   If the grantor has a legal estate less than that which he purports to grant, the grantee obtains an estate in interest (but not by estoppel), and that estate cannot exceed the estate of his grantor: see PARA 168. In such a situation, as there is no estoppel, the grantor's subsequent acquisition of a larger title capable of supporting the estate which he has granted will not enure for the benefit of

the grantee: see *Universal Permanent Building Society v Cooke* [1952] Ch 95, [1951] 2 All ER 893, CA; *First National Bank plc v Thompson* [1996] Ch 231, [1996] 1 All ER 140, CA. See also ESTOPPEL vol 47 (2014) PARA 337.

2 *First National Bank plc v Thompson* [1996] Ch 231, [1996] 1 All ER 140, CA. See further ESTOPPEL vol 47 (2014) PARA 336.

3 *First National Bank plc v Thompson* [1996] Ch 231, [1996] 1 All ER 140, CA. See also *Right d Jeffreys v Bucknell* (1831) 2 B & Ad 278; *General Finance, Mortgage and Discount Co v Liberator Permanent Benefit Building Society* (1878) 10 ChD 15.

4 *First National Bank plc v Thompson* [1996] Ch 231, [1996] 1 All ER 140, CA.

5 *First National Bank plc v Thompson* [1996] Ch 231, [1996] 1 All ER 140, CA.

6 *First National Bank plc v Thompson* [1996] Ch 231, [1996] 1 All ER 140, CA.

7 See *Re Bridgwater's Settlement, Partridge v Ward* [1910] 2 Ch 342; *Re Hoffe's Estate Act 1855* (1900) 82 LT 556.

8 *Seabourne v Powel* (1686) 2 Vern 11; *Noel v Bewley* (1829) 3 Sim 103; *Re Gregory, Gascoigne v Gregory* (1912) 134 LT Jo 106; *Gresham Life Assurance Society v Crowther* [1914] 2 Ch 219 (affd [1915] 1 Ch 214, CA, without reference to this point).

9 *First National Bank plc v Thompson* [1996] Ch 231, [1996] 1 All ER 140, CA. See also ESTOPPEL vol 47 (2014) PARA 336.

C. PROPERTY TO WHICH THE MORTGAGE EXTENDS

168. Effect of mortgagor's want of legal estate. Where a mortgagor purports to mortgage a greater estate in property than that which he possesses, the conveyance[1] or transfer[2] by which the purported mortgage is created passes to the mortgagee such interest as the mortgagor has in the property[3]. Thus where joint owners of a property purport to grant a mortgage but it is void or voidable as against one of the joint owners, the execution of the mortgage by the other takes effect as an equitable charge over his beneficial interest in the property[4]. An imperfect legal mortgage, on the other hand, is treated as an agreement to create a mortgage[5].

Where there is an effective agreement[6] to create a mortgage over a greater estate in property than that which the mortgagor possesses, it may also create an equitable charge over such property as the mortgagor possesses[7], or the court may order the mortgagor to execute a charge over such interest as he has[8].

1 'Conveyance' includes a mortgage, charge, lease, assent, vesting declaration, vesting instrument, disclaimer, release and every other assurance of property or of an interest therein by any instrument, except a will; and 'convey' has a corresponding meaning: see the Law of Property Act 1925 s 205(1)(ii).

2 As to transfers see the Land Registration Act 2002; and REAL PROPERTY AND REGISTRATION vol 87 (2012) PARA 422 et seq.

3 See the Law of Property Act 1925 s 63; and DEEDS AND OTHER INSTRUMENTS vol 32 (2012) PARA 441. This provision does not apply to a mere agreement to create a mortgage.

4 *Ahmed v Kendrick* (1987) 56 P & CR 120, CA. See also *Zandfarid v Bank of Credit and Commerce International SA (in liquidation)* [1996] 1 WLR 1420, [1997] 1 FCR 78; *First National Bank plc v Achampong* [2003] EWCA Civ 487, [2004] 1 FCR 18. No interest passes, however, if the purported mortgage is intended by both parties to it to be a sham transaction: *Penn v Bristol and West Building Society* [1996] 2 FCR 729, [1995] 2 FLR 938.

5 See PARA 218.

6 As to the requirements for a binding agreement see PARA 221.

7 *Murray v Guinness* [1998] NPC 79. See also *United Bank of Kuwait plc v Sahib* [1997] Ch 107, [1996] 3 All ER 215, CA.

8 *Thames Guaranty Ltd v Campbell* [1985] QB 210, [1984] 2 All ER 585, CA; *Bankers Trust Co v Namdar* [1997] NPC 22, CA.

169. Fixtures. A legal mortgage of land comprises, without specific mention, all fixtures which at the date of the mortgage[1] are, or at any time afterwards during its continuance[2] may be, annexed to the land[3]. This rule applies also to an equitable mortgage[4]. So far as fixtures are concerned, mortgages of leaseholds are on the same footing as mortgages of freeholds[5]. If a tenant who has put up fixtures, which as against the landlord he is entitled to remove, mortgages his leasehold interest, the mortgage will pass those fixtures whether they are mentioned or not[6], and whether the security is a legal mortgage or by a deposit of title deeds[7], and whether the articles were affixed before or after the mortgage[8]. In the case of mortgages of freeholds and of leaseholds, where the mortgage includes fixtures or chattels personal, any statutory power of sale and any right to foreclose or take possession extends to the absolute or other interest in them affected by the charge[9].

Where a mortgagor in possession, with the mortgagee's knowledge and acquiescence, lets premises to a tenant who brings upon them trade fixtures, the fixtures do not pass to the mortgagee but may be removed by the tenant[10].

1 *Mather v Fraser* (1856) 2 K & J 536; *Longbottom v Berry* (1869) LR 5 QB 123; *Holland v Hodgson* (1872) LR 7 CP 328, Ex Ch; *Vaudeville Electric Cinema Ltd v Muriset* [1923] 2 Ch 74.
2 *Walmsley v Milne* (1859) 7 CBNS 115; *Tottenham v Swansea Zinc Ore Co Ltd* (1885) 52 LT 738; *Cullwick v Swindell* (1866) LR 3 Eq 249; *Climie v Wood* (1868) LR 3 Exch 257 (affd (1869) LR 4 Exch 328); *Monti v Barnes* [1901] 1 KB 205, CA.
3 See *TSB Bank plc v Botham* [1996] EGCS 149, sub nom *Botham v TSB Bank plc* (1996) 73 P & CR D1, CA (a decision relating to which items in a dwelling house are fixtures); *Hulme v Brigham* [1943] KB 152, [1943] 1 All ER 204 (where printing machines standing by their own weight were held not to be fixtures although the driving apparatus was fixed to the freehold).
4 *Longbottom v Berry* (1869) LR 5 QB 123; *Re Lusty, ex p Lusty v Official Receiver* (1889) 60 LT 160; but see *Re Trethowan, ex p Tweedy* (1877) 5 ChD 559. As to a mortgagee's rights to fixtures as against the mortgagor's trustee in bankruptcy see BANKRUPTCY AND INDIVIDUAL INSOLVENCY vol 5 (2013) PARA 428. As to equitable mortgages see generally PARAS 105, 215 et seq.
5 *Meux v Jacobs* (1875) LR 7 HL 481; *Southport and West Lancashire Banking Co v Thompson* (1887) 37 ChD 64, CA.
6 *Meux v Jacobs* (1875) LR 7 HL 481.
7 *Re Inwood, ex p Cowell* (1848) 17 LJ Bcy 16; *Re Richards, ex p Astbury, ex p Lloyd's Banking Co* (1869) 4 Ch App 630; *Re Gawan, ex p Barclay* (1855) 5 De GM & G 403; *Williams v Evans* (1856) 23 Beav 239; *Boyd v Shorrock* (1867) LR 5 Eq 72. As to the creation of an equitable mortgage by deposit of title deeds see PARA 222 et seq. Since 27 September 1989, however, the mere deposit of title deeds by way of security can no longer create a valid equitable mortgage: see PARA 221.
8 *Meux v Jacobs* (1875) LR 7 HL 481.
9 See the Law of Property Act 1925 s 88(4) (freehold mortgages), s 89(4) (leasehold mortgages). As to the statutory power of sale see PARA 446 et seq. The mortgagee cannot, however, sell the fixtures separately: see PARA 466.
10 *Sanders v Davis* (1885) 15 QBD 218.

170. Accretions and substitutions. The mortgagee is entitled to accretions to the mortgaged property or property received in substitution for it by the mortgagor[1]. Similarly, additions made by a second mortgagee enure to the benefit of the first mortgagee[2]. If the mortgaged property is disposed of in a manner which destroys the mortgagee's estate[3], a security interest automatically arises in the proceeds of sale in favour of the mortgagee[4]. In the case of renewable leaseholds, if either the mortgagor or mortgagee is able to obtain a renewal of the lease, the renewed lease is treated as engrafted upon the old and as forming part of the mortgage security[5]. Where an option to purchase the freehold reversion is part of the mortgage security and the mortgagee exercises the option, he is not entitled to retain the benefit of the exercise of the option; on redemption the mortgagor is entitled to get back the whole of his security and is therefore entitled to a conveyance of the freehold on payment of the principal, interest and the mortgagee's proper expenses, including the purchase price of the reversion[6]. Where a lease subject to a legal charge is forfeited on the mortgagor's default under the lease and an order[7] has vested a new lease in the mortgagee as underlessee, the new lease is a substituted security for the mortgage and subject to the mortgagor's right of redemption[8].

Where a tenant whose interest is mortgaged acquires the freehold[9], the existence of the mortgage will prevent the merger[10] of the enfranchising tenant's leasehold and freehold estates and the mortgagee's security will remain the lease[11]. Where the mortgagor obtains an extended lease[12], it forms part of the mortgage security[13] and the mortgagee who was entitled to possession of the title deeds relating to the original lease is entitled to possession of the deeds relating to the extended lease[14].

1 *Buhr v Barclays Bank plc* [2001] EWCA Civ 1223, [2002] 1 P & CR D1; *Re Kitchin, ex p Punnett* (1880) 16 ChD 226 at 236, CA.

2 *Landowners West of England and South Wales Land Drainage and Inclosure Co v Ashford* (1880) 16 ChD 411 at 433; and see *Maxwell v Ashe* (1752) 1 Bro CC 444n; *Moody v Matthews* (1802) 7 Ves 174 (annuities charged on renewed leases); *Hughes v Howard* (1858) 25 Beav 575 (new lease after a collusive foreclosure); *Sims v Helling* (1851) 21 LJCh 76 (lease following a building agreement).

3 Eg a sale by the mortgagor's trustee in bankruptcy or a sale by the mortgagor to a purchaser against whom an unregistered charge is void: see *Buhr v Barclays Bank plc* [2001] EWCA Civ 1223, [2002] 1 P & CR D1.

4 *Buhr v Barclays Bank plc* [2001] EWCA Civ 1223, [2002] 1 P & CR D1.

5 *Re Biss, Biss v Biss* [1903] 2 Ch 40 at 62, CA; *Leigh v Burnett* (1885) 29 ChD 231; *Rakestraw v Brewer* (1729) 2 P Wms 511. Perpetually renewable leaseholds cannot now exist: see the Law of Property Act 1922 s 145, Sch 15 paras 1(1), 5; and LANDLORD AND TENANT vol 62 (2012) PARA 689.

6 *Nelson v Hannam* [1943] Ch 59, [1942] 2 All ER 680, CA.

7 Ie an order under the Law of Property Act 1925 s 146(4): see LANDLORD AND TENANT vol 63 (2012) PARA 775.

8 *Chelsea Estates Investment Trust Co Ltd v Marche* [1955] Ch 328, [1955] 1 All ER 195.

9 Ie under the Leasehold Reform Acts 1967 and 1979: see the Leasehold Reform Act 1967 ss 8–13; and LANDLORD AND TENANT vol 64 (2012) PARA 1505 et seq. A mortgage term is not capable of enfranchisement: *Re Fairview, Church Street, Bromyard* [1974] 1 All ER 1233, [1974] 1 WLR 579.

10 See PARA 678 et seq.

11 The mortgagor and mortgagee may, of course, agree to substitute the freehold for the lease as the security.

12 See the Leasehold Reform Act 1967 ss 14–16; and LANDLORD AND TENANT vol 64 (2012) PARA 1597 et seq.

13 See the Leasehold Reform, Housing and Urban Development Act 1993 s 58(4); and LANDLORD AND TENANT vol 64 (2012) PARA 1829. Cf also the cases cited in note 5.

14 See the Leasehold Reform Act 1967 s 14(6); the Leasehold Reform, Housing and Urban Development Act 1993 s 58(5); and LANDLORD AND TENANT vol 64 (2012) PARAS 1598, 1829.

171. Compensation money. If, on the compulsory acquisition of mortgaged land, a lump sum is paid into court by the acquiring authority in respect of the interests of the mortgagor and mortgagee, the court will apportion the amount between the mortgagor and mortgagee; usually, however, where the mortgagee is not in possession, the acquiring authority will treat with the mortgagor for the full value of the land, leaving him to discharge the mortgage[1]. Special statutory provision is made entitling the acquiring authority to redeem the mortgagee's interest in the land, including provision for cases where the mortgage debt exceeds the value of the land or part only of the mortgaged land is taken[2].

Money paid as statutory compensation for the licence of a mortgaged public house belongs to the mortgagee as part of the mortgage security[3].

1 See COMPULSORY ACQUISITION OF LAND vol 18 (2009) PARA 711. See also the provisions relating to compensation in the Town and Country Planning Act 1990 ss 107–118, 144, 157, 186, 203–205 (repealed in relation to England), s 282 (see PLANNING vol 83 (2010) PARA 1090); and

the Leasehold Reform Act 1967 ss 1A, 1B, 9A (see LANDLORD AND TENANT vol 64 (2012) PARA 1559 et seq). See further HOUSING vol 56 (2011) PARAS 414, 416.
2 See COMPULSORY ACQUISITION OF LAND vol 18 (2009) PARAS 712–714.
3 *Law Guarantee and Trust Society Ltd v Mitcham and Cheam Brewery Co Ltd* [1906] 2 Ch 98; *Noakes v Noakes & Co Ltd* [1907] 1 Ch 64; *Dawson v Braime's Tadcaster Breweries Ltd* [1907] 2 Ch 359.

172. Business goodwill. There are certain kinds of goodwill[1] to which a mortgagee is entitled. The goodwill which attaches to a particular house increases the value of that house, and therefore the mortgagee is entitled to it[2]. A mortgage of premises comprised in a colliery lease which was subject to a condition that unless the seams of coal were worked the lessor might re-enter was held to charge the business[3]. Goodwill which arises from the personal reputation that a man has made for himself does not pass to the mortgagee of his house, but is a thing personal to the man whose skill and name acquired the goodwill[4]; nor will the goodwill of a business be included where the terms of the security indicate that only the business premises were intended to be charged[5]. A mortgagee of a public house and the goodwill is entitled, as against the mortgagor, to an assignment of the licence[6].

1 As to goodwill generally see PARTNERSHIP vol 79 (2014) PARA 212 et seq; PERSONAL PROPERTY vol 80 (2013) PARA 807 et seq; COMPETITION vol 18 (2009) PARAS 373–376.
2 *Cooper v Metropolitan Board of Works* (1883) 25 ChD 472 at 479, CA. Thus mortgages of an upholsterer's business (*Chissum v Dewes* (1828) 5 Russ 29), of a baker's shop (*King v Midland Rly Co* (1868) 17 WR 113), of a graving dock (*Pile v Pile, ex p Lambton* (1876) 3 ChD 36, CA) and of a public house (*Re Kitchin, ex p Punnett* (1880) 16 ChD 226, CA) have been held to carry the goodwill.
3 *County of Gloucester Bank v Rudry Merthyr Steam and House Coal Colliery Co* [1895] 1 Ch 629, CA. Cf *Hamilton Gas Co Ltd v Hamilton Corpn* [1910] AC 300, PC.
4 *Cooper v Metropolitan Board of Works* (1883) 25 ChD 472, CA.
5 *Whitley v Challis* [1892] 1 Ch 64, CA. See also *Palmer v Barclays Bank Ltd* (1971) 23 P & CR 30 (the mortgage charged merely the property; accordingly, the sale by the mortgagee of the premises without the goodwill of the business was held not to amount to negligence).
6 *Rutter v Daniel* (1882) 30 WR 724 (on appeal 30 WR 801, CA); *Re O'Brien* (1883) 11 LR Ir 213; *Garrett v St Marylebone, Middlesex Justices* (1884) 12 QBD 620. However, the mortgage does not include the proceeds of sale of rights under the licence: see *Re Carr* [1918] 2 IR 448.

173. Insurance money. All money received on an insurance of the mortgaged property effected under the Law of Property Act 1925, or for the maintenance of which the mortgagor is liable under the mortgage deed, must, if the mortgagee so requires, be applied by the mortgagor in making good the loss or damage in respect of which the money is received[1]. Upon the request of any person interested in or entitled to any house or other building burnt down or damaged by fire, the insurance office must apply the insurance money in reinstatement or repair[2], and it has been held that a claim for reinstatement may be made by a mortgagee[3]. On the other hand, and without prejudice to any obligation to the contrary imposed by law or by special contract, a mortgagee may require that all money received under an insurance effected under the Law of Property Act 1925 be applied in or towards discharge of the money due under his mortgage[4]. However, if the mortgagor has effected a further insurance which is independent of the security, the mortgagee will not be entitled to its benefit[5]; if the policy under which the mortgagee is entitled to benefit contains a clause limiting the insurers' liability in the event of the property in question being the subject of any other insurance, the result of the existence of the further insurance may be that the amount payable to the mortgagee is diminished[6]. If the policy is effected in the name of the mortgagee, he is entitled in law to payment of the proceeds but his interest remains by way of charge to secure the mortgage debt and he is accountable to subsequent mortgagees or the mortgagor for the surplus. If the policy is effected in the name of the mortgagor pursuant to a covenant to insure, the mortgagee has an interest in the proceeds by way of a partial equitable assignment which is not destroyed by the failure of the mortgagor to comply with any of his covenants intended to protect that interest[7].

1 See the Law of Property Act 1925 s 108(3). As to the power to insure see PARA 201.
2 See the Fires Prevention (Metropolis) Act 1774 s 83 (which is not confined to the metropolis); *Portavon Cinema Co Ltd v Price and Century Insurance Co Ltd* [1939] 4 All ER 601 at 607; and INSURANCE vol 60 (2011) PARA 611.
3 See INSURANCE vol 60 (2011) PARA 613.
4 See the Law of Property Act 1925 s 108(4).
5 See *Halifax Building Society v Keighley* [1931] 2 KB 248; *Re Doherty* [1925] 2 IR 246.
6 *Halifax Building Society v Keighley* [1931] 2 KB 248. As to contribution clauses in insurance policies see INSURANCE vol 60 (2011) PARAS 233–234.
7 *Colonial Mutual General Insurance Co Ltd v ANZ Banking Group (New Zealand)* [1995] 3 All ER 987, [1995] 1 WLR 1140, PC.

174. Mortgage indemnity policy. Mortgagees commonly take out a mortgage indemnity policy with an insurance company under which the mortgagee is entitled to a specified sum on the happening of events such as a failure by the mortgagor to make payments, a sale by the mortgagee, and the proceeds of sale being less than the outstanding debt[1]. The proceeds of the policy belong to the mortgagee and do not discharge any part of the debt owed by the mortgagor, even though the mortgagor is debited with the premium and the policy is described as additional security in the general conditions applicable to the mortgage[2].

1 As to debt insurance generally see INSURANCE vol 60 (2011) PARA 755 et seq.
2 *Woolwich Building Society v Brown* [1996] CLC 625; *Leeds Building Society v Banfield* [2007] EWCA Civ 1369, [2007] All ER (D) 302 (Dec).

175. Not all rights pass automatically with the mortgage. The benefit of some rights relating to the security, such as appurtenant easements and the benefit of restrictive covenants, pass automatically with the mortgage of the security[1]. Other rights have to be expressly assigned[2].

1 See REAL PROPERTY AND REGISTRATION vol 87 (2012) PARAS 916, 1076 et seq.
2 Eg the benefit of a covenant relating to the making of highways or roads (see HIGHWAYS, STREETS AND BRIDGES vol 55 (2012) PARA 119), the benefit of the National House Builders Registration Council agreement (see BUILDING CONTRACTS vol 6 (2011) PARA 391), and the benefit of some other positive covenant or obligation or a covenant for indemnity.

D. MORTGAGES OF PARTICULAR KINDS OF LAND

176. Charge of registered land. For the purpose only of preventing the title of a disponee being questioned, a person's right to exercise owner's powers in relation to a registered estate[1] is to be taken to be free from any limitation[2] affecting the validity of a disposition[3]. The grant of a legal charge[4] is required to be completed by registration[5] and does not operate at law until the registration requirements[6] are met[7]. The entry is completed by entry on the charges register of the name of the chargee or his successor in title as proprietor of the charge[8]. On completion of the relevant registration requirements, a charge created by means of a registrable disposition[9] of a registered estate has effect, if it would not otherwise do so, as a charge by deed by way of legal mortgage[10].

A charge or mortgage which is not a registered charge takes effect only in equity[11] and is liable to be postponed to a registered disposition by the proprietor unless protected on the register by a notice[12].

1   As to owner's powers and the right to exercise them in relation to a registered estate see the Land Registration Act 2002 ss 23, 24; PARA 127. As to the meaning of 'registered estate' see PARA 142 note 7.
2   Ie any limitation other than a limitation reflected by an entry in the register of title (Land Registration Act 2002 s 26(2)(a)) or imposed by or under the legislation relating to the registration of land (s 26(2)(b)). Such limitations include, for example, limitations on dealing protected by a caution, inhibition or restriction entered under the Land Registration Act 1925: see the Land Registration Act 2002 s 134, Sch 12 paras 1, 2; and REAL PROPERTY AND REGISTRATION vol 87 (2012) PARA 510 et seq. As to the register of title and registration therein see REAL PROPERTY AND REGISTRATION vol 87 (2012) PARA 328 et seq.
3   Land Registration Act 2002 s 26(1), (3); and see REAL PROPERTY AND REGISTRATION vol 87 (2012) PARA 425.
4   As to the meaning of 'charge' see PARA 127 note 5.
5   Land Registration Act 2002 s 27(2)(f); and see REAL PROPERTY AND REGISTRATION vol 87 (2012) PARA 428.
6   As to the registration requirements see REAL PROPERTY AND REGISTRATION vol 87 (2012) PARAS 344 et seq, 569 et seq.
7   See the Land Registration Act 2002 s 27(1); and REAL PROPERTY AND REGISTRATION vol 87 (2012) PARA 427.
8   Land Registration Act 2002 Sch 2 para 8.
9   As to the meaning of 'registrable disposition' see PARA 142 note 8.
10   Land Registration Act 2002 s 51.
11   See the Law of Property Act 1925 s 1(3).
12   See the Land Registration Act 2002 ss 28–30; and REAL PROPERTY AND REGISTRATION vol 87 (2012) PARAS 454–456.

177. Mortgage of commonhold land. The unit-holder of a commonhold unit[1] has owner's powers[2] to charge the whole interest in the unit; a charge cannot be created over part only of an interest in such a unit[3] and an instrument or agreement is of no effect to the extent that it purports to create such a charge[4].

A legal mortgage[5] can be created over the common parts of a commonhold[6] if the creation of the mortgage is approved by a resolution of the commonhold association[7] passed unanimously[8] before it is created[9]. It is not otherwise possible to create a charge over common parts[10] and any instrument or agreement is of no effect to the extent that it purports to create such a charge[11].

1   A person is the unit-holder of a commonhold unit if he is entitled to be registered as the proprietor of the freehold estate in the unit (whether or not he is so registered): Commonhold and Leasehold Reform Act 2002 s 12. For these purposes, a 'commonhold unit' is a commonhold unit specified in a commonhold community statement in accordance with s 11: see s 11(1); and COMMONHOLD vol 13 (2009) PARA 330.
2   As to owner's powers see PARA 127.
3   See the Commonhold and Leasehold Reform Act 2002 s 22(1); and COMMONHOLD vol 13 (2009) PARA 351.
4   See the Commonhold and Leasehold Reform Act 2002 s 22(2); and COMMONHOLD vol 13 (2009) PARA 351.
5   As to the meaning of 'legal mortgage' see PARA 104 note 1; definition applied by the Commonhold and Leasehold Reform Act 2002 s 29(3).
6   Ie every part of the commonhold which is not for the time being a commonhold unit in accordance with the commonhold community statement: Commonhold and Leasehold Reform Act 2002 s 25(1).
7   Commonhold and Leasehold Reform Act 2002 s 29(1). As to commonhold associations see s 34(1), Sch 3; and COMMONHOLD vol 13 (2009) PARAS 305–306.
8   Commonhold and Leasehold Reform Act 2002 s 29(2)(a).
9   Commonhold and Leasehold Reform Act 2002 s 29(2)(b).
10   Commonhold and Leasehold Reform Act 2002 s 28(1).
11   See the Commonhold and Leasehold Reform Act 2002 s 28(2). See further s 28(3), (4); and COMMONHOLD vol 13 (2009) PARA 332.

178. Mortgage of incorporeal hereditaments. Incorporeal hereditaments, such as manors, commons, rentcharges and other property of a like nature existing in gross and apart from the ownership of corporeal property, may be the subject of a mortgage; but only such incorporeal hereditaments as can exist at law[1] can be the subject of a legal mortgage. The mortgage is in the same form, so far as applicable, as in the case of other hereditaments[2], and if it is a legal mortgage it must be by deed[3]. The only profitable parts of a manor which may now exist are mining rights, franchises and sporting rights preserved on the statutory enfranchisement of copyholds[4], and these may be the subject of a mortgage or included in a mortgage of the land with which they are held. An advowson[5] is often appendant to a manor, but cannot now be mortgaged[6]. A right of common in gross is an independent subject of property[7], but is seldom, if ever, met with as the subject of a mortgage. Grants of rentcharges can be mortgaged[8].

1 See the Law of Property Act 1925 s 1(2); and REAL PROPERTY AND REGISTRATION vol 87 (2012) PARA 63.
2 'Land' includes a manor and a rent and other incorporeal hereditaments (see the Law of Property Act 1925 s 205(i)(ix); and PARA 104 note 2); and the provisions of the Act relating to freehold land apply to manors, perpetual rentcharges, and other incorporeal hereditaments, subject only to the qualifications necessarily arising by reason of the inherent nature of the hereditaments affected (see s 201(1) (amended by the Tithe Act 1936 s 48(3), Sch 9)). Thus the method of mortgaging by demise or by legal charge applies, so far as appropriate, to those hereditaments: see PARA 164 et seq.
3 For the statutory provisions rendering a deed necessary in the case of a legal mortgage of land (including an incorporeal hereditament) see PARA 166. As to the necessity of a deed at common law see DEEDS AND OTHER INSTRUMENTS vol 32 (2012) PARA 210 et seq.
4 See REAL PROPERTY AND REGISTRATION vol 87 (2012) PARA 36 et seq. See also COMMONS vol 13 (2009) PARA 556 et seq; CUSTOM AND USAGE vol 32 (2012) PARA 43.
5 As to advowsons generally see ECCLESIASTICAL LAW vol 34 (2011) PARA 550.
6 See the Benefices Act 1898 s 1(1)(b), (7) (repealed); the Law of Property Act 1925 s 201(2); and ECCLESIASTICAL LAW vol 34 (2011) PARA 583.
7 See COMMONS vol 13 (2009) PARA 431 et seq.
8 As to rentcharges see REAL PROPERTY AND REGISTRATION vol 87 (2012) PARA 1104 et seq. As to the general extinguishment of tithe rentcharge see ECCLESIASTICAL LAW vol 34 (2011) PARA 979.

179. Agricultural mortgages and charges. The general law of mortgages and bills of sale applies to mortgages and charges of farms and stock[1]. In addition, there are special provisions for short-term credit by way of charge in favour of a bank on farming stock[2].

1 As to the prohibition on excluding the mortgagor's leasing powers see PARA 350. As to the Agricultural Mortgage Corporation see AGRICULTURAL LAND vol 1 (2008) PARA 618.
2 See AGRICULTURAL PRODUCTION AND MARKETING vol 1 (2008) PARAS 1328–1333.

180. Mortgage of mines. Mortgages of mineral property generally contain provisions similar to those inserted in mortgages of other descriptions of property of the like tenure[1]. However, owing to the wasting nature of the property, it is usual to provide for the repayment by instalments of the sum advanced[2], or by the creation of a sinking fund[3]. It is also desirable to provide that, in case of default, the mortgagee may enter upon the property and work the mine and make all proper expenditure for that purpose[4].

1 See PARA 181 et seq. See also MINES, MINERALS AND QUARRIES vol 76 (2013) PARA 311.
2 As to the effect of a provision for payment by instalments see PARA 185.
3 Similar provision may be made by means of a sinking fund policy.
4 In that case the mortgagee will on taking an account be allowed all proper expenditure, and, in redemption proceedings, will not be deprived of costs if he has refused to furnish an account at his own expense: *Norton v Cooper* (1854) 5 De GM & G 728. See also PARA 755. As to the rights

of a mortgagee in possession to work mines see MINES, MINERALS AND QUARRIES vol 76 (2013) PARA 381. As to the power of a mortgagee to sell minerals separately from the surface see PARA 467.

E. PROVISIONS OF LEGAL MORTGAGE AS TO PRINCIPAL AND INTEREST

181. Main provisions of a legal mortgage. The main provisions of a legal mortgage are:

(1)   a covenant to pay the principal debt and interest on a given date[1];

(2)   a covenant to pay interest in the event of default in payment of the principal on the day named[2];

(3)   the demise or sub-demise of, or the charge by way of legal mortgage on, the mortgaged property[3];

(4)   the proviso for cesser[4]; and

(5)   such variations of the statutory provisions with regard to mortgages as the arrangement between the parties requires[5].

1   See PARA 182 et seq.
2   See PARA 189 et seq.
3   See PARAS 164–165.
4   See PARAS 195–196.
5   See the Law of Property Act 1925 s 101(3); and PARAS 439, 443, 446. Any variations to the relevant statutory provisions can only be made by the mortgage deed itself. In the case of a registered charge, the mortgage deed will not be construed by reference to collateral documents such as the facility letter not available to third parties inspecting the register: *Cherry Tree Investments Ltd v Landmain Ltd* [2012] EWCA Civ 736, [2013] Ch 305, [2013] 2 WLR 481.

182. Covenant for repayment. The first operative part of a mortgage is usually the covenant by the mortgagor to pay the principal and interest on a day named[1]. If there is no covenant and no accompanying bond, there is still an implied promise to pay[2] in the case of a mortgage created by the borrower. In the case of other third party securities whether or not a covenant to pay is implied depends on the construction of the agreement[3]. As every loan transaction implies a right to be repaid, if a person lending money is never to have his principal back, there must be something very definite and clear showing that such was the condition of the contract[4].

The amount repayable may exceed the sum advanced, for example where a sum for interest is added to the principal as a premium[5], or a commission is payable[6], or the mortgage provides for a reasonable increase in the amount of the principal to take account of inflation[7].

1   As to covenants by trustee mortgagors see PARA 157.
2   *Sutton v Sutton* (1882) 22 ChD 511 at 515, CA, per Jessel MR; *Scottish Equitable plc v Thompson* [2003] EWCA Civ 211, [2003] HLR 690; *Wilkinson v West Bromwich Building Society* [2004] EWCA Civ 1063, 148 Sol Jo LB 975 (affd on another point sub nom *West Bromwich Building Society v Wilkinson* [2005] UKHL 44, [2005] 4 All ER 97, [2005] 1 WLR 2303). See also *Ezekiel v Orakpo* [1997] 1 WLR 340 at 346, CA, per Millett LJ. It is, however, possible to agree that repayment will be made exclusively from a particular source: see *Levett v Barclays Bank plc* [1995] 2 All ER 615, [1995] 1 WLR 1260. As to implied terms generally see CONTRACT vol 22 (2012) PARA 364 et seq. As to covenants arising by construction see DEEDS AND OTHER INSTRUMENTS vol 32 (2012) PARA 451 et seq. In the case of a charge registered under the Land Registration Act 1925, there was, in the absence of an entry on the register to the contrary, an implied covenant by the mortgagor to pay the sum secured: see s 28(1) (repealed). The registration of a charge which negatived or modified the implied covenant was deemed a sufficient negative or contrary entry on the register: see the Land Registration Rules 1925, SR & O 1925/1093, r 140 (revoked).
3   *National Provincial Bank Ltd v Liddiard* [1941] Ch 158, sub nom *Re National Provincial Bank Ltd* [1941] 1 All ER 97; *Tam Wing Chuen v Bank of Credit and Commerce Hong Kong Ltd* [1996] 2 BCLC 69, [1996] BCC 388, PC; *Re Bank of Credit and Commerce International SA (No 8)* [1998] AC 214, [1997] 4 All ER 568, HL; *Fairmile Portfolio Management Ltd v Davies Arnold Cooper* [1998] 42 LS Gaz R 34, [1998] EGCS 149.
4   *Hopkins v Worcester and Birmingham Canal Proprietors* (1868) LR 6 Eq 437.

5   Cf *Cityland and Property (Holdings) Ltd v Dabrah* [1968] Ch 166, [1967] 2 All ER 639.
6   As to bonus and commissions see PARA 324.
7   As to index-linking etc see *Multiservice Bookbinding Ltd v Marden* [1979] Ch 84, [1978] 2 All ER
    489; *Nationwide Building Society v Registry of Friendly Societies* [1983] 3 All ER 296, [1983] 1
    WLR 1226.

183.   Date for repayment. Fixing a day for payment does not generally indicate
the parties' intention that actual payment is to be made on the named date, but
only that the mortgagee may call for payment on or at any time after that date if
so minded, but not before[1]. The date fixed is usually six months from the date of
the loan or deed, but may be at the end of three months or any other period, or
the loan may be made repayable upon demand[2]. In general, the mortgagor may
not repay prior to the date fixed for repayment[3].

1   As to a covenant to pay a loan on a fixed day in a named month, without stating the year see
    Grannell v Monck (1889) 24 LR Ir 241. A provision that a term loan is subject to normal banking
    terms and conditions does not make it repayable on demand: *Cryne v Barclays Bank* [1987] BCLC
    548, CA.
2   As to the effect of such a covenant see PARA 539.
3   See PARA 332. As to cancellable regulated agreements under the Consumer Credit Act 1974 see
    ss 67–73; and CONSUMER CREDIT vol 21 (2011) PARA 195 et seq. Those provisions do not apply
    to certain land mortgages: see CONSUMER CREDIT vol 21 (2011) PARA 74.

184.   Length of notice required for payment. At common law, a covenant to pay
the principal money immediately on demand[1] or immediately after notice implies
such reasonable time as would allow the mortgagor to implement the mechanics
of payment but not to raise the money if it is not available[2]. If the demand is by
a person representing himself to be the mortgagee's agent, the mortgagor is
entitled to have time to inquire into the truth of the alleged agency[3]. If the loan is
made by a lender acting for purposes relating to his business to a consumer[4], a
term which was not individually negotiated that enables the lender to terminate a
loan facility of indeterminate duration on demand does not bind the borrower if
it is an unfair term[5]. A term may be regarded as unfair if it enables the lender to
terminate such a facility without reasonable notice except where there are serious
grounds for doing so or unless there is a valid reason (in which case the lender is
required to inform the borrower immediately)[6].

1   As to whether such a covenant requires an actual demand see PARA 539.
2   *Brighty v Norton* (1862) 3 B & S 305; *Toms v Wilson* (1863) 4 B & S 442 (affd 4 B & S 455, Ex
    Ch); *Massey v Sladen* (1868) LR 4 Exch 13; *Re Burghardt, ex p Trevor* (1875) 1 ChD 297; *Cripps
    (Pharmaceuticals) Ltd v Wickenden* [1973] 2 All ER 606, [1973] 1 WLR 944; *Bank of Baroda v
    Panessar* [1987] Ch 335, [1986] 3 All ER 751. As to whether a term can be implied requiring the
    bank to give reasonable notice see *Williams & Glyn's Bank Ltd v Barnes* [1981] Com LR 205;
    Cryne v Barclays Bank [1987] BCLC 548, CA. See also *Lloyds Bank plc v Jeffrey Lampert* [1999]
    Lloyd's Rep Bank 136, [1998] 3 EGLR 109, CA.
3   *Moore v Shelley* (1883) 8 App Cas 285, PC; *Toms v Wilson* (1863) 4 B & S 442 (affd 4 B & S 455,
    Ex Ch).
4   As to the meaning of 'consumer' see PARA 203 note 1.
5   As to the meaning of 'unfair term' and for guidance as to how to assess whether a term is unfair
    see PARA 203.
6   See PARA 203. As to unfair terms in consumer contracts see the Consumer Rights Act 2015 Pt 2
    (ss 61–76), Sch 2; and CONSUMER PROTECTION; CONTRACT.

185.   Payment of principal debt by instalments. The principal may be made
repayable by instalments with a stipulation that if the instalments and interest are
duly paid the repayment of the principal is not to be otherwise enforced[1]. Where
the principal debt is agreed to be repayable by instalments, the parties' intention
is assumed to be that the whole sum is to become immediately payable if default
is made in regular payment of the instalments; and this is provided for either:

(1)   by a covenant to pay the principal sum at a given date, with a proviso that if the sum is to be paid by the instalments mentioned in it the lender will not require payment otherwise; or

(2)   by a direct covenant to pay by instalments, with a proviso that in case of default in payment of any instalment the whole debt is to become immediately payable[2].

Such a proviso is binding and is not in the nature of a penalty[3]. Nor is it caught by the Unfair Contract Terms Act 1977[4].

1   As to commissions and fines on default of repayment by instalments see PARA 737.
2   Where in case of default the whole debt becomes payable on demand, an actual demand is required: *Esso Petroleum Co Ltd v Alstonbridge Properties Ltd* [1975] 3 All ER 358, [1975] 1 WLR 1474.
3   *Strene v Beck* (1863) 1 De GJ & Sm 595; *Thompson v Hudson* (1869) LR 4 HL 1; *Protector Endowment Loan and Annuity Co v Grice* (1880) 5 QBD 592, CA; *Wallingford v Mutual Society* (1880) 5 App Cas 685, HL; *Cityland and Property (Holdings) Ltd v Dabrah* [1968] Ch 166, [1967] 2 All ER 639. See also FINANCIAL INSTITUTIONS vol 48 (2015) PARA 487; EQUITABLE JURISDICTION vol 47 (2014) PARA 222. A provision that interest for the full term would also be payable at once would however be a penalty: *Oresundsvarvet Aktiebolag v Marcos Diamantis Lemos, The Angelic Star* [1988] 1 Lloyd's Rep 122, [1988] CCLR 39, CA.
4   Such a proviso is not caught by the Unfair Contract Terms Act 1977 s 3(2)(a) or (b) (see CONTRACT vol 22 (2012) PARA 411): *Nautch Ltd v Mortgage Express* [2012] EWHC 4136 (Ch), [2013] All ER (D) 115 (Mar).

186. Several mortgagees. Where several persons advance money on mortgage, there is a presumption that the money belongs to them in severalty even though the mortgage was made to them as joint tenants[1]. To obviate this, when trustees lend, it is usual to insert a statement that the money belongs to the lenders on a joint account[2]. Money advanced by more persons than one is deemed, as between them and the mortgagor, to belong to the survivor either where the advance is expressly stated to be on a joint account, or where the security is made to persons jointly[3], but this provision only applies if and so far as a contrary intention is not expressed in the mortgage[4]. An express mention of the joint account is not necessary, although it is convenient as a specific statement of the mortgagees' rights[5].

A statement that the money belongs to the mortgagees on a joint account does not affect their rights among themselves if, in fact, they are entitled to the money as tenants in common[6].

1   *Petty v Styward* (1631) 1 Eq Cas Abr 290; *Rigden v Vallier* (1751) 3 Atk 731 at 734; *Robinson v Preston* (1858) 4 K & J 505 at 511; *Steeds v Steeds* (1889) 22 QBD 537. See also EQUITABLE JURISDICTION vol 47 (2014) PARA 109.
2   See PARA 159.
3   See the Law of Property Act 1925 s 111(1).
4   See the Law of Property Act 1925 s 111(2).
5   As to the discharge of securities in favour of joint mortgagees see PARA 644.
6   *Re Jackson, Smith v Sibthorpe* (1887) 34 ChD 732.

187. Several mortgagors. Where there are several mortgagors the mortgage may, depending on its construction, either secure only joint liabilities or secure the several liabilities of any of the mortgagors; and where the 'mortgagor' is defined as referring to all and/or any one of those persons and their obligation is expressed to be joint and several, all mortgagors are jointly and severally liable for the several liabilities of each of them[1].

1   *AIB Group (UK) plc (formerly Allied Irish Banks plc and AIB Finance Ltd) v Martin* [2001] UKHL 63, [2002] 1 All ER 353, [2002] 1 WLR 94.

188. Agreement not to call in the principal. If a mortgage contains an unqualified stipulation that the principal money is not to be called in for a certain time, it is binding even if the interest falls into arrear, but in general the understanding of the parties is that such an indulgence is conditional upon punctual payment of the interest[1]; and, upon an agreement for a mortgage with a stipulation that the principal is not to be called in for a given period, the mortgage must be framed to make postponement conditional upon punctual payment of interest[2]. Where, under an agreement to forgo the right to call in the debt for a term if the interest is punctually paid, the interest is not paid punctually, the right to call in the principal accrues and there is no equitable relief[3]. The mortgagee does not merely by the subsequent receipt of interest waive his right to call in the principal before the end of the term[4], although receipt of interest is a matter to be taken into account in determining whether there has been a waiver[5].

1   *Seaton v Twyford* (1870) LR 11 Eq 591. A mortgagor who is in arrears for only a day or two cannot take advantage of a clause stipulating that the loan is not to be called in so long as the interest is punctually paid: *Hicks v Gardner* (1837) 1 Jur 541; *Leeds and Hanley Theatre of Varieties v Broadbent* [1898] 1 Ch 343, CA.
2   *Seaton v Twyford* (1870) LR 11 Eq 591 at 598 per Bacon V-C; *Burrowes v Molloy* (1845) 2 Jo & Lat 521 at 526; *Edwards v Martin* (1856) 25 LJCh 284; *Re Theobald, ex p Bignold* (1838) 3 Deac 151. See also *Tate v Crewdson* [1938] Ch 869, [1938] 3 All ER 43.
3   *Hicks v Gardner* (1837) 1 Jur 541; *Leeds and Hanley Theatre of Varieties v Broadbent* [1898] 1 Ch 343, CA. See also *Maclaine v Gatty* [1921] 1 AC 376, HL.
4   *Keene v Biscoe* (1878) 8 ChD 201.
5   *Seal v Gimson* (1914) 110 LT 583.

189. Payment of interest. The covenant fixing the date of payment generally provides for interest in the meantime[1]. This is not, however, necessary in the case of simple interest[2], for a mortgage, whether legal or equitable, carries interest even if interest is not expressly reserved[3] and even if it secures the debt of a third party who is not liable to pay interest to the creditor[4]. A power to charge an estate with a specific sum of money without mentioning interest includes a power to charge with interest[5], and the right to interest is implied where a principal sum is charged on property by court order[6]. Where a security is given by way of indemnity, it will cover interest on sums paid by the guarantor[7]. This, however, does not apply if the instrument expressly provides for cesser on repayment of the principal only[8]. If it is intended that contractual interest should continue to be payable after judgment, express provision should be made to that effect[9]. A charge to secure the payment of principal and interest by a third party secures such interest as is payable by the third party, and is not limited to simple interest[10].

1   As to the allowance of interest in taking accounts see PARA 727 et seq. As to restrictions on the increase of interest on certain mortgages to which the Rent Act 1977 applies see PARAS 532–533.
2   As to compound interest see PARA 191.
3   *Farquhar v Morris* (1797) 7 Term Rep 124; *Anon* (1813) 4 Taunt 876, Ex Ch; *Carey v Doyne* (1856) 5 I Ch R 104; *Re Every, ex p Hirtzel, ex p Hine* (1858) 3 De G & J 464; *Ashwell v Staunton* (1861) 30 Beav 52; *Re Kerr's Policy* (1869) LR 8 Eq 331; *Re King, ex p Furber* (1881) 17 ChD 191 at 196; *Re Drax, Savile v Drax* [1903] 1 Ch 781, CA; *Mendl v Smith* (1943) 112 LJCh 279; *Ezekiel v Orakpo* [1997] 1 WLR 340, CA. See also *Cityland and Property (Holdings) Ltd v Dabrah* [1968] Ch 166 at 182, [1967] 2 All ER 639 at 648 per Goff J.
4   *Al-Wazir v Islamic Press Agency Inc* [2001] EWCA Civ 1276, [2002] 2 P & CR 157, [2002] 1 Lloyd's Rep 410.
5   *Lord Kilmurry v Geery* (1713) 2 Salk 538.
6   *Lippard v Ricketts* (1872) LR 14 Eq 291; *Stoker v Elwell* [1942] Ch 243, [1942] 1 All ER 261; *Ezekiel v Orakpo* [1997] 1 WLR 340, CA.
7   *Fergus' Executors v Gore* (1803) 1 Sch & Lef 107 at 109; *Wainman v Bowker* (1845) 8 Beav 363.
8   *Thompson v Drew* (1855) 20 Beav 49, distinguished in *Mendl v Smith* (1943) 112 LJCh 279.
9   See PARA 735.
10 *Whitbread plc v UCB Corporate Services Ltd* [2000] 3 EGLR 60, [2000] 35 EG 136, CA.

190. Rate of interest. Where a right to interest is implied, interest was formerly allowed at the annual rate of 4 or 5 per cent[1], but now would probably be allowed at a more realistic rate[2]; and in any event the court has general power to re-open extortionate credit agreements[3]. In other cases there is no restriction on the rate of interest which may be charged. Equity does not reform mortgage transactions merely because they are unreasonable[4]. If some other provision in the mortgage relating to the interest could be set aside as an unreasonable collateral advantage, for example if all the interest calculated in advance became payable on early redemption, the court might, however, fix a lower rate of interest[5].

An agreement for interest to be payable at a variable rate determined by the lender from time to time is lawful at common law[6], but it is an implied term of the agreement that the rates of interest will not be set dishonestly, for an improper purpose, capriciously or arbitrarily, although that is not to imply a term that the lender will not set unreasonable rates[7]. It is also not a breach of such an implied term for a lender to increase rates in order to overcome his own financial difficulties[8]. If the loan is made by a lender acting for purposes relating to his business to a consumer[9], a term permitting variation which was not individually negotiated does not bind the borrower if it is an unfair term[10]. A term which has the object or effect of enabling the lender to alter the terms of the contract unilaterally without a valid reason which is specified in the contract is unfair[11]. However, this does not include a term by which a supplier of financial services reserves the right to alter the rate of interest payable by or due to the consumer, or the amount of other charges for financial services without notice where there is a valid reason, if:

(1)   the supplier is required to inform the consumer of the alteration at the earliest opportunity; and

(2)   the consumer is free to dissolve the contract immediately[12].

In the absence of express provision, the rate of interest may not be varied, although, if the money can be called in, this fact will usually be sufficient to make the borrower agree to a variation. Most building society and commercial mortgages explicitly provide for variation[13].

1   *Re Drax, Savile v Drax* [1903] 1 Ch 781, CA (4%); *Mendl v Smith* (1943) 112 LJCh 279 (5%). As to the rate of interest after judgment see PARA 735.
2   *Cityland and Property (Holdings) Ltd v Dabrah* [1968] Ch 166, [1967] 2 All ER 639 (7%); *Mathew v TM Sutton Ltd* [1994] 4 All ER 793, [1994] 1 WLR 1455.
3   See the Consumer Credit Act 1974 ss 140A–140C; and CONSUMER CREDIT vol 21 (2011) PARAS 287–289. See also the Insolvency Act 1986 s 343; and BANKRUPTCY AND INDIVIDUAL INSOLVENCY vol 5 (2013) PARA 697 et seq. Subsequent changes in rates of interest are not relevant to the question whether a credit agreement is extortionate (*Paragon Finance plc v Staunton* [2001] EWCA Civ 1466, [2002] 2 All ER 248, [2002] 1 WLR 685; *Broadwick Financial Services Ltd v Spencer* [2002] EWCA Civ 35, [2002] 1 All ER (Comm) 446), but failure of the lender to inform the borrower of a policy of operating the power to vary interest rates in a certain way, or not varying rates when market rates vary, could be relevant (*Broadwick Financial Services Ltd v Spencer*).
     In the case of moneylenders there was formerly a presumption that interest was excessive where the annual rate exceeded 48% (see the Moneylenders Act 1927 s 10(1) (repealed)), but the court could nevertheless hold that the interest charged, even if less than that rate, was excessive.
4   *Knightsbridge Estates Trust Ltd v Byrne* [1939] Ch 441 at 457, [1938] 4 All ER 618 at 626, CA, per Sir Wilfrid Greene MR.
5   *Cityland and Property (Holdings) Ltd v Dabrah* [1968] Ch 166, [1967] 2 All ER 639 (7% in place of 19% or, as a premium, 57%). See also *United Dominions Trust Ltd v Thomas* (1976) 120 Sol Jo 561 (county court).
6   *Lombard Tricity Finance Ltd v Paton* [1989] 1 All ER 918, 8 Tr LR 129, CA. See *Bank of Scotland v Ladjadj* [2000] 2 All ER (Comm) 583, CA (interpretation of terms in mortgage relating to option to pay interest at stabilised charging rate or fixed payment rate).

7 *Paragon Finance plc v Staunton* [2001] EWCA Civ 1466, [2002] 2 All ER 248, [2002] 1 WLR 685.

8 *Paragon Finance plc v Staunton* [2001] EWCA Civ 1466 at [46]–[48], [2002] 2 All ER 248, [2002] 1 WLR 685 per Dyson LJ.

9 As to the meaning of 'consumer' see PARA 203 note 1.

10 See PARA 203. As to unfair terms in consumer contracts see the Consumer Rights Act 2015 Pt 2 (ss 61–76), Sch 2; and CONSUMER PROTECTION; CONTRACT.

11 See the Consumer Rights Act 2015 s 63(1), Sch 2 Pt 1 para 11; and CONSUMER PROTECTION.

12 See the Consumer Rights Act 2015 s 63(2), Sch 2 Pt 1 para 22; and CONSUMER PROTECTION.

13 As to building societies see FINANCIAL INSTITUTIONS vol 48 (2015) PARA 330 et seq.

191. Compound interest. The mortgagor can validly agree to pay compound interest, and thus he can agree that interest in arrear is to be capitalised and is to bear interest at the same rate as the original advance[1]. Compound interest does not, however, become capital: it retains its character as interest[2]. However, the mortgagee may not charge compound interest except under an agreement to that effect[3]. The agreement may be either express or implied from the nature of the dealings[4]. A mere intimation by the mortgagee that he intends to charge compound interest is not enough; there must be assent by the mortgagor[5], and assent by the mortgagor to the appropriation by the mortgagee as between capital and interest can be inferred from the facts[6] where, for instance, the advances are made in the course of a trade or business in which compound interest is allowed[7]. Thus if the relation of bank and customer exists between mortgagee and mortgagor, and the mortgage is to secure a current account, the mortgagee is entitled to make up the account with yearly or half-yearly rests[8], and charge future interest on the aggregate balance of principal and interest appearing at each rest[9]. The banker's right to compound interest continues until repayment of the debt or judgment, notwithstanding the account ceasing to be current[10]. Similarly, where partnership accounts have been kept on the footing of yearly or half-yearly rests, this method probably continues to be applicable on the dissolution of the partnership[11]. The ordinary rule that receipts are first to be appropriated to payment of interest does not apply to such an account[12]. Under a mortgage to a bank for a fixed sum, however, the accounts must be kept on the footing of simple interest[13], unless otherwise agreed; although where the customer has settled accounts on the footing of compound interest, his executors may not be entitled to reopen them[14]. An agreement to pay interest on arrears existing at a certain date will be inferred where the interest has for a length of time been paid on an aggregate sum made up of the principal and those arrears[15].

1 *Clarkson v Henderson* (1880) 14 ChD 348; *Re Craven's Mortgage, Davies v Craven* [1907] 2 Ch 448; *Re Morris, Mayhew v Halton* [1922] 1 Ch 126, CA. As to the position of a mortgagee in possession in this respect see PARA 193. As to compound interest see further FINANCIAL INSTRUMENTS AND TRANSACTIONS vol 49 (2015) PARA 91. A capitalisation clause may prevent exercise of the power of sale on the ground that two months' interest is in arrears: see *Davy v Turner* (1970) 21 P & CR 967, 114 Sol Jo 884.

2 *IRC v Oswald* [1945] AC 360, [1945] 1 All ER 641, HL; *Whitbread plc v UCB Corporate Services Ltd* [2000] 3 EGLR 60, [2000] 35 EG 136, CA.

3 *Fergusson v Fyffe* (1841) 8 Cl & Fin 121, HL; *Daniell v Sinclair* (1881) 6 App Cas 181, PC; *Procter v Cooper* (1700) Prec Ch 116; *Brown v Barkham* (1720) 1 P Wms 652. Formerly an agreement in the mortgage for capitalising interest in arrear was void, as tending to usury (*Chambers v Goldwin* (1804) 9 Ves 254 at 271; *Mainland v Upjohn* (1889) 41 ChD 126 at 136), although, upon interest falling due, the parties might agree to turn it into principal (*Lord Ossulston v Lord Yarmouth* (1707) 2 Salk 449; *Thornhill v Evans* (1742) 2 Atk 330, where interest charged on arrears at a higher rate than that reserved was not allowed); and, accordingly, accounts might be settled half-yearly on this principle (*Ex p Bevan* (1803) 9 Ves 223; *Blackburn v Warwick* (1836) 2 Y & C Ex 92). The mortgagee may not, however, turn interest into principal against a subsequent incumbrancer of whose incumbrance he has notice: *Digby v Craggs* (1763) Amb 612. See also FINANCIAL INSTITUTIONS vol 48 (2015) PARA 487.

4   *Tompson v Leith* (1858) 4 Jur NS 1091.
5   *Tompson v Leith* (1858) 4 Jur NS 1091.
6   *Yourell v Hibernian Bank Ltd* [1918] AC 372, HL.
7   *Morgan v Mather* (1792) 2 Ves 15 at 20.
8   As to whether more frequent rests are permitted by usage see *National Bank of Greece SA v Pinios Shipping Co* [1990] 1 AC 637, [1990] 1 All ER 78, HL, where it was conceded that compound interest with quarterly rests could be charged. See also *First National Bank plc v Syed* [1991] 2 All ER 250, [1991] CCLR 37, CA (monthly rests).
9   *Lord Clancarty v Latouche* (1810) 1 Ball & B 420; *Rufford v Bishop* (1829) 5 Russ 346; *Thomas v Cooper* (1854) 18 Jur 688 at 690; *Imperial Life Assurance Co of Canada v Efficient Distributors Ltd* [1992] 2 AC 85, [1992] 2 WLR 503, PC. See also FINANCIAL INSTITUTIONS vol 48 (2015) PARA 285.
10   *National Bank of Greece SA v Pinios Shipping Co* [1990] 1 AC 637, [1990] 1 All ER 78, HL; *Bank of Credit and Commerce International SA v Malik* [1996] BCC 15.
11   See *National Bank of Greece SA v Pinios Shipping Co* [1990] 1 AC 637, [1990] 1 All ER 78, HL. Cf *Barfield v Loughborough* (1872) 8 Ch App 1 at 7.
12   *Parr's Banking Co Ltd v Yates* [1898] 2 QB 460, CA.
13   *Mosse v Salt* (1863) 32 Beav 269; *London Chartered Bank of Australia v White* (1879) 4 App Cas 413 at 424, PC. A mortgage for a fixed sum may be, however, in fact intended to cover a current account, and will so operate: *Thomas v Cooper* (1854) 18 Jur 688. See also PARA 732.
14   *Stewart v Stewart* (1891) 27 LR Ir 351 at 363.
15   *M'Carthy v Lord Llandaff* (1810) 1 Ball & B 375.

192. Reduction of interest on punctual payment. To induce punctual payment a proviso is often inserted in the mortgage for reduction of the rate of interest if the interest is paid within the time prescribed[1]. Even an oral agreement to reduce the rate of interest stipulated for in a mortgage may be valid[2]. An agreement for increasing the rate of interest on failure in punctual payment is, however, regarded as a penalty against which the courts will grant relief[3] unless it provides only for a modest increase from the date of default[4]. A proviso for reduction is construed strictly, so that the mortgagor must pay the higher rate unless payment is made within the stipulated time[5]. Unpunctuality on one occasion will not, if the words of the covenant point to payment of interest on any occasion, deprive the mortgagor of the benefit of the proviso for the future[6].

1   See DEEDS AND OTHER INSTRUMENTS vol 32 (2012) PARA 264.
2   *Lord Milton v Edgworth* (1773) 5 Bro Parl Cas 313, HL; *Gregory v Pilkington* (1856) 8 De GM & G 616; cf *Central London Property Trust Ltd v High Trees House Ltd* [1947] KB 130, [1956] 1 All ER 256n; but see also *Re Venning* (1947) 63 TLR 394 at 395, CA; and cf ESTOPPEL vol 47 (2014) PARA 385 et seq.
3   *Wallingford v Mutual Society* (1880) 5 App Cas 685 at 702, HL. See also EQUITABLE JURISDICTION vol 47 (2014) PARA 221.
4   *Lordsvale Finance plc v Bank of Zambia* [1996] QB 752, [1996] 3 All ER 156. As to provisions for the payment of commission or fines in the event of default see PARA 737.
5   *Jory v Cox* (1701) Prec Ch 160; *Stanhope v Manners* (1763) 2 Eden 197; *Wayne v Lewis* (1855) 25 LTOS 264; *Nicholls v Maynard, ex p Marquis of Powis* (1747) 3 Atk 519; *Union Bank of London v Ingram* (1880) 16 ChD 53; *Maclaine v Gatty* [1921] 1 AC 376, HL.
6   *Stanhope v Manners* (1763) 2 Eden 197.

193. Mortgagee in possession. Where the proviso is for reduction of interest on punctual payment[1], a mortgagee in possession may charge the mortgagor with the higher rate even though he receives rent more than sufficient to pay the interest, and even though no interest was in arrear at the time of his taking possession[2]. The receipt of rents by the mortgagee is not a payment by the mortgagor or by anyone on his behalf. The mortgagee receives rents which are his own, subject to the right of redemption[3]; but, under a proviso for the capitalisation of interest if it should be in arrear for 21 days, a mortgagee who enters into possession and has in his hands rents sufficient after deducting proper outgoings for payment of interest cannot claim that the interest is in arrear[4].

1 See PARA 192.
2 *Union Bank of London v Ingram* (1880) 16 ChD 53; *Bright v Campbell* (1889) 41 ChD 388.
3 See *Cockburn v Edwards* (1881) 18 ChD 449 at 457, CA, per Jessel MR, and at 463 per Cotton LJ.
   As to the equity of redemption see PARAS 107, 304 et seq.
4 *Wrigley v Gill* [1906] 1 Ch 165, CA.

194. Payment of interest after repayment date. It is usual to insert in the mortgage a covenant for payment of the interest: this enables the interest to be sued for apart from the principal, although a separate covenant is not absolutely necessary for this purpose[1].

If the mortgage makes provision for payment of the principal on a day certain, with interest at a fixed rate down to that day, there is no implied contract for the continuance of interest at the same rate or at any rate at all after that day; but a stipulation in the mortgage that the mortgagor will not transfer the property until payment in full of principal and interest implies an agreement for the continuance of this original interest until payment[2]. Interest is given in these cases, not as interest payable under the contract, but by way of damages for detention of the debt[3].

The rate of interest given by way of damages was usually 5 per cent[4], but the rate now given will presumably be the current rate of interest on damages which may be awarded by the High Court[5].

In any case a distinct stipulation as to interest will be binding[6].

1 *Dickenson v Harrison* (1817) 4 Price 282. As to payment of interest see PARA 189.
2 *Mathura Das v Raja Narinda Bahadur Pal* (1896) 12 TLR 609, PC.
3 *Cook v Fowler* (1874) LR 7 HL 27 at 32, 37; *Price v Great Western Rly Co* (1847) 16 M & W 244 at 248; *Re Roberts, Goodchap v Roberts* (1880) 14 ChD 49, CA; *Goldstrom v Tallerman* (1886) 18 QBD 1 at 4, CA.
4 *Re Roberts, Goodchap v Roberts* (1880) 14 ChD 49, CA; *Mellersh v Brown* (1890) 45 ChD 225. However, in *Morgan v Jones* (1853) 8 Exch 620 on a mortgage of a ship, the original interest of 10% was allowed. In *Gordillo v Weguelin* (1877) 5 ChD 287 at 303, CA, it was said that the jury would be directed as a matter of law to find damages at the rate of the original interest, but this is questionable. Cf *C and M Matthews Ltd v Marsden Building Society* [1951] Ch 758, [1951] 1 All ER 1053, CA, where the rate of interest was 82½%.
5 See the Senior Courts Act 1981 s 35A; and DAMAGES vol 29 (2014) PARA 635. See also *Cityland and Property (Holdings) Ltd v Dabrah* [1968] Ch 166, [1967] 2 All ER 639.
6 *Re King, ex p Furber* (1881) 17 ChD 191. As to the effect of a proviso limiting the amount to be recovered under a mortgage see PARA 730.

F.   PROVISIONS OF LEGAL MORTGAGE AS TO CESSER

195. Proviso for cesser or discharge. In a legal mortgage by demise[1], the former proviso for redemption[2] has been replaced by a proviso for cesser. This provides that if the mortgagor on a given day pays to the mortgagee the debt and interest the mortgage term is to cease[3]. In the case of a legal charge[4] there is a similar proviso that on payment on the given day the mortgagee will duly discharge the security. Since in the former case the term ceases and in the latter case the legal charge is discharged by payment, the proviso for cesser and the proviso for discharge are not essential, but they are inserted in order to fix the end of the legal right of redemption[5].

1 As to mortgage by demise see PARA 164.
2 The proviso for redemption is, however, still appropriate where a mortgage of an equitable interest in land has been made by conveyance of that interest: see PARA 215.
3 The mortgagor's legal estate is therefore not directly affected.

4   As to mortgage by legal charge see PARA 165.
5   As to the right of redemption see PARAS 107, 304 et seq.

196. Restrictions on the right of redemption. The mortgagor cannot generally compel the mortgagee to accept payment of the mortgage money before the day of payment appointed in the proviso for redemption[1]. A stipulation in a mortgage that the principal debt is not to be called in for a given period is often accompanied by a corresponding stipulation that the mortgagor is not to be entitled without the mortgagee's consent to pay off or redeem the mortgage before the expiration of the period. Although the law will not allow a mortgagor to be precluded from redeeming altogether[2], he may be precluded from redeeming for a fixed period, such as five or seven years[3]; but this does not prohibit the court in a proper case from preventing the application of the clause if it is too large or there are circumstances connected with the proviso which render it, in the court's opinion, unreasonable and oppressive[4]. A proviso against redemption for a period is not binding in the absence of a mutual provision for the continuance of the loan for that period[5].

1   See PARA 332. As to the equity of redemption see PARAS 107, 304 et seq.
2   See PARAS 107, 320 et seq.
3   *Teevan v Smith* (1882) 20 ChD 724 at 729, CA; *Biggs v Hoddinott, Hoddinott v Biggs* [1898] 2 Ch 307 at 311, CA; *Bradley v Carritt* [1903] AC 253 at 259, HL. Although 'five or seven years' was mentioned as permissible in *Teevan v Smith*, eight years was allowed in *Re Hone's Estate* (1873) 8 IR Eq 65, and ten years in *Re Fortesque's Estate* [1916] 1 IR 268, CA. As to unreasonable periods see PARA 321.
4   *Biggs v Hoddinott, Hoddinott v Biggs* [1898] 2 Ch 307, CA; *Davis v Symons* [1934] Ch 442.
5   *Morgan v Jeffreys* [1910] 1 Ch 620.

G.   OTHER PROVISIONS OF LEGAL MORTGAGES

197. Covenants for title. Certain covenants for title will be implied in a mortgage, in different terms according to when the mortgage was granted and the capacity of the mortgagor. In an instrument[1] effecting or purporting to effect a charge or mortgage[2] and expressed to be made with full or limited title guarantee, covenants are implied that the person making the disposition has the right, with the concurrence of any other mortgagor, to dispose of the property as he purports to do[3] and that he will, at his own cost, do all that he reasonably can do to give the mortgagee the title he purports to give[4]. The benefit of the covenants goes with the estate or interest of the person to whom the disposition is made and is capable of being enforced by every person in whom that estate or interest is (in whole or in part) for the time being vested[5]. In the case of leasehold land, covenants will also be implied that the lease is subsisting at the time of the disposition[6]; that there is no subsisting breach of a condition or tenant's obligation and nothing which will render the lease liable to forfeiture[7]; and that the mortgagor will fully and promptly observe and perform all obligations under the lease or any rentcharge to which the property is subject[8]. If the property is a commonhold unit[9], there is implied a covenant that the mortgagor will fully and promptly observe and perform all the obligations under the commonhold community statement[10] that are for the time being imposed on him in his capacity as a unit-holder[11] or as a joint unit-holder[12].

In an instrument effecting or purporting to effect a charge or mortgage and expressed to be made with full title guarantee, covenants are also implied that the mortgagor is creating the mortgage free from all charges and incumbrances and free from all rights exercisable by third parties other than any charges, incumbrances or rights which the mortgagor does not and could not reasonably be expected to know about and certain statutory charges which do not constitute defects in title[13]. Where only a limited title guarantee is given, there is implied a covenant that the mortgagor has not, since the last disposition for value, created any charge or incumbrance or granted any third party rights which subsist at the time of the mortgage, and that the mortgagor has not suffered anyone else to do so and is not aware that anyone else has done so[14].

Such covenants do not impose liability if and in so far as they are expressly limited or excluded, in respect of any matter to which the mortgage is made subject or for anything which is within the actual knowledge of the mortgagee or which is a necessary consequence of facts within his actual knowledge[15].

In a deed of statutory mortgage[16] or of statutory transfer of mortgage[17], made by two or more mortgagors or covenantors, the implied covenant is deemed to be a joint and several covenant by them; and where there are two or more mortgagees or transferees, the implied covenant is deemed to be with them jointly, unless the amount secured is expressed to be secured to them in shares or distinct sums, in which case the implied covenant is deemed to be a covenant with each severally, in respect of the share or distinct sums secured to him[18].

1   'Instrument' includes an instrument which is not a deed: Law of Property (Miscellaneous Provisions) Act 1994 s 1(4). As to what constitutes a deed see DEEDS AND OTHER INSTRUMENTS vol 32 (2012) PARA 201 et seq.

2   The Law of Property (Miscellaneous Provisions) Act 1994 applies to dispositions of property. 'Disposition' includes the creation of a term of years; and 'property' includes a thing in action, and any interest in real or personal property: s 1(4).

3   The mortgagor is presumed to purport to dispose of the whole of the registered title or, in the case of unregistered property, the fee simple or unexpired term, as the case may be: see the Law of Property (Miscellaneous Provisions) Act 1994 s 2(3); and CONVEYANCING vol 23 (2013) PARA 146.

4   See the Law of Property (Miscellaneous Provisions) Act 1994 ss 1(2), 2; and CONVEYANCING vol 23 (2013) PARA 146. This has been the case since 1 July 1995 (ie the date on which the substantive provisions of the Law of Property (Miscellaneous Provisions) Act 1994 were brought into force by the Law of Property (Miscellaneous Provisions) Act 1994 (Commencement No 2) Order 1995, SI 1995/1317).
    In a mortgage created before 1 July 1995 by a mortgagor conveying as beneficial owner, the covenants implied were for the right to convey, for quiet enjoyment after default, for freedom from incumbrances, and for further assurance; and in the case of a mortgage of leasehold property, the further covenants were that the lease was valid and that the rents and covenants had been paid and performed, and for the indemnity of the mortgagee in respect of the rents and covenants in the future: Law of Property Act 1925 s 76(1)(C), (D), Sch 2 Pts III, IV (repealed). No covenants were implied where the person conveying was not expressed to convey in one of the capacities mentioned in the Law of Property Act 1925 s 76 (repealed), which include that of mortgagee: s 76(4) (repealed). The implied covenants are normally deemed to have been made by the mortgagor or each mortgagor, as regards the subject matter or share of subject matter expressed to be mortgaged by him, with the person, if one, to whom the mortgage was made, or with the persons jointly, if more than one, to whom the mortgage was made: see s 76(1) (repealed). The benefit of the covenants was to go with the covenantee's estate or interest and was capable of being enforced by every person in whom that estate or interest was, for the whole or any part thereof, from time to time vested: see s 76(6) (repealed). The implied covenants were variable or extendable by the mortgage deed and, once so varied or extended, would, as far as may be, operate, in the like manner, and with all the like incidents, effects and consequences, as if such variations or extensions were directed by statute to be implied: see s 76(7) (repealed). A person joining in the assurance, but having no beneficial interest in the property, conveys as trustee or as mortgagee, and this will only imply a covenant against incumbrances to which he has been a party: s 76(1)(F), Sch 2 Pt VI (repealed). In the Law of Property Act 1925, 'incumbrance' includes a legal or equitable mortgage and a trust for securing money, and a lien, and a charge of a portion, annuity or other capital or annual sum; and 'incumbrancer' has a corresponding meaning and includes every person entitled to the benefit of an incumbrance or to require its payment or discharge: s 205(1)(vii). As to the meaning of 'legal mortgage' see PARA 104 note 1; and as to the meaning of 'equitable mortgage' see PARA 105. Section 76 and Sch 2 were repealed as regards dispositions of property made after

1 July 1995, subject to transitional provisions for mortgages made pursuant to contracts entered into before that date, by the Law of Property (Miscellaneous Provisions) Act 1994 ss 10(1), (2), 21(2), (3), Sch 2.

As to implied covenants in relation to dispositions of land see further CONVEYANCING vol 23 (2013) PARA 145. As to the effect of the implied covenants in the case of registered land see REAL PROPERTY AND REGISTRATION vol 87 (2012) PARA 485 et seq.

5   Law of Property (Miscellaneous Provisions) Act 1994 s 7.
6   See the Law of Property (Miscellaneous Provisions) Act 1994 ss 1(2), 4(1)(a); and CONVEYANCING vol 23 (2013) PARA 146.
7   See the Law of Property (Miscellaneous Provisions) Act 1994 ss 1(2), 4(1)(b); and CONVEYANCING vol 23 (2013) PARA 146.
8   See the Law of Property (Miscellaneous Provisions) Act 1994 ss 1(2), 5(2), (3); and CONVEYANCING vol 23 (2013) PARA 146. This has been the case since 1 July 1995: see note 4.
9   As to the meaning of 'commonhold unit' see PARA 177 note 1; definition applied by the Law of Property (Miscellaneous Provisions) Act 1994 s 5(4)(a) (s 5(4) substituted by the Commonhold and Leasehold Reform Act 2002 s 68, Sch 5 para 7(1), (4)).
10 As to commonhold community statements see COMMONHOLD vol 13 (2009) PARA 311; definition applied by the Law of Property (Miscellaneous Provisions) Act 1994 s 5(4)(a) (as substituted: see note 9).
11 As to the meaning of 'unit-holder of a commonhold unit' see PARA 177 note 1; definition applied by the Law of Property (Miscellaneous Provisions) Act 1994 s 5(4)(a) (as substituted: see note 9).
12 Law of Property (Miscellaneous Provisions) Act 1994 s 5(3A) (added by the Commonhold and Leasehold Reform Act 2002 s 68, Sch 5 para 7(1), (3)). Two or more persons are joint unit-holders of a commonhold unit if they are entitled to be registered as proprietors of the freehold estate in the unit (whether or not they are registered): Commonhold and Leasehold Reform Act 2002 s 13(1); applied by the Law of Property (Miscellaneous Provisions) Act 1994 s 5(4)(a) (as substituted: see note 9).
13 See the Law of Property (Miscellaneous Provisions) Act 1994 ss 1(2), 3(1), (2); and CONVEYANCING vol 23 (2013) PARA 146. This has been the case since 1 July 1995: see note 4.
14 See the Law of Property (Miscellaneous Provisions) Act 1994 ss 1(2), 3(3); and CONVEYANCING vol 23 (2013) PARA 146. This has been the case since 1 July 1995: see note 4.
15 See the Law of Property (Miscellaneous Provisions) Act 1994 ss 6, 8; and CONVEYANCING vol 23 (2013) PARA 146.
16 See the Law of Property Act 1925 s 117(1); and PARA 166.
17 See the Law of Property Act 1925 s 118(1); and PARA 376.
18 See the Law of Property Act 1925 s 119.

198.   Power of sale. An important incident of a mortgage is the power to sell the property in default of payment of the debt. An express power is seldom now inserted, reliance being placed upon the statutory power[1]. The statutory power may be, and is frequently, varied or extended, and it applies to the mortgage only so far as a contrary intention is not expressed in the mortgage deed[2].

1   As to the statutory power of sale see the Law of Property Act 1925 s 101(1)(i); and PARA 446.
2   See the Law of Property Act 1925 s 101(3), (4); and PARA 446 et seq.

199.   Obligation to repair. There is no statutory obligation on a mortgagor to keep the premises in repair. Provision upon the subject should be made where the nature of the property so requires[1].

1   As to a mortgagor's liability for waste see PARA 360. As to his position as tenant see PARA 344; and LANDLORD AND TENANT vol 62 (2012) PARA 573 et seq.

200.   Powers to grant leases and accept surrenders. A mortgage frequently imposes restrictions upon the exercise of the mortgagor's statutory powers to grant leases[1] and accept surrenders of leases[2], by providing that the powers are not to be exercised without the mortgagee's written consent. In general, the statutory powers apply only so far as a contrary intention is not expressed in the mortgage, and may be extended by written agreement between the parties[3].

1   As to such powers see the Law of Property Act 1925 s 99; and PARA 349 et seq.
2   As to such powers see the Law of Property Act 1925 s 100; and PARA 355.
3   See the Law of Property Act 1925 ss 99(13), (13A), (13B), 100(7), (10); and PARAS 350, 355, 357.

201. Covenant to insure the security. A mortgage deed usually includes a covenant to insure the security. A mortgagee[1] by deed has power[2] at any time after the date of the deed to insure, and keep insured, against fire any building, effects or property of an insurable nature comprised in the mortgage[3], and the premiums paid are a charge on the mortgaged property, in addition to the mortgage money, with the same priority and so as to carry interest at the same rate as the mortgage money[4]. The amount of the insurance effected must not exceed the amount specified in the mortgage deed, or, if no amount is so specified, must not exceed two-thirds of the amount that would be required, in case of total destruction, to restore the property insured[5]. No insurance is to be effected where there is a declaration in the mortgage deed that no insurance is required[6]; nor where an insurance is kept up by or on behalf of the mortgagor[7] in accordance with the mortgage deed[8]; nor where the mortgage deed contains no stipulation respecting insurance, and an insurance is kept up by or on behalf of the mortgagor with the consent of the mortgagee, to the amount to which the mortgagee is authorised[9] to insure[10].

1   As to the meaning of 'mortgagee' see PARA 104 note 1.
2   As regards a mortgagee having an insurable interest see INSURANCE vol 60 (2011) PARA 586.
3   As to the meaning of 'mortgage' see PARA 101 note 4.
4   Law of Property Act 1925 s 101(1)(ii). As to the meaning of 'mortgage money' see PARA 104 note 1. The premiums are only a charge on the property, and cannot be recovered from the mortgagor as a debt, so the practice continues of inserting a covenant for their repayment in the mortgage deed.
5   Law of Property Act 1925 s 108(1). As to the application of insurance money see PARA 173.
6   Law of Property Act 1925 s 108(2)(i).
7   As to the meaning of 'mortgagor' see PARA 104 note 1.
8   Law of Property Act 1925 s 108(2)(ii).
9   Ie by the Law of Property Act 1925.
10 Law of Property Act 1925 s 108(2)(iii).

202. Attornment clause. Sometimes an attornment clause is inserted when the mortgagor is himself in occupation of all or any part of the mortgaged property, but such a clause is of dubious value[1].

1   See PARA 346.

H.   UNFAIR CONTRACT TERMS IN MORTGAGES GRANTED BY CONSUMERS

203. Mortgage terms regarded as unfair. Mortgage terms, like the terms of other contracts between traders and consumers[1], are governed by the Consumer Rights Act 2015 to determine whether they are unfair[2]. An unfair term in a mortgage contract is not binding on the borrower[3], but this does not prevent the borrower from relying on the term if he chooses to do so[4].

A mortgage term is unfair if, contrary to the requirement of good faith, it causes a significant imbalance in the parties' rights and obligations under the contract to the detriment of the borrower[5]. Whether a term is fair is to be determined taking into account the nature of the subject matter of the contract, and by reference to all the circumstances existing when the term was agreed and to all of the other terms of the contract or of any other contract on which it depends[6].

The Consumer Rights Act 2015 sets out an indicative and non-exhaustive list of terms of consumer contracts that may be regarded as unfair[7]. While a term which has the object or effect of enabling the lender to alter the terms of the contract unilaterally without a valid reason which is specified in the contract will be ruled unfair[8], this does not apply to a term by which a supplier of financial services reserves the right to alter the rate of interest payable by or due to the consumer, or the amount of other charges for financial services without notice where there is a valid reason, if:

(1)   the supplier is required to inform the consumer of the alteration at the earliest opportunity; and

(2)   the consumer is free to dissolve the contract immediately[9].

1   Mortgage lenders and borrowers come within the definitions of 'trader' and 'consumer' respectively in the Consumer Rights Act 2015. 'Trader' means a person acting for purposes relating to that person's trade, business, craft or profession, whether acting personally or through another person acting in the trader's name or on the trader's behalf: s 2(2). 'Consumer' means an individual acting for purposes that are wholly or mainly outside that individual's trade, business, craft or profession: s 2(3). A borrower who took out a mortgage for both business and personal purposes was capable of being a consumer for the purposes of the Unfair Terms in Consumer Contracts Regulations 1999, SI 1999/2083 (now revoked and replaced by the Consumer Rights Act 2015): see *Evans v CherryTree Finance Ltd* [2008] EWCA Civ 331, [2008] All ER (D) 86 (Feb).
2   See the Consumer Rights Act 2015 Pt 2 (ss 61–76); and CONSUMER PROTECTION; CONTRACT.
3   See the Consumer Rights Act 2015 s 62(1); and CONSUMER PROTECTION.
4   See the Consumer Rights Act 2015 s 62(3); and CONSUMER PROTECTION.
5   See the Consumer Rights Act 2015 s 62(4); and CONSUMER PROTECTION.
6   See the Consumer Rights Act 2015 s 62(5); and CONSUMER PROTECTION.
7   See the Consumer Rights Act 2015 s 63(1), Sch 2 Pt 1 paras 1–20; and CONSUMER PROTECTION.
8   See the Consumer Rights Act 2015 Sch 2 Pt 1 para 11; and CONSUMER PROTECTION.
9   See the Consumer Rights Act 2015 Sch 2 Pt 2 para 22; and CONSUMER PROTECTION.

204.   Consequences of inclusion of unfair terms in contracts. Where a term of a mortgage contract is not binding on the borrower as a result of its being unfair under the Consumer Rights Act 2015[1], the mortgage contract continues, so far as practicable, to have effect in every other respect[2].

1   Ie under the Consumer Rights Act 2015 Pt 2 (ss 61–76): see PARA 203.
2   See the Consumer Rights Act 2015 s 67; and CONSUMER PROTECTION; CONTRACT.

(iii) Legal Mortgages of Personalty

A.   PERSONAL CHATTELS AND CHOSES IN ACTION

205.   Mortgages of personal chattels. Personal chattels may be made security for repayment of a debt in two ways, namely by pledge[1] or by mortgage[2]. If a mortgage of personal chattels is in writing it is subject to the statutory provisions affecting bills of sale[3], but such a mortgage may be made orally and need not be in writing[4]. A parol mortgage of chattels, completed by actual delivery, is not within the statutory provisions affecting bills of sale[5], and the terms of the mortgage may be proved by oral evidence[6]. A parol mortgage, even without delivery, is good at common law, although as the chattels then remain in the debtor's order and disposition the mortgagee has no priority over the general creditors upon the debtor's bankruptcy[7]. Mortgages of ships and aircraft, debentures of incorporated companies and certain agricultural charges are excluded from the operation of the statutory provisions affecting bills of sale[8].

1   As to the distinction between a mortgage and a pledge see PARA 112.
2   As to the effect of the Consumer Credit Act 1974 see PARA 116.
3   See FINANCIAL INSTRUMENTS AND TRANSACTIONS vol 49 (2015) PARA 403 et seq. As to the meaning of 'personal chattels' for these purposes see the Bills of Sale Act 1878 ss 4, 5; and FINANCIAL INSTRUMENTS AND TRANSACTIONS vol 49 (2015) PARA 445 et seq. As to floating charges of companies see COMPANIES vol 15 (2009) PARA 1269 et seq.
4   Co Litt 225 a, 226a; *Reeves v Capper* (1838) 5 Bing NC 136; *Flory v Denny* (1852) 7 Exch 581.
5   See FINANCIAL INSTRUMENTS AND TRANSACTIONS vol 49 (2015) PARA 422.

6 Cf *Woodgate v Godfrey* (1879) 5 ExD 24, CA; *North Central Wagon Co v Manchester, Sheffield and Lincolnshire Rly Co* (1887) 35 ChD 191 at 203, CA.
7 See BANKRUPTCY AND INDIVIDUAL INSOLVENCY vol 5 (2013) PARA 428.
8 See FINANCIAL INSTRUMENTS AND TRANSACTIONS vol 49 (2015) PARAS 467, 471–473. As to mortgages of ships see PARA 212. As to mortgages of aircraft see PARA 214.

206. Mortgages of choses or things in action. Debts and other legal choses or things in action may be the subject of legal mortgages[1]. The statutory provisions affecting bills of sale do not apply to mortgages of things in action[2].

1 Eg life insurance policies (see PARAS 207–210) or stocks and shares (see PARA 211). As to legal choses in action see CHOSES IN ACTION vol 13 (2009) PARA 3.
2 See the Bills of Sale Act 1878 s 4; and FINANCIAL INSTRUMENTS AND TRANSACTIONS vol 49 (2015) PARA 445. As to charges created by companies see COMPANIES vol 15 (2009) PARA 1256 et seq.

B. LIFE INSURANCE POLICIES

207. Covenants for title. The security for a mortgage of a life insurance policy normally contains express covenants[1] for whatever acts the mortgagee requires the mortgagor to perform or abstain from. The covenants by the mortgagor which are usually inserted are not to permit the policy to become void, and if it becomes void to effect a new policy in lieu of it; and to pay the premiums and deliver receipts to the mortgagee. It is also usual to insert a provision that the mortgagee may keep the policy on foot in case the mortgagor neglects to do so, and that the money advanced for that purpose is to be a charge on the policy. Even without such an express provision, the mortgagee is entitled to charge the property with any sums he may advance for keeping up the policy[2].

1 As to implied covenants for title see PARA 197.
2 *Bellamy v Brickenden* (1861) 2 John & H 137; *Gill v Downing* (1874) LR 17 Eq 316.

208. Priority of mortgages of life insurance policies. The mortgagee of a life insurance policy may sue in his own name[1]. Notice of the mortgage must, however, be given to the insurance office, and the dates on which several notices are received will regulate the priority of all claims under different assignments[2]. A letter by a debtor enclosing a policy on his life and requesting the creditor to instruct his solicitor to prepare the necessary assignment[3], or a memorandum accompanying a deposit of a policy by which the borrower agrees to execute a valid mortgage upon request[4], are not assignments for this purpose[5]. A second mortgagee with notice of a first mortgage does not, however, gain priority over the first mortgagee by giving the first notice to the insurance company[6]; and non-production of the policy to the second mortgagee affects him with constructive notice of the first mortgage[7].

1 See the Policies of Assurance Act 1867 s 1; and INSURANCE vol 60 (2011) PARAS 499–502. The provisions of the Policies of Assurance Act 1867 are not affected by the Law of Property Act 1925 s 136: see s 136(2); and INSURANCE vol 60 (2011) PARA 499.
2 See the Policies of Assurance Act 1867 s 3; and INSURANCE vol 60 (2011) PARA 500.
3 *Crossley v City of Glasgow Life Assurance Co* (1876) 4 ChD 421.
4 *Spencer v Clarke* (1878) 9 ChD 137.
5 Ie for the purposes of the Policies of Assurance Act 1867 s 1.
6 *Newman v Newman* (1885) 28 ChD 674.
7 *Spencer v Clarke* (1878) 9 ChD 137; *Re Weniger's Policy* [1910] 2 Ch 291.

209. Power of sale applies to mortgages by deed of life policies. The statutory power of sale conferred on mortgagees applies to mortgages by deed of policies and other choses or things in action[1].

1 As to the statutory power of sale see PARA 446 et seq.

210. Ownership of the life insurance policy. When an insurance policy is taken out by the creditor on the debtor's life as part of his security, and the premiums are paid by the debtor or charged against him in account, or if it is agreed or can be inferred from the bargain between the parties that the debtor has undertaken to pay the premiums, then the policy, or the balance of the insurance money after discharge of the debt, belongs to the debtor[1]. If the debtor is charged with the premiums in account with the creditor and has not disputed his liability to pay them, his refusal to pay the premiums will not destroy his right to the policy[2]. However, if a mortgagee of an annuity or other property which depends upon a life insures the mortgagor's life merely for his own protection, paying the premiums out of his own pocket, the policy belongs to the mortgagee[3]; and the mere fact that the creditor has charged the premiums against the debtor without the debtor having agreed to pay them does not give the debtor a right to the policy[4].

1 *Holland v Smith* (1806) 6 Esp 11; *Morland v Isaac* (1855) 20 Beav 389; *Re Storie's Will Trusts* (1859) 1 Giff 94; *Lea v Hinton* (1854) 5 De GM & G 823; *Courtenay v Wright* (1860) 2 Giff 337; *Salt v Marquess of Northampton* [1892] AC 1 at 16, HL. As to ownership of joint policies see *Davitt v Titcumb* [1990] Ch 110, [1989] 3 All ER 417; *Smith v Clerical Medical and General Life Assurance Society* [1992] 1 FCR 262, [1993] 1 FLR 47, CA.
2 *Drysdale v Piggott* (1856) 8 De GM & G 546. See also INSURANCE vol 60 (2011) PARA 510.
3 *Gottlieb v Cranch* (1853) 4 De GM & G 440; *Re Jacob's Estate, Lancaster v Gaselee, ex p Lancaster* (1851) 4 De G & Sm 524; *Preston v Neele* (1879) 12 ChD 760. For the analogous case of a mortgage indemnity policy see PARA 174.
4 *Bruce v Garden* (1869) 5 Ch App 32.

C. STOCKS AND SHARES

211. Mortgage of stocks and shares. A mortgagee's legal title to stocks and shares in a public company is given by a transfer and due registration of the stocks or shares in the mortgagee's name[1]. The mortgagor's interest in the shares cannot be noted on the register of members[2], but the transfer is generally accompanied by an independent document setting forth the actual nature of the security and providing for a re-transfer on redemption. In this case the mortgagee becomes a member of the company[3] and is liable for calls if the shares are not fully paid up, but, if the mortgage is under seal, he has a statutory power of sale[4]. Where shares are transferable only by deed[5] and the deed of transfer is invalid, registration of the transferee does not give him any title[6]; nor does he acquire a legal title until all the conditions required by the articles of association of the company have been fulfilled to give him, as between himself and the company, a present, absolute and unconditional right to have the transfer registered[7].

1 As to the transfer of shares see COMPANIES vol 14 (2009) PARA 389 et seq. As to the inclusion of a power of attorney in a mortgage of shares in a private company see *Hunter v Hunter* [1936] AC 222 at 248, HL, per Viscount Hailsham LC. As to the effect of a blank transfer see PARA 244.
2 No notice of any trust, express, implied or constructive, is to be entered on the register, or receivable by the registrar in the case of companies registered in England and Wales: see the Companies Act 2006 s 126; and COMPANIES vol 14 (2009) PARA 343.
3 See *Musselwhite v CH Musselwhite & Son Ltd* [1962] Ch 964, [1962] 1 All ER 201.
4 See the Law of Property Act 1925 ss 101, 103; and PARA 446 et seq.
5 As to the form and execution of transfers see COMPANIES vol 14 (2009) PARA 399 et seq.
6 *France v Clark* (1884) 26 ChD 257, CA; *Hare v London and North-Western Rly Co* (1860) John 722. As to the effect on a transfer of a mis-statement of the consideration or an erroneous stamp see *Powell v London and Provincial Bank* [1893] 2 Ch 555 at 560, CA. See also COMPANIES vol 14 (2009) PARA 401. As to a person obtaining a title against the company by estoppel arising from the issue of a certificate see COMPANIES vol 14 (2009) PARA 387.

7 *Société Général de Paris v Walker* (1885) 11 App Cas 20 at 28, HL; *Roots v Williamson* (1888) 38 ChD 485; *Moore v North Western Bank* [1891] 2 Ch 599; *Nanney v Morgan* (1887) 35 ChD 598 (affd 37 ChD 346, CA). As to the articles of association of a company see COMPANIES vol 14 (2009) PARA 228 et seq.

D. SHIPS, FREIGHT, AIRCRAFT AND HOVERCRAFT

212. Mortgages of ships. Mortgages of ships are governed by statute and are considered elsewhere in this work[1].

1 See the Merchant Shipping Act 1995 s 16, Sch 1; and SHIPPING AND MARITIME LAW vol 93 (2008) PARA 318 et seq.

213. Mortgage of freight. Frequently a statutory mortgage of a ship is accompanied by an independent collateral mortgage by the statutory owner of the freight earnings and the policies of insurance on the ship[1]. With regard to those interests, it is not necessary to comply with the statutory provisions to make a valid security, but the mortgagee should complete his security by giving notice to the persons by whom the freight is payable[2].

The rights of a statutory mortgagee of a ship to freight, and priorities between such a mortgagee and an assignee of freight, are considered elsewhere in this work[3].

1 As to mortgages of ships see PARA 212.
2 *Mestaer v Gillespie* (1805) 11 Ves 621 at 629; *Davenport v Whitmore* (1836) 2 My & Cr 177; *Gardner v Lachlan* (1838) 4 My & Cr 129; *Langton v Horton* (1842) 1 Hare 549.
3 As to the rights of a statutory mortgagee of a ship to freight see SHIPPING AND MARITIME LAW vol 93 (2008) PARA 332; CARRIAGE AND CARRIERS vol 7 (2015) PARAS 581–584, 589. As to the priorities between a statutory mortgagee of a ship and an assignee of freight see SHIPPING AND MARITIME LAW vol 93 (2008) PARA 334.

214. Mortgages of aircraft and hovercraft. A duly registered[1] aircraft or hovercraft[2], or such an aircraft or hovercraft with any store of spares for it, may be made security for a loan or other valuable consideration[3]. Provision is made for the registration of any such mortgage[4]. Whilst registration is voluntary, there is an inducement to register because a registered mortgage has priority over an earlier unregistered mortgage[5]. Mortgages of registered aircraft which would otherwise need to be registered as bills of sale[6] are exempt from the statutory provisions relating to bills of sale[7], although mortgages of unregistered aircraft remain subject to those provisions where appropriate[8].

A mortgage made by a company is registrable under the Companies Act 2006[9].

1 Ie registered in the register maintained under the Civil Aviation Act 1982 s 60 and the Air Navigation Order 2009, SI 2009/3015, art 3: see AIR LAW vol 2 (2008) PARA 366 et seq).
2 Whilst hovercraft rank as ships for most purposes, they rank as aircraft for mortgage purposes: see the Hovercraft (Application of Enactments) Order 1972, SI 1972/971, art 5, Sch 2 Pt A (which, by virtue of the Interpretation Act 1978 ss 17(2)(a), 23(2), applies the Civil Aviation Act 1982 s 86, and hence the Mortgaging of Aircraft Order 1972, SI 1972/1268, to hovercraft). See also the Hovercraft Act 1968 s 1(1)(h), (3); and SHIPPING AND MARITIME LAW vol 93 (2008) PARA 382. As to the meaning of 'hovercraft' see s 4(1); and SHIPPING AND MARITIME LAW vol 93 (2008) PARA 381.
3 See the Mortgaging of Aircraft Order 1972, SI 1972/1268, art 3; and AIR LAW vol 2 (2008) PARA 431.
4 See the Mortgaging of Aircraft Order 1972, SI 1972/1268, arts 4–13; and AIR LAW vol 2 (2008) PARA 431. As to false statements and forgery in connection with registration see art 17; and AIR LAW vol 2 (2008) PARA 431. As to the right of any person who suffers loss by reason of an error or omission in the register to indemnification see art 18; and AIR LAW vol 2 (2008) PARA 431.
5 See the Mortgaging of Aircraft Order 1972, SI 1972/1268, art 14; and AIR LAW vol 2 (2008) PARA 432; FINANCIAL INSTRUMENTS AND TRANSACTIONS vol 49 (2015) PARA 472.
6 See PARA 205.

7   Ie the Bills of Sale Act 1878 and the Bills of Sale Act (1878) Amendment Act 1882: see the
    Mortgaging of Aircraft Order 1972, SI 1972/1268, art 16(1); and FINANCIAL INSTRUMENTS
    AND TRANSACTIONS vol 49 (2015) PARA 472.
8   As to unregistered aircraft see AIR LAW vol 2 (2008) PARA 367.
9   As to the registration of company charges see the Companies Act 2006 Pt 25 Ch A1
    (ss 859A–859Q); and COMPANIES.

(2) EQUITABLE MORTGAGES AND CHARGES

(i) Creation of Equitable Mortgages and Charges

215. How an equitable mortgage may be created. An equitable mortgage passes
only an equitable estate or interest for the purpose of securing the repayment of
a debt[1]. It may be made by:

(1)   a mortgage of an equitable interest[2];
(2)   an agreement to create a legal mortgage[3]; or
(3)   a mortgage which fails to comply with the formalities for a legal
        mortgage[4].

1   See PARA 105.
2   See PARA 216.
3   See PARA 217.
4   See PARA 218.

216. Mortgage of an equitable interest. A mortgage of an equitable interest in
land can be made by assignment of the equitable interest, subject to a proviso for
redemption[1]. Subject to the requirement that a mortgage of an equitable interest
in personalty subsisting at the time of the mortgage must be in writing signed by
the mortgagor or his agent lawfully authorised in writing[2], an equitable mortgage
of personal property is not otherwise required to be in writing[3]. A mortgage of an
equitable interest in land, however, must be in writing[4].

Mortgages of life interests and reversionary interests take the form of equitable
mortgages[5].

1   The restrictions on the creation of mortgages by assignment apply only to mortgages of the legal
    estate: see the Law of Property Act 1925 ss 85, 86; and PARA 164 et seq. As to the
    mortgagor's right to redeem see PARAS 107, 304 et seq.
2   See the Law of Property Act 1925 s 53(1)(c); and PARA 242.
3   See PARAS 242, 247.
4   See PARA 221 et seq.
5   See PARA 163.

217. Agreement to charge. An agreement to charge real or personal estate, made
for valuable consideration[1] by a person who has power to create such a charge,
operates as a valid equitable charge[2], even though the charge extends to all his
existing property[3]; and if, at the date of the agreement, the property agreed to be
charged has been sold, the charge takes effect on the interest which the person
making it has in the purchase money[4]. A covenant to charge property ascertained
or ascertainable creates a binding charge as soon as the property is ascertained[5].
It is sufficient if the land can be ascertained by existing facts and circumstances[6].
A valid agreement to charge will be held effectual notwithstanding any mistake
which may have occurred in the attempt to effect it[7].

A simple agreement or covenant to charge land where no land in particular is
mentioned will not create a charge, neither will an agreement for a personal

security with power to call for a real one, nor is a charge created where it otherwise appears that the intention was to rely on the covenant[8].

1 A voluntary agreement to give a charge is not enforceable: *Re Earl of Lucan, Hardinge v Cobden* (1890) 45 ChD 470. See also EQUITABLE JURISDICTION vol 47 (2014) PARA 216.
2 *Rolleston v Morton* (1842) 1 Dr & War 171 at 195; *Whitworth v Gaugain* (1844) 3 Hare 416 at 424; *Gorringe v Irwell India Rubber and Gutta Percha Works* (1886) 34 ChD 128 at 134, CA.
3 *Re Kelcey, Tyson v Kelcey* [1899] 2 Ch 530. As to charges extending to the whole of the mortgagor's property see generally PARA 103.
4 *Re Selby, ex p Rogers* (1856) 8 De GM & G 271.
5 *Metcalfe v Archbishop of York* (1836) 1 My & Cr 547; *Ravenshaw v Hollier* (1834) 7 Sim 3 (affd (1835) 4 LJCh 119); cf *Legard v Hodges* (1792) 1 Ves 477.
6 *Montagu v Earl of Sandwich* (1886) 32 ChD 525 at 538, CA, per Cotton LJ. See also *Lyde v Mynn* (1833) 1 My & K 683; *Watson v Sadleir* (1829) 1 Mol 585; and LIEN vol 68 (2008) PARAS 878–879.
7 *Re Strand Music Hall Co Ltd, ex p European and American Finance Corpn Ltd* (1865) 3 De GJ & Sm 147; *Ross v Army and Navy Hotel Co* (1886) 34 ChD 43, CA; *Re Queensland Land and Coal Co, Davis v Martin* [1894] 3 Ch 181.
8 *Fremoult v Dedire* (1718) 1 P Wms 429; *Williams v Lucas* (1789) 2 Cox Eq Cas 160; *Collins v Plummer* (1708) 1 P Wms 104; *Berrington v Evans* (1839) 3 Y & C Ex 384.

218. Imperfect mortgage treated as equitable mortgage. An instrument which fails to comply with the formalities for a legal charge[1] is treated as, and must comply with the formalities required for the creation of, an equitable mortgage[2], rather than as an equitable charge[3].

1 As to the formalities for a legal charge see PARA 165.
2 As to equitable mortgages see PARAS 105, 215 et seq. As to the formalities required see PARA 221.
3 *United Bank of Kuwait plc v Sahib* [1997] Ch 107, [1996] 3 All ER 215, CA; and see *Thames Guaranty Ltd v Campbell* [1985] QB 210, [1984] 2 All ER 585, CA. See also *Parker v Housefield* (1834) 2 My & K 419; *Carter v Wake* (1877) 4 ChD 605; *Harrold v Plenty* [1901] 2 Ch 314; *Ex p Wright* (1812) 19 Ves 255 at 258; *Pryce v Bury* (1853) 2 Drew 41; *Featherstone v Fenwick* (1784) 1 Bro CC 270n. As to equitable charges see PARAS 106, 219.

219. Creation of equitable charges. An equitable charge on land or an interest in land must be in writing signed by the chargor or his agent[1]. An instrument which constitutes an agreement to create an equitable charge or formal mortgage is unenforceable unless it either complies with the formalities for an equitable mortgage of land or gives rise to a constructive trust[2]. An equitable charge may be created where a mortgagor purports to mortgage a greater estate in property than that which he possesses[3].

Under the Land Charges Act 1972, a general equitable charge is any equitable charge which:

(1) is not secured by a deposit of documents relating to the legal estate affected; and

(2) does not arise or affect an interest arising under a trust of land or a settlement; and

(3) is not a charge given by way of indemnity against rents equitably apportioned or charged exclusively on land in exoneration of other land and against the breach or non-observance of covenants or conditions; and

(4) is not included in any other class of land charge[4].

1 See the Law of Property Act 1925 s 53(1)(c); and DEEDS AND OTHER INSTRUMENTS vol 32 (2012) PARA 224; REAL PROPERTY AND REGISTRATION vol 87 (2012) PARA 722. See also *Kinane v Mackie-Conteh* [2005] EWCA Civ 45, [2005] 2 P & CR D9, [2005] All ER (D) 229 (May); *Helden v Strathmore Ltd* [2011] EWCA Civ 542, [2011] 2 BCLC 665, [2011] All ER (D) 92 (May). See PARA 106.
2 *Kinane v Mackie-Conteh* [2005] EWCA Civ 45, [2005] 2 P & CR D9, [2005] All ER (D) 229 (May). As to the requirements for the creation of a valid equitable mortgage see *United Bank of Kuwait plc v Sahib* [1997] Ch 107, [1996] 3 All ER 215, CA; and PARA 221.

3 See PARA 168.
4 See the Land Charges Act 1972 s 2(4)(iii); and PARA 262.

220.   Charging orders. A charging order made in favour of a judgment creditor[1] over an asset of the debtor has the like effect and is enforceable in the same manner as an equitable charge created by the debtor by writing under his hand[2]. The Land Charges Act 1972 and the Land Registration Act 2002 apply in relation to charging orders as they apply in relation to other orders or writs issued or made for the purposes of enforcing judgments[3]. In the case of unregistered land, a charging order over the legal estate is registrable but not over a beneficial interest alone[4]. It seems that such a charge takes effect subject to any prior mortgages, whether legal or equitable, affecting the estate or interest charged[5]. In the case of registered land, a charging order may be protected by notice in the same circumstances as apply in the case of unregistered land[6], the priority of such a charge being governed by the general rules relating to interests affecting registered land[7].

A charging order is enforceable by sale[8] or the appointment of a receiver[9] in the same way as an equitable charge.

1 Ie pursuant to the Charging Orders Act 1979. As to the manner of obtaining a charging order, and the circumstances in which, and the assets over which, it may be made see CIVIL PROCEDURE vol 12A (2015) PARA 1462 et seq. As to the discharge of a charging order see PARA 331. The enforcement of a charging order is not subject to loss through being time barred: see *Yorkshire Bank Finance Ltd v Mulhall* [2008] EWCA Civ 1156, [2009] 2 All ER (Comm) 164, [2009] 1 P & CR 345; and PARA 519.
2 See the Charging Orders Act 1979 s 3(4); and CIVIL PROCEDURE vol 12A (2015) PARA 1475. As to priority of charging orders see also PARA 293.
3 See the Charging Orders Act 1979 s 3(2) (amended by the Land Registration Act 2002 s 133, Sch 11 para 15); and CIVIL PROCEDURE vol 12A (2015) PARA 1476.
4 See the Land Charges Act 1972 s 6(1), (1A); and REAL PROPERTY AND REGISTRATION vol 87 (2012) PARA 746. See also *Perry v Phoenix Assurance plc* [1988] 3 All ER 60, [1988] 1 WLR 940.
5 *Whitworth v Gaugain* (1846) 1 Ph 728; *Legg v Mathieson* (1860) 2 Giff 71; *Kinderley v Jervis* (1856) 22 Beav 1; *Eyre v M'Dowell* (1861) 9 HL Cas 619; *Wickham v New Brunswick and Canada Rly Co* (1865) LR 1 PC 64; *Chung Khiaw Bank Ltd v United Overseas Bank* [1970] AC 767, [1970] 2 WLR 858, PC.
6 See the Land Registration Act 2002 s 34; and REAL PROPERTY AND REGISTRATION vol 87 (2012) PARAS 515–516.
7 As to these rules see the Land Registration Act 2002 ss 28–30; and REAL PROPERTY AND REGISTRATION vol 87 (2012) PARAS 454–456.
8 See CPR 73.10; and CIVIL PROCEDURE vol 12A (2015) PARA 1477. As to orders for sale generally see PARA 621 et seq. A judgment creditor holding a charging order over a beneficial interest in land may apply under the Trusts of Land and Appointment of Trustees Act 1996: see s 14; and TRUSTS AND POWERS vol 98 (2013) PARA 479. See also REAL PROPERTY AND REGISTRATION vol 87 (2012) PARAS 106, 224.
9 See the Senior Courts Act 1981 s 37; the County Courts Act 1984 s 107; CPR Pt 69; and CIVIL PROCEDURE vol 12A (2015) PARAS 1493; RECEIVERS vol 88 (2012) PARAS 13, 15.

(ii)   Equitable Mortgages of Land

A.   EQUITABLE MORTGAGES SINCE 1989

221.   Necessity for writing. An equitable mortgage is a specifically enforceable contract to create a legal mortgage in the future[1]. A contract made since 27 September 1989[2] for a mortgage of or charge on land or any interest in land can be made only in writing and by incorporating all the terms which the parties have expressly agreed[3] in one document or, where contracts are exchanged, in each[4]. The document incorporating the terms or, where contracts are exchanged, one of the documents incorporating them (but not necessarily the same one) must be signed by or on behalf of each party to the contract[5]. Accordingly, a facility letter[6] or mortgage deed signed by one party cannot create a valid equitable mortgage[7]. The same requirements apply to a variation of a material term of such a contract[8] but not to a collateral contract which is not itself a contract for the disposition of an interest in land[9]. These formalities do not apply to the actual creation of a charge or mortgage[10] or to the variation of an existing charge or mortgage[11].

Since 27 September 1989 the mere deposit of title deeds by way of security can no longer create a valid equitable mortgage[12].

1   *Swiss Bank Corpn v Lloyds Bank Ltd* [1982] AC 584, [1980] 2 All ER 419, CA; affd [1982] AC 584, [1981] 2 All ER 449, HL. As to equitable mortgages see further PARAS 105, 215 et seq.
2   Ie the date on which the Law of Property (Miscellaneous Provisions) Act 1989 s 2 (see the text to notes 4–5) came into force: see ss 2(7), 5(3), (4). As to the position before that date see PARA 222 et seq.
3   An agreement reached in correspondence is not sufficient: see *Commission for the New Towns v Cooper (GB) Ltd* [1995] Ch 259, [1995] 2 All ER 929, CA. As to the terms of equitable mortgages in writing see also PARAS 236–239.
4   Law of Property (Miscellaneous Provisions) Act 1989 s 2(1), (6) (s 2(6) amended by the Trusts of Land and Appointment of Trustees Act 1996 s 25(2), Sch 4). The terms may be incorporated in a document either by being set out in it or by reference to some other documents: Law of Property (Miscellaneous Provisions) Act 1989 s 2(2). As to incorporation by reference to some other document see *Firstpost Homes Ltd v Johnson* [1995] 4 All ER 355, [1995] 1 WLR 1567, CA.
5   Law of Property (Miscellaneous Provisions) Act 1989 s 2(3). A typed name is not a signature: see *Firstpost Homes Ltd v Johnson* [1995] 4 All ER 355, [1995] 1 WLR 1567, CA.
6   *Lloyds Bank v Bryant* [1996] NPC 31, CA.
7   *Helden v Strathmore Ltd* [2011] EWCA Civ 542, [2011] 2 BCLC 665, [2011] All ER (D) 92 (May).
8   *McCausland v Duncan Lawrie Ltd* [1996] 4 All ER 995, [1997] 1 WLR 38, CA.
9   *Record v Bell* [1991] 4 All ER 471, [1991] 1 WLR 853.
10 *Helden v Strathmore Ltd* [2011] EWCA Civ 542, [2011] 2 BCLC 665, [2011] All ER (D) 92 (May).
11 *Target Holdings Ltd v Priestley* (1999) 79 P & CR 305, [1999] NPC 51, [1999] All ER (D) 341; approved in *Helden v Strathmore Ltd* [2011] EWCA Civ 542, [2011] 2 BCLC 665, [2011] All ER (D) 92 (May).
12 *United Bank of Kuwait plc v Sahib* [1997] Ch 107, [1996] 3 All ER 215, CA. As to the creation of a mortgage by deposit of deeds before 27 September 1989 see PARA 222 et seq.

B.   EQUITABLE MORTGAGES BEFORE 1989

222. Equitable mortgage by deposit of title deeds. Until 27 September 1989[1] a good security in equity could be created by the deposit of the title deeds of freehold or freehold or leasehold property[2]. The deposit could be to secure the debt of a third person[3]. A deposit of title deeds was regarded as an imperfect mortgage which the mortgagee was entitled to have perfected, or as a contract for a legal mortgage which gave to the party entitled all such rights as he would have had if the contract had been completed[4]. By the deposit the mortgagor contracted that his interest in the property comprised in the deeds was to be liable to the debt and bound himself to do everything necessary to effect the vesting in the mortgagee of such interest as a mortgage should create[5]. Where, however, a deposit was made with a surety by way of indemnity, the surety was not, in the absence of agreement, entitled to call for a legal mortgage[6].

1   Ie the date on which the Law of Property (Miscellaneous Provisions) Act 1989 s 2 came into force: see ss 2(7), 5(3), (4); and PARA 221.
2   *Russel v Russel* (1783) 1 Bro CC 269. As to the position where the mortgage is of land abroad see CONFLICT OF LAWS vol 19 (2011) PARA 702.
3   *Re Wallis & Simmonds (Builders) Ltd* [1974] QB 94, [1974] 1 All ER 561.

4 *Parker v Housefield* (1834) 2 My & K 419; *Carter v Wake* (1877) 4 ChD 605; *Harrold v Plenty*
  [1901] 2 Ch 314; *Ex p Wright* (1812) 19 Ves 255 at 258; *Pryce v Bury* (1853) 2 Drew 41;
  Featherstone v Fenwick (1784) 1 Bro CC 270n.
5 *Pryce v Bury* (1853) 2 Drew 41 at 42 per Kindersley V-C; *National Provincial Bank of England
  v Games* (1886) 31 ChD 582 at 587, CA, per Pearson J. Under the Law of Property Act 1925, the
  interest created by the mortgage was a term of years: see PARA 161.
6 *Sporle v Whayman* (1855) 20 Beav 607. See also FINANCIAL INSTRUMENTS AND
  TRANSACTIONS vol 49 (2015) PARA 772.

223. Form of deposit of title deeds. In an equitable mortgage by deposit of deeds
the deposit could be of the deeds alone[1], or might be accompanied by a
memorandum of the terms of the deposit[2] or by an agreement to give a mortgage[3].
The proprietor of any registered land or charge might create a lien on the land by
deposit of the land certificate or charge certificate[4]. One joint tenant could not
deposit the title deeds without the consent of the other[5]. An equitable charge
secured by deposit of documents relating to the legal estate of unregistered land
did not need to be registered as a land charge[6]. A deposit, without writing, or by
word of mouth, might create a charge upon the property notwithstanding the
statutory provision requiring a contract for the disposition of land to be evidenced
in writing[7], since the delivery of the deeds was sufficient part performance of the
implied agreement to give a security[8]. The charge created by the deposit was
contractual, for, although it arose by presumption, it did not arise by operation of
law[9]. Where the deposit was accompanied by a written document, the document
must be referred to in order to ascertain the exact nature of the charge[10]; and oral
evidence is not admitted to contradict the writing[11], although oral evidence of a
subsequent oral agreement may be given[12].

1 *Russel v Russel* (1783) 1 Bro CC 269; *Re Knight, ex p Langston* (1810) 17 Ves 227. Cf *Ex p
  Warner* (1812) 19 Ves 202; *Whitbread v Jordan* (1835) 1 Y & C Ex 303 (cases of deposit of copy
  of court roll). As to equitable mortgage by deposit of deeds see PARA 222. An equitable charge can
  no longer be created by deposit alone: see note 7; and PARA 221.
2 *Ex p Kensington* (1813) 2 Ves & B 79. As to the distinction between a mere memorandum of
  deposit and a memorandum constituting a security see *Hari Sankar Paul v Kedar Nath Saha* [1939]
  2 All ER 737, PC; *Re White Rose Cottage* [1965] Ch 940, [1965] 1 All ER 11, CA.
3 *Lister v Turner* (1846) 5 Hare 281; *National Provincial Bank of England v Games* (1886) 31 ChD
  582, CA.
4 See the Land Registration Act 1925 s 66 (repealed with savings by the Land Registration Act 2002
  ss 134, 135, Schs 12, 13). Such a lien is in the nature of a mortgage or charge rather than a true
  lien: see PARA 113. As to lien see further LIEN.
5 *Thames Guaranty Ltd v Campbell* [1985] QB 210, [1984] 2 All ER 585, CA.
6 See the Land Charges Act 1972 s 2(4)(iii); and REAL PROPERTY AND REGISTRATION vol 87
  (2012) PARAS 720–724. See also the Law of Property Act 1925 s 13; and REAL PROPERTY AND
  REGISTRATION vol 87 (2012) PARA 260. As to the priority of mortgages see generally PARA 260
  et seq. As to the mortgages and charges which are registrable as land charges see PARA 262.
7 See the Law of Property Act 1925 s 40 (replacing in part the Statute of Frauds (1677)) (repealed
  by the Law of Property (Miscellaneous Provisions) Act 1989 ss 2(8), 4, Sch 2, except in relation
  to contracts made before 27 September 1989); and PARA 235. See also PARA 225. Since
  27 September 1989 mortgage contracts must be in writing, not merely evidenced in writing: see
  PARA 221.
8 *Burgess v Moxon* (1856) 2 Jur NS 1059; *Bank of New South Wales v O'Connor* (1889) 14 App
  Cas 273 at 282, PC. See also EQUITABLE JURISDICTION vol 47 (2014) PARA 191 et seq.
9 *Re Wallis & Simmonds (Builders) Ltd* [1974] QB 94, [1974] 1 All ER 561.
10 *Shaw v Foster* (1872) LR 5 HL 321 at 340; *Wylde v Radford* (1863) 33 LJCh 51; *Thames
   Guaranty Ltd v Campbell* [1985] QB 210, [1984] 2 All ER 585, CA.
11 *Ex p Coombe* (1810) 17 Ves 369.
12 *Ede v Knowles* (1843) 2 Y & C Ch Cas 172.

224. Equitable mortgage by deposit and lien mutually exclusive. Where an
equitable mortgage or charge was created by deposit of title deeds[1], there was an
implied contract that the mortgagee or chargee might retain the deeds until he was

paid[2]. When the mortgage or charge was avoided, for example for non-registration as a land charge[3], then everything ancillary to it was avoided, including the right of retention[4].

1   See PARAS 222–223. Since 27 September 1989 the mere deposit of title deeds by way of security can no longer create a valid equitable mortgage: see PARA 221.
2   As to the distinction between mortgages and liens see PARA 113.
3   As to the registration of land charges see generally REAL PROPERTY AND REGISTRATION vol 87 (2012) PARA 693 et seq.
4   *Re Molton Finance Ltd* [1968] Ch 325 at 332–333, [1967] 3 All ER 843 at 845, CA, per Lord Denning MR. See also *Re Wallis & Simmonds (Builders) Ltd* [1974] QB 94, [1974] 1 All ER 561.

225. Memorandum without deposit of title deeds. A memorandum[1] or agreement in writing showing an intention to deposit title deeds by way of mortgage or to charge the property comprised in the deeds was sufficient to create an equitable mortgage even if no deeds were in fact deposited[2], and even if some of the deeds were not executed[3]. A written direction or consent that the deeds might be retained as a security was equally effective[4].

A mere oral agreement to deposit which was not acted upon[5] was not sufficient, but an oral agreement to mortgage with a subsequent delivery of the deeds was, and the security related back to the time of the agreement[6].

A mere promise to give security on deeds to a person who already held them did not of itself create an equitable charge[7].

1   As to the memorandum see further PARA 235.
2   *Re Carter and Justins, ex p Sheffield Union Banking Co* (1865) 13 LT 477; *Re Leathes, ex p Leathes* (1833) 3 Deac & Ch 112; *Re Daintry and Ryle, Re Ravenscroft, ex p Arkwright* (1843) 3 Mont D & De G 129; *Re Blew, ex p Jones* (1835) 4 Deac & Ch 750. As to the creation of an equitable mortgage by deposit of title deeds see PARAS 222–223. Since 27 September 1989 the mere deposit of title deeds by way of security can no longer create a valid equitable mortgage: see PARA 221.
3   *Re Pye, ex p Orrett* (1837) 3 Mont & A 153, where the agreement was to deposit a lease when granted.
4   *Fenwick v Potts* (1856) 8 De GM & G 506.
5   *Re Beavan, ex p Coombe* (1819) 4 Madd 249; *Re Collins, ex p Perry* (1843) 3 Mont D & De G 252; *Re Ridge, ex p Hallifax* (1842) 2 Mont D & De G 544.
6   *Edge v Worthington* (1786) 1 Cox Eq Cas 211.
7   *Re Beetham, ex p Broderick* (1887) 18 QBD 766, CA.

226. Deposit of part of title deeds. To create a valid mortgage by deposit of title deeds[1] it was not necessary that the whole or even the most material of the deeds should be deposited, or that the deeds deposited should show a complete or good title in the depositor: it was sufficient if the deeds deposited bona fide related to the property or were material evidence of title, and were shown to have been deposited with the intention of creating a charge[2]. All the deeds deposited were included in the security, even if the accompanying memorandum only specified some of those deeds[3].

An equitable mortgage could be created by the deposit of a receipt for purchase money containing the terms of the agreement for purchase and attached to a plan[4], or an agreement for a lease[5], even if the lease was afterwards granted on different terms[6], but not, it seems, by a deposit of an attested copy of a lease[7].

1   See PARAS 222–223. Since 27 September 1989 the mere deposit of title deeds by way of security can no longer create a valid equitable mortgage: see PARA 221.
2   *Ex p Wetherell* (1805) 11 Ves 398; *Lacon v Allen* (1856) 3 Drew 579; *Roberts v Croft* (1857) 24 Beav 223; *Re Roche's Estate* (1890) 25 LR Ir 58 (on appeal 25 LR Ir 284, Ir CA). In *Roberts v Croft*, a solicitor made a deposit of the title deeds of his estate with a client, but omitting the conveyance to himself; he afterwards deposited the conveyance with his bank, and it was held that the deposit of the earlier deeds constituted a good equitable mortgage and gave the client priority over the bank. See also *Re Price, ex p Pearse and Prothero* (1820) Buck 525.

3   *Ferris v Mullins* (1854) 2 Sm & G 378. As to a mortgage of shares in a limited company created
    by deposit of certificates see *Harrold v Plenty* [1901] 2 Ch 314. As to the memorandum see further
    PARA 235.
4   *Goodwin v Waghorn* (1835) 4 LJCh 172. See also *Simmons v Montague* [1909] 1 IR 87, where
    the deposit of a plan of the property was held sufficient.
5   *Unity Joint-Stock Mutual Banking Association v King* (1858) 25 Beav 72; *Union Bank of London
    v Kent* (1888) 39 ChD 238, CA; *Tebb v Hodge* (1869) LR 5 CP 73.
6   *Re Buckland, ex p Reid* (1848) De G 600.
7   *Re Borrow, ex p Broadbent* (1834) 1 Mont & A 635.

227. Extent of mortgagee's duty to examine title deeds. In creating an equitable
mortgage by deposit of title deeds[1], it was not negligence to accept the
owner's statement that the deeds deposited were all that were necessary. If the
court was satisfied of the good faith of the person who had a prior equitable
charge, and was satisfied that there had been a positive statement, honestly
believed, that he had the necessary deeds, then he was not bound to examine the
deeds, nor was he bound by constructive notice of their actual contents or of any
deficiencies which by examination he might have discovered in them[2].

1   As to the creation of an equitable mortgage by deposit of title deeds see PARAS 222–223. Since
    27 September 1989 the mere deposit of title deeds by way of security can no longer create a valid
    equitable mortgage: see PARA 221.
2   *Dixon v Muckleston* (1872) 8 Ch App 155 at 161 per Lord Selborne LC. See also PARA 284.

228. Effect of mere deposit of title deeds. A deposit of title deeds did not in itself
create a charge, and the mere possession of deeds without evidence of the contract
under which possession was obtained, or of the manner in which the possession
originated so that a contract might be inferred[1], did not create an equitable
security[2]. The deposit was a fact which admitted evidence of an intention to create
a charge which would otherwise be inadmissible, and raised a presumption of a
charge which threw upon the debtor the burden of rebutting it[3].

A mere deposit of title deeds upon an advance, with intent to create a security
on them, but without a word passing, gave an equitable lien so that, as between
debtor and creditor, the fact of possession of the title deeds raised the presumption
that they were deposited by way of security[4]. As against strangers, however, this
was only the case where possession could be accounted for in no other way[5], and
the mere fact that the title deeds were produced from the custody of a creditor
many years after the deposit, without explanation, did not in itself support a claim
of a mortgage by deposit[6]. There had to be proof of the time when both the loan
and deposit were made[7].

1   *Re McMahon, McMahon v McMahon* (1886) 55 LT 763.
2   *Dixon v Muckleston* (1872) 8 Ch App 155; *Chapman v Chapman* (1851) 13 Beav 308; *Wardle v
    Oakley* (1864) 36 Beav 27. See also *United Bank of Kuwait plc v Sahib* [1997] Ch 107, [1996]
    3 All ER 215, CA.
3   *Russel v Russel* (1783) 1 Bro CC 269; *Burgess v Moxon* (1856) 2 Jur NS 1059.
        As to the creation of an equitable mortgage by deposit of title deeds see PARAS 222–223. Since
    27 September 1989 the mere deposit of title deeds by way of security can no longer create a valid
    equitable mortgage: see PARA 221.
4   *Re Knight, ex p Langston* (1810) 17 Ves 227 at 230; *Ex p Mountfort* (1808) 14 Ves 606;
    Maugham v Ridley (1863) 8 LT 309.
5   *Bozon v Williams* (1829) 3 Y & J 150 at 161.
6   *Chapman v Chapman* (1851) 13 Beav 308.
7   *Kebell v Philpott, Kebell v Daniel* (1838) 7 LJCh 237.

229. Deposit of title deeds by mistake. The delivery by mistake of title deeds to
a creditor did not constitute him an equitable mortgagee, although the delivery
might be prima facie evidence of an intention which threw the burden of proving
the negative on the owner[1]. A deposit of deeds could not create an equitable

mortgage on property to which the deeds did not relate, notwithstanding that by a misapprehension the creditor believed that they related to that property[2].

Where deeds were delivered for a special purpose other than putting them in pledge, the further purpose of creating a security could not be inferred. Thus where they were delivered merely for the purpose of enabling a solicitor to prepare a legal mortgage, an equitable mortgage by deposit was not created[3] unless there was an immediate intention to give a security by the deposit, notwithstanding that a formal legal security was also in contemplation[4]. If, before the money was advanced, the deeds were deposited with a view to preparing a future mortgage, the deposit was not considered as an equitable mortgage by deposit; but it was otherwise where there was an advance and the deeds were deposited under a promise to forbear suing, even though they might be deposited only for the purpose of preparing a future mortgage, and in such a case the deeds were given as part of the security[5].

1   *Wardle v Oakley* (1864) 36 Beav 27 at 30, where the deeds of leaseholds were sent by mistake with the deeds of freeholds which had been mortgaged by deed, and the possession of the former deeds was held to create no lien on the leasehold property.
    As to the creation of an equitable mortgage by deposit of title deeds see PARAS 222–223. Since 27 September 1989 the mere deposit of title deeds by way of security can no longer create a valid equitable mortgage: see PARA 221.
2   *Jones v Williams* (1857) 24 Beav 47.
3   *Norris v Wilkinson* (1806) 12 Ves 192; *Lloyd v Attwood, Attwood v Lloyd* (1859) 3 De G & J 614 at 651.
4   *Edge v Worthington* (1786) 1 Cox Eq Cas 211; *Ex p Bruce* (1813) 1 Rose 374; *Ex p Wright* (1812) 19 Ves 255 at 258; *Hockley v Bantock* (1826) 1 Russ 141.
5   *Keys v Williams* (1838) 3 Y & C Ex 55 at 61 per Lord Abinger CB.

230.   Extent of security created by deposit of title deeds. Where the deposit of title deeds was made for the purpose of obtaining credit, it did not cover money previously advanced and still due[1], unless an intention to cover it appeared from the circumstances[2]. A deposit did, however, cover subsequent advances upon oral evidence of an agreement that the security should be so extended, and notwithstanding that the original deposit was accompanied by a memorandum in writing limiting the purpose of the deposit[3]; but it did not extend to an advance by a third person unless connected with some dealing with the estate[4], or to a subsequent advance made after a legal mortgage had been taken[5].

1   *Mountford v Scott* (1823) Turn & R 274.
    As to the creation of an equitable mortgage by deposit of title deeds see PARAS 222–223. Since 27 September 1989 the mere deposit of title deeds by way of security can no longer create a valid equitable mortgage: see PARA 221.
2   *Re New, ex p Farley, Lavender and Owen* (1841) 1 Mont D & De G 683.
3   *Re Knight, ex p Langston* (1810) 17 Ves 227; *Ex p Kensington* (1813) 2 Ves & B 79; *Re Burkill, ex p Nettleship* (1841) 2 Mont D & De G 124; *James v Rice* (1854) 5 De GM & G 461.
4   *Ex p Whitbread* (1812) 19 Ves 209.
5   *Re Hewett and Hopkins, ex p Hooper* (1815) 19 Ves 477.

231.   With whom the title deeds must be deposited. In order to create an equitable mortgage, when the deposit of title deeds was made without a memorandum[1], the delivery had to be made to the creditor or his agent, being some person other than the debtor. So a memorandum appropriating as security to a creditor a policy which remained in the debtor's possession was not sufficient of itself to create a charge on it[2]. A deposit with the debtor's wife was not sufficient[3]. A deposit with the debtor's solicitor was, however, sufficient, as he was thereby constituted agent and trustee for the creditor[4]; and, in mortgaging, a solicitor might make a deposit by placing his own deeds in a box containing the papers of his client the mortgagee[5].

1   As to the creation of an equitable mortgage by deposit of title deeds see PARAS 222–223. Since 27 September 1989 the mere deposit of title deeds by way of security can no longer create a valid equitable mortgage: see PARA 221. As to the memorandum see further PARA 235.
2   *Adams v Claxton* (1801) 6 Ves 226 at 230. See, however, *Middleton v Pollock, ex p Elliott* (1876) 2 ChD 104, where a memorandum by a solicitor declaring himself trustee for a client of leaseholds of which he was mortgagee was held valid even though the fact of the execution of the memorandum was not known to the client.
3   *Ex p Coming* (1803) 9 Ves 115.
4   *Lloyd v Attwood, Attwood v Lloyd* (1859) 3 De G & J 614 at 652.
5   *Mason v Morley (No 2)* (1865) 34 Beav 475. As to the relation of solicitor and client see generally LEGAL PROFESSIONS vol 66 (2015) PARA 561 et seq.

232.   Extent of property charged by deposit of title deeds. The charge created by a deposit of the title deeds included all the property comprised in the deeds[1], and extended to every estate and interest in the property possessed by the depositor at the time of the deposit, every interest which he afterward acquired[2] and all incidental rights, such as the goodwill of a business carried on upon the premises[3]. Apart from statutory power, a limited owner[4] could charge only his own equitable interest by a deposit, but oral evidence of the remainderman's consent was admissible to charge the legal estate[5].

1   *Ashton v Dalton* (1846) 2 Coll 565. As to the creation of an equitable mortgage by deposit of title deeds see PARAS 222–223. Since 27 September 1989 the mere deposit of title deeds by way of security can no longer create a valid equitable mortgage: see PARA 221.
2   *Re Baker, ex p Bisdee* (1840) 1 Mont D & De G 333; *Bank of New South Wales v O'Connor* (1889) 14 App Cas 273 at 282, PC; *Re Roche's Estate* (1890) 25 LR Ir 58 (on appeal 25 LR Ir 284, Ir CA).
3   *Chissum v Dewes* (1828) 5 Russ 29.
4   As to limited owners see PARA 145 et seq.
5   *Williams v Medlicot* (1819) 6 Price 495.

233.   Parting with or loss of title deeds. The creditor with whom title deeds were deposited did not lose his lien by parting with the deeds for the purpose of allowing a sale to be effected[1], or, if the debtor was the creditor's solicitor and the deeds were in his custody as the creditor's agent, by the debtor wrongfully removing them from the creditor's deed box[2]. Where neither the deeds nor any memorandum of deposit could be produced, secondary evidence of the deposit could be given upon proof that the deeds had been really lost[3].

1   *Ex p Morgan* (1806) 12 Ves 6.
       As to the creation of an equitable mortgage by deposit of title deeds see PARAS 222–223. Since 27 September 1989 the mere deposit of title deeds by way of security can no longer create a valid equitable mortgage: see PARA 221.
2   *Mason v Morley (No 2)* (1865) 34 Beav 475. See also LIEN vol 68 (2008) PARAS 823, 854.
3   *Baskett v Skeel* (1863) 11 WR 1019. As to the memorandum see further PARA 235.

234.   Sub-mortgage by deposit of title deeds. A legal mortgagee might make an equitable sub-mortgage by deposit, and an equitable mortgage by deposit could be sub-mortgaged by redeposit without depositing the memorandum given on the original deposit[1]. The derivative mortgagee had to deliver up the deeds to the original mortgagor upon being paid all that was actually due on the original deposit[2]. A sub-mortgage by deposit of deeds relating to unregistered land did not need to be registered as a land charge[3]. A sub-mortgage of registered land might be created by deposit of a charge certificate[4] or notice of intended deposit[5]. In the case of equitable interests in land or personalty, written notice of dealings had to be given to the trustees[6].

1   *Re Hildyard, ex p Smith* (1842) 2 Mont D & De G 587.

As to the creation of an equitable mortgage by deposit of title deeds see PARAS 222–223. Since 27 September 1989 the mere deposit of title deeds by way of security can no longer create a valid equitable mortgage: see PARA 221. As to the memorandum see further PARA 235.

2   *Matthews v Wallwyn* (1798) 4 Ves 118; *Turner v Smith* [1901] 1 Ch 213.
3   See PARA 223.
4   See PARA 223.
5   See PARA 225.
6   See the Law of Property Act 1925 s 137; and PARA 270.

235.   Equitable mortgage otherwise than by deposit of title deeds. A contract made before 27 September 1989[1] for the mortgage of land or an interest in land[2], except a mortgage by deposit of title deeds[3], is not enforceable unless a memorandum or note of it was made in writing and signed by the party to be charged with it or some person lawfully authorised by him to do so[4], or unless there has been part performance of the contract sufficient to take it out of the statutory requirement as to writing[5].

An offer to give a security, signed by the debtor and accepted orally by the creditor, was sufficient[6].

1   Ie the date on which the Law of Property (Miscellaneous Provisions) Act 1989 s 2 came into force: see ss 2(7), 5(3), (4); and PARA 221.
2   Examples of such an interest are a charge on rent to accrue due (*Re Whitting, ex p Hall* (1879) 10 ChD 615, CA) and a charge on trade fixtures (*Jarvis v Jarvis* (1893) 69 LT 412).
3   As to the creation of an equitable mortgage by deposit of title deeds see PARAS 222–223. Since 27 September 1989 the mere deposit of title deeds by way of security can no longer create a valid equitable mortgage: see PARA 221.
4   See the Law of Property Act 1925 s 40(1) (repealed by the Law of Property (Miscellaneous Provisions) Act 1989 ss 2(8), 4, Sch 2, except in relation to contracts made before 27 September 1989). See also *Lacon v Mertins* (1743) 3 Atk 1 at 4; and CONTRACT vol 22 (2012) PARA 224; CONVEYANCING vol 23 (2013) PARA 151.
5   See CONVEYANCING vol 23 (2013) PARA 151; EQUITABLE JURISDICTION vol 47 (2014) PARA 10. Payment of the consideration is not sufficient part performance: *Re Whitting, ex p Hall* (1879) 10 ChD 615 at 619, CA; *Clinan v Cooke* (1802) 1 Sch & Lef 22 at 40; *Maddison v Alderson* (1883) 8 App Cas 467 at 479, HL. See also *Steadman v Steadman* [1976] AC 536, [1974] 2 All ER 977, HL. As to the deposit of title deeds being sufficient part performance see PARA 223.
    The re-enactment of the part of the Statute of Frauds (1677) s 4 (repealed) relating to contracts for the sale or other disposition of land in the Law of Property Act 1925 s 40 (repealed: see note 4) did not affect the law relating to part performance (see s 40(2) (repealed)), nor does s 53 (see PARA 242; and DEEDS AND OTHER INSTRUMENTS vol 32 (2012) PARAS 224, 347) affect that law (see s 55(d)).
6   *Liverpool Borough Bank v Eccles* (1859) 4 H & N 139; *Warner v Willington* (1856) 3 Drew 523.

C.   TERMS OF EQUITABLE MORTGAGES IN WRITING

236.   General requirements for an equitable mortgage. The equitable mortgage should contain an undertaking by the mortgagor to execute a legal mortgage or charge when called upon to do so[1]. Upon the execution of such a legal mortgage or charge, it seems that the equitable mortgage continues in existence notwithstanding the usual rule of merger of a lower in a higher security[2]. The agreement should state expressly that the property is equitably charged with the repayment of the money advanced and interest, although an equitable mortgage carries interest without such reference[3]. Where the agreement is under seal[4] it should also contain a declaration by the mortgagor that he holds the property on trust for the mortgagee[5] and, in addition or alternatively, a power of attorney[6] for the mortgagee to convey the property in the mortgagor's name. Even without such a power, the equitable mortgagee, on exercising the statutory power of sale, may be able to convey the legal estate[7], but the inclusion of the power makes the mortgagee's position certain.

1   See PARA 221.

2   As to the general rule that the lower security merges with the higher security see PARA 690.
3   *Re Drax, Savile v Drax* [1903] 1 Ch 781 at 794, 796, CA.
4   As to the statutory power of sale arising from a mortgage under seal see the Law of Property Act
    1925 s 101; and PARA 446 et seq.
5   See further PARA 237.
6   See further PARA 238.
7   See *Re White Rose Cottage* [1965] Ch 940 at 951, [1965] 1 All ER 11 at 15, CA, per Lord
    Denning MR.

237. Trust of the legal estate. A declaration[1] by the mortgagor that he holds the
property on trust for the mortgagee enables the mortgagee on exercising the
power of sale[2] to vest the legal estate in the mortgaged property in himself or a
purchaser[3]. The power of appointment of new trustees[4] should be exercisable by
the mortgagee and give the mortgagee and those deriving title under him power to
remove the mortgagor from the trusteeship and to appoint himself or themselves
or any of them as new trustees. On an appointment of new trustees the legal estate
in the mortgaged property will vest in the new trustees[5].

1   Ie a declaration incorporated in the body of the equitable mortgage: see PARAS 221 et seq, 236.
2   As to the power of sale see PARA 443 et seq.
3   *London and County Banking Co v Goddard* [1897] 1 Ch 642.
4   As to the power of appointment of new trustees under the Trustee Act 1925 see s 36; and TRUSTS
    AND POWERS vol 98 (2013) PARA 275 et seq. As to the appointment of new trustees generally see
    TRUSTS AND POWERS vol 98 (2013) PARA 258 et seq.
5   See the Trustee Act 1925 s 40; and TRUSTS AND POWERS vol 98 (2013) PARA 305 et seq.

238. Power of attorney. A power of attorney for the mortgagee to convey the
property in the mortgagor's name may be included in the equitable mortgage as an
alternative or in addition to the declaration of trust[1]. The mortgagor irrevocably[2]
appoints the mortgagee and the persons deriving title under him the attorney or
attorneys of the mortgagor and the persons deriving title under him in his or their
name and on his or their behalf to vest the legal estate in the mortgaged property
in any purchaser or other person in exercise of the statutory powers[3] conferred on
mortgagees free and discharged from the mortgagor's right of redemption[4].
Where, in exercise of the statutory power of sale[5], the mortgagee conveys the
mortgaged property pursuant to such a power of attorney, it seems that the
purchaser will take the property free from subsequent incumbrances as well as the
mortgage in respect of which the power of sale is being exercised[6].

1   As to the power of attorney generally see AGENCY vol 1 (2008) PARA 31 et seq.
2   As to powers of attorney expressed to be irrevocable see the Powers of Attorney Act 1971 s 4; and
    AGENCY vol 1 (2008) PARA 175.
3   As to the statutory powers see PARA 446 et seq.
4   As to the right of redemption see PARA 304 et seq.
5   As to the power of sale see PARA 446 et seq.
6   *Re White Rose Cottage* [1965] Ch 940, [1965] 1 All ER 11, CA.

239. Provisions to be inserted in equitable mortgage in writing. The written
agreement to execute a mortgage must incorporate all terms which the parties
have expressly agreed[1], but need not incorporate those implied by law[2]. An
agreement to execute a legal mortgage, with such powers and provisions and in
such form as the mortgagee may require for further securing the principal money
and interest, only extends to reasonable provisions, and does not enable the
mortgagee to insert terms excluding the operation of the statutory provision[3]
which restricts consolidation of mortgages[4], or extending the subject matter of the
mortgage[5]. The mortgage should, however, contain a covenant for the payment of
the debt and interest[6]; and, even where there is an agreement not to call in the

money for a certain time, the mortgage must contain a proviso that the postponement is to be conditional on the punctual payment of interest[7].

1 See the Law of Property (Miscellaneous Provisions) Act 1989 s 2(1); and PARA 221.
2 *Blackburn v Walker* [1920] WN 291.
3 Ie the Law of Property Act 1925 s 93(1): see PARA 504.
4 *Farmer v Pitt* [1902] 1 Ch 954.
5 *Whitley v Challis* [1892] 1 Ch 64, CA (where an intended lessee agreed, when a lease of a hotel should be granted, to execute a valid second mortgage in such form and to contain such powers, covenants and provisions as the mortgagee's solicitor or counsel should require; it was held that this did not authorise the inclusion of the goodwill of the business in the mortgage).
6 *Saunders v Milsome* (1866) LR 2 Eq 573.
7 *Seaton v Twyford* (1870) LR 11 Eq 591.

D.   REGISTRATION OF EQUITABLE MORTGAGES OF LAND

240. Equitable mortgage of unregistered land. An equitable mortgage of unregistered land, without deposit, should be registered[1], for notice[2] and priority[3] depend on the order of registration. An equitable mortgage secured by a deposit of documents relating to the legal estate affected is not registrable[4].

1 See the Land Charges Act 1972 s 2(4)(iii)(a); and REAL PROPERTY AND REGISTRATION vol 87 (2012) PARA 723. The equitable mortgage would probably be void against a purchaser of a legal estate for money or money's worth as an agreement to create a legal mortgage unless registered as an estate contract under s 2(4)(iv) (see REAL PROPERTY AND REGISTRATION vol 87 (2012) PARA 724). If registered as an equitable charge under s 2(4)(iii), the equitable mortgage would, however, be protected as such and the mortgagee would have the remedies of an equitable chargee: see *United Bank of Kuwait plc v Sahib* [1997] Ch 107, [1996] 3 All ER 215, CA; *Murray v Guinness* [1998] NPC 79. As to charges of unregistered land see PARA 262 et seq.
2 See the Law of Property Act 1925 s 199; and PARA 281.
3 See the Law of Property Act 1925 s 97; the Law of Property Act 1969 s 17(1)(b); and PARA 263 et seq.
4 See the Land Charges Act 1972 s 2(4)(iii)(a); and REAL PROPERTY AND REGISTRATION vol 87 (2012) PARA 723. As to the creation of an equitable mortgage by deposit of title deeds see PARAS 222–223. Since 27 September 1989 the mere deposit of title deeds by way of security can no longer create a valid equitable mortgage: see PARA 221.

241. Equitable mortgage of registered land. Prior to 27 September 1989[1] the registered proprietor of land or of a charge could create a lien of the registered land or charge by the deposit of the land or charge certificate[2]. A notice of deposit could be entered on the register[3], or a notice or a caution might be registered[4]. Similarly an applicant for registration as proprietor of land or of a charge could, whether the land or charge was already registered or not, create a lien on it equivalent to that created by deposit of a certificate by giving to the registrar written notice of intention to deposit the land certificate when issued[5]. Whilst a registered notice of deposit or intended deposit remains uncancelled, it operates as a caution against dealings[6]. A notice will, however, be cancelled in respect of an equitable mortgage created after 27 September 1989 which is not in writing[7].

A notice of deposit or intended deposit cannot now be registered[8].

1 Ie the date on which the Law of Property (Miscellaneous Provisions) Act 1989 s 2 came into force: see ss 2(7), 5(3), (4); and PARA 221.
2 See the Land Registration Act 1925 s 66 (repealed, subject to savings, by the Land Registration Act 2002 ss 134, 135, Schs 12, 13). As to the creation of an equitable mortgage by deposit of deeds see PARA 222 et seq. As to lien see also PARA 113.
3 See the Land Registration Rules 1925, SR & O 1925/1093, r 239 (revoked).
4 See *Re White Rose Cottage* [1965] Ch 940, [1965] 1 All ER 11, CA.
5 See the Land Registration Rules 1925, SR & O 1925/1093, r 240 (revoked).
6 See the Land Registration Rules 1925, SR & O 1925/1093, r 239 (revoked).
7 See *United Bank of Kuwait plc v Sahib* [1997] Ch 107, [1996] 3 All ER 215, CA; and PARA 221.
8 See, however, the Land Registration Act 2002 s 34 (which provides for the registration of an interest: see REAL PROPERTY AND REGISTRATION vol 87 (2012) PARA 515) and s 134, Sch 12

para 2 (which preserves the effect of notices entered before 13 October 2003 under the Land Registration Act 1925 s 49(1) (repealed); and REAL PROPERTY AND REGISTRATION vol 87 (2012) PARA 509 et seq).

(iii) Equitable Mortgages of Personality

242. Necessity for writing. A mortgage of an equitable interest subsisting at the time of the mortgage must be in writing signed by the mortgagor or his agent lawfully authorised in writing[1]. This requirement applies to equitable interests in personalty[2]. Subject to this requirement, an equitable mortgage of personal property is not required to be in writing[3].

1   Law of Property Act 1925 s 53(1)(c).
2   See DEEDS AND OTHER INSTRUMENTS vol 32 (2012) PARAS 223–226. The requirement will apply to a mortgage of an equitable interest in shares: *Grey v IRC* [1960] AC 1, [1959] 3 All ER 603, HL; *Oughtred v IRC* [1960] AC 206, [1959] 3 All ER 623, HL. As to the requirements for an equitable interest in land see PARA 221.
3   *Tibbits v George* (1836) 5 Ad & El 107; *Gurnell v Gardner* (1863) 4 Giff 626; *Riccard v Prichard* (1855) 1 K & J 277 at 279; *Brown, Shipley & Co v Kough* (1855) 29 ChD 848 at 854, CA; *Parish v Poole* (1884) 53 LT 35 at 38. As to oral mortgages of personal chattels, and as to the formalities required where a mortgage of such chattels is in writing, see PARA 205. As to models by which the equitable assignment of choses (or things) in action may be effected see CHOSES IN ACTION vol 13 (2009) PARA 24 et seq.

243. Effect of deposit of share certificate. A deposit of share certificates, with a transfer executed by the registered holders, but in blank as to the date and the names of the transferee, constitutes an equitable mortgage[1]; and, where transfers are not required to be by deed, the transferee as equitable mortgagee has implied authority to complete his security by filling up the transfer and obtaining registration[2].

1   *Stubbs v Slater* [1910] 1 Ch 632, CA; *London and Midland Bank v Mitchell* [1899] 2 Ch 161; *France v Clark* (1884) 26 ChD 257, CA.
2   *France v Clark* (1884) 26 ChD 257, CA; *Re Kimberley North Block Diamond Mining Co, ex p Wernher* (1888) 58 LT 305. See further PARA 211; and FINANCIAL INSTITUTIONS vol 48 (2015) PARA 295 et seq. See also COMPANIES vol 14 (2009) PARA 401.

244. Blank transfers of stocks and shares. Where stocks or shares can be transferred only by deed, a blank transfer does not in itself provide any security to the mortgagee[1] as an instrument containing blanks is not a deed[2]. The mortgagee should obtain authority from the mortgagors to fill in the blanks and deliver the transfer as a deed[3]. Where, however, transfers are not required to be by deed, an equitable mortgagee has an implied authority to complete the transfer for the purpose of perfecting his security[4].

1   See FINANCIAL INSTITUTIONS vol 48 (2015) PARA 297. See also COMPANIES vol 14 (2009) PARA 401. As to the simplified transfer of certain registered securities by means of a stock transfer see the Stock Transfer Act 1963 s 1(2); and COMPANIES vol 14 (2009) PARA 400.
2   As to the delivery of deeds see *Longman v Viscount Chelsea* [1989] 2 EGLR 242, 58 P & CR 189, CA; and DEEDS AND OTHER INSTRUMENTS vol 32 (2012) PARAS 231, 237, 240. The instrument may, however, afford evidence that any deposit of share certificates accompanying it was by way of security: *Colonial Bank v Whinney* (1886) 11 App Cas 426 at 433, HL. As to share certificates generally see COMPANIES vol 14 (2009) PARA 381 et seq. As to the effect of a deposit of share certificates see PARA 112.
3   The authority to fill in the blanks is usually given by means of a power of attorney executed as a deed. However, this is no longer necessary as the rule of law which required authority by one person to another to deliver an instrument as a deed on his behalf to be given by deed was abolished by the Law of Property (Miscellaneous Provisions) Act 1989 s 1(1)(c).
4   See PARA 112. As to the circumstances in which a person who hands over document of title to an agent may be bound by the agent's acts see PARA 286. See also COMPANIES vol 14 (2009) PARA 401; EQUITABLE JURISDICTION vol 47 (2014) PARA 123.

245. Equitable mortgagee of shares. Where a share certificate is deposited without any memorandum, the lender's remedy is an order for transfer and foreclosure[1]. This remedy may be available even though the personal remedy against the mortgagor is barred by statute[2]. Even where the certificate itself is deposited, the equitable mortgagee is not in a safe position, as the mortgagor may be able to obtain a fresh certificate and enable another mortgagee to obtain registration of a transfer, or may subject the shares to a lien having priority over the equitable mortgage[3], or the shares, if not fully paid up, may become liable to be forfeited[4].

1 *Harrold v Plenty* [1901] 2 Ch 314.
2 *London and Midland Bank v Mitchell* [1899] 2 Ch 161, which was decided at a time when there was no limitation period applicable to proceedings for the foreclosure of a mortgage of personal property. A 12 year period is now applicable to such a claim: see LIMITATION PERIODS vol 68 (2008) PARA 1124. However, it seems that the principle laid down in this case still applies where the 12 year period has not elapsed, but the six year period which, in the case of a mortgage not by deed, applies to the personal remedy against the mortgagor has elapsed: cf LIMITATION PERIODS vol 68 (2008) PARA 1105.
3 *Bradford Banking Co v Briggs, Son & Co Ltd* (1886) 12 App Cas 29, HL; *Champagne Perrier-Jouet SA v HH Finch Ltd* [1982] 3 All ER 713, [1982] 1 WLR 1359. As to the effect of a lien for debts incurred after a company has notice of a charge on debts see COMPANIES vol 15 (2009) PARA 1208.
4 See COMPANIES vol 15 (2009) PARA 1213 et seq.

246. Agreement to charge. An agreement to charge personal estate made for valuable consideration operates as a valid equitable charge[1]. Such an agreement will not be enforced in favour of a volunteer[2].

1 See PARA 217.
2 See PARA 217.

247. Mortgages of equitable interests. Personal property in the possession or under the legal dominion of third persons may be the subject of a valid charge by the equitable owner in favour of his creditor[1]. Accordingly, choses or things in action[2], such as debts or funds in the hands of trustees and including future choses in action and after-acquired property, are assignable by way of security[3]. For an equitable assignment by way of charge, notice is necessary as between assignee and debtor but not as between assignor and debtor, and, in order to obtain priority, the notice must be in writing[4]. It seems that an equitable charge may be created over a bank deposit in favour of the bank[5].

1 Formerly at law no possibility, right, title or thing in action could be assigned to a stranger (*Lampet's Case* (1612) 10 Co Rep 46b); but from early times assignments of a mere naked possibility or of a chose in action for valuable consideration were held valid in courts of equity (*Squib v Wyn* (1717) 1 P Wms 378; *Row v Dawson* (1749) 1 Ves Sen 331). See further CHOSES IN ACTION vol 13 (2009) PARA 24 et seq.
2 As to choses or things in action generally see CHOSES IN ACTION vol 13 (2009) PARA 1 et seq; and as to equitable assignments see CHOSES IN ACTION vol 13 (2009) PARA 24 et seq.
3 *Ryall v Rowles* (1750) 1 Ves Sen 348 at 364; 1 White & Tud LC (9th Edn) 90; *Tailby v Official Receiver* (1888) 13 App Cas 523, HL; *Re Clarke, Coombe v Carter* (1887) 36 ChD 348, 352, CA; *Syrett v Egerton* [1957] 3 All ER 331, [1957] 1 WLR 1130, DC; *Elders Pastoral Ltd v Bank of New Zealand (No 2)* [1990] 1 WLR 1478, PC; and see CHOSES IN ACTION vol 13 (2009) PARAS 30–31. Although a general charge purporting to extend to the whole of the mortgagor's after-acquired property may possibly be unenforceable as such, it is enforceable against ascertainable property falling within a class of property specifically included in the charge: see PARA 103.
4 See PARA 269 et seq.
5 *Re Bank of Credit and Commerce International SA (No 8)* [1998] AC 214, [1997] 4 All ER 568, HL. But see *Re Charge Card Services Ltd* [1987] Ch 150, [1986] 3 All ER 289; affd [1989] Ch 497, [1988] 3 All ER 702, CA.

248. Assignment subject to equities. As between the assignor and assignee of a debt[1] or of a fund in the hands of trustees[2], the assignee's title is complete even though no notice is given to the debtor or the trustee. Notice, however, should be given to the debtor or trustee to prevent payment to the assignor, for such payment by the debtor or trustee, without knowledge of the assignment, operates as a satisfaction of the debt or claim[3]. Where the debtor has been released in a general settlement of accounts the release is equally effectual[4]. An assignor can give no greater right in equity than he himself has[5], and a mortgagee of a chose or thing in action takes subject to all equities between the debtor and creditor existing or arising out of circumstances existing before notice is given of the assignment, whether or not the mortgagee has notice of them at the time of taking the assignment[6]. The debtor or holder of the fund may not, however, alter his rights to the prejudice of the assignee after notice of the assignment[7].

1   *Pickering v Ilfracombe Rly Co* (1868) LR 3 CP 235 at 248; *Robinson v Nesbitt* (1868) LR 3 CP 264 at 267; *Re Irving, ex p Brett* (1877) 7 ChD 419 at 421; *Gorringe v Irwell India Rubber and Gutta Percha Works* (1886) 34 ChD 128, CA.
2   *Ward v Duncombe* [1893] AC 369 at 392, HL; and see CHOSES IN ACTION vol 13 (2009) PARA 60 et seq.
3   *Norrish v Marshall* (1821) 5 Madd 475; *Stocks v Dobson* (1853) 4 De GM & G 11; *Re Lord Southampton's Estate, Allen v Lord Southampton, Banfather's Claim* (1880) 16 ChD 178; *Ward v Duncombe* [1893] AC 369 at 392, HL. In order to obtain priority for the assignment, the notice must be in writing (see the Law of Property Act 1925 s 137(3); and PARA 270), although in earlier times it was not essential that the notice should be express notice given by the assignee (*Lloyd v Banks* (1868) 3 Ch App 488).
4   *Stocks v Dobson* (1853) 4 De GM & G 11.
5   *Roxburghe v Cox* (1881) 17 ChD 520 at 526, CA; *Webb v Smith* (1885) 30 ChD 192 at 199, CA.
6   *Brice v Bannister* (1878) 3 QBD 569 at 578, CA, per Cotton LJ; *Cavendish v Geaves* (1857) 24 Beav 163; *Rolt v White* (1862) 31 Beav 520 (affd 3 De GJ & Sm 360); *Stoddart v Union Trust Ltd* [1912] 1 KB 181, CA. See generally CHOSES IN ACTION vol 13 (2009) PARA 60 et seq. As to the special case of a trustee who is also entitled to a share in the trust estate see CHOSES IN ACTION vol 13 (2009) PARA 65.
7   *Bradford Banking Co v Briggs, Son & Co Ltd* (1886) 12 App Cas 29, HL. See also PARA 269.

249. Hire purchase and conditional sale. A mere equitable mortgagee does not gain priority over a hire purchase or conditional sale agreement in respect of the chattels comprised in the agreement[1].

1   *Re Samuel Allen & Sons Ltd* [1907] 1 Ch 575; *Re Morrison, Jones and Taylor Ltd, Cookes v Morrison, Jones and Taylor Ltd* [1914] 1 Ch 50, CA. See also *Hamer v London, City and Midland Bank Ltd* (1918) 87 LJKB 973. As to hire purchase and conditional sale agreements generally see CONSUMER CREDIT vol 21 (2011) PARAS 64, 66.

(iv) Remedies of an Equitable Mortgagee

250. Remedies available to an equitable mortgagee. An equitable mortgagee is entitled to possession if there is a special agreement or the court so orders[1]. He may appoint a receiver if empowered to do so expressly or by statute; otherwise an application to the court is necessary[2]. If an express or statutory power exists he may sell the property[3] and may have express powers enabling him to convey the legal estate[4]. He may obtain an order for sale[5], specific performance[6], or foreclosure[7]; and he may, instead of proceeding against the security, bring a claim on the personal covenant[8].

1   See PARA 405.
2   See PARAS 405, 478 et seq.
3   See PARA 443 et seq. As to completion of share transfers in blank see COMPANIES vol 14 (2009) PARA 401.
4   See PARAS 237–238.

5 See PARA 621 et seq.
6 See PARA 251.
7 See PARA 573. As to foreclosure generally see PARA 571 et seq.
8 See PARA 540.

251. Specific performance. An equitable mortgage is a specifically enforceable contract to create a legal mortgage[1]. Specific performance will normally be ordered of an agreement to execute a legal mortgage of land[2], even though the legal mortgage when executed will confer on the mortgagee an immediate power of sale[3], so long as valuable consideration is given[4]. If the party agreeing to grant a mortgage over property only has a limited interest in the property, the court may order him to execute a charge over such interest as he has[5].

Valuable consideration may be given by the payment of money[6] or forbearance from suing[7]. The court will not, however, grant specific performance of a purely executory agreement to make or take a loan of money[8], whether the loan is to be secured or not[9], except in the case of a contract to take debentures in a limited company[10], but the aggrieved party has a remedy in damages for breach of contract[11].

1 *Swiss Bank Corpn v Lloyds Bank Ltd* [1982] AC 584, [1980] 2 All ER 419, CA; affd [1982] AC 584, [1981] 2 All ER 449, HL. As to the nature of an equitable mortgage see PARA 105.
2 *Swiss Bank Corpn v Lloyds Bank Ltd* [1982] AC 584, [1980] 2 All ER 419, CA; affd [1982] AC 584, [1981] 2 All ER 449, HL.
3 *Hermann v Hodges* (1873) LR 16 Eq 18; *Ashton v Corrigan* (1871) LR 13 Eq 76; *Matthews v Goodday* (1861) 31 LJCh 282.
4 *Jeffreys v Jeffreys* (1841) Cr & Ph 138. A seal is not sufficient: *Houghton v Lees* (1854) 1 Jur NS 862.
5 *Thames Guaranty Ltd v Campbell* [1985] QB 210, [1984] 2 All ER 585, CA; *Bankers Trust Co v Namdar* [1997] NPC 22, CA.
6 See *Hunter v Lord Langford* (1828) 2 Mol 272; *Sichel v Mosenthal* (1862) 30 Beav 371; *Rogers v Challis* (1859) 27 Beav 175; *Western Wagon and Property Co v West* [1892] 1 Ch 271; *Larios v Bonany y Gurety* (1873) LR 5 PC 346. As to payment as part performance see PARA 235.
7 *Alliance Bank Ltd v Broom* (1864) 2 Drew & Sm 289; *Fullerton v Provincial Bank of Ireland* [1903] AC 309, HL.
8 The agreement remains executory if no money has been actually advanced.
9 *Hunter v Lord Langford* (1828) 2 Mol 272; *Sichel v Mosenthal* (1862) 30 Beav 371; *Rogers v Challis* (1859) 27 Beav 175; *Western Wagon and Property Co v West* [1892] 1 Ch 271; *Larios v Bonany y Gurety* (1873) LR 5 PC 346.
10 See the Companies Act 2006 s 740; and COMPANIES vol 15 (2009) PARA 1312.
11 See DAMAGES vol 29 (2014) PARA 499 et seq.

(3) SUB-MORTGAGES

252. Form of sub-mortgage. Where the principal mortgage is a legal mortgage of land[1] by demise or sub-demise[2], a legal sub-mortgage may be effected either by sub-demise for a term that is at least one day shorter than the principal mortgage term or by a charge by deed expressed to be by way of legal mortgage[3]. A sub-mortgage which purports to be by way of assignment of the principal mortgage term takes effect by way of sub-demise but is subject to cesser on redemption[4]. Where the principal mortgage is other than a mortgage by demise or sub-demise, a sub-mortgage may be effected by a transfer of the benefit of the principal mortgage subject to a proviso for redemption[5]. An equitable sub-mortgage may be created in writing but no longer by deposit of deeds alone[6]. Before completing a sub-mortgage the lender should inquire from the original mortgagor as to the actual amount due on the mortgage and should give him notice of the sub-mortgage[7].

1   As to the meaning of 'land' see PARA 104 note 2. As to legal mortgages of land see PARA 161 et seq.
2   See PARA 164.
3   See the Law of Property Act 1925 s 86(1), (3); and PARA 164. See also REAL PROPERTY AND REGISTRATION vol 87 (2012) PARA 422 et seq. In practice, in such a case the sub-mortgage will contain a covenant to pay principal and interest due under the sub-mortgage, a transfer of the principal mortgage debt, a sub-demise or legal charge of the mortgaged property and a provision for cesser or redemption.
4   See the Law of Property Act 1925 s 86(2), (3); and PARA 162.
5   As to the principle that a deed is necessary for a legal mortgage of land or an interest in land see PARA 166. As to the necessity for writing for the disposition of an equitable interest see PARAS 221, 242.
6   See PARAS 221, 234. A memorandum by way of equitable sub-mortgage given by the transferee of a registered bill of sale, accompanied by deposit of the bill of sale and transfer, does not require registration as a bill of sale: see *Re Parker, ex p Turquand* (1885) 14 QBD 636, CA; and FINANCIAL INSTRUMENTS AND TRANSACTIONS vol 49 (2015) PARA 614.
7   See PARA 234.

253. Sub-mortgage of registered land. Because a registered proprietor[1] or a person entitled to be registered as a proprietor is entitled to exercise owner's powers[2], and since those powers in relation to a registered charge[3] consist of power to make a disposition of any kind permitted by the general law in relation to an interest of that description (other than a legal sub-mortgage)[4] and power to charge at law with the payment of money indebtedness secured by the registered charge[5], a sub-mortgage of registered land can be made only by way of a charge on the indebtedness secured by the registered charge[6]. The registered proprietor of a sub-charge[7] has, in relation to the property subject to the principal charge or any intermediate charge, the same powers as the sub-chargor[8].

1   Ie a person who is entered in the register of title: Land Registration Act 2002 s 132(1). As to the register of title and registration therein see REAL PROPERTY AND REGISTRATION vol 87 (2012) PARA 328 et seq.
2   See the Land Registration Act 2002 s 24(a), (b); PARA 127; and REAL PROPERTY AND REGISTRATION vol 87 (2012) PARA 424.
3   As to the meaning of 'charge' see PARA 127 note 5; and as to the meaning of 'registered charge' see PARA 142 note 7.
4   Land Registration Act 2002 s 23(2)(a). As to the meaning of 'legal sub-mortgage' see PARA 127 note 8.
5   Land Registration Act 2002 s 23(2)(b).
6   See the Land Registration Act 2002 ss 23(2), 24; and REAL PROPERTY AND REGISTRATION vol 87 (2012) PARAS 423, 424.
7   'Sub-charge' means a charge under the Land Registration Act 2002 s 23(2)(b) (see the text to note 5): s 132(1).
8   Land Registration Act 2002 s 53.

254. Obligation to sue. On a sub-mortgage of a debt, however secured, the mortgagee should be relieved from any obligation to sue for, or require payment of, the debt or any part of it, or to take any steps for that purpose, unless he thinks fit, and from any liability for loss occasioned by his omission to do so[1].

1   See *Ex p Mure* (1788) 2 Cox Eq Cas 63; *Williams v Price* (1824) 1 Sim & St 581. As to the right of a sub-mortgagee to prove in the administration of the assets of the deceased mortgagor see *Re Burrell, Burrell v Smith* (1869) LR 7 Eq 399.

255. Effect of sub-mortgage by transfer. During its continuance, a sub-mortgage by transfer will place the sub-mortgagee in the position of a transferee of the original mortgage because a deed of transfer operates to transfer the original mortgage debt, the benefit of all securities for it and the mortgagee's estate in the mortgaged property[1]. The transfer of the benefit of all securities includes the power of sale, and this suspends the original mortgagee's power of sale during the continuance of the sub-mortgage[2]. Subject to any stipulations contained in the sub-mortgage, the sub-mortgagee may call in the original mortgage, and may exercise the mortgagee's right to sue for and receive the mortgage money and to realise the security; and the mortgagee, as he is responsible to the sub-mortgagee for the debt due to the sub-mortgagee, may require him to sue for the mortgage debt[3]. If the sub-mortgagee receives the mortgage money, he must reconvey to the mortgagor, and, after satisfying his own debt, must account for the surplus to the mortgagee[4]. If he realises the mortgage security by exercising the power of sale arising under the mortgage, he must set aside the amount due under that mortgage and pay the surplus to the mortgagor[5]; and out of the amount so set aside he must retain the sub-mortgage debt and pay the remainder to the mortgagee[6].

1 See the Law of Property Act 1925 s 114; and PARA 367. In relation to registered land, s 114 takes effect only in equity: see *Paragon Finance plc v Pender* [2003] EWHC 2834 (Ch) at [121], [2003] All ER (D) 346 (Nov) per Peter Smith J (affd on appeal [2005] EWCA Civ 760, [2005] 1 WLR 3412, (2005) Times, 19 July).
2 *Cruse v Nowell* (1856) 25 LJCh 709. As to the power of sale see PARAS 198, 443 et seq. As to application of the statutory power of sale see PARA 446.
3 Cf *Gurney v Seppings* (1846) 2 Ph 40; and see FINANCIAL INSTRUMENTS AND TRANSACTIONS vol 49 (2015) PARA 754 et seq.
4 See the Law of Property Act 1925 ss 105, 107(2); PARA 475; and TRUSTS AND POWERS vol 98 (2013) PARA 16. As to the application of proceeds of sale by a building society see FINANCIAL INSTITUTIONS vol 48 (2015) PARA 501.
5 See PARA 475.
6 See the Law of Property Act 1925 ss 105, 107(2); and TRUSTS AND POWERS vol 98 (2013) PARA 16.

256. Effect of sub-charge by demise or legal charge. A sub-charge creates a new mortgage term of 3000 years less one day, rather than effecting a transfer of the original mortgage term[1]. Whether a sub-charge by demise or legal charge effects a transfer of the rights under the principal charge depends on the terms of the sub-charge[2]. If the principal mortgagee retains his estate he can take possession notwithstanding the transfer of the right to collect the debt and the grant of the sub-charge; if a sub-charge is granted on terms that it is enforceable only after the sub-chargee has made demand, he has no right to possession on the grant of the sub-charge[3].

1 *Credit and Mercantile plc v Marks* [2004] EWCA Civ 568, [2005] Ch 81, [2004] 3 WLR 489, at [29]–[48] per Clarke LJ (citing *Owen v Cornell* (1967) 203 Estates Gazette 29, and the combined effect of the Law of Property Act 1925 ss 86(1), 87(1)(b) (see PARAS 164–165)).
2 *Owen v Cornell* (1967) 203 Estates Gazette 29; *Credit and Mercantile plc v Marks* [2004] EWCA Civ 568 at [35], [2005] Ch 81, [2004] 3 WLR 489 per Clarke LJ.
3 *Credit and Mercantile plc v Marks* [2004] EWCA Civ 568, [2005] Ch 81, [2004] 3 WLR 489.

257. Effect on sub-mortgage of the exercise of power of sale. If the assistance of the court is necessary for a sale, and the original mortgage is to secure an unascertained amount, an account must first be taken of what is due on it[1]. Where a bankrupt mortgagee has purchased the equity of redemption[2], a sub-mortgagee by deposit is entitled to a sale of the bankrupt's entire interest[3]. There may also be a power of sale incident to the sub-mortgage[4], but the exercise of this does not affect the mortgagor. The sub-mortgagee, in pursuance of this power, transfers the mortgage so as to extinguish the mortgagee's equity of redemption, and accounts for the surplus proceeds to the mortgagee; but the mortgagor's equity of redemption continues to exist, and the purchaser under the power of sale holds the mortgaged property subject to it[5].

1 *Re Wright, ex p Mackay* (1841) 1 Mont D & De G 550.
2 As to the equity of redemption see PARAS 107, 304 et seq.

3   *Re Watts, ex p Tuffnell* (1834) 4 Deac & Ch 29. As to an order for sale on the application of an
    equitable sub-mortgagee in the mortgagee's bankruptcy see *Re Vaughan, ex p Powell* (1847) De
    G 405. As to the effect of insolvency see PARA 521 et seq. It is no longer possible to create a
    sub-mortgage by deposit alone: see PARAS 221, 234.
4   As to the power of sale see PARAS 198, 442 et seq; and as to application of the statutory power
    of sale see PARA 446 et seq. As to the effect of conveyance by a sub-mortgagee see PARA 452.
5   See note 4.

258. Sub-mortgagee takes subject to outstanding equities. As the sub-mortgagee
is in the position of a transferee of the mortgage, he takes, like any other
transferee, subject to the accounts between the mortgagor and the mortgagee at
the date of the sub-mortgage[1], and he will be affected by dealings between the
mortgagor and mortgagee until the mortgagor has had notice of the
sub-mortgage[2]. The mortgagor's receipt for the mortgage money, incorporated in
the mortgage or indorsed on it, is, however, usually conclusive in favour of the
sub-mortgagee that the original mortgage money was in fact advanced[3].

1   See *Norrish v Marshall* (1821) 5 Madd 475; *Cockell v Taylor* (1851) 15 Beav 103; *De Lisle v
    Union Bank of Scotland* [1914] 1 Ch 22, CA. See also PARA 382.
2   *Reeve v Whitmore, Martin v Whitmore* (1863) 4 De GJ & Sm 1 at 19.
3   As to the amount originally advanced see PARA 383.

259. Sub-mortgage of securities. By implication of law, a mortgagee of securities
has the right to sub-mortgage the securities to the extent of his own interest in
them without an express agreement to that effect[1]. Any attempt to sub-mortgage
beyond that extent is, however, inoperative, except where negotiable securities are
taken in good faith and for value[2] or where the sub-mortgagee has otherwise
acquired a good legal title, and the original mortgagor can recover the securities
from the sub-mortgagee upon payment of the amount due from him upon them[3].

1   *Donald v Suckling* (1866) LR 1 QB 585; *Re Tahiti Cotton Co, ex p Sargent* (1874) LR 17 Eq 273;
    France v Clark (1884) 26 ChD 257, CA; *Mocatta v Bell* (1857) 24 Beav 585.
2   *London Joint Stock Bank v Simmons* [1892] AC 201, HL; *Fuller v Glyn, Mills, Currie & Co*
    [1914] 2 KB 168.
3   *Donald v Suckling* (1866) LR 1 QB 585; *France v Clark* (1884) 26 ChD 257, CA; *Earl of Sheffield
    v London Joint Stock Bank* (1888) 13 App Cas 333, HL. Cf *Re Burge, Woodall & Co, ex p
    Skyrme* [1912] 1 KB 393.

4. PRIORITY OF MORTGAGES

(1) PRIORITY BETWEEN MORTGAGEES OF LAND

260. Effect of the Law of Property Act 1925. The principles which applied before 1926 with respect to the priorities of legal and equitable mortgages of, and other interests in, land[1] were not abrogated by the Law of Property Act 1925[2], and that Act does not affect any question arising out of or consequent upon any omission to obtain or any other absence of possession by any person of documents relating to a legal estate in land[3]. A mortgagee taking a legal estate still has priority over an earlier equitable incumbrance of which he had no notice when he made his advance[4], and a legal mortgagee may by his conduct in relation to the deeds either lose his priority over an earlier equitable incumbrance or be postponed to a subsequent incumbrance[5]. The operation of these rules is, however, largely modified by the statutory provisions with respect to the registration of land[6] and, in the case of unregistered land, the registration of puisne mortgages, equitable mortgages and general equitable charges, such registration being deemed to constitute actual notice[7].

1 See PARAS 284–288.
2 See *Beddoes v Shaw* [1937] Ch 81, [1936] 2 All ER 1108. See also PARA 264.
3 Law of Property Act 1925 s 13. As to the meaning of 'legal estate' see PARA 105 note 2. As to the meaning of 'land' see PARA 104 note 2.
4 See PARA 265.
5 See PARA 285.
6 As to the registration of land see REAL PROPERTY AND REGISTRATION vol 87 (2012) PARA 232 et seq. The statutory provisions do not, however, affect:
    (1)   priorities between unregistered charges created before 13 October 2003 (ie the date on which the substantive provisions of the Land Registration Act 2002, and the corresponding repeals of the Land Registration Act 1925, were brought into force by the Land Registration Act 2002 (Commencement No 4) Order 2003, SI 2003/1725) which are still governed by the rule that the first in time prevails (see *Mortgage Corpn Ltd v Nationwide Credit Corpn Ltd* [1994] Ch 49 at 56, [1993] 4 All ER 623 at 628, CA, per Dillon LJ);
    (2)   priority between mortgages of equitable interests created before 13 October 2003 which are still governed by the rule in *Dearle v Hall* (1828) 3 Russ 1 (see PARA 269 et seq); or
    (3)   the right of the mortgagor to set aside the mortgage procured by the wrongdoing of the debtor, where the mortgagee must rely on the defence of bona fide purchaser for value without notice (see PARA 119 et seq).
7 See the Law of Property Act 1925 s 198(1); the Land Charges Act 1972 s 2(1), (4)(i), (iii); and PARAS 262–263, 278. In certain circumstances, however, the Law of Property Act 1925 s 198(1) must be disregarded: see the Law of Property Act 1969 ss 24, 25; and CONVEYANCING vol 23 (2013) PARA 53; REAL PROPERTY AND REGISTRATION vol 87 (2012) PARA 709. Thus a general equitable charge (without the deeds) should be registered as a land charge. If it is followed by a legal mortgage (with or without the deeds), the legal mortgagee will have actual notice of it, and cannot gain priority by his legal estate. If the general equitable charge is not registered, it will be void against the legal mortgagee, and he will not have to rely on his legal estate. If the deeds are in the hands of an equitable incumbrancer, the equitable incumbrance need not be registered as a land charge (see PARA 262), but a subsequent legal mortgagee may still be postponed by reason of his negligence in inquiring for them (see PARA 284), and, unless he registers his mortgage as a puisne mortgage, it will be void as against a subsequent incumbrancer. If the legal mortgagee, having obtained the deeds, parts with them, except to some person who holds them on his behalf exclusively, it is possible that his mortgage becomes a puisne mortgage, and unless he registers it as a land charge it may be void against a subsequent incumbrancer whether the subsequent incumbrancer obtains the deeds or not: see the Land Charges Act 1972 s 4(5); and PARA 263. Thus it may be necessary sometimes to resort to the principles which determined priorities before 1926, but in general priorities depend on the statutory provisions which came into operation on 1 January 1926.

261. Priority of charges of registered land. The statutory provisions for the registration of land charges[1] do not apply to charges if and so far as they affect registered land and can be protected under the Land Registration Act 2002[2].

The priority of an interest, such as a charge, affecting a registered estate or charge[3] is not affected by a disposition of the estate or charge[4], save that if a registrable disposition[5] of a registered estate or charge is made for valuable consideration[6], completion of the disposition by registration has the effect of postponing to the interest under the disposition any interest affecting the estate or charge immediately before the disposition whose priority is not protected at the time of registration[7].

Registered charges on the same registered estate, or on the same registered charge, are to be taken to rank as between themselves in the order shown in the register[8].

1 Ie the Land Charges Act 1972: see PARA 262.
2 See the Land Charges Act 1972 s 14; and REAL PROPERTY AND REGISTRATION vol 87 (2012) PARA 697.
3 As to the meanings of 'registered estate' and 'registered charge' see PARA 142 note 7.
4 See the Land Registration Act 2002 s 28(1); and REAL PROPERTY AND REGISTRATION vol 87 (2012) PARA 454. This is the case whether or not the interest or disposition is registered: see s 28(2); and REAL PROPERTY AND REGISTRATION vol 87 (2012) PARA 454.
5 As to the meaning of 'registrable disposition' see PARA 142 note 8.
6 As to the meaning of 'valuable consideration' see PARA 142 note 9. A charging order is not made for valuable consideration: *Hughmans Solicitors v Central Stream Services Ltd (in liquidation)* [2012] EWHC 1222 (Ch), [2012] 2 EGLR 30, [2012] All ER (D) 102 (May).
7 See the Land Registration Act 2002 ss 29(1), 30(1); and REAL PROPERTY AND REGISTRATION vol 87 (2012) PARAS 455–456. For these purposes, the priority of an interest or charge is protected in any case if it is a registered interest or charge or is the subject of a notice on the register, or if it is an overriding interest falling within Sch 3 which has not been the subject of a notice in the register at any time since 13 October 2003 (ie the date on which ss 29, 30 were brought into force by the Land Registration Act 2002 (Commencement No 4) Order 2003, SI 2003/1725), or if it appears from the register to be excepted from the effect of registration: see the Land Registration Act 2002 ss 29(2)(a)(i)–(iii), (3), 30(2)(a)(i)–(iii), (3); and REAL PROPERTY AND REGISTRATION vol 87 (2012) PARAS 455–456. As to the register of title and registration therein see REAL PROPERTY AND REGISTRATION vol 87 (2012) PARA 328 et seq.
8 Land Registration Act 2002 s 48(1). For these purposes, subject to any entry in the individual register to the contrary, the order in which registered charges are entered in an individual register shows the order in which the registered charges rank as between themselves: see the Land Registration Rules 2003, SI 2003/1417, r 101; and REAL PROPERTY AND REGISTRATION vol 87 (2012) PARA 464.

262. Registrable land charges. Among the charges which may be registered in the register of land charges[1] are a puisne mortgage, that is, a legal mortgage which is not protected by a deposit of documents relating to the legal estate affected[2], and a general equitable charge, that is, any equitable charge which is not secured by a deposit of documents relating to the legal estate affected, and does not arise or affect an interest arising under a trust of land or settlement, and is not a charge given by way of indemnity against rents equitably apportioned or charged exclusively on land in exoneration of other land and against the breach or non-observance of covenants or conditions, and is not included in any other class of land charge[3]. Also registrable are estate contracts, that is, contracts by an estate owner (or by a person entitled at the date of the contract to have a legal estate conveyed to him) to convey or create a legal estate, including options to purchase, rights of pre-emption[4] and equitable mortgages[5]. The statutory right of a spouse or civil partner to occupy the matrimonial or partnership home is registrable as a charge on the legal estate[6]. Charges of registered land are not subject to the Land Charges Act 1972[7].

1 See REAL PROPERTY AND REGISTRATION vol 87 (2012) PARAS 720–724. As to other securities of a special nature which may be registered see REAL PROPERTY AND REGISTRATION vol 87 (2012) PARA 714 et seq. As to registration of land charges created by companies see COMPANIES

vol 15 (2009) PARA 1277 et seq; REAL PROPERTY AND REGISTRATION vol 87 (2012) PARA 698. As to local land charges see REAL PROPERTY AND REGISTRATION vol 87 (2012) PARA 763 et seq.

2 See the Land Charges Act 1972 s 2(1), (4)(i); PARA 160 note 5; and REAL PROPERTY AND REGISTRATION vol 87 (2012) PARAS 720–721. For the principle that possession by a mortgagee of documents of title is sufficient to constitute notice of the mortgage to subsequent incumbrancers and to preserve its priority see PARAS 264, 286.

3 See the Land Charges Act 1972 s 2(1), (4)(iii); and REAL PROPERTY AND REGISTRATION vol 87 (2012) PARAS 720, 723. An equitable charge created by deposit of title deeds (see PARA 222 et seq) was not registrable as an estate contract (see s 2(1), (4)(iv); and REAL PROPERTY AND REGISTRATION vol 87 (2012) PARAS 720, 724), even though it was treated as a contract to create a mortgage (see *United Bank of Kuwait v Sahib* [1997] Ch 107, [1996] 3 All ER 215, CA) or contained an ancillary agreement to execute a mortgage (see *Property Discount Corpn Ltd v Lyon Group Ltd* [1981] 1 All ER 379, [1981] 1 WLR 300, CA).

4 See the Land Charges Act 1972 s 2(1), (4)(iv); and REAL PROPERTY AND REGISTRATION vol 87 (2012) PARAS 720, 724.

5 See *United Bank of Kuwait v Sahib* [1997] Ch 107, [1996] 3 All ER 215, CA. An equitable mortgage protected by deposit of title deeds creates an equitable charge which is not registrable: see *United Bank of Kuwait v Sahib*.

6 See the Family Law Act 1996 s 31(13); and REAL PROPERTY AND REGISTRATION vol 87 (2012) PARA 730.

7 See the Land Charges Act 1972 s 14(1); and REAL PROPERTY AND REGISTRATION vol 87 (2012) PARA 697.

263. Priority of registered land charges. The registration of any instrument or matter in any register kept under the Land Charges Act 1972 or any local land charges register, is deemed to constitute actual notice of that instrument or matter to all persons and for all purposes connected with the land affected[1]. Hence, the legal estate will not avail a subsequent legal mortgagee, as he will be deemed to take with notice of any registered charge[2]. On the other hand, if a registrable charge is not registered, it is void as against a purchaser of the land charged (including a subsequent mortgagee or chargee[3]), although an estate contract, including an equitable mortgage, is void only as against a purchaser for money or money's worth[4]. Moreover, even if he has notice of the charge (that is, notice actual or constructive in the ordinary sense as opposed to statutory actual notice arising from registration), a subsequent mortgagee is not prejudicially affected by it[5], whether or not he is a purchaser in good faith[6], and so he has priority over the unregistered incumbrance notwithstanding that he may be in fact well aware of it. When mortgages which require to be registered as land charges (that is, every mortgage, whether legal or equitable, not being a mortgage protected by the deposit of documents relating to the legal estate affected) are registered, they rank according to their date of registration[7].

1 See the Law of Property Act 1925 s 198(1); and EQUITABLE JURISDICTION vol 47 (2014) PARA 131; REAL PROPERTY AND REGISTRATION vol 87 (2012) PARAS 708–709. See also *Williams v Burlington Investments Ltd* (1977) 121 Sol Jo 424, HL, where a legal charge executed pursuant to an agreement to execute a legal charge in an agreement for sale, which had been registered as an estate contract, had priority to, even though executed after, another legal charge executed after the sale.

2 See PARA 265.

3 See the Land Charges Act 1972 s 4(5), (6); and REAL PROPERTY AND REGISTRATION vol 87 (2012) PARA 735. Cf *Khoury v Phillip Said Azar* [1953] 1 WLR 21, PC, where an equitable mortgage not registered in accordance with a local ordinance was held to be of no effect. As to the meaning of 'purchaser' see *McCarthy & Stone Ltd v Julian S Hodge & Co Ltd* [1971] 2 All ER 973, [1971] 1 WLR 1547; and REAL PROPERTY AND REGISTRATION vol 87 (2012) PARA 735.

4 See the Land Charges Act 1972 s 4(6); and REAL PROPERTY AND REGISTRATION vol 87 (2012) PARA 735. Nominal consideration is sufficient: see *Midland Bank Trust Co Ltd v Green* [1981] AC 513, [1981] 1 All ER 153, HL.

5 See the Law of Property Act 1925 s 199(1)(i); PARA 281; and EQUITABLE JURISDICTION vol 47 (2014) PARA 137; REAL PROPERTY AND REGISTRATION vol 87 (2012) PARA 708.

6   *Midland Bank Trust Co Ltd v Green* [1981] AC 513, [1981] 1 All ER 153, HL. As to the meaning of 'a purchaser in good faith' see *Corbett v Halifax plc* [2002] EWCA Civ 1849, [2003] 4 All ER 180, [2003] 1 WLR 964.
7   See the Law of Property Act 1925 s 97; and REAL PROPERTY AND REGISTRATION vol 87 (2012) PARA 721.

264. Effect of possession of title deeds. A first legal mortgagee has the same right to possession of the title deeds of the mortgaged property as if his security either included the fee simple or had been effected by assignment[1]. The Law of Property Act 1925 does not prejudicially affect the right or interest of any person arising out of or consequent on the possession by him of any documents relating to a legal estate in land[2]; and neither the Law of Property Act 1925, the Land Charges Act 1972 nor the Local Land Charges Act 1975 directly interferes with the general rule that possession of the title deeds by a mortgagee is sufficient to give him priority over a subsequent incumbrancer, as the absence of the title deeds from the mortgagor's possession is sufficient to affect the subsequent incumbrancer with actual notice (if he makes proper inquiries as to deeds) or constructive notice (if he fails to make such inquiries) of the existence of the prior mortgage[3].

A legal mortgagee who has possession of the deeds will be bound by prior charges registered at the time when the mortgage accompanied by deposit of deeds was made[4].

1   See the Law of Property Act 1925 ss 85(1) proviso, 86(1) proviso; and PARA 488 et seq. As to the meaning of 'legal mortgagee' see PARA 104 note 1.
2   See the Law of Property Act 1925 s 13. As to the meaning of 'legal estate' see PARA 105 note 2. As to the meaning of 'land' see PARA 104 note 2. As to the effect of the omission to obtain the deeds, which is also preserved by s 13, see PARA 284.
3   See PARA 284 et seq. For the rule that mortgages and charges protected by deposit of documents are not capable of being registered as land charges see PARA 262.
4   See the Law of Property Act 1925 s 97; the Land Charges Act 1972 s 4(5); PARA 263; and REAL PROPERTY AND REGISTRATION vol 87 (2012) PARAS 721, 735.

265. Effect of possession of legal estate. As, since the enactment of the Law of Property Act 1925, it is possible for there to be a succession of legal mortgages, the opportunities for setting up a legal estate against an equitable interest appear to have been increased[1]. In practice, however, the occasions for resorting to the old rules for determining priorities which favour the possessor of the legal estate as such[2] are very much decreased by the provisions of the Law of Property Act 1925, the Land Charges Act 1972 and the Local Land Charges Act 1975 with regard to registration of mortgages and charges which are not accompanied by a deposit of documents relating to the legal estate affected, including the provisions that registration is to be deemed to constitute actual notice and that instruments or matters capable of registration which are not registered are to be void against a purchaser, including a mortgagee[3]. In general a first mortgagee will have a legal term of years and will hold the deeds, and he will have unquestioned priority; but the priorities of other incumbrancers will usually depend on registration or its absence, and on the effect of registration as actual notice.

1   As to obtaining priority by getting in the legal estate see EQUITABLE JURISDICTION vol 47 (2014) PARA 124 et seq. As to the former right of a mortgagee to tack after getting in the legal estate see PARA 266. As to the meaning of 'tacking' see PARA 266.
2   As to the principle that, apart from statute, a purchaser of a legal estate for value without notice obtains priority over an earlier equitable owner see EQUITABLE JURISDICTION vol 47 (2014) PARAS 119–121.
3   See PARA 278 et seq.

266. Partial abolition of tacking. 'Tacking' means the right of a mortgagee to add later advances to earlier advances so as to obtain priority over an intermediate incumbrancer. A mortgagee's right to tack[1] still exists to some extent in relation to further advances made by him[2], but has otherwise been abolished[3].

1   A mortgagee's right to tack formerly existed:
   (1)   where a legal mortgagee made a further advance without having notice at the time when the further advance was made of the existence of an intermediate incumbrance (see eg *Tenison v Sweeny* (1844) 1 Jo & Lat 710; *Wyllie v Pollen* (1863) 3 De GJ & Sm 596);
   (2)   where a third incumbrancer, having made his advance without notice of the second incumbrance, obtained a transfer of the first mortgage so as to obtain the benefit of the first mortgagee's legal estate (see eg *Brace v Duchess of Marlborough* (1728) 2 P Wms 491; *McCarthy and Stone Ltd v Julian S Hodge & Co Ltd* [1971] 2 All ER 973, [1971] 1 WLR 1547); and
   (3)   where a mortgage was made to secure further advances and such advances were made without notice of an intermediate incumbrance (see eg *Hopkinson v Rolt* (1861) 9 HL Cas 514).

   While tacking was based on the special value attached to the legal estate, it was not essential that the mortgagee claiming to tack should have the legal estate actually vested in him. It was sufficient if he had the best right to call for it (see PARA 276). It has been doubted whether the type of tacking referred to in head (3) above depended on the doctrine of estates in land: see *Matzner v Clyde Securities Ltd* [1975] 2 NSWLR 293, NSW SC. Although unsecured debts could not be tacked to mortgage debts as against intermediate incumbrances or the mortgagor, they could be tacked against a person entitled to the equity of redemption on the mortgagor's death so as to entitle the mortgagee to recover all the debts in one action (see eg *Coleman v Winch* (1721) 1 P Wms 775), but not so as to entitle him to give priority in respect of the debts tacked over other creditors (*Pile v Pile* (1875) 23 WR 440).
2   See PARA 267.
3   Law of Property Act 1925 s 94(3). The Law of Property Act 1925 did not affect any priority acquired before 1 January 1926 (ie the commencement of the Act) by tacking, or in respect of further advances made without notice of a subsequent incumbrance or by arrangement with the subsequent incumbrancer: s 94(3) proviso. Section 94 applies to mortgages of land, whether made before or after the commencement of the Act, but not to charges on registered land: s 94(4) (amended by the Land Registration Act 2002 s 133, Sch 11 para 2(1), (9)). The Law of Property Act 1925 s 94 contains no definition of the right to tack and does not distinguish between the right to tack by virtue of the legal estate, and the narrower right to tack by virtue of the contract where the first mortgage contains a provision that it is to extend to further advances. However, s 94 appears to apply to both forms of tacking, and its general effect is to abolish tacking by virtue of the legal estate; to extend tacking to further advances made by a mortgagee, legal or equitable, without notice of a later mortgage; and, where a mortgage is made to cover further advances, to enable these advances to be made without further search. It seems that, provided he does not bring himself within the doctrine of tacking, a mortgagee may still get in the legal estate after his mortgage and use it for his protection if the conveyance to him of the legal estate was not a breach of trust. In the case of land, the principle appears to be limited to cases where the legal estate is obtained by redeeming a prior legal mortgage. The principle also applies in the case of shares: see PARAS 275–276. Cf *Bailey v Barnes* [1894] 1 Ch 25 at 37, CA; *McCarthy and Stone Ltd v Julian S Hodge & Co Ltd* [1971] 2 All ER 973, [1971] 1 WLR 1547.
   As to the modern law of tacking see PARA 267.

267. Modern law of tacking. A prior mortgagee[1] has a right to make further advances to rank in priority to subsequent mortgages[2], whether legal or equitable:
   (1)   if an arrangement to that effect has been made with the subsequent mortgagees[3];
   (2)   if he had no notice of those subsequent mortgages at the time when the further advance was made by him[4]; or
   (3)   whether or not he had such notice, where the mortgage imposes an obligation on him to make further advances[5].

These provisions apply whether or not the prior mortgage was made expressly for securing further advances[6]. As registration of the subsequent incumbrance as a land charge operates as actual notice[7], it is necessary to search the registers before making a further advance, except where the prior mortgage was made expressly for securing a current account or other further advances. If it was so made, then the current account can be operated or further money advanced without further search than that made at the time of the first mortgage, or when the last search, if any, by or on behalf of the mortgagee was made, whichever last happened[8], and the prior mortgage will have priority over subsequent incumbrancers.

Charges on registered land are excluded from these provisions[9].

Where a spouse's or civil partner's estate is subject to a mortgage and the other spouse's or partner's rights of occupation are subsequently registered as a land charge against that estate, the rights of occupation are deemed to be a mortgage subsequent in date to the first mortgage[10].

1 As to the meaning of 'mortgagee' see PARA 104 note 1.
2 As to the meaning of 'mortgage' see PARA 101 note 4. The right of a mortgagee to add later advances to earlier advances so as to obtain priority over an intermediate incumbrancer ('tacking') has been abolished save in regard to the making of further advances as described in the text: see the Law of Property 1925 s 94(3); and PARA 266.
3 Law of Property Act 1925 s 94(1)(a).
4 Law of Property Act 1925 s 94(1)(b). 'Notice' includes constructive notice: s 205(1)(xvii). The requirement that the mortgagee seeking to tack should not have had notice of subsequent incumbrances is in accordance with the principle laid down in *Hopkinson v Rolt* (1861) 9 HL Cas 514. See also *Calisher v Forbes* (1871) 7 Ch App 109; *London and County Banking Co Ltd v Ratcliffe* (1881) 6 App Cas 722, HL; *Bradford Banking Co Ltd v Briggs, Son & Co* (1886) 12 App Cas 29, HL; *Union Bank of Scotland v National Bank of Scotland* (1886) 12 App Cas 53, HL; *Freeman v Laing* [1899] 2 Ch 355. As to the doctrine of notice see EQUITABLE JURISDICTION vol 47 (2014) PARA 130 et seq.
5 Law of Property Act 1925 s 94(1)(c). This provision overrules *West v Williams* [1899] 1 Ch 132, CA, where the principle of *Hopkinson v Rolt* (1861) 9 HL Cas 514 (see note 4) was held to apply even though the mortgagee seeking to tack had been under an obligation to make further advances.
6 Law of Property Act 1925 s 94(1).
7 See PARA 263.
8 See the Law of Property Act 1925 s 94(2) (amended by the Law of Property Act (Amendment) Act 1926 s 7, Schedule; and the Law of Property Act 1969 s 16, Sch 2 Pt I).
9 Law of Property Act 1925 s 94(4) (amended by the Land Registration Act 2002 s 133, Sch 11 para 2(1), (9)). As to further advances in the case of registered land see PARA 268.
10 See the Family Law Act 1996 s 31(12) (amended by the Civil Partnership Act 2004 s 82, Sch 9 Pt 1 para 2(1), (11)); and REAL PROPERTY AND REGISTRATION vol 87 (2012) PARA 730.

268. Further advances in the case of registered land. The proprietor of a registered charge[1] may make a further advance on the security of the charge ranking in priority to a subsequent charge if he has not received from the subsequent chargee notice[2] of the creation of the subsequent charge[3], if the advance is made in pursuance of an obligation which at the time of the creation of the subsequent charge was entered in the register in accordance with rules[4], or if the parties to the prior charge have agreed a maximum amount for which the charge is security and at the time of the creation of the subsequent charge the agreement was entered in the register in accordance with rules[5].

Tacking in relation to a charge over registered land is otherwise possible only with the agreement of the subsequent chargee[6].

1 As to the meaning of 'registered charge' see PARA 142 note 7. As to the meaning of 'registered' see PARA 127 note 3; and as to the meaning of 'charge' see PARA 127 note 5.
2 Notice for these purposes is treated as received at the time when, in accordance with rules, it ought to have been received: see the Land Registration Act 2002 s 49(2). As to the time when notice ought to have been received see the Land Registration Rules 2003, SI 2003/1417, r 107; and REAL PROPERTY AND REGISTRATION vol 87 (2012) PARA 468.
3 See the Land Registration Act 2002 s 49(1); REAL PROPERTY AND REGISTRATION vol 87 (2012) PARA 468.
4 See the Land Registration Act 2002 s 49(3)(a), (b); and REAL PROPERTY AND REGISTRATION vol 87 (2012) PARA 468. As to registration of such obligations see the Land Registration Rules

2003, SI 2003/1417, r 108; and REAL PROPERTY AND REGISTRATION vol 87 (2012) PARA 468. As to the register of title and registration therein see REAL PROPERTY AND REGISTRATION vol 87 (2012) PARA 328 et seq.

5   See the Land Registration Act 2002 s 49(4)(a), (b); and REAL PROPERTY AND REGISTRATION vol 87 (2012) PARA 468. As to registration of such agreements see the Land Registration Rules 2003, SI 2003/1417, r 109; and REAL PROPERTY AND REGISTRATION vol 87 (2012) PARA 468. Rules may disapply the Land Registration Act 2002 s 49(4) in relation to charges of a description specified in the rules or provide for its application to be subject, in the case of charges of a description so specified, to compliance with such conditions as may be so specified: see s 49(5); and REAL PROPERTY AND REGISTRATION vol 87 (2012) PARA 468.

6   See the Land Registration Act 2002 s 49(6); and REAL PROPERTY AND REGISTRATION vol 87 (2012) PARA 468. As to the meaning of 'tacking' see PARA 266.

(2) PRIORITY BETWEEN MORTGAGEES OF PERSONALTY AND OF EQUITABLE INTERESTS IN LAND

(i) Notice or Registration

269. Priority of mortgages of choses or things in action. Where the mortgaged property is a debt or other money owing[1], or an interest in trust funds[2], a mortgagee who gives written notice to the debtor or trustee gains priority over a mortgagee earlier in date who omits to give notice[3]. However, notice to the trustees, without requiring payment of income to the assignees, is not equivalent to taking possession[4], and notice to the trustees will not give priority over advances previously made by them[5]. The omission to give notice leaves the property under the mortgagor's control and deprives the second mortgagee of the chance of ascertaining the existence of the first mortgage by inquiry of the debtor or trustee. The priority of the second mortgagee does not depend on whether in fact he made inquiry; in such a case it depends solely on notice[6]. A second mortgagee will not gain priority if he gave no value[7] or if he had knowledge of a prior mortgage at the time of his advance[8]. A judgment creditor who obtains a charging order is treated as a volunteer and cannot therefore gain priority by giving notice[9]. Where notices are contemporaneous, the incumbrances rank in order of time of creation[10].

1   As to mortgages of choses or things in action see PARA 206.
2   *Dearle v Hall* (1828) 3 Russ 1 at 11–12, 23; cf *Hill v Peters* [1918] 2 Ch 273 at 279. The rule in *Dearle v Hall* has no application where in fact the assignor has no beneficial interest that he can effectively assign: see *BS Lyle Ltd v Rosher* [1958] 3 All ER 597, [1959] 1 WLR 8, HL.
3   As to the necessity for written notice to be given in order to render effectual a legal assignment of a chose in action, and as to the notice which is sufficient, see CHOSES IN ACTION vol 13 (2009) PARAS 72, 80. As to notice in relation to equitable assignments of choses in action see CHOSES IN ACTION vol 13 (2009) PARA 40 et seq. As to whether there is any necessity for a trustee in bankruptcy to give notice of his title see BANKRUPTCY AND INDIVIDUAL INSOLVENCY vol 5 (2013) PARAS 406, 475.
4   *Re Pawson's Settlement, Higgins v Pawson* [1917] 1 Ch 541.
5   *Re Goddard, Hooker v Buckley* (1912) 57 Sol Jo 42, CA.
6   *Ward v Duncombe* [1893] AC 369, HL. See also CHOSES IN ACTION vol 13 (2009) PARA 40 et seq. Notice given to an administrator before he obtains administration is ineffectual: *Re Kinahan's Trusts* [1907] 1 IR 321.
7   *Justice v Wynne* (1860) 12 I Ch R 289, CA. See also CHOSES IN ACTION vol 13 (2009) PARAS 40, 43.
8   *Re Holmes* (1885) 29 ChD 786; *Rhodes v Allied Dunbar Pension Services Ltd, Re Offshore Ventilation Ltd* [1988] 1 All ER 524, [1987] 1 WLR 1703 (revsd on different grounds [1989] 1 All ER 1161, [1989] 1 WLR 800, CA). See also CHOSES IN ACTION vol 13 (2009) PARA 43.

9 *United Bank of Kuwait plc v Sahib* [1997] Ch 107, [1995] 2 All ER 973; affd on different grounds [1997] Ch 107, [1996] 3 All ER 215, CA.
10 *Boss v Hopkinson* (1870) 18 WR 725; *Calisher v Forbes* (1871) 7 Ch App 109.

270. Priority of equitable interests in unregistered land. Before 1926 the doctrine of acquiring priority by notice did not apply to land[1], but it applied to proceeds of sale of real estate and to any interest in land which could reach the assignor's hands only in the form of money[2]. However, it now extends to dealings with equitable interests in unregistered land[3], capital money, and securities representing capital money effected after 31 December 1925[4], so that the doctrine applies now to equitable interests in both real and personal estate. A judgment creditor who obtains a charging order cannot, however, take advantage of the rule[5].

As regards land and the proceeds of sale of land, the persons to whom notice must be given are:

(1)   in the case of a dealing with an equitable interest in settled land, capital money or securities representing capital money, the trustees of the settlement[6];

(2)   in the case of a dealing with an equitable interest in land subject to a trust of land, the trustees[7]; and

(3)   in any other case of a dealing with an equitable interest in land, the estate owner of the land affected[8].

As regards equitable interests in both real and personal property, however, the notice must be in writing or it will not affect the priorities of competing claims of purchasers[9].

1 See EQUITABLE JURISDICTION vol 47 (2014) PARA 122. In *Re Carew's Estate* (1868) 16 WR 1077, it was held that the doctrine did not apply to personalty which by statute was real estate; but this was not followed in *Re Sandes' Trusts* [1920] 1 IR 342, CA, as regards capital money arising under the Settled Land Act 1882 (largely repealed: see now the Settled Land Act 1925).
2 *Re Hughes' Trusts* (1864) 2 Hem & M 89; *Re Roche's Estate* (1890) 25 LR Ir 284 at 292, Ir CA; *Lloyds Bank v Pearson* [1901] 1 Ch 865. See CHOSES IN ACTION vol 13 (2009) PARAS 45, 50.
3 As to equitable interests in registered land see PARA 271.
4 See the Law of Property Act 1925 s 137(1); and CHOSES IN ACTION vol 13 (2009) PARA 45.
5 *United Bank of Kuwait plc v Sahib* [1997] Ch 107, [1995] 2 All ER 973; affd on different grounds [1997] Ch 107, [1996] 3 All ER 215, CA.
6 Law of Property Act 1925 s 137(2)(i); and see CHOSES IN ACTION vol 13 (2009) PARA 50. As to indorsement of a memorandum of assignment on the trust instrument in lieu of notice, and the nomination of a trust corporation to receive notices, see ss 137(4), 138; and CHOSES IN ACTION vol 13 (2009) PARAS 51, 53. Section 137(2) does not apply where the money or securities are in court: see PARA 274.
7 Law of Property Act 1925 s 137(2)(ii) (amended by the Trusts of Land and Appointment of Trustees Act 1996 s 25(1), Sch 3 para 4(1), (15)).
8 Law of Property Act 1925 s 137(2)(iii).
9 Law of Property Act 1925 s 137(3). Before 1926 formal notice was not required; it was sufficient that the trustee had such knowledge of the transaction as an ordinary man of business would act upon (*Lloyd v Banks* (1868) 3 Ch App 488 at 491; *Re Dallas* [1904] 2 Ch 385 at 399, CA; *Ipswich Permanent Money Club Ltd v Arthy* [1920] 2 Ch 257), but the knowledge had to be brought clearly to the trustee's mind (*Saffron Walden Second Benefit Building Society v Rayner* (1880) 14 ChD 406, CA).

271. Priority of equitable interests in registered land. The basic rule governing the priority of an interest affecting a registered estate or charge[1] is that such priority is not affected by a disposition of the estate or charge, although this rule is modified so as to postpone such an interest where a registrable disposition[2] of a registered estate or charge is made for valuable consideration[3].

1 As to the meanings of 'registered estate' and 'registered charge' see PARA 142 note 7.
2 As to the meaning of 'registrable disposition' see PARA 142 note 8.

3 See the Land Registration Act 2002 ss 28–30; PARA 261; and REAL PROPERTY AND REGISTRATION vol 87 (2012) PARAS 454–456.

272. Priority of mortgages of insurance policies. In respect of notice, insurance policies are subject to the same rule as other choses or things in action, and notice to the office or the underwriter by a later incumbrancer will, in the absence of other circumstances, give him priority over an earlier incumbrancer[1]. Companies are not bound to receive notice of assignments of shares, and the priorities of incumbrancers on shares are therefore not regulated by notice[2].

1 *Re Lake, ex p Cavendish* [1903] 1 KB 151; *Re Weniger's Policy* [1910] 2 Ch 291; *Colonial Mutual General Insurance v ANZ Banking Ltd* [1995] 3 All ER 987, [1995] 1 WLR 1140, PC. This result is assisted by the statutory effect of notice under the Policies of Assurance Act 1867 s 3: see PARA 208; and INSURANCE vol 60 (2011) PARAS 496–498.
2 See PARA 275. As to the effect of an incumbrancer serving a stop notice see PARA 277.

273. Priority determined by registration. Where securities on personal property require to be or may be registered, their priority is determined by the order of the dates of registration. This applies to bills of sale[1], mortgages of ships and shares of ships[2], mortgages of aircraft and hovercraft[3], and patents[4].

1 See the Bills of Sale Act 1878 s 10; and FINANCIAL INSTRUMENTS AND TRANSACTIONS vol 49 (2015) PARA 583 et seq.
2 See the Merchant Shipping Act 1995 s 16, Sch 1 para 8; and SHIPPING AND MARITIME LAW vol 93 (2008) PARA 321.
3 See the Mortgaging of Aircraft Order 1972, SI 1972/1268, art 14(2); PARA 214; and AIR LAW vol 2 (2008) PARA 432.
4 See the Patents Act 1977 s 33; and PATENTS AND REGISTERED DESIGNS vol 79 (2014) PARA 587. As to registration generally see s 32; and PATENTS AND REGISTERED DESIGNS vol 79 (2014) PARA 583 et seq.

(ii) Stop Orders on Funds in Court

274. Stop order as notice. Where the subject of the security is a fund in court, the obtaining of a stop order relating to that fund[1] gives the same priority as notice to the trustees with regard to funds in their hands[2] and notice to the trustees is ineffectual[3]; but notice to the trustees before the payment of the fund into court continues to be effectual notwithstanding a stop order obtained by another incumbrancer[4], although the trustee himself will not, without obtaining a stop order, have priority for a charge in his own favour against an incumbrancer who obtains a stop order[5].

1 See CPR 73.13; and CIVIL PROCEDURE vol 12A (2015) PARAS 1482, 1484.
2 *Greening v Beckford* (1832) 5 Sim 195. See also *Montefiore v Guedalla* [1903] 2 Ch 26, CA; and CHOSES IN ACTION vol 13 (2009) PARA 55. As to a stop order on a fund carried to a separate account see CHOSES IN ACTION vol 13 (2009) PARA 55.
3 *Pinnock v Bailey* (1883) 23 ChD 497.
4 *Livesey v Harding* (1856) 23 Beav 141; *Re Marquis of Anglesey, Countess de Galve v Gardner* [1903] 2 Ch 727 at 732. See also CHOSES IN ACTION vol 13 (2009) PARA 55.
5 *Swayne v Swayne* (1848) 11 Beav 463.

(3) PRIORITIES BETWEEN MORTGAGEES OF SHARES

275. Priority of equitable titles to shares. Where several persons claim shares registered in another person's name, the equitable title which is prior in time prevails unless the conduct of the prior claimant disentitles him to priority or a claimant under a subsequent equitable title has, as between him and the company, acquired the full status of a shareholder or an absolute and unconditional right to be registered as the owner[1]. Such a creditor may gain priority[2].

Notice given to the company does not affect the priority of equitable claims in respect of registered shares[3]. Such a notice is not, however, inoperative for all purposes, and the receipt by a company of notice of a charge upon some of its shares will prevent the company from availing itself as against those shares of any lien under its articles of association for a debt to the company incurred subsequently to its receipt of the notice[4]. Although no notice of a trust may be entered in the company's register[5] and the articles of association usually provide that the company need not recognise trusts, if directors know of circumstances showing that a transfer is fraudulent they may be personally liable[6]. Where a board of directors has actual knowledge of an equitable claim by a person to shares in respect of which a transfer to another has been lodged for registration, registration should, as a matter of policy, be delayed to give notice to that person of the proposed transfer[7]. Even the sending of this notice does not protect the company in the case of its acting upon a forged transfer, and the shareholder is not estopped from alleging that the transfer is invalid although he does not reply to the notice[8].

1   *Moore v North Western Bank* [1891] 2 Ch 599 at 602–603 per Romer J. See also *Société Générale de Paris v Walker* (1885) 11 App Cas 20, HL.
2   See PARA 276.
3   *Société Générale de Paris v Walker* (1885) 11 App Cas 20 at 30, HL. See also *Macmillan Inc v Bishopsgate Investment Trust plc (No 3)* [1996] 1 All ER 585, [1996] 1 WLR 387, CA. An equitable mortgagee may nevertheless, by giving notice to the company, prevent a subsequent equitable claimant from obtaining priority by getting a duly executed and stamped transfer registered by the company (*Roots v Williamson* (1888) 38 ChD 485), and he can prevent the company acquiring a lien on the shares having priority to his mortgage in respect of money which becomes due to the company from the shareholder after it has received notice of the mortgage (see COMPANIES vol 15 (2009) PARA 1208). Where a company has no lien on shares, it is not entitled to priority for its claim over an equitable assignee of the shares: *Bank of NT Butterfield & Son Ltd v Golinsky* [1926] AC 733, PC. As to the effect of an incumbrancer serving a stop notice see PARA 277.
4   *Bradford Banking Co v Briggs, Son & Co Ltd* (1886) 12 App Cas 29, HL, applying the principle of *Hopkinson v Rolt* (1861) 9 HL Cas 514. See also *Champagne Perrier-Jouet SA v HH Finch Ltd* [1982] 3 All ER 713, [1982] 1 WLR 1359. Where, however, the company has no lien on the shares, it has no priority over an equitable assignee of those shares: *Bank of NT Butterfield & Son Ltd v Golinsky* [1926] AC 733, PC.
5   See the Companies Act 2006 s 126; and COMPANIES vol 14 (2009) PARA 343. The rule in *Dearle v Hall* (1828) 3 Russ 1 (see PARA 269) does not apply to dealings in shares in an English company: *Société Générale de Paris v Walker* (1885) 11 App Cas 20 at 30–31, HL.
6   *Société Générale de Paris v Tramways Union Co* (1884) 14 QBD 424 at 445, 453, CA; affd without reference to this point sub nom *Société Générale de Paris v Walker* (1885) 11 App Cas 20, HL. See generally PARA 211.
7   *Grundy v Briggs* [1910] 1 Ch 444 at 449; *Re Cadogan and Hans Place Estate Co, ex p Rolt* [1876] WN 91. See also PARA 277.
8   *Barton v London and North Western Rly Co* (1889) 24 QBD 77, CA; *Welch v Bank of England* [1955] Ch 508, [1955] 1 All ER 811.

276. Effect of obtaining legal title. A legal title[1] to securities acquired in perfection of an equitable title when the equitable title has been obtained without notice of prior equities will oust those equities, even though its holder acquired the legal title with notice of the prior equities[2]. If, however, an equitable title is acquired with notice of prior equities, the subsequent getting in of the legal title does not assist the holder and he takes subject to the prior equities[3]. Notice of prior equities is imputed where the circumstances are such as to make it reasonable that inquiry should be made as to the title of the person proposing to deal with the securities[4]; thus a person receiving from another, who is not the registered owner of the securities, a certificate accompanied by a transfer signed in blank by the registered owner is affected with notice of a possible infirmity in the title of the person from whom he receives them[5]. On the other hand, knowledge merely of the fact that the person proposing to deal with the securities is a broker[6], or that the persons so proposing are joint owners of them[7], is not sufficient to raise an imputation of notice of an infirmity in the title.

1   As to what constitutes a legal title to securities see *Macmillan Inc v Bishopsgate Trust (No 3)* [1995] 3 All ER 747 at 768–773, [1995] 1 WLR 978 at 999–1005 per Millett J; affd on different grounds [1996] 1 All ER 585, [1996] 1 WLR 387, CA. See also *Société Générale de Paris v Walker* (1885) 11 App Cas 20 at 28–29, HL, per Lord Selborne, and at 41 per Lord Blackburn; *Roots v Williamson* (1888) 38 ChD 485 at 498 per Stirling J; *Moore v North Western Bank* [1891] 2 Ch 599; *Ireland v Hart* [1902] 1 Ch 522; *Peat v Clayton* [1906] 1 Ch 659; *McCarthy & Stone Ltd v Julian S Hodge & Co Ltd* [1971] 2 All ER 973, [1971] 1 WLR 1547. See further EQUITABLE JURISDICTION vol 47 (2014) PARA 123.
2   *Dodds v Hills* (1865) 2 Hem & M 424; *Blackwood v London Chartered Bank of Australia* (1874) LR 5 PC 92; *Macmillan Inc v Bishopsgate Investment Trust plc (No 3)* [1995] 3 All ER 747 at 772–773, [1995] 1 WLR 978 at 1003–1005 per Millett J (affd on different grounds [1996] 1 All ER 585, [1996] 1 WLR 387, CA).
3   *Earl of Sheffield v London Joint Stock Bank* (1888) 13 App Cas 333, HL.
4   *Earl of Sheffield v London Joint Stock Bank* (1888) 13 App Cas 333, HL.
5   *France v Clark* (1884) 26 ChD 257, CA; *Fox v Martin* (1895) 64 LJCh 473; *Hutchison v Colorado United Mining Co and Hamill* (1886) 3 TLR 265, CA.
6   *Fuller v Glyn, Mills, Currie & Co* [1914] 2 KB 168; *London Joint Stock Bank v Simmons* [1892] AC 201, HL.
7   *Kaemena v Central Bank of London* (1888) 4 TLR 657.

277. Incumbrancer can protect interest in shares with a stop notice. An incumbrancer with an equitable interest in shares can protect his interests by obtaining a stop notice from the High Court[1]. When served on the company this does not give him any priority in respect of his incumbrance, but it prevents the registration of a transfer of the shares without notice to the incumbrancer[2] and until he has had time to obtain a charging order[3] or a stop order[4].

1   See CPR 73.16–73.21; and CIVIL PROCEDURE vol 12A (2015) PARAS 1482, 1487–1491.
2   See CPR 73.18; and CIVIL PROCEDURE vol 12A (2015) PARA 1488.
3   See CPR 73.2–73.10; and CIVIL PROCEDURE vol 12A (2015) PARAS 1462–1480.
4   See CPR 73.11–73.15; and CIVIL PROCEDURE vol 12A (2015) PARAS 1483–1486.

(4) FAILURE TO GAIN, OR LOSS OF, PRIORITY

(i) Priority Barred by Notice of Prior Rights

278. Effect of notice of prior rights. Prima facie an incumbrancer later in point of time may be entitled to priority over an earlier incumbrancer by reason of possession of the legal estate, or by notice to a debtor or to trustees or to an insurance office, by obtaining a stop order[1], or by registration in the register of patents[2]. However, he will fail to gain this priority if he has notice of the earlier incumbrance at the time when he advances his money[3]. The notice may be either actual or constructive, and the registration of an instrument or matter in any register kept under the Land Charges Act 1972[4] or in any local land charges register[5] is deemed to constitute actual notice of the instrument or matter[6].

1   As to stop orders as notice see PARA 274.
2   As to registration of patents determining priority see PARA 273.
3   As to notice avoiding priority in particular cases see eg *Ward v Royal Exchange Shipping Co, ex p Harrison* (1887) 58 LT 174 at 178 (debtor); *Re Ind, Coope & Co Ltd, Fisher v Ind, Coope & Co Ltd, Knox v Ind, Coope & Co Ltd, Arnold v Ind, Coope & Co Ltd* [1911] 2 Ch 223

(debtor); *Ward v Duncombe* [1893] AC 369 at 392, HL, per Lord Macnaghten (trustees); *Montefiore v Guedalla* [1903] 2 Ch 26 at 38, CA (trustees); *Newman v Newman* (1885) 28 ChD 674 (insurance policy); *Re Weniger's Policy* [1910] 2 Ch 291 (insurance policy); *New Ixion Tyre and Cycle Co v Spilsbury* [1898] 2 Ch 484, CA (register of patents). As to cases where the priority of securities on personal property is determined by registration see PARA 273. As to priorities between trustees for debenture holders with a floating charge and specific assignees of a chose or thing in action see *Re Ind, Coope & Co Ltd, Fisher v Ind, Coope & Co Ltd, Knox v Ind, Coope & Co Ltd, Arnold v Ind, Coope & Co Ltd* above. See also *McCarthy and Stone Ltd v Julian S Hodge & Co Ltd* [1971] 2 All ER 973, [1971] 1 WLR 1547.

4   As to the mortgages and charges which may be registered under the Land Charges Act 1972 see PARA 262; and REAL PROPERTY AND REGISTRATION vol 87 (2012) PARA 714 et seq.

5   As to local land charges see REAL PROPERTY AND REGISTRATION vol 87 (2012) PARA 763 et seq.

6   See PARA 263.

279.   Actual notice of prior rights. Actual notice[1] is equally effectual whether it is received by the incumbrancer himself or by a solicitor or other agent[2] employed by him in the matter of the mortgage. Notice to a director is not necessarily notice to the company[3].

1   As to the effect of notice of prior rights on a later incumbrancer see PARA 278. As to constructive notice of prior rights see PARA 280.

2   The extent to which notice to an agent is imputed to a mortgagee is restricted by statute: see the Law of Property Act 1925 s 199(1)(ii); and PARA 281. However, the first question is whether, apart from the statutory restriction, notice to a solicitor or agent would be imputed to the principal: see *Bouts v Stenning* (1892) 8 TLR 600; *Kettlewell v Watson* (1882) 21 ChD 685 at 707; cf *Sharpe v Foy* (1868) 4 Ch App 35; *Sankey v Alexander* (2) (1874) 9 IR Eq 259 at 259n, 300, Ir CA. See also *El Ajou v Dollar Land Holdings plc* [1994] 2 All ER 685, [1994] 1 BCLC 464, CA; *Halifax Mortgage Services Ltd (formerly BNP Mortgages Ltd) v Stepsky* [1996] Ch 1, [1995] 4 All ER 656 (affd on different grounds [1996] Ch 207, [1996] 2 All ER 277, CA); *Barclays Bank plc v Thomson* [1997] 4 All ER 816, [1997] 1 FLR 156, CA; *National Westminster Bank plc v Beaton* (1997) 30 HLR 99, 74 P & CR D19, CA. See further EQUITABLE JURISDICTION vol 47 (2014) PARA 132. As to an agent's knowledge binding his principal see *Blackburn, Low & Co v Vigors* (1887) 12 App Cas 531 at 538, HL; *Muir's Executors v Craig's Trustees* 1913 SC 349; and AGENCY vol 1 (2008) PARA 137.

3   *El Ajou v Dollar Land Holdings plc* [1994] 2 All ER 685, [1994] 1 BCLC 464, CA. See also *Bank of Ireland v Cogry Spinning Co Ltd* [1900] 1 IR 219 at 248; *Re David Payne & Co Ltd, Young v David Payne & Co Ltd* [1904] 2 Ch 608, CA; and COMPANIES vol 14 (2009) PARA 671. See also AGENCY vol 1 (2008) PARA 138.

280.   Constructive notice of prior rights. A mortgagee has constructive notice of an earlier incumbrance if it would have come to his knowledge, or to the knowledge of his solicitor or other agent, if proper inquiries and inspections of deeds had been made[1]. Thus the mortgagee is affected with notice if he omits to make usual and proper inquiries as to the mortgagor's title[2], provided that those inquiries would have disclosed the earlier incumbrance[3]; and there is even more reason for this if he designedly abstains from making inquiry in order to avoid notice, or if he omits to follow up an inquiry suggested by actual notice[4]. Actual notice of an incumbrance is constructive notice of those other matters which the intending mortgagee would have discovered if he had made further inquiries as to the incumbrance[5].

1   Cf the Law of Property Act 1925 s 199(1)(ii): and see PARA 281. As to actual notice of prior rights see PARA 279.

2   See *McCarthy and Stone Ltd v Julian S Hodge & Co Ltd* [1971] 2 All ER 973, [1971] 1 WLR 1547; and EQUITABLE JURISDICTION vol 47 (2014) PARA 136.

3   A mortgagee having notice of a deed forming a link in the mortgagor's title has notice of the contents of the deed (*Patman v Harland* (1881) 17 ChD 353, the actual decision in which cannot survive the Law of Property Act 1925 s 44(5) (see EQUITABLE JURISDICTION vol 47 (2014) PARA 137)), but not of matters which the deed would not have disclosed (*Carter v Williams* (1870) LR 9 Eq 678 at 681; *Wilkes v Spooner* [1911] 2 KB 473 at 487, CA).

4   See EQUITABLE JURISDICTION vol 47 (2014) PARA 136.

5   *Taylor v Baker* (1818) 5 Price 306; *Penny v Watts* (1849) 1 Mac & G 150; *Montefiore v Browne* (1858) 7 HL Cas 241. As to the doctrine of constructive notice generally see EQUITABLE JURISDICTION vol 47 (2014) PARA 130 et seq.

281. Restrictions on constructive and imputed notice of prior rights. A purchaser[1] is not prejudicially affected by notice of any instrument or matter capable of registration under the Land Charges Act 1972 which is void or not enforceable as against him under that Act by reason of its non-registration[2], or by notice of any other instrument or matter, unless it is within his own knowledge or has in the transaction in question[3] come to the knowledge of his counsel or solicitor or other agent as such[4], or would have come to his knowledge or that of his solicitor or other agent if reasonable inquiries and inspections had been made[5].

1   As to the meaning of 'purchaser' in this context see DEEDS AND OTHER INSTRUMENTS vol 32 (2012) PARA 234.
2   See the Law of Property Act 1925 s 199(1)(i); *Diligent Finance Co Ltd v Alleyne* (1972) 23 P & CR 346; *Lloyds Bank plc v Carrick* [1996] 4 All ER 630, 73 P & CR 314, CA; and EQUITABLE JURISDICTION vol 47 (2014) PARA 137.
3   Thus knowledge of the solicitor acquired in relation to a previous transaction is not imputed to the mortgagee: see the Law of Property Act 1925 s 199(1)(ii).
4   As to the effect of the statutory restriction see *Halifax Mortgage Services Ltd (formerly BNP Mortgages Ltd) v Stepsky* [1996] Ch 207, [1996] 2 All ER 277, CA; *Barclays Bank plc v Thomson* [1997] 4 All ER 816, [1997] 1 FLR 156, CA; *National Westminster Bank plc v Beaton* (1997) 30 HLR 99, 74 P & CR D19, CA.
5   See the Law of Property Act 1925 s 199(1)(ii); and EQUITABLE JURISDICTION vol 47 (2014) PARA 137. The inquiries with which s 199(1) are concerned are those which relate to whether the mortgagee will obtain good security, not to other matters such as the credit status of a borrower: see *Abbey National plc v Tufts* [1999] 2 FLR 399, [1999] Fam Law 542, CA.

282. Mortgagee's constructive notice of the rights of persons in occupation of land. A mortgagee will have constructive notice of any existing[1] non-registrable rights reasonably discoverable from inspection of the property and, in particular, from inquiry of any occupier as to his interest and the terms on which he holds it[2]. It is not sufficient to make inquiry solely of the vendor[3]. The mortgagee should ask a tenant in occupation for a copy of his tenancy agreement, but is not obliged to make further inquiry and is entitled to assume that the document represents the agreement between tenant and mortgagor[4]. Inquiry should be made of the spouse of the vendor if in occupation[5], but need not be made of children of the vendor, since their occupation is that of their parents[6]. Where the property to be charged is owned by a company and occupied by its director, the mortgagee is not required to inquire about the rights in the mortgaged property of the director if he negotiates the loan on behalf of the mortgagor[7].

A mortgagee is not prejudicially affected by notice of the registrable but unregistered interest of a person in occupation, such as an estate contract[8] or a claim for a property adjustment order[9]. The equitable interests of a person in occupation under a trust of land may be overreached where the mortgage is granted by at least two trustees of the trust and capital money arising on the mortgage is paid to them or by their direction[10].

1   As to the position where the rights of the occupier are created at the same time as the mortgage see PARA 296.
2   *Hunt v Luck* [1902] 1 Ch 428 at 432–433, CA, per Vaughan Williams LJ. This principle was preserved by the Law of Property Act 1925 s 14: see *City of London Building Society v Flegg* [1988] AC 54, [1987] 3 All ER 435, HL. A mortgagee of registered land is bound by the interests of persons in actual occupation: see the Land Registration Act 2002 Sch 3 para 2; PARA 295; and REAL PROPERTY AND REGISTRATION vol 87 (2012) PARA 482.
3   *Hodgson v Marks* [1971] Ch 892, [1971] 2 All ER 684, CA.
4   *Smith v Jones* [1954] 2 All ER 823, [1954] 1 WLR 1089.

5 See *Williams and Glyn's Bank Ltd v Boland* [1981] AC 487, [1980] 2 All ER 408, HL; *Hodgson v Marks* [1971] Ch 892, [1971] 2 All ER 684, CA (disapproving *Caunce v Caunce* [1969] 1 All ER 722 at 727–728, [1969] 1 WLR 286 at 293 per Stamp J).
6 *Hypo-Mortgage Services Ltd v Robinson* [1997] 2 FCR 422, [1997] 2 FLR 71, CA.
7 *Midland Bank Ltd v Farmpride Hatcheries Ltd* [1981] 2 EGLR 147, CA.
8 *Lloyds Bank plc v Carrick* [1996] 4 All ER 630, 73 P & CR 314, CA. See also PARA 281. As to the incumbrances which are registrable see REAL PROPERTY AND REGISTRATION vol 87 (2012) PARA 714 et seq.
9 *Whittingham v Whittingham* [1979] Fam 9, [1978] 3 All ER 805, CA.
10 See the Law of Property Act 1925 ss 2, 27; *City of London Building Society v Flegg* [1988] AC 54, [1987] 3 All ER 435, HL; and REAL PROPERTY AND REGISTRATION vol 87 (2012) PARA 262.

283. Mortgagee's constructive notice of the rights of the mortgagor to set aside the mortgage. If the mortgagee knows of certain facts which put him on inquiry as to the possible existence of the rights of the mortgagor to set aside the transaction and he fails to make such inquiry or take such other steps as are reasonable to verify whether such earlier right does or does not exist, he will have constructive notice of what he would have discovered if he had made reasonable inquiry[1]. If he does make reasonable inquiry and the results of the inquiries are such as to allay suspicion, he takes free from the rights of the mortgagor[2].

1 *Barclays Bank plc v O'Brien* [1994] 1 AC 180, [1993] 4 All ER 417, HL; *Banco Exterior Internacional SA v Thomas* [1997] 1 All ER 46, [1997] 1 WLR 221, CA; *Royal Bank of Scotland plc v Etridge (No 2)* [2001] UKHL 44, [2002] 2 AC 773, [2001] 4 All ER 449. See also PARA 119 et seq.
2 *Royal Bank of Scotland plc v Etridge (No 2)* [2001] UKHL 44, [2002] 2 AC 773, [2001] 4 All ER 449.

(ii) Priority Barred by Conduct in relation to Title Deeds

284. Mortgagee's duty to obtain title deeds. Apart from the effect of the provisions of the Land Charges Act 1972 and the Law of Property Act 1925 as to registration of puisne mortgages and equitable charges[1], and as to notice[2], a legal mortgagee who, on taking his mortgage, omits to inquire for the title deeds is postponed to an earlier incumbrancer in whose possession they then are[3], and also to a subsequent incumbrancer who inquires for the deeds and gets them or, if he is the third incumbrancer, inquires and finds that they are with the second incumbrancer[4]. The legal mortgagee is not, however, postponed if he makes inquiry and receives a reasonable excuse for the non-delivery of the deeds[5]. Nor is he postponed if he receives only part of the deeds under a reasonable belief that he is receiving all of them[6].

1 See PARA 262.
2 See PARA 278 et seq.
3 As to the right to custody of title deeds see PARA 488 et seq. The mere possession of deeds does not entitle the equitable incumbrancer to priority (*Thorpe v Holdsworth* (1868) LR 7 Eq 139 at 146; and see *Taylor v Russell* [1891] 1 Ch 8 at 19, CA) and in proceedings by the legal mortgagee he can be required to give them up notwithstanding that he is a purchaser for value in good faith without notice: see generally EQUITABLE JURISDICTION vol 47 (2014) PARA 124 et seq. Formerly the omission to make any inquiry for the deeds was treated as evidence of fraud, or gross or wilful negligence, and on this ground the legal mortgagee was postponed (*Hewitt v Loosemore* (1851) 9 Hare 449 at 458; *Hunt v Elmes* (1860) 2 De GF & J 578; *Colyer v Finch* (1856) 5 HL Cas 905 at 928; and see *Northern Counties of England Fire Insurance Co v Whipp* (1884) 26 ChD 482 at 491, CA); and it was said that in order to postpone him it must be possible for the court to infer wilful abstention (*Ratcliffe v Barnard* (1871) 6 Ch App 652, CA). The modern view is that the mere omission to make the ordinary inquiry for title deeds is sufficient to postpone the legal mortgagee, because it gives him constructive notice of the earlier incumbrance (*Berwick & Co v Price* [1905] 1 Ch 632; *Walker v Linom* [1907] 2 Ch 104), or because his negligence deprives him of the benefit of the legal estate (*Oliver v Hinton* [1899] 2 Ch 264, CA), or because his carelessness is of so aggravated a nature as to amount to the neglect of precautions which the ordinarily reasonable man would have observed (*Hudston v Viney* [1921] 1 Ch 98). See also

Lloyd's Banking Co v Jones (1885) 29 ChD 221; *Tsang Chuen v Li Po Kwai* [1932] AC 715, PC (distinguishing *Oliver v Hinton*). The postponement was placed on the ground of notice in *Worthington v Morgan* (1849) 16 Sim 547; *Hipkins v Amery* (1860) 2 Giff 292; *Spencer v Clarke* (1878) 9 ChD 137; *Re Weniger's Policy* [1910] 2 Ch 291. See also *Maxfield v Burton* (1873) LR 17 Eq 15. The negligence of trustees binds their beneficiaries, even if they are minors: *Lloyd's Banking Co v Jones*; *Walker v Linom* above. Where mortgages are contemporaneous, the mortgagee who obtains the title deeds has priority over one who does not inquire for them: *Hopgood v Ernest* (1865) 3 De GJ & Sm 116, where, apparently, the mortgagees were tenants in common or joint tenants of the legal estate.

4 *Clarke v Palmer* (1882) 21 ChD 124. Where the legal mortgagee does not inquire for the deeds, the same principle applies both to prior and subsequent incumbrances (*Walker v Linom* [1907] 2 Ch 104); but there must be some evidence of negligence (*Re Greer, Greer v Greer* [1907] 1 IR 57). A legal mortgagee who took subject to an equitable charge by deposit of the deeds was not negligent in omitting to give notice to the equitable incumbrancer and was not postponed to a subsequent equitable incumbrancer who obtained the deeds on the first equitable incumbrancer being paid off (*Grierson v National Provincial Bank of England Ltd* [1913] 2 Ch 18); but now the legal mortgage would require to be registered as a puisne mortgage, and this case could not arise (see PARA 262). It is no longer possible to create an equitable mortgage by deposit of deeds: see PARA 221. The Law of Property Act 1925 does not affect the consequences of omission to obtain title deeds: see s 13; and PARA 260.

5 *Hewitt v Loosemore* (1851) 9 Hare 449 at 458; *Agra Bank Ltd v Barry* (1874) LR 7 HL 135; *Brown v Stedman* (1896) 44 WR 458. See also *Barnett v Weston* (1806) 12 Ves 130.

6 *Hunt v Elmes* (1860) 2 De GF & J 578; *Colyer v Finch* (1856) 5 HL Cas 905; *Ratcliffe v Barnard* (1871) 6 Ch App 652, CA; *Cottey v National Provincial Bank of England Ltd* (1904) 20 TLR 607. The same principle applies as between successive mortgagees by deposit (*Roberts v Croft* (1857) 2 De G & J 1; *Dixon v Muckleston* (1872) 8 Ch App 155), unless the prior mortgagee has left the substantial part of the deeds with the mortgagor and is otherwise negligent (*Re Lambert's Estate, Lambert Petitioner* (1884) 13 LR Ir 234, Ir CA). See also PARA 226.

285. Effect of conduct of legal mortgagee. A legal mortgagee who gets the title deeds into his custody and subsequently loses or parts with possession of them is not postponed to a subsequent incumbrancer to whom they are delivered on the ground of mere negligence or want of prudence in the custody of them[1], nor is he postponed if he has lent them to the mortgagor upon a reasonable representation made by the mortgagor as to his object in borrowing them[2]. However, he will be postponed on the ground of fraud, that is, where he has assisted in or connived at the fraud which has led to the creation of a subsequent equitable estate without notice of the prior legal estate[3]; and he will also be postponed if he has returned the deeds to, or left them with, the mortgagor for the purposes of enabling the mortgagor to raise money on them[4], notwithstanding that the limit which he has assigned for the loan has been exceeded[5].

1 *Northern Counties of England Fire Insurance Co v Whipp* (1884) 26 ChD 482, CA.

2 *Peter v Russell* (1716) 1 Eq Cas Abr 321; *Martinez v Cooper* (1826) 2 Russ 198. It may be, however, that on the legal mortgagee parting with the deeds, his mortgage would become a puisne mortgage and would require to be registered as a land charge, so that if not registered it would be void as against a subsequent incumbrancer: see the Land Charges Act 1972 ss 2(1), (4)(i), 4(5); and PARAS 262–263.

3 *Northern Counties of England Fire Insurance Co v Whipp* (1884) 26 ChD 482, CA. The judgment in this case was an attempt to give exactness to Lord Eldon's requirement in *Evans v Bicknell* (1801) 6 Ves 174 at 190, of fraud or gross negligence amounting to evidence of fraud as the condition for postponing the legal mortgagee. In *Northern Counties of England Fire Insurance Co v Whipp* above at 494, Fry LJ, while pointing out that negligence and fraud were incompatible, recognised that omission to use ordinary care in the custody of the deeds might be evidence of fraud; but the decision seems to have made it impracticable to postpone the legal mortgage in the case in question except on the ground of actual fraud (*Manners v Mew* (1885) 29 ChD 725). The Law of Property Act 1925 does not affect the consequences of the loss of title deeds: see s 13; and PARA 260.

4 *Briggs v Jones* (1870) LR 10 Eq 92.

5 *Perry Herrick v Attwood* (1857) 2 De G & J 21; *Brocklesby v Temperance Permanent Building Society* [1895] AC 173, HL. The postponement is frequently put on the ground of estoppel (as to which see generally ESTOPPEL). See also *Briggs v Jones* (1870) LR 10 Eq 92; *Marshall v National*

Provincial Bank of England (1892) 61 LJCh 465; *Lloyds Bank Ltd v Cooke* [1907] 1 KB 794, CA; *Robinson v Montgomeryshire Brewery Co* [1896] 2 Ch 841; *Fry and Mason v Smellie and Taylor* [1912] 3 KB 282, CA. Cf *McHenry v Davies* (1870) LR 10 Eq 88; *London Joint Stock Bank v Simmons* [1892] AC 201, HL.

286. Possession of title deeds by equitable incumbrancer. As between equitable incumbrancers the mere possession of the title deeds is not enough to give a subsequent incumbrancer priority over an earlier one[1]: there must be some default on the part of the earlier incumbrancer[2]. If the possession of the title deeds is an essential part of the earlier incumbrancer's security, the same considerations arise as in the case of a legal mortgagee[3], and if he omits to inquire for and get in the deeds[4], or, having got them, allows them by negligence or design to be again, without sufficient reason, in the mortgagor's possession[5], he will be postponed to a subsequent incumbrancer to whom they are delivered. An equitable incumbrancer who enters into an artificial transaction designed to give the impression that the mortgagor is the absolute and unencumbered owner will be postponed to a subsequent incumbrancer[6].

1   See *Evans v Bicknell* (1801) 6 Ves 174 at 183, where Lord Eldon LC corrected the statement of Buller J in *Goodtitle d Norris v Morgan* (1787) 1 Term Rep 755 at 762, that a second mortgagee who took the title deeds without notice was always preferred. In *Bailey v Fermor* (1821) 9 Price 262 at 267, *Goodtitle d Norris v Morgan* above is treated as overruled on this point. See also *Barnett v Weston* (1806) 12 Ves 130 at 132; *Allen v Knight* (1846) 5 Hare 272 at 279 (on appeal (1847) 11 Jur 527). As to the postponement of equitable incumbrancers see EQUITABLE JURISDICTION vol 47 (2014) PARA 123.
2   *Allen v Knight* (1847) 11 Jur 527; *Freeguard v Royal Bank of Scotland* (1998) 79 P & CR 81, CA. He is not in default if the mortgage is of a reversion (*Tourle v Rand* (1789) 2 Bro CC 650), or if he gets the only title deed available at the time (*Union Bank of London v Kent* (1888) 39 ChD 238, CA); and, as a purchaser is not entitled to the deeds until completion, his equitable title under the contract prevails over an equitable incumbrance created by the vendor by deposit of the title deeds after the contract (*Flinn v Pountain* (1889) 58 LJCh 389), at any rate if the contract has been registered as an estate contract under the Land Charges Act 1972 s 2(1), (4)(iv) (see REAL PROPERTY AND REGISTRATION vol 87 (2012) PARAS 720, 724). A mortgagee not immediately entitled to deeds is not, however, bound to take precautions against a future fraud by the mortgagor in respect of them (*Union Bank of London v Kent* above), and if the mortgagee omits to get in the deeds, by reason of a false recital in the mortgage of an existing mortgage by deposit, he is not postponed to a subsequent actual mortgage by deposit (*Frazer v Jones* (1846) 5 Hare 475 (on appeal (1848) 12 Jur 443); and see *Jones v Thomas* (1862) 11 WR 50). It is no longer possible to create a mortgage by deposit of deeds alone: see PARA 221.
3   See PARAS 284–285.
4   *Farrand v Yorkshire Banking Co* (1888) 40 ChD 182. See also EQUITABLE JURISDICTION vol 47 (2014) PARA 123. A blank share transfer should be accompanied by the share certificate, and the later of two transferees, who gets the certificate, will have priority: *Kelly v Munster and Leinster Bank* (1890) 29 LR Ir 19, Ir CA.
5   If they are redelivered to the mortgagor for a particular purpose, it is negligence for the mortgagee not to press for their return after a reasonable time: *Waldron v Sloper* (1852) 1 Drew 193; *Dowle v Saunders* (1864) 2 Hem & M 242; *Layard v Maud* (1867) LR 4 Eq 397.
6   *Freeguard v Royal Bank of Scotland* (1998) 79 P & CR 81, CA.

287. Rights as between equitable mortgagee and unpaid vendor. Where an unpaid vendor hands to the purchaser the title deeds with a conveyance containing a receipt for the purchase money, he thereby enables the purchaser to represent himself as the owner of the property, and he will be postponed to an equitable mortgagee from the purchaser who obtains the deeds[1]; and if the unpaid vendor remains in possession as tenant to the purchaser, there is no notice to a subsequent incumbrancer of his lien for unpaid purchase money[2].

An owner of shares who hands a transfer and the certificate to a broker for the purpose of sale is postponed to an equitable mortgagee from the broker notwithstanding that the broker by mortgaging the shares exceeds his authority[3].

1   *Rice v Rice* (1854) 2 Drew 73; *Smith v Evans* (1860) 28 Beav 59; *Freeguard v Royal Bank of Scotland plc* (1998) 79 P & CR 81, CA. A prior incumbrancer who has been induced by misrepresentation to release his security will not, however, necessarily be postponed: *Beckett v Cordley* (1784) 1 Bro CC 353. In appropriate circumstances, the vendor may be taken to have agreed to postpone his lien: see *Barclays Bank plc v Estates and Commercial Ltd* [1997] 1 WLR 415, 74 P & CR 30, CA; and PARA 290.

2   *White v Wakefield* (1835) 7 Sim 401 at 417.

3   *Rimmer v Webster* [1902] 2 Ch 163 (where the result was treated as an application of the principle of agency); *Tsang Chuen v Li Po Kwai* [1932] AC 715, PC. See also *Perry Herrick v Attwood* (1857) 2 De G & J 21; PARA 286; and COMPANIES vol 14 (2009) PARA 401; EQUITABLE JURISDICTION vol 47 (2014) PARA 123; ESTOPPEL vol 47 (2014) PARAS 353, 370.

288. Beneficiary and trustee's assignees. Where a trust has been constituted, the title deeds are properly left in the trustee's custody, and if he uses them, in breach of trust, for the purpose of creating an equitable incumbrance, the beneficiary's title will prevail over that of the incumbrancer[1]. If, however, the trustee is authorised to dispose of the property, and purports to dispose of it in accordance with his authority, the beneficiary will be postponed to an equitable mortgagee[2] unless the disposition is in substance one not authorised by the trust[3].

1   *Shropshire Union Rlys and Canal Co v R* (1875) LR 7 HL 496; *Bradley v Riches* (1878) 9 ChD 189; *Burgis v Constantine* [1908] 2 KB 484, CA; *Hill v Peters* [1918] 2 Ch 273 at 278; *Coleman v London County and Westminster Bank Ltd* [1916] 2 Ch 353 at 361. See also EQUITABLE JURISDICTION vol 47 (2014) PARA 123. It is otherwise where the conveyance to the trustee contains a representation that he is absolute owner: *Re King's Settlement, King v King* [1931] 2 Ch 294. Where the trustee improperly invests the trust fund in the purchase of land, the beneficiaries are entitled to follow it into the land; and this is not a mere equity, but gives them an equitable interest in the land, so that they will not be postponed to an equitable incumbrancer under the trustee without notice (*Cave v Cave* (1880) 15 ChD 639), although a different view has prevailed in Ireland, and the beneficiaries in such a case are treated as having an inferior equity to the incumbrancer (*Re Ffrench's Estate* (1887) 21 LR Ir 283 at 312, Ir CA; *Re Sloane's Estate* [1895] 1 IR 146 at 165; *Bank of Ireland v Cogry Spinning Co* [1900] 1 IR 219). An executor or trustee disposing of the estate or trust funds to a purchaser for value without notice has generally been treated as giving the purchaser an equity superior to that of the beneficiaries: *Bourke v Lee* [1904] 1 IR 280; *Re Bobbett's Estate, Nugent Petitioner* [1904] 1 IR 461. The Irish decisions were followed with reluctance in *Scott v Scott* [1924] 1 IR 141.

2   *Lloyds Bank Ltd v Bullock* [1896] 2 Ch 192. See also EQUITABLE JURISDICTION vol 47 (2014) PARA 123.

3   *Capell v Winter* [1907] 2 Ch 376.

(iii) Postponement

289. Express postponement. Ordinarily where there are two mortgages of the same property the mortgagees can vary the order of priority of their mortgages without the mortgagor's consent. Since the mortgagor can recover the mortgaged property only on payment of the debts secured by both mortgages, his right to recover the mortgaged property is not adversely affected by a variation in priorities. Although a mortgagor who wishes to have the secured debts satisfied in a particular order can require a specific term to be inserted in the mortgage preventing the priorities of the mortgages from being altered, a reference in the first mortgage to the charge being a first charge merely describes the nature of the security and confers no contractual right on the mortgagor to have that debt satisfied first[1]. A mortgagee of registered land cannot, however, gain priority over an existing protected or statutory tenant in occupation of a dwelling house by inducing him to sign a form of consent[2].

1   *Cheah Theam Swee v Equiticorp Finance Group Ltd* [1992] 1 AC 472, [1991] 4 All ER 989, PC. As to the effect of an agreement postponing a fixed charge to a floating charge see *Re Portbase Clothing Ltd* [1993] Ch 388, [1993] 3 All ER 829. An agreement to limit the priority of a charge to a specific sum with interest thereon gives priority for such interest as is secured by the charge, whether compound or simple: see *Whitbread plc v UCB Corporate Services Ltd* [2000] 3 EGLR 60, [2000] 35 EG 136, CA.
2   *Woolwich Building Society v Dickman* [1996] 3 All ER 204, 72 P & CR 470, CA.

290. Implied postponement. A party with an equitable charge over or an interest in property can be taken to have agreed to the postponement of his interest in favour of any party who is allowed to his knowledge to purchase or take a charge over the land on the faith that it is unincumbered[1]. Thus an unpaid vendor's lien is postponed to the equitable interest of the sub-purchasers where the vendor allows his agent to deal with the land on the footing that the purchasers are selling as absolute owners free from the lien[2], and a person claiming a beneficial interest in a property owned by another is treated as having agreed to postpone his interest to a mortgage which he knows will be granted to secure funds required to provide the purchase price of the property[3], or to that of a replacement mortgage on no less favourable terms effected without his knowledge[4].

1   *Barclays Bank plc v Estates and Commercial Ltd* [1997] 1 WLR 415, 74 P & CR 30, CA; *Bristol and West Building Society v Henning* [1985] 2 All ER 606, [1985] 1 WLR 778, CA. But cf *Skipton Building Society v Clayton* (1993) 66 P & CR 223, 25 HLR 596, CA, where the question was treated as one of estoppel (see PARA 291).
2   *Kettlewell v Watson* (1884) 26 ChD 501, CA, explained in *Barclays Bank plc v Estates and Commercial Ltd* [1997] 1 WLR 415, 74 P & CR 30, CA.
3   *Bristol and West Building Society v Henning* [1985] 2 All ER 606, [1985] 1 WLR 778, CA; *Paddington Building Society v Mendelsohn* (1985) 50 P & CR 244, [1987] Fam Law 121, CA; *Abbey National Building Society v Cann* [1991] 1 AC 56, [1990] 1 All ER 1085, HL (obiter); *Wishart v Credit and Mercantile plc* [2015] EWCA Civ 655, [2015] 2 P & CR 322, [2015] All ER (D) 64 (Jul).
4   *Equity and Law Home Loans Ltd v Prestidge* [1992] 1 All ER 909, [1992] 1 WLR 137, CA.

(iv) Estoppel and Subrogation

291. Estoppel. A person entitled to a charge over or an interest in property who has, knowingly or unknowingly, allowed or encouraged a subsequent incumbrancer to assume to his detriment that his security has priority may be estopped from asserting priority if it would be unconscionable for him to do so[1]. Thus a mortgagee will be postponed if he has returned the deeds to, or left them with, the mortgagor for the purposes of enabling the mortgagor to raise money on them, notwithstanding that the limit which he has assigned for the loan has been exceeded[2]. An agent who negotiates with the mortgagee on behalf of the mortgagor is estopped from asserting any adverse interest of his own in the property which he does not disclose[3]. A person claiming an interest in property who so conducts himself as to give the prospective mortgagee reasonable grounds for believing that he consents to the creation of a charge in priority to his interest will be estopped from asserting priority over the charge[4].

1   *Taylors Fashions Ltd v Liverpool Victoria Trustees Co Ltd* [1982] QB 133n at 151–152, [1981] 1 All ER 897 at 915–916 per Oliver J. See also *Lancashire Mortgage Corpn Ltd v Scottish & Newcastle plc* [2007] EWCA Civ 684, [2007] All ER (D) 68 (Jul) in which the principle in *Taylors Fashions Ltd v Liverpool Victoria Trustees Co Ltd* above was applied.
2   See PARAS 285, 290.
3   *Midland Bank Ltd v Farmpride Hatcheries Ltd* [1981] 2 EGLR 147, CA.

4   *Skipton Building Society v Clayton* (1993) 66 P & CR 223, 25 HLR 596, CA; *Hardy v Fowle*
    [2007] EWHC 2423 (Ch); and see PARAS 285, 290.

292.   Subrogation. A lender who advances money which is used to discharge a
security will be subrogated to the rights under that security and will obtain
priority over incumbrances subsequent to that security if:

(1)   the subsequent incumbrancer has been enriched at the lender's expense;
(2)   such enrichment was unjust; and
(3)   there are no policy reasons for denying a remedy[1].

1   *Banque Financière de la Cité v Parc (Battersea) Ltd* [1999] 1 AC 221, [1998] 1 All ER 737, HL.
    As to the effects of subrogation see further PARAS 386–387.

(5) PRIORITY OF STATUTORY CHARGES

293.   Priority of charging orders. The Land Charges Act 1972 and the Land
Registration Act 2002 apply in relation to charging orders[1] as they apply in
relation to other orders or writs issued or made for the purposes of enforcing
judgments[2]. In the case of unregistered land, a charging order over the legal estate
is registrable but not if it is over a beneficial interest alone[3]. In the case of
registered land, a charging order affecting a registered estate[4] may be protected by
notice[5], but not if it is over a beneficial interest alone[6]. It seems that such a charge
takes effect subject to any prior mortgages, whether legal or equitable, affecting
the estate or interest charged[7]. A caution registered to protect a charging
order confers no priority and the rule in *Dearle v Hall*[8] does not relate to a
judgment creditor[9].

1   As to charging orders see PARA 220.
2   Charging Orders Act 1979 s 3(2) (amended by the Land Registration Act 2002 s 133, Sch 11
    para 15). See PARA 220; and CIVIL PROCEDURE vol 12A (2015) PARA 1476.
3   See the Land Charges Act 1972 s 6(1)(a), (1A); PARA 220; and REAL PROPERTY AND
    REGISTRATION vol 87 (2012) PARA 746. See also *Perry v Phoenix Assurance plc* [1988] 3 All ER
    60, [1988] 1 WLR 940.
4   As to the meaning of 'registered estate' see PARA 142 note 7.
5   See the Land Registration Act 2002 ss 32, 87; and REAL PROPERTY AND REGISTRATION vol 87
    (2012) PARAS 512, 537–538.
6   See the Land Registration Act 2002 s 33(a); and REAL PROPERTY AND REGISTRATION vol 87
    (2012) PARA 513.
7   *Whitworth v Gaugain* (1846) 1 Ph 728; *Legg v Mathieson* (1860) 2 Giff 71; *Kinderley v Jervis*
    (1856) 22 Beav 1; *Eyre v M'Dowell* (1861) 9 HL Cas 619; *Wickham v New Brunswick and
    Canada Rly Co* (1865) LR 1 PC 64; *Chung Khiaw Bank Ltd v United Overseas Bank* [1970] AC
    767, [1970] 2 WLR 858, PC; *United Bank of Kuwait plc v Sahib* [1997] Ch 107, [1995] 2 All ER
    973 (affd on different grounds [1997] Ch 107, [1996] 3 All ER 215, CA). As to priorities of
    equitable interests affecting registered land see the Land Registration Act 2002 ss 28–30; and REAL
    PROPERTY AND REGISTRATION vol 87 (2012) PARAS 454–456.
8   See *Dearle v Hall* (1828) 3 Russ 1; and CHOSES IN ACTION vol 13 (2009) PARA 43.
9   *Clark v Chief Land Registrar* [1994] Ch 370, [1994] 4 All ER 96, CA; *United Bank of Kuwait plc
    v Sahib* [1997] Ch 107, [1996] 3 All ER 215, CA. See also PARA 220.

294.   Priority of other statutory charges. Various statutory rights, liabilities,
claims and penalties are secured by charge upon land, usually as local land
charges[1] which have priority over both existing and future incumbrances[2]. The
nature, effect and priority of a statutory charge depend on the provisions of the
statute in question: statutory charges on 'the land' or 'the premises' confer priority
over existing and future incumbrances[3].

1   See eg the Housing Act 2004 s 37 (improvement notices and prohibition orders); and HOUSING
    vol 56 (2011) PARA 397. As to local land charges generally see REAL PROPERTY AND
    REGISTRATION vol 87 (2012) PARA 763 et seq.

2 See the Local Land Charges Act 1975 s 10(1); the Land Registration Act 2002 ss 29, 30, Sch 3 para 6; and REAL PROPERTY AND REGISTRATION vol 87 (2012) PARAS 482, 785, 786.

3 *Paddington Borough Council v Finucane* [1928] Ch 567; *Bristol Corpn v Virgin* [1928] 2 KB 622; *Westminster City Council v Haymarket Publishing Ltd* [1981] 2 All ER 555, [1981] 1 WLR 677, CA.

(6) PRIORITY BETWEEN MORTGAGEES AND TENANTS OF THE MORTGAGOR

295. Leases created before the mortgage. A mortgagee of registered[1] land is bound only by leases which fall within the categories of overriding interests[2] or are protected by notice[3]. The only legal leases which are now overriding are those granted for a term not exceeding seven years from the date of the grant, except where they are required to be registered[4]. A mortgagee is not bound by a leasehold estate in land granted to take effect in possession after the end of the period of three months beginning with the date of the grant and which has not taken effect in possession at the time of the disposition[5]. A mortgagee of registered land is also bound by an interest belonging at the time of the disposition to a person in actual occupation[6], so far as relating to land of which he is in actual occupation, except for:

(1) an interest under a settlement under the Settled Land Act 1925[7];

(2) an interest of a person of whom inquiry was made before the disposition and who failed to disclose the right when he could reasonably have been expected to do so[8];

(3) an interest which belongs to a person whose occupation would not have been obvious on a reasonably careful inspection of the land at the time of the disposition[9], of which the person to whom the disposition is made does not have actual knowledge at that time[10]; and

(4) a leasehold estate in land granted to take effect in possession after the end of the period of three months beginning with the date of the grant and which has not taken effect in possession at the time of the disposition[11].

An example of such an interest is an agreement for a lease or a statutory tenancy granted by a mortgagor holding the legal estate at the time of the grant of the lease[12]. A mortgagee is not bound by a tenancy if the tenant consents to the grant of the mortgage or is estopped from asserting priority[13], unless the tenancy is statutory or protected[14]. Nor is a mortgagee bound by a tenancy if the mortgage merely replaces and varies a previous mortgage granted before the lease[15]. A legal mortgage of land in lease at the date of the mortgage creates a term of years, and vests in the mortgagee the immediate reversion on the lease[16].

1 As to the meaning of 'registered' see PARA 127 note 3.

2 See the Land Registration Act 2002 ss 28–30, Sch 3 para 1; and REAL PROPERTY AND REGISTRATION vol 87 (2012) PARAS 454–456, 482.

3 See the Land Registration Act 2002 s 32; and REAL PROPERTY AND REGISTRATION vol 87 (2012) PARA 512.

4 See the Land Registration Act 2002 Sch 3 para 1; and REAL PROPERTY AND REGISTRATION vol 87 (2012) PARA 482.

5 See the Land Registration Act 2002 s 4(1)(d), Sch 3 para 1; and REAL PROPERTY AND REGISTRATION vol 87 (2012) PARA 345.

6 Under the Land Registration Act 1925 (see REAL PROPERTY AND REGISTRATION vol 87 (2012) PARA 234) the holder of a registered legal charge upon registered land was not bound by a prior oral agreement for a lease granted by the then prospective mortgagor if the tenant under the agreement had not entered into possession at the date when the charge took effect: see *City Permanent Building Society v Miller* [1952] Ch 840, [1952] 2 All ER 621, CA (where the oral

agreement was held not to constitute an overriding interest within the Land Registration Act 1925 s 70(1)(k) (as originally enacted), despite the definition of lease in s 3(x)); and see also *Hughes v Waite* [1957] 1 All ER 603, [1957] 1 WLR 713.
7   Land Registration Act 2002 Sch 3 para 2(a). As to settlements under the Settled Land Act 1925 see SETTLEMENTS vol 91 (2012) PARA 501 et seq.
8   Land Registration Act 2002 Sch 3 para 2(b).
9   Land Registration Act 2002 Sch 3 para 2(c)(i).
10   Land Registration Act 2002 Sch 3 para 2(c)(ii).
11   Land Registration Act 2002 Sch 3 para 2(d).
12   *Woolwich Building Society v Dickman* [1996] 3 All ER 204, 72 P & CR 470, CA; *Barclays Bank v Zaroovabli* [1997] Ch 321, [1997] 2 All ER 19. Where the mortgagors are themselves in occupation under such a lease at the time when the mortgagee seeks possession against them and against a third person to whom they have conveyed the legal estate in fee simple in the mortgaged land, they are not estopped from setting up the lease merely because in the conveyance to the third person they recited that they were seised in unincumbered fee simple in possession: *District Bank Ltd v Webb* [1958] 1 All ER 126, [1958] 1 WLR 148.
13   *Skipton Building Society v Clayton* (1993) 66 P & CR 223, 25 HLR 596, CA. See also PARAS 291–292.
14   *Woolwich Building Society v Dickman* [1996] 3 All ER 204, 72 P & CR 470, CA.
15   *Walthamstow Building Society v Davies* (1989) 60 P & CR 99, 22 HLR 60, CA.
16   *Rhodes v Allied Dunbar Pension Services Ltd, Re Offshore Ventilation Ltd* [1989] 1 All ER 1161, [1989] 1 WLR 800, CA. Cf *Neale v Mackenzie* (1836) 1 M & W 747, Ex Ch; *Harmer v Bean* (1853) 3 Car & Kir 307. A charge by way of legal mortgage has the same effect: see the Law of Property Act 1925 s 87(1); and PARA 165. As to the rights and liabilities of the mortgagor under the lease see PARAS 299, 355.

296. Purported legal leases granted by a purchaser. Prior to the acquisition of the legal estate, a purchaser cannot grant rights of a proprietary character. Accordingly, if a purchaser purports to grant a legal tenancy[1] before completion, the rights so granted remain personal unless and until the purchaser acquires the legal estate, whereupon the estoppel created by the grant is fed by the legal interest acquired on conveyance and the tenancy becomes a legal tenancy[2].

Where both a mortgage and a tenancy have been granted by a purchaser of property before he has acquired the legal estate, it seems that the doctrine of feeding the estoppel does not operate to render the tenancy valid against the mortgagee[3].

If the purchase is completed simultaneously with a mortgage securing an advance made by the mortgagee to provide part of the purchase price, the mortgagee is not bound by the tenancy since the transactions of acquiring the legal estate and granting the charge are one indivisible transaction and there is no 'scintilla temporis' during which the legal estate vests in the purchaser free of the charge[4]. If, however, the mortgage is not granted until after completion of the purchase, the mortgagee is bound by the tenancy which became a legal tenancy on completion[5].

1   Ie by deed or a valid parol lease: see the Law of Property Act 1925 ss 52, 54(2); and LANDLORD AND TENANT vol 62 (2012) PARA 100 et seq.
2   *Southern Pacific Mortgages Ltd v Scott* [2014] UKSC 52, [2015] 1 AC 385, [2015] 1 All ER 277. See ESTOPPEL vol 47 (2014) PARA 336.
3   *Rust v Goodale* [1957] Ch 33, [1956] 3 All ER 373.
4   *Abbey National Building Society v Cann* [1991] 1 AC 56, [1990] 1 All ER 1085, HL; *Southern Pacific Mortgages Ltd v Scott* [2014] UKSC 52, [2015] AC 385, [2015] 1 All ER 277 (which noted that the ratio of *Abbey National Building Society v Cann* above was limited to those cases where the purchaser required the loan in order to complete his purchase).
5   See PARA 295. See also *First National Bank plc v Thompson* [1996] Ch 231, [1996] 1 All ER 140, CA (registered land).

297. Unauthorised leases granted between execution and registration of the mortgage. A charge of registered land does not vest the legal estate in the mortgagee until completed by registration[1]. A lease of registered land vests a legal estate in the tenant free from an unregistered charge, even if it was granted in breach of the charge[2]. A statutory tenancy arising on the termination of such a lease is also binding on the mortgagee[3]. Accordingly, charges should be lodged for registration promptly[4].

1 *Barclays Bank plc v Zaroovabli* [1997] Ch 321, [1997] 2 All ER 19.
2 *Barclays Bank plc v Zaroovabli* [1997] Ch 321, [1997] 2 All ER 19. See also the Land Registration Act 2002 s 30(2)(b); and REAL PROPERTY AND REGISTRATION vol 87 (2012) PARA 456.
3 *Barclays Bank plc v Zaroovabli* [1997] Ch 321, [1997] 2 All ER 19.
4 *Barclays Bank plc v Zaroovabli* [1997] Ch 321, [1997] 2 All ER 19.

298. Unauthorised leases granted after the mortgage. A lease granted by a mortgagor after a mortgage without statutory or express power is good by estoppel between mortgagor and lessee[1], but void as between mortgagee and lessee[2], although a mortgagee who purchases the equity of redemption may be bound by tenancy agreements made by the mortgagor[3]. The lessee is not protected against a legal mortgagee by the rent restriction legislation[4]. A lease which is void as between the mortgagee and lessee is void against a purchaser on the mortgagee exercising his power of sale without any express assurance of the mortgagee's rights against the mortgagor[5]. A lease may be established against the mortgagee by his conduct[6]. The lessee can, however, protect himself from eviction[7] by the mortgagee by redeeming the mortgage[8]. The reversion by estoppel in the lessor passes by assignment, so that an assignee of the equity of redemption can enforce the lessee's covenants[9]. A mortgagee is not entitled to possession against a tenant if acting in bad faith pursuant to a collusive arrangement with and for the benefit of the lessor who would not otherwise be able to obtain possession[10].

1 *Alchorne v Gomme* (1824) 2 Bing 54; *Doe d Lord Downe v Thompson, Lord Downe v Thompson* (1847) 9 QB 1037; *Cuthbertson v Irving* (1860) 6 H & N 135 at 139, Ex Ch; *Hartcup & Co v Bell* (1883) Cab & El 19.
2 *Keech v Hall* (1778) 1 Doug KB 21; *Pope v Biggs* (1829) 9 B & C 245 at 253; *Trent v Hunt* (1853) 9 Exch 14; *Cuthbertson v Irving* (1860) 6 H & N 135, Ex Ch (explained in *Universal Permanent Building Society v Cooke* [1952] Ch 95 at 102, [1951] 2 All ER 893 at 896–897, CA); *Lows v Telford* (1876) 1 App Cas 414 at 425, HL; *Hassard v Fowler* (1892) 32 LR Ir 49; *Rust v Goodale* [1957] Ch 33 at 44, [1956] 3 All ER 373 at 380; *Hughes v Waite* [1957] 1 All ER 603, [1957] 1 WLR 713; *Taylor v Ellis* [1960] Ch 368, [1960] 1 All ER 549; *Sadiq v Hussain* [1997] NPC 19, CA.
3 *Smith v Phillips* (1837) 1 Keen 694, considered in *Rust v Goodale* [1957] Ch 33, [1956] 3 All ER 373; *O'Loughlin v Fitzgerald* (1873) 7 IR Eq 483.
4 *Dudley and District Benefit Building Society v Emerson* [1949] Ch 707, [1949] 2 All ER 252, CA (protected tenant); *Britannia Building Society v Earl* [1990] 2 All ER 469, [1990] 1 WLR 422, CA (statutory tenant); *Barclays Bank v Zaroovabli* [1997] Ch 321, [1997] 2 All ER 19.
5 *Rust v Goodale* [1957] Ch 33 at 44, [1956] 3 All ER 373 at 380 per Harman J.
6 *Lysaght v Callinan* (1831) Hayes 141.
7 As to the mortgagee's rights against a tenant under a tenancy not binding on the mortgagee see PARA 410.
8 *Tarn v Turner* (1888) 39 ChD 456, CA.
9 *Cuthbertson v Irving* (1860) 6 H & N 135, Ex Ch. See further ESTOPPEL vol 47 (2014) PARA 332 et seq.
10 *Quennell v Maltby* [1979] 1 All ER 568, [1979] 1 WLR 318, CA. See also *Sadiq v Hussain* [1997] NPC 19, CA.

299. Statutory leases granted after the mortgage. The statutory power of leasing[1], if not excluded[2], enables the mortgagor to create a term out of the estate of the mortgagee so as to convert that estate into one expectant on the term granted by the lease[3]. The mortgagee is bound by a lease thus made by the mortgagor[4] so long as the statutory requirements are complied with[5] and, on giving notice to the lessee to pay the rent to him, and on default by the lessee, he can sue for it and bring a claim for breach of any covenant contained in the lease;

and these rights of the mortgagee are not affected by a collateral agreement between the mortgagor and the lessee after the date of the mortgage[6].

1   See PARA 349.
2   See PARA 350.
3   *Municipal Permanent Investment Building Society v Smith* (1888) 22 QBD 70 at 72, CA, per Fry LJ.
4   Eg a mortgagee cannot block the lessee's lights: *Wilson v Queen's Club* [1891] 3 Ch 522; *Turner v Walsh* [1909] 2 KB 484, CA.
5   See PARAS 349–353.
6   See PARA 425. See also *Municipal Permanent Investment Building Society v Smith* (1888) 22 QBD 70, CA.

300. Leases granted for the purpose of prejudicing a mortgagee. A lease granted for the purpose of ensuring that a mortgagee does not obtain possession of the property may be set aside even if the tenant agrees to pay the best rent reasonably obtainable[1].

1   See the Insolvency Act 1986 s 423; *Agricultural Mortgage Corpn plc v Woodward* [1996] 1 FLR 226, [1995] 1 EGLR 1, CA; *Barclays Bank plc v Bean* [2004] 3 EGLR 71, [2004] 41 EG 152; and BANKRUPTCY AND INDIVIDUAL INSOLVENCY vol 5 (2013) PARA 689 et seq.

301. Leases granted with mortgagee's consent. Where leasing is prohibited except with the mortgagee's consent, the onus of proving consent lies with the tenant[1]. A mortgagee who has recognised the tenant as his tenant cannot treat him as a trespasser and evict him[2]. A provision in the mortgage that a lessee is not to be concerned to see that consent for letting had been given may estop the mortgagee from asserting that the lease has been granted without consent[3].

Recognition by the mortgagee of a tenant is a question of fact; receipt of money from a tenant is not conclusive, for it may have been received by the mortgagee as part of the principal, or as interest. An encouragement by the mortgagee to the tenant to spend money may be evidence of a recognition of the lease[4]. No privity can be assumed between the tenant and the mortgagee, but evidence is admissible to prove that the mortgagor in granting the lease acted as agent for the mortgagee[5].

Receipt of rent by a receiver appointed under statute[6] does not create a tenancy between the tenant and mortgagee, but, notwithstanding the receivership, such a tenancy might be created if the facts otherwise show that the mortgagee consented to accept the mortgagor's tenant as his own[7].

Mere inaction by the mortgagee with knowledge of an unauthorised letting does not amount to recognition by conduct[8].

1   *Taylor v Ellis* [1960] Ch 368, [1960] 1 All ER 549.
2   *Underhay v Read* (1887) 20 QBD 209, CA; *Corbett v Plowden* (1884) 25 ChD 678, CA.
3   *Lever Finance Ltd v Needleman Property Trustee* [1956] Ch 375, [1956] 2 All ER 378, distinguishing *Dudley and District Benefit Building Society v Emerson* [1949] Ch 707, [1949] 2 All ER 252, CA.
4   *Doe d Parry v Hughes* (1847) 11 Jur 698; *Doe d Rogers v Cadwallader* (1831) 2 B & Ad 473; *Evans v Elliot* (1838) 9 Ad & El 342. See also *Doe d Whitaker v Hales* (1831) 7 Bing 322; *Doe d Bowman v Lewis* (1884) 13 M & W 241; *Doe d Wilkinson v Goodier* (1847) 10 QB 957; *Barclays Bank Ltd v Kiley* [1961] 2 All ER 849, [1961] 1 WLR 1050.
5   *Corbett v Plowden* (1884) 25 ChD 678 at 681, CA, per Lord Selborne LC.
6   Ie under the Law of Property Act 1925 s 109: see PARA 479.
7   See *Stroud Building Society v Delamont* [1960] 1 All ER 749, [1960] 1 WLR 431; *Chatsworth Properties Ltd v Effiom* [1971] 1 All ER 604, [1971] 1 WLR 144, CA; *Mann v Nijar* (1998) 32 HLR 223, CA.
8   *Re O'Rourke's Estate* (1889) 23 LR Ir 497; *Parker v Braithwaite* [1952] 2 All ER 837, [1952] WN 504; *Taylor v Ellis* [1960] Ch 368, [1960] 1 All ER 549; *Mann v Nijar* (1998) 32 HLR 223, CA.

302. Leases granted by the mortgagee. The mortgagee and tenant may agree to have as between themselves the relationship of landlord and tenant[1]. Such an agreement destroys the old lease between the mortgagor and tenant and creates a tenancy between mortgagee and tenant[2]. Payment of rent by a tenant to the mortgagee is evidence of a new tenancy[3]. The terms of the tenancy are ascertained by evidence and inference from the facts, and are not necessarily those on which the tenant held under the mortgagor[4]. Notice by the mortgagee to the lessee to pay rent to him and payment in accordance with the notice would be such evidence[5]. A mortgagee cannot, however, by notice to a tenant compel him to be his tenant, and the continuance in possession after notice from the mortgagee is no evidence of an agreement that he would become tenant[6].

1 *Brown v Storey* (1840) 1 Man & G 117 at 126 per Tindal CJ.
2 *Corbett v Plowden* (1884) 25 ChD 678 at 681–682, CA.
3 *Partington v Woodcock* (1835) 6 Ad & El 690; *Doe d Higginbotham v Barton* (1840) 11 Ad & El 307 at 315; *Mann v Nijar* (1998) 32 HLR 223, CA. As to the circumstances in which a periodic tenancy arises by implication see now *Cardiothoracic Institute v Shrewdcrest Ltd* [1986] 3 All ER 633, [1986] 1 WLR 368, CA.
4 *Keith v R Gancia & Co Ltd* [1904] 1 Ch 774 at 783, CA; and see *Oakley v Monck* (1866) LR 1 Exch 159, Ex Ch.
5 *Corbett v Plowden* (1884) 25 ChD 678, CA; *Keith v R Gancia & Co Ltd* [1904] 1 Ch 774, CA; *Chatsworth Properties Ltd v Effiom* [1971] 1 All ER 604, [1971] 1 WLR 144, CA (payment to receiver).
6 *Evans v Elliot* (1838) 9 Ad & El 342; *Biner v Walters* (1869) 20 LT 326; *Towerson v Jackson* [1891] 2 QB 484, CA, disapproving on this point *Underhay v Read* (1887) 20 QBD 209, CA. See also *Brown v Storey* (1840) 1 Man & G 117. It seems that *Pope v Biggs* (1829) 9 B & C 245 and *Waddilove v Barnett* (1836) 4 Dowl 347 must be treated as overruled on this point by *Evans v Elliot* above.

303. Lease granted pursuant to statutory right of enfranchisement. A tenant may be entitled to be granted a new lease[1] despite the fact that the grant of the existing lease was subsequent to the creation of a mortgage on the landlord's interest and not authorised as against the persons interested in the mortgage[2]. A lease so granted is deemed to be authorised as against the persons interested in any mortgage on the landlord's interest, however created or arising, and is binding on those persons[3]. However, such a lease is not binding on the persons interested in any such mortgage if the existing lease was granted after 1 November 1993[4] and, being granted subsequent to the creation of the mortgage, would not otherwise[5] be binding on the persons interested in the mortgage[6].

1 As to the statutory right of enfranchisement see LANDLORD AND TENANT vol 64 (2012) PARA 1779 et seq.
2 See the Leasehold Reform, Housing and Urban Development Act 1993 s 58(1); and LANDLORD AND TENANT vol 64 (2012) PARA 1829.
3 See the Leasehold Reform, Housing and Urban Development Act 1993 s 58(1)(a), (b); and LANDLORD AND TENANT vol 64 (2012) PARA 1829.
4 Ie the date on which the Leasehold Reform, Housing and Urban Development Act 1993 Pt I Ch II (ss 39–62) was brought into force by the Leasehold Reform, Housing and Urban Development Act 1993 (Commencement and Transitional Provisions No 1) Order 1993, SI 1993/2134.
5 Ie apart from the Leasehold Reform, Housing and Urban Development Act 1993 s 58(1): see s 58(2).
6 See the Leasehold Reform, Housing and Urban Development Act 1993 s 58(2); and LANDLORD AND TENANT vol 64 (2012) PARA 1829.

5. THE EQUITY OF REDEMPTION

(1) NATURE OF EQUITY OF REDEMPTION

304. The nature of the equity of redemption. At law, a mortgage of land formerly took the form of a conveyance to the creditor on condition that if the money was repaid on the specified date, the creditor would reconvey the land but if the condition was not strictly complied with the debtor would lose the land forever and remain liable for the debt. The Court of Chancery intervened to permit the debtor to redeem the mortgage on performance of the conditions, notwithstanding his failure to do so by the specified date, and this right, known as the 'equity of redemption', arose to provide relief against penalties[1]. This right of a mortgagor to redeem his property was, until the changes made by the Law of Property Act 1925, not a mere right, but an equitable estate or interest in the property mortgaged[2]. Although the mortgagor had mortgaged his property, he might still deal with it in any way consistent with the rights of the mortgagee[3]. It is still true that the mortgagor may deal with the property in any way that is consistent with the rights of the mortgagee. He has still also an equitable right to redeem the property after the day fixed for payment has gone by, but his right or equity of redemption is no longer strictly an equitable estate or interest, although it is still in the nature of an equitable interest[4]. Under the present system of creating legal mortgages, the mortgagee takes only a term of years, leaving the legal freehold reversion expectant on the mortgage term in the mortgagor[5]. Accordingly, the mortgagor retains his legal freehold estate and cannot at the same time have an equitable estate co-extensive with it[6]. Therefore, instead of his equity of redemption constituting an equitable estate or interest, it subsists only as a right in equity to redeem the property, this right being attached to his legal freehold estate.

1 *Kreglinger v New Patagonia Meat and Cold Storage Co Ltd* [1914] AC 25, HL. As to the principle that a right to redeem is a necessary incident of a mortgage see PARA 107. As to the effect of non-payment at common law see Littleton's Tenures s 322; Bac Abr, Mortgage (E) 1. See also REAL PROPERTY AND REGISTRATION vol 87 (2012) PARA 100.
2 *Santley v Wilde* [1899] 2 Ch 474 at 475, CA; *Kreglinger v New Patagonia Meat and Cold Storage Co Ltd* [1914] AC 25 at 48–50, 52, HL; *Re Clancarty* [1921] 2 IR 377; *Re Sir Thomas Spencer Wells, Swinburne-Hanham v Howard* [1933] Ch 29 at 44–48, 52, CA; *Lloyd v Lander* (1821) 5 Madd 282 at 289. See also PARA 107; and REAL PROPERTY AND REGISTRATION vol 87 (2012) PARA 100.
3 *Casborne v Scarfe* (1738) 1 Atk 603; *Heath v Pugh* (1881) 6 QBD 345 at 360, CA (affd sub nom *Pugh v Heath* (1882) 7 App Cas 235, HL); *Jennings v Jordan* (1881) 6 App Cas 698 at 714 per Lord Blackburn; *Tarn v Turner* (1888) 39 ChD 456 at 460 per Kekewich J (affd (1888) 39 ChD 456, CA). See also *Pawlett v A-G* (1667) Hard 465 at 469. A mortgagor was not after execution of a legal mortgage 'seised' of the land according to the common law and, therefore, was not liable to the burdens of tenure incident to customary freeholds, such as a heriot due to the lord of a manor on the death of a tenant seised of a tenement in the manor: *Copestake v Hoper* [1908] 2 Ch 10, CA. As to tenure incident to customary freeholds see CUSTOM AND USAGE vol 32 (2012) PARAS 43–44; REAL PROPERTY AND REGISTRATION vol 87 (2012) PARAS 20 et seq, 37.
4 See the Law of Property Act 1925 s 1(3); and REAL PROPERTY AND REGISTRATION vol 87 (2012) PARA 101.
5 See PARAS 164–165. The legal estate of freehold is an estate in fee simple absolute in possession within the meaning of the Law of Property Act 1925 s 1(1): see REAL PROPERTY AND REGISTRATION vol 87 (2012) PARA 63. The existence of the term does not prevent the reversion on the term being 'in possession': see REAL PROPERTY AND REGISTRATION vol 87 (2012) PARA 63. Under s 1(5), legal estates can exist concurrently, that is, the estate of freehold exists as a legal estate concurrently with the term, and for this purpose it must be treated as in possession

notwithstanding that it is subject to the term: see REAL PROPERTY AND REGISTRATION vol 87 (2012) PARA 64.

6   See *Selby v Alston* (1797) 3 Ves 339; *Re Selous, Thomson v Selous* [1901] 1 Ch 921.

305. Right of redemption on mortgage of chattels. On a mortgage of chattels, even after the mortgagee has seized the goods, the mortgagor can still redeem so long as the goods are in the mortgagee's possession[1]. The right to redemption is incident to the contract of mortgage; it does not depend on the form of the transaction[2], and cannot be negatived by contemporaneous agreement or even clogged[3].

1   *Johnson v Diprose* [1893] 1 QB 512, CA; *Cukurova Finance International Ltd v Alfa Telecom Turkey Ltd* [2013] UKPC 2, [2015] 2 WLR 875, [2013] All ER (D) 21 (Apr). See also PARA 107; and FINANCIAL INSTRUMENTS AND TRANSACTIONS vol 49 (2015) PARA 466. As to the distinction between a mortgage and a pledge of chattels see PARA 112.
2   *Sampson v Pattison* (1842) 1 Hare 533; *Wynne v Styan* (1847) 2 Ph 303; *Kirkwood v Thompson* (1865) 2 De GJ & Sm 613; *Re Alison, Johnson v Mounsey* (1879) 11 ChD 284, CA; *Banner v Berridge* (1881) 18 ChD 254; *Re Duke of Marlborough, Davis v Whitehead* [1894] 2 Ch 133. See also PARA 107. As to redemption of mortgages formerly made by way of trust for sale see *Chambers v Goldwin* (1801) 5 Ves 834; *Wicks v Scrivens* (1860) 1 John & H 215.
3   See PARA 320 et seq.

(2) PERSONS ENTITLED TO REDEEM

306. Persons who can redeem. The mortgagor and all persons having any interest in the property subject to the mortgage or liable to pay the mortgage debt can redeem[1].

Until he has absolutely assigned his equity of redemption, the mortgagor can redeem the mortgaged property, and a mortgagor who has entirely parted with the equity of redemption nevertheless, upon being sued for payment of the mortgage debt by the mortgagee, acquires a new right to redeem[2]. It is immaterial to the mortgagee, so far as the mortgagor's right to redeem is concerned, whether the mortgagor's title to the mortgaged property is good or bad as the mortgagee is not entitled to dispute it[3]. An assignee of a mortgage is in the same position as the mortgagee[4].

1   *Pearce v Morris* (1869) 5 Ch App 227 at 229; *Tarn v Turner* (1888) 39 ChD 456, 57 LJCh 452 (affd (1888) 39 ChD 456, CA); *Green v Wynn* (1869) 4 Ch App 204 at 207. See PARA 107. As to persons claiming under the mortgagor see PARA 307.
2   *Dashwood v Blythway* (1729) 1 Eq Cas Abr 317; *Lockhart v Hardy* (1846) 9 Beav 349; *Palmer v Hendrie* (1859) 27 Beav 349 (subsequent proceedings *Palmer v Hendrie (No 2)* (1860) 28 Beav 341); *Walker v Jones* (1866) LR 1 PC 50 at 61; *Kinnaird v Trollope* (1888) 39 ChD 636 at 645 per Stirling J.
3   *Tasker v Small* (1837) 3 My & Cr 63 at 70 per Lord Cottenham LC.
4   *Walker v Jones* (1866) LR 1 PC 50 at 66. As to the corresponding estoppel binding the mortgagor see ESTOPPEL vol 47 (2014) PARA 336.

307. Persons claiming under the mortgagor. The following persons claiming under the mortgagor can redeem:

(1)   an assignee of the equity of redemption, including a volunteer[1];
(2)   a subsequent incumbrancer[2];
(3)   a tenant for years under a lease made subsequent to the mortgage which the mortgagee refuses to confirm[3]; and
(4)   a surety on payment by himself or refusal by the principal debtor to discharge the mortgage debt, or if the surety has mortgaged his own estate as security for the debt[4], but not where the surety has given up his right to subrogation[5].

A statutory tenant has no right to redeem[6]. Where mortgages on several plots have been consolidated and the mortgagor has conveyed the property to different purchasers, the purchasers are entitled, in foreclosure proceedings by the mortgagee, to redeem in the sequence of the dates of the instruments under which the purchasers acquired their interests[7].

1   *Thorne v Thorne* (1683) 1 Vern 182; *Howard v Harris* (1683) 1 Vern 190 at 193. A voluntary transaction may, however, be set aside if made with the intent to defraud a subsequent purchaser, if made for the purpose of putting assets beyond the reach of, or otherwise prejudicing, a person who is making or may make a claim against him, and in certain circumstances where the donor becomes insolvent: see the Insolvency Act 1986 ss 238, 339, 423; and BANKRUPTCY AND INDIVIDUAL INSOLVENCY vol 5 (2013) PARAS 679, 689; COMPANY AND PARTNERSHIP INSOLVENCY vol 17 (2011) PARA 801 et seq.

2   *Fell v Brown* (1787) 2 Bro CC 276; *Marquis of Chomondeley v Lord Clinton* (1820) 2 Jac & W 1 at 134; *Faulkner v Daniel* (1843) 3 Hare 199; *Peto v Hammond* (1860) 29 Beav 91; *Tomlinson v Gregg* (1866) 15 WR 51. If a subsequent mortgagee loses his status as mortgagee by virtue of the provisions of the Limitation Act 1980 he ceases to be entitled to redeem: see *Cotterell v Price* [1960] 3 All ER 315, [1960] 1 WLR 1097. As to the Limitation Act 1980 see LIMITATION PERIODS vol 68 (2008) PARA 901.

3   *Keech v Hall* (1778) 1 Doug KB 21; *Tarn v Turner* (1888) 57 LJCh 452 (affd (1888) 39 ChD 456, CA).

4   See FINANCIAL INSTRUMENTS AND TRANSACTIONS vol 49 (2015) PARA 767.

5   *Royal Trust Co Mortgage Corpn v Nudnyk Holdings Ltd* (1974) 4 OR (2d) 721, 49 DLR (3d) 169, Ont HC.

6   *Britannia Building Society v Earl* [1990] 2 All ER 469, [1990] 1 WLR 422, CA.

7   *Beevor v Luck, Beevor v Lawson* (1867) LR 4 Eq 537 at 548–549; *Loveday v Chapman* (1875) 32 LT 689.

308. Spouse, civil partner or cohabitant with statutory right of occupation. Where a spouse or civil partner becomes statutorily entitled[1] to occupy a dwelling house or any part of it, any payment or tender by that spouse or civil partner in or towards satisfaction of any liability of the other spouse or civil partner in respect of mortgage payments affecting the dwelling house is as good as if made or done by the other spouse or civil partner[2], but the mortgagee may treat any such payment as having been made by the other spouse or civil partner[3]. A former spouse, former civil partner, cohabitant or former cohabitant in favour of whom an occupation order is made is in the same position as a spouse or civil partner[4]. A spouse or former spouse, civil partner or former civil partner, cohabitant or former cohabitant may apply to be joined to any claim in which a mortgagee of a dwelling house seeks to enforce its security[5]. The statutory provisions do not affect any claim of a spouse or former spouse, civil partner or former civil partner, cohabitant or former cohabitant in occupation and actually making the payment against the other spouse, civil partner, cohabitant or former cohabitant to an interest in the dwelling house by virtue of the payment[6].

1   Ie under the Family Law Act 1996 s 30: see MATRIMONIAL AND CIVIL PARTNERSHIP LAW vol 72 (2015) PARA 304.

2   See the Family Law Act 1996 s 30(3); and MATRIMONIAL AND CIVIL PARTNERSHIP LAW vol 72 (2015) PARA 304.

3   See the Family Law Act 1996 s 30(5); and MATRIMONIAL AND CIVIL PARTNERSHIP LAW vol 72 (2015) PARA 304.

4   See the Family Law Act 1996 ss 35(13), 36(13); and MATRIMONIAL AND CIVIL PARTNERSHIP LAW vol 72 (2015) PARAS 316, 319.

5   See the Family Law Act 1996 ss 54(5), 55; and MATRIMONIAL AND CIVIL PARTNERSHIP LAW vol 72 (2015) PARAS 304, 306.

6   See the Family Law Act 1996 ss 30(5), 35(13), 36(13); and MATRIMONIAL AND CIVIL PARTNERSHIP LAW vol 72 (2015) PARAS 304, 316, 319. See also *Hastings and Thanet Building Society v Goddard* [1970] 3 All ER 954, [1970] 1 WLR 1544, CA.

309. Assignee of the equity of redemption. An assignee of the equity of redemption during proceedings may apply for permission to be made a party to a claim for redemption[1]. If he continues the claim, he is bound by all the proceedings in the claim[2], but he is under no obligation to make himself a party[3].

1 See CPR 19.3; CPR PD 13A—*Addition and Substitution of Parties*; and CIVIL PROCEDURE vol 11 (2015) PARA 481.
2 *Bishop of Winchester v Paine* (1805) 11 Ves 194; *Wood v Surr* (1854) 19 Beav 551; *Campbell v Holyland* (1877) 7 ChD 166; *Re Parbola Ltd Blackburn Ltd, v Parbola Ltd* [1909] 2 Ch 437.
3 *Patch v Ward* (1867) 3 Ch App 203. See, however, *Three Rivers District Council v Governor and Co of the Bank of England* [1996] QB 292, [1995] 4 All ER 312, CA.

310. Judgment creditors' interest in the equity of redemption. A judgment creditor who obtains a charging order[1] is in the same position to redeem as a subsequent incumbrancer[2]. Every judgment creditor to whom the land of his mortgagor has been actually delivered in execution by registration of the order appointing a receiver[3] has an interest in the equity of redemption[4]. He can redeem prior incumbrances, and is a necessary party to foreclosure and redemption[5].

1 As to charging orders see PARA 220. As to the equity of redemption see PARAS 107, 304 et seq.
2 See PARA 307.
3 See PARA 567.
4 *Mildred v Austin* (1869) LR 8 Eq 220; *Earl of Cork v Russell* (1871) LR 13 Eq 210. See also *Hood Barrs v Cathcart* [1895] 2 Ch 411 at 414 per North J.
5 *Bishop of Winchester v Beavor* (1797) 3 Ves 314; *Rolleston v Morton* (1842) 1 Dr & War 171 at 191; *Adams v Paynter* (1844) 1 Coll 530; *Joyce v Joyce* (1846) 10 I Eq R 128. As to foreclosure see PARA 571 et seq.

311. Trustees' right of redemption in respect of land held on trust. Where land is held on trust, the trustees represent the beneficiaries and have in relation to the land subject to the trust the powers of an absolute owner, including the power to redeem a mortgage[1]. This includes the case of an express trust, a former trust for sale[2] or a purported settlement created after 1 January 1997[3], and a trust which arises where land is conveyed to two or more persons as joint tenants or tenants in common[4]. The primary right of redemption is in the trustees, who may bring proceedings claiming redemption without joining the beneficiaries[5]. This appears to be within the rule that he who has the legal estate must redeem, unless a special case is made, such as that the trustees or executors are colluding with the mortgagees[6]. Should the trustees improperly refuse to redeem, any beneficiary may redeem or seek a direction that the trustees do so[7].

1 See the Trusts of Land and Appointment of Trustees Act 1996 s 6; and TRUSTS AND POWERS vol 98 (2013) PARA 476. As to the equity of redemption see PARAS 107, 304 et seq.
2 Land held on trust for sale prior to 1 January 1997 (ie the date on which the Trusts of Land and Appointment of Trustees Act 1996 was brought into force by the Trusts of Land and Appointment of Trustees Act 1996 (Commencement) Order 1996, SI 1996/2974) has since that date been held on a trust of land: see the Trusts of Land and Appointment of Trustees Act 1996 s 1; and REAL PROPERTY AND REGISTRATION vol 87 (2012) PARA 66.
3 See note 2. It is no longer possible to create a settlement for the purposes of the Settled Land Act 1925: see the Trusts of Land and Appointment of Trustees Act 1996 s 2(1); SETTLEMENTS vol 91 (2012) PARA 577.
4 See the Law of Property Act 1925 ss 34, 36; and REAL PROPERTY AND REGISTRATION vol 87 (2012) PARAS 198, 214 et seq.
5 As to representation of beneficiaries by trustees see CPR 19.7A; and CIVIL PROCEDURE vol 12 (2015) PARA 1209. See also *Mills v Jennings* (1880) 13 ChD 639, CA; affd sub nom *Jennings v Jordan* (1881) 6 App Cas 698, HL (trustees of an equity of redemption sufficiently represent their beneficiaries in a redemption claim, if no direction to the contrary has been given by the court).
6 *Troughton v Binkes* (1801) 6 Ves 573 at 575.
7 *Hayim v Citibank NA* [1987] AC 730, [1987] 3 WLR 83, PC. A beneficiary may make an application relating to the exercise by trustees of land of any of their functions: see the Trusts of

Land and Appointment of Trustees Act 1996 s 14; and TRUSTS AND POWERS vol 98 (2013) PARA
479. It does not appear that a beneficiary must necessarily obtain such a direction before exercising
his right to redeem, although he must make out a case for redeeming: see *Troughton v Binkes*
(1801) 6 Ves 573.

312.   Persons with interests in settled land. Where the equity of redemption is
incident to settled land[1], the land will be vested in the tenant for life or statutory
owners as trustees for all persons beneficially interested[2], and the primary right of
redemption is in him or them, although, if he or they improperly refuse to exercise
that right, any persons beneficially interested can redeem[3]. The persons
beneficially interested include life tenants and remaindermen, although perhaps
not remaindermen beyond the first estate of inheritance[4]. A remainderman cannot
redeem a mortgage on the settled property without the consent of the tenant for
life[5].

1   No settlement created after 1 January 1997 (ie the date on which the Trusts of Land and
    Appointment of Trustees Act 1996 was brought into force by the Trusts of Land and Appointment
    of Trustees Act 1996 (Commencement) Order 1996, SI 1996/2974) is a settlement for the purposes
    of the Settled Land Act 1925 although strict settlements in existence on that date continue to exist
    until there is no relevant property: see the Trusts of Land and Appointment of Trustees Act 1996
    s 2; and SETTLEMENTS vol 91 (2012) PARA 577. As to the equity of redemption see PARAS 107,
    304 et seq.
2   See the Settled Land Act 1925 ss 16, 107(1); and SETTLEMENTS vol 91 (2012) PARAS 668–670,
    676.
3   See PARA 311.
4   *Gore v Stacpoole* (1813) 1 Dow 18, HL; *Anderson v Stather* (1845) 2 Coll 209; *Playford v
    Playford* (1845) 4 Hare 546.
5   *Ravald v Russell* (1830) You 9 at 21; *Raffety v King* (1836) 1 Keen 601; *Wicks v Scrivens* (1860)
    1 John & H 215; *Prout v Cock* [1896] 2 Ch 808.

313.   Devolution of the right of redemption on death. On the death of the
mortgagor, the equity of redemption, and with it the right to redeem, devolves on
his personal representatives[1] and is exercisable by them until, by assent or
conveyance, the equity becomes vested in the devisee or other person entitled.

Legatees whose legacies are charged on the mortgaged property can redeem to
protect their legacies[2], but only through the personal representatives, unless a
special case is made for redemption otherwise than through the personal
representatives[3].

If a mortgagor dies without next of kin and intestate in respect of any real
estate, the Crown is beneficially entitled to the equity of redemption as bona
vacantia[4].

1   See the Administration of Estates Act 1925 s 1; and WILLS AND INTESTACY vol 103 (2010) PARA
    944 et seq. See also PARA 151. As to the equity of redemption see PARAS 107, 304 et seq.
2   *Faulkner v Daniel* (1843) 3 Hare 199 at 211; *Batchelor v Middleton* (1848) 6 Hare 75.
3   See CPR 19.7A; and CIVIL PROCEDURE vol 11 (2015) PARA 479.
4   See the Administration of Estates Act 1925 s 46(1)(vi) (now set out in amended form in the
    Intestates' Estates Act 1952 s 4, Sch 1). As to intestate succession generally see WILLS AND
    INTESTACY vol 102 (2010) PARA 479 et seq. As to bona vacantia see CROWN AND CROWN
    PROCEEDINGS vol 29 (2014) PARAS 149–154.

314.   Persons lacking mental capacity. Where the right of redemption[1] is vested
in a person lacking mental capacity, it is exercisable by the court on his behalf[2].

1   See PARAS 107, 304 et seq.
2   See the Mental Capacity Act 2005 Pt 2 (ss 45–61); and MENTAL HEALTH AND CAPACITY vol 75
    (2013) PARA 720 et seq.

315.   Children. A child cannot own a legal estate in land and the right of
redemption[1] will therefore be in the trustees in whom the land is vested[2].

1   See PARAS 107, 304 et seq.

2 See the Trusts of Land and Appointment of Trustees Act 1996 s 2, Sch 1 para 1; and CHILDREN AND YOUNG PERSONS vol 9 (2012) PARA 31; SETTLEMENTS vol 91 (2012) PARA 578.

316. Purchaser of equity of redemption. A person who has contracted to purchase the equity of redemption can redeem, unless his rights under the contract are disputed[1], as can a claimant in proceedings for the administration of the mortgagor's estate who has obtained an order for sale[2].

1 *Pearce v Morris* (1869) 5 Ch App 227. See, however, *Tasker v Small* (1837) 3 My & Cr 63 at 69, where Lord Cottenham LC suggested that the purchase must have been completed. As to the equity of redemption see PARAS 107, 304 et seq.
2 *Christian v Field* (1842) 2 Hare 177.

317. Bankrupts. The bankrupt's estate, of which the equity of redemption of mortgaged property forms part[1], vests in his trustee in bankruptcy on his appointment taking effect[2]. Neither the mortgagor while bankrupt[3], nor his general creditors[4], can redeem property which he has mortgaged. His trustee in bankruptcy has, however, certain powers to redeem such property[5], but he cannot, after a foreclosure order has been made, claim to redeem the mortgaged property at the valuation put upon the security by the mortgagee in the bankruptcy proceedings unless a special direction has been inserted in the foreclosure order[6], nor can he redeem where a secured creditor does not prove[7].

1 See the Insolvency Act 1986 s 283; and BANKRUPTCY AND INDIVIDUAL INSOLVENCY vol 5 (2013) PARA 211. As to the equity of redemption see PARAS 107, 304 et seq.
2 See the Insolvency Act 1986 s 306; and BANKRUPTCY AND INDIVIDUAL INSOLVENCY vol 5 (2013) PARA 398.
3 See *Spragg v Binkes* (1800) 5 Ves 583 at 590; *Rochfort v Battersby* (1849) 2 HL Cas 388. As to the bankrupt's right to redeem after discharge from or annulment of his bankruptcy see the Insolvency Act 1986 ss 281, 281A, 282, 330(5), Sch 4A Pt III; and BANKRUPTCY AND INDIVIDUAL INSOLVENCY vol 5 (2013) PARA 649 et seq.
4 *Troughton v Binkes* (1801) 6 Ves 573; *Heath v Chadwick* (1848) 2 Ph 649.
5 See the Insolvency Rules 1986, SI 1986/1925, r 6.117; and BANKRUPTCY AND INDIVIDUAL INSOLVENCY vol 5 (2013) PARA 578.
6 *Sanguinetti v Stuckey's Banking Co (No 2)* [1896] 1 Ch 502. See generally BANKRUPTCY AND INDIVIDUAL INSOLVENCY vol 5 (2013) PARA 428.
7 *Re Vautin, ex p Saffery* [1899] 2 QB 549. See also BANKRUPTCY AND INDIVIDUAL INSOLVENCY vol 5 (2013) PARA 507 et seq.

318. Dissolved corporation. If a corporation which has executed a mortgage is dissolved, the equity of redemption[1] passes to the Crown as bona vacantia[2].

1 See PARAS 107, 304 et seq.
2 See *Re Sir Thomas Spencer Wells, Swinburne-Hanham v Howard* [1933] Ch 29, CA (equity of redemption in leaseholds); and CORPORATIONS vol 24 (2010) PARA 506. As to the statutory provision by which the rights and property of a company subject to the Companies Act 2006 are on its dissolution to be deemed to be bona vacantia see s 1012; and COMPANY AND PARTNERSHIP INSOLVENCY vol 17 (2011) PARA 892.

319. Persons claiming by possessory title. It seems that a person who has acquired a possessory title against the mortgagor can redeem[1]. A stranger cannot redeem, but if a claimant has a prima facie title to an interest in the equity of redemption, a mortgagee who requires proof of such interest may lose his right to costs[2].

1 *Fletcher v Bird* (1896) Fisher's Law of Mortgage (6th Edn, 1910) 1025. See also LIMITATION PERIODS vol 68 (2008) PARA 1212. As to the equity of redemption see PARAS 107, 304 et seq.
2 *James v Biou* (1819) 3 Swan 234; *Lloyd v Wait* (1842) 1 Ph 61; *Smith v Green* (1844) 1 Coll 555; *Pearce v Morris* (1869) 5 Ch App 227. As to the mortgagee's right to costs see PARA 743 et seq.

(3) RESTRICTIONS ON RIGHT TO REDEEM

320. Clog or fetter on the equity of redemption. On the principle of once a mortgage always a mortgage[1], a clog or fetter on the equity of redemption is void[2]. No agreement between mortgagor and mortgagee contained in the mortgage can make a mortgage irredeemable[3]. This principle does not apply to debentures issued by a company which can be made irredeemable[4], but a forfeiture clause under a lien on fully paid shares may be void as a clog[5]. No contract between a mortgagor and mortgagee made at the time of the mortgage, and as part of the mortgage transaction or, in other words, as one of the terms of the loan, can be valid if it provides that the mortgaged property is to become the absolute property of the mortgagee upon any event whatsoever[6] or that the mortgagee is to have a share in the mortgaged property[7]. Subject to the statutory power to make debentures irredeemable[8], it seems that the rule against clogging the equity of redemption applies to debentures with a floating charge issued by a company[9]; but debenture holders who have been paid off are not precluded by the rule from sharing in surplus assets, if it is so provided[10].

1   See eg *Kreglinger v New Patagonia Meat and Cold Storage Co Ltd* [1914] AC 25, HL; and PARAS 107, 304 et seq.
2   *Newcomb v Bonham* (1681) 1 Vern 7 at 8 per Lord Nottingham LC; *Santley v Wilde* [1899] 2 Ch 474, CA, per Lindley MR; *Salt v Marquess of Northampton* [1892] AC 1, HL; *Noakes & Co Ltd v Rice* [1902] AC 24 at 34, HL; *Samuel v Jarrah Timber and Wood Paving Corpn* [1904] AC 323 at 329, HL; *Kreglinger v New Patagonia Meat and Cold Storage Co Ltd* [1914] AC 25 at 53, HL, per Lord Parker; *Re Rainbow Syndicate Ltd, Owen v Rainbow Syndicate Ltd* [1916] WN 178; *Seton v Slade, Hunter v Seton* (1802) 7 Ves 265; *Jones v Morgan* [2001] EWCA Civ 995, [2001] Lloyd's Rep (Bank) 323. As to the effect of an omission from the deed of a proviso for redemption see PARA 195.
3   *Courtenay v Wright* (1860) 2 Giff 337. Cf *Howard v Harris* (1683) 1 Vern 190, where a restriction of redemption to the heirs male of the body did not prevent the mortgagor from redeeming.
4   See the Companies Act 2006 s 739; and COMPANIES vol 15 (2009) PARA 1305. An ordinary mortgage may be a debenture within this provision: see *Knightsbridge Estates Trust Ltd v Byrne* [1940] AC 613, [1940] 2 All ER 401, HL.
5   *Hopkinson v Mortimer, Harley & Co Ltd* [1917] 1 Ch 646. See also COMPANIES vol 15 (2009) PARA 1214; COMPANIES vol 15 (2009) PARA 1326; LIEN vol 68 (2008) PARA 849.
6   *Mellor v Lees* (1742) 2 Atk 494; *Toomes v Conset* (1745) 3 Atk 261; *Vernon v Bethell* (1762) 2 Eden 110 at 113; *Spurgeon v Collier* (1758) 1 Eden 55; *Courtenay v Wright* (1860) 2 Giff 337; *Re Edwards' Estate* (1861) 11 I Ch R 367; *Lisle v Reeve* [1902] 1 Ch 53, CA (affd sub nom *Reeve v Lisle* [1902] AC 461, HL); *London and Globe Finance Corpn v Montgomery* (1902) 18 TLR 661; *Samuel v Jarrah Timber and Wood Paving Corpn* [1904] AC 323, HL.
7   *Jones v Morgan* [2001] EWCA Civ 995, [2001] Lloyd's Rep (Bank) 323.
8   See note 4.
9   See PARA 322 note 12.
10   *Re Cuban Land Co (1911) Ltd* [1921] 2 Ch 147. See also COMPANIES vol 15 (2009) PARA 1326.

321. Postponement or limitation of right to redeem. A contractual postponement of the right to redeem is enforceable unless:

(1)   it is a clog on the right to redeem[1];
(2)   it is oppressive or unconscionable[2]; or
(3)   it is designed to secure an unreasonable restraint of trade[3].

Mere unreasonableness does not make a term oppressive or unconscionable[4] and the mere length of time of any postponement of the right to redeem is not in itself objectionable[5]. However, the debtor has a right to make payment at any time under a regulated agreement under the Consumer Credit Act 1974[6]. A contractual postponement of the right to redeem may be oppressive if the mortgagee is entitled to call for payment before the mortgagor can redeem[7]. A mortgage can validly secure a contingent liability even if the result is that the mortgagor cannot redeem for an indefinite period[8].

1 Eg as in *Fairclough v Swan Brewery Co Ltd* [1912] AC 565, PC, where in a mortgage of a 20-year lease, redemption was postponed until six weeks before the expiry of the lease. See also *Knightsbridge Estates Trust Ltd v Byrne* [1939] Ch 441, [1938] 4 All ER 618, CA; but see the dictum in *Kreglinger v New Patagonia Meat and Cold Storage Co Ltd* [1914] AC 25 at 53, HL, per Lord Parker of Waddington. On the same principle, a provision limiting the right to redeem to the lifetime of the mortgagor has been held invalid: see *Price v Perrie* (1702) Freem Ch 258; *Salt v Marquess of Northampton* [1892] AC 1, HL. Cf *Bonham v Newcomb* (1684) as reported in 1 Vern 232; affd (1689) 1 Vern 233n, HL (where a provision restricting redemption to the life of the mortgagor was upheld on the ground that it was proved that the mortgagor had intended to make a settlement of the mortgaged property on the mortgagee in case he should not think fit to redeem in his lifetime). As to the equity of redemption see PARAS 107, 304 et seq. As to the concept of a clog or fetter on the right to redeem see PARA 320.
2 *Knightsbridge Estates Trust Ltd v Byrne* [1939] Ch 441, [1938] 4 All ER 618, CA; on appeal [1940] AC 613, [1940] 2 All ER 401, HL (where this question was not dealt with).
3 *Esso Petroleum Co Ltd v Harper's Garage (Stourport) Ltd* [1968] AC 269, [1967] 1 All ER 699, HL; *Re Petrol Filling Station, Vauxhall Bridge Road, London, Rosemex Service Station Ltd v Shell Mex and BP Ltd* (1968) 20 P & CR 1; *Texaco Ltd v Mulberry Filling Station Ltd* [1972] 1 All ER 513, [1972] 1 WLR 814; *Alec Lobb (Garages) Ltd v Total Oil GB Ltd* [1985] 1 All ER 303, [1985] 1 WLR 173, CA. As to restraint of trade see COMPETITION vol 18 (2009) PARA 377 et seq.
4 *Knightsbridge Estates Trust Ltd v Byrne* [1939] Ch 441, [1938] 4 All ER 618, CA; *Multiservice Bookbinding Ltd v Marden* [1979] Ch 84, [1978] 2 All ER 489; *Alec Lobb (Garages) Ltd v Total Oil GB Ltd* [1985] 1 All ER 303, [1985] 1 WLR 173, CA.
5 See *Knightsbridge Estates Trust Ltd v Byrne* [1939] Ch 441, [1938] 4 All ER 618, CA, where postponement for 40 years was upheld.
6 See the Consumer Credit Act 1974 s 94; and CONSUMER CREDIT vol 21 (2011) PARA 264.
7 *Morgan v Jeffreys* [1910] 1 Ch 620; *Davis v Symons* [1934] Ch 442; *Knightsbridge Estates Trust Ltd v Byrne* [1939] Ch 441, [1938] 4 All ER 618, CA.
8 *Re Rudd & Son Ltd* [1991] BCLC 378n, (1986) 2 BCC 98, 955, CA.

322. Collateral benefits. There is no objection to a stipulation that a mortgagee is to have a collateral advantage[1] provided that:

(1)   it is not unfair and unconscionable[2];
(2)   it is not in the nature of a penalty clogging the equity of redemption[3];
(3)   it is not inconsistent with or repugnant to the right to redeem[4]; and
(4)   it is not an unreasonable restraint of trade[5].

So long as these requirements are met, there is no objection to a collateral benefit continuing after redemption, and no rule which permits the mortgagor to redeem merely on payment of principal, interest and costs regardless of the terms of the contract[6]. If a mortgagor wishes to object to a collateral benefit it seems that he must offer to repay the mortgage[7].

Factors to be taken into account in determining whether a provision is unconscionable include the strength of bargaining position of the parties, whether the stronger party has taken advantage of his position, whether he has gained an unequal bargain, whether the weaker party has received independent advice, and the terms of the transaction itself[8]. The conscience of the stronger party must be affected[9].

These rules apply not only to land but also to other forms of property such as shares or stocks[10], insurance policies[11], floating charges[12], and mortgages made by commercial and other companies[13]. The rule forbids an indirect as much as a direct fetter on the property[14]. A tied contract which does not offend these principles will be upheld[15].

Where an option to purchase is granted against the background of a sale of the property by the grantee of the option to the grantor at a price which is to be left outstanding, it is necessary to consider whether the transaction is one of sale and purchase or of mortgage[16].

If the transaction is a mortgage, a contract to sell, if required, to the mortgagee part of the mortgaged property at a fixed price[17], or an option contained in the mortgage deed to the mortgagee to purchase at a fixed price[18], is invalid. Where the property mortgaged is leasehold and the lease contains an option to purchase the freehold reversion, it is doubtful whether the mortgagee can stipulate to have the option transferred to him absolutely by way of collateral benefit[19]. Where the option is assigned to him by way of security only and he exercises it, the mortgagor on redemption is entitled to a conveyance of the reversion[20].

The following contracts have been held not to be enforceable after redemption: a contract to buy back from a brewer-mortgagee[21]; a contract to pay to the mortgagee a share of the profits of a hotel[22]; a contract to employ the mortgagee as auctioneer[23] or broker[24]; and a debenture with a right to the payment of a bonus out of profits after the principal has been paid off[25].

On a sale, where part of the purchase money remains on mortgage, a covenant for pre-emption is good if it is part of the sale and not part of the contract of mortgage[26], but, even in the case of a sale from the mortgagor to the mortgagee, redemption has been allowed on special grounds[27].

An option to call for shares in consideration of a loan may be upheld[28].

1 *Kreglinger v New Patagonia Meat and Cold Storage Co Ltd* [1914] AC 25 at 61, HL, per Lord Parker of Waddington; *Knightsbridge Estates Trust Ltd v Byrne* [1939] Ch 441, [1938] 4 All ER 618, CA; *Multiservice Bookbinding Ltd v Marden* [1979] Ch 84, [1978] 2 All ER 489 (approved in *Alec Lobb (Garages) Ltd v Total Oil GB Ltd* [1985] 1 All ER 303, [1985] 1 WLR 173, CA); *Jones v Morgan* [2001] EWCA Civ 995, [2001] Lloyd's Rep (Bank) 323.

2 The test is not one of reasonableness: see *Multiservice Bookbinding Ltd v Marden* [1979] Ch 84, [1978] 2 All ER 489; approved in *Alec Lobb (Garages) Ltd v Total Oil GB Ltd* [1985] 1 All ER 303, [1985] 1 WLR 173, CA. An unconscionable provision is void, not voidable: see *Brighton and Hove City Council v Audus* [2009] EWHC 340 (Ch), [2010] 1 All ER (Comm) 343, [2009] 2 EGLR 131.

3 As to the concept of a clog or fetter on the right to redeem see PARA 320.

4 As to the right to redeem see PARAS 107, 320.

5 See PARA 321.

6 *Kreglinger v New Patagonia Meat and Cold Storage Co Ltd* [1914] AC 25, HL.

7 *Esso Petroleum Co Ltd v Harper's Garage (Stourport) Ltd* [1968] AC 269 at 299, [1967] 1 All ER 699 at 708, HL, per Lord Reid; *Amoco Australia Pty Ltd v Rocca Bros Motor Engineering Co Pty Ltd* [1975] AC 561, [1975] 1 All ER 968, PC.

8 *Kreglinger v New Patagonia Meat and Cold Storage Co Ltd* [1914] AC 25 at 61, HL, per Lord Parker of Waddington; *Knightsbridge Estates Trust Ltd v Byrne* [1939] Ch 441, [1938] 4 All ER 618, CA; *Multiservice Bookbinding Ltd v Marden* [1979] Ch 84, [1978] 2 All ER 489; *Alec Lobb (Garages) Ltd v Total Oil GB Ltd* [1985] 1 All ER 303, [1985] 1 WLR 173, CA; *Credit Lyonnais Bank Nederland NV v Burch* [1997] 1 All ER 144, 74 P & CR 384, CA; *Portman Building Society v Dusangh* [2000] 2 All ER (Comm) 221, [2000] Lloyd's Rep Bank 197, CA; *Jones v Morgan* [2001] EWCA Civ 995, [2001] Lloyd's Rep Bank 323.

9 *Alec Lobb (Garages) Ltd v Total Oil GB Ltd* [1985] 1 All ER 303, [1985] 1 WLR 173, CA; *Credit Lyonnais Bank Nederland NV v Burch* [1997] 1 All ER 144, 74 P & CR 384, CA.

10 *Bradley v Carritt* [1903] AC 253, HL; *Samuel v Jarrah Timber and Wood Paving Corpn* [1904] AC 323, HL.

11 *Salt v Marquess of Northampton* [1892] AC 1, HL.

12 *Kreglinger v New Patagonia Meat and Cold Storage Co Ltd* [1914] AC 25 at 41, 44, HL, per Lord Haldane LC. The application of the rule to floating charges was left open in *De Beers Consolidated Mines Ltd v British South Africa Co* [1912] AC 52, HL. See also COMPANIES vol 15 (2009) PARA 1269 et seq.

13 *Samuel v Jarrah Timber and Wood Paving Corpn* [1904] AC 323, HL.

14 *Bradley v Carritt* [1903] AC 253, HL.

15 *Esso Petroleum Co Ltd v Harper's Garage (Stourport) Ltd* [1968] AC 269, [1967] 1 All ER 699, HL; *Re Petrol Filling Station, Vauxhall Bridge Road, London, Rosemex Service Station Ltd v Shell Mex and BP Ltd* (1968) 20 P & CR 1; *Texaco Ltd v Mulberry Filling Station Ltd* [1972] 1 All ER 513, [1972] 1 WLR 814; *Alec Lobb (Garages) Ltd v Total Oil GB Ltd* [1985] 1 All ER 303, [1985] 1 WLR 173, CA.

16 *Warnborough Ltd v Garmite Ltd* [2003] EWCA Civ 1544, [2004] 1 P & CR D18, [2003] All ER (D) 52 (Nov); *Warnborough Ltd v Garmite Ltd* [2006] EWHC 10 (Ch), [2007] 1 P & CR 34, [2006] All ER (D) 22 (Jan). See also *Brighton and Hove City Council v Audus* [2009] EWHC 340 (Ch), [2010] 1 All ER (Comm) 343, [2009] 2 EGLR 131.

17 *Jennings v Ward* (1705) 2 Vern 520; *Re Edwards' Estate* (1861) 11 I Ch R 367.

18 *Samuel v Jarrah Timber and Wood Paving Corpn* [1904] AC 323, HL. See also *Lewis v Frank Love Ltd* [1961] 1 All ER 446, [1961] 1 WLR 261.

19 *Nelson v Hannam* [1943] Ch 59 at 61–62, [1942] 2 All ER 680 at 684, CA, per Lord Greene MR.

20 *Nelson v Hannam* [1943] Ch 59, [1942] 2 All ER 680, CA. See also PARA 170.

21 *Noakes & Co Ltd v Rice* [1902] AC 24, HL.

22 *Santley v Wilde* [1899] 2 Ch 474, CA.

23 *Broad v Selfe* (1863) 11 WR 1036; *Browne v Ryan* [1901] 2 IR 653, CA.

24 *Bradley v Carritt* [1903] AC 253, HL.

25 *Re Rainbow Syndicate Ltd, Owen v Rainbow Syndicate Ltd* [1916] WN 178 at 179.

26 *Davies v Chamberlain* (1909) 26 TLR 138, CA; *Re Moore and Texaco Canada Ltd* [1965] 2 OR 253 (Can); *Re Petrol Filling Station, Vauxhall Bridge Road, London, Rosemex Service Station Ltd v Shell Mex and BP Ltd* (1968) 20 P & CR 1. Cf *Orby v Trigg* (1722) 9 Mod Rep 2, where a covenant in a mortgage deed allowing pre-emption was rejected, the mortgagee having concealed it. A mortgagee may not sell to himself in exercise of his power of sale in accordance with a valid option or right of pre-emption: see *Williams v Wellingborough Borough Council* [1975] 3 All ER 462, [1975] 1 WLR 1327, CA.

27 *Bowen v Edwards* (1661) 1 Rep Ch 117 at 221.

28 *London and Globe Finance Corpn v Montgomery* (1902) 18 TLR 661.

323. Subsequent and independent transactions. The rule against clogging the equity of redemption[1] applies to a subsequent transaction which varies the terms on which the mortgagor is entitled to redeem[2] but does not invalidate subsequent and independent transactions between the mortgagor and mortgagee relating to the mortgaged property. Accordingly, the mortgagee may, subsequently to the mortgage, stipulate for an option of purchase of the property[3], or for a sale[4] or release[5] to him of the equity of redemption. Such a sale or release is, however, liable to be set aside if there has been any oppression or unfairness on the part of the mortgagee[6], the burden of proof of such oppression or unfairness being on the mortgagor[7]. Mere inadequacy of price is not, however, in itself ground for setting it aside[8]. Moreover, a contract contemporaneous with a mortgage, but wholly independent of it and forming no part of the consideration for the mortgage, is valid[9].

As regards leases by a mortgagor to his mortgagee, a lease for a long period at an inadequate rent will not be upheld[10], but an ordinary occupation lease at a fair rent is not objectionable[11].

1 As to the equity of redemption see PARAS 107, 304 et seq. As to the rule against clogging the equity of redemption see PARA 320.

2 *Jones v Morgan* [2001] EWCA Civ 995, [2001] Lloyd's Rep (Bank) 323.

3 *Reeve v Lisle* [1902] AC 461, HL; *Bonham v Newcomb* (1684) 1 Vern 232 (affd (1689) 1 Vern 233n, HL); *Kevans v Joyce* [1896] 1 IR 442. Cf *Lewis v Frank Love Ltd* [1961] 1 All ER 446, [1961] 1 WLR 261 (a case on the face of it of transfer of mortgage, but in reality more one of a new loan).

4 *Knight v Marjoribanks* (1849) 2 Mac & G 10 at 14.

5 *Melbourne Banking Corpn v Brougham* (1882) 7 App Cas 307, PC; *Cotterell v Purchase* (1734) Cas *temp* Talb 61. See also *Rushbrook v Lawrence* (1869) 5 Ch App 3, where an agreement for a release was treated as abandoned, since for 12 years no step had been taken to complete the transaction.

6 *Webb v Rorke* (1806) 2 Sch & Lef 661; *Ford v Olden* (1867) LR 3 Eq 461; *Prees v Coke* (1871) 6 Ch App 645. See also MISREPRESENTATION vol 76 (2013) PARA 850 et seq.

7 *Melbourne Banking Corpn v Brougham* (1882) 7 App Cas 307, PC. See also MISREPRESENTATION vol 76 (2013) PARA 850.

8 *Knight v Marjoribanks* (1849) 2 Mac & G 10 at 13; *Purdie v Millett* (1829) Taml 28. See also *Waters v Groom* (1844) 11 Cl & Fin 684 at 699, HL, per Lord Brougham.

9 *De Beers Consolidated Mines Ltd v British South Africa Co* [1912] AC 52 at 67, HL; *Kreglinger v New Patagonia Meat and Cold Storage Co Ltd* [1914] AC 25, HL; *Re Petrol Filling Station, Vauxhall Bridge Road, London, Rosemex Service Station Ltd v Shell Mex and BP Ltd* (1968) 20 P & CR 1. See also PARA 322.
10 *Webb v Rorke* (1806) 2 Sch & Lef 661; *Hickes v Cooke* (1816) 4 Dow 16 at 24–25, HL. See also *Gubbins v Creed* (1804) 2 Sch & Lef 214.
11 *Morony v O'Dea* (1809) 1 Ball & B 109.

324. Bonus payable to the mortgagee. The validity of a provision in a mortgage for a bonus or premium or other such sum must be determined in the same way as any other collateral benefit[1]. A contract for payment to the mortgagee of a bonus in addition to the sum advanced is not inherently objectionable[2]. A valid bonus can be claimed by a mortgagee either in taking account of what is due on his mortgage or under the head of just allowances[3]. Examples of loans with a bonus are debentures issued at a discount and loans by building societies where a premium is charged[4], but a provision in a debenture for payment of a bonus out of profits after the principal has been paid off is not enforceable[5]. A service charge is not inherently objectionable[6].

1 See *Cityland and Property (Holdings) Ltd v Dabrah* [1968] Ch 166, [1967] 2 All ER 639, where such a provision was held to be unconscionable. The older cases are influenced by the old usury laws: see *Kreglinger v New Patagonia Meat and Cold Storage Co Ltd* [1914] AC 25 at 49–50, HL. See also *Multiservice Bookbinding Ltd v Marden* [1979] Ch 84, [1978] 2 All ER 489. As to bonuses see further PARA 729.
2 *Potter v Edwards* (1857) 26 LJCh 468; *James v Kerr* (1889) 40 ChD 449; *Mainland v Upjohn* (1889) 41 ChD 126.
3 *Bucknell v Vickery* (1891) 64 LT 701, PC. See also PARA 729.
4 *Re Anglo-Danubian Steam Navigation and Colliery Co* (1875) LR 20 Eq 339; *Re Phillips, ex p Bath* (1884) 27 ChD 509, CA.
5 *Re Rainbow Syndicate Ltd, Owen v Rainbow Syndicate Ltd* [1916] WN 178 at 179.
6 *Wallingford v Mutual Society* (1880) 5 App Cas 685, HL; *Protector Endowment Loan and Annuity Co v Grice* (1880) 5 QBD 592, CA.

325. Costs charged by mortgagee. A solicitor mortgagee may charge his costs, or those of the firm of which he is a member, for all work done in completing and preparing a mortgage against the security[1]. Consequently no such mortgage can be redeemed except upon payment of such charges and remuneration[2].

1 See the Solicitors Act 1974 s 58; and LEGAL PROFESSIONS vol 66 (2015) PARA 711.
2 See PARA 327.

326. Mortgages temporarily unredeemable. Although in general no contract between a mortgagee and mortgagor can make a mortgage irredeemable[1], the circumstances of the case may make redemption for a time impossible, as for example when a mortgage is made to secure an annuity, or as an indemnity against future liabilities, or for any other object not capable of immediate pecuniary valuation[2].

1 This would be a clog on the equity of redemption: see PARA 320.
2 *Fleming v Self* (1854) 3 De GM & G 997.

(4) TERMS AND INCIDENTS OF REDEMPTION

327. Terms of redemption. The terms on which a mortgagor or those claiming under him are entitled to redeem are the same, whether they are ascertained in a claim for redemption or for foreclosure[1]. These terms are normally: payment to the mortgagee of the principal debt, interest on that debt, all proper costs, charges and expenses incurred by the mortgagee in relation to the mortgage debt or the mortgage security, the costs of litigation properly undertaken by the mortgagee in reference to the mortgage debt or the mortgage security, and the mortgagee's costs of the redemption claim[2]. However small may be the interest in the mortgaged property of the person seeking redemption, he must pay to the mortgagee all that is due[3].

In exceptional circumstances it may be inequitable or unconscionable to insist on redemption taking place on a basis which treats the loan as if it had remained continuously outstanding to date. Equity can and should make a special order as to interest or costs in exceptional situations where the mortgagee has by words or conduct rejected, made impossible or delayed repayment of the mortgage debt, and that such a situation may exist where there is a tender or offer of repayment, particularly one backed by moneys actually paid into court or an account[4].

1   *Sober v Kemp* (1847) 6 Hare 155. As to proceedings for redemption see PARA 661 et seq; and as to foreclosure see PARA 571 et seq. As to the right of a mortgagee to recover arrears of interest see LIMITATION PERIODS vol 68 (2008) PARA 1105 et seq.
2   *Re Wallis, ex p Lickorish* (1890) 25 QBD 176, CA. See also PARA 755 et seq. See further *Gardner v Wainfur* (1919) 89 LJCh 98 (advances made during minority for necessaries and acknowledged after majority must be paid in full on redemption). As to the special rights of a mortgagee under the doctrine of consolidation see PARA 502 et seq. As to the costs of reconveyance see PARA 659.
3   *Palk v Lord Clinton* (1805) 12 Ves 48 at 59; *Marquis of Cholmondeley v Lord Clinton* (1820) 2 Jac & W 1 at 134; *Wilson v Cluer* (1840) 3 Beav 136. Cf *Kinnaird v Trollope* (1889) 42 ChD 610.
4   *Cukurova Finance International Ltd v Alfa Telecom Turkey Ltd* [2013] UKPC 2, [2015] 2 WLR 875, [2013] All ER (D) 21 (Apr).

328.   Incidents of redemption. A mortgagor of personalty, for example securities, may redeem at any time before the actual sale[1]. On redemption the mortgagee must return the identical securities pledged, if capable of identification or, if he has sold them during the currency of the loan, must account to the mortgagor for the proceeds of such sale[2]. The right to a return of the identical securities may be lost by the course of dealing between the mortgagor and the mortgagee, or by acquiescence by the mortgagor, and in these cases the mortgagor's right is a right to have returned to him a corresponding quantity of shares of the same denomination[3].

If, before the right to redeem is lost, the mortgagee by wrongfully parting with the securities has put it out of his power to return the identical securities, he cannot sue for the debt, and his trustee in bankruptcy has no greater right[4].

1   *Re Morritt, ex p Official Receiver* (1886) 18 QBD 222, CA; *Deverges v Sandeman, Clark & Co* [1902] 1 Ch 579, CA. As to mortgages of personalty see PARA 205 et seq.
2   *Langton v Waite* (1868) LR 6 Eq 165, following *Ex p Dennison* (1797) 3 Ves 552.
3   *Crerar v Bank of Scotland* 1921 SC 736, Ct of Sess.
4   *Ellis & Co's Trustee v Dixon-Johnson* [1925] AC 489, HL.

(5) DISPOSAL OR DEVOLUTION OF EQUITY OF REDEMPTION

329.   General power of disposition inter vivos. In as much as the mortgagor after the mortgage is created retains an estate or interest in the mortgaged property[1], he can sell, mortgage or otherwise dispose[2] of it during his life, or dispose of it by will[3]. A mortgagor beneficially entitled to possession of property for a long term of years capable of enlargement can enlarge the term into a fee simple notwithstanding the incumbrances on the term which upon enlargement will affect the fee simple so created[4].

1   Where a legal mortgage or charge of freehold or leasehold property is created, the mortgagor's estate is a legal one: see PARA 164 et seq. As to the powers of a proprietor of registered land see the Land Registration Act 2002 s 26; and REAL PROPERTY AND REGISTRATION vol 87 (2012) PARA 425.
2   See *Pawlett v A-G* (1667) Hard 465; *Casborne v Scarfe* (1738) 1 Atk 603; *Heath v Pugh* (1881) 6 QBD 345 at 360, CA (affd sub nom *Pugh v Heath* (1882) 7 App Cas 235, HL); *Jennings v Jordan* (1881) 6 App Cas 698, HL; *Tarn v Turner* (1888) 39 ChD 456 (affd (1888) 39 ChD 456, CA); *Copestake v Hoper* [1908] 2 Ch 10, CA.
3   See WILLS AND INTESTACY vol 102 (2010) PARA 25 et seq. This power of disposition is usually qualified by a provision in the mortgage requiring the consent of the lender to any disposition. In that case, failure to obtain consent prior to a disposition would be a breach of the terms of the mortgage. Prior consent is also required for the sale of a house purchased with an advance under the Small Dwellings Acquisition Acts 1899 to 1923: see the Housing Act 1985 s 456, Sch 18 (amended by the Insolvency Act 1985 s 235(1), Sch 8 para 39; Insolvency Act 1986 s 439(2), Sch 14; Arbitration Act 1996 s 107(2), Sch 4; Crime and Courts Act 2013 s 17(5), Sch 9 Pt 3 paras 52, 88).
4   See the Law of Property Act 1925 s 153; and REAL PROPERTY AND REGISTRATION vol 87 (2012) PARA 83 et seq. As to the mortgage extending to accretions see PARA 170.

330. Devolution of equity of redemption on death of mortgagor. On the death of the mortgagor intestate the equity of redemption[1] in his mortgaged property devolves on his personal representatives in the same manner as his other estate[2].

1   As to the equity of redemption see PARAS 107, 304 et seq.
2   See PARA 313; and WILLS AND INTESTACY vol 103 (2010) PARA 934 et seq.

(6) RIGHT OF REDEMPTION IN RELATION TO CHARGING ORDERS

331. Discharge of charging orders. A charge imposed by a charging order has the like effect as an equitable charge[1]. The court by which a charging order is made may at any time, on the application of the debtor or any person interested in any property to which the order relates, make an order discharging or varying the charging order[2]. The court may discharge a charging order on the ground that it should not have been made absolute[3], on the ground that the judgment debt is satisfied[4], or on the ground that the creditor proved in the debtor's bankruptcy and failed to evince an intention to realise his security[5]. The debtor cannot obtain a discharge of the charging order merely by paying the judgment debt but must also pay interest and costs as if he were seeking to redeem an equitable charge[6]. The Limitation Act 1980[7] does not apply to the enforcement of a charging order[8].

1   See the Charging Orders Act 1979 s 3(4); and PARA 220; and CIVIL PROCEDURE vol 12A (2015) PARA 1475.
2   See the Charging Orders Act 1979 s 3(5); and CIVIL PROCEDURE vol 12A (2015) PARA 1479.
3   *Howell v Montey* (1990) 61 P & CR 18, CA.
4   See CPR 73.9; and CIVIL PROCEDURE vol 12A (2015) PARA 1480.
5   See *C & W Berry Ltd v Armstrong-Moakes* [2007] EWHC 2101 (QB), [2008] 1 P & CR D2, [2007] All ER (D) 82 (Sep).
6   *Ezekiel v Orakpo* [1997] 1 WLR 340, CA.
7   Ie the Limitation Act 1980 s 20(5): see LIMITATION PERIODS vol 68 (2008) PARA 1111.
8   *Ezekiel v Orakpo* [1997] 1 WLR 340, CA; *Yorkshire Bank Finance Ltd v Mulhall* [2008] EWCA Civ 1156, [2009] 2 All ER (Comm) 164, [2009] 1 P & CR 345.

(7) ENFORCEMENT OF THE EQUITY OF REDEMPTION

332. When right to redeem is enforceable. A mortgagor is not entitled to redeem the mortgaged property before the day fixed in the mortgage contract for payment of the principal[1], unless the mortgagee has taken steps to recover payment by taking possession of the property or otherwise[2]. On that day the mortgagor has a legal right, on payment of what is due, to recover the mortgaged property[3]. After that day has passed and default has been made, he has an equitable right to redeem the property[4].

1 *Brown v Cole* (1845) 14 Sim 427. See also *Harding v Tingey* (1864) 34 LJCh 13.
2 *Bovill v Endle* [1896] 1 Ch 648; *Ex p Wickens* [1898] 1 QB 543 at 548, CA. As to the postponement of the right to redeem see PARA 321. As to early repayment of regulated agreements under the Consumer Credit Act 1974 see s 94; and CONSUMER CREDIT vol 21 (2011) PARA 264 et seq.
3 *Crickmore v Freeston* (1870) 40 LJCh 137; *Cummins v Fletcher* (1880) 14 ChD 699, CA. As to the nature of the mortgagor's rights until the time for payment has arrived see REAL PROPERTY AND REGISTRATION vol 87 (2012) PARA 100.
4 See PARA 107.

333. Notice to pay off mortgage. It was a settled rule of practice that after default has been made by a mortgagor in payment of the principal and interest in accordance with the proviso for redemption, he had either to give the mortgagee six months' notice of his intention to pay off the mortgage, or to pay him six months' interest in lieu of notice[1]; and if the mortgagor, after giving notice of his intention to pay off the mortgage, made default in so doing, and the default was not explained, the mortgagee was entitled to further reasonable notice but not a fresh six months' notice or six months' interest in lieu of notice[2]. Mere delay in drawing up an order directing payment out of a fund in court to a mortgagee was not a ground for demanding a further notice or interest in lieu of notice[3]; and if the default was explained it was sufficient that reasonable notice was given[4]. Neither the nature of the mortgaged property[5], nor the fact that the property had been realised otherwise than by the act of the mortgagee[6], gave rise to any exception from these rules.

However, this practice arose on the basis that a mortgagor who sought an equitable remedy was required to do equity by allowing the mortgagee a reasonable opportunity to find a new investment for his money[7]. The practice has been described as harsh[8] and may be reconsidered in the light of present circumstances where alternative investments are readily available[9]. Most modern mortgages make express provision for the length of notice required to redeem[10].

A mortgagor who has the contractual right to redeem on payment on demand also has an equitable right to redeem without a demand[11].

1 *Smith v Smith* [1891] 3 Ch 550 at 553 per Romer J; *Browne v Lockhart* (1840) 10 Sim 420 at 424; *Johnson v Evans* (1889) 61 LT 18, CA; *Garforth v Bradley* (1755) 2 Ves Sen 675 at 678; 2 Cases with Opinions of Counsel 51; *Cromwell Property Investment Co Ltd v Western and Toovey* [1934] Ch 322.
2 *Cromwell Property Investment Co Ltd v Western and Toovey* [1934] Ch 322.
3 *Sharpnell v Blake* (1737) 2 Eq Cas Abr 603. See also *Harmer v Priestley* (1853) 16 Beav 569.
4 *Cromwell Property Investment Co Ltd v Western and Toovey* [1934] Ch 322, where under the circumstances three months' notice was reasonable.
5 *Smith v Smith* [1891] 3 Ch 550.
6 *Spencer-Bell to London and South Western Rly Co and Metropolitan District Rly Co* (1885) 33 WR 771, where the mortgaged property was acquired by a railway company compulsorily.
7 As to the maxim he who seeks equity must do equity see EQUITABLE JURISDICTION vol 47 (2014) PARAS 110–111.
8 *Cromwell Property Investment Co Ltd v Western and Toovey* [1934] Ch 322 at 332 per Maughan J.

9 Compare the change in the practice of requiring a tenant to pay indemnity costs as a condition of relief from forfeiture: see *Billson v Residential Apartments* [1992] 1 AC 494, [1992] 1 All ER 141, HL. An express term which requires payment of six months' interest in lieu of notice may be regarded as unfair if it requires a consumer who fails to fulfil his obligation to pay a disproportionately high sum in compensation: see PARA 203. As to unfair terms in consumer contracts see the Consumer Rights Act 2015 Pt 2 (ss 61–76), Sch 2; and CONSUMER PROTECTION; CONTRACT.
10 See PARAS 195–196.
11 See *Re Rudd & Son Ltd* [1991] BCLC 378n, (1986) 2 BCC 98, 955, CA.

334. Effect of steps taken by mortgagee. If the mortgagee himself demands payment or takes steps to realise his security, whether the time fixed by the mortgage deed for redemption has arrived or not[1], or consents to a sale of the mortgaged property in administration proceedings[2] or to payment of his debt out of a fund in court[3], he is not entitled to the usual six months' notice or interest even though, after he has taken proceedings to recover his debt, the mortgagor has given him notice of intention to pay in six months[4]. The following are steps taken to realise the security: going into possession of mortgaged property[5] or selling it[6]; bringing a claim for foreclosure[7] or to administer the mortgagor's estate[8]; and giving notice to pay off in such a form as to enable the mortgagee to exercise his statutory power of sale[9]. A mortgagee who has demanded payment cannot refuse a tender of principal and interest to date of payment, even though the time limited in the mortgagee's demand has been exceeded[10]. Where, however, a day for redemption has been fixed by a foreclosure order, the mortgagor, if he wishes to redeem before that day, must pay interest up to the day appointed[11].

The mortgagee is not entitled to notice, or interest in lieu of notice, if his loan is merely of a temporary character, as, for instance, in the case of an equitable mortgage by deposit of title deeds[12]. So also, where the debt is repayable on demand, the mortgagor may redeem at any time and this is apparently so even where the mortgagee has covenanted not to call the mortgage in until a specified date[13].

1 *Bovill v Endle* [1896] 1 Ch 648.
2 *Day v Day* (1862) 31 Beav 270; *Re Fowler, Bishop v Fowler* (1922) 128 LT 620. See also *Matson v Swift* (1841) 5 Jur 645.
3 *Re Moss, Levy v Sewill* (1885) 31 ChD 90.
4 *Re Alcock, Prescott v Phipps* (1883) 23 ChD 372, CA. See also PARA 333.
5 *Bovill v Endle* [1896] 1 Ch 648. See also PARA 404 et seq.
6 *Banner v Berridge* (1881) 18 ChD 254. See also PARA 443 et seq.
7 *Hill v Rowlands* [1897] 2 Ch 361 at 363, CA. See also PARA 571 et seq.
8 *Re Alcock, Prescott v Phipps* (1883) 23 ChD 372, CA.
9 *Edmondson v Copland* [1911] 2 Ch 301 at 306. As to the rules affecting redemption under bills of sale see FINANCIAL INSTRUMENTS AND TRANSACTIONS vol 49 (2015) PARA 579.
10 *Edmondson v Copland* [1911] 2 Ch 301.
11 *Hill v Rowlands* [1897] 2 Ch 361, CA. As to foreclosure orders see PARA 597 et seq.
12 *Fitzgerald's Trustee v Mellersh* [1892] 1 Ch 385. As to the creation of an equitable mortgage by deposit of title deeds see PARAS 222–223. Since 27 September 1989 the mere deposit of title deeds by way of security can no longer create a valid equitable mortgage: see PARA 221.
13 See *GA Investments Pty Ltd v Standard Insurance Co Ltd* [1964] WAR 264, W Aust FC (where it was held that the only notice required was for such period as would enable the mortgagee to receive the money and bank it).

335. Necessity for mortgagor to tender amount due. The mortgagor is entitled to know how much he is liable to pay and how that amount is arrived at[1]. A mortgagor who desires to discharge the mortgage debt must tender to the mortgagee the full amount that is due in legal currency[2] and produce it before the mortgagee unless he waives the production[3], or refuses to accept money then available for immediate payment[4]. Where a mortgagee has unequivocally refused a proposed tender, a formal tender is not necessary, at any rate where the mortgagor has the money or the control of it[5]. The tender must be unconditional, but may be under protest[6].

Unless a place for payment is named in the mortgage deed, the tender must be made to the mortgagee or to some person entitled on his behalf to receive all that is due under the mortgage[7]. Where a debenture does not provide as to the place of payment, the company must seek out the debenture holder in order to pay him[8]. Where more than one person is entitled to the money, a tender is good which, after full notice to all parties, is made at the office of one of them who is a solicitor[9].

A stranger cannot make a valid tender; it must be made by or on behalf of a person having a prima facie right to redeem[10].

1   *Cityland and Property (Holdings) Ltd v Dabrah* [1968] Ch 166 at 172–173, [1967] 2 All ER 639 at 641–642 per Goff J. The mortgagee is obliged only to produce an honest redemption statement, not an accurate one: *Equatorial Corpn v Shah* [1996] NPC 172. As to the rights of a debtor under a regulated agreement under the Consumer Credit Act 1974 see CONSUMER CREDIT vol 21 (2011) PARA 244 et seq.

2   *Rhodes v Buckland* (1852) 16 Beav 212. As to tender generally see CONTRACT vol 22 (2012) PARA 237. A loan in foreign currency may be redeemed in that currency: *Russian Commercial and Industrial Bank v British Bank for Foreign Trade* [1921] 2 AC 438, HL.

3   *Douglas v Patrick* (1790) 3 Term Rep 683; *Powney v Blomberg* (1844) 8 Jur 746 (a letter saying 'DD now tenders', without enclosing any money, was not a good tender, although the mortgagee's solicitor wrote back, 'I decline your tender'); *Blumberg v Life Interests etc Corpn* [1897] 1 Ch 171 (an unsuccessful attempt to establish a tender by cheque to the mortgagee's agent); *Re Farley, ex p Danks* (1852) 2 De GM & G 936.

4   *Robarts v Jefferys* (1830) 8 LJOS Ch 137. As to the effect of refusal of tender see PARA 336.

5   *Chalikani Venkatarayanim v Tuni (Zamindar)* (1922) LR 50 Ind App 41.

6   *Thorpe v Burgess* (1840) 8 Dowl 603; *Manning v Lunn* (1845) 2 Car & Kir 13; *Scott v Uxbridge and Rickmansworth Rly Co* (1866) LR 1 CP 596; *Sweny v Smith* (1869) LR 7 Eq 324; *Greenwood v Sutcliffe* [1892] 1 Ch 1, CA.

7   Co Litt 210a, 210b.

8   *Fowler v Midland Electric Corpn for Power Distribution Ltd* [1917] 1 Ch 656, CA.

9   *Cliff v Wadsworth* (1843) 2 Y & C Ch Cas 598. See also PARA 644.

10 *Pearce v Morris* (1869) 5 Ch App 227.

336. Effect of mortgagee's refusal of tender. A mortgagee may lose his right to receive costs or be ordered to pay the costs if, by refusal of a proper tender, he renders necessary a claim for redemption[1], or after a sufficient tender begins a foreclosure claim[2]. Refusal of a proper tender is not equivalent to payment, but if the money, after the refusal, has been paid into court, or kept ready for immediate payment to the mortgagee, no further interest is payable[3]. For the purpose of stopping interest running, the tender need not be such a tender as would afford a defence at law[4]. If the amount tendered was all that was due, the mortgagee must bear the costs of a subsequent suit for redemption[5]. If it is intended that on receipt of the money the mortgagee should execute a reconveyance or discharge, a draft of the proposed instrument should be sent to him at a reasonable time before the tender[6]. Money extorted by a mortgagee in excess of what is due can be recovered by the mortgagor as money had and received[7]. The duty of the mortgagee on payment of all that is due is to produce and hand over the title deeds and the duly executed reconveyance, and the refusal to do this, when a sufficient tender has been made, amounts to a refusal of the tender[8]. The duty to execute a reconveyance may be performed by the mortgagee indorsing a statutory receipt on the mortgage before handing it over[9].

1   *Bank of New South Wales v O'Connor* (1889) 14 App Cas 273, PC; *Graham v Seal* (1918) 88 LJCh 31, CA; *Cukurova Finance International Ltd v Alfa Telecom Turkey Ltd* [2013] UKPC 2, [2015] 2 WLR 875, [2013] All ER (D) 21 (Apr). As to tender see PARA 335. As to proceedings for redemption see PARA 661 et seq.

2   *Smith v Green* (1844) 1 Coll 555. As to foreclosure see PARA 571 et seq.
3   *Gyles v Hall* (1726) 2 P Wms 378; *Bishop v Church* (1751) 2 Ves Sen 371; *Garforth v Bradley* (1755) 2 Ves Sen 675; *Hodges v Croydon Canal Co* (1840) 3 Beav 86; *Kinnaird v Trollope* (1889) 42 ChD 610; *Barratt v Gough-Thomas* [1951] 2 All ER 48; *Cukurova Finance International Ltd v Alfa Telecom Turkey Ltd* [2013] UKPC 2, [2015] 2 WLR 875, [2013] All ER (D) 21 (Apr).
4   *Manning v Burges* (1663) 1 Cas in Ch 29; *Webb v Crosse* [1912] 1 Ch 323 at 328. As to interest ceasing to run after tender see also PARA 738.
5   *Harmer v Priestley* (1853) 16 Beav 569.
6   *Wiltshire v Smith* (1744) 3 Atk 89; *Rourke v Robinson* [1911] 1 Ch 480; *Webb v Crosse* [1912] 1 Ch 323 at 329. See further PARA 648.
7   *Close v Phipps* (1844) 7 Man & G 586; *Fraser v Pendlebury* (1861) 10 WR 104. See further RESTITUTION vol 88 (2012) PARAS 405, 465 et seq. In appropriate cases money may be recoverable as having been paid under a mistake of fact or law: see MISTAKE vol 77 (2016) PARA 64 et seq; RESTITUTION vol 88 (2012) PARA 428 et seq. As to the binding effect of statements given under the Consumer Credit Act 1974 see s 172; and CONSUMER CREDIT vol 21 (2011) PARA 322.
8   *Rourke v Robinson* [1911] 1 Ch 480; *Walker v Jones* (1866) LR 1 PC 50 at 61.
9   See the Law of Property Act 1925 s 115; and PARA 650.

(8) LOSS OF RIGHT TO REDEEM

337. Loss of right to redeem by sale of equity of redemption. The right of redemption is lost on a sale or release of the equity of redemption by the mortgagor to the mortgagee made by a separate transaction subsequent to the mortgage and entirely independent of any bargain contemporaneous with it[1], or by a valid sale of the property by process of the court[2] or by the mortgagee under his power of sale[3]. The equity of redemption is extinguished by a contract for sale[4].

1   See PARAS 107, 304 et seq, 323.
2   See PARA 621 et seq.
3   See PARA 443 et seq.
4   See *National and Provincial Building Society v Ahmed* [1995] NPC 88, [1995] 2 EGLR 127, CA.

338. Loss of right to redeem by lapse of time or foreclosure. The right of redemption may be lost by lapse of time in the case of a mortgage of land[1], or by the operation of an order for foreclosure[2].

1   When a mortgagee of land has been in possession of any of the mortgaged land for a period of 12 years, no action to redeem the land of which the mortgagee has been so in possession may be brought after the end of that period by the mortgagor or any person claiming through him: see the Limitation Act 1980 s 16; Land Registration Act 2002 s 96(2); and LIMITATION PERIODS vol 68 (2008) PARA 1129.
2   As to foreclosure generally see PARA 571 et seq. As to the order absolute see PARA 612. See also LIMITATION PERIODS vol 68 (2008) PARA 1124 et seq.

[illegible]

4 [illegible]

5 [illegible]

6 [illegible]

7 [illegible]

8 [illegible]

(8) LOSS OF RIGHT TO REDEEM

577. Loss of right to redeem by sale or by release of equity of redemption. The right of redemption is lost on a sale or release of the equity of redemption by the mortgagor to the mortgagee made by a separate transaction subsequent to the mortgage and entirely independent of any bargain or contemporaneous with it, or by a valid sale of the property by process of the court or by the mortgagee under his power of sale. The equity of redemption is extinguished by a contract for sale.

1 See PARA 107; [illegible].

2 See PARA [illegible] et seq.

3 See PARA [illegible] et seq.

4 [illegible]

578. Loss of right to redeem by lapse of time or foreclosure. The right of redemption may be lost by lapse of time in the case of a mortgage of land, or by the operation of an order for foreclosure.

1 Where a mortgagee of land has been in possession of the mortgaged land for [illegible] years, the mortgagor's title to the land of which the mortgagee has been so in possession may be barred [illegible]: see the Limitation Act 1980 s 16; [illegible].

2 As to foreclosure generally see PARA [illegible] et seq.

6. RIGHTS AND LIABILITIES OF THE MORTGAGOR

(1) GENERAL RIGHTS AND LIABILITIES OF THE MORTGAGOR

339. Rights of mortgagor to redeem, to inspect title deeds and to have accounts. The right of a mortgagor to redeem the mortgaged property[1], to inspect title deeds which are in the mortgagee's possession[2], and to the taking of accounts between himself and the mortgagee[3] are considered elsewhere in this title.

1   See PARAS 107, 304 et seq.
2   See PARA 495 et seq.
3   See PARA 709 et seq.

340. Liability of mortgagor to pay principal and interest. The forms of covenant normally included in mortgages for the purpose of providing for the repayment by the mortgagor of the principal money advanced and interest on it, and the effect of such covenants, are considered elsewhere in this title[1].

1   See PARA 182 et seq.

(2) RIGHT TO POSSESSION AND RECEIPT OF RENTS AND PROFITS

341. Mortgagor's right to possession until demand made. When a legal mortgage[1] is executed, the mortgagee has, or is in the same position as if he had, the mortgaged property in possession; and in the absence of express stipulation to the contrary he is entitled to immediate possession or receipt of the rents and profits[2]. However, until the mortgagee demands possession[3], or enters into receipt of the rents and profits of the mortgaged property, it is in accordance with the nature of the transaction that the mortgagor should remain in possession as owner of the legal estate[4], and that possession is rightful[5]. Where a mortgagor[6] is for the time being entitled to the possession or receipt of the rents[7] and profits of any land as to which the mortgagee has not given notice of his intention to take possession or enter into receipt of the rents and profits, the mortgagor may sue for possession or for the recovery of the rents and profits or to prevent or recover damages for trespass or other wrong in relation to the mortgaged property[8], and may rightfully retain possession against the mortgagee's receiver until demand for possession is made, unless the order appointing the receiver directs the mortgagor to obtain or deliver up possession[9].

1   As to the creation of legal mortgages see PARA 161 et seq. As to how far an equitable mortgagee is entitled to possession see PARA 405.
2   See PARA 404 et seq. See also the text to notes 3–9.
3   *Bagnall v Villar* (1879) 12 ChD 812.
4   *Ashe v National Westminster Bank plc* [2008] EWCA Civ 55, [2008] 1 WLR 710, [2008] 2 P & CR 183.
5   *Heath v Pugh* (1881) 6 QBD 345 at 359, CA, per Lord Selborne LC; affd sub nom *Pugh v Heath* (1882) 7 App Cas 235, HL.
6   As to the meaning of 'mortgagor' see PARA 104 note 1.
7   'Rent' includes a rent service or a rentcharge, or other rent, toll, duty, royalty, or annual or periodical payment in money or money's worth, reserved or issuing out of or charged upon land, but does not include mortgage interest; 'rentcharge' includes a fee farm rent; 'fine' includes a premium or foregift and any payment, consideration, or benefit in the nature of a fine, premium or foregift: Law of Property Act 1925 s 205(1)(xxiii).
8   Law of Property Act 1925 s 98(1). The mortgagor may sue in his own name only, unless the cause of action arises upon a lease or other contract made by him jointly with any other person: see

s 98(1). This provision does not prejudice the power of a mortgagor to take proceedings independently in his own name only, either by virtue of any legal estate vested in him or otherwise: see s 98(2). Section 98 applies whenever the mortgage was made: see s 98(3). As to the power of a mortgagor apart from statute see PARA 362. See also PARA 342.

9 *Randfield v Randfield* (1859) 7 WR 651; *Yorkshire Banking Co v Mullan* (1887) 35 ChD 125.

342. Mortgagor in possession entitled to receive rents etc. So long as the mortgagee allows the mortgagor to remain in possession, that is so long as the mortgagee does not give notice to the lessee to pay the rent to him, the mortgagor continues to be entitled to receive the rent, and he is also entitled to enforce and take advantage of the lessee's covenants[1], and, in the absence of any special agreement, damages recovered belong to the mortgagor[2]. Therefore, as the mortgagor, while he remains in possession, is entitled to the income of the land leased, he can enforce the covenants either by bringing proceedings or by re-entry[3].

A tenancy at will is determined by a mortgage of which the tenant has notice, but the creation of a new tenancy may be inferred from the circumstances[4].

The validity of a payment of rent by a tenant before he is given notice of a conveyance of the reversion by the grantee under that conveyance is not prejudiced by the conveyance of the reversion being valid without the tenant's having attorned to the grantee[5]. Although rent paid before it is due is not within this protection[6], the mortgagee, as purchaser, is affected by constructive notice of the tenant's rights and is bound by any settlement made, previous to the mortgage, between mortgagor and lessee, by way of satisfaction of claims for all rent received during the term[7]. Conversely, a bona fide purchaser for value without notice is not affected by constructive notice of a tenant's right to rectification of the tenancy agreement[8].

While rightfully in possession, the mortgagor, so far as is consistent with the mortgagee's rights[9], may cut and sell the crops and underwood[10] in the ordinary course of management[11], remove tenants' fixtures[12], and hold the title deeds against everyone except the mortgagee[13].

1 *Rhodes v Allied Dunbar Pension Services Ltd, Re Offshore Ventilation Ltd* [1989] 1 All ER 1161, [1989] 1 WLR 800, CA. In relation to tenancies granted prior to 1 January 1996, see also the Law of Property Act 1925 s 141(2) (which does not expressly refer to conditions of re-entry); and LANDLORD AND TENANT vol 63 (2012) PARA 715. However, s 141(3) (see PARA 425) shows that the condition of re-entry is regarded as a means of enforcing the lessee's covenants. In relation to tenancies granted on or after 1 January 1996, see the Landlord and Tenant (Covenants) Act 1995 ss 3, 15(1); and LANDLORD AND TENANT vol 63 (2012) PARAS 728, 740. See further PARA 425.

2 *Turner v Walsh* [1909] 2 KB 484, CA. As to re-entry for breach of covenant see LANDLORD AND TENANT vol 63 (2012) PARA 751 et seq.

3 See note 2. In relation to tenancies granted on or after 1 January 1996, a mortgagee in possession can enforce any tenant covenant of a tenancy or any right of re-entry enforceable by the mortgagor: see the Landlord and Tenant (Covenants) Act 1995 s 15(1); PARA 425; and LANDLORD AND TENANT vol 63 (2012) PARA 740.

4 *Jarman v Hale* [1899] 1 QB 994.

5 See the Law of Property Act 1925 s 151(1)(i); and LANDLORD AND TENANT vol 63 (2012) PARA 700.

6 *De Nicholls v Saunders* (1870) LR 5 CP 589; *Cook v Guerra* (1872) LR 7 CP 132.

7 *Green v Rheinberg* (1911) 104 LT 149, CA. See also *Hunt v Luck* [1901] 1 Ch 45 (affd [1902] 1 Ch 428, CA); *Barnhart v Greenshields* (1853) 9 Moo PCC 18 at 23. See further EQUITABLE JURISDICTION vol 47 (2014) PARAS 135–136.

8 *Nurdin & Peacock v DB Ramsden & Co Ltd* [1999] 1 All ER 941, [1999] 1 WLR 1249. See also *Smith v Jones* [1954] 2 All ER 823, [1954] 1 WLR 1089, referring to *Barnhart v Greenshields* (1853) 9 Moo PCC 18.

9 As to the mortgagee's right to possession see PARA 404 et seq.

10 The felling of trees may be subject to restrictions, and a licence may be required: see FORESTRY vol 52 (2014) PARA 121 et seq. As to the preservation of trees and tree preservation orders see PLANNING vol 83 (2010) PARA 1035 et seq.

11 *Hampton v Hodges* (1803) 8 Ves 105 (underwood); *Bagnall v Villar* (1879) 12 ChD 812 (crops); *Re Phillips, ex p National Mercantile Bank* (1880) 16 ChD 104, CA. As to timber see *Hippesley v Spencer* (1820) 5 Madd 422; *Humphreys v Harrison* (1820) 1 Jac & W 581; *King v Smith* (1843) 2 Hare 239 at 243; *Kekewich v Marker* (1851) 3 Mac & G 311 at 329; *Re Phillips, ex p National Mercantile Bank* at 106; *Harper v Aplin* (1886) 54 LT 383.

12 *Gough v Wood & Co* [1894] 1 QB 713, CA; *Huddersfield Banking Co Ltd v Henry Lister & Son Ltd* [1895] 2 Ch 273 at 282, 286, CA; *Ellis v Glover and Hobson Ltd* [1908] 1 KB 388, CA. As to fixtures see PARA 169.

13 *Davies v Vernon* (1844) 6 QB 443; *Newton v Beck* (1858) 3 H & N 220. As to the right of the mortgagee to the title deeds see PARA 488.

343. Who has the right to receipt of rents. Prior to demand for possession, no occupation rent may be charged against the mortgagor for that part of the mortgaged land which is in his occupation, nor may the mortgagee claim back rents[1] or profits[2] accrued due and received before his demand for possession. Back rents received by a sequestrator[3] are in the custody of the law, and can be recovered from him by a mortgagee[4]. A receiver appointed by the mortgagee is entitled to receive the rents as agent of the mortgagor but is not entitled to the rent as against a superior landlord who is seeking commercial rent arrears recovery[5]. Rents received by a receiver appointed by another do not belong to a mortgagee[6], and the mortgagee's remedy is to move to discharge the receiver and enter into possession[7]. Where a mortgage fund was misappropriated, and the mortgagor recovered capital and arrears of income, the mortgagee was held to have no claim to the arrears[8]. The mortgagor receives the profits for his own use and not as agent or trustee for the mortgagee, even though the mortgaged property is a life interest or other wasting security[9].

1 *Jolly v Arbuthnot* (1859) 4 De G & J 224; *Yorkshire Banking Co v Mullan* (1887) 35 ChD 125. See also *Green v Rheinberg* (1911) 104 LT 149, CA (rent paid to mortgagor in advance).

2 *Higgins v York Buildings Co* (1740) 2 Atk 107; *Ex p Wilson* (1813) 2 Ves & B 252; *Hele v Lord Bexley, Whitfield v Bowyer, Whitfield v Knight* (1855) 20 Beav 127.

3 As to writs of sequestration see CONTEMPT OF COURT vol 22 (2012) PARA 97.

4 *Hamblyn v Ley* (1743) 3 Swan 301n; *Walker v Bell* (1816) 2 Madd 21; *Tatham v Parker* (1855) 1 Sm & G 506; *Re Hoare, Hoare v Owen* [1892] 3 Ch 94 at 98.

5 See eg *Rhodes v Allied Dunbar Pension Services Ltd, Re Offshore Ventilation Ltd* [1989] 1 All ER 1161, [1989] 1 WLR 800, CA (concerning notice issued under the Law of Distress Amendment Act 1908 s 6 (now repealed)). The common law right to distrain for arrears of rent was abolished by the Tribunals, Courts and Enforcement Act 2007 s 71. As to the procedure for taking control of goods (including procedure for commercial rent arrears recovery) see the Tribunals, Courts and Enforcement Act 2007 Pt 3 (ss 62–90); and CIVIL PROCEDURE vol 12A (2015) PARA 1342 et seq.

6 See PARA 423. As to the appointment of a receiver out of court see PARA 478 et seq; and as to the appointment of a receiver by the court see PARA 565 et seq.

7 *Thomas v Brigstocke* (1827) 4 Russ 64; *Re Hoare, Hoare v Owen* [1892] 3 Ch 94. As to the right of a mortgagee to enter into possession where the appointment of the receiver has been made subject to a provision preserving his rights see PARA 411. As to the right of a prior incumbrancer to obtain the discharge of a receiver appointed in his absence see PARA 569. As to the appointment of a receiver by a mortgagee already in possession see PARA 418.

8 *Life Association of Scotland v Siddal* (1861) 3 De GF & J 271.

9 *Colman v Duke of St Albans* (1796) 3 Ves 25; *Trent v Hunt* (1853) 9 Exch 14; *Jolly v Arbuthnot* (1859) 4 De G & J 224 at 236; *Markwick v Hardingham* (1880) 15 ChD 339 at 349, CA. See also *Re Marquis of Anglesey's Estate, Paget v Anglesey* (1874) LR 17 Eq 283, where a mortgagee of a life estate who had not entered into possession unsuccessfully claimed an apportioned part of the rents accruing due after the mortgagor's death by virtue of the Apportionment Act 1834.

(3) STATUS OF THE MORTGAGOR IN POSSESSION

344. Position of mortgagor in continued possession without express agreement.
The continued possession of the mortgaged property by the mortgagor by
permission of the mortgagee, without express provision[1], is referable to the
mortgagor's interest in the property not to implied permission[2]. The mortgagor
has a status similar to that of a tenant, but his tenancy differs in some material
respects from any other tenancy[3]. He does not have the rights of a tenant at will[4],
and he may be turned out of possession without notice[5]. The mortgagee may treat
the mortgagor, as against a stranger, as his tenant at will, and as reversioner bring
proceedings for trespass against a third person[6], but the mortgagee is not bound
to recognise such a tenancy and may bring proceedings against the mortgagor as
a trespasser without a previous demand of possession[7].

1   As to cases of express provisions as to tenancies see *Doe d Bastow v Cox* (1847) 11 QB 122
    (mortgagor tenant at will and pleasure of mortgagee at yearly rent); *Walker v Giles* (1848) 6 CB
    662 (mortgagors to retain possession until default, with proviso they should be tenants at will at
    a rent); *Doe d Dixie v Davies* (1851) 7 Exch 89 (covenant for quiet enjoyment by mortgagor as
    tenant at will at yearly rent). As to the position where the mortgagor is in possession by express
    agreement with the mortgagee see PARA 345.
2   See *Ashe v National Westminster Bank plc* [2008] EWCA Civ 55, [2008] 1 WLR 710, [2008] 2
    P & CR 183.
3   See *Rhodes v Allied Dunbar Pension Services Ltd* [1989] 1 All ER 1161, [1989] 1 WLR 800, CA.
4   As to the nature of a tenancy at will see LANDLORD AND TENANT vol 62 (2012) PARA 198 et seq.
5   *Moss v Gallimore* (1779) 1 Doug KB 279 at 285 per Lord Mansfield; *Christophers v Sparke* (1820)
    2 Jac & W 223; *Partridge v Bere* (1822) 5 B & Ald 604; *Hitchman v Walton* (1838) 4 M & W
    409; *Re Knight, ex p Isherwood* (1882) 22 ChD 384 at 392, CA, per Jessel MR.
6   *Partridge v Bere* (1822) 5 B & Ald 604.
7   *Doe d Roby v Maisey* (1828) 8 B & C 767 at 768; *Doe d Higginbotham v Barton* (1840) 11 Ad
    & El 307 at 314.

345. Mortgagor in possession by express agreement. The mortgagor may be
expressly made a tenant of a mortgagee, and an express provision in the mortgage
deed that the mortgagor may remain in possession until some certain event may
create an interest in the nature of a term of years[1]. A demise is implied by a
covenant that the mortgagor may remain in possession until default, but there is
no such implication where the covenant is that the mortgagee may enter after
default[2].

1   *Gibbs v Cruickshank* (1873) LR 8 CP 454 at 461. As to the position where the mortgagor is in
    possession without express agreement with the mortgagee see PARA 344.
2   *Wilkinson v Hall* (1837) 4 Scott 301; *Doe d Roylance v Lightfoot* (1841) 8 M & W 553; *Clowes
    v Hughes* (1870) LR 5 Exch 160; *Gibbs v Cruickshank* (1873) LR 8 CP 454. As to the right of
    entry see PARA 409.

346. Validity of attornment clause. If by the mortgage deed the mortgagor
attorns to the mortgagee, the relationship of landlord and tenant arises between
them[1], but the value of such a clause is doubtful[2]. Such a clause is invalid so far
as it purports to confer a right to distrain upon any chattels unless registered as a
bill of sale[3], but the invalidity does not extend to a case where the mortgagee has
actually entered into possession and demised the land to the mortgagor as his
tenant at a fair and reasonable rent[4].

An attornment by a mortgagor to a second mortgagee has been held to be valid
by estoppel even though the mortgagor has already attorned tenant to the first
mortgagee[5]. If an attornment clause in a mortgage purports to create a yearly
tenancy, the tenancy will not be construed as being a tenancy at will merely

because a power is conferred on the mortgagee to enter and take possession and to determine the tenancy at any time[6].

1   The relationship of landlord and tenant so created is, however, a purely artificial one: see *Steyning and Littlehampton Building Society v Wilson* [1951] Ch 1018, [1951] 2 All ER 452; *Alliance Building Society v Pinwill* [1958] Ch 788, [1958] 2 All ER 408; *Regent Oil Co Ltd v JA Gregory (Hatch End) Ltd* [1966] Ch 402, [1965] 3 All ER 673, CA. As to attornment generally see LANDLORD AND TENANT vol 62 (2012) PARA 3.
2   As to attornment clauses see PARA 202.
3   See FINANCIAL INSTRUMENTS AND TRANSACTIONS vol 49 (2015) PARA 438; LANDLORD AND TENANT vol 62 (2012) PARA 298. See also BANKRUPTCY AND INDIVIDUAL INSOLVENCY vol 5 (2013) PARA 711. Such a clause need not, however, be in the statutory form laid down for a bill of sale by way of security: see FINANCIAL INSTRUMENTS AND TRANSACTIONS vol 49 (2015) PARA 438.
4   See FINANCIAL INSTRUMENTS AND TRANSACTIONS vol 49 (2015) PARA 438; LANDLORD AND TENANT vol 62 (2012) PARA 298. As to what is a fair and reasonable rent see *Re Thompson, ex p Williams* (1877) 7 ChD 138, CA; *Re Bowes, ex p Jackson* (1880) 14 ChD 725, CA; *Re Knight, ex p Voisey* (1882) 21 ChD 442, CA. The rent may be fluctuating in amount: *Re Knight, ex p Voisey*; *Re Stockton Iron Furnace Co* (1879) 10 ChD 335, CA (a mortgage to secure a current account). As to what amounts to possession by a mortgagee see PARA 412 et seq.
5   *Re Kitchin, ex p Punnett* (1880) 16 ChD 226, CA. See also *Morton v Woods* (1869) LR 4 QB 293, Ex Ch; *Jolly v Arbuthnot* (1859) 4 De G & J 224 (attornment to receiver). As to tenancies by estoppel see generally ESTOPPEL vol 47 (2014) PARA 334; LANDLORD AND TENANT vol 62 (2012) PARA 4. In so far as the necessity for invoking an estoppel in the case of attornment to a second mortgagee arose from the fact that the second mortgagee had no legal estate, the position is modified by the fact that a second mortgagee may now have a legal estate: see PARA 164.
6   *Re Threlfall, ex p Queen's Benefit Building Society* (1880) 16 ChD 274, CA. Cf *Walker v Giles* (1848) 6 CB 662, where the scope of the mortgage deed was held to be inconsistent with a tenancy. As to tenancies at will see LANDLORD AND TENANT vol 62 (2012) PARA 198 et seq.

347. Determination of tenancy created by attornment clause. The statutory provision which regulates the length of notice to quit which is required to be given in the case of premises let as a dwelling[1] is intended to protect tenants under true residential lettings and not to protect mortgagors as such against their mortgagees[2], but it seems that the provision may apply where the rent reserved by an attornment clause is not a mere nominal rent but a full rack rent, or where the terms of the mortgage oblige the mortgagor to reside personally on the premises[3]. The tenancy created by an attornment clause in a mortgage of agricultural land is not an agricultural tenancy and the statutory provisions which regulate the length of notices to quit in the case of tenancies of agricultural holdings do not apply to the tenancy so created[4]. Where by a provision in the mortgage deed the tenancy created by an attornment clause is expressly made determinable by re-entry by the mortgagee without notice after default by the mortgagor[5], the taking of proceedings for possession by the mortgagee is equivalent to re-entry and no notice terminating the tenancy need normally[6] be given before proceedings are begun[7]. Where, however, the attornment clause provides that a particular length of notice terminating the tenancy must be given, proceedings cannot be brought until such a notice has been given and has expired[8]. Where the tenancy created by an attornment clause is determined, the mortgagor is no longer a tenant who can claim the benefit of the legislation protecting tenants[9].

1   Ie the Protection from Eviction Act 1977 s 5: see LANDLORD AND TENANT vol 62 (2012) PARA 214.
2   *Alliance Building Society v Pinwill* [1958] Ch 788, [1958] 2 All ER 408; *Peckham Mutual Building Society v Registe* (1980) 42 P & CR 186.
3   *Alliance Building Society v Pinwill* [1958] Ch 788 at 792, [1958] 2 All ER 408 at 410 per Vaisey J. A tenancy or licence is excluded if it is granted otherwise than for money's worth: see the Protection from Eviction Act 1977 s 3A(7)(b); and LANDLORD AND TENANT vol 62 (2012) PARA 215.

4   *Steyning and Littlehampton Building Society v Wilson* [1951] Ch 1018, [1951] 2 All ER 452. See further AGRICULTURAL LAND vol 1 (2008) PARAS 325, 327. As to attornment clauses see PARA 202.
5   As to the effect of such a provision in obviating the necessity for any demand of possession by the mortgagee see PARA 409.
6   As to the statutory provisions which may apply where the rent reserved is a rack rent see the text to notes 1–3.
7   *Woolwich Equitable Building Society v Preston* [1938] Ch 129. See also *Doe d Garrod v Olley* (1840) 12 Ad & El 481; *Doe d Snell v Tom* (1843) 4 QB 615.
8   *Hinckley and Country Building Society v Henny* [1953] 1 All ER 515, [1953] 1 WLR 352.
9   *Portman Building Society v Young* [1951] 1 All ER 191, CA. As to the legislation protecting tenants see PARA 532.

(4) POWER TO GRANT LEASES

348. Express power to grant leases of mortgaged land. The mortgagor and the mortgagee[1] may by agreement in writing, whether or not contained in the mortgage[2] deed, reserve to or confer on the mortgagor or the mortgagee, or both, any further or other powers[3] of leasing or having reference to leasing[4].

1   As to the meanings of 'mortgagor' and 'mortgagee' see PARA 104 note 1.
2   As to the meaning of 'mortgage' see PARA 101 note 4.
3   Ie any further or other powers than those under the Law of Property Act 1925 s 99: see PARA 349 et seq.
4   Law of Property Act 1925 s 99(14). Any further or other powers so reserved or conferred are exercisable, as far as may be, as if they were conferred by the Law of Property Act 1925, and with all the like incidents, effects, and consequences: s 99(14). However, the powers so reserved or conferred do not prejudicially affect the rights of any mortgagee interested under any other mortgage subsisting at the date of the agreement, unless that mortgagee joins in or adopts the agreement: s 99(14) proviso.

349. Statutory power to lease mortgaged land. While in possession[1] a mortgagor[2] of land[3] has statutory power as against every incumbrancer[4] to make from time to time any such lease[5] of the mortgaged[6] land, or any part of it, as is authorised by statute[7]. Also, while in possession a mortgagee[8] of land has a similar statutory power as against all prior incumbrancers, if any, and as against the mortgagor, to make authorised leases of the mortgaged land or any part of it[9]. Every person exercising these powers may execute all necessary assurances[10]. For this purpose, 'mortgagor' does not include an incumbrancer deriving title under the original mortgagor[11]; but a mortgagee who has appointed a receiver of the income of the mortgaged property or any part of it is treated as being in possession so as to entitle him instead of the mortgagor to exercise the statutory powers of leasing as regards the land affected by the receivership so long as the receiver acts, and he may by writing delegate the exercise of any of such powers to the receiver[12]. On going into possession, a mortgagee becomes entitled to the benefits of a lease granted by the mortgagor under his statutory power as if he had been a party to it[13].

A contract for a lease under the statutory power is enforceable by or against every person on whom the lease, if granted, would be binding[14]. As far as circumstances admit, the power extends to any letting or to any agreement, whether in writing or not, for leasing or letting[15].

1   A prospective purchaser who is also a prospective mortgagor is not in possession: see *Hughes v Waite* [1957] 1 All ER 603, [1957] 1 WLR 713.
2   As to the meaning of 'mortgagor' see PARA 104 note 1. See also the text to note 11.
3   As to the meaning of 'land' see PARA 104 note 2.
4   As to the meaning of 'incumbrancer' see PARA 197 note 4.
5   'Lease' includes an underlease or other tenancy: Law of Property Act 1925 s 205(1)(xxiii).

6 As to the meaning of 'mortgage' see PARA 101 note 4.
7 See the Law of Property Act 1925 s 99(1). As to the leases authorised by the Act see PARA 351.
   A mortgagor who has bound himself not to exercise the statutory power of leasing cannot
   authorise a second mortgagee to do so, for the Law of Property Act 1925 s 99 does not confer on
   a mortgagee rights which the mortgagor does not himself have: see *Julian S Hodge & Co Ltd v St
   Helen's Credit Ltd* (1965) 194 Estates Gazette 819. See also the Law of Property Act 1925
   s 99(18); and the text to note 11. As to an oral lease of part of the mortgaged land see *Rhodes v
   Dalby* [1971] 2 All ER 1144, [1971] 1 WLR 1325. As to exclusion or modification of the statutory
   power of leasing see PARA 350.
8 As to the meaning of 'mortgagee' see PARA 104 note 1.
9 See the Law of Property Act 1925 s 99(2).
10 See the Law of Property Act 1925 s 99(4).
11 Law of Property Act 1925 s 99(18).
12 See the Law of Property Act 1925 s 99(19).
13 *Municipal Permanent Investment Building Society v Smith* (1888) 22 QBD 70, CA.
14 Law of Property Act 1925 s 99(12).
15 Law of Property Act 1925 s 99(17). See also PARA 352 note 6. An agreement for a lease of more
   than three years made since 27 September 1989 can only be made in writing: see the Law of
   Property (Miscellaneous Provisions) Act 1989 s 2; and PARA 221.

350. Exclusion or modification of statutory power to lease mortgaged land. The
statutory power of leasing[1] only applies if and so far as a contrary intention is not
expressed in the mortgage[2] or otherwise in writing, and has effect subject to the
terms of the mortgage deed or of any such writing and to the provisions contained
in it[3]. It cannot, however, be modified or excluded in a mortgage of agricultural
land[4], or so as to prevent the carrying out of an order[5] for a grant of a new tenancy
of business premises[6]. A clause excluding the power does not deprive the
mortgagor of his power of creating a lease valid as between himself and the tenant
by estoppel[7], but the statutory provisions for the validation of imperfect leases
granted in intended exercise of powers of leasing[8] do not render such a lease valid
against the mortgagee[9]. Where a mortgage excluded the statutory power of leasing
except with the consent of mortgagees but provided that a lessee should not be
concerned to see that any such consent had been given, the mortgagees were held
to be estopped from denying that a lease had been granted with their consent[10].
The statutory power of leasing may be extended by agreement in writing, without
prejudice to the rights of other mortgagees[11].

   A standard clause in a domestic mortgage by which the mortgagor agrees not
to let the mortgaged property without the consent of the mortgagee does not
contravene the right of workers to freedom of movement within the European
Union[12]; nor can it be implied that the mortgagee will act reasonably in
considering a request by the mortgagor for consent to let the property[13]. A
mortgagee who refuses to consider a request to let the mortgaged property does
not thereby act in bad faith[14]. A proviso that consent is not to be unreasonably
withheld will, however, be implied into a mortgage of a commercial investment
property, and probably a buy-to-let residential mortgage[15].

1 As to the statutory power of leasing see PARA 349. As to the meaning of 'lease' see PARA 349 note
   5.
2 As to the meaning of 'mortgage' see PARA 101 note 4.
3 Law of Property Act 1925 s 99(13) (amended by the Agricultural Tenancies Act 1995 s 31(2)).
4 See the Law of Property Act 1925 s 99(13A) (s 99(13A), (13B) added by the Agricultural Tenancies
   Act 1995 s 31(3)). Section 99(13) does not enable the application of the statutory power of leasing
   to be excluded or restricted in relation to any mortgage of agricultural land made after 1 March
   1948 but before 1 September 1995; and does not enable the power to grant a lease of an
   agricultural holding to which the Agricultural Holdings Act 1986 applies (ie by virtue of the
   Agricultural Tenancies Act 1995) to be excluded or restricted in relation to any mortgage of
   agricultural land made on or after 1 September 1995: Law of Property Act 1925 s 99(13A)(a), (b)
   (as so added). For these purposes, 'agricultural holding' has the same meaning as in the
   Agricultural Holdings Act 1986 (see AGRICULTURAL LAND vol 1 (2008) PARA 323); and

'agricultural land' has the same meaning as in the Agriculture Act 1947 (see AGRICULTURAL LAND vol 1 (2008) PARA 644): Law of Property Act 1925 s 99(13B) (as so added). See also AGRICULTURAL LAND vol 1 (2008) PARA 421. However, an exclusion clause may have a residual effect making the granting of a tenancy under common law powers a breach of the mortgagor's obligations: *Rhodes v Dalby* [1971] 2 All ER 1144, [1971] 1 WLR 1325.

5   Ie under the Landlord and Tenant Act 1954 s 36: see LANDLORD AND TENANT vol 63 (2012) PARAS 873–874.

6   See the Landlord and Tenant Act 1954 s 36(4); and LANDLORD AND TENANT vol 63 (2012) PARA 873.

7   *Iron Trades Employers Insurance Association Ltd v Union House and Land Investors Ltd* [1937] Ch 313, [1937] 1 All ER 481. See also *Rust v Goodale* [1957] Ch 33 at 45, [1956] 3 All ER 373 at 381 per Harman J. As to the creation of leases by estoppel see LANDLORD AND TENANT vol 62 (2012) PARA 4.

8   Ie under the Law of Property Act 1925 s 152: see LANDLORD AND TENANT vol 62 (2012) PARAS 145–146.

9   *Iron Trades Employers Insurance Association Ltd v Union of House and Land Investors Ltd* [1937] Ch 313, [1937] 1 All ER 481, distinguished on this point in *Pawson v Revell* [1958] 2 QB 360, [1958] 3 All ER 233, CA. See also PARA 352 note 6.

10 *Lever Finance Ltd v Needleman Property Trustee* [1956] Ch 375, [1956] 2 All ER 378, distinguishing *Dudley and District Benefit Building Society v Emerson* [1949] Ch 707, [1949] 2 All ER 252, CA. See also *Britannia Building Society v Earl* [1990] 2 All ER 469, [1990] 1 WLR 422, CA. See further ESTOPPEL vol 47 (2014) PARA 334.

11 See PARA 348.

12 *Citibank International plc v Kessler* [1999] 2 CMLR 603, [1999] NPC 32, CA. As to free movement of persons within the European Union see IMMIGRATION AND ASYLUM vol 57 (2012) PARA 256; RIGHTS AND FREEDOMS vol 88A (2013) PARA 88.

13 *Citibank International plc v Kessler* [1999] 2 CMLR 603, [1999] NPC 32, CA; *Starling v Lloyds TSB Bank plc* [2000] Lloyd's Rep Bank 8, [2000] 1 EGLR 101, CA.

14 *Starling v Lloyds TSB Bank plc* [2000] Lloyd's Rep Bank 8, [2000] 1 EGLR 101, CA.

15 *Commercial First Business Ltd v Atkins* [2012] EWHC 4388 (Ch) at [100], [2012] All ER (D) 387 (Jul).

351. Leases of mortgaged land authorised by statute.

The leases authorised by the statutory power[1] are agricultural[2] or occupation[3] leases for any term not exceeding 50 years, and building leases[4] for any term not exceeding 999 years[5]. In the case of a mortgage[6] of leasehold land[7], a lease granted under the statutory power must reserve a reversion of not less than one day[8]. Every such lease must be made to take effect in possession not later than 12 months after its date[9]. It must not be of the mortgaged property and other property at a single rent[10]. It may contain a power for the lessee to determine the lease within the term, and it is not invalidated because it contains an option for the lessee to take a new lease at the end of the term, although the lessee cannot require the mortgagor to grant a renewed lease unless the lease is at the time of renewal a proper one to be granted under the statutory provisions[11].

1   As to the statutory power of leasing see PARA 349. As to the meaning of 'lease' see PARA 349 note 5.

2   An agricultural lease does not cease to be such because of the reservation of sporting rights: *Brown v Peto* [1900] 1 QB 346 at 354 per Bigham J; affd [1900] 2 QB 653, CA.

3   A lease of a house, furniture and sporting rights at a single rent is an occupation lease: *Brown v Peto* [1900] 2 QB 653, CA. See also *Sheehy v Lord Muskerry* (1848) 1 HL Cas 576 at 589; *Edwards v Millbank* (1859) 4 Drew 606 at 613.

4   A 'building lease' is a lease for building purposes or purposes connected therewith; and 'building purposes' include the erecting and improving of, and the adding to, and the repairing of buildings: Law of Property Act 1925 s 205(1)(iii).

5   See the Law of Property Act 1925 s 99(3). Where the mortgage was made before 1 January 1926, the leases authorised are agricultural or occupation leases not exceeding 21 years and building leases not exceeding 99 years: see s 99(3).

6   As to the meaning of 'mortgage' see PARA 101 note 4.

7   As to the meaning of 'land' see PARA 104 note 2.

8   Law of Property Act 1925 s 99(15) proviso.

9   Law of Property Act 1925 s 99(5).

10 *King v Bird* [1909] 1 KB 837.
11 *King v Bird* [1909] 1 KB 837 at 845.

352. Rent payable under leases of mortgaged land. A lease of mortgaged land granted under the statutory power[1] must reserve the best rent[2] that can reasonably be obtained, regard being had to the circumstances of the case, but without any fine being taken[3]. It seems that where a tenant is granted possession on payment of a lump sum, calculated by reference to a rack rent over a period, the payment is not rent for this purpose, but a fine[4]. It must contain a covenant by the lessee[5] for payment of such rent, and a condition of re-entry if the rent is not paid within a period to be specified in the lease, not exceeding 30 days[6]. In the case of a building lease[7], a peppercorn rent or a nominal or other rent less than the rent ultimately payable may be made payable for the first five years, or any less part of the term[8]. The adequacy of the rent reserved must be judged by the particular circumstances[9]. A lessor is justified in taking a rent from a good tenant substantially less than that offered by an inferior tenant, and the court will not, unless it is satisfied that the inadequacy is substantial, interfere with a rent which is the result of a bona fide bargain between the mortgagor and the lessee[10]. However, it seems that the mortgagor cannot accept a lump sum as rent for future years[11], although a mortgagee will be bound by such an arrangement made prior to the mortgage[12]. It is uncertain whether or not the rent can be left to be fixed by a valuer later[13].

1 As to the statutory power of leasing see PARA 349. As to the meaning of 'lease' see PARA 349 note 5.
2 As to the meaning of 'rent' see PARA 341 note 7.
3 Law of Property Act 1925 s 99(6). As to the meaning of 'fine' see PARA 341 note 7.
4 See *Hughes v Waite* [1957] 1 All ER 603, [1957] 1 WLR 713, where a tenancy was purported to be created before the mortgage and before the mortgagor had any title to the property, but it was held that such a tenancy could not have been validly created after the mortgage in exercise of the statutory power. Cf *Grace Rymer Investments Ltd v Waite* [1958] Ch 831, [1958] 2 All ER 777, CA.
5 'Lessee' includes an underlessee and a person deriving title under a lessee or underlessee: Law of Property Act 1925 s 205(1)(xxiii).
6 Law of Property Act 1925 s 99(7). This provision may not be applicable to an oral letting (cf s 99(17); and PARA 349), but even if the oral letting is thereby rendered an ineffective exercise of the statutory power, the letting may be made valid by virtue of s 152 (see LANDLORD AND TENANT vol 62 (2012) PARAS 145–146): see *Pawson v Revell* [1958] 2 QB 360, [1958] 3 All ER 233, CA; *Rhodes v Dalby* [1971] 2 All ER 1144, [1971] 1 WLR 1325.
7 As to the meaning of 'building lease' see PARA 351 note 4.
8 Law of Property Act 1925 s 99(10).
9 *Coutts & Co v Somerville* [1935] Ch 438.
10 Cf *Dowager Duchess of Sutherland v Duke of Sutherland* [1893] 3 Ch 169 at 195.
11 *Municipal Permanent Investment Building Society v Smith* (1888) 22 QBD 70, CA.
12 *Green v Rheinberg* (1911) 104 LT 149, CA. See also *Grace Rymer Investments Ltd v Waite* [1958] Ch 831 at 847, [1958] 2 All ER 777 at 781–782, CA, per Lord Evershed MR.
13 See *Lloyds Bank Ltd v Marcan* [1973] 3 All ER 754 at 761, [1973] 1 WLR 1387 at 1392, CA, per Goulding J.

353. Counterpart required in respect of lease of mortgaged land. A counterpart of every lease[1] of mortgaged land must be executed by the lessee[2] and delivered to the lessor[3]. If the lease is made by the mortgagor[4], then within one month after making the lease, he must deliver to the mortgagee[5] or, where there are more than one, to the mortgagee first in priority, a counterpart of the lease duly executed by the lessee, but the lessee is not concerned to see that this statutory provision is complied with[6].

1 As to the meaning of 'lease' see PARA 349 note 5.
2 As to the meaning of 'lessee' see PARA 352 note 5.

3   See the Law of Property Act 1925 s 99(8). 'Lessor' includes an underlessor and a person deriving title under a lessor or underlessor: s 205(1)(xxiii). Execution of the lease by the lessor is, in favour of the lessee and all persons deriving title under him, sufficient evidence of execution and delivery: see s 99(8). This requirement does not apply to an oral tenancy: see *Rhodes v Dalby* [1971] 2 All ER 1144, [1971] 1 WLR 1325. Cf *Pawson v Revell* [1958] 2 QB 360, [1958] 3 All ER 233, CA.

4   As to the meaning of 'mortgagor' see PARA 104 note 1.

5   As to the meaning of 'mortgagee' see PARA 104 note 1.

6   Law of Property Act 1925 s 99(11). See also *Public Trustee v Lawrence* [1912] 1 Ch 789, where an extended statutory power of leasing was held to be subject to this provision.

(5) SURRENDER OF LEASES

354. Surrender of lease: the position apart from statute. A mortgagor has no general power to accept a surrender of a lease of the mortgaged property even if the lease was made by him under his statutory powers[1]. If a mortgagor has granted a tenancy before a mortgage which prohibits leasing without the mortgagee's consent, and subsequently without the mortgagee's consent purports to grant a new tenancy to the same tenant, the fresh grant is invalid and any surrender of the original tenancy by operation of law is ineffective[2]. If the fresh grant is invalid but there is a separate surrender by deed of the old tenancy, it seems that the surrender may be voidable and liable to be set aside so long as the term granted under the old tenancy would apart from the surrender still be running, but that, otherwise, the surrender is effective[3].

1   *Robbins v Whyte* [1906] 1 KB 125. As to the statutory power of leasing see PARA 349. As to surrender generally see LANDLORD AND TENANT vol 63 (2012) PARA 778 et seq.

2   *Barclays Bank Ltd v Stasek* [1957] Ch 28, [1956] 3 All ER 439, following *Cadle v Moody* (1861) 30 LJ Ex 385 (where the new tenancy was purported to be granted to a fresh tenant); *Doe d Earl of Egremont v Courtenay* (1848) 11 QB 702; *Doe d Biddulph v Poole* (1848) 11 QB 713. For a case where a power authorising the mortgagor to grant leases was held not to enable him to determine pre-existing tenancies see *Miles v Murphy* (1871) IR 5 CL 382.

3   *Rhyl UDC v Rhyl Amusements Ltd* [1959] 1 All ER 257 at 267–268, [1959] 1 WLR 465 at 476–477 per Harman J. A surrender so expressed as to show the intentions of the parties to make the surrender only in consideration of the grant would apparently be a conditional surrender, and void, if the grant should be void: see *Doe d Earl of Egremont v Courtenay* (1848) 11 QB 702; *Doe d Biddulph v Poole* (1848) 11 QB 713.

355. Statutory power of mortgagor to accept surrender of lease. For the purpose only of enabling an authorised lease[1] to be granted, a mortgagor of land[2], while in possession, has power, as against every incumbrancer, to accept a surrender of the whole or any part of the land comprised in the lease, with or without an exception in respect of all or any of the mines and minerals[3] in it, and on a surrender of part of the land, or mines or minerals leased, the rent may be apportioned[4], and the original lease may be varied if the lease so varied would have been an authorised lease if granted by the person accepting the surrender[5]. A mortgagee in possession[6] has, as against prior or other incumbrancers and the mortgagor, similar powers[7].

These powers do not authorise surrenders to a mortgagor without the consent of the incumbrancer or prior incumbrancer for any consideration except an agreement to accept an authorised lease[8].

In order to be valid, the surrender must comply with the statutory requirements[9].

1   'Authorised lease' means a lease authorised under the Law of Property Act 1925 s 99 (see PARA 349 et seq), or under an agreement made pursuant to that provision, or by the mortgage deed: see s 100(1). As to the meaning of 'lease' see PARA 349 note 5. Section 100 may be excluded by the

mortgagor and mortgagee in the mortgage deed or otherwise in writing: see s 100(7). Cf s 99(13) (see PARA 350). For the purposes of s 100, 'mortgagor' does not include an incumbrancer deriving title under the original mortgagor: s 100(12). As to the meanings of 'mortgagor' and 'mortgagee' see PARA 104 note 1. As to the meaning of 'mortgage' see PARA 101 note 4. As to the meaning of 'incumbrancer' see PARA 197 note 4.

2   As to the meaning of 'land' see PARA 104 note 2.
3   As to the meaning of 'mines and minerals' see PARA 104 note 2.
4   Law of Property Act 1925 s 100(1). Section 100 applies only if and as far as a contrary intention is not expressed by the mortgagor and mortgagee in the mortgage deed, or otherwise in writing, and has effect subject to the terms of the mortgage deed or of any such writing and to the provisions contained in it: s 100(7).
5   Law of Property Act 1925 s 100(3). On a surrender and the making of a new or other lease, whether for the same or for any extended or other term, and whether subject or not to the same or to any other covenants, provisions or conditions, the value of the lessee's interest in the lease surrendered may be taken into account in the determination of the amount of the rent to be reserved, and of the nature of the covenants, provisions and conditions to be inserted in the new or other lease: s 100(3). As to the meaning of 'lessee' see PARA 352 note 5. As to the meaning of 'rent' see PARA 341 note 7.
6   A mortgagee who has appointed a receiver of the income of the mortgaged property or any part of it under the statutory powers is, so long as the receiver acts, treated as in possession of the land affected so as to entitle him to exercise the statutory powers of accepting surrenders instead of the mortgagor, and the mortgagee may by writing delegate any such powers to the receiver: see the Law of Property Act 1925 s 100(13). As to the leasing powers of the mortgagee see further PARA 428.
7   See the Law of Property Act 1925 s 100(2).
8   See the Law of Property Act 1925 s 100(4).
9   See the Law of Property Act 1925 s 100(5); and PARA 356.

356. Essentials to validity of surrender of lease. A surrender of a lease of mortgaged land by virtue of the statutory powers[1] is invalid unless:

(1)   an authorised lease[2] is granted of the whole of the land[3] or mines and minerals[4] comprised in the surrender to take effect in possession immediately or within one calendar month after the date of the surrender[5];

(2)   the term certain or other interest granted by the new lease is not less in duration than the unexpired term or interest which would have been subsisting under the old lease if it had not been surrendered[6]; and

(3)   if the whole of the land, mines and minerals originally leased has been surrendered, the rent[7] reserved by the new lease is not less than the rent under the original lease, or, if part only has been surrendered, the aggregate rents remaining payable or reserved under the original and the new lease are not less than the rent payable if there had been no surrender[8].

1   As to the statutory powers of surrender see PARA 355.
2   As to the meaning of 'authorised lease' see PARA 355 note 1. As to the meaning of 'lease' see PARA 349 note 5.
3   As to the meaning of 'land' see PARA 104 note 2.
4   As to the meaning of 'mines and minerals' see PARA 104 note 2.
5   See the Law of Property Act 1925 s 100(5)(a).
6   See the Law of Property Act 1925 s 100(5)(b).
7   As to the meaning of 'rent' see PARA 341 note 7.
8   See the Law of Property Act 1925 s 100(5)(c).

357. Operation of statutory powers authorising surrender of lease. A contract to make or accept an authorised surrender of a lease of mortgaged land[1] may be enforced by or against every person on whom the surrender, if completed, would be binding[2].

The statutory powers of accepting surrenders[3] do not authorise a surrender which could not have been accepted by the mortgagor[4] with the concurrence of all the incumbrancers[5] before 1 January 1912[6], but the mortgagor and mortgagee[7] may by agreement in writing, whether or not contained in the mortgage[8] deed, reserve or confer further powers of accepting surrenders[9]. The statutory powers of accepting surrenders apply, so far as the circumstances admit, to any letting and to an agreement, whether in writing or not, for leasing or letting[10].

1 Ie a surrender authorised under the Law of Property Act 1925 s 100: see PARAS 355–356.
2 Law of Property Act 1925 s 100(6). Cf s 99(12) (see PARA 349).
3 Ie the powers under the Law of Property Act 1925 s 100: see PARAS 355–356.
4 As to the meaning of 'mortgagor' see PARA 104 note 1.
5 As to the meaning of 'incumbrancer' see PARA 197 note 4.
6 See the Law of Property Act 1925 s 100(11).
7 As to the meaning of 'mortgagee' see PARA 104 note 1.
8 As to the meaning of 'mortgage' see PARA 101 note 4.
9 See the Law of Property Act 1925 s 100(10). However, the powers reserved or conferred must not prejudicially affect the rights of any mortgagee interested under any other mortgage subsisting at the date of the agreement, unless that mortgagee joins in or adopts the agreement: see s 100(10) proviso.
10 See the Law of Property Act 1925 s 100(9).

(6) RIGHTS AND LIABILITIES AS REGARDS TENANTS

358. Mortgagor's rights and liabilities as regards validly granted pre-existing leases. The rights and liabilities of the mortgagor and tenant under a lease granted before the mortgage or pursuant to express or statutory powers are considered elsewhere in this title[1].

1 See PARAS 342–343.

359. Leases granted by mortgagor ultra vires. A tenant under a lease granted ultra vires is, until eviction, actual or constructive, by paramount title estopped[1] from denying the mortgagor's title, and therefore is bound to pay the rent to the mortgagor; but payment of the rent to a mortgagee who demands it, and threatens eviction in case of refusal, is a good payment against the mortgagor or his assignee both in respect of rent accruing due after the demand, and of rent which accrued due before the demand but was then unpaid[2]. To constitute an eviction, it is not necessary that the tenant be put out of possession or that proceedings be brought; a threat of eviction directed to anyone in actual occupation is sufficient[3].

A lessee under a lease granted ultra vires may claim damages against the mortgagor for eviction, but may not obtain an order that the mortgagor is to pay off the mortgage and so acquire the legal estate and be able to give effect to the contract[4].

1 As to estoppel see further ESTOPPEL.
2 *Johnson v Jones* (1839) 9 Ad & El 809; *Boodle v Cambell* (1844) 7 Man & G 386; *Delaney v Fox* (1857) 2 CBNS 768; *Underhay v Read* (1887) 20 QBD 209, CA. Notice alone is not sufficient: *Alchorne v Gomme* (1824) 2 Bing 54; *Waddilove v Barnett* (1836) 2 Bing NC 538; *Trent v Hunt* (1853) 9 Exch 14; *Hickman v Machin* (1859) 4 H & N 716. See also *Wilton v Dunn* (1851) 17 QB 294.
3 *Sadiq v Hussain* [1997] NPC 19, CA. See also LANDLORD AND TENANT vol 62 (2012) PARA 271 et seq.
4 *Costigan v Hastler* (1804) 2 Sch & Lef 160; *Carpenter v Parker* (1857) 3 CBNS 206; *Howe v Hunt* (1862) 31 Beav 420.

(7) LIABILITY FOR WASTE

360. Liability of mortgagor for waste. The power of the mortgagor while in possession to exercise all the rights of ownership[1] is subject to the limitation that he may not diminish the security so as to render it insufficient. Waste[2] by a mortgagor in possession, for example by felling timber or pulling down a house, will be restrained by injunction[3] on proof that the security is being made deficient[4], or after order for foreclosure without such proof[5].

1   See PARA 341.
2   As to waste generally see AGRICULTURAL LAND vol 1 (2008) PARA 613; LANDLORD AND TENANT vol 62 (2012) PARAS 577–581; MINES, MINERALS AND QUARRIES vol 76 (2013) PARA 371; SETTLEMENTS vol 91 (2012) PARA 887 et seq.
3   As to injunctions to prevent waste see CIVIL PROCEDURE vol 12 (2015) PARA 1157 et seq.
4   *Usborne v Usborne* (1740) 1 Dick 75; *Hippesley v Spencer* (1820) 5 Madd 422; *Hampton v Hodges* (1803) 8 Ves 105; *King v Smith* (1843) 2 Hare 239 at 243; *Simmins v Shirley* (1877) 6 ChD 173. See further PARA 361.
5   *Goodman v Kine* (1845) 8 Beav 379 (pulling down a house); *Farrant v Lovel* (1750) 3 Atk 723. As to the right of the mortgagee to protect his security see further PARA 395 et seq. As to foreclosure see PARA 571 et seq.

361. Felling of timber and removal of fixtures. The mortgagee's right to restrain the felling of timber on property which is an insufficient security[1] is unaffected by the fact that the timber ought in a prudent course of management to be cut[2].

It seems that a mortgagee might restrain the removal of fixtures if the removal rendered the security insufficient[3].

1   See PARA 360.
2   *Harper v Aplin* (1886) 54 LT 383.
3   *Ellis v Glover and Hobson Ltd* [1908] 1 KB 388, CA; *Ackroyd v Mitchell* (1860) 3 LT 236.

(8) OTHER RIGHTS AND LIABILITIES OF MORTGAGOR

362. Mortgagor's right to prevent or seek redress for injury to property. So long as he is entitled to possession or receipt of rents and profits[1], a mortgagor of land has statutory power to bring proceedings in his own name only to prevent, or recover damages in respect of, any trespass or other wrong in relation to the mortgaged property[2]. Apart from statute, a mortgagor of land in receipt of rents and profits or a mortgagor of personalty has been held to possess sufficient interest, even though the interest may be only equitable[3], to enable him to bring proceedings to restrain or recover damages for an injury to the mortgaged property without joining the mortgagee[4]. If the questions raised in the proceedings concern the mortgagee, so that the whole matter cannot be settled in his absence, the defendant can claim that the mortgagee should be made a party to the proceedings as co-defendant[5].

1   As to the mortgagor's right to possession see PARA 341. As to the mortgagor in possession's right to receive rents and profits see PARAS 342–343.
2   See the Law of Property Act 1925 s 98; and PARA 341.
3   As to the principle that before 1926 the interest of a mortgagor of land in the mortgaged property was merely equitable see PARA 304.
4   *Fairclough v Marshall* (1878) 4 ExD 37, CA (action to restrain breach of covenant relating to land); *Van Gelder, Apsimon & Co v Sowerby Bridge United District Flour Society* (1890) 44 ChD 374, CA (action for damages and injunction for infringement of patent); *Ocean Accident and Guarantee Corpn Ltd v Ilford Gas Co* [1905] 2 KB 493 at 497, CA. Cf *Performing Right Society Ltd v London Theatre of Varieties Ltd* [1924] AC 1 at 14, HL, where the exception in favour of a mortgagor from the rule that the legal owner must be joined in proceedings for a perpetual injunction was treated as possibly based on the statutory power of the mortgagor to sue. See also CIVIL PROCEDURE vol 12 (2015) PARA 1152 et seq.

5   *Fairclough v Marshall* (1878) 4 ExD 37, CA; *Van Gelder, Apsimon & Co v Sowerby Bridge United District Flour Society* (1890) 44 ChD 374, CA. As to the addition of parties to proceedings see CPR Pt 19; and CIVIL PROCEDURE vol 11 (2015) PARA 480 et seq.

Where a mortgagee is in possession, his right of possession relates back to the time when his right to possession accrued, so as to entitle him to sue for trespass committed before his entry: see PARA 400.

363. Mortgagor allowing judgment to go by default. If a mortgagor allows judgment to go against himself in proceedings brought by a stranger to recover possession of the mortgaged property, the mortgagee may apply after judgment for an order setting aside the judgment[1].

1   *Jacques v Harrison* (1884) 12 QBD 165, CA; *Rexhaven Ltd v Nurse* (1995) 28 HLR 241, [1995] EGCS 125. As to obtaining default judgment see CIVIL PROCEDURE vol 12 (2015) PARA 535 et seq. As to setting aside or varying default judgment see CIVIL PROCEDURE vol 12 (2015) PARA 545 et seq.

7. ESTATE AND INTEREST OF THE MORTGAGEE

(1) EXTENT OF THE MORTGAGEE'S INTEREST

364. General extent of the mortgagee's interest. Although a mortgagee under a legal mortgage takes a term of years[1], and a mortgagee under a legal charge has the same protection, powers and remedies as if he had been granted a term of years[2], he takes this only to the extent to which the mortgagor is able to grant it; but, so far as is required to support the demise, all the mortgagor's estate and interest passes[3]. A mortgage of an equitable interest can, however, still be made by conveyance and vests the interest in the mortgagee subject to the mortgagor's equity of redemption[4].

1 See PARA 164 et seq.
2 See PARA 165.
3 See PARA 168.
4 See PARA 215. For the purposes of the Law of Property Act 1925, 'conveyance' includes a mortgage (see s 205(1)(ii); and PARA 168 note 1), and the 'all estate' clause is implied subject to the terms of the conveyance (see s 63(1), (2); and PARA 168). As to 'all estate' clauses see DEEDS AND OTHER INSTRUMENTS vol 32 (2012) PARAS 441–442.

365. Mortgagee's rights and liabilities dependent on nature of interest. The mortgagee has the rights and is subject to the liabilities which are incident to the estate vested in him; hence, if he has acquired a legal estate in the premises, he has, in general, all the rights of a legal owner, both as against the mortgagor and as against third persons[1], and he is subject to the liabilities which fall on a legal owner[2].

In the case of a registered charge[3], the registered proprietor or person entitled to be registered as proprietor is entitled to exercise owner's powers[4]. Owner's powers in relation to a registered charge consist of:

(1) power to make a disposition of any kind permitted by the general law in relation to an interest of that description, other than a legal sub-mortgage[5]; and

(2) power to charge at law with the payment of money indebtedness secured by the registered charge[6].

Thus in the case of a mortgage of shares by actual transfers the mortgagee assumes the shareholder's liability[7], and unless the mortgagor asserts his right of redemption he is under no liability to indemnify the mortgagee against these liabilities[8]. If a mortgagee has acquired an equitable interest only he does not have the rights of a legal owner, and he loses the protection sometimes afforded by the possession of the legal estate[9], but he does not incur a legal owner's liabilities[10].

Where the mortgage is by way of equitable charge only[11], the mortgagee takes no estate in the premises, but he has an equitable interest enforceable by sale and sometimes by foreclosure[12].

1 Note that as long as the mortgagor is in possession he has, by statute, a legal owner's rights for certain purposes: see PARA 341 et seq.
2 As to a mortgagee's liabilities on covenants see PARAS 434–435.
3 As to the meaning of 'registered charge' see PARA 142 note 7. As to the meaning of 'registered' see PARA 127 note 3.
4 See the Land Registration Act 2002 s 24.
5 See the Land Registration Act 2002 s 23(2)(a). As to the meaning of 'legal sub-mortgage' see PARA 127 note 8. As to the meaning of 'legal mortgage' see PARA 104 note 1.
6 See the Land Registration Act 2002 s 23(2)(b).
7 See PARA 211. See also COMPANIES vol 14 (2009) PARA 362 et seq.
8 *Phené v Gillan* (1845) 5 Hare 1.

9 See PARAS 264–265; and EQUITABLE JURISDICTION vol 47 (2014) PARA 124 et seq.
10 The fact that the equitable mortgagee had gone into possession and paid rent did not entitle the lessor to require him to take a legal assignment: *Moore v Greg* (1848) 2 Ph 717. As to the position of an equitable mortgagee of shares see PARA 245.
11 See PARAS 106, 221 et seq. As to legal charges see PARA 165.
12 See PARAS 106, 573.

(2) ASSIGNMENT AND DEVOLUTION

(i) Transfer of Mortgage

366. Mortgagee's right to transfer mortgage. The mortgagee is entitled to transfer his mortgage, and he may do this either absolutely or by way of sub-mortgage[1]. Where a mortgagor[2] is entitled to redeem, he has power[3] to require the mortgagee[4], instead of reconveying or surrendering, to assign the mortgage[5] debt and convey the mortgaged property to any third person, as the mortgagor directs[6]. However, this power cannot be exercised if the mortgagee is or has been in possession[7]. After a mortgagee has been in possession, he cannot with safety transfer his security except under the court's direction, as otherwise he might be liable for the transferee's neglect or default[8].

Where there are subsequent incumbrancers[9], the power can be exercised by any incumbrancer or by the mortgagor notwithstanding any intermediate incumbrance[10]. Any incumbrancer can exercise it in preference to the mortgagor, and as between incumbrancers it is exercisable in the order of their priority[11]; but this does not authorise a first mortgagee to join in a conveyance on sale by the mortgagor to the prejudice of a subsequent incumbrancer[12]. A mortgagee is not safe in transferring to the mortgagor or mortgagor's nominee without the consent of subsequent incumbrancers of whom he has notice[13].

1 *Re Tahiti Cotton Co, ex p Sargent* (1874) LR 17 Eq 273 at 279; *Taylor v Russell* [1892] AC 244 at 255, HL. A mortgagee of shares by blank transfer where the transfer requires to be under hand only has, perhaps, only authority to insert his own name, not that of a sub-mortgagee, and procure registration of himself; although, after he has done this, he can transfer his mortgage title: *France v Clark* (1883) 22 ChD 830; affd (1884) 26 ChD 257, CA. See also PARA 211. As to the right to sub-mortgage see PARA 252 et seq.
2 As to the meaning of 'mortgagor' see PARA 104 note 1.
3 Ie subject to compliance with the terms on compliance with which he would be entitled to require a reconveyance or surrender: see the Law of Property Act 1925 s 95(1).
4 As to the meaning of 'mortgagee' see PARA 104 note 1.
5 As to the meaning of 'mortgage' see PARA 101 note 4.
6 See the Law of Property Act 1925 s 95(1). This applies whenever the mortgage was made, and notwithstanding any stipulation to the contrary: s 95(5). 'Mortgage' includes charge or lien (see PARA 101 note 4), and hence a shareholder can require the company to transfer to his nominee its lien on his shares for a debt due from him (*Everitt v Automatic Weighing Machine Co* [1892] 3 Ch 506).
7 See the Law of Property Act 1925 s 95(3). The case of the mortgagee being in possession is excluded, because he remains liable to account as mortgagee in possession notwithstanding the transfer: see PARA 431.
8 See *Hall v Heward* (1886) 32 ChD 430 at 435, CA; and PARA 634.
9 As to the meanings of 'incumbrancer' and 'incumbrance' see PARA 197 note 4.
10 See the Law of Property Act 1925 s 95(2), which overruled the construction placed on the Conveyancing Act 1881 s 15 (repealed) in *Teevan v Smith* (1882) 20 ChD 724, CA, namely that the mortgagee could only be required to transfer at the direction of a person who could call for a reconveyance, that is, in the case of subsequent incumbrancers, the second mortgagee. Perhaps, in a foreclosure suit, the mortgagee cannot be required to transfer to a person who is not a party: *Smithett v Hesketh* (1890) 44 ChD 161 at 165 per North J.
11 See the Law of Property Act 1925 s 95(2).

12   *West London Commercial Bank v Reliance Permanent Building Society* (1885) 29 ChD 954, CA.
13   *Re Magneta Time Co Ltd, Molden v Magneta Time Co Ltd* (1915) 84 LJCh 814.

367. Nature and form of transfer of mortgage. The mortgage security consists of the debt and the interest in the mortgaged property by which the debt is secured, and a transfer consists of an assignment of the debt and a conveyance of this interest[1].

Unless a contrary intention is expressed in the transfer, and subject to any provisions contained in it, a transfer by deed of the mortgage[2] or the benefit of it operates to convey to the transferee[3]:

(1)   the right to demand, sue for, recover and give receipts for the mortgage money or the unpaid part of it, and the interest then due, if any, and to become due on it[4];

(2)   the benefit of all securities for the same, and the benefit of and the right to sue on all covenants with the mortgagee, and the right to exercise all the mortgagee's powers[5]; and

(3)   all the estate and interest in the mortgaged property then vested in the mortgagee subject to redemption or cesser, but subject to the right of redemption then subsisting[6].

These provisions do not extend to a transfer of a bill of sale of chattels by way of security[7], or of a registered charge of registered land[8], but otherwise they are not restricted, and apply not only to mortgages of freehold and leasehold property, but to mortgages of property generally[9].

There is a statutory form of transfer of mortgage which may be used with such variations and additions, if any, as the circumstances may require[10].

As a transfer of the security carries the benefit of the debt, it is kept alive in favour of a subsequent incumbrancer who pays off the mortgage and takes a conveyance of the property, even though the debt is not expressly assigned[11]; but an express assignment of the benefit of the security will not keep alive the liability of a surety who, by other terms of the deed, is released[12].

1   As to the terms implied in a transfer by deed see heads (1)–(3) in the text. As to the form of transfer see the text to note 10; and PARA 368 et seq. As to the transfer of registered charges see the Land Registration Act 2002 s 27; and REAL PROPERTY AND REGISTRATION vol 87 (2012) PARA 427 et seq.
2   As to the meaning of 'mortgage' see PARA 101 note 4.
3   'Transferee' includes his personal representatives and assigns: Law of Property Act 1925 s 114(2). In general, express powers pass to a transferee by virtue of a definition clause, or by conferring the powers expressly on the mortgagee and his assigns. The statutory powers are vested in him by virtue of the provision that 'mortgagee' includes any person from time to time deriving title under the original mortgagee: see s 205(1)(xvi); and PARA 104 note 1. As to the person entitled to exercise the power of sale see s 106(1); and PARAS 454–455.
4   Law of Property Act 1925 s 114(1)(a). Section 114 applies, whether the mortgage transferred was made before or after 1 January 1926 (ie the commencement date of the Law of Property Act 1925), but applies only to transfers made after that date: s 114(4).
5   Law of Property Act 1925 s 114(1)(b).
6   Law of Property Act 1925 s 114(1)(c).
7   Law of Property Act 1925 s 114(5).
8   See *Paragon Finance plc v Pender* [2005] EWCA Civ 760, [2005] 1 WLR 3412, [2005] All ER (D) 307 (Jun); *Meretz Investments NV v ACP Ltd* [2007] EWCA Civ 1303, [2008] Ch 244, [2007] All ER (D) 156 (Dec). As to the transfer of a registered charge see the Land Registration Act 2002 s 27; and REAL PROPERTY AND REGISTRATION vol 87 (2012) PARA 427 et seq.
9   'Mortgage' includes any charge or lien on any property: see the Law of Property Act 1925 s 205(1)(xvi); and PARA 101 note 4.
10   See the Law of Property Act 1925 s 114(3), Sch 3 Form 1.

11 *Phillips v Gutteridge* (1859) 4 De G & J 531. This seems so notwithstanding the Law of Property Act 1925 s 116 (see PARA 647), although having regard to the present methods of transfer (ie either by transfer in the statutory form or by indorsed receipt: see PARAS 368, 371), the question is not likely to arise.
12 *Bolton v Buckenham* [1891] 1 QB 278, CA.

368. Manner of transfer of mortgage. A transfer of a mortgage is usually made by deed, and this is essential in order to pass the mortgagee's legal estate in unregistered[1] freehold or leasehold property[2], or to obtain the benefit of provisions as to the operation of transfers contained in the Law of Property Act 1925[3]. As regards the mortgage debt, however, an assignment under hand only is effectual, notwithstanding that it was created by deed[4]; and an assignment under hand is effectual to pass any equitable interest in property which is vested in the mortgagee[5].

1 As to the transfer of a registered charge see the Land Registration Act 2002 s 27; and REAL PROPERTY AND REGISTRATION vol 87 (2012) PARA 427 et seq.
2 See the Law of Property Act 1925 s 52(1); and PARA 104.
3 See the Law of Property Act 1925 s 114; and PARA 367. As to the necessity for execution by deed see also DEEDS AND OTHER INSTRUMENTS vol 32 (2012) PARA 214.
4 See the Law of Property Act 1925 s 136; and CHOSES IN ACTION vol 13 (2009) PARA 72 et seq. See also PARA 242.
5 See DEEDS AND OTHER INSTRUMENTS vol 32 (2012) PARAS 339–343, 348.

369. Transfer of equitable mortgage by deposit of title deeds. Since 27 September 1989[1] an equitable mortgage of or charge on land or any interest in land can only be made in writing[2]. In cases where an equitable mortgage has been effectively created by deposit of title deeds[3], any assignment of such an interest should be in writing[4]. A transferee who pays off the mortgagee and takes delivery of the deeds without any assignment in writing may be subrogated to the rights of the mortgagee[5]. A mortgagee by deposit could formerly create a sub-mortgage, effective to the extent of his own charge, by handing over the deeds[6]. Where after a deposit of deeds with a firm of bankers to secure a current account there is a change in the firm, and a continuance of dealings with the new firm, the benefit of the equitable mortgage passes to the new firm[7].

1 Ie the commencement date of the Law of Property (Miscellaneous Provisions) Act 1989 s 2: see s 5.
2 See the Law of Property (Miscellaneous Provisions) Act 1989 s 2; and PARA 221.
3 As to the creation of an equitable mortgage by deposit of title deeds see PARAS 222–223. Since 27 September 1989 the mere deposit of title deeds by way of security can no longer create a valid equitable mortgage: see PARA 221.
4 *Re Richardson, Shillito v Hobson* (1885) 30 ChD 396, CA. See DEEDS AND OTHER INSTRUMENTS vol 32 (2012) PARAS 224, 348.
5 See *Brocklesby v Temperance Permanent Building Society* [1895] AC 173 at 182–183, HL; and PARAS 589–590. As to personal property see *France v Clark* (1884) 26 ChD 257 at 261, CA.
6 *Rayne v Baker* (1859) 1 Giff 241. See also PARA 234.
7 *Re Worters, ex p Oakes* (1841) 2 Mont D & De G 234; *Re O'Brien* (1883) 11 LR Ir 213.

370. Variations in form of mortgage transfer. The form of the mortgage transfer, whether it is in full terms or in short terms authorised by the Law of Property Act 1925[1], varies according as to whether the mortgagor is or is not a party, and may vary according as to whether he has or has not created a subsequent incumbrance. It is desirable for the mortgagor to be a party in order that he may be bound by the recital as to the state of the mortgage debt, and he usually enters into a new covenant with the transferee for payment of the mortgage debt and interest, although the old covenant is in effect extinguished as regards the mortgagor if he enters into a new covenant inconsistent with it[2]. If the mortgagor has not created any subsequent incumbrance, the transfer may include a fresh demise with a new proviso for cesser. Where he has created a subsequent incumbrance, a new demise is not inserted and the transfer relies only on the original demise. If the mortgagor is not a party, the transfer is necessarily restricted to a transfer of the original covenant and mortgage term.

1   As to the statutory form of transfer see PARA 367.
2   *Bolton v Buckenham* [1891] 1 QB 278, CA. If the new covenant postpones the date of payment, a surety who does not concur is released: *Bolton v Buckenham* above; and see FINANCIAL INSTRUMENTS AND TRANSACTIONS vol 49 (2015) PARA 849. The production by the transferor's solicitor or licensed conveyancer of a deed of transfer with a receipt, in the body of the deed or indorsed on it, for the mortgage is a sufficient authority for payment to the solicitor or licensed conveyancer: see the Law of Property Act 1925 s 69; and LEGAL PROFESSIONS vol 66 (2015) PARA 585. See also CONVEYANCING vol 23 (2013) PARA 227; DEEDS AND OTHER INSTRUMENTS vol 32 (2012) PARA 237. In other cases the transferee must inquire as to the solicitor's authority: *Gordon v James* (1885) 30 ChD 249, CA.

371. Transfer of mortgage by indorsed receipt. A mortgage may also be transferred by receipt indorsed on the mortgage stating by whom the money is paid[1]. For the receipt to have this effect, the money must thereby appear to have been paid by a person who was not entitled to the immediate equity of redemption[2].

1   Ie a receipt under the Law of Property Act 1925 s 115: see PARA 650 et seq.
2   See the Law of Property Act 1925 s 115(2); and PARA 654. As to the equity of redemption see PARAS 107, 304 et seq.

372. Mortgage transfer also transfers collateral securities. A transfer by deed of the mortgage[1] or the benefit of it operates to convey collateral securities for the mortgage debt unless a contrary intention is expressed[2]. If the mortgagee holds a negotiable instrument as collateral security and, after a transfer of the mortgage alone for full value, he indorses the instrument to a holder for value in good faith, the holder is able to recover on the instrument[3]. Unless the transferor has agreed to hold the securities for the transferee he will, on being paid off in full by the transferee, hold them in trust for the mortgagor[4].

1   See PARA 366 et seq.
2   See the Law of Property Act 1925 s 114(1)(b); and PARA 367. 'Securities' include stocks, funds and shares: s 205(1)(xxv).
3   *Glasscock v Balls* (1889) 24 QBD 13, CA. As to negotiable instruments see FINANCIAL INSTRUMENTS AND TRANSACTIONS vol 49 (2015) PARA 186 et seq.
4   See *Glasscock v Balls* (1889) 24 QBD 13 at 16, CA.

373. Transfer of building society mortgage. On the transfer of a building society mortgage the mortgagor should be a party, as it is doubtful whether the transferee can exercise the express power of sale which is usually contained in such a mortgage[1], for he is not in the same position as the society in regard generally to the exercise of the society's powers as mortgagee[2]. The necessity for joining the mortgagor is avoided if the mortgage makes provision for transfer[3]. If, however, the loan is made by a mortgagee acting for purposes of his business to a consumer, a term which gives the mortgagee the possibility of transferring his rights and obligations under the contract without the mortgagor's consent is presumed to be unfair[4] where this may serve to reduce the guarantees[5] for the mortgagor[6].

A transfer of a building society mortgage may be made to another society or a commercial company[7], and the rights and powers of the transferor under the mortgage become vested in the transferee[8].

1   *Re Rumney and Smith* [1897] 2 Ch 351, CA. See also FINANCIAL INSTITUTIONS vol 48 (2015) PARA 493.
2   *Sun Permanent Benefit Building Society v Western Suburban and Harrow Road Permanent Building Society* [1921] 2 Ch 438 at 460, 467, CA. See also FINANCIAL INSTITUTIONS vol 48 (2015) PARA 493.

3   *Sun Permanent Benefit Building Society v Western Suburban and Harrow Road Permanent Building Society* [1921] 2 Ch 438 at 460, 467, CA. See also FINANCIAL INSTITUTIONS vol 48 (2015) PARA 493.
4   See PARAS 203–204.
5   Eg guarantees, if any, given by the rules of a building society. As to the rules of a building society see FINANCIAL INSTITUTIONS vol 48 (2015) PARA 351 et seq.
6   See PARA 203. As to unfair terms in consumer contracts see the Consumer Rights Act 2015 Pt 2 (ss 61–76), Sch 2; and CONSUMER PROTECTION; CONTRACT.
7   See the Building Societies Act 1986 ss 93, 94, 97; and FINANCIAL INSTITUTIONS vol 48 (2015) PARA 493.
8   See the Building Societies Act 1986 ss 93, 94, 97; and FINANCIAL INSTITUTIONS vol 48 (2015) PARAS 392 et seq, 493.

374. Transfer of local authority mortgage. A local authority[1] must not dispose of its interest as mortgagee of land[2] without the prior written consent of the mortgagor (or, if there is more than one mortgagor, all of them) specifying the name of the person to whom the interest is to be transferred[3]. A disposal made without this consent is void[4]. The Secretary of State, or, in relation to Wales, the Welsh Ministers[5] may by regulations[6]:

(1)   require a local authority to give to a mortgagor whose consent is sought such information as may be prescribed[7];

(2)   prescribe the form of the document by which a mortgagor's consent is given[8];

(3)   require a local authority making a disposal to secure that notice of the fact that the disposal has been made is given to the mortgagor[9]; and

(4)   prescribe the form of that notice and the period within which it must be given[10].

Consent given for these purposes may be withdrawn by notice in writing to the authority at any time before the disposal is made[11]. It also ceases to have effect if the disposal is not made within six months after it is given[12]. If consent is withdrawn or ceases to have effect the authority must return to the mortgagor any document in its possession by which he gave his consent[13].

If consent has been given and the local authority certifies in the instrument effecting the disposal that it has not been withdrawn or ceased to have effect, the disposal is valid notwithstanding that consent has in fact been withdrawn or ceased to have effect[14]. In such a case, any person interested in the equity of redemption may, within six months of the disposal, by notice in writing served on the local authority, require the authority, the transferee and any person claiming under the transferee, to undo the disposal on such terms as may be agreed between them or determined by the court, and execute any documents and take any other steps necessary to vest back in the local authority the interest disposed of by it to the transferee[15].

1   For these purposes, 'local authority' means: a county, district or London borough council (see LOCAL GOVERNMENT vol 69 (2009) PARA 24 et seq); the Common Council of the City of London (see LONDON GOVERNMENT vol 71 (2013) PARA 34 et seq); a police and crime commissioner (see POLICE AND INVESTIGATORY POWERS vol 84 (2013) PARA 56 et seq); the Mayor's Office for Policing and Crime (see POLICE AND INVESTIGATORY POWERS vol 84 (2013) PARA 78 et seq); a joint authority established by the Local Government Act 1985 Pt IV (ss 23–42) (see LOCAL GOVERNMENT vol 69 (2009) PARA 47); a combined authority established under the Local Democracy, Economic Development and Construction Act 2009 s 103 (see TRADE AND INDUSTRY vol 97 (2015) PARA 1092 et seq); the London Fire and Emergency Planning Authority (see FIRE AND RESCUE SERVICES vol 51 (2013) PARA 17; LONDON GOVERNMENT vol 71 (2013) PARA 315); the Council of the Isles of Scilly (see LOCAL GOVERNMENT vol 69 (2009) PARA 36); or any other authority prescribed for these purposes by regulations made by the Secretary of State or, in relation to Wales, the Welsh Ministers; and includes any authority, board or committee which discharges functions which would otherwise fall to be discharged by two or more such authorities: Local Government Act 1986 s 9(1)(a) (amended

by the Education Reform Act 1988 s 237, Sch 13 Pt I; Police and Magistrates' Courts Act 1994 s 43, Sch 4 Pt I para 30; Police Act 1996 s 103, Sch 7 para 1(2)(y); Police Act 1997 s 88, Sch 6 para 24; Greater London Authority Act 1999 ss 325, 328, Sch 27 para 55, Sch 29 Pt I para 46; Criminal Justice and Police Act 2001 ss 128(1), 137, Sch 6 Pt 2 para 42, Sch 7 Pt 5(1); Local Democracy, Economic Development and Construction Act 2009 s 119, Sch 6 para 71(1), (3); Police Reform and Social Responsibility Act 2011 s 99, Sch 16 Pt 3 paras 172, 174); National Assembly for Wales (Transfer of Functions) Order 1999, SI 1999/672, art 2, Sch 1; Government of Wales Act 2006 s 162(1), Sch 11 paras 30, 32.

Regulations under the Local Government Act 1986 s 9 must be made by statutory instrument which, in the case of regulations made by the Secretary of State, is subject to annulment in pursuance of a resolution of either House of Parliament: see the Local Government Act 1986 s 9(2). At the date at which this volume states the law no such regulations had been made. As to the procedure in relation to subordinate legislation made by the Welsh Ministers see the Government of Wales Act 2006 Sch 11 paras 33–35; and STATUTES AND LEGISLATIVE PROCESS vol 96 (2012) PARA 1033 et seq.

In any enactment, 'Secretary of State' means one of Her Majesty's principal secretaries of state: see the Interpretation Act 1978 s 5, Sch 1. As to the office of Secretary of State see CONSTITUTIONAL AND ADMINISTRATIVE LAW vol 20 (2014) PARA 153. 'Welsh Ministers' means the First Minister and the Welsh Ministers appointed under the Government of Wales Act 2006 s 48: see s 45(2). As to the First Minister and the Welsh Ministers see the Government of Wales Act 2006 ss 46–48; and CONSTITUTIONAL AND ADMINISTRATIVE LAW vol 20 (2014) PARAS 374–375. As to devolved government in Wales generally see CONSTITUTIONAL AND ADMINISTRATIVE LAW vol 20 (2014) PARA 351 et seq. 'Wales' means the combined area of the counties which were created by the Local Government Act 1972 s 20 (as originally enacted) (see LOCAL GOVERNMENT vol 69 (2009) PARAS 5, 37), but subject to any alteration made under s 73 (consequential alteration of boundary following alteration of watercourse) (see LOCAL GOVERNMENT vol 69 (2009) PARA 90): Interpretation Act 1978 Sch 1 (definition substituted by the Local Government (Wales) Act 1994 s 1(3), Sch 2 PARA 9). As to local government areas and councils see LOCAL GOVERNMENT vol 69 (2009) PARA 22 et seq; and as to boundary changes see LOCAL GOVERNMENT vol 69 (2009) PARA 54 et seq.

2   References to a local authority's interest as mortgagee of land include any interest of the authority in the land or in the debt secured; and references to the disposal of such an interest are to any transfer of the interest otherwise than by operation of law; and for these purposes the disposal of an interest in registered land must be taken to occur when the transfer is made and not when it is registered: Local Government Act 1986 s 9(1), (1)(b), (c).

3   Local Government Act 1986 s 7(1). Section 7 applies to disposals on or after 24 July 1985 of a local authority's interest as mortgagee under a housing mortgage, and to disposals on or after 1 April 1986 of a local authority's interest as mortgagee under any description of mortgage, except in either case, where the disposal is carried out in pursuance of a contract entered into before that date: s 7(8).

4   Local Government Act 1986 s 7(3).

5   See the National Assembly for Wales (Transfer of Functions) Order 1999, SI 1999/672, art 2, Sch 1; Government of Wales Act 2006 s 162(1), Sch 11 paras 30, 32.

6   Regulations under the Local Government Act 1986 s 7 are made by statutory instrument which, in the case of regulations made by the Secretary of State, is subject to annulment in pursuance of a resolution of either House of Parliament: see the Local Government Act 1986 s 7(7). As to the regulations made see the Local Authorities (Disposal of Mortgages) Regulations 1986, SI 1986/1028; and notes 7–10).

7   Local Government Act 1986 s 7(6)(a). A local authority must give to a mortgagor whose consent is sought written information as to:

    (1)   the name and address of the intended transferee, and also, where the intended transferee is a company, the name and address of any holding company (Local Authorities (Disposal of Mortgages) Regulations 1986, SI 1986/1028, reg 3(1));

    (2)   the effect which the prospective disposal is likely to have on the rate of interest applicable to the mortgage, the way in which that rate is to be determined, and the places at which and the methods by which amounts payable under the mortgage may be paid (reg 3(2));

    (3)   the policy of the intended transferee with regard to mortgagors who are in arrears or default and a comparison of the policy of the local authority in relation to such matters (reg 3(3));

    (4)   the right of the mortgagor under the Local Government Act 1986 s 7(2)(a) (see the text and note 11) to withdraw his consent, the way in which consent may be withdrawn, and

the fact that, to be effective, notice of the withdrawal must be given before the disposal is made (Local Authorities (Disposal of Mortgages) Regulations 1986, SI 1986/1028, reg 3(4));

(5)   the right of the mortgagor who does not wish to give his consent to the transfer of his mortgage to take no further action, and the fact that a mortgagor who takes no further action will not be treated as having given his consent to the transfer (reg 3(5)); and

(6)   the right of the mortgagor (and others) under the Local Government Act 1986 s 7(5) (see the text to note 15) to require the local authority (and others) to undo a disposal and the steps to be taken by a mortgagor who wishes to exercise that right (Local Authorities (Disposal of Mortgages) Regulations 1986, SI 1986/1028, reg 3(6)).

'Intended transferee' means the person to whom a local authority intends to dispose of its interest as mortgagee of any land: reg 2. 'Prospective disposal' means the prospective disposal by a local authority to the intended transferee: reg 2.

8 Local Government Act 1986 s 7(6)(b). As to the form for consent see the Local Authorities (Disposal of Mortgages) Regulations 1986, SI 1986/1028, reg 4, Schedule.

9 Local Government Act 1986 s 7(6)(c).

10 Local Government Act 1986 s 7(6)(d). This notice is to be given to the mortgagor no later than seven days after the date of the disposal: see the Local Authorities (Disposal of Mortgages) Regulations 1986, SI 1986/1028, reg 5.

11 Local Government Act 1986 s 7(2)(a).

12 Local Government Act 1986 s 7(2)(b).

13 Local Government Act 1986 s 7(2).

14 Local Government Act 1986 s 7(4).

15 Local Government Act 1986 s 7(5).

375. Transfer of mortgage to new trustees. On a mortgage to trustees it is the practice not to disclose the trust, and when a transfer is made to new trustees it is sufficient to recite that they have become entitled in equity to the mortgage debt and securities on a joint account[1]. This justifies the transfer to them and the trust will still be kept off the title[2], and, as a person dealing in good faith with a mortgagee is not concerned with any trust at any time affecting the mortgage money or its income[3], the inconvenient consequences of accidental disclosure of trust are avoided[4].

1 See PARA 159.

2 See *Re Harman and Uxbridge and Rickmansworth Rly Co* (1883) 24 ChD 720; *Carritt v Real and Personal Advance Co* (1889) 42 ChD 263 at 272; *Re Blaiberg and Abrahams* [1899] 2 Ch 340.

3 See the Law of Property Act 1925 s 113(1). This provision is expressed to apply also to a person dealing in good faith with the mortgagor if the mortgage has been discharged, released or postponed as to the whole or any part of the mortgaged property, and to apply whether or not the person in question has notice of the trust: see s 113(1). Unless the contrary is expressly stated in the instruments relating to the mortgage, the person dealing with the mortgagee or mortgagor may assume that:

(1)   the mortgagees (if more than one) are or were entitled to the mortgage money on a joint account (s 113(1)(a)); and

(2)   the mortgagee has or had power to give valid receipts for the purchase money or mortgage money and its income (including any arrears of interest) and to release or postpone the priority of the mortgage debt or any part of it or to deal with the same or the mortgaged property or any part of it (s 113(1)(b)),

without in either case investigating the equitable title to the mortgage debt or the appointment or discharge of trustees in reference to it (s 113(1)). Section 113 applies to mortgages whenever made, but only as respects dealings on or after 1 January 1926: s 113(2). It does not affect the liability of any person in whom the mortgage debt is vested for the purposes of any trust to give effect to that trust: s 113(3). As to the meanings of 'mortgagor' and 'mortgagee' see PARA 104 note 1. As to the meaning of 'mortgage' see PARA 101 note 4.

4 *Re Blaiberg and Abrahams* [1899] 2 Ch 340.

376. Statutory transfer of legal charge. A charge by way of legal mortgage of freehold or leasehold land made by statutory legal charge[1] may be transferred by deed expressed to be made by way of statutory transfer in such one of certain statutory forms as may be appropriate with such variations and additions, if any, as the circumstances may require[2]. A deed of statutory transfer purports to convey and transfer to the transferee the benefit of the mortgage[3], and the effect is to vest in the transferee[4]:

(1)   the right to demand, sue for and recover and give receipts for the mortgage debt, or the unpaid part of it, and interest, and the benefit of all securities for the same, and the benefit of and right to sue on the covenants with, and to exercise all the powers of, the mortgagee[5]; and

(2)   all the mortgagee's term and interest in the mortgaged land, subject to redemption[6].

If a covenantor (normally a surety) joins in the statutory transfer, there will be implied a covenant by him to pay the principal and interest[7]. In all other cases the covenant must be expressed; the covenant for payment on a certain day by implication prevents the covenantor suing before that day[8]. If the transfer is in the form of a statutory transfer and mortgage combined[9], it operates also as a statutory mortgage[10].

1   See PARA 165.
2   See the Law of Property Act 1925 s 118(1). For a statutory form of transfer which is not confined to statutory legal charges see PARA 367.
3   See the Law of Property Act 1925 s 118(2)(i), Sch 4 Form 2 (mortgagor not joining), Form 3 (covenantor joining), Form 4 (statutory transfer and mortgage combined). See also note 6. As to the meaning of 'mortgage' see PARA 101 note 4.
4   This includes his personal representatives and assigns: see the Law of Property Act 1925 s 118(2)(i). See also note 6.
5   See the Law of Property Act 1925 s 118(2)(i). See also note 6. As to the meaning of 'mortgagee' see PARA 104 note 1.
6   See the Law of Property Act 1925 s 118(2)(ii). The words 'benefit of the mortgage' now have statutory effect in all mortgages (see PARA 367), and the transfer would operate under the Law of Property Act 1925 s 117 (see PARA 166): cf the Conveyancing Act 1881 s 27(2)(ii) (repealed); and *Re Beachey, Heaton v Beachey* [1904] 1 Ch 67, CA.
7   See the Law of Property Act 1925 s 118(3).
8   See *Bolton v Buckenham* [1891] 1 QB 278 at 281, CA, per Lord Esher MR.
9   See the Law of Property Act 1925 Sch 4 Form 4.
10 See the Law of Property Act 1925 s 118(4).

377.   Transfer of registered charge. A registered charge of registered land must be transferred in the prescribed form and completed by entry on the register of the name of the new proprietor[1].

1   See the Land Registration Act 2002 s 27, Sch 2 para 10; and REAL PROPERTY AND REGISTRATION vol 87 (2012) PARA 446.

378.   Transfer of statutory mortgage of ship or aircraft. A registered mortgage of a ship or share in a ship may be transferred by an instrument made in the form prescribed by or approved under registration regulations[1].

There is no special form of transfer of mortgage of an aircraft or hovercraft[2].

1   See the Merchant Shipping Act 1995 s 16, Sch 1 paras 11, 12; the Merchant Shipping (Registration of Ships) Regulations 1993, SI 1993/3138, reg 60; and SHIPPING AND MARITIME LAW vol 93 (2008) PARA 323 et seq. As to mortgages of ships see PARA 212.
2   The Bills of Sale Acts 1878 and 1882 do not apply to registered mortgages of aircraft made on or after 1 October 1972: see the Mortgaging of Aircraft Order 1972, SI 1972/1268, arts 2(2), 16(1); and AIR LAW vol 2 (2008) PARA 431. As to mortgages of aircraft and hovercraft see PARA 214.

379.   Transfer of bill of sale. A registered bill of sale can be transferred so as to constitute a valid security in the transferee's favour[1]; but if the bill of sale is unregistered, the transfer, in order to create an effective security, requires the same formalities as an original bill of sale[2].

1 See FINANCIAL INSTRUMENTS AND TRANSACTIONS vol 49 (2015) PARAS 455, 614–615. The provisions of the Law of Property Act 1925 s 114 do not apply to a transfer of a bill of sale of chattels by way of security: see s 114(5); and PARA 367. As to mortgages of personal chattels see PARA 205.
2 *Jarvis v Jarvis* (1893) 63 LJCh 10.

380. Transfer for less than mortgage debt. The value of the mortgage debt to the transferee depends on the soundness of the security, and he may purchase the debt and security at less than the nominal amount of the debt; but, notwithstanding that he has done so, he is entitled to recover the whole amount due at the time of the transfer[1] unless he stands in a position which would make this inequitable[2]. The rule applies not only in favour of a stranger who purchases the mortgage debt[3], but also in favour of a creditor[4] or subsequent incumbrancer[5], or any other person interested in the estate, such as a reversioner, provided that he did not create the charge[6]; and it applies both against the mortgagor[7] and his personal representatives[8] and against a purchaser of, or incumbrancer on, the equity of redemption[9]. If a vendor is bound to clear the property of incumbrances and the purchaser buys them up, he can only recover against the vendor the amount actually paid by him[10]. A trustee of the mortgaged property[11], or the mortgagor's agent[12], or the mortgagor's personal representatives[13] are not, however, allowed to hold the mortgage as a security for more than they gave for it. The disability applies to a solicitor[14] or other person standing in a relation to the mortgagor giving special opportunities of buying up the mortgage[15], and it applies after the agency or other confidential employment has ceased if the purchase of the mortgage is due to knowledge obtained during such an employment[16]. A surety is subject to the same rule as an agent[17]. Moreover, where the transferee of an invalid security has only an equitable right to enforce it, so that relief is given to him on equitable terms, he can recover no more than the sum which he has actually advanced[18].

1 *Anon* (1707) 1 Salk 155; *Davis v Barrett* (1851) 14 Beav 542 at 554.
2 See PARA 382.
3 *Phillips v Vaughan* (1685) 1 Vern 336; *Davis v Barrett* (1851) 14 Beav 542.
4 *Morret v Paske* (1740) 2 Atk 52 at 54.
5 *Darcy v Hall* (1682) 1 Vern 49; *Dobson v Land* (1850) 8 Hare 216 at 220; *Shaw v Bunny* (1865) 2 De GJ & Sm 468 at 472.
6 *Davis v Barrett* (1851) 14 Beav 542.
7 *Dobson v Land* (1850) 8 Hare 216; *Shaw v Bunny* (1865) 2 De GJ & Sm 468.
8 As to the devolution of mortgage estates on personal representatives see PARA 389; and WILLS AND INTESTACY vol 103 (2010) PARA 1020 et seq.
9 *Davis v Barrett* (1851) 14 Beav 542. Originally the purchaser of the mortgage was only allowed to hold it for the amount of his purchase money against a purchaser or subsequent incumbrancer: *Long v Clopton* (1687) 1 Vern 464; *Williams v Springfeild* (1687) 1 Vern 476.
10 *Cane v Lord Allen* (1814) 2 Dow 289 at 296, HL.
11 *Darcy v Hall* (1682) 1 Vern 49; *Anon* (1707) 1 Salk 155; *Morret v Paske* (1740) 2 Atk 52; *Dobson v Land* (1850) 8 Hare 216; *Re Imperial Land Co of Marseilles, ex p Larking* (1877) 4 ChD 566, CA.
12 *Morret v Paske* (1740) 2 Atk 52; *Reed v Norris* (1837) 2 My & Cr 361 at 374; *Lawless v Mansfield* (1841) 1 Dr & War 557 at 629.
13 The rule stated in the text formerly applied to the heir: *Darcy v Hall* (1682) 1 Vern 49; *Morret v Paske* (1740) 2 Atk 52 at 53; *Lancaster v Evors* (1844) 1 Ph 349 at 354; *Lancaster v Evors* (1846) 10 Beav 154 at 165. Apparently a tenant for life who buys up an incumbrance on the inheritance can hold it only for what he has paid: *Hill v Browne* (1844) Drury *temp* Sug 426. Under special circumstances, however, an heir was allowed to recover the full debt: *Darcy v Hall* above.
14 *Nelson v Booth* (1857) 27 LJCh 110; *Macleod v Jones* (1883) 24 ChD 289 at 300, 303, CA.
15 *Hobday v Peters* (1860) 28 Beav 349 at 351.

16 *Carter v Palmer* (1842) 8 Cl & Fin 657 at 705, HL. See also AGENCY vol 1 (2008) PARA 91.
17 *Reed v Norris* (1837) 2 My & Cr 361. See also FINANCIAL INSTRUMENTS AND TRANSACTIONS vol 49 (2015) PARA 785. As to suretyship see PARA 118 et seq.
18 *Re Romford Canal Co, Pocock's Claim, Trickett's Claim, Carew's Claim* (1883) 24 ChD 85 at 93.

381. Effect of mortgage transfer on arrears of rent or interest. The conveyance to the transferee operates in the same manner as an ordinary conveyance of land, and gives the transferee a title to rents in arrear at the date of the transfer[1]. Where interest is in arrear at the date of transfer and the mortgagor does not concur, the transferee, on paying the arrears to the transferor, cannot treat them as principal so as to carry future interest[2]. The mortgagee and the persons claiming under him cannot, without the mortgagor's privity, add to what is due or turn interest into principal[3]. Where a trustee of a mortgaged estate agrees, in excess of his powers, to allow a transferee to capitalise arrears of interest, this will not prejudice the transferee's right to claim the interest as such[4].

1 See PARA 349.
2 *Ashenhurst v James* (1745) 3 Atk 270. See also PARA 742.
3 *Matthews v Wallwyn* (1798) 4 Ves 118 at 128; *Halifax Mortgage Services Ltd v Muirhead* (1997) 76 P & CR 418, [1997] NPC 171, CA.
4 *Cottrell v Finney* (1874) 9 Ch App 541 at 549.

382. Transfer of mortgage subject to outstanding equities. So far as the security consists of the mortgage debt, it is a chose or thing in action, and is only assignable in accordance with the rule that a transferee of a chose in action takes it subject to any equities and rights of set-off existing between the debtor and the transferor[1]. As the mortgage of the property is incident to the debt, the same rule extends to this portion of the security, and the transferee can only hold the property as security for repayment of the amount properly due from the mortgagor to the mortgagee at the date of assignment, allowing for any claims which the mortgagor may on his side have against the mortgagee and which are part of the mortgage transaction[2]. Where a security given by a company is invalid, a transferee who takes after a winding up order cannot maintain it against the liquidator, even if he could have done so against the company[3].

1 *Cockell v Taylor* (1851) 15 Beav 103 at 117; *Smith v Parkes* (1852) 16 Beav 115 at 119; *Roxburghe v Cox* (1881) 17 ChD 520, CA. As to equitable set-off see *Dodd v Lydall* (1841) 1 Hare 333; *Re Poulter, Poulter v Poulter* (1912) 56 Sol Jo 291; *Parker v Jackson* [1936] 2 All ER 281; and CHOSES IN ACTION vol 13 (2009) PARAS 60–67; CIVIL PROCEDURE vol 11 (2015) PARA 406 et seq; EQUITABLE JURISDICTION vol 47 (2014) PARA 244 et seq. Originally the debt was only assignable in equity; the assignee had to sue in the assignor's name, and was therefore liable to be met by any defence or right of set-off available for the mortgagor against the assignor; thus the assignee of a chose in action was not in the position of a purchaser of real estate who took the legal estate for value without notice (*Cockell v Taylor* (1851) 15 Beav 103); and although by statute the debt can now be assigned at law, the statute expressly makes the assignment subject to equities which would, apart from the statute, have priority over the assignee's right (see the Law of Property Act 1925 s 136(1); and CHOSES IN ACTION vol 13 (2009) PARA 72). See also *Re Milan Tramways Co, ex p Theys* (1882) 22 ChD 122 at 127; affd (1884) 25 ChD 587, CA. It has been held, by Bacon V-C, that, where the mortgagor's equity was to set aside the mortgage, a transferee for value had a better equity and was entitled to his security (see *Judd v Green* (1875) 45 LJCh 108; *Nant-y-glo and Blaina Ironworks Co Ltd v Tamplin* (1876) 35 LT 125), but this is opposed to the general principle and is doubtful.
2 *Norrish v Marshall* (1821) 5 Madd 475; *De Lisle v Union Bank of Scotland* [1914] 1 Ch 22, CA; *Halifax Mortgage Services Ltd v Muirhead* (1997) 76 P & CR 418, [1997] NPC 171, CA.
3 *Re Gwelo, Matabeleland, Exploration and Development Co, Williamson's Claim* [1901] 1 IR 38, CA. See further EQUITABLE JURISDICTION vol 47 (2014) PARA 216 et seq.

383. Effect of transfer on amount originally advanced on a mortgage. The effect of a receipt for money is considered generally elsewhere in this work[1]. As regards the amount originally advanced on a mortgage, the mortgagor's receipt contained in or indorsed on the mortgage deed is sufficient evidence of the advance in favour of a transferee of the mortgage for value who has no notice that the money was not advanced[2], even if no money has in fact been advanced[3]. If, however, the mortgage was created in circumstances which call for inquiry, the transferee is bound, if he has notice of those circumstances[4], to inquire whether the advance was made, and cannot recover more than the actual advance[5] unless there are special circumstances depriving the mortgagor of the benefit of this exception, as where a client has handed the mortgage deed containing the receipt to his solicitor for the purpose of enabling the money to be raised by the solicitor, in which case the client is estopped, as against a sub-mortgagee, from saying that the original amount was not advanced[6].

1   See DEEDS AND OTHER INSTRUMENTS vol 32 (2012) PARA 425.
2   See the Law of Property Act 1925 ss 68, 205(1)(xxi).
3   *French v Hope* (1887) 56 LJCh 363. See also *Bickerton v Walker* (1885) 31 ChD 151, CA (overruling *Parker v Clarke* (1861) 30 Beav 54).
4   *Bateman v Hunt* [1904] 2 KB 530, CA.
5   See *Gresley v Mousley* (1862) 3 De GF & J 433; *Saunders v Kent* [1885] WN 147.
6   *Powell v Browne* (1907) 97 LT 854, CA.

384. Dealings with mortgage debt prior to transfer. As regards dealings with the mortgage debt subsequent to the creation of the mortgage, the rule that the transfer is subject to outstanding equities[1] applies, and the transferee of the mortgage takes it, when the mortgagor is not party to the transfer, subject to the state of accounts then subsisting between the mortgagor and mortgagee[2]. He must at his peril inquire what is due on the mortgage, and, if all or part of the principal has been paid off by the mortgagor or has been discharged by receipt of rents and profits, the transferee, although he takes without notice, cannot set up again the whole debt against the mortgagor[3]. Further, whatever the mortgagor can claim by way of set-off or mutual credit against the mortgagee, he can equally claim against the transferee[4]. Hence, for the protection of the transferee, it is proper either to make the mortgagor a party to the transfer or to obtain a written admission from him that the sum claimed by the transferor is really due[5].

1   See PARA 382.
2   *Chambers v Goldwin* (1804) 9 Ves 254 at 264. See also CHOSES IN ACTION vol 13 (2009) PARA 62.
3   *Bradwell v Catchpole* (1700) 3 Swan 78n. As to payment of all the money so that the debt is non-existent see *Turner v Smith* [1901] 1 Ch 213; *Parker v Jackson* [1936] 2 All ER 281 at 288. See also the cases cited in PARA 385 notes 1–3.
4   *Norrish v Marshall* (1821) 5 Madd 475 at 481.
5   See *Matthews v Wallwyn* (1798) 4 Ves 118 at 127.

385. Payment of mortgage debt without notice of transfer. The mortgagor is entitled to make payments to the mortgagee, whether of principal or interest, and to have credit for them as against the transferee after the transfer until he has received notice of it[1]. The notice, which may be actual or constructive[2], stops the mortgagor's right of set-off in respect of matters arising subsequently[3]. The mortgagor is not, by reason of omitting to call for production of the mortgage deed on payment of part of the principal[4], or even on payment of the whole[5], guilty of such negligence as to be postponed to the transferee, the transferee being on his side guilty of negligence in not having given notice of the assignment. A mortgagor executing a new mortgage may be debarred from claiming credit for money realised under an old mortgage which he has allowed to remain outstanding[6]. A payment, to be good against the transferee, need not be made in money; it may be made in any manner which is equivalent to payment, for instance by delivery of goods[7], or by a release founded on any fair and genuine arrangement[8]; and it is sufficient if, on a balance of account between the mortgagor and mortgagee, there is a sum in the mortgagor's favour sufficient to satisfy the debt[9], provided that the balance has been appropriated to the debt before notice of the assignment[10]. The payment must, however, be made to the mortgagee or to a person authorised to receive it on his behalf[11].

1   *Bickerton v Walker* (1885) 31 ChD 151 at 158, CA; *Dixon v Winch* [1900] 1 Ch 736 at 742, CA; *Williams v Sorrell* (1799) 4 Ves 389; *Re Frazer, ex p Monro* (1819) Buck 300 at 303; *Stocks v Dobson* (1853) 4 De GM & G 11; *Wheatley v Bastow* (1855) 7 De GM & G 261 at 275; *Reeve v Whitmore* (1863) 4 De GJ & Sm 1 at 19; *Re Lord Southampton's Estate, Allen v Lord Southampton, Banfather's Claim* (1880) 16 ChD 178 at 186; *Berwick & Co v Price* [1905] 1 Ch 632 at 643.

2   *Dixon v Winch* [1900] 1 Ch 736, CA, where the mortgagee was the mortgagor's solicitor, and the mortgagor left the dealings with the property in his hands. Hence, on a transfer of the mortgage the mortgagor had constructive notice of it, and when, on a subsequent sale, the solicitor, with the mortgagor's consent, retained the mortgage money out of the purchase money, this was not a payment by the mortgagor without notice of the transfer so as to discharge the mortgage in favour of the purchaser as against the transferee. As to the doctrine of notice see EQUITABLE JURISDICTION vol 47 (2014) PARA 130 et seq.

3   *Cavendish v Geaves* (1857) 24 Beav 163; and see CIVIL PROCEDURE vol 11 (2015) PARA 434. Cf *Re Poulter, Poulter v Poulter* (1912) 56 Sol Jo 291.

4   *Stocks v Dobson* (1853) 4 De GM & G 11 at 17; *Berwick & Co v Price* [1905] 1 Ch 632 at 644.

5   *Norrish v Marshall* (1821) 5 Madd 475; *Re Lord Southampton's Estate, Allen v Lord Southampton, Banfather's Claim* (1880) 16 ChD 178. The principle of these decisions was doubted in *Dixon v Winch* [1900] 1 Ch 736 at 743, CA, per Cozens-Hardy J.

6   *Re Ambrose's Estate* [1913] 1 IR 506; affd [1914] 1 IR 123.

7   *Norrish v Marshall* (1821) 5 Madd 475.

8   *Stocks v Dobson* (1853) 4 De GM & G 11 at 16.

9   *Norrish v Marshall* (1821) 5 Madd 475.

10 *Rayne v Baker* (1859) 1 Giff 241.

11 *Withington v Tate* (1869) 4 Ch App 288.

386.   Subrogated rights of person paying off mortgage debt. Subrogation is an equitable remedy to reverse or prevent unjust enrichment[1]. The remedy is available if:

(1)   the defendant has been enriched at the claimant's expense[2];
(2)   such enrichment was unjust[3];
(3)   there are no policy reasons for denying a remedy[4]; and
(4)   there are no defences[5].

A lender who advances money which is used to discharge a security will therefore normally be subrogated to the rights under that security[6] against a borrower and subsequent incumbrancers[7] even though there has been no actual transfer of the security. Frequently in such cases it is intended that the lender will be given a new security, but that security proves to be void or voidable[8]. However, subrogation does not depend on intention, whether common or unilateral, although evidence of an intention that the claimant should be unsecured may prevent the claimant obtaining subrogation to any security[9]. Partial discharge of an earlier security is sufficient to give the lender the benefit of that security as against the defendant, while the holder of an earlier security retains priority over the claimant[10]. The claimant does not need to show that the defendant was at fault. The remedy will not be denied on the ground that the claimant failed to take reasonable steps to protect his position[11]. Thus the claimant may be subrogated to the rights under the security discharged with his funds even though he has actually taken a mortgage of part of the property, as the remedy given by this later mortgage is not co-extensive with that given by the earlier. In such a case there is no merger of the mortgage in the charge[12].

A lender who advances money which is used to discharge an unsecured loan is also, on the above principles, normally subrogated to the rights of the creditor[13].

A lender who advances funds to provide the whole or part of the purchase price of a property may, on the above principles, be subrogated to the vendor's lien over the property[14] as is a lender who releases security over other property, enabling the proceeds of sale to be used to purchase a property[15]. A subsequent lender who pays off such a loan is also subrogated to the vendor's lien[16]. The creator of a charge will not be treated as an assignee against his own subsequent incumbrances[17], and in a case where a purchase is on the terms that the debts due to the purchaser and other mortgagees are to be paid off, the purchaser's own debt is extinguished[18].

However, where two properties are comprised in the same mortgage and the person entitled to the equity of redemption in one pays off the mortgage and takes a reconveyance of both properties, he will be treated as an assignee of the mortgage, at any rate in part, on the other property, notwithstanding that he may not be able to keep it alive on the first-mentioned property against subsequent incumbrancers[19].

1   As to the effect of subrogation see PARA 387. As to subrogation generally see EQUITABLE JURISDICTION vol 47 (2014) PARA 207 et seq. As to the general principles of restitution and defences to claims based on unjust enrichment see RESTITUTION vol 88 (2012) PARA 401 et seq.
2   A defendant is enriched if his financial position is materially improved: see *Filby v Mortgage Express (No 2) Ltd* [2004] EWCA Civ 759, [2004] NPC 98.
3   The enrichment is unjust if the lender does not get the security he bargained for: see *Filby v Mortgage Express (No 2) Ltd* [2004] EWCA Civ 759, [2004] NPC 98.
4   See *Banque Financière de la Cité v Parc (Battersea) Ltd* [1999] 1 AC 221, [1998] 1 All ER 737, HL; *Cheltenham & Gloucester plc v Appleyard* [2004] EWCA Civ 291, [2004] 13 EG 127 (CS).
5   Such as the defence of bona fide purchaser for value without notice: see eg *Halifax plc v Omar* [2002] EWCA Civ 121, [2002] All ER (D) 271 (Feb); *Bank of Scotland plc v Joseph* [2014] EWCA Civ 28, [2014] 1 P & CR 302, [2014] All ER (D) 170 (Jan).
6   *Banque Financière de la Cité v Parc (Battersea) Ltd* [1999] 1 AC 221, [1998] 1 All ER 737, HL. See also *Chetwynd v Allen* [1899] 1 Ch 353; *Butler v Rice* [1910] 2 Ch 277; *Ghana Commercial Bank v Chandiram* [1960] AC 732, [1960] 2 All ER 865, PC; *Orakpo v Manson Investments Ltd* [1978] AC 95, [1977] 3 All ER 1, HL; *Boscawen v Bajwa* [1995] 4 All ER 769, [1996] 1 WLR 328, CA.
7   *Banque Financière de la Cité v Parc (Battersea) Ltd* [1999] 1 AC 221, [1998] 1 All ER 737, HL. See also *Whiteley v Delaney* [1914] AC 132, HL; *Ghana Commercial Bank v Chandiram* [1960] AC 732, [1960] 2 All ER 865, PC.
8   *Butler v Rice* [1910] 2 Ch 277; *Cheltenham and Gloucester plc v Appleyard* [2004] EWCA Civ 291, [2004] 13 EG 127 (CS). See also *Whiteley v Delaney* [1914] AC 132, HL; *Ghana Commercial Bank v Chandiram* [1960] AC 732, [1960] 2 All ER 865, PC. An equitable chargee of a policy who pays the premiums and interest on them can add these to his charge with interest on the sum so paid: *Re City of Glasgow Life Assurance Co, Clare's Policy* (1914) 84 LJCh 684; and see PARA 689. See also *Halifax Mortgage Services Ltd v Muirhead* (1997) 76 P & CR 418, [1997] NPC 171, CA.
9   *Banque Financière de la Cité v Parc (Battersea) Ltd* [1999] 1 AC 221, [1998] 1 All ER 737, HL. See also *Paul v Speirway Ltd* [1976] Ch 220, [1976] 2 All ER 587; *Boscawen v Bajwa* [1995] 4 All ER 769, [1996] 1 WLR 328, CA; *Filby v Mortgage Express (No 2) Ltd* [2004] EWCA Civ 759, [2004] NPC 98. Thus a lender may be subrogated to the rights of a prior mortgagee over jointly owned property even if one of the co-owners was unaware of the discharge: *National Guardian Mortgage Corpn v Roberts* [1993] NPC 149, CA.
10 *Banque Financière de la Cité v Parc (Battersea) Ltd* [1999] 1 AC 221, [1998] 1 All ER 737, HL. See also *Chetwynd v Allen* [1899] 1 Ch 353.
11 *Banque Financière de la Cité v Parc (Battersea) Ltd* [1999] 1 AC 221, [1998] 1 All ER 737, HL. See also *Chetwynd v Allen* [1899] 1 Ch 353. Applying this principle, a lender which failed to protect a charge by registration against a subsequent charge was nonetheless entitled to be subrogated to a prior charge which it discharged: see *Anfield (UK) Ltd v Bank of Scotland plc* [2010] EWHC 2374 (Ch), [2011] 1 All ER 708, [2011] 1 WLR 2414.
12 *Chetwynd v Allen* [1899] 1 Ch 353. See also *Bell v Banks* (1841) 3 Man & G 258.
13 *Filby v Mortgage Express (No 2) Ltd* [2004] EWCA Civ 759, [2004] NPC 98.
14 *Boodle Hatfield & Co v British Films Ltd* [1986] FLR 134, 2 BCC 99, 221. As to the vendor's lien see LIEN vol 68 (2008) PARA 859.

15   *Menelaou v Bank of Cyprus UK Ltd* [2013] EWCA Civ 1960, [2014] 1 WLR 854, [2013] All ER (D) 33 (Jul).
16   *UCB Bank plc v Hedworth* [2003] EWCA Civ 1717, [2002] 3 EGLR 76, [2002] 46 EG 200.
17   See PARA 678. Cf *Mackenzie v Gordon* (1839) 6 Cl & Fin 875 at 883, HL. The trustee in bankruptcy of the mortgagor, who acquires a charge on the estate, is, however, entitled to hold the charge for the benefit of creditors: *Squire v Ford* (1851) 9 Hare 47 at 60; *Adams v Angell* (1876) 5 ChD 634 at 647, CA; *Cracknall v Janson* (1877) 6 ChD 735; *Bell v Sunderland Building Society* (1883) 24 ChD 618.
18   *Brown v Stead* (1832) 5 Sim 535; but see *Squire v Ford* (1851) 9 Hare 47.
19   *Taws v Knowles* [1891] 2 QB 564 at 572, CA; *Re City of Glasgow Life Assurance Co, Clare's Policy* (1914) 84 LJCh 684. See also PARAS 678, 688.

387. Effect of subrogation. The effect of subrogation to a security is that the relations between the claimant and a defendant who would otherwise be unjustly enriched are regulated as if the benefit of the security had been assigned to him[1]. The claimant is not to be treated as an assignee in relation to someone who would not be unjustly enriched[2].

A claimant is entitled to enforce the subrogated security to recover payment of the secured debt which was discharged together with interest at the rate, compounded if appropriate, which would have been payable under it[3] up to the rate which the claimant agreed to accept[4]. The court should not make an order for possession without determining what sums would have been due under the subrogated security. This may require consideration of what repayments by the borrower should be attributed to the subrogated security, and the effect of subsequent events such as an agreement to extend time for repayments or a variation of the amount of repayments[5]. It is not necessary for the creditor to make a demand or take steps to enforce its rights pursuant to the terms of the subrogated security so long as those rights would have been available[6].

A secured creditor whose debt has been repaid by another owes a duty to the payer not to destroy or prejudice any right or remedy the payer may have by way of subrogation and is liable to pay damages for any loss caused to the payer as a result of a breach of that duty[7].

1   As to subrogation see PARA 386. As to unjust enrichment see RESTITUTION vol 88 (2012) PARA 401 et seq.
2   *Banque Financière de la Cité v Parc (Battersea) Ltd* [1999] 1 AC 221, [1998] 1 All ER 737, HL. See also PARA 689.
3   *Western Trust Savings Ltd v Rock* [1993] NPC 89, CA.
4   *Halifax Mortgage Services Ltd v Muirhead* [1997] NPC 171, 76 P & CR 418, CA. See also *Kali Ltd v Chawla; Advani v Chawla* [2007] EWHC 2357 (Ch), [2008] BPIR 415, [2007] All ER (D) 90 (Sep).
5   *Halifax Mortgage Services Ltd v Muirhead* [1997] NPC 171, 76 P & CR 418, CA.
6   *Day v Tiuta International Ltd (in administration)* [2014] EWCA Civ 1246, [2015] 1 P & CR D25, [2014] All ER (D) 06 (Oct).
7   *Faircharm Investments Ltd v Citibank International plc* (1998) Times, 20 February, CA.

388. Securitisation of mortgages. Securitisation is the sale of a package of mortgage debts to a corporate vehicle (the 'issuer') established for the purpose of issuing securities usually in bearer form such as bonds. One or more mortgagees (the 'originator') may agree to sell debts and related security to the issuer. This effects an equitable assignment of the mortgages which is not perfected by notice to the mortgagors or by registration. The issuer is entitled to call for a legal transfer of legal title to the mortgages in certain circumstances such as the persistent default or insolvency of the originator. The issuer is given an irrevocable power of attorney to effect the transfer and for certain other purposes[1]. The originator retains the powers of the mortgagee, including the right to possession[2], but agrees to act in accordance with the instructions of the issuer in relation to matters such as interest rates and enforcement. The undertaking and assets of the issuer, including the mortgages, are in turn charged in favour of a security trustee for the benefit of the holders of notes or bonds issued by the issuer[3]. The security trustee is given custody of the charge certificates or, in the case of unregistered land, mortgages and title deeds, and is given an irrevocable power of attorney to effect a legal transfer of the mortgages[4].

1 See the Powers of Attorney Act 1971 s 4; and AGENCY vol 1 (2008) PARA 175.
2 See *Paragon Finance plc v Pender* [2005] EWCA Civ 760, [2005] All ER (D) 307 (Jun).
3 The charge takes effect as an equitable sub-charge. As to equitable charges see PARAS 106, 221 et seq.
4 As to transfer of mortgages see PARA 366 et seq.

(ii) Devolution on Death of Mortgagee

389. Devolution of mortgagee's estate or interest. It has long been settled that a mortgage security is personal estate, as the mortgagee's principal right is to the money, and his right to the land is only security for the money[1]. On the mortgagee's death leaving a will, both the mortgage debt and the mortgagee's estate or interest in the mortgaged property, whether it is of freehold tenure or consists of leaseholds or other personal property, vest, in the first instance, in the executors, notwithstanding any disposition in the will, and the executors can exercise the mortgagee's powers under the mortgage[2]. Hence, provided that the executors have not assented to any bequest of the mortgage, they hold the legal estate in freehold mortgaged property, and can reconvey or transfer or, if they exercise the power of sale, convey.

The personal representatives for the time being are to be deemed in law the mortgagee's heirs and assigns within the meaning of all trusts and powers[3]. Further, by virtue of the definition of 'mortgagee' as including any person from time to time deriving title under the original mortgagee[4], personal representatives can exercise the mortgagee's statutory powers[5]. The devolution of a mortgage on land is governed by the law of the place where it is situated[6].

1 *Thornborough v Baker* (1675) 3 Swan 628 at 630; *Canning v Hicks* (1686) 1 Vern 412; *Tabor v Grover* (1699) 2 Vern 367; and see *Winn v Littleton* (1681) 1 Vern 3 at 4 note (1). See also REAL PROPERTY AND REGISTRATION vol 87 (2012) PARA 100. Formerly the mortgaged property, if it was real estate, might devolve on one person, while the mortgage debt devolved on another, in which case he who took the mortgaged estate by devise or by descent was a trustee for the person entitled to the mortgage debt: *A-G v Meyrick* (1750) 2 Ves Sen 44 at 46.
2 Personal estate (including leaseholds) vests in the personal representatives at common law, and real estate (including leaseholds and mortgage estates) vests in them by virtue of the Administration of Estates Act 1925 ss 1(1), 3(1): see WILLS AND INTESTACY vol 103 (2010) PARAS 952–954.
3 Administration of Estates Act 1925 s 1(2). Thus personal representatives can exercise all express powers conferred in a mortgage made before 1926 on the mortgagee, his heirs and assigns.
4 As to the meaning of 'mortgagee' in the Law of Property Act 1925 see PARA 104 note 1.
5 Eg the statutory power of sale: see PARA 446 et seq.
6 *Re Hoyles, Row v Jagg* [1911] 1 Ch 179, CA; cf *Haque v Haque (No 2)* (1965) 114 CLR 98, Aust HC. This does not, apparently, apply for revenue purposes: see *Lawson v IRC* [1896] 2 IR 418; *Re Hoyles, Row v Jagg* at 182 per Farwell LJ. See also *New York Life Insurance Co v Public Trustee* [1924] 2 Ch 101, CA. As to the circumstances rendering it necessary to consider the division of property into movables and immovables see *Re Hoyles, Row v Jagg* above at 185 per Farwell LJ. See also CONFLICT OF LAWS vol 19 (2011) PARAS 677, 683; INHERITANCE TAXATION vol 59A (2014) PARA 217.

390. Effect of specific bequest of mortgage. A specific bequest of the mortgage entitles the legatee both to the mortgage debt and to the mortgaged property, subject to the executors' assent[1]. Upon this assent being given, the legal title to the debt and all the mortgagee's interest in the mortgaged property, legal or otherwise, vests in the legatee[2]. Where a testator has by his will devised or bequeathed property and sells it during his lifetime, leaving part of the purchase money on mortgage, the mortgage does not pass to the devisee or legatee of the property[3]. Mortgages can be bequeathed for charitable purposes[4].

1   *Martin d Weston v Mowlin* (1760) 2 Burr 969 at 978; *Renvoize v Cooper* (1822) 6 Madd 371; *Mather v Thomas* (1833) 10 Bing 44; *Doe d Guest v Bennett* (1851) 6 Exch 892.

2   It is, however, better for the executors to transfer the mortgage to the legatee by short deed of transfer. As to assents see WILLS AND INTESTACY vol 103 (2010) PARA 1141 et seq.

3   *Moor v Raisbeck* (1841) 12 Sim 123; *Farrar v Lord Winterton* (1842) 5 Beav 1; *Re Clowes* [1893] 1 Ch 214, CA; *Re Richards, Jones v Rebbeck* (1921) 90 LJCh 298.

4   This could not be done before the enactment of the Mortmain and Charitable Uses Act 1891 s 3 (repealed): see CHARITIES vol 8 (2015) PARAS 83–84. See also *Re Hoyles, Row v Jagg* [1911] 1 Ch 179, CA.

391. Circumstances causing property to devolve as realty. So long as the equity of redemption[1] is not released or foreclosed or extinguished by lapse of time, the mortgagee's interest continues to be personal estate, notwithstanding that he may have entered into possession[2], and will not pass under a general devise of real estate[3] unless such an intention is shown[4] or where there is no other estate or interest to which the description can refer[5]. If, in addition to his mortgage interest, the mortgagee has an estate in the property, a specific devise of the property will pass his proprietary estate only and not his interest as mortgagee. Thus, if he is mortgagee of a term and also reversioner, a specific devise does not carry the mortgage, notwithstanding that the term has at law merged in the reversion[6]. If, however, he has entered into possession, a specific devise of the property will pass all his interest and will consequently include the mortgage debt[7].

If, at the time of the mortgagee's death, the equity of redemption is already extinguished, the property is real estate in his hands and devolves as such[8]. If in his will he disposes of the property as though his interest were still that of mortgagee only, the property none the less passes under the disposition[9].

1   As to the equity of redemption see PARAS 107, 304 et seq.

2   *Noy v Ellis* (1677) 2 Cas in Ch 220; *Re Loveridge, Drayton v Loveridge* [1902] 2 Ch 859.

3   *Strode v Russel* (1707) 2 Vern 621; *Casborne v Scarfe* (1738) 1 Atk 603; *Bowen v Barlow* (1872) 8 Ch App 171; *Davy v Redington* [1917] 1 IR 250, Ir CA.

4   *Mackesy v Mackesy* [1896] 1 IR 511; *Kilkelly v Powell* [1897] 1 IR 457.

5   *Re Lowman, Devenish v Pester* [1895] 2 Ch 348, CA.

6   *Bowen v Barlow* (1872) 8 Ch App 171.

7   *Woodhouse v Meredith* (1816) 1 Mer 450; *Re Carter, Dodds v Pearson* [1900] 1 Ch 801.

8   See WILLS AND INTESTACY vol 103 (2010) PARA 944 et seq. As to extinguishment of title by lapse of time see LIMITATION PERIODS vol 68 (2008) PARA 1105 et seq.

9   *Silberschildt v Schiott* (1814) 3 Ves & B 45, where the equity of redemption had been extinguished by foreclosure.

392. Death of proprietor of registered charge over land. On the death of a sole proprietor or the survivor of two or more proprietors of a registered charge on registered land, his personal representatives are entitled to be registered in his place[1]. They have power to transfer the registered charge without themselves being registered[2].

1   See the Land Registration Rules 2003, SI 2003/1417, r 163; and REAL PROPERTY AND REGISTRATION vol 87 (2012) PARA 440. Cf the position on bankruptcy of the proprietor see rr 165–170; and REAL PROPERTY AND REGISTRATION vol 87 (2012) PARA 441.

2   See REAL PROPERTY AND REGISTRATION vol 87 (2012) PARA 440.

393. Devolution of mortgage debt on mortgagee's intestacy. On a mortgagee's death intestate both the mortgage debt and the mortgaged property devolve on the administrator[1], whose duty it is to get in the mortgage money and apply it in due course of administration, the beneficial interest in any surplus being in the persons entitled under the rules for the distribution of the residuary estate[2].

1 See the Administration of Estates Act 1925 ss 1(1), 3(1); and PARA 389. As to the devolution of estate on intestacy generally see WILLS AND INTESTACY vol 102 (2010) PARA 479 et seq. As to devolution on the representative see WILLS AND INTESTACY vol 103 (2010) PARA 916 et seq. As to the role of the administrator see WILLS AND INTESTACY vol 103 (2010) PARA 643 et seq.

2 As to the distribution of the residuary estate on intestacy see WILLS AND INTESTACY vol 103 (2010) PARA 1137 et seq.

8. RIGHTS AND LIABILITIES OF THE MORTGAGEE

(1) DUTIES OWED BY THE MORTGAGEE

394. Duties owed by mortgagee. A mortgagee owes duties in equity to the mortgagor arising out of the particular relationship between them[1]. This duty extends to any subsequent incumbrancer[2] or surety[3]. The duties cannot be replaced or supplemented by a liability in negligence[4] or extended to others such as beneficiaries under a trust of the mortgaged property[5]. They can be excluded by agreement[6]. The mortgagee is not obliged to exercise his powers even if advised to do so, although the mortgaged property is depreciating and however advantageous it might be to the mortgagor[7]. He can decide if and when to exercise his powers on the basis of his own interests[8]. He is not obliged to enforce his security and may rely on the personal covenant for payment[9].

The mortgagee does, however, owe a general duty to exercise his powers in good faith[10] for the purpose of obtaining repayment[11] which flows from the equitable principles for the enforcement of mortgages and the protection of borrowers, that a mortgage is security for the repayment of a debt and that a security for repayment of a debt is only a mortgage[12]. He also owes specific duties once he exercises his powers[13]. It has been said that he owes a duty to act fairly towards the mortgagor[14].

A mortgagee owes no duty to explain the security to the mortgagor[15]. However, he may have to explain the security or ensure the mortgagor obtains independent legal advice to avoid being fixed with constructive notice of the right of a mortgagor who is securing the debts of another to set the transaction aside[16].

A mortgagee also owes specific duties to a surety[17].

The limitation period for a claim for breach of the duty in equity owed by a mortgagee is six years[18].

1   *Parker-Tweedale v Dunbar Bank plc* [1991] Ch 12, [1990] 2 All ER 577, CA; *Silven Properties Ltd v Royal Bank of Scotland plc* [2003] EWCA Civ 1409, [2004] 4 All ER 484, [2004] 1 WLR 997.

2   If there is a subsequent incumbrancer who is able to obtain full repayment notwithstanding a breach of duty by the prior mortgagee, the mortgagor can make a claim in respect of such breach of duty: *Downsview Nominees Ltd v First City Corpn Ltd* [1993] AC 295, [1993] 3 All ER 626, PC.

3   *China and South Sea Bank Ltd v Tan Soon Gin (alias George Tan)* [1990] 1 AC 536, [1989] 3 All ER 839, PC. The guarantor's liability is reduced by the amount by which the property was sold at an undervalue: see *Skipton Building Society v Stott* [2001] QB 261, [2000] 2 All ER 779, CA.

4   *Downsview Nominees Ltd v First City Corpn Ltd* [1993] AC 295, [1993] 3 All ER 626, PC. See also *Parker-Tweedale v Dunbar Bank plc* [1991] Ch 12, [1990] 2 All ER 577, CA. Dicta in earlier cases (see eg *Standard Chartered Bank Ltd v Walker* [1982] 3 All ER 938, [1982] 1 WLR 1410, CA; *American Express International Banking Corpn v Hurley* [1985] 3 All ER 564, 2 BCC 98, 993; *Knight v Lawrence* [1991] 1 EGLR 143, [1991] BCC 411) that the mortgagee owes a duty of care in tort must be read in the light of these authorities.

5   *Parker-Tweedale v Dunbar Bank plc* [1991] Ch 12, [1990] 2 All ER 577, CA. A beneficiary can sue on behalf of the trust if the trustee unreasonably refuses to do so or has committed some breach of his duties to the beneficiaries: *Parker-Tweedale v Dunbar Bank plc* above.

6   *Bishop v Bonham* [1988] 1 WLR 742, [1988] BCLC 656, CA; *Armitage v Nurse* [1998] Ch 241, [1997] 2 All ER 705, CA (exemption clause in trust deed); cf *Barclays Bank plc v Kingston* [2006] EWHC 533 (QB), [2006] 1 All ER (Comm) 519, [2006] 2 Lloyd's Rep 59 (bank's standard terms did not relieve it of the duty). The Unfair Contracts Terms Act 1977 does not apply to contracts for the disposition of an interest in land: see s 1(2), Sch 1 para 1(b). An exclusion clause contained in a mortgage to which the provisions of the Consumer Rights Act 2015 apply may, however, be regarded as unfair: see PARA 203. As to unfair terms in consumer contracts see the Consumer Rights Act 2015 Pt 2 (ss 61–76), Sch 2; and CONSUMER PROTECTION; CONTRACT.

7 *Palk v Mortgage Services Funding plc* [1993] Ch 330, [1993] 2 All ER 481, CA; *Lloyd's Bank v Bryant* [1996] NPC 31, CA. See also *China and South Sea Bank Ltd v Tan Soon Gin (alias George Tan)* [1990] 1 AC 536, [1989] 3 All ER 839, PC.
8 *Routestone Ltd v Minories Finance Ltd* [1997] 1 EGLR 123, [1997] BCC 180. As to the right to choose between remedies see PARA 518.
9 *Cheah Theam Swee v Equiticorp Finance Group Ltd* [1992] 1 AC 472, [1991] 4 All ER 989, PC.
10 The duty of good faith is not breached by conduct which is not dishonest or otherwise tainted by bad faith: *Medforth v Blake* [2000] Ch 86, CA, [1999] 3 All ER 97.
11 *Downsview Nominees Ltd v First City Corpn Ltd* [1993] AC 295, [1993] 3 All ER 626, PC; *China and South Sea Bank Ltd v Tan Soon Gin (alias George Tan)* [1990] 1 AC 536, [1989] 3 All ER 839, PC; *Silven Properties Ltd v Royal Bank of Scotland plc* [2003] EWCA Civ 1409, [2004] 4 All ER 484, [2004] 1 WLR 997. For examples of breach of this duty see *Downsview Nominees Ltd v First City Corpn Ltd; Albany Home Loans Ltd v Massey* [1997] 2 All ER 609, 29 HLR 902, CA; *Quennell v Maltby* [1979] 1 All ER 568, [1979] 1 WLR 318, CA; *Sadiq v Hussain* [1997] NPC 19, 73 P & CR D44, CA.
12 *Downsview Nominees Ltd v First City Corpn Ltd* [1993] AC 295, [1993] 3 All ER 626, PC. If a chargee enforces his security for the proper purpose of satisfying the debt, the mere fact that he may have additional purposes, however significant, which are collateral to that object, cannot vitiate his enforcement of the security: *Cukurova Finance International Ltd v Alfa Telecom Turkey Ltd* [2013] UKPC 2, [2015] 2 WLR 875, [2013] All ER (D) 21 (Apr).
13 As to the liabilities of a mortgagee in possession, for example, see PARA 430 et seq.
14 *Palk v Mortgage Services Funding plc* [1993] Ch 330, [1993] 2 All ER 481, CA; *AIB Finance Ltd v Debtors* [1998] 2 All ER 929, [1998] 1 BCLC 665, CA (but cf *Starling v Lloyds TSB Bank plc* [2000] Lloyd's Rep Bank 8, [2000] 1 EGLR 101); *Yorkshire Bank plc v Hall* [1999] 1 All ER 879, [1999] 1 WLR 1713, CA.
15 *Barclays Bank plc v Khaira* [1992] 1 WLR 623, [1991] NPC 141; on appeal on another point [1993] 1 FLR 343, [1993] Fam Law 124, CA.
16 See PARA 122 et seq.
17 See FINANCIAL INSTRUMENTS AND TRANSACTIONS vol 49 (2015) PARA 767 et seq.
18 See *Raja v Lloyds TSB Bank plc* [2001] EWCA Civ 210, 82 P & CR 191, [2001] Lloyd's Rep Bank 113; and LIMITATION PERIODS vol 68 (2008) PARAS 953–954.

(2) RIGHT TO PROTECT SECURITY

(i) Mortgagee's Rights as against the Mortgagor

395. Mortgagee's rights as regards title. As regards the title to the mortgaged property, if the mortgagee has in the first instance taken an equitable title[1], but with an agreement for a legal mortgage[2], he is entitled to have a legal mortgage executed on request, and will be allowed any charges and expenses properly incurred in preparing the mortgage[3]. If the mortgagor has conveyed to the mortgagee a defective title and subsequently acquires an interest which enables him to cure the defect, the mortgagee can call upon him to perfect the mortgage title[4]. Subject to the statutory provisions which relate to the effect of the registration of a mortgage or the failure to register a mortgage upon its priority[5], the mortgagee's right to have his title perfected gives him an equitable interest which will prevail against a subsequent incumbrancer who takes the legal estate with notice[6], but not if he takes without notice[7].

1 See PARAS 105, 215 et seq.
2 See PARA 105.
3 *National Provincial Bank of England v Games* (1886) 31 ChD 582, CA; and see PARA 748. As to mortgage by estoppel see PARA 167.
4 *Smith v Osborne* (1857) 6 HL Cas 375 at 390 per Lord Cranworth. As to mortgages see *Seabourne v Powel* (1686) 2 Vern 11. As to sales cf *Taylor v Debar* (1675) 1 Cas in Ch 274; *Smith v Baker* (1842) 1 Y & C Ch Cas 223.
5 See PARA 260 et seq.
6 *Jennings v Moore* (1708) 2 Vern 609; affd sub nom *Blenkarne v Jennens* 2 Bro Parl Cas 278.

7   *Oxwick v Plumer* (1708) 5 Bac Abr Mortgage (E) 3. Where the mortgagor had no title at all at the time of the mortgage, and subsequently acquired a title, it was doubted whether his heir was bound to convey: *Morse v Faulkner* (1792) 1 Anst 11.

396. Mortgagee's rights as regards value of property. As regards the value of the property itself, the mortgagee's rights possibly depend to some extent upon the circumstance that the mortgagor while in possession is a quasi-tenant[1], but, more substantially, they depend on the general principle that the mortgagee is entitled to have the security kept unimpaired. Hence, the mortgagor must not deal with the property so as to diminish its value[2]. Moreover, the mortgagee, if in possession, is entitled to lay out any money necessary for the maintenance of the property[3]. The mortgagee is not, however, obliged to preserve the mortgaged property prior to taking possession[4].

1   See *Partridge v Bere* (1822) 5 B & Ald 604 at 605 note (a); *Hitchman v Walton* (1838) 4 M & W 409. See also PARA 344.
2   As to the mortgagor's liability for waste see PARA 360.
3   *Sandon v Hooper* (1843) 6 Beav 246; affd (1844) 14 LJCh 120. As to repairs and improvements see PARA 749.
4   *AIB Finance Ltd v Debtors* [1998] 2 All ER 929, [1998] 1 BCLC 665, CA.

397. Mortgagee's right to restrain conduct prejudicing security. Apart from the doctrine of waste[1], the mortgagee is entitled to restrain the mortgagor from conduct which would prejudice the mortgage security[2]. Upon a mortgage of goods where the mortgagor retains the right of possession until default, an improper sale by him determines his right, and gives the immediate right to possession to the mortgagee who can then sue for conversion[3].

1   See PARAS 360–361.
2   Thus under a mortgage of tolls by the trustees of a road, the trustees might be restrained from reducing the tolls: *Lord Crewe v Edleston* (1857) 1 De G & J 93 at 110. Where a company has mortgaged a call on its shares, it cannot make a second call and get it in first at the mortgagee's expense (*Re Humber Ironworks Co, ex p Warrant Finance Co* (1868) 16 WR 667); and where property is subject to a vendor's lien, a sale of part will be restrained (*Blakely v Dent, Re Blakely Ordnance Co* (1867) 15 WR 663). See also CIVIL PROCEDURE vol 12 (2015) PARAS 1153–1154. As to claims in conversion see TORT vol 97 (2015) PARA 604 et seq.
3   *Fenn v Bittleston* (1851) 7 Exch 152.

(ii) Mortgagee's Rights as against Third Persons

398. Mortgagee's right to protect title against third persons. As against third persons, the mortgagee is entitled to protect his own or the mortgagor's title to the mortgaged property, and to maintain the value of that property. Thus if the mortgagor's title is impeached, the mortgagee may take any step necessary to support it[1]. If he is an equitable mortgagee, and a third person with an inferior title proposes to dispose of the legal estate, the mortgagee can obtain an injunction to restrain him[2]. As a rule, questions between the mortgagee and mortgagor can be determined without bringing in third persons[3], but where, as in redemption and foreclosure, other persons claiming an interest in the equity of redemption are affected, they must be made parties[4]. In general, however, the mortgagee will have to defend, at his own expense, proceedings brought by third persons to impeach the mortgage security[5]; and the first mortgagee cannot as against the second mortgagee deduct from the proceeds of sale by the first mortgagee costs caused by the mortgagor's contesting the sale, as costs 'incident to the sale'[6]. Where, however, in proceedings for the execution of trusts, the beneficiaries desire to impeach a mortgage by the trustees, and for that purpose make the mortgagee a party, he will apparently, if successful, be allowed his costs[7].

1 *Godfrey v Watson* (1747) 3 Atk 517 at 518; *Sandon v Hooper* (1843) 6 Beav 246 at 248. See also PARAS 771–772.
2 *London and County Banking Co v Lewis* (1882) 21 ChD 490, CA. As to equitable mortgages see PARAS 105, 215 et seq.
3 See eg *Petre v Duncombe* (1848) 7 Hare 24.
4 *Evans v Jones* (1853) Kay 29. As to the equity of redemption see PARAS 107, 304 et seq. As to foreclosure see PARA 571 et seq.
5 *Parker v Watkins* (1859) John 133; *Parker-Tweedale v Dunbar Bank plc (No 2)* [1991] Ch 26, [1990] 2 All ER 588, CA.
6 Ie under the Law of Property Act 1925 s 105: see PARA 475. See also *Re Smith's Mortgage, Harrison v Edwards* [1931] 2 Ch 168; and PARA 772. For the right of mortgagees to apply to the court to mitigate any financial hardship caused on enfranchisement under the Leasehold Reform Act 1967 see s 36; and LANDLORD AND TENANT vol 64 (2012) PARA 1580.
7 See *Langton v Langton* (1855) 7 De GM & G 30.

399. Mortgagee's right to recover and maintain property. As regards the recovery or preservation of the mortgaged property, the mortgagee may be entitled to bring proceedings against third persons either by virtue of his immediate legal estate in the property, or of his possession or immediate right to possession. In relation to tenancies granted on or after 1 January 1996[1], a mortgagee in possession can enforce any covenant or any right of re-entry enforceable by the mortgagor[2]. In relation to land, the mortgagor retains a legal estate and while in possession has the statutory right to bring certain proceedings in his own name[3]. In other cases a mortgagor can usually sue in his own name by virtue of his beneficial interest, subject to the mortgagee's security[4]. Even though the mortgagor of personalty can sue alone by virtue of his equitable ownership, it may be necessary to join the mortgagee, if, for instance, it is necessary for the legal estate to be before the court, or if accounts have to be taken which are to be made binding on the mortgagee[5].

1 Ie the commencement date of the Landlord and Tenant (Covenants) Act 1995: see the Landlord and Tenant (Covenants) Act 1995 (Commencement) Order 1995, SI 1995/2963, art 2.
2 See the Landlord and Tenant (Covenants) Act 1995 s 15(1)(b); PARA 419; LANDLORD AND TENANT vol 63 (2012) PARA 740. By implication a mortgagee cannot enforce any covenant or any right of re-entry until in possession.
3 See the Law of Property Act 1925 ss 98(1), 141(2). See also the Landlord and Tenant (Covenants) Act 1995 ss 3, 15; and PARAS 341–342.
4 *Fairclough v Marshall* (1878) 4 Ex D 37, CA; *Van Gelder, Apsimon & Co v Sowerby Bridge United District Flour Society* (1890) 44 ChD 374, CA.
5 As to accounts see PARA 709 et seq.

400. Mortgagee's right to sue for trespass to land. Where the mortgagee is in possession of land he can sue a third person in trespass[1], and, after entry, his right of possession relates back to the time when his right to possession accrued, so as to enable him to maintain a claim for trespass committed by a stranger before his entry. This is so whether the mortgagee has a legal estate or not[2].

1 It seems that he may also be able to sue if he has the immediate right to possession as against the mortgagor, for it has been said that a lessor at will can sue in trespass: see *Harper v Charlesworth* (1825) 4 B & C 574 at 583; *Geary v Bearecroft* (1667) 1 Lev 202; and TORT vol 97 (2015) PARA 576. Formerly, if the security was by way of demise, the mortgagee could not sue in trespass before he had entered: *Wheeler v Montefiore* (1841) 2 QB 133 at 142; *Doe d Parsley v Day* (1842) 2 QB 147 at 156. However, this was altered by the Law of Property Act 1925 s 149(2): see REAL PROPERTY AND REGISTRATION vol 87 (2012) PARA 77. See also LANDLORD AND TENANT vol 62 (2012) PARA 119.
2 *Ocean Accident and Guarantee Corpn Ltd v Ilford Gas Co* [1905] 2 KB 493, CA.

401. Mortgagee's right to sue for trespass or conversion of goods. Where the mortgagee is in possession, or has the immediate right to possession, of goods, he can sue for trespass or conversion, or to recover the goods[1], and is the proper person to do so[2], but the mortgagor, on tendering the amount due, is entitled to sue the mortgagee in conversion[3]. Similarly, a vendor who retains possession of goods subject to his lien is the proper person to sue in conversion in the event of the conversion of the goods by a stranger[4]. The lawful holder of a bill of lading, to whom the property in the goods mentioned in it passes, has transferred to and vested in him all rights of suit under the contract of carriage[5]. Proceedings for trespass or conversion are not open to the mortgagee if the mortgagor is entitled under the mortgage to retain possession till a certain event, such as demand of payment and default, and that event has not happened[6]; although, if goods are mortgaged by way of assignment to the mortgagee upon trust to allow the mortgagor to remain in possession till demand of payment, the mortgagee is considered to have the right to immediate possession upon the analogy of the case of trustee and beneficiary[7]. Where the mortgagee is entitled to sue in conversion, he can recover as damages the full value of the goods[8], whether he is or is not liable to account for any surplus to the mortgagor[9].

1 Trespass, trover and detinue were all possessory actions, and the plaintiff had to show either actual possession or the right to immediate possession: *Gordon v Harper* (1796) 7 Term Rep 9. As to the abolition of detinue and the introduction of the concept of wrongful interference with goods see the Torts (Interference with Goods) Act 1977 ss 1, 2; and TORT vol 97 (2015) PARAS 602–603. As to claims in conversion see further TORT vol 97 (2015) PARA 604 et seq.
2 *Sewell v Burdick* (1884) 10 App Cas 74 at 92, HL; *Bristol and West of England Bank v Midland Rly Co* [1891] 2 QB 653, CA.
3 *Franklin v Neate* (1844) 13 M & W 481 at 484. See also note 1; and TORT vol 97 (2015) PARA 635.
4 *Lord v Price* (1874) LR 9 Exch 54; and see TORT vol 97 (2015) PARA 634.
5 See the Carriage of Goods by Sea Act 1992 s 2; and CARRIAGE AND CARRIERS vol 7 (2015) PARA 339 et seq. Under the Bills of Lading Act 1855, the rights and liabilities of the shipper were transferred only to a person who obtained full property and not to an indorsee who was a mere pledgee: see *Sewell v Burdick* (1884) 10 App Cas 74 at 96, HL; and CARRIAGE AND CARRIERS vol 7 (2015) PARA 352. See also *Burgos v Nascimento* (1908) 100 LT 71; and SALE OF GOODS AND SUPPLY OF SERVICES vol 91 (2012) PARAS 239, 379.
6 *Bradley v Copley* (1845) 1 CB 685.
7 *White v Morris* (1852) 11 CB 1015; cf *Barker v Furlong* [1891] 2 Ch 172.
8 *Brierly v Kendall* (1852) 17 QB 937 at 943.
9 *The Winkfield* [1902] P 42, CA (overruling *Claridge v South Staffordshire Tramway Co* [1892] 1 QB 422, DC). See also DAMAGES vol 29 (2014) PARA 408 et seq; TORT vol 97 (2015) PARA 662 et seq.

402. Mortgagee's general right to prevent deterioration of security. In general, a mortgagee is entitled to bring proceedings to prevent the deterioration of his security[1]. Where the property is to be compulsorily acquired, notice to treat must be served on him as well as on the mortgagor[2]. If the property consists of licensed premises, the mortgagee can appeal to the Crown Court against non-renewal of the licence[3]. A prior mortgagee is also entitled to an injunction to prevent the mortgaged property being taken or dealt with by a subsequent incumbrancer[4], but the mortgagee cannot obtain an injunction unless he is prejudiced by the conduct complained of. Thus if the mortgage comprises the goodwill of a business and the right to use a name, the mortgagee, if he does not intend to use the name, cannot prevent the mortgagor's assignees from using it[5]. A mortgagee is entitled to bring proceedings against a prior mortgagee and a receiver appointed by him to prevent any breach of the equitable duty owed to subsequent mortgagees as well as to the mortgagor, or claim damages for any breach which occurs[6]. A mortgagee is justified in procuring a breach of contract between the mortgagor and a third party in defence and protection of his right to repayment of the secured indebtedness[7].

1   See *Western Bank Ltd v Schindler* [1977] Ch 1 at 9–10, [1976] 2 All ER 393 at 396, CA, per Buckley LJ. As to the liability of the mortgagor for waste and other liabilities see PARA 360 et seq.
2   *Cooke v LCC* [1911] 1 Ch 604. See also COMPULSORY ACQUISITION OF LAND vol 18 (2009) PARA 619. As to the position of mortgagees in regard to compulsory purchase see COMPULSORY ACQUISITION OF LAND vol 18 (2009) PARA 711 et seq.
3   *Garrett v St Marylebone, Middlesex, Justices* (1884) 12 QBD 620. See also the Licensing Act 2003 s 178 (notification of licensing matters); and LICENSING AND GAMBLING vol 67 (2008) PARA 39.
4   *Legg v Mathieson* (1860) 2 Giff 71; *Wildy v Mid-Hants Rly Co* (1868) 16 WR 409.
5   *Beazley v Soares* (1882) 22 ChD 660. See also CIVIL PROCEDURE vol 12 (2015) PARAS 1153–1154. As to goodwill generally see COMPETITION vol 18 (2009) PARAS 373–376; PARTNERSHIP vol 79 (2014) PARA 212 et seq; PERSONAL PROPERTY vol 80 (2013) PARA 807 et seq.
6   *Downsview Nominees Ltd v First City Corpn Ltd* [1993] AC 295, [1993] 3 All ER 626, PC. As to the duties owed by a mortgagee and receiver see PARA 426 et seq.
7   *Edwin Hill & Partners v First National Finance Corpn plc* [1989] 1 WLR 225, [1989] BCLC 89, CA.

403.   Mortgagee's right to relief from forfeiture. A mortgagee[1] is entitled to apply for relief from forfeiture for non-payment of rent as the lessee[2] or to apply for a vesting order[3]. In cases of forfeiture for other breaches of covenant, the court has a discretion to grant a mortgagee of the property relief from forfeiture or to make a vesting order[4]. Even if the landlord obtains an order for possession, a mortgagee can apply after execution to intervene in the proceedings to seek relief, but such an application is unlikely to succeed if the mortgagee was notified of the proceedings before judgment was obtained but failed to intervene until after judgment[5]. The effect of an order for relief from forfeiture is to restore the lease as if it had never been forfeited, and with it any underlease[6]. Where a vesting order is made, a new lease is granted as from the date of the order granting it[7], and the new lease is regarded as a substituted security in the mortgagee's hands[8]. The court does not have power to grant relief from forfeiture for breaches of covenant other than for the payment of rent under its inherent equitable jurisdiction[9].

1   No distinction is to be drawn between a mortgagee by sub-demise or a mortgagee by way of legal charge: *Grand Junction Co Ltd v Bates* [1954] 2 QB 160, [1954] 2 All ER 385; *Belgravia Insurance Co Ltd v Meah* [1964] 1 QB 436, [1963] 3 All ER 828, CA. An equitable mortgagee or chargee is treated as an underlessee and thus as a lessee: see the Law of Property Act 1925 s 146(5)(d); and the County Courts Act 1984 s 140. See also *Re Good's Lease, Good v Wood* [1954] 1 All ER 275, [1954] 1 WLR 309; *Escalus Properties Ltd v Robinson* [1996] QB 231, [1995] 4 All ER 852, CA; *United Dominions Trust Ltd v Shellpoint Trustees Ltd* [1993] 4 All ER 310, 67 P & CR 18, CA.
2   See the Common Law Procedure Act 1852 s 210; the Senior Courts Act 1981 s 38; the County Courts Act 1984 s 138; and LANDLORD AND TENANT vol 63 (2012) PARAS 776–777. See also the Law of Property Act 1925 s 146; and LANDLORD AND TENANT vol 63 (2012) PARA 767 et seq. See further *Doe d Wyatt v Byron* (1845) 1 CB 623; *Belgravia Insurance Co Ltd v Meah* [1964] 1 QB 436, [1963] 3 All ER 828, CA; *United Dominions Trust Ltd v Shellpoint Trustees Ltd* [1993] 4 All ER 310, 67 P & CR 18, CA; *Escalus Properties Ltd v Robinson* [1996] QB 231, [1995] 4 All ER 852, CA. As to the circumstances in which and the terms on which relief is available see *Escalus Properties Ltd v Robinson* above.
3   See the Law of Property Act 1925 s 146(4); the County Courts Act 1984 s 138(9C); and COURTS AND TRIBUNALS vol 24 (2010) PARA 773; LANDLORD AND TENANT vol 63 (2012) PARA 775.
4   See the Law of Property Act 1925 s 146(2), (4); and *Escalus Properties Ltd v Robinson* [1996] QB 231, [1995] 4 All ER 852, CA. The court has jurisdiction to grant relief under the Law of Property Act 1925 s 146(4) notwithstanding a disclaimer of the lease before forfeiture: *Barclays Bank plc v Prudential Assurance Co Ltd* [1998] BCC 928, [1998] 1 EGLR 44.
5   *Rexhaven Ltd v Nurse and Alliance and Leicester* (1995) 28 HLR 241, [1995] EGCS 125.
6   *Dendy v Evans* [1910] 1 KB 263, CA. This is usually more advantageous to the mortgagee than a vesting order since there is no period in respect of which the landlord can claim mesne profits: see *Escalus Properties Ltd v Robinson* [1996] QB 231, [1995] 4 All ER 852, CA.

7   *Cadogan v Dimovic* [1984] 2 All ER 168, [1984] 1 WLR 609, CA; *Official Custodian for Charities v Mackey* [1985] Ch 168, [1984] 3 All ER 689.
8   *Chelsea Estates Investment Trust Co Ltd v Marche* [1955] Ch 328, [1955] 1 All ER 195.
9   *Ladup Ltd v Williams & Glyn's Bank plc* [1985] 2 All ER 577, [1985] 1 WLR 851; *Billson v Residential Apartments Ltd* [1991] 3 All ER 265, [1991] 1 EGLR 70, CA (revsd on another point [1992] 1 AC 494, [1992] 1 All ER 141, HL).

(3) RIGHT TO POSSESSION OF THE MORTGAGED PROPERTY

(i) When the Mortgagee's Right to Possession Arises

404. Right of legal mortgagee or chargee to possession. Where a legal mortgage has been created, whether by demise or by legal charge[1], and no provision is made for retention of possession by the mortgagor[2], the mortgagee is entitled as against the mortgagor to immediate possession[3] or receipt of the rents and profits[4] at any time after the execution of the mortgage; and equity does not interfere[5], notwithstanding that there has been no default on the mortgagor's part[6], or that a bill of exchange has been given for the debt[7], or that considerable time has elapsed, provided a claim for possession is not statute-barred[8]. A mere power of sale on default does not, it seems, give a right of entry except on default, and then only for the purpose of a sale[9]. A mortgagee can choose whether to take possession or not, and he can foreclose without taking possession[10]. This applies to a second mortgagee as well as to the first mortgagee, as the second mortgage is now made by demise or legal charge, but a second mortgagee can only take possession subject to the first mortgagee's rights. The mere existence of a sub-charge does not deprive a principal chargee of the right to possession[11].

1   As to mortgage by demise see PARA 164. As to the rights conferred upon the mortgagee by a charge by way of legal mortgage see the Law of Property Act 1925 s 87(1); and PARA 165.
2   See *National Westminster Bank plc v Skelton* [1993] 1 All ER 242, [1993] 1 WLR 72n, CA; *Keech v Hall* (1778) 1 Doug KB 21; *Gibbs v Cruikshank* (1873) LR 8 CP 454 at 461; *Moore v Shelley* (1883) 8 App Cas 285, PC. The change in the nature of legal mortgages, from a conveyance of the fee simple to a demise for a term of years, did not alter this incident of the security: see the Law of Property Act 1925 s 95(4), which provides that nothing in the Act affects prejudicially the right of a mortgagee of land, whether or not his charge is secured by a legal term of years absolute, to take possession of the land. It is expressly recognised that a legal charge gives this right: see s 87(1); and PARA 165. As to the effect of a re-demise by the mortgagee of the mortgaged property to the mortgagor either expressly or by implication see PARAS 344–347. Where the advance is repayable by instalments it may be implied that the mortgagor is to retain possession unless he defaults: see *Birmingham Citizens Permanent Building Society v Caunt* [1962] Ch 883 at 890, [1962] 1 All ER 163 at 168 per Russell J; *Esso Petroleum Co Ltd v Alstonbridge Properties Ltd* [1975] 3 All ER 358 at 367–368, [1975] 1 WLR 1474 at 1483–1484 per Walton J.
3   *Four-Maids Ltd v Dudley Marshall (Properties) Ltd* [1957] Ch 317, [1957] 2 All ER 35; *Western Bank Ltd v Schindler* [1977] Ch 1, [1976] 2 All ER 393, CA; *Centrax Trustees Ltd v Ross* [1979] 2 All ER 952.
4   *Pope v Biggs* (1829) 9 B & C 245.
5   *Marquis of Cholmondeley v Lord Clinton* (1817) 2 Mer 171; *London Permanent Benefit Building Society v De Baer* [1969] 1 Ch 321, [1968] 1 All ER 372.
6   *Doe d Roylance v Lightfoot* (1841) 8 M & W 553; *Rogers v Grazebrook* (1846) 8 QB 895; *Green v Burns* (1879) 6 LR Ir 173; *Western Bank Ltd v Schindler* [1977] Ch 1, [1976] 2 All ER 393, CA.
7   *Bramwell v Eglinton* (1864) 5 B & S 39.
8   *Wright v Pepin* [1954] 2 All ER 52, [1954] 1 WLR 635. As to the effect of lapse of time on a mortgagee's right to bring a claim for possession see LIMITATION PERIODS vol 68 (2008) PARA 1016 (12 year period for proceedings to recover land). As to the limitation period in relation to foreclosure claims see LIMITATION PERIODS vol 68 (2008) PARA 1124 et seq. As to the extension or postponement of limitation periods see LIMITATION PERIODS vol 68 (2008) PARA 1168 et seq.

9   *Watson v Waltham* (1835) 2 Ad & El 485.
10 *Lord Penrhyn v Hughes* (1799) 5 Ves 99 at 106. As to foreclosure see PARA 571 et seq.
11 *Credit and Mercantile plc v Marks* [2004] EWCA Civ 568, [2005] Ch 81, [2004] 3 WLR 489.

405. Position of equitable incumbrancer. An incumbrancer who has no legal mortgage has no right to enter into possession of the land until he obtains a court order[1], but if his charge is created by instrument under seal he can appoint a receiver[2], and if his charge arises otherwise he can obtain the appointment of a receiver by the court[3]. The mortgagee may expressly give an equitable incumbrancer the right to take possession[4]; and if the incumbrancer gives notice to the tenant to pay the rent to him, this, by virtue of the agreement, entitles the mortgagee to the rents as against a judgment creditor apart from the question of the mortgagee's right to recover possession[5]. The appointment of a receiver does not, however, give priority over a judgment creditor if the receiver has not given notice to the tenant, or claimed payment, before judgment is recovered against the mortgagor[6].

1   *Barclays Bank Ltd v Bird* [1954] Ch 274, [1954] 1 All ER 449. Cf *Vacuum Oil Co Ltd v Ellis* [1914] 1 KB 693, CA; *Garfitt v Allen, Allen v Longstaffe* (1887) 37 ChD 48 at 50; but see *Spencer v Mason* (1931) 75 Sol Jo 295.
2   As to the appointment of a receiver out of court see PARAS 478 et seq.
3   As to the appointment of a receiver by the court see PARAS 565 et seq. As to possible equitable incumbrancers see PARA 105.
4   *Ocean Accident and Guarantee Corpn Ltd v Ilford Gas Co* [1905] 2 KB 493 at 497, CA.
5   *Campion v Palmer* [1896] 2 IR 445, Ir CA.
6   *Vacuum Oil Co Ltd v Ellis* [1914] 1 KB 693, CA.

406. Date from which equitable mortgagee is entitled to rents and profits. If a receiver is not appointed, but the equitable incumbrancer obtains an order for sale, he is entitled to the rents at least from the date of the order[1]. It is not clearly settled whether the equitable mortgagee is entitled to rents from the date of the order for sale or from the date of the application on which the order for sale is made. In some cases the rents have been allowed from the date of the order for sale[2], notwithstanding that the mortgagee did not establish his title until subsequently[3]. However, a mortgagee has been held entitled to the produce of the mortgaged property from the time of presenting a petition for sale[4], and to the rents from the date of an order for inquiry as to title, and not only from the date when the title was affirmed and an order for sale made[5]. A mortgagee does not entitle himself to the rents before the order for sale by giving notice to the tenants to pay the rents to him[6], unless, of course, his mortgage entitles him to go into possession. Where a receiver is appointed, the relevant date is neither the date of the institution of proceedings to raise the money secured, nor the date of the order for sale, but the date of the appointment[7]. An equitable mortgagee by deposit who gives notice to, and receives rent from, the tenant can retain it as against him[8].

1   *Vacuum Oil Co Ltd v Ellis* [1914] 1 KB 693, CA. As to possible equitable incumbrancers see PARA 105. As to the mortgagee in possession's right to rents and profits see PARA 419 et seq.
2   *Rele, ex p Bignold* (1835) 4 Deac & Ch 259; *Re Tombs, ex p Living* (1835) 2 Mont & A 223; *Re Birks, ex p Carlon* (1837) 3 Mont & A 328; *Re Norman, ex p Burrell* (1838) 3 Mont & A 439; *Re Pearson, ex p Scott* (1838) 3 Mont & A 592. In *Re Keer, ex p Bignold* (1832) 2 Deac & Ch 398, the mortgagee only asked for the rents from the date of the order for sale. In *Re Tills, ex p Alexander* (1827) 2 Gl & J 275, Lord Eldon LC held that the mortgagor's assignees in bankruptcy took the rents till the actual sale, but this ruling has not been followed.
3   *Re Teesdale and Swales, ex p Thorpe* (1838) 3 Mont & A 441.
4   *Re Harvey, ex p Bignold* (1827) 2 Gl & J 273.
5   *Re Feaver, ex p Smith* (1844) 3 Mont D & De G 680.
6   *Re Pearson, ex p Scott* (1838) 3 Mont & A 592.

7   *Butler v Butler* [1925] 1 IR 185, where the position of the equitable mortgagee when the
    mortgagor is bankrupt was distinguished. As to the appointment of a receiver out of court see
    PARA 478 et seq. As to the appointment of a receiver by the court see PARA 565 et seq.
8   *Re Freeman, ex p Williams* (1865) 13 WR 564; *Finck v Tranter* [1905] 1 KB 427. As to the
    creation of an equitable mortgage by deposit of title deeds see PARAS 222–223. Since 27 September
    1989 the mere deposit of title deeds by way of security can no longer create a valid equitable
    mortgage: see PARA 221.

407.   Effect of cross-claim by mortgagor on the mortgagee's right to possession.
A legal mortgagee's right to possession cannot, in the absence of some contractual
or statutory provision to the contrary, be defeated by a cross-claim for damages
made by a mortgagor, even if the cross-claim is liquidated and admitted and in
excess of the mortgage arrears, or is for unliquidated damages giving rise to a right
of equitable set-off[1]. However, in the case of a dwelling house, the court may
adjourn proceedings for possession, stay or suspend an order for possession, or
postpone the date for possession[2], if the existence and prospects of success of the
mortgagor's cross-claim could be regarded as enabling the sums due to be paid
within a reasonable time[3].

1   *Mobil Oil Co Ltd v Rawlinson* (1981) 43 P & CR 221, 126 Sol Jo 15; *National Westminster
    Bank plc v Skelton* [1993] 1 All ER 242, [1993] 1 WLR 72n, CA; *Ashley Guarantee plc v Zacaria*
    [1993] 1 All ER 254, [1993] 1 WLR 62, CA; *Midland Bank plc v McGrath* [1996] EGCS 61, CA.
    As to the right to set off generally see CIVIL PROCEDURE vol 11 (2015) PARA 382 et seq.
2   As to the powers of the court to suspend orders for possession see PARAS 557 et seq.
3   *Ashley Guarantee plc v Zacaria* [1993] 1 All ER 254, [1993] 1 WLR 62, CA; *National
    Westminster Bank plc v Skelton* [1993] 1 All ER 242, [1993] 1 WLR 72n, CA.

408.   Mortgagee's right of entry arising on default of payment on demand.
Where the mortgagee's right of entry is to arise only on default in payment of the
mortgage debt on demand, such time as may be required should be allowed for
compliance with the demand before the mortgagee enters[1]. If a mortgagee of
goods seizes them too soon, the mortgagor recovers as damages, not the value of
the goods, but the value of his interest in them[2]; but a premature taking of
possession does not prevent the mortgagee from taking possession in due time[3].

1   *Toms v Wilson* (1863) 4 B & S 442, Ex Ch.
2   *Brierly v Kendall* (1852) 17 QB 937; *Chinery v Viall* (1860) 5 H & N 288; *Toms v Wilson* (1863)
    4 B & S 442, Ex Ch.
3   *Bramwell v Eglinton* (1864) 5 B & S 39.

(ii)   Exercise of the Mortgagee's Right to Possession

409.   When entry can be made or proceedings brought without notice. When the
mortgagee has a right of entry and allows the mortgagor to remain in possession,
he is not bound to give any notice to the mortgagor before entering[1]; similarly he
can bring proceedings to recover the land without any previous notice or demand
of possession[2]. The court will not interfere with the mortgagee's right to
possession on account of the pendency of administration proceedings[3], but the
exercise of the right of entry may be subject to restriction under the Insolvency Act
1986[4].

A mortgagor has been described as a tenant at will[5], but this analogy is
misleading, and it is, perhaps, more correct to say that he remains at the
mortgagee's will, or that the mortgagee is entitled at any moment to treat him as
a trespasser[6]. If, however, the mortgagor is indeed made tenant at will by the
contract, he holds subject to the legal incidence of that relation[7]. Where the
mortgagor has attorned tenant to the mortgagee[8], the necessity for any notice or

demand previous to entry[9] is usually avoided by express provision that the mortgagee is to be entitled to enter without notice at any time after default in payment of the principal money[10].

1   *Keech v Hall* (1778) 1 Doug KB 21; 1 Smith LC (13th Edn) 562; *Birch v Wright* (1786) 1 Term Rep 378 at 383. See also PARA 344.
2   *Doe d Fisher v Giles* (1829) 5 Bing 421; *Jolly v Arbuthnot* (1859) 4 De G & J 224 at 236. See also PARAS 541–543. As to proceedings for the delivery of possession see PARA 549 et seq.
3   *Crowle v Russell* (1878) 27 WR 84, CA.
4   See PARA 521 et seq; and BANKRUPTCY AND INDIVIDUAL INSOLVENCY vol 5 (2013) PARA 672 et seq. As to the effect of the Administration of Justice Act 1970 s 36 (see PARA 557) see *Ropaigealach v Barclays Bank plc* [2000] QB 263, (1998) 77 P & CR D32, CA.
5   See *Keech v Hall* (1778) 1 Doug KB 21.
6   *Doe d Roby v Maisey* (1828) 8 B & C 767; *Jolly v Arbuthnot* (1859) 4 De G & J 224; and see PARAS 344–347.
7   *Re Skinner, ex p Temple and Fishe* (1822) 1 Gl & J 216. As to tenancies at will see LANDLORD AND TENANT vol 62 (2012) PARA 198 et seq.
8   As to attornment clauses see PARA 346.
9   As to the principle that notice is normally necessary before the mortgagor goes into possession where there is an attornment clause see *Four-Maids Ltd v Dudley Marshall (Properties) Ltd* [1957] Ch 317 at 320, [1957] 2 All ER 35 at 36 per Harman J.
10   *Doe d Garrod v Olley* (1840) 12 Ad & El 481; *Doe d Snell v Tom* (1843) 4 QB 615; *Jolly v Arbuthnot* (1859) 4 De G & J 224; *Metropolitan Counties Assurance Society v Brown* (1859) 4 H & N 428. As to the principle that the reservation of a right of re-entry without notice does not in itself convert a yearly tenancy into a tenancy at will see PARA 346. As to the effect of such a provision on the mortgagee's right to take proceedings for possession see PARA 347.

410. Exercise of mortgagee's right of entry. Where the mortgaged property is in the occupation of the mortgagor or of a tenant of the mortgagor whose tenancy is not binding on the mortgagee[1], the mortgagee exercises his right to possession either by entering on the land if this can be done peaceably[2], or by making a claim in the County Court or, where that court does not have jurisdiction[3], the Chancery Division of the High Court, for delivery of possession of the land[4]. If the mortgaged property is in the occupation of a tenant whose tenancy is binding[5] on the mortgagee, the mortgagee exercises his right by giving the tenant notice to pay the rent to him.

1   See PARA 295 et seq.
2   See *Ropaigealach v Barclays Bank plc* [2000] QB 263, (1998) 77 P & CR D32, CA. As to criminal penalties for forcible entry see CRIMINAL LAW vol 26 (2010) PARA 553 et seq. See also LANDLORD AND TENANT vol 63 (2012) PARA 800. As to the right to possession of a mortgagee who has entered forcibly see PARA 413.
3   See PARA 549.
4   See PARA 549 et seq. A claim for possession is simply a claim for the recovery of land and is not proceedings for enforcing the mortgage: *Esso Petroleum Co Ltd v Alstonbridge Properties Ltd* [1975] 3 All ER 358 at 365, [1975] 1 WLR 1474 at 1481 per Walton J. Nothing in the Protection from Eviction Act 1977 affects the jurisdiction of the High Court in proceedings to enforce a lessor's right of re-entry or forfeiture or to enforce a mortgagee's right of possession in a case where the former tenancy was not binding on the mortgagee: s 9(3).
5   See PARA 295 et seq. As to spouses', civil partners' and cohabitants' occupation rights where a dwelling house is subject to a mortgage see the Family Law Act 1996 ss 54–56; and MATRIMONIAL AND CIVIL PARTNERSHIP LAW vol 72 (2015) PARA 304 et seq.

411. Effect of prior possession by receiver. If, at a time when the mortgagee wishes to go into possession, he finds a receiver appointed by the court in possession[1], and the rights of prior incumbrancers have not been preserved, he must apply in the proceedings in which the receiver was appointed for the receiver's discharge and for liberty to take possession[2]; and the mortgagee is not entitled to rents collected by the receiver before the mortgagee's application to the court[3]. If, however, the existence of prior incumbrancers is known, the order is made subject to, or with a proviso that it is not to affect, their right to take possession. Tenants will then be justified in paying their rents to the mortgagee after notice from him, and he is entitled to possession as against the receiver[4]; but if any difficulty arises in asserting his right he should apply to the court in the proceedings in which the receiver was appointed[5].

1   See PARA 569.
2   *Angel v Smith* (1804) 9 Ves 335; *Thomas v Brigstocke* (1827) 4 Russ 64; *Langton v Langton* (1855) 7 De GM & G 30; *Walmsley v Munday* (1884) 13 QBD 807, CA; and see *Searle v Choat* (1884) 25 ChD 723, CA.
3   *Re Metropolitan Amalgamated Estates Ltd, Fairweather v Metropolitan Amalgamated Estates Ltd* [1912] 2 Ch 497.
4   *Davis v Duke of Marlborough* (1819) 2 Swan 108 at 137; *Underhay v Read* (1887) 20 QBD 209 at 219, CA.
5   *Searle v Choat* (1884) 25 ChD 723.

(iii)   What Amounts to Possession

412.   Mortgagee entering on part. A mortgagee who is entitled to vacant possession of the property acquires possession of the whole of the property by entering on part, provided that the property is so bounded and defined that entry on part can be regarded as entry on the whole[1]. However, a mortgagee is entitled to limit his possession to part of the property, and, if that is his intention, he will not be charged as being constructively in possession of the whole[2]. Thus where a farm is let to a tenant without the shooting or timber, notice to pay rent to the mortgagee will put him in possession of the farm only, and not of the shooting and timber[3].

1   Cf *Low Moor Co v Stanley Coal Co Ltd* (1876) 34 LT 186, CA.
2   *Soar v Dalby* (1852) 15 Beav 156.
3   *Simmins v Shirley* (1877) 6 ChD 173.

413.   Forcible entry by mortgagee. Even if the mortgagee's entry is forcible so as to subject him to penalties under the criminal law[1], once he has entered his right to possession gives him the possession for civil purposes, and he can treat the mortgagor or any other person who is on the property as a trespasser[2].

1   See CRIMINAL LAW vol 26 (2010) PARA 553 et seq.
2   *Lows v Telford* (1876) 1 App Cas 414, HL; and see *Harvey v Brydges* (1845) 14 M & W 437 (affd (1847) 1 Ex Ch 261); *Beddall v Maitland* (1881) 17 ChD 174 at 188. As to the tort of trespass to land see further TORT vol 97 (2015) PARA 563 et seq.

414.   Who may be treated as being in possession. A solicitor who pays off a mortgage for a client and receives the rents receives them as agent for the client, and is not a mortgagee in possession[1]. If necessary, an inquiry as to the fact of possession will be directed[2], but not where the mortgagee has admitted this on his statements of case[3].

1   *Ward v Carttar* (1865) LR 1 Eq 29. See also AGENCY vol 1 (2008) PARA 96.
2   *Dobson v Lee* (1842) 1 Y & C Ch Cas 714. See also *Wills v Palmer* (1904) 53 WR 169. Where land is not suitable for occupation, possession is gained by doing such acts of ownership as are possible: see *Lord Advocate v Young* (1887) 12 App Cas 544, HL; *Kirby v Cowderoy* [1912] AC 599, PC. As to possession by a receiver see *Re R W Hill Ltd and Simmons' Contract* [1920] WN 386.
3   *Parker v Watkins* (1859) John 133 at 137.

415.   Mortgagee taking actual possession. Where a mortgagee takes actual possession of the property, there is no doubt as to his intention to take possession, and he thereby assumes the liability of a mortgagee in possession[1]. Where he gives notice to the tenants to pay their rents to him, it is equally clear that he intends to go into receipt of rents and profits, and this, as regards the liability to account, is equivalent to taking possession[2]. This is also the case if the mortgagee gives notice to the tenants not to pay rent to the mortgagor[3]. The mortgagee must either take possession or leave the mortgagor in possession[4]. A receiver who, on being discharged, continues to receive the rents and pays them to the mortgagee will become the mortgagee's agent so as to put the mortgagee into possession[5].

1   As to taking possession of goods situated on different premises see *Re Eslick, ex p Phillips, ex p Alexander* (1876) 4 ChD 496.
2   See *Horlock v Smith* (1842) 11 LJCh 157. As to the right of the mortgagee in possession to rents and profits see PARA 419 et seq.
3   See *Mexborough UDC v Harrison* [1964] 2 All ER 109 at 111, [1964] 1 WLR 733 at 736–737 per Pennycuick J.
4   *Heales v M'Murray* (1856) 23 Beav 401.
5   *Horlock v Smith* (1842) 11 LJCh 157. As to the appointment of a receiver out of court see PARA 478 et seq. As to the appointment of a receiver by the court see PARA 565 et seq.

416.   Mortgagee substituted for mortgagor in the control of the estate. If a mortgagee merely receives from the mortgagor's agent a sum equal to the rents which the agent has collected, while the agent has not served on the tenants any notice on the mortgagee's behalf, this is not enough to render the mortgagee chargeable as a mortgagee in possession[1]. In order to burden himself with the liability of a mortgagee in possession, the mortgagee must act in such a manner as to substitute himself for the mortgagor in the control and management of the estate[2]. A mortgagee does not assume possession by insuring the property nor by merely making arrangements with the tenants, if they do not recognise him as landlord[3].

1   *Noyes v Pollock* (1886) 32 ChD 53, CA. See also *Mexborough UDC v Harrison* [1964] 2 All ER 109 at 111, [1964] 1 WLR 733 at 736–737 per Pennycuick J.
2   See *Mexborough UDC v Harrison* [1964] 2 All ER 109 at 111, [1964] 1 WLR 733 at 736–737 per Pennycuick J.
3   *Ward v Carttar* (1865) LR 1 Eq 29.

417.   Tenancy created by mortgage deed. Where the mortgage deed creates a tenancy in the mortgagor under the mortgagee at a rent[1], this does not put the mortgagee in possession so as to make him liable to account to subsequent incumbrancers for the amount of the rent reserved[2]; nor is the mortgagee liable in such a case to account as mortgagee in possession to the mortgagor[3].

1   See PARA 345.
2   *Stanley v Grundy* (1883) 22 ChD 478; and see *Re Knight, ex p Isherwood* (1882) 22 ChD 384 at 392, CA. However, there have been several dicta to the contrary: see *Re Stockton Iron Furnace Co* (1879) 10 ChD 335 at 356, CA; *Re Kitchin, ex p Punnett* (1880) 16 ChD 226, CA; *Re Betts, ex p Harrison* (1881) 18 ChD 127 at 135, CA; *Green v Marsh* [1892] 2 QB 330 at 336, CA.
3   *Re Betts, ex p Harrison* (1881) 18 ChD 127, CA.

418.   Appointment of receiver by mortgagee. A mortgagee in possession may relieve himself of his position and responsibility by appointing a receiver under his statutory power[1]; and the court may appoint a receiver after a mortgagee has taken possession if the circumstances render it just and convenient[2].

1   *Anchor Trust Co v Bell* [1926] Ch 805 at 817; *Refuge Assurance Co v Pearlberg* [1938] Ch 687, [1938] 3 All ER 231, CA. As to the statutory power to appoint a receiver out of court see PARA 479.
2   As to the appointment of a receiver by the court see PARA 565 et seq.

(iv) Rights of the Mortgagee in Possession

A. RIGHT TO RENT AND BENEFIT OF COVENANTS

419. When mortgagee becomes entitled to rents and profits. So long as the mortgagee allows the mortgagor to remain in possession, the mortgagor, if in occupation, takes the profits of the land and, if the property is let, takes the rents, in either case for his own use and without liability to account to the mortgagee[1]. The mortgagee, however, on going into possession is entitled to take the rents and profits by virtue of the legal or equitable ownership which the mortgage confers upon him[2].

1   *Trent v Hunt* (1853) 9 Exch 14 at 22. As to the mortgagor's right to receipt of rent and profits see PARAS 341–343.
2   See *Cockburn v Edwards* (1881) 18 ChD 449 at 457, CA. See PARA 406. In relation to tenancies granted on or after 1 January 1996, a mortgagee in possession can enforce any covenant or any right of re-entry enforceable by the mortgagor: see the Landlord and Tenant (Covenants) Act 1995 s 15(1); Landlord and Tenant (Covenants) Act 1995 (Commencement) Order 1995, SI 1995/2963, art 2; and LANDLORD AND TENANT vol 63 (2012) PARA 740. As to rights to crops on agricultural holdings see AGRICULTURAL LAND vol 1 (2008) PARA 369.

420. Rent from tenancies binding on mortgagee. As regards tenancies created before the mortgage or created by the mortgagor after the mortgage under an express or statutory power[1], the mortgagee, as he is entitled to the reversion, may require payment to himself of all arrears of rent existing when he goes into possession[2]. He is entitled to arrears of rent, whether falling due before or after the mortgage was granted, and the claim of the mortgagee will prevail over the claim of persons to whom the rents have been assigned by the mortgagor[3]. The mortgagee can recover also an increased rent which the tenant has agreed with the mortgagor to pay after the date of the mortgage[4]. The rule is restricted to rents proper; it does not extend, in a mortgage of warehouses, to charges for warehousing goods, even though called rents, and recoverable by statute by distraint and sale of the goods[5], or to freight[6]. A mortgagee is not bound by a collateral agreement between the mortgagor and a lessee under a lease created before 1 January 1996 and before the mortgage[7], but if he takes his mortgage with knowledge that the land is used for a particular purpose, he cannot object to that user[8]. A tenant cannot set off a claim for damages against a mortgagor against a mortgagee's claim for rent[9].

1   As to the mortgagor's power to grant leases see PARA 348 et seq.
2   As to tenancies granted before 1 January 1996 see the Law of Property Act 1925 s 141(3); and PARA 425. See also *London and County (A & D) Ltd v Wilfred Sportsman Ltd (Greenwoods (Hosiers and Outfitters) Ltd, third party)* [1971] Ch 764, [1970] 2 All ER 600, CA; *Kataria v Safeland plc* (1997) 75 P & CR D30, [1998] 1 EGLR 39, CA. As to tenancies granted on or after 1 January 1996 see the Landlord and Tenant (Covenants) Act 1995 s 15(1); and PARA 419. As to the mortgagor's right to rent while in possession see PARAS 341–343. See also LANDLORD AND TENANT vol 63 (2012) PARA 718.
3   *Re Ind, Coope & Co Ltd, Fisher v Ind, Coope & Co Ltd, Knox v Ind, Coope & Co Ltd, Arnold v Ind, Coope & Co Ltd* [1911] 2 Ch 223. See also *Rhodes v Allied Dunbar Pension Services Ltd, Re Offshore Ventilation Ltd* [1989] 1 All ER 1161, [1989] 1 WLR 800, CA.
4   *Burrowes v Gradin* (1843) 1 Dow & L 213. See also LANDLORD AND TENANT vol 62 (2012) PARA 246.
5   *Anderson v Butler's Wharf Co Ltd* (1879) 48 LJCh 824.
6   *Rusden v Pope* (1868) LR 3 Exch 269 at 275.
7   *Thomas v Jennings* (1896) 66 LJQB 5. In relation to tenancies granted on or after 1 January 1996, a mortgagee in possession is bound by a covenant that falls to be complied with by the landlord even if contained in a collateral agreement: see the Landlord and Tenant (Covenants) Act 1995 s 15(3); Landlord and Tenant (Covenants) Act 1995 (Commencement) Order 1995, SI 1995/2963, art 2.

8   *Moreland v Richardson* (1857) 24 Beav 33.
9   *Reeves v Pope* [1914] 2 KB 284, CA.

421. Rent from tenancies not binding on mortgagee. Where after the mortgage a tenancy is created which is not binding on the mortgagee[1], he is not entitled to demand payment of the rents as such, but after notice from him to the tenants to pay the rents to him they must not pay rents to the mortgagor, and they are justified in paying the rents to the mortgagee, as otherwise, on recovering possession, he would be entitled to recover the rents as mesne profits[2]. Technically, the claim for mesne profits is for trespass and requires that the mortgagee is to have been in possession during the time for which mesne profits are claimed[3], but on entry by the mortgagee or judgment and possession taken his possession relates back to the date of the mortgage[4], and he can recover the rent accrued due within six years[5] during that period[6]. The mortgagee may include a claim for mesne profits in his claim for recovery of possession of land[7], and he will be allowed to prove when his title to possession accrued, and to recover from the tenant the rents, accrued within six years before proceedings, which have not been paid to the mortgagor.

1   See PARA 295 et seq.
2   *Pope v Biggs* (1829) 9 B & C 245 at 257; *Wyse v Myers* (1854) 4 ICLR 101; *Underhay v Read* (1887) 20 QBD 209, CA. See also *Rusden v Pope* (1868) LR 3 Exch 269 at 275. As to mesne profits see LANDLORD AND TENANT vol 62 (2012) PARA 285.
3   *Turner v Cameron's Coalbrook Steam Coal Co* (1850) 5 Exch 932.
4   See PARA 400.
5   As to the six-year limitation period applicable to the recovery of arrears of rent see LIMITATION PERIODS vol 68 (2008) PARA 1033.
6   *Barnett v Earl of Guildford* (1855) 11 Exch 19 (overruling *Litchfield v Ready* (1850) 5 Exch 939); *Ocean Accident and Guarantee Corpn Ltd v Ilford Gas Co* [1905] 2 KB 493 at 498, CA. See also *Harris v Mulkern* (1875) 1 ExD 31.
7   *Dunlop v Macedo* (1891) 8 TLR 43. See also *Brandreth v Shears* [1883] WN 89.

422. Right where rent paid is advance to mortgagor. If the tenant has paid rent to the mortgagor before it was due, this is not a good payment against the mortgagee as regards rent accruing due after notice of the mortgage has been given to the tenant, and the tenant is liable to pay that rent over again to the mortgagee[1]; but if before the mortgage the tenant has paid a lump sum in satisfaction of all rents accruing during the term, and the mortgagee makes no inquiry of the tenant, he is bound by this payment[2].

1   *De Nicholls v Saunders* (1870) LR 5 CP 589; *Cook v Guerra* (1872) LR 7 CP 132; *Lord Ashburton v Nocton* [1915] 1 Ch 274 at 282, CA; *Smallman Ltd v Castle* [1932] IR 294.
2   *Green v Rheinberg* (1911) 104 LT 149, CA.

423. Rents in hands of receiver. Where a receiver has been appointed by the court, the mortgagee may obtain possession by applying for his discharge[1]. Whether rents then received by and remaining in the receiver's hands belong to the mortgagee or not depends on the object of the receiver's appointment[2]. If he has been appointed in proceedings only affecting the title to the equity of redemption, for example, in proceedings to administer the trusts of the mortgagor's will[3], or in other proceedings in which the mortgagee's title is not in question[4], the mortgagee is not entitled to past rents, but only to rents paid after he applied to discharge the receiver[5]. Where a mortgagee has let the mortgagor remain in possession and rents are received by the receiver appointed in a debenture holders' claim to which the mortgagee is not a party, any rents which as between the parties to the claim turn out to have been received for the mortgagor will not be paid over by the receiver to the mortgagee[6]. If, however, the receiver is appointed on behalf of incumbrancers on the property generally, or to settle a dispute as to title in which the mortgagee is interested, the mortgagee is entitled to rents in the receiver's hands[7]; and where sequestrators have been appointed, the mortgagee is entitled to rents received by the sequestrators and remaining in their hands when he makes his claim[8].

1 See PARAS 343, 411. As to a mortgagee's right to possession where his rights have been expressly preserved by the order appointing the receiver see PARA 569. As to appointment of a receiver by the court see PARA 565 et seq.
2 *Re Hoare, Hoare v Owen* [1892] 3 Ch 94 at 103. See also *Re Metropolitan Amalgamated Estates Ltd, Fairweather v Metropolitan Amalgamated Estates Ltd* [1912] 2 Ch 497 at 503.
3 *Thomas v Brigstocke* (1827) 4 Russ 64.
4 *Gresley v Adderley, Gresley v Heathcoat* (1818) 1 Swan 573 at 579. See also *Bertie v Earl of Abingdon* (1817) 3 Mer 560.
5 Ie after the date of service of his application: *Preston v Tunbridge Wells Opera House Ltd* [1903] 2 Ch 323. See also *Re Metropolitan Amalgamated Estates Ltd, Fairweather v Metropolitan Amalgamated Estates Ltd* [1912] 2 Ch 497 at 502.
6 *Re Lands Securities Co, ex p Norwich Life Insurance Society* (1894) 13 R 48.
7 *Gresley v Adderley, Gresley v Heathcoat* (1818) 1 Swan 573; *Re Hoare, Hoare v Owen* [1892] 3 Ch 94.
8 See PARA 343.

424. Application of rents received by mortgagee. The rents received by a mortgagee in possession are applicable in the first instance in paying the current outgoings such as rents, rates and taxes, repairs, insurance premiums and the interest on prior incumbrances[1]. The balance is then applicable, first, in payment of interest on the mortgage debt, and on expenses of improvements and otherwise, which the mortgagee is entitled to add to principal; and, secondly, in payment of the principal and of capital expenditure added to principal[2]. The mortgagee is not restricted to paying his interest out of the rents unless special provision to that effect is made by the mortgage deed[3]. The mode in which the rents are thus applied depends on whether the accounts are taken with or without rests[4].

1 As to the application of money received by a mortgagee's receiver see the Law of Property Act 1925 s 109(8); and PARA 486. See also *Bompas v King* (1886) 33 ChD 279, CA.
2 See the order in *Webb v Rorke* (1806) 2 Sch & Lef 661 at 676.
3 *Re Betts, ex p Harrison* (1881) 18 ChD 127 at 136, CA; *Re Knight, ex p Isherwood* (1882) 22 ChD 384 at 392, CA.
4 See PARA 722.

425. Mortgagee's right to benefit of covenants. A mortgagee of premises subject to a lease granted before 1 January 1996[1] is entitled to enforce and take advantage of covenants having reference to the subject matter of a lease given by the lessee and rights of re-entry[2]. The mortgagee can also re-enter for breaches of covenant committed since the mortgage, and breaches of covenant committed before the mortgage unless they had been waived or released at the time of the mortgage[3]. A mortgagee in possession of leasehold premises is entitled to the benefit of covenants by the lessor which touch and concern the land[4].

A mortgagee in possession of premises subject to a lease granted on or after 1 January 1996 can enforce any tenant covenant[5] or right of re-entry which is enforceable by the mortgagor[6]. A landlord covenant[7] which is enforceable against a landlord is also enforceable by a mortgagee in possession of the tenant's interest[8].

1 Ie the commencement date of the Landlord and Tenant (Covenants) Act 1995: see the Landlord and Tenant (Covenants) Act 1995 (Commencement) Order 1995, SI 1995/2963, art 2.
2 See the Law of Property Act 1925 s 141(1), (2); Landlord and Tenant (Covenants) Act 1995 s 30(4). See also *Greenaway v Hart* (1854) 14 CB 340; *Yellowly v Gower* (1855) 11 Exch 274; *Municipal Permanent Investment Building Society v Smith* (1888) 22 QBD 70, CA. As to the rights of a mortgagor in possession see PARA 341 et seq.

3 See the Law of Property Act 1925 s 141(3); Landlord and Tenant (Covenants) Act 1995 s 30(4).
4 *Spencer's Case* (1583) 5 Co Rep 16a. See also the Law of Property Act 1925 s 78; and LANDLORD AND TENANT vol 63 (2012) PARA 714; REAL PROPERTY AND REGISTRATION vol 87 (2012) PARA 1081.
5 'Tenant covenant', in relation to a tenancy, means a covenant falling to be complied with by the tenant of premises demised by the tenancy: see the Landlord and Tenant (Covenants) Act 1995 s 28(1).
6 See the Landlord and Tenant (Covenants) Act 1995 s 15(1). This right appears to extend to rent in arrears and existing breaches. See further LANDLORD AND TENANT vol 63 (2012) PARA 740.
7 'Landlord covenant', in relation to a tenancy, means a covenant falling to be complied with by the landlord of premises demised by the tenancy: see the Landlord and Tenant (Covenants) Act 1995 s 28(1).
8 See the Landlord and Tenant (Covenants) Act 1995 s 15(3). For these purposes, 'mortgagee' includes a chargee: s 15(6). See further LANDLORD AND TENANT vol 63 (2012) PARA 740.

B. CONDUCT OF BUSINESS

426. Mortgagee's power to carry on business. Where the mortgage security includes a business carried on upon the mortgaged premises[1], the mortgagee on entering is entitled to carry on the business for a reasonable time with a view to sale[2]. The mortgagee would, however, normally appoint a receiver to carry on the business[3] or apply to the court for an appointment of a receiver and manager[4].

1 As to whether the mortgage includes the business see *Whitley v Challis* [1892] 1 Ch 64, CA; *County of Gloucester Bank v Rudry Merthyr Steam and House Coal Colliery Co* [1895] 1 Ch 629, CA; *Re Leas Hotel Co, Salter v Leas Hotel Co* [1902] 1 Ch 332; *Leney & Sons Ltd v Callingham and Thompson* [1908] 1 KB 79, CA; and see *Re Bennett, Clarke v White* [1899] 1 Ch 316. As to goodwill see PARA 172.
2 *Cook v Thomas* (1876) 24 WR 427. As to the liabilities and powers of the mortgagee carrying on business see PARA 427. As to the duties of a mortgagee who does decide to carry on a business see PARA 429 et seq.
3 As to the appointment of a receiver out of court see PARA 478 et seq.
4 As to the appointment of a receiver by the court see PARA 565 et seq.

427. Liabilities and powers of mortgagee carrying on business. By carrying on the business the mortgagee does not render himself liable on the existing contracts of the business[1] unless he adopts them so as to effect a novation[2], but he is personally liable on any new contracts into which he enters[3]. He becomes owner of the business, and stands, as regards his powers, in the mortgagor's place[4]. The power may be exercised although the consequences are disadvantageous to the mortgagor[5]. The mortgagee is not, however, obliged to appoint a receiver to run the business, nor is he under any duty to preserve the goodwill prior to taking possession[6]. A receiver owes more extensive duties[7].

1 As to the mortgagee's power to carry on business on the mortgaged premises see PARA 426.
2 As to novation see CONTRACT vol 22 (2012) PARA 598 et seq. It seems that the entry by the mortgagee normally operates as a dismissal of the employees employed in the business: *Reid v Explosives Co Ltd* (1887) 19 QBD 264 at 267, 269, CA. As to the position where the court appoints a receiver and manager of a company's business see COMPANIES vol 15 (2009) PARA 1372 et seq.
3 Cf *Burt, Boulton and Hayward v Bull* [1895] 1 QB 276, CA.
4 *Chaplin v Young* (1864) 33 Beav 330 at 337.
5 *Downsview Nominees Ltd v First City Corpn Ltd* [1993] AC 295, [1993] 3 All ER 626, PC.
6 *AIB Finance Ltd v Debtors* [1998] 2 All ER 929, [1998] 1 BCLC 665, CA. As to goodwill generally see COMPETITION vol 18 (2009) PARAS 373–376; PARTNERSHIP vol 79 (2014) PARA 212 et seq; PERSONAL PROPERTY vol 80 (2013) PARA 807 et seq. As to the duties of a mortgagee who does decide to carry on a business see PARA 429 et seq.
7 See PARA 482.

C.　LEASING POWERS OF THE MORTGAGEE IN POSSESSION

428.　Mortgagee's leasing powers. A mortgagee who is in possession[1], or who has appointed a receiver of the rents and profits of the mortgaged property[2], has the same statutory powers of leasing and accepting surrenders of leases as are enjoyed by a mortgagor in possession[3]. A lease by the mortgagee not made under the statutory power or under any express power contained in the mortgage deed or with the mortgagor's consent[4] is not binding on the mortgagor after redemption[5]. Consequently, where the lease is not made under the statutory power, nor under an express power of leasing, both mortgagor and mortgagee should concur to grant it[6]. The lease operates then as a demise by the mortgagee and confirmation by the mortgagor[7]. The lease should treat the mortgagee as the actual lessor[8].

1　See the Law of Property Act 1925 ss 99(2), 100(2); and PARAS 349, 355. See also *Berkshire Capital Funding Ltd v Street* (1999) Times, 27 May, CA.
2　See the Law of Property Act 1925 ss 99(19), 100(13); and PARAS 349, 355.
3　As to the statutory powers of leasing see PARA 349 et seq.
4　The consent need not be under seal in order to render the lease binding on the mortgagor: *Chapman v Smith* [1907] 2 Ch 97 at 102. A lease granted by the mortgagee is binding on a purchaser from the mortgagee: *Chapman v Smith* above at 103.
5　*Franklinski v Ball* (1864) 33 Beav 560. It may, perhaps, be otherwise where the granting of the lease was urgent: *Hungerford v Clay* (1722) 9 Mod Rep 1 at 2.
6　*Doe d Barney v Adams* (1832) 2 Cr & J 232; cf *Smith v Pocklington* (1831) 1 Cr & J 445.
7　*Doe d Barney v Adams* (1832) 2 Cr & J 232; cf *Smith v Pocklington* (1831) 1 Cr & J 445.
8　See *Webb v Russell* (1789) 3 Term Rep 393; *Saunders v Merryweather* (1865) 3 H & C 902.

(v)　Liabilities of the Mortgagee in Possession

A.　GENERAL DUTIES OF THE MORTGAGEE IN POSSESSION

429.　General duties of the mortgagee in possession. A mortgagee who goes into possession becomes the manager of the charged property[1]. He thereby assumes a duty to take reasonable care of the property[2]. This requires him to be active in protecting and exploiting the security, maximising the return, but without taking undue risks[3].

1　*Kendle v Melsom* (1998) 193 CLR 46, Aust HC; *Silven Properties Ltd v Royal Bank of Scotland plc* [2003] EWCA Civ 1409, [2004] 4 All ER 484, [2004] 1 WLR 997.
2　*Downsview Nominees Ltd v First City Corpn Ltd* [1993] AC 295, [1993] 3 All ER 626, PC; *Silven Properties Ltd v Royal Bank of Scotland plc* [2003] EWCA Civ 1409, [2004] 4 All ER 484.
3　*Palk v Mortgage Services Funding plc* [1993] Ch 330, [1993] 2 All ER 481, CA; *Silven Properties Ltd v Royal Bank of Scotland plc* [2003] EWCA Civ 1409, [2004] 4 All ER 484, [2004] 1 WLR 997.

B.　MORTGAGEE'S LIABILITY TO ACCOUNT

430.　Mortgagee's liability to account for wilful default. A mortgagee who goes into possession of the mortgaged property, and thereby excludes the mortgagor from control of it, is bound to account to the mortgagor, not only for the rents and profits which he actually receives, but also for the rents and profits which, but for his wilful default or neglect, he might have received[1]; that is, for everything which he has received, or might or ought to have received, while he continued in possession[2]. The usual form of order is for an account of the rents and profits of the hereditaments comprised in the mortgage received by the mortgagee, or by any other person for the order or use of the mortgagee, or which, without the mortgagee's wilful default, might have been so received[3]. The rule as to the footing on which accounts are to be taken applies both to tangible property and to the goodwill of a business[4], and not only to rents and profits, such as the rents and profits of land, or the profits of a business[5], but also to the corpus of the mortgaged property. It seems that, where stock is mortgaged, and the mortgagee makes a profit by selling and repurchasing, he must account for this[6].

A co-owner of a patent who is also mortgagee of the share of another co-owner, while bound to account to his mortgagor for royalties, need not account for the profits derived from his own use of the patent, as he is entitled to this use as co-owner[7].

If the assignee of a judgment debt issues execution on it, thereby in effect going into possession, but omits to proceed with the execution and the debt is lost, he must account for it[8]. So, also, an assignee of a debt who is empowered to sue for it but fails to do so must account for any loss incurred by his forbearance[9], but this principle does not apply to a mere equitable assignee[10]. Where a lease is forfeited through the mortgagee's default, he is liable in respect of the forfeiture[11]. An account against a mortgagee in possession who has sold the mortgaged property is on the footing of wilful default[12].

The rule as to the footing on which accounts are to be taken is based on the principle that, as the property is only a security for the money, the mortgagee must be diligent in realising the amount due in order that he may restore the property to the mortgagor[13]. He does not, however, account for profits arising from business done in connection with the mortgaged premises which do not arise from the premises[14]. The duties owed by the mortgagee are equitable, and cannot be replaced or supplemented by a liability in negligence[15].

1   *Hughes v Williams* (1806) 12 Ves 493; *Quarrell v Beckford* (1816) 1 Madd 269 at 274; *Rowe v Wood* (1822) 2 Jac & W 553 at 556; *Williams v Price* (1824) 1 Sim & St 581 at 587; *Parkinson v Hanbury* (1867) LR 2 HL 1 at 14; *National Bank of Australasia v United Hand-in-Hand and Band of Hope Co* (1879) 4 App Cas 391 at 409, PC; *Gaskell v Gosling* [1896] 1 QB 669 at 691, CA. There is an early decision to the contrary: *Anon* (1675) 1 Cas in Ch 258.
        As to how far the mortgagee's liability for wilful default account extends see PARA 431. As to accounts between mortgagee and mortgagor generally see PARA 709 et seq. As to accounts by the mortgagee in possession see further PARA 718 et seq.
2   *Chaplin v Young* (1864) 33 Beav 330 at 337.
3   See the note to *Harnard v Webster* (1725) Cas *temp* King (2nd Edn) 53. See also PARA 598 et seq.
4   *Mayer v Murray* (1878) 8 ChD 424. As to goodwill generally see COMPETITION vol 18 (2009) PARAS 373–376; PARTNERSHIP vol 79 (2014) PARA 212 et seq; PERSONAL PROPERTY vol 80 (2013) PARA 807 et seq.
5   *Chaplin v Young* (1864) 33 Beav 330.
6   *Langton v Waite* (1868) LR 6 Eq 165; revsd on another point (1869) 4 Ch App 402.
7   *Steers v Rogers* [1892] 2 Ch 13, CA (affd [1893] AC 232, HL); cf *Heyl Dia v Edmunds* (1899) 48 WR 167.
8   *Williams v Price* (1824) 1 Sim & St 581 at 587.
9   *Ex p Mure* (1788) 2 Cox Eq Cas 63 at 75.
10 *Glyn v Hood* (1860) 1 De G F & J 334 at 348.
11 *Perry v Walker* (1855) 3 Eq Rep 721.
12 *Mayer v Murray* (1878) 8 ChD 424; *National Bank of Australasia v United Hand-in-Hand and Band of Hope Co* (1879) 4 App Cas 391 at 409, PC.
13 *Lord Kensington v Bouverie* (1855) 7 De GM & G 134 at 157; and see *Sherwin v Shakespear* (1854) 5 De GM & G 517 at 536.
14 *White v City of London Brewery Co* (1889) 42 ChD 237, CA (mortgagees' profits as brewers from sale of beer to tenant to whom they had let the premises).
15 *Downsview Nominees Ltd v First City Corpn Ltd* [1993] AC 295, [1993] 3 All ER 626, PC.

431. How far the mortgagee's liability for wilful default account extends. The mortgagee accounts on the same footing to all persons interested in the equity of redemption, and remains liable to account notwithstanding that he has assigned the mortgage[1], unless he has assigned it under court order[2]. The rule as to the footing on which a mortgagee must account[3] applies, however, only when the mortgagee enters in his character as mortgagee, so that he knows that he is in possession and chargeable accordingly[4]. Thus a mortgagee in occupation as tenant does not account as mortgagee in possession[5], but, where a tenancy is created in favour of the mortgagee after a second mortgage, the prior mortgagee accounts as mortgagee in possession to the second mortgagee[6]. A person, therefore, who enters as a purchaser and who, on the sale going off, has a lien for purchase money which he has paid is not liable to account as mortgagee in possession[7]. A vendor in possession with a lien for the unpaid purchase money is not ordinarily chargeable as a mortgagee in possession[8], although he may become so chargeable by insisting on retaining possession when he might properly give it up[9]. A mortgagee can escape the liabilities of a mortgagee in possession by entering as agent for a prior incumbrancer, but not, it seems, as agent for the mortgagor[10]. The mortgagee must account notwithstanding that the agent who received the rents for him is dead[11].

1   *Hinde v Blake* (1841) 11 LJCh 26; *Hall v Heward* (1886) 32 ChD 430, CA. See also *Venables v Foyle* (1661) 1 Cas in Ch 2. As to the rule that the mortgagee in possession is liable to account for wilful default see PARA 430.
2   *Hall v Heward* (1886) 32 ChD 430, CA. The rule as to the footing on which a mortgagee must account was applied to a mortgage by way of trust for sale, and the mortgagee accounted as mortgagee in possession from the time when he entered into possession, but not before: *Beare v Prior* (1843) 6 Beav 183. The mortgagee accounted as such and not as trustee: *Chambers v Goldwin* (1801) 5 Ves 834 at 837; on appeal (1804) 9 Ves 254. As to these mortgages see *Re Alison, Johnson v Mounsey* (1879) 11 ChD 284, CA; *Re Metropolis and Counties Permanent Investment Building Society, Gatfield's Case* [1911] 1 Ch 698. A legal mortgage in this form cannot now be made as a mortgage of land by conveyance or trust for sale now takes effect as a mortgage by demise: see the Law of Property Act 1925 s 85(2), (3); and PARA 161. As to a trustee's liability to account see TRUSTS AND POWERS vol 98 (2013) PARA 693. A trust for sale is now referred to as a trust of land: see the Trusts of Land and Appointment of Trustees Act 1996 s 1; and REAL PROPERTY AND REGISTRATION vol 87 (2012) PARA 105.
3   See PARA 430.
4   *Parkinson v Hanbury* (1867) LR 2 HL 1 at 14.
5   *Page v Linwood* (1837) 4 Cl & Fin 399 at 434, HL; cf *Morony v O'Dea* (1809) 1 Ball & B 109 at 117. A mortgagee of the inheritance who was in possession as purchaser of the life estate did not account as a mortgagee in possession: *Whitbread v Smith* (1854) 3 De GM & G 727 at 741; cf *Lord Kensington v Bouverie* (1855) 7 De GM & G 134 at 144; and see *Blennerhassett v Day* (1812) 2 Ball & B 104 at 125.
6   *Gregg v Arrott* (1835) L & G temp Sugd 246.
7   *Parkinson v Hanbury* (1867) LR 2 HL 1 at 14 (where, however, the contrary decision in *Adams v Sworder* (1864) 2 De GJ & Sm 44 at 60 was not mentioned).
8   *Sherwin v Shakespear* (1854) 5 De GM & G 517.
9   *Phillips v Silvester* (1872) 8 Ch App 173. See also EQUITABLE JURISDICTION vol 47 (2014) PARAS 214–215; LIEN vol 68 (2008) PARA 855 et seq.
10 *Refuge Assurance Co Ltd v Pearlberg* [1938] Ch 687, [1938] 3 All ER 231, CA.
11 *Noyes v Pollock* (1885) 30 ChD 336, CA.

432. Amount charged when property let or unlet. Where the mortgaged property is let at the time of the mortgagee taking possession, he is charged with the rents at the rate reserved[1], if he could with due diligence have recovered them[2]. A mortgagee must use the usual means to recover the rents if they are likely to prove effectual[3]. When the property is not let, he must use due diligence to let it[4], and, if it remains unlet through his default, he is charged with the rents which ought to have been obtained. The mortgagee is under no duty to let the property if a letting might hinder or interfere with an intended sale of the property[5]. It has been said that the rent obtained will be deemed to be the same throughout the time during which the mortgagee is in possession, unless he shows to the contrary[6]. The burden of proving wilful default is, in the first instance, on the person alleging it, but if he shows that the premises were capable of being let and were left vacant the burden is shifted, and the mortgagee must prove that no tenant could be obtained[7]. If resident at a distance, the mortgagee is justified in acting on an agent's advice as to letting the property[8]. If the mortgagor is a party to any act to prevent the letting, this is an answer to the charge of wilful default[9]; if he knows that the property is let at an undervalue, he should give notice of the fact to the mortgagee[10] unless the mortgagee already knows that a better rent could be obtained[11]. If by obtaining an advantage for himself[12], or by underhand dealing with the tenant[13], or by wantonly changing the tenant[14], the mortgagee lets the property at less than the full rent, he is charged with the full rent. Similarly, if the mortgagee turns out or refuses to accept a suitable tenant he is chargeable with the rent which he might have received[15].

If the mortgagee goes into actual occupation himself[16], he will be charged with a fair occupation rent[17], but he is not to be charged a higher rent on account of improvements effected by himself, unless he is allowed the expense of the improvements[18]. Unless the mortgagee admits occupation, an inquiry will be directed[19]. The mortgagee is not chargeable with an occupation rent on the ground that on selling the property he has let the purchaser into possession before the date for completion[20].

It has been said that the mortgagee is charged with the utmost value the property is proved to be worth[21], but it seems that this statement is too wide; if the mortgagee occupies under a lease from the mortgagor, he is chargeable only with the rent reserved if the amount is proper, notwithstanding that the lease is set aside[22].

The mortgagee is not liable for rent while the property, from its ruinous condition or otherwise, is incapable of beneficial occupation[23].

1 *Lord Trimleston v Hamill* (1810) 1 Ball & B 377 at 385.
2 *Noyes v Pollock* (1886) 32 ChD 53 at 61, CA. See also *Brandon v Brandon* (1862) 10 WR 287.
3 *Duke of Bucks v Gayer* (1684) 1 Vern 258. The common law right to distrain for arrears of rent was abolished by the Tribunals, Courts and Enforcement Act 2007 s 71 and replaced with a system of commercial rent arrears recovery: see LANDLORD AND TENANT vol 62 (2012) PARA 419 et seq.
4 *Blacklock v Barnes* (1725) Cas *temp* King 53.
5 See *Downsview Nominees Ltd v First City Corpn Ltd* [1993] AC 295, [1993] 3 All ER 626, PC; *China and South Sea Bank Ltd v Tan Soon Gin (alias George Tan)* [1990] 1 AC 536, [1989] 3 All ER 839, PC; *Huish v Ellis* [1995] BCC 462, [1995] NPC 3. A mortgagee is entitled to choose when to sell the property and is not obliged to exercise other powers in the meantime: *Kennedy v General Credits* (1982) 2 BPR 9456.
6 *Metcalf v Campion* (1828) 1 Mol 238; *Brandon v Brandon* (1862) 10 WR 287.
7 *Brandon v Brandon* (1862) 10 WR 287.
8 *Brandon v Brandon* (1862) 10 WR 287.
9 *Metcalfe v Campion* (1828) 1 Mol 238.
10 *Hughes v Williams* (1806) 12 Ves 493.
11 *Shepherd v Spanheath Ltd* [1988] EGCS 35, CA.
12 *White v City of London Brewery Co* (1889) 42 ChD 237, CA, where brewers who were mortgagees let a public house with a tied house covenant.
13 *Metcalfe v Campion* (1828) 1 Mol 238.
14 *Hughes v Williams* (1806) 12 Ves 493.
15 *Anon* (1682) 1 Vern 45.
16 See *Trulock v Robey* (1846) 15 Sim 265 at 273; *Shepard v Jones* (1882) 21 ChD 469 at 475, CA.
17 *Metcalfe v Campion* (1828) 1 Mol 238; *Fee v Cobine* (1847) 11 I Eq R 406 at 410; *Marriott v Anchor Reversionary Co Ltd* (1861) 3 De GF & J 177 at 193. See also *Fyfe v Smith* [1975] 2 NSWLR 408.
18 *Bright v Campbell* (1885) 54 LJCh 1077, CA.
19 3 Seton's Form of Decrees, Judgments and Orders (7th Edn, 1912) 1887.
20 *Shepard v Jones* (1882) 21 ChD 469, CA.
21 *Lord Trimleston v Hamill* (1810) 1 Ball & B 377 at 385.

22   *Gubbins v Creed* (1804) 2 Sch & Lef 214 at 224; *Webb v Rorke* (1806) 2 Sch & Lef 661 at 674.
23   *Marshall v Cave* (1824) 3 LJOS Ch 57.

433. Mortgagee's liability to subsequent incumbrancer. If he has surplus rents in hand after satisfying his interest, the mortgagee in possession can pay them to the mortgagor, provided that he has received no notice of any subsequent incumbrance, and neither he nor the mortgagor is liable to account for them to a subsequent incumbrancer[1]. This is in accordance with the rule that the mortgagor is not bound to account for rents which the mortgagee allows him to receive[2]. The rule applies to a mortgage for a term[3] and of a life estate[4], and notwithstanding that a receiver is in possession appointed otherwise than on the mortgagee's behalf[5]. It applies also to receipt by the mortgagor's trustee in bankruptcy, unless he has retained the rents in violation of an agreement to apply them in payment of interest[6]. However, once the mortgagee has notice of a subsequent incumbrance entitling the subsequent incumbrancer to the rents and profits, he will be liable to the subsequent incumbrancer for any surplus rents paid to the mortgagor[7]. The taking by a second incumbrancer of proceedings to which the first mortgagee is made a party for the purpose of enforcing the second incumbrancer's security amounts to notice to the first mortgagee of the second incumbrancer's right to receive surplus rents[8].

Where separate properties subject to separate mortgages are included in the same lease, the rent is apportioned between the two mortgagees notwithstanding that by error the whole has been reserved to one of them[9].

1   See PARA 343. See also *Drummond v Duke of St Albans* (1800) 5 Ves 433 at 438.
2   See PARAS 342–343. See also *Drummond v Duke of St Albans* (1800) 5 Ves 433 at 438.
3   *Gresley v Adderley, Gresley v Heathcoat* (1818) 1 Swan 573 at 579.
4   *Colman v Duke of St Albans* (1796) 3 Ves 25.
5   *Flight v Camac* (1856) 25 LJCh 654.
6   *Ex p Calwell* (1828) 1 Mol 259.
7   *Berney v Sewell* (1820) 1 Jac & W 647 at 650; *Archdeacon v Bowes* (1824) 13 Price 353 at 368. See also *Maddocks v Wren* (1680) 2 Rep Ch 209; *Holton v Lloyd* (1827) 1 Mol 30 at 31; *Clark v Cook* (1849) 3 De G & Sm 333 at 336.
8   *Parker v Calcraft* (1821) 6 Madd 11 at 12. The taking of those proceedings by the second incumbrancer amounts to the taking of equitable possession: *Parker v Calcraft* at 12. As to the principle that the second incumbrancer, where he has a legal mortgage, is entitled to take actual possession subject to the first mortgagee's rights see PARA 404.
9   *Harryman v Collins* (1854) 18 Beav 11.

C.   LIABILITY UNDER COVENANTS

434. Burden of leasehold covenants. In relation to leases granted before 1 January 1996[1], the relationship of lessor and lessee is not affected by a mortgage, so that the lessee remains liable to perform the covenants whether or not a mortgagee takes possession[2].

In relation to tenancies granted on or after 1 January 1996, where any landlord covenant[3] of a tenancy is enforceable against the reversioner in respect of any premises demised by the tenancy, it is also enforceable against either any person (other than the reversioner) who, as the holder of the immediate reversion in those premises, is for the time being entitled to the rents and profits under the tenancy in respect of those premises, or any mortgagee in possession of the reversion in those premises who is so entitled[4]. Any landlord covenant of a tenancy which is enforceable by the tenant in respect of any premises demised by the tenancy is also enforceable by any mortgagee in possession of those premises under a mortgage granted by the tenant[5]. Any tenant covenant[6] of a tenancy, or right of re-entry contained in a tenancy, which is enforceable against the tenant in respect of any premises demised by the tenancy is also enforceable against any mortgagee in possession of the tenant's interest[7]. Covenants which are expressed to be personal or are unenforceable for non-registration are not enforceable against a mortgagee in possession[8].

1   Ie the commencement date of the Landlord and Tenant (Covenants) Act 1995: see the Landlord and Tenant (Covenants) Act 1995 (Commencement) Order 1995, SI 1995/2963, art 2.
2   *Bonner v Tottenham and Edmonton Permanent Investment Building Society* [1899] 1 QB 161; *Smith v Spaul* [2002] EWCA Civ 1830, [2003] QB 983, [2003] 1 All ER 509. However, cf the Law of Property Act 1925 s 142(1); *Wilson v Queen's Club* [1891] 3 Ch 522; and LANDLORD AND TENANT vol 63 (2012) PARA 719. Cf *Municipal Permanent Investment Building Society v Smith* (1888) 22 QBD 70, CA. As to the benefit of covenants see PARA 425. As to the transmission of the burden of covenants see LANDLORD AND TENANT vol 63 (2012) PARA 719.
3   As to the meaning of 'landlord covenant' see PARA 425 note 7.
4   Landlord and Tenant (Covenants) Act 1995 s 15(1), (2).
5   Landlord and Tenant (Covenants) Act 1995 s 15(3). 'Mortgagee' includes chargee: see s 15(6).
6   As to the meaning of 'tenant covenant' see PARA 425 note 5.
7   See the Landlord and Tenant (Covenants) Act 1995 s 15(4).
8   See the Landlord and Tenant (Covenants) Act 1995 s 15(5) (amended by the Land Registration Act 2002 s 133, Sch 11 para 33(1), (2)).

435.   Burden of freehold covenants. The burden of a positive covenant does not run with the land so as to bind a mortgagee[1], but the burden of a restrictive covenant is in certain circumstances enforceable in equity against successors in title of a covenantor[2].

1   A mortgagee who seeks to take the benefit of a deed may be liable to assume the burdens under it: *Halsall v Brizell* [1957] Ch 169, [1957] 1 All ER 371.
2   See REAL PROPERTY AND REGISTRATION vol 87 (2012) PARA 1081. As to restrictive covenants running with the land see REAL PROPERTY AND REGISTRATION vol 87 (2012) PARA 1076 et seq.

D.   MORTGAGEE'S LIABILITY TO EXECUTE REPAIRS

436.   Extent of mortgagee's liability to execute repairs. The mortgagee's liability to keep the mortgaged premises in repair depends on the considerations that by taking possession he has excluded the mortgagor from control of the property, and that the rents are the proper fund out of which to provide for repairs. The mortgagee is not, however, judged by the degree of care which a person would take of his own property. He is chargeable in respect of gross negligence[1]; and if his default may cause a forfeiture of leasehold property, he is bound to act as a provident owner and to do what is necessary to prevent the forfeiture[2]. He must, at any rate to the extent of surplus rents in his hands after the interest due on his mortgage is satisfied, do such repairs as are required to maintain the premises in a proper state of preservation[3]. On a prima facie case being made out, an inquiry as to deterioration will be directed[4].

The mortgagee is not bound, however, to keep the premises in as good repair as that in which he found them, and when he has done ordinary repairs he will not be charged with deterioration due to the lapse of time[5]; nor, where the buildings are in such a state that a prudent owner would pull them down and rebuild, is the mortgagee bound to do this[6]. The mortgagee must not pull down buildings[7] except to substitute new buildings for decayed old buildings without changing their purpose[8].

1   *Wragg v Denham* (1836) 2 Y & C Ex 117; *Silven Properties Ltd v Royal Bank of Scotland plc* [2003] EWCA Civ 1409, [2004] 4 All ER 484, [2004] 1 WLR 997.
2   *Perry v Walker* (1855) 3 Eq Rep 721. As to depreciation of a ship owing to improper working by mortgagees see *Marriott v Anchor Reversionary Co Ltd* (1861) 3 De GF & J 177.
3   *Richards v Morgan* (1753) 4 Y & C Ex 570 (Appendix); and see *Moore v Painter* (1842) 6 Jur 903.

4   Cf *Batchelor v Middleton* (1848) 6 Hare 75 at 85, where an inquiry was directed whether the
    mortgagee, to the damage and injury of the mortgagor, had allowed buildings to fall down.
5   *Russel v Smithies* (1794) 1 Anst 96; *Wragg v Denham* (1836) 2 Y & C Ex 117.
6   *Moore v Painter* (1842) 6 Jur 903.
7   *Sandon v Hooper* (1843) 6 Beav 246.
8   *Marshall v Cave* (1824) 3 LJOS Ch 57. As to insurance by the mortgagee see PARA 201.

437. Extent of repair authorised. The mortgagee must not burden the equity of
redemption[1] so as to make it more difficult for the mortgagor to redeem, and on
redemption he must be able to hand back the property as far as possible in its
original condition. The mortgagee must not improve the mortgagor out of his
estate[2]. Hence, he must not make a large outlay on permanent improvements
unless he obtains the mortgagor's consent, or unless the mortgagor, after notice,
acquiesces[3], nor may he change the character of the property, even though such
change constitutes an improvement[4], but he may make reasonable improvements
without notice to the mortgagor[5]. On the other hand, the mortgagee is not bound
to rebuild or to lay out large sums beyond the rent, for this would be to lend more
money upon, perhaps, a deficient security[6]. Expenditure properly made is allowed
to the mortgagee in his accounts[7].

1   As to the equity of redemption see PARAS 107, 304 et seq.
2   *Sandon v Hooper* (1843) 6 Beav 246.
3   *Sandon v Hooper* (1843) 6 Beav 246; *Shepard v Jones* (1882) 21 ChD 469 at 479, CA; cf *Gubbins
    v Creed* (1804) 2 Sch & Lef 214 at 227. Mere notice does not affect the mortgagor if he does
    nothing; there must be some specific sign of acquiescence: *Shepard v Jones* at 479.
4   *Moore v Painter* (1842) 6 Jur 903; *Bright v Campbell* (1885) 54 LJCh 1077, CA.
5   *Shepard v Jones* (1882) 21 ChD 469 at 479, CA.
6   *Richards v Morgan* (1753) 4 Y & C Ex 570 (Appendix).
7   See PARA 749.

E.   MORTGAGEE'S LIABILITY FOR WASTE

438. General rule as regards mortgagee's liability for waste. A mortgagee who
formerly took the legal estate in fee simple became the absolute owner at law, and
hence could not strictly commit waste[1], and a mortgage by demise under the
present law[2] is expressed to be without impeachment of waste[3]. In equity the
mortgagee is subject to the rule that he must on redemption give back the property
unimpaired, and, therefore, unless his security is deficient, he may not destroy any
part of the inheritance. If he does so, he must make good the loss to the mortgagor
in taking the accounts[4].

1   See PARA 161. As to the mortgagor's liability for waste see PARAS 360–361.
2   As to mortgage by demise see PARAS 164. For mortgages of freeholds before 1926 see PARA 161.
3   As to a legal charge see PARA 165.
4   *Millett v Davey* (1862) 9 Jur NS 92; and see *Re Yates, Batcheldor v Yates* (1888) 38 ChD 112 at
    117, CA. As to accounts see PARA 709 et seq. As to the rights of a mortgagee in possession of mines
    see PARA 180.

439. Mortgagee's statutory power to cut and sell timber. A mortgagee in
possession has statutory power to cut and sell timber and other trees ripe for
cutting and not planted or left standing for shelter or ornament, and he may
contract for any such cutting and sale, to be completed within any time not
exceeding 12 months from the making of the contract[1]. The power may, however,
be varied or excluded by the mortgage deed[2], and in certain cases a felling licence
may be necessary[3]. The proceeds of any such cutting or sale are applied as rents
and profits[4].

1   Law of Property Act 1925 s 101(1)(iv). Under the former system of mortgages (see PARA 161) and
    apart from the statutory power, the mortgagee of the fee simple might cut timber by virtue of his

ownership without committing waste at law (see PARA 438), but in equity he would be restrained unless his security was defective: *Withrington v Banks* (1725) Cas *temp* King 30. In that case he might cut the timber and sell it (*Millett v Davey* (1862) 31 Beav 470 at 476), provided he applied the proceeds in payment of principal and interest (*Farrant v Lovel* (1750) 3 Atk 723). This applies, apart from the statutory power, to a term mortgage. As to the meaning of 'timber' see FORESTRY vol 52 (2014) PARA 55; LANDLORD AND TENANT vol 62 (2012) PARA 187 et seq. As to trees planted or left standing for shelter or ornament see *Weld-Blundell v Wolseley* [1903] 2 Ch 664; and SETTLEMENTS vol 91 (2012) PARA 899.

2 See the Law of Property Act 1925 s 101(3), (4).
3 See FORESTRY vol 52 (2014) PARA 121 et seq. As to preservation of trees and tree preservation orders see PLANNING vol 83 (2010) PARA 1035 et seq.
4 As to the mortgagee in possession's right to rents and profits see PARA 419 et seq.

440. Mortgagee liable for damage to cultivation. A mortgagee in possession of agricultural land is liable for damage occasioned by his gross negligence in regard to cultivation[1] and should take proper means for preventing damage by strangers, but is not liable for waste committed under a claim of right which he has not authorised[2].

1 *Wragg v Denham* (1836) 2 Y & C Ex 117.
2 *Anon* (1823) 1 LJOS Ch 119. As to the mortgagee in possession's liability for waste see PARAS 438–439.

441. Remedies for wrongful waste. Waste committed by the mortgagee which is not justified by the terms or the deficiency of his security, in addition to rendering him liable to an injunction, may be a ground for depriving him of possession, either by replacing the mortgagor in possession or by the appointment of a receiver[1]. Conversely, a mortgagee may restrain by injunction a mortgagor in possession from committing waste which would render the security insufficient[2].

1 *Hanson v Derby* (1700) 2 Vern 392.
2 *King v Smith* (1843) 2 Hare 239; *Harper v Aplin* (1886) 54 LT 383. As to the mortgagor's liability for waste see PARAS 360–361.

(4) SALE OUT OF COURT

(i) Express, Implied and Statutory Powers of Sale

442. Express, implied and statutory powers of sale. So long as the equity of redemption remains vested in the mortgagor[1], the mortgagee may not sell the property except under an express[2] or implied power of sale[3], or under a statutory power[4], or with the mortgagor's concurrence[5].

1 As to the equity of redemption see PARAS 107, 304 et seq.
2 As to express powers of sale see PARAS 443–444.
3 As to implied powers of sale see PARA 445.
4 As to statutory powers of sale see PARAS 446–453.
5 Where the mortgagor sells and obtains the mortgagee's concurrence, a deposit paid to their common agent who absconds is well paid as between the mortgagee and the purchaser (*Rowe v May* (1854) 18 Beav 613), but the mortgagee cannot be charged with it by the mortgagor or by a subsequent incumbrancer (*Barrow v White* (1862) 2 John & H 580). As to the appropriation of proceeds of sale received by the mortgagee see PARAS 474–477. As to the statutory restrictions on the enforcing of his security by a mortgagee in certain circumstances see PARAS 532–533.

(ii) Express Power of Sale

443. Terms of express power of sale. It was usual to insert in mortgages executed before 1 January 1882[1] an express power of sale[2]. The statutory power of sale[3] renders express powers unnecessary, although in practice it remains common to include an express power of sale in the mortgage in addition to the statutory power of sale[4]. A variation or extension of the statutory power operates as if it were a part of the statutory power[5], and a conveyance on sale by a mortgagee is deemed to have been made in exercise of the statutory power of sale unless a contrary intention appears[6].

1 Ie the date of commencement of the Conveyancing Act 1881: see s 1(2) (repealed).
2 It was not until the latter part of the nineteenth century that the insertion of a power of sale became a matter of course. In 1857 it was said not to be a universal practice: *Clarke v Royal Panopticon of Science and Art* (1857) 4 Drew 26 at 30. The insertion of the express power continued until 1882, notwithstanding the statutory power given by 23 & 24 Vict c 145 (1860) (known as Lord Cranworth's Act) (repealed).
3 As to the statutory power of sale see PARA 446 et seq.
4 There is nothing in the Law of Property Act 1925 s 101 (see PARA 446) or s 103 (see PARA 456) which restricts express powers conferred on the mortgagee in the mortgage deed itself: *The Maule* [1997] 1 WLR 528, [1997] 1 Lloyds Rep 419, PC.
5 See the Law of Property Act 1925 s 101(3). This provision is designed to counter arguments that a purchaser under a sale pursuant to an express power is not afforded the statutory protection given by s 104 (see PARA 471). See *Horsham Properties Group Ltd v Clark* [2008] EWHC 2327 (Ch), [2009] 1 All ER (Comm) 745, [2009] 1 P & CR 153.
6 Law of Property Act 1925 s 104(3).

444. Paramount effect of power of sale. The power of sale is paramount to any subsequent arrangement between the mortgagee and mortgagor for the management of the premises. Thus where, by a deed subsequent to the mortgage, the mortgagee with power of sale and the mortgagor demised the mortgaged property to a receiver upon trust to grant leases, but the trusts were not declared to be subject to the power of sale, it was held that they were so in effect, and that the receiver must join in the conveyance to a purchaser from the mortgagee under the power of sale[1]. The power is not extinguished by an ineffectual attempt to exercise it[2]; and even though the mortgagee believes himself to be absolute owner, and sells as such, the sale can be supported as a sale under the power[3]. When duly exercised, the power extinguishes the mortgagor's equity of redemption, and he is from then onwards only interested in the surplus proceeds of sale[4].

1 *King v Heenan* (1853) 3 De GM & G 890.
2 *Henderson v Astwood* [1894] AC 150, PC.
3 *Henderson v Astwood* [1894] AC 150, PC; *Deverges v Sandeman, Clark & Co* [1902] 1 Ch 579 at 596, CA.
4 See PARAS 107, 474. See also *Duke v Robson* [1973] 1 All ER 481, [1973] 1 WLR 267, CA, where mortgagors contracted to sell only their equity of redemption so the plaintiff purchasers were in no better position than their vendor mortgagors to restrain a sale by the mortgagee.

(iii) Implied Power of Sale

445. Implied power of sale in mortgages of chattels and choses in action. A mortgagee of personal chattels, when possession has been delivered to him[1], and a mortgagee of stocks and shares, including a mortgagee by deposit of the share certificates with a blank transfer[2], has, in the absence of an express power of sale, an implied power to sell the mortgaged property, where a day for payment is fixed by the mortgage, at any time after default, and, where no day for payment is fixed, after reasonable notice has been given to the mortgagor and default made in payment in pursuance of that notice[3]. The notice must be in all respects reasonable having regard to the circumstances of the case[4]. It is desirable that, in addition to fixing a day for payment, the notice should intimate that if the mortgagor fails to avail himself of the opportunity given to redeem, the mortgagee will be in a position to enforce his rights[5] but it is not necessary that it should state that the mortgagee will sell[6]. In the case of shares, a month's or perhaps a fortnight's notice is reasonable[7]. The mortgagee does not prejudice his implied power of sale by claiming more than is due to him[8], but he refuses at his own risk a tender of the amount actually due, although the mortgagee will not be restrained from selling unless the mortgagor pays into court the amount claimed to be due[9].

1   See *Re Morritt, ex p Official Receiver* (1886) 18 QBD 222 at 233, CA; and FINANCIAL INSTRUMENTS AND TRANSACTIONS vol 49 (2015) PARA 525. As to the distinction between mortgages and pledges see PARA 112.
2   *Stubbs v Slater* [1910] 1 Ch 632, CA (where it is pointed out that the headnote to *Pigot v Cubley* (1864) 15 CBNS 701, in so far as it states that a notice that the pledgee will sell unless an excessive sum is paid immediately is not such a notice as will justify the sale of a pledge, is not borne out by the judgment). As to mortgages of stocks and shares see PARA 211.
3   *Re Morritt, ex p Official Receiver* (1886) 18 QBD 222 at 233, CA; *Deverges v Sandeman, Clark & Co* [1902] 1 Ch 579, CA; *Wilson v Tooker* (1714) 5 Bro Parl Cas 193, HL; *Lockwood v Ewer* (1742) 2 Atk 303; *Kemp v Westbrook* (1749) 1 Ves Sen 278; *France v Clark* (1883) 22 ChD 830 (affd (1884) 26 ChD 257, CA). See also *McHugh v Union Bank of Canada* [1913] AC 299, PC; *The Odessa* [1916] 1 AC 145 at 159, PC.
4   *Deverges v Sandeman, Clark & Co* [1902] 1 Ch 579 at 593, CA.
5   *Deverges v Sandeman, Clark & Co* [1902] 1 Ch 579 at 593–594, CA.
6   *Deverges v Sandeman, Clark & Co* [1902] 1 Ch 579 at 596, CA.
7   *Deverges v Sandeman, Clark & Co* [1902] 1 Ch 579 at 595, 597, CA.
8   *Stubbs v Slater* [1910] 1 Ch 632, CA.
9   *Stubbs v Slater* [1910] 1 Ch 632 at 640, CA. As to payments into court see CIVIL PROCEDURE vol 12A (2015) PARA 1653 et seq.

(iv)   Statutory Power of Sale

446.   Application of the statutory power of sale. A power of sale is conferred by statute[1]. The mortgage must be made by deed, but, subject to this, the power applies to any mortgage, charge or lien on real or personal property or any interest in it, or any thing in action[2], except certain bills of sale[3], and possibly debentures upon a statutory public utility company[4].

The registered proprietor of a registered charge over registered land is entitled to exercise owners' powers[5], which include power to make a disposition of any kind permitted by the general law in relation to an interest of that description, other than a legal sub-mortgage[6]. A person is not entitled to exercise owner's powers merely as a result of being entitled to be registered as proprietor of a registered charge[7].

An equitable mortgagee under a memorandum of charge by deed containing an appropriate power of attorney[8] can convey the legal estate on sale by him in exercise of the statutory power of sale[9]. An equitable assignee of a registered charge is, however, entitled to exercise owner's powers by virtue of being entitled to give a discharge for the mortgage money[10]. The power of sale does not affect the right of foreclosure[11], may be varied or extended by the mortgage deed, applies to the mortgage only so far as a contrary intention is not expressed in it, and has effect subject to the terms of the mortgage deed and to the provisions contained in it[12].

1   See the Law of Property Act 1925 s 101(1)(i), (5). The power in s 101(1)(i) is subject to the Commonhold and Leasehold Reform Act 2002 s 21 (no disposition of part-units: see COMMONHOLD vol 13 (2009) PARA 350): Law of Property Act 1925 s 101(1A) (added by the Commonhold and Leasehold Reform Act 2002 s 68, Sch 5 para 2). As to mortgages of commonhold land see PARA 177.
2   See the Law of Property Act 1925 s 205(1)(xvi), (xx).
3   Ie bills of sale subject to the Bills of Sale Act 1878 (Amendment) Act 1882: see *Calvert v Thomas* (1887) 19 QBD 204, CA. See also FINANCIAL INSTRUMENTS AND TRANSACTIONS vol 49 (2015) PARA 525.

4   In *Blaker v Herts and Essex Waterworks Co* (1889) 41 ChD 399 at 406, debentures of all companies were thought to be excluded; but *Deyes v Wood* [1911] 1 KB 806 at 818, CA, suggests that the exclusion is limited as stated in the text. As to enforcing a security under the Consumer Credit Act 1974 see CONSUMER CREDIT vol 21 (2011) PARA 229 et seq.

5   See the Land Registration Act 2002 s 24; and REAL PROPERTY AND REGISTRATION vol 87 (2012) PARA 424.

6   See the Land Registration Act 2002 s 23(2); and REAL PROPERTY AND REGISTRATION vol 87 (2012) PARA 423. As to sub-mortgages see PARA 252 et seq.

7   *Skelwith (Leisure) Ltd v Armstrong* [2015] EWHC 2830 (Ch), [2015] All ER (D) 98 (Oct) (such a person may be able to sell).

8   See PARA 236.

9   See *Re White Rose Cottage* [1965] Ch 940, [1965] 1 All ER 11, CA.

10   *Skelwith (Leisure) Ltd v Armstrong* [2015] EWHC 2830 (Ch), [2015] All ER (D) 98 (Oct). See also PARA 454.

11   Law of Property Act 1925 s 106(2). As to foreclosure see PARA 571 et seq.

12   See the Law of Property Act 1925 s 101(3), (4). Any variations to the statutory provisions can only be made by the mortgage deed itself. In the case of a registered charge, the mortgage deed will not be construed by reference to collateral documents such as the facility letter not available to third parties inspecting the register: see *Cherry Tree Investments Ltd v Landmain Ltd* [2012] EWCA Civ 736, [2013] Ch 305, [2013] 2 WLR 481.

447. Mode of sale under the statutory power of sale. The statutory power of sale[1] authorises the mortgagee[2], when the mortgage[3] money has become due[4], to sell, or to concur with any other person in selling, the mortgaged property[5] or any part of it either subject to prior charges or not, and either together or in lots, by public auction or private contract[6], subject to such conditions of title as he thinks fit[7]. The mortgagee exercising the power of sale has also power to vary any contract of sale, and to buy in at an auction, and to rescind any contract of sale, and to re-sell, without being answerable for any loss occasioned by it[8]. A mortgagee exercising the power of sale also has power by deed to convey the property sold for such estate or interest as he is by the Law of Property Act 1925 authorised to sell or convey or as may be the subject of the mortgage, freed from all estates, interests and rights to which the mortgage has priority, but subject to all estates, interests and rights which have priority to the mortgage[9].

1   Ie the power of sale under the Law of Property Act 1925 s 101(1)(i): see PARA 446 et seq. As to the restrictions on the exercise of the power see PARA 456.

2   As to the meaning of 'mortgagee' see PARA 104 note 1.

3   As to the meaning of 'mortgage' see PARA 101 note 4.

4   Ie when the legal date for redemption, if any, has passed or in the case of an instalment mortgage as soon as each instalment becomes due: see *Payne v Cardiff RDC* [1932] 1 KB 241. The power may be excluded before a specified date: see *Twentieth Century Banking Corpn Ltd v Wilkinson* [1977] Ch 99, [1976] 3 All ER 361, where the express provision that the mortgage money was to become due on a specified date excluded the statutory power to sell at any previous time.

5   The mortgaged property is the property over which the mortgage deed purports to extend: *Re White Rose Cottage* [1964] Ch 483, [1964] 1 All ER 169; on appeal [1965] Ch 940, [1965] 1 All ER 11, CA.

6   A retaking by a local authority under a right of pre-emption in its mortgage is not a sale either by public auction or private contract, as a mortgagee cannot sell to himself: *Williams v Wellingborough Borough Council* [1975] 3 All ER 462, [1975] 1 WLR 1327, CA.

7   See the Law of Property Act 1925 s 101(1)(i). See *Property and Bloodstock Ltd v Emerton* [1968] Ch 94, [1967] 3 All ER 321, CA. The statutory power of sale includes such power of selling the fee simple or any leasehold reversion as is conferred by the provisions of the Law of Property Act 1925 relating to realisation of mortgages: s 101(6). As to the realisation of mortgages see ss 88–89; and PARAS 449–452. Exercise of statutory power of sale under s 101, after default by the mortgagor, is not a deprivation of possessions within meaning of the Convention for the Protection of Human Rights and Fundamental Freedoms (ie the European Convention on Human Rights) (Rome, 4 November 1950; TS 71 (1953); Cmd 8969) First Protocol art 1: *Horsham Properties Group Ltd v Clark* [2008] EWHC 2327 (Ch), [2009] 1 All ER (Comm) 745, [2009] 1 P & CR 153. As to the right to property protected under the European Convention on Human Rights First Protocol art 1 see RIGHTS AND FREEDOMS vol 88A (2013) PARA 534 et seq.

8   See the Law of Property Act 1925 s 101(1)(i).

9   Law of Property Act 1925 s 104(1). Nothing in the Consumer Credit Act 1974 affects the
    operation of the Law of Property Act 1925 s 104(1): see the Consumer Credit Act 1974 s 177(2).

448. Effect of disposition by mortgagee of registered land. If a registrable
disposition[1] of a registered estate[2] is made for valuable consideration by a
mortgagee entitled to do so[3], completion of the disposition by registration has the
effect of postponing to the interest under the disposition any interest affecting the
estate immediately before the disposition whose priority is not protected at the
time of registration[4].

1   As to the meaning of 'registrable disposition' see PARA 142 note 8.
2   As to the meaning of 'registered estate' see PARA 142 note 7.
3   As to the mortgagee's power to make a registered disposition see PARA 446.
4   Land Registration Act 2002 s 29(1); and see REAL PROPERTY AND REGISTRATION vol 87 (2012)
    PARA 455.

449. Effect of conveyance by mortgagee by demise. On a sale by a mortgagee by
demise[1] of an estate in fee simple, the conveyance by the mortgagee operates to
vest the fee simple in the purchaser[2], and the mortgage term or the charge by way
of legal mortgage[3] and any subsequent mortgage terms or charges merge or are
extinguished as respects the land conveyed[4]. The conveyance, under a mortgage of
freeholds, has the same statutory operation whether it is made under an express
power of sale or under the statutory power[5].

Thus it is sufficient for the mortgagee to be named alone as the conveying
party[6], although as regards the fee simple the conveyance may be made in the
name of the estate owner in whom the fee simple is vested[7]. Usually the mortgagee
is named alone.

The vesting of the fee simple in the purchaser is subject to any legal mortgage
(including a legal charge) which has priority to the mortgage in right of which the
sale is made and to any money secured by it[8]. Thus the purchaser takes the fee
simple clear of the mortgage term[9].

On a sale by the mortgagee by sub-demise under his statutory power of sale or
on express power of sale in a leasehold mortgage, the conveyance by him operates
to convey to the purchaser, not only the mortgage term, but also (unless expressly
excepted by the permission of the court[10]) the leasehold reversion[11]; and the
mortgage term and any subsequent mortgage term or charge merge in the
leasehold reversion or are extinguished (unless excepted by leave of the court)[12].
The vesting of the leasehold reversion is subject to any legal mortgage (including
a legal charge) which has priority to the mortgage in right of which the sale is
made and to any money secured by it[13]. The conveyance of the leasehold reversion
may be made in the name of the estate owner in whom it is vested[14]; and where
a licence to assign is required on a sale by a mortgagee, the licence is not to be
unreasonably refused[15].

1   As to the meaning of 'mortgagee' see PARA 104 note 1. As to mortgage by demise see PARA 164.
    The power of sale is effectively exercised as soon as there is an enforceable contract for sale of the
    mortgaged property: *Lord Waring v London and Manchester Assurance Co Ltd* [1935] Ch 310;
    Property and Bloodstock Ltd v Emerton [1968] Ch 94, [1967] 3 All ER 321, CA; *National and
    Provincial Building Society v Ahmed* [1995] NPC 88, [1995] 2 EGLR 127, CA; *Corbett v
    Halifax plc* [2002] EWCA Civ 1849, [2003] 4 All ER 180, [2003] 1 WLR 964.
2   See the Law of Property Act 1925 s 88(1)(a).
3   As to the meaning of 'legal mortgage' see PARA 104 note 1.
4   See the Law of Property Act 1925 s 88(1)(b).
5   See the Law of Property Act 1925 s 88(1). As to the statutory power of sale see PARA 446 et seq.
    As to express powers of sale see PARA 443–444.
6   See the Law of Property Act 1925 s 9; and REAL PROPERTY AND REGISTRATION vol 87 (2012)
    PARA 259.
7   See the Law of Property Act 1925 s 88(1).

8 See the Law of Property Act 1925 s 88(1)(a).
9 The effect is the same as when under the former system the mortgagee conveyed the fee simple free
   from any equity of redemption (see PARA 161). This included the equity of redemption of the
   mortgagor and of his subsequent incumbrancers. As to the equity of redemption see PARAS 107,
   304 et seq.
10 The Law of Property Act 1925 gives no direction as to the grounds on which the nominal reversion
   will be excepted. The object of excepting it would be to save the purchaser from becoming liable
   on the lessee's covenants. These might be so onerous as to be unfair to the purchaser or prevent
   a beneficial realisation by the mortgagee.
11 See the Law of Property Act 1925 s 89(1)(a).
12 See the Law of Property Act 1925 s 89(1)(b).
13 See the Law of Property Act 1925 s 89(1)(a).
14 See the Law of Property Act 1925 s 89(1).
15 See the Law of Property Act 1925 s 89(1). As to the general provision to this effect made by the
   Landlord and Tenant Act 1927 s 19(1) see LANDLORD AND TENANT vol 62 (2012) PARA 635 et
   seq.

450. Effect of conveyance by mortgagee by legal charge. Where the mortgage is
created by charge[1] by deed expressed to be by way of legal mortgage, the
mortgagee[2] has the same statutory power of sale as if the mortgage were by
demise[3]. There is in this case, however, no term which requires to be merged in the
freehold or leasehold reversion, and it is provided that the conveyance by the
mortgagee is to operate, as in the case of a mortgage by demise, to vest in the
purchaser the fee simple or the lease, and the legal charge is extinguished[4].

Where the mortgage, whether freehold or leasehold, includes fixtures or
chattels personal, the statutory power of sale extends to the absolute or other
interest in them affected by the charge[5], but trade machinery may not be sold by
the mortgagee separately from the land[6].

1 As to the meaning of 'mortgage' see PARA 101 note 4. As to mortgage by way of charge see PARA
   165.
2 As to the meaning of 'mortgagee' see PARA 104 note 1.
3 See the Law of Property Act 1925 s 87(1); and PARA 165. As to mortgage by demise see PARA 164.
4 See the Law of Property Act 1925 ss 88(1), 89(1). As to the corresponding provisions which apply
   in the case of foreclosure see ss 88(2), 89(2); and PARA 612. As to provisions which apply in the
   case of the mortgagee acquiring title by the running of time see ss 88(3), 89(3); and LIMITATION
   PERIODS vol 68 (2008) PARA 1099.
5 See the Law of Property Act 1925 ss 88(4), 89(4).
6 See PARA 466.

451. Extent of the interest conveyed under statutory power of sale. The
statutory provisions relating to the effect of conveyances by mortgagees[1] apply
whether the mortgage[2] was created before or after the commencement of the Law
of Property Act 1925[3], and to mortgage terms created by that Act[4]. In the case of
a mortgage of freeholds, the provisions do not operate to confer a better title to
the fee simple than would have been acquired if the statutory restrictions on the
effect and creation of mortgages[5] had not been in force and the fee simple had
been validly conveyed by the mortgage and all prior mortgages, if any, not being
merely equitable charges had been created by demise or legal charge[6]. In the case
of mortgages of leaseholds, the provisions take effect without prejudice to any
incumbrance[7] or trust affecting the leasehold reversion which has priority over the
mortgage in right of which the sale, foreclosure, or title is made or acquired, and
do not apply where the mortgage term does not comprise the whole of the land[8]
included in the leasehold reversion, unless the rent, if any, payable in respect of
that reversion has been apportioned as respects the land affected, or the rent is of
no money value, or no rent is reserved, and unless the lessee's[9] covenants and
conditions, if any, have been apportioned, either expressly or by implication, as

respects the land affected[10]. For this purpose, an equitable apportionment made without the lessor's[11] consent is sufficient[12].

1 Ie the Law of Property Act 1925 ss 88(1), 89(1): see PARAS 449–450. As to the meaning of 'mortgagee' see PARA 104 note 1.
2 As to the meaning of 'mortgage' see PARA 101 note 4.
3 Ie 1 January 1926: see the Law of Property Act 1925 s 209(2) (repealed).
4 See the Law of Property Act 1925 ss 88(6), 89(6).
5 See PARAS 164–166.
6 See the Law of Property Act 1925 s 88(6).
7 As to the meaning of 'incumbrance' see PARA 197 note 4.
8 As to the meaning of 'land' see PARA 104 note 2.
9 As to the meaning of 'lessee' see PARA 352 note 5.
10 See the Law of Property Act 1925 s 89(6).
11 As to the meaning of 'lessor' see PARA 353 note 3.
12 See the Law of Property Act 1925 s 89(6) (amended by the Law of Property (Amendment) Act 1926 s 7, Schedule). A legal apportionment of rent can now be made: see LANDLORD AND TENANT vol 62 (2012) PARA 279 et seq.

452. Effect of conveyance by sub-mortgagee under statutory power of sale. The provisions as to the realisation of freehold and leasehold mortgages by sale[1] are adapted to freehold and leasehold sub-mortgages[2] as follows. In the case of a sub-mortgage by sub-demise of a long term (less a nominal period) itself limited out of an estate in fee simple, the provisions operate as if the derivative term, if any, created by the sub-term had been limited out of the fee simple, and so as to enlarge the principal term and extinguish the derivative term created by the sub-mortgage and to enable the sub-mortgagee to convey the fee simple[3]. In the case of a sub-mortgage by sub-demise of a term (less a nominal period) itself limited out of a leasehold reversion, the provisions operate as if the derivative term created by the sub-mortgage had been limited out of the leasehold reversion, and so as to merge the principal mortgage term in it as well as the derivative term created by the sub-mortgage and to enable the sub-mortgagee to convey the leasehold reversion[4].

1 Ie the Law of Property Act 1925 ss 88, 89: see PARAS 449–451.
2 As to sub-mortgages see PARA 252 et seq.
3 See the Law of Property Act 1925 s 88(5).
4 See the Law of Property Act 1925 s 89(5).

453. Power of sale exercisable by mortgagee of ship or aircraft. A registered mortgagee[1] of a ship or a share in a ship has power absolutely to dispose of the ship or share and to give effectual receipts for the purchase money[2], but, where two or more mortgagees are registered in respect of the same ship or share, a subsequent mortgagee, except under the order of a court of competent jurisdiction, may not exercise this power without the concurrence of every prior mortgagee[3].

The mortgagee of an aircraft or hovercraft has the statutory power of sale where the mortgage is by deed[4].

1 As to the meaning of 'mortgagee' see PARA 104 note 1.
2 Merchant Shipping Act 1995 s 16(1), Sch 1 para 9(1); and see SHIPPING AND MARITIME LAW vol 93 (2008) PARA 333. As to mortgages of ships generally see SHIPPING AND MARITIME LAW vol 93 (2008) PARA 318 et seq. As to duties owed by a mortgagee in exercising the power of sale see *Den Norske Bank ASA v Acemex Management Co Ltd (The Tropical Reefer)* [2003] EWCA Civ 1559, [2004] 1 All ER (Comm) 904, [2005] 1 BCLC 274.
3 Merchant Shipping Act 1995 Sch 1 para 9(2); and see SHIPPING AND MARITIME LAW vol 93 (2008) PARA 333.
4 See PARA 446.

(v) Who may Exercise the Power of Sale

454. Devolution of statutory powers of sale. The statutory power of sale under the Law of Property Act 1925[1] is exercisable by any person for the time being entitled to receive and give a discharge for the mortgage money[2]; that is, by persons who are mortgagees[3], or have the mortgaged property vested in them (such as executors) or are equitable assignees of a legal charge[4]. Persons deriving title under the original mortgagee can also exercise the power of sale[5]. The mortgagee's agent under a power of attorney may not sell by virtue of an authority to receive the money, although he may sell if the power of attorney expressly authorises him to exercise the power of sale[6].

In relation to registered land, the power may be exercised by the registered proprietor of a registered charge or by the person entitled to be registered as proprietor[7].

1　Ie the power of sale under the Law of Property Act 1925 s 101(1)(i): see PARA 446 et seq.
2　Law of Property Act 1925 s 106(1). As to the meaning of 'mortgage money' see PARA 104 note 1.
3　As to the meaning of 'mortgagee' see PARA 104 note 1.
4　*Skelwith (Leisure) Ltd v Armstrong* [2015] EWHC 2830 (Ch), [2015] All ER (D) 98 (Oct).
5　See the Law of Property Act 1925 s 205(1)(xvi) (definition of 'mortgagee'); and PARA 104 note 1. See also PARA 366 et seq.
6　*Re Dowson and Jenkins's Contract* [1904] 2 Ch 219, CA.
7　See the Land Registration 2002 s 24; and REAL PROPERTY AND REGISTRATION vol 87 (2012) PARA 424.

455. Who may exercise an express power of sale. An express power of sale[1] is exercisable only by the persons who are designated for that purpose by the power[2].

A power of sale in a mortgage to two mortgagees who are expressed to advance the money on a joint account[3] is exercisable by the survivor[4], but a power of sale in a mortgage to partners is not exercisable by one unless it is so expressed in the mortgage[5].

1　As to express powers of sale see PARA 443–444.
2　*Re Crunden and Meux's Contract* [1909] 1 Ch 690 at 695; WILLS AND INTESTACY vol 103 (2010) PARA 950. As to devolution of powers and trusts see the Trustee Act 1925 s 18; and TRUSTS AND POWERS vol 98 (2013) PARA 257.
3　See PARA 186. As to the meaning of 'mortgagee' see PARA 104 note 1.
4　*Hind v Poole* (1855) 1 K & J 383.
5　*Warr v Jones* (1876) 24 WR 695. As to the power of partners to lend on mortgage see PARA 137.

(vi) Conditions of Exercise of the Power of Sale

456. Restrictions on exercise of statutory powers of sale. The time when the power of sale arises is fixed in the manner already stated[1], but restrictions are placed on the time when it is exercisable. The statutory power of sale is not exercisable until:

(1)　notice[2] requiring payment of the mortgage money[3] has been served on the mortgagor[4] or one of two or more mortgagors, and default has been made in payment of it, or of part of it, for three months[5] after such service[6];

(2)　some interest under the mortgage is in arrear[7] and unpaid for two months after becoming due[8]; or

(3) there has been a breach of some provision in the mortgage deed or in the Law of Property Act 1925 on the part of the mortgagor, or of some person concurring in making the mortgage, to be observed or performed, other than the covenant for payment of principal or interest[9].

The restrictions may, however, be negatived or varied[10]. In a bank mortgage to secure all moneys due, the restrictions are generally excluded and the power of sale is exercisable following demand or default. Where a charge provides a specific date for the mortgage money to become due, the statutory power of sale may not be exercised before that date even if the mortgagor is in default[11]. It has been held that where in a bank mortgage the power was to be exercisable on default in payment of the balance due on current account for one month after the closing of the account, and the account was closed by notice of insolvency, the month ran from the receipt of the notice[12].

An express power of sale is usually subject to restrictions similar to the restrictions mentioned above[13]. The exercise of the power of sale is not contrary to the right to protection of property under the European Convention on Human Rights[14].

1 As to express powers of sale see PARA 443–444; as to implied powers of sale see PARA 445; and as to the statutory power of sale see PARAS 446 et seq.
2 As to such notice see PARAS 457–458.
3 As to the meaning of 'mortgage money' see PARA 104 note 1. As to the meaning of 'mortgage' see PARA 101 note 4.
4 As to the meaning of 'mortgagor' see PARA 104 note 1.
5 'Month' means calendar month: see the Interpretation Act 1978 ss 5, 22(1), Sch 1, Sch 2 para 4(1); and TIME vol 97 (2015) PARA 309.
6 Law of Property Act 1925 s 103(i).
7 The capitalisation of arrears may make this inapplicable: see *Davy v Turner* (1970) 21 P & CR 967, 114 Sol Jo 884.
8 Law of Property Act 1925 s 103(ii). It is sufficient if an instalment which includes interest is in arrear for two months: *Walsh v Derrick* (1903) 19 TLR 209, CA. See also *Payne v Cardiff RDC* [1932] 1 KB 241.
9 Law of Property Act 1925 s 103(iii). The breach may have been waived: see eg *Braithwaite v Winwood* [1960] 3 All ER 642, [1960] 1 WLR 1257.
10 See PARA 446. The power of sale under the Law of Property Act 1925 (see PARA 446) can be made immediate by providing in the mortgage that the mortgagee is to have the statutory power but without the restrictions imposed by s 103. In the case of a bankrupt mortgagor, the permission of the court may be necessary under s 110(1): see PARA 528.
11 *Twentieth Century Banking Corpn Ltd v Wilkinson* [1977] Ch 99, [1976] 3 All ER 361.
12 *Berry v Halifax Commercial Banking Co Ltd* [1901] 1 Ch 188.
13 As to express powers of sale see PARA 443–444.
14 *Horsham Properties Group Ltd v Clark* [2008] EWHC 2327 (Ch), [2009] 1 All ER (Comm) 745, [2009] 1 WLR 1255. As to the right to the protection of property see the European Convention on Human Rights (ie the Convention for the Protection of Human Rights and Fundamental Freedoms (Rome, 4 November 1950; TS 71 (1953); Cmd 8969)) First Protocol art 1; and RIGHTS AND FREEDOMS vol 88A (2013) PARA 534 et seq.

457. Notice to mortgagor requiring payment. A notice to the mortgagor requiring payment of the mortgage money[1] for the purpose of complying with the statutory restrictions on the exercise of power of sale or a notice required by the mortgage to be served[2] must be in writing[3].

Such a notice is sufficient although only addressed to the mortgagor[4] by that designation without his name, or generally to the persons interested, without any name, and notwithstanding that any person to be affected is absent, under disability, unborn or unascertained[5].

The notice is sufficiently served[6] if left at the mortgagor's last-known place of abode or business in the United Kingdom[7], or if it is affixed or left for him on the land[8] or any house or building comprised in the mortgage[9], or if it is sent in a registered letter, or by recorded delivery service, addressed to the mortgagor at his place of abode or business, and is not returned undelivered by the postal operator concerned[10]. Service by registered letter is deemed to be made at the time when the letter would in the ordinary course be delivered[11].

Where there are several mortgagors it is sufficient if the notice is served on one of them[12]. Where the mortgagor is dead it should be served on the person entitled to redeem[13]. Where an express power provided for notice to the mortgagor, his heirs, executors or administrators, or any of them, notice to the executors alone has been held to be sufficient[14]. Where there are subsequent incumbrancers, it may be that it is sufficient to serve only the mortgagor, but the first subsequent incumbrancer should also be served[15]. When an express power of sale provides for notice to the mortgagor, or his assigns, notice to a second mortgagee is necessary, although it is doubtful whether it must also be given to the mortgagor[16]. To ascertain the subsequent incumbrancers, search should be made in the land charges register for puisne mortgages[17]. Where an express power is stated to be exercisable immediately with a proviso that it is not to be exercised until default under the covenant for payment, a second mortgagee is not entitled to notice, as he is not liable under the covenant[18].

1 Ie a notice under the Law of Property Act 1925 s 103(i): see PARA 456. As to the form of such notices see PARA 458.
2 *Wandsworth London Borough Council v Attwell* [1996] 1 EGLR 57, [1995] NPC 67, CA.
3 Law of Property Act 1925 s 196(1). 'Writing' includes typing, printing, lithography, photography and other modes of representing or reproducing words in a visible form, and expressions referring to writing are construed accordingly: Interpretation Act 1978 s 5, Sch 1.
4 As to the meaning of 'mortgagor' see PARA 104 note 1.
5 Law of Property Act 1925 s 196(2). It has been held sufficient to put a notice through the letterbox of the premises even though the premises were vacant and the tenant in prison and the landlord knew that the tenant could be contacted through his solicitor: *Van Haarlam v Kasner* (1992) 64 P & CR 214, [1992] 2 EGLR 59.
6 Service is presumed if the requirements of the Law of Property Act 1925 s 196 are complied with, even though the notice is never received: see *R v Westminster Unions Assessment Committee, ex p Woodward & Sons* [1917] 1 KB 832, DC. Where one is considering a notice in writing there can be no difference between 'serving' the notice and 'giving' the notice: *Re 88, Berkeley Road, NW 9, Rickwood v Turnsek* [1971] Ch 648, [1971] 1 All ER 254.
7 Under a similar provision in an express power it is sufficient to fix the notice on the door of the mortgagor's last known place of abode: *Major v Ward* (1847) 5 Hare 598. A notice left at the furthest place to which a member of the public or a postman could go, constituted service at the place of abode: *Henry Smith's Charity Trustees v Kyriakou* [1989] RVR 106, [1989] 2 EGLR 110, CA. As to the meaning of 'United Kingdom' means Great Britain and Northern Ireland: Interpretation Act 1978 s 5, Sch 1. 'Great Britain' means England, Scotland and Wales: Union with Scotland Act 1706, preamble art I; Interpretation Act 1978 s 22(1), Sch 2 para 5(a). Neither the Isle of Man nor the Channel Islands are within the United Kingdom. See further CONSTITUTIONAL AND ADMINISTRATIVE LAW vol 20 (2014) PARA 3. 'England' means, subject to any alteration of boundaries of local government areas, the area consisting of the counties established by the Local Government Act 1972 s 1 (see LOCAL GOVERNMENT vol 69 (2009) PARAS 5, 22), Greater London and the Isles of Scilly: Interpretation Act 1978 s 5, Sch 1. As to the meaning of 'Wales' see PARA 374 note 1.
8 As to the meaning of 'land' see PARA 104 note 2.
9 Law of Property Act 1925 s 196(3).
10 See the Law of Property Act 1925 s 196(4) (amended by SI 2001/1149); Recorded Delivery Service Act 1962 s 1. The text refers to postal operators within the meaning of the Postal Services Act 2011 Pt 3 (ss 27–67) (see POSTAL SERVICES vol 85 (2012) PARA 243 note 3): Law of Property Act 1925 s 196(4) (further amended by the Postal Services Act 2011 s 91(1), (2), Sch 12 Pt 3 para 75). See also *Stephenson & Son v Orca Properties Ltd* [1989] 2 EGLR 129, [1989] 44 EG 81; and note 6.
11 Law of Property Act 1925 s 196(4).
12 See the Law of Property Act 1925 s 103(i); and PARA 456.

13 See the Law of Property Act 1925 s 205(1)(xvi) (definition of 'mortgagor'); and PARA 104 note 1. Service will be on the personal representatives until by assent or conveyance they have vested the property in some person entitled: see the Administration of Estates Act 1925 s 36(1); and WILLS AND INTESTACY vol 103 (2010) PARA 1145. Where no grant of representation has been filed, the notice should be addressed to 'The Personal Representatives of' the deceased and left at or sent by to his last known place of residence or business in the United Kingdom and a copy of it, similarly addressed, should be served on the Public Trustee: see the Law of Property (Miscellaneous Provisions) Act 1994 s 18(1). Note that the offices of the Public Trustee and the Official Solicitor have been reorganised, and the trust division of the Public Trust Office has merged with the office of the Official Solicitor: see TRUSTS AND POWERS vol 98 (2013) PARA 206 et seq. Service of a notice which would be effective but for the death of the intended recipient is effective despite his death if the mortgagee had no reason to believe that he had died: see s 17(1).

14 *Gill v Newton* (1866) 14 WR 490.

15 'Mortgagor' includes any person deriving title under the original mortgagor: see the Law of Property Act 1925 s 205(1)(xvi); and PARA 104 note 1. Thus the persons to whom notice may be given appear to be the mortgagor and all the incumbrancers; and if these are treated as 'several mortgagors', notice to the first incumbrancer who has given notice of his security to the mortgagee who sells is sufficient. On the other hand, as long as the mortgagor retains an equity of redemption, it may be that he remains sole mortgagor for the purposes of s 103 (see the text to note 12), so that notice to him is necessary and sufficient.

16 *Hoole v Smith* (1881) 17 ChD 434. However, it seems proper to give the notice to the mortgagor and the first of the subsequent incumbrancers.

17 See the Land Charges Act 1972 s 2(1), (4)(i); PARA 262; and REAL PROPERTY AND REGISTRATION vol 87 (2012) PARAS 720–721. As to puisne mortgages see PARA 160 note 5.

18 *Tozer v Buxton* (1888) 5 TLR 7.

458. Form of notice requiring payment of mortgage money. A notice requiring payment of the mortgage money[1] may be in the form of a demand for immediate payment, with an intimation that if the money is not paid before the expiration of three months from the date of service the mortgagee will proceed to sell; but it is equally effectual if it is in the form of a notice to pay at the expiration of that period, as the three months' default begins to run forthwith[2]. Under an express power of sale the notice is good if in effect it gives the mortgagor the prescribed period of warning[3]. A notice is not rendered ineffective if it overstates the principal[4].

1 As to such notices see PARA 457.
2 *Barker v Illingworth* [1908] 2 Ch 20, distinguishing *Selwyn v Garfit* (1888) 38 ChD 273, CA, where it was held that a notice was bad because it was given before the legal date for payment of the mortgage money had arrived.
3 *Metters v Brown* (1863) 33 LJCh 97. As to express powers of sale see PARAS 443–444.
4 *Clyde Properties Ltd v Tasker* [1970] NZLR 754.

459. When power of sale may be exercised. The mortgagee may not exercise the power of sale until the notice, where notice is required[1], has expired, or until such other event as makes it immediately exercisable; but he may enter into a conditional contract to sell on the power becoming exercisable, and may carry that contract into effect provided that the price is then proper[2]. The acceptance of a bill of exchange for the amount due only suspends the notice, and on the dishonour of the bill the notice revives and the mortgagee may sell without a fresh notice[3].

1 As to the required notice see PARAS 457–458.
2 *Major v Ward* (1847) 5 Hare 598 at 604; *Farrar v Farrars Ltd* (1888) 40 ChD 395 at 412, CA.
3 *Wood v Murton* (1877) 47 LJQB 191.

460. When mortgagee may be restrained from exercising power of sale. The mortgagee will not be restrained from exercising his power of sale because the amount due is in dispute[1], or because the mortgagor has begun a redemption claim[2], or because the mortgagor objects to the manner in which the sale is being arranged[3]. He will be restrained, however, if the mortgagor pays the amount claimed into court[4], that is, normally, the amount which the mortgagee claims to be due to him[5], unless, on the terms of the mortgage, the claim is excessive[6]; but where he was the mortgagor's solicitor at the time of the mortgage, the court will fix a sum probably sufficient to cover his claim[7]. The mortgagee will also be restrained if, upon a subsequent incumbrancer offering to pay off the first mortgage, the mortgagee denies his title to redeem[8], and possibly where the validity of the mortgage or the availability of the power of sale is in issue[9]. The extent to which a mortgagee of a ship is bound to a charterparty entered into by the mortgagor is considered elsewhere in this work[10]. The sale is improper if at the time of sale the mortgagor tenders the amount due for principal and interest, even though without costs[11].

Where a mortgage deed conferring an express power of sale contains a covenant that the power is not to be exercised without a specified notice, but that the only remedy for breach of the covenant is to be in damages against the mortgagee, it has been held that the court cannot restrain the sale on the ground of want of notice[12]; but it seems that, ordinarily, want of due notice in accordance with the terms of an express power of sale, as it is a ground for setting aside a sale against a purchaser with knowledge, is a ground for restraining a sale[13]. If the mortgagee has, in exercise of his statutory power of sale, entered into a contract for the sale of the property, the court will not, upon tender of the money due under the mortgage, interfere to stop the completion of the sale by conveyance unless the contract was entered into in bad faith[14]. The fact that the contract is at an undervalue is not by itself proof of bad faith[15].

1 *Cockell v Bacon* (1852) 16 Beav 158; *Gill v Newton* (1866) 14 WR 490. As to restraining the sale where it involves a breach of trust see *Merest v Murray* (1866) 14 LT 321. As to a sale after a winding up petition by the mortgagee see *Re Cambrian Mining Co Ltd, ex p Fell* (1881) 50 LJCh 836.
2 *Gomba Holdings UK Ltd v Homan* [1986] 1 WLR 1301, 2 BCC 99, 102. See also *Adams v Scott* (1859) 7 WR 213. As to proceedings for redemption see PARA 661 et seq.
3 *Anon* (1821) 6 Madd 10.
4 *Jones v Matthie* (1847) 11 Jur 504; *Whitworth v Rhodes* (1850) 20 LJCh 105; *Warner v Jacob* (1882) 20 ChD 220 at 224; *Cavenagh v Cohen* (1919) 147 LT Jo 252; *Duke v Robson* [1973] 1 All ER 481, [1973] 1 WLR 267, CA. As to payments into court see CIVIL PROCEDURE vol 12A (2015) PARA 1653 et seq.
5 *Hill v Kirkwood* (1880) 28 WR 358, CA. This is a rule of practice, which may no longer be applied as inflexibly as before: see *Rottenburg v Monjack* [1992] BCC 688, [1992] NPC 89; *Eltran Prty Ltd v Westpac Banking Corpn* (1988) 32 FCR 195.
6 *Hickson v Darlow* (1883) 23 ChD 690, CA.
7 *Macleod v Jones* (1883) 24 ChD 289, CA.
8 *Rhodes v Buckland* (1852) 16 Beav 212.
9 *Ashley Guarantee plc v Zacaria* [1993] 1 All ER 254, [1993] 1 WLR 62, CA. See also *Allfox Building Pty Ltd v Bank of Melbourne* (1992) NSW Conv R 55-634, 66 ALJ 863.
10 See SHIPPING AND MARITIME LAW vol 93 (2008) PARA 331.
11 *Jenkins v Jones* (1860) 2 Giff 99.
12 *Prichard v Wilson* (1864) 10 Jur NS 330. As to express powers of sale see PARAS 443–444.
13 *Selwyn v Garfit* (1888) 38 ChD 273, CA; and see PARA 458. See also CIVIL PROCEDURE vol 12 (2015) PARAS 1152–1154.
14 *Lord Waring v London and Manchester Assurance Co Ltd* [1935] Ch 310; *Property and Bloodstock Ltd v Emerton* [1968] Ch 94, [1967] 3 All ER 321, CA; *Corbett v Halifax plc* [2002] EWCA Civ 1849, [2003] 4 All ER 180, [2003] 1 WLR 964. As to statutory power of sale see PARA 446 et seq.
15 *Lord Waring v London and Manchester Assurance Co Ltd* [1935] Ch 310.

(vii) Mode of Exercise of the Power

461. Duty of mortgagee on exercise of power of sale. A mortgagee is not a trustee for the mortgagor as regards the exercise of the power of sale[1]. He is not obliged to exercise the power of sale even if advised to do so, or if the asset is depreciating, however advantageous a sale might be to the mortgagor[2]. He is not obliged to delay in the hope of obtaining a higher price[3], or if redemption is imminent[4] or until after the pursuit of an application for planning permission or the grant of a lease of the mortgaged property, though the outcome of the application and the effect of the grant of the lease may be to increase the market value of the mortgaged property and price obtained on sale. A mortgagee is entitled to sell the property in the condition in which it stands without investing money or time in increasing its likely sale value. He is entitled to discontinue efforts already undertaken to increase the likely sale value in favour of such a sale[5]. He can decide if and when to sell on the basis of his own interests[6].

A mortgagee owes a duty in equity to exercise the power in good faith for the purpose of obtaining repayment[7] and to take reasonable precautions to secure a proper price[8]. The duty is not breached where the mortgagee has mixed motives for a sale, one of which is to secure repayment[9]. Nor is the duty breached by a mortgagee's assessment of the market value of the mortgaged property which falls within an acceptable margin of error[10]. The duty is owed to the mortgagor, subsequent mortgagees[11], and a surety[12] but not to others such as beneficiaries under a trust of the mortgaged property[13]. The duty cannot be replaced or supplemented by a liability in negligence[14]. It can, however, be excluded by agreement[15].

The limitation period for a claim against the mortgagee for breach of its duty in equity is six years[16].

If the mortgagor seeks relief promptly[17], a sale will be set aside if there is some element of impropriety or bad faith on the part of the mortgagee in the exercise of its power of sale[18], but not on the ground of undervalue alone[19], and still less if the mortgagor has in some degree sanctioned the proceedings leading up to the sale[20] or if it would be inequitable as between the mortgagor and the purchaser for the sale to be set aside[21]. However, if the mortgagee does not sell with proper precautions, he will be charged in taking the accounts with any loss resulting from it[22] or liable for damages. The prima facie measure of damage is the reduction in the value of the equity of redemption[23].

1 *Cuckmere Brick Co Ltd v Mutual Finance Ltd* [1971] Ch 949, [1971] 2 All ER 633, CA; *Silven Properties Ltd v Royal Bank of Scotland plc* [2003] EWCA Civ 1409, [2004] 4 All ER 484, [2004] 1 WLR 997. As to express powers of sale see PARAS 443–444. As to the statutory power of sale see PARA 446 et seq.
2 *Lloyd's Bank plc v Bryant* [1996] NPC 31; *Palk v Mortgage Services Funding plc* [1993] Ch 330, [1993] 2 All ER 481, CA; *China and South Sea Bank Ltd v Tan Soon Gin (alias George Tan)* [1990] 1 AC 536, [1989] 3 All ER 839, PC. If the mortgagor wishes the property to be sold he should apply for an order for sale under the Law of Property Act 1925 s 91: see PARAS 621 et seq, 676. See also PARA 577.
3 *Tse Kwong Lam v Wong Chit Sen* [1983] 3 All ER 54, [1983] 1 WLR 1349, PC; *Silven Properties Ltd v Royal Bank of Scotland plc* [2003] EWCA Civ 1409, [2004] 4 All ER 484, [2004] 1 WLR 997.
4 *Routestone Ltd v Minories Finance Ltd* [1997] 1 EGLR 123, [1996] NPC 83.
5 *Silven Properties Ltd v Royal Bank of Scotland plc* [2003] EWCA Civ 1409, [2004] 4 All ER 484, [2004] 1 WLR 997.
6 *China and South Sea Bank Ltd v Tan Soon Gin (alias George Tan)* [1990] 1 AC 536, [1989] 3 All ER 839, PC; *Silven Properties Ltd v Royal Bank of Scotland plc* [2003] EWCA Civ 1409, [2004] 4 All ER 484, [2004] 1 WLR 997.
7 *Downsview Nominees Ltd v First City Corpn Ltd* [1993] AC 295, [1993] 3 All ER 626, PC; *Silven Properties Ltd v Royal Bank of Scotland plc* [2003] EWCA Civ 1409, [2004] 4 All ER 484, [2004] 1 WLR 997. See also *Mortgage Express v Mardner* [2004] EWCA Civ 1859, [2004] All ER (D) 299 (Dec); *Bradford and Bingley plc v Ross* [2005] EWCA Civ 394, (2005) Times, 2 May, [2005] All ER (D) 210 (Mar).

8   *Cuckmere Brick Co Ltd v Mutual Finance Ltd* [1971] Ch 949, [1971] 2 All ER 633; *Downsview Nominees Ltd v First City Corpn Ltd* [1993] AC 295, [1993] 3 All ER 626, PC; *Tse Kwong Lam v Wong Chit Sen* [1983] 3 All ER 54, [1983] 1 WLR 1349, PC. See also *Alpstream AG v PK Airfinance Sarl* [2013] EWHC 2370 (Comm), [2014] 1 All ER (Comm) 441 (deliberate loss caused by unlawful acts of mortgagee).

9   *Meretz Investments NV v ACP Ltd* [2006] EWHC 74 (Ch), [2007] Ch 197, [2006] 3 All ER 1029 (partly revsd on other grounds [2007] EWCA Civ 1303, [2008] Ch 244, [2007] All ER (D) 156 (Dec)).

10 *Michael v Miller* [2004] EWCA Civ 282, [2004] 2 EGLR 151.

11 *Downsview Nominees Ltd v First City Corpn Ltd* [1993] AC 295, [1993] 3 All ER 626, PC.

12 *Standard Chartered Bank Ltd v Walker* [1982] 3 All ER 938, [1982] 1 WLR 1410, CA; *China and South Sea Bank Ltd v Tan Soon Gin (alias George Tan)* [1990] 1 AC 536, [1989] 3 All ER 839, PC.

13 *Parker-Tweedale v Dunbar Bank plc* [1991] Ch 12, [1990] 2 All ER 577, CA. A beneficiary can sue on behalf of the trust if the trustee unreasonably refuses to do so or has committed some breach of his duties to the beneficiaries: *Parker-Tweedale v Dunbar Bank plc* above.

14 *Downsview Nominees Ltd v First City Corpn Ltd* [1993] AC 295, [1993] 3 All ER 626, PC.

15 *Bishop v Bonham* [1988] 1 WLR 742, [1988] BCLC 656, CA.

16 See *Raja v Lloyds TSB Bank plc* [2001] EWCA Civ 210, 82 P & CR 191, [2001] Lloyd's Rep Bank 113; and LIMITATION PERIODS vol 68 (2008) PARAS 953–954.

17 *Nutt v Easton* [1900] 1 Ch 29, CA. As to such relief see CIVIL PROCEDURE vol 12 (2015) PARAS 1126–1127.

18 *Corbett v Halifax Building Society* [2002] EWCA Civ 1849, [2003] 4 All ER 180, [2003] 1 WLR 964; *Warner v Jacob* (1882) 20 ChD 220 at 224; *Haddington Island Quarry Co Ltd v Huson* [1911] AC 722, PC; *Jones v Matthie* (1847) 11 Jur 504; *Davey v Durrant, Smith v Durrant* (1857) 1 De G & J 535 at 538; *Adams v Scott* (1859) 7 WR 213.

19 *Corbett v Halifax Building Society* [2002] EWCA Civ 1849, [2003] 4 All ER 180, [2003] 1 WLR 964; *Lord Waring v London and Manchester Assurance Co Ltd* [1935] Ch 310.

20 *Newport Farm Ltd v Damesh Holdings Ltd* [2003] UKPC 54, 147 Sol Jo LB 1117; *Ferrand v Clay* (1837) 1 Jur 165.

21 *Tse Kwong Lam v Wong Chit Sen* [1983] 3 All ER 54, [1983] 1 WLR 1349, PC.

22 *Wolff v Vanderzee* (1869) 17 WR 547; 3 Seton's Form of Decrees, Judgments and Orders in Equity (7th Edn, 1912) 1890.

23 *Adamson v Halifax plc* [2002] EWCA Civ 1134, [2003] 4 All ER 423, [2003] 1 WLR 60, CA. As to the equity of redemption see PARAS 107, 304 et seq.

462. Mode of sale. The burden is on the mortgagor to show that the mortgagee has breached the duty to take reasonable precautions to secure a proper price, unless the sale is to a company in which the mortgagee is interested or a similarly connected purchaser[1]. There is no general obligation upon a mortgagee to sell the whole of the mortgaged property if he does not choose to, but he must not, in selling what he does sell, deliberately destroy its value by failing to sell what would normally and naturally form part of what he does sell[2]. The mortgagee is not bound to postpone the sale in the hope of obtaining a better price nor to adopt a piecemeal method of sale which could only be carried out over a substantial period or at some risk of loss[3]. A mortgagee selling specialist property should take specialist advice as to its value, advertising and the mode of sale[4]. Although the mortgagee can choose the time of sale he should normally ensure that the property is exposed to the market for an adequate length of time[5], in appropriate publications[6], and should obtain an open market valuation[7]. It is not necessarily sufficient for the mortgagee to advertise the property and sell it at auction[8].

It is an open question whether a mortgagee discharges his duty by instructing a competent agent[9]. An agent is not negligent in his handling of the sale merely because another agent would have acted differently[10] and a mortgagee who has instructed an agent is unlikely to have breached his duty to the mortgagor merely because a different agent would have given different advice.

The mortgagee may sell on the terms that a substantial part, or even the whole, is to remain on mortgage[11].

1 *Tse Kwong Lam v Wong Chit Sen* [1983] 3 All ER 54, [1983] 1 WLR 1349, PC. There is no such burden on the mortgagee simply because the selling agents are connected to the mortgagee: *Morgan v Lloyds Bank plc* [1998] Lloyd's Rep Bank 72, CA. The mortgagee cannot sell to himself: see PARA 469.
2 *Huish v Ellis* [1995] BCC 462, [1995] NPC 3; *Champagne Perrier-Jouet SA v HH Finch Ltd* [1982] 3 All ER 713, [1982] 1 WLR 1359.
3 *Tse Kwong Lam v Wong Chit Sen* [1983] 3 All ER 54, [1983] 1 WLR 1349, PC; *Bell v Long* [2008] EWHC 1273 (Ch), [2008] 2 BCLC 706, [2008] BPIR 1211, [2008] All ER (D) 179 (Jun).
4 *American Express International Banking Corpn v Hurley* [1985] 3 All ER 564, [1986] BCLC 52.
5 *Predeth v Castle Phillips Finance Co Ltd* [1986] 2 EGLR 144, 279 Estates Gazette 1355, CA, where a period of three months was held to be appropriate. See also *Routestone Ltd v Minories Finance Ltd* [1997] 1 EGLR 123, [1996] NPC 83.
6 *American Express International Banking Corpn v Hurley* [1985] 3 All ER 564, [1986] BCLC 52.
7 *Predeth v Castle Phillips Finance Co Ltd* [1986] 2 EGLR 144, 279 Estates Gazette 1355, CA.
8 *Tse Kwong Lam v Wong Chit Sen* [1983] 3 All ER 54, [1983] 1 WLR 1349, PC.
9 See *Routestone Ltd v Minories Finance Ltd* [1997] 1 EGLR 123, [1996] NPC 83. See also *Huish v Ellis* [1995] BCC 462, [1995] NPC 3, where it was suggested that the weight of authority was in favour of a mortgagee being liable where he employs an agent who is negligent.
10 *Routestone Ltd v Minories Finance Ltd* [1997] 1 EGLR 123, [1996] NPC 83.
11 *Davey v Durrant, Smith v Durrant* (1857) 1 De G & J 535 at 553; *Thurlow v Mackeson* (1868) LR 4 QB 97; *Bettyes v Maynard* (1883) 31 WR 461, CA; *Farrar v Farrars Ltd* (1888) 40 ChD 395 at 413, CA; *Kennedy v De Trafford* [1897] AC 180, HL. See also *Belton v Bass, Ratcliffe and Gretton Ltd* [1922] 2 Ch 449, where the purchaser was given a right to call on the mortgagee to repurchase. In *Thurlow v Mackeson* above, the whole purchase price, except the deposit, was left on mortgage.

463. Different securities held by one mortgagee. Where different properties are mortgaged by different mortgagors to the same mortgagee, and a sale of the two properties together is beneficial, both may be sold together and the purchase money apportioned[1]. Where the properties are quite separate, evidence is required that the joint sale will produce a higher price; where they are united, for example a house and a garden, or are undivided shares of the same property, this is not necessary; and the apportionment must be made on the advice of a competent person[2].

1 *Hiatt v Hillman* (1871) 19 WR 694; *Re Cooper and Allen's Contract for Sale to Harlech* (1876) 4 ChD 802.
2 *Re Cooper and Allen's Contract for Sale to Harlech* (1876) 4 ChD 802 at 816.

464. Conditions of sale. A mortgagee is entitled to sell upon such conditions as he thinks suitable for securing a sale of the property, and the sale is not invalidated by the insertion of any condition in ordinary use, notwithstanding that in a sense it may be depreciatory[1]. He is entitled to use stringent conditions if these are required by the state of the title[2]. Express powers usually provide for the mortgagee selling subject to such conditions as he thinks fit[3], and similar provision is made in regard to the statutory powers[4]. The mortgagee is not answerable for any involuntary loss happening in or about the exercise or execution of the statutory power of sale or of any trust connected with it or of any power or provision contained in the mortgage deed[5].

1 *Falkner v Equitable Reversionary Society* (1858) 4 Drew 352. See also *Hobson v Bell* (1839) 2 Beav 17.
2 *Kershaw v Kalow* (1855) 1 Jur NS 974. As to conditions of sale see generally CONVEYANCING vol 23 (2013) PARAS 168–169.
3 As to express powers of sale see PARAS 443–444.
4 See the Law of Property Act 1925 s 101(1)(i); and PARA 447.
5 Law of Property Act 1925 s 106(3). The practical value of this statutory protection is doubtful as the mortgagee is only liable in any event for loss caused by a breach of its duty.

465. Right of sale as between successive incumbrancers. Where there are successive mortgages, the first mortgagee may exercise his power of sale without the concurrence of the subsequent mortgagees, but he must account to them for the surplus sale money[1]. A first mortgagee may buy a subsequent incumbrance at a reduced price without communicating to the subsequent incumbrancer an anticipated advantageous sale; and the sale, if afterwards effected, will be valid[2]. If the second mortgagee exercises his power of sale, he can sell subject to the first mortgage[3]; or he can sell free from it[4], either with the consent of the first mortgagee, who will be paid off out of the purchase money and will concur in the conveyance to the purchaser, or under the statutory power of sale[5]. In the latter case, application[6] should be made to the court to allow payment into court of an amount sufficient to meet the mortgage debt and any interest due on it[7], and of such additional amount as the court considers will be sufficient to meet the contingency of further costs, expenses and interest, and any other contingency, except depreciation of investments[8]. The further sum must not exceed one-tenth of the original amount paid in, unless the court for special reason thinks fit to require a larger additional amount[9]. Although the additional sum to be paid in is not intended to cover depreciation of investments, it seems that this risk can be taken into account[10]. If the sum paid in proves deficient, the mortgagee can follow the remainder of the proceeds of sale[11]. On the application being made, the court may, if it thinks fit, direct or allow payment into court[12]. Thereupon the court may, if it thinks fit, and either after or without any notice to the incumbrancer[13], as it thinks fit, declare the land to be freed from the mortgage[14], and make any order for conveyance, or vesting order, proper for giving effect to the sale or exchange[15]; but the vendor is not estopped from alleging subsequently that the incumbrance is statute-barred[16].

1 As to the application of proceeds of sale see PARAS 474–477.
2 *Dolman v Nokes* (1855) 22 Beav 402; affd (1856) 27 LTOS 178, CA.
3 See *Manser v Dix* (1857) 8 De GM & G 703.
4 *Kaolim Private Ltd v United Overseas Land Ltd* [1983] 1 WLR 472, 127 Sol Jo 241, PC.
5 See the Law of Property Act 1925 s 101(1); and PARA 446.
6 The court may dispense with service of notice of the application on the vendor or purchaser: see the Law of Property Act 1925 s 50(4). As to the procedure on an application see PARA 631.
7 See the Law of Property Act 1925 s 50(1)(b). The amount to be paid in is not limited to the bare amount of mortgage debt; the court may direct payment in of such amount as in the court's opinion is sufficient when invested in government securities to meet the mortgage debt and any interest on it: *Re Wilberforce's Trusts, Wilberforce v Wilberforce* [1915] 1 Ch 94.
8 See the Law of Property Act 1925 s 50(1). Section 50 applies to sales or exchanges whenever made, and to incumbrances whether created by statute or otherwise: see s 50(6). Application may be made under s 50 where land subject to any incumbrance, whether immediately realisable or payable or not, is sold or exchanged by the court or out of court and may be made by any party to the sale or exchange: see s 50(1). As to the meaning of 'incumbrance' see PARA 197 note 4. As to the meaning of 'land' see PARA 104 note 2.
9 See the Law of Property Act 1925 s 50(1); and *Milford Haven Rly and Estate Co v Mowatt, Re Lake and Taylor's Mortgage, Spain v Mowatt* (1884) 28 ChD 402.
10 See the Law of Property Act 1925 s 50(1); and *Milford Haven Rly and Estate Co v Mowatt, Re Lake and Taylor's Mortgage, Spain v Mowatt* (1884) 28 ChD 402.
11 *Re Wilberforce's Trusts, Wilberforce v Wilberforce* [1915] 1 Ch 94.
12 See the Law of Property Act 1925 s 50(1). The court's discretion ought not, it seems, to be exercised by a master, at least where the amount involved is large: *Re Wilberforce's Trusts, Wilberforce v Wilberforce* [1915] 1 Ch 94 at 100.
13 As to the meaning of 'incumbrancer' see PARA 197 note 4.
14 As to the meaning of 'mortgage' see PARA 101 note 4.
15 Law of Property Act 1925 s 50(2); and see *Dickin v Dickin* (1882) 30 WR 887; cf *Re Uplands, Portmore Road, Weybridge, Surrey* [1948] WN 165. The court may also:

(1) give directions for the retention and investment of the money in court and for the payment or application of its income (Law of Property Act 1925 s 50(2));

(2) declare all other land, if any, affected by the incumbrance (besides the land sold or exchanged) to be freed from the incumbrance, and this power may be exercised either after or without notice to the incumbrancer, and notwithstanding that on a previous occasion an order relating to the same incumbrance has been made by the court which was confined to the land then sold or exchanged (s 50(3));

(3) after notice served on the persons interested in or entitled to the money or fund in court, direct its payment or transfer to the persons entitled to receive or give a discharge for the same, and generally give directions for the application or distribution of the capital or its income (s 50(5)).

16 *Re M'Swiney and Hartnett's Contract* [1921] 1 IR 178.

466. Sale of fixtures. The sale of fixtures separately from the land is not authorised by a statutory power to sell the mortgaged property[1] or any part of it, or by an express power of sale[2] which does not in terms give that power, whether the fixtures are expressly mentioned in the mortgage[3] or not[4]. Trade fixtures pass as part of the mortgaged property[5].

1 As to the statutory power of sale see PARA 446 et seq.
2 As to express powers of sale see PARAS 443–444.
3 *Re Brooke* [1894] 2 Ch 600.
4 *Re Yates, Batchelor v Yates* (1888) 38 ChD 112, CA. See also *Re Joyce, ex p Barclay* (1874) 9 Ch App 576; *Re Rogerstone Brick and Stone Co, Southall v Wescomb* [1919] 1 Ch 110, CA; *Hunter v Hunter* [1936] AC 222 at 248–249, HL, per Lord Hailsham LC; *Kay's Leasing Corpn Pty Ltd v CSR Provident Fund Nominees Pty Ltd* [1962] VR 429.
5 *Southport and West Lancashire Banking Co v Thompson* (1887) 37 ChD 64, CA (mortgage of leaseholds by sub-demise). See also PARA 169. As to the statutory power of sale extending to fixtures see PARA 450.

467. Sale of minerals. In a mortgage deed executed after 31 December 1911 the mortgagee's statutory power of sale[1] includes power to sell the mortgaged[2] property or any part of it with an exception or reservation of all or any mines or minerals[3], or to sell all or any mines and minerals apart from the surface[4]. The sale may be made with or without an exception or reservation of all or any of the mines and minerals in or under the mortgaged property, and with or without a grant or reservation of powers of working, wayleaves or rights of way, rights of water and drainage and other powers, easements, rights and privileges for or connected with mining purposes in relation to the property remaining unsold or any part of it or to any property sold[5]. These powers apply, however, only if and so far as a contrary intention is not expressed in the mortgage deed and have effect subject to its terms and provisions[6]. In the absence of express or statutory power the mortgagee is not entitled to effect such sales[7].

Where a mortgagee has a power of sale which has become exercisable but does not extend to the separate dealing with the land and the minerals[8], the court may on his application authorise him and the persons deriving title under him to dispose: (1) of the land[9] with the exception or reservation of all or any mines and minerals[10]; or (2) of all or any mines and minerals separately from the land[11], and with or without rights and powers of or incidental to the working, getting or carrying away of the minerals[12]. The power so conferred has effect as if the same were contained in the mortgage[13].

1 As to the meaning of 'mortgagee' see PARA 104 note 1. As to the statutory power of sale see PARA 446 et seq.
2 As to the meaning of 'mortgage' see PARA 101 note 4.
3 See the Law of Property Act 1925 s 101(2)(i). As to the meaning of 'mines and minerals' see PARA 104 note 2.
4 See the Law of Property Act 1925 s 101(2)(ii).

5　Law of Property Act 1925 s 101(2)(ii)(b). As to the power to impose restrictions and grant or reserve easements see PARA 468.
6　See the Law of Property Act 1925 s 101(4). The statutory forms may be varied or extended by the mortgage deed: see s 101(3).
7　*Buckley v Howell* (1861) 29 Beav 546. See also *Re Gladstone, Gladstone v Gladstone* [1900] 2 Ch 101 at 105, CA.
8　Eg where the mortgage was executed before 1 January 1912: see the Law of Property Act 1925 s 92(1) (s 92(1) numbered as such by the County Courts Act 1984 s 148(1), Sch 2 Pt II para 3); and the text to notes 1–3.
9　As to the meaning of 'land' see PARA 104 note 2.
10　See the Law of Property Act 1925 s 92(1)(a) (s 92(1) as so numbered: see note 8).
11　See the Law of Property Act 1925 s 92(1)(b) (s 92(1) as so numbered: see note 8).
12　See the Law of Property Act 1925 s 92(1)(a), (b) (s 92(1) as so numbered: see note 8).
13　Law of Property Act 1925 s 92(1) (as so numbered: see note 8).

468. Easements and covenants. In the absence of statutory power, the mortgagee may not, on a sale of part of the property, grant easements over, or impose restrictive covenants upon, the part remaining unsold, or reserve easements or the benefit of covenants over the part sold[1], save that a conveyance made in pursuance of such a sale has its ordinary effect with regard to apparent continuous easements. Hence it will give to the purchaser such rights of light and other easements as he would take without express mention if the mortgagee were selling as absolute owner[2].

Where the mortgage[3] deed is executed after 31 December 1911, the mortgagee may, on the exercise of his statutory power of sale[4] create restrictive covenants or conditions against either the part sold or the part remaining unsold[5], and may on sale of the mortgaged property or any part of it, or of mines and minerals apart from the surface, grant or reserve rights of way and water, easements, rights and privileges for or connected with building or other purposes in relation to the property remaining in mortgage or any part of it or any property sold[6], and may impose covenants on the purchaser to expend money on the land sold[7]. These powers apply only if and as far as a contrary intention is not expressed in the mortgage deed and have effect subject to its terms and conditions[8].

1　See *Dayrell v Hoare* (1840) 12 Ad & El 356; *Born v Turner* [1900] 2 Ch 211. As to the creation of easements see REAL PROPERTY AND REGISTRATION vol 87 (2012) PARA 846 et seq. As to restrictive covenants see REAL PROPERTY AND REGISTRATION vol 87 (2012) PARA 1076 et seq.
2　*Born v Turner* [1900] 2 Ch 211. See also REAL PROPERTY AND REGISTRATION vol 87 (2012) PARAS 916, 1024.
3　As to the meaning of 'mortgage' see PARA 101 note 4.
4　As to the statutory power of sale see PARA 446 et seq.
5　See the Law of Property Act 1925 s 101(2)(i). The covenants may be with respect to building on, or other user of land, or with respect to mines and minerals, or for the purpose of the more beneficial working thereof, or with respect to any other thing: see s 101(2)(i). As to the meanings of 'land' and 'mines and minerals' see PARA 104 note 2.
6　See the Law of Property Act 1925 s 101(2)(ii)(a).
7　See the Law of Property Act 1925 s 101(2)(ii)(c).
8　Law of Property Act 1925 s 101(4). The powers may be varied or extended by the mortgage deed: see s 101(3).

(viii) Who may Purchase

469. Mortgagee cannot sell to himself. A mortgagee cannot sell to himself, either alone or with others, nor to a trustee for himself[1]. Unless there are different persons filling the positions of vendor and purchaser the transaction is not a sale at all, and is not an exercise of the power. The interposition of a trustee does not affect the substance of the transaction[2]. The same principle prevents a sale to an agent, solicitor[3] or employee acting for the mortgagee in the matter of the sale[4];

consequently, on a sale by a building society as mortgagee, a purchase by the secretary[5] or other officer concerned with the conduct of the sale may be set aside[6]. If there is in fact no conflict between the interests of the purchaser and his duty to the mortgagee, the sale is not to be set aside[7]. The mortgagee may, however, sell to an employee[8] or a solicitor who does not have conduct of the sale[9]. A sale where the purchaser employed the mortgagee's clerk to bid has been set aside[10]. A sale by the mortgagee to a company in which he is interested will not be impugned if the mortgagee exercises the power in good faith for the purpose of obtaining repayment and shows that he took reasonable precautions to secure a proper price[11]. Where the mortgagee fails to satisfy the court that he took all reasonable steps to obtain the best price reasonably obtainable and that his company bought at the best price, the court will, as a general rule, set aside the sale; but the mortgagor will be left to his remedy in damages against the mortgagee for the failure of the mortgagee to secure the best price if it will be inequitable as between a mortgagor and the purchaser for the sale to be set aside[12]. If the sale is ordered by the court[13], the mortgagee may be given liberty to make an offer for the property[14].

1   *Downes v Grazebrook* (1817) 3 Mer 200; *Robertson v Norris* (1857) 1 Giff 421; *National Bank of Australasia v United Hand-in-Hand and Band of Hope Co* (1879) 4 App Cas 391 at 404, PC; *Henderson v Astwood, Astwood v Cobbold, Cobbold v Astwood* [1894] AC 150, PC; *Williams v Wellingborough Borough Council* [1975] 3 All ER 462, [1975] 1 WLR 1327, CA (right of pre-emption in favour of local authority); *Australian and New Zealand Banking Group Ltd v Bangadilly Pastoral Co Pty Ltd* (1978) 19 ALR 519, Aust HC.
2   *Farrar v Farrars Ltd* (1888) 40 ChD 395 at 409, CA.
3   *Whitcomb v Minchin* (1820) 5 Madd 91; *Orme v Wright* (1839) 3 Jur 19; *Re Bloye's Trust* (1849) 1 Mac & G 488 at 494 (affd sub nom *Lewis v Hillman* (1852) 3 HL Cas 607); *Martinson v Clowes* (1882) 21 ChD 857 at 860. But see *York Buildings Co v MacKenzie* (1795) 8 Bro Parl Cas 42, HL, cited in *Tse Kwong Lam v Wong Chit Sen* [1983] 3 All ER 54, [1983] 1 WLR 1349, as to the position of an agent for the creditors who purchased an estate of the insolvent debtor at auction.
4   *Corbett v Halifax plc* [2002] EWCA Civ 1849, [2003] 4 All ER 180, [2003] 1 WLR 964.
5   *Martinson v Clowes* (1882) 21 ChD 857; affd (1885) 52 LT 706, CA.
6   *Hodson v Deans* [1903] 2 Ch 647.
7   *Corbett v Halifax plc* [2002] EWCA Civ 1849, [2003] 4 All ER 180, [2003] 1 WLR 964.
8   *Corbett v Halifax plc* [2002] EWCA Civ 1849, [2003] 4 All ER 180, [2003] 1 WLR 964.
9   *Guest v Smythe* (1870) 5 Ch App 551, where the solicitor's name appeared on the conditions of sale, but he was only solicitor to the mortgagee's creditor; *Nutt v Easton* [1899] 1 Ch 873, where the solicitor had acted for the mortgagee, but was not employed to effect a sale (affd on the question of laches [1900] 1 Ch 29, CA).
10 *Parnell v Tyler* (1833) 2 LJCh 195. See also *Orme v Wright* (1839) 3 Jur 19, questioning the validity of a purchase by an agent who had acted in effecting the mortgage and receiving interest.
11 *Tse Kwong Lam v Wong Chit Sen* [1983] 3 All ER 54, [1983] 1 WLR 1349, PC. See also *Mortgage Express v Mardner* [2004] EWCA Civ 1859, [2001] All ER (D) 299 (Dec); *Bradford and Bingley plc v Ross* [2005] EWCA Civ 394, (2005) Times, 2 May, [2005] All ER (D) 210 (Mar).
12 *Tse Kwong Lam v Wong Chit Sen* [1983] 3 All ER 54, [1983] 1 WLR 1349, PC (inexcusable delay by the mortgagor in prosecuting his claim, and therefore the only remedy available was damages, and not an order to set the sale aside).
13 Ie under the Law of Property Act 1925 s 91(2): see PARA 621.
14 *Palk v Mortgage Services Funding plc* [1993] Ch 330, [1993] 2 All ER 481, CA.

470. Later mortgagee may purchase. There is no fiduciary relation between co-owners of the equity of redemption so as to prevent one from purchasing the property on his own account from the mortgagee[1], and for this purpose a second mortgagee is in the same position as a stranger, and obtains under the purchase a title free from any equity of redemption[2]. It makes no difference that the second mortgagee is in possession[3].

1   *Kennedy v De Trafford* [1897] AC 180, HL. See also *Nunes v District Registrar of Winnipeg Land Titles Office* [1971] 5 WWR 427, 21 DLR (3d) 97. As to the equity of redemption see PARAS 107, 304 et seq.
2   *Parkinson v Hanbury* (1860) 1 Drew & Sm 143 at 146 (this point was not dealt with on appeal (1865) 2 De GJ & Sm 450; affd (1867) LR 2 HL 1); *Shaw v Bunny* (1864) 33 Beav 494 (affd (1865) 2 De GJ & Sm 468); *Kirkwood v Thompson* (1865) 2 De GJ & Sm 613 at 618. See also *Rajah Kishendatt Ram v Rajah Mumtaz Ali Khan* (1879) LR 6 Ind App 145 at 160, PC; *Flower & Sons Ltd v Pritchard* (1908) 53 Sol Jo 178.
3   *Kirkwood v Thompson* (1865) 2 De GJ & Sm 613 at 619.

(ix) Protection of Purchasers

471. Protection of purchasers from irregularity in sale. In the absence of any provision for the protection of purchasers, evidence must be furnished that the event on which the power of sale is to arise has happened[1]. Where a sale is made in exercise of the statutory power[2], the purchaser's title is not impeachable on the ground that:

(1)   no case had arisen to authorise the sale[3];
(2)   due notice was not given[4];
(3)   the permission of the court, when required, was not obtained[5]; or
(4)   the power was otherwise improperly or irregularly exercised[6].

A purchaser is also, whether before or on conveyance[7], not concerned to see or inquire whether a case has arisen to authorise the sale, or due notice has been given, or whether the power is otherwise properly and regularly exercised[8]. A purchaser for value who does not have notice of an impropriety connected with the exercise of the power of sale is not affected by that impropriety merely because of a lack of good faith unconnected with the impropriety[9].

However, any person damnified by the unauthorised, improper or irregular exercise of the power has his remedy in damages against the person exercising the power[10]. Unless a contrary intention appears, a conveyance on sale by a mortgagee[11] is deemed to have been made in exercise of the statutory power of sale[12].

The written receipt of the mortgagee is a sufficient discharge for any money arising from the exercise of his statutory power of sale or for any money or securities comprised in his mortgage[13] or arising under it[14].

1   *Hobson v Bell* (1839) 2 Beav 17 at 22, where the mortgagee's unsupported statutory declaration was held insufficient.
2   As to the statutory power of sale see PARA 446 et seq.
3   Law of Property Act 1925 s 104(2)(a). See also *Haddington Island Quarry Co Ltd v Huson* [1911] AC 722, PC.
4   Law of Property Act 1925 s 104(2)(b). As to notice see PARAS 457–458.
5   Law of Property Act 1925 s 104(2)(c).
6   Law of Property Act 1925 s 104(2)(d).
7   As to the meaning of 'conveyance' see PARA 168 note 1.
8   See the Law of Property Act 1925 s 104(2). As to the effect of notice of irregularity see PARA 472.
9   *Corbett v Halifax plc* [2002] EWCA Civ 1849, [2003] 4 All ER 180, [2003] 1 WLR 964. As to the doctrine of notice see EQUITABLE JURISDICTION vol 47 (2014) PARA 130 et seq.
10   See the Law of Property Act 1925 s 104(2).
11   As to the meaning of 'mortgagee' see PARA 104 note 1.
12   Law of Property Act 1925 s 104(3). Cf *Re Statutory Trusts Declared by Section 105 of the Law of Property Act 1925 affecting the Proceeds of Sale of Moat House Farm, Thurlby* [1948] Ch 191 at 194, sub nom *Young v Clarey* [1948] 1 All ER 197 at 199, per Harman J; *Re White*

Rose Cottage [1965] Ch 940, [1965] 1 All ER 11, CA (applied in *Swift 1st Ltd v Colin* [2011] EWHC 2410 (Ch), [2012] Ch 206, [2012] 2 WLR 186). As to the purchaser's lien see LIEN vol 68 (2008) PARA 866.

13   As to the meaning of 'mortgage' see PARA 101 note 4.

14   See the Law of Property Act 1925 s 107(1). See also s 113; and PARA 375. A person paying or transferring that money or those securities to the mortgagee is not concerned to inquire whether any money remains due on the mortgage: s 107(1). As to the payment to a solicitor or licensed conveyancer producing a deed containing a receipt see s 69; and PARA 370. See also LEGAL PROFESSIONS vol 66 (2015) PARA 585. See further CONVEYANCING vol 23 (2013) PARA 227; DEEDS AND OTHER INSTRUMENTS vol 32 (2012) PARA 237.

472.   Effect of notice of irregularity. The effect of the statutory protection to purchasers from irregularity in sale[1] is that the purchaser is exempted from any duty to make inquiries; and, provided that he has no notice of any irregularity, he is protected notwithstanding that an event giving rise to the power of sale has not occurred, and even though at the time of the sale the mortgage has been paid off[2]. He is not, however, protected if he has actual notice[3] of the irregularity[4]; consequently, he is not protected if the exercise of the power depends on a notice being given which in the circumstances cannot have been given[5], although he is, perhaps, protected if the want of notice might have been waived by the mortgagor[6], and he is protected if the want of notice has been in fact waived by the persons to whom it should have been given[7]. If the persons concerned propose to join in the conveyance in order to show the waiver, it seems that the purchaser cannot refuse to complete on the ground that the title offered is different from that which he had contracted to take[8].

1   See PARA 471.

2   *Dicker v Angerstein* (1876) 3 ChD 600.

3   Actual notice includes 'blind eye' knowledge and imputed knowledge; constructive notice is not enough: see *Meretz Investments NV v ACP Ltd* [2006] EWHC 74 (Ch), [2007] Ch 197, [2006] 3 All ER 1029 (partly revsd on other grounds [2007] EWCA Civ 1303, [2008] Ch 244, [2008] 2 WLR 904). But see *Bailey v Barnes* [1894] 1 Ch 25 at 30, 34, CA (a decision on the Conveyancing Act 1881 s 21 (repealed) where constructive notice was regarded as sufficient). As to the doctrine of notice see EQUITABLE JURISDICTION vol 47 (2014) PARA 130 et seq.

4   See *Lord Waring v London and Manchester Assurance Co Ltd* [1935] Ch 310 at 318.

5   *Parkinson v Hanbury* (1860) 1 Drew & Sm 143, where the mortgagor, to whom a three months' notice was to be given, was dead, and no representative had been appointed (the point was not dealt with on appeal (1865) 2 De GJ & Sm 450; affd (1867) LR 2 HL 1). See also *Selwyn v Garfit* (1888) 38 ChD 273, CA (notice could only be given after default, and the necessary period had not elapsed); and PARA 458.

6   *Selwyn v Garfit* (1888) 38 ChD 273 at 285, CA, per Bowen LJ.

7   *Re Thompson and Holt* (1890) 44 ChD 492.

8   *Re Thompson and Holt* (1890) 44 ChD 492; but cf *Forster v Hoggart* (1850) 15 QB 155, where it was held that the purchaser was not bound to take a title depending on waiver.

473.   Protection of purchasers of registered land. For the purpose of preventing the title of a disponee of registered land being questioned, a person's right to exercise owner's powers[1] in relation to a registered estate is to be taken to be free from any limitation affecting the validity of the disposition which is not reflected by an entry on the register or imposed by or under the Land Registration Act 2002[2].

1   As to a mortgagee's right to exercise owner's powers see PARA 446.

2   See the Land Registration Act 2002 s 26; and REAL PROPERTY AND REGISTRATION vol 87 (2012) PARA 425.

(x)   Application of Proceeds of Sale

474.   Effect of sale. A sale under a power of sale destroys the equity of redemption in the mortgaged property[1]. Consequently, the sale defeats the rights of all subsequent incumbrancers, whose remedy then is only against the proceeds of sale[2]. The sale constitutes the mortgagee exercising the power of sale as trustee of the surplus proceeds, if any, after satisfying his own charge, first for the subsequent incumbrancers, and ultimately for the mortgagor[3]. A mortgagee who has contracted to sell but, before the land has become vested in the purchaser, has rescinded the contract is not accountable to the mortgagor for purchase money which he has never received[4]. In the absence of special provision in the power of sale, the above principles determine the application of the proceeds, but such provision is contained in the statutory powers and usually in express powers[5].

1   See PARAS 107, 337. As to the effect of the conveyance see PARAS 448–450. As to the equity of redemption see PARAS 107, 304 et seq. As to the power of sale see PARA 442 et seq.
2   *Directors etc of South Eastern Rly Co v Jortin* (1857) 6 HL Cas 425 at 435.
3   *Wilson v Tooker* (1714) 5 Bro Parl Cas 193, HL (mortgage of exchequer annuities); *Rajah Kishendatt Ram v Rajah Mumtaz Ali Khan* (1879) LR 6 Ind App 145 at 160, PC (mortgage of land). See also *Harrison v Hart* (1726) 2 Eq Cas Abr 6 (mortgage of stock); *Samuel Keller (Holdings) Ltd v Martins Bank Ltd* [1970] 3 All ER 950, [1971] 1 WLR 43, CA.
4   *Wright v New Zealand Farmers Co-operative Association of Canterbury Ltd* [1939] AC 439, [1939] 2 All ER 701, PC.
5   See further PARAS 475–477. As to the statutory power of sale see PARA 446 et seq. As to express powers of sale see PARAS 443–444.

475. Application of money from sale under statutory powers. Money arising from a sale is applicable in the first instance to the discharge of any prior incumbrances to which the sale is not made subject or to the payment into court of a sum to meet any prior incumbrance[1]. The balance or the whole, as the case may be, is held by the mortgagee[2] in trust to be applied, first, in payment of all costs, charges and expenses properly incurred by him as incident to the sale, or any attempted sale, or otherwise and, secondly, in discharge of the mortgage money[3], interest and costs, and other money, if any, due under the mortgage[4]; and the residue is to be paid to the person entitled to the mortgaged property or authorised to give receipts for the proceeds of sale[5]. For the purposes of this requirement, in its application to the proceeds of sale of registered land, a person is taken to have notice of anything in the register immediately before the disposition on sale[6].

A mortgagee can abandon or waive his security and rely on the personal covenant for payment. The mortgagor has no right to insist that a mortgagee enforce his debt against the security, or to insist on the order in which successive mortgaged debts are satisfied unless he has the benefit of an express provision precluding the alteration of priorities of mortgages[7]. A mortgagee who sells under his statutory power of sale after the rights of the mortgagor and puisne mortgagees have become statute-barred is entitled to retain the whole proceeds; he is the only person entitled to the property and to give a good receipt[8]. A second mortgagee who is unable to enforce his claim by bringing proceedings is not entitled to the property or authorised to give a good receipt[9]. A mortgagee is not, however, entitled to retain the whole proceeds on the ground that he has a claim against the mortgagor other than for the debt secured by the mortgage[10].

Money received by a mortgagee under his mortgage, or from the proceeds of securities comprised in his mortgage, is to be applied in the same manner as proceeds of sale, except that for costs incident to the sale are substituted costs of recovering and receiving the money or securities or the conversion of the securities into money[11]. In the case of a mortgage of trust funds, the trustees are not bound to pay a mortgagee more than the amount due on his mortgage[12].

1 See the Law of Property Act 1925 s 50; and PARA 465. As to the meaning of 'incumbrance' see PARA 197 note 4.
2 As to the meaning of 'mortgagee' see PARA 104 note 1.
3 As to the meaning of 'mortgage money' see PARA 104 note 1.
4 The mortgagee is entitled to appropriate the proceeds of sale between different secured liabilities in such a way as it may choose: *West Bromwich Building Society v Crammer* [2002] EWHC 2618 (Ch), [2003] BPIR 783, [2002] All ER (D) 343 (Oct); *Chubb v Dean* [2013] EWHC 1282 (Ch). As to the meaning of 'mortgage' see PARA 101 note 4.
5 See the Law of Property Act 1925 s 105. As to costs of a vexatious claim after sale see *Re Smith's Mortgage, Harrison v Edwards* [1931] 2 Ch 168. Where a mortgagee sells property of a company subject to a fixed charge, the surplus is payable in accordance with the Law of Property Act 1925 s 105 and not to the preferential creditors even though the charge is contained in a debenture which also creates floating charges: *Re GL Saunders Ltd (in liquidation)* [1986] 1 WLR 215, [1986] BCLC 40. See also *Re H & K (Medway) Ltd, Mackay v IRC* [1997] 2 All ER 321, [1997] 1 WLR 1422; and COMPANIES vol 15 (2009) PARA 1334.
6 Land Registration Act 2002 s 54. As to the register see REAL PROPERTY AND REGISTRATION vol 87 (2012) PARA 328.
7 *Cheah Theam Swee v Equiticorp Finance Group Ltd* [1992] 1 AC 472, [1991] 4 All ER 989, PC.
8 *Re Statutory Trusts Declared by Section 105 of the Law of Property Act 1925 affecting the Proceeds of Sale of Moat House Farm, Thurlby* [1948] Ch 191, sub nom *Young v Clarey* [1948] 1 All ER 197. As to puisne mortgages see PARA 160 note 5.
9 *C & M Matthews Ltd v Marsden Building Society* [1951] Ch 758, sub nom *Re Martin's Mortgage Trusts, C & M Matthews Ltd v Marsden Building Society* [1951] 1 All ER 1053, CA.
10 *Halifax Building Society v Thomas* [1996] Ch 217, [1995] 4 All ER 673, CA.
11 See the Law of Property Act 1925 s 107(2).
12 See *Re Bell, Jeffery v Sayles* [1896] 1 Ch 1, CA; *Hockey v Western* [1898] 1 Ch 350, CA; *Re Lloyd, Lloyd v Lloyd* [1903] 1 Ch 385 at 403, CA. See also TRUSTS AND POWERS vol 98 (2013) PARA 169.

476. Satisfaction of claims of subsequent mortgagees. Where there are subsequent incumbrancers, their claim to receive the surplus proceeds of sale is prior to that of the mortgagor, and if the first mortgagee has notice, he is liable to them if he pays the proceeds to the mortgagor[1]. It seems that knowledge of the existence of a subsequent incumbrance acquired by the first mortgagee's solicitor does not necessarily constitute constructive notice to the first mortgagee unless the solicitor acquired his knowledge in his capacity as such[2]. The mortgagee should, however, search the register in the case of registered land or, in the case of unregistered land, the land charges register for puisne mortgages[3], as registration in the land charges register constitutes actual notice[4]. If there is a second mortgagee, the whole of the proceeds must be paid to him, and his receipt is a good discharge[5].

If there is any doubt as to the persons entitled to the surplus proceeds, the first mortgagee may pay the surplus into court[6].

A mortgagee may be liable for breach of duty if he allows the surplus to remain in his solicitor's hands without the authority of the mortgagor or subsequent incumbrancer[7].

1 *West London Commercial Bank v Reliance Building Society* (1885) 29 ChD 954 at 962, CA.
2 *Thorne v Heard and Marsh* [1895] AC 495 at 501, 505, HL. Cf the Law of Property Act 1925 s 199(1)(ii); and PARA 281. As to constructive notice see EQUITABLE JURISDICTION vol 47 (2014) PARAS 134–137.
3 Ie under the Land Charges Act 1972 s 2(1), (4)(i): see PARA 262; and REAL PROPERTY AND REGISTRATION vol 87 (2012) PARAS 720–721.
4 See the Law of Property Act 1925 s 198(1); and PARA 263.

5 See the Law of Property Act 1925 s 107(1). See also *Re Thomson's Mortgage Trusts, Thomson v Bruty* [1920] 1 Ch 508, distinguished in *C & M Matthews Ltd v Marsden Building Society* [1951] Ch 758, sub nom *Re Martin's Mortgage Trusts, C & M Matthews Ltd v Marsden Building Society* [1951] 1 All ER 1053, CA.

6 See *Re Walhampton Estate* (1884) 26 ChD 391. See also *Samuel Keller (Holdings) Ltd v Martins Bank Ltd* [1970] 3 All ER 950, [1971] 1 WLR 43, CA.

7 *Thorne v Heard* [1893] 3 Ch 530 at 534; affd sub nom *Thorne v Heard and Marsh* [1895] AC 495, HL (see note 2). See also LEGAL PROFESSIONS vol 66 (2015) PARA 589. As to the nature of the duty owed by the mortgagee see PARA 394.

477. Mortgagee as express or constructive trustee. Where the power of sale, whether express or statutory[1], provides that the surplus proceeds are to be held in trust for the mortgagor[2], the mortgagee becomes a trustee of the surplus proceeds in his hands[3]; otherwise he becomes a trustee only on proof that there is a surplus in his hands[4]. The mortgagee is not a trustee of the surplus for the mortgagor or subsequent incumbrancers if before the sale their rights had become statute-barred[5]. On the sale being completed, interest ceases to run against the mortgagor[6], unless otherwise agreed[7], and the mortgagee is charged interest in equity on the balance in his hands[8]. Interest is likely to be awarded either at a rate linked to some independent rate such as bank base rate[9], the short term investment account rate[10], or at the rate of return which the mortgagee was able to obtain in his business[11].

1 As to express power of sale see PARAS 443–444. As to statutory power of sale see PARA 446 et seq.

2 As to the application of money resulting from the exercise of the statutory power of sale see PARA 475.

3 *Locking v Parker* (1872) 8 Ch App 30 at 40; *Banner v Berridge* (1881) 18 ChD 254 at 269; *Re Bell, Lake v Bell* (1886) 34 ChD 462; *Re Thomson's Mortgage Trusts, Thomson v Bruty* [1920] 1 Ch 508, distinguished in *C & M Matthews Ltd v Marsden Building Society* [1951] Ch 758, sub nom *Re Martin's Mortgage Trusts, C & M Matthews Ltd v Marsden Building Society* [1951] 1 All ER 1053, CA. See also *Thorne v Heard and Marsh* [1895] AC 495, HL; and LIMITATION PERIODS vol 68 (2008) PARA 1152.

4 *Banner v Berridge* (1881) 18 ChD 254 at 269; and see *Gouthwaite v Rippon* (1838) 8 LJCh 139; *Tanner v Heard* (1857) 23 Beav 555; *Charles v Jones* (1887) 35 ChD 544. See also *Ocean Accident and Guarantee Corpn Ltd and Hewett v Collum and Archdall* [1913] 1 IR 328. As to such a trust being sufficient to prevent time running see LIMITATION PERIODS vol 68 (2008) PARA 1152.

5 *Re Statutory Trusts Declared by Section 105 of the Law of Property Act 1925 affecting the Proceeds of Sale of Moat House Farm, Thurlby* [1948] Ch 191, sub nom *Young v Clarey* [1948] 1 All ER 197. As to the principle that the rights of a mortgagor of land and of persons claiming through him are normally barred and their titles extinguished after the mortgagee has been in possession for 12 years see LIMITATION PERIODS vol 68 (2008) PARAS 1095, 1129.

6 *West v Diprose* [1900] 1 Ch 337 at 340.

7 As to contractual provisions regarding interest see PARAS 189–194.

8 *Mathew v TM Sutton Ltd* [1994] 4 All ER 793, [1994] 1 WLR 1455. Interest will run from a time after the sale sufficient to enable the mortgagee to ascertain the surplus. As to interest on money generally see FINANCIAL INSTRUMENTS AND TRANSACTIONS vol 49 (2015) PARA 90 et seq.

9 *Wallersteiner v Moir (No 2)* [1975] QB 373, 508n, [1975] 1 All ER 849.

10 See *Bartlett v Barclays Bank Trust Co Ltd (No 2)* [1980] Ch 515, [1980] 2 All ER 92.

11 *Mathew v TM Sutton Ltd* [1994] 4 All ER 793, [1994] 1 WLR 1455.

(5) APPOINTMENT OF RECEIVER OUT OF COURT

478. Appointment of receiver under express power. In order to give the mortgagee the advantages, without the liabilities, of being in possession, a receiver may be appointed at the time of the mortgage and as part of the security, or, more commonly, subsequently under an express power in the mortgage deed. In the former case the appointment is made by the mortgagor with the mortgagee's concurrence either by a separate deed, which can be given to the receiver as evidence of his authority, or in the mortgage deed. In the latter case the appointment is made by the mortgagee, either by writing under hand or by deed, according to the terms of the power, and in either case it is provided that the receiver is to be the mortgagor's agent[1]. Receivers are more commonly appointed under mortgages and debentures over the property of companies, and such receiverships are subject to statutory regulation[2]. Although a mortgagee may have a receiver at the mortgagor's expense, he cannot stipulate to be receiver of the rents and profits himself with a commission[3].

The deed of appointment, or the power and appointment under the power, now usually:

(1)   gives the receiver the power to do anything the mortgagor might do;

(2)   contains an irrevocable power of attorney enabling him to execute deeds and sell the mortgaged property[4]; and

(3)   provides for application of sums received.

Where successive incumbrancers join in a deed appointing a receiver and declaring trusts of the receipts, with an ultimate trust for the mortgagor, an incumbrancer subsequent to the deed is entitled to the benefit of it, but in proceedings for an account or for the execution of the trusts he must make all the prior incumbrancers parties[5].

1   *Jefferys v Dickson* (1866) 1 Ch App 183 at 190; *Law v Glenn* (1867) 2 Ch App 634 at 641; *Jones v Smith* (1841) 1 Hare 43 at 71; *Lord Kensington v Bouverie* (1855) 7 De GM & G 134 at 157; *Owen & Co v Cronk* [1895] 1 QB 265, CA; *Bissell v Ariel Motors (1906) Ltd and Walker* (1910) 27 TLR 73. As to the practice of making the receiver the mortgagor's agent see *Gaskell v Gosling* [1896] 1 QB 669 at 692, CA, per Rigby LJ. As to persons for whom a receiver appointed by debenture holders acts as agent see *Deyes v Wood* [1911] 1 KB 806, CA; and COMPANIES vol 15 (2009) PARA 1340. As to the position of a receiver appointed by the court see COMPANIES vol 15 (2009) PARA 1361 et seq; RECEIVERS vol 88 (2012) PARA 9 et seq. As to the law relating to agent and principal see generally AGENCY.

2   See the Insolvency Act 1986 ss 33–49; and COMPANIES vol 15 (2009) PARA 1340 et seq; COMPANY AND PARTNERSHIP INSOLVENCY vol 16 (2011) PARAS 352 et seq, 377–378.

3   *Bonithon v Hockmore* (1685) 1 Vern 316; *Chambers v Goldwin* (1801) 9 Ves 254 at 271; *Langstaffe v Fenwick, Fenwick v Langstaffe* (1805) 10 Ves 405; *Lord Trimleston v Hamill* (1810) 1 Ball & B 377; *Leith v Irvine* (1833) 1 My & K 277; *Eyre v Hughes* (1876) 2 ChD 148 at 161. See also PARA 752.

4   See eg *Phoenix Properties v Wimpole Street Nominees* [1992] BCLC 737.

5   *Ford v Rackham* (1853) 17 Beav 485; *Jefferys v Dickson* (1866) 1 Ch App 183.

479. General statutory powers to appoint a receiver. The mortgagee[1] has statutory power, when the mortgage money[2] has become due, to appoint a receiver of the income of the mortgaged property or of any part of it[3]. If a mortgaged property consists of an interest in income or of a rentcharge[4] or an annual or other periodical sum, a receiver may be appointed of that property or any part of it[5]. The statutory power may be excluded[6] or varied or extended by the mortgage deed[7]. It is now usually varied to remove the statutory restrictions and to give extensive powers to the receiver[8]. The power to appoint a receiver must not be exercised until the mortgagee has become entitled to exercise the statutory power of sale[9]. The appointment of such person as the mortgagee thinks fit may be made by writing under the mortgagee's hand[10], and the receiver may be removed and a new receiver appointed from time to time in like manner[11]. The power is exercisable even where the mortgagee has gone into possession[12].

1   As to the meaning of 'mortgagee' see PARA 104 note 1.

2   As to the meaning of 'mortgage money' see PARA 104 note 1.

3   See the Law of Property Act 1925 s 101(1)(iii). Save as otherwise provided, s 101 applies where the mortgage deed is executed after 31 December 1881: s 101(5). As to the meaning of 'mortgage'

see PARA 101 note 4. In the case of a registered charge, the power is not exercisable until the charge is registered: *Lever Finance Ltd v Needleman Property Trustee* [1956] Ch 375, [1956] 2 All ER 378.

4   As to the meaning of 'rentcharge' see PARA 341 note 7.
5   Law of Property Act 1925 s 101(1)(iii).
6   See the Law of Property Act 1925 s 101(4).
7   See the Law of Property Act 1925 s 101(3). Any variations to the statutory provisions can only be made by the mortgage deed itself. In the case of a registered charge, the mortgage deed will not be construed by reference to collateral documents such as the facility letter not available to third parties inspecting the register: see *Cherry Tree Investments Ltd v Landmain Ltd* [2012] EWCA Civ 736, [2013] Ch 305, [2013] 2 WLR 481.
8   This power of sale is not an extension of the statutory powers, but an express power: see *Phoenix Properties v Wimpole Street Nominees* [1992] BCLC 737.
9   See the Law of Property Act 1925 s 109(1). As to when the statutory power of sale is exercisable see PARAS 456–460. See also PARA 621.
10   See the Law of Property Act 1925 s 109(1). As to the meaning of 'writing' see PARA 457 note 3.
11   See the Law of Property Act 1925 s 109(5).
12   *Refuge Assurance Co Ltd v Pearlberg* [1938] Ch 687, [1938] 3 All ER 231, CA.

480. Duties of mortgagee in appointing receiver. A mortgagee owes a general duty to subsequent incumbrancers and to the mortgagor to use his powers for the sole purpose of securing repayments of the moneys owing under his mortgage and a duty to act in good faith[1]. The mortgagee can choose when to appoint a receiver having regard to his own interests even though the timing of the appointment may be disadvantageous to the mortgagor or unsecured creditors[2]. It may well be that a mortgagee who appoints a receiver and manager, knowing that the receiver and manager intends to exercise his powers for the purpose of frustrating the activities of a second mortgagee or for some other improper purpose or who fails to revoke the appointment of a receiver and manager when the mortgagee knows that the receiver and manager is abusing his powers, may himself be guilty of bad faith[3]. The mortgagee is not otherwise responsible for what a receiver does whilst he is the mortgagor's agent unless the mortgagee directs or interferes with the receiver's activities[4]. The mortgagee is responsible for what a receiver does whilst he is the mortgagee's agent and acting as such[5].

1   *Downsview Nominees Ltd v First City Corpn Ltd* [1993] AC 295, [1993] 3 All ER 626, PC. As to the general duties owed by a mortgagee see PARA 394.
2   *Shamji v Johnson Matthey Bankers Ltd* [1986] BCLC 278, 2 BCC 98, 910 (on appeal [1991] BCLC 36, [1986] 1 FTLR 329, CA); *Re Potters Oils Ltd (No 2)* [1986] 1 All ER 890, [1986] 1 WLR 201.
3   *Downsview Nominees Ltd v First City Corpn Ltd* [1993] AC 295, [1993] 3 All ER 626, PC.
4   *American Express International Banking Corpn v Hurley* [1985] 3 All ER 564, [1986] BCLC 52; *Standard Chartered Bank v Walker* [1982] 3 All ER 938, [1982] 1 WLR 1410, CA.
5   *American Express International Banking Corpn v Hurley* [1985] 3 All ER 564, [1986] BCLC 52. The receiver may become the mortgagee's agent following the bankruptcy or liquidation of the mortgagor: see *American Express International Banking Corpn v Hurley* above; and PARA 483. As to the law of agent and principal see generally AGENCY.

481. Receiver's position. A receiver appointed under the statutory power[1] is deemed to be the mortgagor's agent[2] and the mortgagor is solely responsible for his acts or defaults unless the mortgage[3] deed otherwise provides[4], but the agency may be modified by the terms of the mortgage deed[5]. A receiver who, although originally appointed by the mortgagee under the statutory power, is subsequently appointed by the court[6], ceases to be the mortgagor's agent[7].

The mortgagor's death does not operate as a revocation of the power to appoint a receiver[8]. The receiver may be permitted to sue in the name of the mortgagor's personal representatives on giving indemnity[9].

The agency of a receiver is not an ordinary agency[10]. It is primarily a device to protect the mortgagee or debenture holder[11]. Thus the receiver acts as agent for the mortgagor in that he has power to affect the mortgagor's position by acts which, though done for the benefit of the debenture holder, are treated as if they were the acts of the mortgagor[12]. The relationship set up by the debenture and the appointment of the receiver is tripartite and involves the mortgagor, the receiver and the debenture holder[13]. The receiver is appointed by the debenture holder, but the mortgagor will have to pay the receiver's fees[14]. Further, the mortgagor cannot dismiss the receiver since that power is reserved to the debenture holder as another of the contractual terms of the loan[15]. The mortgagor cannot instruct the receiver how to act in the conduct of the receivership[16]. There is no contractual relationship or duty owed in tort by the receiver to the mortgagor: the relationship and duties owed by the receiver are equitable only[17]. The equitable duty is owed to the mortgagee as well as the mortgagor[18]. Although the receiver is the agent of the mortgagor he owes fiduciary duties to the debenture holder who has a right, as against the receiver, to be put in possession of all the information concerning the receivership available to the receiver[19].

1   As to the statutory power of appointment see PARA 479.
2   As to the meaning of 'mortgagor' see PARA 104 note 1. As to the law relating to agent and principal see generally AGENCY.
3   As to the meaning of 'mortgage' see PARA 101 note 4.
4   Law of Property Act 1925 s 109(2). See also *Portman Building Society v Gallwey* [1955] 1 All ER 227, [1955] 1 WLR 96. A receiver is not the 'owner' of the mortgaged premises within the meaning of the London Building Act 1930: see *Solomons v R Gertzenstein Ltd* [1954] 2 QB 243, [1954] 2 All ER 625, CA.
5   *Richards v Kidderminster Overseers* [1896] 2 Ch 212 at 220.
6   As to the appointment of a receiver by the court see PARA 565 et seq.
7   *Hand v Blow* [1901] 2 Ch 721 at 732, CA. Cf *Lever Finance Ltd v Needleman Property Trustee* [1956] Ch 375, [1956] 2 All ER 378, where the receiver was held to be the mortgagee's agent until the mortgagee was registered as proprietor of the charge. As to the effect of payment of interest out of rent by the receiver see LIMITATION PERIODS vol 68 (2008) PARA 1099.
8   *Re Hale, Lilley v Foad* [1899] 2 Ch 107 at 117, CA.
9   *Fairholme and Palliser v Kennedy* (1890) 24 LR Ir 498.
10 *Gomba Holdings UK Ltd v Minories Finance Ltd* [1989] 1 All ER 261, [1988] 1 WLR 1231, CA.
11 *Gomba Holdings UK Ltd v Minories Finance Ltd* [1989] 1 All ER 261, [1988] 1 WLR 1231, CA; *Silven Properties Ltd v Royal Bank of Scotland plc* [2003] EWCA Civ 1409, [2004] 4 All ER 484, [2004] 1 WLR 997.
12 *Gomba Holdings UK Ltd v Minories Finance Ltd* [1989] 1 All ER 261, [1988] 1 WLR 1231, CA.
13 *Gomba Holdings UK Ltd v Minories Finance Ltd* [1989] 1 All ER 261, [1988] 1 WLR 1231, CA.
14 *Gomba Holdings UK Ltd v Minories Finance Ltd* [1989] 1 All ER 261, [1988] 1 WLR 1231, CA.
15 *Gomba Holdings UK Ltd v Minories Finance Ltd* [1989] 1 All ER 261, [1988] 1 WLR 1231, CA.
16 *Gomba Holdings UK Ltd v Minories Finance Ltd* [1989] 1 All ER 261, [1988] 1 WLR 1231, CA.
17 *Medforth v Blake* [2000] Ch 86; *Raja v Austin Gray* [2002] EWCA Civ 1965, [2003] Lloyd's Rep PN 126, [2003] 1 EGLR 91; *Silven Properties Ltd v Royal Bank of Scotland plc* [2003] EWCA Civ 1409, [2004] 4 All ER 484, [2004] 1 WLR 997.
18 *Silven Properties Ltd v Royal Bank of Scotland plc* [2003] EWCA Civ 1409, [2004] 4 All ER 484, [2004] 1 WLR 997.
19 *Re Magadi Soda Co Ltd* (1925) 41 TLR 297, 94 LJCh 217. As to the ownership of documents created by receivers see *Gomba Holdings Ltd v Minories Finance Ltd* [1989] 1 All ER 261, [1988] 1 WLR 1231, CA.

482. Duties of receivers to mortgagor and others. A receiver and manager owes the same duty in equity to the mortgagor, all subsequent incumbrancers and guarantors as the mortgagee[1] to exercise his powers in good faith and for the purpose of obtaining repayment of the debt owing to the mortgagee. In a number of respects however, a receiver is in a very different position to the mortgagee: whilst a mortgagee has no duty at any time to exercise his powers to enforce his security, a receiver has no right to remain passive if that course would be damaging to the interests of the mortgagor or mortgagee[2]. In the absence of a provision to the contrary in the mortgage or in his appointment, the receiver is to be active in the protection and preservation of the charged property over which he is appointed[3]. Thus if the mortgaged property is let, the receiver is duty bound to inspect the lease and if the lease contains an upward only rent review, to trigger that rent review in due time[4]. His management duties ordinarily impose on him no general duty to exercise the power of sale[5]. However a duty may arise if for example the goods are perishable and a failure to do so would cause loss to the mortgagee and the mortgagor[6].

A receiver exercising his power of sale also owes the same specific duties as the mortgagee[7]. The receiver is entitled (like the mortgagee) to sell the property in the condition in which it is without awaiting or effecting any increase in value or improvement in the property. The receiver is not obliged before sale to spend money on repairs[8] to make the property more attractive before marketing it[9] or to 'work' an estate by refurbishing it[10] or to apply for planning permission[11].

A receiver does not owe the mortgagor any duty comparable to the duty owed to a company by its own directors or managers[12]. He is entitled, but not bound, to allow the company's business to be continued by himself or by the existing or other executives[13]. The decisions of the receiver and manager whether to continue the business or close down the business and sell assets chosen by him cannot be impeached if those decisions are taken in good faith while protecting the interests of the debenture holder in recovering the moneys due under the debenture, even though the decisions of the receiver and manager may be disadvantageous for the company[14]. The duties owed by a receiver and manager do not compel him to adopt any particular course of action, such as selling the whole or part of the mortgaged property, carrying on the business of the company or exercising any other powers and discretions vested in him[15]. The primary duty of the receiver is to the debenture holders and not to the company[16]. The primary objective of the receivership is to enforce the security by recouping the moneys which it secures from the income or assets of the company subject to the security, and when recoupment is complete to hand the remaining property back to the control of the company[17].

If the receiver does decide to carry on the business, he owes a duty to take reasonable steps to do so profitably[18].

Where a receiver is in breach of his duty to the mortgagor or guarantor while acting as agent of the mortgagee, he is liable to indemnify the mortgagee against his liability to the mortgagor or guarantor unless such liability is excluded in the contract of agency[19].

1   As to the general duties owed by a mortgagee see PARA 394. As to the appointment of a receiver see PARAS 478 et seq.
2   *Silven Properties Ltd v Royal Bank of Scotland plc* [2003] EWCA Civ 1409, [2004] 4 All ER 484, [2004] 1 WLR 997.
3   *Silven Properties Ltd v Royal Bank of Scotland plc* [2003] EWCA Civ 1409, [2004] 4 All ER 484, [2004] 1 WLR 997.
4   *Knight v Lawrence* [1991] 1 EGLR 143, [1993] BCLC 215; *Silven Properties Ltd v Royal Bank of Scotland plc* [2003] EWCA Civ 1409, [2004] 4 All ER 484, [2004] 1 WLR 997.
5   See *Routestone Ltd v Minories Finance Ltd* [1997] BCC 180, 187g; *Silven Properties Ltd v Royal Bank of Scotland plc* [2003] EWCA Civ 1409, [2004] 4 All ER 484, [2004] 1 WLR 997; *Bell v Long* [2008] EWHC 1273 (Ch), [2008] 2 BCLC 706, [2008] BPIR 1211, [2008] All ER (D) 179 (Jun).
6   *Silven Properties Ltd v Royal Bank of Scotland plc* [2003] EWCA Civ 1409, [2004] 4 All ER 484, [2004] 1 WLR 997.
7   *Downsview Nominees Ltd v First City Corpn Ltd* [1993] AC 295, [1993] 3 All ER 626, PC; *Standard Chartered Bank v Walker* [1982] 3 All ER 938, [1982] 1 WLR 1410, CA; *Silven Properties Ltd v Royal Bank of Scotland plc* [2003] EWCA Civ 1409, [2004] 4 All ER 484, [2004] 1 WLR 997. As to the nature of the duty see PARA 461.

8 *Meftah v Lloyds TSB Bank plc* [2001] 2 All ER (Comm) 741, 744, 766 per Lawrence Collins J;
   Silven Properties Ltd v Royal Bank of Scotland plc [2003] EWCA Civ 1409, [2004] 4 All ER 484,
   [2004] 1 WLR 997.
9 *Garland v Ralph Pay & Ransom* [1984] 2 EGLR 147, 151 per Nicholls J; *Silven Properties Ltd
   v Royal Bank of Scotland plc* [2003] EWCA Civ 1409, [2004] 4 All ER 484, [2004] 1 WLR 997.
10 *Routestone Ltd v Minories Finance Ltd* [1997] BCC 180, 195 per Jacob J; *Silven Properties Ltd
   v Royal Bank of Scotland plc* [2003] EWCA Civ 1409, [2004] 4 All ER 484, [2004] 1 WLR 997.
11 *Silven Properties Ltd v Royal Bank of Scotland plc* [2003] EWCA Civ 1409, [2004] 4 All ER 484,
   [2004] 1 WLR 997.
12 *Re B Johnson & Co (Builders) Ltd* [1955] Ch 634 at 661–663, [1955] 2 All ER 775 at 790–791,
   CA, per Jenkins LJ; *Downsview Nominees Ltd v First City Corpn Ltd* [1993] AC 295, [1993]
   3 All ER 626, PC. As to a director's duty to a company see COMPANIES vol 14 (2009) PARA 532
   et seq.
13 *Downsview Nominees Ltd v First City Corpn Ltd* [1993] AC 295 at 312–313, [1993] 3 All ER
   626 at 635, PC. See also *Gomba Holdings UK Ltd v Minories Finance Ltd* [1989] 1 All ER 261,
   [1988] 1 WLR 1231, CA.
14 *Downsview Nominees Ltd v First City Corpn Ltd* [1993] AC 295 at 312–313, [1993] 3 All ER
   626 at 635, PC. See also *Gomba Holdings UK Ltd v Minories Finance Ltd* [1989] 1 All ER 261,
   [1988] 1 WLR 1231, CA.
15 *Downsview Nominees Ltd v First City Corpn Ltd* [1993] AC 295 at 314, [1993] 3 All ER 626 at
   636, PC. See also *Gomba Holdings UK Ltd v Minories Finance Ltd* [1989] 1 All ER 261, [1988]
   1 WLR 1231, CA.
16 *Downsview Nominees Ltd v First City Corpn Ltd* [1993] AC 295 at 315, [1993] 3 All ER 626 at
   635, PC; *Silven Properties Ltd v Royal Bank of Scotland plc* [2003] EWCA Civ 1409, [2004]
   4 All ER 484, [2004] 1 WLR 997. See also *Gomba Holdings UK Ltd v Minories Finance Ltd*
   [1989] 1 All ER 261, [1988] 1 WLR 1231, CA.
17 *Downsview Nominees Ltd v First City Corpn Ltd* [1993] AC 295 at 315, [1993] 3 All ER 626 at
   637, PC; *Silven Properties Ltd v Royal Bank of Scotland plc* [2003] EWCA Civ 1409, [2004]
   4 All ER 484, [2004] 1 WLR 997.
18 *Medforth v Blake* [2000] Ch 86, [1999] 3 All ER 97, CA.
19 *American Express International Banking Corpn v Hurley* [1985] 3 All ER 564, [1986] BCLC 52.

483. Termination of receivership. The mortgagor cannot dismiss the receiver
since that power is reserved to the mortgagee[1]. The receiver will, however, be
displaced by the appointment of a receiver by a prior mortgagee. Liquidation of
a company mortgagor does not terminate the receiver's appointment or powers,
but does terminate his agency for the mortgagor[2]. If the receiver continues to act,
he normally acts as principal[3] but may become the agent of a mortgagee who
treats him as such[4]. Where an administration order has been made, any receiver
of part of the company's property must vacate office on being required to do so
by the administrator[5].

1 *Gomba Holdings UK Ltd v Minories Finance Ltd* [1989] 1 All ER 261, [1988] 1 WLR 1231, CA.
2 *Gosling v Gaskell* [1897] AC 575; *Sowman v David Samuel Trust Ltd (in liquidation)* [1978]
   1 All ER 616, [1978] 1 WLR 22, CA; *American Express International Banking Corpn v Hurley*
   [1985] 3 All ER 564, [1986] BCLC 52, CA. See also COMPANIES vol 15 (2009) PARA 1355.
3 *Gosling v Gaskell* [1897] AC 575, HL. As to the law of agent and principal see generally AGENCY.
4 *Re Wood Application* [1941] Ch 112, [1940] 4 All ER 306; *American Express International
   Banking Corpn v Hurley* [1985] 3 All ER 564, [1986] BCLC 52.
5 See the Insolvency Act 1986 s 8, Sch B1 para 41; and COMPANY AND PARTNERSHIP
   INSOLVENCY vol 16 (2011) PARA 209. Provision is also made for the rights and liabilities of a
   receiver who vacates office at the request of the administrator: see COMPANY AND PARTNERSHIP
   INSOLVENCY vol 16 (2011) PARA 209.

484. Statutory powers of receivers. The receiver has statutory power to demand
and recover all the income of which he is appointed receiver by bringing
proceedings, by commercial rent arrears recovery[1] or otherwise, in the name either
of the mortgagor or mortgagee[2], to the full extent of the estate or interest which
the mortgagor could dispose of, and to give effectual receipts and to exercise any
powers which may have been delegated to him by the mortgagee[3]. After the
appointment of a receiver the mortgagor cannot distrain, even though he alleges

negligence on the receiver's part[4]; and a distress by him is illegal[5]. A person paying money to the receiver is not concerned to inquire whether any case has happened to authorise the receiver to act[6]. The receiver's power to distrain ceases, however, when the mortgagee's interest is determined[7]. The powers conferred on the administrative receiver[8] of a company by the debentures by virtue of which he was appointed are deemed to include (except in so far as they are inconsistent with any of the provisions of those debentures) certain statutory powers[9]. An administrative receiver may apply to the court for an order permitting him to dispose of property free from certain securities[10].

1 Ie by action under the Tribunals, Courts and Enforcement Act 2007 s 72(1): see the Law of Property Act 1925 s 109(3) (amended by the Tribunals, Courts and Enforcement Act 2007 s 86, Sch 14 paras 21, 22). As to commercial rent arrears recovery see LANDLORD AND TENANT vol 62 (2012) PARA 419 et seq.
2 As to the meanings of 'mortgagor' and 'mortgagee' see PARA 104 note 1.
3 Law of Property Act 1925 s 109(3).
4 *Bayly v Went* (1884) 51 LT 764.
5 *Woolston v Ross* [1900] 1 Ch 788. As to estoppel by payment of rent by a tenant to a receiver see *Serjeant v Nash, Field & Co* [1903] 2 KB 304, CA; and ESTOPPEL vol 47 (2014) PARA 340.
6 Law of Property Act 1925 s 109(4).
7 *Serjeant v Nash, Field & Co* [1903] 2 KB 304, CA (mortgage of leaseholds in breach of covenant in lease; lease determined by lessor; subsequent distraint by receiver appointed by mortgagee held illegal).
8 An administrative receiver is:
   (1) a receiver or manager of the whole (or substantially the whole) of a company's property appointed by or on behalf of the holders of any debentures of the company secured by a charge which, as created, was a floating charge, or by such a charge and one or more other securities (see the Insolvency Act 1986 s 29(2)(a); and COMPANIES vol 15 (2009) PARA 1337); or
   (2) a person who would be such a receiver or manager but for the appointment of some other person as the receiver of part of the company's property (see the Insolvency Act 1986 s 29(2)(b); and COMPANIES vol 15 (2009) PARA 1337).
9 See the Insolvency Act 1986 s 42(1); and COMPANY AND PARTNERSHIP INSOLVENCY vol 16 (2011) PARA 345. The powers referred to are those specified in Sch 1: see COMPANY AND PARTNERSHIP INSOLVENCY vol 16 (2011) PARA 345.
10 See the Insolvency Act 1986 s 43(1); and COMPANY AND PARTNERSHIP INSOLVENCY vol 16 (2011) PARA 347.

485. Express powers of receiver. A receiver appointed otherwise than under statute has only the powers conferred on him by his appointment, and, unless specially empowered to do so, may not sue or exercise commercial rent arrears recovery in the name of the person so entitled, that is either the mortgagor or mortgagee according to the circumstances[1]. A receiver appointed by debenture holders who, under the terms of the debentures, is entitled to take possession will be put into possession by the court as against the liquidator, even though if the court were asked to appoint a receiver it would appoint the liquidator[2]. Receivers are usually given extensive powers in modern mortgages.

1 Where the receiver was empowered to distrain and the mortgagor attorned tenant to the receiver, this was held to justify distress by the receiver against the mortgagor in the receiver's own name: *Jolly v Arbuthnot* (1859) 4 De G & J 224. Attornment clauses are now in general invalid for the purpose of conferring powers of distress unless registered as bills of sale: see PARA 346. See also FINANCIAL INSTRUMENTS AND TRANSACTIONS vol 49 (2015) PARA 438. As to the abolition of distress and the introduction of commercial rent arrears recovery see LANDLORD AND TENANT vol 62 (2012) PARAS 288, 419 et seq.
2 *Re Henry Pound, Son and Hutchins* (1889) 42 ChD 402, CA; *Re Joshua Stubbs Ltd, Barney v Joshua Stubbs Ltd* [1891] 1 Ch 475, CA.

486. Receiver's powers as to insurance and application of income. If appointed under the statutory power[1], the receiver must, if so directed in writing[2] by the mortgagee[3], insure to the extent, if any, to which the mortgagee might have insured and keep insured against loss or damage by fire, out of the money received by him, any building, effects or property comprised in the mortgage[4], whether affixed to the freehold or not, being of an insurable nature[5].

Subject to the statutory provisions as to the application of insurance money[6], the receiver must apply all money received by him as follows[7]:

(1)   in discharge of all rents, taxes[8], rates[9] and outgoings affecting the mortgaged property[10];

(2)   in keeping down annual sums or other payments, and interest on all principal sums, having priority to the mortgage in right of which he is receiver[11];

(3)   in payment of his commission, and of premiums on fire, life and other insurances, if any, properly payable under the mortgage deed or the Law of Property Act 1925, and the cost of executing necessary or proper repairs directed in writing by the mortgagee[12];

(4)   in payment of interest accruing due in respect of any principal money due under the mortgage[13]; and

(5)   in or towards discharge of the principal money, if so directed in writing by the mortgagee[14].

The receiver pays the residue, if any, to the person who, but for the receiver's possession, would have been entitled to receive the income of which he is appointed receiver, or who is otherwise entitled to the mortgaged property[15]. The statutory application of income may be extended by the mortgage deed so as, for instance, to authorise the receiver and manager of a business to pay unsecured debts[16]. The statutory duties in heads (4) and (5) above are for the mortgagee's benefit as well as the mortgagor's, and he may maintain a claim against the receiver for failure to perform them[17]. A receiver appointed by a mortgagee of a lease which the landlord claims to have forfeited is entitled to receive the income from the property and discharge current outgoings, but his title to the balance is liable to be divested by a declaration that the lease has been forfeited[18].

1   See the Law of Property Act 1925 s 109(1); and PARA 479.
2   As to the meaning of 'writing' see PARA 457 note 3.
3   As to the meaning of 'mortgagee' see PARA 104 note 1.
4   As to the meaning of 'mortgage' see PARA 101 note 4.
5   Law of Property Act 1925 s 109(7).
6   See the Law of Property Act 1925 s 108; and PARA 173.
7   Law of Property Act 1925 s 109(8). See *Portman Building Society v Gallwey* [1955] 1 All ER 227, [1955] 1 WLR 96. Appointments of receivers under receivership deeds or express powers contain similar provisions.
8   Tax includes VAT on rent paid to the receiver in respect of mortgaged property: *Sargent v Customs and Excise Comrs* [1994] 1 WLR 235, [1993] NPC 142; affd in part [1995] 1 WLR 821, [1995] 2 BCLC 34, CA.
9   The non-payment of rates by a receiver is not a breach of statutory duty for which the local authority can sue: *Liverpool Corpn v Hope* [1938] 1 KB 751, [1938] 1 All ER 492, CA. See also *Ratford v Northavon District Council* [1987] QB 357, [1986] 3 All ER 193, CA. The position would be different if the receiver had dispossessed the mortgagor or taken possession in an independent capacity: *Ratford v Northavon District Council* above.
10   Law of Property Act 1925 s 109(8)(i). The purpose of s 109(8)(i) is to preserve the property in the interest of both the mortgagee and the mortgagor by ensuring that the normal outgoings are duly discharged: *Sargent v Customs and Excise Comrs* [1994] 1 WLR 235, [1993] NPC 142; affd in part [1995] 1 WLR 821, [1995] 2 BCLC 34, CA.
11   Law of Property Act 1925 s 109(8)(ii).
12   Law of Property Act 1925 s 109(8)(iii). See *White v Metcalf* [1903] 2 Ch 567; and PARA 749.
13   Law of Property Act 1925 s 109(8)(iv). The receiver must pay arrears of interest due at the time of his appointment, as well as interest accruing subsequently: *National Bank v Kenney* [1898] 1 IR 197.

14 Law of Property Act 1925 s 109(8)(v).
15 See the Law of Property Act 1925 s 109(8).
16 *Re Hale, Lilley v Foad* [1899] 2 Ch 107 at 118, CA.
17 *Leicester Permanent Building Society v Butt* [1943] Ch 308, [1943] 2 All ER 523, where the
    mortgagee was held entitled to an account.
18 *Official Custodian for Charities v Mackey (No 2)* [1985] 2 All ER 1016, [1985] 1 WLR 1308.

487. Remuneration of receiver. A receiver appointed under the statutory power[1] is entitled to retain out of any money received by him a commission at such rate, not exceeding 5 per cent on the gross amount of all money received, as is specified in his appointment, and, if no rate is specified, then at the rate of 5 per cent on that gross amount, or at such other rate as the court thinks fit to allow, on the receiver's application[2]. The rate thus determined covers the receiver's remuneration and all costs, charges and expenses incurred by him as receiver[3]. Appointments made otherwise than under the statutory provisions usually provide specially as to remuneration, and, if they do not, the receiver will be entitled to a proper remuneration as a quantum meruit[4]. The statutory limit on the remuneration of a receiver is usually excluded. The court can fix the remuneration of a receiver of the property of a company in liquidation on an application by the liquidator[5] or on the taking of an account between the mortgagor and the mortgagee[6].

1 See the Law of Property Act 1925 s 109(1); and PARA 479.
2 See the Law of Property Act 1925 s 109(6). Under this provision, where no rate has been provided
   for, the receiver is entitled to commission at the rate of 5% without making an application to court:
   Marshall v Cottingham [1982] Ch 82, [1981] 3 All ER 8.
3 See the Law of Property Act 1925 s 109(6). See also *Marshall v Cottingham* [1982] Ch 82, [1981]
   3 All ER 8, where a receiver was appointed under a debenture which provided for payment of the
   'costs of realisation' out of sums realised, and such costs did not fall to be paid out of the receivers
   commission as part of the 'costs, charges and expenses' incurred by him as receiver.
4 *Re Vimbos Ltd* [1900] 1 Ch 470.
5 See the Insolvency Act 1986 s 36; and COMPANIES vol 15 (2009) PARA 1356.
6 See *Gomba Holdings UK Ltd v Minories Finance Ltd (No 2)* [1993] Ch 171, [1992] 4 All ER 588,
   CA.

(6) MORTGAGEE'S RIGHTS AS REGARDS TITLE DEEDS

(i) Right to Custody of Title Deeds

488. Mortgagee or chargee of freeholds or leaseholds. Where freeholds are mortgaged, whether by demise or legal charge[1], a first mortgagee[2] has the same right to possession of documents as if his security included the fee simple[3]; and where leaseholds are mortgaged, whether by sub-demise or legal charge[4], a first mortgagee has the same right to possession of documents as if his security had been effected by assignment[5]. A legal mortgagee who omits to inquire for the title deeds may be postponed to an earlier or subsequent incumbrancer[6]. The mortgage gives the mortgagee a property in all the deeds relating to the mortgaged land[7], and a mortgagee with a good title to whom a forged copy of a genuine deed has been delivered can recover the genuine deed from a subsequent incumbrancer[8].

1 As to mortgage by demise see PARA 164. As to mortgage by legal charge see PARA 165.
2 As to the meaning of 'mortgagee' see PARA 104 note 1.
3 See the Law of Property Act 1925 s 85(1) proviso.
4 See PARAS 164–165.
5 See the Law of Property Act 1925 s 86(1) proviso.
6 See PARA 284.

7   *Newton v Beck* (1858) 3 H & N 220 at 222.
8   *Newton v Beck* (1858) 3 H & N 220.

489. Right as between tenant for life and mortgagee. Where the property is settled land, the legal estate in fee simple is vested in the tenant for life, who holds it as trustee for all the persons entitled under the settlement[1], and he is entitled to possession of the title deeds[2]. The court may, however, take charge of the deeds when they are in danger in the custody of the tenant for life[3], and the trustees of the settlement are entitled to retain title deeds which they require for the purposes of their trusts[4]. A mortgagee of the beneficial life interest of a tenant for life, which is an equitable interest, is not entitled to the deeds and the tenant for life is prohibited from handing them over to him unless he is a mortgagee of the whole of the settled land to which the documents relate[5]. The mortgagee of the life interest has, however, the same rights with respect to the deeds as if the tenant for life had given to him a statutory acknowledgment and undertaking for production and safe custody of the deeds[6].

1   See the Settled Land Act 1925 s 107(1); and SETTLEMENTS vol 91 (2012) PARA 676. No settlement created after 1 January 19971 is a settlement for the purposes of the Settled Land Act 1925. As to the continued existence of settlements created before 1 January 1997 see PARA 145; and SETTLEMENTS vol 91 (2012) PARA 576.
2   He had the same right under the previous law when his legal estate was a life estate: *Garner v Hannyngton* (1856) 22 Beav 627. See also Sugden's Law of Vendors and Purchasers (14th Edn, 1862) 445n. As to the right to custody of title deeds see REAL PROPERTY AND REGISTRATION vol 87 (2012) PARA 15. The trustees of the settlement are not liable in any way on account of documents of title being placed in the possession of the tenant for life: see the Settled Land Act 1925 s 98(3); and SETTLEMENTS vol 91 (2012) PARA 793.
3   See *Leathes v Leathes* (1877) 5 ChD 221.
4   See *Clayton v Clayton* [1930] 2 Ch 12; and SETTLEMENTS vol 91 (2012) PARA 672; TRUSTS AND POWERS vol 98 (2013) PARA 156. See also REAL PROPERTY AND REGISTRATION vol 87 (2012) PARA 15.
5   See the Settled Land Act 1925 ss 111 proviso, 117(1)(xxi); and SETTLEMENTS vol 91 (2012) PARA 674. Under a mortgage of his life estate by the tenant for life before 1926, the mortgagee was entitled to have the deeds of the settled land handed to him.
6   See the Settled Land Act 1925 ss 111 proviso, 117(1)(xxi); and note 5.

490. Right to custody of title deeds as between co-owners and mortgagee. Apart from the statutory trusts affecting land held by co-owners[1], whichever one of them obtains the deeds is entitled to hold them, subject to the right of the others to have the deeds produced[2]. Accordingly, a mortgagee of the interest of a co-owner is not entitled to the custody of the deeds as against another co-owner who has them in his possession[3]. Nor is a mortgagee entitled to custody of the deeds deposited by one co-owner by way of security without the consent of the other[4]. The trustees under the statutory trusts are, however, entitled to hold the deeds, and a mortgagee will take them only when the mortgage is made by the trustees or by all the co-owners by virtue of their beneficial interests[5].

1   See the Law of Property Act 1925 s 34; and REAL PROPERTY AND REGISTRATION vol 87 (2012) PARA 219.
2   *Foster v Crabb* (1852) 12 CB 136; *Wright v Robotham* (1886) 33 ChD 106, CA; Sugden's Law of Vendors and Purchasers (14th Edn, 1862) 443. See also *Lambert v Rogers* (1817) 2 Mer 489. But see *Thames Guaranty Ltd v Campbell* [1985] QB 210, [1984] 2 All ER 585, CA, where each joint tenant was entitled to joint custody.
3   See *Yea v Field* (1788) 2 Term Rep 708 (although the actual decision in that case may not have been correct: see Sugden's Law of Vendors and Purchasers (14th Edn, 1862) 441).
4   *Thames Guaranty v Campbell* [1985] QB 210, [1984] 2 All ER 585, CA.
5   See REAL PROPERTY AND REGISTRATION vol 87 (2012) PARA 219.

491. Right to title deeds when power of sale exercisable. As soon as the statutory power of sale has become exercisable[1], the mortgagee may demand and recover from any person, other than a person entitled in priority to himself, all the deeds and documents relating to the property or its title which a purchaser under the power of sale would be entitled to demand and recover from him[2].

1　As to the statutory power of sale see PARA 446 et seq. As to the conditions on which it becomes exercisable see PARAS 456–460.
2　Law of Property Act 1925 s 106(4). The reference in the text is apparently a reference to the deeds which the purchaser could recover from the holder of them after the sale.

492. Right of equitable mortgagee by deposit to retain title deeds. An equitable mortgagee by deposit of title deeds[1] is entitled to retain the deeds until payment or tender of the amount due on his security[2], and until then the mortgagor has no direct claim to recover the deeds; but if a proper tender has been made and refused, the mortgagor, in a claim for redemption or other suitable proceeding, may obtain an order for delivery of the deeds on payment into court of a stated sum sufficient to cover principal, interest and costs[3].

1　As to the creation of an equitable mortgage by deposit of title deeds see PARAS 222–223. Since 27 September 1989 the mere deposit of title deeds by way of security can no longer create a valid equitable mortgage: see PARA 221.
2　*Re Molton Finance Ltd* [1968] Ch 325 at 332–333, [1967] 3 All ER 843 at 845, CA, per Lord Denning MR.
3　*Bank of New South Wales v O'Connor* (1889) 14 App Cas 273 at 283, PC. See also *Mills v Finlay* (1839) 1 Beav 560.

493. Right of mortgagee with bad title to retain mortgage deed. A mortgagee who has taken a bad title and is compelled to deliver up the title deeds may keep the mortgage deed so as to be able to avail himself of the covenant for payment[1].

1　*Opie v Godolphin* (1720) Prec Ch 548. As to the mortgagee's rights as regards a defective title see PARA 395.

494. Contractual right to mortgage documents. The contractual documentation between mortgagor and mortgagee may contain an authority by the mortgagor to his conveyancer[1] to disclose documents relating to the transaction to the mortgagee at its request. If, on the proper construction of the agreement, the authority is irrevocable and privilege[2] has been waived, the court will order delivery up of the whole file including privileged documents[3].

1　As to solicitors and licensed conveyancers see further LEGAL PROFESSIONS.
2　As to legal professional privilege see CONFIDENCE AND INFORMATIONAL PRIVACY vol 19 (2011) PARAS 35–36; CIVIL PROCEDURE vol 12 (2015) PARAS 647 et seq, 799; CRIMINAL PROCEDURE vol 28 (2015) PARA 468; LEGAL PROFESSIONS vol 65 (2015) PARAS 538–539; LEGAL PROFESSIONS vol 66 (2015) PARA 877.
3　*Mortgage Express v Sawali* [2010] EWHC 3054 (Ch), [2011] 1 EGLR 58, [2010] All ER (D) 254 (Nov); *Capital Home Loans Ltd v Bennett Griffin LLP* [2013] EWHC 2613 (Ch).

(ii) Liability for Production of Title Deeds

495. Statutory liability of mortgagee to produce title deeds. A mortgagor[1], so long as his right to redeem subsists, is entitled from time to time, at reasonable times, on his request and at his own cost and on payment of the mortgagee's[2] costs and expenses in this behalf, to inspect and make copies of or extracts from the documents of title relating to the mortgaged property in the mortgagee's custody or power[3]. This right cannot be excluded by contract[4]. It seems that, where the mortgagee has sub-mortgaged, he must arrange for production by the sub-mortgagee[5]. Documents in a solicitor's possession are under his client's control[6]. Where a mortgagor is subject to a bankruptcy order, or an interim receiver has been appointed[7], the mortgagee can be required to produce the deeds in bankruptcy proceedings[8].

1   As to the meaning of 'mortgagor' see PARA 104 note 1.
2   As to the meaning of 'mortgagee' see PARA 104 note 1.
3   Law of Property Act 1925 s 96(1). Where in proceedings for the detention of title deeds the defendants pleaded that they held the deeds as equitable mortgagees, the plaintiffs were held entitled to inspect a memorandum of deposit of the deeds alleged to be held by the defendants: see *Owen v Nickson* (1861) 7 Jur NS 497 (a decision under the Evidence Act 1851 s 6 (now repealed)).
    As to disclosure and the inspection of documents in proceedings see CIVIL PROCEDURE vol 12 (2015) PARA 621 et seq. As to production of the deeds on a sale by the court see *Armstrong v Dixon* [1911] 1 IR 435. As to handing the deeds over on payment of debt see PARA 656.
4   See the Law of Property Act 1925 s 96(1).
5   See *Rogers v Rogers* (1842) 6 Jur 497. As to sub-mortgages see PARA 252 et seq.
6   *Fenwick v Reed* (1816) 1 Mer 114; *Bligh v Benson* (1819) 7 Price 205 at 207. As to the relationship between solicitor and client see LEGAL PROFESSIONS vol 66 (2015) PARA 561 et seq.
7   Ie under the Insolvency Act 1986 s 286: see BANKRUPTCY AND INDIVIDUAL INSOLVENCY vol 5 (2013) PARA 218 et seq.
8   See the Insolvency Act 1986 ss 366, 368; *Re White, ex p Caldecott* (1830) Mont 55; *Re Marks' Trust Deed* (1866) 1 Ch App 429; and BANKRUPTCY AND INDIVIDUAL INSOLVENCY vol 5 (2013) PARA 305.

496. Statutory liability of estate owner to produce title deeds. The owner of the legal estate is liable to produce the deeds and furnish information to a mortgagee of an equitable interest in the land[1].

1   See the Law of Property Act 1925 s 137(9); and CHOSES IN ACTION vol 13 (2009) PARA 58. See also *Compton v Earl Grey* (1826) 1 Y & J 154; *Re Cowin, Cowin v Gravett* (1886) 33 ChD 179.

497. Non-statutory liability to produce title deeds. Apart from the statutory liability to produce title deeds[1], a mortgagee, when the day fixed for redemption is past, is not bound to produce the deeds to the mortgagor except on payment of all money secured by the mortgage[2]. Moreover, the mortgagee may refuse to produce the deeds in proceedings between the mortgagor and a third person[3], in which case secondary evidence of them can be given[4]. Although in general a mortgagee cannot be required to disclose the mortgagor's title, production may sometimes be ordered in favour of a third person in the mortgagor's absence[5]; and, similarly, a mortgagor may be ordered to produce copies of deeds to a third person[6]. Where, however, the mortgagee loses all title to the mortgaged land by lapse of time, the mortgagor can recover possession of the mortgage and other title deeds[7].

1   Ie under the Law of Property Act 1925 s 96(1): see PARA 495.
2   *Browne v Lockhart* (1840) 10 Sim 420; *Greenwood v Rothwell* (1844) 7 Beav 291; *Cannock v Jauncey* (1853) 1 Drew 497 at 507; *Chichester v Marquis of Donegall* (1870) 5 Ch App 497; and see *Senhouse v Earl* (1752) 2 Ves Sen 450; *Sparke v Montriou* (1834) 1 Y & C Ex 103; *Jones v Jones* (1853) Kay App vi; *Burn v London and South Wales Coal Co and Risca Investment Co* (1890) 7 TLR 118. The decision in *Latimer v Neate* (1837) 4 Cl & Fin 570, HL, which appears to be authority to the contrary, was explained in *Browne v Lockhart* (1840) 10 Sim 420 and in *Glover v Hall* (1848) 2 Ph 484 at 490. Payment into court of the utmost amount due was not sufficient to give a right to production (*Postlethwaite v Blythe* (1818) 2 Swan 256; but see *Bank of New South Wales v O'Connor* (1889) 14 App Cas 273 at 283, PC); nor was the mortgagee bound to show the deeds to an intending purchaser (*Postlethwaite v Blythe* above) or transferee (*Damer v Earl of Portarlington* (1846) 15 Sim 380) unless the sale was being made in court (*Livesey v Harding* (1839) 1 Beav 343), or out of court with his consent (*Anon* (1729) Mos 246). A beneficiary who had mortgaged his interest to the trustee lost his ordinary right to production as against the trustee: *Johnston v Tucker* (1847) 11 Jur 382.
    This rule was treated as an instance of the general rule that a defendant is not bound to produce his title deeds, and it therefore extended to the mortgage deed itself (*Beaumont v Foster* (1835) 5 LJCh 4; *Crisp v Platel* (1844) 8 Beav 62; *Dendy v Cross* (1848) 11 Beav 91), and to a transfer (*Gill v Eyton* (1843) 7 Beav 155; *Lewis v Davies* (1853) 17 Jur 253). The attempt in *Patch v Ward*

(1865) LR 1 Eq 436 to revive the early right to production of the mortgage deed itself (2 Cases with Opinions of Counsel 53; *Anon* (1729) Mos 246; *Re White, ex p Caldecott* (1830) Mont 55 at 59) was not approved (*Carter v Hubback* (1876) 24 WR 354, CA), possibly because the mortgage deed belongs to the mortgagee (see *Sheffield v Eden* (1878) 10 ChD 291, CA). The rule applied, notwithstanding that the mortgagor was contesting the mortgage's validity (*Crisp v Platel*; *Dendy v Cross* above) and was not excluded by a mere allegation of fraud (*Bassford v Blakesley* (1842) 6 Beav 131; *Gill v Eyton* above); but in such a case production might be ordered if the circumstances under which the mortgage was obtained, or other circumstances, made this reasonable (*Balch v Symes* (1823) Turn & R 87; *Bassford v Blakesley*; *Costa Rica Republic v Erlanger* (1874) LR 19 Eq 33 at 45). The rule applied notwithstanding that the mortgagee in his statements of case had craved leave to refer to the deeds (*Howard v Robinson* (1859) 4 Drew 522), and it extended to drafts and copies (*Bycroft v Sibel* (1852) 1 WR 96) but not necessarily to vouchers (*Gibson v Hewett* (1846) 9 Beav 293; *Freeman v Butler* (1863) 33 Beav 289); and a mortgage deed might be ordered to be produced for inspection of an indorsement on it (*Phillips v Evans* (1843) 2 Y & C Ch Cas 647). Where a trustee had mortgaged, and had then released the equity of redemption to the mortgagee who had notice of the trust, the beneficiary was entitled to production against the mortgage: *Smith v Barnes* (1865) LR 1 Eq 65.

3   *Schlenker v Moxey* (1824) 1 C & P 178.
4   *Mills v Oddy* (1834) 6 C & P 728; *Doe d Gilbert v Ross* (1840) 7 M & W 102 at 122; *Phelps v Prew* (1854) 3 E & B 430; contra *Doe d Bowdler v Owen* (1837) 8 C & P 110.
5   *Gough v Offley* (1852) 5 De G & Sm 653.
6   *Hercy v Ferrers* (1841) 4 Beav 97. As to secondary evidence generally see CIVIL PROCEDURE vol 12 (2015) PARAS 695–696, 936 et seq.
7   *Lewis v Plunket* [1937] Ch 306, [1937] 1 All ER 530.

498. Liability of mortgagee of limited interest to produce title deeds. A tenant for life holds the title deeds subject to liability to produce them for the inspection of remaindermen with a vested, but not with a contingent, interest; and the mortgagee from the tenant for life, if he takes the deeds, takes them subject to the same liability[1]. This rule does not seem to be affected by the legal estate in fee simple being now vested in the tenant for life[2]. If the mortgage is paramount to the settlement, the remainderman cannot as such require production[3], but, as he has a right to redeem, he would have the statutory right to production[4]. Generally, the mortgagee of a partial interest in property who obtains the deeds is bound to produce them to other persons interested[5]. Thus the mortgagee of a lease of which there is no counterpart is bound to produce it at the lessor's request[6].

1   *Noel v Ward* (1816) 1 Madd 322; *Davis v Earl of Dysart* (1855) 20 Beav 405. As to the power of mortgage of a tenant for life see PARA 146.
2   See the Settled Land Act 1925 s 38; and SETTLEMENTS vol 91 (2012) PARA 728.
3   *Chichester v Marquis of Donegall* (1870) 5 Ch App 497. See also PARA 514.
4   See PARAS 488, 495.
5   In *Lambert v Rogers* (1817) 2 Mer 489, it was held that a mortgagee of the share of a co-owner was not bound to produce the deeds to another co-owner, as a mortgagee could not be compelled to disclose his mortgagor's title; but the other co-owner's rights cannot be prejudiced by the mortgage; and now the deeds should be held by the trustees of the statutory trusts. See also PARA 128.
6   *Doe d Morris v Roe* (1836) 1 M & W 207; *Balls v Margrave* (1841) 4 Beav 119.

(iii) Liability for Loss of Title Deeds

499. Nature of mortgagor's remedy for loss of title deeds. Upon redeeming, the mortgagor is entitled to a discharge and to delivery of the title deeds and writings relating to the property, including copies[1], and if they have been lost he is justified in instituting proceedings for redemption[2] in order that the fact of the loss may be ascertained for the satisfaction of future purchasers. In such proceedings, the mortgagee is directed to give an indemnity against the consequences of the loss of the deeds, and he is liable to pay the costs[3]; and the rule is the same if the mortgagor redeems in the mortgagee's foreclosure claim[4]. Where the deeds are known to be in a third person's possession, the mortgagor will be allowed to bring proceedings to recover them at the mortgagee's expense[5]. The mortgagor may also be entitled to compensation for the loss of the deeds[6], but not until redemption[7].

1 The mortgagee is not entitled to keep fair copies made at the mortgagor's expense, nor, it seems, copies made at his own expense: *Re Wade and Thomas* (1881) 17 ChD 348 at 352.
2 As to proceedings for redemption see PARA 661 et seq.
3 *Lord Midleton v Eliot* (1847) 15 Sim 531; *James v Rumsey* (1879) 11 ChD 398; *Caldwell v Matthews* (1890) 62 LT 799. An inquiry as to the loss of the deeds will be directed: *Smith v Bicknell* (1805) 3 Ves & B 51n; *Stokoe v Robson* (1814) 3 Ves & B 51; *Shelmardine v Harrop* (1821) 6 Madd 39. For forms of indemnity see *Shelmardine v Harrop*; *James v Rumsey* above. The form, in case of difference, is settled in chambers; but unreasonable opposition by the mortgagor to the indemnity offered will, perhaps, make him liable for costs thereby occasioned: cf *Macartney v Graham* (1831) 2 Russ & M 353. Where the mortgage deed has been destroyed, eg by fire, the mortgage may be confirmed.
4 *Stokoe v Robson* (1815) 19 Ves 385; *Shelmardine v Harrop* (1821) 6 Madd 39. As to foreclosure see PARA 571 et seq.
5 *Hornby v Matcham* (1848) 16 Sim 325; *Brown v Sewell* (1853) 11 Hare 49.
6 *Hornby v Matcham* (1848) 16 Sim 325; *Brown v Sewell* (1853) 11 Hare 49.
7 *Gilligan and Nugent v National Bank Ltd* [1901] 2 IR 513; *Browning v Handiland Group Ltd and Bush Investments Trust Ltd (third party)* (1976) 35 P & CR 345; cf *James v Rumsey* (1879) 11 ChD 398, where compensation was refused on special grounds.

500. Delay of redemption through loss of title deeds. Interest will cease to run at the date when the mortgagor is ready to redeem if redemption is delayed through the loss of the title deeds[1]. The mortgagor cannot be sued for the debt if there is a danger of his not getting back his title deeds on payment[2], but it is otherwise if the deeds are in fact lost[3].

1 *Lord Midleton v Eliot* (1847) 15 Sim 531; *James v Rumsey* (1879) 11 ChD 398.
2 *Schoole v Sall* (1803) 1 Sch & Lef 176.
3 *Baskett v Skeel* (1863) 11 WR 1019.

(iv) Delivery of Title Deeds on Extinguishment of Mortgage Debt

501. To whom title deeds delivered. On being paid off, the mortgagee delivers the title deeds to the mortgagor, or, if he has notice of other incumbrancers, to the incumbrancer ranking next after himself[1], but he is not liable for delivering them to the person not having the best right to them unless he has notice of the right or claim of a person having a better right[2]. As registration of a later mortgage as a land charge is notice to all the world[3], the mortgagee would not have been safe in handing over the deeds without searching the land charges register against the mortgagor. To avoid this, it is provided that notice in this connection does not include notice by reason of registration under the Land Charges Act 1972[4]. Where the mortgagee loses all title to the mortgaged land by lapse of time, the mortgagor can recover possession of the mortgage and other title deeds[5].

1 See *Corbett v National Provident Institution* (1900) 17 TLR 5.
2 Law of Property Act 1925 s 96(2). As to the meaning of 'mortgagor' see PARA 104 note 1. As to the meaning of 'mortgagee' see PARA 104 note 1.
3 See PARA 263.
4 Law of Property Act 1925 s 96(2) (amended by the Law of Property (Amendment) Act 1926 s 7, Schedule; Law of Property Act 1969 s 16(2), Sch 2 Pt I; Land Charges Act 1972 s 18(6)). As to the registration of puisne mortgages and general equitable charges see PARA 262.
5 *Lewis v Plunket* [1937] Ch 306, [1937] 1 All ER 530.

(7) RIGHT OF CONSOLIDATION

(i) Nature of the Right of Consolidation

502. General principle of consolidation. A mortgagee who holds several distinct mortgages over different properties owned by the same mortgagor which are redeemable, not under the right of redemption expressly reserved by the mortgage deeds, but only by virtue of the equity of redemption arising after default in payment at the fixed day[1], may, within certain limits, and against certain persons who are entitled to redeem all or some of the mortgages, consolidate the mortgages, that is, treat them as one, and decline to be redeemed as to any unless he is redeemed as to all[2]. This is an application of the maxim that he who seeks equity must do equity[3]. After the original day for redemption is past[4], the mortgagor can only redeem by the assistance of equity, and this assistance is given upon the terms that he is to pay the money due both in respect of the estate which he seeks to redeem and in respect of the other mortgaged estates[5]. Where two estates are subject to distinct mortgages, and a second mortgage is granted of both estates, the second mortgagee is not bound to redeem both the first mortgages if he wishes to redeem one[6].

The right of consolidation is excluded by statute unless the contrary intention is expressed in the mortgage deed[7].

1   As to enforcement of the equity of redemption see PARA 332 et seq. The right to consolidate arises in equity after default: see PARA 503.
2   *Jennings v Jordan* (1881) 6 App Cas 698 at 700, HL, per Lord Selborne LC; and see the same case in the Court of Appeal sub nom *Mills v Jennings* (1880) 13 ChD 639 at 646, CA. See also *Griffith v Pound* (1890) 45 ChD 553 at 560.
3   *Chesworth v Hunt* (1880) 5 CPD 266 at 271. See also EQUITABLE JURISDICTION vol 47 (2014) PARAS 110–111.
4   See PARAS 332, 571.
5   *Willie v Lugg* (1761) 2 Eden 78 at 80; *Jones v Smith* (1794) 2 Ves 372 at 377; *Cummins v Fletcher* (1880) 14 ChD 699 at 708, CA; *Mills v Jennings* (1880) 13 ChD 639 at 646, CA (on appeal sub nom *Jennings v Jordan* (1881) 6 App Cas 698, HL); *Minter v Carr* [1894] 3 Ch 498 at 501, CA. For early statements of the rule see *Shuttleworth v Laycock* (1684) 1 Vern 245; *Margrave v Le Hooke* (1690) 2 Vern 207; *Pope v Onslow* (1692) 2 Vern 286; *Cator v Charlton* (1775) cited in 2 Ves at 377; *Collett v Munden* (1786) cited in 2 Ves at 377. The courts of law recognised the doctrine in proceedings where the equity of redemption incidentally fell within their jurisdiction: *Roe d Kaye v Soley* (1770) 2 Wm Bl 726; and see *Marcon v Bloxam* (1856) 11 Exch 586.
6   *Pelly v Wathen* (1849) 7 Hare 351 at 365.
7   See the Law of Property Act 1925 s 93; and PARA 504.

503. Right of consolidation arises only after default. As the right of consolidation[1] is equitable, it only arises after there has been default on all the securities in respect of which it is claimed; that is, the days fixed for redemption must have passed, so that the mortgagor has lost his legal right and is bound to come into equity to redeem[2].

1   As to the right of consolidation see PARA 502.
2   *Crickmore v Freeston* (1870) 40 LJCh 137; *Cummins v Fletcher* (1880) 14 ChD 699, CA. See also *Jones v Smith* (1794) 2 Ves 372 at 376; *Jennings v Jordan* (1881) 6 App Cas 698 at 717, HL.

504. Statutory exclusion of consolidation. A mortgagor[1] seeking to redeem any one mortgage[2] is entitled to do so without paying any money due under any separate mortgage made by him, or by any person through whom he claims, solely on property other than that comprised in the mortgage which he seeks to redeem[3]. This applies only if and so far as a contrary intention is not expressed in the mortgage deeds or one of them[4]. Apart from this, nothing in the Law of Property

Act 1925 in reference to mortgages affects any right of consolidation or renders inoperative a stipulation in relation to any mortgage, whenever made, reserving a right to consolidate[5]. Where it is intended to exclude the statutory rule, this is usually done by a clause expressly providing that the rule is not to apply to the security, although a clause providing for the preservation of the right of consolidation is equally effective[6]. A clause which refers to mortgages only will not give a right to consolidate a vendor's lien with a mortgage[7]. A clause excluding the statutory provision contained in the first of several mortgages of different properties effectively preserves the right of consolidation under all the mortgages, even though it is not contained in the subsequent mortgages[8]; and, similarly, a clause in a subsequent mortgage is effective as to previous mortgages[9].

1   As to the meaning of 'mortgagor' see PARA 104 note 1.
2   As to the meaning of 'mortgage' see PARA 101 note 4.
3   Law of Property Act 1925 s 93(1).
4   Law of Property Act 1925 s 93(1).
5   Law of Property Act 1925 s 93(3). As to the right of consolidation see PARA 502 et seq.
6   *Hughes v Britannia Permanent Benefit Building Society* [1906] 2 Ch 607 at 611.
7   *Re Pearce* [1909] 2 Ch 492 at 495, CA. As to the vendor's lien see LIEN vol 68 (2008) PARA 859.
8   *Re Salmon, ex p Trustee* [1903] 1 KB 147.
9   *Griffith v Pound* (1890) 45 ChD 553.

505. Right of consolidation in relation to registered land. A chargee who has the right of consolidation in relation to a registered charge[1] may apply to the registrar for an entry to be made in respect of that right in the individual register in which that charge is registered[2]. The registrar must make an entry in the individual register in such terms as he considers appropriate to give effect to such an application[3].

1   As to the right of consolidation see PARA 502 et seq. As to the meaning of 'registered charge' see PARA 142 note 7.
2   Land Registration Rules 2003, SI 2003/1417, r 110(1). The application must be made in Form CC: r 110(2). As to registered land generally see REAL PROPERTY AND REGISTRATION vol 87 (2012) PARA 232 et seq.
3   Land Registration Rules 2003, SI 2003/1417, r 110(3).

(ii) When the Right of Consolidation Exists

506. Right to consolidation where mortgages made by same mortgagor. The right of consolidation[1] only exists where the mortgages have been made originally by the same mortgagor[2], and can be asserted only to the extent of the mortgagor's own interest in the properties[3], although it is possible that the right exists where one mortgage is made by the mortgagor and another by persons claiming by devolution from him on his death[4]. The right does not exist where one mortgage is by a sole mortgagor and the other mortgage is by the same mortgagor jointly with another[5]. Hence a security given by a partner for his private debt cannot be consolidated with a security given by himself and the other partners for a partnership debt[6], and a mortgage by a co-owner of his share of the estate cannot be consolidated with a mortgage of the entirety[7]. As, for the purpose of ascertaining the right of consolidation, the mortgagee is not entitled to look into any transactions between the mortgagor and third persons, a mortgage by a trustee cannot be consolidated with a mortgage by the beneficiary[8], nor can a mortgage by a surety be consolidated with a mortgage given by the principal debtor for another debt[9].

1   As to the right of consolidation see PARA 502 et seq.
2   *Sharp v Rickards* [1909] 1 Ch 109.

3   See *Lord Kensington v Bouverie* (1854) 19 Beav 39; on appeal (1859) 7 HL Cas 557.
4   See *White v Hillacre* (1839) 3 Y & C Ex 597. As to the exercise of the right against an assignee of one of the equities of redemption see PARA 512.
5   *Jones v Smith* (1794) 2 Ves 372 at 376. See also *Marcon v Bloxam* (1856) 11 Exch 586 at 600.
6   *Cummins v Fletcher* (1880) 14 ChD 699 at 710, CA, per James LJ (disagreeing with *Beevor v Luck, Beevor v Lawson* (1867) LR 4 Eq 537 at 543). As to mortgages by partners see PARA 134 et seq.
7   *Thorneycroft v Crockett* (1848) 2 HL Cas 239 at 245–255.
8   *Re Raggett, ex p Williams* (1880) 16 ChD 117 at 119, CA, per James LJ; *Sharp v Rickards* [1909] 1 Ch 109.
9   See FINANCIAL INSTRUMENTS AND TRANSACTIONS vol 49 (2015) PARA 769.

507. Consolidation where securities are of different natures. For the purposes of the right to consolidate[1], it is immaterial that the securities comprise properties of different natures, or that one or both are equitable mortgages; hence a mortgage of real estate can be consolidated with a mortgage of personal estate[2], and a legal mortgage can be consolidated with an equitable mortgage[3], and an equitable mortgage with another equitable mortgage[4]. The right to consolidate does not depend, as the right to tack formerly did[5], upon the possession of the legal estate[6].

1   As to the right to consolidate see PARA 502 et seq.
2   *Tassell v Smith* (1858) 2 De G & J 713. See also *Watts v Symes* (1851) 1 De GM & G 240 (revsg the judgment of Shadwell V-C (1849) 16 Sim 640 at 647); *Spalding v Thompson* (1858) 26 Beav 637; *Cracknall v Janson* (1879) 11 ChD 1, CA. As to bills of sale see FINANCIAL INSTRUMENTS AND TRANSACTIONS vol 49 (2015) PARAS 438, 452.
3   See *Watts v Symes* (1851) 1 De GM & G 240. As to legal mortgages see PARAS 104, 160 et seq. As to equitable mortgages see PARAS 105, 215 et seq.
4   *Tweedale v Tweedale* (1857) 23 Beav 341.
5   As to the meaning of 'tacking' see PARA 266.
6   *Neve v Pennell, Hunt v Neve* (1863) 2 Hem & M 170 at 183. See, however, dicta to the contrary in *Jones v Smith* (1794) 2 Ves 372 at 376; *White v Hillacre* (1839) 3 Y & C Ex 597 at 609.

508. Consolidation where securities originally in favour of different mortgagees. For the purposes of the right of consolidation[1] it is not necessary that the securities should have been created originally in favour of the same mortgagee. The right exists where mortgages given to different mortgagees subsequently become vested in the same person[2]. There must be, however, an actual union of the securities in one person. A mortgage to one mortgagee will not be treated as consolidated with a mortgage to the same person and another on a joint account[3].

1   As to the right of consolidation see PARA 502 et seq.
2   *Tweedale v Tweedale* (1857) 23 Beav 341; *Vint v Padget* (1858) 2 De G & J 611; *Selby v Pomfret* (1861) 3 De GF & J 595; *Jennings v Jordan* (1881) 6 App Cas 698 at 700, HL; *Pledge v White* [1896] AC 187, HL. The contrary decision in *Fosbrooke v Walker* (1832) 2 LJCh 161 is clearly wrong. As to *Selby v Pomfret* above see *Cummins v Fletcher* (1880) 14 ChD 699 at 709, CA, per James LJ.
3   *Riley v Hall* (1898) 79 LT 244.

509. Securities must be in existence at time of consolidation. Both the securities which the mortgagee claims to consolidate must be in existence at the time when the claim is made[1]. There is no right to apply a surplus on an existing mortgage to make good a debt secured by a mortgage which has ceased to exist by reason of the determination of its subject matter, such as a life interest[2] or a lease[3]. In such a case, the debt formerly secured by the mortgage has ceased to be a secured debt, and a mortgagee who has in his hands a surplus from a realised security may not, as against other creditors, apply it in payment of a debt which has become a simple contract debt[4]. Where a mortgagee has been redeemed as to one mortgage by an incumbrancer against whom he could not consolidate, he loses any right to consolidation he had against subsequent incumbrancers[5].

Notwithstanding this rule, however, a mortgagee who has sold one of his securities and paid off the debt primarily charged on that security is not thereby debarred from exercising the right of consolidation, and can apply the balance of the proceeds in payment of the debt owing on his other security[6], and where a mortgagee has given notice to pay off one mortgage with a view to acquiring the right to exercise his power of sale, he may nevertheless consolidate and may refuse a tender of the money due under that mortgage alone[7].

1   As to the right of consolidation see PARA 502 et seq.
2   *Re Gregson, Christison v Bolam* (1887) 36 ChD 223.
3   *Re Raggett, ex p Williams* (1880) 16 ChD 117, CA. Similarly, a subsequent debt could not be tacked to a mortgage which had been paid off: *Brecon Corpn v Seymour* (1859) 26 Beav 548. Tacking by virtue of a legal estate has now been abolished: see PARA 266.
4   *Talbot v Frere* (1878) 9 ChD 568; *Re Gregson, Christison v Bolam* (1887) 36 ChD 223 (disagreeing with *Spalding v Thompson* (1858) 26 Beav 637; *Re Haselfoot's Estate, Chauntler's Claim* (1872) LR 13 Eq 327; *Re General Provident Assurance Co, ex p National Bank* (1872) LR 14 Eq 507).
5   *Jennings v Jordan* (1881) 6 App Cas 698 at 707, HL. As to the persons against whom the mortgagee may consolidate see PARAS 510–515.
6   *Selby v Pomfret* (1861) 1 John & H 336; *Cracknall v Janson* (1879) 11 ChD 1, CA.
7   *Griffith v Pound* (1890) 45 ChD 553.

(iii) Against whom the Mortgagee may Consolidate

510.   Consolidation against mortgagor. The right of consolidation[1] is exercisable primarily against the mortgagor, and may be asserted in any proceeding in which the right of redemption comes in question; for this purpose foreclosure and redemption claims are on the same footing[2].

1   As to the right of consolidation see PARA 502 et seq.
2   *Watts v Symes* (1851) 1 De GM & G 240 at 246; *Selby v Pomfret* (1861) 1 John & H 336 at 338 (affd on appeal 3 De G F & J 596 at 598); *Tribourg v Lord Pomfret* (1773) cited in Amb at 733; *Re Loosemore, ex p Berridge* (1843) 3 Mont D & De G 464. As to terms and incidents of redemption see PARAS 327–328. As to foreclosure see PARA 571 et seq. Formerly the view was held that consolidation was confined to redemption suits: *Holmes v Turner* (1843) 7 Hare 367n; *Smeathman v Bray (or Gray)* (1851) 15 Jur 1051. As to the amount of arrears of interest to which a mortgagee is entitled in a foreclosure claim see LIMITATION PERIODS vol 68 (2008) PARA 1128. As to the amount of arrears of interest to which a mortgagee is entitled in a redemption claim see LIMITATION PERIODS vol 68 (2008) PARA 1137.

511.   Consolidation against mortgagor's successors in title. So long as the equities of redemption are not severed[1], the right of consolidation[2] may be asserted against successors in title to the mortgagor[3]. For this purpose, it is immaterial whether the mortgages were originally made to the same mortgagee, or whether they have merely become united in the same person[4]; and in the latter case the right may be asserted even though the union of the mortgages has taken place after the change in the title to the equities of redemption. Thus the right of consolidation exists where the mortgages become united after a mortgagor's bankruptcy[5] or after the sale or further mortgage of both the estates to the same person[6], provided that the sale or further mortgage of the two estates is effected as one transaction[7]. The right may be asserted even though the union of the mortgages has taken place with notice of a change in the title to the equity of redemption[8]. The mortgages must, however, both be prior to the change of title[9].

1   As to the effect of severance of the equities of redemption see PARA 512. As to the equity of redemption see PARAS 107, 304 et seq.
2   As to the right of consolidation see PARA 502 et seq.

3 *Willie v Lugg* (1761) 2 Eden 78; *Jones v Smith* (1794) 2 Ves 372 at 376. Thus it might be asserted against the heir, and may now be asserted against the mortgagor's personal representatives (*Margrave v Le Hooke* (1690) 2 Vern 207), or against his trustee in bankruptcy (*Pope v Onslow* (1692) 2 Vern 286; *Re Breeds, ex p Alsager* (1841) 2 Mont D & De G 328; *Cracknall v Janson* (1879) 11 ChD 1, CA). As to consolidation against sureties see FINANCIAL INSTRUMENTS AND TRANSACTIONS vol 49 (2015) PARA 769.
4 See PARA 508.
5 *Selby v Pomfret* (1861) 3 De GF & J 595; *Re Salmon, ex p Trustee* [1903] 1 KB 147.
6 *Tweedale v Tweedale* (1857) 23 Beav 341; *Vint v Padget* (1858) 2 De G & J 611; *Pledge v White* [1896] AC 187, HL. See also *Bovey v Skipwich* (1671) 1 Cas in Ch 201.
7 *Pledge v White* [1896] AC 187, HL.
8 *Vint v Padget* (1858) 2 De G & J 611.
9 See *Squire v Pardoe* (1891) 40 WR 100, CA.

512. Effect of severance of equities of redemption. Where the equities of redemption[1] have been severed, whether by sale or further mortgage, or by settlement, voluntary or otherwise[2], the existence of the right of consolidation[3] against the assignee of one equity of redemption depends on whether it had attached before the severance. This may be either because both mortgages were prior to the severance and were made to the same mortgagee[4], or because, although made to different mortgagees, they had become vested in the same person before the severance[5]. In these cases, the assignee of one mortgaged property, even though he has given valuable consideration[6], and without notice of the mortgage on the other property[7], takes subject to the existing right of consolidation, and must submit to give effect to it[8]. Hence he cannot redeem his own property without paying off the mortgage on the other property also[9], but, if he does this, he is entitled to have both properties conveyed to him[10].

1 As to the equity of redemption see PARA 107, 304 et seq.
2 See *Re Walhampton Estate* (1884) 26 ChD 391, where it was held that the avoidance by a mortgage of a prior voluntary settlement under 27 Eliz 1 c 4 (1584–5) did not let in the right to consolidate that mortgage with a subsequent mortgage of other property. That Act, which was amended by the Voluntary Conveyances Act 1893, is now reproduced in the Law of Property Act 1925 s 173: see MISREPRESENTATION vol 76 (2013) PARA 864 et seq.
3 As to the right of consolidation see PARA 502 et seq.
4 *Tribourg v Lord Pomfret* (1773) cited in Amb 733; *Re—, ex p Carter* (1773) Amb 733; *Ireson v Denn* (1796) 2 Cox Eq Cas 425. See also *Titley v Davies* (1743) 2 Y & C Ch Cas 399n; *Jones v Smith* (1794) 2 Ves 372 at 376–377.
5 *Jennings v Jordan* (1881) 6 App Cas 698, HL; *Hughes v Britannia Permanent Benefit Building Society* [1906] 2 Ch 607.
6 *Re, ex p Carter* (1773) Amb 733 (purchase on sale); *Tribourg v Lord Pomfret* (1773) cited in Amb 733 (subsequent mortgage).
7 *Ireson v Denn* (1796) 2 Cox Eq Cas 425.
8 See *Neve v Pennell, Hunt v Neve* (1863) 2 Hem & M 170 at 183.
9 *Jennings v Jordan* (1881) 6 App Cas 698 at 701, HL.
10 *Mutual Life Assurance Society v Langley* (1886) 32 ChD 460 at 466, CA.

513. Right to consolidate must have attached before severance. Where the right of consolidation[1] has not attached at the date of severance[2], it does not attach subsequently. Thus the assignee of an equity of redemption does not become subject to consolidation by reason of a subsequent mortgage by the assignor of different property[3], or by reason of the subsequent union of mortgages which were created before the assignment in favour of different mortgagees[4]. An express right of consolidation contained in the first mortgage does not enable the mortgagee to consolidate it with subsequent mortgages of other properties as against a second mortgagee of the first property, such subsequent mortgages being made after the date of the second mortgage of the first property and with notice of it[5].

1 As to the right of consolidation see PARA 502 et seq.

2   As to the alternative position see PARA 512.
3   *Jennings v Jordan* (1881) 6 App Cas 698 at 702, HL, overruling *Tassell v Smith* (1858) 2 De G & J 713. The principle stated in the text applies even more strongly where the mortgagee of the second estate takes a transfer of the mortgage of the first estate with notice of the assignment of the equity of redemption of that estate: *Baker v Gray* (1875) 1 ChD 491. Where there is a mortgage of leasehold property, A, first to X, and secondly to Y; subsequently a mortgage of property, B, to X; and then substituted mortgages to X and Y successively of a renewed lease of A, the substituted mortgages to X and Y are not treated as new mortgages so as to give to X a right of consolidation against Y, especially if the priority of X for his first mortgage, and for a further advance to enable the new lease to be taken, is expressly reserved: *Bird v Wenn* (1886) 33 ChD 215.
4   *White v Hillarce* (1839) 3 Y & C Ex 597 at 609; *Harter v Colman* (1882) 19 ChD 630; *Minter v Carr* [1894] 3 Ch 498, CA. See, contra, *Beevor v Luck, Beevor v Lawson* (1867) LR 4 Eq 537, where it was considered that, if at the time of assignment of one equity of redemption a mortgage by the same mortgagor was existing on another estate, the assignee took subject to the possibility of the two mortgages uniting, and in that case would be subject to consolidation; but this was questioned in *Jennings v Jordan* (1881) 6 App Cas 698 at 701, 718, HL, and must be taken to be overruled (*Pledge v White* [1896] AC 187 at 195, HL).
5   *Hughes v Britannia Permanent Benefit Building Society* [1906] 2 Ch 607. To allow such a claim would be contrary to the principle of *Hopkinson v Rolt* (1861) 9 HL Cas 514: see PARA 267 note 4. In *Andrews v City Permanent Benefit Building Society* (1881) 44 LT 641, the mortgagee was allowed to consolidate against a second mortgagee of one property taking with notice of an express covenant for consolidation.

514. Right of consolidation where severance occurs by devise. Similar considerations apply where the equities of redemption are severed by devise to different devisees[1]. If the mortgages are not united until after the testator's death, the right of consolidation does not arise[2].

1   As to the effect of severance of the equities of redemption on the right to consolidate see PARAS 512–513. As to the right of consolidation see PARA 502 et seq.
2   *White v Hillacre* (1839) 3 Y & C Ex 597.

515. Effect of intervening incumbrancers' right to marshal. Where the mortgagee of two properties is entitled to a further charge on one, and there are intervening incumbrances on that property, then, after his first mortgage has been paid off out of that property exclusively the mortgagee may not exercise his right of consolidation[1] so as to throw his further charge on the other property and defeat the intervening incumbrancers' right to marshal[2].

1   As to the right of consolidation see PARA 502 et seq.
2   *Ford v Tynte* (1872) 41 LJCh 758. As to marshalling of assets see PARAS 637–640.

(iv) Who may Exercise the Right of Consolidation

516. Person in whom mortgages are united. Where mortgages over distinct properties have been granted by the same mortgagor, the right of consolidation[1] may be exercised by the person in whom the mortgages are united, whether he is the original mortgagee, or whether the mortgages or one of them have come to him by assignment or devolution[2]. It is immaterial whether he holds on his own account or as trustee[3]. Although he may consolidate notwithstanding that such union has taken place after the mortgagor's bankruptcy[4], he cannot, to the prejudice of other creditors, consolidate, with a prior security held by him, a security for an advance taken after notice of insolvency[5].

An incumbrancer on the equity of redemption in one of two mortgaged estates who pays off a mortgage on the other estate becomes an equitable assignee of that mortgage, and is entitled to consolidate what he so pays with his own debt[6]. Moreover, if a first mortgagee has two debts, secured on separate properties, and the second mortgagee of one property sells that property and, in pursuance of the first mortgagee's claim to consolidate, pays off both the first mortgagee's debts out of the proceeds, the second mortgagee is entitled to consolidate the first mortgagee's debt secured on the unsold property with his own debt and to recover it against a third property included in his security[7].

1   As to the right of consolidation see PARA 502 et seq.
2   *Jennings v Jordan* (1881) 6 App Cas 698 at 700, HL.
3   *Tassell v Smith* (1858) 2 De G & J 713, overruled on another point (see PARA 513 note 3).
4   See PARA 528.
5   *Re Softley, ex p Hodgkin* (1875) LR 20 Eq 746 at 757 per Bacon CJ.
6   *Titley v Davies* (1743) 2 Y & C Ch Cas 399n. As to the subrogated rights of a person paying off a mortgage debt see PARA 386.
7   *Cracknall v Janson* (1879) 11 ChD 1, CA. In such a case the payment of the debt owed to the first mortgagee and secured on the unsold property is made out of money which, if the first mortgagee had not claimed the right to consolidate, would have belonged to the second mortgagee; the payment is therefore treated as a payment by the second mortgagee out of his own money and the second mortgagee becomes an equitable transferee of the mortgage on the unsold property: *Cracknall v Janson* (1879) 11 ChD 1 at 17–18, CA.

517.   Assignee of right takes subject to equities. As the right of consolidation[1] is an equitable right, the ordinary incidents of equitable rights attach to it. Consequently, the mortgagee's assignee stands in no better position than his assignor; and if, by arrangement between the assignor and a subsequent incumbrancer, the assignor has waived his right of consolidation, the right is not exercisable by the assignee[2].

1   As to the right of consolidation see PARA 502 et seq.
2   *Bird v Wenn* (1886) 33 ChD 215.

9. REMEDIES OF MORTGAGEES

(1) GENERAL RIGHT TO PURSUE REMEDIES

(i) Right to Pursue Remedies Concurrently

518. Mortgagee's right to exercise remedies concurrently. Once the mortgagor has made default[1] in payment of the mortgage debt, the mortgagee is entitled to pursue any or all of his remedies, subject, as regards the powers of sale and appointing a receiver, to the restrictions imposed by agreement or by statute, according as the powers are express or statutory[2]. Accordingly, the mortgagee can at the same time sue for payment on the covenant to pay principal and interest, for possession of the mortgaged estate, and for foreclosure[3], and can combine these in the same claim[4]; and until judgment nisi has been obtained in his foreclosure claim, he can exercise his power of sale[5]. The mortgagee does, however, owe a general duty to exercise his powers in good faith for the purpose of obtaining repayment[6].

If the mortgagee realises part of the debt by his claim on the covenant, or by sale of part of the property, he must give credit in the foreclosure claim for the amount realised, and if, after foreclosure, he proceeds on the covenant, he reopens the foreclosure[7]. The mortgagee may not sue on the covenant if he has sold the property to a third party, since the foreclosure cannot be reopened[8]. A realisation of the whole debt gives the mortgagor an immediate right to reconveyance of the mortgaged property remaining unsold[9]. It follows that where there are collateral securities the mortgagee should realise these first, and then foreclose in respect of the balance of his debt[10].

1 Where a day for payment is fixed by the mortgage deed, the default occurs when this day has elapsed without payment (see PARAS 107, 332). Where no day is fixed, there is default when the money is not paid on demand (see PARA 539).
2 As to the mortgagee's powers of sale see PARA 443 et seq. As to the appointment of receivers see PARA 478 et seq.
3 *China and South Sea Bank Ltd v Tan Soon Gin (alias George Tan)* [1990] 1 AC 536, [1989] 3 All ER 839, PC; *Re Bank of Credit and Commerce International SA (No 8)* [1998] AC 214, [1997] 4 All ER 568, HL. See also *Cheah Theam Swee v Equiticorp Finance Group Ltd* [1992] 1 AC 472, [1991] 4 All ER 989, PC. As to foreclosure see PARA 571 et seq.
4 *Dymond v Croft* (1876) 3 ChD 512; *Greenough v Littler* (1880) 15 ChD 93; *Farrer v Lacy, Hartland & Co* (1885) 31 ChD 42, CA. As to joining a claim for possession with the claim for foreclosure see PARA 592.
5 After judgment for foreclosure nisi (see PARA 599 et seq) and before foreclosure absolute (see PARA 608 et seq), a mortgagee cannot sell without the permission of the court, but the power of sale is merely suspended and not extinguished so that a purchaser for value without notice may get a good title: see *Stevens v Theatres Ltd* [1903] 1 Ch 857. See also PARA 619.
6 See PARA 394.
7 As to opening foreclosure see PARA 616 et seq.
8 *Lloyds and Scottish Trust Ltd v Britten* (1982) 44 P & CR 249, 79 LS Gaz 1291 (applying *Kinnaird v Trollope* (1888) 39 ChD 636).
9 *Cheah Theam Swee v Equiticorp Finance Group Ltd* [1992] 1 AC 472, [1991] 4 All ER 989, PC; *Lockhart v Hardy* (1846) 9 Beav 349 at 355. See also PARA 647 et seq.
10 *Dyson v Morris* (1842) 1 Hare 413 at 423.

(ii) Loss of Right to Sue

519. Loss of right to sue by running of time. A mortgagee's claim (other than a foreclosure claim in respect of mortgaged land) to recover the principal money secured by a mortgage or other charge on property, whether real or personal, which existed when the cause of action accrued[1], may not be brought after 12 years from the date when the right to receive the money accrued[2]. The statutory provisions relating to the limitation of actions to recover land apply to a foreclosure claim in respect of land[3] or a claim by a mortgagee of land for possession[4]; but not to a claim for possession by an equitable chargee[5]. The period of limitation applicable is normally 12 years from the date when the right of action accrued, and at the end of the period the mortgagee's title is extinguished[6]. A foreclosure claim in respect of mortgaged personal property may not be brought more than 12 years from the date when the right to foreclose accrued[7].

In general, not more than six years' arrears of interest can be recovered by a mortgagee[8], but this restriction does not apply to a foreclosure claim in respect of land[9]. Where a mortgagee sells the mortgaged property or brings proceedings to enforce his security he is entitled to retain all principal and arrears of interest, whether or not statute barred, before accounting to the mortgagor for the surplus[10]. A mortgagor is not entitled to redeem a mortgage unless he tenders the full amount of the principal and interest due, whether or not any part of it is statute barred[11]. If a mortgagee sues on the covenant and obtains a judgment for the debt, not more than six years' arrears of interest in respect of the judgment debt can be recovered by bringing proceedings or by execution[12].

These periods of limitation are subject to certain extensions or postponements in the case of disability, acknowledgment[13], part payment[14], fraud or mistake[15].

No statutory limitation period applies to the execution of a judgment[16] or to a charging order[17].

1   The cause of action accrues when there is a breach of an express or implied covenant to repay the advance (see PARA 182), regardless of whether there was an antecedent loan contract, and regardless of whether there is an express covenant to pay the shortfall following sale. In the case of an instalment mortgage the cause of action normally accrues on failure to pay an instalment, whether or not there is an express covenant to repay the capital advance: see *Bristol & West plc v Bartlett* [2002] EWCA Civ 1181, [2002] 4 All ER 544, [2003] 1 WLR 284; *Scottish Equitable plc v Thompson* [2003] EWCA Civ 211, [2003] HLR 690; *West Bromwich Building Society v Wilkinson* [2005] UKHL 44, [2005] 4 All ER 97, [2005] 1 WLR 2303.
2   See the Limitation Act 1980 s 20(1); and LIMITATION PERIODS vol 68 (2008) PARA 1105. This provision applies whether or not the mortgagee has exercised his power of sale before proceedings are commenced and whether or not there is a covenant in the mortgage to pay any shortfall following sale: see *Bristol & West plc v Bartlett* [2002] EWCA Civ 1181, [2002] 4 All ER 544, [2003] 1 WLR 284.
3   See the Limitation Act 1980 s 20(4); and LIMITATION PERIODS vol 68 (2008) PARA 1105.
4   See LIMITATION PERIODS vol 68 (2008) PARA 1124 et seq.
5   *Yorkshire Bank Finance Ltd v Mulhall* [2008] EWCA Civ 1156, [2009] 2 All ER (Comm) 164, [2009] 1 P & CR 345.
6   See the Limitation Act 1980 ss 15, 17; and LIMITATION PERIODS vol 68 (2008) PARAS 1025, 1095. The cause of action arises on the grant of the mortgage where the mortgagor remains in possession without express permission: see *Ashe v National Westminster Bank plc* [2008] EWCA Civ 55, [2008] 1 WLR 710, [2008] 2 P & CR 183.
7   See the Limitation Act 1980 s 20(2); and LIMITATION PERIODS vol 68 (2008) PARA 1124.
8   See the Limitation Act 1980 s 20(5); and LIMITATION PERIODS vol 68 (2008) PARA 1111. As to the rights of mortgagees of future interests or life insurance policies see s 20(7); and LIMITATION PERIODS vol 68 (2008) PARA 1117.
9   See the Limitation Act 1980 s 20(4); and LIMITATION PERIODS vol 68 (2008) PARA 1104.
10 *Edmunds v Waugh* (1866) LR 1 Eq 418; *Re Marshfield, Marshfield v Hutchings* (1887) 34 ChD 721; *Re Lloyd, Lloyd v Lloyd* [1903] 1 Ch 385, CA; *Holmes v Cowcher* [1970] 1 All ER 1224, [1970] 1 WLR 834; *Ezekiel v Orakpo* [1997] 1 WLR 340, CA.
11 *Dingle v Coppen* [1899] 1 Ch 726.
12 See the Limitation Act 1980 s 24(2); and LIMITATION PERIODS vol 68 (2008) PARA 1010. See also *Lowsley v Forbes* [1999] 1 AC 329, [1998] 3 All ER 897, HL.
13 See *Bradford & Bingley plc v Rashid* [2006] UKHL 37, [2006] 4 All ER 705, [2006] 2 All ER (Comm) 951; and LIMITATION PERIODS vol 68 (2008) PARAS 1183–1184.

14 See *UCB Corporate Services Ltd v Kohli* [2004] EWHC 1126 (Ch), [2004] 2 All ER (Comm) 422; *Ashcroft v Bradford & Bingley plc* [2010] EWCA Civ 223, [2010] 2 P & CR 193, [2010] All ER (D) 94 (Mar).
15 See LIMITATION PERIODS vol 68 (2008) PARA 1168 et seq.
16 See *National Westminster Bank plc v Powney* [1991] Ch 339, [1990] 2 All ER 416, CA; and LIMITATION PERIODS vol 68 (2008) PARA 915 et seq.
17 *Yorkshire Bank Finance Ltd v Mulhall* [2008] EWCA Civ 1156, [2009] 2 All ER (Comm) 164, [2009] 1 P & CR 345. As to charging orders see PARA 220.

520. Loss of right to sue by cause of action estoppel. It may be an abuse of process for a party in subsequent proceedings to raise a ground of claim or defence which could have been but was not raised in earlier proceedings[1]. Therefore, a mortgagee who obtains judgment for possession and for the sums expressed to be due under the mortgage cannot bring a subsequent claim for sums due under a guarantee which were also secured by the mortgage[2]. A mortgagee is not, however, necessarily required to enforce all his rights in one action: if he brings a claim for possession or payment alone, or if he obtains an unopposed order for possession alone in proceedings for possession and payment, he is not estopped from claiming the other remedy in a subsequent proceeding[3].

1 See *Johnson v Gore Wood & Co (a firm)* [2002] 2 AC 1, [2001] 1 All ER 481. HL; *Arnold v National Westminster Bank plc* [1991] 2 AC 93, [1991] 3 All ER 41, HL; and CIVIL PROCEDURE vol 12A (2015) PARA 1627.
2 *Lloyds Bank v Hawkins* [1998] Lloyd's Rep Bank 379, [1998] 47 EG 137, CA.
3 See *UCB Bank plc v Chandler* (1999) 79 P & CR 270, CA; *Securum Finance Ltd v Ashton* [2001] Ch 291, [2000] 3 WLR 1400, CA; and CIVIL PROCEDURE vol 12A (2015) PARA 1627.

(iii) Effect of Insolvency of Companies and Partnerships

521. Effect of mortgagor in administration. While a company is in administration[1] a mortgagee is not entitled to take any steps to enforce any security over the company's property except with the consent of the administrator or the permission of the court[2]. An administrator may also dispose of or take action relating to property which is subject to a floating charge as if the property were not subject to the charge[3]. In the case of any other type of security, the administrator may apply to the court for an order for disposal of property subject to the security as if it were not so subject, although any such order is subject to the condition that there be applied towards discharging the sums secured by the security:

(1)   the net proceeds of the disposal; and
(2)   any additional sum required to be added to the net proceeds so as to produce the amount determined by the court as the net amount which would be realised on a sale of the property at market value[4].

The provisions described above also apply to limited liability partnerships[5]. Similar provisions apply in respect of a partnership which is in administration[6].

1 Ie is subject to an administration order pursuant to the Insolvency Act 1986 s 8, Sch B1: see COMPANY AND PARTNERSHIP INSOLVENCY vol 16 (2011) PARA 158 et seq. These provisions also apply to limited liability partnerships: see the Limited Liability Partnerships Regulations 2001, SI 2001/1090, reg 5(1); and PARTNERSHIP vol 79 (2014) PARA 244.
2 See the Insolvency Act 1986 Sch B1 para 43(2) (Sch B1 added by the Enterprise Act 2002 s 248(2)); and COMPANY AND PARTNERSHIP INSOLVENCY vol 16 (2011) PARAS 171, 178, 186. The provisions of the Insolvency Act 1986 Sch B1 apply to any administration commencing after 15 September 2003 apart from an administration operated under a special administration regime: see the Enterprise Act 2002 ss 248, 249; the Enterprise Act 2002 (Commencement No 4 and Transitional Provisions and Savings) Order 2003, SI 2003/2093; and COMPANY AND PARTNERSHIP INSOLVENCY vol 16 (2011) PARA 158. Similar, but not identical, provisions have effect in relation to administrations commencing before 15 September 2003 and administrations

operated under special administration regimes: see the Insolvency Act 1986 s 11(3)(c) (saved for these purposes, and modified in its application to special administration regimes); and COMPANY AND PARTNERSHIP INSOLVENCY vol 16 (2011) PARA 158.

3   See the Insolvency Act 1986 Sch B1 para 70; and COMPANY AND PARTNERSHIP INSOLVENCY vol 16 (2011) PARA 304. For the application of these provisions see note 2. As to the appointment of an administrator by the holder of a floating charge see Sch B1 paras 2(b), 14; and COMPANY AND PARTNERSHIP INSOLVENCY vol 16 (2011) PARAS 175–182. Similar, but not identical, provision has effect in relation to administrations commencing before 15 September 2003 and administrations operated under special administration regimes: see s 15(1), (3), (4); and COMPANY AND PARTNERSHIP INSOLVENCY vol 16 (2011) PARA 158.

4   See the Insolvency Act 1986 Sch B1 para 71; and COMPANY AND PARTNERSHIP INSOLVENCY vol 16 (2011) PARA 305. For the application of these provisions see note 2. For similar provisions in relation to hire-purchase property see Sch B1 para 72; and COMPANY AND PARTNERSHIP INSOLVENCY vol 16 (2011) PARA 306. Similar, but not identical, provision has effect in relation to administrations commencing before 15 September 2003 and administrations operated under special administration regimes: see s 15(2), (5); and COMPANY AND PARTNERSHIP INSOLVENCY vol 16 (2011) PARA 158.

5   See note 1.

6   See the Insolvent Partnerships Order 1994, SI 1994/2421, art 6; and COMPANY AND PARTNERSHIP INSOLVENCY vol 17 (2011) PARA 1235 et seq.

522. Effect of voluntary arrangement. A company[1] may enter a voluntary arrangement with its creditors for a composition in satisfaction of its debts or a scheme of arrangement of its affairs[2]. The proposal must state how it is proposed to deal with creditors who are, or claim to be, secured[3]. The meeting of the company and its creditors summoned to consider the proposal may not approve any proposal or modification which affects the right of a secured creditor to enforce his security, except with his concurrence[4].

The provisions described above also apply to limited liability partnerships[5]. Similar provisions have effect in relation to insolvent partnerships[6].

1   The Insolvency Act 1986 Pt I (ss 1–7B) also applies to limited liability partnerships: see the Limited Liability Partnerships Regulations 2001, SI 2001/1090, reg 5(1); and PARTNERSHIP vol 79 (2014) PARA 244.

2   See the Insolvency Act 1986 Pt I (ss 1–7B); Limited Liability Partnerships Regulations 2001, SI 2001/1090, reg 5(1); and COMPANY AND PARTNERSHIP INSOLVENCY vol 16 (2011) PARA 83 et seq. As to the difference between a composition in satisfaction of debts and a scheme of arrangement see *March Estates plc v Gunmark Ltd* [1996] 2 BCLC 1 at 5, [1996] 2 EGLR 38 at 39 per Lightman J.

3   See the Insolvency Rules 1986, SI 1986/1925, r 1.3(2)(c)(i); and COMPANY AND PARTNERSHIP INSOLVENCY vol 16 (2011) PARA 121. As to the meanings of 'security' and 'secured creditor' for these purposes see the Insolvency Act 1986 s 248; and COMPANY AND PARTNERSHIP INSOLVENCY vol 16 (2011) PARA 121. See also *March Estates plc v Gunmark Ltd* [1996] 2 BCLC 1, [1996] 2 EGLR 38 (right to re-entry and forfeit lease renders the lessor a secured creditor for the purposes of the Insolvency Act 1986 s 4(3)).

4   See the Insolvency Act 1986 s 4(3); and COMPANY AND PARTNERSHIP INSOLVENCY vol 16 (2011) PARA 135.

5   See note 1.

6   See the Insolvent Partnerships Order 1994, SI 1994/2421, art 4; and COMPANY AND PARTNERSHIP INSOLVENCY vol 17 (2011) PARA 1212 et seq.

523. Effect of moratorium. Where company directors intend to make a proposal for a voluntary arrangement[1], they may take steps to obtain a moratorium for the company[2], and during the period for which the moratorium is in force[3] no steps may be taken to enforce any security over company property[4] and no proceedings, execution or other legal process may be commenced or continued against the company or its property except with the leave of the court and subject to such terms as the court may impose[5].

A company in respect of which a moratorium is in force may dispose of property which is subject to a security if either the holder of the security consents or the court gives leave[6]; in relation to a charge other than a floating charge, it is a condition of any such consent or leave that the net proceeds of the disposal and, where those proceeds are less than such amount as may be agreed or determined by the court to represent market value, such sums as may be required to make good any deficiency, be applied towards discharging the sums secured by the security[7].

The provisions described above also apply to moratoriums in force in respect of insolvent limited liability partnerships and partnerships[8].

1   The Insolvency Act 1986 Pt I (1–7B) also applies to limited liability partnerships: see the Limited Liability Partnerships Regulations 2001, SI 2001/1090, reg 5(1); and PARTNERSHIP vol 79 (2014) PARA 244. The Insolvency Act 1986 Pt I (1–7B) is also modified and extended to apply to partnerships too: see the Insolvent Partnerships Order 1994, SI 1994/2421, art 4, Sch 1 Pts I, II; and PARTNERSHIP vol 79 (2014) PARA 98.

2   See the Insolvency Act 1986 s 1A(1); and COMPANY AND PARTNERSHIP INSOLVENCY vol 16 (2011) PARA 85; COMPANY AND PARTNERSHIP INSOLVENCY vol 17 (2011) PARA 1215. Not every type of company, LLP or partnership is eligible for a moratorium: see the Insolvency Act 1986 Sch A1 paras 2–4, 4A–4K, 5; and COMPANY AND PARTNERSHIP INSOLVENCY vol 16 (2011) PARAS 85–86; COMPANY AND PARTNERSHIP INSOLVENCY vol 17 (2011) PARA 1216.

3   A moratorium comes into force when the directors file the required documents with the court: see the Insolvency Act 1986 Sch A1 para 8(1); and COMPANY AND PARTNERSHIP INSOLVENCY vol 16 (2011) PARA 90; COMPANY AND PARTNERSHIP INSOLVENCY vol 17 (2011) PARA 1215. Provision is also made for the duration and extension of moratoriums: see Sch A1 paras 8–11, 32; and COMPANY AND PARTNERSHIP INSOLVENCY vol 16 (2011) PARAS 90–94; COMPANY AND PARTNERSHIP INSOLVENCY vol 17 (2011) PARA 1215.

4   See the Insolvency Act 1986 Sch A1 para 12(1)(g); and COMPANY AND PARTNERSHIP INSOLVENCY vol 16 (2011) PARA 100; COMPANY AND PARTNERSHIP INSOLVENCY vol 17 (2011) PARA 1217.

5   See the Insolvency Act 1986 Sch A1 para 12(1)(h); and COMPANY AND PARTNERSHIP INSOLVENCY vol 16 (2011) PARA 100; COMPANY AND PARTNERSHIP INSOLVENCY vol 17 (2011) PARA 1217.

6   See the Insolvency Act 1986 Sch A1 para 20(1)(a), (2); and COMPANY AND PARTNERSHIP INSOLVENCY vol 16 (2011) PARA 103; COMPANY AND PARTNERSHIP INSOLVENCY vol 17 (2011) PARA 1218.

7   See the Insolvency Act 1986 Sch A1 para 20(6); and COMPANY AND PARTNERSHIP INSOLVENCY vol 16 (2011) PARA 103; COMPANY AND PARTNERSHIP INSOLVENCY vol 17 (2011) PARA 1218. Where such a condition relates to two or more securities, it must require such proceeds and sums to be applied towards discharging the sums secured by those securities in the order of their priorities: see the Insolvency Act 1986 Sch A1 para 20(7); and COMPANY AND PARTNERSHIP INSOLVENCY vol 16 (2011) PARA 103; COMPANY AND PARTNERSHIP INSOLVENCY vol 17 (2011) PARA 1218.

8   See note 1.

524. Effect of mortgagor in liquidation. A mortgagee is entitled to enforce his security notwithstanding the liquidation of the mortgagor[1]. However, on the making of a winding-up order or the appointment of a provisional liquidator, no action or proceeding is to be proceeded with or commenced against a company[2] or its property except by leave of the court and subject to such terms as the court may impose[3]. Leave will normally be granted to a secured creditor seeking to enforce his security[4]. If a claim or proceeding is pending against a company after the presentation of a winding-up petition but before a winding-up order has been made, an application can be made by the company or any creditor or contributory for a stay of the proceedings[5].

If a mortgagee realises his security, he may prove for the balance of his debt, after deducting the amount realised[6]. If he voluntarily surrenders his security for the general benefit of creditors, he may prove for his whole debt, as if it were unsecured[7]. A mortgagee may, with the agreement of the liquidator or the permission of the court, at any time alter the value which he has, in his proof of debt, put upon his security[8]. However, if a secured creditor being the petitioner, has in the petition put a value on his security, or has voted in respect of the unsecured balance of his debt, he may re-value his security only with permission of the court[9].

If a mortgagee omits to disclose his security in his proof of debt, he must surrender his security for the general benefit of creditors, unless the court, on application by him, relieves him on the ground that the omission was inadvertent or the result of honest mistake[10]. If the court grants that relief, it may require or allow the mortgagee's proof of debt to be amended, on such terms as may be just[11].

The provisions described above also apply to limited liability partnerships[12].

1 *Re David Lloyd & Co, Lloyd v David Lloyd & Co* (1877) 6 ChD 339, CA.
2 The Insolvency Act 1986 Pt IV (ss 73–220) also applies to limited liability partnerships: see the Limited Liability Partnerships Regulations 2001, SI 2001/1090, reg 5(1); and PARTNERSHIP vol 79 (2014) PARA 244.
3 See the Insolvency Act 1986 s 130(2); and COMPANY AND PARTNERSHIP INSOLVENCY vol 16 (2011) PARAS 440, 441; COMPANY AND PARTNERSHIP INSOLVENCY vol 17 (2011) PARA 851 et seq. As to applications to the court see COMPANY AND PARTNERSHIP INSOLVENCY vol 16 (2011) PARA 387; COMPANY AND PARTNERSHIP INSOLVENCY vol 17 (2011) PARA 1016 et seq. The position where proceedings are started without leave after a winding-up order has been made was considered in *Re National Employers Mutual General Insurance Association Ltd (in liquidation)* [1995] 1 BCLC 232, [1995] BCC 774, where it was held that retrospective leave could not be granted. This approach was not followed in *Re Saunders (a bankrupt)* [1997] Ch 60, [1997] 3 All ER 992 (a personal insolvency case concerning the application of the Insolvency Act 1986 s 285(3): see PARA 529).
4 *Re Joshua Stubbs Ltd, Barney v Joshua Stubbs Ltd* [1891] 1 Ch 187; *Re David Lloyd & Co, Lloyd v David Lloyd & Co* (1877) 6 ChD 339, CA.
5 See the Insolvency Act 1986 s 126(1); and COMPANY AND PARTNERSHIP INSOLVENCY vol 17 (2011) PARA 845. If the claim or proceeding is pending in the High Court or the Court of Appeal, the application must be made in that court; otherwise the application must be made to the court having jurisdiction to wind up the company: see s 126(1)(a), (b); and COMPANY AND PARTNERSHIP INSOLVENCY vol 17 (2011) PARA 845. See also note 2.
6 See the Insolvency Rules 1986, SI 1986/1925, r 4.88(1); and COMPANY AND PARTNERSHIP INSOLVENCY vol 17 (2011) PARA 752.
7 See the Insolvency Rules 1986, SI 1986/1925, r 4.88(2); and COMPANY AND PARTNERSHIP INSOLVENCY vol 17 (2011) PARA 752. Inadvertent proof for the whole debt is not to be treated as an express surrender: see *C & W Berry Ltd v Armstrong-Moakes* [2007] EWHC 2101 (QB), [2008] 1 P & CR D2, [2007] All ER (D) 82 (Sep).
8 See the Insolvency Rules 1986, SI 1986/1925, r 4.95(1); and COMPANY AND PARTNERSHIP INSOLVENCY vol 17 (2011) PARA 753.
9 See the Insolvency Rules 1986, SI 1986/1925, r 4.95(2); and COMPANY AND PARTNERSHIP INSOLVENCY vol 17 (2011) PARA 753.
10 See the Insolvency Rules 1986, SI 1986/1925, r 4.96(1); and COMPANY AND PARTNERSHIP INSOLVENCY vol 17 (2011) PARA 754.
11 See the Insolvency Rules 1986, SI 1986/1925, r 4.96(2); and COMPANY AND PARTNERSHIP INSOLVENCY vol 17 (2011) PARA 754.
12 See note 2.

525. Disclaimer by a liquidator. Where a company[1] is being wound up, the liquidator may disclaim onerous property[2] by giving notice even if he has taken possession of it, endeavoured to sell it or otherwise exercised rights of ownership in relation to it[3]. Disclaimer determines the rights, interests and liabilities of the company in or in respect of the property disclaimed, as from the date of disclaimer[4]. Except so far as is necessary to release the company from liability, disclaimer does not affect the rights or liabilities of any other person[5]. Accordingly, where the liquidator disclaims a lease, the rights and liabilities of a subtenant or a mortgagee are not affected[6].

The liquidator must send or give a copy of the notice of disclaimer to a mortgagee of the disclaimed property[7]. The disclaimer of any leasehold property does not take effect until such a notice has been served on every person claiming under the company as mortgagee and either no application is made for a vesting order within 14 days or, where such an application has been made, the court directs that the disclaimer is to take effect[8].

On an application by any person who either claims an interest in the disclaimed property or who is under any liability in respect of that property, not being a liability discharged by the disclaimer, the court may make an order on such terms as it thinks fit for the vesting of the disclaimed property in or for its delivery to a person entitled to it, a person subject to such a liability or a trustee for such a person[9]. Accordingly, the landlord of a disclaimed lease which has been mortgaged by the bankrupt can apply for an order vesting the property in the mortgagee[10]. The court may not make an order vesting leasehold property in a mortgagee except on terms making him subject to the same liabilities and obligations as those to which the company was subject under the lease at the commencement of the winding up or, if the court thinks fit, to the same liabilities and obligations as the mortgagee would be subject to if the lease had been assigned to him at that time[11]. The court may attach conditions to an order vesting a lease in a mortgagee to ensure that he only receives what is due under the mortgage and to direct what is to be done with the surplus[12]. If the mortgagee declines to accept the terms of that order, he is excluded from all interest in the property[13].

Any person sustaining loss or damage as a result of a disclaimer may prove for the loss or damage in the winding up as a deemed creditor of the company[14]. In assessing such loss and damage, the effect of a vesting order must be taken into account[15]. An order vesting disclaimed property need not be completed by a conveyance, assignment or transfer[16].

The provisions described above also apply to limited liability partnerships[17].

1 The Insolvency Act 1986 Pt IV (ss 73–220) also applies to limited liability partnerships: see the Limited Liability Partnerships Regulations 2001, SI 2001/1090, reg 5(1); and PARTNERSHIP vol 79 (2014) PARA 244.
2 Onerous property is any unprofitable contract and any other property of the company which is unsaleable or not readily saleable, or is such that it may give rise to a liability to pay money or perform any other onerous act: see the Insolvency Act 1986 s 178(3); and COMPANY AND PARTNERSHIP INSOLVENCY vol 17 (2011) PARA 825.
3 See the Insolvency Act 1986 s 178; and COMPANY AND PARTNERSHIP INSOLVENCY vol 17 (2011) PARA 824 et seq.
4 See the Insolvency Act 1986 s 178(4)(a); and COMPANY AND PARTNERSHIP INSOLVENCY vol 17 (2011) PARA 826.
5 See the Insolvency Act 1986 s 178(4)(b); and COMPANY AND PARTNERSHIP INSOLVENCY vol 17 (2011) PARA 826.
6 *Hindcastle Ltd v Barbara Attenborough Associates Ltd* [1997] AC 70, [1996] 1 All ER 737, HL; *Barclays Bank plc v Prudential Assurance Co Ltd* [1998] 1 EGLR 44, [1998] 10 EG 159.
7 See the Insolvency Rules 1986, SI 1986/1925, r 4.188; and COMPANY AND PARTNERSHIP INSOLVENCY vol 17 (2011) PARA 828.
8 See the Insolvency Act 1986 s 179; and COMPANY AND PARTNERSHIP INSOLVENCY vol 17 (2011) PARA 832.
9 See the Insolvency Act 1986 s 181; and COMPANY AND PARTNERSHIP INSOLVENCY vol 17 (2011) PARA 834. The court will not make such an order unless it appears just to do so for the purpose of compensating that person: see s 181(4); and COMPANY AND PARTNERSHIP INSOLVENCY vol 17 (2011) PARA 834.
10 See *Re Finley, ex p Clothworkers' Co* (1888) 21 QBD 475, CA.
11 See the Insolvency Act 1986 s 182; and COMPANY AND PARTNERSHIP INSOLVENCY vol 17 (2011) PARA 835. The latter course will be adopted provided it does not prejudice the lessor, or give undue advantage to the mortgagee: *Re Carter and Ellis, ex p Savill Bros Ltd* [1905] 1 KB 735, CA; *Re Walker, ex p Mills* (1895) 64 LJQB 783.
12 *Lee v Lee* [1998] 1 FLR 1018, [1998] 2 BCLC 219 (a bankruptcy case).
13 See the Insolvency Act 1986 s 182(4); and COMPANY AND PARTNERSHIP INSOLVENCY vol 17 (2011) PARA 835. See also *Re Finley, ex p Clothworkers' Co* (1888) 21 QBD 475, CA. Where a

mortgagee assigns his interest to a nominee for the purpose of escaping liability under a lease on disclaimer, he remains a person entitled to the property, and must accept the terms of the vesting order or be excluded: *Re Smith, ex p Hepburn* (1890) 25 QBD 536, CA.

14 See the Insolvency Act 1986 s 178(6); and COMPANY AND PARTNERSHIP INSOLVENCY vol 17 (2011) PARA 837.

15 See the Insolvency Act 1986 s 181(5); and COMPANY AND PARTNERSHIP INSOLVENCY vol 17 (2011) PARA 834.

16 See the Insolvency Act 1986 s 181(6); and COMPANY AND PARTNERSHIP INSOLVENCY vol 17 (2011) PARA 834.

17 See note 1.

526. Preferences and transactions at an undervalue. Where a company[1] enters administration[2] or goes into liquidation[3], and that company has entered into a transaction at an undervalue[4] or has given a preference[5] at a relevant time[6], the administrator or liquidator may apply to the court for such order as it thinks fit[7] for restoring the position to what it would have been if the transaction had not been entered into or the preference had not been given[8]. However, in the case of a transaction at an undervalue, such an order may not be made if the company entered into the transaction in good faith and for the purpose of carrying out its business and there were reasonable grounds for believing that it would benefit the company[9]. Similarly, in the case of a preference, an order may not be made unless, in giving the preference, the company was influenced by a desire to place the recipient in a better position in the event of it going into insolvent liquidation than he would have been otherwise[10].

The provisions described above also apply to limited liability partnerships[11].

There are provisions similar to those governing corporate insolvency which govern the treatment of preferences and transactions in the case of personal insolvency[12].

1 The Insolvency Act 1986 Pt VI (ss 230–246C) also applies to limited liability partnerships: see the Limited Liability Partnerships Regulations 2001, SI 2001/1090, reg 5(1); and PARTNERSHIP vol 79 (2014) PARA 244.

2 Ie becomes subject to an administration order pursuant to the Insolvency Act 1986 s 8, Sch B1: see COMPANY AND PARTNERSHIP INSOLVENCY vol 16 (2011) PARA 158 et seq.

3 Ie pursuant to the Insolvency Act 1986 Pt IV (ss 73–219): see COMPANY AND PARTNERSHIP INSOLVENCY vol 16 (2011) PARA 381 et seq.

4 As to the meaning of 'transaction at an undervalue' see the Insolvency Act 1986 s 238(4); and COMPANY AND PARTNERSHIP INSOLVENCY vol 17 (2011) PARA 802. In *Re MC Bacon Ltd* [1990] BCLC 324 at 340, [1990] BCC 78 at 92, Millett J held that the creation of a security (a debenture) over a company's assets in favour of an existing creditor was not a transaction at an undervalue.

5 As to the meaning of 'preference' see the Insolvency Act 1986 s 239(4); and COMPANY AND PARTNERSHIP INSOLVENCY vol 17 (2011) PARA 804.

6 As to the relevant time for these purposes see the Insolvency Act 1986 s 240; and COMPANY AND PARTNERSHIP INSOLVENCY vol 17 (2011) PARA 808.

7 For a non-exhaustive list of the type of orders the court may make see the Insolvency Act 1986 s 241(1); and COMPANY AND PARTNERSHIP INSOLVENCY vol 17 (2011) PARA 809. The power to order the release or discharge (in whole or in part) of any security given by the company is specifically included: see s 241(1)(c).

8 See the Insolvency Act 1986 ss 238(3), 239(3); and COMPANY AND PARTNERSHIP INSOLVENCY vol 17 (2011) PARAS 803, 805.

9 See the Insolvency Act 1986 s 238(5); and COMPANY AND PARTNERSHIP INSOLVENCY vol 17 (2011) PARA 803.

10 See the Insolvency Act 1986 s 239(5); and COMPANY AND PARTNERSHIP INSOLVENCY vol 17 (2011) PARA 805. See also *Re MC Bacon Ltd* [1990] BCLC 324, [1990] BCC 78; *Re Fairway Magazines Ltd, Fairbairn v Hartigan* [1993] BCLC 643, [1992] BCC 924; *Re Agriplant Services Ltd (in liquidation)* [1997] 2 BCLC 598, [1997] BCC 842. Therefore, where a debenture is granted by a company within the relevant time which has the effect of giving a creditor security and preference over other creditors, it can be the subject of a court order only if the company was actually influenced by a desire that the creditor be so benefitted: see *Re MC Bacon Ltd* above (grant of debenture to bank was actuated by proper commercial considerations and was not a preference). See also *Re Mistral Finance Ltd (in liquidation)* [2001] BCC 27. However, where the

company gives a preference to a person connected to the company (other than by reason only of being its employee) at the time of the preference, it is presumed, unless the contrary is shown, to have been influenced by such a desire: see the Insolvency Act 1986 s 239(6); and COMPANY AND PARTNERSHIP INSOLVENCY vol 17 (2011) PARA 806. See also eg *Wills v Corfe Joinery Ltd (in liquidation)* [1998] 2 BCLC 75, [1997] BCC 511. As to the objective test under previous legislation see COMPANY AND PARTNERSHIP INSOLVENCY vol 17 (2011) PARA 805.
11 See note 1.
12 See the Insolvency Act 1986 ss 339–342; and BANKRUPTCY AND INDIVIDUAL INSOLVENCY vol 5 (2013) PARAS 678–687.

(iv) Effect of Insolvency of Individual Mortgagors

527. Effect of mortgagor's individual voluntary arrangement. A debtor who wishes to make a proposal for a voluntary arrangement may apply for an interim order[1] to enable him to put a scheme of arrangement to his creditors[2]. While an interim order is in force no proceedings and no execution or other legal process may be commenced or continued, and no distress may be levied, against the debtor or his property except with the leave of the court[3]. A mortgagee therefore needs leave to bring proceedings for possession, but does not appear to need leave to exercise the power of sale without the assistance of the court[4]. The proposed voluntary arrangement is considered at a creditors meeting, but the meeting cannot approve a proposal which affects the right of a secured creditor of the debtor to enforce his security, except with the concurrence of the creditor concerned[5]. Any interim order in force ceases to have effect 28 days after a report of a meeting approving the proposed voluntary arrangement is filed at court[6].

In the absence of an express term or necessary inference[7] in the voluntary arrangement, the court will be slow to imply a term that by participating in and accepting payment of a dividend under the arrangement a secured creditor has agreed to treat that part of his debt as unsecured[8].

1 Ie an order under the Insolvency Act 1986 s 252: see BANKRUPTCY AND INDIVIDUAL INSOLVENCY vol 5 (2013) PARA 45 et seq.
2 See the Insolvency Act 1986 s 253; and BANKRUPTCY AND INDIVIDUAL INSOLVENCY vol 5 (2013) PARA 46.
3 See the Insolvency Act 1986 s 252(2)(b); and BANKRUPTCY AND INDIVIDUAL INSOLVENCY vol 5 (2013) PARA 45.
4 Cf the Insolvency Act 1986 Sch B1 para 43(2) (which specifically refers to the enforcement of security); and PARA 521. As to the mortgagee's power of sale see PARA 443 et seq.
5 See the Insolvency Act 1986 s 258(4); and BANKRUPTCY AND INDIVIDUAL INSOLVENCY vol 5 (2013) PARA 62. As to the meaning of 'secured creditor' for these purposes see s 383; and BANKRUPTCY AND INDIVIDUAL INSOLVENCY vol 5 (2013) PARA 574.
6 See the Insolvency Act 1986 s 260(4); and BANKRUPTCY AND INDIVIDUAL INSOLVENCY vol 5 (2013) PARA 69.
7 See eg *Khan v Permayer* [2001] BPIR 95.
8 *Whitehead v Household Mortgage Corpn plc* [2002] EWCA Civ 1657, [2003] 1 All ER 319, [2003] 1 WLR 1173.

528. Rights in mortgagor's bankruptcy. In the case of the goods of an undischarged bankrupt which are held by any person by way of pledge, pawn or other security, the official receiver may give notice that he intends to inspect the goods[1]. If the official receiver has served no such notice, the trustee in bankruptcy may do so[2]. The effect of service of such a notice is that the secured creditor may not realise his security without the leave of the court unless he has given the trustee of the bankrupt's estate a reasonable opportunity to inspect the goods and to exercise the bankrupt's right of redemption[3]. Subject to that, the bankruptcy of the debtor does not affect the right of a secured creditor to enforce his security[4]; and for this purpose a person to whom a debt is owed who holds any security for the debt, whether a mortgage, charge, lien or other security over any property of the person by whom the debt is owed, is a secured creditor[5]. Where, however, the statutory or express power for a mortgagee either to sell[6] or to appoint a receiver[7] is made exercisable by reason of the mortgagor being adjudicated a bankrupt, the power is not to be exercised only on account of the adjudication, without the leave of the court[8].

If a mortgagee realises his security, he may prove for the balance of his debt, after deducting the amount realised[9]. If a mortgagee voluntarily surrenders his security for the general benefit of creditors, he may prove for his whole debt, as if it were unsecured[10]. A mortgagee may, with the agreement of the trustee or the leave of the court, at any time alter the value which he has, in his proof of debt, put upon his security[11]. However, if a mortgagee:

(1)   being the petitioner, has in the petition put a value on his security; or

(2)   has voted in respect of the unsecured balance of his debt,

he may re-value his security only with leave of the court[12].

If a mortgagee omits to disclose his security in his proof of debt, he must surrender his security for the general benefit of creditors, unless the court, on application by him, relieves him on the ground that the omission was inadvertent or the result of honest mistake[13]. If the court grants that relief, it may require or allow the mortgagee's proof of debt to be amended, on such terms as may be just[14].

The mortgagee may allocate his security to that part of his debt in respect of which he has no right of proof[15]; but, as against the trustee in bankruptcy, he may not apply any part of the proceeds of sale to interest accruing due[16] after the date of the bankruptcy order, although he may so apply subsequent income[17].

If a mortgagee applies to the court for an order that the land belonging to the bankrupt be sold[18], the proceeds of sale go first to pay the costs and expenses of the trustee, of and occasioned by the application to the court, and then in payment of the principal, interest and costs of the mortgagee, and any balance is retained by or paid to the trustee[19]. If the proceeds are insufficient to pay the amount due to the mortgagee, he is entitled to prove for the deficiency as a creditor[20].

1   See the Insolvency Act 1986 s 285(5); and BANKRUPTCY AND INDIVIDUAL INSOLVENCY vol 5 (2013) PARA 214.

2   See the Insolvency Act 1986 s 311(5); and BANKRUPTCY AND INDIVIDUAL INSOLVENCY vol 5 (2013) PARA 411.

3   See the Insolvency Act 1986 ss 285(5), 311(6); and BANKRUPTCY AND INDIVIDUAL INSOLVENCY vol 5 (2013) PARAS 214, 411. As to the equity of redemption see PARAS 107, 304 et seq.

4   See the Insolvency Act 1986 s 285(3), (4); and BANKRUPTCY AND INDIVIDUAL INSOLVENCY vol 5 (2013) PARAS 214, 507. Cf the position of an unsecured creditor under s 285(3): see BANKRUPTCY AND INDIVIDUAL INSOLVENCY vol 5 (2013) PARA 214. As to the rights of a secured creditor on the bankruptcy of the debtor see BANKRUPTCY AND INDIVIDUAL INSOLVENCY vol 5 (2013) PARA 574 et seq.

5   See the Insolvency Act 1986 s 383(1), (2); and BANKRUPTCY AND INDIVIDUAL INSOLVENCY vol 5 (2013) PARA 574. Such a security does not include a lien on books, papers or other records, except to the extent that they consist of documents which give a title to property and are held as such: see s 383(4); and BANKRUPTCY AND INDIVIDUAL INSOLVENCY vol 5 (2013) PARA 574. As to liens on books see also s 349; and BANKRUPTCY AND INDIVIDUAL INSOLVENCY vol 5 (2013) PARA 721. See further *Re William Hall (Contractors) Ltd* [1967] 2 All ER 1150, [1967] 1 WLR 948; *Re Rushton (a bankrupt), ex p National Westminster Bank Ltd v Official Receiver* [1972] Ch 197, [1971] 2 All ER 937, DC.

6   As to powers of sale see PARA 443 et seq.

7   See PARA 478.

8   Law of Property Act 1925 s 110(1) (amended by the Insolvency Act 1985 s 235(3), Sch 10 Pt III). This provision applies only where the mortgage deed is executed after 31 December 1925: Law of Property Act 1925 s 110(2).

9 See the Insolvency Rules 1986, SI 1986/1925, r 6.109(1); and BANKRUPTCY AND INDIVIDUAL INSOLVENCY vol 5 (2013) PARA 575.
10 See the Insolvency Rules 1986, SI 1986/1925, r 6.109(2); and BANKRUPTCY AND INDIVIDUAL INSOLVENCY vol 5 (2013) PARA 575. Inadvertent proof for the whole debt is not to be treated as an express surrender: see *C & W Berry Ltd v Armstrong-Moakes* [2007] EWHC 2101 (QB), [2008] 1 P & CR D2, [2007] All ER (D) 82 (Sep).
11 See the Insolvency Rules 1986, SI 1986/1925, r 6.115(1); and BANKRUPTCY AND INDIVIDUAL INSOLVENCY vol 5 (2013) PARA 576.
12 See the Insolvency Rules 1986, SI 1986/1925, r 6.115(2); and BANKRUPTCY AND INDIVIDUAL INSOLVENCY vol 5 (2013) PARA 576.
13 See the Insolvency Rules 1986, SI 1986/1925, r 6.116(1); and BANKRUPTCY AND INDIVIDUAL INSOLVENCY vol 5 (2013) PARA 577.
14 See the Insolvency Rules 1986, SI 1986/1925, r 6.116(2); and BANKRUPTCY AND INDIVIDUAL INSOLVENCY vol 5 (2013) PARA 577.
15 *Ex p Hunter* (1801) 6 Ves 94; *Re Medley, ex p Glyn* (1840) 1 Mont D & De G 25; *Re Bulmer, ex p Johnson* (1853) 3 De GM & G 218 at 235; *Re Fox and Jacobs, ex p Discount Banking Co of England and Wales* [1894] 1 QB 438.
16 *Re London, Windsor and Greenwich Hotels Co, Quartermaine's Case* [1892] 1 Ch 639 (where the earlier cases were discussed, and *Re Talbott, King v Chick* (1888) 39 ChD 567 was not followed). As to administration see *Ross v Ross* (1890) 25 LR Ir 362.
17 *Re London, Windsor and Greenwich Hotels Co, Quartermaine's Case* [1892] 1 Ch 639. See also *Re Barker, ex p Penfold* (1851) 4 De G & Sm 282.
18 See the Insolvency Rules 1986, SI 1986/1925, r 6.197; and BANKRUPTCY AND INDIVIDUAL INSOLVENCY vol 5 (2013) PARA 428. Any person claiming to be the legal or equitable mortgagee of land belonging to the bankrupt may apply: see r 6.197. An application will be necessary only if the mortgagee is seeking to enforce an equitable charge or mortgage.
19 See the Insolvency Rules 1986, SI 1986/1925, r 6.199(1); and BANKRUPTCY AND INDIVIDUAL INSOLVENCY vol 5 (2013) PARA 428.
20 See the Insolvency Rules 1986, SI 1986/1925, r 6.199(2); and BANKRUPTCY AND INDIVIDUAL INSOLVENCY vol 5 (2013) PARA 428.

529. Proceedings against a bankrupt mortgagor. At any time when proceedings on a bankruptcy petition are pending or an individual mortgagor has been adjudged bankrupt, the court may stay any action, execution or legal process against the property or person of the debtor or, as the case may be, of the bankrupt[1]. Any court in which proceedings are pending against any individual may, on proof that a bankruptcy petition has been presented in respect of that individual or that he is an undischarged bankrupt, either stay the proceedings or allow them to continue on such terms as it thinks fit[2]. Although these provisions in theory apply to proceedings which concern non-provable debts, the court is unlikely to prevent a secured creditor from pursuing a remedy which would in any event survive the discharge of the bankrupt[3].

After the making of a bankruptcy order, no person who is a creditor of the bankrupt in respect of a debt provable in the bankruptcy has any remedy against the property or person of the bankrupt in respect of the debt, and no proceedings may be commenced by him against the bankrupt without the leave of the court[4]. It has been held that if proceedings are commenced without leave after the making of the bankruptcy order, leave to commence can, on a later application, be granted with retrospective effect[5].

1 See the Insolvency Act 1986 s 285(1); and BANKRUPTCY AND INDIVIDUAL INSOLVENCY vol 5 (2013) PARA 214. Note that as from a day to be appointed, s 285 is amended by the Enterprise and Regulatory Reform Act 2013 s 71(3), Sch 19, paras 1, 16 so that, inter alia, references to being 'adjudged bankrupt' are replaced by the words 'made bankrupt'. At the date at which this volume states the law no such day had been appointed.
2 See the Insolvency Act 1986 s 285(2); and BANKRUPTCY AND INDIVIDUAL INSOLVENCY vol 5 (2013) PARA 214.
3 *Re Blake* (1875) 10 Ch App 652; *Re Hutton (a bankrupt), Mediterranean Machine Operations Ltd v Haigh* [1969] 2 Ch 201. Cf *Cobham v Dalton* (1875) 10 Ch App 655.
4 See the Insolvency Act 1986 s 285(3); and BANKRUPTCY AND INDIVIDUAL INSOLVENCY vol 5 (2013) PARA 214. Subject to s 285(5) (inspection of goods by official receiver: see PARA 528), this

does not affect the right of a secured creditor to enforce his security: see s 285(4); and BANKRUPTCY AND INDIVIDUAL INSOLVENCY vol 5 (2013) PARA 214.

5 *Re Saunders (a bankrupt)* [1997] Ch 60, [1997] 3 All ER 992; *Re Linkrealm Ltd* [1998] BCC 478. Since the Insolvency Act 1986 s 285(3) refers only to the commencement of proceedings, it is not possible to treat a later application as an application to continue earlier proceedings. In *Re Saunders* above the plaintiffs would have met with limitation problems had they been forced to start afresh: see PARA 519.

530. Disclaimer by a trustee in bankruptcy. Where a mortgagor is declared insolvent, the trustee in bankruptcy may disclaim onerous property in the same way as a liquidator of a company[1], subject to the proviso that:

(1)   a notice of disclaimer may not be given without leave of the court in respect of property claimed for the estate in the form of after-acquired property, personal property of the bankrupt exceeding reasonable replacement value or certain tenancies protected by statute[2]; and

(2)   where the trustee seeks to disclaim any property in a dwelling house, every person in occupation of or claiming a right to occupy the dwelling house must be served with a copy of the notice of disclaimer and is entitled to apply for a vesting order[3].

1 See PARA 525. As to what constitutes onerous property see the Insolvency Act 1986 s 315(2); and BANKRUPTCY AND INDIVIDUAL INSOLVENCY vol 5 (2013) PARA 491.

2 See the Insolvency Act 1986 s 315(4); and BANKRUPTCY AND INDIVIDUAL INSOLVENCY vol 5 (2013) PARAS 491, 496.

3 See the Insolvency Act 1986 ss 318, 320; and BANKRUPTCY AND INDIVIDUAL INSOLVENCY vol 5 (2013) PARAS 500, 503.

531. Rights against insolvent estate of deceased mortgagor. The administration of the insolvent estate of a deceased mortgagor must be carried out under the general insolvency legislation, subject to certain modifications[1]. For these purposes, an estate of a deceased person is insolvent if, when realised, it will be insufficient to meet in full all the debts and other liabilities to which it is subject[2]. Whether an estate is insolvent must be decided on the facts, and if there is any uncertainty, administration should proceed on the basis that it is insolvent until debts and liabilities are discharged[3]. The provisions currently in force cover the administration of estates both in and out of bankruptcy[4]. In either case the same rules apply as to the respective rights of secured and unsecured creditors, and as to debts and liabilities provable, as are in force for the time being in regard to bankrupts' estates[5].

1 See the Administration of Insolvent Estates of Deceased Persons Order 1986, SI 1986/1999; and BANKRUPTCY AND INDIVIDUAL INSOLVENCY vol 5 (2013) PARA 830 et seq. As to the administration of insolvent estates generally see WILLS AND INTESTACY vol 103 (2010) PARA 980 et seq.

2 See the Insolvency Act 1986 s 421(4); and BANKRUPTCY AND INDIVIDUAL INSOLVENCY vol 5 (2013) PARA 831. Funeral, testamentary and administration expenses are included as liabilities of the estate: see the Administration of Insolvent Estates of Deceased Persons Order 1986, SI 1986/1999, art 4(2); and BANKRUPTCY AND INDIVIDUAL INSOLVENCY vol 5 (2013) PARA 838; WILLS AND INTESTACY vol 103 (2010) PARA 980.

3 *Re Pink, Elvin v Nightingale* [1927] 1 Ch 237 at 241 per Clauson J. See also *Re Hopkins, Williams v Hopkins* (1881) 18 ChD 370 at 377, CA, per Jessel MR.

4 See the Administration of Insolvent Estates of Deceased Persons Order 1986, SI 1986/1999, arts 3, 4; and BANKRUPTCY AND INDIVIDUAL INSOLVENCY vol 5 (2013) PARAS 831, 838.

5 See BANKRUPTCY AND INDIVIDUAL INSOLVENCY vol 5 (2013) PARA 838. As to the time when the security must be valued see *Cooper v Teahan* (1889) 23 LR Ir 203. As to the procedure where a mortgagor has made a composition to which the mortgagees were not parties and then died insolvent see *Re Hardy, Hardy v Farmer* [1896] 1 Ch 904.

(2) REGULATED MORTGAGES

532. Regulation of certain mortgages by the Rent Act 1977. A mortgage is a regulated mortgage for the purposes of the Rent Act 1977[1] if it is a legal mortgage[2] of land consisting of or including a dwelling house which is let on or subject to a regulated tenancy[3], and the regulated tenancy is binding on the mortgagee[4]. However, a mortgage is not a regulated mortgage for these purposes if either the rateable value of the dwelling house[5] is less than 10 per cent of the rateable value of the whole of the land comprised in the mortgage[6], or the mortgagor is in breach of covenant[7].

1 The provisions of the Rent Act 1977 which regulate mortgages (ie Pt X (ss 129–136)) apply to all regulated mortgages created before the relevant date: Rent Act 1977 s 129(1)(a). For these purposes, 'relevant date':
  (1) in a case where, on 28 November 1967, land consisting of or including a dwelling house was subject to a long tenancy which became a regulated tenancy on that date by virtue of the Leasehold Reform Act 1967 s 39 (see LANDLORD AND TENANT vol 63 (2012) PARA 1227 et seq), means, in relation to that land, 28 November 1967 (Rent Act 1977 s 129(2)(a));
  (2) in a case where, on 22 March 1973, land consisting of or including a dwelling house was subject to a tenancy which became a regulated tenancy by virtue of the Counter-Inflation Act 1973 s 14 (repealed) (see LANDLORD AND TENANT vol 63 (2012) PARA 964), means, in relation to that land, 22 March 1973 (Rent Act 1977 s 129(2)(b));
  (3) in the case of land consisting of or including a dwelling house subject to a regulated furnished tenancy, means, in relation to that land, 14 August 1974 (s 129(2)(c)); and
  (4) in any other case, means 8 December 1965 (s 129(2)(d)).
  As to the meaning of 'regulated furnished tenancy' see s 152(1); and LANDLORD AND TENANT vol 63 (2012) PARA 961.
2 For the purposes of the Rent Act 1977 Pt X, except where the context otherwise requires, 'legal mortgage', in relation to regulated mortgages, includes any registered charge within the meaning of the Land Registration Act 2002 (see PARA 142 note 7) (Rent Act 1977 s 136(b) (amended by the Housing Act 1980 Sch 25 para 50; and the Land Registration Act 2002 s 133, Sch 11 para 14)); and, for the purposes of the Rent Act 1977 s 131, includes a charge by way of legal mortgage (s 131(4)). As to the meaning of 'legal mortgage' generally see PARA 104 note 1.
3 Rent Act 1977 ss 129(1)(b) (substituted by the Housing Act 1980 s 152, Sch 25 para 48); Rent Act 1977 s 131(1)(a) (amended by the Housing Act 1980 s 152, Sch 26). As to the meaning of 'regulated tenancy' see LANDLORD AND TENANT vol 63 (2012) PARA 963.
4 Rent Act 1977 s 131(1)(b). 'Mortgagee' and 'mortgagor' include any person from time to time deriving title under the original mortgagee or mortgagor: s 136(a). As to the meanings of 'mortgagee' and 'mortgagor' generally see PARA 104 note 1.
5 Or, if there is more than one such dwelling house comprised in the mortgage, the aggregate of the rateable values of those dwelling houses: Rent Act 1977 s 131(2)(a). As to the meaning of 'rateable value' for these purposes see s 25; and LANDLORD AND TENANT vol 63 (2012) PARA 964.
6 Rent Act 1977 s 131(2)(a). The rateable value for these purposes is assessed on the appropriate day. As to the appropriate day see s 25; and LANDLORD AND TENANT vol 63 (2012) PARA 964. Section 131(2)(a) has effect, in the case of land consisting of or including a dwelling house which on 22 March 1973 was subject to a tenancy which became a regulated tenancy by virtue of the Counter-Inflation Act 1973 s 14 (repealed), as if for reference to the appropriate day there were substituted a reference to 7 March 1973: Rent Act 1977 s 131(3).
7 Rent Act 1977 s 131(2)(b). For this purpose, a breach of the covenant for the repayment of the principal money otherwise than by instalments is disregarded: s 131(2)(b).

533. Mitigation of hardship under regulated mortgages. The power of the court[1] to mitigate hardship under regulated mortgages[2] becomes exercisable only on an application made by the mortgagor[3] within 21 days, or such longer time as the court may allow, after the rate of interest payable in respect of the mortgage being increased[4], a rent for a dwelling house comprised in the mortgage being registered[5] (provided such registered rent is lower than the rent payable immediately before the registration)[6], or the mortgagee demanding payment of the principal money secured by the mortgage or taking any steps for exercising any right of foreclosure or sale or otherwise enforcing his security[7].

If the court is satisfied on any such application that, by reason of the event in question and of the operation of the Rent Act 1977, the mortgagor would suffer severe financial hardship unless relief were given, the court may by order[8] make such provision as it thinks appropriate, limiting the rate of interest[9], extending the time for repayment of the principal money[10], or otherwise varying the terms of the mortgage or imposing any limitation or condition on the exercise of any right or remedy in respect of it[11]. Where the court makes such an order in relation to a mortgage which comprises other land as well as a dwelling house or dwelling houses subject to a regulated tenancy[12], then, if the mortgagee so requests, the order may make provision for apportioning the money secured by the mortgage between that other land and the dwelling house or dwelling houses[13]. Where such an apportionment is made, the other provisions of the order do not apply in relation to the other land, and the mortgage has effect for all purposes as two separate mortgages of the apportioned parts[14].

1 For the purposes of the Rent Act 1977 s 132, the court is the County Court, except that where an application is made in pursuance of any step taken by the mortgagee in the High Court, it is the High Court: s 132(6) (amended by the Crime and Courts Act 2013 s 17(5), Sch 9 Pt 3 para 52(1)(b), (2)). As to the meaning of 'mortgagee' for these purposes see PARA 532 note 4.
2 As to the meaning of 'regulated mortgage' see PARA 532.
3 As to the meaning of 'mortgagor' for these purposes see PARA 532 note 4.
4 Rent Act 1977 s 132(1)(a) (s 132(1) amended by the Housing Act 1980 s 152, Sch 25 para 49).
5 Ie registered under the Rent Act 1977 Pt IV (ss 62–75): see LANDLORD AND TENANT vol 63 (2012) PARA 1009 et seq.
6 Rent Act 1977 s 132(1)(b). Section 132(1)(b) does not apply to a case falling within s 129(2)(b) (see PARA 532 note 1): s 132(1).
7 Rent Act 1977 s 132(1)(c). The mortgagee must not be a mortgagee who was in possession on the relevant date: s 132(1)(c). As to the relevant date see PARA 532 note 1.
8 Where the court has made an order under the Rent Act 1977 s 132 it may vary or revoke it by a subsequent order: s 132(5).
9 Rent Act 1977 s 132(2)(a).
10 Rent Act 1977 s 132(2)(b).
11 Rent Act 1977 s 132(2)(c).
12 As to the meaning of 'regulated tenancy' see LANDLORD AND TENANT vol 63 (2012) PARA 963.
13 Rent Act 1977 s 132(3).
14 Rent Act 1977 s 132(4).

(3) LEGAL PROCEEDINGS IN GENERAL

(i) Jurisdiction of the Courts in relation to Mortgage Proceedings

534. Jurisdiction of High Court and County Court. In general, the High Court has jurisdiction to determine any proceedings by a mortgagor or mortgagee to enforce the terms of a mortgage, although in practice most mortgage claims are brought in the County Court[1]. The High Court does not have jurisdiction to hear and determine proceedings in which a mortgagee claims possession and the mortgaged property consists of or includes a dwelling house[2], as those proceedings must, except where any part of the land is situated in Greater London[3], be brought in the County Court[4]. The County Court also has exclusive jurisdiction to hear and determine any action by the creditor to enforce any security relating to an agreement regulated under the Consumer Credit Act 1974[5]. By virtue of its general jurisdiction in contract, the County Court has unlimited jurisdiction to hear and determine a claim by a mortgagee for payment of principal and interest[6].

The County Court has all the jurisdiction of the High Court to hear and determine proceedings for foreclosure or redemption of any mortgage, or for enforcing any charge or lien, where the amount owing in respect of the mortgage, charge or lien does not exceed the county court limit[7]. Where the original loan exceeds that limit but has been reduced below that amount by payment or otherwise, the County Court has jurisdiction[8]. The County Court also has all the jurisdiction of the High Court to hear and determine proceedings for relief against fraud or mistake, where the damage sustained or the estate or fund in respect of which relief is sought does not exceed in amount or value the county court limit[9]. The jurisdiction may be extended beyond the financial limits by agreement[10]. Even where the loan or the amount of the loan outstanding exceeds the county court limit, the County Court has unlimited jurisdiction to hear and determine any claim for possession by a mortgagee, as it is a claim for the recovery of land[11].

Under the statutory provisions which relate to the power of the court to except the leasehold reversion from the conveyance on the realisation of a leasehold mortgage[12], the realisation of equitable charges by the court[13], the sale of mortgaged property in claims for redemption or foreclosure[14], and the power of the court to authorise land and minerals to be dealt with separately[15], the County Court has jurisdiction where the amount owing in respect of the mortgage or charge at the date of the commencement of the proceedings does not exceed a specified sum[16].

The County Court also has unlimited jurisdiction to make an order on the application of a person who has an interest in a property subject to a trust of land[17], such as a chargee of an equitable interest seeking an order for sale[18].

1   As to allocation of proceedings between the High Court and the County Court see PARA 535.
2   'Dwelling house' includes any building or part of a building which is used as a dwelling (County Courts Act 1984 s 21(7)); and the fact that part of the premises comprised in a dwelling house is used as a shop or office or for business, trade or professional purposes does not prevent the dwelling house from being a dwelling house (s 21(8)).
3   As to the area comprising Greater London see LONDON GOVERNMENT vol 71 (2013) PARA 14.
4   County Courts Act 1984 s 21(3) (amended by the Crime and Courts Act 2013 s 17(5), Sch 9 Pt 1 paras 1, 10); and see COURTS AND TRIBUNALS vol 24 (2010) PARA 772. For the procedure relating to possession claims see PARA 549 et seq. This exclusive jurisdiction of the County Court does not apply, however, to proceedings for foreclosure or sale in which a claim for possession of the mortgaged property is also made: see s 21(4); and COURTS AND TRIBUNALS vol 24 (2010) PARA 772. The claim for foreclosure or sale must be a genuine one for that relief and not merely added as a colourable device to take the proceedings outside the County Court's exclusive jurisdiction: see *Trustees of Manchester Unity Life Insurance Collecting Society v Sadler* [1974] 2 All ER 410, [1974] 1 WLR 770; *Lord Marples of Wallasey v Holmes* (1975) 31 P & CR 94; *PB Frost Ltd v Green* [1978] 2 All ER 206, [1978] 1 WLR 949. It is commonplace to claim payment, possession, foreclosure or sale and other relief in the same proceedings, but the mere claim for foreclosure or sale does not make the action one for foreclosure or sale; the test is what is the claimant genuinely seeking: see *Trustees of Manchester Unity Life Insurance Collecting Society v Sadler* above. If a claimant abandons his claim for possession, leaving a claim for payment outstanding, the High Court has jurisdiction: see *National Westminster Bank Ltd v Oceancrest Ltd* (1985) Times, 24 April, CA. A claim for money in which the County Court has jurisdiction may be commenced in the High Court only if the financial value of the claim exceeds £100,000: see the High Court and County Courts Jurisdiction Order 1991, SI 1991/724, art 4A (added by SI 1999/1014; substituted by SI 2009/577; and amended by SI 2014/821); and COURTS AND TRIBUNALS vol 24 (2010) PARA 863; CIVIL PROCEDURE vol 11 (2015) PARA 135. Whether the matter is heard in the County Court or the High Court, the court has the powers of adjournment given by the Administration of Justice Act 1970: see PARA 557 et seq.
5   See the Consumer Credit Act 1974 s 141; and CONSUMER CREDIT vol 21 (2011) PARA 307.
6   County Courts Act 1984 s 15(1) (amended by SI 1991/724; and by the Crime and Courts Act 2013 Sch 9 Pt 1 paras 1, 10); and see COURTS AND TRIBUNALS vol 24 (2010) PARA 769.
7   County Courts Act 1984 s 23(c) (s 23 amended by the Crime and Courts Act 2013 Sch 9 Pt 1 paras 1, 10); and see COURTS AND TRIBUNALS vol 24 (2010) PARA 776. As to the county court

limit see COURTS AND TRIBUNALS vol 24 (2010) PARA 767. As to the transfer of proceedings from the High Court to the County Court see s 40; and CIVIL PROCEDURE vol 11 (2015) PARA 108.

8   *Shields, Whitley and District Amalgamated Model Building Society v Richards* (1901) 84 LT 587.

9   See the County Courts Act 1984 s 23(g); and COURTS AND TRIBUNALS vol 24 (2010) PARA 776.

10   See the County Courts Act 1984 s 24(1), (2)(g); and COURTS AND TRIBUNALS vol 24 (2010) PARA 776.

11   See the County Courts Act 1984 s 21(1); and COURTS AND TRIBUNALS vol 24 (2010) PARA 772. A claim for possession is a claim for the recovery of land: *R v Judge Dutton Briant, ex p Abbey National Building Society* [1957] 2 QB 497, [1957] 2 All ER 625; *West Penwith RDC v Gunnell* [1968] 2 All ER 1005, [1968] 1 WLR 1153, CA; *Esso Petroleum Co Ltd v Alstonbridge Properties Ltd* [1975] 3 All ER 358 at 365, [1975] 1 WLR 1474 at 1481 per Walton J; cf *Redditch Benefit Building Society v Roberts* [1940] Ch 415 at 420, [1940] 1 All ER 342 at 345, CA, per Clayson LJ.

12   See PARA 449.

13   See PARA 575.

14   See PARAS 575–577, 671.

15   See PARA 467.

16   See the High Court and County Courts Jurisdiction Order 1991, SI 1991/724, art 2(4) (amended by SI 2014/821). The sum specified is £30,000: High Court and County Courts Jurisdiction Order 1991, SI 1991/724, art 2(4). The sum specified for the equity jurisdiction under the County Courts Act 1984 s 23 is £350,000: County Court Jurisdiction Order 2014, SI 2014/503, art 3.

17   Ie under the Trusts of Land and Appointment of Trustees Act 1996 s 14: see TRUSTS AND POWERS vol 98 (2013) PARA 479.

18   See the High Court and County Courts Jurisdiction Order 1991, SI 1991/724, art 2(1)(p); and CIVIL PROCEDURE vol 11 (2015) PARA 48. As to orders for sale see PARA 621 et seq.

535. Allocation between High Court and County Court. Generally, proceedings in which both the County Court and the High Court have jurisdiction may be commenced in either court[1], and may be tried in the High Court or in the County Court[2].

Where the claim includes a possession claim[3] brought by a mortgagee[4] the claimant may make the claim at any County Court hearing centre, unless:

(1)   the claim is started in the High Court and the claimant files with his claim form a certificate stating the reasons for bringing the claim in that court verified by a statement of truth; or

(2)   an enactment provides otherwise[5].

In the County Court the claim will be issued by the hearing centre where the claim is made[6]. If the claim is not made at the County Court hearing centre which serves the address where the land is situated, the claim will be sent to the hearing centre serving that address when it is issued[7].

Only exceptional circumstances justify starting such a claim in the High Court[8]. Circumstances which may, in an appropriate case, justify starting a claim in the High Court are if:

(a)   there are complicated disputes of fact;

(b)   there are points of law of general importance; or

(c)   the claim is against trespassers and there is a substantial risk of public disturbance or of serious harm to persons or property which properly require immediate determination[9].

1   See the High Court and County Courts Jurisdiction Order 1991, SI 1991/724, arts 4, 4A, 5, 6, 6A; CIVIL PROCEDURE vol 11 (2015) PARAS 48, 135; COURTS AND TRIBUNALS vol 24 (2010) PARA 863. Proceedings (other than those which include a claim for damages in respect of personal injury) may not be started in the High Court unless the value of the claim is £100,000 or more: art 4A (added by SI 1999/1014; substituted by SI 2009/577; and amended by SI 2014/821); and CIVIL PROCEDURE vol 11 (2015) PARA 135; COURTS AND TRIBUNALS vol 24 (2010) PARA 863.

2   As to case management see also CPR Pts 26, 29; CPR PD 29—*The Multi-Track* paras 2.1–2.7; and CIVIL PROCEDURE vol 11 (2015) PARA 233 et seq; CIVIL PROCEDURE vol 12 (2015) PARA 506 et seq. An undue influence claim is suitable for trial in the High Court: see CPR PD 29—*The Multi-Track* para 2.6(3); and CIVIL PROCEDURE vol 11 (2015) PARA 234. As to undue influence

generally see MISREPRESENTATION vol 76 (2013) PARA 834 et seq. As to the criteria for a transfer see CPR 30.3; and CIVIL PROCEDURE vol 11 (2015) PARAS 105, 108.
3 For these purposes, 'possession claim' means a claim for the recovery of possession of land (including buildings or parts of buildings): CPR 55.1(a).
4 CPR 55.2(1)(a)(ii). For these purposes, 'mortgage' includes a legal or equitable mortgage and a legal or equitable charge; and 'mortgagee' is to be interpreted accordingly: CPR 55.1(c).
5 CPR 55.3(1)(a), (2). As to statements of truth see CIVIL PROCEDURE vol 11 (2015) PARA 363 et seq. As to the limitation on the jurisdiction of the County Court to hear possession claims see PARA 534. For the procedure relating to possession claims see PARA 549 et seq.
6 CPR 55.3(1)(b).
7 CPR 55.3(1)(c).
8 CPR PD 55A—*Possession Claims* para 1.1(1); and see CIVIL PROCEDURE vol 11 (2015) PARA 135.
9 CPR PD 55A—*Possession Claims* para 1.3. The value of the property and the amount of any financial claim may be relevant circumstances, but these factors alone will not normally justify starting the claim in the High Court: CPR PD 55A—*Possession Claims* para 1.4. If a claimant starts a claim in the High Court and the court decides that it should have been started in the County Court, the court will normally either strike the claim out or transfer it to the County Court on its own initiative. This is likely to result in delay and the court will normally disallow the costs of starting the claim in the High Court and of any transfer: CPR PD 55A—*Possession Claims* para 1.2.

(ii) Procedure for Mortgage Claims Generally

536. Procedure for mortgage claims is governed by Civil Procedure Rules. Most legal proceedings falling within the scope of this title are governed by the general procedural code set out in the Civil Procedure Rules[1]. The only types of mortgage claim which are subject to specific procedural rules are possession claims[2] by a mortgagee[3] and claims to enforce charging orders by sale[4]. All other mortgage claims are brought under the Part 8 alternative procedure[5], as appropriately modified[6].

1 As to the Civil Procedure Rules see CIVIL PROCEDURE vol 11 (2015) PARA 6 et seq.
2 As to the meaning of 'possession claim' see PARA 535 note 3. For the procedure relating to possession claims see PARA 549 et seq.
3 As to the meaning of 'mortgagee' see PARA 535 note 4.
4 As to enforcement of charging orders by sale see CPR 73.10; and CIVIL PROCEDURE vol 12A (2015) PARA 1477.
5 See CIVIL PROCEDURE vol 11 (2015) PARA 150 et seq.
6 See CPR PD 8A—*Alternative Procedure for Claims*; and CIVIL PROCEDURE vol 11 (2015) PARA 150 et seq.

537. Commencement of mortgage claim in the High Court. A mortgage possession claim[1] in the High Court will be assigned to the Chancery Division[2]. Other mortgage claims in the High Court are also normally commenced there[3], although claims in respect of a mortgage or charge on a ship or any share in a ship lie within the Admiralty jurisdiction of the High Court[4].

1 As to the meaning of 'possession claim' see PARA 535 note 3.
2 CPR PD 55A—*Possession Claims* para 1.6; and see CIVIL PROCEDURE vol 11 (2015) PARA 135. For the procedure relating to possession claims see PARA 549 et seq.
3 See CPR PD 7—*How to Start Proceedings* para 2.5; and CIVIL PROCEDURE vol 11 (2015) PARA 135.
4 See the Senior Courts Act 1981 Sch 1 para 2(c); and COURTS AND TRIBUNALS vol 24 (2010) PARA 706; SHIPPING AND MARITIME LAW vol 93 (2008) PARA 91.

(4) CLAIM ON COVENANT FOR PAYMENT

(i) When Right to Claim on Covenant for Payment Arises

538. Covenant to pay on or on or after a certain day. Where a day for payment is fixed by the mortgage covenant[1], the right to claim arises upon non-payment on that day, as the affirmative covenant implies that the lender will not sue before that day[2]. Consequently, a substituted covenant taken by the mortgagee for payment at a date subsequent to that originally fixed is a binding arrangement to give time, and ordinarily discharges a surety[3]. If the covenant also fixes a place for payment, the creditor must attend there to receive payment, and there is no default unless he does so[4]. The claim on the covenant is for principal and interest only and any other sums which the mortgagor has covenanted to pay, not for expenses incurred by the mortgagee outside the covenant, although he may be entitled to these in a redemption or foreclosure claim[5]. If a bond has been given for the mortgage debt, the amount recoverable for principal and interest is, in general, limited to the amount of the penalty, and no more is recoverable against the mortgaged property if the mortgage is to secure the bond debt[6], but it is otherwise if the mortgage is for the principal sum and interest without reference to the bond[7]. A covenant to pay on or after a certain date gives the covenantee the right to payment at any time after that date, although possibly demand must first be made[8].

1 As to the effect of a covenant to repay the principal by instalments see PARA 185.
2 *Bolton v Buckenham* [1891] 1 QB 278 at 281, CA; *Twentieth Century Banking Corpn Ltd v Wilkinson* [1977] Ch 99, [1976] 3 All ER 361.
3 See FINANCIAL INSTRUMENTS AND TRANSACTIONS vol 49 (2015) PARA 849.
4 *Thorn v City Rice Mills* (1889) 40 ChD 357. See also CONTRACT vol 22 (2012) PARA 509.
5 *Re Sneyd, ex p Fewings* (1883) 25 ChD 338, CA. See further PARAS 597, 672.
6 *Hughes v Wynne* (1832) 1 My & K 20.
7 *Clarke v Lord Abingdon* (1810) 17 Ves 106; *Mathews v Keble* (1867) LR 4 Eq 467 (on appeal (1868) 3 Ch App 691).
8 *Re Tewkesbury Gas Co, Tysoe v Tewkesbury Gas Co* [1911] 2 Ch 279; affd [1912] 1 Ch 1, CA. As to an implied demand see *The Halcyon Skies (No 2)* [1977] 1 Lloyd's Rep 22.

539. Principal mortgage debt payable on demand. When the principal sum is payable on demand, and there is no provision, express or implied, for notice to be given, the necessity for notice depends on whether the covenant is direct or collateral. If it is direct, that is, if it secures the covenantor's own debt and is not merely a collateral security for that debt, no actual demand is required and the right of action accrues immediately on the money being advanced[1]. If, however, the covenant is collateral, where, for instance, it is to secure the debt of another or to secure an ordinary banking overdraft between the covenantor and his banker, it seems that the claim may not be brought until after actual demand[2].

Where on the true construction of the mortgage deed there is a provision, express or implied, for notice to be given, actual demand in writing must be made before the right to claim arises[3], and any other condition prescribed as a preliminary to suing on the covenant must be observed[4]. In the case of an instalment mortgage, a demand is necessary, because of the change in the nature of the debtor's obligation from instalments to lump sum[5]. Any mode of service is sufficient which brings home to the mortgagor the fact that the demand has been made[6]. A notice is still an effective demand even if it overstates the amount due[7].

Where a loan is repayable on demand, the mortgage may provide for a demand to be deemed to have been duly made, even if not received, if certain formalities are observed. However, where a demand is actually made and effectively communicated, it is not necessary to observe any formalities and consequently an implied demand will be effective[8]. A demand is made by any clear intimation that payment is required[9].

1 *Norton v Ellam* (1837) 2 M & W 461; *Jackson v Ogg* (1859) John 397; *Re Brown's Estate, Brown v Brown* [1893] 2 Ch 300 at 304; *Esso Petroleum Co Ltd v Alstonbridge Properties Ltd* [1975] 3 All ER 358, [1975] 1 WLR 1474. See also LIMITATION PERIODS vol 68 (2008) PARA 958. As to the covenant for repayment see PARA 182.

2 *Birks v Trippet* (1666) 1 Wms Saund 28; *Re Brown's Estate, Brown v Brown* [1893] 2 Ch 300; *Lloyds Bank Ltd v Margolis* [1954] 1 All ER 734, [1954] 1 WLR 644; *Habib Bank Ltd v Tailor* [1982] 3 All ER 561, [1982] 1 WLR 1218, CA. See also LIMITATION PERIODS vol 68 (2008) PARAS 968, 977, 1125. It has been held that a bond to secure money payable on demand is not forfeited until after demand (*Carter v Ring* (1813) 3 Camp 459), but the distinction is doubtful (see *Re Brown's Estate, Brown v Brown*).

3 *Lloyds Bank Ltd v Margolis* [1954] 1 All ER 734, [1954] 1 WLR 644. As to the length of notice required see PARA 184. See also LIMITATION PERIODS vol 68 (2008) PARA 1125.

4 See *Rogers & Co v British and Colonial Colliery Supply Association* (1898) 68 LJQB 14, where a debenture stockholder's right to claim depended on previous notice to the debenture stock trustees and default by them in suing. As to the allowance of a reasonable time for obtaining the money from the debtor's bankers see PARAS 183–184.

5 *Esso Petroleum Co Ltd v Alstonbridge Properties Ltd* [1975] 3 All ER 358, [1975] 1 WLR 1474. As to payment by instalments see PARA 185.

6 *Worthington & Co Ltd v Abbott* [1910] 1 Ch 588. See also *Belding v Read* (1865) 3 H & C 955 at 963; *Massey v Sladen* (1868) LR 4 Exch 13 (demand either personally or by service at place of business).

7 *Campbell v Commercial Bank of Sydney* (1879) 40 LT 137, PC; *Fox v Jolly* [1916] 1 AC 1, HL; *Clyde Properties Ltd v Tasker* [1970] NZLR 754. As to the binding effect of statements given under the Consumer Credit Act 1974 see s 172; and CONSUMER CREDIT vol 21 (2011) PARA 322.

8 *The Halcyon Skies (No 2)* [1977] 1 Lloyd's Rep 22.

9 *Re Colonial Finance, Mortgage, Investment and Guarantee Corpn Ltd* (1905) 6 SR NSW 6, NSW SC; *Re a Company* [1985] BCLC 37.

(ii) Who may Sue on Covenant for Payment

540. Claim by mortgagee and those claiming under him. A claim on the covenant for payment[1] contained in the mortgage deed can be brought by the mortgagee and those claiming the mortgage security under him, whether by devolution on death[2] or by alienation inter vivos. Accordingly, if the mortgagee has not assigned the mortgage, the right to sue passes on his death to his personal representatives, and, if he has specifically bequeathed the mortgage, the mortgage debt and the right to sue for it will vest in the legatee upon the executors' assent to the bequest being given[3], although it is usual for the executors to transfer the mortgage security to the legatee in the short statutory form[4]. If the mortgagee or his personal representatives transfer the mortgage, the right to sue on the covenant vests in the transferee on his giving notice in writing of the transfer to the mortgagor[5].

1 As to the implied personal obligation on the mortgagor in the express covenant see PARA 182.

2 See the Administration of Estates Act 1925 ss 1(1), 3(1)(ii), 36; and PARAS 389–393.

3 See WILLS AND INTESTACY vol 103 (2010) PARA 952.

4 See PARA 376.

5 See CHOSES IN ACTION vol 13 (2009) PARA 76 et seq. It is not open to a party seeking to recover payment of money secured by a mortgage or charge to claim at the hearing that the money was payable only under a bare covenant: see *William Hill (Park Lane) Ltd v Hofman* [1950] 1 All ER 1013.

541. Claim by mortgagees as trustees. Where the mortgagees are trustees, the beneficiaries are not entitled to sue on the covenant for payment unless it appears that the beneficiaries were intended to have the benefit of the contract of mortgage[1] or if the trustees fail in their duty to protect the trust estate or the interests of the beneficiaries in the trust estate[2]. The beneficiaries must call upon the trustees either to sue, or to allow the beneficiaries to sue[3]. Alternatively, a beneficiary may make an application seeking an order that the trustees bring a claim[4]. Similarly, where debentures or debenture stock are secured by a trust deed, the right to claim is in the trustees and not in the debenture holders or debenture stockholders[5], unless there is a direct covenant with the holders[6].

1 *Gandy v Gandy* (1885) 30 ChD 57, CA; *Kelly v Larkin and Carter* [1910] 2 IR 550. See also CONTRACT vol 22 (2012) PARAS 339–340. As to the covenant for repayment see PARA 182.
2 *Hayim v Citibank NA* [1987] AC 730, [1987] 3 WLR 83, PC. See also CPR 19.7A; and CIVIL PROCEDURE vol 11 (2015) PARA 493; TRUSTS AND POWERS vol 98 (2013) PARAS 54, 524.
3 *Re Booth and Kettlewell's Contract* (1892) 67 LT 550. See also TRUSTS AND POWERS vol 98 (2013) PARA 524.
4 Ie under the Trusts of Land and Appointment of Trustees Act 1996 s 14: see TRUSTS AND POWERS vol 98 (2013) PARA 479.
5 *Re Uruguay Central and Hygueritas Rly Co of Monte Video* (1879) 11 ChD 372 at 383; *Re Dunderland Iron Ore Co Ltd* [1909] 1 Ch 446.
6 *Re Olathe Silver Mining Co* (1884) 27 ChD 278 at 283. See also COMPANIES vol 15 (2009) PARA 1299 et seq.

(iii) Who may be Sued under Covenant for Payment

542. Mortgagor and his surety. The claim on the covenant for payment may be brought against the mortgagor and against any person who has joined with him in the covenant or has given a separate covenant as surety[1]. The mortgagor cannot without the mortgagee's consent rid himself of his liability under the covenant for payment of the mortgage debt by transferring the equity of redemption[2]. Words added to a covenant excluding personal liability may be repugnant, and the full liability may remain[3], but it is permissible to qualify the covenant, and accordingly a covenant by a trustee may in terms limit his liability to the time while he is a trustee[4].

1 See *Esso Petroleum Co Ltd v Alstonbridge Properties Ltd* [1975] 3 All ER 358, [1975] 1 WLR 1474. As to suretyship see PARA 118 et seq. As to the covenant for repayment see PARA 182.
2 See PARA 543; and CONTRACT vol 22 (2012) PARA 335. Cf *West Bromwich Building Society v Bullock* [1936] 1 All ER 887 (mortgage to building society; rules of the society provided that on transfer of the equity of redemption the board of the society might grant the original mortgagor release from future liability; the mortgagor was liable despite a transfer in absence of release). See also FINANCIAL INSTITUTIONS vol 48 (2015) PARA 493. As to the equity of redemption see PARAS 107, 304 et seq.
3 *Furnivall v Coombes* (1843) 5 Man & G 736.
4 *Williams v Hathaway* (1877) 6 ChD 544. See also PARA 157.

543. Assignee of equity of redemption. The covenant for payment of the mortgage debt does not run with the land, and so the assignee of the equity of redemption is not liable to be sued on it by the mortgagee[1]. This is in accordance with the rules that, except as between lessor and lessee, the burden of the covenant does not run with the land at law and the burden of a positive covenant does not run with the land in equity[2]. If, however, the assignee is a purchaser on sale, he usually enters into a covenant to indemnify the mortgagor against the debt, and, in the absence of an express covenant[3], a covenant of indemnity is implied[4]. The benefit of the covenant of indemnity is in general assignable[5]. The assignee may make himself directly liable by entering into a fresh covenant with the mortgagee, but such liability is not implied from the mere payment of interest[6].

1 *Re Errington, ex p Mason* [1894] 1 QB 11. As to the equity of redemption see PARAS 107, 304 et seq. As to the covenant for repayment see PARA 182.

2 See REAL PROPERTY AND REGISTRATION vol 87 (2012) PARA 1078 et seq; LANDLORD AND
   TENANT vol 63 (2012) PARA 702 et seq. See also CONVEYANCING vol 23 (2013) PARA 70. The
   bringing of a claim against the mortgagor gives him a new right to redeem: see PARA 306. See also
   Re Richardson, ex p Governors of St Thomas's Hospital [1911] 2 KB 705, CA, where proceedings
   were brought in the joint names of a lessor and a lessee to enforce a covenant of indemnity.
3 *Waring v Ward* (1802) 7 Ves 332 at 337; *Bridgman v Daw* (1891) 40 WR 253; *Adair v Carden*
   (1892) 29 LR Ir 469; *Dodson v Downey* [1901] 2 Ch 620.
4 *Mills v United Counties Bank Ltd* [1912] 1 Ch 231, CA, doubting on this point [1911] 1 Ch 669
   (decision of Eve J). The implied covenant is excluded by an express covenant for indemnity: *Mills
   v United Counties Bank Ltd* above.
5 See *Shore v Shore* (1847) 2 Ph 378.
6 *Re Errington, ex p Mason* [1894] 1 QB 11.

544. Personal representatives and beneficiaries. On the death of the mortgagor,
a claim on the covenant for payment lies against his personal representatives, and
the judgment can be enforced against them to the extent of the assets remaining
unadministered[1]. The mortgagee also has the remedies of a creditor against any
person to whom any beneficial interest of the mortgagor not comprised in the
mortgage devolves or is given[2], and the remedy, common to specialty and simple
contract creditors, of having the mortgagor's real and personal estate
administered by the court and applied rateably in satisfaction of debts of both
classes[3]. If personal estate of the mortgagor has been paid to legatees, the
mortgagee can follow it in their hands and make them refund[4]. The mortgagee
may sue in his own name alone for administration of real or personal estate[5].

1 See WILLS AND INTESTACY vol 103 (2010) PARA 952. As to the covenant for repayment see
   PARA 182.
2 Ie under the Administration of Estates Act 1925 s 32(2): see WILLS AND INTESTACY vol 103
   (2010) PARA 969. See also *Re Lacey, Howard v Lightfoot* [1907] 1 Ch 330 at 347, CA;
   Worthington & Co Ltd v Abbott [1910] 1 Ch 588 at 598, where the terms of the order are set out.
   As to the effect of an acknowledgment given by the devisee see LIMITATION PERIODS vol 68
   (2008) PARA 1216.
3 See the Administration of Estates Act 1925 s 32; and EQUITABLE JURISDICTION vol 47 (2014)
   PARAS 61–62; WILLS AND INTESTACY vol 103 (2010) PARAS 968–969.
4 See eg *Re Eustace, Lee v McMillan* [1912] 1 Ch 561. See also EQUITABLE JURISDICTION vol 47
   (2014) PARA 259; WILLS AND INTESTACY vol 103 (2010) PARA 1100. An assent or conveyance
   by a personal representative to a person other than a purchaser does not prejudice the right to
   follow property: see the Administration of Estates Act 1925 s 38(1); and WILLS AND INTESTACY
   vol 103 (2010) PARA 969. As to the mortgagee being barred by acquiescence in the distribution
   of the assets see EQUITABLE JURISDICTION vol 47 (2014) PARA 259.
5 *Re James, James v Jones* [1911] 2 Ch 348. See also WILLS AND INTESTACY vol 103 (2010) PARA
   968. As to proof by the mortgagee against an insolvent estate see PARA 531.

(iv) Loss of Right to Claim under Covenant for Payment

545. Loss of right by foreclosure and sale. A mortgagee who has foreclosed and
subsequently sold the property is precluded from suing on the covenant for
payment[1], but this principle does not apply to a sale under the mortgagee's power
of sale[2] or under the order of the court[3], and, if it does not realise enough to pay
off the mortgage, he may sue for the deficiency[4]. The mortgagee may be restrained
from suing if he cannot hand back the title deeds[5]. These principles are applicable
not only to real property, but also to shares deposited as security with a broker,
so that, if they have been wrongfully sold, the broker may not sue for the balance
due, but if the shares are readily purchasable their money value may be
substituted[6].

The mortgagee is not prevented from suing if his inability to restore the
property is due to the intervention of a third person, as in the case of a forfeiture
of leasehold property by the landlord, not due to the mortgagee's default[7]. If the

mortgagee holds bills of exchange as collateral security and retains them on transferring the mortgage, he may not sue on them pending a claim for redemption[8].

1 *Lloyds and Scottish Trust Ltd v Britten* (1982) 44 P & CR 249, [1982] LS Gaz R 1291. As to foreclosure see PARA 571 et seq.
2 See PARA 619.
3 *Gordon Grant & Co v Boos* [1926] AC 781, PC.
4 *Rudge v Richens* (1873) LR 8 CP 358; *Re McHenry, McDermott v Boyd Barker's Claim* [1894] 3 Ch 290, CA; *Bristol & West plc v Bartlett* [2002] EWCA Civ 1181, [2002] 4 All ER 544, [2003] 1 WLR 284.
5 *Schoole v Sall* (1803) 1 Sch & Lef 176. As to the delivery of title deeds see PARA 656.
6 *Ellis & Co's Trustee v Dixon-Johnson* [1925] AC 489, HL. As to the deposit of share certificates see PARA 243.
7 *Re Burrell, Burrell v Smith* (1869) LR 7 Eq 399. As to forfeiture of leasehold property see LANDLORD AND TENANT vol 63 (2012) PARA 751 et seq.
8 *Walker v Jones* (1866) LR 1 PC 50. As to bills of exchange see generally FINANCIAL INSTRUMENTS AND TRANSACTIONS vol 49 (2015) PARA 184 et seq.

546. Loss of right by lapse of time. The right to claim on the mortgage covenant for payment[1] for principal money is liable to be barred by lapse of time[2]. The period applicable will normally be a period of six years from the date when the cause of action arose[3].

1 As to the covenant for repayment see PARA 182.
2 See PARA 519.
3 See the Limitation Act 1980 s 20; and PARA 519.

(v) Procedure for Claims on Covenant for Payment

547. Procedure in the High Court for claims on covenant for payment. If the claim for payment under the mortgage covenant includes a claim for possession of land, the procedure applicable to a possession claim[1] applies[2].

If the claim for payment does not include such a claim, the claim is brought under the Part 8 alternative procedure[3], as appropriately modified[4].

1 As to the meaning of 'possession claim' see PARA 535 note 3.
2 See CPR Pt 55; and PARAS 535, 549 et seq.
3 As to the alternative procedure for commencing claims under CPR Pt 8 see CIVIL PROCEDURE vol 11 (2015) PARA 150 et seq.
4 See CPR PD 8A—*Alternative Procedure for Claims*; PARA 536; and CIVIL PROCEDURE vol 11 (2015) PARA 150 et seq.

548. Procedure in the County Court for claims on covenant for payment. If the claim for payment under the mortgage covenant includes a claim for possession of land, the procedure applicable to a possession claim[1] applies[2].

If the claim for payment does not include such a claim, the claim is brought under the Part 8 alternative procedure[3], as appropriately modified[4].

1 As to the meaning of 'possession claim' see PARA 535 note 3.
2 See CPR Pt 55; and PARAS 535, 549 et seq.
3 As to the alternative procedure for commencing claims under CPR Pt 8 see CIVIL PROCEDURE vol 11 (2015) PARA 150 et seq.
4 See CPR PD 8A—*Alternative Procedure for Claims*; PARA 536; and CIVIL PROCEDURE vol 11 (2015) PARA 150 et seq.

(5) PROCEEDINGS FOR POSSESSION

549. Jurisdiction and procedure for possession proceedings. Most claims by a mortgagee for possession must be brought under the Civil Procedure Rules[1] in the County Court[2] and what is, in essence, a possession claim is treated as such, notwithstanding that the relief claimed includes foreclosure or other relief[3]. Only in exceptional circumstances may claims for possession be brought in the Chancery Division of the High Court[4].

Before proceedings are begun it should be confirmed that the right to possession has arisen[5] and any necessary notice given[6].

1 See CPR 55.2(1)(a)(ii). See further CPR 55.1–55.10; and PARA 551 et seq. The application of these provisions is subject to any enactment or practice direction which sets out special provisions with regard to any particular category of claim: CPR 55.2(2)(a); CPR PD 55A—*Possession Claims*; and PARA 551 et seq.
2 See PARAS 534–535.
3 See PARA 534. As to foreclosure see PARA 571 et seq.
4 See PARAS 534–535.
5 As to the mortgagee's right to possession see PARA 404 et seq.
6 Eg a notice to quit might be necessary: see PARA 347. A subsequent mortgagee should give notice to any prior mortgagee of his intention to apply for possession. As to transfers of prior mortgages see PARA 366 et seq. A mortgagee who seeks possession of land which consists of or includes residential property must, within five days of receiving notification of the date of the hearing by the court, send a notice in the specified form to the tenant or occupier of the property: see CPR 55.10; and PARA 553. See also the CPR Pre-action Protocol for Possession Claims based on Mortgage or Home Purchase Plan Arrears in respect of Residential Property.

550. Necessary parties to possession proceedings. If there are several mortgagors in a claim for possession[1] they should all be joined[2], but, if they are not all in occupation and it is not possible to serve[3] any or all of those not in occupation, only those in occupation and the others on whom service can be effected without difficulty need be served[4]. Where the mortgagor is bankrupt, his trustee in bankruptcy should not be joined, unless the court directs otherwise[5].

The only other persons who need to be made defendants are those persons having an independent right to remain in occupation[6]. A spouse or civil partner who asserts that he or she is entitled[7] to take over the obligations of the mortgage and shows that there is a real prospect in the near future of him or her redeeming the mortgage should be made a defendant[8]. If the mortgagor is not in occupation, the occupier should normally be made defendant[9]. If, after proceedings properly begun against the mortgagor alone, the mortgagee discovers another person in occupation, the mortgagee may be ordered to give notice of his application to that other person[10].

1 For the procedure relating to possession claims see PARAS 549, 551 et seq.
2 After the original mortgagor has parted with the property, he should not be made a defendant in respect of a claim for possession: *Esso Petroleum Co Ltd v Alstonbridge Properties Ltd* [1975] 3 All ER 358, [1975] 1 WLR 1474.
3 As to the methods by which service may be made see CPR Pt 6; and CIVIL PROCEDURE vol 11 (2015) PARA 244 et seq.
4 *Alliance Building Society v Yap* [1962] 3 All ER 6n, [1962] 1 WLR 857. As to the need to give notice to occupiers see PARA 553.
5 *Alliance Building Society v Shave* [1952] Ch 581, [1952] 1 All ER 1033.
6 *Brighton and Shoreham Building Society v Hollingdale* [1965] 1 All ER 540, [1965] 1 WLR 376.
7 Ie under the Family Law Act 1996 s 30(3): see PARA 308; and MATRIMONIAL AND CIVIL PARTNERSHIP LAW vol 72 (2015) PARA 304.
8 See *Hastings and Thanet Building Society v Goddard* [1970] 3 All ER 954, [1970] 1 WLR 1544, CA.
9 *Leicester Permanent Building Society v Shearley* [1951] Ch 90, [1950] 2 All ER 738; *Esso Petroleum Co Ltd v Alstonbridge Properties Ltd* [1975] 3 All ER 358, [1975] 1 WLR 1474. See also *Barclays Bank Ltd v Kiley* [1961] 2 All ER 849, [1961] 1 WLR 1050, where the mortgagor was dead and no personal representatives had been appointed. See further *Bristol and West Building Society v Henning* [1985] 2 All ER 606, [1985] 1 WLR 778, CA; *Equity and Law Home Loans Ltd v Prestridge* [1992] 1 All ER 909, [1992] 1 WLR 137, CA.
10 *Alliance Building Society v Shave* [1952] Ch 581, [1952] 1 All ER 1033. See also PARA 553.

551. Commencing the claim for possession of the mortgaged property. In proceedings for possession of the mortgaged property, the claim form and particulars of claim must be in the prescribed forms[1], and must be filed and served together[2]. The particulars of claim must:

(1)   identify the land to which the claim relates[3];

(2)   state whether the claim relates to residential property[4];

(3)   state the ground on which possession is claimed[5];

(4)   give full details about any mortgage[6] or tenancy agreement[7];

(5)   give details of every person who, to the best of the claimant's knowledge, is in possession of the property[8];

(6)   describe the state of the mortgage account[9];

(7)   provide details of arrears of payment, where relevant[10];

(8)   state whether or not the loan which is secured by the mortgage is a regulated consumer credit agreement[11];

(9)   set out, if appropriate, details that show that the property is not one in relation to which claims are required to be brought in the County Court[12];

(10)   give relevant information about the defendant's circumstances[13];

(11)   give details of any tenancy entered into between the mortgagor and the mortgagee[14]; and

(12)   state any previous steps which the claimant has taken to recover either the money secured by the mortgage or the mortgaged property[15].

1   CPR 55.3(5); CPR PD 55A—*Possession Claims* para 1.5. For the prescribed claim form see CPR PD 4—*Forms* Table 1, Form N5; and for the prescribed form of particulars of claim for mortgaged residential premises see CPR PD 4—*Forms* Table 1, Form N120. As to forms generally see CIVIL PROCEDURE vol 11 (2015) PARA 20.

2   CPR 55.4.

3   CPR PD 55A—*Possession Claims* para 2.1(1).

4   CPR PD 55A—*Possession Claims* para 2.1(2). If the claim relates to residential property, the particulars of claim must additionally state whether a Class F land charge (ie a land charge which has been registered under the Matrimonial Homes Act 1967 s 2(7) (repealed), a notice under the Matrimonial Homes Act 1983 s 2(8) or s 8(3) (repealed) or a notice under the Family Law Act 1996 s 31(10): see MATRIMONIAL AND CIVIL PARTNERSHIP LAW vol 72 (2015) PARA 305) has been registered, and where relevant on whose behalf, and if so, that the claimant will serve notice of the claim on the persons on whose behalf the charge is registered or the notice or caution entered: CPR PD 55A—*Possession Claims* para 2.5(1). As to Class F land charges see the Land Charges Act 1972 s 2(7); and REAL PROPERTY AND REGISTRATION vol 87 (2012) PARA 730.

5   CPR PD 55A—*Possession Claims* para 2.1(3).

6   As to the meaning of 'mortgage' see PARA 535 note 4. See also *Practice Direction (Chancery 1/91)* [1991] 3 All ER 768, [1991] 1 WLR 782, which provides that:

(1)   most building society mortgages incorporate standard mortgage conditions, and that in such cases a copy of the relevant conditions must also be exhibited;

(2)   some standard forms of building society mortgage are so abbreviated that they give no particulars of the amount of the advance, the term of the loan, the rate of interest or the amount of the instalments, but that all these matters are defined in the mortgage conditions by reference to the offer letter and where the offer letter is thus in effect incorporated into the mortgage by reference, that also should be exhibited to the particulars; and

(3)   many bank mortgages, although expressed in the usual bank 'all monies' form, are also qualified by an offer letter or other side letter, providing for repayment of the advance by instalments, and in these cases also the relevant letter should be exhibited to the particulars.

As to building society mortgages generally see FINANCIAL INSTITUTIONS vol 48 (2015) PARA 479 et seq.

7   CPR PD 55A—*Possession Claims* para 2.1(4).

8   CPR PD 55A—*Possession Claims* para 2.1(5).

9   CPR PD 55A—*Possession Claims* para 2.5(2). Particulars must include:

(1)   the amounts of the advance, any periodic repayment, and any payment of interest required to be made (CPR PD 55A—*Possession Claims* para 2.5(2)(a));

(2)   the amount which would have to be paid (after taking into account any adjustment for early settlement) in order to redeem the mortgage at a stated date not more than 14 days after the claim started, specifying the amount of solicitor's costs and administration charges which would be payable (in which regard see also *Nationwide Building Society v Bateman* [1978] 1 All ER 999, [1978] 1 WLR 394) (CPR PD 55A—*Possession Claims* para 2.5(2)(b));

(3)   if the loan which is secured by the mortgage is a regulated consumer credit agreement (see CONSUMER CREDIT vol 21 (2011) PARA 51 et seq), the total amount outstanding under the terms of the mortgage (CPR PD 55A—*Possession Claims* para 2.5(2)(c)); and

(4)   the rate of interest payable at the commencement of the mortgage, immediately before any arrears (see the text to note 10) accrued, and at the commencement of the proceedings (CPR PD 55A—*Possession Claims* para 2.5(2)(d)).

10 See CPR PD 55A—*Possession Claims* para 2.5(3). If the claim is brought because of failure to pay the periodic payments when due, the particulars must:

(1)   state in schedule form, the dates and amounts of all payments due and payments made under the mortgage agreement or mortgage deed for a period of two years immediately preceding the date of issue, or if the first date of default occurred less than two years before the date of issue from the first date of default and a running total of the arrears (CPR PD 55A—*Possession Claims* para 2.5(3)(a)); and

(2)   give details of any other payments required to be made as a term of the mortgage (eg for insurance premiums, legal costs, default interest, penalties, administrative or other charges), any other sums claimed, stating the nature and amount of each such charge, and whether any of these payments is in arrears and whether or not it is included in the amount of any periodic payment (CPR PD 55A—*Possession Claims* para 2.5(3)(b)).

11 CPR PD 55A—*Possession Claims* para 2.5(4). If the loan is a regulated consumer credit agreement, particulars must specify the date on which any notice required by the Consumer Credit Act 1974 s 76 or s 87 (see CONSUMER CREDIT vol 21 (2011) PARAS 242, 281) was given: CPR PD 55A—*Possession Claims* para 2.5(4).

12 CPR PD 55A—*Possession Claims* para 2.5(5). Such properties are those to which the Consumer Credit Act 1974 s 141: see CONSUMER CREDIT vol 21 (2011) PARA 307) applies.

13 CPR PD 55A—*Possession Claims* para 2.5(6). In particular, information must be give as to whether the defendant is in receipt of social security benefits and whether any payments are made on his behalf directly to the claimant under the Social Security Contributions and Benefits Act 1992: CPR PD 55A—*Possession Claims* para 2.5(6).

14 CPR PD 55A—*Possession Claims* para 2.5(7). Such details must include details of any notices served: CPR PD 55A—*Possession Claims* para 2.5(7).

15 CPR PD 55A—*Possession Claims* para 2.5(8). If such steps involved court proceedings, particulars must state the dates when the claim started and concluded and the dates and terms of any orders made: CPR PD 55A—*Possession Claims* para 2.5(8).

552. Possession claims: hearing date, service and response. On issuing the claim form the court fixes a date for the hearing[1]. However, if the claim is not made at the County Court hearing centre which serves the address where the land is situated, a date will be fixed for hearing when the claim is received by that hearing centre[2].

The date must be not less than 28 days from the date of issue of the form[3], and the defendant must be served with the claim form and particulars of claim not less than 21 days before the hearing date[4]. An acknowledgment of service is not required[5], although the defendant is as a rule required to file a defence within 14 days after service of the particulars[6]. In the case of a claim for possession of mortgaged residential premises the prescribed form of defence must be used[7]. Where the defendant does not file a defence within the time specified[8], he may take part in any hearing but the court may take his failure to do so into account when deciding what order to make about costs[9]. The court cannot give judgment in default[10] nor, in the case of residential premises, summary judgment[11].

1   CPR 55.5(1). As to the commencement of the claim for possession see PARA 551.
2   CPR 55.5(1A).
3   CPR 55.5(3)(a). The standard period between the issue of the claim form and the hearing must be not more than eight weeks (CPR 55.5(3)(b)), although the court is empowered to extend or shorten the time for compliance with any rule (see CPR 3.1(2)(a); and CIVIL PROCEDURE vol 12 (2015)

PARAS 507, 511; CIVIL PROCEDURE vol 12A (2015) PARA 1524). As to the exercise of the court's powers in this regard so far as relating to possession claims see CPR PD 55A—*Possession Claims* para 3.

4   CPR 55.5(3)(c).
5   CPR 55.7(1). Therefore, CPR Pt 10 (which is concerned with acknowledgment of service: see CIVIL PROCEDURE vol 11 (2015) PARA 311 et seq) is inapplicable: CPR 55.7(1).
6   See CPR 15.4(1)(a), (2); and CIVIL PROCEDURE vol 11 (2015) PARA 315.
7   See CPR 55.3(5); CPR PD 55A—*Possession Claims* para 1.5. For the prescribed form see CPR PD 4—*Forms* para 3.1, Table 1, Form N11M. As to forms generally see CIVIL PROCEDURE vol 11 (2015) PARA 20.
8   Ie the time specified in CPR 15.4: see CIVIL PROCEDURE vol 11 (2015) PARA 315.
9   CPR 55.7(3).
10 CPR 55.7(4). Therefore, CPR Pt 12 (which is concerned with default judgment: see CIVIL PROCEDURE vol 12 (2015) PARA 535 et seq) inapplicable: see CPR 55.7(4).
11 See CPR 24.3(2)(a); and CIVIL PROCEDURE vol 12 (2015) PARA 549.

553. Persons to be notified of possession claim. Where a mortgagee[1] seeks possession of land which consists of or includes residential property[2], the claimant must, within five days of receiving notification of the date of the hearing by the court, send a notice to:

(1)   the property, addressed to 'the tenant or the occupier'[3];

(2)   the housing department of the local authority within which the property is located[4]; and

(3)   any registered proprietor (other than the claimant) of a registered charge over the property[5].

The notice must state that a possession claim for the property has started[6], show the name and address of the claimant, the defendant and the court which issued the claim form[7], and give details of the hearing[8]. The notice to the local authority must also state the full address of the property in question[9].

The claimant must produce at the hearing a copy of the notices[10] and evidence that they have been sent[11].

1   As to the meaning of 'mortgagee' see PARA 535 note 4.
2   CPR 55.10(1).
3   CPR 55.10(2)(a).
4   CPR 55.10(2)(b). As to local housing authorities see HOUSING vol 56 (2011) PARA 9.
5   CPR 55.10(2)(c).
6   CPR 55.10(3)(a). As to the meaning of 'possession claim' see PARA 535 note 3.
7   CPR 55.10(3)(b). As to the commencement of a possession claim see PARA 551.
8   CPR 55.10(3)(c). As to the hearing see PARA 554.
9   CPR 55.10(3A).
10 CPR 55.10(4)(a).
11 CPR 55.10(4)(b).

554. Possession claims: the hearing. Each party to possession proceedings should, wherever possible, include all the evidence he wishes to present in his statement of case, verified by a statement of truth[1]. Where relevant, the claimant's evidence should include the amount of any rent or mortgage arrears and interest on those arrears[2], and the defendant should give evidence of the amount of any outstanding social security or housing benefit payments relevant to rent or mortgage arrears[3], as well as the status of pending social security claims and applications[4]. Where the claimant serves the claim form and particulars of claim[5] he must produce at the hearing a certificate of service of those documents[6]; and he must also produce at the hearing a copy of the notices to tenants or occupiers and the local authority housing department and evidence that they have been sent[7].

At the hearing[8], the court may either decide the claim[9] or give case management directions[10]. Unless either the claim is allocated to the fast track or the multi-track[11] or the court orders otherwise, any fact that needs to be proved by the evidence of witnesses at a hearing may be proved by evidence in writing[12]. Provision is also made for the adjournment of a hearing in order that oral evidence can be given in circumstances where the maker of a witness statement does not attend a hearing and the other party disputes material evidence contained in his statement[13].

1   CPR PD 55A—*Possession Claims* para 5.1. As to statements of truth see CIVIL PROCEDURE vol 11 (2015) PARA 363 et seq. Witness statements must be filed and served at least two days before the hearing: see CPR 55.8(4).
2   CPR PD 55A—*Possession Claims* para 5.2. Such amounts should, if possible, be up to date to the date of the hearing (if necessary by specifying a daily rate of arrears and interest), although CPR 55.8(4) (see note 1) does not prevent such evidence being brought up to date orally or in writing on the day of the hearing if necessary: CPR PD 55A—*Possession Claims* para 5.2.
3   CPR PD 55A—*Possession Claims* para 5.3(1).
4   CPR PD 55A—*Possession Claims* para 5.3(2). Pursuant to this requirement, the defendant should give evidence of the status of any claims for social security or housing benefit about which a decision has not yet been made and any applications to appeal against or review a social security or housing benefit decision where that appeal or review has not yet concluded: CPR PD 55A—*Possession Claims* para 5.3(2).
5   See PARA 551.
6   CPR 55.8(6). CPR 6.17(2)(a) (certificate of service of claim form: see CIVIL PROCEDURE vol 11 (2015) PARA 260) does not apply in these circumstances: CPR 55.8(6).
7   See CPR 55.10(4); and PARA 553.
8   Ie a hearing fixed in accordance with CPR 55.5(1) (see PARA 552) or at any adjournment of that hearing: see CPR 55.8(1).
9   CPR 55.8(1)(a).
10 CPR 55.8(1)(b). As to the giving of case management directions see CIVIL PROCEDURE vol 12 (2015) PARA 506 et seq. Where the claim is genuinely disputed on grounds which appear to be substantial, case management directions given under CPR 55.8(1)(b) will include the allocation of the claim to a track or directions to enable it to be allocated: CPR 55.8(2). As to the allocation of defended cases to case management tracks see CIVIL PROCEDURE vol 11 (2015) PARA 200 et seq.
11 As to the matters to which the court will have regard when it decides on allocation see CIVIL PROCEDURE vol 11 (2015) PARA 200 et seq.
12 CPR 55.8(3). As to the rules about witness evidence in this context see CPR 32.2(1), (2); and CIVIL PROCEDURE vol 12 (2015) PARA 768.
13 CPR PD 55A—*Possession Claims* para 5.4. The claimant must bring two completed copies of Form N123 to the hearing: CPR PD 55A—*Possession Claims* para 5.5. As to adjournments see further PARA 555.

555. Power to adjourn proceedings for possession.

Apart from the power of adjournment in the absence of a witness[1] or where a dwelling house is involved[2], the court has no general jurisdiction to stand an undefended claim for possession over, whether on terms of making payments or paying arrears, unless the mortgagee agrees: it is not in principle legitimate for the court to order an adjournment designed to achieve a result which the law in force at the date of the hearing would not permit[3]. An adjournment may be ordered for a short time to afford the mortgagor a chance of paying off the mortgage in full, or otherwise satisfying the mortgagee, but this will not be done if there is no reasonable prospect of this occurring[4]. Thus the court has a limited jurisdiction to postpone the giving of possession to enable the property to be sold[5].

1   See CPR PD 55A—*Possession Claims* para 5.4; and PARA 554.
2   See PARA 557 et seq.
3   *North British Housing Association Ltd v Matthews* [2004] EWCA Civ 1736, [2005] 2 All ER 667.
4   *Birmingham Citizens Permanent Building Society v Caunt* [1962] Ch 883, [1962] 1 All ER 163; *Royal Trust Co of Canada v Markham* [1975] 3 All ER 433, [1975] 1 WLR 1416, CA. See also *London Permanent Benefit Building Society v De Baer* [1969] 1 Ch 321, [1968] 1 All ER 372 (where it was held that the rules of court do not confer on the court any power to grant a stay of execution of an order of possession).

5   See *Cheltenham and Gloucester plc v Booker* (1996) 73 P & CR 412, 29 HLR 597, CA; and PARA
    561.

556. Restrictions on mortgagee's ability to obtain possession order. A mortgagee
will be restrained from obtaining possession except when it is sought bona fide for
the purpose of enforcing the security[1]. Likewise, although the court has a power
to make an order for possession against one of two joint mortgagors, it would not
in general be appropriate to do so where it would be of no benefit to the
mortgagee, especially where the mortgagors are husband and wife[2]. The
mortgagee's ability to enforce his security is also restricted by the application for
and existence of an administration order[3], or a moratorium in advance of a
voluntary arrangement[4], in relation to a corporate or partnership mortgagor, and
by an interim order obtained by an individual mortgagor who wishes to enter a
voluntary arrangement[5]. The mortgagee needs leave to bring proceedings for
possession against a company in liquidation[6] or a bankrupt[7]. Any order for
possession made in favour of a second mortgagee must respect the interest of the
prior mortgagee, including his interests as landlord[8].

1   *Quennell v Maltby* [1979] 1 All ER 568 at 571, [1979] 1 WLR 318 at 322, CA, per Lord
    Denning MR; *Sadiq v Hussain* [1997] NPC 19, CA. See also PARA 394.
2   *Albany Home Loans Ltd v Massey* [1997] 2 All ER 609, [1997] 2 FLR 305, CA.
3   See PARA 521. See also *Bristol Airport plc v Powdrill* [1990] Ch 744, [1990] 2 All ER 493, CA;
    Re Atlantic Computer Systems plc [1992] Ch 505, [1992] 1 All ER 476, CA.
4   See PARA 523.
5   See PARA 527.
6   See PARA 524.
7   See PARA 529.
8   See *Berkshire Capital Funding Ltd v Street* (1999) Times, 27 May, CA. As to the leasing power of
    a mortgagee see PARA 428.

**557. Power to suspend or adjourn possession order in the case of a dwelling
house.** Where a mortgagee under a mortgage[1] of land which consists of or includes
a dwelling house[2] brings proceedings in which he claims possession of the
mortgaged property, not being a claim for foreclosure[3] in which a claim for
possession of the mortgaged property is also made, the court may adjourn the
proceedings[4] or, on giving judgment or making an order for delivery of possession
of the mortgaged property or at any time before the execution of the judgment or
order, may stay or suspend execution of the judgment or order, or postpone the
date for delivery of possession[5], for such period or periods as it thinks reasonable[6].

The court may exercise these powers only where it appears to it that in the
event of its exercising them the mortgagor is likely to be able within a reasonable
period to pay any sums due[7] under the mortgage or to remedy a default[8] consisting
of a breach[9] of any other obligation arising under or by virtue of the mortgage[10];
and it may also suspend any order it makes in order to enable the mortgagor to
effect a sale[11]. Repeat applications may be made but a judge may reject a repeat
application if he considers that it amounts to an abuse of process[12].

A suspended possession order conditional on both payment of the arrears and
payment of current instalments under the mortgage remains enforceable
throughout the term of the mortgage notwithstanding payment or consolidation
of the arrears[13].

The County Court cannot set aside or suspend a warrant for possession of a
dwelling house let under a secure tenancy after execution unless either:

(1)   the possession order on which it was issued was itself set aside; or
(2)   the warrant had been obtained by fraud; or
(3)   there had been an abuse of process or oppression in its execution[14].

The court has further statutory power to postpone delivery of possession, or stay or suspend an order for delivery of possession, in the case of a dwelling house subject to an unauthorised tenancy[15].

1 Ie other than a mortgage securing an agreement which is a regulated agreement within the meaning of the Consumer Credit Act 1974 (see CONSUMER CREDIT vol 21 (2011) PARA 51): Administration of Justice Act 1970 s 38A (added by the Consumer Credit Act 1974 s 192(3)(a), Sch 4 Pt 1 para 30). For these purposes, 'mortgage' includes a charge; and 'mortgagor' and 'mortgagee' are to be construed accordingly and include any person deriving title under the original mortgagor or mortgagee: Administration of Justice Act 1970 s 39(1). A statutory tenant of a mortgagor is not a 'person deriving title under the original mortgagor': *Britannia Building Society v Earl* [1990] 2 All ER 469, [1990] 1 WLR 422, CA.
2 'Dwelling house' includes any building or part of a building which is used as a dwelling: Administration of Justice Act 1970 s 39(1). The fact that part of the premises comprised in a dwelling house is used as a shop or office or for business, trade or professional purposes does not prevent the dwelling house from being a dwelling house for these purposes: s 39(2). Premises consist of or include a dwelling house for these purposes if they include such a house on the date when the mortgagee brings the claim for possession: see *Royal Bank of Scotland plc v Miller* [2001] EWCA Civ 344, [2002] QB 255, [2001] 3 WLR 523.
3 As to foreclosure see PARA 571 et seq.
4 See the Administration of Justice Act 1970 s 36(1), (2)(a). Any such adjournment, stay, suspension or postponement (see the text to notes 5–6) may be made subject to such conditions with regard to the payment by the mortgagor of any sum secured by the mortgage or the remedying of any default as the court thinks fit: s 36(3). The court may from time to time vary or revoke any condition imposed: s 36(4).
5 Administration of Justice Act 1970 s 36(2)(b). See also note 4. The court has no jurisdiction once an order or judgment has been executed or once the mortgagee has extinguished the mortgagor's equity: *National and Provincial Building Society v Ahmed* [1995] 2 EGLR 127, [1995] NPC 88, CA.
6 Administration of Justice Act 1970 s 36(2). Execution of an order may not be suspended for an indefinite period: *Royal Trust Co of Canada v Markham* [1975] 3 All ER 433, [1975] 1 WLR 1416, CA; *Bristol and West Building Society v Ellis and Ellis* (1996) 73 P & CR 158, 29 HLR 282, CA. As to the principles applicable on the determination of a reasonable period see PARAS 560–561.
7 The court can order its own inquiry as to the amounts due: *Shirlstar Container Transport Ltd v Re-Enforce Trading Co Ltd* [1990] NPC 76, CA.
8 This provision does not apply only to breaches of obligations affecting the mortgagee's security; a breach consisting of an unlawful letting by the mortgagor without the mortgagee's consent can only be remedied by the departure of those tenants: see *Britannia Building Society v Earl* [1990] 2 All ER 469, [1990] 1 WLR 422, CA.
9 This provision also applies where there is no default: *Western Bank Ltd v Schindler* [1977] Ch 1, [1976] 2 All ER 393, CA.
10 See the Administration of Justice Act 1970 s 36(1).
11 See PARAS 561–562.
12 *Abbey National Mortgages plc v Bernard* (1995) 71 P & CR 257, [1995] NPC 118, CA.
13 *Bank of Scotland plc v Zinda* [2011] EWCA Civ 706, [2011] 2 All ER (Comm) 839, [2012] 1 WLR 728.
14 *Cheltenham and Gloucester Building Society v Obi* (1994) 28 HLR 22, CA; *Mortgage Express v Da Rocha-Afodu* [2007] EWHC 297 (QB), [2007] All ER (D) 276 (Feb).
15 See the Mortgage Repossessions (Protection of Tenants etc) Act 2010 s 1; and PARA 558.

558. Power to postpone, suspend or stay possession order in the case of a dwelling house subject to an unauthorised tenancy. Where the mortgagee[1] under a mortgage of land which consists of or includes a dwelling house[2] brings an action (other than an action for foreclosure[3]) in which the mortgagee claims possession of the mortgaged property, and there is an unauthorised tenancy[4] of all or part of the property, when making an order for delivery of possession of the property, the court may, on the application of the tenant[5], postpone the date for delivery of possession for a period not exceeding two months[6].

Where an order for delivery of possession of the property has been made but not executed, the court may, on the application of the tenant ('the applicant'), stay or suspend execution of the order for a period not exceeding two months if:

(1)   the court did not exercise its powers of postponement[7] when making the order or, if it did, the applicant was not the tenant when it exercised those powers;

(2)   the applicant has asked the mortgagee to give an undertaking in writing not to enforce the order for two months beginning with the date the undertaking is given; and

(3)   the mortgagee has not given such an undertaking[8].

When considering whether to exercise its powers of postponement[9], the court must have regard to the circumstances of the tenant and, if there is an outstanding breach by the tenant of a term of the unauthorised tenancy, the nature of that breach and whether the tenant might reasonably be expected to have avoided breaching that term or to have remedied the breach[10]. A postponement, stay or suspension may be made conditional on the making of payments to the mortgagee in respect of the occupation of the property (or part of the property) during the period of the postponement, stay or suspension[11].

Where the mortgagee under a mortgage of land which consists of or includes a dwelling-house has obtained an order for possession of the mortgaged property, the order may be executed only:

(a)   if the mortgagee gives notice at the property of any prescribed[12] step taken for the purpose of executing the order[13]; and

(b)   after the end of a prescribed period beginning with the day on which such notice is given[14].

1 'Mortgage' includes a charge; 'mortgagee' is to be read accordingly, and includes any person deriving title under the original mortgagee: Mortgage Repossessions (Protection of Tenants etc) Act 2010 s 3(4), (5).
2 'Dwelling house' includes any building, or part of a building, that is used as a dwelling, and the fact that part of the premises comprised in a dwelling house is used as a shop or office, or for other business, trade or professional purposes, does not prevent it from being a dwelling house: Mortgage Repossessions (Protection of Tenants etc) Act 2010 s 3(2), (3).
3 As to foreclosure see PARA 571 et seq.
4 There is an 'unauthorised tenancy' if:
   (1)   an agreement has been made which, as between the parties to it, or their successors in title, is or gives rise to an assured tenancy within the meaning of the Housing Act 1988, or a protected or statutory tenancy within the meaning of the Rent Act 1977 (Mortgage Repossessions (Protection of Tenants etc) Act 2010 s 1(8)(a)); and
   (2)   the mortgagee's interest in the property is not subject to the tenancy (s 1(8)(b)).
5 'The tenant', in relation to an unauthorised tenancy, means the person who is, as between the parties to the agreement in question, or their successors in title, the tenant under the unauthorised tenancy or, if there is more than one tenant, any of them: Mortgage Repossessions (Protection of Tenants etc) Act 2010 s 1(9).
6 Mortgage Repossessions (Protection of Tenants etc) Act 2010 s 1(1), (2); CPR 55.10(4A).
7 Ie its power under the Mortgage Repossessions (Protection of Tenants etc) Act 2010 s 1(2): see the text and notes 1–6.
8 Mortgage Repossessions (Protection of Tenants etc) Act 2010 s 1(3), (4). The making of any payment pursuant to a condition of an undertaking of a kind mentioned in head (3) in the text is not to be regarded as creating (or as evidence of the creation of) any tenancy or other right to occupy the property: s 1(7).
9 Ie under the Mortgage Repossessions (Protection of Tenants etc) Act 2010 s 1: see the text and notes 1–8.
10 Mortgage Repossessions (Protection of Tenants etc) Act 2010 s 1(5).
11 Mortgage Repossessions (Protection of Tenants etc) Act 2010 s 1(6). The making of any payment pursuant to a condition imposed by virtue of s 1(6) is not to be regarded as creating (or as evidence of the creation of) any tenancy or other right to occupy the property: s 1(7).
12 Ie prescribed by regulations in the form of a statutory instrument made by the Secretary of State with the consent of the Lord Chancellor: Mortgage Repossessions (Protection of Tenants etc) Act 2010 s 2(3), (6), (7), (8). Such regulations may prescribe the form of notices and the way in which they must be given and may make supplementary, incidental, transitional or saving provision:

s 2(4), (5). In exercise of this power, the Dwelling Houses (Execution of Possession Orders by Mortgagees) Regulations 2010, SI 2010/1809, have been made (see reg 1). They provide that the mortgagee's notice of execution of the possession order must be in the form set out in the Dwelling Houses (Execution of Possession Orders by Mortgagees) Regulations 2010, SI 2010/1809, reg 4, Schedule. The mortgagee's notice may be given in any of the following ways:

   (1)   by sending the notice to the property by first class post or registered post in an envelope addressed to the tenant by name, or if the tenant's name is not known, to 'The Tenant or Occupier' (reg 5(1)(a));

   (2)   by leaving the notice at the property in an envelope addressed as described in head (1), or affixed to and displayed in a prominent place where its contents can be read by a person entering the property (reg 5(1)(b)); or

   (3)   by personal service upon a person who appears to be in residence at the property (reg 5(1)(c)).

13   Mortgage Repossessions (Protection of Tenants etc) Act 2010 s 2(1), (2)(a). The step that has been prescribed for these purposes is the mortgagee making an application to the court for a warrant for possession of the property: Dwelling Houses (Execution of Possession Orders by Mortgagees) Regulations 2010, SI 2010/1809, reg 2.

14   Mortgage Repossessions (Protection of Tenants etc) Act 2010 s 2(1), (2)(b). The prescribed period for these purposes is 14 days: Dwelling Houses (Execution of Possession Orders by Mortgagees) Regulations 2010, SI 2010/1809, reg 3.

559.   Extension of powers where payment is deferred with provision for earlier payment in certain circumstances. Where by a mortgage[1] of land which consists of or includes a dwelling house[2], or by any agreement between the mortgagee and the mortgagor[3] under such a mortgage, the mortgagor may pay the principal sum secured by instalments or otherwise defer[4] payment in whole or in part, but provision is also made for earlier payment in the event of any default by the mortgagor or of a demand by the mortgagee or otherwise, then for the purposes of its powers to delay giving possession[5] the court may treat as due under the mortgage on account of the principal sum secured and interest on it only such amounts as the mortgagor would have expected to be required to pay if there had been no such provision for earlier payment[6]. The court may not exercise any of its powers unless it appears to it not only that the mortgagor is likely to be able within a reasonable period to pay the amounts he would have expected to be required to pay if there had been no provision for earlier payment, together with interest, but also that he is likely to be able by the end of that period to pay any further amounts that he would have expected to be required to pay by then on account of that sum and the interest on it if there had been no provision for earlier payment[7].

The power to attach conditions with regard to payment by the mortgagor of any sum secured by the mortgage[8] is not confined to the arrears of the instalments due to date or to the future instalments accruing during the reasonable period referred to in the legislation[9]. It extends to 'any' sum secured by the mortgage, including, for example, the totality of the future instalments accruing due throughout the remaining life of the mortgage[10].

Where, pursuant to these provisions, a court could, in proceedings in which the mortgagee only claimed possession of the mortgaged property, treat as due under the mortgage only such amounts as the mortgagor would have expected to pay had there been no provision for earlier payment, and the mortgagee brings proceedings for foreclosure[11] (with or without also claiming possession of the property), the court may exercise its statutory powers as if the mortgagee were only claiming possession of the mortgaged property, except that the court's power to stay or suspend execution of a judgment or order for delivery or to postpone the date for delivery of possession may only be exercised in relation to any claim for possession[12].

1   As to the meaning of 'mortgage' see PARA 557 note 1; definition applied by the Administration of Justice Act 1973 s 8(4).
2   As to the meaning of 'dwelling house' see PARA 557 note 2; definition applied by the Administration of Justice Act 1973 s 8(4).
3   As to the meanings of 'mortgagee' and 'mortgagor' see PARA 557 note 1; definition applied by the Administration of Justice Act 1973 s 8(4).
4   See *Habib Bank Ltd v Tailor* [1982] 3 All ER 561, [1982] 1 WLR 1218, CA, where it was held that the Administration of Justice Act 1973 s 8 presupposes an existing liability to pay which is deferred by the terms of the mortgage or covenant, and accordingly, it was held that s 8 does not apply in a case where demand is a precondition to liability such as on a running account between banker and customer. See also *Rees Investments Ltd v Groves* [2002] 1 P & CR D15. However, the provision applies in the case of a mortgage financed by an endowment policy where there is no obligation to repay the capital until the end of the term (*Bank of Scotland v Grimes* [1985] QB 1179, [1985] 2 All ER 254, CA) and in the case of a mortgage repayable at the end of a fixed period (*Royal Bank of Scotland plc v Miller* [2001] EWCA Civ 344, [2002] QB 255, [2001] 3 WLR 523).
5   Ie the court's powers under the Administration of Justice Act 1970 s 36: see PARA 557. As to exercising suspensory powers see PARA 562.
6   Administration of Justice Act 1973 s 8(1). This statutory provision effectively reversed the decision in *Halifax Building Society v Clark* [1973] Ch 307, [1973] 2 All ER 33. See also *Centrax Trustees Ltd v Ross* [1979] 2 All ER 952.
7   Administration of Justice Act 1973 s 8(2).
8   Ie under the Administration of Justice Act 1970 s 36(3): see PARA 557.
9   Ie the period referred to in the Administration of Justice Act 1970 s 36(1): see PARA 557.
10 *Bank of Scotland plc v Zinda* [2011] EWCA Civ 706, [2011] 2 All ER (Comm) 839, [2012] 1 WLR 728.
11 As to foreclosure see PARA 571 et seq.
12 Administration of Justice Act 1973 s 8(3).

560.   Mortgagor must be likely to be able to pay sums due within a reasonable period. The court may exercise its powers to suspend or adjourn a possession order only where it appears to it that in the event of its exercising them the mortgagor is likely to be able within a reasonable period to pay the sums due under the mortgage[1]. The starting point for assessing what is a reasonable period[2] is the remaining term of the mortgage[3]. It is not proper for the court to make an order for payments which the mortgagor cannot afford and has no foreseeable prospects of being able to afford within a reasonable time, and neither is it proper for the court to make an order for payments which the mortgagor can afford if those will not be enough to pay off the arrears within a reasonable period and also cover the current instalments[4]. Where the mortgagor asserts a cross-claim, the court should consider whether its existence and prospects of success could be regarded as enabling the sums due to be paid within a reasonable time[5]. The court has a discretion as to whether or not to require sworn evidence in deciding upon the debtor's ability to pay off the arrears in a reasonable time[6].

1   See PARA 557.
2   Ie for the purposes of the Administration of Justice Act 1970 s 36: see PARA 557.
3   See *Cheltenham and Gloucester Building Society v Norgan* [1996] 1 All ER 449, [1996] 1 WLR 343, CA (disapproving the former practice of the courts of imposing a shorter period of two or more years). See also *Western Bank Ltd v Schindler* [1977] Ch 1, [1976] 2 All ER 393, CA.
4   *First National Bank v Syed* [1991] 2 All ER 250, [1991] CCLR 37, CA; *Abbey National Mortgages plc v Bernard* (1995) 71 P & CR 257, [1995] NPC 118, CA. See also *Town and Country Building Society v Julien* (1991) 24 HLR 312, CA.
5   *National Westminster Bank plc v Skelton* [1993] 1 All ER 242, [1993] 1 WLR 72n, CA; *Ashley Guarantee plc v Zacaria* [1993] 1 All ER 254, [1993] 1 WLR 62, CA. Cf *Household Mortgage Corpn plc v Pringle* (1997) 30 HLR 250, CA, where the court disregarded a cross-claim for unliquidated damages in considering what sum was due for the purpose of exercising the

statutory discretion to suspend a judgment for possession. As to the rule that the existence of a counterclaim does not affect the mortgagee's right to possession see PARA 407.
6 *Cheltenham and Gloucester Building Society v Grant* (1994) 26 HLR 703, CA. The court is entitled to infer from the mortgagor's poor payment record that he is unlikely to pay: *Abbey National v Mewton* [1995] CLY 3598, CA.

561. Court may suspend order for possession to allow mortgagor to effect a sale. The court may suspend an order for possession[1] where a mortgagor's only prospect of repaying the entire mortgage loan and accrued interest is from a sale of the property[2], if such a sale would be more readily achieved where the dwelling house is occupied rather than repossessed[3]. In such cases the relevant factors will be the extent to which the mortgage debt arrears are secured by the value of the property and the effect of the passing of time on that security[4]. There should be evidence before the court of the likelihood of a proposed sale and the period within which such a sale is likely to be achieved[5]. There is no rule of law to the effect that an order for possession is to be adjourned or suspended only if a sale would take place within a short period of time, and in each case the question of what is a reasonable period is one for the court[6]. The court cannot suspend an order for possession where the proceeds of such a sale would be insufficient to discharge the mortgage debt unless other funds would be available to make up the shortfall[7]. The court also has power to defer possession for a short time to enable the mortgagee to sell the property while allowing the mortgagor to remain in occupation pending completion, although such orders will be rare[8].

1 Ie an order made under the Administration of Justice Act 1970 s 36(2): see PARA 557. See also PARA 559. As to exercising suspensory powers see PARA 562.
2 *Royal Trust Co of Canada v Markham* [1975] 3 All ER 433, [1975] 1 WLR 1416, CA; *Citibank Trust Ltd v Ayivor* [1987] 3 All ER 241, [1987] 1 WLR 1157; *National and Provincial Building Society v Lloyd* [1996] 1 All ER 630, 28 HLR 459, CA. As to the jurisdiction of the court to make an order for sale see the Law of Property Act 1925 s 91(2); and PARA 621 et seq.
3 *Target Home Loans Ltd v Clothier* [1994] 1 All ER 439, (1992) 25 HLR 48, CA.
4 *Bristol and West Building Society v Ellis* (1996) 73 P & CR 158, 29 HLR 282, CA.
5 *National and Provincial Building Society v Lloyd* [1996] 1 All ER 630, 28 HLR 459, CA; *Bristol and West Building Society v Ellis* (1996) 73 P & CR 158, 29 HLR 282, CA; *Cheltenham and Gloucester Building Society v Johnson* (1996) 73 P & CR 293, 28 HLR 885, CA.
6 *National and Provincial Building Society v Lloyd* [1996] 1 All ER 630, 28 HLR 459, CA. See also PARA 560.
7 *Cheltenham and Gloucester plc v Krausz* [1997] 1 All ER 21, [1997] 1 WLR 1558, CA. See also PARA 622.
8 *Cheltenham and Gloucester plc v Booker* (1996) 73 P & CR 412, 29 HLR 634, CA.

562. Power to suspend order for money judgment must be exercised consistently with power to suspend possession order. The discretion to suspend an order for payment on proceedings for money judgment[1] should be exercised consistently with the exercise of discretion to suspend or stay an order or judgment for possession[2], and therefore, if the court suspends an order for possession of the mortgage property it should in the normal course of events also suspend execution of an order for money judgment on the same terms as and in line with the suspension of the possession order[3].

1 Ie under the County Courts Act 1984 s 71(2): see CIVIL PROCEDURE vol 12A (2015) PARA 1272.
2 Ie under the Administration of Justice Act 1970 s 36 (see PARA 557) and the Administration of Justice Act 1973 s 8 (see PARA 559).
3 *Cheltenham and Gloucester Building Society v Grattidge and Grattidge* (1993) 25 HLR 454, CA. There may be instances where special circumstances justify a departure from the usual practice: *Cheltenham and Gloucester Building Society v Johnson* (1997) 73 P & CR 293, 28 HLR 885, CA.

563. The order for possession. There is a prescribed form of order for possession to be used[1], which requires delivery of possession[2] by a specified time and date[3].

There is also a prescribed form for suspended orders for possession of residential mortgaged property[4].

A writ or warrant of possession must not be issued without the permission of the court where:

(1) six years or more have elapsed since the date of the judgment or order;

(2) any change has taken place, whether by death or otherwise, in the parties entitled to enforce the judgment or order, or liable to have it enforced against them[5].

The court's permission is not required for the issue of a writ of possession to enforce a judgment or order for the giving of possession of any land where the judgment or order was given or made in proceedings in which there is a claim for:

(a) payment of moneys secured by the mortgage[6];

(b) sale of the mortgaged property;

(c) foreclosure;

(d) delivery of possession (whether before or after foreclosure or without foreclosure) to the mortgagee by the mortgagor or by any other person who is alleged to be in possession of the property;

(e) redemption;

(f) reconveyance of the land or its release from the security; or

(g) delivery of possession by the mortgagee[7].

Where two or more mortgagors are in occupation an order for possession should not be made against one of them alone: the proceedings against the one mortgagor should be adjourned with permission to restore if the other mortgagor leaves the property or an order for possession is made against that other mortgagor[8].

If the mortgagor unlawfully retakes possession after a writ of possession has been executed, permission is required to issue a writ of restitution[9].

1 See CPR Pt 4; CPR PD 4—*Forms* para 3.1, Table, Form N26. As to forms generally see CIVIL PROCEDURE vol 11 (2015) PARA 20.

2 This means vacant possession: see *Norwich Union Life Insurance Society v Preston* [1957] 2 All ER 428, [1957] 1 WLR 813.

3 See CPR 2.9; and CIVIL PROCEDURE vol 11 (2015) PARA 122. See also *Barclays Bank Ltd v Bird* [1954] Ch 274 at 282, [1954] 1 All ER 449 at 453 per Harman J; *Four-Maids Ltd v Dudley Marshall (Properties) Ltd* [1957] Ch 317, [1957] 2 All ER 35; *London Permanent Benefit Building Society v De Baer* [1969] 1 Ch 321, [1968] 1 All ER 372.

4 See CPR Pt 4; CPR PD 4—*Forms* para 3.1, Table, Form N31.

5 See CPR 83.1(2)(l), 83.2(3); and CIVIL PROCEDURE vol 12A (2015) PARA 1372.

6 For these purposes, 'mortgage' includes a legal or equitable mortgage and a legal or equitable charge, and reference to a mortgagor, a mortgagee and mortgaged land is to be interpreted accordingly: CPR 83.13(7).

7 See CPR 83.13(6); and CIVIL PROCEDURE vol 12A (2015) PARA 1382.

8 *Albany Home Loans v Massey* [1997] 2 All ER 609, 73 P & CR 509, CA.

9 See CPR 83.13(5); and CIVIL PROCEDURE vol 12A (2015) PARA 1382. For the prescribed form see CPR PD 4—*Forms* para 3.1, Table, Form N68.

564. Mortgagee's rights and responsibilities in relation to chattels. The mortgagor is subject to an obligation to deliver up vacant possession of the property on the execution of a warrant for possession[1]. A mortgagee who finds himself in possession of chattels on the execution of a warrant for possession is in law an involuntary bailee[2]. The duty of an involuntary bailee is to do what is right and reasonable[3], and what is right and reasonable depends upon the findings of fact in each case. The relevant conditions of the mortgage provide a framework within which the common law duty of care, which is imposed on an involuntary bailee, is to operate. Further, any of the trigger events in the mortgage conditions is merely a starting point. The court has to go on and ask whether what the mortgagee did was, in the particular circumstances of the case, right and reasonable[4].

1   As to warrants of possession see PARA 563; and CIVIL PROCEDURE vol 12A (2015) PARAS 1327 et seq, 1392.
2   See BAILMENT AND PLEDGE vol 4 (2011) PARA 111 et seq.
3   As to the obligations of a bailee see BAILMENT AND PLEDGE vol 4 (2011) PARAS 121–125.
4   *Da Rocha-Afodu v Mortgage Express Ltd* [2014] EWCA Civ 454, [2014] 2 P & CR D25, [2014] All ER (D) 212 (Mar); applied in *Campbell v Redstone Mortgages Ltd* [2014] EWHC 3081 (Ch), [2015] 1 P & CR D49, [2014] All ER (D) 193 (Oct).

(6) APPOINTMENT OF RECEIVER BY THE COURT

565. Object of receiver's appointment. Where there has been a breach of the mortgagor's obligations, or where, without such actual breach, the security is in jeopardy[1], the mortgagee may obtain an order for the appointment of a receiver by the court, provided the circumstances render it just and convenient[2]. However, because mortgagees already have statutory powers to appoint a receiver[3], it is not usually necessary for a mortgagee to apply to the court for such an order[4].

It is sufficient that interest is in arrear[5] even though principal is not yet payable[6]. In the case of a floating security where the breach relied on is non-payment of principal, it is sufficient if it is due before the application, even if it was not due when the claim form was issued[7]. The appointment is made with a view to preserving the property if it is in danger or, by intercepting the income, to provide a fund for payment of the mortgage; and it is made either as a step in proceedings brought to enforce the security, or in proceedings having the appointment of a receiver as the sole object[8]. A receiver will not be appointed to sell a business carried on at the mortgaged property, but not included in the mortgage[9].

1   *Re Victoria Steamboats Ltd, Smith v Wilkinson* [1897] 1 Ch 158; *Edwards v Standard Rolling Stock Syndicate* [1893] 1 Ch 574; *Re London Pressed Hinge Co Ltd, Campbell v London Pressed Hinge Co Ltd* [1905] 1 Ch 576. See also *Higginson v German Athenaeum Ltd* (1916) 32 TLR 277, where the property was in effect derelict. As to the mortgagor's rights and liabilities see PARA 339 et seq.
2   See the Senior Courts Act 1981 s 37(1); the County Courts Act 1984 s 38(1); CPR Pt 69; and RECEIVERS vol 88 (2012) PARAS 13, 15. See also *Re Prytherch, Prytherch v Williams* (1889) 42 ChD 590. As to the appointment of receivers by the court see RECEIVERS vol 88 (2012) PARA 9 et seq. As to the appointment of receivers of the assets of companies see COMPANIES vol 15 (2009) PARA 1340.
3   Ie under the Law of Property Act 1925 ss 101(1)(iii), 109: see PARA 479.
4   See eg *Bank of Credit and Commerce International SA v BRS Kumar Bros Ltd* [1994] 1 BCLC 211.
5   *Strong v Carlyle Press* [1893] 1 Ch 268, CA.
6   *Burrowes v Molloy* (1845) 2 Jo & Lat 521; *Bissill v Bradford Tramways Co* [1891] WN 51.
7   *Re Carshalton Park Estate Ltd, Graham v Carshalton Park Estate Ltd, Turnell v Carshalton Park Estate Ltd* [1908] 2 Ch 62.
8   As to the circumstances in which a receiver will be appointed, the stage of the proceedings at which the application may be made, and generally as to receivers appointed by the court and their duties and liabilities see RECEIVERS vol 88 (2012) PARA 1 et seq. As to the appointment of receivers on behalf of mortgagees and debenture stockholders of companies established for public purposes see COMPANIES vol 15 (2009) PARA 1333 et seq. On its true construction, a security may give the creditor only the right to have a receiver appointed: see *Taylor v Emerson* (1843) 6 I Eq R 224.
9   *Britannia Building Society v Crammer* [1997] BPIR 596.

566. Who applies to the court for the appointment of receiver. It is the practice of the court to appoint a receiver on the application of a legal as well as of an equitable mortgagee[1]. Where proceedings are pending, an appointment by the court is the proper procedure, notwithstanding that the mortgagee has power to appoint a receiver himself[2]. The appointment will not be made after judgment for foreclosure absolute[3].

1   *Pease v Fletcher* (1875) 1 ChD 273; *Truman & Co v Redgrave* (1881) 18 ChD 547; *Tillett v Nixon* (1883) 25 ChD 238; *Duke of Grafton v Taylor, Earl Manvers v Taylor* (1891) 7 TLR 588. See also *Re Pope* (1886) 17 QBD 743 at 749, CA; *Re Whiteley, Whiteley v Learoyd* (1887) 56 LT 846 at 847. Cf *Anglo-Italian Bank v Davies* (1878) 9 ChD 275 at 286, CA. The practice is certainly applicable where the mortgage includes both legal estates and equitable interests: *Pease v Fletcher* above. As to legal mortgages see PARAS 104, 160 et seq. As to equitable mortgages see PARAS 105, 215 et seq.
2   *Tillett v Nixon* (1883) 25 ChD 238. See also *Bord v Tollemache* (1862) 1 New Rep 177. A receiver already appointed is not displaced by the commencement of foreclosure proceedings (as to which see PARA 571 et seq).
3   *Wills v Luff* (1888) 38 ChD 197 (on the ground that the proceedings are at an end, although a conveyance of the property has still to be settled). As to foreclosure absolute see PARA 608 et seq.

567. Registration of appointment of receiver. An order for the appointment of a receiver is registrable as a land charge in the case of unregistered land[1], and is capable of being protected by a restriction in the case of registered land[2].

In the case of an order for the appointment of a receiver or manager of company property, the person obtaining the order must give notice to the registrar of companies so that he can register that fact on the register of charges[3].

1   See the Land Charges Act 1972 s 6(1)(b); and REAL PROPERTY AND REGISTRATION vol 87 (2012) PARA 746. See also *Clayhope Properties Ltd v Evans* [1986] 2 All ER 795, [1986] 1 WLR 1223, CA.
2   See the Land Registration Act 2002 ss 42, 43; and REAL PROPERTY AND REGISTRATION vol 87 (2012) PARAS 525–526.
3   As to the registration of company charges see the Companies Act 2006 Pt A1 (ss 859A–859Q); and COMPANIES.

568. Functions of receiver; appointment of receiver and manager. A receiver's functions are limited to receipt of income and payment of ascertained outgoings[1]. He has no general powers of management[2], but where the mortgage, expressly or by implication, includes a business[3], a receiver and manager may be appointed[4]. It seems that if the business is not included in the security the court has no jurisdiction to appoint a manager[5]. An appointment of a manager may be made even if this is with a view to the sale of the business as a going concern[6]. Consequently, if the security is a public undertaking which the receiver has no power to sell, a manager will not be appointed[7]. A receiver and manager will, if necessary, be appointed of land[8].

1   See RECEIVERS vol 88 (2012) PARA 99 et seq.
2   *Re Manchester and Milford Rly Co, ex p Cambrian Rly Co* (1880) 14 ChD 645 at 653, CA.
3   See *Truman & Co v Redgrave* (1881) 18 ChD 547 (mortgage to brewers of licensed premises, together with the trade fixtures, goodwill and licences); *Taylor v Soper* (1890) 62 LT 828 (where the brewers' mortgage was in similar terms); *Re Victoria Steamboats Ltd, Smith v Wilkinson* [1897] 1 Ch 158 (debenture of a trading company charging its undertaking and all its property). See also *Chaplin v Young* (1862) 6 LT 97 (mortgage of a newspaper); *Peek v Trinsmaran Iron Co* (1876) 2 ChD 115 (debentures charging real and personal estate, assets, plant, machinery and effects of mining company); *Makins v Percy Ibotson & Sons* [1891] 1 Ch 133 (debentures of trading company charging all property including uncalled capital); *Campbell v Lloyd's, Barnett's and Bosanquet's Bank Ltd* [1891] 1 Ch 136n (mortgage of freehold and leasehold collieries but not, in terms, of colliery business); *Edwards v Standard Rolling Stock Syndicate* [1893] 1 Ch 574 (mortgage of whole of company's undertaking); *County of Gloucester Bank v Rudry Merthyr Steam and House Coal Colliery Co* [1895] 1 Ch 629, CA (mortgage of land, mines, beds, and seams of coal, and all buildings and erections, fixed motive power, plant etc); *Fairfield Shipbuilding and Engineering Co Ltd v London and East Coast Express Steamship Co Ltd* [1895] WN 64 (statutory mortgage of a ship); *Re A Boynton Ltd, Hoffmann v A Boynton Ltd* [1910] 1

Ch 519 at 520 (debenture charging all the property and assets of an hotel company); *Re Leas Hotel Co, Salter v Leas Hotel Co* [1902] 1 Ch 332 (debenture charging all the buildings, property, stock-in-trade, furniture, chattels and effects of a hotel company).

4   *County of Gloucester Bank v Rudry Merthyr Steam and House Coal Colliery Co* [1895] 1 Ch 629, CA. See also PARA 172. See further RECEIVERS vol 88 (2012) PARA 184 et seq.

5   *Whitley v Challis* [1892] 1 Ch 64, CA; *Re Victoria Steamboats Ltd, Smith v Wilkinson* [1897] 1 Ch 158; *Re Leas Hotel Co, Salter v Leas Hotel Co* [1902] 1 Ch 332. See also *Waters v Taylor* (1808) 15 Ves 10, where the appointment of a manager was refused partly on the ground that the plaintiff in his capacity as mortgagee was suing for foreclosure only, and not for sale. As to foreclosure see PARA 571 et seq.

6   *Gardner v London, Chatham and Dover Rly Co (No 1), Drawbridge v London, Chatham and Dover Rly Co, Gardner v London, Chatham and Dover Rly Co (No 2), Imperial Mercantile Credit Association v London, Chatham and Dover Rly Co* (1867) 2 Ch App 201 at 212; *Whitley v Challis* [1892] 1 Ch 64 at 69–70, CA; *Securities and Properties Corpn Ltd v Brighton Alhambra Ltd* (1893) 62 LJCh 566; *Re Victoria Steamboats Ltd, Smith v Wilkinson* [1897] 1 Ch 158 at 162; *Re Newdigate Colliery Ltd, Newdigate v Newdigate Colliery Ltd* [1912] 1 Ch 468 at 472, CA. See also PARA 426.

7   *Marshall v South Staffordshire Tramways Co* [1895] 2 Ch 36, CA.

8   *Duke of Grafton v Taylor, Earl Manvers v Taylor* (1891) 7 TLR 588. It has been said not to be the practice of the courts in appointing receivers and managers of mortgaged hereditaments to make any order for delivery of possession of the land, as distinct from the possession of stock-in-trade and effects; the ground of this practice was stated to be that possession of mortgaged premises would not be ordered in a mortgage action until after foreclosure absolute: *National Provincial Bank of England Ltd v United Electric Theatres Ltd* (1916) as reported in 85 LJCh 106 at 113. See, however, the cases cited in PARA 570 note 3. As to foreclosure absolute see PARA 608 et seq.

569.   Appointment of receiver on behalf of subsequent mortgagee or persons equitably interested. The appointment of a receiver at the instance of a subsequent incumbrancer is without prejudice to the rights of prior incumbrancers[1]. Therefore, if a prior mortgagee whose existence is known is not in possession, the appointment is made subject to his right to take possession[2], and, accordingly, the first mortgagee can take possession without the permission of the court[3], although formerly it was considered that permission was required[4], and application for permission was usually made[5]. Permission is, however, necessary where there has been no express reservation of the mortgagee's rights in the order[6]. If a prior mortgagee is in possession, an appointment of a receiver at the instance of a subsequent incumbrancer will not be made so long as anything remains due to the prior mortgagee, unless he refuses to accept a tender of what he alleges to be due[7]. To avoid the appointment being made he must claim that something is due, though he need not claim a specific sum[8]. If the prior mortgagee's accounts are in such a state that he cannot claim that anything is due, a receiver will be appointed[9]. If a receiver has been appointed in the absence of a prior incumbrancer, he will be discharged and the prior incumbrancer, although only equitable, let into possession[10]; and where other incumbrances are known to exist, the appointment may be accompanied by an inquiry as to the priorities of the several incumbrancers[11]. A receiver will be appointed against the owner of the legal estate who refuses to satisfy equitable interests[12], or if there is a strong prima facie case for setting the conveyance to him aside[13]; but not otherwise, unless the rents and profits are in danger[14].

1   *Davis v Duke of Marlborough* (1819) 2 Swan 108 at 137, 165; *Berney v Sewell* (1820) 1 Jac & W 647.

2   *Bryan v Cormick* (1788) 1 Cox Eq Cas 422; *Dalmer v Dashwood* (1793) 2 Cox Eq Cas 378 at 383; *Davis v Duke of Marlborough* (1819) 2 Swan 108; *Berney v Sewell* (1820) 1 Jac & W 647; *Tanfield v Irvine* (1826) 2 Russ 149 at 151; *Liverpool Marine Credit Co v Wilson* (1872) 7 Ch App 507 at 511, CA; *Cadogan v Lyric Theatre Ltd* [1894] 3 Ch 338, CA. As to the mortgagee's right to possession see PARA 404 et seq.

3 *Underhay v Read* (1887) 20 QBD 209 at 219, CA; *Engel v South Metropolitan Brewing and Bottling Co* [1891] WN 31. See also PARA 411.
4 See *Davis v Duke of Marlborough* (1819) 2 Swan 108 at 138n.
5 *Preston v Tunbridge Wells Opera House Ltd* [1903] 2 Ch 323; *Re Metropolitan Amalgamated Estates Ltd, Fairweather v Metropolitan Amalgamated Estates Ltd* [1912] 2 Ch 497, 502.
6 *Re Henry Pound, Son and Hutchins* (1889) 42 ChD 402 at 422, CA.
7 *Berney v Sewell* (1820) 1 Jac & W 647.
8 *Chambers v Goldwin* (1804) 9 Ves 254; *Quarrell v Beckford* (1807) 13 Ves 377 at 378; *Rowe v Wood* (1822) 2 Jac & W 553 at 557.
9 *Codrington v Parker* (1810) 16 Ves 469; *Hiles v Moore* (1852) 15 Beav 175.
10 *Langton v Langton* (1855) 7 De GM & G 30. A first mortgagee is entitled to back rents paid to a receiver after service of notice of motion for his discharge: *Preston v Tunbridge Wells Opera House Ltd* [1903] 2 Ch 323.
11 *Davis v Duke of Marlborough* (1819) 2 Swan 108 at 138; *Metcalfe v Archbishop of York* (1835) 6 Sim 224 (affd (1836) 1 My & Cr 547); *Hiles v Moore* (1852) 15 Beav 175 at 179. As to the priority of mortgages see PARA 260 et seq.
12 *Pritchard v Fleetwood* (1815) 1 Mer 54. See also RECEIVERS vol 88 (2012) PARA 41.
13 *Hugonin v Baseley* (1806) 13 Ves 105; *Stilwell v Wilkins* (1821) Jac 280; *George v Evans* (1840) 4 Y & C Ex 211. Fraud must be clearly proved: see *Lloyd v Passingham* (1809) 16 Ves 59 at 70.
14 *Lancashire v Lancashire* (1845) 9 Beav 120 at 129.

570. Position of tenants or mortgagor in possession on appointment of receiver. On a receiver of real or leasehold property being appointed, the tenants are directed to attorn and pay their rents in arrear and becoming due to him[1]. If it does not appear in what right possession is held, application should be made that the person in possession should attorn, and then he must explain his possession to the court[2]. If the mortgagor is in possession, prima facie the mortgagee is entitled to an order that the mortgagor deliver up possession of the premises to the receiver[3], but the matter is within the discretion of the court, which may give the mortgagor an opportunity to attorn tenant to the mortgagee[4]. If the mortgagor is ordered to attorn, the liability to pay rent commences from the date of the order[5]. If there is no order for the mortgagor in occupation to give up possession or to attorn, he must pay rent from the date of demand by the receiver[6].

1 *Davis v Duke of Marlborough* (1819) 2 Swan 108 at 116; *Hawkes v Holland* [1881] WN 128, CA. See also RECEIVERS vol 88 (2012) PARA 75 et seq.
2 *Reid v Middleton* (1823) Turn & R 455. Cf *Randfield v Randfield* (1859) 7 WR 651.
3 *Pratchett v Drew* [1924] 1 Ch 280, following *Hawkes v Holland* [1881] WN 128, CA, and *Edgell v Wilson* [1893] WN 145, and distinguishing as due to special circumstances *Taylor v Soper* (1890) 62 LT 828 (where it was held that an order for possession could not be granted until judgment in foreclosure proceedings). As to foreclosure see PARA 571 et seq.
4 *Pratchett v Drew* [1924] 1 Ch 280 at 286. See also *Re Burchnall, Walker v Lacey* (1893) 38 Sol Jo 59.
5 *Lloyd v Mason* (1837) 2 My & Cr 487; *Re Burchnall, Walker v Lacey* (1893) 38 Sol Jo 59.
6 *Yorkshire Banking Co v Mullan* (1887) 35 ChD 125.

(7) FORECLOSURE

(i) Nature of Right to Foreclose

571. Effect of foreclosure order on legal mortgage. Under a legal mortgage by demise[1] the mortgagee becomes absolute owner of the mortgage term at law as soon as the day fixed for redemption is past, and the equity of redemption arises by virtue of the interference of equity to allow the mortgagor to redeem, notwithstanding that his legal right of redemption is gone[2]. The effect is the same in the case of a legal mortgage created by way of legal charge for, although there is no mortgage term, the mortgagee's rights are enforced in the same way as if a mortgage term had been created, and the legal right to redeem and so to terminate the legal charge lasts until the day fixed for payment[3]. By foreclosure a mortgagee may make his ownership effectual, for, on his bringing proceedings for foreclosure, a further day is appointed for payment, and if the money is not then paid the court leaves the parties to their legal rights[4].

There is no foreclosure, however, against the Crown[5]; the established practice is to direct a sale and rely on the Crown conveying[6]. Where it appears that the Crown has no interest, the Attorney General is dismissed from the proceedings[7].

By permitting foreclosure, the court removes the stop it has itself put on[8]; the property belongs to the mortgagee absolutely[9], not only for the mortgage term, but also for the mortgagor's whole interest so that, if he has the fee simple, the order absolute operates to vest the fee simple in the mortgagee and the mortgage term is merged in the fee simple; the vesting in the mortgagee is subject to any prior legal mortgage, but any subsequent legal mortgage is extinguished[10]. In the case of a legal leasehold mortgage, the nominal reversion vests in the mortgagee, and the mortgage sub-term is merged[11].

1 See PARA 164.
2 As to the equity of redemption see PARAS 107, 304 et seq.
3 See PARAS 165, 195.
4 *Sampson v Pattison* (1842) 1 Hare 533 at 536. As to foreclosure under a building society mortgage see FINANCIAL INSTITUTIONS vol 48 (2015) PARA 505. As to land abroad see CONFLICT OF LAWS vol 19 (2011) PARA 692 et seq; EQUITABLE JURISDICTION vol 47 (2014) PARA 103.
5 Formerly the order was that the mortgagee should hold and enjoy the mortgaged property until the Crown thought fit to redeem: *Lutwich's Case* (circa 1729), cited in 2 Atk at 223; *Hodge v A-G* (1839) 3 Y & C Ex 342. A sale might be ordered if the Crown had only an equitable interest, but not where the legal estate was vested in the Crown, as the court could not compel the Crown to convey: *Hodge v A-G* above.
6 *Hancock v A-G* (1864) 10 Jur NS 557; *Bartlett v Rees* (1871) LR 12 Eq 395. See also *Rogers v Maule* (1841) 1 Y & C Ch Cas 4; *Scott v Robarts* (1856) 4 WR 499. Cf *Prescott v Tyler* (1837) 1 Jur 470; *Prescott v Tyler* (1838) 2 Jur 870, where the Crown had no legal estate, and declined either to claim or disclaim.
7 *Prescott v Tyler* (1837) 1 Jur 470.
8 *Carter v Wake* (1877) 4 ChD 605.
9 *Silberschildt v Schiott* (1814) 3 Ves & B 45 at 49; *Le Gros v Cockerell* (1832) 5 Sim 384 at 389.
10 Law of Property Act 1925 s 88(2). Formerly, the effect of the order for foreclosure was, when the mortgagee took a legal fee simple estate, to vest a new title in the mortgagee. Previously he had been, in the view of equity, a mere incumbrancer. Under the order the beneficial ownership for the first time vested in him, and this principle seems to be applicable also to the change in the mortgagee's title from the holding of a term as an incumbrance to the beneficial ownership of the fee simple: see *Heath v Pugh* (1881) 6 QBD 345 at 360, CA, per Lord Selborne LC. As to the statutory effect of a foreclosure order see PARA 612. As to the mortgagee's liability in respect of leaseholds see PARA 365; and cf *Re Loom, Fulford v Reversionary Interest Society Ltd* [1910] 2 Ch 230.
11 See the Law of Property Act 1925 s 89(2); and PARA 612. As to the application of this provision to leaseholds where the mortgage affects only part of the land comprised in the lease see PARA 451.

572. Loss of right to foreclose. The right to bring proceedings for foreclosure may be lost by effluxion of time. The periods of limitation applicable to foreclosure claims in respect of land or personalty and the length of the areas of interest recoverable in foreclosure claims are considered elsewhere[1].

1 See PARA 519.

573. Foreclosure of equitable mortgage. The right of foreclosure exists in the case of an equitable mortgagee[1] who has taken an agreement for a legal mortgage[2] whether the charge relates to land[3] or to personal estate[4]. The judgment in such a case is prefaced by a declaration of charge and, in order to complete the mortgagee's title, it directs a conveyance to him of the legal estate[5] or, if necessary in the case of a chose or thing in action, the execution by the mortgagor of a power of attorney[6]. The remedy of foreclosure is available in respect of policies of insurance[7], stocks and shares[8], debentures charging uncalled capital[9] and pensions[10], reversionary as well as present interests[11], and a partnership share[12].

1   As to foreclosure or sale by a trustee under a charge in his own favour see *Darke v Williamson* (1858) 25 Beav 622. Cf *Tennant v Trenchard* (1869) 4 Ch App 537.
2   *Perry v Keane, Perry v Partridge* (1836) 6 LJCh 67; *Cox v Toole* (1855) 20 Beav 145. As to equitable mortgages see PARAS 105, 215 et seq. As to the effect of dismissal of a claim for redemption see PARA 675.
3   See *Tylee v Webb* (1843) 6 Beav 552; *Pryce v Bury* (1854) LR 16 Eq 153n; *James v James* (1873) LR 16 Eq 153; *Re Owen* [1894] 3 Ch 220 at 227.
4   See *London and Midland Bank v Mitchell* [1899] 2 Ch 161; *Harrold v Plenty* [1901] 2 Ch 314 (cases of the deposit of share certificates); *Re Kerr's Policy* (1869) LR 8 Eq 331 at 336 (policy of insurance). In this respect the position of a mortgagee by deposit of share certificates differs from that of a mere pledgee of chattels who has no right of foreclosure: see eg *Harrold v Plenty* above at 316; *Stubbs v Slater* [1910] 1 Ch 632 at 639, CA. In *Carter v Wake* (1877) 4 ChD 605 (approved in *Gilligan and Nugent v National Bank Ltd* [1901] 2 IR 513 at 538), a person with whom bearer bonds were deposited by way of security was held to be a mere pledgee and therefore not entitled to foreclosure, but it seems doubtful whether this decision can be considered to be of authority in so far as it decides that deposited bearer securities are the subject of pledge and not of mortgage in view of the comments in *Sadler v Worley* [1894] 2 Ch 170 at 175; *Harrold v Plenty* above at 316; and *Stubbs v Slater* above at 639. As to the distinction between a mortgage and a pledge see PARA 112.
5   *Marshall v Shrewsbury* (1875) 10 Ch App 250 at 254.
6   *James v Ellis* (1871) 19 WR 319 (power of attorney to receive pension). See also CHOSES IN ACTION vol 13 (2009) PARA 76. As to powers of attorney see AGENCY vol 1 (2008) PARA 31 et seq.
7   See note 4.
8   *Booking v Rendell* (1852) 3 Seton's Form of Decrees, Judgments and Orders in Equity (7th Edn, 1912) 1923; *General Credit and Discount Co v Glegg* (1883) 22 ChD 549 at 553–554. See also note 4.
9   See *Sadler v Worley* [1894] 2 Ch 170. See also COMPANIES vol 15 (2009) PARA 1379.
10 *James v Ellis* (1871) 19 WR 319.
11 *Slade v Rigg* (1843) 3 Hare 35; *Wayne v Hanham* (1851) 9 Hare 62. The terms of the mortgage may, however, show that the mortgagee is entitled to neither foreclosure nor sale, but only to repayment out of the fund when it falls into possession: *Stamford, Spalding and Boston Banking Co v Ball* (1862) 4 De GF & J 310.
12 *Redmayne v Forster* (1866) LR 2 Eq 467. See also PARTNERSHIP vol 79 (2014) PARA 125.

(ii) Where Sale is Appropriate Remedy

574. Where foreclosure is not available. Where there is a mere charge without an agreement for a legal mortgage[1], or a charging order[2] or where the circumstances give rise to an equitable lien, such as a vendor's lien[3], the remedy is by sale[4] and foreclosure is not possible.

1   *Tennant v Trenchard* (1869) 4 Ch App 537 at 542; *Re Owen* [1894] 3 Ch 220 at 227; *Shea v Moore* [1894] 1 IR 158, CA. See also PARA 106. Foreclosure was, however, treated as the remedy for the charge in *Hugill v Wilkinson* (1888) 38 ChD 480, perhaps because the security was more than a mere charge and operated as an equitable conveyance.
2   As to the nature and effect of a charging order see CIVIL PROCEDURE vol 12A (2015) PARA 1462 et seq.
3   *Neate v Duke of Marlborough* (1838) 3 My & Cr 407 at 417; *Munns v Isle of Wight Rly Co* (1870) 5 Ch App 414; *Marshall v South Staffordshire Tramways Co* [1895] 2 Ch 36 at 50, CA. The lien must, however, first be judicially declared: see LIEN vol 68 (2008) PARA 880.
4   As to orders for sale see PARA 621 et seq.

575. Statutory jurisdiction to order sale in foreclosure proceedings. In proceedings for foreclosure, the court may direct a sale[1] of the mortgaged property on the request of the mortgagee or of any person interested either in the mortgage money or in the right of redemption, notwithstanding the dissent of any other person, and notwithstanding that the mortgagee or any person so interested does not appear in the proceedings[2].

1   As to orders for sale see PARA 621 et seq.
2   See the Law of Property Act 1925 s 91(2); and PARA 621.

576. When sale may be directed. A sale may be directed at any time before the foreclosure has become absolute[1]. Where an application to enlarge the time for payment is pending, the sale may be enforced on application for foreclosure absolute[2]. Similarly, an order for foreclosure absolute may be made after an order for sale[3]. The only condition is that request must be made by one of the persons specified. This gives rise to the court's discretionary power, and accordingly the order may be made on an interim application[4]. If, however, the claim requests foreclosure only and the mortgagor does not appear, an order for sale will not be made unless he has had notice[5].

1   *Union Bank of London v Ingram* (1882) 20 ChD 463, CA. As to the foreclosure order absolute see PARA 608 et seq. The authorities referred to in this paragraph must be read in the light of the Civil Procedure Rules: see CIVIL PROCEDURE vol 11 (2015) PARA 6 et seq.
2   *Weston v Davidson* [1882] WN 28.
3   *Lloyds Bank Ltd v Colston* [1912] WN 26. As to orders for sale see PARA 621 et seq.
4   *Woolley v Colman* (1882) 21 ChD 169. Cf *London and County Banking Co v Dover* (1879) 11 ChD 204. As to interim applications see CPR Pt 25; and CIVIL PROCEDURE vol 12 (2015) PARA 566 et seq.
5   *South Western District Bank v Turner* (1882) 31 WR 113.

577. When sale is directed. A sale is generally directed where the property is worth more than the amount secured by the mortgage, to enable a mortgagor who cannot raise the sum required to redeem to get the benefit of the surplus[1]. It may also be directed to avoid the delay and expense which is occasioned by foreclosure and redemption in a case where there are a great number of successive mortgages[2]. An order for sale will not be made in the absence of any evidence as to the value[3], nor against the claimant's wish if the property is situated in several places and cannot be advantageously sold in one lot[4], nor where the order would necessarily include property not subject to the mortgage[5]. An order for sale will be refused if the security is deficient and the mortgagor's application is based only on a possible rise in value[6], or where the value of the property is reduced because the mortgagee is an assured tenant of the property[7] with a right to retain possession after any sale[8]. A sale is likely to be refused where the principal motivation of the mortgagor is to avoid eviction rather than to achieve any financial benefit for themselves[9]. A sale may, however, be ordered on the terms of the subsequent mortgagee or the mortgagor requesting a sale paying a sum into court to guarantee the claimant against loss[10].

1   *Palk v Mortgage Services Funding plc* [1993] Ch 330, [1993] 2 All ER 481, CA. As to orders for sale see PARA 621 et seq.
2   *Palk v Mortgage Services Funding plc* [1993] Ch 330, [1993] 2 All ER 481, CA.
3   *Smithett v Hesketh* (1890) 44 ChD 161 at 163.
4   *Provident Clerks' Mutual etc Association v Lewis* (1892) 62 LJCh 89.
5   *Gibbs v Haydon* (1882) 30 WR 726.
6   *Hurst v Hurst* (1852) 16 Beav 372 at 375; *Merchant Banking Co of London v London and Hanseatic Bank* (1886) 55 LJCh 479; *Palk v Mortgage Services Funding plc* [1993] Ch 330, [1993] 2 All ER 481, CA. As to ordering foreclosure in lieu of sale, where, owing to the value of the property, it would be a useless expense to direct a sale see *Lloyds Bank Ltd v Colston* [1912] WN 26.
7   Ie under the Housing Act 1988 Pt I (ss 1–45): see LANDLORD AND TENANT vol 63 (2012) PARA 1098 et seq. This also applies to statutory tenants under the Rent Act 1977: see LANDLORD AND TENANT vol 63 (2012) PARA 944 et seq.

8   *Silsby v Holliman* [1955] Ch 552, [1955] 2 All ER 373. See LANDLORD AND TENANT vol 63 (2012) PARAS 953 et seq, 1150 et seq.
9   *Toor v State Bank of India* [2010] EWHC 1097 (Ch).
10 *Norman v Beaumont* [1893] WN 45; *Cripps v Wood* (1882) 51 LJCh 584.

(iii) When Right to Foreclose Arises

578. Time when right to foreclose arises depends on proviso for redemption. So long as the mortgagor has a legal right of redemption there can be no foreclosure; but when the time for repayment of the loan is past, the right to commence foreclosure proceedings arises unless the mortgagee has by special stipulation postponed the right[1]. Consequently, the time when the right arises depends on the form of the proviso for redemption, if any[2]. If a day is fixed for redemption, the right arises on default in payment on that day; if the proviso is for redemption on payment of the principal on demand, the right arises after demand and a reasonable time to comply with it[3].

1   See *Bonham v Newcomb* (1689) 1 Vern 233n, HL (proviso for redemption at any time during the mortgagor's life). The right of foreclosure is not affected by the mortgagee's statutory power of sale: see the Law of Property Act 1925 s 106(2); and PARA 446 et seq. As to the equity of redemption see PARAS 107, 304 et seq.
2   See PARA 195. Where there is no express proviso, it is a question of construction whether a breach of covenant by the mortgagor is such as to debar him at law from recovering his property: see *Twentieth Century Banking Corpn Ltd v Wilkinson* [1977] Ch 99, [1976] 3 All ER 361.
3   See *Balfe v Lord* (1842) 2 Dr & War 480. See also PARA 195.

579. Effect where proviso for redemption conditional on payment of interest. The proviso for redemption usually refers to the covenant for payment and makes the right of redemption depend on payment of principal and interest in accordance with that covenant[1]. Where it does not do so, the proviso is independent of the covenant, and, if there is a proviso for redemption on payment of the principal at a distant date with interest in the meantime, there can be no foreclosure before the day fixed, notwithstanding that there is a covenant for periodical payment of interest and that the mortgagor is in default as to a payment[2]. The question is, it seems, one of construction of the mortgage[3], and if the proviso for redemption is conditional on payment of intermediate interest, where, for instance, it is a proviso for redemption on payment of principal on a fixed day with interest half-yearly in the meantime, or on payment of principal and interest in accordance with the covenant, the right to foreclose arises upon default in payment of interest[4].

1   As to the covenant for repayment see PARA 182. As to the equity of redemption see PARAS 107, 304 et seq.
2   *Re Turner, Turner v Spencer* (1894) 43 WR 153; *Williams v Morgan* [1906] 1 Ch 804; and see PARA 181 et seq.
3   See *Mohamedali Jaffer Karachiwalla v Noorally Rattanshi Rajan Nanji* [1959] AC 518, [1959] 1 All ER 137, PC (distinguishing *Williams v Morgan* [1906] 1 Ch 804).
4   *Burrowes v Molloy* (1845) 2 Jo & Lat 521 at 526; *Edwards v Martin* (1856) 25 LJCh 284. See also *Gladwyn v Hitchman* (1690) 2 Vern 135; *Kidderminster Mutual Benefit Building Society v Haddock* [1936] WN 158.

580. Loan for a term conditional on payment of interim interest. Instead of fixing a distant date for redemption, it is usual, when the loan is to continue for a term certain, to fix the usual period of six months, and then to provide that the money is not to be called in or steps to be taken to enforce the mortgage for the agreed term or until after a specified notice has been given[1]. The benefit of such a provision is, however, lost if the mortgagor gives charges for further advances without the provision, and agrees that the further charges are not to be redeemed except on payment of all the advances[2]. Moreover, such a provision is made conditional on payment of interest and observance of the mortgagor's covenants, and the right of foreclosure arises on default in such payment or observance[3]. The default is not waived merely by subsequent acceptance of interest[4], but may be waived otherwise[5]. In the absence of such a condition, however, default in payment of interest does not accelerate the time for foreclosure[6].

1 See PARA 183. As to the equity of redemption see PARAS 107, 304 et seq.
2 *Haywood v Gregg* (1875) 24 WR 157.
3 *Stanhope v Manners* (1763) 2 Eden 197; *Seaton v Twyford* (1870) LR 11 Eq 591. As to non-payment of premiums in a mortgage of a policy of insurance see *Sapio v Hackney* (1907) 51 Sol Jo 428.
4 *Keene v Biscoe* (1878) 8 ChD 201. See also *Stanhope v Manners* (1763) 2 Eden 197; and PARA 188.
5 *Re Taaffe's Estate* (1864) 14 I Ch R 347. See also *Langridge v Payne* (1862) 2 John & H 423; *Seal v Gimson* (1914) 110 LT 583 (where receipt of interest was treated as one of the facts relevant to determining whether the mortgagee had exercised his right to call in the money before the stipulated period for breach of covenant).
6 *Burrowes v Molloy* (1845) 2 Jo & Lat 521.

581. Equitable mortgages and charges. Where there is no actual mortgage, but only an agreement to execute a mortgage[1], the right of foreclosure arises on non-payment of the money at the time agreed upon, or, if no time is agreed upon, then on non-payment within a reasonable time after demand[2].

1 See PARA 215 et seq.
2 See *Fitzgerald's Trustee v Mellersh* [1892] 1 Ch 385 at 390; cf as to sale *France v Clark* (1883) 22 ChD 830 (affd (1884) 26 ChD 257, CA); *Deverges v Sandeman, Clark & Co* [1902] 1 Ch 579, CA. See also *Jones v Woodward* (1917) 116 LT 378; *London County and Westminster Bank Ltd v Tompkins* [1918] 1 KB 515, CA.

(iv) Who may Institute Foreclosure Proceedings

582. Mortgagee or his assignee instituting foreclosure proceedings. The mortgagee may institute foreclosure proceedings so long as he remains entitled to the mortgage. After the mortgagee has assigned the mortgage security, the assignee is entitled to bring the proceedings[1], but he is subject to the state of the accounts between the mortgagor and the mortgagee at the date of the transfer, and also to any equities then existing in the mortgagor's favour[2]. A subsequent mortgagee can sue to foreclose the mortgagor and incumbrancers subsequent to himself[3].

1 *Platt v Mendel* (1884) 27 ChD 246 at 247. As to the effect of an assignment of the debt apart from the security see PARA 367.
2 See *Withington v Tate* (1869) 4 Ch App 288; *Turner v Smith* [1901] 1 Ch 213. See also PARA 382.
3 *Rose v Page* (1829) 2 Sim 471; *Slade v Rigg* (1843) 3 Hare 35 at 38.

583. Personal representatives and trustees instituting foreclosure proceedings. On the mortgagee's death without having transferred the mortgage, the debt and security devolve upon his personal representatives, who can institute foreclosure proceedings until they have transferred the mortgage to a beneficiary or a transferee for value[1]. Where the legal estate is in a trustee for the mortgagee, he must be a party[2]; he should, if possible, be joined as claimant[3]. Trustees sufficiently represent their beneficiaries for the purpose of suing for foreclosure[4].

1 See PARA 390.
2 *Wood v Williams* (1819) 4 Madd 186. See also *Bartle v Wilkin* (1836) 8 Sim 238.
3 *Smith v Chichester* (1842) 2 Dr & War 393 at 404. See also *Browne v Lockhart* (1840) 10 Sim 420 at 426.
4 See CPR 19.7A; and CIVIL PROCEDURE vol 11 (2015) PARAS 479, 493; TRUSTS AND POWERS vol 98 (2013) PARAS 54, 524.

584. Co-mortgagees instituting foreclosure proceedings. Where there are co-mortgagees, they may institute foreclosure proceedings jointly, or, if some are unwilling to be joined as claimants or have done some act precluding them from suing in that capacity, one may sue by himself, provided he makes all the others defendants[1]. A mortgagee entitled to part only of the mortgage money, however, may not sue alone and obtain foreclosure of a corresponding part of the mortgaged estate[2]. Unless the advance is made on a joint account, the mortgagees are tenants in common of the mortgage money, and, on the death of one, his representatives are necessary parties[3].

1 *Davenport v James* (1847) 7 Hare 249; *Luke v South Kensington Hotel Co* (1879) 11 ChD 121, CA. See also *Remer v Stokes* (1856) 4 WR 730. As to mortgages of tolls or rates see *Mellish v Brooks* (1840) 3 Beav 22; *Watts v Lord Eglinton* (1846) 15 LJCh 412.
2 *Palmer v Earl of Carlisle* (1823) 1 Sim & St 423. See also *Lowe v Morgan* (1784) 1 Bro CC 368.
3 *Vickers v Cowell* (1839) 1 Beav 529. As to advances on joint account see PARA 186. The co-mortgagees cannot now at law be tenants in common of the mortgaged property: see PARA 128. As to foreclosure or sale by debenture holders see COMPANIES vol 15 (2009) PARA 1378 et seq.

(v) Parties to Foreclosure Proceedings

585. Persons interested in equity of redemption. The judgment in foreclosure proceedings gives to all persons interested in the equity of redemption[1] the opportunity of redeeming. In default of their doing so, they are foreclosed. All those persons, therefore, must be parties, or be sufficiently represented by persons who are parties[2].

1 As to the equity of redemption see PARAS 107, 304 et seq.
2 *Tylee v Webb* (1843) 6 Beav 552 at 557; *Gedye v Matson* (1858) 25 Beav 310; *Caddick v Cook* (1863) 32 Beav 70; *Griffith v Pound* (1890) 45 ChD 553 at 567. See also *Audsley v Horn* (1858) 26 Beav 195 at 197 (the parties to the mortgage deed, and those claiming under them, should alone be parties to the cause). As to the parties to foreclosure where several mortgagors have mortgaged their interests see *Gee v Liddell* [1913] 2 Ch 62.

586. Subsequent incumbrancers. In foreclosure proceedings by the first mortgagee all subsequent incumbrancers are necessary parties, otherwise they will not be bound[1]. If they are discovered pending the proceedings they must be added as parties[2]. If the claimant mortgagee is himself interested in the subsequent incumbrance, he must not be made a defendant; the same person cannot be claimant and defendant[3]. Persons entitled to contribution out of the mortgaged property, by reason of being interested in other property comprised in a later incumbrance, are also necessary parties[4]. A later mortgagee can bring proceedings to foreclose those behind him and the mortgagor, and to such proceedings the subsequent incumbrancers are necessary parties, but not the prior incumbrancers[5].

1 *Ormsby v Thorpe* (1808) 2 Mol 503.
2 *Keith v Butcher* (1884) 25 ChD 750; *Burgess v Sturges* (1851) 14 Beav 440.
3 *Wavell v Mitchell* (1891) 64 LT 560; *Re Phillips, Public Trustee v Meyer* (1931) 101 LJCh 338.
4 See *Gee v Liddell* [1913] 2 Ch 62. As to parties to an application for permission to realise the security where this is necessary see *Re Hill's Application* (1918) 88 LJCh 136, CA.
5 *Rose v Page* (1829) 2 Sim 471; *Brisco v Kenrick* (1832) 1 Coop temp Cott 371; *Richards v Cooper* (1842) 5 Beav 304; *Slade v Rigg* (1843) 3 Hare 35 at 38; *Johnson v Holdsworth* (1850) 1 Sim NS 106. As to the necessary parties in proceedings to redeem prior incumbrancers see PARA 664.

587. Persons having a direct charge on the property. Generally all persons having a direct charge on the equity of redemption[1] are necessary parties to foreclosure proceedings[2]. Thus debenture holders[3], or, if there is a debenture trust deed, the trustees[4], are necessary parties to foreclosure by a prior mortgagee.

Where there are numerous persons having the same interest, one or more of them may represent them all[5]. A judgment creditor of the mortgagor must be joined if he has obtained an order charging the judgment debt on the land affected by the mortgage[6]. Where a partnership share is mortgaged, and by the articles of partnership the partners have a right of pre-emption over each other's shares, the other partners are necessary parties to foreclosure of the share[7].

1   As to the equity of redemption see PARAS 107, 304 et seq.
2   See eg *Gedye v Matson* (1858) 25 Beav 310 at 311 (surety who has paid part of mortgage debt). For the principle that a surety who has paid off the mortgage debt has a charge on the mortgaged property see FINANCIAL INSTRUMENTS AND TRANSACTIONS vol 49 (2015) PARAS 644, 767. It seems that a surety who has not paid off the mortgage debt in whole or in part, and is bound only by his personal covenant, is not a necessary party to foreclosure proceedings: *Newton v Earl of Egmont* (1831) 4 Sim 574 at 584; *Gedye v Matson*; *Gee v Liddell* [1913] 2 Ch 62 at 73. For the rule that only one period of redemption is allowed to a mortgagor and his surety see FINANCIAL INSTRUMENTS AND TRANSACTIONS vol 49 (2015) PARA 767. See also PARA 606.
3   *Wallace v Evershed* [1899] 1 Ch 891. See also COMPANIES vol 15 (2009) PARA 1382. Although general provision is made for the making of a representation order where there are numerous persons having the same interest in proceedings (see CPR 19.6; and CIVIL PROCEDURE vol 11 (2015) PARA 491), it seems that, in the case of foreclosure proceedings brought by a mortgagee where debenture holders are necessary parties, the better view is that all the debenture holders must be joined: see *Griffith v Pound* (1890) 45 ChD 553; *Westminster Bank Ltd v Residential Properties Improvement Co Ltd* [1938] Ch 639, [1938] 2 All ER 374; but contrast *Fairfield Shipbuilding and Engineering Co Ltd v London and East Coast Express Steamship Co Ltd* [1895] WN 64 (where a representation order was made in such a case); and cf *Re Wilcox & Co (late WH Fox and Co) Ltd, Hilder v Wilcox & Co Ltd* [1903] WN 64 (representative of subsequent debenture holders appointed in proceedings by first debenture holders).
4   *Cox v Dublin City Distillery Co Ltd (No 3)* [1917] 1 IR 203, CA.
5   See CPR 19.6; and CIVIL PROCEDURE vol 11 (2015) PARA 491. It seems that an order will not be made under this rule appointing one debenture holder to represent the class of debenture holders: see note 2.
6   See *Earl of Cork v Russell* (1871) LR 13 Eq 210 (disapproving *Mildred v Austin* (1869) LR 8 Eq 220, and holding that a judgment creditor is not a necessary party until he has an actual charge on the land). For the court's power to impose a charge on the land of a judgment debtor see PARA 111; and CIVIL PROCEDURE vol 12A (2015) PARA 1462 et seq. As to the necessity for the registration of a charging order see PARA 293.
7   *Redmayne v Forster* (1866) LR 2 Eq 467. As to mortgages by partners see PARA 134 et seq.

588. Several properties in one mortgage. The mortgagee cannot in general foreclose part only of the mortgaged property. If several properties are mortgaged together, and are afterwards incumbered or disposed of separately, the incumbrancers on and persons interested in the equity of redemption of each property are necessary parties to the first mortgagee's foreclosure proceedings[1]. If, however, the two properties are subject to separate prior mortgages, the later mortgagee of both can redeem one by itself, and then he may foreclose the mortgagor as to that only[2] unless there is a right to consolidation in respect of the prior mortgages[3]. A later mortgagee of one property can foreclose those behind him on that property without making the persons who are interested in the equity of redemption of the other property parties to the proceedings[4].

1   See eg *Payne v Compton* (1837) 2 Y & C Ex 457. As to the equity of redemption see PARAS 107, 304 et seq.
2   See PARA 673.
3   See *Ireson v Denn* (1796) 2 Cox Eq Cas 425; and PARA 664. See also PARA 586.
4   See PARA 586.

(vi) Foreclosure Proceedings: The Procedure

589. Form of proceedings in a foreclosure claim. A mortgage claim for foreclosure is begun by claim form in the Chancery Division of the High Court[1] or, subject to the amount owing, in the County Court of the district in which the mortgaged property is situate[2].

1 See PARA 534 et seq. Claims for foreclosure in respect of different mortgages by the same mortgagor can be consolidated: see CPR 3.1(2)(g), (h); and CIVIL PROCEDURE vol 12 (2015) PARA 507. See also *Holden v Silkstone and Dodworth Coal and Iron Co Ltd* (1881) 30 WR 98.
2 See PARAS 534–535. As to the commencement of a claim in the County Court see PARA 535. The County Court's exclusive jurisdiction in relation to dwelling houses outside Greater London does not apply to proceedings for foreclosure or sale in which a claim for possession of the mortgaged property is also made: see the County Courts Act 1984 s 21(4); and PARA 534. As to claims for possession see PARA 549 et seq.

590. Foreclosure or sale. Where the mortgagee is suing for foreclosure only, the claim is that an account may be taken of what is due to him on the mortgage, which must be specifically described, for principal, interest and costs, and that the mortgage may be enforced by foreclosure[1]. If the mortgagee is willing to have a sale directed by the court, he will claim foreclosure or sale, but even if foreclosure only is claimed the court may still direct a sale[2].

1 As to procedure under the old law see *Bake v French* [1907] 1 Ch 428; *Weymouth v Davis* [1908] 2 Ch 169; *Practice Note* [1932] WN 6. These authorities should now be read in the light of the Civil Procedure Rules: see CIVIL PROCEDURE vol 11 (2015) PARA 6 et seq.
2 As to the jurisdiction to order a sale see PARAS 575–577. As to orders for sale see PARA 621 et seq.

591. Mortgagee's request for an account of rents and profits. If the mortgagee is in possession[1], he will ask for an account of rents and profits received and for the allowance of any special expenses[2].

1 As to the rights of the mortgagee in possession see PARA 419 et seq.
2 See PARAS 597–598, 771–772. As to accounts generally see PARA 709 et seq; and as to costs, charges and expenses see PARA 743 et seq.

592. Mortgagee's claim for possession. If the mortgagee is not in possession and there is likely to be any difficulty as to obtaining possession, he may claim also delivery of possession, although this is not necessary. A claim for foreclosure includes a claim for possession, and delivery of possession may be ordered as against the mortgagor even though not asked for by the claim[1], notwithstanding that the mortgagor does not appear[2], but will not be ordered without notice where not asked for[3]. The order may be made after foreclosure absolute[4], even if not asked for by the claim[5]. Where foreclosure has taken place by reason of the failure of the claimant in a mortgage claim for redemption[6] to redeem, the defendant in whose favour the foreclosure has taken place may apply for an order for delivery to him of possession of the mortgaged property and the court may make such order as it thinks fit[7].

1 See CPR 16.2(5); and CIVIL PROCEDURE vol 11 (2015) PARA 343. See also *Manchester and Liverpool Bank v Parkinson* (1889) 60 LT 258. As to proceedings for possession see PARA 549 et seq. The authorities referred to in this paragraph should be read in the light of the Civil Procedure Rules: see CIVIL PROCEDURE vol 11 (2015) PARA 6 et seq.
2 *Salt v Edgar* (1886) 54 LT 374; *Lacon v Tyrrell* (1887) 56 LT 483; *Best v Applegate* (1887) 37 ChD 42.
3 *Le Bas v Grant* (1895) 64 LJCh 368.
4 *Keith v Day* (1888) 39 ChD 452, CA. As to foreclosure absolute see PARA 608 et seq.
5 *Jenkins v Ridgley* (1893) 41 WR 585.
6 As to proceedings for redemption see PARA 661 et seq.
7 As to proceedings relating to possession see CPR Pt 55; and PARA 549 et seq.

593. Mortgagee's claim for payment on covenant. In a claim for foreclosure, the mortgagee may include a claim for payment under the covenant in the mortgage deed[1].

1   *Dymond v Croft* (1876) 3 ChD 512; *Farrer v Lacy, Hartland & Co* (1885) 31 ChD 42, CA. These authorities should be read in the light of the Civil Procedure Rules: see CIVIL PROCEDURE vol 11 (2015) PARA 6 et seq.

594. Mortgagee's claim for declaration of title. If the mortgagee is claiming enforcement by foreclosure or sale of a charge created by deposit of title deeds[1], or to enforce by sale a charge or equitable lien, he may claim in the first instance a declaration that he is to be considered as a mortgagee, or that he is entitled to a charge or lien, and will then go on to claim an account and the enforcement of the security[2].

1   As to the creation of an equitable mortgage by deposit of title deeds see PARAS 222–223. Since 27 September 1989 the mere deposit of title deeds by way of security can no longer create a valid equitable mortgage: see PARA 221.
2   See *Marshall v Shrewsbury* (1875) 10 Ch App 250 at 254. This authority should be read in the light of the Civil Procedure Rules: see CIVIL PROCEDURE vol 11 (2015) PARA 6 et seq.

595. Procedure to be adopted in a foreclosure claim. The Civil Procedure Rules[1] make no specific provision for the procedure to be adopted in a foreclosure claim. If the claim expressly or impliedly includes a claim for possession, the procedure applicable to such a claim should be followed[2].

1   See CIVIL PROCEDURE vol 11 (2015) PARA 6 et seq.
2   For the procedure relating to possession claims see PARA 549 et seq.

596. Powers of adjournment etc. The application of the additional statutory powers of adjournment, stay, suspension or postponement to foreclosure proceedings in respect of instalment mortgages is considered elsewhere in this title[1]. Where the only claim is for foreclosure, there is a statutory power of adjournment; where the claim is for foreclosure and possession there is power, in appropriate circumstances, to adjourn the foreclosure claim, or adjourn the possession claim, or stay or suspend any order for possession or postpone the date for delivery of possession[2].

1   See the Administration of Justice Act 1973 s 8; and PARA 559.
2   See the Administration of Justice Act 1970 ss 36(1), (2), 38A (see PARA 556); the Administration of Justice Act 1973 s 8(3) (see PARA 559).

(vii) The Foreclosure Order

A. ACCOUNTS AND INQUIRIES

597. Covenant account and mortgage account. The order made in foreclosure proceedings directs, in the first instance, that the necessary accounts are to be taken, and any inquiries made which are essential to taking the accounts or required for ascertaining the parties' rights. If payment is claimed, two accounts may have to be taken, as the sum recoverable on the covenant for payment and the sum which must be paid as the price of redemption are different. The former sum is limited to principal and interest, and to so much of the costs of the proceedings as would have been incurred if the proceedings had been brought for payment only[1]. Accordingly, the covenant account is of principal and interest, and there follows judgment for the amount certified to be due and for the assessed and apportioned costs.

If the amount of debt and interest is proved, admitted or agreed at the trial, the mortgagee is entitled to judgment for immediate payment; otherwise an account is taken, and he is entitled to judgment for payment immediately the amount is certified, but the judge has a discretion to suspend the judgment[2]. In certain circumstances, immediate payment may not be directed if the particulars of claim ask for an account[3]. The sum in respect of costs does not include expenses which the mortgagee is entitled to charge against the mortgaged property but which are not payable by the mortgagor personally[4].

The mortgage account is an account of what is due to the claimant under and by virtue of his mortgage, and for his assessed costs in the proceedings. In taking this account, anything which has been recovered under the order for payment is deducted and the balance due to the claimant is certified[5]. If there is no claim for payment, only the mortgage account is directed to be taken.

1   *Farrer v Lacy, Hartland & Co* (1885) 31 ChD 42, CA. The authorities referred to in this paragraph should be read in the light of the Civil Procedure Rules: see CIVIL PROCEDURE vol 11 (2015) PARA 6 et seq.
2   As to an order nisi see PARA 599.
3   *Faithfull v Woodley* (1889) 43 ChD 287. As to the form of judgment where the debt is payable by instalments see *Greenough v Littler* (1880) 15 ChD 93. As to arrears of interest recoverable see LIMITATION PERIODS vol 68 (2008) PARA 1128.
4   See PARA 743 et seq.
5   *Lee v Dunsford* (1884) 45 LJCh 108.

598. Account of rents and profits. If the mortgagee is in possession, the order directs an account of rents and profits received by him or by any other persons by his order or for his use, or which without his wilful default might have been so received[1]. The amount due from him on this account is directed to be deducted from the aggregate amount due on the mortgage account and the balance certified. The order also contains a direction for any further accounts and inquiries which the circumstances require, such as an account of proceeds of sale of part of the property; an inquiry as to deterioration in value, or loss through an improper sale; and an inquiry as to priority of incumbrancers[2].

1   As to the taking of an account on the footing of wilful default see PARA 430. As to taking the account with rests see PARA 720 et seq.
2   As to accounts between mortgagor and mortgagee see PARA 709 et seq. Where the account is agreed, or is so simple that the sum can be ascertained in court, an order may be made without directing the amount to be ascertained by an account. As to master's orders see PARA 601.

B.   FORECLOSURE NISI

599. Form of foreclosure order nisi. In foreclosure proceedings by the mortgagee against the mortgagor alone, the order usually allows six months from the date of the master's order[1] as the period within which the defendant may redeem. The order directs that upon payment of the specified sum at the time and place appointed[2], the claimant is to give a receipt[3] and deliver up the title deeds to the defendant or as he appoints, but that in default of payment the defendant is to be foreclosed. Therefore, the order is not an absolute order for foreclosure[4], but only for foreclosure nisi, that is, unless the defendant redeems within the time allowed. If the mortgagee applies for possession[5], the order will direct the mortgagor to deliver up possession to him describing the property as in the parcels in the mortgage deed. Application for possession may also be made subsequently[6].

1   As to the master's order see PARA 601.
2   See PARA 601.
3   Ie pursuant to the Law of Property Act 1925 s 115: see PARA 650.
4   As to foreclosure absolute see PARA 608 et seq.
5   As to when an order for possession can be made see PARA 592.
6   *Keith v Day* (1888) 39 ChD 452, CA. Cf PARA 610.

600. Directions for avoiding unnecessary expense. In order to make it unnecessary to go to the expense of preparing deeds, powers of attorney and form of receipt to hand over in case a mortgagor should attend to redeem at the time and place appointed by the master's order[1] for redemption, all orders for foreclosure[2], unless the court otherwise directs, should provide that:

(1)   the mortgagor must give seven days' notice of his intention to attend and redeem; and

(2)   if no such notice is given but the mortgagor in fact attends at the appointed time and place then at the mortgagee's option the time for redemption must be extended for one week, thus giving the mortgagee's solicitor time to prepare the necessary documents[3].

1   As to the master's order see PARA 601.
2   The provisions set out in the text also apply to orders for redemption: see *Practice Directions* [1955] 1 All ER 30, [1955] 1 WLR 36; and PARA 671. This should be read in the light of the Civil Procedure Rules: see CIVIL PROCEDURE vol 11 (2015) PARA 6 et seq.
3   *Practice Directions* [1955] 1 All ER 30, [1955] 1 WLR 36.

601. Master's order. The master's order calculates further interest for six months from its date and fixes a time on the day at the expiration of six months when, and a place where, the aggregate sum made up of the certified balance and the further interest is to be paid[1]. The mortgagor is not entitled to redeem before the appointed day on payment of principal and interest only until the date of payment together with costs[2].

1   The result of the account before the master is expressed in the form of a notice of decision: see CPR Pt 40; PD 40A—*Accounts and Inquiries* para 13; and CIVIL PROCEDURE vol 12A (2015) PARA 1252 et seq.
2   *Hill v Rowlands* [1897] 2 Ch 361, CA.

602. Order against second mortgagee and mortgagor. Where proceedings are brought by a first mortgagee against a second mortgagee and the mortgagor, successive periods may be allowed for redemption, and in that case the first right of redemption is given to the second mortgagee and in default he is foreclosed[1]. The claimant's subsequent interest and costs are then computed and assessed, and a further three months may be allowed for the mortgagor to pay the original and additional amount, and in default he also is foreclosed; but the second mortgagee must be foreclosed absolutely before proceedings are taken to foreclose the mortgagor[2]. This completes the foreclosure contemplated.

1   If the mortgagor is bankrupt, and the mortgagee has valued his security, the trustee in bankruptcy is entitled to redeem at that value, and the order must show this: *Knowles v Dibbs* (1889) 37 WR 378. In *Hayes and Harlington UDC v Williams's Trustee* [1936] Ch 315 (where the order was made in the form of 3 Seton's Form of Decrees, Judgments and Orders in Equity (7th Edn, 1912) 1892), the mortgagees, who alleged that they had undervalued their security, obtained a discharge of the order and a fresh order with a declaration that they were entitled to hold the mortgaged property as against the mortgagor's trustee in bankruptcy for the amount due to them on the mortgage. This was to enable them to apply to amend their proof in bankruptcy.
2   *Whitbread v Lyall* (1856) 8 De GM & G 383; *Webster v Patteson* (1884) 25 ChD 626.

603. Successive redemptions. If the second mortgagee redeems, proceedings are thereafter for foreclosure between him and the mortgagor; subsequent interest is computed on the amount paid to the claimant; and the ordinary account is taken of the second mortgage[1]. The amount paid to the claimant, with subsequent interest, and the amount certified to be due to the second mortgagee under his mortgage and his costs, give the aggregate sum at which the mortgagor can redeem within three months, and in default he is foreclosed. The result is to clear the property of all incumbrances in favour of one of the parties to the proceedings, either the first mortgagee, the second mortgagee or the mortgagor, according as the rights of redemption are exercised or not[2].

The successive rights were formerly worked out on the same principle where there were third and subsequent mortgages, and the property was in the same manner cleared of all incumbrances[3], but now the excessive complication of such an order, and the delay consequent on successive redemptions, is usually avoided by giving only one time for redemption to all the later incumbrancers with liberty, on any of them redeeming, to apply to determine their rights among themselves[4]. By voluntarily submitting to foreclosure, a later mortgagee does not necessarily lose his remedy on the covenant against the mortgagor[5].

1   As to accounts see PARA 597.
2   As to rights of redemption see PARA 304 et seq.
3   As to the order of redemption where the claimant is a mortgagee who has consolidated his mortgages, and the equities of redemption of the properties are in the hands of different assignees see *Beevor v Luck, Beevor v Lawson* (1867) LR 4 Eq 537; *Loveday v Chapman* (1875) 32 LT 689. As to consolidation see PARA 502.
4   See PARA 606.
5   *Worthington & Co Ltd v Abbott* [1910] 1 Ch 588.

604. Foreclosure limited to later incumbrancers. A later incumbrancer may limit his claim to foreclosure against incumbrancers subsequent to himself and against the mortgagor, and, in this case, the prior incumbrancers are not affected by the order, as it operates only on the equity of redemption subsequent to those prior incumbrancers[1]. Each incumbrancer subsequent to the claimant, and also the mortgagor, must redeem or be foreclosed, so that in the result the property is clear of the claimant's, and all the subsequent, incumbrances[2].

1   *Rose v Page* (1829) 2 Sim 471. See also PARA 603. As to the equity of redemption see PARAS 107, 304 et seq.
2   See PARA 603.

605. Redemption by intervening incumbrancers. Proceedings by the second mortgagee to redeem the first are in effect proceedings for foreclosure against the incumbrancers subsequent to himself and against the mortgagor. As regards the first mortgagee, the order is the same as that made in redemption proceedings[1]. The account under the first mortgage is taken, and, if the claimant redeems, the order then proceeds, as in foreclosure proceedings, to give the subsequent incumbrancers, and ultimately the mortgagor, the chance of redeeming, and in default they are successively foreclosed[2]. Therefore, if the claimant redeems and is not in his turn redeemed, he obtains the property free from incumbrances, at the price of the aggregate of the first mortgage and his own. If the claimant does not redeem, the proceedings are dismissed with costs, and this means that he has to pay the mortgagor's costs also[3]. In proceedings by an intervening incumbrancer against prior incumbrancers, the right of redemption is given to the mortgagees subsequent to the first in succession, and accordingly all mortgagees prior to the claimant must redeem or be foreclosed; after redemption by any one of them, those subsequent to him must likewise redeem or be foreclosed. If, however, the claimant fails to redeem, the proceedings are dismissed. If he redeems, then the successive rights of redemption, with foreclosure in default, are continued as in foreclosure proceedings[4].

1   See PARAS 671, 673.
2   See PARA 604.
3   *Pelly v Wathen* (1849) 7 Hare 351; *Hallett v Furze* (1885) 31 ChD 312. See also PARA 674.
4   *Duberley v Waring* (1776) 3 Seton's Form of Decrees, Judgments and Orders in Equity (7th Edn, 1912) 1909. If the proceedings are dismissed, the claimant is foreclosed; but it is questionable whether the foreclosure of the prior intermediate incumbrances remains operative.

606. When one period of redemption is fixed. The rights of redemption of successive mortgagees[1] are not always preserved. The mortgagor himself is not entitled to any further period for redemption beyond the ordinary six months because he has incumbered the equity of redemption[2]. When questions of priority arise between incumbrancers which do not affect the claimant, these need not be determined in his presence, and therefore, to avoid doing so, only one period of redemption is fixed for all the incumbrancers and the mortgagor, and the order is made without prejudice to the priority of the incumbrancers among themselves[3]. Similarly, where they, or some of them, do not appear, or do not put in a defence, only one period is allowed, as to do otherwise would be to fix their priorities in their absence[4]. It is the same whether the particulars of claim allege that the defendants are entitled, or only that they claim to be entitled, to incumbrances[5].

Where a sale is ordered, only one time is allowed for redemption if the margin for subsequent incumbrancers will be small[6]. Established practice now is, generally, to fix only one period of redemption[7], but subsequent incumbrancers, if their priorities are proved or admitted, although not the mortgagor, may obtain successive periods on showing a case for this indulgence[8]. If any of the defendants redeem, there is liberty to apply, and their respective rights will be worked out without notice to the claimant.

1 See PARAS 602–605.
2 *Platt v Mendel* (1884) 27 ChD 246 at 248. See also PARA 599. As to the equity of redemption see PARAS 107, 304 et seq.
3 *Bartlett v Rees* (1871) LR 12 Eq 395; *General Credit and Discount Co v Glegg* (1883) 22 ChD 549; *Lewis v Aberdare and Plymouth Co* (1884) 53 LJCh 741; *Tufdnell v Nicholls* (1887) 56 LT 152.
4 *Doble v Manley* (1885) 28 ChD 664.
5 *Doble v Manley* (1885) 28 ChD 664; *Smithett v Hesketh* (1890) 44 ChD 161 at 164.
6 *Cripps v Wood* (1882) 51 LJCh 584.
7 *Smith v Olding* (1884) 25 ChD 462; *Platt v Mendel* (1884) 27 ChD 246 at 248; *Smithett v Hesketh* (1890) 44 ChD 161. Formerly the allowance of successive periods was usual (*Lewis v Aberdare and Plymouth Co* (1884) 53 LJCh 741), except in the case of judgment creditors (*Stead v Banks* (1852) 5 De G & Sm 560; *Bates v Hillcoat* (1852) 16 Beav 139).
8 *Platt v Mendel* (1886) 27 ChD 246 at 249; *Mutual Life Assurance Society v Langley* (1884) 26 ChD 686 at 692 (one additional period of three months allowed); *Bertlin v Gordon* [1886] WN 31 (one additional period of one month; the mortgage was of a reversionary interest likely to fall in soon); *Smithett v Hesketh* (1890) 44 ChD 161 (two additional periods of three months).

607. Foreclosure of equitable securities. In proceedings for foreclosure of an equitable mortgage by deposit[1], the order is prefaced by a declaration that the claimant is entitled to be considered as a mortgagee of the premises comprised in the deeds[2]. The order directs the usual accounts and foreclosure of the mortgagor in default of payment, and there is a direction for conveyance of the property to the claimant[3].

1 As to the creation of an equitable mortgage by deposit of title deeds see PARAS 222–223. Since 27 September 1989 the mere deposit of title deeds by way of security can no longer create a valid equitable mortgage: see PARA 221.
2 *Parker v Sidney* [1897] WN 135. The authorities referred to in this paragraph should be read in the light of the Civil Procedure Rules: see CIVIL PROCEDURE vol 11 (2015) PARA 6 et seq.
3 *Lees v Fisher* (1882) 22 ChD 283, CA. As to the usual form of order see PARA 599.

C. FORECLOSURE ABSOLUTE

608. Procedure to obtain foreclosure order absolute. On non-payment of the amount stated to be due under the mortgage at the time and place described[1], the mortgagee is entitled to an order for foreclosure absolute as against the person or persons in default. The application is made to the master[2].

1 Ie as described in the master's order: see PARA 601. It was previously held that there is no requirement that a master's order or a foreclosure nisi order should be served on the mortgagor: see *Lancashire and Yorkshire Reversionary Interest Co Ltd v Crowe* (1970) 114 Sol Jo 435. However the Civil Procedure Rules now provide that, unless the court directs otherwise, any order made otherwise than at trial must be served on the applicant and the respondent and any other person on whom the court orders it to be served: see CPR 40.4(2); and CIVIL PROCEDURE vol 12A (2015) PARA 1222.
2 As to making such an application see CPR Pt 23; and CIVIL PROCEDURE vol 12 (2015) PARA 554 et seq.

609. Evidence in support of application foreclosure absolute. On application for foreclosure absolute there must be a witness statement made by the mortgagee, or, if he attended by an agent, by the agent, of attendance at the prescribed time and place[1] and non-payment of the money[2], and also a witness statement by the mortgagee of non-payment since the appointed time[3].

The statement of attendance should prove attendance during the whole of the appointed time by the mortgagee or his agent authorised by power of attorney to receive the money[4], but a want of strict compliance with these formalities is not necessarily a ground for refusing the order[5]. These irregularities, however, prevent the order being of course, and the matter must be mentioned to the judge[6]. If one joint mortgagee is abroad, it is sufficient for the others to make the witness statement or affidavit[7].

Where the mortgagee has received rents after default, the usual form of witness statement or affidavit must be altered[8].

1 See PARAS 599, 601.
2 See *Docksey v Else* (1891) 64 LT 256. The authorities referred to in this paragraph should be read in the light of the Civil Procedure Rules: see CIVIL PROCEDURE vol 11 (2015) PARA 6 et seq. As to the mode of making an application see CPR Pt 23; and CIVIL PROCEDURE vol 12 (2015) PARA 554 et seq. If an applicant wishes to rely on matters set out in his application notice as evidence, the application notice must be verified by a statement of truth: see CPR 22.1(3); and CIVIL PROCEDURE vol 11 (2015) PARA 363; CIVIL PROCEDURE vol 12 (2015) PARA 769.
3 *Barrow v Smith* (1885) 52 LT 798; *Docksey v Else* (1891) 64 LT 256. Cf *Frith v Cooke* (1885) 52 LT 798, where the mortgagee's personal affidavit of non-payment was dispensed with. All mortgagees in the jurisdiction should join in the witness statement or affidavit: *Bostock v Shaw* (1848) 10 LTOS 481; *Kinnaird v Yorke* (1889) 60 LT 380; *Docksey v Else* (1891) 64 LT 256. See also the text to note 7.
4 As to powers of attorney see AGENCY vol 1 (2008) PARA 31 et seq.
5 The order has been granted where the mortgagees attended during part of the appointed time only (see *Anon* (1844) 1 Coll 273; *Bernard v Norton* (1864) 10 LT 183), and even where the attendance was by an agent and he did not have a power of attorney to receive the money if the mortgagor did attend (see *Lechmere v Clamp (No 3)* (1862) 31 Beav 578; *London Monetary Advance and Assurance Society v Brown* (1868) 16 WR 782; *Macrae v Evans* (1875) 24 WR 55; *Cox v Watson* (1877) 7 ChD 196). The order was certainly granted where the agent had a power of attorney but omitted to bring it with him: see *Hart v Hawthorne* (1880) 42 LT 79; *Crawley v Fuller* [1890] WN 35. See also *Frith v Cooke* (1885) 52 LT 798 (defendant had never appeared in the proceedings; affidavit by the solicitors' clerk who attended to receive the money was accepted as sufficient).
6 *King v Hough* [1895] WN 60. As to the form of order under these circumstances see *Moore and Robinson's Nottinghamshire Banking Co v Horsfield* [1882] WN 43.
7 *Kinnaird v Yorke* (1889) 60 LT 380. See also note 3.
8 See *National Permanent Mutual Benefit Building Society v Raper* [1892] 1 Ch 54. See also PARA 726.

610. Form of foreclosure order absolute. The order for foreclosure absolute recites the order for an account in the order nisi, the certificate showing the sum found due, the time and place appointed for payment, and the evidence of attendance by the claimant or his agent and of non-payment; and orders that the mortgagor, or other defendant against whom it is made, is to stand from that time absolutely debarred and foreclosed of and from all equity of redemption in the mortgaged premises[1]. If necessary an order for delivery of possession will be added, or this may be obtained subsequently[2]. The order for foreclosure absolute does not by itself entitle the mortgagee to a writ of possession[3].

In the case of an equitable mortgage of land or stock or a chose or thing in action, if a conveyance cannot be obtained from the mortgagor, then on the footing that the mortgagor is a trustee the court may under its statutory powers[4] make a vesting order in relation to the mortgaged property[5]. The procedure by application for a vesting order has the advantage of avoiding cost and delay as compared with the alternative procedure[6] of seeking the appointment of a third person to execute the conveyance[7]. If the defendant has in his possession any deeds affecting the title to the claimant's mortgage, these will be ordered to be given up, but a later mortgagee will not be ordered to deliver up deeds, subsequent to the claimant's mortgage, which affect only the equity of redemption[8].

1 As to the order for foreclosure nisi see PARA 599. As to the equity of redemption see PARAS 107, 304 et seq.
2 *Keith v Day* (1888) 39 ChD 452, CA; *Manchester and Liverpool Bank v Parkinson* (1889) 60 LT 258; *Jenkins v Ridgley* (1893) 41 WR 585. See also PARA 592. The authorities referred to in this paragraph should be read in the light of the Civil Procedure Rules: see CIVIL PROCEDURE vol 11 (2015) PARA 6 et seq. As to orders generally see CPR Pt 40; and CIVIL PROCEDURE vol 12A (2015) PARA 1219 et seq.
3 *Wood v Wheater* (1882) 22 ChD 281; *Wood v Smallpiece* [1942] Ch 190, [1942] 1 All ER 252, CA. Where an order was not properly indorsed, because it omitted to name any time within which possession was to be given, and the claimants applied on motion for leave to issue a writ of attachment for non-compliance with the order, and the defendant appeared in person, the court ordered that the writ of attachment should issue, but should lie in the office for a week: *Re Higg's Mortgage, Goddard v Higg* [1894] WN 73.
4 Ie under the Trustee Act 1925 ss 44, 51: see TRUSTS AND POWERS vol 98 (2013) PARA 315 et seq. As to jurisdiction see PARAS 534–535.
5 See eg *Lechmere v Clamp (No 2)* (1861) 30 Beav 218; *Lechmere v Clamp (No 3)* (1862) 31 Beav 578 (where the mortgagor could not be found); *Jones v Davies* [1940] WN 174 (where the mortgagor refused to convey). See also *Re Crowe's Mortgage* (1871) LR 13 Eq 26; *Re D Jones & Co's Mortgage* (1888) 59 LT 859. Cf *Smith v Boucher* (1852) 1 Sm & G 72. Formerly, the court might make a vesting order in the case of a mortgage by sub-demise of leasehold property which contained a declaration of trust by the mortgagor of his reversion: see *British Empire Mutual Life Assurance Co v Sugden* (1878) 47 LJCh 691, where the court refused to make such an order until foreclosure absolute. In the case of a mortgage by sub-demise, the leasehold reversion now vests automatically on foreclosure absolute: see PARA 612.
6 Ie under the Senior Courts Act 1981 s 39(1): see CIVIL PROCEDURE vol 12A (2015) PARA 1219. As to the procedure under this provision see *Savage v Norton* [1908] 1 Ch 290; and SPECIFIC PERFORMANCE vol 95 (2013) PARA 460.
7 See *Jones v Davies* [1940] WN 174. As to the power of the court to appoint a person to convey in a case where a vesting order can be made see the Trustee Act 1925 ss 50, 51(2); and TRUSTS AND POWERS vol 98 (2013) PARAS 319, 326. See also *Foster v Parker* (1878) 8 ChD 147.
8 *Greene v Foster* (1882) 22 ChD 566.

611. Stamp duty land tax. An order for foreclosure absolute is a land transaction[1] effected by operation of law, and as such is subject to stamp duty land tax[2]. All such orders are required to be notified to the Commissioners for Her Majesty's Revenue and Customs, by delivery of a land transaction return, before the end of the period of 30 days after the effective date[3] of the transaction[4], and the Commissioners for Her Majesty's Revenue and Customs confirm that stamp duty land tax has been accounted for on the transaction by issuing a return certificate (a 'revenue certificate'), which accompanies the application to the land registry[5].

1 For the purposes of the Finance Act 2003 Pt 4 (ss 42–124) 'land transaction' means any acquisition of a chargeable interest: see ss 43(1), 48; and STAMP TAXES vol 96 (2012) PARA 426.

2   See the Finance Act 2003 s 42 (which provides that stamp duty land tax is charged on all land transactions whether or not effected by instrument and regardless of the place of execution of the instrument and the residence of any party to the transaction); and STAMP TAXES vol 96 (2012) PARA 425.
3   Ie the date of completion: see the Finance Act 2003 s 119(1).
4   See the Finance Act 2003 s 76; the Commissioners for Revenue and Customs Act 2005 s 50(1); and STAMP TAXES vol 96 (2012) PARA 477.
5   See the Finance Act 2003 s 79; the Commissioners for Revenue and Customs Act 2005 s 50(1); and STAMP TAXES vol 96 (2012) PARA 481.

612. Effect of foreclosure order absolute. The mortgagee under a legal mortgage of freehold has a term of years or a legal interest instead of the fee simple estate, and the fee simple is in the mortgagor[1]. The vesting of the fee simple in the mortgagee on foreclosure is effected automatically in the case of unregistered land[2]; the foreclosure order absolute operates to vest the fee simple in the mortgagee, subject to any legal mortgage having priority, and the mortgage term, if any, merges in the fee simple, any subsequent mortgage term or legal charge being extinguished[3]. This also applies to a sub-mortgage[4].

A foreclosure order absolute of a leasehold mortgage by sub-demise or legal charge operates, unless it otherwise provides, to vest the nominal reversion and any subsequent mortgage term, subject to any legal mortgage having priority, in the mortgagee, and the mortgage term or legal charge merges in the nominal reversion or is extinguished[5]. This also applies to a sub-mortgage[6].

In relation to registered land, foreclosure effects a transfer by operation of law of the registered estate[7] over which the charge was held, and must be completed by registration[8]. The registrar must cancel the registration of the charge in respect of which the foreclosure order was made, cancel all entries in respect of interests over which the charge has priority, and enter the mortgagee as proprietor of the registered estate[9].

Trustees who have foreclosed mortgaged lands hold them in trust[10]. A release of the equity of redemption after default under the order nisi is equivalent to final foreclosure[11].

1   See PARAS 164–165.
2   Formerly, the effect of the order for foreclosure absolute was to transfer the mortgagor's equitable estate to the mortgagee and the mortgagor then had no interest in the property: *Heath v Pugh* (1881) 6 QBD 345 at 360, CA; affd (1882) 7 App Cas 235, HL. The mortgagee held the mortgaged property as absolute owner in lieu of the mortgage money, and if it was real estate, he held it as such and not as personalty: *Thompson v Grant* (1819) 4 Madd 438; *Re Loveridge, Pearce v Marsh* [1904] 1 Ch 518 at 523.
3   See the Law of Property Act 1925 s 88(2); and PARA 571.
4   See the Law of Property Act 1925 s 88(5); and PARA 452.
5   See the Law of Property Act 1925 s 89(2).
6   See the Law of Property Act 1925 s 89(5).
7   As to the meaning of 'registered estate' see PARA 142 note 7.
8   See the Land Registration Act 2002 s 27(5); and REAL PROPERTY AND REGISTRATION vol 87 (2012) PARA 430.
9   See the Land Registration Rules 2003, SI 2003/1417, r 112(2)(a)–(c); and REAL PROPERTY AND REGISTRATION vol 87 (2012) PARA 477. See also PARA 613.
10 See the Law of Property Act 1925 s 31(1); and TRUSTS AND POWERS vol 98 (2013) PARA 469. As to opening foreclosure see PARA 616 et seq.
11 As to the order nisi see PARA 599 et seq. Formerly, if made by a tenant in tail it bound those in remainder (*Reynoldson v Perkins* (1769) Amb 564), but now the tenant in tail would have the legal estate, and the release would be by conveyance of the legal estate. As to entailed interests see REAL PROPERTY AND REGISTRATION vol 87 (2012) PARA 112 et seq.

613. Foreclosure in respect of registered land. Where a mortgagee has foreclosed in respect of registered land and become registered as proprietor of the mortgagor's estate[1], a mortgagor who wishes to redeem must apply for alteration of the register[2]. Alteration cannot be ordered against a proprietor in possession without his consent unless he has by fraud or lack of proper care caused or substantially contributed to the mistake, or it would for any other reason be unjust for the alteration not to be made[3].

1   Ie pursuant to the Land Registration Rules 2003, SI 2003/1417, r 112; see PARA 612.
2   As to alteration of the register see the Land Registration Act 2002 s 65, Sch 4; and REAL PROPERTY AND REGISTRATION vol 87 (2012) PARA 493 et seq.
3   See the Land Registration Act 2002 Sch 4 para 3(1), (2); and REAL PROPERTY AND REGISTRATION vol 87 (2012) PARA 498.

(viii) Costs

614. Mortgagee's costs added to mortgage debt. In foreclosure proceedings the mortgagee's costs are not, in the absence of special circumstances, payable by the mortgagor personally; the mortgagee adds them to his debt, and the mortgagor only pays them if he redeems[1]. Moreover, the mortgagee is not liable in general to pay the costs of any other party to the proceedings[2]. A defendant who disclaims interest is, however, entitled to his costs if he has been needlessly made a party to the proceedings, or to costs subsequent to disclaimer if the proceedings are needlessly continued against him[3].

1   See PARAS 677, 755 et seq.
2   See PARA 769.
3   See PARA 615.

615. Rules as to defendant's costs. On the question of costs in foreclosure proceedings the following rules have been recognised:

(1)   if a defendant has no interest[1], and claims no interest, at the commencement of the claim or afterwards, he is not properly made a party[2]. If he disclaims either before or after[3] the commencement of the claim in terms which shows this to be the case, he is entitled to his costs against the claimant[4].

(2)   if a person has an interest, he is prima facie a necessary party, but if he disclaims or offers to disclaim before proceedings are brought, and the disclaimer is known to the mortgagee or would have been known had he used ordinary care and prudence[5], that person ceases to be a necessary party and, if made a defendant, is entitled to his costs against the claimant[6].

(3)   if a person has an interest, and does not disclaim or offer to disclaim before proceedings are brought, he is properly made a defendant and is not entitled to be paid his costs[7]. If he disclaims during the proceedings and does not ask for costs, but is brought to the trial for some special purpose of the claimant, he is entitled to be paid his costs subsequent to the disclaimer[8], but not if he appears of his own accord without being required for such a special purpose[9] even though he has been served with notice of subsequent proceedings[10]. A disclaimer should be made immediately on notice of the claim[11], and the defendant must not plead or appear at the hearing to claim costs[12].

1   This includes the case where he has had an interest, but has assigned it before proceedings are brought (*Glover v Rogers* (1847) 11 Jur 1000; *Hurst v Hurst* (1852) 22 LJCh 538), but not the case where he has only agreed to assign his interest (*Roberts v Hughes* (1868) LR 6 Eq 20). As to disclaimer by a trustee who has never acted see *Benbow v Davies* (1848) 11 Beav 369. The authorities referred to in this paragraph should be read in the light of the Civil Procedure Rules: see CIVIL PROCEDURE vol 11 (2015) PARA 6 et seq. As to general rules about costs see CPR Pt 44; and CIVIL PROCEDURE vol 12A (2015) PARA 1688 et seq.

2   *Furber v Furber* (1862) 30 Beav 523 at 524.

3   *Bellamy v Brickenden* (1858) 4 K & J 670; *Day v Gudgen* (1876) 2 ChD 209.

4   *Ford v Earl of Chesterfield* (1853) 16 Beav 516 (where rules substantially the same as those stated in the text were first enunciated). See also *Tipping v Power* (1842) 1 Hare 405 at 408; *Gabriel v Sturgis* (1846) 5 Hare 97 at 101; *Hiorns v Holtom, Fortnam v Holtom* (1852) 16 Jur 1077; *Ward v Shakeshaft* (1860) 1 Drew & Sm 269; *Ridgway v Kynnersley* (1865) 2 Hem & M 565; *Earl of Cork v Russell* (1871) LR 13 Eq 210.

5   See *Ridgway v Kynnersley* (1865) 2 Hem & M 565.

6   *Ford v Earl of Chesterfield* (1853) 16 Beav 516. See also *Thompson v Kendall* (1840) 9 Sim 397; *Lock v Lomas* (1851) 15 Jur 162.

7   *Land v Wood* (1823) 1 LJOS Ch 89; *Grigg v Sturgis* (1846) 5 Hare 93; *Ohrly v Jenkins* (1847) 1 De G & Sm 543; *Buchanan v Greenway* (1848) 11 Beav 58; *Staffurth v Pott* (1848) 2 De G & Sm 571; *Ford v Earl of Chesterfield* (1853) 16 Beav 516; *Furber v Furber* (1862) 30 Beav 523 at 524. See also *Gibson v Nicol* (1846) 9 Beav 403. A statement by the defendant that if he had been applied to before proceedings were brought he would have released or disclaimed his right does not entitle him to costs: *Collins v Shirley* (1830) 1 Russ & M 638; *Ford v White* (1852) 16 Beav 120. Cf *Gurney v Jackson* (1852) 1 Sm & G 97.

8   *Talbot v Kemshead* (1858) 4 K & J 93; *Dillon v Ashwin* (1864) 10 Jur NS 119; *Jones v Rhind, Rhind v Jones* (1869) 17 WR 1091 per James V-C; *Greene v Foster* (1882) 22 ChD 566 at 569. See also *Lewin v Jones* (1884) 53 LJCh 1011.

9   *Gowing v Mowberry (Mowbray)* (1863) 11 WR 851, 8 LT 531; *Lewin v Jones* (1884) 53 LJCh 1011.

10 *Clarke v Toleman* (1872) 42 LJCh 23 (disapproving *Davis v Whitmore* (1860) 28 Beav 617).

11 See *Bradley v Borlase* (1858) 7 WR 125.

12 See *Maxwell v Wightwick* (1866) LR 3 Eq 210.

(ix) Opening Foreclosure

616. General principle as to enlargement of time. Neither an order for foreclosure nisi, which directs foreclosure in the event of non-payment at a prescribed date[1], nor an order for foreclosure absolute[2], is conclusive as regards the mortgagor's right to redeem[3]. After an order for foreclosure nisi, whether or not followed by an order for foreclosure absolute, the mortgagor may apply for, and, in suitable circumstances and on certain conditions, obtain, an order enlarging the time for redemption[4] and, if there has been foreclosure absolute, opening the foreclosure and giving a new right of redemption[5]; and the same results may follow from acts of the mortgagee.

Enlargement of the time is not a matter of course[6]. It will not be granted in favour of an assignee added as a defendant after judgment nisi[7]. There must be some reason for it, such as that the security is ample, and that the mortgagor has a reasonable probability of obtaining the money to pay the mortgage debt[8], but on a first application before the day fixed for payment[9] the reason need not be a strong one[10].

1   As to foreclosure nisi see PARA 599 et seq.

2   As to foreclosure absolute see PARA 608 et seq.

3   *Cukurova Finance International Ltd v Alfa Telecom Turkey Ltd* [2013] UKPC 2, [2015] 2 WLR 875, [2013] All ER (D) 21 (Apr). As to the mortgagor's right to redeem see PARA 304 et seq.

4   As to enlarging time for redemption in a redemption claim see PARA 674.

5   See *Campbell v Holyland* (1877) 7 ChD 166; *Re Power and Carton's Contract* (1890) 25 LR Ir 459.

6   *Quarles v Knight* (1820) 8 Price 630. As to the circumstances that the court will consider on an application for relief from any sanction imposed for failure to comply with any court order see CPR 3.9; and CIVIL PROCEDURE vol 12 (2015) PARA 521.

7   *Re Parbola Ltd, Blackburn v Parbola Ltd* [1909] 2 Ch 437.

8   *Forrest v Shore* (1884) 32 WR 356.

9   *Patch v Ward* (1867) 3 Ch App 203 at 212. See also *Lancashire and Yorkshire Reversionary Interest Co Ltd v Crowe* (1970) 114 Sol Jo 435.

10 *Nanny v Edwards* (1827) 4 Russ 124; *Eyre v Hanson* (1840) 2 Beav 478.

617. Effect of a joint mortgagee's death. Where under the order for foreclosure and master's order[1] the debt is payable to mortgagees on a joint account, and one of them dies before the day fixed for payment, this operates as a postponement of the time for redemption, and a new day must be appointed[2].

1 As to the master's order see PARA 601.
2 *Blackburn v Caine* (1856) 22 Beav 614; *Kingsford v Poile* (1859) 8 WR 110. See, however, *Browell v Pledge* [1888] WN 166.

618. Receipt of rents by mortgagee in possession or receiver. The time for redemption will be enlarged if the mortgagee is in possession and receives rents between the date of the master's order and the day appointed for payment[1]. The receipt reopens the account, and a fresh order must be made and a further day appointed[2]; in this case, the mortgagor is not put upon terms of paying interest and costs[3]. A mortgagee is not allowed to reopen the account for the purpose of letting in the costs of other proceedings on the ground of consolidation[4] but after default on the day appointed for payment the mortgagee receives the rents on his own account and the time is not by that enlarged[5].

Receipt of rents by a receiver has the same effect as receipt by the mortgagee if the mortgagee claims them, that is, the account is reopened if the rents are received before the day for payment, but not if they are received after that day[6]. The expense of further account may, however, be saved by the mortgagee filing a witness statement or affidavit as to the amount due for principal, interest and costs, after allowing for receipts, down to the day for which notice is given of application to fix another day for redemption[7]. The account is not reopened if in the order nisi the mortgagee submits to be charged with a certain sum in respect of rents in the receiver's hands or which may come into his hands prior to the order absolute, and if the amount received does not exceed that sum[8], or if the amount received is not sufficient to cover the receiver's expenses and remuneration[9]. This effect is given to the receipt of rents by a receiver on the ground that until default the rents belong to the mortgagor and must be credited to him. It is otherwise where receipts represent capital and in that case they belong to the party redeeming, or, if no person redeems, to the mortgagee foreclosing, and the account is not reopened[10]. Accordingly, the judgment should give permission to apply in chambers as to payment of the money[11]; but the direction giving permission to apply implies that the account is not to be reopened, and it will not be inserted unless the nature of the receipts justifies it[12]. Where a receiver omits from his accounts certain rents received, this does not, without proof that the mortgagee received those rents, reopen the foreclosure[13].

1 See PARA 601.
2 *Geldard v Hornby* (1841) 1 Hare 251; *Garlick v Jackson* (1841) 4 Beav 154; *Alden v Foster* (1842) 5 Beav 592; *Ellis v Griffiths* (1844) 7 Beav 83; *Holford v Yate* (1855) 1 K & J 677; *Patch v Ward* (1867) 3 Ch App 203 at 209; *Prees v Coke* (1871) 6 Ch App 645; *Allen v Edwards* (1873) 42 LJCh 455. The authorities referred to in this paragraph should be read in the light of the Civil Procedure Rules: see CIVIL PROCEDURE vol 11 (2015) PARA 6 et seq.
3 *Buchanan v Greenway* (1849) 12 Beav 355.
4 *Barron v Lancefield* (1853) 17 Beav 208.
5 *Constable v Howick* (1858) 5 Jur NS 331; *Prees v Coke* (1871) 6 Ch App 645; *National Permanent Mutual Benefit Building Society v Raper* [1892] 1 Ch 54. See also *Webster v Patteson* (1884) 25 ChD 626. As to the effect of the rule where successive periods are fixed for redemption see *Bird v Gandy* (1715) 7 Vin Abr 45 pl 20.
6 *Jenner-Fust v Needham* (1886) 32 ChD 582, CA; *Peat v Nicholson* (1886) 54 LT 569. Cases allowing a further month (eg *Hoare v Stephens* (1886) 32 ChD 194; *Ross Improvement Comrs v Usborne* [1890] WN 92) have been overruled (see *National Permanent Mutual Benefit Building Society v Raper* [1892] 1 Ch 54). As to the appointment of a receiver see PARAS 478 et seq, 565 et seq.

7 *Jenner-Fust v Needham* (1886) 32 ChD 582, CA.
8 *Barber v Jeckells* [1893] WN 91; *Christy v Godwin* (1893) 38 Sol Jo 10; *Simmons v Blandy* [1897] 1 Ch 19. Cf *Lusk v Sebright* (1894) 71 LT 59.
9 *Ellenor v Ugle* [1895] WN 161.
10 *Welch v National Cycle Works Co Ltd* (1886) 55 LT 673, CA.
11 *Coleman v Llewellin* (1886) 34 ChD 143, CA; *Smith v Pearman* (1888) 58 LT 720.
12 *Cheston v Wells* [1893] 2 Ch 151. As to takings in the hands of a receiver and manager see *Holt & Co v Beagle* (1886) 55 LT 592.
13 *Ingham v Sutherland* (1890) 63 LT 614.

619. Effect of foreclosure proceedings on covenant, or sale under power, or fraud. An order for foreclosure absolute will be reopened if, after foreclosure, the mortgagee sues the mortgagor on his covenant for payment[1]. It will be reopened also if the mortgagee sells under his power of sale and not as absolute owner, although the effect is only to make him liable to account for the surplus proceeds of sale, and the purchaser's title is not disturbed[2]. Further, like any other judgment, the order can be set aside if it has been obtained by fraud[3], where, for instance, the mortgagee has misled the court as to the persons interested in the equity of redemption[4]; but mere constructive fraud is not sufficient[5]. The foreclosure may be reopened in a suitable case as against a purchaser[6], but it is not reopened by sale to a party to the proceedings[7] or by the mortgagee bequeathing the security as a debt[8].

1 *Lockhart v Hardy* (1846) 9 Beav 349; *Re Power and Carton's Contract* (1890) 25 LR Ir 459 at 469. See also *Dashwood v Blythway* (1729) 1 Eq Cas Abr 317. See further PARA 514. Where a second mortgagee has been foreclosed, and the mortgagor acquires the estate by devise from the first mortgagee, this may revive the second mortgage: *Cook v Sadler* (1691) 2 Vern 235. See also *Mexborough UDC v Harrison* [1964] 2 All ER 109, [1964] 1 WLR 733. However, where the mortgagee has sold the foreclosed property to a third party he cannot sue the mortgagor or guarantor on the covenant: see *Lloyds and Scottish Trust Ltd v Britten* (1982) 44 P & CR 249, [1982] LS Gaz R 129; and PARA 545.
2 See *Watson v Marston* (1853) 4 De GM & G 230; *Stevens v Theatres Ltd* [1903] 1 Ch 857. Cf *Re Alison, Johnson v Mounsey* (1879) 11 ChD 284, CA.
3 *Loyd v Mansell* (1722) 2 P Wms 73. As to setting aside judgments obtained by fraud see CIVIL PROCEDURE vol 12A (2015) PARA 1225; MISREPRESENTATION vol 76 (2013) PARAS 780, 811 et seq.
4 *Gore v Stacpoole* (1813) 1 Dow 18, HL; *Harvey v Tebbutt* (1820) 1 Jac & W 197.
5 *Patch v Ward* (1867) 3 Ch App 203. As to constructive fraud see MISREPRESENTATION vol 76 (2013) PARA 834 et seq.
6 *Campbell v Holyland* (1877) 7 ChD 166 at 172–173.
7 *Re Power and Carton's Contract* (1890) 25 LR Ir 459.
8 *Tooke v Bishop of Ely* (1705) 5 Bro Parl Cas 181; *Re Power and Carton's Contract* (1890) 25 LR Ir 459 at 470. As to reopening foreclosure when it is contrary to agreement between the parties see *Cox v Peele* (1788) 2 Bro CC 334. As to the bequest of securities as a debt see WILLS AND INTESTACY vol 102 (2010) PARA 27.

620. Effect of acquiescence or delay in reopening foreclosure absolute. An application to reopen a foreclosure absolute must be made promptly[1]. The mortgagor loses his right by acquiescing in the mortgagee's ownership[2], especially if there have been dealings with or expenditure on the estate[3].

1 *Thornhill v Manning* (1851) 1 Sim NS 451 at 454; *Campbell v Holyland* (1877) 7 ChD 166.
2 See *Fleetwood v Jansen* (1742) 2 Atk 467.
3 See *Stuckville v Dolben* (undated) cited in 5 Vin Abr 476 pl 1; *Ord v Smith* (1725) Cas *temp* King 9. See also EQUITABLE JURISDICTION vol 47 (2014) PARA 252.

10. ORDERS FOR SALE

(1) ORDER FOR SALE IN MORTGAGE PROCEEDINGS

621. Statutory jurisdiction to order sale. In any proceedings, whether for foreclosure[1], or for redemption[2], or for sale, or for the raising and payment in any manner of mortgage money[3], the court[4] may direct a sale[5] of the mortgaged property[6] on the request of the mortgagee or of any person interested either in the mortgage money or the right of redemption[7], notwithstanding the dissent of any other person[8], and notwithstanding that the mortgagee or any person so interested does not appear in the proceedings[9]. This provision extends to equitable mortgages and charges[10]. Any person entitled to redeem mortgaged property may have a judgment or order for sale instead of for redemption in proceedings brought by him either for redemption alone, or for sale alone, or for sale or redemption in the alternative[11]. The sale may be directed without allowing any time for redemption or for payment of any mortgage money, and may be directed on such terms as the court thinks fit, including the deposit in court of a reasonable sum, fixed by the court, to meet the expenses of the sale and to secure performance of the terms[12]. The court may direct a sale without previously determining the priorities of incumbrancers[13]. In favour of a purchaser, the court may make a vesting order conveying the mortgaged property, or appoint a person to do so, subject or not to any incumbrance, as the court may think fit; alternatively, in the case of an equitable mortgage, the court may create and vest a mortgage term in the mortgagee to enable him to carry out the sale as if the mortgage had been made by deed by way of legal mortgage[14]. The court's discretion is unfettered but must be exercised judicially by having due regard to the interests of all concerned[15].

1   As to foreclosure see PARA 571 et seq.
2   As to redemption proceedings see PARA 661 et seq.
3   As to the meaning of 'mortgage money' see PARA 104 note 1.
4   As to the jurisdiction of the High Court and County Court see PARAS 534–535. As to procedure generally see PARA 536 et seq.
5   See *Twentieth Century Banking Corpn Ltd v Wilkinson* [1977] Ch 99, [1976] 3 All ER 361.
6   'Mortgaged property' includes the estate or interest which a mortgagee would have had power to convey if the statutory power of sale were applicable: Law of Property Act 1925 s 91(6). As to the meaning of 'mortgagee' see PARA 104 note 1. As to the application of the statutory power of sale see PARA 446.
7   As to the right of the person entitled to redeem to have a sale see further the Law of Property Act 1925 s 91(1); and PARA 676. Thus a person claiming a beneficial interest in the property may apply for a sale: *Halifax Building Society v Stansfield* [1993] EGCS 147, CA. In proceedings by a person interested in the right of redemption and seeking a sale, the court may, on the application of any defendant, direct the claimant to give security for costs: see PARA 676.
8   Law of Property Act 1925 s 91(2)(a).
9   Law of Property Act 1925 s 91(2)(b).
10 'Mortgage' is defined as including any charge or lien by the Law of Property Act 1925 s 205(xvi): see PARA 101 note 4. See also *Oldham v Stringer* (1884) 33 WR 251.
11 Law of Property Act 1925 s 91(1). See also CPR 40.16; and CIVIL PROCEDURE vol 12A (2015) PARA 1256. See also *Woolley v Colman* (1882) 21 ChD 169 (an order can be made even on an interim application).
12 Law of Property Act 1925 s 91(2).
13 Law of Property Act 1925 s 91(4). Cf s 90(1): see PARA 630. As to the meaning of 'incumbrancer' see PARA 197 note 4.
14 Law of Property Act 1925 s 91(7). Cf s 90(1): see PARA 630.
15 *Palk v Mortgage Services Funding plc* [1993] Ch 330, [1993] 2 All ER 481, CA; *Arab Bank plc v Merchantile Holdings Ltd* [1994] Ch 71, [1994] 2 All ER 74.

622. Order for sale against wishes of mortgagee. The court will normally only order a sale at the request of a mortgagor against the wishes of a mortgagee if the court can protect the mortgagee against the loss of his right to repayment of the loan with interest, either by ordering the mortgagor to put up sufficient security to ensure full repayment of the mortgage debt[1], or by imposing a sufficiently high reserve price on the property so as to preclude a sale unless it achieves this result[2]. Where a mortgagee seeks foreclosure, an order for sale will be refused if the security is deficient and the mortgagor's application is based only on a possible rise in value, or where the value of the property is reduced because the mortgagee is a statutory tenant of the property with a right to retain possession after any sale[3].

Only in exceptional circumstances will the power be exercised against the mortgagee's wishes when a substantial part of the mortgage debt will remain outstanding following a sale[4]. Accordingly, no order for sale will be made in favour of the mortgagor where the mortgagee is taking active steps to enforce its security by sale[5] or where a mortgagee can demonstrate a real possibility that a refusal or postponement of a sale would be financially beneficial because of the likely increase in value of the property or because of the extent of the revenue which it would generate in the interim[6].

Where a mortgagee seeks possession but has no wish to realise his security in the near future, and wishes to retain the property to speculate on an increase in value notwithstanding an income shortfall, the court may order a sale even though the proceeds of sale would be insufficient to discharge the mortgage debt and the mortgagor cannot pay the deficit[7]. However, once the mortgagee has an order for possession and the warrant takes effect the court will not suspend that order to enable the mortgagor to make an application for sale[8].

1   *Cripps v Wood* (1882) 51 LJCh 584; *Norman v Beaumont* [1893] WN 45. See also *Palk v Mortgage Services Funding plc* [1993] Ch 330, [1993] 2 All ER 481, CA.
2   *Woolley v Colman* (1882) 21 ChD 169. See also *Palk v Mortgage Services Funding plc* [1993] Ch 330, [1993] 2 All ER 481, CA.
3   See PARA 577. As to foreclosure see PARA 571 et seq.
4   *Palk v Mortgage Services Funding plc* [1993] Ch 330, [1993] 2 All ER 481, CA.
5   *Cheltenham and Gloucester plc v Krausz* [1997] 1 All ER 21, [1997] 1 WLR 1558, CA.
6   *Palk v Mortgage Services Funding plc* [1993] Ch 330 at 343, [1993] 2 All ER 481 at 491, CA, per Sir Michael Kerr. See, however, *Polonski v Lloyds Bank Mortgages Ltd* [1998] 1 FCR 282, [1998] 1 FLR 896, where an order for sale was made notwithstanding the financial detriment to the mortgagee because the mortgagor wished to move house.
7   *Palk v Mortgage Services Funding plc* [1993] Ch 330, [1993] 2 All ER 481, CA; *Polonski v Lloyds Bank Mortgages Ltd* [1998] 1 FCR 282, [1998] 1 FLR 896. The mortgagee may be given liberty to bid for the property: see *Polonski v Lloyds Bank Mortgages Ltd*.
8   See *Cheltenham and Gloucester plc v Krausz* [1997] 1 All ER 21, [1997] 1 WLR 1558, CA (doubting the correctness of the decision in *Barrett v Halifax Building Society* (1995) 28 HLR 634, [1995] NPC 146, ChD).

623. Order for sale in favour of legal mortgagee. The court has jurisdiction[1] to make an order for sale in favour of a legal mortgagee, the effect of which is to render the sale unimpeachable[2]. Such an order will be made only in exceptional circumstances and the mortgagee must make out a proper case that the proposed sale is necessary and that the court must exercise its discretion rather than leave it to the mortgagee to exercise his own power of sale; and the mortgagee must adduce sufficient evidence to enable the court to exercise its jurisdiction[3]. Such an order may be made where the court is satisfied:

(1)   that the prospects of the mortgagor successfully impeaching the sale are utterly remote;

(2)   that the mortgagor's conduct, during the application as well as before it, justifies the apprehension that he will not hesitate to threaten proceedings against the purchaser if that will spoil the sale; and

(3)   that the mortgagee's fear that the sale will be lost unless an order is obtained is not unreasonable[4].

1   Ie under the Law of Property Act 1925 s 91: see PARAS 575, 621.
2   Ie by virtue of the Law of Property Act 1925 s 104(2): see PARA 471.
3   *Arab Bank plc v Merchantile Holdings Ltd* [1994] Ch 71, [1994] 2 All ER 74.
4   See *Arab Bank plc v Merchantile Holdings Ltd* [1994] Ch 71, [1994] 2 All ER 74.

(2) ORDER FOR SALE IN FAVOUR OF CHARGEE OF EQUITABLE INTEREST

624. Statutory jurisdiction to order sale in favour of equitable chargee. Any person who has an interest in property subject to a trust of land may apply for an order for the sale of the land[1]. Thus an equitable chargee[2] of the share of a co-owner of land may apply to court for an order for sale[3]. The court must have regard to the intentions of the person who created the trust, the purposes for which the property is held, the welfare of any child occupying the property as his home, and the interests of any secured creditor of any beneficiary[4].

A powerful consideration is whether the creditor is receiving proper recompense for being kept out of his money, repayment of which is overdue[5].

Where an application was made before 1997[6], the interests of creditors would usually prevail over the other beneficiaries of the trust[7] unless there was a subsisting collateral purpose of the trust other than the provision of a home for the chargor and his spouse[8]. It made no difference that the chargee held a legal charge which was subject to the overriding interest of the other beneficiary[9]. These authorities are still useful but not decisive[10].

1   See the Trusts of Land and Appointment of Trustees Act 1996 s 14; and REAL PROPERTY AND REGISTRATION vol 87 (2012) PARA 106. As to the jurisdiction of the High Court and County Court see PARAS 534–535. As to the procedure for bringing a claim to order sale in favour of equitable chargee see PARA 625. As to procedure generally see PARA 536 et seq.
2   This includes the holder of a charging order, which is enforceable in the same manner as an equitable charge created by the debtor by writing under his hand: see the Charging Orders Act 1979 s 3(2); and PARAS 220, 293.
3   *Midland Bank plc v Pike* [1988] 2 All ER 434; *Lloyds Bank plc v Byrne* [1993] 2 FCR 41, [1993] 1 FLR 369, CA.
4   See the Trusts of Land and Appointment of Trustees Act 1996 s 15; and REAL PROPERTY AND REGISTRATION vol 87 (2012) PARA 106.
5   *Bank of Ireland Home Mortgages Ltd v Bell* [2001] 2 All ER (Comm) 920, [2001] 2 FLR 809; *Mortgage Corpn Ltd v Shaire* [2001] Ch 743, [2001] 4 All ER 364; *Close Invoice Finance Ltd v Pile* [2008] EWHC 1580 (Ch), [2009] 1 FLR 873, [2008] BPIR 1465; *Putnam & Sons v Taylor* [2009] EWHC 317 (Ch), [2009] BPIR 769, [2009] All ER (D) 242 (Mar). The adequacy of the security may justify a postponement of the sale even if no interest is being paid: see *Edwards v Lloyds TSB Bank plc* [2004] EWHC 1745 (Ch), [2005] 1 FCR 139, [2004] BPIR 1190.
6   Ie under the Law of Property Act 1925 s 30 (repealed) and before the commencement of the Trusts of Land and Appointment of Trustees Act 1996.
7   See *Re Citro (a bankrupt)* [1991] Ch 142, [1990] 3 All ER 952, CA; *Lloyds Bank plc v Byrne* [1993] 2 FCR 41, [1993] 1 FLR 369, CA; *Zandfarid v Bank of Credit and Commerce International SA (in liquidation)* [1996] 1 WLR 1420, [1997] 1 FCR 78; *Bank of Baroda v Dhillon* [1998] 1 FLR 524, 30 HLR 845, CA.
8   *Abbey National plc v Moss* [1994] 1 FLR 307, 26 HLR 249, CA.
9   *Bank of Baroda v Dhillon* [1998] 1 FLR 524, 30 HLR 845, CA.
10 *Mortgage Corpn Ltd v Shaire* [2001] Ch 743, [2001] 4 All ER 364.

625. Procedure for bringing claim to order sale in favour of equitable chargee.
A claim for an order for sale should be made to the court which made the charging
order unless that court does not have jurisdiction to order a sale[1]. A claim in the
High Court must be started in the Chancery Chambers at the Royal Courts of
Justice or a Chancery District Registry[2]. The claimant must use the Part 8
procedure[3]. A copy of the charging order must be filed with the claim form[4].
Sample forms of order are provided in the Civil Procedure Rules[5].

1 See CPR 73.10(2); and CIVIL PROCEDURE vol 12A (2015) PARA 1477. The County Court has
   jurisdiction where the charged judgment debt does not exceed £350,000 (the 'County Court
   limit'): see the County Courts Act 1984 s 23(g); the County Court Jurisdiction Order 2014, SI
   2014/503, art 3. See also PARA 534. As to the County Court limit see further COURTS AND
   TRIBUNALS vol 24 (2010) PARA 767.
2 See CPR PD 73—*Charging Orders, Stop Orders and Stop Notices* para 4.2; and CIVIL
   PROCEDURE vol 12A (2015) PARA 1477. As to procedure generally see PARA 536 et seq.
3 See CPR 73.10(3); and CIVIL PROCEDURE vol 12A (2015) PARA 1477.
4 See CPR 73.10(4); and CIVIL PROCEDURE vol 12A (2015) PARA 1477.
5 See CPR PD 73—*Charging Orders, Stop Orders and Stop Notices* Appendix A; and CIVIL
   PROCEDURE vol 12A (2015) PARA 1477.

626. Evidence required for enforcement of charging order by sale. A witness
statement in support of a claim to enforce a charging order by sale of the property
charged[1] must:

(1) identify the charging order and the property sought to be sold[2];
(2) state the amount in respect of which the charge was imposed and the
     amount due at the date of issue of the claim[3];
(3) verify, so far as known, the debtor's title to the property charged[4];
(4) state, so far as the claimant is able to identify, the names and addresses
     of any other creditors who have a prior charge or other security over the
     property and the amount owed to each such creditor[5];
(5) give an estimate of the price which would be obtained on sale of the
     property[6]; and
(6) if the claim relates to land, give details of every person who to the best
     of the claimant's knowledge is in possession of the property[7]; and
(7) in the case of residential property, state certain required information[8].

1 See CPR PD 73—*Charging Orders, Stop Orders and Stop Notices* para 4.3; and CIVIL
   PROCEDURE vol 12A (2015) PARA 1477. As to the statutory jurisdiction to order sale in favour
   of equitable chargee see PARA 624.
2 CPR PD 73—*Charging Orders, Stop Orders and Stop Notices* para 4.3(1).
3 CPR PD 73—*Charging Orders, Stop Orders and Stop Notices* para 4.3(2).
4 CPR PD 73—*Charging Orders, Stop Orders and Stop Notices* para 4.3(3).
5 CPR PD 73—*Charging Orders, Stop Orders and Stop Notices* para 4.3(4).
6 CPR PD 73—*Charging Orders, Stop Orders and Stop Notices* para 4.3(5).
7 CPR PD 73—*Charging Orders, Stop Orders and Stop Notices* para 4.3(6).
8 The information to be stated is whether a Class F land charge or a notice under the Family Law
   Act 1996 s 31(10) (MATRIMONIAL AND CIVIL PARTNERSHIP LAW vol 72 (2015) PARA 305), or
   under any provision of an Act which preceded that section, has been registered, and, if so, on
   whose behalf; and that the claimant will serve notice of the claim on that person: CPR PD
   73—*Charging Orders, Stop Orders and Stop Notices* para 4.3(7)(a), (b). As to Class F land charges
   see REAL PROPERTY AND REGISTRATION vol 87 (2012) PARA 730.

(3) ORDER FOR SALE IN PROCEEDINGS RELATING TO LAND

627. Jurisdiction to order sale in any proceedings relating to land. In any proceedings relating to any land[1], the court may order that land or part of it to be sold[2].

1 For these purposes, 'land' includes any interest in, or right over, land: CPR 40.15(2).
2 See CPR 40.16; and CIVIL PROCEDURE vol 12A (2015) PARAS 1256–1257. As to the mode of carrying out the sale see PARA 629 et seq.

(4) SALE OF LAND BELONGING TO BANKRUPT

628. Statutory jurisdiction to order sale of bankrupt's land. The trustee in bankruptcy of a person who has an interest in property subject to a trust of land may apply for an order for the sale of the land[1]. On such an application the court will make such order as it thinks just and reasonable having regard to:
(1)   the interests of the bankrupt's creditors[2];
(2)   in certain circumstances, the conduct of the spouse or civil partner or former spouse or civil partner, so far as contributing to the bankruptcy, and his or her needs and financial resources;
(3)   the needs of the children; and
(4)   all the circumstances of the case other than the needs of the bankrupt[3].
Where such an application is made after the end of one year from the date of the first vesting of the bankrupt's estate in a trustee, the court will assume, unless the circumstances are exceptional[4], that the interests of the bankrupt's creditors outweigh all other considerations[5]. It is an abuse of process for the trustee to make such an application for the sole benefit of a secured creditor who could himself make an application for sale[6].

Any person claiming to be the legal or equitable mortgagee of land belonging to the bankrupt may apply to the court for an order that the land be sold[7]. The proceeds of sale go first to pay the costs and expenses of the trustee of and occasioned by the application to the court and the sale and attendance at court, and then in payment of the principal, interest and costs of the mortgagee; if there is any balance, it is to be retained by or paid to the trustee[8]. If the proceeds are insufficient to pay the amount due to the mortgagee, he is entitled to prove for the deficiency as a creditor[9].

1 See PARA 624. As to the procedure for such a sale see BANKRUPTCY AND INDIVIDUAL INSOLVENCY vol 5 (2013) PARA 428.
2 'Creditors' means both secured and unsecured creditors: see *Judd v Brown* [1998] 2 FLR 360, [1998] Fam Law 514. The bankrupt's creditors have an interest in an order for sale even if the proceeds of sale are only sufficient to discharge bankruptcy expenses: *Eric Bowe (Trustee) v Bowe* [1998] 2 FLR 439, [1998] Fam Law 515.
3 See the Insolvency Act 1986 s 335A(2); and BANKRUPTCY AND INDIVIDUAL INSOLVENCY vol 5 (2013) PARA 672.
4 As to what constitutes exceptional circumstances see *Judd v Brown* [1998] 2 FLR 360, [1998] Fam Law 514; *Eric Bowe (Trustee) v Bowe* [1998] 2 FLR 439, [1998] Fam Law 515; *Re Raval* [1998] 2 FLR 718, [1998] Fam Law 590. As to the effect of the Human Rights Act 1998 s 1, Sch 1 Pt I art 8 (right to respect for private and family life) see *Barca v Mears* [2004] EWHC 2170 (Ch), [2005] 2 FLR 1, [2005] BPIR 15.
5 See the Insolvency Act 1986 s 335A(3); and BANKRUPTCY AND INDIVIDUAL INSOLVENCY vol 5 (2013) PARA 672.
6 *Re Ng (a bankrupt), Ng v Ng (trustee)* [1998] 2 FLR 386, [1998] Fam Law 515; *Judd v Brown* [1998] 2 FLR 360, [1998] Fam Law 514.

7   See the Insolvency Rules 1986, SI 1986/1925, r 6.197; and BANKRUPTCY AND INDIVIDUAL
    INSOLVENCY vol 5 (2013) PARA 428.
8   See the Insolvency Rules 1986, SI 1986/1925, r 6.199(1); and BANKRUPTCY AND INDIVIDUAL
    INSOLVENCY vol 5 (2013) PARA 428.
9   See the Insolvency Rules 1986, SI 1986/1925, r 6.199(2); and BANKRUPTCY AND INDIVIDUAL
    INSOLVENCY vol 5 (2013) PARA 428.

(5) PROCEDURE FOR CARRYING OUT ORDER FOR SALE

629. Conduct of sale following court order. Where the court has made an
order for sale[1], it may give any other directions it considers appropriate for giving
effect to the order[2].

Where a sale has been directed by the court, any party who wishes to bid
should, before the sale, apply to the court for permission to do so[3].

The conduct of the sale is often given to the mortgagor if the sale is likely to
produce a surplus for him, as it is in his interest to secure the best price for the
property[4], and, as he will be liable for the expenses of the sale, it is not necessary
to require him to give security for them[5]. There is, however, no general rule that
the conduct of the sale will be given to the mortgagor or a subsequent
incumbrancer[6]. Where the proceeds of sale are unlikely to be sufficient to
discharge the debts secured over it, conduct of the sale should normally be given
to the mortgagee[7]. The parties having the conduct of the sale are not chargeable
with any impropriety in connection with the sale on the part of other persons in
which they are not implicated[8].

1   As to the jurisdiction to make such an order see PARA 627.
2   See CPR PD 40D—*Court's Powers in Relation to Land* para 2; and CIVIL PROCEDURE vol 12A
    (2015) PARA 1256.
3   See CPR PD 40D—*Court's Powers in Relation to Land* para 3; and CIVIL PROCEDURE vol 12A
    (2015) PARA 1256. If all parties are given permission to bid, the conduct of the sale may be given
    to an independent person (usually a solicitor): CPR PD 40D—*Court's Powers in Relation to Land*
    para 3.3.
4   *Cheltenham and Gloucester plc v Krausz* [1997] 1 All ER 21, [1997] 1 WLR 1558, CA.
5   *Davies v Wright* (1886) 32 ChD 220. See also *Manchester and Salford Bank v Scowcroft* (1883)
    27 Sol Jo 517; *Woolley v Colman* (1882) 21 ChD 169.
6   *Christy v Van Tromp* [1886] WN 111. As to the court's power, in proceedings by the person
    interested in the right of redemption, on the defendant's application to give conduct of the sale to
    the defendant and to give directions as to costs see PARA 673.
7   *Cheltenham and Gloucester plc v Krausz* [1997] 1 All ER 21, [1997] 1 WLR 1558, CA.
8   *Union Bank of London v Munster* (1887) 37 ChD 51.

630. Form of order for sale by equitable mortgagee or chargee. Where the
security is an equitable charge[1], the order for sale declares the charge, directs an
account[2] and gives the mortgagor the opportunity to redeem. If he does so, the
deeds are to be handed back to him; in default, the direction for sale follows[3].
Where an order for sale is made by the court in reference to an equitable
mortgage[4] on land[5] not secured by a legal term of years absolute or by a charge
by way of legal mortgage, the court may, in favour of a purchaser, make a vesting
order conveying the land or may appoint a person to convey the land or create and
vest in the mortgagee[6] a legal term of years absolute to enable him to carry out the
sale, as the case may require, in like manner as if the mortgage had been created
by deed by way of legal mortgage, but without prejudice to prior incumbrancers[7]
unless they consent to the sale[8].

1   As to equitable mortgages and charges see PARAS 105, 215 et seq.
2   As to the appropriate accounts see PARAS 597–598.
3   As to the premises comprised in the sale see *Simmons v Montague* [1909] 1 IR 87.

4   As to the meaning of 'mortgage' see PARA 101 note 4.
5   As to the meaning of 'land' see PARA 104 note 2.
6   As to the meaning of 'mortgagee' see PARA 104 note 1.
7   As to the meaning of 'incumbrancer' see PARA 197 note 4.
8   Law of Property Act 1925 s 90(1). This provision applies to equitable mortgages, but not to a
    mortgage which has been overreached under the powers conferred by the Law of Property Act
    1925 or otherwise: s 90(2). As to the power to make vesting orders, appoint persons to convey, and
    create mortgage terms see s 91(7); and PARA 621. See also the Trustee Act 1925 s 47; and TRUSTS
    AND POWERS vol 98 (2013) PARA 322.

631. Procedure to provide for sale free from incumbrances. If the land to be sold
is subject to any incumbrance, the court may[1] direct that a sum (sufficient to
provide for the incumbrance and for further costs and expenses) be paid into
court[2]. The land may then be sold free from the incumbrance[3].

1   Ie on an application under the Law of Property Act 1925 s 50 (see PARA 465): see CPR PD
    40D—*Court's Powers in Relation to Land* para 1.2; and CIVIL PROCEDURE vol 12A (2015)
    PARA 1256. Any application under the Law of Property Act 1925 s 50 should, if made in existing
    proceedings, be made in accordance with CPR Pt 23, otherwise by claim form under CPR Pt 8: see
    CPR PD 40D—*Court's Powers in Relation to Land* para 1.5; and CIVIL PROCEDURE vol 12A
    (2015) PARA 1256.
2   See CPR PD 40D—*Court's Powers in Relation to Land* para 1.3; and CIVIL PROCEDURE vol 12A
    (2015) PARA 1256.
3   See the Law of Property Act 1925 s 50(2); and PARA 465. See also CPR PD 40D—*Court's Powers
    in Relation to Land* para 1.4; and CIVIL PROCEDURE vol 12 (2015) PARA 1215.

632. Certifying the result of the sale. If the court has directed the purchase
money to be paid into court, or if the court has directed that the result of the sale
be certified, then the result of the sale must be certified by the person having
conduct of the sale[1]. Unless the court directs otherwise, the certificate must give
details of:

(1)   the amount of the purchase price;
(2)   the amount of the fees and expenses payable to any auctioneer or estate
      agent[2];
(3)   the amount of any other expenses of the sale;
(4)   the net amount received in respect of the sale,

and must be verified by a statement of truth[3].

If the proceedings are being dealt with in the Royal Courts of Justice, the
certificate must be filed in Chancery Chambers; if the proceedings are being dealt
with anywhere else, the certificate must be filed in the court where the proceedings
are being dealt with[4].

1   See CPR PD 40D—*Court's Powers in Relation to Land* para 4.1; and CIVIL PROCEDURE vol 12A
    (2015) PARA 1256.
2   As to the estate agent and auctioneer's fees and expenses which may be claimed see CPR PD
    40D—*Court's Powers in Relation to Land* para 5; and CIVIL PROCEDURE vol 12A (2015) PARA
    1256.
3   See CPR PD 40D—*Court's Powers in Relation to Land* para 4.2; and CIVIL PROCEDURE vol 12A
    (2015) PARA 1256.
4   See CPR PD 40D—*Court's Powers in Relation to Land* para 4.3; and CIVIL PROCEDURE vol 12A
    (2015) PARA 1256.

633. Order for possession following order for sale. Where the court has made an
order for sale it may order any party to deliver up to the purchaser or any other
person possession of the land, receipt of rents or profits relating to it, or both[1]. In
order to protect the position of other co-owners as far as possible, it is not usual
to order possession until necessary to effect the sale[2].

1   See CPR 40.17; and CIVIL PROCEDURE vol 12A (2015) PARA 1256. As to proceedings for
    possession see PARA 549 et seq.

2   As to when possession is necessary see *Cheltenham and Gloucester plc v Booker* (1997) 73 P & CR 412, 29 HLR 597, CA.

11. DISCHARGE OF MORTGAGES

(1) BURDEN OF DISCHARGE

(i) Where Several Persons or Properties Liable

A. EXAMPLES OF MULTIPLE LIABILITIES

634. Liability for repayment where there are several mortgagors. Mortgagors may either agree between themselves[1] who is to be responsible for repayment[2], or such an agreement may be inferred[3]. If they have had the benefit of the money in specific shares, or for the purpose of a joint adventure, they must contribute to the repayment of the debt in the proportions of their shares in the mortgage money[4], or in the joint adventure[5]. Alternatively, one may have had the exclusive benefit of it, so as to be the principal debtor, while the others are sureties[6], in which case the sureties are entitled to be exonerated by the principal debtor[7], save in respect of advances applied for their joint benefit[8], and, as between themselves, they must contribute equally to the debt unless it has been otherwise agreed[9].

Where one mortgagor has paid more than his share of the mortgage debt or instalments, he is entitled to be credited with the amount he has paid in respect of the mortgagor's liability before division of the proceeds of sale, although where the other mortgagor has been excluded from the property he may be debited with an occupation rent[10].

1 Where there are several mortgagors the mortgage may, depending on its construction, secure either joint or several liabilities of any of the mortgagors, and mortgagors may be jointly and severally liable: see *AIB Group (UK) plc (formerly Allied Irish Banks plc and AIB Finance Ltd) v Martin* [2001] UKHL 63, [2002] 1 All ER 353, [2002] 1 WLR 94; and PARA 187.
2 *Harwood v Harwood* [1992] 1 FCR 1, [1991] 2 FLR 274, CA; *Huntingford v Hobbs* (1992) 24 HLR 652, [1992] NPC 39, CA.
3 *Bernard v Josephs* [1982] Ch 391, [1982] 3 All ER 162, CA; *Re Pittortou (a bankrupt), ex p the Trustee of the Property of the Bankrupt v Bankrupt* [1985] 1 All ER 285, [1985] 1 WLR 58. See also note 1.
4 As to apportionment of a charge between joint tenants or tenants in common see *Re Rushton (a bankrupt), ex p National Westminster Bank Ltd v Official Receiver* [1972] Ch 197, [1971] 2 All ER 937. Oral evidence is admissible to show for whose benefit the money was advanced: *Gray v Dowman* (1858) 27 LJCh 702.
5 As to joint adventure see eg PARTNERSHIP vol 79 (2014) PARA 11.
6 See PARA 118 et seq.
7 As to a surety's right to the transfer of the mortgage on payment by him of the debt see FINANCIAL INSTRUMENTS AND TRANSACTIONS vol 49 (2015) PARA 767; and as to a surety's right against the principal debtor see FINANCIAL INSTRUMENTS AND TRANSACTIONS vol 49 (2015) PARA 772 et seq.
8 *Re Pittortou (a bankrupt), ex p the Trustee of the Property of the Bankrupt v Bankrupt* [1985] 1 All ER 285, [1985] 1 WLR 58.
9 As to a surety's right to contribution see FINANCIAL INSTRUMENTS AND TRANSACTIONS vol 49 (2015) PARA 790 et seq; and as to rights to securities held by a creditor or co-surety see FINANCIAL INSTRUMENTS AND TRANSACTIONS vol 49 (2015) PARA 802 et seq.
10 *Bernard v Josephs* [1982] Ch 391, [1982] 3 All ER 162, CA; *Re Gorman (a bankrupt), ex p the Trustee of the Bankrupt v Bankrupt* [1990] 1 All ER 717, [1990] 1 WLR 616; *Re Pavlou (a bankrupt)* [1993] 3 All ER 955, [1993] 1 WLR 1046; *Byford v Butler* [2003] EWHC 1267 (Ch), [2004] 1 P & CR 159, [2004] 1 FLR 56. In some cases the occupation rent is set off against the interest element of the repayments to save the expense of an account: see eg *Sutill v Graham* [1977] 3 All ER 1117, [1977] 1 WLR 819, CA; *Brassford v Patel* [2007] BPIR 1049, [2007] All ER (D) 256 (Feb). See also REAL PROPERTY AND REGISTRATION vol 87 (2012) PARA 205.

635. Liability for repayment on mortgagor's death. On the mortgagor's death the mortgagee may pursue his rights and remedies against the mortgagor's estate[1].

As between the persons interested in the mortgaged property and those interested in the general personal estate, the mortgaged property is, unless the deceased has signified a contrary intention, primarily liable to bear the debt[2]. This principle does not apply if the mortgagor is a surety only, and the debt is paid off by the principal debtor after his death[3].

1   See PARAS 395 et seq, 518 et seq.
2   See the Administration of Estates Act 1925 s 35; and WILLS AND INTESTACY vol 103 (2010) PARAS 1005–1007. Written evidence that a testator had intended that the mortgage be repaid by another means, such as an insurance policy or endowment, may be sufficient to establish a 'contrary or other intention': see *Ross v Perrin-Hughes* [2004] EWHC 2559 (Ch), 7 ITELR 405, [2004] All ER (D) 159 (Nov). See also *Re Biss, Heasman v Biss* [1956] Ch 243, [1956] 1 All ER 89 (property comprised in residuary devise).
3   See *Re Hawkes, Reeve v Hawkes* [1912] 2 Ch 251 at 255. For the example of a mortgage of a wife's property to secure the husband's debt see *Hall v Hall* [1911] 1 Ch 487; and MATRIMONIAL AND CIVIL PARTNERSHIP LAW vol 72 (2015) PARAS 279. As to the discharge of guarantees see generally FINANCIAL INSTRUMENTS AND TRANSACTIONS vol 49 (2015) PARA 814 et seq.

636. Where several properties liable on the same mortgage. Where several properties of the same mortgagor which have been charged with a single debt become severed in title, they must, as between themselves, bear the mortgage debt rateably in proportion to their respective values[1] unless, by special agreement in the mortgage itself or by declaration on the mortgagor's part, one property has been made liable to bear the whole debt in exoneration of the others[2]. The rule does not apply where one property is subject to a specific charge and the other to a general lien for the debt[3]; but it applies as between real and personal property charged with the same debt[4], and it applies where additional properties are brought into the security on the occasion of further advances[5]. Property which is only charged in aid of the property in the primary security is entitled to exoneration[6], but property described in a mortgage as a collateral security is not necessarily a secondary security so as to be entitled to be exonerated[7].

1   See *Ker v Ker* (1869) 4 IR Eq 15 at 25, CA; *Re Darby's Estate, Rendall v Darby* [1907] 2 Ch 465; and cf *Galton v Hancock* (1742) 2 Atk 424 at 426.
2   *Marquis of Bute v Cunynghame* (1826) 2 Russ 275 at 299; *Leonino v Leonino* (1879) 10 ChD 460 at 465; *Re Dunlop, Dunlop v Dunlop* (1882) 21 ChD 583 at 588 (on appeal 21 ChD 583 at 592, CA). As to exoneration see PARAS 641–643.
3   *Re Dunlop, Dunlop v Dunlop* (1882) 21 ChD 583, CA.
4   *Lipscomb v Lipscomb* (1868) LR 7 Eq 501 (and as to this case see *Leonino v Leonino* (1879) 10 ChD 460 at 465–466); *Trestrail v Mason* (1878) 7 ChD 655.
5   *Leonino v Leonino* (1879) 10 ChD 460.
6   *Stringer v Harper* (1858) 26 Beav 33.
7   *Early v Early* (1878) 16 ChD 214n; *Re Athill, Athill v Athill* (1880) 16 ChD 211, CA; and see FINANCIAL INSTRUMENTS AND TRANSACTIONS vol 49 (2015) PARA 638.

B.   MARSHALLING OF ASSETS

637. Application of marshalling to mortgages. The doctrine of marshalling applies to the case of securities, whether mortgages, charges or liens, so as to prevent one claimant arbitrarily depriving another of his only security[1]. The doctrine applies where one creditor has a charge or lien on two funds and another has a charge or lien on only one of the funds, although if the double creditor has merely a right of set-off against the second fund, he cannot be required to abandon his charge on the first fund in favour of the second incumbrance on that fund and rely on his right of set-off[2]. If, however, one incumbrancer has a security on two properties of the same mortgagor, and another mortgagee has a security on one property only, the two properties will be marshalled, so as to throw the first incumbrance as far as possible on the property not included in the second security[3]. The securities need not have been created at the same time, and may be successive securities for the same debt[4]. There must, however, normally be two funds or securities, both originally the same owner's property[5]. Possibly there may be cases where the two securities have not been actually subject to the same ownership, but at least the owners of the security against which the claim is made must not be entitled to throw the paramount liability on the claimant's security[6]. A fund and a right of action are not marshalled[7].

Marshalling is not available to a second mortgagee where the common property does not secure a debt from the mortgagor[8]. It is, however, available where the doubly secured creditor has security over properties owned by different debtors if one has an equity of exoneration against the other, for example as guarantor[9].

The doctrine of marshalling does not entitle the single creditor to interfere with the double creditor's right to resort to whichever security he chooses[10] but, if the double creditor satisfies his incumbrance out of the property included in the single creditor's security, the single creditor is subrogated to the double creditor's rights against the other security[11].

The doctrine of marshalling is not available where the parties expressly agree to exclude it, or its exclusion is necessarily implied[12]. It will be applied if at any time during the proceedings the court sees occasion for it, even if marshalling has not been claimed by the statements of case[13].

1   For the general principle of marshalling see EQUITABLE JURISDICTION vol 47 (2014) PARA 195 et seq; and see *Galton v Hancock* (1742) 2 Atk 424 at 427, 430, 435, 438; *A-G v Tyndall* (1764) Amb 614 at 615; *Averall v Wade* (1835) L & G temp Sugd 252, 262.
2   *Webb v Smith* (1885) 30 ChD 192, CA.
3   *Lanoy v Duke of Athol* (1742) 2 Atk 444 at 446; *Gibson v Seagrim* (1855) 20 Beav 614; *Victoria and Grey Trust Co v Brewer* [1970] 3 OR 704, 14 DLR (3d) 28. See also EQUITABLE JURISDICTION vol 47 (2014) PARA 197.
4   *Gwynne v Edwards* (1825) 2 Russ 289n.
5   *Douglas v Cooksey* (1868) 2 IR Eq 311; *The Chioggia* [1898] P 1.
6   See *Douglas v Cooksey* (1868) 2 IR Eq 311.
7   *The Arab* (1859) 5 Jur NS 417.
8   *National Crime Agency v Szepietowski* [2013] UKSC 65, [2014] AC 338, [2014] 1 All ER 225.
9   *Re Dawes, ex p Kendall* (1811) 17 Ves 514 at 520 (applied in *Highbury Pension Fund Management Co v Zirfin Investments Ltd* [2013] EWCA Civ 1283, [2014] Ch 359, [2014] 1 All ER 674).
10   *Wallis v Woodyear* (1855) 2 Jur NS 179 at 180; *Noyes v Pollock* (1886) 32 ChD 53 at 70, CA; *Manks v Whiteley* [1911] 2 Ch 448 at 466 (on appeal but not affecting this point [1912] 1 Ch 735, CA, sub nom *Whiteley v Delaney* [1914] AC 132, HL). See also EQUITABLE JURISDICTION vol 47 (2014) PARA 195. The contrary dictum in *Lawrance v Galsworthy* (1857) 3 Jur NS 1049 is erroneous.
11   See eg *Aldrich v Cooper* (1803) 8 Ves 382 at 395–397; *Noyes v Pollock* (1886) 32 Ch D 53 at 70, CA. Marshalling fastens on the conduct and the conscience of the doubly secured creditor. It is the fact that he has the choice which fund to resort to and the power at law to disappoint the singly secured creditor which brings equity into play: *Highbury Pension Fund Management Co v Zirfin Investments Ltd* [2013] EWCA Civ 1283 at [18], [2014] Ch 359, [2014] 1 All ER 674.
12   *National Crime Agency v Szepietowski* [2013] UKSC 65, [2014] AC 338, [2014] 1 All ER 225.
13   See CPR 16.2(5); and CIVIL PROCEDURE vol 11 (2015) PARA 343. See also *Gibbs v Ougier* (1806) 12 Ves 413 at 416. See further the Senior Courts Act 1981 s 49(2); and EQUITABLE JURISDICTION vol 47 (2014) PARA 98.

638. In whose favour marshalling applies. The doctrine of marshalling[1] applies in favour of persons claiming one of the properties subject to the double creditor's charge, whether they claim by assignment or charge by the mortgagor for value as in a case where they are mortgagees[2], or claim as volunteers under a settlement made by the mortgagor[3]. Hence, where settled and unsettled estates are comprised in the mortgage, the mortgage will be thrown as far as possible on the unsettled estate, although not as against a subsequent mortgagee, unless the settlement contains a covenant against incumbrances or the mortgage is made subject to it so that the settled property is entitled to be exonerated⁴. The doctrine does not, however, apply in favour of the mortgagor himself or in favour of persons claiming under him otherwise than by assignment or charge, that is, his trustee in bankruptcy, his judgment creditors⁵ unless they have by judgment a charge on the estate⁶, his unsecured creditors⁷ or his personal representatives.

A surety who has given his property as security for a debt may require the creditor to resort to the debtor's other property comprised in the security in order to exonerate the surety's property⁸ or to marshall securities in the surety's favour⁹. Where an agent has pledged property, on which his principal has a lien, with property of his own as security for his own debt, the principal is entitled to have the debt thrown on the agent's property¹⁰.

1 As to the application of marshalling to mortgages see PARA 637.
2 *Aldrich v Cooper* (1803) 8 Ves 382 at 395–396.
3 *Hales v Cox* (1863) 32 Beav 118; *Anstey v Newman* (1870) 39 LJCh 769; *Mallott v Wilson* [1903] 2 Ch 494.
4 *Re Roche's Estate* (1890) 25 LR Ir 284, Ir CA; *Re Lysaght's Estate* [1903] 1 IR 235. See also PARAS 639–640; and MISREPRESENTATION vol 76 (2013) PARA 871.
5 See *Averall v Wade* (1835) L & G *temp* Sugd 252, 262.
6 *Re Fox* (1856) 5 I Ch R 541 PC.
7 *Anstey v Newman* (1870) 39 LJCh 769.
8 *Re Westzinthus* (1833) 5 B & Ad 817. See also *Spalding v Ruding* (1843) 6 Beav 376; *Kemp v Falk* (1882) 7 App Cas 573, HL; and FINANCIAL INSTRUMENTS AND TRANSACTIONS vol 49 (2015) PARA 760.
9 See FINANCIAL INSTRUMENTS AND TRANSACTIONS vol 49 (2015) PARAS 761, 764.
10 *Broadbent v Barlow* (1861) 3 De GF & J 570; *Re Holland, ex p Alston* (1868) 4 Ch App 168. As to marshalling securities given by a partnership firm and also by one of the partners separately see *Re Stratton, ex p Salting* (1883) 25 ChD 148, CA. See also *Re Burge, Woodall & Co, ex p Skyrme* [1912] 1 KB 393, where relief analogous to marshalling was granted.

639. Against whom marshalling applies. The doctrine of marshalling¹ applies against the owner of the two properties, if the mortgage or charge on both was created by himself; and it applies against persons claiming the property, or part of it, under him otherwise than by actual assignment or charge, that is, it applies against the mortgagor's trustee in bankruptcy², against his judgment creditors³, and against his personal representatives⁴. The right to marshal exists notwithstanding that the two estates or funds have become vested by devolution in different persons⁵. The right to marshall may apply in favour of a second mortgagee against a surety of the first mortgagee⁶; and it applies against the mortgagor's wife who has charged her own property for the prior debt⁷. The doctrine does not, however, otherwise apply to the prejudice of third persons' rights⁸; and it does not apply, therefore, against persons claiming part of the property by assignment or charge, whether for value⁹ or as volunteers¹⁰, unless the assignment or charge was made at a time when the other part had already been disposed of with a right of exoneration against the double creditor's mortgage as, for example, where the assignment of the part first disposed of contained a covenant against incumbrances¹¹.

1 As to the application of marshalling to mortgages see PARA 637.
2 *Baldwin v Belcher, Re Cornwall* (1842) 3 Dr & War 173; *Re Tristram, ex p Hartley* (1835) 1 Deac 288; *Re Holland, ex p Alston* (1868) 4 Ch App 168; *Heyman v Dubois* (1871) LR 13 Eq 158.
3 *Gray v Stone and Funnell* (1893) 69 LT 282.
4 *Flint v Howard* [1893] 2 Ch 54 at 73, CA. The right to marshal existed against the heir: see *Lanoy v Duke of Athol* (1742) 2 Atk 444 at 446.
5 *Lanoy v Duke of Athol* (1742) 2 Atk 444.
6 See *South v Bloxam* (1865) 2 Hem & M 457. See also EQUITABLE JURISDICTION vol 47 (2014) PARA 196; FINANCIAL INSTRUMENTS AND TRANSACTIONS vol 49 (2015) PARA 768.

7 *Tidd v Lister* (1853) 3 De GM & G 857.
8 *Webb v Smith* (1885) 30 ChD 192 at 202, CA; *Aldrich v Cooper* (1803) 8 Ves 382 at 391; *Averall v Wade* (1835) L & G temp Sugd 252, 262 at 258; *Flint v Howard* [1893] 2 Ch 54 at 73, CA; *The Chioggia* [1898] P 1 at 6; cf *Douglas v Cooksey* (1868) 2 IR Eq 311. See also EQUITABLE JURISDICTION vol 47 (2014) PARA 196.
9 *Barnes v Racster* (1842) 1 Y & C Ch Cas 401; *Flint v Howard* [1893] 2 Ch 54 at 73, CA.
10 *Dolphin v Aylward* (1870) LR 4 HL 486 at 501; cf *Mallott v Wilson* [1903] 2 Ch 494. See also MISREPRESENTATION vol 76 (2013) PARA 871.
11 See the cases cited in PARA 642 notes 5–7. The decisions in *Finch v Shaw, Colyer v Finch* (1854) 19 Beav 500 (affd sub nom *Colyer v Finch* (1856) 5 HL Cas 905 at 922) and *Haynes v Forshaw* (1853) 11 Hare 93 suggest that subsequent alienation of another part is necessarily subject to the right of marshalling, but this is inconsistent with *Barnes v Racster* (1842) 1 Y & C Ch Cas 401 and other cases cited in PARA 640 note 2.

640. Illustration of application of marshalling. Where two properties are mortgaged to A, and then one of them is mortgaged to B, and afterwards the other to C, there is no right of marshalling[1] in favour of B against C, so as to throw the whole of the first mortgage on C's security, notwithstanding that C took with notice of the prior mortgages. As between B and C, however, the first mortgage is apportioned between the two properties according to their value[2], unless C's mortgage is expressed to be subject to and after satisfaction of both the previous mortgages in which case B can marshal against him[3], or unless the mortgage to B was made on the footing that it was a first mortgage and the mortgage to C is subsequent in date. In the last case C takes subject to B's right to exoneration[4] out of the property retained by the mortgagor.

1 As to the application of marshalling to mortgages see PARA 637.
2 *Barnes v Racster* (1842) 1 Y & C Ch Cas 401; *Bugden v Bignold* (1843) 2 Y & C Ch Cas 377; *Moxon v Berkeley Mutual Benefit Building Society* (1890) 59 LJCh 524; *Flint v Howard* [1893] 2 Ch 54, CA; *Baglioni v Cavalli* (1900) 83 LT 500; *Smyth v Toms* [1918] 1 IR 338 (differing from *Re Archer's Estate* [1914] 1 IR 285, where marshalling in the second mortgagee's favour was allowed). See also EQUITABLE JURISDICTION vol 47 (2014) PARA 197.
3 *Re Mower's Trusts* (1869) LR 8 Eq 110; *Aldridge v Forbes* (1839) 4 Jur 20; cf *Re Lysaght's Estate* [1903] 1 IR 235.
4 *Tighe v Dolphin* [1906] 1 IR 305. As to exoneration see PARA 641.

C. EXONERATION

641. Nature of exoneration. The application of the doctrine of marshalling[1] often has the effect of giving an incumbrancer a claim against a fund not comprised in his security in substitution for his claim against a fund comprised in it, but of the benefit of which he is deprived by the overriding claim of an incumbrancer on both funds[2]. The same principle is, however, applied in cases where the person entitled to one fund or property claims, against the person entitled to the other fund or property, either complete exoneration or indemnity from or against the overriding charge, or contribution towards the charge[3]. Whether such a claim will be allowed depends on whether the owner of the two properties prior to their severance was himself the creator of the first charge on both, or whether that charge was paramount to his title; and also on whether, upon the severance of title, he gave the part alienated or charged a right of exoneration by the part retained[4].

1 As to the application of marshalling to mortgages see PARA 637.
2 See PARA 637.
3 See PARA 642.
4 See PARA 643.

642. Assignment of part of property by mortgagor. If the owner of two properties has mortgaged both and assigned one of them, whether for value or not, without reference to the mortgage on both[1], and he or his representatives pay it off, there is no right of contribution in his or their favour against the assignee[2]; but where the mortgagor assigns part of the mortgaged property by an assignment which is expressly made subject to the mortgage, there is a right of contribution between the property assigned and that retained[3]. If, in a case where the mortgagor has no right of contribution, the mortgagee enforces the debt against the assignee, the assignee is entitled to be exonerated out of the property retained by the mortgagor[4]; and where the assignment contains a covenant against incumbrances or for further assurance[5], or where it is taken upon a representation, even if only oral, that the estate is free from incumbrances[6], this gives the assignee an equity to exoneration or marshalling which will prevail against a subsequent purchaser of the other property who does not take the legal estate for value and without notice[7].

1   *Re Repington, Wodehouse v Scobell* [1904] 1 Ch 811.
2   *Re Darby's Estate, Rendall v Darby* [1907] 2 Ch 465. See also *Ker v Ker* (1869) 4 IR Eq 15, CA; *Hollinshead v Devane* (1914) 49 ILT 87.
3   *Re Mainwaring, Mainwaring v Verden* [1937] Ch 96, [1936] 3 All ER 540, CA.
4   *Re Best, Parker v Best* [1924] 1 Ch 42. As to the nature of exoneration see PARA 641.
5   *Averall v Wade* (1835) L & G *temp* Sugd 252, 262; *Hughes v Williams* (1852) 3 Mac & G 683; *Chappell v Rees* (1852) 1 De GM & G 393; *Re Roddy's Estate, ex p Fitzgerald* (1861) 11 I Ch R 369; *Re Roche's Estate* (1890) 25 LR Ir 284, Ir CA; *Re Jones, Farrington v Forrester* [1893] 2 Ch 461 at 470. In a voluntary settlement a covenant for further assurance does not have this effect: *Ker v Ker* (1869) 4 IR Eq 15, CA.
6   *Tighe v Dolphin* [1906] 1 IR 305. As to an erroneous recital that the prior incumbrance has been paid see *Stronge v Hawkes* (1859) 4 De G & J 632.
7   *M'Carthy v M'Cartie (No 2)* [1904] 1 IR 100 at 115, CA. See also *Finch v Shaw, Colyer v Finch* (1854) 19 Beav 500 (on appeal sub nom *Colyer v Finch* (1856) 5 HL Cas 905); *Re Chute's Estate* [1914] 1 IR 180.

643.   Assignment of part of property subject to paramount charge. If the owner of the two properties at the time of severance was not the creator of the prior charge, but that charge is paramount to his title, then he can claim the benefit of the rule of equality as between himself and his assignee, whether for value or not; and if he or his representatives pay off the first mortgage, the assignee must contribute[1]. It is otherwise if the assignor has on the assignment attached to the property assigned a right of exoneration[2], in which case the assignee is entitled to the benefit of marshalling[3] against the property retained until it comes to a purchaser for value without notice who obtains the legal estate[4].

1   *Ker v Ker* (1869) 4 IR Eq 15, CA, as explained in *Re Darby's Estate, Rendall v Darby* [1907] 2 Ch 465.
2   As to the nature of exoneration see PARA 641.
3   As to the application of marshalling to mortgages see PARA 637.
4   *Ocean Accident and Guarantee Corpn Ltd and Hewitt v Collum* [1913] 1 IR 337; and see PARA 642.

(ii)   What Constitutes a Good Discharge of Mortgage Debt

644.   Discharge of mortgage debt by payment. Any person may redeem who is beneficially interested in the equity of redemption or liable to pay the mortgage debt[1]. The mortgage debt may be discharged by payment to the mortgagee[2], or to a person authorised to receive it. There must be actual payment; the giving of a cheque is not conditional payment of a secured debt so as to release the security[3], and payment of substantial sums by registered post which were stolen in transit cannot be relied on[4]. The mortgagor cannot unilaterally appropriate a cross-claim for unliquidated damages in discharge of the debt[5] even if it gives rise to an equitable set-off[6].

An agent's authority to receive the debt may be express or implied[7]. The authority of a mortgagee's solicitor to receive money secured by the mortgagee is considered elsewhere in this work[8].

Where the advance is expressed to be made by several persons out of money belonging to them on a joint account, or the mortgage is made to more than one person jointly, the written receipt of the survivors or the last survivor of them, or of the personal representatives of the last survivor, is a complete discharge for the mortgage money, notwithstanding any notice to the payer of a severance of the joint account[9].

Where a charge[10] is registered[11] in the name of two or more proprietors, a valid receipt for the money secured by the charge may be given by the registered proprietors, the survivors or survivor of the registered proprietors, or the personal representative of the last survivor of the registered proprietors[12].

1   As to redemption see PARAS 107, 304 et seq. As to the persons entitled to redeem see PARA 306 et seq.
2   Where the mortgage is not by deed, the claim for the debt may be barred by lapse of time, but the creditor may nevertheless be entitled to enforce the charge: see LIMITATION PERIODS vol 68 (2008) PARA 1105.
3   *Re J Defries & Sons Ltd, Eichholz v J Defries & Sons Ltd* [1909] 2 Ch 423. See also *Henderson v Arthur* [1907] 1 KB 10 at 13–14, CA, per Farwell LJ.
4   *Mitchell-Henry v Norwich Union Life Insurance Society* [1918] 2 KB 67, CA.
5   *Samuel Keller (Holdings) Ltd v Martins Bank Ltd* [1970] 3 All ER 950, [1971] 1 WLR 43, CA; *Mobil Oil v Rawlinson* (1981) 43 P & CR 221, 126 Sol Jo 15.
6   *National Westminster Bank plc v Skelton* [1993] 1 All ER 242, [1993] 1 WLR 72n, CA. A claim to a quantified sum by way of equitable set-off might discharge the mortgage debt: see *National Westminster Bank plc v Skelton.* See also *Ashley Guarantee plc v Zacaria* [1993] 1 All ER 254, [1993] 1 WLR 62, CA.
7   As to an agent's implied authority see generally AGENCY vol 1 (2008) PARA 37 et seq.
8   See *Wilkinson v Candlish* (1850) 5 Exch 91; and LEGAL PROFESSIONS vol 66 (2015) PARA 589. As to receipts in deeds produced by solicitors see PARAS 368 note 2, 641. The receipt of the mortgagee's solicitor in a claim to recover the debt is a good discharge: *Bourton v Williams* (1870) 5 Ch App 655.
9   See the Law of Property Act 1925 s 111(1); and PARA 186.
10 As to the meaning of 'charge' see PARA 127 note 5.
11 As to the meaning of 'registered' see PARA 127 note 3.
12 See the Land Registration Act 2002 s 56; and REAL PROPERTY AND REGISTRATION vol 87 (2012) PARA 473.

645.   Discharge of mortgage debt by accord and satisfaction. The mortgage debt may be discharged by accord and satisfaction[1] where, for example, the creditor accepts some consideration in full discharge, not being payment after the debt has become due of a smaller sum than the debt[2], or where the mortgagee agrees to discharge the security as part of a voluntary arrangement[3].

A release of a debt is binding without consideration if made under seal, but otherwise must be made for consideration[4].

1   As to accord and satisfaction see CONTRACT vol 22 (2012) PARAS 605–614. If the mortgagee accepts worthless debentures in a company formed by the mortgagor in substitution for his mortgage, he cannot subsequently rely on the mortgage: *Re Goldburg, ex p Silverstone* [1912] 1 KB 384.
2   *Foakes v Beer* (1884) 9 App Cas 605, HL, following *Pinnel's Case* (1602) 5 Co Rep 117a. See also CONTRACT vol 22 (2012) PARAS 607, 614.
3   See PARAS 522, 527.
4   See DEEDS AND OTHER INSTRUMENTS vol 32 (2012) PARAS 231, 259.

646.   Repayment of mortgage: evidence of receipt. A mortgagor is entitled to a receipt at the time he makes repayment[1]. Where a solicitor produces a mortgage deed indorsed with a receipt signed by the mortgagee or a deed signed by the mortgagee containing a receipt, the deed is sufficient authority for payment to the solicitor[2]. If it is proposed to pay the sums required to a solicitor on his undertaking to procure the discharge of the mortgage, the cheque or draft should be made payable to the mortgagee rather than to the solicitor unless the mortgagee provides authority to the solicitor to receive payment[3].

1 See *Rourke v Robinson* [1911] 1 Ch 480; and PARA 648.
2 See the Law of Property Act 1925 s 69; DEEDS AND OTHER INSTRUMENTS vol 32 (2012) PARA 426; LEGAL PROFESSIONS vol 66 (2015) PARA 585.
3 *Edward Wong Finance Co Ltd v Johnson Stokes & Master (a firm)* [1984] AC 296, [1984] 2 WLR 1, PC. The assertion of the solicitor that he has authority is not sufficient.

(2) EFFECT OF PAYMENT, RECEIPTS AND TRANSFERS AND DELIVERY OF DEEDS

(i) Effect of Payment of Mortgage

647. Effect of payment of mortgage in general. When money secured by the mortgage has been discharged, a mortgage, other than a registered charge[1], becomes a satisfied term and ceases unless the money was paid by a person having a limited interest in the equity of redemption who requires the mortgage to be kept alive by transfer or otherwise[2]. Hence there is no need for a reconveyance of freeholds or reassignment of leaseholds; and, although a surrender of the mortgage term is appropriate where a mortgage is discharged as to part only of the property comprised in it[3], where it is completely discharged a surrender has no operation, as the mortgage term ceases upon discharge. All that is required, therefore, to discharge a legal charge or mortgage created by demise, is evidence that the principal money, with interest and costs, has been paid[4]. Evidence of payment is sufficient to discharge an equitable mortgage in whatever form it was created[5].

In general, where a mortgage has been paid off, the mortgagee is a trustee for the mortgagor, so that if necessary a vesting order can be made under the appropriate statutory provision or a person may be appointed to convey[6].

1 As to discharge of registered charges see PARA 652.
2 See the Law of Property Act 1925 s 116. In the case of a legal mortgage of land by demise, the term of years merges in the reversion where the purpose for which it was created is satisfied: see s 5; and REAL PROPERTY AND REGISTRATION vol 87 (2012) PARA 88. As to mortgage by demise see PARA 164. As to the equity of redemption see PARAS 107, 304 et seq.
3 A trustee-mortgagee may release part of his security on receipt of the whole of the purchase money produced thereby: *Re Morrell and Chapman's Contract* [1915] 1 Ch 162.
4 See *Edwards v Marshall-Lee* (1975) 119 Sol Jo 506, 235 Estates Gazette 901, CA. As to legal mortgages see PARAS 104, 160 et seq.
5 As to equitable mortgages see PARAS 105, 215 et seq.
6 In the case of a trustee, an order can be made under the Trustee Act 1925 ss 41, 51, 54: see *Holme v Fieldsend* [1911] WN 111, 55 Sol Jo 552 (one of two joint mortgagees wilfully refusing or neglecting to convey). See also TRUSTS AND POWERS vol 98 (2013) PARAS 47, 56 et seq. In the case of a minor an order can be made in the like manner as in the case of a trustee under a disability: see the Trustee Act 1925 s 46; and TRUSTS AND POWERS vol 98 (2013) PARA 321. As to the power of the Court of Protection to make decisions concerning the property and affairs of a mortgagee who lacks mental capacity see the Mental Capacity Act 2005 Pt 2 (ss 45–61); and MENTAL HEALTH AND CAPACITY vol 75 (2013) PARAS 727–728.

648. Rights of person making payment of mortgage. On payment of all money secured by the mortgage, the mortgagor is entitled to have the property restored to him free from the mortgagee's security. For that purpose, the mortgagee must execute any discharge or reconveyance that may be appropriate (although no express reconveyance is now normally required in the case of a mortgage of land[1]), and he must deliver up the title deeds[2] to the mortgagor, if he is the person making the payment[3]. If the payment is made by some person interested in the equity of redemption other than the mortgagor and it is desired to keep the mortgage alive, a transfer of the mortgage should be taken[4].

Thus a second mortgagee who redeems is entitled to a transfer[5]; and so is the mortgagor himself, after he has assigned the equity of redemption, if he is sued on his covenant for payment and pays the debt[6], but in this case the transfer is made subject to such equity of redemption as may be vested in any person other than himself[7]. The person claiming to redeem must at his own expense prove a prima facie title to do so[8]. Where there has been a sub-mortgage, both the mortgagee and the sub-mortgagee must give a discharge or reconvey[9]. If the accounts between the mortgagee and sub-mortgagee have not been settled, the mortgagor can require a reconveyance from them on payment into court of the amount due from him[10].

If a purchaser from the mortgagor redeems, he is entitled to have transferred to him any securities held by the mortgagee for the debt, including a personal judgment which the mortgagee has obtained against the mortgagor[11].

1   As to the principle that a mortgage term ceases on payment of all money secured see PARA 647. As to the effect of a receipt given by the mortgagee see PARAS 649–651. As to reassignment in the case of a mortgage of personalty see PARA 651.
2   As to the delivery of title deeds on discharge of the mortgage see further PARAS 656–658.
3   *Tasker v Small* (1837) 3 My & Cr 63 at 70; *Thornton v Court* (1854) 3 De GM & G 293; *Palmer v Hendrie* (1859) 27 Beav 349; *Palmer v Hendrie (No 2)* (1860) 28 Beav 341; *Walker v Jones* (1866) LR 1 PC 50 at 61; *Rourke v Robinson* [1911] 1 Ch 480; *Webb v Crosse* [1912] 1 Ch 323. As to terms of redemption see PARA 327. As to tender see further PARAS 335–336. As to the mortgagor's right to call for a transfer to a third person instead of a conveyance to himself see PARA 366.
4   A statutory receipt may operate as a transfer: see PARA 650. See also *Pearce v Morris* (1869) 5 Ch App 227; and PARA 316.
5   *Smith v Green* (1844) 1 Coll 555 at 563.
6   *Kinnaird v Trollope* (1888) 39 ChD 636.
7   *Kinnaird v Trollope* (1888) 39 ChD 636 at 645.
8   *James v Biou* (1819) 3 Swan 234 at 237. See also PARA 319.
9   *Lysaght v Westmacott* (1864) 33 Beav 417. As to sub-mortgages see PARAS 252 et seq.
10 *Lysaght v Westmacott* (1864) 33 Beav 417.
11 *Greenough v Littler* (1880) 15 ChD 93.

(ii) Forms of Receipt and Discharge

649.   Ordinary receipt given by the mortgagee. A receipt given by the mortgagee or his successor in title for all principal, interest and costs is sufficient evidence that all money secured by the mortgage has been paid and that the mortgagee or his successor in title has no further interest in or claim against the mortgaged property. This is so whether the mortgage is a legal mortgage, by demise or legal charge, or an equitable mortgage[1]. Usually, however, the receipt is given in the form which is known as a 'statutory receipt'[2].

1   See *Edwards v Marshall-Lee* (1975) 119 Sol Jo 506, 235 Estates Gazette 901, CA. As to legal mortgages see PARAS 104, 160 et seq. As to mortgage by demise see PARA 164. As to mortgage by legal charge see PARA 165. As to equitable mortgages see PARAS 105, 215 et seq.
2   See PARA 650.

650.   Statutory receipt given by the mortgagee. A receipt given by the mortgagee or his successor in title for all principal, interest and costs is usually in the form of a 'statutory receipt'. A statutory receipt must be indorsed on, written[1] at the foot of, or annexed to the mortgage[2], and must be for all the money thereby secured[3]. Where the mortgage consists of a mortgage and further charge, or of more than one deed, it is sufficient if the receipt refers either to all the deeds or to the aggregate amount of the mortgage money[4] secured by them and for the time being owing, and is indorsed on, written at the foot of, or annexed to, one of the mortgage deeds[5]. The receipt must state the name of the person who pays the money[6], and must be executed[7] by the chargee by way of legal mortgage[8] or by the person in whom the mortgaged property[9] is vested and who is legally entitled to give a receipt for the mortgage money[10].

A receipt so given operates, without any reconveyance, surrender or release:

(1)   where a mortgage takes effect by demise or sub-demise, as a surrender of the term, so as to determine the term or merge the same in the reversion immediately expectant on it[11];

(2)   where the mortgage does not take effect by demise or sub-demise, as a reconveyance thereof, to the extent of the interest which is the subject matter of the mortgage, to the person who immediately before the execution of the receipt was entitled to the equity of redemption[12]; and

(3)   in either case, as a discharge of the mortgaged property from all principal money and interest secured by, and from all claims under, the mortgage, but without prejudice to any term or other interest which is paramount to the estate or interest of the mortgagee or other person in whom the mortgaged property was vested[13].

In a statutory receipt the same covenants will be implied as if the person who executes the receipt had by deed been expressed to convey the property as mortgagee[14], subject to any interest which is paramount to the mortgage[15].

1   As to the meaning of 'written' see PARA 457 note 3.
2   As to the meaning of 'mortgage' see PARA 101 note 4.
3   Law of Property Act 1925 s 115(1). Where part only of the money is repaid, an ordinary receipt or surrender is appropriate: see PARA 649.
4   As to the meaning of 'mortgage money' see PARA 104 note 1.
5   Law of Property Act 1925 s 115(7).
6   If it does not state the payer's name it takes effect as an ordinary receipt: see *Edwards v Marshall-Lee* (1975) 119 Sol Jo 506, 235 Estates Gazette 901, CA.
7   It need be made only under hand: *Simpson v Geoghegan* [1934] WN 232.
8   As to the meaning of 'legal mortgage' see PARA 104 note 1.
9   Ie the property remaining subject to the mortgage at the date of the receipt: Law of Property Act 1925 s 115(11). As to the meaning of 'property' see PARA 101 note 5. The reference in s 115(1) to a 'chargee by way of legal mortgage' shows that this provision applies to legal charges; and this is expressly provided for: see s 115(8).
10   Law of Property Act 1925 s 115(1). For the form of statutory receipt see s 115(5), Sch 3 Form 2 (s 115(5) amended by the Finance Act 1971 s 69(7), Sch 14 Part VI). A receipt in the statutory form may be given with such variations and additions, if any, as may be deemed expedient: Law of Property Act 1925 s 115(5). As to the addition to the form where the money is paid by personal representatives or trustees see PARA 654.
11   Law of Property Act 1925 s 115(1)(a). As a receipt for all money secured, whether given in statutory form or not, has the effect of terminating the legal demise, legal charge or equitable mortgage or charge (see PARA 647), this provision as to the operation of a statutory receipt appears to have no effect, and it seems that it was inserted merely to show that, as a matter of conveyancing, the property is cleared of the incumbrance.
12   Law of Property Act 1925 s 115(1)(b).
13   Law of Property Act 1925 s 115(1).
14   As to the meaning of 'mortgagee' see PARA 104 note 1.
15   Law of Property Act 1925 s 115(6). As to the covenant so implied see PARA 197.

651. When statutory receipt available. A statutory receipt can generally be used for mortgages[1], except bills of sale[2], and registered charges[3]. Personal property is, however, usually mortgaged by assignment, and on payment off is reassigned by deed or instrument under hand. Where stock has been mortgaged by joint mortgagors, the reassignment must be to or at the direction of all; otherwise the mortgagee will be liable for any loss thereby arising[4]. A statutory mortgage[5] may be surrendered or discharged by the prescribed form of receipt[6].

The discharge of mortgages over ships, aircraft and hovercraft is dealt with elsewhere in this work[7].

1 See the Law of Property Act 1925 s 115(8); and PARA 650.
2 See the Law of Property Act 1925 s 114(5). As to entering satisfaction of a bill of sale see FINANCIAL INSTRUMENTS AND TRANSACTIONS vol 50 (2015) PARA 619.
3 See the Law of Property Act 1925 s 115(10) (amended by the Land Registration Act 2002 s 133, Sch 11 para 2(1), (11)). As to the meaning of 'registered charge' see PARA 142 note 7. As to the discharge of a registered charge see PARA 652.
4 *Magnus v Queensland National Bank* (1887) 36 ChD 25; affd (1888) 37 ChD 466, CA. As to mortgages of stocks and shares see PARA 211. As to the redemption of a loan made in foreign currency see *British Bank for Foreign Trade Ltd v Russian Commercial and Industrial Bank* (1921) 38 TLR 65; *Feist v Société Intercommunale Belge d'Électricité* [1934] AC 161, HL. As to foreign money obligations see FINANCIAL INSTRUMENTS AND TRANSACTIONS vol 49 (2015) PARA 25 et seq.
5 See PARA 166.
6 See the Law of Property Act 1925 s 120, Sch 4 Form 5.
7 See AIR LAW vol 2 (2008) PARAS 431, 432; SHIPPING AND MARITIME LAW vol 93 (2008) PARAS 335–336.

652. Charges on registered land continue until discharged. The legal estate created by a charge over registered land is deemed to be vested in the registered proprietor as a result of the registration, and therefore continues to subsist until discharged, notwithstanding payment[1]. A registered charge may be discharged either by documentary proof of satisfaction of the charge[2], or in electronic form[3]. Documentary discharge must be in the prescribed form[4], executed as a deed or authenticated in such other manner as the registrar may approve[5], although the registrar is entitled to accept and act upon any other proof of satisfaction of a charge he may regard as sufficient[6]. An application to register a discharge must be made in the prescribed form[7].

Electronic notification of the discharge of or the release of part of a registered estate in a registered title may be given by the mortgagee with the same effect as a prescribed form of discharge[8]. The discharge of a registered charge does not affect accrued rights under the contractual obligations contained in the charge[9].

A discharge given by mistake can be set aside[10].

1 See the Land Registration Act 2002 s 58; and REAL PROPERTY AND REGISTRATION vol 87 (2012) PARA 384.
2 See the Land Registration Rules 2003, SI 2003/1417, r 114; and REAL PROPERTY AND REGISTRATION vol 87 (2012) PARA 479.
3 See the Land Registration Rules 2003, SI 2003/1417, r 115; and REAL PROPERTY AND REGISTRATION vol 87 (2012) PARA 479.
4 See the Land Registration Rules 2003, SI 2003/1417, r 114(1), (2); and REAL PROPERTY AND REGISTRATION vol 87 (2012) PARA 479.
5 Land Registration Rules 2003, SI 2003/1417, r 114(3); and REAL PROPERTY AND REGISTRATION vol 87 (2012) PARA 479.
6 Land Registration Rules 2003, SI 2003/1417, r 114(4); and REAL PROPERTY AND REGISTRATION vol 87 (2012) PARA 479.
7 See the Land Registration Rules 2003, SI 2003/1417, r 114(5); and REAL PROPERTY AND REGISTRATION vol 87 (2012) PARA 479.
8 See the Land Registration Rules 2003, SI 2003/1417, r 115; and REAL PROPERTY AND REGISTRATION vol 87 (2012) PARA 479.
9 See *Bristol & West plc v Bartlett* [2002] EWCA Civ 1181, [2002] 4 All ER 544, [2003] 1 WLR 284.
10 *Garwood v Bank of Scotland plc* [2013] EWHC 415 (Ch), [2013] All ER (D) 14 (Mar); *NRAM plc v Evans* [2015] EWHC 1543 (Ch), [2015] BPIR 888, [2015] All ER (D) 13 (Jun).

(iii) Discharge of Mortgage as Transfer

653. Discharge of building society mortgages. The provisions relating to statutory receipts[1] apply (in substitution for the like provisions relating to receipts given by or on behalf of a building society[2]) to the discharge of a mortgage made to any building society, provided that the receipt is executed in the manner required by the statute relating to the society[3]. However, when all the money intended to be secured by the mortgage given to the building society has been fully paid or discharged, the society may endorse on or annex to the mortgage one or other of:

(1)   a receipt in the prescribed form signed by any person acting under the authority of the board of directors[4];

(2)   a reconveyance of the mortgaged property to the mortgagor[5];

(3)   a reconveyance of the mortgaged property to such person of full age, and on such trusts (if any), as the mortgagor may direct[6],

and the provisions relating to statutory receipts[7] do not apply to a receipt in the prescribed form so indorsed or annexed[8].

1   Ie the provisions of the Law of Property Act 1925 s 115: see PARA 650.
2   See FINANCIAL INSTITUTIONS vol 48 (2015) PARAS 494–495.
3   Law of Property Act 1925 s 115(9) (amended by the Industrial and Provident Societies Act 1965 s 77(1), Sch 5; the Friendly Societies Act 1971 s 14(2), Sch 3; and the Finance Act 1971 s 64, Sch 14 Pt VI). As to the manner required by the statute relating to the society see note 8.
4   Building Societies Act 1986 Sch 2A para 1(1)(a) (Sch 2A added by the Building Societies Act 1997 s 7(2), Sch 2). See further FINANCIAL INSTITUTIONS vol 48 (2015) PARA 495.
5   Building Societies Act 1986 Sch 2A para 1(1)(b) (as added: see note 4).
6   Building Societies Act 1986 Sch 2A para 1(1)(c) (as added: see note 4).
7   See note 1.
8   See the Building Societies Act 1986 Sch 2A para 1(3) (as added: see note 4); and FINANCIAL INSTITUTIONS vol 48 (2015) PARA 495. Where a receipt is so indorsed or annexed to a mortgage, and is not a registered charge within the meaning of the Land Registration Act 2002 (see PARA 142 note 7), the receipt operates in accordance with the Law of Property Act 1925 s 115(1), (3), (6), (8) (see PARA 650), in the like manner as a receipt that fulfils the requirements of s 115(1): see the Building Societies Act 1986 Sch 2A para 1(2) (as so added; and amended by the Land Registration Act 2002 s 133, Sch 11 para 19(1), (2)).

   In the application of the Law of Property Act 1925 s 115(9) (see the text to notes 1–3) to a receipt so indorsed or annexed but not in the prescribed form, the receipt is taken to be executed in the manner required by the statute relating to the society (see the text to note 3) if it is signed by any person acting under the authority of the board of directors: see the Building Societies Act 1986 Sch 2A para 1(3) (as so added). As to the position regarding registered charges see PARA 652.

654. Transfer of benefit of mortgage by statutory receipt. Where a statutory receipt may be used[1] and by the receipt the money appears to have been paid by a person who is not entitled to the immediate equity of redemption[2], the receipt operates (save in the case of registered land) as if the benefit of the mortgage[3] had by deed been transferred to him[4], unless either it is otherwise expressly provided[5] or the mortgage is paid off out of capital money or other money in the hands of a personal representative or trustee properly applicable for the discharge of the mortgage, and it is not expressly provided that the receipt is to operate as a transfer[6].

It is essential to a receipt operating as a transfer that it should appear by the receipt that the person making the payment is not entitled to the immediate equity of redemption. A statement in the receipt that he is not so entitled will suffice, but is not strictly necessary as that fact may be indicated by the receipt[7]. If the persons paying the money are the personal representatives of the deceased mortgagor, the equity of redemption will normally be vested in them, so that no special statement as to the source of payment is required; but if the money is paid out of capital money by trustees of a settlement, the equity of redemption being vested in the tenant for life, there should be a statement that the payment is made out of a fund applicable to the discharge of the mortgage[8].

The operation of a statutory receipt as a transfer does not affect the right of any person to require a reassignment, surrender, release or transfer to be executed in lieu of a receipt[9]; and where there is no right to keep the mortgage alive the receipt does not operate as a transfer[10]. The mortgagor[11] himself cannot keep the mortgage alive as against subsequent incumbrancers[12]. Hence, where there are subsequent incumbrancers, the receipt cannot operate as a transfer to the mortgagor. The mortgagee cannot safely transfer his mortgage to the mortgagor or his nominee without the consent of intermediate incumbrancers of whom he has notice[13].

1 See PARA 651. As to statutory receipts see PARA 650.
2 As to the equity of redemption see PARAS 107, 304 et seq.
3 As to the meaning of 'mortgage' see PARA 101 note 4.
4 Law of Property Act 1925 s 115(2). Thus the receipt operates as if there were a transfer under s 114: see PARA 367; and *Simpson v Geoghegan* [1934] WN 232; *Cumberland Court (Brighton) Ltd v Taylor* [1964] Ch 29, [1963] 2 All ER 536.
5 Law of Property Act 1925 s 115(2)(a). See *Pyke v Peters* [1943] KB 242 (mortgage of annuity and policies of insurance; sale by mortgagor of part of annuity and of insurance policies and redemption of mortgage out of purchase money by purchasers; sale intended to supersede mortgage; purchasers not transferees of mortgage).
6 Law of Property Act 1925 s 115(2)(b).
7 *Simpson v Geoghegan* [1934] WN 232; *Pyke v Peters* [1943] KB 242.
8 See the Law of Property Act 1925 s 115(5), Sch 3 Form 2 Note. The receipt will then operate as a discharge. If it is desired to keep the mortgage alive, the words 'and this receipt shall operate as a transfer', should be added.
9 Law of Property Act 1925 s 115(4). The statutory form of transfer (see s 114(3), Sch 3 Form 1) is quite short and avoids the difficulties which may arise in respect of a transfer by indorsed receipt.
10 Law of Property Act 1925 s 115(3). See also *Cumberland Court (Brighton) Ltd v Taylor* [1964] Ch 29, [1963] 2 All ER 536.
11 As to the meaning of 'mortgagor' see PARA 104 note 1.
12 See the Law of Property Act 1925 s 115(3). See also *Otter v Lord Vaux* (1856) 6 De GM & G 638; and PARA 678. As to the meaning of 'incumbrancer' see PARA 197 note 4.
13 *Re Magneta Time Co Ltd, Molden v Magneta Time Co Ltd* (1915) 84 LJCh 814. See also PARA 366.

655. Subrogation. Even if there is no statutory receipt[1] which operates as a transfer[2] so that the mortgage or charge is discharged, it may be treated as having been assigned in equity by the doctrine of subrogation[3].

1 As to statutory receipts see PARAS 650–651.
2 As to the statutory receipt operating as a transfer of the benefit of the mortgage see PARA 654.
3 As to the doctrine of subrogation see PARAS 386–387; and EQUITABLE JURISDICTION vol 47 (2014) PARA 207 et seq.

(iv) Delivery of Title Deeds

656. Delivery of title deeds on discharge of mortgage. In general, on discharge of the mortgage, all deeds relating to the title to the mortgaged property, including the mortgage deed and transfers of the mortgage, must be given up[1]. Where there has been a former mortgage to the same mortgagee, followed by reconveyance, these deeds form part of the mortgagor's title and must be given up[2]. If the mortgage deed comprises other property, the mortgagor is entitled to a reconveyance of the mortgaged property, but not, it seems, to delivery of the mortgage deed[3], although he is entitled to a covenant for production[4]. Where several trust mortgages have been transferred to trustees by one deed, the mortgagor first redeeming is entitled to have the transfer deed delivered to him on giving the trustees a covenant or acknowledgment for production[5]. Where the mortgagee has lost all title to the mortgaged land through lapse of time[6], the mortgagor is entitled to recover possession of the title deeds[7].

1 *Re Wade and Thomas* (1881) 17 ChD 348. The documents which had to be given up included, formerly, a settlement of the mortgage money which had been allowed to get on the title (see *Dobson v Land* (1851) 4 De G & Sm 575 at 581); but on a transfer to trustees the trust should not be disclosed (see PARA 375); and even if a trust of the mortgage money should be disclosed, the mortgagor is not concerned with it (see the Law of Property Act 1925 s 113(1); and PARA 375). As to the mortgagor's right to delivery of title deeds upon payment of all money secured see PARA 648. As to the custody of deeds during the continuance of the security see PARA 488 et seq. Tender of the mortgage money alone does not entitle the mortgagor to delivery of the deeds: see PARA 657.
2 *Hudson v Malcolm* (1862) 10 WR 720.
3 See *Young v Whitchurch and Ellesmere Banking Co* (1867) 37 LJCh 186 (where, however, the report is not clear as to the retention of the original conveyance).
4 *Yates v Plumbe* (1854) 2 Sm & G 174.
5 *Capper v Terrington* (1844) 13 LJCh 239. Before tacking became restricted (see PARAS 266–267), the mortgagee could not retain the deeds until payment of a sum not covered by the mortgage (*Chilton v Carrington* (1854) 15 CB 95), where at the time of payment no right to tack the further sum had arisen (*Brecon Corpn v Seymour* (1859) 5 Jur NS 1069).
6 See the Limitation Act 1980 ss 15, 17, 20; and PARA 519. See also LIMITATION PERIODS vol 68 (2008) PARAS 1025, 1095, 1124.
7 *Lewis v Plunket* [1937] Ch 306, [1937] 1 All ER 530. See also LIMITATION PERIODS vol 68 (2008) PARA 992.

657. Effect of tender of mortgage money. Tender of the mortgage money[1], even though improperly refused, does not entitle the mortgagor to delivery of the deeds[2]. However, an order may be obtained giving him liberty to pay into court a stated sum sufficient to cover principal, interest, and the probable costs of proceedings; and upon that payment the mortgagee will be ordered to deliver up the deeds[3].

1 As to tender see PARAS 335–336.
2 *Bank of New South Wales v O'Connor* (1889) 14 App Cas 273 at 283, PC; and see *Johnson v Diprose* [1893] 1 QB 512, CA. See also PARA 488 et seq. As to delivery of title deeds on discharge of the mortgage see PARAS 501, 656.
3 *Bank of New South Wales v O'Connor* (1889) 14 App Cas 273, PC.

658. Effect of subsequent incumbrances. If the mortgagee has notice of subsequent incumbrances, he is not bound to redeliver the deeds to the mortgagor without being satisfied that the subsequent incumbrancers have been paid off[1]. However, unless he has notice of the right or claim of a person having a better right, he is not liable for delivering the deeds to a person not having the best right to them[2]; and although the registration of another incumbrance under the Land Charges Act 1972 is actual notice of the incumbrance[3], this is not so in the case of a mortgagee who delivers the title deeds on his mortgage being surrendered or otherwise extinguished[4].

1 *Corbett v National Provident Institution* (1900) 17 TLR 5.
2 Law of Property Act 1925 s 96(2). See also PARA 501.
3 See PARA 263.
4 See the Law of Property Act 1925 s 96(2) (amended by the Law of Property (Amendment) Act 1926 s 7, Schedule). As to delivery of title deeds on discharge of mortgage see PARAS 501, 656.

(v) Costs of Reconveyance and Delivery of Deeds

659. By whom costs of reconveyance borne. The costs of reconveyance are borne by the mortgagor[1]. They include not only the ordinary costs where the mortgage title has not been changed by assignment[2] or devolution, but also any extraordinary costs rendered necessary by a change of title or other event, such as the cost of obtaining a vesting order where the person who should reconvey cannot be found or is under disability[3], or where the legal estate is in a trustee-mortgagee who has absconded[4]. They do not, however, include the costs of any order required where the mortgagee himself has become mentally disordered, these being normally paid out of his estate[5], nor costs occasioned by the mortgagee mixing the title to the mortgaged estate with other property[6].

1   *King v Smith* (1848) 6 Hare 473 at 475.
2   See *Wetherell v Collins* (1818) 3 Madd 255.
3   *Ex p Ommaney* (1841) 10 Sim 298; *King v Smith* (1848) 6 Hare 473; and see *Re Stuart, ex p Marshall* (1859) 4 De G & J 317.
4   *Webb v Crosse* [1912] 1 Ch 323.
5   See eg *Re Lewis, ex p Richards* (1820) 1 Jac & W 264; *Re Townsend* (1847) 2 Ph 348; but contrast *Re Marrow* (1841) Cr & Ph 142.
6   *King v Smith* (1848) 6 Hare 473 at 475; and see *Capper v Terrington* (1844) 1 Coll 103.

660.   Costs of getting deeds out of court. Where the deeds have come into the court's custody in the course of the reasonable and proper administration of the mortgagee's estate, the costs of getting them out must be paid by the mortgagor[1], but not if the advance was made by the executors and the mortgagor had no notice of their character or of the proceedings[2].

1   *Burden v Oldaker* (1844) 1 Coll 105.
2   *Reed v Freer* (1844) 13 LJCh 417.

(3) PROCEEDINGS FOR REDEMPTION

(i) Parties to Redemption Proceedings

661.   Necessary parties to redemption proceedings. All persons entitled to redeem[1], and all persons entitled to any part of the security or debt, are necessary parties to redemption proceedings[2], but the court will not stop redemption on account of the absence of a party who cannot be found if the mortgagee runs no risk[3], and it can protect the rights of the absent party by preserving them in the judgment[4]. The rule requiring the presence of all parties is based on the mortgagee's right to account once for all, which can only be done if the account is taken in the presence of all parties who could demand an account. A person entitled to redeem cannot be omitted because his interest is small[5]. The mortgagee after assignment and intermediate assignees are not necessary parties unless they have been in possession and the mortgagor, alleging receipts in excess of the debt, claims personal repayment[6].

1   As to the persons entitled to redeem the mortgage see PARA 306.
2   *Fell v Brown* (1787) 2 Bro CC 276; *Farmer v Curtis* (1829) 2 Sim 466; *Marquis of Cholmondeley v Lord Clinton* (1820) 2 Jac & W 1 at 134; *Audsley v Horn* (1858) 26 Beav 195; *Hood v Easton* (1856) 2 Jur NS 729, where a stranger had, by the mortgagee's authority, obtained possession of part of the mortgaged property.
3   *Faulkner v Daniel* (1843) 3 Hare 199 at 212.
4   *Francis v Harrison* (1889) 43 ChD 183; *Griffith v Pound* (1890) 45 ChD 553; *Hall v Heward* (1886) 32 ChD 430, CA.
5   *Hunter v Macklew* (1846) 5 Hare 238.
6   *Chambers v Goldwin* (1804) 9 Ves 254 at 269; *Hall v Heward* (1886) 32 ChD 430, CA.

662.   Sub-mortgagee as party to redemption proceedings. Where a mortgage has been sub-mortgaged, both the original mortgagee and the sub-mortgagee are necessary parties in a claim for redemption by the original mortgagor[1], but the original mortgagee may redeem the sub-mortgagee without making the original mortgagor a party[2].

1 *Chambers v Goldwin* (1804) 9 Ves 254 at 269; *Re Burrell, Burrell v Smith* (1869) LR 7 Eq 399; *Hobart v Abbot* (1731) 2 P Wms 643.
2 As to sub-mortgages see PARAS 252 et seq.

663. Personal representatives and trustees as parties to redemption proceedings. On the death of a mortgagee of freehold or leasehold land, his personal representatives are necessary parties to proceedings for redemption[1]. Where the equity of redemption[2] is settled, the tenant for life in whom the legal estate is vested will be the proper party to represent the settled land; in other cases of land held on trust, the beneficiaries are sufficiently represented by trustees, executors or administrators, but the court may direct beneficiaries to be added at any stage of the proceedings[3]. Beneficiaries are not bound if under the circumstances the trustees do not represent their interests[4].

Notwithstanding anything to the contrary in the trust instrument, the trustees' written receipt is a sufficient discharge for the money when the mortgage debt has been paid[5].

1 See the Administration of Estates Act 1925 s 1(1); and WILLS AND INTESTACY vol 103 (2010) PARA 944.
2 As to the equity of redemption see PARAS 107, 304 et seq.
3 *Jennings v Jordan* (1881) 6 App Cas 698, HL; *Re Cooper, Cooper v Vesey* (1882) 20 ChD 611, CA. See also CPR 19.1, 19.3, 19.7A; CPR PD 19A—*Addition and Substitution of Parties*; and CIVIL PROCEDURE vol 11 (2015) PARAS 480, 481.
4 *Re De Leeuw, Jakens v Central Advance and Discount Corpn* [1922] 2 Ch 540. As to the creditors' rights under deeds of assignment to trustees for payment of debts see *Slade v Rigg* (1843) 3 Hare 35; *Smith v Baker* (1842) 1 Y & C Ch Cas 223 at 229; *Morley v Morley* (1858) 25 Beav 253; *Troughton v Binkes* (1801) 6 Ves 573; *Yeatman v Yeatman* (1877) 7 ChD 210.
5 See the Trustee Act 1925 s 14(1), (3); and TRUSTS AND POWERS vol 98 (2013) PARA 517.

664. Claim by later incumbrancer. In the case of successive mortgages, a later mortgagee must make all mortgagees subsequent to himself, as well as the mortgagor, parties in proceedings to redeem a prior mortgage[1]. If he seeks to redeem any other mortgage than the one immediately prior to himself he must make parties all mortgagees between himself and the mortgage he seeks to redeem[2], but he need not make a mortgagee prior to that mortgage a party unless the amount due cannot be ascertained in his absence. As between himself and all behind him, a later mortgagee has a prior right to redeem a prior mortgage[3].

1 *Fell v Brown* (1787) 2 Bro CC 276; *Johnson v Holdsworth* (1850) 1 Sim NS 106 at 109; *Farmer v Curtis* (1829) 2 Sim 466; *Rose v Page* (1829) 2 Sim 471; *Ramsbottom v Wallis* (1835) 5 LJCh 92; *Richards v Cooper* (1842) 5 Beav 304; *Slade v Rigg* (1843) 3 Hare 35; *Teevan v Smith* (1882) 20 ChD 724, CA.
2 *Teevan v Smith* (1882) 20 ChD 724, CA.
3 *Lord Kensington v Bouverie* (1852) 16 Beav 194. As to where the subsequent mortgagee cannot make the mortgagor a party, eg by reason of a covenant not to foreclose for a certain period see *Ramsbottom v Wallis* (1835) 5 LJCh 92; *Rhodes v Buckland* (1852) 16 Beav 212.

665. Mortgage on two properties. Where two properties are subject to the same mortgage, the owner of the equity of redemption[1] of the one property is a necessary party in a claim to redeem the other property[2].

1 As to the equity of redemption see PARAS 107, 304 et seq.
2 *Palk v Lord Clinton* (1805) 12 Ves 48 at 59; *Marquis of Cholmondeley v Lord Clinton* (1820) 2 Jac & W 1 at 134; *Hall v Heward* (1886) 32 ChD 430, CA. As to consolidation see PARA 502 et seq.

(ii) Institution of Redemption Proceedings

666. Jurisdiction and procedure for redemption proceedings. The jurisdiction of the High Court and County Court, and the procedure for redemption proceedings are dealt with elsewhere in this title[1].

1 See PARA 534 et seq.

(iii) Statements of Case and Disclosure

667. Particulars or evidence in support of claim for redemption. The claimant must set forth in his particulars of claim, or in a witness statement in support of the claim, the mortgage contract and all the material facts, showing, if he is not the original mortgagor, how he derives his right to redeem; and he should also state briefly any special circumstances, such as that the defendant mortgagee has been in possession[1]. The mortgagee may deny the claimant's right to redeem[2], or any of the allegations in the particulars of claim or in a witness statement.

1 As to procedure generally see PARAS 536–537. As to the persons entitled to redeem see PARA 306 et seq.
2 This denial, if unfounded, may be a ground for depriving the mortgagee of his costs: *Incorporated Society in Dublin v Richards* (1841) 1 Dr & War 258 at 334.

668. When offer to redeem unnecessary. Every claim against a mortgagee by the owner of the equity of redemption[1] who admits the mortgage must expressly or by implication contain an offer to redeem[2], except where a person entitled to redeem[3] asks for a sale of the mortgaged property instead of redemption[4], or where the question raised is one merely of construction arising under the mortgage deed[5], or where the mortgagee has become a party to trusts affecting the equity of redemption, in which case any person interested in those trusts may enforce their due performance without offering to redeem[6], or, possibly, where the mortgagee proposes to make an improper sale[7].

1 As to the equity of redemption see PARAS 107, 304 et seq.
2 *Troughton v Binkes* (1801) 6 Ves 573; *Dalton v Hayter* (1844) 7 Beav 313; *Tasker v Small* (1837) 3 My & Cr 63; *Inman v Wearing* (1850) 3 De G & Sm 729; *Harding v Tingey* (1864) 34 LJCh 13; *Hughes v Cook* (1865) 34 Beav 407; *Gordon v Horsfall* (1847) 5 Moo PCC 393. It seems, however, that there is no rule that an annuitant whose annuity is repurchasable may only be sued for purposes of redemption: *Knight v Bowyer* (1858) 2 De G & J 421 at 446.
3 As to persons entitled to redeem see PARA 306 et seq.
4 See the Law of Property Act 1925 s 91; and PARA 676. Under the old practice an offer to redeem had to be pleaded expressly or in substance, but if the statements of case made a case for redemption the court would give permission to amend (*Palk v Lord Clinton* (1805) 12 Ves 48), and would require the mortgagor to undertake to redeem (*Balfe v Lord* (1842) 2 Dr & War 480).
5 *Re Nobbs, Nobbs v Law Reversionary Interest Society* [1896] 2 Ch 830.
6 *Dalton v Hayter* (1844) 7 Beav 313; *Jefferys v Dickson* (1866) 1 Ch App 183.
7 *Murad v National Provincial Bank Ltd* (1966) 198 Estates Gazette 117.

669. Redemption in proceedings brought to impeach mortgage. Under the old Chancery practice, a mortgagor who did not admit the mortgage, and failed in an action, containing no claim for redemption, brought to impeach the mortgage, would not be allowed in that action to redeem a mortgagee who had relied wholly on his title as mortgagee, but had to commence a new action for redemption[1]. He could, however, redeem in the same action if the mortgagee did not rely solely on his title as mortgagee, but claimed that he had become absolute owner[2].

1 *Martinez v Cooper* (1826) 2 Russ 198 at 215; *Johnson v Fesenmeyer* (1858) 25 Beav 88; *Crenver etc Mining Co Ltd v Willyans* (1866) 35 Beav 353; cf *Jervis v Berridge* (1873) 8 Ch App 351 at 358 per Lord Selborne LC. The authorities referred to in this paragraph must be read in the light of the Civil Procedure Rules: see CIVIL PROCEDURE vol 11 (2015) PARA 6 et seq. As to procedure generally see PARAS 536–537.

2 *National Bank of Australasia v United Hand-in-Hand and Band of Hope Co* (1879) 4 App Cas 391, PC. See note 1.

670. Disclosure in redemption claim. In a claim for redemption, disclosure can be enforced of the amount claimed to be due[1], of the mortgagee's securities[2] and of the incumbrancers' names[3]. Such disclosure should now be given or obtained by order before proceedings are commenced[4]. So long as his right to redeem[5] subsists, a mortgagor is entitled at his own cost to inspect and make copies or abstracts of or extracts from the documents of title in the mortgagee's custody or power relating to the mortgaged property[6].

1 *Bridgwater v De Winton* (1863) 33 LJCh 238; *Elmer v Creasy* (1873) 9 Ch App 69; *Beavan v Cook* (1869) 17 WR 872. As to disclosure and inspection of documents generally see CPR Pt 31; and CIVIL PROCEDURE vol 12 (2015) PARA 621 et seq.
2 *West of England and South Wales Bank v Nickolls* (1877) 6 ChD 613.
3 *Union of Bank of London v Manby* (1879) 13 ChD 239, CA.
4 See CPR Pt 31; and CIVIL PROCEDURE vol 12 (2015) PARA 621 et seq.
5 See PARA 306 et seq.
6 See the Law of Property Act 1925 s 96(1); and PARA 495. It seems that inspection can be enforced by a mortgagor by proceedings in the Chancery Division: see *Burn v London and South Wales Coal Co and Risca Investment Co* (1890) 7 TLR 118.

(iv) Order for Redemption or Sale

671. Order for redemption. The common form order for redemption directs an account of what is due to the mortgagee under and by virtue of the mortgage, and for his assessed costs of the redemption claim, and directs that, on the mortgagor paying to the mortgagee the amount certified to be due within six months[1] after the date of the master's order[2], at a time and place to be appointed by that order, the mortgagee is to surrender or give a statutory receipt[3] and deliver up the title deeds; and it further directs that if the mortgagor makes default in that payment his claim is to stand dismissed with costs. If one of two mortgagees has disappeared, the costs of obtaining a vesting order to get his interest must be borne, in the absence of misconduct by the other mortgagee, by the mortgagor[4]. If the mortgagee has been in possession, the order directs as against the mortgagee an account of the rents and profits of the mortgaged property on the footing of wilful default[5]; and if the mortgagor alleges that nothing is due on the mortgage, a direction is added for surrender within 21 days after the date of the certificate, if on taking the accounts it appears that nothing is in fact due[6].

1 This means calendar months: see the Law of Property Act 1925 s 61(a); CPR 2.10; and CIVIL PROCEDURE vol 11 (2015) PARA 123. A longer or shorter time may be given in special circumstances: *Lewis v Aberdare and Plymouth Co* (1884) 53 LJCh 741.
2 As to the master's order see PARA 601.
3 Ie pursuant to the Law of Property Act 1925 s 115: see PARA 650.
4 *Webb v Crosse* [1912] 1 Ch 323.
5 As to wilful default see PARA 430 et seq.
6 *Reed v Cooper* (1884) 3 Seton's Form of Decrees, Judgments and Orders in Equity (7th Edn, 1912) 1853–1854.

672. Special directions in order for redemption. Special directions are sometimes added as to improvements or substantial repairs by the mortgagee, but sums expended in necessary repairs, and any sums properly included under the mortgage contract, may be allowed without special directions[1]. Special directions may also be added to charge the mortgagee with wilful neglect in allowing the mortgaged property to deteriorate, or for improper management[2], waste[3], or improper sale, or to bring out any special circumstances, such as a valuation of the security in the mortgagor's bankruptcy[4], and accounts may be directed to be taken with rests. If the order for redemption is made after tender, the account is directed of what was due on the date of the tender, with consequential directions to meet the alternative results of the amount due exceeding or not exceeding the amount tendered[5].

1   *Blackford v Davis* (1869) 4 Ch App 304; *Wilkes v Saunion* (1877) 7 ChD 188; *Tipton Green Colliery Co v Tipton Moat Colliery Co* (1877) 7 ChD 192; *Shepard v Jones* (1882) 21 ChD 469, CA. See also PARA 749.
2   *Wragg v Denham* (1836) 2 Y & C Ex 117; *Batchelor v Middleton* (1848) 6 Hare 75 at 85.
3   See PARAS 438–441.
4   *Knowles v Dibbs* (1889) 37 WR 378 (for the form of order in this case see 3 Seton's Form of Decrees, Judgments and Orders in Equity (7th Edn, 1912) 1892); *Sanguinetti v Stuckey's Banking Co (No 2)* [1896] 1 Ch 502.
5   See the judgment in *Greenwood v Sutcliffe* [1892] 1 Ch 1, CA (for the form of judgment in this case see 3 Seton's Form of Decrees, Judgments and Orders in Equity (7th Edn, 1912) 1854). As to tender see PARAS 335–336.

673.   Successive incumbrancers. Where there are successive incumbrancers, the order directs redemption by them according to their priorities[1], a later mortgagee on redeeming the prior mortgagees being given the right to foreclose subsequent mortgagees and the mortgagor unless they in their turn redeem him[2]. The order may declare the priorities of the various incumbrancers[3], or direct an inquiry as to priorities[4]. If the claim is brought by a later mortgagee to redeem the first mortgagee and he fails to redeem, the claim will be dismissed with costs as against the mortgagor as well as the first mortgagee[5], but a later mortgagee of two properties, separately mortgaged to different prior incumbrancers, is entitled on redeeming the prior incumbrance on one property to foreclose the mortgagor as regards that property, although the prior incumbrance on the other property remains unredeemed[6].

1   As to priority between mortgagees see generally PARA 260 et seq.
2   See PARA 605.
3   *Jones v Griffith* (1845) 2 Coll 207.
4   *Duberly v Day* (1851) 14 Beav 9.
5   *Pelly v Wathen* (1849) 7 Hare 351; *Hallett v Furze* (1885) 31 ChD 312.
6   *Pelly v Wathen* (1849) 7 Hare 351. As to foreclosure see PARA 571 et seq.

674.   Effect of failure to redeem. Failure by a mortgagor to pay the amount certified due to the mortgagee within the time fixed by the order for redemption involves the dismissal of the claim[1], unless the court for good cause extends the time[2]. The court will not readily extend the time in a redemption claim[3], but it will do so in a case of genuine mistake[4].

1   *Faulkner v Bolton* (1835) 7 Sim 319. As to the effect of dismissal see PARA 675.
2   *Jones v Creswicke* (1839) 9 Sim 304.
3   *Novosielski v Wakefield* (1811) 17 Ves 417; *Faulkner v Bolton* (1835) 7 Sim 319.
4   *Collinson v Jeffery* [1896] 1 Ch 644.

675.   Effect of dismissal of redemption claim. Dismissal for any cause, except want of prosecution[1], of a claim for the redemption of a legal mortgage, is equivalent to a final order of foreclosure against the claimant[2]. In the case of successive mortgages, if the mortgagor is the claimant the effect of excluding his interest is that the last of the incumbrancers becomes quasi-mortgagor, the prior mortgagees ranking according to their priorities[3]. The dismissal forecloses not only the mortgagor and his successors in title, but also a person who has purchased the equity of redemption after the date of the claim form if the claim has been duly registered as pending[4], but the trustee in bankruptcy of a mortgagor who becomes bankrupt after the issue of the claim form is not foreclosed unless he has been made a party to the claim[5].

1 *Hansard v Hardy* (1812) 18 Ves 455. The authorities referred to in this paragraph must be read in the light of the Civil Procedure Rules: see CIVIL PROCEDURE vol 11 (2015) PARA 6 et seq. As to dismissal for want of prosecution see CIVIL PROCEDURE vol 12 (2015) PARA 516.

2 *Cholmley v Countess Dowager of Oxford* (1741) 2 Atk 267; *Bishop of Winchester v Paine* (1805) 11 Ves 194; *Inman v Wearing* (1850) 3 De G & Sm 729; *Re Alison, Johnson v Mounsey* (1879) 11 ChD 284 at 293, CA. It is not, however, so equivalent against other persons entitled to redeem: *Re Gleaves, ex p Paine* (1863) 3 De GJ & Sm 458 at 463; *Chappell v Rees* (1852) 1 De GM & G 393. As to foreclosure see PARA 571 et seq.

3 *Cottingham v Earl of Shrewsbury* (1843) 3 Hare 627 at 637. As to priority between mortgagees see generally PARA 260 et seq.

4 *Garth v Ward* (1741) 2 Atk 174.

5 *Wood v Surr* (1854) 19 Beav 551. As to foreclosing a surety who has mortgaged his own property see *Beckett v Micklethwaite* (1821) 6 Madd 199; *Aldworth v Robinson* (1840) 2 Beav 287.

676. Order for sale. Any person entitled to redeem[1] mortgaged property may have a judgment or order for sale instead of for redemption[2] in proceedings brought by him either for redemption alone, or for sale alone, or for sale or redemption in the alternative[3]. In proceedings brought by a person interested in the right of redemption and seeking a sale, on the application of any defendant the court may direct the claimant to give security for costs, and may give the conduct of the sale to any defendant, and may give directions as to the costs of any defendant[4]. The court may direct a sale without previously determining the priorities of incumbrancers[5].

1 As to persons entitled to redeem see PARA 306 et seq.

2 As to orders for redemption see PARA 671 et seq.

3 Law of Property Act 1925 s 91(1). As to the general statutory jurisdiction to order sale see s 91(2); and PARA 621. As to the court's discretion to make an order see *Polonski v Lloyd's Bank Mortgages Ltd* [1998] 1 FCR 282 (which must now be read in the light of the Civil Procedure Rules: see CIVIL PROCEDURE vol 11 (2015) PARA 6 et seq).

4 Law of Property Act 1925 s 91(3). As to security for costs see CIVIL PROCEDURE vol 12 (2015) PARA 617 et seq.

5 Law of Property Act 1925 s 91(4). As to the meaning of 'incumbrancer' see PARA 197 note 4. As to the power to make a vesting order or appoint a person to convey, or to create and vest a mortgage term in the mortgagee, see s 91(7); and PARA 621. Cf s 90(1); and see PARA 630. As to priority between mortgagees see generally PARA 260 et seq.

677. Costs in redemption proceedings. In a claim for redemption the mortgagor, as a rule, pays his own costs. The mortgagee may add all costs, charges and expenses properly incurred in relation to the mortgaged property to his mortgage debt[1].

1 *Hewitt v Loosemore* (1851) 9 Hare 449; *Dunstan v Patterson* (1847) 2 Ph 341; *Cotterell v Stratton* (1872) 8 Ch App 295; *Re Sneyed, ex p Fewings* (1883) 25 ChD 338, CA; *Parker-Tweedale v Dunbar Bank plc* [1991] Ch 12, [1990] 2 All ER 577, CA; *Gomba Holdings (UK) Ltd v Minories Finance Ltd (No 2)* [1993] Ch 171, [1992] 4 All ER 588, CA. As to the mortgagee's proper costs, charges and expenses, his right to them and the circumstances in which he may be deprived of them if ordered to pay the mortgagor's costs made necessary by the mortgagee's misconduct see PARA 743 et seq.

(4) MERGER

(i) When Merger takes Place

A. NATURE OF MERGER IN GENERAL

678. Nature of merger. Merger may take the form of a merger of estates or of a merger of charges in the land[1].

Where a charge on land and the ownership of the land become united in the same person, merger does not necessarily follow in equity[2], and the equitable rule now prevails[3].

In general, merger of charges, like the merger of estates, is in equity a question of intention and this intention may be actual or presumed[4]. The sole exception to this rule is that where the owner of land pays off a charge which he is personally liable to pay, he is not allowed to set up the charge against subsequent incumbrancers to whom he is liable[5]. He may, however, do so when he has been discharged by bankruptcy from personal liability[6]; and where the first mortgage is also secured on property other than that of the person redeeming, it may be kept alive as to the other property[7]. In general, even though a charge is expressed to be extinguished, it may be treated as still in existence for the protection of the person finding the money to pay it off[8]; and where it has been extinguished under a misapprehension of title, it may be treated as in existence if this will be more in accordance with the general intention of the owner[9]. Where money advanced on the understanding that the lender is to have a first mortgage has been used to pay off an existing first mortgage, but owing to a mistake in the form of conveyance adopted the first mortgage has been discharged, it will nevertheless be treated as kept on foot for the protection of the new lender against a second mortgagee[10].

1 2 Bl Com (14th Edn) 177; *Capital and Counties Bank Ltd v Rhodes* [1903] 1 Ch 631 at 652, CA. There is no merger if the estates are held in different rights: *Lady Platt v Sleap* (1611) Cro Jac 275; *Chambers v Kingham* (1878) 10 ChD 743; *Re Radcliffe, Radcliffe v Bewes* [1892] 1 Ch 227, CA. An estate of freehold is, in law, greater than a term of years, however long (3 Preston's Conveyancing 219); and where the reversion on a lease for 1,000 years has been granted for 500 years, this reversion is the greater estate, and the 1,000 years can be swallowed up in it (*Stephens v Bridges* (1821) 6 Madd 66). Now that the only estates capable of existing at law are the fee simple and a term of years (see the Law of Property Act 1925 s 1(1); and REAL PROPERTY AND REGISTRATION vol 87 (2012) PARA 63), the question can arise only with regard to the merger of a term of years in the fee, or of one term in another. As to merger generally see EQUITABLE JURISDICTION vol 47 (2014) PARA 201 et seq.
2 See EQUITABLE JURISDICTION vol 47 (2014) PARAS 203–205.
3 This is because in any conflict or variance between the rules of equity and the rules of common law with reference to the same matter, the rules of equity prevail: see the Senior Courts Act 1981 s 49(1); and EQUITABLE JURISDICTION vol 47 (2014) PARA 99.
4 As to such actual or presumed intention see *Tyrwhitt v Tyrwhitt* (1863) 32 Beav 244 at 249; *Thorne v Cann* [1895] AC 11 at 18–19, HL, per Lord Macnaghten; *Re Gibbon, Moore v Gibbon* [1909] 1 Ch 367 at 373. See also *Forbes v Moffatt* (1811) 18 Ves 384 at 390–392, per Grant MR. See further PARA 682 et seq; and EQUITABLE JURISDICTION vol 47 (2014) PARAS 202, 204–205.
5 See *Otter v Lord Vaux* (1853) 6 De GM & G 638 at 642; *Platt v Mendel* (1884) 27 ChD 246 at 251; *Re W Tasker & Sons Ltd, Hoare v W Tasker & Sons Ltd* [1905] 2 Ch 587, CA; *Morrison v Guaranty Trust Co of Canada* [1972] 3 OR 448, 28 DLR (3d) 458. A statutory receipt does not operate as a transfer where there is no right to keep the mortgage alive: see the Law of Property Act 1925 s 115(3); and PARA 654.
6 *Re Howard's Estate* (1892) 29 LR Ir 266, CA.
7 *Taws v Knowles* [1891] 2 QB 564 at 572, CA.
8 *Irby v Irby (No 3)* (1858) 25 Beav 632; *Lord Gifford v Lord Fitzhardinge* [1899] 2 Ch 32. See also *Banque Financière de la Cité v Parc (Battersea) Ltd* [1999] 1 AC 221, [1998] 1 All ER 737, HL.
9 *Earl of Buckinghamshire v Hobart* (1818) 3 Swan 186 at 202.

10 *Whiteley v Delaney* [1914] AC 132, HL. See also *Banque Financière de la Cité v Parc (Battersea) Ltd* [1999] 1 AC 221, [1998] 1 All ER 737, HL.

679. Union of beneficial interests sufficient for merger. As merger depends on intention, and not on the mere legal union of the charge and the estate, it may take place even though the charge is supported by an outstanding legal estate[1]. For merger to take place it is sufficient that the beneficial interest in the charge and the beneficial estate in the land meet in the same person, whether in either case they are accompanied by the legal interest or estate or not[2].

1 *Astley v Milles* (1827) 1 Sim 298 at 344; *Pitt v Pitt* (1856) 22 Beav 294. As to the nature of merger see PARA 678.
2 *Forbes v Moffatt* (1811) 18 Ves 384 at 390 per Grant MR; *Donisthorpe v Porter* (1762) 2 Eden 162 at 164 per Lord Henley LC.

B.   MERGER IN PARTICULAR CASES

680. Charge united with fee simple. The presumption in favour of merger arises when the absolute interest in the charges is united with the estate in fee simple in the land, whether the owner of the land acquired the charge before[1], or at the same time as[2], or after[3], he became entitled to the land, unless the estate in fee simple is subject to an executory devise or is otherwise defeasible[4], or the title is in dispute[5]. There is no advantage in keeping the charge alive[6], and its extinguishment simplifies the title to the land[7].

The presumption in favour of merger arises in these cases not only where the charge and estate devolve upon the same person, but also where the owner of the estate purchases[8] or pays off[9] the charge.

1 *Forbes v Moffatt* (1811) 18 Ves 384; *Swinfen v Swinfen (No 3)* (1860) 29 Beav 199 at 203. As to the nature of merger see PARA 678. As to the presumption of merger see EQUITABLE JURISDICTION vol 47 (2014) PARAS 204–205.
2 *Grice v Shaw* (1852) 10 Hare 76 at 79.
3 *Price v Gibson* (1762) 2 Eden 115; *Hood v Phillips* (1841) 3 Beav 513; *Pitt v Pitt* (1856) 22 Beav 294; *Tyrwhitt v Tyrwhitt* (1863) 32 Beav 244 at 249. In *Swabey v Swabey* (1846) 15 Sim 106, the mortgage was treated as existing for the purpose of probate and legacy duty, though merged as between heir and next of kin. See also *Re French-Brewster's Settlements, Walters v French-Brewster* [1904] 1 Ch 713.
4 *Drinkwater v Combe* (1825) 2 Sim & St 340.
5 *Re Pride, Shackell v Colnett* [1891] 2 Ch 135.
6 *Forbes v Moffatt* (1811) 18 Ves 384.
7 See *Donisthorpe v Porter* (1762) 2 Eden 162 at 163. Merger has been held to have taken place where the owner of the land was entitled to the charge, a portion, as next of kin to the portioner, and had not taken out administration to him (*Re French-Brewster's Settlements, Walters v French-Brewster* [1904] 1 Ch 713); and merger may result from the mortgagor taking the mortgage as the mortgagee's executor and having sufficient as beneficiary to pay off the mortgage (*Re Greg, Fordham v Greg* [1921] 2 Ch 243).
8 *Astley v Milles* (1827) 1 Sim 298.
9 *Earl of Buckinghamshire v Hobart* (1818) 3 Swan 186.

681. Where limited owner acquires charge, or charge is not absolute. The presumption is against merger where a tenant for life or other limited owner (not being tenant in tail[1]) acquires or pays off a charge, as the merger would operate as a gift to those in remainder[2]. This presumption against merger has been held to exist notwithstanding that the reconveyance to the tenant for life was expressed to be absolutely discharged from the mortgage debt[3]. A presumption against merger also applies where the charge is subject to limitations which prevent the full union of the charge and the estate in the lifetime of the owner (for example, where the charge is subject to a prior life interest which does not terminate during the life of the owner in fee simple)[4]. In such cases, it is not necessary to take an assignment of the charge[5], or to prove any intention on the part of the tenant for life to keep the charge alive[6].

Where the tenant for life has had an ultimate remainder in fee simple, which, by the failure of intermediate estates, falls into possession on his death, there is no merger. The presumption against merger raised by his tenancy for life continues in the absence of any proof to the contrary[7].

1   *Morley v Morley* (1855) 5 De GM & G 610 at 620. As to the presumptions as to merger see EQUITABLE JURISDICTION vol 47 (2014) PARAS 204–205. As to entailed interests see REAL PROPERTY AND REGISTRATION vol 87 (2012) PARA 112 et seq.
2   *Burrell v Earl of Egremont* (1844) 7 Beav 205 at 232; *Pitt v Pitt* (1856) 22 Beav 294; *Lindsay v Earl of Wicklow* (1873) 7 IR Eq 192 at 204; *Williams v Williams-Wynn* (1915) 84 LJCh 801. As to merger generally see PARA 678.
3   *Lord Gifford v Lord Fitzhardinge* [1899] 2 Ch 32.
4   *Jones v Morgan* (1783) 1 Bro CC 206; *Wilkes v Collin* (1869) LR 8 Eq 338.
5   *Morley v Morley* (1855) 5 De GM & G 610 at 626; and see *Redington v Redington* (1809) 1 Ball & B 131.
6   *Lindsay v Earl of Wicklow* (1873) 7 IR Eq 192 at 204.
7   *Wyndham v Earl of Egremont* (1775) Amb 753; *Trevor v Trevor* (1833) 2 My & K 675. Where, however, the tenancy for life and the remainder in fee were separated only by special powers to appoint to issue and general powers vested in the tenant for life, and the tenant for life was at her death a spinster over 70 years of age, an intention to merge was presumed: *Re Toppin's Estate* [1915] 1 IR 330, CA.

     C.   SUFFICIENT REBUTTAL OF PRESUMPTION IN FAVOUR OF OR AGAINST MERGER

682. Rules as to presumption regarding merger yield to intention. The rules as to the presumption in favour of or against merger yield to the intention, and this may be actual or presumed[1]. The actual intention is to be gathered either from express declaration or the person's acts, and the presumed intention by considering what is most for his benefit[2].

1   *Forbes v Moffatt* (1811) 18 Ves 384 at 390; *Grice v Shaw* (1852) 10 Hare 76 at 79. As to merger generally see PARA 678. As to the presumptions as to merger see EQUITABLE JURISDICTION vol 47 (2014) PARAS 204–205.
2   *Tyrwhitt v Tyrwhitt* (1863) 32 Beav 244 at 249. This applies both to the original presumption and to the rebutting presumption. Where a tenant in fee simple pays off a charge, the original presumption is in favour of merger: see PARA 680. Where under the circumstances it is for his advantage to keep the charge alive, there may be a rebutting presumption which prevents merger: see PARA 686.

683. Express declaration as to merger. The clearest way of causing or preventing merger is by express declaration in the instrument which effects the union of the charge and the estate[1]. However, even an express declaration against merger will not keep the charge alive if there are circumstances pointing conclusively to merger[2].

1   See *Re Gibbon, Moore v Gibbon* [1909] 1 Ch 367 at 373. In this case, although the declaration was expressed to keep the charge alive for the benefit of the owner, his heirs and assigns, it passed on his death as personal estate (*Re Gibbon, Moore v Gibbon* at 378–379); and where, subsequently to a proviso in a conveyance of the land that the land is to be the primary fund for payment of the charge, the grantor pays it off, it will be kept alive as part of his personal estate (*Pears v Weightman* (1856) 2 Jur NS 586). Cf *Johnson v Webster* (1854) 4 De GM & G 474. As to merger generally see PARA 678.
2   *Re Gibbon, Moore v Gibbon* [1909] 1 Ch 367 at 374. See also *Swabey v Swabey* (1846) 15 Sim 106.

684. Intention as to merger inferred from circumstances attending union. Where there is no express declaration as to merger[1], an actual intention can be inferred from the circumstances attending the union of the charge and the estate. The contemporaneous transfer of the charge to a trustee is one of the grounds on which an actual intention can be inferred and the presumption in favour of merger rebutted[2], but by itself it is not decisive against merger[3].

1   As to merger generally see PARA 678. As to express declaration as to merger see PARA 683.
2   *Earl of Buckinghamshire v Hobart* (1818) 3 Swan 186 at 199. As to the presumptions as to merger see EQUITABLE JURISDICTION vol 47 (2014) PARAS 204–205.
3   *Hood v Phillips* (1841) 3 Beav 513; *Tyrwhitt v Tyrwhitt* (1863) 32 Beav 244; *Re Lloyd's Estate* [1903] 1 IR 144 at 148. As to a merger of a lease cf *Gunter v Gunter* (1857) 23 Beav 571.

685. Intention as to merger inferred from indications occurring subsequent to union. Where the union of the interests takes place otherwise than by the intended acquisition of the charge or estate, or payment off of the charge, so that no indications of intention can exist at the time of union, it is permissible to rely on any such indications occurring subsequently during the life of the owner[1], but apparently not on expressions of intention previous to the union of the interests[2]. Merger will be prevented by any acts done by the owner which are only consistent with the charge being kept on foot[3]. Similarly, merger will be effected where the owner has disposed of the land free from incumbrances, whether by sale[4], mortgage[5] or marriage settlement[6]. In such cases, he cannot set up the charge notwithstanding a clear expression of intention to keep it alive at the time he took it[7]. There will also be a merger where he has devised the estate in such a manner as to show that he treated the charge as non-existing[8], but a devise of the estate in such terms as to merge charges will not merge them so far as they form a security for subsequent charges made by the owner[9]. Where a tenant for life pays off an incumbrance, intending to discharge the inheritance, he cannot afterwards revive it[10].

1   *Redington v Redington* (1809) 1 Ball & B 131 at 143; *Swinfen v Swinfen (No 3)* (1860) 29 Beav 199 at 204; *Re Godley's Estate* [1896] 1 IR 45 at 51. As to merger generally see PARA 678. As to the presumptions as to merger see EQUITABLE JURISDICTION vol 47 (2014) PARAS 204–205.
2   *Tyrwhitt v Tyrwhitt* (1863) 32 Beav 244 at 251.
3   *Tyrwhitt v Tyrwhitt* (1863) 32 Beav 244. See also *Hatch v Skelton* (1855) 20 Beav 453; *Lea v Thursby* [1904] 2 Ch 57 at 65; *Re Fletcher, Reading v Fletcher* [1917] 1 Ch 339, CA.
4   *Bulkeley v Hope* (1855) 1 K & J 482 at 489. See also EQUITABLE JURISDICTION vol 47 (2014) PARA 205.
5   *Tyler v Lake* (1831) 4 Sim 351; *Re Gibbon, Moore v Gibbon* [1909] 1 Ch 367 at 374.
6   *Countess Dowager of Gower v Earl of Gower* (1783) 1 Cox Eq Cas 53.
7   *Countess Dowager of Gower v Earl of Gower* (1783) 1 Cox Eq Cas 53.
8   See *Hood v Phillips* (1841) 3 Beav 513; *Re Lloyd's Estate* [1903] 1 IR 144 at 149.
9   *Re Nunn's Estate* (1888) 23 LR Ir 286 at 300, CA.
10 *Morley v Morley* (1855) 5 De GM & G 610 at 626; *Re Godley's Estate* [1896] 1 IR 45 at 52.

686. Presumption where merger not beneficial to owner. Where there is no evidence of any actual intention, an intention to keep the charge alive, notwithstanding that it would prima facie merge[1], may be presumed where this is for the benefit of the owner[2] (for example, where the merger of the charge would let in subsequent charges[3], unless the subsequent charges have been created by the owner himself[4]). The result is in fact based directly on the advantage to the owner, but technically it is based on the presumed intention[5].

1   As to merger generally see PARA 678. As to the presumptions as to merger see EQUITABLE JURISDICTION vol 47 (2014) PARAS 204–205.
2   *Swinfen v Swinfen (No 3)* (1860) 29 Beav 199 at 204. See also *Earl of Clarendon v Barham* (1842) 1 Y & C Ch Cas 688 at 703.
3   *Forbes v Moffatt* (1811) 18 Ves 384; *Davis v Barrett* (1851) 14 Beav 542; *Whiteley v Delaney* [1914] AC 132, HL; *Ghana Commercial Bank v Chandiram* [1960] AC 732, [1960] 2 All ER 865, PC.
4   *Johnson v Webster* (1854) 4 De GM & G 474 at 488.

5   *Grice v Shaw* (1852) 10 Hare 76 at 80; *Byam v Sutton* (1854) 19 Beav 556 at 562. See also PARA 682.

687. Presumed intention operative despite owner's ignorance or incapacity. The fact that the owner of the estate is ignorant of his rights prevents him from having any actual intention as to merger, but the presumed intention may still operate, according to the circumstances, either to effect or to prevent merger[1].

Where the owner is under an incapacity, the question of merger as a rule depends technically on the presumed intention but actually on considering what is most advantageous to him[2].

1   *Burrell v Earl of Egremont* (1844) 7 Beav 205 at 232; but see *Whiteley v Delaney* [1914] AC 132, HL. As to merger generally see PARA 678. As to the presumptions as to merger see EQUITABLE JURISDICTION vol 47 (2014) PARAS 204–205.
2   *Forbes v Moffatt* (1811) 18 Ves 384 at 392.

688. Right of purchaser to keep charge alive. Prima facie where a mortgagee purchases the equity of redemption[1], or where, on a purchase, part of the purchase money is applied in paying off a mortgage, or where the mortgage and the equity of redemption become united by purchase in the same person, the mortgage is merged in the land[2]; but the person thus entitled to both interests can have the mortgage kept alive for his benefit[3]. A person advancing money to pay off a charge is entitled to have the charge kept alive and transferred to himself[4], and such a transfer should be a transfer both of the debt and the security[5].

1   As to the equity of redemption see PARAS 107, 304 et seq.
2   See *Smith v Phillips* (1837) 1 Keen 694. As to merger generally see PARA 678.
3   *Clark v May* (1852) 16 Beav 273; *Cooper v Cartwright* (1860) John 679.
4   *Manks v Whiteley* [1912] 1 Ch 735 at 743, CA, per Cozens-Hardy MR; revsd on other grounds sub nom *Whiteley v Delaney* [1914] AC 132, HL. As to forms of transfer see PARA 367 et seq. As to transfer by statutory receipt see PARA 654.
5   *Medley v Horton* (1844) 14 Sim 222 at 229.

689. Acquisition of charge by subrogation. Where the purchase money is applied in paying off a mortgage, but the mortgage is not transferred, it may be treated as subsisting to prevent unjust enrichment under the doctrine of subrogation[1].

1   As to the circumstances in which the remedy of subrogation is available see PARAS 386–387.

(ii) Merger of Lower in Higher Security

690. Merger of lower in higher security; the general rule. As a general rule, by taking or acquiring a security of a higher nature in legal valuation than one he already possesses, a person merges and extinguishes his legal remedies upon the inferior security or cause of action; thus the taking of a bond or covenant, or the obtaining of a judgment for a simple contract debt, merges and extinguishes the simple contract debt[1]. For this purpose, however, the superior security must be co-extensive with the inferior security and between the same parties[2]. A security given by one of two co-debtors to secure a simple contract debt does not merge the simple contract debt[3].

1   *Owen v Homan* (1851) 3 Mac & G 378 at 407; affd (1853) 4 HL Cas 997. As to interest recoverable see PARA 735. A judgment does not prevent a petition in bankruptcy on the original debt: see *Re Mostyn, ex p Griffiths* (1853) 3 De GM & G 174. See also BANKRUPTCY AND INDIVIDUAL INSOLVENCY vol 5 (2013) PARA 139.
2   *Holmes v Bell* (1841) 3 Man & G 213; *Norfolk Rly Co v M'Namara* (1849) 3 Exch 628.
3   *Bell v Banks* (1841) 3 Man & G 258; *Ansell v Baker* (1850) 15 QB 20; *Sharpe v Gibbs* (1864) 16 CBNS 527; *Boaler v Mayor* (1865) 19 CBNS 76; *Westmoreland Green and Blue Slate Co v Feilden* [1891] 3 Ch 15 at 26, CA.

691. Effect of judgment for mortgage debt. The obtaining of a judgment for the mortgage debt does not, while the judgment remains unsatisfied[1], prevent the mortgagee from enforcing his security[2].

1 *Lloyd v Mason* (1845) 4 Hare 132 at 138; *O'Brien v Lewis* (1863) 3 De GJ & Sm 606. See also *Re Lonergan, ex p Sheil* (1877) 4 ChD 789 at 793, CA.
2 A mortgagee is entitled to pursue his remedies simultaneously: see PARA 518.

692. Effect of legal mortgage on equitable charge. A mere charge or equitable mortgage[1] is extinguished by the taking of a formal mortgage[2], even though the mortgage does not confer a legal estate, and the sum from then on secured is the sum mentioned in the mortgage notwithstanding that other sums were covered by the deposit[3]. However, an equitable security is not merged by taking a security which is ineffectual[4].

1 As to equitable mortgages and charges see PARAS 105–106, 215 et seq.
2 As to legal mortgages see PARAS 104, 160 et seq.
3 *Vaughan v Vanderstegen* (1854) 2 Drew 289; *Bristol & West plc v Bartlett* [2002] EWCA Civ 1181, [2002] 4 All ER 544, [2003] 1 WLR 284.
4 *Re Emery, ex p Harvey* (1839) Mont & Ch 261. See also *Ghana Commercial Bank v Chandiram* [1960] AC 732, [1960] 2 All ER 865, PC.

693. Merger prevented by the contract. Merger may be prevented by an express or implied intention to the contrary[1]. Thus an assignment made by way of further security cannot prejudice the continuance of any existing security for the same debt[2], and a mortgage is not merged by the taking of a new mortgage on the same property to cover the original debt and further advances[3]. A covenant to pay interest can be so expressed as not to merge in a judgment[4].

1 As to merger generally see PARA 678.
2 *Twopenny v Young* (1824) 3 B & C 208; *Boaler v Mayor* (1865) 19 CBNS 76 at 83; and see *Re Warwick and Clagett, ex p Whitmore* (1838) 3 Deac 365. It seems, however, that a covenant to pay a simple contract debt necessarily turns it into a specialty debt (see *Stamps Comr v Hope* [1891] AC 476, PC); and an agreement under seal to execute a mortgage to secure a simple contract debt turns it into a specialty debt (see *Saunders v Milsome* (1866) LR 2 Eq 573; and DEEDS AND OTHER INSTRUMENTS vol 32 (2012) PARA 452). See also FINANCIAL INSTRUMENTS AND TRANSACTIONS vol 49 (2015) PARA 824.
3 *Tenison v Sweeny* (1844) 1 Jo & Lat 710 at 717; *Re James, ex p Harris* (1874) LR 19 Eq 253; cf *Re Dix, ex p Whitbread* (1841) 2 Mont D & De G 415.
4 As to covenants to pay interest see PARA 735.

(5) RELEASE

694. Release of the mortgage debt. By releasing the debt the security for the debt is released[1]. To be binding a release of a debt must generally be made for consideration[2], or, if not so made, under seal[3]. While an alleged release or forgiveness of the debt cannot be established merely by showing that the creditor had expressed an intention to release the debt, where the creditor has so acted that the debtor has done acts by which his position has been altered the creditor will not be allowed to enforce his security[4]. Moreover, a declaration of present forgiveness of the debt, even though only oral and unsupported by consideration, may be effective to release the debt, if it is accompanied by the delivery of the deeds to the debtor[5]; and if the mortgagee declares himself a trustee of the mortgaged premises for the mortgagor this is equivalent to a release[6].

A release of the debt is usually made on the disposition of the whole of the equity of redemption, either on sale, or, for example, on its transfer to new trustees[7]. The purchaser or other assignee of the equity of redemption is not liable on the covenant for payment[8], and the mortgagor remains liable, but the assignee will be liable to indemnify the mortgagor even if there is no express indemnity covenant[9]. On a disposition of the equity of redemption the mortgagee may release the mortgagor or his successor in title from the mortgage debt in consideration of a covenant by the purchaser or donee, or, if applicable, the new trustees, for payment and to observe and perform the mortgagor's covenants in the mortgage deed. The release and covenant may be included in the transfer or be effected by a separate document[10].

1 Shep Touch 342; *Cowper v Green* (1841) 7 M & W 633. As to release see also EQUITABLE JURISDICTION vol 47 (2014) PARAS 249, 251.
2 See eg *Taylor v Manners* (1865) 1 Ch App 48. As to consideration see CONTRACT vol 22 (2012) PARA 308.
3 As to deeds under seal see DEEDS AND OTHER INSTRUMENTS vol 32 (2012) PARA 227 et seq. See also CONTRACT vol 22 (2012) PARAS 216, 308.
4 *Yeomans v Williams* (1865) LR 1 Eq 184. This will be more readily applied to the release of interest than principal, because the intention to release the principal would probably be evidenced by the giving up of the security.
5 Such an oral declaration may also be effective where the debtor becomes the creditor's personal representative (*Strong v Bird* (1874) LR 18 Eq 315), so long as the intention to forgive continued until the creditor's death (*Re Wale, Wale v Harris* [1956] 3 All ER 280, [1956] 1 WLR 1346).
6 *Re Hancock, Hancock v Berrey* (1888) 57 LJCh 793.
7 As to the equity of redemption see PARAS 107, 304 et seq.
8 *Re Errington, ex p Mason* [1894] 1 QB 11. See also PARA 543.
9 *Waring v Ward* (1802) 7 Ves 332. See also PARA 543.
10 As to release of debts by will see WILLS AND INTESTACY vol 102 (2010) PARA 299. The appointment of a debtor as executor may extinguish the cause of action in debt, but the executor may remain liable under an equitable obligation to account to those interested in the estate for the amount of the debt: see *Stamp Duties Comr v Bone* [1977] AC 511, [1976] 2 All ER 354, PC.

695. Release of the security. On payment of the mortgage money, a mortgage term becomes a satisfied term and a legal charge is discharged[1]. Strictly speaking, therefore, where the whole of the mortgage money is paid, no further documentation is required although this is desirable from the practical point of view of proof of the intent to discharge.

In the case of a mortgage by demise, the legal estate may be released or surrendered only by deed or by operation of law[2] although an agreement to surrender which complies with the required formalities is effective in equity[3]. An informal surrender may be effective where, for example, the mortgagee hands back the mortgage deed and treats the mortgage as at an end[4].

The form of the release of property secured by legal mortgage depends on the circumstances. Usually it is made for value to enable the mortgagor to sell the property. In such circumstances the mortgagee may join in the conveyance rather than making a statutory receipt, where that is appropriate, or a separate deed of surrender or release followed by the conveyance. Where the mortgagee joins in the conveyance, then unless the property, if any, remaining in mortgage is sufficient security for the mortgage debt he will usually require the whole or part of the purchase money to be paid to him in discharge or reduction of the mortgage debt.

Where a sale of the property to be released is not contemplated, the appropriate Land Registry form should be used in the case of registered land[5]. Where the land is not registered a statutory receipt should be used, if the release is in consideration of the repayment of the money secured by the mortgage, but otherwise a deed of surrender, where the mortgage was by demise or sub-demise, or release, in the case of charge, is appropriate[6].

1 See PARA 647.
2 See the Law of Property (Miscellaneous Provisions) Act 1989 s 2; and PARA 221. As to mortgage by demise see PARA 164.

3   *Walsh v Lonsdale* (1882) 21 ChD 9, CA.
4   *Haigh v Brooks* (1839) 10 Ad & El 309. This decision may now be regarded as an example of estoppel or an equitable surrender which did not need to be in writing.
5   See PARA 652.
6   Debentures are released in the appropriate manner according to what sort of charge had been created (ie legal charge, equitable charge or floating charge). Any land charge registration in respect of the mortgage should be cancelled. As to statutory receipts see PARA 650.

696.   Release of security under equitable mortgage. An equitable mortgage does not create any legal estate or interest in favour of the mortgagee and no formal deed of release is required[1]. A release of the whole of the security may be effected by the cancellation of the mortgage or a simple receipt[2]. The release of part of equitably mortgaged property is generally effected by a written statement or letter from the mortgagee that he has no charge on the particular property[3].

1   As to equitable mortgages see PARAS 105, 215 et seq.
2   See PARA 649.
3   But see 26 Conv (NS) (1962) 449–453. For property subject to a floating charge, a letter of non-crystallisation from some officer of the company or its solicitor suffices. As to floating charges see COMPANIES vol 15 (2009) PARA 1269 et seq.

697.   Partial discharge of security by trustee-mortgagee. A trustee-mortgagee may release part of his security on receipt of the whole of the purchase money produced thereby[1].

1   *Re Morrell and Chapman's Contract* [1915] 1 Ch 162. As to the position of a purchaser of mortgaged land who has notice that the mortgagees are trustees see the Law of Property Act 1925 s 113; and PARA 375.

698.   Partial discharge of leasehold property. The statutory provisions as to the realisation of leasehold mortgages[1] do not apply where the mortgage term does not comprise the whole of the land included in the leasehold reversion, unless the rent, if any, payable in respect of that reversion has been apportioned, either legally or informally, as respects the land affected, or the rent is of no money value or no rent is reserved, and unless the lessee's covenants and the conditions, if any, have been apportioned either expressly or by implication, as respects the land affected[2]. Accordingly a release should never be executed as to part of mortgaged leaseholds without such an apportionment.

1   Ie the Law of Property Act 1925 s 89: see PARAS 449–451.
2   See the Law of Property Act 1925 s 89(6); and PARA 451.

699.   Release from judgment of part of land affected. A release from a judgment, including a charging order, of part of any land[1] charged with it does not affect the judgment charge as respects any land not specifically released[2].

1   As to the meaning of 'land' see PARA 104 note 2.
2   Law of Property Act 1925 s 71(1). These provisions operate without prejudice to the rights of any persons interested in the property remaining unreleased and not concurring in or confirming the release: s 71(2).

700.   Release of surety. The fact that a creditor accepts further security from the principal debtor does not release a surety[1], but a surety is entitled to the benefit of a collateral security[2]. A release of the collateral security will release the surety[3]. The rights of the surety may be, and usually are, modified or excluded by agreement[4].

1   *Twopenny v Young* (1824) 3 B & C 208; *Eyre v Everett* (1826) 2 Russ 381 at 384.
2   *Dixon v Steel* [1901] 2 Ch 602.
3   *Pearl v Deacon* (1857) 1 De G & J 461.
4   See generally FINANCIAL INSTRUMENTS AND TRANSACTIONS vol 49 (2015) PARA 846 et seq.

(6) WAIVER

701. Waiver of mortgage debt. As regards the mortgage debt itself, a waiver is ineffectual unless it amounts to a release[1], but the rights of the creditor under his security may be varied by waiver, provided he is cognisant of his rights[2]. Waiver may be express or implied[3].

1   A mere waiver signifies nothing more than an expression of intention not to insist on the right and as such is unenforceable: *Stackhouse v Barnston* (1805) 10 Ves 453. But the claimant's conduct may be such as to estop him from asserting the continuance of the liability: *Yeomans v Williams* (1865) LR 1 Eq 184. As to release see PARAS 694–700. As to waiver and release see further EQUITABLE JURISDICTION vol 47 (2014) PARAS 249–251.
2   *Vyvyan v Vyvyan* (1861) 30 Beav 65 (affd 4 De GF & J 183). See also *Peyman v Lanjani* [1985] Ch 457, [1984] 3 All ER 703, CA. See further EQUITABLE JURISDICTION vol 47 (2014) PARA 251.
3   See EQUITABLE JURISDICTION vol 47 (2014) PARA 250. As to express waiver see PARA 702. As to implied waiver see PARA 703.

702. Express waiver of mortgage debt. The extent of an express waiver is governed by the language used[1]. If the waiver is clearly limited to part of the security, the mortgagee's rights over the remainder of the security will be unaffected. Accordingly, where a mortgagee surrendered his legal interest in a leasehold security to enable the mortgagor to provide another security, but stipulated that the surrender was without prejudice to any other security he might have for his debt, he and his assignee were held to be still entitled to the benefit of the covenants in the mortgage, the legal interest only, and not the covenants, being within the operation of the surrender[2]. If the waiver is on the face of it clearly a general one, it will not be restricted on the representation of one of the parties that a more limited one was intended[3].

1   See PARA 701; and EQUITABLE JURISDICTION vol 47 (2014) PARA 250.
2   *Greenwood v Taylor* (1845) 14 Sim 505; revsd sub nom *A-G v Cox, Pearce v A-G* (1850) 3 HL Cas 240.
3   *Drought v Jones* (1840) 4 Dr & War 174.

703. Implied waiver of mortgage debt. There can be a waiver of a debt only if the creditor is aware of his rights[1]. The court will not be anxious to imply waiver from a mere omission, or other circumstances, from which the intention cannot fairly be inferred[2]. Thus where it was provided by the mortgage deed that, as between the mortgagor and his surety, a certain part of the security given by the principal should be primarily liable to the debt, without mentioning the rest, it was held that on paying off the debt the surety had not lost, by the omission, the right to a transfer of the whole security[3].

1   See PARA 701; and EQUITABLE JURISDICTION vol 47 (2014) PARA 251.
2   The sale by a mortgagee of mortgaged chattels discharged a collateral security of land in *Greenberg v Rapoport* (1970) 10 DLR (3d) 737.
3   *Bowker v Bull* (1850) 1 Sim NS 29.

704. Taking additional security for mortgage debt. If a creditor having a security on the funds of his debtor for part of his debt takes another security on the same funds for his whole debt, the earlier debt keeps its force and may be separately dealt with[1]. Similarly, where a creditor, having a security upon his debtor's funds takes afterwards, either alone (but on behalf of himself and another creditor), or jointly with such other creditor, a security for both debts on the same funds, the separate security keeps its force and may be separately dealt with. Where the surety pays off the debt or interest in arrear and his payment has been included in the security of a subsequent mortgagee, the surety having taken a note from that mortgagee to that effect, an intention by the surety to take an additional security, and not a waiver of his old right, is to be inferred[2].

1   See *Miln v Walton* (1843) 2 Y & C Ch Cas 354, where a lien on the freight of a ship arose from the discounting of bills of exchange.
2   *Beckett v Booth* (1708) 2 Eq Cas Abr 595; and see *Martin v Sedgwick* (1846) 9 Beav 333. As to waiver see PARA 701 et seq; and EQUITABLE JURISDICTION vol 47 (2014) PARAS 250–251.

705. Taking substituted security. Where it is contended that the benefit of a security has been waived by the acceptance of another security in its place, it is for the owner of the estate to show that it was discharged by the taking of the new security and not for the creditor to disprove the substitution of the new security for the old[1]. The mere acceptance of a personal security for interest in arrear, or other charge whether express or implied, is therefore not a waiver of the original security, even if a receipt is given for the amount[2]. The absence of any mention of the original security, and the reservation of interest at a different rate from that which was secured by it, have been treated as evidence that the new security was taken by way of substitution[3].

1   As to waiver see PARA 701 et seq; and EQUITABLE JURISDICTION vol 47 (2014) PARAS 250–251.
2   *Barret v Wells* (1700) Prec Ch 131; *Hardwick v Mynd* (1793) 1 Anst 109; *Curtis v Rush* (1814) 2 Ves & B 416; *Saunders v Leslie* (1814) 2 Ball & B 509. It is uncertain whether this rule applies as against a purchaser for value of a subsequent interest in the estate on the faith of an assurance, supported by the receipt, that no interest was due: see *Kemmis v Stepney* (1828) 2 Mol 85.
3   *Re Brettle, Brettle v Burdett* (1864) 2 De GJ & Sm 244.

(7) DISCHARGE OR MODIFICATION BY STATUTE

706. Compulsory acquisition by tenants of landlord's interest. In some circumstances, where a landlord has disposed of property, certain tenants have a right to serve a notice on the purchaser requiring him to dispose of the estate or interest that was the subject matter of the original disposal to the tenants[1]. If the property has at any time since the original disposal become subject to any charge or mortgage, then, unless the court directs otherwise, the instrument by virtue of which the property is disposed of by the purchaser operates to discharge the property from that charge or mortgage[2].

Other categories of tenant[3] may apply to the court for an acquisition order enabling a person nominated by them to acquire their landlord's interest in the premises without his consent[4]. Where the landlord's interest in any premises is acquired in pursuance of an acquisition order, the instrument by virtue of which it is acquired operates to discharge from the premises any existing charge or mortgage[5].

1   See the Landlord and Tenant Act 1987 s 12B; and LANDLORD AND TENANT vol 64 (2012) PARAS 1880–1881. As to the tenants who are qualifying tenants for these purposes see LANDLORD AND TENANT vol 64 (2012) PARA 1856.
2   See the Landlord and Tenant Act 1987 s 12B(5)(a), (6), Sch 1 Pt I; and LANDLORD AND TENANT vol 64 (2012) PARA 1881.
3   As to the qualifying tenants for these purposes see LANDLORD AND TENANT vol 64 (2012) PARA 1856.
4   See the Landlord and Tenant Act 1987 s 25(1); and LANDLORD AND TENANT vol 64 (2012) PARA 1891.
5   See the Landlord and Tenant Act 1987 s 32, Sch 1 Pt II; and LANDLORD AND TENANT vol 64 (2012) PARA 1898 et seq.

707. Compulsory acquisition of mortgaged land. Where land which is to be acquired compulsorily is subject to a mortgage, the undertakers or acquiring authority may purchase or redeem the mortgagee's interest in the land, whether or not they have previously purchased the equity of redemption[1], or the mortgagee is a trustee, or he is in possession of the land, or the mortgage includes other land in addition to that to be acquired[2]. An acquiring authority is under no obligation to redeem the mortgage, although it is entitled to[3]. On redemption of the mortgage, the mortgagee must convey or release his interest in the land to the undertakers or acquiring authority or as the undertakers or authority may direct[4].

1 As to the equity of redemption see PARAS 107, 304 et seq.
2 See the Lands Clauses Consolidation Act 1845 ss 108–114 (where that Act is incorporated: see COMPULSORY ACQUISITION OF LAND vol 18 (2009) PARA 509); the Compulsory Purchase Act 1965 ss 14–17 (where that Act applies: see COMPULSORY ACQUISITION OF LAND vol 18 (2009) PARA 513); and COMPULSORY ACQUISITION OF LAND vol 18 (2009) PARA 712. As to the compulsory acquisition of mortgaged land see further COMPULSORY ACQUISITION OF LAND vol 18 (2009) PARAS 711–714.
3 *Shewu v Hackney London Borough Council* (1999) 79 P & CR 47, CA. As to persons entitled to redeem see PARA 306 et seq.
4 See the Lands Clauses Consolidation Act 1845 s 108; the Compulsory Purchase Act 1965 s 14(2), (3); and COMPULSORY ACQUISITION OF LAND vol 18 (2009) PARA 712.

708. Enfranchisement of leaseholds where freehold mortgaged. Where a conveyance is executed in pursuance of a tenant's statutory right[1] to acquire the freehold of the leasehold house occupied by him, it operates to discharge the property from any charge on the landlord's estate to secure the payment of money, and to extinguish any term of years created for the purpose of the charge, and it does so without the persons entitled to or interested in the charge or term of years becoming parties to the conveyance[2].

Where a conveyance is executed in pursuance of the statutory right of tenants of flats to have the freehold acquired on their behalf[3], it is effective to:

(1)   discharge the interest from the mortgage, and from the order made by a court for the enforcement of the mortgage; and

(2)   extinguish any term of years created for the purposes of the mortgage[4].

1 Ie under the Leasehold Reform Act 1967: see LANDLORD AND TENANT vol 64 (2012) PARA 1505 et seq.
2 See the Leasehold Reform Act 1967 s 12(1); and LANDLORD AND TENANT vol 64 (2012) PARA 1578. As to the effect of such discharge and the tenant's duties and powers with respect to the application of the purchase money see ss 12, 13; and LANDLORD AND TENANT vol 64 (2012) PARAS 1578–1580. As to the relief available in certain circumstances to the landlord or mortgagee see s 36; and LANDLORD AND TENANT vol 64 (2012) PARA 1580.
3 Ie under the Leasehold Reform, Housing and Urban Development Act 1993 Pt 1 (ss 1–103): see LANDLORD AND TENANT vol 64 (2012) PARA 1663 et seq.
4 See the Leasehold Reform, Housing and Urban Development Act 1993 s 35, Sch 8; and LANDLORD AND TENANT vol 64 (2012) PARA 1760 et seq.

12. ACCOUNTS BETWEEN THE MORTGAGOR AND MORTGAGEE

(1) GENERAL ACCOUNTS BETWEEN THE MORTGAGOR AND MORTGAGEE

709. Nature of general accounts between mortgagor and mortgagee. The relationship of mortgagor and mortgagee is terminated by redemption, foreclosure, or the accounting for the proceeds of realisation, and proceedings for any of these purposes involve the taking of an account between the mortgagor and mortgagee[1]. In such an account the mortgagor is debited with principal and interest[2], and also with the costs, charges and expenses incurred by the mortgagee in relation to the mortgage security[3]. It may be necessary first to construe the mortgage deed, and in the case of a building society mortgage also the society's rules[4], in order to settle the basis of the account.

The mortgagor is not debited with rents and profits which he has received while allowed to continue in possession[5], nor, on the other hand, is he credited with any money which he has expended on the repair or improvement of the property[6]. Where, however, the mortgagee is restrained from taking possession and a receiver is appointed adversely to him, the receiver may be charged with an occupation rent[7]. The mortgagor is credited with any sums which the mortgagee has received on account of the security, and the balance appearing to his debit is the sum at which he is entitled to redeem in a redemption claim[8], or to redeem, so as to prevent foreclosure, in a foreclosure claim[9]. If the property has been realised, the balance, if any, appearing to his credit is the sum which the mortgagee must pay over to him[10].

Although the direction to account does not in terms extend to future receipts, sums subsequently received must be brought into the account[11]. Where the foreclosure is reopened the mortgagee is not necessarily bound to account for rents and profits received since the foreclosure[12].

1   See PARAS 575, 597–598, 621, 672. As to proceedings for redemption see PARA 661 et seq. As to foreclosure generally see PARA 571 et seq. As to the jurisdiction to order an account see EQUITABLE JURISDICTION vol 47 (2014) PARAS 49 et seq, 103. As to the time for which an account will be granted see LIMITATION PERIODS vol 68 (2008) PARAS 952, 1008. As to the procedure for taking an account see CPR PD 40A—*Accounts and Inquiries*; and CIVIL PROCEDURE vol 12A (2015) PARA 1250 et seq.
2   As to accounts of principal and interest see PARA 727 et seq.
3   See *Re Wallis, ex p Lickorish* (1890) 25 QBD 176 at 181, CA; and PARA 743 et seq.
4   As to the rules of building societies see FINANCIAL INSTITUTIONS vol 48 (2015) PARA 351 et seq.
5   See PARA 344 et seq. As to the account taken against a mortgagee in possession see PARA 718.
6   *Norris v Caledonian Insurance Co* (1869) 17 WR 954.
7   *Re Joyce, ex p Warren* (1875) 10 Ch App 222. As to the appointment of receivers out of court see PARA 478 et seq; and as to the appointment of receivers by the court see PARA 565 et seq.
8   See PARA 327 et seq.
9   See PARA 571 et seq.
10 See PARA 475.
11 *Bulstrode v Bradley* (1747) 3 Atk 582.
12 *Bird v Gandy* (1715) 2 Eq Cas Abr 251 note (4).

710. Form of the account between mortgagor and mortgagee. The ordinary form of judgment for foreclosure or redemption[1] contains a direction that an account be taken of what is due to the mortgagee under his mortgage, and for the costs of the claim[2]. A judgment in proceedings to recover surplus proceeds of sale requires the like account, and also an account of the proceeds of sale. A claim involving an account against a mortgagee as such must be limited to the mortgage account[3]. Where an account is asked for, the mortgagee is not generally ordered to give particulars of his claim[4], but this may be done if he is in effect claiming a definite sum[5]. In each case, it has to be considered whether any special inquiries or accounts are required[6], such as accounts of rents and profits against the mortgagee in possession[7], of costs, charges and expenses[8], of sums expended in lasting improvements[9], as to deterioration of mortgaged property[10] or as to sale at insufficient price[11]. A full general account may be refused on proportionality grounds[12]. In foreclosure proceedings the prosecution of accounts and inquiries may be stayed until security is given if, owing to the sum due and a deficiency in the value of the property, they will be useless[13]. The mortgagee of a partner's share is entitled to an account[14].

1   As to foreclosure generally see PARA 571 et seq. As to the equity of redemption see PARAS 107, 304 et seq. As to proceedings for redemption see PARA 661 et seq. As to the procedure for taking an account see CPR PD 40A—*Accounts and Inquiries*; and CIVIL PROCEDURE vol 12A (2015) PARA 1250 et seq.
2   See PARA 597 et seq.
3   *Pearse v Hewitt* (1835) 7 Sim 471.
4   *Augustinus v Nerinckx* (1880) 16 ChD 13, CA; *Blackie v Osmaston* (1884) 28 ChD 119, CA.
5   *Kemp v Goldberg* (1887) 36 ChD 505.
6   See PARAS 597–598.
7   See PARAS 718–726.
8   See PARA 743 et seq.
9   See PARAS 436–437, 672, 749.
10 See PARAS 438–441, 672.
11 See PARA 461.
12 *Nautch Ltd v Mortgage Express* [2012] EWHC 4136 (Ch), [2013] All ER (D) 115 (Mar).
13 *Exchange and Hop Warehouses Ltd v Association of Land Financiers* (1886) 34 ChD 195; *Taylor v Mostyn* (1883) 25 ChD 48, CA.
14 *Watts v Driscoll* [1901] 1 Ch 294, CA. As to a mortgage of a partnership share see PARA 138.

711. Account taken by second mortgagee. An account taken against a first mortgagee at the instance of a second mortgagee must be taken in all respects as though the mortgagor were taking it[1]. If the mortgagor would have an equity to exclude any item in the account, this equity can be asserted by the second mortgagee[2].

1   *Mainland v Upjohn* (1889) 41 ChD 126 at 136. See also *Melbourne Banking Corpn v Brougham* (1882) 7 App Cas 307 at 311, PC.
2   *Mainland v Upjohn* (1889) 41 ChD 126 at 136. See also *Melbourne Banking Corpn v Brougham* (1882) 7 App Cas 307 at 311, PC.

712. General principle as to application of money received by virtue of mortgage. When a mortgagor makes a payment, he has the first right to appropriate it between different secured liabilities including interest and capital. If he does so, then the mortgagee is bound to apply the monies in that way; but if he does not do so, then the mortgagee is entitled to appropriate the funds in such a way as it may choose[1].

Where the mortgagor is indebted to the mortgagee on accounts other than the mortgage, the mortgagee is not at liberty to appropriate sums received by virtue of the mortgage to those other accounts[2]. An incumbrancer is bound to apply what he receives by virtue of his security to that security[3]. Money received by a mortgagee on a sale by the mortgagor in which he concurs is received by virtue of the security[4]. Money received from a third person who is liable to make good a deficiency on the first mortgage is not, however, retained for the benefit of subsequent incumbrancers if ultimately it appears that there is no deficiency, but instead will be repaid to the third person[5].

1 *West Bromwich Building Society v Crammer* [2002] EWHC 2618 (Ch), [2003] BPIR 783, [2002] All ER (D) 343 (Oct); *Chubb v Dean* [2013] EWHC 1282 (Ch).
2 See *Knight v Bowyer* (1859) 4 De G & J 619.
3 See *Knight v Bowyer* (1859) 4 De G & J 619 at 629.
4 *Johnson v Bourne* (1843) 2 Y & C Ch Cas 268; *Young v English* (1843) 7 Beav 10.
5 *Sawyer v Goodwin* (1875) 1 ChD 351 at 358, CA.

713. When settled accounts may be reopened. A settled account[1] between mortgagor and mortgagee is prima facie binding on both parties, but in certain circumstances it will be reopened[2] and taken again from the beginning, or the less drastic remedy may be allowed of giving leave to surcharge and falsify, that is to take exception to particular omissions or entries in the account[3].

1 As to settled accounts see EQUITABLE JURISDICTION vol 47 (2014) PARA 52. As to a settlement of account constituting a payment so as to discharge a right of action for breach of contract see CONTRACT vol 22 (2012) PARA 605 et seq. As to the effect of an account stated see CONTRACT vol 22 (2012) PARAS 611–613.
2 As to reopening a settled account see EQUITABLE JURISDICTION vol 47 (2014) PARA 53.
3 As to surcharge and falsification see EQUITABLE JURISDICTION vol 47 (2014) PARA 54. In addition to the equitable remedy, the Civil Procedure Rules also provide for the notification of objections to the accounting party in circumstances where the account is perceived to be inaccurate: see CPR PD 40A—*Accounts and Inquiries* para 3; and CIVIL PROCEDURE vol 12A (2015) PARA 1252.

714. Claim to reopen account or to surcharge and falsify must be distinctly alleged and proved. Whether it is desired to reopen the account[1] or only to surcharge and falsify[2], the ground on which relief is claimed must be distinctly alleged and proved as alleged[3]. Where there are several accounts, errors in some will render all liable to be reopened or objected to, if the relationship subsisting between the parties, the character of the errors and the connection of the accounts lead to the inference that the errors proved in some cases may be expected to appear in all[4].

1 As to reopening settled accounts see PARA 713.
2 As to liberty to surcharge and falsify see PARA 713; and EQUITABLE JURISDICTION vol 47 (2014) PARA 54.
3 *Taylor v Haylin* (1788) 2 Bro CC 310; *Drew v Power* (1803) 1 Sch & Lef 182 at 192; *Davies v Spurling* (1829) Taml 199 (cited sub nom *Davis v Starling* (1829) in 1 Coop *temp* Cott at 551); *Shepherd v Morris* (1841) 4 Beav 252; *Parkinson v Hanbury* (1867) LR 2 HL 1 at 19.
4 *Cheese v Keen* [1908] 1 Ch 245 at 251. See also *Lawless v Mansfield* (1841) 1 Dr & War 557 at 604.

715. Setting off and correcting errors in accounts between mortgagor and mortgagee. The accounting party cannot avoid liability by setting off against each other errors in different accounts[1]. He may escape an order to surcharge and falsify[2] by correcting particular errors before proceedings are commenced[3], but not in the course of the proceedings[4].

1 *Lawless v Mansfield* (1841) 1 Dr & War 557 at 615. As to set-off generally see CIVIL PROCEDURE vol 11 (2015) PARA 382 et seq.
2 As to liberty to surcharge and falsify see PARA 713; and EQUITABLE JURISDICTION vol 47 (2014) PARA 54.
3 *Davies v Spurling* (1829) Taml 199 at 214 (now to be read in the light of the Civil Procedure Rules: see CIVIL PROCEDURE vol 11 (2015) PARA 6 et seq).
4 *Lawless v Mansfield* (1841) 1 Dr & War 557 at 623 (now to be read in the light of the Civil Procedure Rules: see CIVIL PROCEDURE vol 11 (2015) PARA 6 et seq).

716. Persons bound by the mortgagee's account. An account taken, whether in or out of court, between the mortgagee and the person immediately interested in the equity of redemption[1] is prima facie binding on other persons interested[2]. Thus an account between mortgagee and mortgagor binds a second mortgagee[3]. An account taken in the presence of a bankrupt will bind him if he afterwards procures a reassignment of the property, even though his trustee was not a party[4]. An account between a mortgagee and the tenant for life of the equity of redemption binds both vested and contingent remaindermen[5].

1   As to the equity of redemption see PARAS 107, 304 et seq.
2   See the cases cited in notes 3–5.
3   *Needler v Deeble* (1677) 1 Cas in Ch 299; *Williams v Day* (1680) 2 Cas in Ch 32; *Knight v Bampfeild* (1683) 1 Vern 179; cf *Dick v Butler* (1827) 1 Mol 42. A first mortgagee is under no duty to inform a second mortgagee of the state of account between himself and the mortgagor: *Weld-Blundell v Synott* [1940] 2 KB 107, [1940] 2 All ER 580.
4   *Byrne v Lord Carew* (1849) 13 I Eq R 1.
5   *Allen v Papworth* (1731) 1 Ves Sen 163; *Wrixon v Vize* (1842) 2 Dr & War 192.

717. Persons not bound by the account. Persons who are not parties to the account are not bound if fraud or collusion and also particular errors are alleged and proved[1]. Apart from fraud or collusion, proof of particular errors will entitle the absent party to an order to surcharge and falsify[2]. An account taken between the mortgagee and a transferee of the mortgage does not bind the mortgagor[3]. An account taken in court at the instance of a claimant is not binding as between co-defendants, unless the claimant cannot obtain the object of the proceedings without determining the rights of the defendants among themselves[4], but in proceedings by a second mortgagee against the mortgagor and the first mortgagee, if the first mortgagee's debt is established, the mortgagor is bound so long as the judgment remains unimpeached[5].

1   *Needler v Deeble* (1677) 1 Cas in Ch 299; *Knight v Bampfeild* (1683) 1 Vern 179; *Hall v Heward* (1886) 32 ChD 430 at 435, CA. The authorities referred to in this paragraph must be read in the light of the Civil Procedure Rules: see CIVIL PROCEDURE vol 11 (2015) PARA 6 et seq.
2   *Wrixon v Vize* (1842) 2 Dr & War 192 at 205; cf *Badham v Odell* (1742) 4 Bro Parl Cas 349, HL. As to liberty to surcharge and falsify see PARA 713; and EQUITABLE JURISDICTION vol 47 (2014) PARA 54.
3   *Earl of Macclesfield v Fitton* (1683) 1 Vern 168; *Mangles v Dixon* (1852) 3 HL Cas 702 at 737; cf *Jamieson v English* (1820) 2 Mol 337.
4   *Cottingham v Earl of Shrewsbury* (1843) 3 Hare 627 at 638. See also *North West Water v Binnie & Partners* [1990] 3 All ER 547.
5   *Farquharson v Seton* (1828) 5 Russ 45 at 62.

(2) ACCOUNTS BY THE MORTGAGEE IN POSSESSION

718. Continuous account. In the absence of special direction, the account taken against a mortgagee in possession is a continuous debtor and creditor account[1]. The mortgagee is debited with all sums which he has received or which he is to be treated as having received[2] by virtue of the mortgage, whether rents and profits, or accidental payments, such as proceeds of sale[3]; and he is credited with the principal money, with interest accruing due from time to time[4], and with costs, charges and expenses[5], including all expenditure upon the mortgaged property which he is entitled to charge against it[6]. The nature of the account requires that it is to be taken without limit[7], that is, from the commencement of the possession, or, if there has already been a settled account, from that account[8].

1   *Wrigley v Gill* [1905] 1 Ch 241 at 253. As to account taken with rests see PARA 720 et seq.
2   As to wilful default account see PARA 430.
3   As to the application of the proceeds of sale see PARA 474 et seq.
4   As to accounts of principal and interest see PARA 727 et seq.

5   See *Re Wallis, ex p Lickorish* (1890) 25 QBD 176, CA; and PARA 743 et seq.
6   See *Thompson v Hudson* (1870) LR 10 Eq 497 at 498; *Union Bank of London v Ingram* (1880)
     16 ChD 53; *Cockburn v Edwards* (1881) 18 ChD 449 at 456, CA. In *Thompson v Hudson* above,
     the account was taken in three columns, showing the sums received in one column, the interest due
     and the costs in a second column and the capital debt in the third. If, however, the whole account
     is presented as a debtor and creditor account, it is necessarily restricted to two columns. In fact,
     however, where the mortgagee is in possession, the order to account normally requires that
     separate single column accounts are to be taken of:
     (1)   what is due to the mortgagee for principal, interest and costs;
     (2)   money laid out by the mortgagee in necessary repairs and lasting improvements, with,
            in the case of lasting improvements, interest from the date of outlay; and
     (3)   the rents and profits received by the mortgagee or which without wilful default might
            have been received.
     The aggregates of the accounts in heads (1) and (2) are added together, and that of the account in
     head (3) is subtracted, and the balance is the amount due to the mortgagee.
7   See *Hood v Easton* (1856) 2 Giff 692; and LIMITATION PERIODS vol 68 (2008) PARA 1118. Cf
     Forster v Forster [1918] 1 IR 95, where the defendant was held not to have been a mortgagee in
     possession.
8   As to partnership accounts see *Miller v Miller* (1869) LR 8 Eq 499; *Betjemann v Betjemann* [1895]
     2 Ch 474, CA; and PARTNERSHIP vol 79 (2014) PARA 149 et seq.

719. Effect of surplus receipts or deficiency in receipts. If the rents and other
receipts from time to time derived from the mortgaged property are more than the
interest[1], the mortgagee, where the account is taken continuously, does not apply
the excess in reduction of principal, and so at the same time reduce the subsequent
interest; he keeps it in hand, paying no interest on it, and thereby gains an
incidental advantage[2]. If, on the other hand, the rents and other receipts are less
than the interest, the deficiency means an accumulation of interest overdue, and
this is a further debt owing by the mortgagor on which he pays no interest[3]. The
rents and receipts are not appropriated to interest separately, but go generally in
reduction of principal and interest, and this method favours either mortgagee or
mortgagor according to the state of the account[4].

1   As to accounts of principal and interest see PARA 727 et seq.
2   See *Union Bank of London v Ingram* (1880) 16 ChD 53.
3   See *Union Bank of London v Ingram* (1880) 16 ChD 53.
4   See *Union Bank of London v Ingram* (1880) 16 ChD 53.

720. Taking account with rests. So far as the continuous account favours the
mortgagor, it is not interfered with[1]. If the current excess of interest due over
receipts were turned into capital and so made to bear interest, this would be to
give compound interest against the mortgagor, which can only be done when the
mortgage contract provides for compound interest[2]. So far as the continuous
account favours the mortgagee, however, the court interferes in certain
circumstances and deprives him of the advantage so gained by directing the
account to be taken with rests, that is, when the receipts for the year or other
period exceed the interest and current expenses, the surplus is credited in
reduction of principal, and interest runs from then onwards only on the reduced
amount[3].

This may be done either by taking a separate revenue account, and carrying the
balance to the credit of principal, or by simply striking a balance in the ordinary
account which includes principal[4], the balance thus showing the reduced
principal. Rests, it has been said, are only directed in the case of real estate[5], but
there seems to be no reason for this distinction. They may be directed where the
mortgagee is charged with an occupation rent[6], but the mortgagee must be in
possession as such, and not as tenant[7]. Where rests have been directed in a
redemption claim[8] which is abandoned and a foreclosure claim[9] is subsequently
brought, the accounts must be taken with rests, at any rate up to the date of the

earlier order[10]. Although rests are not directed, it may be necessary to find out from time to time whether the mortgagee has rents in hand sufficient to cover interest; where, for instance, this is required to avoid a claim for capitalisation of interest in arrear[11].

1   See PARA 719. As to continuous account see PARA 718.
2   As to compound interest see PARA 191; and FINANCIAL INSTRUMENTS AND TRANSACTIONS vol 49 (2015) PARA 91.
3   See PARA 719.
4   See PARA 719.
5   *Robinson v Cumming* (1742) 2 Atk 409 at 410.
6   *Donovan v Fricker* (1821) Jac 165; *Wilson v Metcalfe* (1826) 1 Russ 530. See also PARA 432.
7   *Page v Linwood* (1837) 4 Cl & Fin 399, HL.
8   See PARA 672. As to proceedings for redemption see PARA 661 et seq. As to the equity of redemption see PARAS 107, 304 et seq.
9   As to foreclosure generally see PARA 571 et seq.
10 *Morris v Islip* (1855) 20 Beav 654.
11 *Wrigley v Gill* [1906] 1 Ch 165, CA. See also PARA 193.

721.   Effect of rests after satisfaction of mortgage debt. After the mortgage debt is satisfied, the effect of the rests is to make interest payable by the mortgagee. For each period in which there is an excess of receipts over expenses, there is a balance owing from the mortgagee to the mortgagor; and these balances carry compound interest[1], that is, the interest due for any period is added to the balance due at the end of the period, and the interest for the ensuing period is reckoned on the aggregate sum. As long as there is principal due, the rests may be made either from time to time, whenever the mortgagee has an excess of receipts over interest and expenses in hand, or at stated intervals[2]. The former method is suitable if there are likely to be substantial sums in hand, and it has been ordered[3], but more usually the account is directed to be taken with yearly or half-yearly rests and then only the periodical balance in the mortgagee's hands is struck off the principal[4]. When there is no longer any principal due, the direction for annual rests is equivalent to a direction that the mortgagee is to be charged with compound interest, and operates in the same way as in other cases where an accounting party (for example, an executor) has money in hand[5]; but this may be made more explicit by a direction that, in taking the periodic rests (except the first), the interest of each preceding balance is to be included in the new balance, so as to charge the mortgagee with compound interest[6]. Under special circumstances the order may direct each receipt to carry interest from the time of receipt in addition to periodic rests[7]. If a mortgagee, who has not been in possession, has surplus sale money in hand, he is charged simple interest at the same rate[8]. A mortgagee, although not in possession, will be charged compound interest on money in his hands if he improperly resists redemption[9].

1   As to compound interest see PARA 191; and FINANCIAL INSTRUMENTS AND TRANSACTIONS vol 49 (2015) PARA 91.
2   As to taking account with rests see PARA 720 et seq.
3   *Binnington v Harwood* (1825) Turn & R 477.
4   See the form of decree in *Yates v Hambly* (1742) 2 Atk 360 (cited in *Webber v Hunt* (1815) 1 Madd 13 at 14). See also *Wilson v Cluer* (1840) 3 Beav 136; *Thorneycroft v Crockett* (1848) 2 HL Cas 239 at 256. In *Binnington v Harwood* (1825) Turn & R 477, the decree combined both these methods, but they appear to be incompatible.
5   See *Raphael v Boehm* (1805) 11 Ves 92 (affd (1807) 13 Ves 407; subsequent proceedings as to costs 13 Ves 590); *Heighington v Grant* (1840) 5 My & Cr 258; and WILLS AND INTESTACY vol 103 (2010) PARA 1259.
6   See the orders in *Cotham v West* (1839) 1 Beav 380; *Ashworth v Lord* (1887) 36 ChD 545 at 552.
7   See *Raphael v Boehm* (1805) 11 Ves 92; *Lloyd v Jones* (1842) 12 Sim 491. The rate of interest was usually 4% per annum: *Ashworth v Lord* (1887) 36 ChD 545 at 552; *Quarrell v Beckford* (1816)

1 Madd 269 at 285; *Wilson v Metcalfe* (1826) 1 Russ 530 at 537; *Lewes v Morgan* (1829) 3 Y &
J 394 at 399; *Montgomery v Calland* (1844) 14 Sim 79 at 82; *Horlock v Smith* (1844) 1 Coll 287
at 297. Presumably a more realistic rate would be allowed today. As to interest generally see
FINANCIAL INSTRUMENTS AND TRANSACTIONS vol 49 (2015) PARA 90 et seq.
8   *Smith v Pilkington* (1859) 1 De GF & J 120 at 136; *Eley v Read* (1897) 76 LT 39, CA.
9   *Smith v Pilkington* (1859) 1 De GF & J 120. As to the equity of redemption see PARAS 107, 304
    et seq.

722.   When rests ordered in the taking of account. The account is not taken with
rests unless a special direction to that effect is inserted in the order[1], and such a
direction is not inserted as a matter of course[2]. A mortgagee is not bound to accept
payment of his money by driblets[3], and the direction is not given unless the
mortgagee has impliedly elected to be paid in this manner, or has so acted as to
forfeit his usual immunity. He impliedly elects to be paid by driblets if he enters
into possession when no interest is in arrear[4], and there are no special
circumstances to account for his taking this step[5]. Hence the account will usually
be taken with rests if there was no interest in arrear when the mortgagee entered[6],
but without rests if interest was in arrear[7]. For this purpose, a half-year's arrear of
interest is sufficient[8]. Where bills for arrears of interest are current when the
mortgagee takes possession and are dishonoured at maturity, the interest is in
arrear all the time, and no rests will be directed[9]. Apparently, mere excess of
receipts is not sufficient to render the mortgagee liable to rests[10]. If special burdens
have been imposed upon the mortgagee by the mortgagor's conduct, rests will not
be directed even though no interest was in arrear[11]; and the mortgagee need not
account with rests if he enters on leasehold premises to avoid a forfeiture[12].

1   *Webber v Hunt* (1815) 1 Madd 13; *Donovan v Fricker* (1821) Jac 165 at 168. As to taking account
    with rests see PARA 720 et seq.
2   *Davis v May* (1815) 19 Ves 383; *Donovan v Fricker* (1821) Jac 165; *Scholefield v Ingham*
    (1838) Coop Pr Cas 477. See also *Neesom v Clarkson* (1845) 4 Hare 97 at 105.
3   *Nelson v Booth* (1858) 3 De G & J 119 at 122; *Wrigley v Gill* [1905] 1 Ch 241 at 254 (on appeal
    [1906] 1 Ch 165 at 175, CA).
4   *Nelson v Booth* (1858) 3 De G & J 119; *Ashworth v Lord* (1887) 36 ChD 545. As to the
    circumstances entitling the mortgagee to take possession see PARA 404 et seq.
5   *Horlock v Smith* (1844) 1 Coll 287 at 297.
6   *Shephard v Elliot* (1819) 4 Madd 254; *Scholefield v Ingham* (1838) Coop Pr Cas 477; *Wilson v
    Cluer* (1840) 3 Beav 136.
7   *Stephens v Wellings* (1835) 4 LJCh 281; *Wilson v Cluer* (1840) 3 Beav 136; *Finch v Brown* (1840)
    3 Beav 70; *Nelson v Booth* (1858) 3 De G & J 119 at 122; *Scholefield v Lockwood (No 3)* (1863)
    32 Beav 439.
8   *Moore v Painter* (1842) 6 Jur 903.
9   *Dobson v Land* (1851) 4 De G & Sm 575.
10 *Baldwin v Lewis* (1835) 4 LJCh 113. See also *Nelson v Booth* (1858) 3 De G & J 119. Formerly
    it was considered that any considerable excess of receipts over interest was a ground for directing
    rests (*Gould v Tancred* (1742) 2 Atk 533; *Donovan v Fricker* (1821) Jac 165); and this was treated
    as correct in *Carter v James* (1881) 29 WR 437, although rests were not directed where the excess
    was slight (*Gould v Tancred* above; *Donovan v Fricker* above; *Scholefield v Ingham* (1838) Coop
    Pr Cas 477).
11 *Horlock v Smith* (1844) 1 Coll 287 at 297.
12 *Patch v Wild* (1861) 30 Beav 99.

723.   Effect of mortgagee setting up adverse title. The mortgagee forfeits an
ordinary mortgagee's immunities if he unsuccessfully sets up a title as owner
adverse to the mortgagor and denies his right to redeem[1], and he will be ordered
to account with rests[2] even though interest was in arrear when he took
possession[3].

1   As to the equity of redemption see PARAS 107, 304 et seq. As to persons entitled to redeem see
    PARA 306 et seq.
2   As to taking account with rests see PARA 720 et seq.

3   *Incorporated Society in Dublin v Richards* (1841) 1 Dr & War 258 at 334; *National Bank of Australasia v United Hand-in-Hand and Band of Hope Co* (1879) 4 App Cas 391 at 409, PC; *Wrigley v Gill* [1905] 1 Ch 241 at 254. See also *Montgomery v Calland* (1844) 14 Sim 79; *Douglas v Culverwell* (1862) 4 De GF & J 20.

724. Effect of subsequent payment of arrears of interest. If interest was in arrear when the mortgagee took possession, so that he was not in the first instance liable to account with rests[1], he does not become liable so to account from the date when the arrears were paid off out of the rents[2]. If, however, while the mortgagee is in possession under circumstances which do not subject him to account with rests, an account is settled between the parties which shows that no interest is due, or that arrears of interest have been turned into principal, the mortgagee is from then onwards liable to account with rests[3]. Moreover, when the mortgage has been satisfied, the mortgagee must from then onwards account with rests, and a direction to that effect may be given subsequently to the original order to account[4]. The direction may be given at any time after the account shows that the mortgage is paid off, although not asked for originally[5]; or the mortgagee may be charged with interest on money received from the times of receipt[6].

1   As to taking account with rests see PARA 720 et seq.
2   *Davis v May* (1815) 19 Ves 383; *Latter v Dashwood* (1834) 6 Sim 462; *Finch v Brown* (1840) 3 Beav 70; *Wilson v Cluer* (1840) 3 Beav 136 at 140; *Scholefield v Lockwood (No 3)* (1863) 32 Beav 439.
3   *Wilson v Cluer* (1840) 3 Beav 136. As to the arrears of interest recoverable by a mortgagee in possession see PARA 193.
4   *Wilson v Metcalfe* (1826) 1 Russ 530; *Wilson v Cluer* (1840) 3 Beav 136; *Montgomery v Calland* (1844) 14 Sim 79; *Ashworth v Lord* (1887) 36 ChD 545. See also *Quarrell v Beckford* (1816) 1 Madd 269.
5   *Wilson v Metcalfe* (1826) 1 Russ 530.
6   *Lloyd v Jones* (1842) 12 Sim 491.

725. Application of proceeds of sale of part of mortgaged property. Where a sale of part of the mortgaged property is effected, the net proceeds are applied first in payment of interest then due, and the surplus is carried to the credit of principal as at the date of receipt, so as to reduce the amount on which interest runs from then; but no rest[1] is made at the same time in the account of rents and profits. If the account is being taken without rests[2], the account of rents and profits will go on continuously as though there had been no special receipt of capital money. If the account is being taken with rests, the usual rest will be made at the next period[3].

1   As to taking account with rests see PARA 720 et seq.
2   See PARA 718.
3   *Wrigley v Gill* [1905] 1 Ch 241 at 253–254; *Ainsworth v Wilding* [1905] 1 Ch 435 (explaining *Thompson v Hudson* (1870) LR 10 Eq 497).

726. When fresh account necessary. Where the mortgagee receives rents after the account has been taken, he must render a fresh account verified by witness statement or affidavit up to the time when the matter is finally settled[1].

1   *Oxenham v Ellis* (1854) 18 Beav 593 at 595. This authority must be read in the light of the Civil Procedure Rules (see CIVIL PROCEDURE vol 11 (2015) PARA 6 et seq). See also CPR 40; CPR PD 40A—*Accounts and Inquiries*; and CIVIL PROCEDURE vol 12A (2015) PARA 1250 et seq.

(3) ACCOUNTS OF PRINCIPAL AND INTEREST

727. Special matters must be pleaded or set out. The first account to be taken under a mortgage is the account of principal and interest. If there is any special matter affecting the amount at which the mortgagor or a person claiming under him is entitled to redeem, such as a valuation of the security in bankruptcy[1], this must be pleaded or otherwise brought to the court's attention before the judgment directing the account is given, in which case an appropriate direction can be inserted. If this is not done, the question cannot be subsequently raised on taking the account[2]. If the account of interest is not taken owing to an expected deficiency, and payments are ordered to be made on account of principal, this does not prevent the subsequent calculation of interest in the event of a surplus[3].

1 See PARA 602 note 1.
2 *Sanguinetti v Stuckey's Banking Co (No 2)* [1896] 1 Ch 502.
3 *Re Calgary and Medicine Hat Land Co Ltd, Pigeon v Calgary and Medicine Hat Land Co Ltd* [1908] 2 Ch 652 at 658, 662, CA.

728. Proof of principal mortgage debt. Where a mortgage is given for a specific sum stated to be then advanced, the receipt of which is acknowledged by the mortgagor, the mortgage deed is prima facie evidence of the amount of the advance[1], and, accordingly, the principal debt is proved by production of the deed, with the receipt contained in the deed or indorsed on it[2]. The receipt is not conclusive, however, and the mortgagor is entitled to show by oral evidence that the sum named was not in fact advanced[3]. The burden of proving the advance strictly is on the mortgagee in certain cases, namely where the mortgagee was at the time the mortgagor's solicitor or agent[4], or where there is evidence of pressure[5] or fraud[6]. Where a security is given for a bill of costs, the court will inquire whether the charges were fair and reasonable[7].

1 As to the effect of the receipt see further PARA 383; and DEEDS AND OTHER INSTRUMENTS vol 32 (2012) PARA 425; ESTOPPEL vol 47 (2014) PARA 328.
2 *Piddock v Brown* (1734) 3 P Wms 288; *Goddard v Complin* (1699) 1 Cas in Ch 119; *Holt v Mill* (1692) 2 Vern 279. A transfer of a mortgage, reciting that a certain sum is due on the security, has been held to estop the transferee from subsequently having costs which were included assessed on an ordinary application, although a contemporaneous receipt ended with 'accounts hereafter to be adjusted': see *Re Forsyth* (1865) 11 Jur NS 213 at 615; and DEEDS AND OTHER INSTRUMENTS vol 32 (2012) PARA 425; ESTOPPEL vol 47 (2014) PARA 328. Account books of a deceased mortgagee containing entries against his interest are evidence of the state of the accounts: see *Hudson and Humphrey v Owners of Swiftsure* (1900) 82 LT 389. The authorities referred to in this paragraph must now be read in the light of the Civil Procedure Rules: see CIVIL PROCEDURE vol 11 (2015) PARA 6 et seq.
3 *Minot v Eaton* (1826) 4 LJOS Ch 134 at 135; *Mainland v Upjohn* (1889) 41 ChD 126 at 136; *Close Asset Finance Ltd v Taylor* [2006] EWCA Civ 788, 150 Sol Jo LB 708, [2006] All ER (D) 304 (May); *Vickers v Jackson* [2011] EWCA Civ 725, [2011] 3 EGLR 65, [2011] All ER (D) 236 (May). See also DEEDS AND OTHER INSTRUMENTS vol 32 (2012) PARA 425; ESTOPPEL vol 47 (2014) PARA 328.
4 *Lewes v Morgan* (1817) 5 Price 42 at 83; *Lewes v Morgan* (1829) 3 Y & J 230 at 249, Ex Ch (subsequent proceedings (1829) 3 Y & J 394 at 398); *Lawless v Mansfield* (1841) 1 Dr & War 557 at 608; *Gresley v Mousley* (1862) 8 Jur NS 320. As to entries in the mortgagor's solicitor's books of the receipt of the mortgage money being evidence of the advance see *Clark v Wilmot* (1841) 1 Y & C Ch Cas 53; 2 Y & C Ch Cas 259 note (h). As to the relationship of solicitor and client see generally LEGAL PROFESSIONS vol 66 (2015) PARA 561 et seq.
5 Eg in a post-obit security: *Tottenham v Green* (1863) 32 LJCh 201.
6 *Piddock v Brown* (1734) 3 P Wms 288.
7 *Wragg v Denham* (1836) 2 Y & C Ex 117 at 121.

729. Mortgagee's bonus or commission. The mortgagee may stipulate for a commission of an amount reasonable, having regard to the risk run[1]. If, on making the advance, he deducts this commission from the sum stated in the mortgage deed, and pays only the balance, the full sum so stated will be allowed as the principal debt in his account[2]. If the commission is not deducted at the time of the advance, it will be allowed subsequently in the accounts under the head of just allowances, provided that it is stipulated for in the mortgage contract, and that the bargain is deliberately entered into while the parties are on equal terms[3]. An agreement in consideration of a present advance to pay a larger sum in the future is valid[4].

1 See PARA 324.
2 *Mainland v Upjohn* (1889) 41 ChD 126; *Potter v Edwards* (1857) 26 LJCh 468; *Biggs v Hoddinott, Hoddinott v Biggs* [1898] 2 Ch 307 at 322, CA. The doctrine laid down in *Re Edwards' Estate* (1861) 11 I Ch R 367 at 369, that an onerous contract entered into as part of the mortgage transaction is presumed to be made under pressure, is not correct: *Biggs v Hoddinott, Hoddinott v Biggs* above.
3 *Bucknell v Vickery* (1891) 64 LT 701, PC; *The Benwell Tower* (1895) 72 LT 664 at 670. So far as to the contrary, *Broad v Selfe* (1863) 11 WR 1036 and *James v Kerr* (1889) 40 ChD 449 at 459 appear now not to be law.
4 *Wallingford v Mutual Society* (1880) 5 App Cas 685 at 702, HL.

730. Future advances; current account. The security may be given to cover future advances whether in addition to an immediate advance or not, or to cover a current account, or to cover present or future liabilities[1]. A security for advances will generally, if the surrounding circumstances favour the construction, include past as well as future advances[2]. A charge on a policy of insurance for notes cashed may cover the balance due at the mortgagor's death[3], but a security to cover the mortgagor's liabilities to the mortgagee refers only to direct liabilities and does not include liability on a bill which the mortgagee has purchased[4]. A mortgage to a bank to cover debts due or growing due from the mortgagor covers his liability on bills drawn by him and accepted by a third person which are then under discount with the bank and subsequently dishonoured[5]; and a mortgage of a public house to brewers to cover the debts due from the mortgagor or his assigns will cover the business debt of his devisee[6]. There may be a further advance even though no money is paid directly to the mortgagor[7]. Sometimes an express limit on the amount recoverable under the security is inserted, and, according to the construction of the deed, this may be a limit on principal only, leaving interest and outgoings to be recovered in addition[8], or it may be a limit on the aggregate sum recoverable for principal, interest and costs[9].

1 As to the right of a solicitor mortgagee to add certain costs to his security see PARA 325. As to further advances by an executor-mortgagee see *Gannon v Gannon* [1909] 1 IR 47, CA.
2 *Hibernian Bank v Gilbert* (1890) 23 LR Ir 321.
3 *Jones v Consolidated Investment Assurance Co* (1858) 26 Beav 256.
4 *Calisher v Forbes* (1871) 7 Ch App 109 at 114.
5 *Merchants Bank of London v Maud* (1871) 19 WR 657.
6 *Re Watts, Smith v Watts* (1882) 22 ChD 5, CA.
7 *Re Smith, Lawrence v Kitson* [1918] 2 Ch 405.
8 See *White v City of London Brewery Co* (1889) 42 ChD 237, CA.
9 *Blackford v Davis* (1869) 4 Ch App 304 at 309 (proviso 'that the total moneys to be secured by and ultimately recoverable under these presents shall not exceed the sum of £1,200').

731. Proof as to amount secured by way of mortgage. By agreement between the parties, a mortgage for a specific sum may be in fact a mortgage to secure a current account up to the limit of that sum, but the burden of proof is on the party who seeks to establish that it is a running security[1]. The actual amount due on a mortgage to secure a current account, or a mortgage covering further advances, may be proved by evidence outside the deed or by receipts on the deed[2].

1 *Re Boys, Eedes v Boys, ex p Hop Planters Co* (1870) LR 10 Eq 467. See also *Henniker v Wigg* (1843) 4 QB 792; *Melland v Gray* (1843) 2 Y & C Ch Cas 199.
2 See *Melland v Gray* (1843) 2 Y & C Ch Cas 199.

732. Appropriation of payments in current account. Prima facie, in the case of a mortgage to secure a current account[1], unless there has been express appropriation by either party[2], sums paid by the mortgagor are applied in satisfaction of the items on the debit side in order, beginning with the earliest in date[3]. In as much, however, as the security does not, for purposes of priority as against a second mortgage, include advances made after notice of the second mortgage[4] unless the security imposes an obligation to make those advances, the result is that the mortgage becomes a mortgage for the fixed amount of the balance then outstanding, and subsequent payments will go to satisfy it, while subsequent advances will, as against the second mortgagee, be unsecured[5].

1 See PARAS 730–731.
2 *The Mecca* [1897] AC 286, HL; and see *Williams v Rawlinson* (1825) 3 Bing 71.
3 *Devaynes v Noble, Clayton's Case* (1816) 1 Mer 529 at 572; and see *Bodenham v Purchas* (1818) 2 B & Ald 39. This rule is usually referred to as 'the rule in *Clayton's Case*'. See FINANCIAL INSTITUTIONS vol 48 (2015) PARA 185; CONTRACT vol 22 (2012) PARAS 525–529.
4 *Hopkinson v Rolt* (1861) 9 HL Cas 514. See also *Gordon v Graham* (1716) 7 Vin Abr 52 pl 3; and FINANCIAL INSTITUTIONS vol 48 (2015) PARA 289.
5 See *London and County Banking Co v Ratcliffe* (1881) 6 App Cas 722, HL; *Deeley v Lloyds Bank Ltd* [1912] AC 756 at 774, HL, per Lord Atkinson; *Re Chute's Estate* [1914] 1 IR 180.

733. Mortgage security implies agreement to pay interest. Apart from express stipulation[1], a mortgage security implies an agreement to pay interest[2]. The first mortgagee is not accountable to a second mortgagee for extra interest stipulated for and received after notice of the second mortgage[3].

1 As to express stipulations for payment of interest see PARAS 189–191. As to a proviso for reduction of interest on punctual payment see PARA 192. As to set-off of interest where the mortgagor takes a legacy from the mortgagee see *Pettat v Ellis* (1804) 9 Ves 563. As to set-off generally see CIVIL PROCEDURE vol 11 (2015) PARA 382 et seq. In mortgage transactions, 'month' formerly meant 'calendar month' (*Hutton v Brown* (1881) 45 LT 343 per Fry J; *Schiller v Petersen & Co Ltd* [1924] 1 Ch 394, CA); and this is its meaning in all documents made or coming into operation after 1925, unless the context otherwise requires (see the Law of Property Act 1925 s 61(a); CPR 2.10; and CIVIL PROCEDURE vol 11 (2015) PARA 123; TIME vol 97 (2015) PARA 307 et seq).
2 See PARAS 182, 189.
3 *Law v Glenn* (1867) 2 Ch App 634 at 639.

734. Interest on mortgage loan as damages for delay in payment. Where the mortgage provides for interest up to the day fixed for payment but not beyond, a contract for the continuance of the same rate of interest until payment is not implied, but subsequent interest will be given by way of damages for breach of contract, and the current rate of interest on damages will generally be adopted as a proper measure of damages for the subsequent delay[1]. This rule applies both to proceedings on the covenant, and to accounts taken in redemption or foreclosure[2]. In taking those accounts, interest may not be ascertained as damages but will be awarded on the same footing as consideration for allowing the loan to remain unpaid[3].

1 See PARA 194.
2 As to proceedings for redemption see PARA 661 et seq. As to foreclosure generally see PARA 571 et seq.
3 *Wallington v Cook* (1878) 47 LJCh 508 (where, in a 60% loan, interest at 5% was allowed subsequent to the day for payment). Dicta in *Re Roberts, Goodchap v Roberts* (1880) 14 ChD 49 at 52, CA, *Mellersh v Brown* (1890) 45 ChD 225 at 230 and, perhaps, *Economic Life Assurance Society v Usborne* [1902] AC 147 at 154, HL, per Lord Davey, suggest that full interest at the original rate will be allowed, but the procedure in *Wallington v Cook* above seems correct.

735. Interest on covenant merges in judgment. Where the mortgage deed provides for payment of interest on the principal debt after default and judgment for the principal debt is obtained, the mortgage debt is merged in the judgment, and, if the covenant to pay interest was merely incidental to the covenant to pay the principal debt, the interest will no longer be recoverable under the covenant to pay interest, but interest at the statutory rate[1] is recoverable on the judgment[2].

Similarly, where the mortgage does not provide for interest after default, only the statutory rate is recoverable after judgment[3]. If the covenant is to pay interest on principal remaining unpaid, it ceases to be operative on the judgment being obtained, as the principal due under the covenant is merged in the judgment debt, and is no longer, so it has been said, unpaid[4]. If the covenant is to pay interest on the principal money remaining due on the security of the mortgage, the effect is different, and the covenant remains operative notwithstanding the judgment[5]. The covenant likewise remains operative despite the judgment if it expressly binds the mortgagor to pay interest at the agreed rate on the principal sum or any judgment recovered for it[6].

1   As to the covenant for repayment in the mortgage deed see PARA 182. As provision for payment of interest in the mortgage deed see PARA 189 et seq. As to the interest on judgment debts see CIVIL PROCEDURE vol 12A (2015) PARA 1235 et seq.
2   *Re Sneyd, ex p Fewings* (1883) 25 ChD 338 at 355, CA; *Arbuthnot v Bunsilall* (1890) 62 LT 234; *Economic Life Assurance Society v Usborne* [1902] AC 147 at 149, HL. As to money and interest on money see FINANCIAL INSTRUMENTS AND TRANSACTIONS vol 49 (2015) PARA 1 et seq.
3   *Re European Central Rly Co, ex p Oriental Financial Corpn* (1876) 4 ChD 33, CA. See also CIVIL PROCEDURE vol 12A (2015) PARA 1235 et seq.
4   *Re Sneyd, ex p Fewings* (1883) 25 ChD 338 at 353, CA.
5   *Popple v Sylvester* (1882) 22 ChD 98, where the action was to obtain personal payment, and not, as suggested in *Re Sneyd, ex p Fewings* (1883) 25 ChD 338 at 345, CA, to realise the security. See also *Economic Life Assurance Society v Usborne* [1902] AC 147 at 152, HL; *Ealing London Borough Council v El Isaac* [1980] 2 All ER 548, [1980] 1 WLR 932, CA. As to the rate of interest on costs ordered to be added to the security see PARA 746.
6   See *Re Sneyd, ex p Fewings* (1883) 25 ChD 338 at 355, CA. After judgment a new agreement may be made continuing the old rate of interest: *Re Agriculturist Cattle Insurance Co, ex p Hughes* (1872) 4 ChD 34n.

736. Rate of interest recoverable in foreclosure or redemption. The rule as to merger of interest in the judgment[1] applies only to claims for interest made against the mortgagor personally under his covenants for payment of principal and interest[2]. The amount for the time being recoverable under those covenants is independent of the amount for which the mortgaged property is a security[3]. The security stands for the amount of the principal and the full interest, that is interest at the agreed rate, and, in taking the accounts in redemption or foreclosure[4], or for purposes incident to the realisation of the security, it is immaterial that personal judgment has been obtained[5]. Similarly, where the debt is secured by bond, the full interest can be recovered against the mortgaged property, even though the principal and interest recoverable on the bond is limited to the amount of the penalty[6].

1   See PARA 735; and CIVIL PROCEDURE vol 12A (2015) PARA 1235 et seq.
2   *Economic Life Assurance Society v Usborne* [1902] AC 147, HL. As to the covenant for repayment in the mortgage deed see PARA 182. As provision for payment of interest in the mortgage deed see PARA 189 et seq.
3   *Economic Life Assurance Society v Usborne* [1902] AC 147, HL.
4   As to proceedings for redemption see PARA 661 et seq. As to foreclosure see PARA 571 et seq.
5   *Economic Life Assurance Society v Usborne* [1902] AC 147, HL. See also *Lowry v Williams* [1895] 1 IR 274, CA.
6   *Clarke v Lord Abingdon* (1810) 17 Ves 106. As to bonds see PARA 126.

737. Commission or fines on default of mortgage repayment by instalments. A loan secured by mortgage may be made payable by instalments of a specified amount covering both principal and interest[1]. This is usually done in the case of bank and building society mortgages[2], and may be done in bills of sale[3]. Additional sums, whether under the name of commission[4] or fines[5], and prospective, but not retrospective, default interest rate increases[6] may be agreed to be paid in the event of instalments being in arrear, and these will be allowed against the mortgagor in the accounts. As a second mortgagee is not in any better position than the mortgagor, commission will also be allowed against him[7]. Interest on fines may not, however, be charged[8] unless (for instance, on the construction of the building society rules) the fines are to be added to principal[9]; nor may fines for non-payment of fines be charged (unless the rules so provide)[10].

1　As to payment by instalments see PARA 185. As to the exercise of the mortgagee's statutory powers of sale in such a case see PARA 456.
2　See FINANCIAL INSTITUTIONS vol 48 (2015) PARAS 288, 489 et seq.
3　See FINANCIAL INSTRUMENTS AND TRANSACTIONS vol 49 (2015) PARA 515 et seq.
4　*General Credit and Discount Co v Glegg* (1883) 22 ChD 549; *The Benwell Tower* (1895) 72 LT 664. See FINANCIAL INSTITUTIONS vol 48 (2015) PARA 286.
5　*Parker v Butcher* (1867) LR 3 Eq 762.
6　*Lordsvale Finance plc v Bank of Zambia* [1996] QB 752, [1996] 3 All ER 156. As to interest rate increases as penalties see PARA 192.
7　*The Benwell Tower* (1895) 72 LT 664 at 669.
8　*Parker v Butcher* (1867) LR 3 Eq 762; *Ingoldby v Riley* (1873) 28 LT 55.
9　*Provident Permanent Building Society v Greenhill* (1878) 9 ChD 122.
10　*Re Middlesbrough Building Society* (1884) 54 LJCh 592. See also FINANCIAL INSTITUTIONS vol 48 (2015) PARA 376.

738. Mortgage interest ceasing to run after tender. A tender of the amount due on the mortgage at a time when the mortgagee is bound to receive it stops interest from running if the mortgagor keeps the money ready to pay over to the mortgagee[1]. For this purpose, there must be an actual tender[2]. Even if there has been a tender by a borrower of the amount due for principal and interest, that tender does not stop interest running after the date of the tender unless there is evidence that the sum has been set aside and is ready for payment at any time[3]. The mortgagor should pay the money into court if there are any proceedings pending in which this can be done; if he makes profit, as by placing the money on deposit, he must account for this to the mortgagee[4]. A mortgagee is not entitled to interest if by his own default he delays payment off[5], but unavoidable delay in revesting the property in the mortgagor is not such a default[6].

If the mortgagee fails to attend on the day fixed for payment in a redemption suit, a new day is appointed and subsequent interest is not allowed[7].

1　*Gyles v Hall* (1726) 2 P Wms 378; *Bank of New South Wales v O'Connor* (1889) 14 App Cas 273 at 284, PC; *Rourke v Robinson* [1911] 1 Ch 480; *Lutton v Rodd* (1675) 2 Cas in Ch 206; *Cliff v Wadsworth* (1843) 2 Y & C Ch Cas 598. As to the necessity to tender the amount due see PARA 335. As to the payment of six months' interest in lieu of notice, and the cases where this is excused, see PARAS 333–334. As to interest being stopped on loss of title deeds see PARA 500.
2　*Bishop v Church* (1751) 2 Ves Sen 371 at 372; *Garforth v Bradley* (1755) 2 Ves Sen 675 at 678; *Kinnaird v Trollope* (1889) 42 ChD 610; *Graham v Seal* (1918) 88 LJCh 31, CA. See also *Webb v Crosse* [1912] 1 Ch 323; and PARA 335.
3　*Barratt v Gough-Thomas* [1951] 2 All ER 48 at 49, [1951] WN 309 at 309 per Danckwerts J.
4　*Edmondson v Copland* [1911] 2 Ch 301 at 310. Cf *Robarts v Jefferys* (1830) 8 LJOS Ch 137.
5　See *Thornton v Court* (1854) 3 De GM & G 293 at 301.
6　*Webb v Crosse* [1912] 1 Ch 323.
7　*Hughes v Williams* (1853) Kay, App iv. See also PARA 671. As to the equity of redemption see PARAS 107, 304 et seq. As to proceedings for redemption see PARA 661 et seq.

739. Time limit on recovery of mortgage interest arrears. The statutory limitation on proceedings for the recovery of arrears of interest by a mortgagee[1], and the exclusion from this limitation of foreclosure claims in respect of land[2] and claims in which the mortgagor is seeking to redeem[3], are dealt with elsewhere in this work.

1　See LIMITATION PERIODS vol 68 (2008) PARA 1111 et seq.
2　See LIMITATION PERIODS vol 68 (2008) PARA 1128. As to foreclosure generally see PARA 571 et seq.

3   See LIMITATION PERIODS vol 68 (2008) PARA 1137. As to proceedings for redemption see PARA
    661 et seq.

740. Interest on mortgage of settled property. Where the mortgaged property is
in settlement subject to the mortgage, it is the duty of the tenant for life to keep
down the interest[1], but this is a duty only as between himself and the
remainderman. If he makes good a deficiency out of his own money, he has no
charge for the amount on the inheritance, unless in some way he has intimated his
intention to charge it[2]. Subsequent rents during the life of a tenant for life are
applicable to liquidate arrears during the same life tenancy, but he is not liable to
make good arrears of a previous life tenancy[3]. Where several estates are included
in the same settlement, the tenant for life is bound, out of the whole rents and
profits, to keep down the interest on charges on all the estates[4]. The mortgagee is
not affected, and, unless he has allowed interest to remain unpaid by collusion
with the remainderman or other misconduct, he can recover against the
inheritance arrears which have accumulated during the life tenancy[5]. The principle
applies equally whether the mortgage is made before or after the estate is settled.
The mortgagor cannot by putting the equity of redemption in settlement affect the
mortgagee's rights, and mere laches[6] on the mortgagee's part does not prejudice
his claim against the remainderman[7]. The remainderman has his remedy by
proceedings to compel the tenant for life to keep down the interest[8]. Similarly, all
arrears of interest are chargeable by the first mortgagee as against a second
mortgagee[9], unless the first mortgagee has been in possession and has allowed the
mortgagor to have the rents without paying interest[10].

1   *Revel v Watkinson* (1748) 1 Ves Sen 93; *Burges v Mawbey* (1823) Turn & R 167 at 174; *Marshall
    v Crowther* (1874) 2 ChD 199. See also SETTLEMENTS vol 91 (2012) PARA 862 et seq.
2   *Lord Kensington v Bouverie* (1859) 7 HL Cas 557.
3   *Caulfield v Maguire* (1845) 2 Jo & Lat 141 at 160; *Honywood v Honywood* [1902] 1 Ch 347.
4   *Frewen v Law Life Assurance Society* [1896] 2 Ch 511; *Honywood v Honywood* [1902] 1 Ch 347.
5   *Aston v Aston* (1750) 1 Ves Sen 264; *Loftus v Swift and Governors of St Patrick's Hospital* (1806)
    2 Sch & Lef 642 at 654; *Roe v Pogson* (1816) 2 Madd 457; *Wrixon v Vize* (1842) 2 Dr & War
    192 at 202; *Re Morley, Morley v Saunders* (1869) LR 8 Eq 594.
6   As to laches see EQUITABLE JURISDICTION vol 47 (2014) PARA 253 et seq.
7   *Wrixon v Vize* (1842) 2 Dr & War 192; *Hill v Browne* (1844) Drury *temp* Sug 426 at 435.
8   *Lord Kensington v Bouverie* (1859) 7 HL Cas 557 at 596; *Makings v Makings* (1860) 1 De GF &
    J 355 at 358; but see *Scholefield v Lockwood (No 2)* (1863) 4 De GJ & Sm 22 at 31, where it was
    said that no right arises to the remainderman until the death of the tenant for life.
9   *Aston v Aston* (1749) 1 Ves Sen 264.
10 *Bentham v Haincourt* (1691) Prec Ch 30; *Loftus v Swift and Governors of St Patrick's Hospital*
    (1806) 2 Sch & Lef 642 at 655.

741. Overpayments and underpayments of mortgage interest. Where interest
has been paid on a sum greater than that ultimately held to be charged on the
property, the overpayment is not treated as paid in reduction of principal
mortgage debt[1]. In appropriate circumstances an overpayment of interest may be
refunded to the mortgagor[2], or an underpayment made good to the mortgagee[3].

1   *Blandy v Kimber (No 2)* (1858) 25 Beav 537.
2   *Tyler v Manson, Manson v Tyler* (1826) 5 LJOS Ch 34 at 38 per Leach V-C. See *Re Jones's Estate*
    [1914] 1 IR 188, where payments of interest in full had been made in ignorance of a provision for
    reduction for punctual payment, and the mortgagor was allowed credit for the amounts overpaid
    within six years.
3   *Gregory v Pilkington* (1856) 8 De GM & G 616; *Universities Superannuation Scheme Ltd v Marks
    & Spencer plc* [1999] 1 EGLR 13, [1999] 04 EG 158, CA (underpayment of service charges due
    from tenant to landlord).

742. Capitalisation of interest on transfer, or on redemption by later mortgagee.
Where at the time of the transfer of a mortgage there are arrears of interest due

which the transferee pays to the transferor, he can add these to the principal so that from that time they will carry interest, if the transfer is made with the mortgagor's concurrence, but not otherwise[1]. In a foreclosure claim[2] where successive periods of redemption[3] are directed, interest is in effect capitalised[4]. Where, in a claim by a first mortgagee against subsequent incumbrancers and the mortgagor, successive redemptions are directed[5], and the second mortgagee redeems the first but the third mortgagee fails to redeem the second and is foreclosed, it seems that the aggregate amount which the third mortgagee would have had to pay for principal, interest and costs carries interest against the mortgagor[6].

1   *Ashenhurst v James* (1745) 3 Atk 270; *Agnew v King* [1902] 1 IR 471. See also *Gladwyn v Hitchman* (1690) 2 Vern 135; *Earl of Macclesfield v Fitton* (1683) 1 Vern 168.
2   As to foreclosure see PARA 571 et seq.
3   As to the equity of redemption see PARAS 107, 304 et seq. As to proceedings for redemption see PARA 661 et seq.
4   See PARA 603.
5   Only one time for redemption will now be allowed to the later incumbrancers: see PARAS 606, 664.
6   *Elton v Curteis* (1881) 19 ChD 49.

13. COSTS, CHARGES AND EXPENSES

(1) GENERAL PRINCIPLES REGARDING COSTS

743. Mortgagee's general right to reimbursement of costs from the security. A mortgagee is allowed to reimburse himself out of the mortgaged property for all costs, charges and expenses reasonably and properly incurred in enforcing or preserving his security[1], including the costs of litigation properly undertaken by him[2]. The right extends to equitable mortgagees and chargees[3]. There is, however, no implied contract by the mortgagor to pay any such costs, charges and expenses, and they are not, in the absence of express agreement, recoverable against him personally[4].

1   See *Parker-Tweedale v Dunbar Bank plc (No 2)* [1991] Ch 26, [1990] 2 All ER 588, CA; *Gomba Holdings Ltd v Minories Finance Ltd (No 2)* [1993] Ch 171, [1992] 4 All ER 588, CA.
2   See PARAS 771–772.
3   *Ezekiel v Orakpo* [1997] 1 WLR 340, CA; *Connell v Hardie* (1839) 3 Y & C Ex 582; *R v Chambers* (1840) 4 Y & C Ex 54. As to equitable mortgages and charges see PARAS 105–106, 215 et seq.
4   *Re Sneyd, ex p Fewings* (1883) 25 ChD 338 at 352, CA, per Cotton LJ; *Sinfield v Sweet* [1967] 3 All ER 479, [1967] 1 WLR 1489.

744. Provisions as to costs in the mortgage deed. The mortgage deed may contain express provisions varying or extending the mortgagee's general right to reimbursement from the security of costs properly incurred[1]. There may, for example, be agreement that the mortgagor is personally liable for payment of costs[2]; or that costs should be payable on the indemnity basis[3]; or that the mortgagee is entitled to the costs of proceedings where a third party impugns the title to the mortgage, or the enforcement or exercise of some right or power accruing to the mortgagee[4]. However, express contractual provisions are not normally construed so as to require the mortgagor to pay all costs, charges and expenses even if improperly or unreasonably incurred or improper or unreasonable in amount, and the enforceability of a provision which did so provide would be open to serious questions on public policy grounds[5].

1   As to the mortgagee's general right to reimbursement of costs from the security see PARA 743.
2   See eg *Gomba Holdings Ltd v Minories Finance Ltd (No 2)* [1993] Ch 171, [1992] 4 All ER 588, CA.
3   *Gomba Holdings Ltd v Minories Finance Ltd (No 2)* [1993] Ch 171, [1992] 4 All ER 588, CA, where a contractual provision for costs on a full indemnity basis in favour of the mortgagee was construed to require taxation on that basis. (Note that under the Civil Procedure Rules, taxation is now referred to as 'detailed assessment of costs': see CPR Pt 47; and CIVIL PROCEDURE vol 12A (2015) PARA 1749 et seq). The effect of a provision for payment of 'full costs' or 'all costs' is the subject of conflicting decisions. In *Re Adelphi Hotel (Brighton) Ltd, District Bank Ltd v Adelphi Hotel (Brighton) Ltd* [1953] 2 All ER 498 at 501, [1953] 1 WLR 955 at 958–959 per Vaisey J, it was held that such an expression did not require taxation on the solicitor and own client basis. This decision was not cited in *Bank of Baroda v Panessar* [1987] Ch 335, [1986] 3 All ER 751, where it was held that the expression required taxation on the indemnity basis. The decision in *Re Adelphi Hotel (Brighton) Ltd, District Bank Ltd v Adelphi Hotel (Brighton) Ltd* was doubted in *Gomba Holdings Ltd v Minories Finance Ltd (No 2)* [1992] BCLC 851 at 856–860 per Vinelott J (although no view on the issue was expressed in the subsequent Court of Appeal hearing: see [1993] Ch 171, [1992] 4 All ER 588).
4   Such costs are not normally allowable (see *Parker-Tweedale v Dunbar Bank plc (No 2)* [1991] Ch 26, [1990] 2 All ER 588, CA) but express contractual provisions may alter what would otherwise have been the position (see *Gomba Holdings Ltd v Minories Finance Ltd (No 2)* [1993] Ch 171 at 185, [1992] 4 All ER 588 at 600, CA, per Scott LJ).
5   *Gomba Holdings Ltd v Minories Finance Ltd (No 2)* [1993] Ch 171 at 187–188, [1992] 4 All ER 588 at 601–602, CA, per Scott LJ. As to unfair terms in mortgages see PARA 203. As to unfair terms in consumer contracts generally see further the Consumer Rights Act 2015 Pt 2 (ss 61–76), Sch 2; and CONSUMER PROTECTION; CONTRACT.

745. Assessment of costs relating to mortgage. The mortgagee does not need to apply for an order for those costs that he has a contractual right to recover out of the mortgage funds, and nor do those costs have to be assessed[1]. The mortgagor may make an application for the court to direct that an account of the mortgagee's costs be taken, and may then dispute an amount in the mortgagee's account on the basis that it has been unreasonably incurred or is unreasonable in amount[2]. Where a mortgagor disputes an amount, the court may make an order that the disputed costs be assessed[3]; and where the court assesses costs payable under the terms of the mortgage, the costs payable are, unless the contract expressly provides otherwise, to be presumed to be costs which have been reasonably incurred, and are reasonable in amount, and the court will assess them accordingly[4]. The court may make an order that all or part of the costs payable under the contract be disallowed if it is satisfied by the paying party that costs have been unreasonably incurred or are unreasonable in amount[5].

A mortgagor is also entitled to apply for an assessment of a bill of costs rendered to the mortgagee by his solicitor if the mortgagor is liable to pay it[6].

1 See CPR 44.5; CPR PD 44—*General Rules About Costs* para 7.1; and PARA 759. As to the assessment of costs payable pursuant to a contract see CIVIL PROCEDURE vol 12A (2015) PARA 1740.

2 See CPR PD 44—*General Rules About Costs* para 7.3(1), (2); and PARA 759.

3 See CPR PD 44—*General Rules About Costs* para 7.3(3); and PARA 759.

4 See CPR 44.5(1); and CIVIL PROCEDURE vol 12A (2015) PARA 1740.

5 See CPR 44.11; and CIVIL PROCEDURE vol 12A (2015) PARA 1712.

6 See the Solicitors Act 1974 ss 70, 71(1); and LEGAL PROFESSIONS vol 66 (2015) PARA 743 et seq. See further *Re Griffith, Jones & Co* (1883) 50 LT 434, CA; *Re Longbotham & Sons* [1904] 2 Ch 152, CA; *Re Paice and Cross* (1914) 58 Sol Jo 593. If such an application is made after 12 months from the delivery of the bill, or after judgment for recovery of the costs has been obtained or after it is paid, no order can be made except in special circumstances (see the Solicitors Act 1974 s 70(3); and LEGAL PROFESSIONS vol 66 (2015) PARA 746), including those which affect the mortgagor but not the mortgagee (see s 71(2); and LEGAL PROFESSIONS vol 66 (2015) PARA 745). Such an assessment is on the indemnity basis: see CPR 44.3; and CIVIL PROCEDURE vol 12A (2015) PARA 1704.

746. Interest on costs and expenses. Interest at the rate reserved by the mortgage[1] is usually allowed on outlays of a permanent nature, such as renewal fines[2] or expenses of lasting improvements[3], and expenses which there is no income to meet, such as premiums of life policies[4], but not on the expense of ordinary repairs where the mortgagee is in receipt of the rents and profits[5] except, perhaps, where the expense exceeds the balance of rents after payment of interest[6].

The mortgagee is not entitled to interest on costs of proceedings, unless an order is made by which the costs are to be added to his security[7]. If such an order is made they will carry interest from the date of the order at the statutory rate[8], notwithstanding that a higher rate is reserved by the mortgage[9]. Interest is recoverable[10] only on costs ordered to be paid by one party to the other, not on costs payable out of an estate[11], unless the mortgage deed otherwise provides.

1 *Woolley v Drag* (1795) 2 Anst 551; *Townley v Moore* (1856) 3 Seton's Form of Decrees, Judgments and Orders in Equity (7th Edn, 1912) 1885; *Glencross v Pulman* (1859) 3 Seton's Form of Decrees, Judgments and Orders in Equity (7th Edn, 1912) 1887.

2 *Manlove v Bale and Bruton* (1688) 2 Vern 84; *Lacon v Mertins* (1743) 3 Atk 1 at 4. As to the conversion of renewal fines on perpetually renewable leases see the Law of Property Act 1922 s 145, Sch 15 paras 5(1), 6, 7(1), 12; and LANDLORD AND TENANT vol 62 (2012) PARA 689.

3 *Webb v Rorke* (1806) 2 Sch & Lef 661 at 676; *Quarrell v Beckford* (1807) 14 Ves 177 at 179. See also *Procter v Cooper* (1700) Prec Ch 116; *Townley v Moore* (1856) 3 Seton's Form of Decrees, Judgments and Orders in Equity (7th Edn, 1912) 1885; *Glencross v Pulman* (1859) 3 Seton's Form of Decrees, Judgments and Orders in Equity (7th Edn, 1912) 1887.

4   *Hodgson v Hodgson* (1837) 2 Keen 704; *Marshall v Nunn* (1853) 3 Seton's Form of Decrees,
    Judgments and Orders in Equity (7th Edn, 1912) 1885; *Bates v Johnson* (1859) 3 Seton's Form of
    Decrees, Judgments and Orders in Equity (7th Edn, 1912) 1885.
5   In the cases cited in note 1, interest on expenses of repairs was not allowed, but sometimes it has
    been allowed: see *Eyre v Hughes* (1876) 2 ChD 148 at 164; *King v Kitchener* (1871) 3
    Seton's Form of Decrees, Judgments and Orders in Equity (7th Edn, 1912) 1886, CA. See also
    Seton's Form of Decrees, Judgments and Orders in Equity (7th Edn, 1912) 1906.
6   See 3 Seton's Form of Decrees, Judgments and Orders in Equity (7th Edn, 1912) 1906. See also
    Wrigley v Gill [1906] 1 Ch 165 at 169, CA, where the dictum that the allowance of interest on
    necessary repairs and lasting improvements was very unusual seems erroneous so far as it refers to
    lasting improvements.
7   *Eardley v Knight* (1889) 41 ChD 537.
8   See PARA 735; and CIVIL PROCEDURE vol 12A (2015) PARA 1235 et seq.
9   *Eardley v Knight* (1889) 41 ChD 537. See also *Lippard v Ricketts* (1872) LR 14 Eq 291.
10 As to the interest on judgment debts see CIVIL PROCEDURE vol 12A (2015) PARA 1235 et seq.
11 *A-G v Nethercote* (1841) 11 Sim 529.

(2) COSTS AND EXPENSES WHICH MAY BE ADDED TO SECURITY

747. Costs of negotiating the loan and preparing the mortgage. The
mortgagee's costs, charges and expenses which he may add to his security do not,
in the absence of special stipulation, include the costs of negotiating the loan and
preparing the mortgage as, for these, the mortgagor is personally liable[1]. Where
the mortgage is to cover every sum advanced or paid by the mortgagee to the
mortgagor, or to become owing to the mortgagee by the mortgagor, this does not
cover costs[2].

Where, however, in proceedings, the court ordered that money should be raised
by mortgage, a direction was given that the mortgagee should be allowed his
costs, including the costs of settling the security[3].

1   *Wales v Carr* [1902] 1 Ch 860. See also *Gregg v Slater* (1856) 22 Beav 314; *Field v Hopkins* (1890)
    44 ChD 524, CA. The costs of negotiating the loan and preparing the mortgage are normally
    deducted from the initial advance.
2   *Field v Hopkins* (1890) 44 ChD 524, CA. As to costs of reconveyance see PARA 659.
3   *Nicholson v Jeyes* (1853) 22 LJCh 833.

748. Costs of completing the mortgage security. The costs of completing the
security, such as the costs of obtaining a legal mortgage in pursuance of an
agreement accompanying a mortgage by deposit of deeds[1], may be added to the
security, but not the costs of investigating the mortgagor's title for the purpose of
the legal mortgage[2]. Where the security is on a fund in court and the mortgagee
is empowered by the mortgage to apply for a stop order[3], the costs of the
application are allowed[4].

1   As to legal mortgages see PARAS 104, 160 et seq. As to the creation of an equitable mortgage by
    deposit of title deeds see PARA 222–223. Since 27 September 1989, however, the mere deposit of
    title deeds by way of security can no longer create a valid equitable mortgage: see PARA 221.
2   See *National Provincial Bank of England v Games* (1886) 31 ChD 582, CA, where the items
    allowed included costs of correspondence as to the legal mortgage. Similarly, the costs of a
    surrender of copyholds were allowed: see *Pryce v Bury* (1853) 2 Drew 41 (affd (1854) 22 LTOS
    324); *Lane v King* (1799) 3 Seton's Form of Decrees, Judgments and Orders (7th Edn, 1912) 1886.
    However, the costs of an order appointing trustees under the Settled Land Act 1882 (largely
    repealed: see now the Settled Land Act 1925) for the purpose of leasing the property were not
    allowed: see *Field v Hopkins* (1890) 44 ChD 524, CA.
3   As to stop orders see PARA 274; and CIVIL PROCEDURE vol 12A (2015) PARA 1483 et seq.
4   *Waddilove v Taylor* (1848) 6 Hare 307. See also *Hoole v Roberts* (1848) 12 Jur 108, where the
    costs of a needless application were disallowed.

749. Expenses of maintenance and repair of mortgaged property. Expenses of maintenance and improvement of the mortgaged property incurred by the mortgagee[1], such as caretaker's wages[2], expenses of necessary repairs[3], and of permanent improvements properly undertaken[4], and payments to agricultural tenants[5], are allowed to be added to his security. Expenses of repairs are allowed as just allowances without express mention in the order for redemption[6], but repairs done without the mortgagee's written authority by a receiver[7] appointed by him under his statutory power[8] cannot be included in his account[9]. To obtain expenses of permanent improvements the mortgagee must allege and prove some expenditure of this nature, and then an inquiry as to money properly[10] laid out in lasting improvements will be directed[11]. To obtain an inquiry it is sufficient to give general proof of expenditure, and prima facie proof that it has been laid out in lasting improvements; if the proof establishes that the works are improvements proper to be allowed, an account of money so laid out will be directed[12]. A similar direction may be given where an adverse possessor has to yield up possession[13]. Where the mortgagor is seeking not redemption but an account of proceeds of sale, the mortgagee's right to an inquiry as to improvements is stronger, as he is of course entitled to the expenses to the extent that they have increased the selling value of the property[14]. The mortgagee is also allowed extraordinary expenses incurred for the protection of the property, but the mortgagor should be informed of the outlay as soon as possible[15]. A second mortgagee in possession is not entitled as against the first mortgagee to a charge for money expended in preserving or permanently improving the property[16].

1 *White v City of London Brewery Co* (1889) 42 ChD 237 at 243, CA.
2 *Brandon v Brandon* (1862) 10 WR 287.
3 *Godfrey v Watson* (1747) 3 Atk 517; *Sandon v Hooper* (1843) 6 Beav 246. See also LIEN vol 68 (2008) PARA 877.
4 *Shepard v Jones* (1882) 21 ChD 469 at 476, CA. See also *Spurgeon v Collier* (1758) 1 Eden 55 at 63; *Davey v Durrant, Smith v Durrant* (1857) 1 De G & J 535 at 554; and PARAS 437, 672.
5 See *Oxenham v Ellis* (1854) 18 Beav 593, where payments for which the mortgagee was liable to an outgoing tenant were allowed after certificate and payment of the amount due. In *Barron v Lancefield* (1853) 17 Beav 208, however, further expenses were not allowed after certificate. As to the mortgagee's liability to tenants see LANDLORD AND TENANT vol 62 (2012) PARA 34.
6 See *Tipton Green Colliery Co v Tipton Moat Colliery Co* (1877) 7 ChD 192; and PARA 672. As to redemption orders see PARA 671 et seq.
7 As to the appointment of receivers out of court see PARAS 478–487.
8 As to the statutory power to appoint a receiver see PARA 479.
9 *White v Metcalf* [1903] 2 Ch 567.
10 *Houghton v Sevenoaks Estate Co* (1884) 33 WR 341.
11 *Tipton Green Colliery Co v Tipton Moat Colliery Co* (1877) 7 ChD 192; 3 Seton's Form of Decrees, Judgments and Orders in Equity (7th Edn, 1912) 1885. See also *Webb v Rorke* (1806) 2 Sch & Lef 661 at 676; *Quarrell v Beckford* (1807) 14 Ves 177 at 179; *Scholefield v Lockwood (No 2)* (1863) 11 WR 555. As to objecting to the allowance see *Powell v Trotter* (1861) 1 Drew & Sm 388.
12 *Shepard v Jones* (1882) 21 ChD 469, CA.
13 See *Pelly v Bascombe* (1863) 4 Giff 390.
14 *Shepard v Jones* (1882) 21 ChD 469 at 478, CA; *Henderson v Astwood, Astwood v Cobbold, Cobbold v Astwood* [1894] AC 150 at 163, PC.
15 *Lord Trimleston v Hamill* (1810) 1 Ball & B 377 at 385.
16 See *Landowners West of England and South Wales Land Drainage and Inclosure Co v Ashford* (1880) 16 ChD 411 at 433; and PARA 170.

750. Mortgagee's expenditure incurred in making profits. Where a mortgagee has to account for profits, he is allowed all expenditure necessary for obtaining them[1]. If by the terms of the mortgage deed this expenditure is authorised and the mortgagor has covenanted to pay it, it may, in case of deficiency, be charged against the property[2] or allowed out of the proceeds of sale[3].

1 *Bompas v King* (1886) 33 ChD 279 at 288, CA; *White v City of London Brewery Co* (1889) 42 ChD 237 at 243, CA.
2 *Norton v Cooper* (1854) 5 De GM & G 728.
3 *Bompas v King* (1886) 33 ChD 279 at 288, CA; *White v City of London Brewery Co* (1889) 42 ChD 237 at 243, CA.

751. Insurance premiums and other salvage payments. So far as no contrary intention is expressed in the mortgage deed, the mortgagee is allowed the premiums in respect of fire insurance, with the same priority and with interest at the same rate as the mortgage money[1]. Where the mortgagor has covenanted to insure and has neglected to do so, the mortgagee, except by virtue of a statutory or express power, may not insure and charge the premiums as against a second mortgagee[2]. Except under a power conferred by the terms of the mortgage or by statute, the mortgagee may not charge such premiums in his accounts[3] unless he is in possession, in which case the premiums fall under just allowances[4].

Where the security covers a life policy[5], the mortgagee is allowed premiums paid by him for keeping the policy on foot[6]. A covenant by the mortgagee to pay the premiums does not deprive him of the right to add the premiums to his debt[7]. Where the insurance company is the mortgagee and the policy has been actually issued[8], the company may, if so authorised under the mortgage, debit the mortgagor with the premiums and add to the mortgage debt[9].

Where a shipowner had mortgaged ships to a firm of merchants, and had also insured ships[10] through the firm's agency, and accounts were directed between the mortgagors and mortgagees, the mortgagees were held entitled to charge in the accounts the full insurance premiums without deducting customary commission allowed to them by the insurance offices[11].

In general, the mortgagee will be allowed sums which are properly expended for the preservation of the mortgaged property, such as fines for the renewal of leases[12] and ground rent[13]. Such advances, however, follow the principal debt, and, if the right to recover this is postponed, the right to recover salvage payments out of the property is also postponed[14].

1 See the Law of Property Act 1925 s 101(1)(ii), (4); and PARA 201. As to the application of the insurance money see PARA 173; and as to a joint insurance by mortgagor and mortgagee see *Rogers v Grazebrooke* (1842) 12 Sim 557.
2 *Brooke v Stone* (1865) 34 LJCh 251.
3 *Dobson v Land* (1850) 8 Hare 216; *Bellamy v Brickenden* (1861) 2 John & H 137.
4 *Scholefield v Lockwood (No 2)* (1863) 11 WR 555.
5 As to life policies generally see INSURANCE vol 60 (2011) PARA 476 et seq.
6 *Bellamy v Brickenden* (1861) 2 John & H 137; *Gill v Downing* (1874) LR 17 Eq 316.
7 *Shaw v Scottish Widows' Fund Assurance Society* (1917) 87 LJCh 76.
8 *Grey v Ellison* (1856) 1 Giff 438.
9 *Earl of Fitzwilliam v Price* (1858) 4 Jur NS 889. See also *Browne v Price* (1858) 4 Jur NS 882. For a direction for account of premiums paid by the mortgagee see 3 Seton's Form of Decrees, Judgments and Orders in Equity (7th Edn, 1912) 1885. In Ireland, where salvage payments are more readily recognised, a second mortgagee may have priority for premiums paid by him: see *Re Power's Policies* [1899] 1 IR 6, CA; and cf LIEN vol 68 (2008) PARAS 870–877. As to lien by payment of premiums see INSURANCE vol 60 (2011) PARA 511.
10 As to marine insurance generally see INSURANCE vol 60 (2011) PARA 238 et seq.
11 *Baring v Stanton* (1876) 3 ChD 502, CA. See also *Leete v Wallace* (1888) 58 LT 577 (agreement that premiums on policy effected on mortgagor's life be secured on mortgaged premises; full amount of premiums paid allowed to mortgagees, without deducting commission received by their solicitor from insurance offices).
12 *Manlove v Bale and Bruton* (1688) 2 Vern 84; *Lacon v Mertins* (1743) 3 Atk 1 at 4; *Woolley v Drag* (1795) 2 Anst 551; *Bishop v Mantell* (1807) 3 Seton's Form of Decrees, Judgments and Orders in Equity (7th Edn, 1912) 1886; *Hamilton v Denny* (1809) 1 Ball & B 199 at 202. As to

the conversion of renewal fines on perpetually renewable leases see the Law of Property Act 1922 s 145, Sch 15 paras 5(1), 6, 7(1), 12; and LANDLORD AND TENANT vol 62 (2012) PARA 689.
13 *Hill v Browne* (1844) Drury *temp* Sug 426; *Brandon v Brandon* (1862) 10 WR 287.
14 *Burrowes v Molloy* (1845) 2 Jo & Lat 521.

752. Mortgagee's expenses incurred in management of the property. In the absence of special agreement a mortgagee is not entitled to any remuneration for his special trouble in relation to the mortgaged property and, therefore, when in possession may not charge for work done by himself in collection of rents and management[1], but he may employ a house or land agent or a bailiff at commission or a salary where the work is so troublesome that in the ordinary course he would do this if the property were his own, and he is allowed the expense so incurred in his accounts[2]. It is not a matter of course to allow the expense of a collector[3]. The mortgagee may, however, stipulate for payment for his own work[4] and, if the stipulation is free from any circumstances of oppression or unfair dealing, effect will be given to it[5]. Effect will not be given to such a stipulation as between solicitor-mortgagee and mortgagor where the mortgagor has had no independent advice[6]. Where the mortgagee is a company, it may employ its own directors at remuneration to do work in connection with the property and charge this against the mortgagor in addition to its own agreed remuneration[7].

1 *Langstaffe v Fenwick, Fenwick v Langstaffe* (1805) 10 Ves 405; *Sclater v Cottam* (1857) 5 WR 744; *Re Wallis, ex p Lickorish* (1890) 25 QBD 176 at 182, CA. See also *Nicholson v Tutin (No 2)* (1857) 3 K & J 159.
2 *Bonithon v Hockmore* (1685) 1 Vern 316; *Godfrey v Watson* (1747) 3 Atk 517; *Davis v Dendy* (1818) 3 Madd 170; *Leith v Irvine* (1833) 1 My & K 277 at 295–296; *Sclater v Cottam* (1857) 5 WR 744; *Eyre v Hughes* (1876) 2 ChD 148 at 161; *Re Wallis, ex p Lickorish* (1890) 25 QBD 176, CA.
3 *Union Bank of London v Ingram* (1880) 16 ChD 53 at 56.
4 Formerly such a stipulation was void as tending to oppression or usury, and as a collateral advantage (*French v Baron* (1740) 2 Atk 120; *Scott v Brest* (1788) 2 Term Rep 238 at 241; *Chambers v Goldwin* (1804) 9 Ves 254 at 271; *Barrett v Hartley* (1866) LR 2 Eq 789 at 795; *Comyns v Comyns* (1871) 5 IR Eq 583; *Eyre v Hughes* (1876) 2 ChD 148; *Field v Hopkins* (1890) 44 ChD 524 at 530 per Kay J (on appeal (1890) 44 ChD 524, CA)), although the mortgagee might stipulate for the appointment of a receiver to be paid by the mortgagor (see *Chambers v Goldwin*; *Langstaffe v Fenwick, Fenwick v Langstaffe* (1805) 10 Ves 405). In principle, however, there is now no objection to it (*Biggs v Hoddinott, Hoddinott v Biggs* [1898] 2 Ch 307, CA; *Bath v Standard Land Co Ltd* [1911] 1 Ch 618, CA), so far as the stipulation is confined to the continuance of the mortgage security (*Browne v Ryan* [1901] 2 IR 653, CA; *Noakes & Co Ltd v Rice* [1902] AC 24, HL; *Bradley v Carritt* [1903] AC 253, HL). Cf *Maxwell v Tipping* [1903] 1 IR 499. As to collateral benefits see PARA 322.
5 See *Barrett v Hartley* (1866) LR 2 Eq 789.
6 *Eyre v Hughes* (1876) 2 ChD 148. See also LEGAL PROFESSIONS vol 66 (2015) PARA 606.
7 *Bath v Standard Land Co Ltd* [1911] 1 Ch 618, CA, disapproving *Kavanagh v Workingman's Benefit Building Society* [1896] 1 IR 56, CA.

753. Expenses of sale of the mortgaged property. The mortgagee is entitled to charge the expenses of any actual[1] or attempted[2] sale. In taking the accounts the mortgagor may be allowed credit for loss on realisation due to the mortgagee's negligence[3], but acceptance of a cheque for the deposit which is dishonoured is not negligence so as to deprive the mortgagee of his right to the expenses[4]. The mortgagee cannot charge remuneration for his personal services in connection with the sale[5] unless this is expressly agreed with the mortgagor[6]. Thus an auctioneer[7] or a broker mortgagee[8] may not charge a commission for selling.

1 *White v City of London Brewery Co* (1889) 42 ChD 237 at 243, CA.
2 *Farrer v Lacy, Hartland & Co* (1885) 31 ChD 42, CA. See also *Thompson v Rumball* (1839) 3 Jur 53; *Sutton v Rawlings* (1849) 3 Exch 407; *Batten v Wedgwood Coal and Iron Co* (1884) 28 ChD 317.
3 *McHugh v Union Bank of Canada* [1913] AC 299, PC.

4   *Farrer v Lacy, Hartland & Co* (1885) 31 ChD 42, CA.
5   See PARA 752.
6   Formerly such an agreement was void, as giving the mortgagee a collateral advantage: *Leith v Irvine* (1833) 1 My & K 277; *Broad v Selfe* (1863) 11 WR 1036; *James v Kerr* (1889) 40 ChD 449 at 459; *Field v Hopkins* (1890) 44 ChD 524 at 530 per Kay J (on appeal (1890) 44 ChD 524, CA); *The Benwell Tower* (1895) 72 LT 664. This reason does not now exist, but the agreement will not be enforceable after the redemption of the mortgage: see *Brown v Ryan* [1901] 2 IR 653, CA; and PARA 322.
7   *Matthison v Clarke* (1854) 3 Drew 3; *Furber v Cobb* (1887) 18 QBD 494 at 509, CA.
8   *Arnold v Garner* (1847) 2 Ph 231. As to the right of a solicitor-mortgagee to charge profit costs see the Solicitors Act 1974 s 58; and LEGAL PROFESSIONS vol 66 (2015) PARA 711.

754. Costs of transfer of mortgage. A transferee of a mortgage may add the costs of the transfer to his security if the mortgagor has been required to pay the debt or if interest was in arrear; otherwise he may not[1].

1   See *Re Radcliffe* (1856) 22 Beav 201; *Bolingbroke v Hinde* (1884) 25 ChD 795.

(3) COSTS OF PROCEEDINGS BETWEEN THE MORTGAGEE AND THE MORTGAGOR OR SURETY

755. Mortgagee's costs reasonably and properly incurred. The mortgagee's costs, reasonably and properly incurred, of proceedings between himself and the mortgagor or his surety are allowable[1]. The classic examples are proceedings for payment, sale, foreclosure or redemption[2] but nowadays the most common are those for possession of the mortgaged property preliminary to an exercise of the mortgagee's statutory power of sale out of court[3] and those in which the mortgagor contends that the mortgage is void or voidable[4].

Where, however, the mortgagee has sold the property, a claim brought by the mortgagor for an account of surplus proceeds of sale is not within the general rule as to costs[5]. The mortgagee must pay the costs if the proceedings have been occasioned by his refusal to render accounts or by his understating the amount due from him[6].

Costs of proceedings relating to two mortgages which the mortgagee is not entitled to consolidate are apportioned rateably between the two estates[7].

1   *Parker-Tweedale v Dunbar Bank plc (No 2)* [1991] Ch 26 at 33, [1990] 2 All ER 588 at 591, CA, per Nourse LJ. See also *Millar v Major* (1818) Coop *temp* Cott 550, sub nom *Millard v Magor* 3 Madd 433; *Lewis v John* (1838) 9 Sim 366; *Sandon v Hooper* (1843) 6 Beav 246 at 250; *Owen v Crouch* (1857) 5 WR 545; and see *Horlock v Smith* (1844) 1 Coll 287.
2   As to foreclosure see PARA 571 et seq. As to proceedings for redemption see PARA 661 et seq.
3   *Parker-Tweedale v Dunbar Bank plc (No 2)* [1991] Ch 26 at 33, [1990] 2 All ER 588 at 591, CA, per Nourse LJ. As to the statutory power of sale see PARA 446 et seq.
4   *Ramsden v Langley* (1705) 2 Vern 536; *Samuel v Jones* (1862) 7 LT 760. See also *Clark v Hoskins* (1868) 37 LJCh 561 at 569, CA; *Re Baldwin's Estate* [1900] 1 IR 15. See further *Sinfield v Sweet* [1967] 3 All ER 479, [1967] 1 WLR 1489; *Saunders v Anglia Building Society (No 2)* [1971] AC 1039, [1971] 1 All ER 243, HL (legal aid cases).
5   See *Parker-Tweedale v Dunbar Bank plc (No 2)* [1991] Ch 26, [1990] 2 All ER 588. See also *Millar v Major* (1818) Coop *temp* Cott 550, sub nom *Millard v Magor* 3 Madd 433; *Lewis v John* (1838) 9 Sim 366; *Sandon v Hooper* (1843) 6 Beav 246 at 250; *Owen v Crouch* (1857) 5 WR 545; and see *Horlock v Smith* (1844) 1 Coll 287.
6   *Williams v Jones* (1911) 55 Sol Jo 500. See also *Tanner v Heard* (1857) 23 Beav 555; *Charles v Jones* (1887) 35 ChD 544.
7   *De Caux v Skipper, Tee v De Caux* (1886) 31 ChD 635, CA (overruling *Clapham v Andrews* (1884) 27 ChD 679). As to consolidation see PARA 502 et seq.

756. Mortgagee's costs of recovery of debt. The mortgagee is allowed the costs of a claim to recover the mortgage debt, whether brought against the mortgagor[1] or a surety, and notwithstanding that the claim is unproductive through the surety's insolvency[2] or that the contract of suretyship is subsequent to the mortgage[3]. The mortgagee may also recover costs incidental to the dishonour of a bill or note[4], and the costs of administration of a deceased mortgagor's estate if this is required for recovering the debt[5].

1 *National Provincial Bank of England v Games* (1886) 31 ChD 582, CA. On this point *Lewis v John* (1838) 9 Sim 366 is overruled (*National Provincial Bank of England v Games* above at 593), although it has been objected that these costs are not costs in relation to the mortgage security (*Merriman v Bonner* (1864) 12 WR 461).
2 *Ellison v Wright* (1827) 3 Russ 458.
3 *Sachs v Ashby & Co* (1903) 88 LT 393.
4 *Aberdeen v Chitty* (1839) 3 Y & C Ex 379 at 382.
5 *Ramsden v Langley* (1705) 2 Vern 536; *Ward v Barton* (1841) 11 Sim 534. Costs of administration necessary for enabling the mortgagee to enforce his rights against the property are allowed (*Hunt v Fownes* (1803) 9 Ves 70) but costs of administration incurred by the mortgagor's representative without the mortgagee's request do not take priority to the mortgage (*Saunders v Dunman* (1878) 7 ChD 825).

757. The court's statutory discretion as to costs. The mortgagee does not usually require an order for costs since he is entitled to add his costs to the security[1]. He may, however, wish to seek an order for costs if, for example, the security is inadequate or the mortgagor has obtained an order for costs against him: the court has a statutory discretion to award costs as between the parties to proceedings[2]. A mortgagee also has the right in equity to reimbursement from the security of his costs, reasonably and properly incurred, of proceedings between himself and the mortgagor or his surety[3]. The mortgage deed also usually makes provision as to costs.

The following principles apply to costs relating to a mortgage[4]:

(1) an order for the payment of costs of proceedings by one party to another party is always a discretionary order[5];

(2) where there is a contractual right to the costs, the discretion should ordinarily be exercised so as to reflect that contractual right[6];

(3) the power of the court to disallow a mortgagee's costs sought to be added to the mortgage security is a power that does not derive from statute but from the power of courts of equity to fix the terms on which redemption will be allowed[7];

(4) a decision by a court to refuse costs, in whole or in part, to a mortgagee may be:
  (a) a decision in the exercise of the statutory discretion;
  (b) a decision in the exercise of the power to fix the terms on which redemption will be allowed;
  (c) a decision as to the extent of a mortgagee's contractual right to add the mortgagee's costs to the security; or
  (d) a combination of two or more of these things[8].

(5) a mortgagee is not to be deprived of a contractual or equitable right to add costs to the security merely by reason of an order for payment of costs made without reference to the mortgagee's contractual or equitable rights and without any adjudication as to whether or not the mortgagee should be deprived of those costs[9].

1 See PARAS 743–744.
2 See the Senior Courts Act 1981 s 51; CPR 44.2; and CIVIL PROCEDURE vol 12A (2015) PARA 1698 et seq; JUDICIAL REVIEW vol 61 (2010) PARA 681.

3   See *Parker-Tweedale v Dunbar Bank plc (No 2)* [1991] Ch 26, [1990] 2 All ER 588, CA; *Gomba Holdings Ltd v Minories Finance Ltd (No 2)* [1993] Ch 171, [1992] 4 All ER 588, CA; and PARAS 743, 755. The right is reflected in, but not extended by, CPR 48.3: see CIVIL PROCEDURE vol 12A (2015) PARA 1704.

4   CPR PD 44—*General Rules About Costs* para 7.2(1). See also *Gomba Holdings Ltd v Minories Finance Ltd (No 2)* [1993] Ch 171, [1992] 4 All ER 588, CA.

5   Supreme Court Act 1981 s 51 (substituted by the Courts and Legal Services Act 1990 s 4); CPR PD 44—*General Rules About Costs* para 7.2(2). See also *Parker-Tweedale v Dunbar Bank plc (No 2)* [1991] Ch 26, [1990] 2 All ER 588, CA; *Gomba Holdings Ltd v Minories Finance Ltd (No 2)* [1993] Ch 171, [1992] 4 All ER 588, CA; and JUDICIAL REVIEW vol 61 (2010) PARA 681. As to the exercise of the court' discretion in awarding costs and the amount of costs see CPR 44.2; and CIVIL PROCEDURE vol 12A (2015) PARA 1698 et seq.

6   CPR PD 44—*General Rules About Costs* para 7.2(3). As to the assessment of costs payable pursuant to a contract see PARA 744; and CIVIL PROCEDURE vol 12A (2015) PARA 1740.

7   CPR PD 44—*General Rules About Costs* para 7.2(4). See also *Parker-Tweedale v Dunbar Bank plc (No 2)* [1991] Ch 26, [1990] 2 All ER 588, CA; *Gomba Holdings Ltd v Minories Finance Ltd (No 2)* [1993] Ch 171, [1992] 4 All ER 588, CA; and CIVIL PROCEDURE vol 12A (2015) PARA 1740. As to the equity of redemption see PARAS 107, 304 et seq.

8   CPR PD 44—*General Rules About Costs* para 7.2(5). See also *Parker-Tweedale v Dunbar Bank plc (No 2)* [1991] Ch 26, [1990] 2 All ER 588, CA; *Gomba Holdings Ltd v Minories Finance Ltd (No 2)* [1993] Ch 171, [1992] 4 All ER 588, CA; and CIVIL PROCEDURE vol 12A (2015) PARA 1740.

9   CPR PD 44—*General Rules About Costs* para 7.2(6). See also *Parker-Tweedale v Dunbar Bank plc (No 2)* [1991] Ch 26, [1990] 2 All ER 588, CA; *Gomba Holdings Ltd v Minories Finance Ltd (No 2)* [1993] Ch 171, [1992] 4 All ER 588, CA; and CIVIL PROCEDURE vol 12A (2015) PARA 1740. See also PARAS 743–744.

758. When costs are payable personally. A mortgagor, or subsequent incumbrancer, who raises an untenable defence must pay personally any costs so occasioned for which the mortgagee's security is insufficient[1]. In a redemption claim, if the mortgagor fails to redeem, the claim is dismissed with costs to be paid by him personally[2].

1   *Liverpool Marine Credit Co v Wilson* (1872) 7 Ch App 507 at 512, CA; *Guardian Assurance Co v Lord Avonmore* (1873) 7 IR Eq 496. See also *Sharples v Adams* (1863) 1 New Rep 460.

2   See *Mutual Life Assurance Society v Langley* (1886) 32 ChD 460 at 475, CA, where a first mortgagee was also third mortgagee. See also PARA 673. As to costs payable by a later mortgagee who fails to redeem see PARAS 673–674, 677. As to proceedings for redemption see PARA 661 et seq.

759. Assessment of contractual costs. Where the court assesses costs which are payable by the paying party to the receiving party under the terms of a contract, the costs payable under those terms are, unless the contract expressly provides otherwise, to be presumed to be costs which have been reasonably incurred; and are reasonable in amount, and the court will assess them accordingly[1].

Where the contract entitles a mortgagee to:

(1)   add the costs of litigation relating to the mortgage to the sum secured by it; or

(2)   require a mortgagor to pay those costs,

the mortgagor may make an application for the court to direct that an account of the mortgagee's costs be taken[2].

The mortgagor may then dispute an amount in the mortgagee's account on the basis that it has been unreasonably incurred or is unreasonable in amount[3]. Where a mortgagor disputes an amount, the court may make an order that the disputed costs are to be assessed[4].

1   See CPR 44.5(1). These presumptions are rebuttable, and the court may order otherwise: see CPR PD 44—*General Rules About Costs*; and CIVIL PROCEDURE vol 12A (2015) PARA 1689 et seq. As to the assessment of costs payable pursuant to a contract see CIVIL PROCEDURE vol 12A (2015) PARA 1740.

2   CPR PD 44—*General Rules About Costs* para 7.3(1). The court may direct that a party file an account: see CPR 25.1(1)(n); and CIVIL PROCEDURE vol 12 (2015) PARA 566; CIVIL PROCEDURE vol 12A (2015) PARA 1251.
3   CPR PD 44—*General Rules About Costs* para 7.3(2).
4   CPR PD 44—*General Rules About Costs* para 7.3(3). Such assessment is made under CPR 44.5: see the text and note 1. As to assessment see further PARA 745.

760.   Summary assessment of costs by the court. The general rule is that the court should make a summary assessment of the costs unless there is good reason not to do so (for example where the paying party shows substantial grounds for disputing the sum claimed for costs that cannot be dealt with summarily)[1]. However, this general rule does not apply to a mortgagee's costs incurred in mortgage possession proceedings or other proceedings relating to a mortgage unless the mortgagee asks the court to make an order for the mortgagee's costs to be paid by another party[2].

1   CPR PD 44—*General Rules About Costs* para 9.2; and see CIVIL PROCEDURE vol 12A (2015) PARA 1748.
2   CPR PD 44—*General Rules About Costs* para 9.3.

761.   Forfeiture of mortgagee's right to costs. A mortgagee will not be allowed costs or expenses unreasonably or improperly incurred[1] or incurred otherwise than in enforcing or preserving his security[2]. In these cases he may either be made to pay costs or merely be deprived of costs[3]. An order for an account to be taken including the mortgagee's assessed costs of the claim does not prevent an adverse order as to costs if reason for this subsequently appears[4].

1   See *Gomba Holdings Ltd v Minories Finance Ltd (No 2)* [1993] Ch 171, [1992] 4 All ER 588, CA. See also CPR 44.11; PARA 745; and CIVIL PROCEDURE vol 12A (2015) PARA 1712. The mortgagee will forfeit his right to costs if there is such inequitable conduct on his part as to amount to a violation or culpable neglect of duty under the mortgage contract, or if his conduct as mortgagee is otherwise improper: see *Cotterell v Stratton* (1872) 8 Ch App 295 at 302 per Lord Selborne LC; *Cottrell v Finney* (1874) 9 Ch App 541 at 551; *Kinnaird v Trollope* (1889) 42 ChD 610 at 619; *Graham v Seal* (1918) 88 LJCh 31, CA. See also *Dunstan v Patterson* (1847) 2 Ph 341; *Re Watts, Smith v Watts* (1882) 22 ChD 5, CA. The authorities referred to in this paragraph must be read in the light of the Civil Procedure Rules: see CIVIL PROCEDURE vol 11 (2015) PARA 6 et seq.
2   *Wickenden v Rayson* (1856) 25 LJCh 641. As to the mortgagor's right to apply for the assessment of a bill of costs rendered to the mortgagee by his solicitor if the mortgagor is liable to pay see the Solicitors Act 1974 ss 70, 71; and LEGAL PROFESSIONS vol 66 (2015) PARA 743 et seq. See also *Re Griffith, Jones & Co* (1883) 50 LT 434, CA; *Re Longbotham & Sons* [1904] 2 Ch 152, CA; *Re Paice and Cross* (1914) 58 Sol Jo 593.
3   See *Detillin v Gale* (1802) 7 Ves 583; *Harvey v Tebbutt* (1820) 1 Jac & W 197 at 202; *Kinnaird v Trollope* (1889) 42 ChD 610; and PARA 766.
4   *Ashworth v Lord* (1887) 36 ChD 545 at 551 (disagreeing on this point with *Wilson v Metcalfe* (1826) 1 Russ 530). See also *Quarrell v Beckford* (1816) 1 Madd 269 at 285.

762.   Costs ensuing from mortgagee's refusal of tender. If the mortgagor makes an unconditional tender of a sum sufficient to cover the amount secured by the mortgage, at a time when he is entitled to pay off the mortgage[1], and the mortgagee refuses to accept it, the mortgagee must pay the costs of a redemption claim thus made necessary[2]. If he fails on part of his case, he may be disallowed costs of that part[3]. In order to throw the costs on the mortgagee, the mortgagor must make an actual tender[4], notwithstanding that there is a dispute on a question of law[5]. In the absence of a tender, the mortgagee does not forfeit his right to costs merely by claiming more than is due to him[6], or by bringing before the court a question as to the amount due, even though he is unsuccessful in his contention[7]. Such a claim is not necessarily vexatious, so as to deprive the mortgagee of the benefit of the general rule as to reimbursement of costs[8]. The fact that a deed contains a receipt for more than the sum actually advanced is not a ground for depriving the mortgagee of costs[9].

1 *Edmondson v Copland* [1911] 2 Ch 301. The authorities referred to in this paragraph must now be read in the light of the Civil Procedure Rules: see CIVIL PROCEDURE vol 11 (2015) PARA 6 et seq. As to tender see PARAS 335–336.
2 *Harmer v Priestley* (1853) 16 Beav 569. See also *Wilson v Cluer* (1841) 4 Beav 214; *Smith v Green* (1844) 1 Coll 555; *Roberts v Williams* (1844) 4 Hare 129; *Morley v Bridges* (1846) 2 Coll 621; *Hosken v Sincock* (1865) 12 LT 262; *Cottrell v Finney* (1874) 9 Ch App 541 at 551; *Graham v Seal* (1918) 88 LJCh 31, CA. As to redemption proceedings see PARA 661 et seq.
3 *Kinnaird v Trollope* (1889) 42 ChD 610 at 621.
4 *Gammon v Stone* (1749) 1 Ves Sen 339.
5 *Hodges v Croydon Canal Co* (1840) 3 Beav 86.
6 *Loftus v Swift and Governors of St Patrick's Hospital* (1806) 2 Sch & Lef 642 at 657; *Cotterell v Stratton* (1872) 8 Ch App 295; *Re Watts, Smith v Watts* (1882) 22 ChD 5, CA; *Kinnaird v Trollope* (1889) 42 ChD 610 at 619.
7 *Re Watts, Smith v Watts* (1882) 22 ChD 5 at 14, CA; *Stone v Lickorish* [1891] 2 Ch 363 at 370.
8 *Norton v Cooper* (1854) 5 De GM & G 728. As to the general rule that the mortgagee has a right to reimbursement of costs from the security see PARA 743.
9 *Dunstan v Patterson* (1847) 2 Ph 341 at 345.

763. Proceedings instituted by mortgagee when nothing due. If the mortgagee brings a claim for foreclosure[1], or resists redemption proceedings[2], when there is nothing due to him, he will have to pay, or will be deprived of, costs. If he is paid off before the claim is heard and carries it to a hearing, he may have his costs up to payment but must pay those incurred subsequently[3].

1 *Binnington v Harwood* (1825) Turn & R 477 at 485; *Morris v Islip* (1856) 23 Beav 244. As to foreclosure generally see PARA 571 et seq. The authorities referred to in this paragraph must now be read in the light of the Civil Procedure Rules: see CIVIL PROCEDURE vol 11 (2015) PARA 6 et seq.
2 *Barlow v Gains* (1856) 23 Beav 244; *National Bank of Australasia v United Hand-in-Hand and Band of Hope Co* (1879) 4 App Cas 391 at 412, PC; *Wilson v Cluer* (1841) 4 Beav 214. If any money is due the mortgagee may have his costs: see *Barlow v Gains*; *Cassidy v Sullivan* (1878) 1 LR Ir 313; but see PARA 766. If the mortgagee has gone into possession, he may be deprived of his costs for failing to render accounts when required to do so: *Powell v Trotter* (1861) 1 Drew & Sm 388; *Cassidy v Sullivan*. As to the liability of a mortgagee in possession see PARA 429 et seq. As to proceedings for redemption see PARA 661 et seq. As to the equity of redemption see PARAS 107, 304 et seq.
3 *Gregg v Slater* (1856) 22 Beav 314; *Seal v Kemsley* [1883] WN 122, CA. See also *Montgomery v Calland* (1844) 14 Sim 79.

764. Unsuccessful denial of mortgagor's right or untenable claim. If the mortgagee unsuccessfully denies or resists the mortgagor's right to redeem, whether on the ground that it has been extinguished[1], or otherwise[2], he is liable for the costs so occasioned. Usually the costs will not be payable to the mortgagor personally; they will be set off on his redeeming[3]. A first mortgagee must pay the costs if he sets up an unsuccessful claim to consolidate[4], or refuses to allow the mortgagor to redeem on the ground that a subsequent incumbrancer wishes to do so[5], or on any other ground involving an untenable claim on his part[6]. The mortgagee is, however, entitled to his costs so far as proceedings were necessary for redemption[7], and he will not be deprived of costs if a specific, but unsuccessful, charge of fraud is made against him[8].

1 *Baker v Wind* (1748) 1 Ves Sen 160; *Harvey v Tebbutt* (1820) 1 Jac & W 197 at 202; *National Bank of Australasia v United Hand-in-Hand and Band of Hope Co* (1879) 4 App Cas 391 at 412, PC. See also *Henderson v Astwood, Astwood v Cobbold, Cobbold v Astwood* [1894] AC 150 at 162, PC. The authorities referred to in this paragraph must now be read in the light of the Civil Procedure Rules: see CIVIL PROCEDURE vol 11 (2015) PARA 6 et seq. As to the equity of redemption see PARAS 107, 304 et seq. As to persons with the right to redeem see PARA 306 et seq.

2   See *England v Codrington* (1758) 1 Eden 169, where a mortgagee who wrongfully claimed that the conveyance to him was an absolute one was held liable to pay the costs of redemption. See also *Robarts v Jefferys* (1830) 8 LJOS Ch 137; *Fleming v Self* (1854) 3 De GM & G 997 at 1029; *Cowdry v Day* (1859) 1 Giff 316 at 325.

3   *Wheaton v Graham* (1857) 24 Beav 483; *Forbes v Jackson* (1882) 19 ChD 615 at 623.

4   *Squire v Pardoe* (1891) 40 WR 100, CA. As to consolidation see PARA 502 et seq. A mortgagee was also formerly liable to pay the costs where he set up an unsuccessful claim to tack: see *Lacey v Ingle* (1847) 2 Ph 413 at 424; *Credland v Potter* (1874) 10 Ch App 8 (where, however, as there had been a want of caution on the part of the second mortgagee, the first mortgagee was only deprived of costs); *Kinnaird v Trollope* (1889) 42 ChD 610 at 621 (where the mortgagees were not allowed costs of their unsuccessful claim). See also *Forbes v Jackson* (1882) 19 ChD 615 at 622. As to the statutory restriction of the right to tack see PARAS 266–267.

5   *Tomlinson v Gregg* (1866) 15 WR 51. As to the costs of successive incumbrancers see PARA 768.

6   *Hall v Heward* (1886) 32 ChD 430, CA (where the mortgagee of real and personal estate insisted that the mortgagor's executrix was entitled to redeem only the personal estate); *Heath v Chinn* (1908) 98 LT 855 at 858. The mortgagee is not deprived of his costs if he brings forward a case which is fairly open to argument: *Bird v Wenn* (1886) 33 ChD 215 at 219. Cf *Tarn v Turner* (1888) 39 ChD 456 at 467, CA; *Deeley v Lloyds Bank Ltd (No 2)* (1909) 53 Sol Jo 419.

7   *Detillin v Gale* (1802) 7 Ves 583; *Harvey v Tebbutt* (1820) 1 Jac & W 197. As to proceedings for redemption see PARA 661 et seq.

8   *Hayward v Kersey* (1866) 14 WR 999.

765. Default in reconveyance to the mortgagor. Upon a proper tender being made to him, the mortgagee is bound to give a statutory receipt[1], or, if appropriate, to execute a reconveyance[2] to the mortgagor or other person entitled. If a reconveyance is required, the draft must be previously submitted to the mortgagee's solicitor for approval and the engrossment then left for execution[3]. If the reconveyance is not ready to be handed over on the tender being made, the mortgagee loses his right to costs[4].

1   As to statutory receipts see PARAS 650–651.
2   As to the costs of reconveyance see PARA 659.
3   See note 4.
4   *Rourke v Robinson* [1911] 1 Ch 480; *Graham v Seal* (1918) 88 LJCh 31, CA. See also *Cliff v Wadsworth* (1843) 2 Y & C Ch Cas 598, where the mortgagee had occasioned difficulties as to reconveyance. Cf *Webb v Crosse* [1912] 1 Ch 323, where the draft reconveyance was submitted at the same time as the intended payment. As to the mortgagee being deprived of costs where he has lost the title deeds see PARA 499. The authorities referred to in this paragraph must now be read in the light of the Civil Procedure Rules: see CIVIL PROCEDURE vol 11 (2015) PARA 6 et seq.

766. Mortgagee's unreasonable or oppressive conduct. In general, the mortgagee must pay the costs if his conduct has been unreasonable or oppressive, for example where he has withheld accounts[1], or the transaction is tainted with fraud[2], or only a small sum remains due to him and his conduct has been vexatious[3], or he attempts to get the estate into his own hands[4]. Even though the mortgagee obtains the general costs, he will not get costs occasioned by charges against the mortgagor of fraud or other misconduct which fail[5], or by unnecessary proceedings, such as the joinder of unnecessary parties, or the adducing of unnecessary evidence[6]. Where the mortgagor is allowed costs, these include the costs which he has to pay to a necessary party[7].

1   *Detillin v Gale* (1802) 7 Ves 583. The authorities referred to in this paragraph must now be read in the light of the Civil Procedure Rules: see CIVIL PROCEDURE vol 11 (2015) PARA 6 et seq.
2   *Morony v O'Dea* (1809) 1 Ball & B 109.
3   *Snagg v Frith* (1846) 9 I Eq R 285, sub nom *Snagg v Frizell* 3 Jo & Lat 383; but see PARA 763 note 2.
4   See — *v Trecothick* (1813) 2 Ves & B 181; but cf *Thornhill v Evans* (1742) 2 Atk 330.
5   See *West v Jones* (1851) 1 Sim NS 205 at 218; *Cockell v Taylor* (1851) 15 Beav 103 at 127.
6   *Audsley v Horn* (1858) 26 Beav 195; *Jones v Harris* (1887) 55 LT 884.
7   *Cockell v Taylor* (1851) 15 Beav 103.

767. Effect of institution of administration proceedings by mortgagee. Where the mortgagee, instead of relying on his security only, institutes a suit for the administration of the mortgagor's estate, he subjects himself to the ordinary rule in administration that the costs of all necessary and proper parties are a first charge upon the estate[1], and consequently these costs, including the expenses of sale, rank before the mortgage[2]. If, however, the mortgagee institutes a suit to realise his security, and also for administration of the mortgagor's estate with a view to realising any deficiency out of the general estate, he is entitled, subject to the expenses of sale, to the entire produce of the mortgaged property towards payment of his debt and costs, and, as regards the general assets, the costs of all parties will be paid in the first place as in an ordinary administration suit[3].

1   See WILLS AND INTESTACY vol 103 (2010) PARA 1205.
2   *Armstrong v Storer* (1851) 14 Beav 535 at 538; *Walter v Stanton* (1862) 10 WR 570; *Re Spensley's Estate, Spensley v Harrison* (1872) LR 15 Eq 16; *Leonard v Kellett* (1891) 27 LR Ir 418 at 427. In a mortgagee's suit the expenses of sale are usually part of his own costs. The authorities referred to in this paragraph must now be read in the light of the Civil Procedure Rules: see CIVIL PROCEDURE vol 11 (2015) PARA 6 et seq.
3   *Tipping v Power* (1842) 1 Hare 405; *Tuckley v Thompson* (1860) 1 John & H 126; *Pinchard v Fellows* (1874) LR 17 Eq 421; *Leonard v Kellett* (1891) 27 LR Ir 418. Cf *White v Gudgeon* (1862) 30 Beav 545, where the costs of the administrator's suit were given priority on the ground of an overclaim by the mortgagee.

768. Costs of successive incumbrancers. Where there are successive incumbrancers, the rule as to the right of a mortgagee to reimbursement[1] in general prevails, and each incumbrancer adds his costs to his security[2]. Accordingly, the costs are repayable in the same priority as the debts[3], and in a priority suit the costs usually follow the mortgages, but the court has a discretion and may order one or other of the claimants to pay the costs if a case is made for it[4]. If a second mortgagee makes an unsuccessful claim to priority in the first mortgagee's foreclosure claim, the first mortgagee will add his ordinary foreclosure costs to his security, and the second mortgagee will pay the extra costs occasioned by the claim[5]. Where, however, a subsequent incumbrancer institutes proceedings, not in his own interest only, but to secure or to realise and distribute the mortgaged property[6] or to ascertain the priority of the incumbrancers[7], he is entitled to his costs, so far as incurred for these objects, as a first charge on the fund. This principle has been applied to administration proceedings brought by a subsequent incumbrancer[8].

1   As to the mortgagee's general right to reimbursement of costs from the security see PARA 743.
2   *Ford v Earl of Chesterfield (No 3)* (1856) 21 Beav 426 at 428; *Wright v Kirby* (1857) 23 Beav 463 at 467; *Johnstone v Cox* (1881) 19 ChD 17 at 19, CA; *Bird v Wenn* (1886) 33 ChD 215 at 219; *Pollock v Lands Improvement Co* (1888) 37 ChD 661 at 668. The authorities referred to in this paragraph must now be read in the light of the Civil Procedure Rules: see CIVIL PROCEDURE vol 11 (2015) PARA 6 et seq.
3   *Barnes v Racster* (1842) 1 Y & C Ch Cas 401 at 403; cf *Re Baldwin's Estate* [1900] 1 IR 15; *O'Meagher v Daly* [1917] 1 IR 341 (affd [1917] 1 IR 493, CA).
4   *Harpham v Shacklock* (1881) 19 ChD 207 at 215, CA.
5   *Northern Counties of England Fire Insurance Co v Whipp* (1884) 26 ChD 482 at 496, CA. As to foreclosure generally see PARA 571 et seq.
6   *White v Bishop of Peterborough* (1821) Jac 402; *Ford v Earl of Chesterfield (No 3)* (1856) 21 Beav 426; *Wright v Kirby* (1857) 23 Beav 463.
7   *Batten, Proffitt and Scott v Dartmouth Harbour Comrs* (1890) 45 ChD 612; *Carrick v Wigan Tramways Co* [1893] WN 98. See also the cases cited in note 2.
8   *Re Barne, Lee v Barne* (1890) 62 LT 922.

769. Costs of parties claiming under mortgagee. Where a sub-mortgagee[1] is a necessary party, he has his costs against the mortgagee, and the mortgagee adds them to his own debt[2]. This rule applies, however, only to costs due to persons claiming under the mortgagee[3]. The mortgagee is not bound to pay, and add to his security, the costs of necessary parties claiming under the mortgagor, such as a trustee in bankruptcy[4].

1 As to sub-mortgages see PARA 252 et seq.
2 *Smith v Chichester* (1842) 2 Dr & War 393 at 404. Where possible, the sub-mortgagee should be joined as co-claimant: *Smith v Chichester* above at 404. When a mortgagee adopts the claim of a later mortgagee, the later mortgagee's costs are payable before those of the earlier mortgagee: *Hutchinson v Cummins* (1920) 54 ILT 168. The authorities referred to in this paragraph must now be read in the light of the Civil Procedure Rules: see CIVIL PROCEDURE vol 11 (2015) PARA 6 et seq.
3 See note 4.
4 *Hunter v Pugh* (1839) 1 Hare 307n; *Appleby v Duke* (1842) 1 Hare 303 (affd (1843) 1 Ph 272, where earlier decisions to the contrary were discussed); *Clarke v Wilmot* (1843) 1 Ph 276. As to the costs of disclaiming defendants see PARA 615.

770. Priority of mortgagee's costs. The mortgagee's right to costs extends to the costs of a claim in which his security is realised by sale[1], but his priority for his debt and costs over the costs of other parties depends on the object of the claim. If the claim is designed to give the mortgagee no benefit beyond the realisation of his security, or if the matter within the court's jurisdiction is in effect the equity of redemption only[2], the mortgagee is entitled to priority over the costs of other parties; this is so in an administration suit if it becomes necessary to sell the property but the mortgagee is not otherwise interested in the suit[3]. The proceeds of sale will be paid to the mortgagee so far as required for satisfaction of his principal, interest and costs, without deduction except of the expenses of sale[4]. As the mortgagee gets the benefit of the sale, the expenses of sale are a first charge[5]. This is so notwithstanding that he consents to[6] or asks for[7] a sale. Similarly, where the mortgagee comes in under an administration judgment and submits to have his rights determined, he will be entitled to principal, interest and costs out of the net proceeds of the property in priority to the costs of other parties[8].

A mortgagee does not adopt a suit, so as to let in the costs in priority to his mortgage, by allowing his rights to be ascertained in it[9], but, if he is a party to the proceedings, he must allow the costs of realisation to be first paid out of the proceeds of sale[10].

1 *Wade v Ward* (1859) 4 Drew 602. It seems that an equitable mortgagee by deposit was entitled to costs, even though there was not an accompanying memorandum: *Connell v Hardie* (1839) 3 Y & C Ex 582; *R v Chambers* (1840) 4 Y & C Ex 54. Cf *Re v Gawan, ex p Barclay* (1855) 5 De GM & G 403 at 407. Formerly, he was not allowed the costs of establishing his right to a sale where there was no memorandum (*Re Wells, ex p Brightwen* (1818) 1 Swan 3; *Ex p Trew* (1818) 3 Madd 372; *Re Evans, ex p Robinson* (1832) 1 Deac & Ch 119), unless it had been dispensed with under a trade custom (*Re Davies, ex p Moss* (1849) 3 De G & Sm 599). The authorities referred to in this paragraph must now be read in the light of the Civil Procedure Rules: see CIVIL PROCEDURE vol 11 (2015) PARA 6 et seq.
2 See *Armstrong v Storer* (1851) 14 Beav 535 at 538. As to the equity of redemption see PARAS 107, 304 et seq.
3 *Hepworth v Heslop* (1844) 3 Hare 485; *Wonham v Machin* (1870) LR 10 Eq 447; *Hilliard v Moriarty* [1894] 1 IR 316, CA. See also *Clark v Doherty* [1916] 1 IR 257.
4 See note 5.
5 *Dighton v Withers* (1862) 31 Beav 423; *Re Oriental Hotels Co, Perry v Oriental Hotels Co* (1871) LR 12 Eq 126; *Batten v Wedgwood Coal and Iron Co* (1884) 28 ChD 317; *Lathom v Greenwich Ferry Co* (1895) 72 LT 790. This has not, however, always been recognised: see *Upperton v Harrison* (1835) 7 Sim 444; *Re Johnston, Millar v Johnston* (1888) 23 LR Ir 50; *Ross v Ross* (1892) 29 LR Ir 318. See also *Re Mackinlay, Ward v Mackinlay* (1864) 2 De GJ & Sm 358. As to costs in debenture holders' actions see COMPANIES vol 15 (2009) PARA 1387.
6 *Wild v Lockhart* (1847) 10 Beav 320; *Cutfield v Richards* (1858) 26 Beav 241; *Wade v Ward* (1859) 4 Drew 602; *Cook v Hart* (1871) LR 12 Eq 459. See also *Crosse v General Reversionary and Investment Co* (1853) 3 De GM & G 698.
7 *Wonham v Machin* (1870) LR 10 Eq 447.

8   *Re Marine Mansions Co* (1867) LR 4 Eq 601.
9   *Langton v Langton* (1855) 7 De GM & G 30 at 37.
10 *Re Regent's Canal Ironworks Co, ex p Grissell* (1875) 3 ChD 411 at 427, CA.

(4) COSTS OF PROCEEDINGS BETWEEN THE MORTGAGEE AND THIRD PARTIES

771. Mortgagee's costs reasonably and properly incurred. The mortgagee is entitled to add to his security the costs, reasonably and properly incurred, of proceedings between himself and a third party where what is impugned is the title to the estate[1]. In such a case the mortgagee acts for the benefit of the equity of redemption as much as for that of the security[2]. However, where a third party impugns the title to the mortgage, or the enforcement or exercise of some right or power accruing to the mortgagee thereunder, the mortgagee's costs of the proceedings, even though they be reasonably and properly incurred, are not allowable[3]. Costs needlessly incurred are not allowed[4]. In order that costs properly incurred may be included, they must be claimed at the hearing[5], and, if the claim is supported by proper evidence, an inquiry will be directed as to costs, charges and expenses properly incurred by the mortgagee in respect of his mortgage security, not being costs of the claim[6].

1   *Parker-Tweedale v Dunbar Bank plc (No 2)* [1991] Ch 26, [1990] 2 All ER 588, CA.
2   *Parker-Tweedale v Dunbar Bank plc (No 2)* [1991] Ch 26, [1990] 2 All ER 588, CA. As to the equity of redemption see PARAS 107, 304 et seq.
3   *Parker-Tweedale v Dunbar Bank plc (No 2)* [1991] Ch 26, [1990] 2 All ER 588, CA. See also *Dryden v Frost* (1838) 3 My & Cr 670 at 675. However, as to the alteration of this position by express contractual provisions see *Parker-Tweedale v Dunbar Bank plc (No 2)* above; *Gomba Holdings Ltd v Minories Finance Ltd (No 2)* [1993] Ch 171, [1992] 4 All ER 588, CA; and PARA 744. See also *Saunders v Anglia Building Society (No 2)* [1971] AC 1039, [1971] 1 All ER 243, HL (legal aid case).
4   Cf *Macken v Newcomen* (1844) 2 Jo & Lat 16.
5   *Millard v Magor* (1818) 3 Madd 433, sub nom *Millar v Major* (1818) Coop temp Cott 550; *Ward v Barton* (1841) 11 Sim 534. Generally, when the account is to include more than principal, interest and costs of the proceedings, a special case must be made (*Bolingbroke v Hinde* (1884) 25 ChD 795), save that costs, charges and expenses, which are expressly included in the security, may be allowed without mention in the order: see *Blackford v Davis* (1869) 4 Ch App 304. The expenses of recovering possession (see PARA 755), and of necessary repairs and ordinary outgoings (see PARA 749) may be similarly allowed. As to accounts and inquiries see CPR PD 40A—*Accounts and Inquiries*; and CIVIL PROCEDURE vol 12A (2015) PARA 1250 et seq.
6   *Merriman v Bonner* (1864) 12 WR 461. See also PARA 756. Where property which was the subject of a foreclosure claim was purchased by a public body under statutory powers and the compensation paid into court, and the mortgagee alleged that he had incurred costs in relation to the assessment of compensation beyond those which had been paid to him by the public body, he was held not to be entitled to an express direction for the allowance of the extra costs out of the fund in court, but merely to an order for inquiry in the ordinary form, as the costs, if found on the inquiry to have been properly incurred, would be allowable in taking the accounts without any express direction: *Rees v Metropolitan Board of Works* (1880) 14 ChD 372.

772–800. Costs incurred by mortgagee in defending title. Costs incurred in asserting or defending the mortgagor's title to the mortgaged property are allowed[1], but not costs incurred in defending the mortgagee's title to the mortgage against a third person[2] unless provided for in the mortgage[3]. Similarly, the mortgagee may not charge the costs of defending proceedings for trespass brought by a third person unless those costs were incurred in protecting the title to the estate[4]. Where in proceedings properly taken to protect the security the mortgagee has already received costs from a third party, he is entitled to add any deficiency to his security[5]. The proceedings must, however, be reasonably undertaken[6]. An equitable mortgagee may not have the costs of proceedings which are only suitable for a legal mortgagee[7]. The proceedings must not fail through the mortgagee's neglect[8], so that a mortgagee who has sold under a contract which is unenforceable for misdescription may not charge the costs of a suit for specific performance[9].

1   *Parker-Tweedale v Dunbar Bank plc (No 2)* [1991] Ch 26, [1990] 2 All ER 588, CA. See also *Godfrey v Watson* (1747) 3 Atk 517 at 518; *Sandon v Hooper* (1843) 6 Beav 246; *Sclater v Cottam* (1857) 5 WR 744. A mortgagee has been allowed the costs of defending proceedings caused by the mortgagor including in the mortgage property which did not belong to him, but not the costs of an appeal: *Re Hofmann, ex p Carr* (1879) 11 ChD 62, CA. See also PARA 395. In a redemption claim the costs of a pending foreclosure claim must be provided for: *Ainsworth v Roe* (1850) 14 Jur 874. As to the equity of redemption see PARAS 107, 304 et seq. As to proceedings for redemption see PARA 661 et seq. As to foreclosure see PARA 571 et seq.

2   *Parker-Tweedale v Dunbar Bank plc (No 2)* [1991] Ch 26, [1990] 2 All ER 588, CA. See also *Parker v Watkins* (1859) John 133; *Re Smith's Mortgage, Harrison v Edwards* [1931] 2 Ch 168.

3   *Credit & Mercantile plc v Wishart* [2015] EWCA Civ 655, [2015] 2 P & CR 322, [2015] All ER (D) 64 (Jul) (where costs of defending a claim by a person claiming a beneficial interest in the property were secured by the mortgage).

4   *Parker-Tweedale v Dunbar Bank plc (No 2)* [1991] Ch 26, [1990] 2 All ER 588, CA. See also *Owen v Crouch* (1857) 5 WR 545. As to the right to protect title against third persons see PARA 398.

5   *Ramsden v Langley* (1705) 2 Vern 536. See also *Re Love, Hill v Spurgeon* (1885) 29 ChD 348, CA. See further PARA 753.

6   *Parker-Tweedale v Dunbar Bank plc (No 2)* [1991] Ch 26, [1990] 2 All ER 588, CA.

7   *Dryden v Frost* (1838) 3 My & Cr 670. As to equitable mortgages see PARAS 105, 215 et seq. As to legal mortgages see PARAS 104, 160 et seq.

8   *Burke v O'Connor* (1855) 4 I Ch R 418, where a claim for rent failed through being brought in the wrong person's name.

9   *Peers v Ceeley* (1852) 15 Beav 209. As to specific performance see SPECIFIC PERFORMANCE vol 95 (2013) PARA 301 et seq.

NATIONAL CULTURAL HERITAGE

1. SCOPE OF TITLE

801. Scope of national cultural heritage. This title covers cultural institutions[1], moveable cultural heritage[2], immoveable cultural heritage[3] and provisions relating to the international protection of cultural heritage[4].

The cultural institutions covered include those established either by statute or royal charter and comprise those of a general cultural nature[5], museums and galleries[6], libraries[7], and other institutions of a literary, scientific or cultural nature[8], including the Ordnance Survey[9]. Theatres, cinemas and performances of sound and video recordings are covered elsewhere in this work[10].

The material in this title relating to moveable cultural heritage covers treasure[11], the loan[12], import and export of cultural objects[13], and the control of illicit trade in cultural objects[14]. The material relating to immoveable cultural heritage covers world heritage sites[15], archaeological sites and ancient monuments[16], historic shipwrecks and military remains[17], and historic buildings[18], gardens[19] and battlefields[20]. Whereas certain footpaths and open spaces may be managed under the auspices of a specific cultural body[21], general rights of access for recreational purposes are covered elsewhere in this work[22].

1 See PARA 803 et seq.
2 See PARA 1088 et seq.
3 See PARA 1004 et seq.
4 See PARA 1108 et seq. See also PARAS 1004–1005, 1072, 1096 et seq.
5 See PARA 803 et seq. As to the National Trust for Places of Historic Interest or Natural Beauty (the 'National Trust') see PARA 973 et seq.
6 See PARA 817 et seq. As to the Royal Collection of pictures and works of art in the ownership of the monarch see CROWN AND CROWN PROCEEDINGS vol 29 (2014) PARA 289.
7 See PARA 894 et seq. As to the Royal Library which is included in the Royal Archives at Windsor Castle see CROWN AND CROWN PROCEEDINGS vol 29 (2014) PARA 289.
8 See PARA 932 et seq. The British Broadcasting Corporation (BBC) is covered elsewhere in this work: see BROADCASTING vol 4 (2011) PARA 603 et seq. As to the public purposes of the British Broadcasting Corporation (BBC) see the *Royal Charter for the Continuance of the British Broadcasting Corporation* (Cm 6925) (2006) art 4; and BROADCASTING vol 4 (2011) PARA 603. As to the BBC's archive obligations and research and development activities see BROADCASTING vol 4 (2011) PARA 618.
9 See PARA 994 et seq.
10 See LICENSING AND GAMBLING vol 67 (2008) PARA 234 et seq. However, as to the deposit of scripts of new plays see PARA 826. See also note 8.
11 See PARA 1088 et seq. As to the Crown jewels see CROWN AND CROWN PROCEEDINGS vol 29 (2014) PARA 288. As to Crown chattels generally see CROWN AND CROWN PROCEEDINGS vol 29 (2014) PARA 282 et seq. See also as to swans and royal fish CROWN AND CROWN PROCEEDINGS vol 29 (2014) PARAS 143–144.
12 See PARA 1094 et seq.
13 See PARAS 1096–1097.
14 See PARA 1098 et seq.
15 See PARA 1004.
16 See PARA 1005 et seq.
17 See PARA 1068 et seq. As to war memorials see HIGHWAYS, STREETS AND BRIDGES vol 55 (2012) PARA 574; LOCAL GOVERNMENT vol 69 (2009) PARA 614.
18 See PARA 1076 et seq. Royal palaces are covered elsewhere in this work: see CROWN AND CROWN PROCEEDINGS vol 29 (2014) PARAS 278–281. The Palace of Westminster is a royal palace but is managed by the two houses of Parliament themselves: see CROWN AND CROWN PROCEEDINGS vol 29 (2014) PARA 279. As to parliament generally see PARLIAMENT vol 78 (2010) PARA 801 et seq. As to the care and conservation of cathedrals generally see ECCLESIASTICAL LAW vol 34 (2011) PARA 356 et seq. As to consecrated churches and churchyards generally see ECCLESIASTICAL LAW vol 34 (2011) PARA 821 et seq.
19 See PARAS 1084–1086. As to royal parks see CROWN AND CROWN PROCEEDINGS vol 29 (2014) PARA 281.
20 See PARA 1087. See note 17.

21 Eg the Historic Buildings and Monuments Commission for England ('the Commission') (see
    PARAS 803–809) or the National Trust (see PARA 973 et seq).
22 See OPEN SPACES AND COUNTRYSIDE vol 78 (2010) PARA 501 et seq. As to footpaths and other
    rights of way see HIGHWAYS, STREETS AND BRIDGES vol 55 (2012) PARA 590 et seq. As to
    long-distance routes and coastal access see HIGHWAYS, STREETS AND BRIDGES vol 55 (2012)
    PARA 702 et seq. As to inland waterways see WATER AND WATERWAYS vol 101 (2009) PARA 713
    et seq.

2. INSTITUTIONS

(1) THE SECRETARY OF STATE AND THE WELSH MINISTERS

802. The Secretary of State and the Welsh Ministers. Although administrative responsibility for the matters within the scope of this title[1] has over the years rested with a number of different ministers it is now almost entirely vested in the Secretary of State[2].

Under the arrangements originally made[3] for devolved government in Wales[4], a number of ministerial functions relating to the matters covered by this title were transferred, subject to prescribed exceptions and qualifications, to the National Assembly for Wales[5]. Following the re-organisation of devolved government in Wales under the Government of Wales Act 2006, the functions transferred to the Assembly are now exercisable by the Welsh Ministers[6].

Her Majesty may by Order in Council:

(1)   provide for the transfer to the Welsh Ministers, the First Minister or the Counsel General of any function so far as exercisable by a Minister of the Crown in relation to Wales or the Welsh zone;

(2)   direct that any function so far as so exercisable is to be exercisable by the Welsh Ministers, the First Minister or the Counsel General concurrently with the Minister of the Crown; or

(3)   direct that any function so far as exercisable by a Minister of the Crown in relation to Wales or the Welsh zone is to be exercisable by the Minister of the Crown only with the agreement of, or after consultation with, the Welsh Ministers, the First Minister or the Counsel General[7].

1   As to the scope of this title see PARA 801.
2   In any enactment, 'Secretary of State' means one of Her Majesty's principal secretaries of state: see the Interpretation Act 1978 s 5, Sch 1. As to the office of Secretary of State see CONSTITUTIONAL AND ADMINISTRATIVE LAW vol 20 (2014) PARA 153. Where administrative responsibility remains vested in a particular Minister of the Crown this is stated in the text in the paragraph in this title concerned.
3   Ie under the Government of Wales Act 1998.
4   'Wales' means the combined area of the counties which were created by the Local Government Act 1972 s 20 (as originally enacted) (see LOCAL GOVERNMENT vol 69 (2009) PARAS 5, 37), but subject to any alteration made under s 73 (consequential alteration of boundary following alteration of watercourse) (see LOCAL GOVERNMENT vol 69 (2009) PARA 90): Interpretation Act 1978 Sch 1 (definition substituted by the Local Government (Wales) Act 1994 s 1(3), Sch 2 para 9). As to local government areas see LOCAL GOVERNMENT vol 69 (2009) PARA 22 et seq; and as to boundary changes see LOCAL GOVERNMENT vol 69 (2009) PARA 54 et seq.
        For the purposes of the Government of Wales Act 1998 and the Government of Wales Act 2006 (see the text to note 6), 'Wales' includes the sea adjacent to Wales out as far as the seaward boundary of the territorial sea: Government of Wales Act 1998 s 155 (definition substituted by the Government of Wales Act 2006 s 160(1), Sch 10 paras 41, 54(1), (4)); Government of Wales Act 2006 s 158(1). The Secretary of State may by order determine, or make provision for determining, for the purposes of this definition of 'Wales' and the definition of the Welsh zone, any boundary between waters which are to be treated as parts of the sea adjacent to Wales, or sea within British fishery limits adjacent to Wales, and those which are not: s 158(3) (substituted by the Marine and Coastal Access Act 2009 s 43(1), (3)). For the purposes of this definition the boundary between those parts of the sea within the Severn and Dee Estuaries which are to be treated as adjacent to Wales and those which are not is, in each case, a line drawn between the co-ordinates set out in the National Assembly for Wales (Transfer of Functions) Order 1999, SI 1999/672, Sch 3: art 6; Government of Wales Act 2006 Sch 11 para 26. An Order in Council transferring ministerial functions under the Government of Wales Act 2006 s 58 (see the text to note 7) may include any provision that may be included in an order under s 158(3): s 158(4). 'Welsh zone' means the sea adjacent to Wales which is within British fishery limits (that is, the limits set by or under the Fishery Limits Act 1976 s 1: see FISHERIES AND AQUACULTURE vol 51 (2013) PARA

214), and specified in an Order in Council under the Government of Wales Act 2006 s 58 (see the text to note 7) or an order under s 158(3): s 158(1) (definition added by the Marine and Coastal Access Act 2009 s 43(1), (3)). As to territorial waters see WATER AND WATERWAYS vol 100 (2009) PARA 31.

5 See the National Assembly for Wales (Transfer of Functions) Order 1999, SI 1999/672, art 2, Sch 1. As to the National Assembly for Wales see CONSTITUTIONAL AND ADMINISTRATIVE LAW vol 20 (2014) PARA 351.

6 See the Government of Wales Act 2006 Sch 11 para 30. 'Welsh Ministers' means the First Minister and the Welsh Ministers appointed under the Government of Wales Act 2006 s 48: see s 45(2). Where any function is transferred to the Welsh Ministers this is referred to in the specific paragraph or paragraphs dealing with that function in this title. As to the First Minister and the Welsh Ministers see the Government of Wales Act 2006 ss 46–48; and CONSTITUTIONAL AND ADMINISTRATIVE LAW vol 20 (2014) PARA 373 et seq. As to devolved government in Wales generally see CONSTITUTIONAL AND ADMINISTRATIVE LAW vol 20 (2014) PARA 351 et seq. As to the exercise of transferred functions and the bringing of subordinate legislation made by the Welsh Ministers before the National Assembly for Wales see Sch 11 paras 33–35 (in the case of functions transferred to the Assembly by Order in Council under the Government of Wales Act 1998 s 22) or the Government of Wales Act 2006 Sch 3 para 9 (in the case of functions transferred to the Welsh Ministers by Order in Council under s 58: see the text to note 7); and CONSTITUTIONAL AND ADMINISTRATIVE LAW vol 20 (2014) PARA 380.

7 See the Government of Wales Act 2006 s 58, Sch 3; and CONSTITUTIONAL AND ADMINISTRATIVE LAW vol 20 (2014) PARA 380. See also note 4.

(2) THE HISTORIC BUILDINGS AND MONUMENTS COMMISSION FOR ENGLAND

803. Constitution of the Historic Buildings and Monuments Commission for England. A body known as the Historic Buildings and Monuments Commission for England ('the Commission') (commonly known as 'Historic England')[1] was established in 1983[2]. It is a body corporate[3] whose members are appointed by the Secretary of State[4].

The Commission must appoint, with the Secretary of State's approval, a chief officer who is responsible for the general exercise of the Commission's functions[5]; and may appoint such other employees as it thinks fit[6]. The Commission may regulate its own procedure, including its quorum[7]. The validity of any proceedings of the Commission is not affected by any vacancy among the members, or by any defect in the appointment of any person as a member or chairman or deputy chairman, or by a failure to comply with disclosure provisions[8]. A document purporting to be duly executed under the seal of the Commission, or to be signed on the Commission's behalf, must be received in evidence and, unless the contrary is proved, be deemed to be so executed or signed[9].

The Commission must constitute at least one committee to advise it on ancient monuments and at least one to advise it on historic buildings, and may constitute other committees to advise it on those or other aspects of its functions[10].

The Commission must keep proper accounts and records[11] and prepare an annual statement of accounts[12]. It must also make to the Secretary of State an annual report on the exercise of its functions[13], which must include a copy of the statement of accounts and of the report thereon of the Comptroller and Auditor General[14], and a statement of action taken by the Commission to promote the enjoyment of ancient monuments and buildings by disabled members of the public[15]. The Secretary of State must lay a copy of each such report before each House of Parliament[16].

The Commission must furnish the Secretary of State with such information relating to its property and the discharge and proposed discharge of its functions as he may require, and for that purpose it must permit any person[17] authorised by him to inspect and make copies of any accounts or other documents of the Commission and must give such explanation of them as that person or the Secretary of State may require[18].

1   Historic England was commonly known as English Heritage until 1 April 2015. On 1 April 2015 English Heritage changed its name to Historic England and a new charity, the English Heritage Trust, took the name of English Heritage. English Heritage looks after the National Heritage Collection which it cares for and opens to the public under a licence from Historic England. As to the registration of charities see CHARITIES vol 8 (2015) PARA 307 et seq.

2   National Heritage Act 1983 s 32(1). On 1 April 1999 the Royal Commission on the Historical Monuments of England was merged with English Heritage. See note 1. As to the historic environment in Wales see PARA 810. As to the meaning of 'England' see PARA 804 note 2. As to the meaning of 'Wales' see PARA 802 note 4.

3   National Heritage Act 1983 Sch 3 para 1. The Commission is not to be regarded as the servant or agent of the Crown or as enjoying any status, immunity or privilege of the Crown; and the members of the Commission and of their staff are not regarded as civil servants and the Commission's property is not regarded as property of, or held on behalf of, the Crown: see Sch 3 para 2 (amended by SI 1997/2971). The National Heritage Act 1983 Sch 3 para 2(1) is subject to the National Heritage Act 2002 s 3(5) (see PARA 805): see s 3(6). As to the legal status of bodies not to be regarded as the servant or agent of the Crown or as enjoying any status, immunity or privilege of the Crown see CONSTITUTIONAL AND ADMINISTRATIVE LAW vol 20 (2014) PARA 311 et seq. As to the civil service see CONSTITUTIONAL AND ADMINISTRATIVE LAW vol 20 (2014) PARA 285 et seq.
        The Commission is a public body for the purposes of the Local Authorities (Goods and Services) Act 1970 in its application to England and Wales; and agreements which may be entered into by the Commission are restricted to agreements with a local authority for the supply of goods or materials, or the provision of administrative, professional or technical services, by that authority to the Commission: see the Local Authorities (Goods and Services) (Public Bodies) (English Heritage) Order 1997, SI 1997/1835, arts 2, 3; and LOCAL GOVERNMENT vol 69 (2009) PARA 495.

4   See the National Heritage Act 1983 Sch 3 para 3 (amended by SI 2012/2404). As to the Secretary of State see PARA 802 note 2. As to the remuneration of members see Sch 3 para 11. Members of the Commission are disqualified for membership of the House of Commons: see the House of Commons Disqualification Act 1975 s 1, Sch 1 Pt III (amended by the National Heritage Act 1983 Sch 3 para 14); and PARLIAMENT vol 78 (2010) PARA 908.

5   See the National Heritage Act 1983 Sch 3 para 4(1), (2). As to the Commission's functions see PARA 804.

6   See the National Heritage Act 1983 Sch 3 paras 4(3)–(8), 5 (amended by the Employment Rights Act 1996 s 240, Sch 1 para 23; and the Employment Rights (Dispute Resolution) Act 1998 s 1(2)(a)).

7   National Heritage Act 1983 Sch 3 para 6. However, a member of the Commission who is in any way directly or indirectly interested in a contract made or proposed to be made by the Commission, or in any other matter which falls to be considered by the Commission, must disclose the nature of his interest at a meeting of the Commission: Sch 3 para 7(1). As to provisions relating to such disclosure see Sch 3 para 7(2)–(5).

8   National Heritage Act 1983 Sch 3 para 8.

9   National Heritage Act 1983 Sch 3 para 10(2). The fixing of the seal of the Commission must be authenticated by the signature of the chairman or of some other person authorised either generally or specially by the Commission to act for that purpose: Sch 3 para 10(1).

10 National Heritage Act 1983 Sch 3 para 9(1). The Commission may include as members of committees persons who are not members of the Commission: Sch 3 para 9(2).

11 National Heritage Act 1983 Sch 3 para 12(1).

12 See the National Heritage Act 1983 Sch 3 para 12(2)–(4). The accounts and statement of accounts must be audited by persons appointed in respect of each financial year by the Secretary of State (see Sch 3 para 12(5), (6) (Sch 3 para 12(5) amended by SI 2003/1326; National Heritage Act 1983 Sch 3 para 12(6) amended by SI 2008/948)). The Commission must send a copy of the statement of accounts prepared by it in each financial year to the Comptroller and Auditor General who must examine, certify and report thereon: see the National Heritage Act 1983 Sch 3 para 12(6A), (6B) (both added by SI 2003/1326). As soon as may be after receiving any report made by the auditors or the Comptroller and Auditor General the Commission must send a copy of the report to the Secretary of State: see the National Heritage Act 1983 Sch 3 para 13(5) (amended by SI 2003/1326). 'Financial year' means the period commencing with the day of the Commission's establishment and ending with the second 31 March following that day, and

each successive period of 12 months: National Heritage Act 1983 Sch 3 para 12(7). 'Month' means calendar month: Interpretation Act 1978 s 5, Sch 1. As to the Comptroller and Auditor General see CONSTITUTIONAL AND ADMINISTRATIVE LAW vol 20 (2014) PARAS 494–496.

13 See the National Heritage Act 1983 Sch 3 para 13(1).

14 See the National Heritage Act 1983 Sch 3 para 13(2) (amended by SI 2003/1326).

15 See the National Heritage Act 1983 Sch 3 para 13(3) (amended by SI 2003/1326). As to the prohibition against discrimination in the provision of goods, facilities and services to disabled persons see DISCRIMINATION vol 33 (2013) PARA 78 et seq.

16 National Heritage Act 1983 Sch 3 para 13(4) (amended by SI 2003/1326). As to the laying of documents before Parliament see STATUTES AND LEGISLATIVE PROCESS vol 96 (2012) PARA 1052.

17 'Person', unless the contrary intention appears, includes a body of persons corporate or unincorporate: Interpretation Act 1978 s 5, Sch 1. As to bodies corporate see COMPANIES vol 14 (2009) PARA 2; CORPORATIONS vol 24 (2010) PARA 301 et seq.

18 National Heritage Act 1983 Sch 3 para 13(6).

804. General functions of the Commission. It is the duty of the Historic Buildings and Monuments Commission for England ('the Commission')[1] so far as practicable:

(1)   to secure the preservation of ancient monuments[2] and historic buildings[3] situated in England[4];

(2)   to promote the preservation and enhancement of the character and appearance of conservation areas[5] situated in England[6]; and

(3)   to promote the public's enjoyment of, and advance the public's knowledge of, ancient monuments and historic buildings situated in England and their preservation[7],

in exercising the functions conferred on it[8]; but in the event of a conflict between those functions and that duty, those functions will prevail[9].

The Commission must, so far as practicable, provide educational facilities and services, instruction and information to the public in relation to ancient monuments and historic buildings, with particular reference to those in England, and in relation to conservation areas situated in England[10]. It may give advice to any person in relation to ancient monuments, historic buildings and conservation areas situated in England, whether or not it has been consulted[11]. It may, for the purpose of exercising its functions, carry out, or defray or contribute towards the cost of, research in relation to ancient monuments, historic buildings and conservation areas situated in England[12]; and it may, for the purpose of exercising its functions, make and maintain records in relation to ancient monuments and historic buildings situated in England[13]. It may produce souvenirs relating to ancient monuments or historic buildings situated in England and sell souvenirs[14]; and may defray or contribute to the cost of any activity undertaken by another person if the activity relates to ancient monuments or historic buildings[15], and is of a kind which the Commission may itself undertake[16].

Certain enactments[17] are amended for the purpose of conferring functions on the Commission in relation to England, including functions of making grants in relation to historic buildings and conservation areas, acquiring historic buildings, acquiring or becoming guardian of ancient monuments, providing information and other services to the public in connection with affording them access to ancient monuments, and undertaking archaeological investigation and publishing the results, and for connected purposes, which include allowing the Secretary of State to approve lists of historic buildings compiled by the Commission, and imposing requirements for him to consult with the Commission before he includes a monument in the schedule of monuments or grants scheduled monument consent or designates an area of archaeological importance[18].

The Commission may: (a) produce and publish, or sell, books, films or other informative material relating to foreign ancient monuments or foreign historic buildings[19]; (b) produce or sell souvenirs relating to such monuments or buildings[20]; (c) provide (whether on payment or otherwise) advice, assistance or other services in respect of, or information relating to, such monuments or buildings[21]. The Commission may[22] exploit any intellectual property[23], or any other intangible asset, relating to ancient monuments or historic buildings[24]. The Commission may defray or contribute towards the cost of: (i) any survey, excavation or other investigation undertaken in respect of any protected wreck[25]; (ii) the removal of any protected wreck or of any part of any protected wreck to another place for the purpose of preserving it[26]; or (iii) the preservation and maintenance of any protected wreck[27].

For the purpose of exercising its functions the Commission may[28] enter into contracts and other agreements[29]; acquire and dispose of property other than land[30]; with the Secretary of State's consent, acquire land for providing the Commission with office or other accommodation and dispose of the land when no longer required for such accommodation[31]; and do such other things as the Commission thinks necessary or expedient[32]. With the Secretary of State's consent, the Commission may borrow temporarily by way of overdraft such sums as it may require for meeting its obligations and discharging its functions[33].

1   As to the Historic Buildings and Monuments Commission for England ('the Commission') see PARA 803.
2   'Ancient monument' means any structure, work, site (including any site comprising, or comprising the remains of, any vehicle, vessel, aircraft or other moveable structure or part thereof), garden or area which in the Commission's opinion is of historic, architectural, traditional, artistic or archaeological interest: National Heritage Act 1983 s 33(8) (definition amended by the National Heritage Act 2002 s 1(1), (2)). In the National Heritage Act 1983 s 33 references to ancient monuments in England include ancient monuments in, on or under the seabed within the seaward limits of the United Kingdom territorial waters adjacent to England: s 33(9) (s 33(9)–(10) added by the National Heritage Act 2002 s 1(1), (3)). For this purpose the Secretary of State may, by order, determine (or make provision for determining) any boundary between the parts of the United Kingdom territorial waters which are to be treated as adjacent to England, and those which are not: National Heritage Act 1983 s 33(10) (as so added). In exercise of this power, the National Heritage (Territorial Waters Adjacent to England) Order 2002, SI 2002/2427, has been made. As to territorial waters see WATER AND WATERWAYS vol 100 (2009) PARA 31. As to the Secretary of State see PARA 802 note 2.
    'United Kingdom' means Great Britain and Northern Ireland: Interpretation Act 1978 s 5, Sch 1. 'Great Britain' means England, Scotland and Wales: Union with Scotland Act 1706, preamble art I; Interpretation Act 1978 s 22(1), Sch 2 para 5(a). Neither the Isle of Man nor the Channel Islands are within the United Kingdom. See further CONSTITUTIONAL AND ADMINISTRATIVE LAW vol 20 (2014) PARA 3. 'England' means, subject to any alteration of boundaries of local government areas, the area consisting of the counties established by the Local Government Act 1972 s 1 (see LOCAL GOVERNMENT vol 69 (2009) PARAS 5, 22), Greater London and the Isles of Scilly: Interpretation Act 1978 s 5, Sch 1. However, references to 'England' in Acts passed before 1967 include references to Wales (see the Interpretation Act 1978 Sch 2 PARA 5(a)). As to the meaning of 'Wales' see PARA 802 note 4. As to local government areas see LOCAL GOVERNMENT vol 69 (2009) PARA 22 et seq; and as to boundary changes see LOCAL GOVERNMENT vol 69 (2009) PARA 54 et seq. As to Greater London see LONDON GOVERNMENT vol 71 (2013) PARA 14.
3   'Historic building' means any building which in the Commission's opinion is of historic or architectural interest: National Heritage Act 1983 s 33(8).
4   National Heritage Act 1983 s 33(1)(a). As to the historic environment in Wales see PARA 810.
5   'Conservation area' means an area designated as a conservation area under the Planning (Listed Buildings and Conservation Areas) Act 1990 s 69 (see PLANNING vol 83 (2010) PARA 1318): National Heritage Act 1983 s 33(8) (definition amended by the Planning (Consequential Provisions) Act 1990 s 4, Sch 2 para 60).
6   National Heritage Act 1983 s 33(1)(b).

7   National Heritage Act 1983 s 33(1)(c).
8   Ie by the National Heritage Act 1983 s 33(2)–(4) (see the text to notes 10–18), s 34 (see PARA 805).
9   National Heritage Act 1983 s 33(1). The Commission is a designated regulator for the purposes of the Regulatory Enforcement and Sanctions Act 2008 s 37(1), Sch 5: see CONSTITUTIONAL AND ADMINISTRATIVE LAW vol 20 (2014) PARA 331.
10 National Heritage Act 1983 s 33(2)(a). The Commission may make such charges as it may from time to time determine in respect of anything so provided to any person other than a Minister of the Crown: s 33(6). As to the meaning of 'person' see PARA 803 note 17.
11 National Heritage Act 1983 s 33(2)(b). Without prejudice to the generality of this provision, the Commission may advise the Secretary of State with regard to the exercise of functions exercisable by him in relation to England under the Historic Buildings and Ancient Monuments Act 1953 and the Ancient Monuments and Archaeological Areas Act 1979, whether or not it has been consulted: National Heritage Act 1983 s 33(4). The Commission may make such charges as it may from time to time determine in respect of anything given under s 33(2)(b) to any person other than a Minister of the Crown: s 33(6).
    In relation to England, the Commission has the power to prosecute offences under the Ancient Monuments and Archaeological Areas Act 1979 Pt I (ss 1–32) (see ss 2, 19, 28; and PARAS 1016, 1041, 1046), the Town and Country Planning Act 1990 s 196D (see PLANNING vol 83 (2010) PARA 1323), or the Planning (Listed Buildings and Conservation Areas) Act 1990 (see PLANNING vol 83 (2010) PARA 1263) and to institute proceedings in its own name for an injunction to restrain any contravention of the Ancient Monuments and Archaeological Areas Act 1979 Pt I or the Planning (Listed Buildings and Conservation Areas) Act 1990: National Heritage Act 1983 s 33(2A) (added by the Planning and Compensation Act 1991 s 29(1); and amended by the Enterprise and Regulatory Reform Act 2013 Sch 17, para 1(1), (2)). In relation to England, the Commission may make, or join in the making of, applications under the Leasehold Reform, Housing and Urban Development Act 1993 s 73(1) (see LANDLORD AND TENANT vol 64 (2012) PARA 1847), and may exercise, or participate in the exercise of, any rights or powers conferred by a scheme approved under s 70 (see LANDLORD AND TENANT vol 64 (2012) PARA 1844): National Heritage Act 1983 s 33(2B) (added by the Leasehold Reform, Housing and Urban Development Act 1993 s 187(1), Sch 21 para 9). Such references to provisions of the Leasehold Reform, Housing and Urban Development Act 1993 include references to those provisions as they have effect by virtue of the Housing Act 1996 s 118(1) (see LANDLORD AND TENANT vol 64 (2012) PARA 1618): National Heritage Act 1983 s 33(2C) (added by the Housing Act 1996 s 118(6)). See further LANDLORD AND TENANT vol 64 (2012) PARAS 1844–1847.
12 National Heritage Act 1983 s 33(2)(c).
13 National Heritage Act 1983 s 33(2)(d). As to powers of entry for these purposes see PARA 807.
14 National Heritage Act 1983 s 33(2)(e) (added by the National Heritage Act 2002 s 4(1)).
15 National Heritage Act 1983 s 33(2)(f)(i) (s 33(2)(f) added by the National Heritage Act 2002 s 7).
16 National Heritage Act 1983 s 33(2)(f)(ii) (as added: see note 15).
17 Ie the Historic Buildings and Ancient Monuments Act 1953, the Pastoral Measure 1968, the Ancient Monuments and Archaeological Areas Act 1979 and the Mission and Pastoral Measure 2011: see the National Heritage Act 1983 Sch 4.
18 National Heritage Act 1983 s 33(3). As to ancient monuments and archaeological areas see PARA 1006 et seq.
19 National Heritage Act 1983 s 33A(1)(a) (ss 33A, 33B added by the National Heritage Act 2002 s 4(2)). For this purpose 'ancient monument' and 'historic building' have the meanings given in the National Heritage Act 1983 s 33(8) (see notes 2, 3); and an ancient monument or historic building is 'foreign' if it is not situated in the United Kingdom, or in the case of a monument, in, on or under the seabed within the seaward limits of the territorial waters of the United Kingdom: s 33A(2) (as so added).
20 National Heritage Act 1983 s 33A(1)(b) (as added: see note 19).
21 National Heritage Act 1983 s 33A(1)(c) (as added: see note 19).
22 Ie without prejudice to any power of the Commission to do anything authorised by the National Heritage Act 1983 s 33B by virtue of s 33 (see the text to notes 1–18, 28–33) or s 33A (see the text to notes 19–21): s 33B(5) (as added: see note 19).
23 'Intellectual property' means (1) any patent, trade mark, registered design, copyright, design right, right in performance or plant breeder's right; and (2) any rights under the law of a country outside the United Kingdom which correspond or are similar to those rights: National Heritage Act 1983 s 33B(4) (as added: see note 19). As to patents see PATENTS AND REGISTERED DESIGNS vol 79 (2014) PARA 301 et seq. As to trade marks see TRADE MARKS AND TRADE NAMES vol 97A (2014) PARA 1 et seq. As to registered designs see PATENTS AND REGISTERED DESIGNS vol 79 (2014) PARA 657 et seq. As to copyright see COPYRIGHT vol 23 (2013) PARA 653 et seq. As to design right see COPYRIGHT vol 23 (2013) PARA 1048 et seq. As to rights in performance see

COPYRIGHT vol 23 (2013) PARA 1151 et seq. As to plant breeder's right see AGRICULTURAL PRODUCTION AND MARKETING vol 1 (2008) PARA 1175 et seq.

24 National Heritage Act 1983 s 33B(1) (as added: see note 19). In s 33B(1) the references to 'ancient monuments' and 'historic buildings' are to ancient monuments and historic buildings within the meaning of s 33(8) (see notes 2, 3) that are (1) situated in England, or in the case of monuments, in, on or under the seabed within the seaward limits of the United Kingdom territorial waters adjacent to England (s 33B(2)(a) (as so added)); or (2) are foreign ancient monuments or foreign historic buildings within the meaning of s 33A(2) (see note 19) (s 33B(2)(b) (as so added)). An order under s 33(10) (see note 2) applies for the purposes of s 33B(2) as it applies for the purposes of s 33(9) (see note 2): s 33B(3) (as so added).

25 National Heritage Act 1983 s 33C(1)(a) (s 33C added by the National Heritage Act 2002 s 6). 'Protected wreck' means any site which (1) comprises, or comprises the remains of, any vessel or part thereof which is protected by an order under the Protection of Wrecks Act 1973 s 1 (see PARA 1068) designating an area round the site as a restricted area (National Heritage Act 1983 s 33C(2)(a) (as so added)); and (2) is in, on or under the seabed within the seaward limits of the United Kingdom territorial waters adjacent to England (s 33C(2)(b) (as so added)). An order under s 33(10) (see note 2) applies for the purposes of head (2) above as it applies for the purposes of s 33(9) (see note 2): s 33C(3) (as so added).

26 National Heritage Act 1983 s 33C(1)(b) (as added: see note 25).

27 National Heritage Act 1983 s 33C(1)(c) (as added: see note 25). 'Maintenance' includes repairing and covering in of a protected wreck and the doing of any other act or thing which may be required for the purpose of repairing the wreck or protecting it from decay or injury: s 33C(2) (as so added).

28 Subject to the provisions of the National Heritage Act 1983 and any other Act: see s 33(5).

29 National Heritage Act 1983 s 33(5)(a).

30 National Heritage Act 1983 s 33(5)(b). In any Act, unless the contrary intention appears, 'land' includes buildings and other structures, land covered with water, and any estate, interest, easement, servitude or right in or over land: Interpretation Act 1978 s 5, Sch 1.

31 National Heritage Act 1983 s 33(5)(c).

32 National Heritage Act 1983 s 33(5)(d).

33 National Heritage Act 1983 s 33(7). As to the finance of the Commission see PARA 809.

805. Ministerial functions exercised by the Commission. If the Secretary of State for Culture, Media and Sport[1] directs the Historic Buildings and Monuments Commission for England ('the Commission')[2] to exercise certain functions which are specified in the direction in relation to any monument, building or land[3] so specified, the Commission must exercise them on his behalf in such manner as he may from time to time direct[4]. The functions which may be so specified are:

(1)   functions of management exercisable by the Secretary of State, whether by virtue of an enactment[5] or otherwise, in relation to any ancient monument[6] or historic building[7] situated in England[8]; and

(2)   such functions exercisable by him for purposes connected with such a monument or building, in relation to any land which is situated in England and which adjoins or is in the vicinity of the monument or building[9].

This provision does not apply to a function of making regulations or other instruments of a legislative character[10], or a function exercisable in relation to any royal palace or land adjoining it or in its vicinity[11].

If the Secretary of State[12] directs the Commission to exercise functions[13] which are specified in the direction[14], in relation to any ancient monument or class of ancient monument so specified, the Commission must exercise them on his behalf in such manner as he may from time to time direct[15]. The Commission must comply with any such direction given to it[16]. In relation to any matter as respects which the Commission acts by virtue of such a direction, the Commission enjoys the same privileges, immunities and exemptions as those enjoyed in relation to that matter by the Secretary of State[17].

1   As to the Secretary of State see PARA 802 note 2.

2 As to the Historic Buildings and Monuments Commission for England ('the Commission') see PARA 803.

3 As to the meaning of 'land' see PARA 804 note 30.

4 National Heritage Act 1983 s 34(2) (s 34(1), (2) amended by virtue of SI 1997/1744).

5 'Enactment' does not include an enactment comprised in, or in an instrument made under, an Act of the Scottish Parliament: Interpretation Act 1978 s 5, Sch 1. As to the Scottish Parliament see CONSTITUTIONAL AND ADMINISTRATIVE LAW vol 20 (2014) PARA 66.

6 'Ancient monument' means any structure, work, site (including any site comprising, or comprising the remains of, any vehicle, vessel, aircraft or other moveable structure or part thereof), garden or area which in the opinion of the Secretary of State for Culture, Media and Sport is of historic, architectural, traditional, artistic or archaeological interest: National Heritage Act 1983 s 34(3) (definition amended by the National Heritage Act 2002 s 2(1)(a); and SI 1997/1744).

7 'Historic building' means any building which in the opinion of the Secretary of State for Culture, Media and Sport is of historic or architectural interest: see National Heritage Act 1983 s 34(3) (amended by SI 1997/1744).

8 National Heritage Act 1983 s 34(1)(a) (as amended: see note 4). References to ancient monuments in England include ancient monuments in, on or under the seabed within the seaward limits of the United Kingdom territorial waters adjacent to England; and an order under the National Heritage Act 1983 s 33(10) (see PARA 804 note 2) applies for these purposes as it applies for the purposes of s 33(9) (see PARA 804 note 2): s 33(3A) (added by the National Heritage Act 2002, s 2(1)(b)). As to the meanings of 'England' and 'United Kingdom' see PARA 804 note 2. As to territorial waters see WATER AND WATERWAYS vol 100 (2009) PARA 31.

9 National Heritage Act 1983 s 34(1)(b) (as amended: see note 4).

10 National Heritage Act 1983 s 34(4)(a).

11 National Heritage Act 1983 s 34(4)(b).

12 The National Heritage Act 2002 s 3 refers to the Secretary of State. As to the Secretary of State see PARA 802 note 2.

13 The National Heritage Act 2002 s 3 applies to any administrative function exercisable by the Secretary of State (whether by virtue of an enactment or otherwise) in relation to any ancient monument which is in, on or under the seabed within the seaward limits of the United Kingdom territorial waters: s 3(1). However it does not apply to a function of making regulations or other instruments of a legislative character (s 3(4)(a)); or a function to which the National Heritage Act 1983 s 34 (see the text to notes 1–11) applies (National Heritage Act 2002 s 3(4)(b)). In s 3 'ancient monument' means any structure, work, site (including any site comprising, or comprising the remains of, any vehicle, vessel, aircraft or other moveable structure or part thereof) or area which in the opinion of the Secretary of State is, or may be, of historic, architectural, traditional, artistic or archaeological interest: s 3(3).

14 Any direction must be in writing: National Heritage Act 2002 s 3(7). Any power conferred by s 3 to give a direction includes a power to vary or revoke the direction: s 3(8). 'Writing' includes typing, printing, lithography, photography and other modes of representing or reproducing words in a visible form, and expressions referring to writing are construed accordingly: Interpretation Act 1978 s 5, Sch 1.

15 National Heritage Act 2002 s 3(2).

16 National Heritage Act 2002 s 3(9).

17 National Heritage Act 2002 s 3(5). The National Heritage Act 1983 Sch 3 para 2(1) (Commission not to be regarded as servant or agent of the Crown) (see PARA 803) is subject to the National Heritage Act 2002 s 3(5): s 3(6).

806. Power of the Commission to form companies. The Historic Buildings and Monuments Commission for England ('the Commission')[1] may form or take part in forming one or more bodies corporate which, or each of which, has as its main object or objects one or more of the following particular objects[2]:

(1) the production and publication or sale of books, films and other informative material relating to ancient monuments or historic buildings[3];

(2) the provision (whether on payment or otherwise) of advice, assistance or other services in respect of, or information relating to, ancient monuments or historic buildings[4];

(3) the production of souvenirs relating to ancient monuments or historic buildings, or sale of souvenirs[5];

(4)   the exploitation of any intellectual property[6], or any other intangible asset, relating to ancient monuments or historic buildings[7]; and

(5)   the provision in England of catering or car parking or other services or facilities for members of the public visiting ancient monuments or historic buildings[8],

or any other object or objects incidental to the Commission's functions[9].

The Commission may hold interests in any such body, exercise rights conferred by the holding of interests in it, and provide financial or other assistance to or in respect of it, including assistance by way of guarantee of its obligations[10].

These provisions are without prejudice to any power of the Commission to undertake any of the above functions by virtue of its general powers[11].

1   As to the Historic Buildings and Monuments Commission for England ('the Commission') see PARA 803.
2   National Heritage Act 1983 s 35(1)(a) (s 35(1)(a), (1)(b) substituted by the Public Bodies Act 2011 s 32(1), (5)). The reference in the text to particular objects is to those particular objects mentioned in the National Heritage Act 1983 s 35(2) (see the text and notes 3–8).
3   National Heritage Act 1983 s 35(2)(a) (amended by the National Heritage Act 2002 s 5(1), (2)(a); and the Public Bodies Act 2011 s 32(1), (5)). 'Ancient monument' and 'historic building' have the same meanings as in the National Heritage Act 1983 s 33 (see PARA 804 notes 2, 3). References to 'ancient monuments' and 'historic buildings' are to those which (1) are situated in England or, in the case of monuments, in, on or under the seabed within the seaward limits of the United Kingdom territorial waters adjacent to England; or (2) are foreign ancient monuments or foreign historic buildings within the meaning of the National Heritage Act 1983 s 33A(2)(b) (see PARA 804): s 35(3A) (s 35(3A)–(3C) added by the National Heritage Act 2002 s 5(1), (3)). An order under the National Heritage Act 1983 s 33(10) (see PARA 804 note 2) applies for the purposes of s 35(3A) as it applies for the purposes of s 33(9) (see PARA 804 note 2): s 35(3B) (as so added). As to the meanings of 'England' and 'United Kingdom' see PARA 804 note 2. As to territorial waters see WATER AND WATERWAYS vol 100 (2009) PARA 31.
4   National Heritage Act 1983 s 35(2)(ab) (added by the National Heritage Act 2002 s 5(1), (2)(b)).
5   National Heritage Act 1983 s 35(2)(b) (amended by the National Heritage Act 2002 s 5(1), (2)(c)).
6   'Intellectual property' means (1) any patent, trade mark, registered design, copyright, design right, right in performance or plant breeder's right; and (2) any rights under the law of a country outside the United Kingdom which correspond or are similar to those rights falling within head (1): National Heritage Act 1983 s 35(3C) (as added: see note 3). As to patents see PATENTS AND REGISTERED DESIGNS vol 79 (2014) PARA 301 et seq. As to trade marks see TRADE MARKS AND TRADE NAMES vol 97A (2014) PARA 1 et seq. As to registered designs see PATENTS AND REGISTERED DESIGNS vol 79 (2014) PARA 657 et seq. As to copyright see COPYRIGHT vol 23 (2013) PARA 653 et seq. As to design right see COPYRIGHT vol 23 (2013) PARA 1048 et seq. As to rights in performance see COPYRIGHT vol 23 (2013) PARA 1151 et seq. As to plant breeder's right see AGRICULTURAL PRODUCTION AND MARKETING vol 1 (2008) PARA 1175 et seq.
7   National Heritage Act 1983 s 35(2)(ca) (added by the National Heritage Act 2002 s 5(1), (2)(d)).
8   National Heritage Act 1983 s 35(2)(d).
9   National Heritage Act 1983 s 35(1)(b) (as substituted: see note 2).
10 National Heritage Act 1983 s 35(3).
11 National Heritage Act 1983 s 35(5). The general powers referred to are those in s 33 (see PARA 804).

807.   Power of entry to inspect land. Any person[1] duly authorised in writing[2] by the Historic Buildings and Monuments Commission for England ('the Commission')[3] may at any reasonable time enter any land in England[4] to inspect it with a view to obtaining information for inclusion in the Commission's records[5]. Such a person may take with him any assistance or equipment reasonably required and may do there anything reasonably necessary for the purpose[6]. The Commission may not give an authorisation unless it knows or has reason to believe there is in, on or under the land an ancient monument or historic building[7]. An authorised person may not enter a dwelling house without the occupier's consent[8], or demand admission to any land which is occupied unless 24 hours' notice has been given[9]; and if so required by or on behalf of the owner or occupier of the land, he must produce evidence of his authority before entering[10]. Where any works are being carried out on the land, a person acting in the exercise of the power must comply with any reasonable requirements or conditions imposed by the person by whom the works are being carried out for the purpose of preventing interference with or delay to the works[11].

Any person who intentionally obstructs an authorised person is guilty of an offence[12].

Where damage has been caused to land or chattels on land by the exercise of this power, any interested person may recover compensation from the Commission[13]. Any question of disputed compensation must be referred to and determined by the Upper Tribunal[14].

1 As to the meaning of 'person' see PARA 803 note 17.
2 As to the meaning of 'writing' see PARA 805 note 14.
3 As to the Historic Buildings and Monuments Commission for England ('the Commission') see PARA 803.
4 As to the meaning of 'land' see PARA 804 note 30. As to the meaning of 'England' see PARA 804 note 2.
5 National Heritage Act 1983 s 36(1). The records referred to are those made under s 33(2)(d) (see PARA 804).
6 See the National Heritage Act 1983 s 36(2).
7 See the National Heritage Act 1983 s 36(3). As to the meanings of 'ancient monument' and 'historic building' see PARA 804 notes 2, 3 (definitions applied by s 36(3)).
8 See the National Heritage Act 1983 s 36(4)(a).
9 See the National Heritage Act 1983 s 36(4)(b).
10 National Heritage Act 1983 s 36(5).
11 National Heritage Act 1983 s 36(6). However, any requirements or conditions imposed are not regarded as reasonable for this purpose if compliance with them would in effect frustrate the exercise of the power or the purpose of the entry: s 36(6).
12 National Heritage Act 1983 s 36(7). The penalty for such an offence is, on summary conviction, a fine not exceeding level 3 on the standard scale: s 36(7) (amended by the Statute Law (Repeals) Act 1993). As to the standard scale and magistrates' powers to levy unlimited fines see SENTENCING vol 92 (2015) PARA 176.
13 See the National Heritage Act 1983 s 36(8). Any such claim for compensation must be made within the time and in the manner prescribed by the regulations made by the Secretary of State for that purpose: s 36(9). As to the provision made see the Ancient Monuments (Claims for Compensation) (England) Regulations 1991, SI 1991/2512, reg 3. As to the Secretary of State see PARA 802 note 2.
14 National Heritage Act 1983 s 36(10) (amended by SI 2009/1307). In relation to the determination of any such question the Land Compensation Act 1961 s 4 (see COMPULSORY ACQUISITION OF LAND vol 18 (2009) PARAS 716–717) applies (construing the references in that section to the acquiring authority as references to the Commission): National Heritage Act 1983 s 36(10) (as so amended). As to the Upper Tribunal see COMPULSORY ACQUISITION OF LAND vol 18 (2009) PARA 720.

808. Functions in relation to monuments etc partly in England. The Secretary of State[1] may by order[2] provide that the Historic Buildings and Monuments Commission for England ('the Commission')[3] is to have such functions as he thinks appropriate, having regard to its functions in relation to monuments, buildings, gardens, areas or sites situated in England[4], and as are specified in the order[5], in relation to the parts situated in England of any such monuments etc which are only partly so situated and which are specified in the order[6]. However, nothing in these provisions permits the Commission to be given a function of making regulations or other instruments of a legislative character[7].

1 As to the Secretary of State see PARA 802 note 2.
2 Any such order may contain (1) amendments of the National Heritage Act 1983 s 33 (see PARA 804) or s 34 (see PARA 805) (s 37(2)(a)); and (2) amendments of any section or Schedule amended by Sch 4 (see PARA 804) (including consequential amendments relating to the parts of monuments, buildings, gardens, areas or sites not situated in England) (s 37(2)(b)). Any such order has effect

subject to such supplementary provisions (which may include savings and transitionals) as may be specified in the order: s 37(3). At the date at which this volume states the law no such order had been made. As to the meaning of 'England' see PARA 804 note 2.

3   As to the Historic Buildings and Monuments Commission for England ('the Commission') see PARA 803.
4   National Heritage Act 1983 s 37(1)(a). As to the Commission's functions see PARA 804.
5   National Heritage Act 1983 s 37(1)(b).
6   National Heritage Act 1983 s 37(1).
7   National Heritage Act 1983 s 37(4).

809. Expenditure of the Commission. The Secretary of State[1] may, out of money provided   by   Parliament[2],   pay   to   the   Historic   Buildings   and Monuments Commission for England ('the Commission')[3] such sums towards its expenditure as the Treasury[4] may approve and defray such of its expenditure as the Treasury may approve[5]. The payment may be made on such conditions as the Secretary of State imposes with the Treasury's approval[6].

1   As to the Secretary of State see PARA 802 note 2.
2   As to the provision of money by Parliament see PARLIAMENT vol 78 (2010) PARA 804.
3   As to the Historic Buildings and Monuments Commission for England ('the Commission') see PARA 803.
4   'Treasury' means the Commissioners of Her Majesty's Treasury: Interpretation Act 1978 s 5, Sch 1. As to the Treasury see CONSTITUTIONAL AND ADMINISTRATIVE LAW vol 20 (2014) PARAS 262–265.
5   National Heritage Act 1983 s 38(1). As to the duty of the Commission to keep accounts see PARA 803.
6   National Heritage Act 1983 s 38(2).

(3) HISTORIC ENVIRONMENT IN WALES

810. Welsh Government and the historic environment. The Welsh Ministers[1] may do anything which they consider appropriate to support archaeological remains[2], ancient monuments[3], buildings and places of historical or architectural interest[4], historic wrecks[5], and museums and galleries in Wales[6]; and arts and crafts[7], libraries[8] archives and historical records[9], and cultural activities and projects relating to Wales[10].

The Welsh Government[11] maintains an historic environment division known as 'Cadw[12]' which aims to protect and sustain, encourage community engagement in, and improve access to, the historic environment of Wales, which includes historic buildings, ancient monuments, historic parks, gardens and landscapes, and underwater archaeology[13].

There is also a Royal Commission on the Ancient and Historical Monuments of Wales[14].

1   As to the Welsh Ministers see PARA 802.
2   See the Government of Wales Act 2006 s 61(a).
3   See the Government of Wales Act 2006 s 61(b).
4   See the Government of Wales Act 2006 s 61(c).
5   See the Government of Wales Act 2006 s 61(d).
6   Government of Wales Act 2006 s 61(f). As to the meaning of 'Wales' see PARA 802 note 4.
7   See the Government of Wales Act 2006 s 61(e).
8   See the Government of Wales Act 2006 s 61(g).
9   See the Government of Wales Act 2006 s 61(h).
10   Government of Wales Act 2006 s 61(i).
11   As to the Welsh Government see CONSTITUTIONAL AND ADMINISTRATIVE LAW vol 20 (2014) PARA 351 et seq.
12   Cadw promotes the conservation of Wales's historic environment and gives (1) advice on the conserving and maintaining historic buildings, ancient monuments, historic landscapes and underwater archaeology; (2) grants for conserving and repairing for the historic environment; and

(3) comments on applications for development or demolition that effect the historic environment: see the Cadw website which, at the date at which this volume states the law, can be found at www.cadw.wales.gov.uk.

13 See the Cadw website which, at the date at which this volume states the law, can be found at www.cadw.wales.gov.uk.

14 See PARA 811.

811. Royal Commission on the Ancient and Historical Monuments of Wales. The Royal Commission on the Ancient and Historical Monuments of Wales (Comisiwn Brenhinol Henebion Cymru) was first appointed by royal warrant dated 10 August 1908[1]. The current provisions are contained in the royal warrant dated 12 July 2000, which revoked the previous warrant[2].

The Commission is appointed to provide for the survey and recording of ancient and historical monuments and constructions[3] connected with, or illustrative of, the contemporary culture, civilisation and conditions of the life of the people in Wales from the earliest times by the following:

(1) compiling, maintaining and curating the National Monuments Record of Wales as the basic national record of the archaeological and historical environment;

(2) identifying, surveying, interpreting and recording all buildings, sites and ancient monuments of archaeological, architectural and historic interest in Wales or within the territorial sea adjacent to Wales, in order both to enhance and update the National Monuments Record of Wales, and also to respond to statutory needs[4];

(3) providing advice and information relevant to the preservation and conservation of such buildings, sites and ancient monuments of archaeological, architectural and historic interest:

(4) collecting and exchanging data with other record holders and providing an index to data from other sources:

(5) promoting the public use of information available in the National Monuments Record of Wales by all appropriate means:

(6) establishing and maintaining national standards in surveying, recording and curating of records relating to archaeology and historical architecture and providing guidance on these matters to other bodies and by exercising responsibility for the oversight of local sites and monuments records[5].

The Commission consists of a chairman and not more than ten other persons, appointed by Her Majesty The Queen, on the advice of the Welsh Government and the Secretary of State for Wales[6]. The Commission may act notwithstanding a vacancy amongst its commissioners, and the validity of any of its proceedings is not affected by any defect in the appointment of all or any of the commissioners[7].

Subject as provided by the royal warrant, the Commission may regulate its own procedure[8]. The Commission must publish an annual report; and has power to require persons with information likely to be needed for the National Monuments Record of Wales to provide such information as it may request, and may make inquiries about any premises by all other lawful ways and means whatsoever[9]. The Commission is funded by the Welsh Government, and must report periodically on its proceedings to the Welsh Government at such times and in such manner as might be directed[10].

The Commission may appoint a secretary and other officers; and anything authorised or required to be done by the Commission may be done by any commissioner or officer who is authorised (generally or specifically) for that purpose[11].

1 As to royal warrants and other public documents see CONSTITUTIONAL AND ADMINISTRATIVE LAW vol 20 (2014) PARA 580 et seq.
2 Ie the royal warrant of 6 April 1992: see the royal warrant of 12 July 2000. All property, rights and liabilities of the Commission appointed under the 1992 warrant and subsequent warrants were transferred to the commission: and any agreement, transaction or other thing which had been made, effected or done by or in relation to the Commission appointed under previous warrants, has effect as if made, effected or done by the commission appointed under the 2000 warrant: see the royal warrant of 12 July 2000.
3 This includes ancient and historical monuments and constructions in, on or under, the sea bed within the United Kingdom territorial sea adjacent to Wales: see the royal warrant of 12 July 2000. As to the United Kingdom's territorial sea see WATER AND WATERWAYS vol 100 (2009) PARA 31.
4 As to the statutory protection and recording of ancient monuments and archaeological areas see PARA 1006 et seq.
5 See the royal warrant of 12 July 2000.
6 See the royal warrant of 12 July 2000 (amended by virtue of the Government of Wales Act 2006 s 85; and the Wales Act 2014 s 4(4)(a)). Provision is made as to tenure of office and removal from office, the payment of the commissioners' expenses, and as to the declaration of financial interests in matters for consideration by the Commission: see the royal warrant of 12 July 2000. As to the Welsh Government and the Secretary of State for Wales see CONSTITUTIONAL AND ADMINISTRATIVE LAW vol 20 (2014) PARAS 79, 351 et seq.
7 See the royal warrant of 12 July 2000.
8 See the royal warrant of 12 July 2000.
9 See the royal warrant of 12 July 2000.
10 See the royal warrant of 12 July 2000 (amended by virtue of the Wales Act 2014 s 4(4)(a)).
11 See the royal warrant of 12 July 2000. Every commissioner and officer is indemnified against all costs and expenses and losses for which he may become liable by reason of any act or thing done by him in the proper discharge of his office or duty: see the royal warrant of 12 July 2000.

(4) THE ROYAL COMMISSION ON HISTORICAL MANUSCRIPTS

812. Establishment and terms of reference of the Royal Commission on Historical Manuscripts. The Royal Commission on Historical Manuscripts was first appointed by royal warrant of 2 April 1869[1]. By royal warrant of 1 April 2003 the responsibilities of the Commission were transferred to be exercised by a sole Historical Manuscripts Commissioner[2]. The commissioner must:

(1)   make inquiry as to the existence and location of manuscripts, including records or archives of all kinds, of value for the study of history, other than records which are for the time being public records by virtue of the Public Records Acts[3];

(2)   with the consent of the owners or custodians inspect and report on them;

(3)   with the consent of the owners or custodians reproduce and publish or assist the publication of such reports;

(4)   record particulars of such manuscripts and records in a national register thereof;

(5)   promote and assist the proper preservation and storage of such manuscripts and records;

(6)   assist those wishing to use such manuscripts or records for study or research;

(7)   consider and advise upon general questions relating to the location, preservation and use of such manuscripts and records; and

(8)   promote the co-ordinated action of all professional and other bodies concerned with the preservation and use of such manuscripts and records[4].

The Historical Manuscripts Commission now forms part of the National Archives[5].

Special provision is made as to the keeping and preservation of manorial documents[6].

1   See the royal warrant of 2 April 1869 appointing commissioners to make inquiry as to the places in which various collections of manuscripts and papers of general public interest in the possession of institutions and private families, a knowledge of which would be of great utility in the illustration of history, constitutional law, science and general literature, were deposited, and for any of the other purposes therein mentioned; and the royal warrants of 18 December 1897 and 27 March 1919. By royal warrant of 5 December 1959 the terms of reference of the Commission were revised and extended. As to royal warrants and other public documents see CONSTITUTIONAL AND ADMINISTRATIVE LAW vol 20 (2014) PARA 580 et seq.

2   The responsibilities were transferred to the last holder of the office of Keeper of Public Records, and any persons who succeed her in that office, for so long as they hold it, to act as sole Historical Manuscripts Commissioner: see the royal warrant of 1 April 2003. As to the office of Keeper of Public Records see CONSTITUTIONAL AND ADMINISTRATIVE LAW vol 20 (2014) PARA 346.

3   As to the Public Records Acts see CONSTITUTIONAL AND ADMINISTRATIVE LAW vol 20 (2014) PARA 343.

4   See the royal warrant of 1 April 2003.

5   The National Archives is a non-ministerial government department and an executive agency of the Ministry of Justice bringing together the Public Record Office, the Historical Manuscripts Commission, the Office of Public Sector Information and Her Majesty's Stationery Office. As to the Ministry of Justice see CONSTITUTIONAL AND ADMINISTRATIVE LAW vol 20 (2014) PARAS 252–254. As to the Public Record Office see CONSTITUTIONAL AND ADMINISTRATIVE LAW vol 20 (2014) PARA 346.

6   See the Manorial Documents Rules 1959, SI 1959/1399. 'Manorial documents' means court rolls, surveys, maps, terriers, documents and books of every description relating to the boundaries, wastes, customs or courts of a manor, but does not include the deeds or other instruments required for evidencing the title to a manor or agreements or draft agreements relating to compensation, or any documents which came into being after 31 December 1925: r 1.

     The lord of the manor must cause all manorial documents in his possession or under his control to be kept and used under conditions suitable for their safe and proper preservation and must upon request furnish to the Master of the Rolls particulars of all such documents: r 2. He must inform the secretary of the Historical Manuscripts Commission whether any manorial documents in his possession or under his control are damaged or decayed, or whether he is unable to preserve them under proper conditions, in order that proposals may be made for the repair or better preservation of the documents; and the lord of the manor must, so far as he is able, give effect to any such proposals: r 3. Every change in the ownership of manorial documents must be notified by the new owner to the secretary of the Commission: r 4. The lord of the manor may deposit manorial documents for their better preservation in a repository approved by the Master of the Rolls, and documents so deposited are deemed to remain under the control of the lord of the manor: r 5. The controlling authority of the repository must furnish to the lord of the manor and to the secretary of the Commission an inventory in the prescribed form of any documents so deposited: r 6, Schedule. 'Lord of the manor' means the lord for the time being of the manor, or any person entitled to manorial documents: r 1. As to the preservation of manorial records see further PARA 929. As to manors see CUSTOM AND USAGE vol 32 (2012) PARA 95 et seq.

(5) THE NATIONAL ART COLLECTIONS FUND

813.   Establishment and functions of the National Art Collections Fund. The National Art Collections Fund[1] was formally constituted in 1903[2] and was incorporated by royal charter in 1928[3]. The fund is a body corporate with perpetual succession and a common seal and may, in its name, plead or defend an action in all courts and has power to do all things generally incidental to or appertaining to a body corporate[4].

The government and control of the fund is vested in the executive committee[5] which appoints an advisory council[6]. The fund may have permanent officers with such functions, tenure and terms of office as are prescribed by the byelaws of the fund[7].

The fund is a registered charity[8] whose main objects are:

(1)   to secure by purchase, gift, exchange, bequest or otherwise works of art, and objects of national and historical importance for presentation or loan to public art collections in the United Kingdom and Commonwealth and to the National Trust for Places of Historic Interest or Natural Beauty (the 'National Trust') and the National Trust for Scotland for public exhibition[9];

(2)   to make grants in aid of opening and maintaining public or private exhibitions or works of art and objects of national and historical importance wherever held[10]; and

(3)   to promote and obtain support for Acts of Parliament and other legislative measures which are conducive to promoting or furthering the objects and interests of the fund[11].

In pursuance of its objects the fund may purchase, take on lease or in exchange, hire or otherwise acquire or hold any real or personal property thought necessary or convenient for its purposes and may likewise erect, alter, improve and maintain any buildings for those purposes[12].

The fund's sources of income include commercial sponsorship, membership subscriptions, donations, legacies and investment income[13]. The fund may not carry on any trade or business or engage in any transactions with a view to the pecuniary gain or profit of its members[14] but this does not preclude commercial operations for the benefit of the fund itself and the fund has a wholly owned trading subsidiary, Art Fund Services Limited, a company incorporated in England and Wales, which donates all its profits in the year to the fund[15].

Gifts to the fund are specifically exempted from inheritance tax[16]; and the fund enjoys other tax advantages and privileges[17].

1   In May 2006 the National Art Collections Fund adopted the name 'The Art Fund' as its public and trading name but its full name has been retained for legal purposes. The National Art Collections Fund ('The Art Fund') is registered as a charity with the Charity Commission for England and Wales under number 209174: see the Art Fund's Report of Activities 2014–2015. As to the registration of charities see CHARITIES vol 8 (2015) PARA 307 et seq.

2   See National Art-Collections Fund *Twenty-five Years of the National Art-Collections Fund 1903–1928* (1928) University Press, Glasgow, p 2.

3   See the Charter of Incorporation of the National Art-Collections Fund, 19 December 1928. The charter was amended by resolutions passed in 1976, 1978, 1990 and 1991. As to incorporation by royal charter see CORPORATIONS vol 24 (2010) PARA 329 et seq.

4   See the Charter of Incorporation of the National Art-Collections Fund, 19 December 1928, art 1.

5   See Charter of Incorporation of the National Art-Collections Fund, 19 December 1928, art 10, Schedule paras 33–38.

6   See Charter of Incorporation of the National Art-Collections Fund, 19 December 1928, art 10, Schedule para 10.

7   See Charter of Incorporation of the National Art-Collections Fund, 19 December 1928, art 8. The byelaws are set out in the Schedule to the charter of incorporation and may be altered or revoked by the executive committee with the approval of a general meeting of the fund, provided that such alterations or revocations have been allowed by the Privy Council: see art 13. As to the Privy Council see CONSTITUTIONAL AND ADMINISTRATIVE LAW vol 20 (2014) PARAS 268–272.

8   See note 1.

9   See the Charter of Incorporation of the National Art-Collections Fund, 19 December 1928, art 3(a). As to the National Trust see PARA 973 et seq. As to the Commonwealth see COMMONWEALTH vol 13 (2009) PARA 701 et seq.

10   Charter of Incorporation of the National Art-Collections Fund, 19 December 1928, art 3(c).

11 Charter of Incorporation of the National Art-Collections Fund, 19 December 1928, art 3(g).
12 Charter of Incorporation of the National Art-Collections Fund, 19 December 1928, art 3(f).
13 See the Art Fund's Report of Activities 2014–2015.
14 See the Charter of Incorporation of the National Art-Collections Fund, 19 December 1928, art 4.
15 See the Art Fund's Report of Activities 2014–2015.
16 See the Inheritance Tax Act 1984 s 25, Sch 3; and INHERITANCE TAXATION vol 59A (2014) PARA 137.
17 See generally PARAS 1003, 1112–1114.

(6) THE NATIONAL HERITAGE MEMORIAL FUND

814. Establishment and constitution of the National Heritage Memorial Fund.
The National Heritage Memorial Fund was established in succession to the National Land Fund as a memorial to those who have died for the United Kingdom[1]. It is vested in and administered by a body corporate known as the trustees of the National Heritage Memorial Fund[2] consisting of a chairman[3] and not more than 14 other members appointed by the Prime Minister[4]. They must include persons with knowledge, experience or interests relevant to the purposes for which the fund may be applied[5] and who are connected by residence or otherwise with England, Wales, Scotland and Northern Ireland respectively[6].

The trustees may appoint such officers and servants as they think fit[7]. The trustees discharge their functions in accordance with their own arrangements[8]. The validity of any proceedings of the trustees is not affected by any vacancy among them or by any defect in the appointment of a trustee[9].

Her Majesty may by Order in Council[10] provide for the transfer to the trustees of certain functions[11] exercisable by the Secretary of State[12].

1 National Heritage Act 1980 s 1(1). The National Heritage Memorial Fund has adopted the acronym 'NHMF': see the NMHF website which, at the date at which this volume states the law, can be found at www.nmhf.org.uk. As to the abolition of the National Land Fund see s 15 (repealed). As to the meaning of 'United Kingdom' see PARA 804 note 2.
2 National Heritage Act 1980 s 1(2). The trustees are not to be regarded as acting on behalf of the Crown and neither they nor their officers or servants are to be regarded as Crown servants: s 1(4), Sch 1 para 1. References to the trustees in Pt I (ss 1–7) are to the body constituted by s 1(2): s 1(4). As to the legal status of bodies not to be regarded as the servant or agent of the Crown or as enjoying any status, immunity or privilege of the Crown see CONSTITUTIONAL AND ADMINISTRATIVE LAW vol 20 (2014) PARA 311 et seq.
3 The Prime Minister must consult the Scottish Ministers before appointing the chairman of the trustees: National Heritage Act 1980 s 1(3A)(a) (s 1(3A) added by SI 2000/1102). As to the tenure of office of the chairman see the National Heritage Act 1980 Sch 1 para 4. As to the Scottish Ministers see CONSTITUTIONAL AND ADMINISTRATIVE LAW vol 20 (2014) PARA 67.
4 National Heritage Act 1980 s 1(2) (amended by the National Lotteries etc Act 1993 s 36, Sch 4 para 1). As to the tenure of office of trustees see the National Heritage Act 1980 Sch 1 para 3 (amended by SI 2000/1102; and SI 2012/2404). As to the remuneration of trustees see the National Heritage Act 1980 Sch 1 para 4A (added by the National Heritage Act 1997 s 2(a)). As to the payment of expenses and allowances see the National Heritage Act 1980 Sch 1 para 5 (amended by the National Lottery etc Act 1993 Sch 4 para 7; National Heritage Act 1997 s 2(b)). As to the Prime Minister see CONSTITUTIONAL AND ADMINISTRATIVE LAW vol 20 (2014) PARAS 203–208.
5 As to the purposes of the fund see PARA 815.
6 National Heritage Act 1980 s 1(3). The Prime Minister must consult the Scottish Ministers before appointing any person on the ground that he is connected by residence or otherwise with Scotland: s 1(3A)(b) (as added: see note 3). As to the meaning of 'England' see PARA 804 note 2. As to the meaning of 'Wales' see PARA 802 note 4.
7 See the National Heritage Act 1980 Sch 1 para 6 (amended by the National Heritage Act 1997, s 2(c)).
8 See the National Heritage Act 1980 Sch 1 para 7(1)(a), (4) (amended by SI 1992/1311). Those arrangements may provide for any function to be discharged under the general direction of the

trustees by a committee or committees consisting of three or more trustees: National Heritage Act 1980 Sch 1 para 7(1)(b). Anything done by a committee has effect as if done by the trustees if the arrangements so provide: Sch 1 para 7(2).
9 National Heritage Act 1980 Sch 1 para 7(3).
10 As to Orders in Council see CONSTITUTIONAL AND ADMINISTRATIVE LAW vol 20 (2014) PARA 581.
11 Ie functions under any provisions of the National Heritage Act 1980 Pt II (ss 8–15) or under the Inheritance Tax Act 1984 s 230 (see PARA 1112). Such an order may contain incidental, consequential and supplemental provisions in order to give it effect: National Heritage Act 1980 s 14(2).
12 National Heritage Act 1980 s 14(1) (amended by the Inheritance Tax Act 1984 s 276, Sch 8 para 16; and SI 1992/1311). As to the Secretary of State see PARA 802 note 2.

815. Financial assistance from the National Heritage Memorial Fund and other expenditure out of the fund. The powers of the trustees of the National Heritage Memorial Fund[1] to give financial assistance[2] are exercisable in the case of things of any kind which are of scenic, historic, archaeological, aesthetic, architectural, engineering, artistic or scientific interest, including animals and plants which are of zoological or botanical interest[3]. The trustees may, for the purpose of:

(1) securing the preservation or enhancement of such things[4];
(2) encouraging the study and understanding of them and the compilation and dissemination of information about them[5];
(3) securing or improving access to them, or their display[6];
(4) encouraging enjoyment of them[7]; or
(5) encouraging the maintenance and development of the skills required for their preservation or enhancement[8],

or for any purpose ancillary to those purposes, give financial assistance for any project which appears to them to be of public benefit[9]. The projects for which financial assistance may be so given for any of the above purposes include (among others) projects for any person[10] to whom the assistance is to be given to acquire property of any kind (including land[11]); to construct or convert buildings[12]; to carry out other works[13]; or to provide education or training[14]. Before giving any financial assistance for any project, the trustees must obtain any expert advice about the project they consider appropriate[15], and must be satisfied that the project is of importance to the national heritage[16].

The trustees may also give financial assistance[17] for any projects for any person to whom the assistance is to be given to set up and maintain a public exhibition[18], to compile and maintain an archive[19], to publish archive material[20], or to compile and publish a comprehensive work of reference (or publish a comprehensive work of reference that has previously been compiled)[21], or to do any ancillary thing[22], which appears to them to relate to an important aspect of the history, natural history or landscape of the United Kingdom[23] and to be of public benefit[24].

The trustees may apply the fund for any purpose, other than making grants and loans, which is a purpose connected with the acquisition, maintenance or preservation of property falling within heads (a) to (e) below, including its acquisition, maintenance or preservation by the trustees[25]. The property referred to is:

(a) any land, building or structure which in the opinion of the trustees is of outstanding scenic, historic, archaeological, aesthetic, architectural, engineering or scientific interest[26];
(b) any object which in their opinion is of outstanding historic, artistic or scientific interest[27];

(c)   any collection or group of objects, being a collection or group which taken as a whole is in their opinion of outstanding historic, artistic or scientific interest[28];

(d)   any land or object not falling within head (a), (b) or (c) above the acquisition, maintenance or preservation of which is in their opinion desirable by reason of its connection with land or a building or structure falling within head (a) above[29]; or

(e)   any rights in or over land the acquisition of which is in their opinion desirable for the benefit of land or a building or structure falling within head (a) or (d) above[30].

The trustees must not, however, apply the fund for any such purpose in respect of any property unless they are of the opinion, after obtaining any expert advice they consider appropriate, that the property[31] is of importance to the national heritage[32]. Notwithstanding that an object such as is mentioned in head (b) above or a collection or group of objects such as is mentioned in head (c) above is not of itself of importance to the national heritage, the trustees may apply the fund for any purpose connected with its acquisition if they are satisfied that after the acquisition it will form part of a collection or group of objects such as is mentioned in head (c) above[33], and, after obtaining any expert advice they consider appropriate, they are of the opinion that that collection or group is of importance to the national heritage[34]. The trustees must not, however, retain any property acquired by them under these provisions[35] except in such cases and for such period as the Secretary of State[36] may allow[37].

1   As to the National Heritage Memorial Fund and its trustees see PARA 814.
2   Ie the powers under the National Heritage Act 1980 s 3 (see the text to notes 3–16).
3   National Heritage Act 1980 s 3(1) (s 3 substituted by the National Heritage Act 1997 s 1(1)). Financial assistance under this provision must be given by way of grant or loan out of the fund, and in giving such assistance the trustees may impose any conditions they think fit: National Heritage Act 1980 s 3(5) (as so substituted). The conditions that may be imposed in giving such assistance may relate (among other things) to:
    (1)   maintenance, repair, insurance and safekeeping (s 3(6)(a) (as so substituted));
    (2)   means of access or display (s 3(6)(b) (as so substituted));
    (3)   disposal or lending (s 3(6)(c) (as so substituted)); or
    (4)   repayment of grant or loan (s 3(6)(d) (as so substituted)).
   References in the National Heritage Act 1980 to the making of a grant or loan or the transfer or conveyance of any property to any institution or body include references to the making of a grant or loan or the transfer or conveyance of property to trustees for that institution or body: s 18(4).
4   National Heritage Act 1980 s 3(2)(a) (as substituted: see note 3). In giving any financial assistance for any project for the preservation or enhancement of anything, or determining the conditions on which such assistance is to be given, the trustees must bear in mind the desirability of public access to, or the public display of, the thing in question and of its enjoyment by the public: s 3(7) (as so substituted).
5   National Heritage Act 1980 s 3(2)(b) (as substituted: see note 3).
6   National Heritage Act 1980 s 3(2)(c) (as substituted: see note 3).
7   National Heritage Act 1980 s 3(2)(d) (as substituted: see note 3).
8   National Heritage Act 1980 s 3(2)(e) (as substituted: see note 3).
9   National Heritage Act 1980 s 3(2) (as substituted: see note 3).
10 As to the meaning of 'person' see PARA 803 note 17.
11 National Heritage Act 1980 s 3(3)(a) (as substituted: see note 3). As to the meaning of 'land' see PARA 804 note 30.
12 National Heritage Act 1980 s 3(3)(b) (as substituted: see note 3).
13 National Heritage Act 1980 s 3(3)(c) (as substituted: see note 3).
14 National Heritage Act 1980 s 3(3)(d) (as substituted: see note 3).
15 National Heritage Act 1980 s 3(4)(a) (as substituted: see note 3).
16 National Heritage Act 1980 s 3(4)(b) (as substituted: see note 3).
17 Before giving any financial assistance under the National Heritage Act 1980 s 3A for any project, the trustees must obtain any expert advice about the project they consider appropriate: s 3A(4)

(s 3A added by the National Heritage Act 1997 s 1(2)). National Heritage Act 1980 s 3(5), (6) (see note 3) applies for the purposes of s 3A as it applies for the purposes of s 3: see s 3A(5) (as so added).

18 National Heritage Act 1980 s 3A(2)(a) (as added: see note 17).

19 National Heritage Act 1980 s 3A(2)(b) (as added: see note 17). In giving any financial assistance for any project to compile or maintain an archive, or determining the conditions on which such assistance is to be given, the trustees must bear in mind the desirability of public access to the archive: s 3A(6) (as so added). For these purposes, 'archive' includes any collection of sound recordings, images or other information, however stored: s 3A(3) (as so added).

20 National Heritage Act 1980 s 3A(2)(c) (as added: see note 17).

21 National Heritage Act 1980 s 3A(2)(d) (as added: see note 17).

22 National Heritage Act 1980 s 3A(2) (as added: see note 17).

23 National Heritage Act 1980 s 3A(1)(a) (as added: see note 17). As to the meaning of 'United Kingdom' see PARA 804 note 2.

24 National Heritage Act 1980 s 3A(1)(b) (as added: see note 17).

25 National Heritage Act 1980 s 4(1) (amended by the National Heritage Act 1997 s 3, Schedule para 1(1), (2)). The National Heritage Act 1980 s 3(7) (see note 4) has effect in relation to the application of any sums out of the fund under s 4 as it has in relation to the making of a grant or loan under s 3: see s 4(2C) (s 4(2) substituted, s 4(2A)–(2C) added, by the National Heritage Act 1997 Schedule para 1(1), (3)).

26 National Heritage Act 1980 s 4(2)(a) (as substituted: see note 25).

27 National Heritage Act 1980 s 4(2)(b) (as substituted: see note 25).

28 National Heritage Act 1980 s 4(2)(c) (as substituted: see note 25).

29 National Heritage Act 1980 s 4(2)(d) (as substituted: see note 25).

30 National Heritage Act 1980 s 4(2)(e) (as substituted: see note 25).

31 Ie or, in the case of land or an object falling within the National Heritage Act 1980 s 4(2)(d) (see head (d) in the text) the land, building or structure with which it is connected, or in the case of rights falling within s 4(2)(e) (see head (e) in the text) the land, building or structure for whose benefit they are acquired: s 4(2A) (as added: see note 25).

32 National Heritage Act 1980 s 4(2A) (as added: see note 25).

33 National Heritage Act 1980 s 4(2B)(a) (as added: see note 25).

34 National Heritage Act 1980 s 4(2B)(b) (as added: see note 25).

35 Ie under the National Heritage Act 1980 s 4: see the text to notes 25–34.

36 As to the Secretary of State see PARA 802 note 2.

37 National Heritage Act 1980 s 4(3) (amended by SI 1992/1311).

816. Property, finance and information in relation to the National Heritage Memorial Fund. The Secretary of State[1] must pay into the National Heritage Memorial Fund[2] in the first month of each financial year[3] a sum determined by him before the beginning of the year; and he may at any time pay into the fund such further sums as he may from time to time determine[4]. There must also be paid into the fund any other sums received by the trustees in consequence of the discharge of their functions[5] or which they receive under the National Lottery[6].

The trustees of the fund may accept gifts[7] of money or other property[8] if it is either unconditional or on conditions which enable it, and any income or proceeds of sale arising from it, to be applied for a purpose for which the fund may[9] be applied[10]. The trustees must not retain any property, other than money, accepted by way of gift except in such cases and for such period as the Secretary of State may allow[11].

Any sums in the fund not immediately required for any other purpose may be invested by the trustees subject to the following conditions[12]. Sums directly or indirectly representing money paid into the fund[13] may be invested in any manner approved by the Treasury[14]. The trustees must not invest any amount available for investment which represents such money except with the consent of the Treasury[15]; and must, if required by the Treasury, invest any such amount specified by the Treasury in such manner as it directs[16].

As soon as practicable after the end of each financial year the trustees must make a report on their activities for that year to the Secretary of State who must publish the report and lay copies of it before Parliament[17].

The trustees must keep proper accounts and proper records in relation to them[18]. In respect of each financial year, they must prepare a statement of account in such form as the Secretary of State may direct with Treasury approval[19], and they must send copies of the statement to the Secretary of State and the Comptroller and Auditor General[20] before the end of the following November[21]. The Comptroller and Auditor General must examine, certify and report on each statement and lay copies of it and of his report before Parliament[22].

1   As to the Secretary of State see PARA 802 note 2.
2   As to the National Heritage Memorial Fund see PARA 814.
3   'Financial year' means the 12 months ending with 31 March: National Heritage Act 1980 s 18(2).
4   National Heritage Act 1980 s 2(1) (amended by SI 1981/207; SI 1992/1311).
5   National Heritage Act 1980 s 2(2). As to the trustees see PARA 814; and as to their functions see PARAS 814–815.
6   The trustees must pay into the fund any sums paid to them under the National Lottery etc Act 1993 s 24 (see LICENSING AND GAMBLING vol 68 (2008) PARA 721): National Heritage Act 1980 s 2(1A) (added by the National Lottery etc Act 1993 s 36, Sch 4 para 2). The trustees are a distributing body for the purposes of the National Lottery Distribution Fund: see the National Lottery etc Act 1993 s 23(3); and LICENSING AND GAMBLING vol 68 (2008) PARA 721.
7   'Gifts' includes bequests and devises: National Heritage Act 1980 s 5(4).
8   National Heritage Act 1980 s 5(1). As to property accepted in satisfaction of tax see PARA 1112. As to relief from rates see s 1(4), Sch 1 para 2 (amended by the Rating (Empty Properties) Act 2007 s 2(1), Sch 1 para 7; and SI 1990/776).
9   Ie under the National Heritage Act 1980 Pt I (ss 1–7) (see PARA 815).
10 National Heritage Act 1980 s 5(2). The conditions must also enable the trustees to comply with s 5(3) (see the text to note 11) and s 2(2) (see the text to note 5): s 5(2).
11 National Heritage Act 1980 s 5(3) (amended by SI 1992/1311).
12 See the National Heritage Act 1980 s 6(1).
13 Ie under the National Heritage Act 1980 s 2(1) or s 2(1A) (see the text to notes 4, 6).
14 National Heritage Act 1980 s 6(2) (amended by the National Lottery etc Act 1993 Sch 4 para 5). As to the meaning of 'Treasury' see PARA 809 note 4. The trustees may invest any sums to which the National Heritage Act 1983 s 6(2) does not apply in any investments in which trustees may invest under the general power of investment in the Trustee Act 2000 s 3 (as restricted by s 4 and s 5 of that Act) (see TRUSTS AND POWERS vol 98 (2013) PARA 453 et seq): National Heritage Act 1980 s 6(3) (substituted by the Trustee Act 2000 s 40(1), Sch 2 Pt II para 39).
15 National Heritage Act 1980 s 6(2)(a).
16 National Heritage Act 1980 s 6(2)(b).
17 National Heritage Act 1980 s 7(1) (amended by SI 1992/1311). As to the laying of documents before Parliament see STATUTES AND LEGISLATIVE PROCESS vol 96 (2012) PARA 1052.
18 National Heritage Act 1980 s 7(2)(a).
19 National Heritage Act 1980 s 7(2)(b) (amended by SI 1992/1311).
20 As to the Comptroller and Auditor General see CONSTITUTIONAL AND ADMINISTRATIVE LAW vol 20 (2014) PARAS 494–496.
21 National Heritage Act 1980 s 7(2)(c) (amended by SI 1992/1311).
22 National Heritage Act 1980 s 7(3).

(7) MUSEUMS AND GALLERIES

(i) Transfers and Loans

817. Transfer of objects or related documents between museum and gallery institutions. Any specified body[1] may, by way of sale, gift or exchange, transfer an object[2] the property in which is vested in it and which is comprised in its collection, if the transfer is to any other specified body[3]. Where the property in an object has become vested in a body subject to a trust or condition, the power so conferred is exercisable in a manner inconsistent with the trust or condition if the person[4] who first imposed the trust or condition has, or his personal representatives[5] have, consented to the exercise of the power in that manner[6].

Where a body in whom an object has become vested subject to a trust or condition transfers the object to another body under these provisions, the object must be held by that other body subject to the same trust or condition[7].

The powers so conferred on a body are in addition to any other powers of transfer which that body may have[8].

1 The specified bodies are: the Board of Trustees of the Armouries; the British Library Board; the trustees of the British Museum; the trustees of the Imperial War Museum; the Board of Governors of the Museum of London; the Board of Trustees of the National Gallery; the Board of Trustees of the National Galleries of Scotland; the National Library of Scotland; the trustees of the National Maritime Museum; the Board of Trustees of the National Museums and Galleries on Merseyside; the Board of Trustees of the National Museums of Scotland; the Board of Trustees of the National Portrait Gallery; the trustees of the Natural History Museum; the Board of Trustees of the Science Museum; the Board of Trustees of the Tate Gallery; the Board of Trustees of the Victoria and Albert Museum; the Historic Buildings and Monuments Commission for England ('the Commission'): Museums and Galleries Act 1992 Sch 5 Pt I (amended by the National Library of Scotland Act 2012 Sch 2 para 3(a); and SI 2000/2955). The Secretary of State may by order amend the Museums and Galleries Act 1992 Sch 5 by adding any body in the United Kingdom to those for the time being specified therein: s 6(6) (amended by SI 1992/1311). The functions of the Secretary of State under the Museums and Galleries Act 1992 s 6(6) are transferred to the Welsh Ministers so far as they relate to the Court of Governors of the National Library of Wales and the Council of the National Museum of Wales: see the National Assembly for Wales (Transfer of Functions) Order 1999, SI 1999/672, art 2, Sch 1; and the Government of Wales Act 2006 Sch 11 para 30. The power of the Secretary of State to make an order under the Museums and Galleries Act 1992 s 6(6) may, for the purpose of the application of s 6 to transfers of objects by bodies in Scotland, be exercised separately: s 6(8) (added by SI 1999/1756). As to the Secretary of State and the Welsh Ministers see PARA 802. As to the meaning of 'United Kingdom' see PARA 804 note 2. As to the Board of Trustees of the Armouries see PARA 873. As to the British Library and the National Library of Wales see PARA 902. As to the British Museum and the Natural History Museum see PARA 822 et seq. As to the Imperial War Museum see PARA 841. As to the Museum of London see PARA 854. As to the National Gallery, the National Portrait Gallery and the Tate Gallery see PARA 832 et seq. As to the trustees of the National Maritime Museum see PARA 847. As to the Board of Trustees of the Science Museum see PARA 867. As to the Board of Trustees of the Victoria and Albert Museum see PARA 861. As to the Commission see PARA 803 et seq. As to the National Museum of Wales see PARA 889.
2 These provisions apply in relation to a document as they apply in relation to an object other than a document: Museums and Galleries Act 1992 s 6(2).
3 Museums and Galleries Act 1992 s 6(1).
4 As to the meaning of 'person' see PARA 803 note 17.
5 As to personal representatives see WILLS AND INTESTACY vol 103 (2010) PARA 605 et seq.
6 Museums and Galleries Act 1992 s 6(3).
7 Museums and Galleries Act 1992 s 6(4).
8 Museums and Galleries Act 1992 s 6(5).

818. Gifts of works of art to the nation. In any case where a work of art is given for the benefit of the public or the nation[1], and the donor has made no provision as to the person[2] responsible for its care[3], it will vest in such specified bodies[4] as the Secretary of State may direct[5]. If, however, the body in whom a gift by will would otherwise so vest determines that the work of art is not fit to be part of its collection, the work of art, unless otherwise disposed of by the testator, becomes part of his residuary estate[6].

1 Museums and Galleries Act 1992 s 7(1)(a).
2 As to the meaning of 'person' see PARA 803 note 17.
3 Museums and Galleries Act 1992 s 7(1)(b).
4 The bodies concerned are those specified in the Museums and Galleries Act 1992 Sch 5: see s 7(1). As to the bodies specified in Sch 5 Pt I see PARA 817 note 1. For these purposes only, the following additional bodies are specified: the Court of Governors of the National Library of Wales;

the Council of the National Museum of Wales; the trustees of the Ulster Museum; the trustees of the Ulster Folk and Transport Museum; the Board of Trustees of the National Museums and Galleries of Northern Ireland; Historic Royal Palaces; and the National Trust for Places of Historic Interest or Natural Beauty: Sch 5 Pt II (amended by SI 1998/613; SI 2000/2955). As to the National Trust see PARA 973. As to the power of the Secretary of State by order to amend the Museums and Galleries Act 1992 Sch 5 see s 6(6)–(8); and PARA 817 note 1. As to the Secretary of State see PARA 802 note 2.

5   Museums and Galleries Act 1992 s 7(1) (amended by SI 1992/1311). Such gifts are exempt from inheritance tax: see the Inheritance Tax Act 1984 s 25, Sch 3; and INHERITANCE TAXATION vol 59A (2014) PARA 137.
6   Museums and Galleries Act 1992 s 7(2).

819. Transfers of land occupied by specified museums or galleries. Where any land[1] occupied wholly or partly for the purposes of any specified institution[2] is vested in the Secretary of State[3], he may, notwithstanding any prohibition or restriction to the contrary, transfer the land to the body specified[4] in relation to that institution[5]. Stamp duty will not be chargeable on any instrument certified to the Commissioners for Her Majesty's Revenue and Customs[6] by the Secretary of State as having been made or executed for the purpose of giving effect to a transfer by him of land occupied wholly or partly for the purposes of any such specified institution to the body specified in relation to that institution[7].

1   As to the meaning of 'land' see PARA 804 note 30.
2   Ie an institution specified in the Museums and Galleries Act 1992 Sch 6 col 1: see s 8(1); and note 4.
3   As to the Secretary of State see PARA 802 note 2.
4   Ie a body specified in the Museums and Galleries Act 1992 Sch 6 col 2: s 8(1). The specified institutions and the bodies specified in relation to them are:
    (1)   the British Library and the British Library Board;
    (2)   the British Museum and the trustees of the British Museum;
    (3)   the Imperial War Museum and the trustees of the Imperial War Museum;
    (4)   the National Gallery and the Board of Trustees of the National Gallery;
    (5)   the National Galleries of Scotland and the Board of Trustees of the National Galleries of Scotland;
    (6)   the National Library of Scotland and the National Library of Scotland;
    (7)   the National Maritime Museum and the trustees of the National Maritime Museum;
    (8)   the National Museums of Scotland and the Board of Trustees of the National Museums of Scotland;
    (9)   the National Portrait Gallery and the Board of Trustees of the National Portrait Gallery;
    (10)   the Natural History Museum and the trustees of the Natural History Museum;
    (11)   the Science Museum and the Board of Trustees of the Science Museum;
    (12)   the Tate Gallery and the Board of Trustees of the Tate Gallery;
    (13)   the Victoria and Albert Museum and the Board of Trustees of the Victoria and Albert Museum; and
    (14)   the Wallace Collection and the Board of Trustees of the Wallace Collection: Sch 6 (amended by the National Library of Scotland Act 2012 Sch 2 para 3(b)).
    As to the British Library see PARA 902. As to the British Museum and the Natural History Museum see PARA 822 et seq. As to the Imperial War Museum see PARA 841. As to the National Gallery, the National Portrait Gallery, the Tate Gallery and the Wallace Collection see PARA 832 et seq. As to the National Maritime Museum see PARA 847. As to the Science Museum see PARA 867. As to the Victoria and Albert Museum see PARA 861.
5   Museums and Galleries Act 1992 s 8(1).
6   As to the Commissioners for Her Majesty's Revenue and Customs see INCOME TAXATION vol 58 (2014) PARAS 33–34.
7   Museums and Galleries Act 1992 s 8(2) (amended by virtue of the Commissioners for Revenue and Customs Act 2005 s 50). An instrument such as is mentioned in the Museums and Galleries Act 1992 s 8(2) is not duly stamped unless (1) it has, in accordance with the provisions of the Stamp Act 1891 s 12, been stamped with a particular stamp denoting that it is not chargeable with any duty or that it has been duly stamped (Museums and Galleries Act 1992 s 8(3)(a)); or (2) it has been stamped with the duty to which it would otherwise be liable (see s 8(3)(b)). See further STAMP TAXES.

(ii) Human Remains in Museums

820. Care of human remains in specified museums and galleries. The specified bodies[1] may transfer from their collection any human remains which they reasonably believe to be remains of a person who died less than 1000 years before 3 October 2005[2] if it appears to them to be appropriate to do so for any reason, whether or not relating to their other functions[3]. If, in relation to any human remains in their collection, it appears to such a body that the human remains are mixed or bound up with something other than human remains[4], and that it is undesirable, or impracticable, to separate them[5], this power includes power to transfer the thing with which the human remains are mixed or bound up[6].

The government has issued non-statutory guidance for the care of human remains in museums which is intended to provide guidance, and to set out best practice, on the care of human remains for all museums and not just the specified bodies[7].

1 The specified bodies are: the Board of Trustees of the Armouries; the trustees of the British Museum; the trustees of the Imperial War Museum; the Board of Governors of the Museum of London; the trustees of the National Maritime Museum; the Board of Trustees of the National Museums and Galleries on Merseyside; the trustees of the Natural History Museum; the Board of Trustees of the Science Museum; and the Board of Trustees of the Victoria and Albert Museum: Human Tissue Act 2004 s 47(1). As to the Armouries see PARA 873. As to the British Museum and the Natural History Museum see PARA 822 et seq. As to the Imperial War Museum see PARA 841. As to the Museum of London see PARA 854. As to the National Maritime Museum see PARA 847. As to the Science Museum see PARA 867. As to the Victoria and Albert Museum see PARA 861.
2 Ie the day on which the Human Tissue Act 2004 s 47 came into force: see ss 47(2), 60(2); Human Tissue Act 2004 (Commencement No 2) Order 2005, SI 2005/2632, art 2.
3 Human Tissue Act 2004 s 47(2). The power conferred by s 47(2) does not affect any trust or condition subject to which a specified body holds anything in relation to which the power is exercisable: s 47(4). The power is an additional power: s 47(5).
4 Human Tissue Act 2004 s 47(3)(a).
5 Human Tissue Act 2004 s 47(3)(b).
6 Human Tissue Act 2004 s 47(3).
7 See *Guidance for the Care of Human Remains in Museum Collections*: Department for Culture, Media and Sport, 2005.

821. Public display of human remains. No person[1] may use, for the purpose of public display, the body of a deceased person or relevant material which has come from the body of a deceased person, otherwise than under the authority of a licence granted by the Human Tissue Authority for the purpose[2].

1 As to the meaning of 'person' see PARA 803 note 17.
2 See the Human Tissue Act 2004 s 16(1), (2)(f). This does not apply to the body of a person who died before 1 September 2006 or to material which has come from the body of such a person, and at least 100 years have elapsed since the date of the person's death: see s 16(4). See further MEDICAL PROFESSIONS vol 74 (2011) PARA 83 et seq. As to the Human Tissue Authority see MEDICAL PROFESSIONS vol 74 (2011) PARA 55 et seq.

(iii) Particular Museums and Galleries

A. THE BRITISH MUSEUM AND THE NATURAL HISTORY MUSEUM

822. The British Museum Act 1963. The British Museum Act 1963 repealed and replaced almost all the legislation relating to the British Museum[1]. It also provides for the separation of the Natural History Museum from the British Museum[2].

1 See the British Museum Act 1963 s 13(5), Sch 4 (repealed). The British Museum was established in 1753. The British Museum Act 1753 (repealed) incorporated the trustees of the British Museum,

vested the management of the museum in them, and authorised the purchase of the museum or collection of Sir Hans Sloane for £20,000 and the Harleian collection of manuscripts for £10,000. It further provided for the erection of a general repository for the reception of the collections mentioned above and all additions, and of the Cottonian Library, for preservation for public use. The necessary money was raised by lottery: see ss 22–49 (repealed). The Cottonian Library, consisting of manuscripts and other writings, was acquired by the nation, with a number of coins, medals and other rarities, from Sir Robert Cotton in 1700: see 12 & 13 Will 3 c 7 (British Museum) (1700) (repealed); and 6 Anne c 30 (British Museum) (1706) (repealed). Other special collections forming part of the British Museum include the Townley collection (see the British Museum Act 1805 (repealed)); the Elgin Marbles (see the British Museum Act 1816 (repealed)); the Payne Knight collection of coins etc (see the British Museum (No 2) Act 1824 (repealed)); the Rothschild Zoological Collection (see the British Museum Act 1938 (repealed)); and books, manuscripts etc presented by George II, George III and George IV. In 1755 Old Montagu House, Great Russell Street, Bloomsbury, subsequently known as the British Museum, was vested in the museum trustees for the purposes of a general repository by 28 Geo 2 c iii (Vesting of Montagu House in trustees of British Museum) (1755) (repealed); and see the British Museum Act 1753 ss 9, 21 (repealed). The acquisition of other land for the enlargement of the museum was authorised by the British Museum Act 1824 (repealed); the British Museum Act 1838 (repealed); and the British Museum (Purchase of Land) Act 1894 (largely repealed).

2 See the British Museum Act 1963 s 8; and PARA 823. As to the transfer of the British Museum Library see the British Library Act 1972 s 3; and PARA 903.

823. Separation of Natural History Museum. On 30 September 1963[1] the functions of the trustees of the British Museum[2] with respect to the Natural History Museum were transferred to the trustees of the Natural History Museum (known as the 'Natural History trustees') who now have the general management and control of that museum[3]. The Natural History trustees are a body corporate, with perpetual succession and a common seal[4].

On 30 September 1963 the following property vested in the Natural History trustees[5]: (1) the objects vested immediately before that date in the trustees of the British Museum and comprised in the collections of the British Museum (Natural History)[6]; and (2) the land and buildings at Tring referred to in the British Museum Act 1938[7]. Such of those objects as became vested in the trustees of the British Museum by virtue of a gift or bequest must be treated for the purposes of the British Museum Act 1963 as vested in the Natural History trustees by virtue of a like gift or bequest[8].

1 Ie the date of commencement of the British Museum Act 1963: see ss 8(1), 13(2); and the British Museum Act 1963 (Commencement) Order 1963, SI 1963/1546.

2 As to the trustees of the British Museum see PARA 824.

3 See the British Museum Act 1963 s 8(1) (amended by the Museums and Galleries Act 1992 Sch 8 para 1(1), (2), (3)(a)). The Natural History Museum consists of the collections of the British Museum departments of zoology, geology and palaeontology, mineralogy and botany which were moved to South Kensington (see the British Museum Act 1878 (repealed)) and the collection at Tring bequeathed by the second Lord Rothschild (see the British Museum Act 1938 (repealed)).

4 British Museum Act 1963 s 8(1) (as amended: see note 3). As to the appointment of the trustees see s 8(2) (amended by SI 1988/1836; and SI 1992/1311). The British Museum Act 1963 ss 2–7 (see PARAS 826–827, 829–830) and Sch 1 (see PARA 824) apply in relation to the Natural History Museum and the trustees thereof as they apply in relation to the British Museum and the trustees thereof, with adaptations: see s 8(3) (amended by the Museums and Galleries Act 1992 Sch 8 para 1(3)(a)).

5 See the British Museum Act 1963 Sch 2 para 1(1).

6 British Museum Act 1963 Sch 2 para 1(1)(a). See also note 3.

7 British Museum Act 1963 Sch 2 para 1(1)(b). The British Museum Act 1938 is repealed: see note 3.

8 British Museum Act 1963 Sch 2 para 1(2). Subject to the provisions of the British Museum Act 1963, all matters and things having effect in relation to the British Museum (Natural History) immediately before 30 September 1963 continue as nearly as may be to have effect in relation to the Natural History Museum thereafter: Sch 2 para 4 (amended by the Museums and Galleries Act 1992 Sch 8 para 1(2), (3)(b)).

824. Trustees of the British Museum. The trustees of the British Museum are a body corporate with perpetual succession and a common seal, having the general management and control of the British Museum[1]. They consist of 25 persons:

(1)   one appointed by Her Majesty[2];

(2)   15 appointed by the Prime Minister[3];

(3)   four appointed by the Secretary of State on the nominations of the Presidents of the Royal Society, the Royal Academy, the British Academy, and the Society of Antiquaries of London, respectively[4]; and

(4)   five appointed by the trustees of the British Museum[5].

The trustees' functions may be exercised notwithstanding vacancies in their number[6]. The trustees may make rules for regulating their proceedings and for other matters relevant to the exercise of their functions[7].

1   See the British Museum Act 1963 s 1(1).
2   British Museum Act 1963 s 1(1)(a).
3   British Museum Act 1963 s 1(1)(b). As to the Prime Minister see CONSTITUTIONAL AND ADMINISTRATIVE LAW vol 20 (2014) PARAS 203–208.
4   British Museum Act 1963 s 1(1)(c) (amended by SI 1992/1311). As to the Secretary of State see PARA 802 note 2.
5   British Museum Act 1963 s 1(1)(d). As to the tenure of office of the trustees see s 1(2), Sch 1 paras 1, 2.
6   British Museum Act 1963 Sch 1 para 3.
7   British Museum Act 1963 Sch 1 para 5. The quorum at the meetings of trustees is six: see Sch 1 para 4.

825. Director and staff of the British Museum and the Natural History Museum. There is a Director of the British Museum and a Director of the Natural History Museum, who must be persons appointed respectively by the trustees of the British Museum[1] and the Natural History trustees[2] with the approval of the Prime Minister[3], and who hold office on such terms and subject to such conditions as the Secretary of State[4] may direct[5]. They are responsible to the trustees for the care of all property in their possession and for the general administration of the museum[6].

Subject to the Secretary of State's consent as to numbers and conditions of service, the trustees may appoint such other officers and servants as they think fit; and there must be paid to the director and officers and servants so appointed such salaries, allowances and other remuneration as the Secretary of State may determine[7]. Museum staff may be included in a civil service pension scheme under the Superannuation Act 1972[8].

1   As to the trustees of the British Museum see PARA 824.
2   As to the meaning of 'Natural History trustees' see PARA 823.
3   As to the Prime Minister see CONSTITUTIONAL AND ADMINISTRATIVE LAW vol 20 (2014) PARAS 203–208.
4   As to the Secretary of State see PARA 802 note 2.
5   See the British Museum Act 1963 s 6(1) (s 6(1), (2) amended by SI 2011/1213), the British Museum Act 1963 s 8(3) (amended by the Museums and Galleries Act 1992 Sch 8 para 1(1), (2), (3)(a)).
6   See the British Museum Act 1963 ss 6(1), 8(3) (both as amended: see note 5).
7   See the British Museum Act 1963 ss 6(2), 8(3) (both as amended: see note 5).
8   See the Superannuation Act 1972 s 1(4), Sch 1; and PARA 893. See also *Tucker v British Museum Trustees* (1967) 112 Sol Jo 70, CA, where it was held under the British Museum Act 1753 s 15 (repealed), that an employee was not entitled to have the proceedings for his dismissal conducted judicially.

826. Powers of trustees of the British Museum and the Natural History trustees. The trustees of the British Museum[1] and the Natural History trustees[2] have power, subject to the restrictions imposed on them by virtue of any enactment[3], to enter into contracts and other agreements, to acquire and hold land and other property and to do all other things that appear to them necessary or expedient for the purposes of their functions[4].

At intervals of not more than three years, the trustees must prepare and lay before each House of Parliament a report on the museums[5].

Byelaws, ordinances, statutes or rules in force[6] immediately before 30 September 1963[7] are not invalidated by the repeal of their enabling provision but have effect in relation to each museum, with such modifications as may be necessary in consequence of the British Museum Act 1963, as if they were rules made[8] by the trustees of the relevant museum[9].

Notwithstanding anything in any enactment, the trustees of the British Museum and the Natural History trustees may make such charges for admission to their museums as they may determine[10].

There is a statutory obligation to deliver to the trustees of the British Museum free of charge a copy of the actual script[11] on which the public performance of a new play[12] is based[13], but in practice this obligation is satisfied by the delivery of such scripts to the British Library[14].

1　As to the trustees of the British Museum see PARA 824.
2　As to the meaning of 'Natural History trustees' see PARA 823.
3　Ie whether contained in the British Museum Act 1963 or not: see s 2. As to the meaning of 'enactment' see PARA 805 note 5. The Secretary of State may transfer land to the trustees: see the Museums and Galleries Act 1992 s 8, Sch 6; and PARA 819. As to the Secretary of State see PARA 802 note 2.
4　British Museum Act 1963 ss 2, 8(3) (amended by the Museums and Galleries Act 1992 Sch 8 para 1(1), (2), (3)(a)). Certain records of the British Museum and the Natural History Museum are public records for the purposes of the Public Records Act 1958: see s 10, Sch 1 para 3, Table Pt II; and CONSTITUTIONAL AND ADMINISTRATIVE LAW vol 20 (2014) PARA 343.
5　See the British Museum Act 1963 ss 7, 8(3) (as amended: see note 4). As to the laying of documents before Parliament see STATUTES AND LEGISLATIVE PROCESS vol 96 (2012) PARA 1052.
6　Ie under the British Museum Act 1753 s 14 or s 15 (repealed).
7　Ie the date of commencement of the British Museum Act 1963: see s 13(2), (6); and the British Museum Act 1963 (Commencement) Order 1963, SI 1963/1546.
8　Ie under the British Museum Act 1963 Sch 1 para 5 (see PARA 824).
9　British Museum Act 1963 s 13(6).
10　See the Museums and Galleries Admission Charges Act 1972 s 1 (amended by the Museums and Galleries Act 1992 Sch 8 para 1(1), (2), (6)).
11　'Script', in relation to a play, means the text of the play, whether expressed in words or in musical or other notation, together with any stage or other directions for its performance, whether contained in a single document or not: Theatres Act 1968 s 9(2).
12　'Public performance of a new play' means a public performance of a play of which no previous public performance has ever been given in Great Britain, but does not include a public performance of a play which is (1) based on a script substantially the same as that on which a previous public performance of a play given there was based; or (2) based substantially on a text of the play which has been published in the United Kingdom: Theatres Act 1968 s 11(3). A performance of a play given solely or primarily for one or more of the specified purposes is, however, to be disregarded: s 11(4). The specified purposes are: (a) rehearsal; (b) to enable (i) a record or cinematograph film to be made from or by means of the performance; or (ii) the performance to be broadcast; or (iii) the performance to be included in a programme service within the meaning of the Broadcasting Act 1990 (see BROADCASTING vol 4 (2011) PARA 507), other than a sound or television broadcasting service: Theatres Act 1968 s 7(2)(a), (b) (amended by the Broadcasting Act 1990 s 203(1), Sch 20 para 13; applied by the Theatres Act 1968 s 11(4)). 'Record' means any record or similar contrivance for reproducing sound, including the soundtrack of a cinematograph film; 'cinematograph film' means any print, negative, tape or other article on which a performance of a play or any part of such a performance is recorded for the purposes of visual reproduction; and 'broadcast' means broadcast by wireless telegraphy (within the meaning of the Wireless Telegraphy Act 2006: see BROADCASTING vol 4 (2011) PARA 510), whether by way of sound broadcasting or television: Theatres Act 1968 s 7(3) (definition amended the Wireless Telegraphy Act 2006 s 123, Sch 7 para 3; and as so applied). As to the meanings of 'Great Britain' and 'United Kingdom' see PARA 804 note 2.

13 Theatres Act 1968 s 11(1). The copy must be delivered within one month from the date of the performance and the trustees must give a written receipt for every script so delivered to them: see s 11(1). If these requirements are not complied with in the case of any performance to which they apply, any person who presented that performance is liable on summary conviction to a fine not exceeding level 1 on the standard scale: s 11(2) (amended by virtue of the Criminal Justice Act 1982 ss 38, 46). As to the meaning of 'month' see PARA 803 note 12. As to the meaning of 'written' see PARA 805 note 14. As to the standard scale and magistrates' powers to levy unlimited fines see SENTENCING vol 92 (2015) PARA 176.

14 As to the British Library see PARA 902 et seq.

827. Keeping of the collections by trustees. Subject to the provisions of the British Museum Act 1963, it is the duty of the trustees of the British Museum[1] and of the Natural History trustees[2] to keep the objects comprised in the collections of the British Museum and the Natural History Museum within the authorised repositories of the museums[3], except in so far as they may consider it expedient to remove them temporarily for any purpose connected with the administration of the museums and the care of their collections[4]. When it appears to the trustees that any such objects cannot conveniently be kept within the authorised repositories, they may store them at other premises in Great Britain[5] if satisfied that they can be stored in those premises without detriment to the museums' purposes[6].

The trustees must secure, so far as appears to them to be practicable, that the objects comprised in the collections of each museum, including those stored under these provisions, are, when required for inspection by members of the public, made available in one or other of the authorised repositories under such conditions as the trustees think fit to impose for preserving the collections' safety and ensuring the museums' proper administration[7]. Objects vested in the trustees as part of the museums' collections must not be disposed of by them otherwise than under the statutory provisions[8] authorising disposal and transfer[9].

1   As to the trustees of the British Museum see PARA 824.
2   As to the meaning of 'Natural History trustees' see PARA 823.
3   As to the authorised repositories see the British Museum Act 1963 s 10; and PARA 828.
4   British Museum Act 1963 ss 3(1), 8(3) (amended by the Museums and Galleries Act 1992 Sch 8 para 1(2), (2), (3)(a)).
5   As to the meaning of 'Great Britain' see PARA 804 note 2.
6   British Museum Act 1963 ss 3(2), 8(3) (as amended: see note 4).
7   British Museum Act 1963 ss 3(3), 8(3) (as amended: see note 4).
8   Ie the British Museum Act 1963 s 5 (see PARA 830) or s 9 (see PARA 831) or the Museums and Galleries Act 1992 s 6 (see PARA 817). As to the transfer of the British Museum Library see the British Library Act 1972 s 3; and PARA 903. As to lending objects for exhibition see PARA 829.
9   British Museum Act 1963 s 3(4), s 8(3) (s 3(4) amended by the Museums and Galleries Act 1992 Sch 8 para 5(a); British Museum Act 1963 s 8(3) as amended (see note 4)). In *A-G v Trustees of the British Museum (Commission for Looted Art in Europe intervening)* [2005] EWHC 1089 (Ch), [2005] Ch 397, (2005) Times, 2 June, [2005] All ER (D) 463 (May) (concerning a claim by the heirs of the owner of paintings looted by the Nazis) the following points were decided: (1) no moral obligation can justify a disposition by the trustees of an object forming part of the collection of the museum in breach of the British Museum Act 1963 s 3(4); some statutory authority is required; (2) the existence of the express exceptions in s 3(4) negatives the recognition of further but implied exceptions; (3) the word 'disposition' in s 3(4) is not limited to acts but may include omissions as well; (4) the bona fide compromise of a claim by persons to be entitled to objects forming part of the museum's collection may not involve any breach of s 3(4) if it involves a recognition that the objects have never been part of the collection, as s 3(4) applies only to objects which are part of the collection. As to Nazi spoliation and the Spoliation Advisory Panel see PARA 1106. See also the Holocaust (Return of Cultural Objects) Act 2009; and PARA 1107.

828. Authorised repositories for the collections of the British Museum and the Natural History Museum. The buildings for the time being occupying certain sites in London are the authorised repositories[1] for the collections of the British

Museum[2], and the buildings for the time being occupying certain sites in London and in Tring, Hertfordshire are the authorised repositories for the collections of the Natural History Museum[3].

A building or a site vested in the trustees of either museum, being an authorised repository or the site of an authorised repository, must not be sold or otherwise disposed of by them[4].

1 It is the duty of the trustees of the museums to keep the collections of the museums at the authorised repositories: see the British Museum Act 1963 s 3; and PARA 827.

2 See the British Museum Act 1963 s 10(1). The specified sites are: (1) the British Museum, Great Russell Street, London; (2) 6 Burlington Gardens, London W1; (3) 38–56 Orsman Road, London N1 (even numbers only); (4) the former Office Savings Bank Building, Blythe Road, London W14; and (5) 23 Blythe Road, London W14: see Sch 3 Pt I (amended by SI 1973/1126; SI 1984/1181; and SI 1995/1224). The Secretary of State may, with the agreement of the trustees concerned, by order amend the British Museum Act 1963 Sch 3 by adding a reference to a further site, or deleting the reference to the whole or any part of a site, or altering the description of a site; and any such order must be made by statutory instrument subject to annulment in pursuance of a resolution of either House of Parliament: s 10(2) (amended by SI 1988/1836; and SI 1992/1311). The orders made are referred to in the references to the British Museum Act 1963 Sch 3 Pt I above and Pt II in note 3. As to the Secretary of State see PARA 802 note 2. As to the trustees of the British Museum see PARA 824. As to the trustees of the Natural History Museum see PARA 823. As to the annulment of statutory instruments see STATUTES AND LEGISLATIVE PROCESS vol 96 (2012) PARA 1049.

3 See the British Museum Act 1963 s 10(1) (amended by the Museums and Galleries Act 1992 Sch 8 para 1(1), (2), (3)(a)). The specified sites are:

    (1)   the Natural History Museum, South Kensington, London but excluding the part of that site known as the 'Central Boiler House';

    (2)   the site in Tring lying to the east of Akeman Street and occupied by the museum on 30 September 1963 but excluding:

        (a)   the part of that site known as the 'Boiler Room' and located on the ground floor of the Rothschild Building at that site;

        (b)   the part of that site known as the 'Roof Plant Area' and located on the roof of the Ornithology building of that site;

    (3)   the site in Tring lying to the west of Akeman Street known as 67–69 Akeman Street; and

    (4)   the site in Wandsworth known as 75 Kimber Road, London SW18 4NX excluding:

        (a)   the part of that site known as the 'Boiler Room' and located on the ground floor of that site;

        (b)   the part of that site known as the 'Plant Area' and located on the ground floor of that site;

        (c)   the part of that site known as the 'Chiller Compound Area' and located on the roof of that site;

        (d)   the site known as 249–251 Merton Road, London SW18 5EB: see the British Museum Act 1963 Sch 3 Pt II (amended by SI 1982/1238; SI 1985/462; SI 1995/654; SI 2004/1392; SI 2006/1547; and SI 2011/1682).

As to the power of the Secretary of State to amend the British Museum Act 1963 Sch 3 see note 2.

4 British Museum Act 1963 s 10(3).

829. Lending of objects from the British Museum and the Natural History Museum. The trustees of the British Museum[1] and the Natural History trustees[2] may lend for public exhibition or, in the case of the Natural History trustees, for research, in the United Kingdom[3] or elsewhere, any object comprised in the museums' collections[4]. In deciding whether or not to lend any such object, and in determining the time for which, and the conditions subject to which, any such object is to be lent, the trustees must have regard to the interests of students and other persons visiting the museums, to the physical condition and degree of rarity of the object in question and to any risks to which it is likely to be exposed[5].

1 As to the trustees of the British Museum see PARA 824.
2 As to the meaning of 'Natural History trustees' see PARA 823.
3 As to the meaning of 'United Kingdom' see PARA 804 note 2.

4   British Museum Act 1963 ss 4, 8(3)(a) (s 8(3) amended by the Museums and Galleries Act 1992 Sch 8 para 1(1), (2), (3)(a)).
5   British Museum Act 1963 ss 4 proviso, 8(3) (as amended: see note 4). As to the government indemnity scheme in respect of objects on loan see PARA 1094. As to overseas loans see PARAS 1095, 1096.

830. Disposal of objects by trustees. The trustees of the British Museum[1] and the Natural History trustees[2] may sell, exchange, give away or otherwise dispose of any object vested in them and comprised in their collections[3] if: (1) the object is a duplicate of another such object[4]; (2) the object appears to them to have been made not earlier than the year 1850, and substantially consists of printed matter of which a copy made by photography or a process akin to photography is held by them[5]; or (3) in their opinion the object is unfit to be retained in the collections of the museum concerned and can be disposed of without detriment to the interests of students[6]. However, where an object has become vested in the trustees by virtue of a gift or bequest these powers of disposal are not exercisable as respects that object in a manner inconsistent with any condition attached to the gift or bequest[7].

The trustees may destroy or otherwise dispose of any object vested in them and comprised in their collections if satisfied that it has become useless for the purposes of their respective museums by reason of damage, physical deterioration, or infestation by destructive organisms[8].

Money accruing to the trustees by virtue of an exercise of these powers or of their powers to transfer objects to certain other institutions[9] must be laid out by them in the purchase of objects to be added to the museums' collections[10].

In certain circumstances the trustees may also transfer an object from their collections under the Holocaust (Return of Cultural Objects) Act 2009[11].

1   As to the trustees of the British Museum see PARA 824.
2   As to the meaning of 'Natural History trustees' see PARA 823.
3   As to the general prohibition on the disposal of objects in the museums' collections see the British Museum Act 1963 s 3; and PARA 827.
4   British Museum Act 1963 ss 5(1)(a), 8(3) (amended by the Museums and Galleries Act 1992 Sch 8 para 1(1), (2), (3)(a)).
5   British Museum Act 1963 ss 5(1)(b), 8(3) (as amended: see note 4).
6   British Museum Act 1963 ss 5(1)(c), 8(3) (as amended: see note 4).
7   British Museum Act 1963 ss 5(1) proviso, 8(3) (as amended: see note 4).
8   British Museum Act 1963 ss 5(2), 8(3) (as amended: see note 4).
9   Ie the powers contained in the Museums and Galleries Act 1992 s 6 (see PARA 817).
10 British Museum Act 1963 ss 5(3), 8(3) (s 5(3) amended by the Museums and Galleries Act 1992 Sch 8 para 5(b); British Museum Act 1963 s 8(3) as amended (see note 4)).
11 See PARA 1107.

831. Transfers of moveable property to other institutions. Any moveable property vested in the trustees of the British Museum[1] or the Natural History trustees[2] may be transferred by one to the other[3]. The trustees are specified transferors and transferees for the purposes of the general powers of transfer between collections[4] and for the purposes of the statutory provision for vesting of gifts to the nation where the donor has not specified a destination[5].

1   As to the trustees of the British Museum see PARA 824.
2   As to the meaning of 'Natural History trustees' see PARA 823.
3   See the British Museum Act 1963 s 9(1) (amended by the Museums and Galleries Act 1992 Sch 9). As to the general prohibition on the disposal of objects in the museums' collections see the British Museum Act 1963 s 3; and PARA 827.
4   See the Museums and Galleries Act 1992 s 6, Sch 5; and PARA 817.
5   See the Museums and Galleries Act 1992 s 7; and PARA 818.

B.   THE NATIONAL GALLERY, THE NATIONAL PORTRAIT GALLERY, THE TATE GALLERY AND
·THE WALLACE COLLECTION

832.   Establishment of the National Gallery, the National Portrait Gallery, the Tate Gallery and the Wallace Collection. The National Gallery was established in 1824[1] and the National Portrait Gallery was established in 1856[2].

The Tate Gallery was opened in 1897 as a result of private benefaction[3], and was originally operated as a branch of the National Gallery. It subsequently acquired its own trustees, but its contents remained vested in the National Gallery Trustees[4]. However, on 14 February 1955 the responsibility for the collection at the Tate Gallery passed from the National Gallery Trustees to the Tate Gallery Trustees[5] and the pictures and other works of art which on that day formed part of the collection vested in them[6]. The Tate Gallery collection is intended to be a national collection of British paintings, modern foreign art and modern sculpture[7].

Dame Amelie Julie Charlotte Wallace, the widow of Sir Richard Wallace, by her will dated 23 May 1894[8], bequeathed to the British nation her pictures, porcelain, bronzes, artistic furniture, armour, miniatures, snuffboxes and works of art placed on the ground and first floors and in the galleries of Hertford House, Manchester Square, and the Louis XIV balustrade at Hertford House, on condition that the government for the time being should agree to give a site in a central part of London and build on it a special museum to contain the collection, which should be always kept together unmixed with other objects of art, and should be styled 'The Wallace Collection'. The Treasury accepted the bequest on behalf of the nation and subsequently acquired Hertford House for the purpose of housing and maintaining the collection in it. It was agreed between the Treasury and the residuary legatee under the will that the collection should remain at Hertford House and that no other site should be given or acquired or building erected for the purpose of containing it. The residuary legatee waived any claim he might otherwise have had or have been entitled to raise to the collection as forming part of the residuary estate by reason or on account of the non-fulfilment of the condition to build a special museum. The first trustees were appointed by the Treasury by Treasury Minute dated 28 July 1897[9].

The National Gallery Act 1856 and the National Gallery and Tate Gallery Act 1954, which formerly regulated most of the activities of the National Gallery and the Tate Gallery, were repealed in 1992[10]. The Museums and Galleries Act 1992 now provides for the establishment of incorporated Boards of Trustees of the National Gallery, Tate Gallery, National Portrait Gallery and Wallace Collection, the transfer of property to them and the conferring of functions on them[11].

1   See Treasury Minute, 24 March 1824.
2   See Treasury Minute, 2 December 1856.
3   The cost of erecting the gallery and the nucleus of the present collection were donated by Sir Henry Tate.
4   Under the terms of a Treasury letter of 24 March 1917, a separate board for the Tate Gallery was constituted.
5   See the National Gallery and Tate Gallery Act 1954 ss 1(1), 8(3) (repealed); the National Gallery and Tate Gallery Act 1954 (Commencement) Order 1955, SI 1955/230 (spent).
6   National Gallery and Tate Gallery Act 1954 s 1(2) (repealed).
7   Treasury Minute, 5 February 1955.
8   See the trust deed of 27 July 1899.
9   See the trust deed of 27 July 1899.
10 Museums and Galleries Act 1992 Sch 9.
11 See the Museums and Galleries Act 1992 s 11(4); the Museum and Galleries Act 1992 (Commencement) Order 1992, SI 1992/1874; and PARA 833 et seq. As to transfers to and from

certain specified institutions see PARA 817. As to financial provision see PARA 892. As to the government indemnity scheme for loans see PARA 1094.

833. Establishment of Boards of Trustees for the National Gallery, the Tate Gallery, the National Portrait Gallery and the Wallace Collection. Bodies corporate[1] known as: (1) the Board of Trustees of the National Gallery (the 'National Gallery Board')[2]; (2) the Board of Trustees of the Tate Gallery (the 'Tate Gallery Board')[3]; (3) the Board of Trustees of the National Portrait Gallery (the 'National Portrait Gallery Board')[4]; and (4) the Board of Trustees of the Wallace Collection (the 'Wallace Collection Board')[5] have been established[6]. On 1 September 1992[7] all the property and rights which immediately before that day were held by any of the new boards' predecessor trustees[8] in their capacity as such, and any liabilities or obligations to which, immediately before that day, any of those trustees were subject in that capacity, were transferred to and vested in the relevant new board[9].

The new boards are not to be regarded as the servants or agents of the Crown or as enjoying any status, immunity or privilege of the Crown[10]; nor are the trustees and their staff to be regarded as civil servants[11]. The new boards' property is not to be regarded as property of, or held on behalf of, the Crown[12].

The validity of any proceedings of each new board is not affected by any vacancy among the trustees or by any defect in the appointment of any trustee[13]. The fixing of the seal of each new board must be authenticated by the signature of the chairman or of some other person authorised either generally or specially by the board to act for that purpose[14]. A document purporting to be duly executed under the seal of a new board, or to be signed on that board's behalf, is receivable in evidence and, unless the contrary is proved, is deemed to be so executed or signed[15].

1   As to bodies corporate see COMPANIES vol 14 (2009) PARA 2; CORPORATIONS vol 24 (2010) PARA 301 et seq.
2   Museums and Galleries Act 1992 s 1(1)(a). As to the constitution of the board and staff see s 1(2)(a), Sch 1 paras 2, 3 (amended by SI 1992/1311). As to the proceedings of the board see the Museums and Galleries Act 1992 Sch 1 para 4. As to the payment of allowances see Sch 1 para 5 (amended by SI 1992/1311).
3   Museums and Galleries Act 1992 s 1(1)(b). As to the constitution of the board and staff see s 1(2)(b), Sch 2 paras 2, 3 (amended by SI 1992/1311; SI 2008/919). As to the proceedings of the board see the Museums and Galleries Act 1992 Sch 2 para 4. As to the payment of allowances see Sch 2 para 5 (amended by SI 1992/1311).
4   Museums and Galleries Act 1992 s 1(1)(c). As to the constitution of the board see Sch 3 para 2 (amended by SI 1992/1311). As to the proceedings of the board see the Museums and Galleries Act 1992 Sch 3 para 4. As to the payment of allowances see Sch 3 para 5 (amended by SI 1992/1311).
5   Museums and Galleries Act 1992 s 1(1)(d). As to the constitution of the board and staff see s 1(2)(d), Sch 4 paras 2, 3 (amended by SI 1992/1311). As to the proceedings of the board see the Museums and Galleries Act 1992 Sch 4 para 4. As to the payment of allowances see Sch 4 para 5 (amended by SI 1992/1311).
6   Museums and Galleries Act 1992 s 1(1). Any reference in the Museums and Galleries Act 1992 to a 'new board' is a reference to any of these boards: see s 1(1). Each of the new boards, so far as it is a charity, and any institution which is administered by or on its behalf and established for general or special purposes, is an exempt charity for the purposes of the Charities Act 2011: see s 22, Sch 3 paras 19–22; and CHARITIES vol 8 (2015) PARA 318.
7   Ie the vesting day for each new board: see the Museums and Galleries Act 1992 ss 1(10), 11(4); and the Museums and Galleries Act 1992 (Commencement) Order 1992, SI 1992/1874.
8   'Predecessor trustees' means (1) in relation to the National Gallery Board, the National Gallery Trustees; (2) in relation to the Tate Gallery Board, the Tate Gallery Trustees; (3) in relation to the National Portrait Gallery Board, the National Portrait Gallery Trustees; and (4) in relation to the Wallace Collection Board, the Trustees of the Wallace Collection: Museums and Galleries Act 1992 s 1(10).
9   See the Museums and Galleries Act 1992 s 1(3). References in s 1(3) to property, rights, liabilities and obligations are references to any property, rights, liabilities or obligations whether or not

capable of being transferred or assigned: s 1(4). For further provision as to the transfer of property, rights, liabilities and obligations to the new boards see s 1(5)–(9) (s 1(7) amended by the Employment Rights Act 1996 Sch 1 para 55).

10 Museums and Galleries Act 1992 Sch 1 para 1(1), Sch 2 para 1(1), Sch 3 para 1(1), Sch 4 para 1(1). However, in relation to any matter as respects which the new board acts by virtue of a direction under s 2(7) (see PARA 835), the board enjoys the same privileges, immunities and exemptions as those enjoyed in relation to that matter by the minister giving the direction: Sch 1 para 1(3), Sch 2 para 1(3), Sch 3 para 1(3), Sch 4 para 1(3). As to the legal status of bodies not to be regarded as the servant or agent of the Crown or as enjoying any status, immunity or privilege of the Crown see CONSTITUTIONAL AND ADMINISTRATIVE LAW vol 20 (2014) PARA 311 et seq.

11 Museums and Galleries Act 1992 Sch 1 para 1(2), Sch 2 para 1(2), Sch 3 para 1(3), Sch 4 para 1(2). As to staff pensions, however, see PARA 893. As to the civil service see CONSTITUTIONAL AND ADMINISTRATIVE LAW vol 20 (2014) PARA 285 et seq.

12 Museums and Galleries Act 1992 Sch 1 para 1(2), Sch 2 para 1(2), Sch 3 para 1(3), Sch 4 para 1(2).

13 See the Museums and Galleries Act 1992 Sch 1 para 4(8), Sch 2 para 4(8), Sch 3 para 4(8), Sch 4 para 4(8).

14 See the Museums and Galleries Act 1992 Sch 1 para 6(1), Sch 2 para 6(1), Sch 3 para 6(1), Sch 4 para 6(1). As to the corporate seal see CORPORATIONS vol 24 (2010) PARA 323 et seq.

15 See the Museums and Galleries Act 1992 Sch 1 para 6(2), Sch 2 para 6(2), Sch 3 para 6(2), Sch 4 para 6(2). Certain records of each of the National Gallery, Tate Gallery, National Portrait Gallery and the Wallace Collection are public records for the purposes of the Public Records Act 1958: see s 10, Sch 1 para 3, Table Pt II; and CONSTITUTIONAL AND ADMINISTRATIVE LAW vol 20 (2014) PARA 343.

834. Directors and staff appointed by new board. There is a director of the National Gallery, a director of the Tate Gallery, a director of the National Portrait Gallery and a director of the Wallace Collection, each appointed by the relevant new board[1] with the approval of the Prime Minister[2]. Each director is responsible to the relevant board for the general exercise of that board's functions[3].

Each new board may appoint such other employees as it thinks fit[4]. Subject to such conditions as the Secretary of State[5] may impose with the consent of the Treasury[6], each new board must pay to its employees such remuneration and allowances as the board may determine[7], and the employees are appointed on such other terms and conditions as the board may determine[8].

1 As to the meaning of 'new board' see PARA 833 note 6.
2 See the Museums and Galleries Act 1992 Sch 1 para 3(1), Sch 2 para 3(1), Sch 3 para 3(1), Sch 4 para 3(1). For transitional provisions relating to the appointment of the directors see Sch 1 para 3(5), Sch 2 para 3(5), Sch 3 para 3(5), Sch 4 para 3(5). As to the Prime Minister see CONSTITUTIONAL AND ADMINISTRATIVE LAW vol 20 (2014) PARAS 203–208.
3 See the Museums and Galleries Act 1992 Sch 1 para 3(2), Sch 2 para 3(2), Sch 3 para 3(2), Sch 4 para 3(2). As to the general functions of the boards see PARA 835.
4 See the Museums and Galleries Act 1992 Sch 1 para 3(3), Sch 2 para 3(3), Sch 3 para 3(3), Sch 4 para 3(3).
5 As to the Secretary of State see PARA 802 note 2.
6 As to the meaning of 'Treasury' see PARA 809 note 4.
7 See the Museums and Galleries Act 1992 Sch 1 para 3(4)(a), Sch 2 para 3(4)(a), Sch 3 para 3(4)(a), Sch 4 para 3(4)(a) (all amended by SI 1992/1311).
8 See the Museums and Galleries Act 1992 Sch 1 para 3(4)(b), Sch 2 para 3(4)(b), Sch 3 para 3(4)(b), Sch 4 para 3(4)(b). As to staff pensions see PARA 893.

835. General functions of new boards. So far as practicable and subject to the provisions of the Museums and Galleries Act 1992:

(1)   the National Gallery Board must maintain a collection of works of art, principally consisting of pictures, of established merit or significance, and of documents relating to those works[1];

(2)   the Tate Gallery Board must maintain a collection of British works of art and of documents relating to those works, and a collection of twentieth century and contemporary works of art and of documents relating to those works[2];

(3) the National Portrait Gallery Board must maintain a collection of portraits of the most eminent persons in British history, of other works of art relevant to portraiture and of documents relating to those portraits and other works of art[3]; and

(4) the Wallace Collection Board must maintain the collection of objects known as the Wallace Collection[4].

The Wallace Collection Board must:

(a) care for and preserve the objects in its collection[5];

(b) secure that they are exhibited to the public[6];

(c) secure that they are available to persons[7] seeking to inspect them in connection with study or research[8]; and

(d) generally promote the public's enjoyment and understanding of fine and applied art both by means of the board's collection and by such other means as the board considers appropriate[9].

Each of the other new boards[10] must:

(i) care for, preserve and add to the works of art (including, in the case of the National Portrait Gallery, the portraits) and the documents in their collection[11];

(ii) secure that the works of art (or, in the case of the National Portrait Gallery, the portraits) are exhibited to the public[12];

(iii) secure that the works of art (including, in the case of the National Portrait Gallery, the portraits) and the documents are available to persons seeking to inspect them in connection with study or research[13]; and

(iv) generally promote the public's enjoyment and understanding of:

(A) in the case of the National Gallery, painting and other fine art[14];

(B) in the case of the Tate Gallery, British art, and of twentieth century and contemporary art[15]; and

(C) in the case of the National Portrait Gallery, portraiture of British persons and British history through portraiture[16]

both by means of their collections and by such other means as they consider appropriate[17].

For the purposes of the above provisions, a new board may provide education, instruction and advice and carry out research[18]; may enter into contracts and other agreements[19]; may acquire and dispose of land[20] and other property[21]; and has other incidental powers[22].

If a Minister of the Crown directs a new board to exercise functions which are exercisable by him (whether by virtue of an enactment or otherwise)[23], in his opinion can appropriately be exercised by that new board, having regard to its functions and resources[24], and are specified in the direction[25], the new board must exercise them on his behalf in such manner as he may from time to time direct[26].

1 Museums and Galleries Act 1992 s 2(1). As to the National Gallery Board see PARA 833.
2 Museums and Galleries Act 1992 s 2(2). As to the Tate Gallery Board see PARA 833.
3 Museums and Galleries Act 1992 s 2(3). As to the National Portrait Gallery Board see PARA 833.
4 Museums and Galleries Act 1992 s 2(4). The Wallace Collection Board may neither add to, nor dispose of any object comprised in, its collection: see s 4(6); and PARA 839. As to the Wallace Collection Board see PARA 833. As to the Wallace Collection see PARA 832.
5 Museums and Galleries Act 1992 s 2(4)(a).
6 Museums and Galleries Act 1992 s 2(4)(b).
7 As to the meaning of 'person' see PARA 803 note 17.
8 Museums and Galleries Act 1992 s 2(4)(c).
9 Museums and Galleries Act 1992 s 2(4)(d).
10 As to the meaning of 'new board' see PARA 833 note 6.

11 See the Museums and Galleries Act 1992 s 2(1)(a), (2)(a), (3)(a).
12 See the Museums and Galleries Act 1992 s 2(1)(b), (2)(b), (3)(b).
13 See the Museums and Galleries Act 1992 s 2(1)(c), (2)(c), (3)(c).
14 Museums and Galleries Act 1992 s 2(1)(d).
15 Museums and Galleries Act 1992 s 2(2)(d).
16 Museums and Galleries Act 1992 s 2(3)(d).
17 See the Museums and Galleries Act 1992 s 2(1)(d), (2)(d), (3)(d).
18 Museums and Galleries Act 1992 s 2(5)(a).
19 Museums and Galleries Act 1992 s 2(5)(b). The agreements may include agreements for the new board's occupation or management of its principal building or of other premises: see s 2(5)(b). A new board may allow premises occupied or managed by it to be used by other persons (for payment or otherwise) for purposes not connected with the functions mentioned in whichever of s 2(1)–(4) (see the text to notes 1–17) has effect in relation to that new board, if the new board is satisfied that to do so would not conflict unduly with those functions: s 2(9). The reference in s 2(5)(b) to a new board's 'principal building' is a reference: (1) in the case of the National Gallery Board, to the premises known as the National Gallery (s 2(10)(a)); (2) in the case of the Tate Gallery Board, to the premises known as the Tate Gallery (s 2(10)(b)); (3) in the case of the National Portrait Gallery Board, to the premises known as the National Portrait Gallery (s 2(10)(c)); and (4) in the case of the Wallace Collection Board, to the premises known as Hertford House (s 2(10)(d)).
20 A new board must not acquire or dispose of land without the consent of the Secretary of State: Museums and Galleries Act 1992 s 2(8) (amended by SI 1992/1311). As to the meaning of 'land' see PARA 804 note 30. As to the Secretary of State see PARA 802 note 2.
21 Museums and Galleries Act 1992 s 2(5)(c).
22 See Museums and Galleries Act 1992 s 2(6). Subject to the provisions of the Museums and Galleries Act 1992, a new board may do such things (including requiring payment for admission or for other services or for goods provided by the board) as it thinks necessary or expedient:
    (1)   for preserving, and increasing the utility of, its collection (s 2(6)(a));
    (2)   for securing the due administration of anything vested in or acquired by the board, and any premises occupied or managed by the board, under or by virtue of the Museums and Galleries Act 1992 (s 2(6)(b)); and
    (3)   otherwise for the purposes of its functions (s 2(6)(c)).
23 Museums and Galleries Act 1992 s 2(7)(a). As to the meaning of 'enactment' see PARA 805 note 5.
24 Museums and Galleries Act 1992 s 2(7)(b).
25 Museums and Galleries Act 1992 s 2(7)(c).
26 Museums and Galleries Act 1992 s 2(7). However, nothing in this provision authorises the new board to exercise a function of making regulations or other instruments of a legislative character: s 2(7). In relation to any matter as respects which a new board acts by virtue of a direction under s 2(7), the board enjoys the same privileges, immunities and exemptions as those enjoyed in relation to that matter by the minister giving the direction: see Sch 1 para 1(3), Sch 2 para 1(3), Sch 3 para 1(3), Sch 4 para 1(3), and PARA 833.

836. Reports to the Secretary of State. Each new board[1] must make to the Secretary of State[2] a report on the exercise of its functions[3] since the making of its last report[4]. The first such report was to be made not later than the end of the period of three years (or such shorter period as the Secretary of State directed) beginning with the day of the new board's establishment[5]; and each subsequent report must be made not later than three years (or such shorter period as the Secretary of State may direct) after the last was made[6].

The Secretary of State must lay a copy of each report before each House of Parliament[7].

1 As to the meaning of 'new board' see PARA 833 note 6.
2 As to the Secretary of State see PARA 802 note 2.
3 As to the general functions of the boards see PARA 835.
4 See the Museums and Galleries Act 1992 Sch 1 para 7(1), Sch 2 para 7(1), Sch 3 para 7(1), Sch 4 para 7(1) (all amended by SI 1992/1311).
5 See the Museums and Galleries Act 1992 Sch 1 para 7(2), Sch 2 para 7(2), Sch 3 para 7(2), Sch 4 para 7(2) (all amended by SI 1992/1311). The new boards were established on 1 September 1992 (see PARA 833).

6   See the Museums and Galleries Act 1992 Sch 1 para 7(3), Sch 2 para 7(3), Sch 3 para 7(3), Sch 4
    para 7(3) (all amended by SI 1992/1311).
7   Museums and Galleries Act 1992 Sch 1 para 7(4), Sch 2 para 7(4), Sch 3 para 7(4), Sch 4 para 7(4)
    (all amended by SI 1992/1311). As to laying documents before Parliament see STATUTES AND
    LEGISLATIVE PROCESS vol 96 (2012) PARA 1052.

837. Power of new boards to form companies. With the consent of the Secretary
of State[1] and subject to any conditions he may impose, each new board[2] may
form, or take part in forming, one or more bodies corporate which, or each of
which, has as its main object or objects one or more of those mentioned below[3]
in relation to that new board[4], or any other object or objects incidental to the new
board's functions[5]. A new board so authorised to form or take part in forming any
such body may hold interests in any such body, exercise rights conferred by the
holding of interests in it, and provide financial or other assistance to or in respect
of it (including assistance by way of guarantee of its obligations)[6].
     The specified objects are:
(1)   the production and publication of books, films or other informative
       material relating:
       (a)   in the case of the National Gallery Board, to fine art[7];
       (b)   in the case of the Tate Gallery Board, to British art or twentieth
              century or contemporary art[8];
       (c)   in the case of the National Portrait Gallery Board, to portraiture
              of British persons or British history through portraiture[9]; and
       (d)   in the case of the Wallace Collection Board, to fine or applied
              art[10];
(2)   the production of replicas or reproductions of works of art, or of
       souvenirs (or, in the case of the National Portrait Gallery Board, of
       replicas or reproductions of portraits of eminent British persons)[11];
(3)   in the case of the Tate Gallery Board, the commissioning of works of
       art[12];
(4)   in the case of the National Portrait Gallery Board, the commissioning of
       portraits of eminent British persons[13];
(5)   the sale[14] of informative material relating to those fields of art with
       which the board's collection is concerned, and of replicas or productions
       of works of art (or, in the case of the National Portrait Gallery Board,
       of replicas or reproductions of portraits of eminent British persons) or
       of souvenirs or other goods[15]; and
(6)   the provision[16] of catering or car parking or other services or facilities
       for the public at any premises occupied or managed by the board[17].

1   As to the Secretary of State see PARA 802 note 2.
2   As to the meaning of 'new board' see PARA 833 note 6.
3   Ie mentioned in the Museums and Galleries Act 1992 s 3(2)–(5) (see heads (1)–(6) in the text).
4   Museums and Galleries Act 1992 s 3(1)(a) (s 3(1) amended by SI 1992/1311).
5   Museums and Galleries Act 1992 s 3(1)(b) (as amended: see note 4).
6   Museums and Galleries Act 1992 s 3(6). Section 3 is without prejudice to any power of a new
    board to undertake by virtue of s 2 (see PARA 835) anything mentioned in s 3(1)(b) (see the text
    to note 5) or in whichever of s 3(2)–(5) (see heads (1)–(6) in the text) has effect in relation to that
    new board: s 3(7).
7   See the Museums and Galleries Act 1992 s 3(2)(a). As to the National Gallery Board see PARA 833.
8   See the Museums and Galleries Act 1992 s 3(3)(a). As to the Tate Gallery Board see PARA 833.
9   See the Museums and Galleries Act 1992 s 3(4)(a). As to the National Portrait Gallery Board see
    PARA 833.
10 See the Museums and Galleries Act 1992 s 3(5)(a). As to the Wallace Collection Board see PARA
    833.
11 See the Museums and Galleries Act 1992 s 3(2)(b), (3)(c), (4)(c), (5)(b).
12 Museums and Galleries Act 1992 s 3(3)(b).

13 Museums and Galleries Act 1992 s 3(4)(b).
14 Ie whether or not at an hour when the collection is open to the public for viewing: see the Museums and Galleries Act 1992 s 3(2)(c), (3)(d), (4)(d), (5)(c).
15 See the Museums and Galleries Act 1992 s 3(2)(c), (3)(d), (4)(d), (5)(c).
16 Ie whether or not at an hour when the collection is open to the public for viewing: see the Museums and Galleries Act 1992 s 3(2)(d), (3)(e), (4)(e), (5)(d).
17 Museums and Galleries Act 1992 s 3(2)(d), (3)(e), (4)(e), (5)(d).

838. Acquisition of land in relation to the National Gallery. The Secretary of State[1] may acquire land for the enlargement or improvement of the National Gallery[2]. He may also transfer land to the National Gallery, the Tate Gallery, the National Portrait Gallery or the Wallace Collection[3].

1 As to the Secretary of State see PARA 802 note 2.
2 See the National Gallery Enlargement Act 1866 s 16.
3 See the Museums and Galleries Act 1992 s 8, Sch 6; and PARA 819.

839. Acquisition and disposal of pictures and other objects. The National Gallery Board, the Tate Gallery Board and the National Portrait Gallery Board[1] may, in particular, acquire (whether by purchase, exchange or gift) any relevant objects[2] which, in the opinion of the board concerned, it is desirable to add to that board's collection[3].

The National Gallery Board may not, however, dispose of a relevant object the property in which is vested in the board and which is comprised in its collection unless the disposal is an exercise of the statutory power[4] of transfer[5]. Nor may the Tate Gallery Board dispose of a relevant object the property in which is vested in that board and which is comprised in its collections unless the disposal[6]:

(1) is an exercise of the statutory power of transfer[7]; or
(2) is of a relevant object which, in the board's opinion, is unsuitable for retention in its collections and can be disposed of without detriment to the interests of students or other members of the public[8]; or
(3) is (by whatever means, including destruction) of a relevant object which the board is satisfied has become useless for the purposes of its collections by reason of damage, physical deterioration, or infestation by destructive organisms[9].

The National Portrait Gallery Board may not dispose of a relevant object the property in which is vested in the board and which is comprised in its collection unless the disposal:

(a) is an exercise of the statutory power of transfer[10]; or
(b) is by way of sale, exchange or gift of a relevant object which is a duplicate of another relevant object the property in which is so vested and which is so comprised[11]; or
(c) is (by whatever means) of a portrait and the board is satisfied that the identification formerly accepted by the board of the person portrayed has been discredited[12]; or
(d) is (by whatever means, including destruction) of a relevant object which the board is satisfied has become useless for the purposes of its collection by reason of damage, physical deterioration or infestation by destructive organisms[13].

The Wallace Collection Board may neither add any object to its collection nor dispose of any object the property in which is vested in the board and which is comprised in its collection[14].

Money accruing to a new board[15] by virtue of any disposal mentioned above must be applied by the board in the acquisition of relevant objects to be added to its collection[16].

The National Gallery Board, the Tate Gallery Board, the National Portrait Gallery Board and the Wallace Collection Board may, in certain circumstances, transfer an object from their collections under the Holocaust (Return of Cultural Objects) Act 2009[17].

1   As to the National Gallery Board, the Tate Gallery Board and the National Portrait Gallery Board see PARA 833.
2   For these purposes, 'relevant objects' means: (1) in the case of the National Gallery Board, works of art (Museums and Galleries Act 1992 s 4(2)(a)); (2) in the case of the Tate Gallery Board, works of art (s 4(2)(b)); and (3) in the case of the National Portrait Gallery Board, portraits or other works of art relevant to portraiture (s 4(2)(c)); and, in each case, includes any documents relating to a relevant object which falls, or has at any time fallen, within head (1), (2) or (3) above, as the case may be, and which is, or at that time was, comprised in the board's collection (s 4(2)).
3   Museums and Galleries Act 1992 s 4(1). As to the general functions of the boards see PARA 835.
4   Ie the power conferred by the Museums and Galleries Act 1992 s 6 (see PARA 817).
5   Museums and Galleries Act 1992 s 4(3).
6   The Museums and Galleries Act 1992 s 4(4) is without prejudice to any trust or condition (express or implied) prohibiting or restricting disposal of the relevant object: s 4(4).
7   Museums and Galleries Act 1992 s 4(4)(a). The statutory power of transfer referred to is that conferred by s 6 (see PARA 817).
8   Museums and Galleries Act 1992 s 4(4)(b).
9   Museums and Galleries Act 1992 s 4(4)(c).
10 Museums and Galleries Act 1992 s 4(5)(a). The statutory power of transfer referred to is that conferred by s 6 (see PARA 817).
11 Museums and Galleries Act 1992 s 4(5)(b).
12 Museums and Galleries Act 1992 s 4(5)(c).
13 Museums and Galleries Act 1992 s 4(5)(d). A relevant object may be disposed of by the board as mentioned in this provision notwithstanding a trust or condition (express or implied) prohibiting or restricting the disposal of the relevant object: s 4(5).
14 Museums and Galleries Act 1992 s 4(6). As to the Wallace Collection Board see PARA 833.
15 As to the meaning of 'new board' see PARA 833 note 6.
16 Museums and Galleries Act 1992 s 4(7).
17 See PARA 1107.

840. Lending and borrowing of pictures and other objects. The National Gallery Board, the Tate Gallery Board and the National Portrait Gallery[1] Board may lend any relevant object[2] the property in which is vested in the board and which is comprised in the board's collection, whether the loan is for purposes of public exhibition or not and whether, under the terms of the loan, the relevant object is to remain in the United Kingdom[3] or not[4]. This power is, however, subject to the requirements that, in deciding whether or not to lend a relevant object, and in determining the time for which, and the conditions subject to which, a relevant object is to be lent, the board[5]:

(1)   must give special consideration to a request for the loan of a relevant object for public exhibition[6]; and

(2)   subject to that, must have regard to the interests of students and other persons[7] visiting the board's collection, the suitability of the prospective borrower, the purpose of the loan, the physical condition and degree of rarity of the relevant object, and any risks to which it is likely to be exposed[8].

Where the property in a relevant object has become vested in the board subject to a trust or condition, this power to lend may be exercised in a manner inconsistent with the trust or condition if either:

(a)   50 years have elapsed since the date on which the property became so vested in the board or in any person through whom the board derives title to the relevant object[9]; or

(b)   the person who first imposed the trust or condition has, or his personal representatives[10] have, consented in writing[11] to the exercise of the power in that manner[12].

The National Gallery Board, the Tate Gallery Board and the National Portrait Gallery Board may accept loans of relevant objects for the purpose (depending on the terms of the loan) of exhibiting them, or of study or research by the board or by persons seeking to inspect them[13]. Those boards are specified transferors and transferees for the purposes of the general powers of transfer between collections[14] and the statutory provision for vesting of gifts to the nation where the donor has not specified a destination[15].

1   As to the National Gallery Board, the Tate Gallery Board and the National Portrait Gallery Board see PARA 833.
2   As to the meaning of 'relevant object' see PARA 839 note 2: definition applied by the Museums and Galleries Act 1992 s 5(5).
3   As to the meaning of 'United Kingdom' see PARA 804 note 2.
4   Museums and Galleries Act 1992 s 5(1). As to the government indemnity scheme in relation to loans see PARA 1094. As to the return of cultural objects unlawfully removed from member states see PARA 1099 et seq. As to overseas loans see PARAS 1095, 1096.
5   See the Museums and Galleries Act 1992 s 5(1), (2).
6   Museums and Galleries Act 1992 s 5(2)(a).
7   As to the meaning of 'person' see PARA 803 note 17.
8   Museums and Galleries Act 1992 s 5(2)(b).
9   Museums and Galleries Act 1992 s 5(3)(a).
10 As to personal representatives see WILLS AND INTESTACY vol 103 (2010) PARA 605 et seq.
11 As to the meaning of 'writing' see PARA 805 note 14.
12 Museums and Galleries Act 1992 s 5(3)(b).
13 Museums and Galleries Act 1992 s 5(4).
14 See the Museums and Galleries Act 1992 s 6; and PARA 817.
15 See the Museums and Galleries Act 1992 s 7; and PARA 818.

C.   THE IMPERIAL WAR MUSEUM

841. Board of Trustees of the Imperial War Museum. The Imperial War Museum[1] was established by statute in 1920[2]. For the purpose of managing the museum, and for the other purposes of the Imperial War Museum Act 1920, a board of trustees is established, which is a body corporate[3] (by the name of the 'Trustees of the Imperial War Museum') with perpetual succession and a common seal[4]. The powers of the board may be exercised notwithstanding any vacancy in its number[5].

The board may make rules, with the consent of the Secretary of State[6], for regulating its proceedings, and the constitution of, and delegation to, committees[7]. The seal of the board must be authenticated in the prescribed manner and any document purporting to be sealed with the seal so authenticated is receivable in evidence of the particulars so stated in that document[8].

1   'Imperial War Museum' means the institution established in 1917 under the name of the 'National War Museum' and known on the passing of the Imperial War Museum Act 1920 as the Imperial War Museum, and includes all collections, galleries and museums, wherever situated, which from time to time form or are administered as part of the Imperial War Museum: s 6(2).
2   The Acts regulating the Imperial War Museum are the Imperial War Museum Act 1920 and the Imperial War Museum Act 1955. The two Acts may be cited together as the Imperial War Museum Acts 1920 and 1955: Imperial War Museum Act 1955 s 3.
3   As to bodies corporate see COMPANIES vol 14 (2009) PARA 2; CORPORATIONS vol 24 (2010) PARA 301 et seq.
4   See the Imperial War Museum Act 1920 s 1(1) (amended by the Charities Act 1960 s 48(2), Sch 7 Pt II). As to the constitution of the board and tenure of office of the trustees see the Imperial War Museum Act 1920 s 1(2), Schedule paras 1–5, 7 (amended by the Pakistan Act 1990 s 1, Schedule para 2; the South Africa Act 1995 s 1, Schedule para 2(1); SI 1986/2239; SI 1988/253; SI

1997/1744; SI 2010/1551; and SI 2012/2590). Her Majesty may from time to time by Order in Council make further provision with respect to the membership of the board: see the Imperial War Museum Act 1955 s 1(2). A draft of any such Order in Council must be laid before each House of Parliament: s 1(3). The orders made are referred to above in relation to the Imperial War Museum Act 1920 Schedule. As to Orders in Council see CONSTITUTIONAL AND ADMINISTRATIVE LAW vol 20 (2014) PARA 581. As to the laying of documents before Parliament see STATUTES AND LEGISLATIVE PROCESS vol 96 (2012) PARA 1052. The Board of Trustees, so far as it is a charity, and any institution which is administered by or on its behalf and established for general or special purposes, is an exempt charity for the purposes of the Charities Act 2011: see s 22, Sch 3 para 23; and CHARITIES vol 8 (2015) PARA 318.
5   Imperial War Museum Act 1920 Schedule para 6.
6   As to the Secretary of State see PARA 802 note 2.
7   See the Imperial War Museum Act 1920 Schedule para 8 (amended by SI 1992/1311).
8   See the Imperial War Museum Act 1920 s 1(3). As to the corporate seal see CORPORATIONS vol 24 (2010) PARA 323 et seq. Certain records of the Imperial War Museum are public records for the purposes of the Public Records Act 1958: see s 10, Sch 1 para 3, Table Pt II; and CONSTITUTIONAL AND ADMINISTRATIVE LAW vol 20 (2014) PARA 343.

842.   Director general and staff of the Imperial War Museum. There is a director general of the Imperial War Museum[1] and a curator of the Imperial War Museum who are appointed by the Board of Trustees[2] with the approval of the Prime Minister[3], and who hold office on such terms and conditions as the board may determine subject to such conditions as the Secretary of State[4] may impose with the consent of the Treasury[5]. Subject to the board's directions, the director general is responsible generally for the museum's management, and the curator is charged with the care of the museum and the objects collected there, subject to the director general's control and direction[6]. The director general, curator and any officers of the board[7] are to be paid such salaries or remuneration as the board may determine, subject to such conditions as the Secretary of State may impose with the consent of the Treasury[8].

1   As to the meaning of 'Imperial War Museum' see PARA 841 note 1.
2   As to the board see PARA 841.
3   As to the Prime Minister see CONSTITUTIONAL AND ADMINISTRATIVE LAW vol 20 (2014) PARAS 203–208.
4   As to the Secretary of State see PARA 802 note 2.
5   Imperial War Museum Act 1920 s 4(1) (amended by the Museums and Galleries Act 1992 Sch 8 para 7(4); and SI 1992/1311). As to the meaning of 'Treasury' see PARA 809 note 4.
6   See the Imperial War Museum Act 1920 s 4(2). The curator acts as secretary to the board: s 4(3).
7   As to the board's power to appoint officers see PARA 843.
8   See the Imperial War Museum Act 1920 s 4(4) (amended by the Museums and Galleries Act 1992 Sch 8 para 7(5); and SI 1992/1311).

843.   General powers and duties of Board of Trustees of the Imperial War Museum. The Board of Trustees[1] of the Imperial War Museum[2] has the general management and control of the museum and for that purpose may make such rules as it thinks necessary for securing the due administration of the museum and preserving the objects in it, including rules requiring payment to be made for admission[3]. Subject to the consent of the Secretary of State[4], the board may appoint officers on such terms and subject to such conditions as it thinks fit[5]; and subject to the provisions of the Imperial War Museum Act 1920, it may do such other things as appear to it necessary or expedient for furthering the interests and increasing the utility of the museum[6].

With the consent of the Secretary of State, the board may apply any money received by it on the exchange, sale or disposal of any objects[7] or on the sale or other disposition of any land, or by way of payment for admission to the museum, or by way of gift or grant or otherwise, in the purchase of any object which the board thinks it desirable to acquire for the museum, or otherwise in defraying the expenses of the board[8].

1 As to the board see PARA 841.
2 As to the meaning of 'Imperial War Museum' see PARA 841 note 1.
3 Imperial War Museum Act 1920 s 2(1)(a) (s 2(1) renumbered as such by the Museums and Galleries Act 1992 Sch 8 para 7(2)).
4 As to the Secretary of State see PARA 802 note 2.
5 Imperial War Museum Act 1920 s 2(1)(f) (s 2(1) as renumbered (see note 3); amended by SI 2011/1213). As to the payment of salaries or remuneration to such officers see PARA 842.
6 Imperial War Museum Act 1920 s 2(1)(g) (s 2(1) as renumbered: see note 3).
7 As to the disposal of objects see PARA 846.
8 Imperial War Museum Act 1920 s 2(1)(d) (s 2(1) as renumbered (see note 3); s 2(1)(d) amended by the Museums and Galleries Act 1992 Sch 8 para 7(1); and SI 1992/1311).

844. Power of Board of Trustees of the Imperial War Museum to form companies. With the consent of the Secretary of State[1], and subject to any conditions he may impose, the Board of Trustees[2] of the Imperial War Museum[3] may form, or take part in forming, one or more bodies corporate which, or each of which, has as its main object or objects one or more of the following[4]:

(1)   the production and publication of books, films or other informative material relating to the museum's collection or theme[5];

(2)   the production of replicas or reproductions of objects relating to the museum's collection or theme, or of souvenirs[6];

(3)   the sale (whether or not at an hour when the collection is open to the public for viewing) of informative material relating to the museum's collection or theme, or of souvenirs or other goods[7];

(4)   the provision (whether or not at such an hour) of catering or car parking or other services or facilities for the public at any premises occupied or managed by the board[8]; and

(5)   any other object or objects incidental to the board's functions[9].

The board may hold interests in any such body, exercise rights conferred by the holding of interests in it, and provide financial or other assistance to or in respect of it, including assistance by way of guarantee of its obligations[10].

These provisions are without prejudice to any other statutory power of the board[11] to undertake anything mentioned in heads (1) to (5) above[12].

1 As to the Secretary of State see PARA 802 note 2.
2 As to the board see PARA 841.
3 As to the meaning of 'Imperial War Museum' see PARA 841 note 1.
4 Imperial War Museum Act 1920 s 2A(1) (s 2A added by the Museums and Galleries Act 1992 Sch 8 para 7(3); Imperial War Museum Act 1920 s 2A(1) amended by SI 1992/1311).
5 Imperial War Museum Act 1920 s 2A(2)(a) (as added: see note 4).
6 Imperial War Museum Act 1920 s 2A(2)(b) (as added: see note 4).
7 Imperial War Museum Act 1920 s 2A(2)(c) (as added: see note 4).
8 Imperial War Museum Act 1920 s 2A(2)(d) (as added: see note 4).
9 Imperial War Museum Act 1920 s 2A(2)(e) (as added: see note 4). As to the board's functions see PARA 841.
10 Imperial War Museum Act 1920 s 2A(3) (as added: see note 4).
11 Ie by virtue of the Imperial War Museum Act 1920 s 2 (see PARAS 843, 845, 846).
12 Imperial War Museum Act 1920 s 2A(4) (as added: see note 4).

845. Power of Board of Trustees of the Imperial War Museum to hold land. The Board of Trustees[1] of the Imperial War Museum[2] has power, with the consent of the Secretary of State[3], to acquire land for the purposes of the museum and to sell or make other dispositions of any land vested in it which is not required for that purpose[4]. The Secretary of State may transfer land to the board[5].

The board may allow premises occupied or managed by it to be used by other persons[6] (for payment or otherwise) for purposes not connected with the board's functions, if the board is satisfied that to do so would not unduly conflict with those functions[7].

1   As to the board see PARA 841.
2   As to the meaning of 'Imperial War Museum' see PARA 841 note 1.
3   As to the Secretary of State see PARA 802 note 2.
4   Imperial War Museum Act 1920 s 2(1)(b) (s 2(1) renumbered as such by the Museums and Galleries Act 1992 Sch 8 para 7(2); Imperial War Museum Act 1920 s 2(1)(b) amended by the Museums and Galleries Act 1992 Sch 8 para 7(1)(a); and SI 1992/1311). As to the application of the proceeds of sale see PARA 843.
5   See the Museums and Galleries Act 1992 s 8, Sch 6; and PARA 819.
6   As to the meaning of 'person' see PARA 803 note 17.
7   Imperial War Museum Act 1920 s 2(2) (added by the Museums and Galleries Act 1992 Sch 8 para 7(2)). As to the board's functions see PARA 841.

846. Vesting, lending and disposal of objects held for purposes of the Imperial War Museum. All objects given, bequeathed or otherwise acquired for the purposes of the Imperial War Museum[1] at the time of the establishment of the Board of Trustees[2] were vested in the board for the museum's purposes[3]; and all objects which are at any subsequent time expressly given or bequeathed to the public, or to the nation, or to the board for the purposes of the museum, or given or bequeathed by words showing an intention that the gifts should inure to or for the benefit of the museum, or which are acquired by purchase or otherwise for the purposes of the museum, vest in the board and are held by it for the museum's purposes[4].

The board may lend any objects belonging to the museum for public exhibition in the United Kingdom or elsewhere[5], or to any government department or other authority or institution in the United Kingdom or elsewhere[6]. The board must give special consideration to any application for a loan for public exhibition[7], or for display in any permanent headquarters or other establishment belonging to the armed forces of the Crown[8]. A loan may be made on such terms and subject to such conditions as the board may think fit[9]. In the case of an object which has been given or bequeathed to the museum, these powers to lend are not, however, exercisable: (1) until 15 years after the date of the gift or bequest, unless the donor or his personal representatives, or the personal representatives of the testator, as the case may be, have consented to the exercise of the powers[10]; or (2) in any manner inconsistent with any condition attached to the gift or bequest unless either 25 years have elapsed since the date of the gift or bequest, or the donor or his personal representatives, or the personal representatives of the testator, as the case may be, have consented to the exercise of the board's powers in that manner[11].

The board may exchange, sell or otherwise dispose of any duplicate objects belonging to the museum, and with the consent of the Secretary of State[12] may exchange, sell or otherwise dispose of any objects belonging to the museum which the board considers unfit to be preserved or not required for its purposes[13].

The trustees of the British Museum[14] or the Secretary of State may lend to the Imperial War Museum, at any time and on such terms and subject to such conditions as they think fit, any pictures or other objects vested in them respectively[15]. The board is a specified transferor and transferee for the purposes of the general powers of transfer between collections[16] and the statutory provision for vesting of gifts to the nation where the donor has not specified a destination[17].

In certain circumstances the board may transfer an object from its collections under the Holocaust (Return of Cultural Objects) Act 2009[18].

1 As to the meaning of 'Imperial War Museum' see PARA 841 note 1.
2 The board was established on 2 July 1920 being the day on which the Imperial War Museum Act 1920 received royal assent. As to the board see PARA 841.
3 See the Imperial War Museum Act 1920 s 3(1).
4 See the Imperial War Museum Act 1920 s 3(1).
5 Imperial War Museum Act 1955 s 2(1)(a) (s 2(1) amended by the Museums and Galleries Act 1992 Sch 8 para 9(1), Sch 9). As to the meaning of 'United Kingdom' see PARA 804 note 2.
6 Imperial War Museum Act 1955 s 2(1)(b) (s 2(1) as amended: see note 5).
7 Imperial War Museum Act 1955 s 2(2)(a).
8 Imperial War Museum Act 1955 s 2(2)(b).
9 Imperial War Museum Act 1955 s 2(3) (amended by the Museums and Galleries Act 1992 Sch 8 para 9(2), Sch 9).
10 Imperial War Museum Act 1955 s 2(4)(a). As to personal representatives see WILLS AND INTESTACY vol 103 (2010) PARA 605 et seq.
11 Imperial War Museum Act 1955 s 2(4)(b). As to overseas loans see PARAS 1095, 1096.
12 As to the Secretary of State see PARA 802 note 2.
13 Imperial War Museum Act 1920 s 2(1)(c) (s 2(1) renumbered as such by the Museums and Galleries Act 1992 Sch 8 para 7(2); Imperial War Museum Act 1920 s 2(1)(c) amended by SI 1992/1311).
14 As to the trustees of the British Museum see PARA 824.
15 Imperial War Museum Act 1920 s 3(2) (amended by the National Gallery and Tate Gallery Act 1954 s 8(2), Sch 2; the Museums and Galleries Act 1992 Sch 9; and SI 1992/1311).
16 See the Museums and Galleries Act 1992 s 6, Sch 5; and PARA 817.
17 See the Museums and Galleries Act 1992 s 7: and PARA 818.
18 See PARA 1107.

D.   THE NATIONAL MARITIME MUSEUM

847. Board of Trustees of the National Maritime Museum. The National Maritime Museum at Greenwich was established in 1934[1]. A Board of Trustees was established for the purpose of managing the museum[2]. The board is a body corporate with perpetual succession and a common seal[3]. The powers of the board may be exercised notwithstanding any vacancy in its number[4]. The board may make rules for regulating its proceedings[5].

The site of the museum is vested in the board[6]. The board:

(1)   may make such alterations as may be necessary to adapt any buildings on that land for use for the purposes of the museum[7];

(2)   may for those purposes reconstruct any such buildings or demolish any such buildings and construct new buildings[8]; and

(3)   must at all times maintain any buildings on that land in a proper condition for the purposes of the museum[9].

If at any time the Secretary of State by order made by statutory instrument declares that the buildings on the land have ceased to be used for the purposes of the museum, the land will vest in the Minister of the Crown at that time entrusted with responsibility for defence and be held by him in trust for Her Majesty for the benefit of Greenwich Hospital[10].

1 See the National Maritime Museum Act 1934 s 1(1) (amended by the National Maritime Museum Act 1989 s 3(2)).
2 See the National Maritime Museum Act 1934 s 2(1). As to the constitution of the board see s 2(2), Sch 2 paras 1–3 (amended by the Museums and Galleries Act 1992 Sch 8 para 8(4)). The Board of Trustees, so far as it is a charity, and any institution which is administered by or on its behalf and established for general or special purposes, is an exempt charity for the purposes of the Charities Act 2011: see s 22, Sch 3 para 24; and CHARITIES vol 8 (2015) PARA 318.
3 See the National Maritime Museum Act 1934 s 2(1). As to bodies corporate see COMPANIES vol 14 (2009) PARA 2; CORPORATIONS vol 24 (2010) PARA 301 et seq. As to the corporate seal see CORPORATIONS vol 24 (2010) PARA 323 et seq.

4   National Maritime Museum Act 1934 Sch 2 para 4.
5   See the National Maritime Museum Act 1934 Sch 2 para 5.
6   See the National Maritime Museum Act 1989 ss 1(1), (7), 3(3); National Maritime Act 1934 Sch
    1; National Maritime Museum Act 1989 (Commencement) Order 1989, SI 1989/1028. As to the
    description of land and buildings comprised in the museum see the National Maritime Museum
    Act 1934 Sch 1. Additionally, the Secretary of State may transfer land to the museum: see the
    Museums and Galleries Act 1992 s 8, Sch 6; and PARA 819. The vesting of the site in the board
    does not affect the application to that land of the Parks Regulation Acts 1872 to 1974 (ie the Parks
    Regulation Act 1872, the Parks Regulation (Amendment) Act 1926 and the Parks Regulation
    (Amendment) Act 1974: see s 1(2)); and OPEN SPACES AND COUNTRYSIDE vol 78 (2010) PARAS
    561–563: see the National Maritime Museum Act 1989 s 1(2). As to the Secretary of State see
    PARA 802 note 2.
7   National Maritime Museum Act 1989 s 1(3)(a). However, nothing in s 1(3):
    (1)   authorises the demolition of the ancient monument consisting of the Queen's House and
          the colonnades on the east and west sides of it (see s 1(3));
    (2)   exempts the board from the provisions of the Town and Country Planning Act 1990, the
          Planning (Listed Buildings and Conservation Areas) Act 1990 (see PLANNING vol 83
          (2010) PARAS 1233 et seq, 1263 et seq), the Ancient Monuments and Archaeological
          Areas Act 1979 (see PARA 1006) or any other enactment relating to the preservation of
          buildings or the execution of building work (see the National Maritime Museum Act
          1989 s 1(4) (amended by the Planning (Consequential Provisions) Act 1990 Sch 2
          para 80)). As to the meaning of 'enactment' see PARA 805 note 5.
8   National Maritime Museum Act 1989 s 1(3)(b). See also note 7.
9   National Maritime Museum Act 1989 s 1(3)(c). See also note 7.
10 National Maritime Museum Act 1989 s 1(5) (amended by SI 1992/1311). At the date at which this
    volume states the law no such order had been made by the Secretary of State.

848. Staff appointed by Board of Trustees of the National Maritime Museum.
There is a director of the National Maritime Museum, appointed by the Board of
Trustees[1] with the approval of the Prime Minister[2], who holds office on such terms
and conditions as the board determines, subject to such conditions as the
Secretary of State[3] may impose with the consent of the Treasury[4]. Subject to the
board's control and direction, the director is charged with the care of the museum
and of the objects collected there[5].

The board may appoint such officers and servants as it thinks fit, and there
must be paid to the director of the museum and to any officers so appointed such
salaries or remuneration as the board may determine subject to such conditions as
the Secretary of State imposes with the consent of the Treasury[6].

1   As to the National Maritime Museum and the board see PARA 847.
2   As to the Prime Minister see CONSTITUTIONAL AND ADMINISTRATIVE LAW vol 20 (2014)
    PARAS 203–208.
3   As to the Secretary of State see PARA 802 note 2.
4   National Maritime Museum Act 1934 s 5(1) (amended by the Museums and Galleries Act 1992
    Sch 8 para 8(1); and SI 1992/1311). As to the meaning of 'Treasury' see PARA 809 note 4.
5   See the National Maritime Museum Act 1934 s 5(1) (as amended: see note 4).
6   National Maritime Museum Act 1934 s 5(2) (amended by the Museums and Galleries Act 1992
    Sch 8 para 8(2), Sch 9; and SI 1992/1311).

849. General powers of Board of Trustees of the National Maritime Museum.
The Board of Trustees of the National Maritime Museum[1] has the general
management and control of the museum[2] and for that purpose may make such
regulations as it thinks necessary for securing the due administration of the
museum and preserving the objects collected in it, including regulations requiring
payment to be made for admission to the museum[3].

The board may expend any money available for the purpose[4] in the purchase
of any object which in the board's opinion it is desirable to acquire for the
museum[5]. Money received by the board on the sale, exchange or disposal of
objects[6] or by way of gift or bequest may be invested by the board and with the
interest may be used for the purchase of objects or otherwise for the

museum's purposes in the discretion of the board[7]. The board may, in exercising its functions, enter into contracts and other agreements, including those for their occupation or management of land[8], and acquire or dispose of land and other property[9]; but it may not acquire and dispose of land without the consent of the Secretary of State[10]. If the board is satisfied that to do so would not conflict unduly with its functions[11], it may allow premises owned, occupied or managed by it to be used by other persons[12], for payment or otherwise, for purposes not connected with those functions[13].

Subject to the provisions of the National Maritime Museum Act 1934, the board may do such other things as appear to it necessary or expedient for furthering the interests and increasing the utility of the museum[14].

1 As to the National Maritime Museum and the board see PARA 847.
2 National Maritime Museum Act 1934 s 2(3).
3 National Maritime Museum Act 1934 s 2(3)(a). Any such regulations made are outside the scope of this work. As to the appointment of a director general and officers see s 5; and PARA 848.
4 The money referred to is money available in accordance with the provisions of the National Maritime Museum Act 1934: see s 2(3)(c).
5 National Maritime Museum Act 1934 s 2(3)(c).
6 As to the disposal of objects see PARA 850.
7 See the National Maritime Museum Act 1934 s 6(2) (amended by the Museums and Galleries Act 1992 Sch 8 para 8(3)(b)). No money received by the board by way of gift or bequest may, however, be spent in any way inconsistent with any condition attached to the gift or bequest: National Maritime Museum Act 1934 s 6(2) proviso.
8 National Maritime Museum Act 1989 s 2(1)(a). Section 2(1) is without prejudice to the board's powers under the National Maritime Museum Act 1934 and the National Maritime Museum Act 1989 s 1 (see PARA 847): see s 2(1), (4). As to the meaning of 'land' see PARA 804 note 30.
9 National Maritime Museum Act 1989 s 2(1)(b). See note 8.
10 National Maritime Museum Act 1989 s 2(2) (amended by SI 1992/1311). As to the Secretary of State see PARA 802 note 2.
11 Ie its functions under the National Maritime Museum Act 1934 and the National Maritime Museum Act 1989 s 1 (see PARA 847): see s 2(3), (4).
12 As to the meaning of 'person' see PARA 803 note 17.
13 National Maritime Museum Act 1989 s 2(3).
14 National Maritime Museum Act 1934 s 2(3)(f).

850. Vesting, lending and disposal of objects held for purposes of the National Maritime Museum. All objects which at the time of the establishment of the Board of Trustees of the National Maritime Museum[1] formed part of the Naval Museum of the Royal Naval College at Greenwich[2], or were in the possession of certain specified trusts[3], are vested in the board for the museum's purposes[4], as are all objects which (1) are expressly given or bequeathed to the public or to the nation or to the board for the museum's purpose[5]; (2) are given or bequeathed by words showing an intention that the gifts should inure to, or for the benefit of, the museum[6]; or (3) are acquired by purchase or otherwise for the purposes of the museum[7].

Specific power is given to any government department or to the trustees or other persons[8] having the management of any gallery, museum or other institution in Great Britain[9] in receipt of money provided by Parliament, with the consent of the Secretary of State[10], to transfer or lend any objects under their control or management to the board on such terms and subject to such conditions as may be agreed, where it is considered that such objects would more properly form part of the collection in the National Maritime Museum[11]. The board has an equivalent power, subject to the Secretary of State's consent, to lend to such persons any objects vested in the board for the purposes of the museum which, in the board's opinion, would more properly be under the control or management of those persons[12].

The museum's trustees are specified transferors and transferees for the purposes of the general powers of transfer between collections[13] and the statutory provision for vesting of gifts to the nation where the donor has not specified a destination[14].

The board may lend any objects vested in it for the purposes of the museum to any gallery, museum or exhibition approved by the Secretary of State, on such terms and conditions as the board thinks fit[15]. The board may exchange, sell or otherwise dispose of any duplicate objects vested in it for the purposes of the museum, and may with the consent of the Secretary of State exchange, sell or otherwise dispose of any objects so vested which the board considers are not required for the museum's purposes[16]. These powers[17] of selling or otherwise disposing of, or of lending or transferring, any object must not, however, be exercised in any manner inconsistent with any condition attached to any gift or bequest by virtue or in consequence of which that object was vested in the board for the purposes of the museum[18].

In certain circumstances the board may transfer an object from its collections under the Holocaust (Return of Cultural Objects) Act 2009[19].

1 The board was established on 25 July 1934 being the day on which the National Maritime Museum Act 1934 received royal assent. As to the National Maritime Museum and the board see PARA 847.
2 See the National Maritime Museum Act 1934 s 3(a).
3 See the National Maritime Museum Act 1934 s 3(b). As to the specified trusts see Sch 3.
4 See the National Maritime Museum Act 1934 s 3.
5 See the National Maritime Museum Act 1934 s 3(c).
6 See the National Maritime Museum Act 1934 s 3(d).
7 See the National Maritime Museum Act 1934 s 3(e).
8 As to the meaning of 'person' see PARA 803 note 17.
9 As to the meaning of 'Great Britain' see PARA 804 note 2.
10 As to the Secretary of State see PARA 802 note 2.
11 See the National Maritime Museum Act 1934 s 4 (amended by SI 1992/1311). This power to transfer or lend must not be exercised in any manner inconsistent with any condition attached to the gift or bequest of the objects transferred or lent: National Maritime Museum Act 1934 s 4 proviso.
12 See the National Maritime Museum Act 1934 s 2(3)(e) (amended by SI 1992/1311). This power is subject to the National Maritime Museum Act 1934 s 2(3) proviso: see the text to notes 17–18.
13 See the Museums and Galleries Act 1992 s 6, Sch 5; and PARA 817.
14 See the Museums and Galleries Act 1992 s 7; and PARA 818.
15 National Maritime Museum Act 1934 s 2(3)(d) (amended by SI 1992/1311).
16 National Maritime Museum Act 1934 s 2(3)(b) (amended by SI 1992/1311).
17 Ie the powers under the National Maritime Museum Act 1934 s 2(3) (see the text to notes 12, 15–16).
18 National Maritime Museum Act 1934 s 2(3) proviso.
19 See PARA 1107.

E.   THE WELLINGTON MUSEUM

851. Establishment of the Wellington Museum. The Wellington Museum was established in 1947 by the transfer of Apsley House to the then Minister of Works[1]; and by the transfer to the then Minister of Education[2], under an agreement made between him and the seventh Duke of Wellington, of certain chattels held as heirlooms, together with other chattels formerly belonging to the first Duke of Wellington which had become the property of the seventh Duke of Wellington[3].

1 See the Wellington Museum Act 1947 s 1(1) (as originally enacted). The functions of the Minister of Public Buildings and Works have been transferred to the Secretary of State: s 1(1) (amended by SI 1970/1681). As to the Secretary of State see PARA 802 note 2.
2 The functions of the Minister of Education have been transferred to the Secretary of State: see the Wellington Museum Act 1947 s 1(2) (amended by SI 1992/1311).
3 See the Wellington Museum Act 1947 s 1(2) (as originally enacted).

852. Use of Apsley House as a museum. Certain portions of Apsley House[1] are, subject to rights reserved to the Secretary of State[2], to be maintained and used as a museum for the preservation and exhibition to the public of the chattels now vested[3] in the Secretary of State and such other chattels as the seventh Duke of Wellington or any other person[4] may think fit from time to time to permit to be exhibited in it, being chattels associated with the first Duke of Wellington or his times, which in the opinion of the Secretary of State should be exhibited[5]. The Secretary of State has power temporarily to remove from, or from exhibition in, the museum any of the chattels which for any reason it appears to him desirable ought not for the time being to be kept, or kept and exhibited, in it[6]. The museum portions of Apsley House may also be used for the purpose of any entertainment given on the government's behalf[7] or, with the consent of the Duke of Wellington, for any other public purpose not inconsistent with the continued use of it as the Wellington Museum[8].

1 Ie those portions specified in the Wellington Museum Act 1947 s 2(1), Sch 2 Pt I. Rights of occupation in respect of the remainder of Apsley House are reserved to the Duke of Wellington for the time being and his successors: see s 3(1), Sch 2 Pt II. Those rights include a right of access to the portions which he is entitled to occupy by specified routes (see s 3(2), Sch 2 Pt II); and a right to occupy the garden, but not to assign, let or part with possession of the whole or any part of it (s 3(4)). On the extinction of the Dukedom, the portions of the house not used as a museum, and the garden, may be used or dealt with in such manner as the Secretary of State thinks fit: s 3(6) (amended by SI 1970/1681). As to the Secretary of State see PARA 802 note 2. The Inheritance Tax Act 1984 does not apply to the rights conferred by the Wellington Museum Act 1947 s 3: see the Inheritance Tax Act 1984 s 156(a); and INHERITANCE TAXATION vol 59A (2014) PARA 231.
2 The Secretary of State has a power to discontinue the use of Apsley House as a museum if owing to fire or any cause beyond his control it is destroyed or so damaged that in his opinion it could not be restored so as to preserve its association with the first Duke of Wellington: see the Wellington Museum Act 1947 s 6(1) (s 6(1) amended by SI 1970/1681). Notice in writing must be given to the Duke of Wellington for the time being of any such decision, he must be given reasonable compensation and Apsley House and the site, forecourt and garden may either be used for such public purposes as the Secretary of State thinks fit or may be sold or otherwise disposed of: see the Wellington Museum Act 1947 s 6(1)(a)–(c) (as so amended). As to the meaning of 'writing' see PARA 805 note 14. No compensation is payable to the then Duke of Wellington if the destruction or damage is due to his negligence or that of his servants or agents: s 6(1) proviso. Any fire originating in the portions of Apsley House which the Duke of Wellington for the time being is entitled to occupy is presumed to be due to his negligence or that of his servants or agents unless the contrary is proved: s 6(3).
    The Secretary of State also has power to redesignate the portions of the house used as a museum, by varying the provisions of Sch 2 by order made with the consent of the Duke of Wellington: see s 7(1) (s 7 amended by SI 1970/1681).
3 Ie by virtue of the Wellington Museum Act 1947.
4 As to the meaning of 'person' see PARA 803 note 17.
5 Wellington Museum Act 1947 s 2(1) (amended by SI 1992/1311).
6 Wellington Museum Act 1947 s 2(1) proviso (amended by SI 1992/1311).
7 Wellington Museum Act 1947 s 2(2)(a).
8 Wellington Museum Act 1947 s 2(2)(b).

853. Maintenance of Apsley House. The general responsibility for maintaining Apsley House[1] lies with the Secretary of State[2], subject to a duty placed on the Duke of Wellington for the time being to keep the portions of the house which he is entitled to occupy[3] in good and tenantable repair and to maintain the garden[4]. If any of the Dukes of Wellington fails to comply with the obligation so imposed on him, the Secretary of State, on giving reasonable notice of his intention to do so, may himself do such repairs to the portions of Apsley House which the Duke is entitled to occupy, and do such work on the garden, as appear to him to be necessary; and any expenses reasonably incurred by the Secretary of State in so doing are recoverable by him from the Duke[5].

If, owing to fire or any other cause, Apsley House is damaged or any of the contents of it which are the property of the Crown, other than chattels which are being or have been or are to be exhibited in the museum, are damaged or destroyed, and the damage or destruction is due to the negligence of the Duke of Wellington for the time being or his servants or agents[6], then if no notice discontinuing the use of the house as a museum is given[7], the Duke must repay to the Secretary of State such expenses as may be reasonably incurred by him in making good the damage or in replacing any of the contents which are destroyed[8].

1 As to Apsley House see PARA 852.
2 It is the duty of the Secretary of State to maintain the forecourt of Apsley House in a proper condition, to maintain the whole of the fabric of the exterior of the house in a proper state of repair and to carry out and maintain such works as are necessary for separating the portions of Apsley House to be used as a museum from the remainder of the house and adapting those portions to that use: see the Wellington Museum Act 1947 s 5(1) (amended by SI 1970/1681). As to the Secretary of State see PARA 802 note 2.
3 As to the right of the Duke of Wellington to occupy part of the property see PARA 852. The right of occupation includes a right to carry out such internal alterations, renewals, repairs and decorations in the portions of the house which the Duke is entitled to occupy as he may think fit (Wellington Museum Act 1947 s 3(1) (amended by SI 1970/1681)); but nothing may be done which affects the fabric of the house except with the consent of the Secretary of State (Wellington Museum Act 1947 s 3(1) proviso (amended by SI 1970/1681)). The Secretary of State and the Duke of Wellington or any of his successors may enter into and carry out agreements with respect to the heating and lighting of the house: see the Wellington Museum Act 1947 s 3(5) (amended by SI 1970/1681).
4 See the Wellington Museum Act 1947 ss 3(4), 5(2).
5 See the Wellington Museum Act 1947 s 5(3) (s 5(3), (4) amended by SI 1970/1681). There is a power of entry and inspection for this purpose: see the Wellington Museum Act 1947 s 5(4) (as so amended). As to the responsibility for rates and taxes see s 4 (amended by the Finance Act 1982 Sch 22 Pt XI).
6 As to the burden of proof see the Wellington Museum Act 1947 s 6(3); and PARA 852 note 2.
7 Ie notice under the Wellington Museum Act 1947 s 6(1) (see PARA 852).
8 Wellington Museum Act 1947 s 6(2) (amended by SI 1970/1681).

F. THE MUSEUM OF LONDON

854. Establishment of the Museum of London. The Museum of London was established by the Museum of London Act 1965[1]. There is a Board of Governors of the Museum of London[2] which is a body corporate with perpetual succession and a common seal[3]. The board may determine its own quorum and procedure[4]. The board may act notwithstanding a vacancy amongst the governors, and no act of the board must be deemed to be invalid by reason only of a defect in the appointment of any of the governors[5]. The application of the seal of the board must be authenticated by the signatures of the chairman of the board or some other governors authorised by the board to authenticate the application or the seal and of the secretary or some other person authorised by the board to act in his stead in that behalf[6].

1 See the Museum of London Act 1965 s 2. The Museum of London Act 1965 s 2 made provision for the transfer to the Board of Governors of the Museum of London of the collections of the London and Guildhall Museums (see s 2(1) (amended by SI 1992/1311)) and the benefit of certain funds (see the Museum of London Act 1965 s 2(2)) and the transfer of functions from the London

Museum Trustees and the Corporation of the City of London to the board (see s 2(3)). See also s 12 (substitution, in certain devises and bequests, of board in place of London Museum and Guildhall Museum).

2 See the Museum of London Act 1965 s 1(1). As to the constitution of the board see s 1(2) (amended by the Museum of London Act 1986 s 1(1); the Greater London Authority Act 2007 s 45(1)). As to tenure of office of governors and the appointment of a chairman see the Museum of London Act 1965 Schedule paras 2–6 (paras 2–4 amended by the Local Government Act 1985 s 43(5), Sch 17; Museum of London Act 1965 Schedule para 2 further amended by the Greater London Authority Act 2007 ss 45(2) 46(1)).

3 See the Museum of London Act 1965 Schedule para 1. As to bodies corporate see COMPANIES vol 14 (2009) PARA 2; CORPORATIONS vol 24 (2010) PARA 301 et seq. As to the corporate seal see CORPORATIONS vol 24 (2010) PARA 323 et seq.

4 See the Museum of London Act 1965 Schedule para 7. This provision is expressed to be subject to the provisions of the Schedule paras 1–6 (see note 2 and the text to note 3).

5 Museum of London Act 1965 Schedule para 8.

6 Museum of London Act 1965 Schedule para 9.

855. Director and staff of the Museum of London. There is a director of the Museum of London who is appointed by the Board of Governors[1] with the approval of the Greater London Authority[2] and the Corporation of the City of London[3]. The director holds office on such terms and subject to such conditions as the Greater London Authority and the corporation may jointly direct, and is responsible to the board for the care of all property in its possession and for the general administration of the collections vested in it and any place where those collections are kept and for the administration of any services provided by the board in the exercise of its functions[4].

With the corporation's consent the board must, from among the corporation's officers, appoint persons who must, while remaining corporation officers, act as the board's secretary and treasurer[5].

Subject to the consent of the Greater London Authority and the corporation as to numbers, and without prejudice to the provisions above relating to the secretary and the treasurer, the board may appoint such officers and such servants as it thinks fit; and any officer and any servant so appointed holds office on such terms and subject to such conditions as the corporation may direct[6]. There are paid to the director and any officers and servants appointed under these provisions such salaries, allowances and other remuneration as the corporation, with the approval of the Greater London Authority, may determine[7].

1 As to the Museum of London and the Board of Governors see PARA 854.

2 As to the Greater London Authority see LONDON GOVERNMENT vol 71 (2013) PARAS 19, 67 et seq.

3 See the Museum of London Act 1965 s 9(1) (amended by the Local Government Act 1985 s 43(3); the Greater London Authority Act 2007 s 48(2); and SI 1992/1311). As to the Corporation of the City of London see LONDON GOVERNMENT vol 71 (2013) PARA 23 et seq.

4 Museum of London Act 1965 s 9(1) (as amended (see note 3); further amended by the Museum of London Act 1986 s 2(3)). This provision is expressed to be subject to the provisions of the Museum of London Act 1965 s 9 (see the text and notes 1–3, 5–7) and s 10 (repealed).

5 Museum of London Act 1965 s 9(2). The persons so appointed act on such terms and such conditions as may be agreed between the board and the corporation, except that no salaries, allowances or other remuneration may be paid to them by the board, but in respect of their service to the board, there are due to the corporation from the board such sums as the corporation and the board may agree: s 9(2).

6 Museum of London Act 1965 s 9(3) (amended by the Local Government Act 1985 s 43(3); the Greater London Authority Act 2007 s 48(2); and SI 1992/1311).

7 Museum of London Act 1965 s 9(4) (amended by the Local Government Act 1985 Sch 17; the Greater London Authority Act 2007 s 48(2); and SI 1992/1311). In making such a determination, the corporation must have regard to any recommendations that may be made by the board: Museum of London Act 1965 s 9(4). As to staff pensions see PARA 893.

856. General powers of Board of Governors of the Museum of London. The Board of Governors of the Museum of London[1] has a duty, so far as practicable, to care for, preserve and add to the objects in its collections[2]; to secure that those objects are exhibited to the public and made available to persons seeking to inspect them for study or research[3]; and generally to promote understanding and appreciation of historic and contemporary London[4] and of its society and culture, both by means of its collections and by such other means as the board considers appropriate[5]. The board may[6] do all such things as it thinks necessary or expedient for these purposes and its functions under the Museum of London Act 1965[7]. The board may also provide archaeological services, and undertake archaeological investigations and research in connection with land in London, and publish information concerning such activities and promote the provision of such services, the undertaking of such investigations and research and the publishing of such information[8].

The board may acquire or dispose of any land or any estate or interest in land[9]; but the board must not acquire or dispose of any land or estate or interest in land without the consent of the Greater London Authority[10] and the Corporation of the City of London[11].

1   As to the board see PARA 854.
2   Museum of London Act 1965 s 3(1)(a) (s 3 substituted by the Museum of London Act 1986 s 2(1)). As to the keeping of collections see PARA 857. As to the acquisition and disposal of objects see PARA 858.
3   Museum of London Act 1965 s 3(1)(b) (as substituted: see note 2).
4   For these purposes, 'London' includes Greater London and the surrounding region: Museum of London Act 1965 s 3(5) (as substituted: see note 2). 'Greater London' means the area comprising the areas of the London boroughs, the City and the Temples: see the London Government Act 1963 s 2(1); and LONDON GOVERNMENT vol 71 (2013) PARA 14.
5   Museum of London Act 1965 s 3(1)(c) (as substituted: see note 2).
6   Ie subject to the provisions of the Museum of London Act 1965.
7   Museum of London Act 1965 s 3(2) (as substituted: see note 2).
8   Museum of London Act 1965 s 3(3)(a) (as substituted: see note 2). As to the making of grants to the board for these purposes see the Museum of London Act 1986 s 4; and PARA 860.
9   Museum of London Act 1965 s 3(3)(b) (as substituted: see note 2).
10 As to the Greater London Authority see LONDON GOVERNMENT vol 71 (2013) PARAS 19, 67 et seq.
11 Museum of London Act 1965 s 3(4) (s 3 as substituted (see note 2); s 3(4) amended by the Greater London Authority Act 2007 s 48(1); and SI 1992/1311). Such consent may be given subject to such conditions as the Greater London Authority and the corporation consider appropriate: Museum of London Act 1965 s 3(4) (as so substituted and amended).

857. Keeping of collections for the Museum of London. The Board of Governors of the Museum of London[1] must take steps to acquire premises for the purpose of maintaining its collections in them and holding exhibitions in them of its collections, or so much of them as from time to time it thinks fit, being premises situated within Greater London[2] and, so long as they are held by the board, to be known as the Museum of London[3]. The board must[4], as soon as practicable after it has acquired the premises, keep the objects comprised in its collections in those premises, or, if those premises cease to be held by the board, in other premises within Greater London held by it[5].

However, nothing in these provisions is be taken as precluding the board from exhibiting any of the objects comprised in the collections at any place, wherever situated, other than such premises as are mentioned above, or from removing any of those objects for any purpose, other than exhibition, connected with the administration of any such premises or the care of the board's collections[6]. Where it appears to the board that any objects comprised in its collections cannot conveniently be kept within any such premises as are mentioned above[7] it may store those objects at such other premises, wherever situated, as appear to it to be suitable[8].

The board may make such charges as it may determine for admission to its premises[9]. The board may use the premises known as the Museum of London for any educational or cultural purpose whether or not connected with the board's functions under the Museum of London Act 1965[10]; and may allow any premises occupied or managed by it to be used by other persons[11] for purposes not connected with such functions if it is satisfied that to do so would not conflict with those functions[12].

1   As to the Museum of London and the board see PARA 854.
2   As to the meaning of 'Greater London' see PARA 856 note 4.
3   Museum of London Act 1965 s 4(1) (amended by SI 2004/1939).
4   Ie subject to the provisions of the Museum of London Act 1965 ss 5–16 (see the text and notes 10–12; and PARAS 855, 858–860).
5   Museum of London Act 1965 s 4(2) (amended by SI 2004/1939).
6   Museum of London Act 1965 s 4(3). As to the power to lend objects see PARA 859.
7   Ie as are mentioned in the Museum of London Act 1965 s 4(2) (see the text to notes 4–5).
8   Museum of London Act 1965 s 4(4).
9   Museum of London Act 1965 s 4(5) (added by the City of London (Various Powers) Act 1979 s 18).
10 Museum of London Act 1965 s 8(1) (s 8 substituted by the Museum of London Act 1986 s 2(2)).
11 As to the meaning of 'person' see PARA 803 note 17.
12 Museum of London Act 1965 s 8(2) (as substituted: see note 10).

858. Power of Board of Governors of the Museum of London to acquire, dispose of and transfer objects. The Board of Governors of the Museum of London[1] may[2] acquire any objects which in its opinion it is desirable to add to its collections[3]. The board may[4] sell, exchange, give away or otherwise dispose of any object vested in it and comprised in its collections if the object is a duplicate of another such object or is for any other reason not, in its opinion, required for retention in those collections[5]. These powers are only exercisable with the approval as respects that object of not less than two-thirds of the governors for the time being[6]. Where an object has become vested in the board subject to any trust or condition, the powers of disposal are not exercisable as respects that object in a manner inconsistent with that trust or condition[7].

The board is a specified transferor and transferee for the purposes of the general powers of transfer between collections[8]; but the powers of transfer are not exercisable by the board as respects an object except with the approval of their exercise as respects that object of not less than two-thirds of the governors for the time being[9]. The board is also a specified body for the purposes of the statutory provisions for the vesting of gifts to the nation where the donor has not specified a destination[10].

1   As to the Museum of London and the board see PARA 854.
2   Ie subject to the Museum of London Act 1965 ss 6–16 (see the text and notes 8–10; and PARAS 855, 857, 859–860).
3   Museum of London Act 1965 s 5(1). As to the keeping of collections see PARA 857. As to the power to lend objects see PARA 859.
4   See note 2.
5   Museum of London Act 1965 s 5(2).
6   See the Museum of London Act 1965 s 5(3).
7   Museum of London Act 1965 s 5(4).
8   See the Museums and Galleries Act 1992 s 6, Sch 5; and PARA 817.
9   Museum of London Act 1965 s 7(3) (amended by the Museums and Galleries Act 1992 Sch 8 para 11(b)).
10 See the Museums and Galleries Act 1992 s 7; and PARA 818.

859. Power of Board of Governors of the Museum of London to lend objects.
Any object vested in the Board of Governors of the Museum of London[1] may be
lent by it on such terms and conditions as it thinks fit, to any person[2] for any
purpose, whether the purpose is to be carried out in the United Kingdom[3] or
elsewhere[4]. However, in exercising the power to lend in the case of any object, the
board must have regard to the interests of students and other persons visiting the
collections vested in it, to the physical condition and degree of rarity of the object
and to any risks to which the object is likely to be exposed[5].

1 As to the Museum of London and the board see PARA 854.
2 As to the meaning of 'person' see PARA 803 note 17.
3 As to the meaning of 'United Kingdom' see PARA 804 note 2.
4 Museum of London Act 1965 s 6(1).
5 Museum of London Act 1965 s 6(2). As to the government indemnity scheme in respect of loans
   see PARA 1094. As to overseas loans see PARAS 1095, 1096.

860. Finance in respect of the Museum of London. The Historic Buildings and
Monuments Commission for England ('the Commission')[1] may make grants to
the Board of Governors of the Museum of London[2], subject to such conditions as
the commission may think fit to impose[3], for the purpose of assisting the board:
(1)   in providing archaeological services and undertaking archaeological
        investigations and research in connection with land in London[4] and
        publishing information concerning such investigations and research[5]; or
(2)   in promoting the provision of such services or the undertaking of such
        investigations and research or the publishing of such information by
        another person[6] or body[7].
From time to time the board must submit to the Greater London Authority[8]
and the Corporation of the City of London[9] an estimate of the expenditure which,
during the period to which the estimate relates, the board proposes to incur in
carrying the Museum of London Act 1965 into effect, being expenditure which it
proposes should be defrayed in accordance with the relevant statutory
provisions[10]; and the estimate must specify the matters in respect of which it is
proposed that the expenditure to which it relates should be incurred, and the
amount proposed to be incurred in respect of those matters[11]. Expenditure
incurred in accordance with an estimate thus submitted must, if the estimate is
approved by the authority and the corporation, be defrayed in the first instance by
the corporation, but the corporation and the authority may make payments to the
board in respect of such part of the expenditure incurred or to be incurred or in
respect of such expenditure of a particular description, as the corporation or (as
the case may be) the authority may determine, and in that event that part of such
expenditure, or, as the case may be, such expenditure of that description, must be
defrayed by the board itself instead of by the corporation[12].
    The total of the payments made by the authority under the above provisions
must equal the total expended by the corporation under those provisions[13].
However, in the case of particular amounts paid in respect of particular expenses,
the corporation and the authority may agree that the proportion of expenditure
paid for by the authority is other than one half[14].
    Money received by the board[15] otherwise than:
(a)   in accordance with estimates of expenditure approved by the Greater
        London Authority and the Corporation of the City of London under the
        above provisions[16];
(b)   in respect of the disposal of objects vested in it and comprised in its
        collections[17];
(c)   by way of gift or bequest[18]; or

(d)   by way of grant[19],

must not, except with the approval of the authority and the corporation, be applied by the board otherwise than in defraying expenses of the general administration of its collections and of any place where those collections are, or any part of them is, kept[20]. However, these provisions[21] do not authorise the application by the board of any money received by it by way of gift or bequest in a manner inconsistent with any condition attached to the gift or bequest[22].

1   As to the Historic Buildings and Monuments Commission for England ('the Commission') see PARA 803.
2   As to the Museum of London and the board see PARA 854.
3   See the Museum of London Act 1986 s 4(2).
4   For these purposes, 'London' includes all Greater London and the surrounding region: Museum of London Act 1986 s 4(3). As to the meaning of 'Greater London' see PARA 856 note 4.
5   Museum of London Act 1986 s 4(1). As to the power of the board to provide archaeological services and undertake archaeological investigations and research see the Museum of London Act 1965 s 3(3); and PARA 856.
6   As to the meaning of 'person' see PARA 803 note 17.
7   Museum of London Act 1986 s 4(1).
8   As to the Greater London Authority see LONDON GOVERNMENT vol 71 (2013) PARAS 19, 67 et seq.
9   As to the Corporation of the City of London see LONDON GOVERNMENT vol 71 (2013) PARA 23 et seq.
10   Ie in accordance with the Museum of London Act 1965 s 15 (see the text to notes 11–14).
11   Museum of London Act 1965 s 15(1) (amended by the Local Government Act 1985 s 43(3); the Greater London Authority Act 2007 s 47(2), (3); and SI 1992/1311).
12   Museum of London Act 1965 s 15(2) (amended by the Local Government Act 1985 s 43(3); the Greater London Authority Act 2007 s 47(2), (4); and SI 1992/1311).
13   Museum of London Act 1965 s 15(3) (s 15(3) substituted by, and s 15(4) added by, the Greater London Authority Act 2007 s 47(2), (5)).
14   Museum of London Act 1965 s 15(4) (as added: see note 13).
15   Any interest received by the board on the investment of any money received by it in any way must be treated, for these purposes, as forming part of the money received in that way: Museum of London Act 1965 s 14(3).
16   See the Museum of London Act 1965 s 14(1)(a) (amended by the Museum of London Act 1985 ss 4(4), 7(3), Schedule).
17   Museum of London Act 1965 s 14(1)(b). Moneys received by the board in such a way must not be applied by them, except with the approval of the authority and the corporation, otherwise than in the exercise of the power conferred on the board by s 5(1) (see PARA 858): s 14(2) (amended by the Local Government Act 1985 s 43(3); the Greater London Authority Act 2007 s 47(1); and SI 1992/1311).
18   Museum of London Act 1965 s 14(1)(c). This includes money received under s 2(2) (see PARA 854): see s 14(1)(c).
19   See the Museum of London Act 1965 s 14(1)(d) (added by the Museum of London Act 1985 ss 4(4), 7(3), Schedule). The text refers to a grant made under the Museum of London Act 1986 s 4 (see the text to notes 1–7).
20   Museum of London Act 1965 s 14(1) (amended by the Local Government Act 1985 s 43(3); the Greater London Authority Act 2007 s 47(1); and SI 1992/1311). As to the keeping of collections see PARA 857.
21   Ie the Museum of London Act 1965 s 14(1)–(3) (see the text to notes 15–20).
22   See the Museum of London Act 1965 s 14(4).

G.   THE VICTORIA AND ALBERT MUSEUM

861. Board of Trustees of the Victoria and Albert Museum. There is a body known as the Board of Trustees of the Victoria and Albert Museum[1]. The board is a body corporate[2]. The board is not to be regarded as the servant or agent of the Crown or as enjoying any status, immunity or privilege of the Crown[3], and the trustees and their staff are not to be regarded as civil servants and the board's property is not to be regarded as property of, or held on behalf of, the

Crown[4]. Subject to the provisions of any enactment[5], the board is not exempt from any tax, duty, rate, levy or other charge whatever (whether general or local)[6].

The board may regulate its own procedure[7], and may make arrangements for any of its functions, other than the power to acquire or dispose of land[8], to be discharged by committees[9]. The validity of any proceedings of the board is not affected by any vacancy among the trustees or by any defect in the appointment of any trustee[10].

The fixing of the seal of the board must be authenticated by the signature of the chairman or of some other person authorised either generally or specially by the board to act for that purpose[11]. A document purporting to be duly executed under the seal of the board, or to be signed on the board's behalf, is receivable in evidence and, unless the contrary is proved, is deemed to be so executed or signed[12].

1 National Heritage Act 1983 s 1(1). As to the membership of the board see Sch 1 para 3. As to the payment of allowances to the trustees and members of any committee see Sch 1 para 7 (amended by SI 1992/1311). The Board of Trustees, so far as it is a charity, and any institution which is administered by or on its behalf and established for general or special purposes, is an exempt charity for the purposes of the Charities Act 2011: see s 22, Sch 3 para 12; and CHARITIES vol 8 (2015) PARA 318. As to the vesting of objects in the board see PARA 866.
2 National Heritage Act 1983 Sch 1 para 1. As to bodies corporate see COMPANIES vol 14 (2009) PARA 2; CORPORATIONS vol 24 (2010) PARA 301 et seq.
3 National Heritage Act 1983 Sch 1 para 2(1). However, in relation to any matter as respects which the board acts by virtue of a direction by a Minister of the Crown under s 2(4) (see PARA 863), the board enjoys the same privileges, immunities and exemptions as those enjoyed in relation to that matter by the minister giving the direction: Sch 1 para 2(3). As to the legal status of bodies not to be regarded as the servant or agent of the Crown or as enjoying any status, immunity or privilege of the Crown see CONSTITUTIONAL AND ADMINISTRATIVE LAW vol 20 (2014) PARA 311 et seq.
4 National Heritage Act 1983 Sch 1 para 2(2). As to the power to appoint staff see PARA 862. As to the civil service see CONSTITUTIONAL AND ADMINISTRATIVE LAW vol 20 (2014) PARA 285 et seq.
5 As to the meaning of 'enactment' see PARA 805 note 5.
6 National Heritage Act 1983 Sch 1 para 2(4) (amended by the Local Government and Rating Act 1997 Sch 3 para 18(2)(a)).
7 See the National Heritage Act 1983 Sch 1 para 6(1). As to quorum see Sch 1 para 6(1), (7).
8 As to the meaning of 'land' see PARA 804 note 30.
9 See the National Heritage Act 1983 Sch 1 para 6(2)–(6).
10 National Heritage Act 1983 Sch 1 para 6(8).
11 National Heritage Act 1983 Sch 1 para 8(1). As to the corporate seal see CORPORATIONS vol 24 (2010) PARA 323 et seq.
12 National Heritage Act 1983 Sch 1 para 8(2). Certain records of the board are public records for the purposes of the Public Records Act 1958: see s 10, Sch 1 para 3, Table Pt II; and CONSTITUTIONAL AND ADMINISTRATIVE LAW vol 20 (2014) PARA 343.

862. Director and staff of the Victoria and Albert Museum. There is a director of the Victoria and Albert Museum who is appointed by the Board of Trustees of the museum[1] with the approval of the Prime Minister[2], and who is responsible to the board for the general exercise of the board's functions[3].

The board may appoint such other employees as it thinks fit[4]. The board must pay to them such remuneration and allowances as it may determine[5], and the employees are appointed on such other terms and conditions as the board may determine[6].

1 As to the board see PARA 861.
2 National Heritage Act 1983 Sch 1 para 4(1). As to the Prime Minister see CONSTITUTIONAL AND ADMINISTRATIVE LAW vol 20 (2014) PARAS 203–208.
3 National Heritage Act 1983 Sch 1 para 4(2). As to the functions of the board see PARA 863.
4 National Heritage Act 1983 Sch 1 para 4(3).

5   National Heritage Act 1983 Sch 1 para 4(4). A determination under Sch 1 para 4(4) or 4(5) (see
the text to note 6) is ineffective unless made with the approval of the Secretary of State given with
the Treasury's consent: Sch 1 para 4(6) (amended by SI 1992/1311). As to the Secretary of State
see PARA 802 note 2. As to the meaning of 'Treasury' see PARA 809 note 4.
6   National Heritage Act 1983 Sch 1 para 4(5). See also note 5. Employment with the board is
included among the kinds of employment to which a scheme under the Superannuation Act 1972
s 1 can apply: National Heritage Act 1983 Sch 1 para 4(7). See further PARA 893. As to the
provision made in respect of the employment by the board of staff formerly employed in the civil
service for the purposes of the museum see Sch 1 para 5 (amended by the Employment Rights Act
1996 s 240, Sch 1 para 23; the Employment Rights (Dispute Resolution) Act 1998 s 1(2)(a); and
SI 1992/1311).

863.   General functions of Board of Trustees of the Victoria and Albert Museum.
So far as practicable, and subject to the provisions of the National Heritage Act
1983, the Board of Trustees of the Victoria and Albert Museum[1] must:

(1)   care for, preserve and add to the objects in its collections[2];
(2)   secure that the objects are exhibited to the public[3];
(3)   secure that the objects are available to persons[4] seeking to inspect them
in connection with study or research[5]; and
(4)   generally promote the public's enjoyment and understanding of art,
craft and design, both by means of the board's collections and by such
other means as the board considers appropriate[6].

For those purposes the board may[7]:

(a)   provide education, instruction and advice and carry out research[8];
(b)   enter into contracts and other agreements (including agreements for the
board's occupation or management of the building known as the
Victoria and Albert Museum or other premises)[9];
(c)   acquire and dispose of land[10] and other property[11];
(d)   do such things, including requiring payment for admission or for other
services or for goods provided by it, as it thinks necessary or expedient:
(i)   for preserving, and increasing the utility of, its collections[12];
(ii)   for securing the due administration of anything vested in or
acquired by the board, and any premises occupied or managed
by it, under or by virtue of the National Heritage Act 1983[13]; and
(iii) otherwise for the purposes of its functions[14].

If a Minister of the Crown directs the board to exercise functions which are
exercisable by him (whether by virtue of an enactment[15] or otherwise), which in
his opinion can appropriately be exercised by the board having regard to its
functions and resources, and which are specified in the direction, the board must
exercise them on his behalf in such manner as he may from time to time direct[16].

The board may allow premises occupied or managed by it to be used by other
persons (for payment or otherwise) for purposes not connected with its functions
in heads (1) to (4) above, if the board is satisfied that to do so would not conflict
unduly with those functions[17].

The board must make a report to the Secretary of State on the exercise of its
functions since the last report was made, not later than three years (or such
shorter period as the Secretary of State may direct) since the last report was
made[18]. Each report must include a statement of action taken by the board to
enable disabled members of the public to use any services or facilities provided by
the board[19]; and a statement of the total amount received by the board by way of
admission charges in the period covered by the report[20]. The Secretary of State
must lay a copy of each report before each House of Parliament[21].

1   As to the board see PARA 861.
2   National Heritage Act 1983 s 2(1)(a).

3 National Heritage Act 1983 s 2(1)(b). As to the vesting of objects in the board see PARA 866.
4 As to the meaning of 'person' see PARA 803 note 17.
5 National Heritage Act 1983 s 2(1)(c).
6 National Heritage Act 1983 s 2(1)(d).
7 Ie subject to the provisions of the National Heritage Act 1983: see s 2(2), (3).
8 National Heritage Act 1983 s 2(2)(a).
9 National Heritage Act 1983 s 2(2)(b).
10 As to the meaning of 'land' see PARA 804 note 30.
11 National Heritage Act 1983 s 2(2)(c). The board may not acquire or dispose of land without the
   Secretary of State's consent: s 2(5) (amended by SI 1992/1311). As to the power of the Secretary
   of State to transfer land vested in him to the board see the Museums and Galleries Act 1992 s 8,
   Sch 6; and PARA 819. As to the Secretary of State see PARA 802 note 2.
12 National Heritage Act 1983 s 2(3)(a).
13 National Heritage Act 1983 s 2(3)(b).
14 National Heritage Act 1983 s 2(3)(c).
15 As to the meaning of 'enactment' see PARA 805 note 5.
16 National Heritage Act 1983 s 2(4). However, nothing in this provision authorises the board to
   exercise a function of making regulations or other instruments of a legislative character: s 2(4). In
   relation to any matter as respects which the board acts by virtue of a direction under s 2(4), the
   board enjoys the same privileges, immunities and exemptions as those enjoyed in relation to that
   matter by the minister giving the direction: see Sch 1 para 2(3); and PARA 861.
17 National Heritage Act 1983 s 2(6).
18 See the National Heritage Act 1983 Sch 1 para 10(1), (3) (s 10(1)–(3) amended by SI 1992/1311).
   The first report was to be made not later than the expiry of the period of three years (or such
   shorter period as the Secretary of State directed), commencing with the day of the
   board's establishment (ie 30 September 1983): see the National Heritage Act 1983 ss 1(1), 41(1),
   Sch 1 para 10(2) (as so amended); National Heritage Act 1983 (Commencement No 1) Order
   1983, SI 1983/1062, art 3, Sch 2.
19 National Heritage Act 1983 Sch 1 para 10(4). As to the prohibition against discrimination in the
   provision of goods, facilities and services to disabled persons see DISCRIMINATION vol 33 (2013)
   PARA 78 et seq.
20 National Heritage Act 1983 Sch 1 para 10(5). Such statement must include information, in such
   detail as the board thinks fit, about rates of, exemptions from and reductions in admission charges
   made by the board: Sch 1 para 10(5).
21 National Heritage Act 1983 Sch 1 para 10(6) (amended by SI 1992/1311). As to the laying of
   documents before Parliament see STATUTES AND LEGISLATIVE PROCESS vol 96 (2012) PARA
   1052.

**864. Power of Board of Trustees of the Victoria and Albert Museum to form
companies.** Without prejudice to its general powers[1], the Board of Trustees of the
Victoria and Albert Museum may, with the consent of the Secretary of State[2] and
subject to any conditions he may impose, form or take part in forming one or
more bodies corporate which, or each of which, has as its main object or objects[3]:

    (1)   one or more of the following particular objects[4]:

        (a)   the production and publication of books, films or other
informative material relating to art, craft or design[5];

        (b)   the commissioning of works of art, craft or design[6];

        (c)   the production of replicas or reproductions of works of art, craft
or design, or of souvenirs[7];

        (d)   the sale of informative material relating to art, craft or design, of
works of art, craft or design, of replicas or reproductions of such
works, or of souvenirs[8];

        (e)   the provision of catering or car parking or other services or
facilities for the public at any premises occupied or managed by
the board[9]; or

    (2)   any other object or objects incidental to the board's functions[10].

The board may hold interests in any such body, exercise rights conferred by the holding of interests in it, and provide financial or other assistance to or in respect of it, including assistance by way of guarantee of its obligations[11].

1 The National Heritage Act 1983 s 3 is without prejudice to any power of the Board of Trustees of the Victoria and Albert Museum to undertake anything mentioned in s 3(2) (see the text to notes 4–9) by virtue of s 2 (see PARA 863): s 3(5). As to the board see PARA 861.
2 As to the Secretary of State see PARA 802 note 2.
3 See the National Heritage Act 1983 s 3(1) (amended by SI 1992/1311).
4 National Heritage Act 1983 s 3(1)(a), (2) (s 3(1)(a), (b) substituted by, and s 3(2) amended by, the Public Bodies Act 2011 s 32(1), (2)(a)).
5 National Heritage Act 1983 s 3(2)(a).
6 National Heritage Act 1983 s 3(2)(b). For these purposes, references to works of design are to works illustrating the principles of design: s 3(4).
7 National Heritage Act 1983 s 3(2)(c).
8 National Heritage Act 1983 s 3(2)(d).
9 National Heritage Act 1983 s 3(2)(e).
10 National Heritage Act 1983 s 3(1)(b) (as substituted: see note 4).
11 National Heritage Act 1983 s 3(3).

865. Power of Board of Trustees of the Victoria and Albert Museum to acquire and dispose of objects. The Board of Trustees of the Victoria and Albert Museum[1] may acquire (whether by purchase, exchange or gift) any objects which in its opinion it is desirable to add to its collections[2]. Without prejudice to any power apart from this provision, a Minister of the Crown may transfer to the board any object (whether or not he acquired it before the board's establishment) if in his opinion it would appropriately form part of its collections[3].

The board may not dispose of an object the property in which is vested in the board and which is comprised in its collections unless:

(1)   the disposal is by way of sale, exchange or gift of an object which is a duplicate of another object the property in which is so vested and which is so comprised[4]; or

(2)   the disposal is by way of sale, exchange or gift of an object which in the board's opinion is unsuitable for retention in its collections and can be disposed of without detriment to the interests of students or other members of the public[5]; or

(3)   the disposal is an exercise of the statutory power of transfer[6]; or

(4)   the disposal, by whatever means, including destruction, is of an object which the board is satisfied has become useless for the purposes of its collections by reason of damage, physical deterioration, or infestation by destructive organisms[7].

Money accruing to the board by virtue of any such disposal must be applied by the board in the acquisition of objects to be added to its collections[8].

The board is a specified transferor and transferee for the purposes of the general powers of transfer between collections[9], and a specified body for the purposes of the statutory provision for vesting of gifts to the nation where the donor has not specified a destination[10].

In certain circumstances the board may transfer an object from its collections under the Holocaust (Return of Cultural Objects) Act 2009[11].

1 As to the board see PARA 861.
2 National Heritage Act 1983 s 6(1). As to the vesting of objects in the board see PARA 866.
3 National Heritage Act 1983 s 6(2). The board was established on 30 September 1983: see ss 1(1), 41(1); National Heritage Act 1983 (Commencement No 1) Order 1983, SI 1983/1062, art 3, Sch 2.
4 National Heritage Act 1983 s 6(3)(a).
5 National Heritage Act 1983 s 6(3)(b).

6 See the National Heritage Act 1983 s 6(3)(c) (amended by the Museums and Galleries Act 1992 Sch 8 para 13(1)). The statutory power of transfer is that under the Museums and Galleries Act 1992 s 6 (see PARA 817): see the National Heritage Act 1983 s 6(3)(c) (as so amended).

7 National Heritage Act 1983 s 6(3)(d). An object may be disposed of as mentioned in this provision notwithstanding a trust or condition, express or implied, prohibiting or restricting the disposal of the object: s 6(5).

8 National Heritage Act 1983 s 6(6).

9 See the Museums and Galleries Act 1992 s 6, Sch 5; and PARA 817.

10 See the Museums and Galleries Act 1992 s 7; and PARA 818.

11 See PARA 1107.

866. Vesting, lending and borrowing of objects held for purposes of the Victoria and Albert Museum. Where, immediately before 1 April 1984 (the 'vesting day)[1], the property in an object was vested in a Minister of the Crown and the object:

(1) then formed part of the collections of the institution known as the Victoria and Albert Museum[2]; or

(2) was then in use in respect of the collections or solely for the purposes of the administration of the institution[3],

then the property on that day became vested instead in the Board of Trustees of the Victoria and Albert Museum[4]. Similar provision was made for the transfer to the board of any interest in a fund or share in a fund (whether or not of money) held for the purposes of the institution vested in a Minister of the Crown immediately before the vesting day[5]. On the vesting day any right, power, duty or liability which was immediately before that day exercisable by or incumbent on a Minister of the Crown:

(a) in relation to any object mentioned in head (1) or (2) above[6]; or

(b) by virtue of his having any such interest as is mentioned above[7],

instead became exercisable by or incumbent on the board[8].

The board may lend any object the property in which is vested in it and which is comprised in its collections, whether or not the loan is for purposes of public exhibition, and whether or not under the terms of the loan the object is to remain in the United Kingdom[9]. However, in deciding whether or not to lend an object, and in determining the time for which and the conditions subject to which an object is to be lent, the board:

(i) must give special consideration to a request for the loan of an object for public exhibition[10]; and

(ii) subject to that, must have regard to the interests of students and other persons visiting the board's collections, the suitability of the prospective borrower, the purpose of the loan, the physical condition and degree of rarity of the object, and any risks to which it is likely to be exposed[11].

Where the property in an object has become vested in the board subject to a condition, this power to lend the object is exercisable in a manner inconsistent with the condition if either: (A) 25 years have elapsed since the date on which the property became vested in the board or, where it became vested in the board under the initial vesting provisions above[12], the minister[13]; or (B) the person[14] who first imposed the condition or his personal representatives[15] has or have consented in writing[16] to the exercise of the power in that manner[17].

The board may accept loans of objects for the purpose (depending on the terms of the loan) of exhibiting them, or of study or research by the board or by persons seeking to inspect them[18].

1 See the National Heritage Act 1983 ss 4(8), 5(3), 41(1); National Heritage Act 1983 (Commencement No 6) Order 1984, SI 1984/225.

2 National Heritage Act 1983 s 4(1)(a). In the case of an object mentioned in s 4(1)(a), it is immaterial that, immediately before the vesting day, it was situated elsewhere than at premises managed for the purposes of the institution (as where it was on loan): s 4(2).
3 National Heritage Act 1983 s 4(1)(b).
4 National Heritage Act 1983 s 4(1). As to the board see PARA 861. Section 4(1), (4)(a) (see head (a) in the text) does not apply as regards an object excepted from those provisions by an order made by the Secretary of State and coming into force before the vesting day (s 4(5) (s 4(5), (6) amended by SI 1992/1311)); and nothing in the National Heritage Act 1983 s 4(1) or s 4(4)(a) affects chattels vested in the Secretary of State by virtue of the Wellington Museum Act 1947 (see PARA 852), but he and the board may make agreements for the board to perform, on his behalf, functions exercisable by him in relation to the chattels mentioned in s 2(1) of that Act (see PARA 852) (National Heritage Act 1983 s 4(6) (as so amended)). In exercise of the power under s 4(5), the Victoria and Albert Museum (Excepted Objects) Order 1984, SI 1984/226, has been made. As to the Secretary of State see PARA 802 note 2.
5 See the National Heritage Act 1983 s 4(3).
6 See the National Heritage Act 1983 s 4(4)(a). See also note 4.
7 See the National Heritage Act 1983 s 4(4)(b).
8 National Heritage Act 1983 s 4(4). Any gift, by will or otherwise, which is contained in an instrument made or executed before the vesting day but coming into effect on or after that day, and which would otherwise have vested an interest in property (of any nature) in a Minister of the Crown for the purposes of the Victoria and Albert Museum, has effect so as to vest the interest in the board in place of the minister in the absence of any contrary intention expressed in that or another instrument made by the testator or donor: see the National Heritage Act 1983 s 5(1), (2).
9 National Heritage Act 1983 s 7(1). As to the meaning of 'United Kingdom' see PARA 804 note 2. As to the government indemnity scheme for loans see PARA 1094. As to overseas loans see PARAS 1095, 1096.
10 National Heritage Act 1983 s 7(2)(a).
11 National Heritage Act 1983 s 7(2)(b).
12 Ie under the National Heritage Act 1983 s 4(1) (see the text to notes 1–4).
13 National Heritage Act 1983 s 7(3)(a).
14 As to the meaning of 'person' see PARA 803 note 17.
15 As to personal representatives see WILLS AND INTESTACY vol 103 (2010) PARA 605 et seq.
16 As to the meaning of 'writing' see PARA 805 note 14.
17 National Heritage Act 1983 s 7(3)(b).
18 National Heritage Act 1983 s 7(4).

H. THE SCIENCE MUSEUM

867. Board of Trustees of the Science Museum. There is a body known as the Board of Trustees of the Science Museum[1]. The board is a body corporate[2]. The board is not to be regarded as the servant or agent of the Crown or as enjoying any status, immunity or privilege of the Crown[3], and the trustees and their staff are not to be regarded as civil servants and the board's property is not to be regarded as property of, or held on behalf of, the Crown[4]. Subject to the provisions of any enactment[5], the board is not exempt from any tax, duty, rate, levy or other charge whatever (whether general or local)[6].

The board may regulate its own procedure[7], and may make arrangements for any of its functions, other than the power to acquire or dispose of land[8], to be discharged by committees[9]. The validity of any proceedings of the board is not affected by any vacancy among the trustees or by any defect in the appointment of any trustee[10].

The fixing of the seal of the board must be authenticated by the signature of the chairman or of some other person authorised either generally or specially by the board to act for that purpose[11]. A document purporting to be duly executed under the seal of the board, or to be signed on the board's behalf, is receivable in evidence and, unless the contrary is proved, is deemed to be so executed or signed[12].

1 National Heritage Act 1983 s 9(1). The board, so far as it is a charity, and any institution which is administered by or on its behalf and established for general or special purposes, is an exempt

charity for the purposes of the Charities Act 2011: see s 22, Sch 3 para 13; and CHARITIES vol 8 (2015) PARA 318.
2 National Heritage Act 1983 Sch 1 para 11. As to the constitution of the board see Sch 1 para 13. As to the payment of allowances to the trustees and members of committees see Sch 1 para 17 (amended by SI 1992/1311). As to bodies corporate see COMPANIES vol 14 (2009) PARA 2; CORPORATIONS vol 24 (2010) PARA 301 et seq.
3 National Heritage Act 1983 Sch 1 para 12(1). However, in relation to any matter as respects which the board acts by virtue of a direction given by a Minister of the Crown under s 10(4) (see PARA 869), the board enjoys the same privileges, immunities and exemptions as those enjoyed in relation to that matter by the minister giving the direction: Sch 1 para 12(3). As to the legal status of bodies not to be regarded as the servant or agent of the Crown or as enjoying any status, immunity or privilege of the Crown see CONSTITUTIONAL AND ADMINISTRATIVE LAW vol 20 (2014) PARA 311 et seq.
4 National Heritage Act 1983 Sch 1 para 12(2). As to the power to appoint staff see PARA 868. As to the civil service see CONSTITUTIONAL AND ADMINISTRATIVE LAW vol 20 (2014) PARA 285 et seq.
5 As to the meaning of 'enactment' see PARA 805 note 5.
6 National Heritage Act 1983 Sch 1 para 12(4) (amended by the Local Government and Ratings Act 1997 s 33(1), Sch 3 para 18(3)(a)).
7 See the National Heritage Act 1983 Sch 1 para 16(1). As to quorum see Sch 1 para 16(1), (7).
8 As to the meaning of 'land' see PARA 804 note 30.
9 See the National Heritage Act 1983 Sch 1 para 16(2)–(6). As to the general functions of the board see PARA 869.
10 National Heritage Act 1983 Sch 1 para 16(8).
11 National Heritage Act 1983 Sch 1 para 18(1). As to the corporate seal see CORPORATIONS vol 24 (2010) PARA 323 et seq.
12 National Heritage Act 1983 Sch 1 para 18(2). Certain records of the board are public records for the purposes of the Public Records Act 1958: see s 10, Sch 1 para 3, Table Pt II; and CONSTITUTIONAL AND ADMINISTRATIVE LAW vol 20 (2014) PARA 343.

868. Director and staff of the Science Museum. There is a director of the Science Museum who is appointed by the Board of Trustees of the museum[1] with the approval of the Prime Minister[2]. The director is responsible to the board for the general exercise of the board's functions[3].

The board may appoint such other employees as it thinks fit[4] and must pay to them such remuneration and allowances as it may determine[5]. The employees are appointed on such other terms and conditions as the board may determine[6].

1 As to the board see PARA 867.
2 National Heritage Act 1983 Sch 1 para 14(1). As to the Prime Minister see CONSTITUTIONAL AND ADMINISTRATIVE LAW vol 20 (2014) PARAS 203–208.
3 National Heritage Act 1983 Sch 1 para 14(2). As to the functions of the board see PARA 869.
4 National Heritage Act 1983 Sch 1 para 14(3).
5 National Heritage Act 1983 Sch 1 para 14(4). A determination under Sch 1 para 14(4) or (5) (see the text to note 6) is ineffective unless made with the approval of the Secretary of State given with the Treasury's consent: Sch 1 para 14(6) (amended by SI 1992/1311). As to the Secretary of State see PARA 802 note 2. As to the meaning of 'Treasury' see PARA 809 note 4.
6 National Heritage Act 1983 Sch 1 para 14(5). See also note 5. Employment with the board is included among the kinds of employment to which a scheme under the Superannuation Act 1972 s 1 can apply: National Heritage Act 1983 Sch 1 para 14(7). See further PARA 893. As to the provision made in respect of the employment by the board of staff formerly employed in the civil service for the purposes of the museum see Sch 1 para 15 (amended by the Employment Rights Act 1996 s 240, Sch 1 para 23; the Employment Rights (Dispute Resolution) Act 1998 s 1(2)(a); and SI 1992/1311).

869. General functions of Board of Trustees of the Science Museum. So far as practicable and subject to the provisions of the National Heritage Act 1983, the Board of Trustees of the Science Museum[1] must:

(1) care for, preserve and add to the objects in its collections[2];
(2) secure that the objects are exhibited to the public[3];
(3) secure that the objects are available to persons[4] seeking to inspect them in connection with study or research[5]; and

(4)	generally promote the public's enjoyment and understanding of science and technology and of the development of those subjects, both by means of the board's collections and by such other means as the board considers appropriate[6].

For those purposes the board may[7]:

(a)	provide education, instruction and advice and carry out research[8];

(b)	enter into contracts and other agreements (including agreements for the board's occupation or management of the building known as the Science Museum or other premises)[9];

(c)	acquire and dispose of land[10] and other property[11];

(d)	do such things, including requiring payment for admission or for other services or for goods provided by it, as it thinks necessary or expedient:

    (i)	for preserving, and increasing the utility of, its collections[12];

    (ii)	for securing the due administration of anything vested in or acquired by the board, and any premises occupied or managed by it, under or by virtue of the National Heritage Act 1983[13]; and

    (iii)	otherwise for the purposes of its functions[14].

If a Minister of the Crown directs the board to exercise functions which are exercisable by him (whether by virtue of an enactment[15] or otherwise), which in his opinion can appropriately be exercised by the board having regard to its functions and resources, and which are specified in the direction, the board must exercise them on his behalf in such manner as he may from time to time direct[16].

The board may allow premises occupied or managed by it to be used by other persons (for payment or otherwise) for purposes not connected with its functions in heads (1) to (4) above, if the board is satisfied that to do so would not conflict unduly with those functions[17].

The board must make a report to the Secretary of State on the exercise of its functions since the last report was made[18], not later than three years (or such shorter period as the Secretary of State may direct) since that last report was made[19]. Each report must include: (A) a statement of action taken by the board to enable disabled members of the public to use any services or facilities provided by the board[20]; and (B) a statement of the total amount received by the board by way of admission charges in the period covered by the report[21]. The Secretary of State must lay a copy of each report before each House of Parliament[22].

1	As to the board see PARA 867.
2	National Heritage Act 1983 s 10(1)(a).
3	National Heritage Act 1983 s 10(1)(b).
4	As to the meaning of 'person' see PARA 803 note 17.
5	National Heritage Act 1983 s 10(1)(c).
6	National Heritage Act 1983 s 10(1)(d).
7	Ie subject to the provisions of the National Heritage Act 1983: s 10(2), (3) (see the text and notes 8–14).
8	National Heritage Act 1983 s 10(2)(a).
9	National Heritage Act 1983 s 10(2)(b).
10	As to the meaning of 'land' see PARA 804 note 30.
11	National Heritage Act 1983 s 10(1)(c). The board may not acquire or dispose of land without the Secretary of State's consent: s 10(5) (amended by SI 1992/1311). As to the Secretary of State see PARA 802 note 2. As to the power of the Secretary of State to transfer land vested in him to the board see the Museums and Galleries Act 1992 s 8, Sch 6; and PARA 819.
12	National Heritage Act 1983 s 10(3)(a).
13	National Heritage Act 1983 s 10(3)(b).
14	National Heritage Act 1983 s 10(3)(c).
15	As to the meaning of 'enactment' see PARA 805 note 5.
16	National Heritage Act 1983 s 10(4). Nothing in this provision authorises the board to exercise a function of making regulations or other instruments of a legislative character: s 10(4). In relation

to any matter as respects which the board acts by virtue of a direction given by a Minister of the Crown under s 10(4), the board enjoys the same privileges, immunities and exemptions as those enjoyed in relation to that matter by the minister giving the direction: see Sch 1 para 12(3); and PARA 867.
17 National Heritage Act 1983 s 10(6).
18 See the National Heritage Act 1983 Sch 1 para 20(1) (Sch 1 para 20(1)–(3), (6) amended by SI 1992/1311). The first report was to be made not later than the expiry of the period of three years (or such shorter period as the Secretary of State directed), commencing with the day of the board's establishment (ie 30 September 1983): see the National Heritage Act 1983 ss 1(1), 41(1), Sch 1 para 20(2) (as so amended); National Heritage Act 1983 (Commencement No 1) Order 1983, SI 1983/1062, art 3, Sch 2.
19 See the National Heritage Act 1983 Sch 1 para 20(3) (as amended: see note 18).
20 National Heritage Act 1983 Sch 1 para 20(4). As to the prohibition against discrimination in the provision of goods, facilities and services to disabled persons see DISCRIMINATION vol 33 (2013) PARA 78 et seq.
21 National Heritage Act 1983 Sch 1 para 20(5). This statement must include information, in such detail as the board thinks fit, about rates of, exemptions from and reductions in admission charges made by the board: Sch 1 para 20(5).
22 National Heritage Act 1983 Sch 1 para 20(6) (as amended: see note 18). As to the laying of documents before Parliament see STATUTES AND LEGISLATIVE PROCESS vol 96 (2012) PARA 1052.

870. Power of Board of Trustees of the Science Museum to form companies. Without prejudice to its general powers[1], the Board of Trustees of the Science Museum may, with the consent of the Secretary of State[2] and subject to any conditions he may impose, form or take part in forming one or more bodies corporate which, or each of which, has as its main object or objects[3]:

(1)   one or more of the following particular objects[4]:
  (a)   the production and publication of books, films or other informative material relating to science and technology[5];
  (b)   the production of replicas or reproductions of objects relating to science and technology, or of souvenirs[6];
  (c)   the sale of informative material relating to science and technology, or of replicas or reproductions of objects relating to science and technology, or of souvenirs[7];
  (d)   the provision of catering or car parking or other services or facilities for the public at any premises occupied or managed by the board[8]; or
(2)   any other object or objects incidental to the board's functions[9].

The board may hold interests in any such body, exercise rights conferred by the holding of interests in it, and provide financial or other assistance to or in respect of it, including assistance by way of guarantee of its obligations[10].

1   The National Heritage Act 1983 s 11 is without prejudice to any power of the Board of Trustees of the Science Museum to undertake anything mentioned in s 11(2) (see heads (1)(a)–(d) in the text) by virtue of s 10 (see PARA 869): s 11(5). As to the board see PARA 867.
2   As to the Secretary of State see PARA 802 note 2.
3   National Heritage Act 1983 s 11(1) (amended by SI 1992/1311).
4   National Heritage Act 1983 s 11(1)(a), (2) (s 11(1)(a), (b) substituted by, and s 11(2) amended by, the Public Bodies Act 2011 s 32(1), (3)(a), (b)).
5   National Heritage Act 1983 s 11(2)(a). References in s 11 to science and technology include references to the development of those subjects: s 11(4).
6   National Heritage Act 1983 s 11(2)(b).
7   National Heritage Act 1983 s 11(2)(c).
8   National Heritage Act 1983 s 11(2)(d).
9   National Heritage Act 1983 s 11(1)(b) (as substituted: see note 4).
10 National Heritage Act 1983 s 11(3).

871. Power of Board of Trustees of the Science Museum to acquire and dispose of objects. The Board of Trustees of the Science Museum[1] may acquire (whether by purchase, exchange or gift) any objects which in its opinion it is desirable to add to its collections[2]. Without prejudice to any power apart from this provision, a Minister of the Crown may transfer to the board any object (whether or not he acquired it before the board's establishment) if in his opinion it would appropriately form part of its collections[3].

The board may not dispose of an object the property in which is vested in the board and which is comprised in its collections unless:

(1)   the disposal is by way of sale, exchange or gift of an object which is a duplicate of another object the property in which is so vested and which is so comprised[4]; or

(2)   the disposal is by way of sale, exchange or gift of an object which in the board's opinion is unsuitable for retention in its collections and can be disposed of without detriment to the interests of students or other members of the public[5]; or

(3)   the disposal is an exercise of the statutory power of transfer[6]; or

(4)   the disposal, by whatever means, including destruction, is of an object which the board is satisfied has become useless for the purposes of its collections by reason of damage, physical deterioration, or infestation by destructive organisms[7].

Money accruing to the board by virtue of any such disposal must be applied by the board in the acquisition of objects to be added to its collections[8].

The board is a specified transferor and transferee for the purposes of the general powers of transfer between collections[9], and a specified body for the purposes of the statutory provision for vesting of gifts to the nation where the donor has not specified a destination[10].

In certain circumstances the board may transfer an object from its collections under the Holocaust (Return of Cultural Objects) Act 2009[11].

1   As to the board see PARA 867.
2   National Heritage Act 1983 s 14(1). As to the vesting of objects in the board, and as to the board's power to lend or borrow objects, see PARA 872.
3   National Heritage Act 1983 s 14(2). The board was established on 30 September 1983: see ss 9(1), 41(1); National Heritage Act 1983 (Commencement No 1) Order 1983, SI 1983/1062, art 3, Sch 2.
4   National Heritage Act 1983 s 14(3)(a).
5   National Heritage Act 1983 s 14(3)(b).
6   National Heritage Act 1983 s 14(3)(c) (amended by the Museums and Galleries Act 1992 Sch 8 para 13(1)). The statutory power of transfer is that under the Museums and Galleries Act 1992 s 6 (see PARA 817).
7   National Heritage Act 1983 s 14(3)(d). An object may be disposed of as mentioned in this provision notwithstanding a trust or condition, express or implied, prohibiting or restricting the disposal of the object: s 14(5).
8   National Heritage Act 1983 s 14(6).
9   See the Museums and Galleries Act 1992 s 6, Sch 5; and PARA 817.
10 See the Museums and Galleries Act 1992 s 7; and PARA 818.
11 See PARA 1107.

872. Vesting, lending and borrowing of objects held for purposes of the Science Museum. Where, immediately before 1 April 1984 (the 'vesting day')[1], the property in an object was vested in a Minister of the Crown and the object:

(1)   then formed part of the collections of the institution known as the Science Museum or the institution known as the Patent Museum[2]; or

(2)   was then in use in respect of the collections or solely for the purposes of the administration of the institutions[3],

then the property on that day became vested instead in the Board of Trustees of the Science Museum[4]. Similar provision was made for the transfer to the board of any interest in a fund or share in a fund (whether or not of money) held for the purposes of the institution known as the Science Museum vested in a Minister of the Crown immediately before the vesting day.[5] On the vesting day any right, power, duty or liability which was immediately before that day exercisable by or incumbent on a Minister of the Crown:

    (a)   in relation to any object mentioned in head (1) or (2) above[6]; or

    (b)   by virtue of his having any such interest as is mentioned above[7],

instead became exercisable by or incumbent on the board[8].

The board may lend any object the property in which is vested in the board and which is comprised in its collections, whether or not the loan is for purposes of public exhibition, and whether or not under the terms of the loan the object is to remain in the United Kingdom[9]. However, in deciding whether or not to lend an object, and in determining the time for which and the conditions subject to which an object is to be lent, the board:

    (i)   must give special consideration to a request for the loan of an object for public exhibition[10]; and

    (ii)   subject to that, must have regard to the interests of students and other persons[11] visiting the board's collections, the suitability of the prospective borrower, the purpose of the loan, the physical condition and degree of rarity of the object, and any risks to which it is likely to be exposed[12].

Where the property in an object has become vested in the board subject to a condition, this power to lend the object is exercisable in a manner inconsistent with the condition if either: (A) 25 years have elapsed since the date on which the property became vested in the board or, where it vested in it under the initial vesting provisions above[13], in the minister[14]; or (B) the person who first imposed the condition or his personal representatives[15] has or have consented in writing[16] to the exercise of the power in that manner[17].

The board may accept loans of objects for the purpose (depending on the terms of the loan) of exhibiting them, or of study or research by the board or by persons seeking to inspect them[18].

1   See the National Heritage Act 1983 ss 12(7), 13(3), 41(1); and the National Heritage Act 1983 (Commencement No 6) Order 1984, SI 1984/225.

2   National Heritage Act 1983 s 12(1)(a). In the case of an object mentioned in this provision, it is immaterial that, immediately before the vesting day, it was situated elsewhere than at premises managed for the purposes of the institutions (as where it was on loan): s 12(2).

3   National Heritage Act 1983 s 12(1)(b).

4   National Heritage Act 1983 s 12(1). Section 12(1), (4)(a) (see head (a) in the text) did not apply as regards an object excepted from those provisions by an order made by the Secretary of State and coming into force before the vesting day: see s 12(5) (amended by SI 1992/1311). No such order was made before the vesting day.

5   See the National Heritage Act 1983 s 12(3).

6   National Heritage Act 1983 s 12(4)(a). See also note 4.

7   National Heritage Act 1983 s 12(4)(b).

8   National Heritage Act 1983 s 12(4). Any gift, by will or otherwise, contained in an instrument made or executed before the vesting day but coming into effect on or after that day, and which would otherwise have vested an interest in property (of any nature) in a Minister of the Crown for the purposes of the institution known as the Science Museum or the institution known as the Patent Museum, has effect so as to vest the interest in the board in place of the minister in the absence of any contrary intention expressed in that or another instrument made by the testator or donor: s 13(1), (2).

9   National Heritage Act 1983 s 15(1). As to the meaning of 'United Kingdom' see PARA 804 note 2. As to the government indemnity scheme for loans see PARA 1094. As to overseas loans see PARAS 1095, 1096.

10 National Heritage Act 1983 s 15(2)(a).

11 As to the meaning of 'person' see PARA 803 note 17.
12 National Heritage Act 1983 s 15(2)(b).
13 Ie under the National Heritage Act 1983 s 12(1): see the text to notes 1–4.
14 National Heritage Act 1983 s 15(3)(a).
15 As to personal representatives see WILLS AND INTESTACY vol 103 (2010) PARA 605 et seq.
16 As to the meaning of 'writing' see PARA 805 note 14.
17 National Heritage Act 1983 s 15(3)(b).
18 National Heritage Act 1983 s 15(4).

I. THE ARMOURIES

873. The Board of Trustees of the Armouries. There is a body known as the Board of Trustees of the Armouries[1]. The board is a body corporate[2]. The board is not to be regarded as the servant or agent of the Crown or as enjoying any status, immunity or privilege of the Crown[3]; the trustees and their staff are not to be regarded as civil servants, and the board's property is not to be regarded as property of, or held on behalf of, the Crown[4]. Subject to the provisions of any enactment[5], the board is not exempt from any tax, duty, rate, levy or other charge whatever (whether general or local)[6].

The board may regulate its own procedure[7], and may make arrangements for any of its functions, other than the power to acquire or dispose of land[8], to be discharged by committees[9]. The validity of any proceedings of the board is not affected by any vacancy among the trustees or by any defect in the appointment of any trustee[10].

The fixing of the seal of the board must be authenticated by the signature of the chairman or of some other person authorised either generally or specially by the board to act for that purpose[11]. A document purporting to be duly executed under the seal of the board, or to be signed on the board's behalf, is receivable in evidence and, unless the contrary is proved, is deemed to be so executed or signed[12].

1 National Heritage Act 1983 s 17(1). The board, so far as it is a charity, and any institution which is administered by or on its behalf and established for general or special purposes, is an exempt charity for the purposes of the Charities Act 2011: see s 22, Sch 3 para 14; and CHARITIES vol 8 (2015) PARA 318.
2 National Heritage Act 1983 Sch 1 para 21. As to the membership of the board see Sch 1 para 23. As to the payment of allowances to trustees and members of committees see Sch 1 para 27. As to bodies corporate see COMPANIES vol 14 (2009) PARA 2; CORPORATIONS vol 24 (2010) PARA 301 et seq.
3 As to the legal status of bodies not to be regarded as the servant or agent of the Crown or as enjoying any status, immunity or privilege of the Crown see CONSTITUTIONAL AND ADMINISTRATIVE LAW vol 20 (2014) PARA 311 et seq.
4 National Heritage Act 1983 Sch 1 para 22(1). As to the power to appoint staff see PARA 874. As to the civil service see CONSTITUTIONAL AND ADMINISTRATIVE LAW vol 20 (2014) PARA 285 et seq.
5 As to the meaning of 'enactment' see PARA 805 note 5.
6 National Heritage Act 1983 Sch 1 para 22(2) (amended by the Local Government and Rating Act 1997 s 33(1), Sch 3 para 18(4)(a)).
7 See the National Heritage Act 1983 Sch 1 para 26(1). As to quorum see Sch 1 para 26(1), (7).
8 As to the meaning of 'land' see PARA 804 note 30.
9 See the National Heritage Act 1983 Sch 1 para 26(2)–(6). As to the board's functions see PARA 875.
10 National Heritage Act 1983 Sch 1 para 26(8).
11 National Heritage Act 1983 Sch 1 para 28(1). As to the corporate seal see CORPORATIONS vol 24 (2010) PARA 323 et seq.
12 National Heritage Act 1983 Sch 1 para 28(2). Certain records of the board are public records for the purposes of the Public Records Act 1958: see s 10, Sch 1 para 3, Table Pt II; and CONSTITUTIONAL AND ADMINISTRATIVE LAW vol 20 (2014) PARA 343.

874. Director and staff of the Armouries. There is a director of the Armouries who is appointed by the Board of Trustees of the Armouries[1] with the approval of the Secretary of State[2]. The director is responsible to the board for the general exercise of the board's functions[3].

The board may appoint such other employees as it thinks fit[4] and must pay to them such remuneration and allowances as it may determine[5]. The employees are appointed on such other terms and conditions as the board may determine[6].

1   As to the board see PARA 873. In the National Heritage Act 1983 the director is entitled 'Master of the Armouries': see Sch 1 para 24.
2   National Heritage Act 1983 Sch 1 para 24(1). As to the Secretary of State see PARA 802 note 2.
3   National Heritage Act 1983 Sch 1 para 24(2). As to the functions of the board see PARA 875. See note 1.
4   National Heritage Act 1983 Sch 1 para 24(3).
5   National Heritage Act 1983 Sch 1 para 24(4). A determination under Sch 1 para 24(4) or (5) (see the text to note 6) is ineffective unless made with the approval of the Secretary of State given with the Treasury's consent: Sch 1 para 24(6). As to the meaning of 'Treasury' see PARA 809 note 4.
6   National Heritage Act 1983 Sch 1 para 24(5). See also note 5. Employment with the board is included among the kinds of employment to which a scheme under the Superannuation Act 1972 s 1 can apply: see the National Heritage Act 1983 Sch 1 para 24(7). See further PARA 893. As to the provision made in respect of the employment by the board of staff formerly employed in the civil service for the purposes of the Armouries see the National Heritage Act 1983 Sch 1 para 25 (amended by the Employment Rights Act 1996 s 240, Sch 1 para 23; Employment Rights (Dispute Resolution) Act 1998 s 1(2)).

875. General functions of Board of Trustees of the Armouries. The Board of Trustees of the Armouries[1] must perform its functions for the general purpose of maintaining and exhibiting a national collection of arms, armour and associated objects, and of maintaining a record relating to arms and armour and to the Tower of London[2]. So far as practicable and subject to the provisions of the National Heritage Act 1983, the board must:

(1)   care for, preserve and add to the objects in its collection of arms, armour and associated objects[3];

(2)   secure that the objects are exhibited to the public[4];

(3)   secure that the objects are available to persons[5] seeking to inspect them in connection with study or research[6];

(4)   maintain a record, which may include books, pictures and other articles, relating to its collection, to arms and armour generally and to the Tower[7]; and

(5)   generally promote the public's enjoyment and understanding of arms and armour, both by means of the board's collection and by such other means as the board considers appropriate[8].

For the purpose of fulfilling its duties under heads (1) to (5) above, the board may[9]:

(a)   provide education, instruction and advice and carry out research[10];

(b)   enter into contracts and other agreements (including agreements for the board's occupation or management of premises in the Tower or elsewhere)[11];

(c)   acquire and dispose of land[12] and other property[13];

(d)   with the consent of the Secretary of State and subject to such conditions as he may impose, make grants to any person for the purpose of promoting enjoyment, knowledge or understanding of arms and armour[14];

(e)   do such things as it thinks necessary or expedient:
        (i)   for preserving, and increasing the utility of, its collection[15];

(ii)   for securing the due administration of anything vested in or acquired by the board, and any premises occupied or managed by it, under or by virtue of the National Heritage Act 1983[16]; and

(iii)   otherwise for the purposes of its functions[17];

(f)   require payment for admission to objects in the board's collection and objects exhibited with them, but only while the objects are exhibited at a place other than the Tower, and require payment for goods or for services other than admission provided by the board[18].

For so long as the board has a right to occupy premises in the Tower, and so far as otherwise practicable, it must secure that an exhibition of arms, armour and associated objects from among its collection is maintained and open to the public in those premises[19]. The board may[20] allow premises occupied or managed by it to be used by other persons (for payment or otherwise) for purposes not connected with its functions under heads (1) to (5) above, if the board is satisfied that to do so would not conflict unduly with those functions[21].

The board must make a report to the Secretary of State on the exercise of its functions since the last report was made[22], not later than three years (or such shorter period as the Secretary of State may direct) since that last report was made[23]. Each report must include a statement of action taken by the board to enable disabled members of the public to use any services or facilities provided by the board[24], and a statement of the total amount received by the board by way of admission charges in the period covered by the report[25]. The Secretary of State must lay a copy of each report before each House of Parliament[26].

The board must furnish the Secretary of State with such information relating to its property and the discharge and proposed discharge of its functions as he may require, and for that purpose the board must permit any person authorised by him to inspect and make copies of any accounts or other documents of the board and must give such explanation of them as that person or the Secretary of State may require[27].

1 As to the board see PARA 873.
2 National Heritage Act 1983 s 18(1). As to the vesting of objects in the board see PARA 878.
3 National Heritage Act 1983 s 18(2)(a).
4 National Heritage Act 1983 s 18(2)(b).
5 As to the meaning of 'person' see PARA 803 note 17.
6 National Heritage Act 1983 s 18(2)(c).
7 National Heritage Act 1983 s 18(2)(d).
8 National Heritage Act 1983 s 18(2)(e).
9 Ie subject to the provisions of the National Heritage Act 1983: s 18(3), (4).
10 National Heritage Act 1983 s 18(3)(a).
11 National Heritage Act 1983 s 18(3)(b) (amended by the Museums and Galleries Act 1992 Sch 8 para 13(2), Sch 9).
12 As to the meaning of 'land' see PARA 804 note 30.
13 National Heritage Act 1983 s 18(3)(c). The board must not acquire or dispose of land without the Secretary of State's consent: s 18(6). As to the Secretary of State see PARA 802 note 2.
14 National Heritage Act 1983 s 18(3)(d) (amended by the Museums and Galleries Act 1992 Sch 8 para 13(2), Sch 9).
15 National Heritage Act 1983 s 18(4)(a).
16 National Heritage Act 1983 s 18(4)(b).
17 National Heritage Act 1983 s 18(4)(c).
18 See the National Heritage Act 1983 s 18(7).
19 National Heritage Act 1983 s 18(5).
20 Ie whether or not for the general purposes mentioned in the National Heritage Act 1983 s 18(1) (see the text to notes 1–2).
21 National Heritage Act 1983 s 18(8) (added by the Museums and Galleries Act 1992 Sch 8 para 13(3)).
22 See the National Heritage Act 1983 Sch 1 para 30(1).

23 National Heritage Act 1983 Sch 1 para 30(3). The first report was to be made not later than the expiry of the period of three years (or such shorter period as the Secretary of State directed), commencing with the day of the board's establishment (ie 1 October 1983): see ss 17(1), 41(1), Sch 1 para 30(2); National Heritage Act 1983 (Commencement No 3) Order 1983, SI 1983/1437, art 2(a).

24 National Heritage Act 1983 Sch 1 para 30(5). As to the prohibition against discrimination in the provision of goods, facilities and services to disabled persons see DISCRIMINATION vol 33 (2013) PARA 78 et seq.

25 National Heritage Act 1983 Sch 1 para 30(6). Such statement must include information, in such detail as the board thinks fit, about rates of, exemptions from and reductions in admission charges made by the board: Sch 1 para 30(6).

26 National Heritage Act 1983 Sch 1 para 30(4). As to the laying of documents before Parliament see STATUTES AND LEGISLATIVE PROCESS vol 96 (2012) PARA 1052.

27 National Heritage Act 1983 Sch 1 para 30(7). As to accounts see PARA 879.

876. Power of Board of Trustees of the Armouries to form companies. Without prejudice to any general power[1], the Board of Trustees of the Armouries may, with the consent of the Secretary of State[2] and subject to any conditions he may impose, form or take part in forming one or more bodies corporate which, or each of which, has as its main object or objects one or more of the following[3]:

(1)   the production and publication of books, films or other informative material relating to the board's collection and record[4];

(2)   the production of replicas or reproductions of objects comprised in its collection or of documents forming part of its record, or of souvenirs[5];

(3)   the sale, whether or not at an hour when the collection is open to the public for viewing, of informative material relating to its collection or record, of replicas or reproductions of objects comprised in its collection or of documents forming part of its record, or of souvenirs or other goods[6];

(4)   the provision, whether or not at such an hour, of catering or car parking or other services or facilities for the public at any premises occupied or managed by the board[7]; and

(5)   any other object or objects incidental to the board's functions[8].

The board may hold interests in any such body, exercise rights conferred by the holding of interests in it, and provide financial or other assistance to or in respect of it, including assistance by way of guarantee of its obligations[9].

1   The National Heritage Act 1983 s 18A is without prejudice to any power of the Board of Trustees of the Armouries to undertake anything mentioned in s 18A(2) (see heads (1)–(5) in the text) by virtue of s 18 (see PARA 875): s 18A(4) (s 18A added by the Museums and Galleries Act 1992 Sch 8 para 13(4)). As to the board see PARA 873.

2   As to the Secretary of State see PARA 802 note 2.

3   National Heritage Act 1983 s 18A(1) (as added: see note 1).

4   National Heritage Act 1983 s 18A(2)(a) (as added: see note 1).

5   National Heritage Act 1983 s 18A(2)(b) (as added: see note 1).

6   National Heritage Act 1983 s 18A(2)(c) (as added: see note 1).

7   National Heritage Act 1983 s 18A(2)(d) (as added: see note 1).

8   National Heritage Act 1983 s 18A(2)(e) (as added: see note 1). As to the board's functions see PARA 875.

9   National Heritage Act 1983 s 18A(3) (as added: see note 1).

877. Power of Board of Trustees of the Armouries to acquire and dispose of objects. The Board of Trustees of the Armouries[1] may acquire (whether by purchase, exchange or gift) any objects which in its opinion it is desirable to add to its collection[2]. Without prejudice to any power apart from this provision, a Minister of the Crown may transfer to the board any object (whether or not he acquired it before the board's establishment) if in his opinion it would appropriately form part of its collection[3].

The board may not dispose of an object the property in which is vested in the board and which is comprised in its collection unless:

(1)   the disposal is by way of sale, exchange or gift of an object which is a duplicate of another object the property in which is so vested and which is so comprised[4]; or

(2)   the disposal is by way of sale, exchange or gift of an object which in the board's opinion is unsuitable for retention in its collections and can be disposed of without detriment to the interests of students or other members of the public[5]; or

(3)   the disposal is an exercise of the statutory power of transfer[6]; or

(4)   the disposal, by whatever means, including destruction, is of an object which the board is satisfied has become useless for the purposes of its collections by reason of damage, physical deterioration, or infestation by destructive organisms[7].

Money accruing to the board by virtue of any such disposal must be applied by the board in the acquisition of objects to be added to its collections[8].

The board is a specified transferor and transferee for the purposes of the general powers of transfer between collections[9], and a specified body for the purposes of the statutory provision for vesting of gifts to the nation where the donor has not specified a destination[10].

In certain circumstances the board may transfer an object from its collections under the Holocaust (Return of Cultural Objects) Act 2009[11].

1   As to the board see PARA 873.
2   National Heritage Act 1983 s 20(1). As to the vesting of objects in the board, and as to the power to lend or borrow objects, see PARA 878.
3   National Heritage Act 1983 s 20(2). The board was established on 1 October 1983: see ss 17(1), 41(1); National Heritage Act 1983 (Commencement No 3) Order 1983, SI 1983/1437, art 2(a).
4   National Heritage Act 1983 s 20(3)(a).
5   National Heritage Act 1983 s 20(3)(b).
6   National Heritage Act 1983 s 20(3)(c) (amended by the Museums and Galleries Act 1992 Sch 8 para 13(1)). The statutory power of transfer is that under the Museums and Galleries Act 1992 s 6 (see PARA 817).
7   National Heritage Act 1983 s 20(3)(d).
8   National Heritage Act 1983 s 20(5). As to finance see PARA 879.
9   See the Museums and Galleries Act 1992 s 6, Sch 5; and PARA 817.
10   See the Museums and Galleries Act 1992 s 7; and PARA 818.
11   See PARA 1107.

878. Vesting, lending and borrowing of objects held for purposes of the Armouries. Where, immediately before 1 April 1984 (the 'vesting day')[1], the property in an object was vested in the Secretary of State for the Environment[2] and the object:

(1)   then formed part of the collection of arms, armour and associated objects of the institution known as the Armouries or of their record (including books, pictures and other articles)[3]; or

(2)   was then in use in respect of the collection or solely for the purposes of the administration of the institution[4],

then the property on that day became vested instead in the Board of Trustees of the Armouries[5]. On the vesting day any right, power, duty or liability which was immediately before that day exercisable by or incumbent on the Secretary of State for the Environment in relation to any object mentioned in head (1) or (2) above instead became exercisable by or incumbent on the board[6].

The board may lend any object the property in which is vested in it and which is comprised in its collection, whether or not the loan is for purposes of public exhibition, and whether or not under the terms of the loan the object is to remain in the United Kingdom[7]. In deciding whether or not to lend an object, and in determining the time for which and the conditions subject to which an object is to be lent, the board:

  (a)   must give special consideration to a request for the loan of an object for public exhibition[8]; and

  (b)   subject to that, must have regard to the interests of students and other persons[9] visiting the board's collections, the suitability of the prospective borrower, the purpose of the loan, the physical condition and degree of rarity of the object, and any risks to which it is likely to be exposed[10].

Where the property in an object has become vested in the board subject to a condition, this power to lend the object is exercisable in a manner inconsistent with the condition if either (i) 25 years have elapsed since the date on which the condition was first imposed on any person[11]; or (ii) the person who first imposed the condition or his personal representatives[12] has or have consented in writing[13] to the exercise of the power in that manner[14].

The board may accept loans of objects for the purpose (depending on the terms of the loan) of exhibiting them, or of study or research by the board or by persons seeking to inspect them[15].

1   See the National Heritage Act 1983 ss 19(6), 41(1); and the National Heritage Act 1983 (Commencement No 4) Order 1984, SI 1984/208.
2   As to the Secretary of State generally see PARA 802 note 2.
3   National Heritage Act 1983 s 19(1)(a). In the case of an object mentioned in s 19(1)(a), it is immaterial that, immediately before the vesting day, it was situated elsewhere than at premises managed for the purposes of the institution (as where it was on loan): s 19(2).
4   National Heritage Act 1983 s 19(1)(b).
5   National Heritage Act 1983 s 19(1). Section 19(1), (3) (see the text to note 6) did not apply as regards an object excepted from those provisions by an order made by the Secretary of State and coming into force before the vesting day: see s 19(4). No such order was made before the vesting day.
6   National Heritage Act 1983 s 19(3). See also note 5.
7   National Heritage Act 1983 s 21(1). As to the meaning of 'United Kingdom' see PARA 804 note 2. As to the government indemnity scheme for loans see PARA 1094. As to overseas loans see PARAS 1095, 1096.
8   National Heritage Act 1983 s 21(2)(a).
9   As to the meaning of 'person' see PARA 803 note 17.
10 National Heritage Act 1983 s 21(2)(b).
11 National Heritage Act 1983 s 21(3)(a).
12 As to personal representatives see WILLS AND INTESTACY vol 103 (2010) PARA 605 et seq.
13 As to the meaning of 'writing' see PARA 805 note 14.
14 National Heritage Act 1983 s 21(3)(b).
15 National Heritage Act 1983 s 21(4).

879.   Finance and accounts of Board of Trustees of the Armouries. The Secretary of State[1] may pay to the Board of Trustees of the Armouries[2], out of money provided by Parliament, such sums towards its expenditure as the Treasury may approve[3]. The payment may be made on such conditions as the Secretary of State imposes with the Treasury's approval[4].

The board must keep proper accounts and proper records in relation to them[5], and must prepare a statement of accounts in respect of each financial year[6]. The statement must give a true and fair view of the state of the board's affairs at the end of the financial year and of the board's income and expenditure in the financial year[7]; and it must comply with any directions given by the Secretary of State with the Treasury's consent as to the information to be contained in the statement, the manner in which the information is to be presented or the methods and principles according to which the statement is to be prepared[8]. The board must send the statement to the Secretary of State at such time as he may direct[9] and the Secretary of State must, on or before 31 August in any year, send to the Comptroller and Auditor General the statement prepared by the board under these provisions for the financial year last ended[10]. The Comptroller and Auditor General must examine, certify and report on the statement so sent to him and must lay copies of it and of his report before each House of Parliament[11].

1 As to the Secretary of State see PARA 802 note 2.
2 As to the board see PARA 873.
3 National Heritage Act 1983 s 22(1). As to the meaning of 'Treasury' see PARA 809 note 4. As to the provision of money by Parliament see PARLIAMENT vol 78 (2010) PARA 804.
4 National Heritage Act 1983 s 22(2).
5 National Heritage Act 1983 Sch 1 para 29(1).
6 National Heritage Act 1983 Sch 1 para 29(2). 'Financial year' means the period commencing with the day of the board's establishment and ending with the second 31 March following that day, and each successive period of 12 months: Sch 1 para 29(8). The board was established on 1 October 1983: see ss 17(1), 41(1); National Heritage Act 1983 (Commencement No 3) Order 1983, SI 1983/1437, art 2(a). As to the meaning of 'month' see PARA 803 note 12.
7 National Heritage Act 1983 Sch 1 para 29(3).
8 National Heritage Act 1983 Sch 1 para 29(4).
9 National Heritage Act 1983 Sch 1 para 29(5).
10 National Heritage Act 1983 Sch 1 para 29(6). As to the Comptroller and Auditor General see CONSTITUTIONAL AND ADMINISTRATIVE LAW vol 20 (2014) PARAS 494–496.
11 National Heritage Act 1983 Sch 1 para 29(7). As to the laying of documents before Parliament see STATUTES AND LEGISLATIVE PROCESS vol 96 (2012) PARA 1052.

J.   THE ROYAL BOTANIC GARDENS, KEW

880.   **Board of Trustees of the Royal Botanic Gardens, Kew.** There is a body known as the Board of Trustees of the Royal Botanic Gardens, Kew[1]. The board is a body corporate[2]. The board is not to be regarded as the servant or agent of the Crown or as enjoying any status, immunity or privilege of the Crown[3], the trustees and their staff are not to be regarded as civil servants and the board's property is not to be regarded as property of, or held on behalf of, the Crown[4]. Subject to the provisions of any enactment[5], the board is not exempt from any tax, duty, rate, levy or other charge whatever (whether general or local)[6].

The board may regulate its own procedure[7], and may make arrangements for any of its functions, other than the power to acquire or dispose of land[8], to be discharged by committees[9]. The validity of any proceedings of the board is not affected by any vacancy among the trustees or by any defect in the appointment of any trustee[10].

The fixing of the seal of the board must be authenticated by the signature of the chairman or of some other person authorised either generally or specially by the board to act for that purpose[11]. A document purporting to be duly executed under the seal of the board, or to be signed on the board's behalf, is receivable in evidence and, unless the contrary is proved, is deemed to be so executed or signed[12].

1 National Heritage Act 1983 s 23(1). As to the membership of the board see Sch 1 para 33 (Sch 1 paras 33, 37 amended by SI 2002/794). As to the payment of allowances to the trustees and members of committees see the National Heritage Act 1983 Sch 1 para 37 (as so amended). The board, so far as it is a charity, and any institution which is administered by or on its behalf and established for general or special purposes, is an exempt charity for the purposes of the Charities Act 2011: see s 22, Sch 3 para 15; and CHARITIES vol 8 (2015) PARA 318. The board is a designated body for the purposes of the Natural Environment and Rural Communities Act 2006 Pt 8 Ch 1 (ss 78–86) with which the Secretary of State may enter into an agreement authorising it to perform certain ministerial functions: see s 80, Sch 7 para 5; and OPEN SPACES AND COUNTRYSIDE vol 78 (2010) PARA 520.

2 National Heritage Act 1983 Sch 1 para 31. As to bodies corporate see COMPANIES vol 14 (2009) PARA 2; CORPORATIONS vol 24 (2010) PARA 301 et seq.
3 National Heritage Act 1983 Sch 1 para 32(1). However, in relation to any matter as respects which the board acts by virtue of a direction of a Minister of the Crown under s 24(5) (see PARA 882), the board enjoys the same privileges, immunities and exemptions as those enjoyed in relation to that matter by the minister giving the direction: see Sch 1 para 32(3). As to the legal status of bodies not to be regarded as the servant or agent of the Crown or as enjoying any status, immunity or privilege of the Crown see CONSTITUTIONAL AND ADMINISTRATIVE LAW vol 20 (2014) PARA 311 et seq.
4 National Heritage Act 1983 Sch 1 para 32(2). As to the power of the board to appoint staff see PARA 881. As to the civil service see CONSTITUTIONAL AND ADMINISTRATIVE LAW vol 20 (2014) PARA 285 et seq.
5 As to the meaning of 'enactment' see PARA 805 note 5.
6 National Heritage Act 1983 Sch 1 para 32(4) (amended by the Local Government and Rating Act 1997 s 33(1), Sch 3 para 18(5)(a)).
7 See the National Heritage Act 1983 Sch 1 para 36(1). As to quorum see Sch 1 para 36(1), (7).
8 As to the meaning of 'land' see PARA 804 note 30.
9 See the National Heritage Act 1983 Sch 1 para 36(2)–(6). As to the board's functions see PARA 882.
10 National Heritage Act 1983 Sch 1 para 36(8).
11 National Heritage Act 1983 Sch 1 para 38(1). As to the corporate seal see CORPORATIONS vol 24 (2010) PARA 323 et seq.
12 National Heritage Act 1983 Sch 1 para 38(2). Certain records of the board are public records for the purposes of the Public Records Act 1958: see s 10, Sch 1 para 3, Table Pt II; and CONSTITUTIONAL AND ADMINISTRATIVE LAW vol 20 (2014) PARA 343.

881. Director and staff of the Royal Botanic Gardens, Kew. There is a director of the Royal Botanic Gardens, Kew who is appointed by the Board of Trustees of the Royal Botanic Gardens[1] with the approval of the Secretary of State[2]. The director is responsible to the board for the general exercise of the board's functions[3].

The board may appoint such other employees as it thinks fit[4] and must pay to them such remuneration and allowances as it may determine[5]. The employees are appointed on such other terms and conditions as the board may determine[6].

1 As to the board see PARA 880.
2 National Heritage Act 1983 Sch 1 para 34(1) (Sch 1 para 34(1), (6) amended by SI 2002/794). As to the Secretary of State see PARA 802 note 2.
3 National Heritage Act 1983 Sch 1 para 34(2). As to the functions of the board see PARA 882.
4 National Heritage Act 1983 Sch 1 para 34(3).
5 National Heritage Act 1983 Sch 1 para 34(4). A determination under Sch 1 para 34(4) or (5) (see the text to note 6) is ineffective unless made with the approval of the Secretary of State given with the Treasury's consent: Sch 1 para 34(6) (as amended: see note 2). As to the meaning of 'Treasury' see PARA 809 note 4.
6 National Heritage Act 1983 Sch 1 para 34(5). See also note 5. Employment with the board is included among the kinds of employment to which a scheme under the Superannuation Act 1972 s 1 can apply: National Heritage Act 1983 Sch 1 para 34(7). See further PARA 893. As to the provision made in respect of the employment by the board of staff formerly employed in the civil service for the purposes of the Royal Botanic Gardens see Sch 1 para 35 (amended by the Employment Rights Act 1996 s 240, Sch 1 para 23; Employment Rights (Dispute Resolution) Act 1998 s 1(2)(a)).

882. General functions of the Board of Trustees of the Royal Botanic Gardens, Kew. So far as practicable and subject to the provisions of the National Heritage Act 1983, the Board of Trustees of the Royal Botanic Gardens, Kew[1] must:

(1) carry out investigation and research into the science of plants and related subjects, and disseminate the results of the investigation and research[2];

(2) provide advice, instruction and education in relation to those aspects of the science of plants with which the board is for the time being in fact concerned[3];

(3)   provide other services (including quarantine) in relation to plants[4];

(4)   care for their collections of plants, preserved plant material, other objects relating to plants, books and records[5];

(5)   keep the collections as national reference collections, secure that they are available to persons[6] for the purposes of study, and add to and adapt them as scientific needs and the board's resources allow[7]; and

(6)   afford to members of the public opportunities to enter any land[8] occupied or managed by the board, for the purpose of gaining knowledge and enjoyment from the board's collections[9].

For these purposes, the board may[10]:

(a)   enter into contracts and other agreements (including agreements for the board's occupation or management of land)[11];

(b)   acquire and dispose of land and other property[12];

(c)   require payment for any advice, instruction, education or other service provided by the board or for any goods provided by the board or for entry to any land occupied or managed by the board[13];

(d)   do such things as it thinks necessary or expedient:

   (i)   for preserving, and increasing the utility of, its collections[14];

   (ii)   for securing the due administration of anything vested in or acquired by the board, and any land occupied or managed by it, under or by virtue of the National Heritage Act 1983[15]; and

   (iii)   otherwise for the purposes of its functions[16].

If a Minister of the Crown directs the board to exercise functions which are exercisable by him (whether by virtue of an enactment[17] or otherwise) in relation to the management of Kew Gardens or other land and which in his opinion can appropriately be exercised by the board having regard to its functions and resources[18], and which are specified in the direction, the board must exercise them on his behalf in such manner as he may from time to time direct[19].

The board's name is not to be taken to confine its activities to Kew[20].

The board must make a report to the Secretary of State on the exercise of its functions since the last report was made[21], not later than three years (or such shorter period as the Secretary of State may direct) since the last report was made[22]. Each report must include a statement of action taken by the board to enable disabled members of the public to use any services or facilities provided by the board[23]. The Secretary of State must lay a copy of each report before each House of Parliament[24].

The board must furnish the Secretary of State with such information relating to its property and the discharge and proposed discharge of its functions as he may require, and for that purpose the board must permit any person authorised by him to inspect and make copies of any accounts or other documents of the board and must give such explanation of them as that person or the minister may require[25].

1   As to the board see PARA 880.
2   National Heritage Act 1983 s 24(1)(a).
3   National Heritage Act 1983 s 24(1)(b).
4   National Heritage Act 1983 s 24(1)(c).
5   National Heritage Act 1983 s 24(1)(d).
6   As to the meaning of 'person' see PARA 803 note 17.
7   National Heritage Act 1983 s 24(1)(e).
8   As to the meaning of 'land' see PARA 804 note 30.
9   National Heritage Act 1983 s 24(1)(f).
10 Ie subject to the provisions of the National Heritage Act 1983: see s 24(2), (3).
11 National Heritage Act 1983 s 24(2)(a).

12 National Heritage Act 1983 s 24(2)(b). The board may not acquire or dispose of land without the consent of the Secretary of State; but that restriction does not apply to the grant of a lease of, or a licence or concession in respect of, land if the term of the proposed grant is less than one year: s 24(6) (amended by SI 2002/794). As to the Secretary of State see PARA 802 note 2.
13 National Heritage Act 1983 s 24(2)(c).
14 National Heritage Act 1983 s 24(3)(a).
15 National Heritage Act 1983 s 24(3)(b). As to the vesting of property in the board see PARA 885.
16 National Heritage Act 1983 s 24(3)(c).
17 As to the meaning of 'enactment' see PARA 805 note 5.
18 See the National Heritage Act 1983 s 24(4).
19 See the National Heritage Act 1983 s 24(5). However, nothing in this provision authorises the board to exercise a function of making regulations or other instruments of a legislative character: see s 24(5). In relation to any matter as respects which the board acts by virtue of a direction under s 24(5), it enjoys the same privileges, immunities and exemptions as those enjoyed in relation to that matter by the minister giving the direction: see Sch 1 para 32(3); and PARA 880. The Board of Trustees may make arrangements with other persons to provide administrative, professional or technical services for purposes relating to the exercise of public functions in or as regards England and Wales: see Public Bodies Act 2011 s 28; and CONSTITUTIONAL AND ADMINISTRATIVE LAW vol 20 (2014) PARA 330.
20 National Heritage Act 1983 s 24(9).
21 See the National Heritage Act 1983 Sch 1 para 40(1) (Sch 1 para 40 amended by SI 2002/794).
22 See the National Heritage Act 1983 Sch 1 para 40(3) (as amended: see note 21). The first report was to be made not later than the expiry of the period of three years (or such shorter period as the Secretary of State directed), commencing with the day of the board's establishment: Sch 1 para 40(2) (as amended: see note 21). The board was established on 8 August 1983: see ss 23(1), 41(2); National Heritage Act 1983 (Commencement No 2) Order 1983, SI 1983/1183, art 2(a).
23 National Heritage Act 1983 Sch 1 para 40(5). As to the prohibition against discrimination in the provision of goods, facilities and services to disabled persons see DISCRIMINATION vol 33 (2013) PARA 78 et seq.
24 National Heritage Act 1983 Sch 1 para 40(4) (as amended: see note 21). As to the laying of documents before Parliament see STATUTES AND LEGISLATIVE PROCESS vol 96 (2012) PARA 1052.
25 National Heritage Act 1983 Sch 1 para 40(6) (as amended: see note 21). As to accounts see PARA 886.

883. Power of Board of Trustees of the Royal Botanic Gardens, Kew to form companies. Without prejudice to any general power[1], the Board of Trustees of the Royal Botanic Gardens, Kew may, with the consent of the Secretary of State[2] and subject to any conditions he may impose, form or take part in forming one or more bodies corporate which, or each of which, has as its main object or objects[3]:

(1)   one or more of the following particular objects[4]:

(a)   the production and publication of books, films or other informative material relating to the science of plants or related subjects or to the board and its functions[5];

(b)   the production of souvenirs relating to plants or to the board's activities[6];

(c)   the sale of plants produced by the board or objects relating to plants, of informative material relating to the science of plants or related subjects, or of souvenirs relating to plants or to the board's activities[7]; and

(d)   the provision of catering or car parking or other services or facilities for the public at any land[8] occupied or managed by the board[9]; or

(2)   any other object or objects incidental to the board's functions[10].

The board may hold interests in any such body, exercise rights conferred by the holding of interests in it, and provide financial or other assistance to or in respect of it, including assistance by way of guarantee of its obligations[11].

1   The National Heritage Act 1983 s 25 is without prejudice to any power of the Board of Trustees of the Royal Botanic Gardens, Kew to undertake anything mentioned in s 25(2) (see heads (1)(a)–(1)(d) in the text) by virtue of s 24 (see PARA 882): s 25(4). As to the board see PARA 880.
2   As to the Secretary of State see PARA 802 note 2.
3   National Heritage Act 1983 s 25(1) (amended by SI 2002/794).
4   National Heritage Act 1983 s 25(1)(a) (s 25(1)(a), (b) substituted by the Public Bodies Act 2011 s 32(4)).
5   National Heritage Act 1983 s 25(2)(a). As to the board's functions see PARA 882.
6   National Heritage Act 1983 s 25(2)(b).
7   National Heritage Act 1983 s 25(2)(c).
8   As to the meaning of 'land' see PARA 804 note 30.
9   National Heritage Act 1983 s 25(2)(d).
10 National Heritage Act 1983 s 25(1)(b) (as substituted: see note 4).
11 National Heritage Act 1983 s 25(3).

884.   Power of Board of Trustees of the Royal Botanic Gardens, Kew to acquire and dispose of objects. The Board of Trustees of the Royal Botanic Gardens, Kew[1] may acquire (whether by purchase, exchange or gift) any objects which in its opinion it is desirable to add to its collections[2].

The board may not dispose of an object the property in which is vested in the board and which is comprised in its collections unless:

(1)   the disposal is by way of sale, exchange or gift of an object which is a duplicate of another object the property in which is so vested and which is so comprised[3]; or

(2)   the disposal is by way of sale, exchange or gift of an object which in the board's opinion is unsuitable for retention in its collections and can be disposed of without detriment to the interests of students or other members of the public[4]; or

(3)   the disposal, by whatever means, including destruction, is of an object which the board is satisfied has become useless for the purposes of its collections by reason of damage, physical deterioration, or infestation by destructive organisms[5].

In certain circumstances the board may transfer an object from its collections under the Holocaust (Return of Cultural Objects) Act 2009[6].

1   As to the board see PARA 880.
2   National Heritage Act 1983 s 27(1). As to the vesting of property in the board see PARA 885. As to the functions of the board see PARA 882.
3   National Heritage Act 1983 s 27(2)(a).
4   National Heritage Act 1983 s 27(2)(b).
5   National Heritage Act 1983 s 27(2)(c). An object may be disposed of as mentioned in this provision notwithstanding a trust or condition, express or implied, prohibiting or restricting the disposal of the object: s 27(3).
6   See PARA 1107.

885.   Vesting, lending and borrowing of objects at the Royal Botanic Gardens, Kew. Where, immediately before 1 April 1984 (the 'vesting day')[1], the property in an object was vested in the Minister of Agriculture, Fisheries and Food and the object:

(1)   then formed part of the collections of plants (other than those growing in land[2]), preserved plant material, other objects relating to plants, or books or records, of the institution known as the Royal Botanic Gardens[3]; or

(2)   was then in use in respect of the collections or solely for the purposes of
         the administration of the institution[4],

then the property on that day became vested instead in the Board of Trustees of
the Royal Botanic Gardens, Kew[5]. On the vesting day any right, power, duty or
liability which was immediately before that day exercisable by or incumbent on
the minister in relation to any object mentioned in head (1) or (2) above instead
became exercisable by or incumbent on the board[6].

The board may lend any object the property in which is vested in it and which
is comprised in its collections, whether or not the loan is for purposes of public
exhibition, and whether or not under the terms of the loan the object is to remain
in the United Kingdom[7]. In deciding whether or not to lend an object, and in
determining the time for which and the conditions subject to which an object is to
be lent, the board:

(a)   must give special consideration to a request for the loan of an object for
         public exhibition[8]; and

(b)   subject to that, must have regard to the interests of students and other
         persons[9] visiting the board's collections, the suitability of the
         prospective borrower, the purpose of the loan, the physical condition
         and degree of rarity of the object, and any risks to which it is likely to
         be exposed[10].

The board may accept loans of objects for the purpose (depending on the terms
of the loan) of exhibiting them, or of study or research by the board or by persons
seeking to inspect them[11].

1 See the National Heritage Act 1983 ss 26(4), 41(2); and the National Heritage Act 1983
   (Commencement No 5) Order 1984, SI 1984/217.
2 As to the meaning of 'land' see PARA 804 note 30.
3 National Heritage Act 1983 s 26(1)(a). In the case of an object mentioned in this provision, it is
   immaterial that, immediately before the vesting day, it was situated elsewhere than at premises
   managed for the purposes of the institution (as where it was on loan): s 26(2).
4 National Heritage Act 1983 s 26(1)(b).
5 National Heritage Act 1983 s 26(1). As to the board see PARA 880.
6 National Heritage Act 1983 s 26(3).
7 National Heritage Act 1983 s 28(1). As to the meaning of 'United Kingdom' see PARA 804 note
   2. As to the government indemnity scheme for loans see PARA 1094. As to overseas loans see
   PARAS 1095, 1096.
8 National Heritage Act 1983 s 28(2)(a).
9 As to the meaning of 'person' see PARA 803 note 17.
10 National Heritage Act 1983 s 28(2)(b).
11 National Heritage Act 1983 s 28(3).

886. Finance and accounts of Board of Trustees of the Royal Botanic Gardens, Kew.
The Secretary of State[1] may pay to the Board of Trustees of the Royal
Botanic Gardens, Kew[2], out of money provided by Parliament, such sums towards
its expenditure as the Treasury may approve[3]. The payment may be made on such
conditions as the Secretary of State imposes with the Treasury's approval[4].

The board must keep proper accounts and proper records in relation to them[5]
and must prepare a statement of accounts in respect of each financial year[6]. The
statement must give a true and fair view of the state of the board's affairs at the
end of the financial year and of the board's income and expenditure in the
financial year[7]; and it must comply with any directions given by the Secretary
of State with the Treasury's consent as to the information to be contained in the
statement, the manner in which the information is to be presented or the methods
and principles according to which the statement is to be prepared[8]. The board
must send the statement to the Secretary of State at such time as he may direct[9],

and the Secretary of State must, on or before 31 August in any year, send to the Comptroller and Auditor General the statement prepared by the board under these provisions for the financial year last ended[10]. The Comptroller and Auditor General must examine, certify and report on the statement so sent to him and must lay copies of it and of his report before each House of Parliament[11].

1　As to the Secretary of State see PARA 802 note 2.
2　As to the board see PARA 880.
3　National Heritage Act 1983 s 29(1) (s 29, Sch 1 para 39 amended by SI 2002/794). As to the meaning of 'Treasury' see PARA 809 note 4. As to the provision of money by Parliament see PARLIAMENT vol 78 (2010) PARA 804.
4　National Heritage Act 1983 s 29(2) (as amended: see note 3).
5　National Heritage Act 1983 Sch 1 para 39(1).
6　National Heritage Act 1983 Sch 1 para 39(2). 'Financial year' means the period commencing with the day of the board's establishment and ending with the second 31 March following that day, and each successive period of 12 months: Sch 1 para 39(8). As to the meaning of 'month' see PARA 803 note 12. The board was established on 8 August 1983: see ss 23(1), 41(2); National Heritage Act 1983 (Commencement No 2) Order 1983, SI 1983/1183, art 2(a).
7　National Heritage Act 1983 Sch 1 para 39(3).
8　National Heritage Act 1983 Sch 1 para 39(4) (as amended: see note 3).
9　National Heritage Act 1983 Sch 1 para 39(5) (as amended: see note 3).
10　National Heritage Act 1983 Sch 1 para 39(6) (as amended: see note 3). As to the Comptroller and Auditor General see CONSTITUTIONAL AND ADMINISTRATIVE LAW vol 20 (2014) PARAS 494–496.
11　National Heritage Act 1983 Sch 1 para 39(7). As to laying documents before Parliament see STATUTES AND LEGISLATIVE PROCESS vol 96 (2012) PARA 1052.

K.　ARMED FORCES MUSEUMS

887. Designation and funding of armed forces museums. In relation to any institution which has as its object, or as one of its main objects, the collection, exhibition or retention of articles relating to the history and traditions of some section of the armed forces of the Crown[1], the Secretary of State[2] may out of money provided by Parliament pay to the governing body of any such institution such sums towards its expenditure as the Treasury may approve[3]. The payment may be made on such conditions as the Secretary of State imposes with the Treasury's approval[4].

The Secretary of State may designate by order[5] any such institution which, immediately before the making of the order, was staffed by persons at least one of whom was employed in the civil service of the state[6].

The following institutions have been designated under these provisions:

(1)　The Council of the National Army Museum[7];
(2)　the Royal Air Force Museum[8];
(3)　the Portsmouth Royal Naval Museum and the Submarine Branch Collection[9];
(4)　the Fleet Air Arm Museum[10]; and
(5)　the Royal Marine Corps Museum[11].

1　National Heritage Act 1983 s 30(1).
2　As to the Secretary of State see PARA 802 note 2.
3　National Heritage Act 1983 s 30(2). As to the meaning of 'Treasury' see PARA 809 note 4. As to the provision of money by Parliament see PARLIAMENT vol 78 (2010) PARA 804.
4　National Heritage Act 1983 s 30(3).
5　See the National Heritage Act 1983 s 31(1). As to the orders made see notes 7–11.
6　See the National Heritage Act 1983 s 31(2). Not later than such date as the Secretary of State determines, the governing body of a designated institution must make an offer of employment by the body concerned to each person employed immediately before that date in the civil service of the state for the purposes of the institution concerned (Sch 2 paras 1, 2(1)), on terms which, taken as a whole, are not less favourable to the person to whom the offer is made than the terms on which

he is employed at the date on which the offer is made (Sch 2 para 2(2)). The offer is not revocable during the period of three months commencing with the date on which it is made Sch 2 para 2(4). As to the meaning of 'month' see PARA 803 note 12. As to the civil service see CONSTITUTIONAL AND ADMINISTRATIVE LAW vol 20 (2014) PARA 285 et seq.

In determining whether the terms of the offer are any more or less favourable to that person than those enjoyed by him on the date of the offer, no account may be taken of the fact that employment with the body is not employment in the service of the Crown: Sch 2 para 2(3). Any dispute arising under this provision as to whether or not the terms of any employment offered by a body are, taken as a whole, less favourable than those applying to a person's employment in the civil service of the state must be referred to and determined by an employment tribunal: Sch 2 para 2(6) (Sch 2 para 2(6)–(8) amended by the Employment Rights (Dispute Resolution) Act 1998 s 1(2)(a)). An employment tribunal may not consider a complaint whereby such a dispute is referred to it unless the complaint is presented to the tribunal before the end of the period of three months beginning with the date of the offer of employment or within such further period as the tribunal considers reasonable in a case where it is satisfied that it was not reasonably practicable for the complaint to be presented before the end of the period of three months: National Heritage Act 1983 Sch 2 para 2(7) (as so amended). An appeal lies to the Employment Appeal Tribunal on a question of law arising from any decision of, or arising in proceedings before, an employment tribunal under this provision; and no appeal lies except to the Employment Appeal Tribunal from any decision of an employment tribunal under this provision: Sch 2 para 2(8) (as so amended). As to employment tribunals and the Employment Appeal Tribunal see EMPLOYMENT vol 41A (2014) PARA 1399 et seq.

Where a person becomes an employee of the governing body of a designated institution in consequence of these provisions, then, for the purposes of the Employment Rights Act 1996, his period of employment in the civil service of the state counts as a period of employment by the body and the change of employment does not break the continuity of the period of employment: National Heritage Act 1983 Sch 2 para 2(5) (amended by the Employment Rights Act 1996 s 240, Sch 1 para 23). Employment with the governing body of a designated institution is included among the kinds of employment to which a pension scheme under the Superannuation Act 1972 (see PARA 893) can apply: see the National Heritage Act 1983 Sch 2 para 3. As to continuity of employment see EMPLOYMENT vol 39 (2014) PARA 130 et seq.

7   See the Armed Forces Museums (Designation of Institutions) Order 1983, SI 1983/1780, art 2.
8   See the Armed Forces Museums (Designation of Institutions) Order 1984, SI 1984/422, art 2.
9   See the Armed Forces Museums (Designation of Institutions) (No 2) Order 1984, SI 1984/1850, art 2.
10 See the Armed Forces Museums (Designation of Institutions) Order 1985, SI 1985/1818, art 2.
11 See the Armed Forces Museums (Designation of Institutions) Order 1987, SI 1987/1945, art 2.

888.   Grants for the preservation of the Royal Naval College site. The Secretary of State[1] may out of money provided by Parliament[2] make grants towards expenditure in connection with the repair or maintenance of the land[3] and buildings on the site known as the Royal Naval College[4], or any object of historical interest situated on that land or in those buildings[5]. Any such grants made may be paid to such persons[6] and on such conditions as the Secretary of State considers appropriate[7].

1   As to the Secretary of State see PARA 802 note 2.
2   As to the provision of money by Parliament see PARLIAMENT vol 78 (2010) PARA 804.
3   As to the meaning of 'land' see PARA 804 note 30.
4   National Heritage Act 1983 s 31A(1)(a) (s 31A added by the Armed Forces Act 1996 s 31).
5   National Heritage Act 1983 s 31A(1)(b) (as added: see note 4).
6   As to the meaning of 'person' see PARA 803 note 17.
7   National Heritage Act 1983 s 31A(2) (as added: see note 4).

L.   THE NATIONAL MUSEUM OF WALES

889.   Establishment and objects of the National Museum of Wales. The National Museum of Wales is a body corporate with perpetual succession and a common seal with power to sue and be sued and to do all other matters and things incidental or appertaining to a body corporate[1]. There is a board of trustees of the museum[2] which is the governing body of the museum responsible for the management and administration of the finances and property of the museum[3].

The objects of the museum are the advancement of the education of the public: (1) primarily, by the comprehensive representation of science, art, industry, history and culture of, or relevant to, Wales; and (2) generally, by the collection, recording, preservation, elucidation and presentation of objects and things and associated knowledge, whether connected or not with Wales, which are calculated to further the enhancement of understanding and the promotion of research[4].

There is a chief executive of the museum who is responsible for the management and administration of the museum on behalf of the Trustees[5].

Every year, the Welsh Government issues the museum with a remit letter setting out the museum's role in relation to the government's strategic agenda, including details of the priorities and outputs expected as well as how much funding will be provided[6].

1   Supplemental Charter of the National Museum of Wales, 2006, art 1. The museum was originally incorporated by royal charter in 1907. The museum operates seven sites: National Museum, Cardiff; St Fagans National History Museum; National Slate Museum, Llanberis; Big Pit: National Coal Museum, Blaenafon; National Wool Museum, Dre-fach Felindre, Carmarthenshire; National Roman Legion Museum, Caerleon; National Waterfront Museum, Swansea. The Welsh Government introduced free entry to national museums in April 2001. As to the Welsh Government see CONSTITUTIONAL AND ADMINISTRATIVE LAW vol 20 (2014) PARA 373 et seq.
2   Supplemental Charter of the National Museum of Wales, 2006, art 3.
3   See the Supplemental Charter of the National Museum of Wales, 2006, art 6.
4   Supplemental Charter of the National Museum of Wales, 2006, art 4.
5   See the Supplemental Charter of the National Museum of Wales, 2006, art 7.
6   A copy of the remit letter is available on the National Museum of Wales website which, at the date at which this volume states the law, can be found at www.museumwales.ac.uk.

M.   THE COMMONWEALTH INSTITUTE

890. The Commonwealth Institute. The Commonwealth Institute was the successor to the Imperial Institute[1] which was incorporated in 1888[2] and reconstituted in 1925[3]. On 7 January 2003[4] the enactments[5] which made provision in connection with the management of the Commonwealth Institute ceased to have effect[6], and the money constituting the capital of the endowment fund[7] was transferred to and became vested in a company limited by guarantee known as the Commonwealth Institute free from any restrictions as to the purposes for which it must be held[8].

The Commonwealth Institute has been succeeded by the Commonwealth Education Trust, a charity registered in England and Wales, which has been established to ensure that the assets of the Commonwealth Institute are protected and are applied in a manner that is congruent with the purposes of the original trust which has its origins in the donations first made by individual citizens of the now Commonwealth to the Prince of Wales in 1886 in celebration of the Golden Jubilee of Queen Victoria[9]. The objects of the trust are to advance education in the Commonwealth, and the focus of the work of the trust is on supporting primary and secondary education and the training and development of teachers across the Commonwealth[10].

1   See the Commonwealth Institute Act 1958 s 1(1) (repealed).
2   Incorporation was by royal charter dated 12 May 1888, and administration was regulated by the Imperial Institute (Transfer) Act 1902 (repealed): see the Imperial Institute Act 1925, preamble.
3   See the Imperial Institute Act 1925 s 1 (repealed).
4   See the Commonwealth Act 2002 ss 1, 4(2).
5   Ie the Imperial Institute Act 1925 and the Commonwealth Institute Act 1958: Commonwealth Act 2002 s 1(1)(a), (b).
6   See the Commonwealth Act 2002 s 1(1).
7   Ie the fund referred to by that name in the Imperial Institute Act 1925: Commonwealth Act 2002 s 1(3).

8   Commonwealth Act 2002 s 1(2). As to companies limited by guarantee see COMPANIES vol 14 (2009) PARAS 79, 102.
9   See the website of the Commonwealth Education Trust which, at the date at which this volume states the law, can be found at www.cet1886.org. As to the Commonwealth see COMMONWEALTH vol 13 (2009) PARA 701 et seq.
10 See the website of the Commonwealth Education Trust which, at the date at which this volume states the law, can be found at www.cet1886.org.

(iv) Local Authority Museums and Art Galleries

891. Museums and art galleries maintained by local authorities. A local authority[1] may provide and maintain museums and art galleries within its administrative area or elsewhere in England or Wales[2], and may do all such things as may be necessary or expedient for or in connection with their provision or maintenance[3]. A local authority so maintaining a museum or art gallery may enter into an agreement with any other local authority empowered to maintain it for the transfer of the museum or gallery and its collections to that authority[4].

A local authority may make a charge for admission to a museum or art gallery maintained under these provisions[5]. In determining whether, and in what manner, to exercise its powers to make such a charge, the authority must take into account the need to secure that the museum or gallery plays its full part in the promotion of education in the area, and must have particular regard to the interests of children and students[6]. A local authority maintaining museum or art gallery premises may use the premises or allow them to be used (whether or not in return for payment) for the holding of meetings and exhibitions, the showing of films and slides, the giving of musical performances and the holding of other events of an educational or cultural nature and in connection therewith may make or authorise the making of a charge for admission[7].

A local authority may make byelaws regulating the use of facilities provided by the authority and the conduct of persons[8] in the premises where those facilities are provided[9]. A local authority[10] may make contributions towards expense incurred by any person:

(1)   in providing or maintaining a museum or art gallery in any place within England or Wales[11]; or

(2)   in providing advisory or other services or financial assistance for the benefit of a museum or art gallery in any such place[12].

A local authority maintaining or proposing to provide a museum or art gallery under these provisions may establish a fund to be used for the purchase of objects for exhibition in any museum or art gallery which it maintains or proposes to provide[13]. Where at the time such a fund is established, a local authority maintains under a local Act[14] a fund which it is authorised to use for the purchase of such objects, it may amalgamate the funds, but without prejudice to the effect of any condition attached to any particular gift received by the authority[15]. The following provisions apply with respect to the management of a fund so established[16]:

(a)   no payment may be made into the fund (the 'art fund') unless it is authorised or required to be made by these provisions[17];

(b)   there may be paid into the art fund from the county fund, council fund or, as the case may be, the general fund or, in the case of the Common Council of the City of London, the City fund, such sums as the local authority determines[18];

(c)   where any object previously kept for exhibition in a museum or art gallery maintained by the local authority is sold by it, and the proceeds of sale are not subject to any trust the terms of which prevent their being used for the purchase of other objects for exhibition either in that museum or gallery or in any other museum or art gallery for the time being so maintained, the proceeds of sale or any part of them may be paid into the art fund[19];

(d)   until it is required for the purposes of the art fund, money in the fund may be invested by the local authority in the same investments as trustees are for the time being by law authorised to make[20];

(e)   income made from investments so made must be carried to the county fund, council fund or the general fund, or, in the case of the Common Council of the City of London, the City fund as the case may be, and an equivalent sum must be paid from that fund into the art fund[21].

A local authority museum or art gallery is an eligible recipient for a grant or loan from the trustees for the National Heritage Fund in accordance with the provisions of the National Heritage Act 1980 and the trustees may also apply the fund for purposes connected with the acquisition, maintenance or preservation of property for purposes specified in the Act[22]. A local authority museum or art gallery comes within the government indemnity scheme for loans of objects to other institutions[23].

1   As to the meaning of 'local authority' see PARA 922.
2   As to the meaning of 'England' see PARA 804 note 2. As to the meaning of 'Wales' see PARA 802 note 4.
3   Public Libraries and Museums Act 1964 s 12(1) (s 12 amended by the Local Government Act 1972 s 272(1), Sch 30). It is not necessary for a local authority to obtain the consent of the Secretary of State or, in relation to Wales, the Welsh Ministers to the provision of a museum or art gallery under the Public Libraries and Museums Act 1964 s 12(1) or to the transfer of a museum or art gallery and its collections under s 12(2) (see the text to note 4): see the Local Government Act 1972 s 208(1); National Assembly for Wales (Transfer of Functions) Order 1999, SI 1999/672, art 2, Sch 1; Government of Wales Act 2006 Sch 11 para 30. As to the Secretary of State and the Welsh Ministers see PARA 802.
4   Public Libraries and Museums Act 1964 s 12(2) (as amended: see note 3). See also note 3.
5   Public Libraries and Museums Act 1964 s 13(1).
6   Public Libraries and Museums Act 1964 s 13(2).
7   Public Libraries and Museums Act 1964 s 20.
8   As to the meaning of 'person' see PARA 803 note 17.
9   See the Public Libraries and Museums Act 1964 s 19; and PARA 930.
10 The powers conferred by the Public Libraries and Museums Act 1964 s 14 are exercisable by every local authority whether or not it is a library authority or maintains a museum or art gallery: see the Local Government Act 1972 s 208(2). As to the meaning of 'library authority' see PARA 922.
11 Public Libraries and Museums Act 1964 s 14(a) (s 14 amended by the Local Government Act 1972 Sch 30).
12 Public Libraries and Museums Act 1964 s 14(b).
13 Public Libraries and Museums Act 1964 s 15(1) (s 15(1), (2) amended by the Local Government Act 1972 s 208(3)(g)).
14 As to local Acts see STATUTES AND LEGISLATIVE PROCESS vol 96 (2012) PARA 626.
15 Public Libraries and Museums Act 1964 s 15(2) (as amended: see note 13). It is not necessary for the local authority to apply to the Secretary of State or, in relation to Wales, the Welsh Ministers for an order before amalgamating the funds: see the Local Government Act 1972 s 208(1); National Assembly for Wales (Transfer of Functions) Order 1999, SI 1999/672, art 2, Sch 1; Government of Wales Act 2006 Sch 11 para 30.
16 See the Public Libraries and Museums Act 1964 s 15(3).
17 Public Libraries and Museums Act 1964 Sch 2 para 1.
18 Public Libraries and Museums Act 1964 Sch 2 para 2(1) (amended by the Local Government Act 1972 s 208(3)(k), Sch 30; Local Government (Wales) Act 1994 s 66(6), Sch 16 para 24(4); and SI 1990/1285). As to the county, council, general and City funds see generally LOCAL GOVERNMENT FINANCE vol 70 (2012) PARA 491 et seq.
19 Public Libraries and Museums Act 1964 Sch 2 para 3.

20 Public Libraries and Museums Act 1964 Sch 2 para 4. For this purpose, the Trustee Investments
    Act 1961 s 7 (which applies ss 1–6 to persons, other than trustees, having trustee investment
    powers: see TRUSTS AND POWERS vol 98 (2013) PARA 460 et seq) has effect as if the Public
    Libraries and Museums Act 1964 had been passed before the 1961 Act, provided that, for the
    purpose of the making of investments by the authority, the Trustee Investments Act 1961 s 1(1),
    Sch 1 Pt II para 9 does not apply to the authority or a joint board comprising the authority and
    established under the Public Libraries and Museums Act 1964 s 5 (see PARA 923): Sch 2 para 4.
21 Public Libraries and Museums Act 1964 Sch 2 para 5 (amended by the Local Government (Wales)
    Act 1994 Sch 16 para 24(4)).
22 See the National Heritage Act 1980 ss 3, 4; and PARA 815.
23 See the National Heritage Act 1980 s 16; and PARA 1094.

(v) Finance, Accounts and Staff Pensions

892. Finance and accounts of specified museums and galleries. The Secretary
of State[1] may out of money provided by Parliament pay to specified bodies[2] such
sums towards their expenditure as the Treasury may approve[3]. Each of the
specified bodies must keep proper accounts and proper records in relation to those
accounts[4], and must prepare a statement of accounts in respect of each financial
year[5] which must give a true and fair view of the state of the body's affairs at the
end of the financial year and of the body's income and expenditure in the financial
year[6]. The statement must comply with any directions given by the Secretary
of State, with the Treasury's consent[7], as to (1) the information which is to be
contained in the statement[8]; (2) the form which the statement is to take[9]; (3) the
manner in which the information is to be presented[10]; or (4) the methods and
principles according to which the statement is to be prepared[11].

Each of the bodies must send their statement to the Secretary of State at such
time as he may direct[12], and the Secretary of State must, on or before 31 August
in any year, send to the Comptroller and Auditor General the statements so
prepared for the financial year last ended[13]. The Comptroller and Auditor General
must examine, certify and report on each statement so sent to him, and must lay
copies of it and of his report before each House of Parliament[14].

1   The functions of the Secretary of State under the Museums and Galleries Act 1992 s 9, so far as
    they relate to the Court of Governors of the National Library of Wales and the Council of the
    National Museum of Wales, are transferred to the Welsh Ministers: see the National Assembly for
    Wales (Transfer of Functions) Order 1999, SI 1999/672, art 2, Sch 1; Government of Wales Act
    2006 Sch 11 para 30. In relation to those bodies the Treasury consent requirement under the
    Museums and Galleries Act 1992 s 9(5) (see the text to notes 7–11) continues in effect: see the
    National Assembly for Wales (Transfer of Functions) Order 1999, SI 1999/672, art 2, Sch 1;
    Government of Wales Act 2006 Sch 11 para 30. The functions of the Comptroller and Auditor
    General in the Museums and Galleries Act 1992 s 9(7), (8) (see the text to notes 13–14) are, in
    relation to statements of account prepared by those bodies for financial years beginning in and
    after 1999, transferred to the Auditor General for Wales and in relation thereto s 9(8) has effect
    so that for the requirement to lay before Parliament the documents referred to therein, there is
    substituted a requirement for the Auditor General for Wales to lay those documents before the
    National Assembly for Wales: see the National Assembly for Wales (Transfer of Functions) Order
    1999, SI 1999/672, art 2, Sch 1. As to the Secretary of State and the Welsh Ministers see PARA 802.
    As to the National Library of Wales see PARA 902. As to the National Museum of Wales see PARA
    889. As to the National Assembly for Wales and the Auditor General for Wales see
    CONSTITUTIONAL AND ADMINISTRATIVE LAW vol 20 (2014) PARAS 351 et seq, 400 et seq.
2   The specified bodies are: the trustees of the British Museum; the trustees of the Imperial War
    Museum; the Board of Trustees of the National Gallery; the trustees of the National Maritime
    Museum; the Board of Trustees of the National Portrait Gallery; the trustees of the Natural
    History Museum; the Board of Trustees of the Science Museum; the Board of Trustees of the Tate
    Gallery; the Board of Trustees of the Victoria and Albert Museum; the Board of Trustees of the
    Wallace Collection; the Museums and Galleries Commission: see the Museums and Galleries Act
    1992 Sch 7 Pt I (amended by SI 1992/1311). The specified bodies also include the Court of
    Governors of the National Library of Wales and the Council of the National Museum of Wales:

see the Museums and Galleries Act 1992 Sch 7 Pt II; and note 1. As to the British Museum and the Natural History Museum see PARA 822 et seq. As to the trustees of the Imperial War Museum see PARA 841. As to the Boards of Trustees of the National Gallery, the National Portrait Gallery, the Tate Gallery and the Wallace Collection see PARA 833. As to the trustees of the National Maritime Museum see PARA 847. As to the Board of Trustees of the Science Museum see PARA 867. As to the Board of Trustees of the Victoria and Albert Museum see PARA 861. As to the Museums and Galleries Commission (replaced by the Museums, Libraries and Archives Council) see now the Arts Council and the National Archives (functions having been transferred to both bodies following the abolition of the Museums, Libraries and Archives Council); and PARA 957.

3 Museums and Galleries Act 1992 s 9(1) (s 9 amended by SI 1992/1311). Payments may be made on such conditions as the Secretary of State may impose with the approval of the Treasury: Museums and Galleries Act 1992 s 9(2) (as so amended). As to the meaning of 'Treasury' see PARA 809 note 4.

4 Museums and Galleries Act 1992 s 9(3).

5 'Financial year' means, in relation to any body, the period beginning with the day appointed under the Museums and Galleries Act 1992 s 11(4) for the commencement of s 9 in relation to that body and ending with 31 March following that day, and each successive period of 12 months: s 9(9). The appointed day was 1 April 1993: see the Museums and Galleries Act 1992 (Commencement) Order 1992, SI 1992/1874. As to the meaning of 'month' see PARA 803 note 12.

6 Museums and Galleries Act 1992 s 9(4).

7 Museums and Galleries Act 1992 s 9(5) (as amended: see note 3).

8 Museums and Galleries Act 1992 s 9(5)(a).

9 Museums and Galleries Act 1992 s 9(5)(b).

10 Museums and Galleries Act 1992 s 9(5)(c).

11 Museums and Galleries Act 1992 s 9(5)(d).

12 Museums and Galleries Act 1992 s 9(6) (as amended: see note 3).

13 Museums and Galleries Act 1992 s 9(7) (as amended: see note 3). As to the Comptroller and Auditor General see CONSTITUTIONAL AND ADMINISTRATIVE LAW vol 20 (2014) PARAS 494–496.

14 Museums and Galleries Act 1992 s 9(8). As to the laying of documents before Parliament see STATUTES AND LEGISLATIVE PROCESS vol 96 (2012) PARA 1052.

893. Staff pensions of employees of museums and galleries, commissions and other cultural bodies.

The Minister for the Civil Service[1] may:

(1) make, maintain and administer schemes, whether contributory or not, by which provision is made with respect to the pensions, allowances or gratuities which, subject to the fulfilment of such requirements and conditions as may be prescribed by the scheme, are to be paid, or may be paid, by him to or in respect of such of the persons to whom these provisions apply as he may determine[2];

(2) in relation to such persons as any such scheme may provide, pay or receive transfer values[3];

(3) in such circumstances as any such scheme may provide, make payments by way of a return of contributions, with or without interest[4]; and

(4) make such payments as he thinks fit towards the provision, otherwise than by virtue of such a scheme, of superannuation benefits for or in respect of such of the persons to whom these provisions apply as he may determine[5].

To such extent and subject to such conditions as he thinks fit, the minister may delegate to any other minister or officer of the Crown any functions exercisable by him under these provisions or any scheme made under them[6]. Before making a scheme, the minister, or if he so directs in relation to a particular scheme, another minister of the Crown specified in the direction, must consult with persons appearing to the minister concerned to represent persons likely to be affected by the scheme or with those persons themselves[7]. These provisions apply[8] to persons, inter alia, serving in employment with specified museums and galleries[9], royal and other commissions[10] and other bodies[11] falling within the scope of this title[12].

Persons employed by local library authorities[13] may be superannuable under the Local Government Pension Scheme[14].

1 By the Transfer of Functions (Treasury and Minister for the Civil Service) Order 1995, SI 1995/269, art 3, Schedule para 6, the minister's functions under these provisions, which were transferred to the Treasury by the Transfer of Functions (Minister for the Civil Service and Treasury) Order 1981, SI 1981/1670, again became functions of the minister with effect from 1 April 1995. As to the Minister for the Civil Service see CONSTITUTIONAL AND ADMINISTRATIVE LAW vol 20 (2014) PARA 235.

2 Superannuation Act 1972 s 1(1)(a). Section 1(1) is subject to ss 18, 19 of the Public Service Pensions Act 2013 (restrictions on benefits provided under existing schemes: see CONSTITUTIONAL AND ADMINISTRATIVE LAW vol 20 (2014) PARA 298): Superannuation Act 1972 s 1(1A) (s 1(1A), (4A) added by the Public Service Pensions Act 2013 Sch 8 para 7). As to the meaning of 'person' see PARA 803 note 17.

3 Superannuation Act 1972 s 1(1)(b). See note 2.

4 Superannuation Act 1972 s 1(1)(c). See note 2.

5 Superannuation Act 1972 s 1(1)(d). See note 2.

6 See the Superannuation Act 1972 s 1(2); and CONSTITUTIONAL AND ADMINISTRATIVE LAW vol 20 (2014) PARA 298. As to where a money purchase scheme under s 1 includes provision enabling a member to elect for the benefits which are to be provided to or in respect of him to be purchased from any authorised provider whom he may specify, see s 1(2A) (added by the Pensions (Miscellaneous Provisions) Act 1990 s 8(1); and CONSTITUTIONAL AND ADMINISTRATIVE LAW vol 20 (2014) PARA 298).

7 Superannuation Act 1972 s 1(3) (amended by SI 2000/2040).

8 The Superannuation Act 1972 s 1 also applies to persons serving in employment or in an office, not being service in employment or in an office of a kind mentioned in section 1(4) (see note 9), where the employment or office is specified in a list produced for the purposes of s 1(4A) (see s 1A): ss 1(4A) (as added: see note 2), 1A (added by the Public Service Pensions Act 2013 s 29, Sch 9, paras 1, 3); and the Superannuation (Specification of Employments and Offices) Regulations 2013, SI 2013/1564, reg 3.

9 Ie persons in employment with the Armouries, the British Museum, the Natural History Museum, the Imperial War Museum, the London Museum, the National Gallery, the National Maritime Museum, the National Museums and Galleries on Merseyside, the National Museum of the Royal Navy, the National Portrait Gallery, the Royal Botanic Gardens, Kew, the Science Museum, Sir John Soane's Museum, the Tate Gallery, the Victoria and Albert Museum and the Wallace Collection: Superannuation Act 1972 s 1(4)(b), Sch 1 (amended by the National Heritage Act 1983 ss 1, 9, 17, 23, Sch 1 paras 4(7), 14(7), 24(7), 34(7); the Museums and Galleries Act 1992 Sch 8 para 1(1), (2), (5); SI 1990/757; SI 2003/1073; and SI 2011/2257). As to the appointment of staff at the Armouries see PARA 874; at the British Museum and the Natural History Museum see PARA 825; at the Imperial War Museum see PARA 842; at the London Museum see PARA 855; at the National Gallery, the National Portrait Gallery, the Tate Gallery and the Wallace Collection see PARA 834; at the National Maritime Museum see PARA 848; at the Royal Botanic Gardens, Kew see PARA 881; at the Science Museum see PARA 868; at the Victoria and Albert Museum see PARA 862.

10 Ie persons in employment with the Historic Buildings and Monuments Commission for England ('the Commission'), the Historical Manuscripts Commission, and the Royal Commission on Ancient and Historical Monuments of Wales: see the Superannuation Act 1972 Sch 1 (amended by SI 1986/2119; SI 2000/108; SI 2003/1073; and SI 2013/1609). As to the Commission see PARA 803. As to the Historical Manuscripts Commission see PARA 812. As to the Royal Commission on Ancient and Historical Monuments of Wales see PARA 811.

11 Ie persons in employment with the British Council, the British Library and the Trustees of the National Heritage Memorial Fund: see the Superannuation Act 1972 Sch 1 (amended by the British Council and Commonwealth Institute Superannuation Act 1986 s 1(1); the Higher Education Act 2004 s 5(2); SI 2000/108; SI 2000/1728; SI 2003/1073; SI 2011/2257; and SI 2013/2352). As to the Arts and Humanities Research Council see PARA 972. As to the British Council see PARA 962. As to the British Library see PARA 902. As to the National Heritage Memorial Fund see PARA 814.

12 As to the scope of this title see PARA 801.

13 As to the meaning of 'library authority' see PARA 922.

14 See LOCAL GOVERNMENT vol 69 (2009) PARA 448 et seq.

(8) LIBRARIES

(i) Public Lending Right

894. The Public Lending Right Act 1979 and the public lending right scheme.
The Public Lending Right Act 1979 provides that, in accordance with a scheme to
be known as the public lending right scheme, there is conferred on authors a right,
known as public lending right, to receive from time to time out of a central fund
payment in respect of loans of their books to the public by local library authorities
in the United Kingdom[1]. The scheme is administered by the British Library
Board[2]. The provisions of the Act and the public lending right scheme are covered
in detail elsewhere in this work[3].

1 See the Public Lending Right Act 1979 s 1(1) (amended by SI 1992/1311). As to the meaning of
'United Kingdom' see PARA 804 note 2. The scheme is the Public Lending Right Scheme 1982 as
set out in the Public Lending Right Scheme 1982 (Commencement) Order 1982, SI 1982/719,
Appendix: see COPYRIGHT vol 23 (2013) PARA 1295.
2 See the Public Lending Right Act 1979 Schedule (amended by SI 2013/2352). The scheme was
formerly administered by the Registrar of Public Lending Right which was abolished on 1 October
2013 and the functions transferred to the British Library Board: see the Public Bodies (Abolition
of the Registrar of Public Lending Right) Order 2013, SI 2013/2352, arts 2–6. As to the British
Library Board see PARAS 904–908.
3 See COPYRIGHT vol 23 (2013) PARA 1291 et seq.

(ii) Delivery of Books to Libraries

895. Deposit of publications with libraries. A person[1] who publishes[2] in the
United Kingdom[3] a specified work must at his own expense deliver a copy of it to
an address[4] specified (generally or in a particular case) by any deposit library[5]
entitled to delivery under these provisions[6].

The specified works are:
(1) subject to any prescribed exception, in the case of a work published in
  print[7]:
  (a) a book (including a pamphlet, magazine or newspaper)[8];
  (b) a sheet of letterpress or music[9];
  (c) a map, plan, chart or table[10]; and
  (d) a part of any such work[11];
(2) in the case of a work published in a medium[12] other than print, a work
  of a prescribed description[13].

The obligation is to deliver a copy of the work in the medium in which it is
published[14].

These provisions do not apply to works published before 1 February 2004[15],
nor to a work which is substantially the same as one already published in the same
medium in the United Kingdom[16].

Where a person (the 'publisher') is required[17] to deliver anything to an address
specified by a deposit library, or to a deposit library, has failed to comply with that
obligation[18], the library may, in accordance with rules of court, apply to
the County Court for an order requiring the publisher to comply with the
obligation[19]. If on such an application it appears that the publisher is unable to
comply with the obligation[20], or for any other reason it is not appropriate to make
an order[21], the court may instead make an order requiring the publisher to pay to

the library an amount which is not more than the cost of making good the failure to comply[22].

1   As to the meaning of 'person' see PARA 803 note 17.

2   'Publication', in relation to a work: (1) means the issue of copies of the work to the public; and (2) includes making the work available to the public by means of an electronic retrieval system; and related expressions are to be interpreted accordingly: Legal Deposit Libraries Act 2003 s 14.

3   As to the meaning of 'United Kingdom' see PARA 804 note 2.

4   'Address' means an address in the United Kingdom or an electronic address: Legal Deposit Libraries Act 2003 s 1(7).

5   'Deposit library' means any of: (1) the British Library Board; and (2) the National Library of Scotland; and (3) the authorities controlling (a) the National Library of Wales; (b) the Bodleian Library, Oxford; (c) the University Library, Cambridge; (d) the Library of Trinity College, Dublin: Legal Deposit Libraries Act 2003 s 14 (definition amended by the National Library of Scotland Act 2012 Sch 2 para 7(b)(i), (ii)). As to the British Library and the National Library of Wales see PARA 902.

6   Legal Deposit Libraries Act 2003 s 1(1). If a deposit library other than the authority controlling the Library of Trinity College, Dublin has not specified an address, the copy is to be delivered to the library: s 1(2).

7   See the Legal Deposit Libraries Act 2003 s 1(3). 'Prescribed' means prescribed by regulations made by the Secretary of State: s 14. As to the making of regulations see PARA 900. As to the Secretary of State see PARA 802 note 2. At the date at which this volume states the law no such regulations had been made. As to the deposit of printed publications see further PARAS 897, 898.

8   Legal Deposit Libraries Act 2003 s 1(3)(a).

9   Legal Deposit Libraries Act 2003 s 1(3)(b).

10   Legal Deposit Libraries Act 2003 s 1(3)(c).

11   Legal Deposit Libraries Act 2003 s 1(3)(d).

12   'Medium' means any medium of publication, including in particular any form of on line or off line publication: Legal Deposit Libraries Act 2003 s 14.

13   Legal Deposit Libraries Act 2003 s 1(4). A prescribed description may not include works consisting only of (1) a sound recording or film or both (s 1(5)(a)); or (2) such material and other material which is merely incidental to it (s 1(5)(b)). Work published off line and work that is published on line is the description of work prescribed for these purposes but does not include work which contains personal data and which is only made available to a restricted group of persons or work published before the following regulations were made: see the Legal Deposit Libraries (Non-Print Works) Regulations 2013, SI 2013/777, reg 13(1), (2). As to exemptions for micro-businesses and new businesses see Pt 2 (regs 4–12). 'Personal data' has the same meaning as in the Data Protection Act 1998 s 1 (see CONFIDENCE AND INFORMATIONAL PRIVACY vol 19 (2011) PARA 97): reg 2. 'Sound recording' means:

    (1)   a recording of sounds, from which the sounds may be reproduced, or

    (2)   a recording of the whole or any part of a literary, dramatic or musical work, from which sounds reproducing the work or part may be produced,

regardless of the medium on which the recording is made or the method by which the sounds are reproduced or produced: see the Copyright, Designs and Patents Act 1988 s 5A(1) (s 5A added by SI 1995/3297); definition applied by the Legal Deposit Libraries Act 2003 s 14. 'Film' means a recording on any medium from which a moving image may by any means be produced; and the sound track accompanying a film is treated as part of the film for these purposes: see the Copyright, Designs and Patents Act 1988 s 5B(1), (2) (s 5B added by SI 1995/3297); definition applied by the Legal Deposit Libraries Act 2003 s 14. As to the deposit of non print publications see further PARA 896.

14   Legal Deposit Libraries Act 2003 s 1(6). This provision is expressed to be subject to s 6(2)(h) (see PARA 896). Where substantially the same work is published in the United Kingdom in more than one medium: (1) s 1(1) (see the text to notes 1–6) applies only in relation to its publication in one of those media (s 2(2)(a)); and (2) that medium is to be determined in accordance with regulations made by the Secretary of State (s 2(2)(b)). Where substantially the same work is published in the United Kingdom in print and in one or more non-print media, the duty under s 1(1) (see the text and notes 1–6) applies only in relation to its publication in print unless the publisher and the deposit library agree that instead the duty applies in relation to its publication in one of the non-print media in which the work is published: see the Legal Deposit Libraries (Non-Print Works) Regulations 2013, SI 2013/777, reg 14(1). Where substantially the same work is published in the United Kingdom in two or more non-print media (and is not published in print), the publisher and the deposit library may agree one of those non-print media as the medium in relation to which the duty applies and, in the absence of agreement, the publisher may decide the non-print medium (which must be one in which the work is published) in relation to which the duty applies: see reg 14(2). As to delivery of non-print publications see PARA 896. As to exemptions for

micro-businesses and new businesses see Pt 2. The Secretary of State may by regulations make provision as to circumstances in which works are or are not to be regarded for the purposes of the Legal Deposit Libraries Act 2003 s 2 as substantially the same: s 2(3). At the date at which this volume states the law no such provision had been made. As to exemptions from liability arising from the deposit of publications see PARA 899.

15 Legal Deposit Libraries Act 2003 s 16(4). 1 February 2004 is the date of the commencement of s 1: see s 16(1), (4); Legal Deposit Libraries Act 2003 (Commencement) Order 2004, SI 2004/130, art 2.

16 See the Legal Deposit Libraries Act 2003 s 2(1). See note 14.

17 Ie by or under the Legal Deposit Libraries Act 2003.

18 Legal Deposit Libraries Act 2003 s 3(1).

19 Legal Deposit Libraries Act 2003 s 3(2). As to the County Court see COURTS AND TRIBUNALS vol 24 (2010) PARA 758 et seq.

20 Legal Deposit Libraries Act 2003 s 3(3)(a).

21 Legal Deposit Libraries Act 2003 s 3(3)(b).

22 Legal Deposit Libraries Act 2003 s 3(3).

896. Delivery of non print publications to libraries. The Secretary of State[1] may make regulations[2] supplementing the provisions relating to the deposit of publications[3] as they apply to works published in media[4] other than print[5]. Such regulations may in particular:

(1) make provision about the time at which or the circumstances in which any deposit library[6] becomes or ceases to be entitled[7] to delivery[8];

(2) require the person who publishes the work[9] to deliver, with the copy of the work, a copy of any computer program and any information necessary in order to access the work, and a copy of any manual and other material that accompanies the work and is made available to the public[10];

(3) require delivery within a time prescribed in the regulations by reference to publication or another event[11];

(4) permit or require delivery by electronic means[12];

(5) where a work is produced for publication in copies of differing quality, specify the quality of copies to be delivered[13];

(6) where a work is published or made available to the public in different formats, provide for the format in which any copy is to be delivered to be determined in accordance with requirements specified (generally or in a particular case) by the deposit libraries or any of them[14];

(7) make provision as to the circumstances in which works published on line are or are not to be treated as published in the United Kingdom[15];

(8) specify the medium in which a copy of a work published on line is to be delivered[16].

A relevant person[17] may not do any of the following activities in relation to relevant material[18]. The activities are: (a) using the material (whether or not such use necessarily involves the making of a temporary copy of it)[19]; (b) copying the material (other than by making a temporary copy where this is necessary for the purpose of using the material)[20]; (c) in the case of relevant material comprising or containing a computer program or database, adapting it[21]; (d) lending the material to a third party (other than lending by a deposit library to a reader for use by the reader on library premises controlled by the library)[22]; (e) transferring the material to a third party[23]; (f) disposing of the material[24]. However, the Secretary of State may by regulations make provision permitting relevant persons to do any of these activities in relation to relevant material, subject to such conditions as may be prescribed[25]. A contravention of these provisions[26] is actionable at the suit of a person who suffers loss as a result of the contravention, subject to the defences and other incidents applying to actions for breach of statutory duty[27].

1   As to the Secretary of State see PARA 802 note 2.
2   As to the making of regulations see PARA 900.
3   Ie the Legal Deposit Libraries Act 2003 ss 1, 2 (see PARA 895). As to the meaning of 'publication' see PARA 895 note 2.
4   As to the meaning of 'medium' see PARA 895 note 12.
5   Legal Deposit Libraries Act 2003 s 6(1). As to the regulations made see the Legal Deposit Libraries (Non-Print Works) Regulations 2013, SI 2013/777; and the text and notes 8, 10.
6   As to the meaning of 'deposit library' see PARA 895 note 5.
7   Ie under the Legal Deposit Libraries Act 2003 s 1 (see PARA 895).
8   Legal Deposit Libraries Act 2003 s 6(2)(a). As to the regulations made see the Legal Deposit Libraries (Non-Print Works) Regulations 2013, SI 2013/777, regs 15, 16.
9   Ie the person mentioned in the Legal Deposit Libraries Act 2003 s 1(1) (see PARA 895). As to the meaning of 'person' see PARA 803 note 17.
10 Legal Deposit Libraries Act 2003 s 6(2)(b). As to the regulations made see the Legal Deposit Libraries (Non-Print Works) Regulations 2013, SI 2013/777, reg 17. As to exemptions from liability arising from the delivery, pursuant to regulations under the Legal Deposit Libraries Act 2003 s 6, of a copy of a computer program or material within s 6(2)(b) see PARA 899.
11 Legal Deposit Libraries Act 2003 ss 6(2)(c), 14.
12 Legal Deposit Libraries Act 2003 s 6(2)(d).
13 Legal Deposit Libraries Act 2003 s 6(2)(e).
14 Legal Deposit Libraries Act 2003 s 6(2)(f). As to where substantially the same work is published in two or more non-print media see the Legal Deposit Libraries (Non-Print Works) Regulations 2013, SI 2013/777, reg 14(2); and PARA 895 note 14.
15 Legal Deposit Libraries Act 2003 s 6(2)(g). As to the meaning of 'United Kingdom' see PARA 804 note 2.
16 Legal Deposit Libraries Act 2003 s 6(2)(h). See PARA 895 note 14.
17 'Relevant person' means a deposit library or person acting on its behalf, or a reader: Legal Deposit Libraries Act 2003 s 7(5)(c). 'Reader' means a person who, for the purposes of research or study and with the permission of a deposit library, is on library premises controlled by it: s 7(5)(a). References in s 7 to a deposit library include references to the Faculty of Advocates: s 7(5)(d).
18 Legal Deposit Libraries Act 2003 s 7(1). 'Relevant material' means: (1) a copy delivered under s 1 (see PARA 895) of a work published in a medium other than print (s 7(5)(b)(i)); (2) a copy delivered pursuant to regulations under s 6 (see the text to notes 1–16) of a computer program or material within s 6(2)(b) (s 7(5)(b)(ii)); (3) a copy of a work to which s 10(6) (see PARA 899) applies (s 7(5)(b)(iii)); (4) a copy (at any remove) of anything within any of heads (1)–(3) above (s 7(5)(b)(iv)).
19 Legal Deposit Libraries Act 2003 s 7(2)(a). As to exemptions from liability arising out of the doing by a relevant person of an activity listed in s 7(2) see PARA 899.
20 Legal Deposit Libraries Act 2003 s 7(2)(b).
21 Legal Deposit Libraries Act 2003 s 7(2)(c).
22 Legal Deposit Libraries Act 2003 s 7(2)(d).
23 Legal Deposit Libraries Act 2003 s 7(2)(e).
24 Legal Deposit Libraries Act 2003 s 7(2)(f).
25 Legal Deposit Libraries Act 2003 s 7(3). Such regulations may in particular make provision about: (1) the purposes for which relevant material may be used or copied (s 7(4)(a)); (2) the time at which or the circumstances in which readers may first use relevant material (s 7(4)(b)); (3) the description of readers who may use relevant material (s 7(4)(c)); (4) the limitations on the number of readers who may use relevant material at any one time (whether by limiting the number of terminals in a deposit library from which readers may at any one time access an electronic publication or otherwise) (s 7(4)(d)). As to the regulations made see the Legal Deposit Libraries (Non-Print Works) Regulations 2013, SI 2013/777, Pt 4 (regs 19–31), Schedule. 'Electronic publication' means an on line or off line publication including any publication in electronic form (within the meaning given by the Copyright, Designs and Patents Act 1988 s 178: see COPYRIGHT vol 23 (2013) PARA 778): Legal Deposit Libraries Act 2003 s 14. Neither copyright, nor database right in a database, is infringed by the doing of anything in relation to relevant material permitted to be done under regulations under s 7: see the Copyright, Designs and Patents Act 1988 s 44A(2); Copyright and Rights in Databases Regulations 1997, SI 1997/3032, reg 20A(2); and INFORMATION TECHNOLOGY LAW vol 57 (2012) PARA 573.
26 Ie the Legal Deposit Libraries Act 2003 s 7 (see the text to notes 17–25).

27 Legal Deposit Libraries Act 2003 s 7(6). As to breach of statutory duty see TORT vol 97 (2015) PARA 500 et seq.

897. Printed publications: the British Library. The British Library Board[1] is entitled to delivery[2] of a copy of every work published[3] in print[4]. The copy must be delivered within one month[5] beginning with the day of publication[6], and is to be of the same quality as the best copies which, at the time of delivery, have been produced for publication in the United Kingdom[7]. The Board must give a receipt in writing[8] (whether sent by electronic or other means)[9].

1 As to the British Library Board see PARA 904.
2 Ie under the Legal Deposit Libraries Act 2003 s 1 (see PARA 895).
3 As to the meaning of 'publish' see PARA 895 note 2.
4 Legal Deposit Libraries Act 2003 s 4(1).
5 As to the meaning of 'month' see PARA 803 note 12.
6 Legal Deposit Libraries Act 2003 s 4(2).
7 Legal Deposit Libraries Act 2003 s 4(3). As to the meaning of 'United Kingdom' see PARA 804 note 2.
8 As to the meaning of 'writing' see PARA 805 note 14.
9 Legal Deposit Libraries Act 2003 s 4(4).

898. Printed publications: other libraries. Each deposit library[1], other than the British Library Board[2], is entitled to delivery[3] of a copy of any work published[4] in print which it requests[5]. A request must be in writing[6] (whether sent by electronic or other means)[7], may be made before publication[8], and, in particular, may relate to all future numbers or parts of an encyclopaedia, newspaper, magazine or other work[9]. However, no request may be made after the end of 12 months[10] beginning with the day of publication[11].

The copy must be delivered within one month beginning with the day of publication[12] or, if later, the day on which the request is received[13]. The copy is to be of the same quality as the largest number of copies which, at the time of delivery, have been produced for publication in the United Kingdom[14].

1 As to the meaning of 'deposit library' see PARA 895 note 5.
2 As to the British Library Board see PARA 904. As to the delivery of printed publications to the British Library Board see PARA 897.
3 Ie under the Legal Deposit Libraries Act 2003 s 1 (see PARA 895).
4 As to the meaning of 'publish' see PARA 895 note 2.
5 Legal Deposit Libraries Act 2003 s 5(1).
6 As to the meaning of 'writing' see PARA 805 note 14.
7 Legal Deposit Libraries Act 2003 s 5(2).
8 Legal Deposit Libraries Act 2003 s 5(3)(a).
9 Legal Deposit Libraries Act 2003 s 5(3)(b).
10 As to the meaning of 'month' see PARA 803 note 12.
11 Legal Deposit Libraries Act 2003 s 5(4).
12 Legal Deposit Libraries Act 2003 s 5(5)(a).
13 Legal Deposit Libraries Act 2003 s 5(5)(b).
14 Legal Deposit Libraries Act 2003 s 5(6). As to the meaning of 'United Kingdom' see PARA 804 note 2.

899. Exemptions from liability for deposit libraries. The delivery by a person[1] of a copy of a work is to be taken:

(1)   not to breach any contract relating to any part of the work to which that person is a party[2]; and

(2)   not to infringe copyright, publication right or database right in relation to any part of the work or any patent[3].

A deposit library[4], or a person acting on its behalf, is not liable in damages for defamation arising out of the doing by a relevant person[5] of a prescribed activity[6] in relation to a copy of a work delivered[7] to the library[8]. However, this does not apply to the liability of a deposit library where:

(a)   it knows, or it knows of facts or circumstances from which it ought to know, that the copy contains a defamatory statement[9]; and

(b)   it has had a reasonable opportunity since obtaining that knowledge to prevent the doing of the activity in relation to the copy[10].

Where[11] a person (the 'publisher') has delivered a copy of a work to an address specified by a deposit library, the publisher is not liable in damages for defamation arising out of the doing by a relevant person of a prescribed activity[12] in relation to the copy[13]. However, this does not apply where:

(i)   the publisher knows, or the publisher knows of facts or circumstances from which it ought to know, that the copy contains a defamatory statement[14]; and

(ii)   it has had a reasonable opportunity since obtaining that knowledge to inform the library of the matter, facts or circumstances known to it and has not done so[15].

Where a work is published on the internet and certain conditions are met[16]:

(A)   no person other than the library is liable in damages for defamation arising out of the doing by a relevant person of a prescribed activity[17] in relation to a copy of the work[18]; and

(B)   the above provisions[19] apply in relation to the doing of an activity in relation to the copy as they apply in relation to the doing of the activity in relation to a copy of a work delivered[20].

The Secretary of State[21] may by regulations provide for these provisions[22], as they apply in relation to liability in damages for defamation, to apply in relation to liability (including criminal liability) of any description prescribed in the regulations, subject to such modifications as may be prescribed[23].

Nothing in these provisions[24] imposes liability on any person[25].

1   Ie pursuant to the Legal Deposit Libraries Act 2003 s 1 (see PARA 895). Section 9(1) applies to the delivery, pursuant to regulations under s 6, of a copy of a computer program or material within s 6(2)(b) (see PARA 896) as it applies to the delivery of a copy of a work pursuant to s 1: s 9(2). As to the meaning of 'person' see PARA 803 note 17.

2   Legal Deposit Libraries Act 2003 s 9(1)(a).

3   Legal Deposit Libraries Act 2003 s 9(1)(b). 'Database right' has the meaning given by the Copyright and Rights in Databases Regulations 1997, SI 1997/3032, reg 13(1) (see INFORMATION TECHNOLOGY LAW vol 57 (2012) PARA 546): Legal Deposit Libraries Act 2003 s 14. As to copyright see COPYRIGHT vol 23 (2013) PARA 653 et seq. As to publication right see COPYRIGHT vol 23 (2013) PARA 1044 et seq. As to patents see PATENTS AND REGISTERED DESIGNS vol 79 (2014) PARA 301 et seq.

4   As to the meaning of 'deposit library' see PARA 895 note 5. References in the Legal Deposit Libraries Act 2003 s 10 to a deposit library include references to the Faculty of Advocates: s 10(7)(c).

5   As to the meaning of 'relevant person' see PARA 896 note 17: definition applied by the Legal Deposit Libraries Act 2003 s 10(7)(a).

6   Ie an activity listed in the Legal Deposit Libraries Act 2003 s 7(2) (see PARA 896). References in s 10 to activities listed in s 7(2) are references to those activities whether or not done in relation to relevant material (as defined in s 7: see PARA 896 note 18): s 10(7)(b).

7   Ie under the Legal Deposit Libraries Act 2003 s 1 (see PARA 895).

8   Legal Deposit Libraries Act 2003 s 10(1) (amended by the Coroners and Justice Act 2009 Sch 23 Pt 2). Where the Legal Deposit Libraries Act 2003 s 10 applies to the doing of an activity in relation to a copy of a work it also applies to the doing of the activity in relation to a copy (at any remove) of that copy: s 10(9). As to liability for defamatory statements see DEFAMATION vol 32 (2012) PARA 510.

9   Legal Deposit Libraries Act 2003 s 10(2)(a) (amended by the Coroners and Justice Act 2009 Sch 23 Pt 2).

10 Legal Deposit Libraries Act 2003 s 10(2)(b).

11 Ie pursuant to the Legal Deposit Libraries Act 2003 s 1 (see PARA 895).

12 See note 6.

13 Legal Deposit Libraries Act 2003 s 10(3) (amended by the Coroners and Justice Act 2009 Sch 23 Pt 2).

14 Legal Deposit Libraries Act 2003 s 10(4)(a) (amended by the Coroners and Justice Act 2009 Sch 23 Pt 2).

15 Legal Deposit Libraries Act 2003 s 10(4)(b).

16 See the Legal Deposit Libraries Act 2003 s 10(5). The conditions are: (1) the work is of a description prescribed by regulations (Legal Deposit Libraries Act 2003 s 10(5)(a)); (2) the publication of the work on the internet, or a person publishing it there, is connected with the United Kingdom in a manner so prescribed (s 10(5)(b)); and (3) the copy was made by a deposit library or person acting on its behalf copying the work from the internet in accordance with any conditions so prescribed (s 10(5)(c)). The description of work that is prescribed for the purposes of s 10(5)(a) is work that is published on the internet but does not include: (a) work consisting only of a sound recording or film or both or such material and other material which is merely incidental to it; or (b) work which contains personal data and which is only made available to a restricted group of persons: see the Legal Deposit Libraries (Non-Print Works) Regulations 2013, SI 2013/777, reg 13(2)(a), (b), (3). For the purposes of the Legal Deposit Libraries Act 2003 s 10(5)(b), where work is published on line, the publication of that work or a person publishing it there is connected with the United Kingdom in the prescribed manner where the work published on the internet is made available to the public from a website with a domain name which relates to the United Kingdom or to a place within the United Kingdom; or it is made available to the public by a person and any of that person's activities relating to the creation or the publication of the work take place within the United Kingdom: see the Legal Deposit Libraries (Non-Print Works) Regulations 2013, SI 2013/777, reg 18(1), (3). However, a work published on line is not to be treated as published in the United Kingdom for these purposes if access to the work is only made available to persons outside the United Kingdom: see reg 18(2), (3). Neither copyright, nor database right in a database, is infringed by the copying of a work from the internet by a deposit library or person acting on its behalf if the work is of a description prescribed by such regulations, its publication on the internet, or a person publishing it there, is connected with the United Kingdom in a manner so prescribed, and the copying is done in accordance with any conditions so prescribed: see the Copyright, Designs and Patents Act 1988 s 44A(1); Copyright and Rights in Databases Regulations 1997, SI 1997/3032, reg 20A(1); and INFORMATION TECHNOLOGY LAW vol 57 (2012) PARA 573. As to the making of regulations see PARA 900. As to the meaning of 'personal data' see PARA 895 note 13. As to the meaning of 'United Kingdom' see PARA 804 note 2.

17 See note 6.

18 See the Legal Deposit Libraries Act 2003 s 10(6)(a) (amended by the Coroners and Justice Act 2009 Sch 23 Pt 2). See also note 8.

19 Ie the Legal Deposit Libraries Act 2003 s 10(1), (2) (see the text to notes 4–10).

20 See the Legal Deposit Libraries Act 2003 s 10(6)(b). See also note 8.

21 As to the Secretary of State see PARA 802 note 2.

22 Ie for the Legal Deposit Libraries Act 2003 s 10 (see the text to notes 4–20).

23 Legal Deposit Libraries Act 2003 s 10(8) (amended by the Coroners and Justice Act 2009 Sch 23 Pt 2). At the date at which this volume states the law no such regulations had been made.

24 Ie nothing in the Legal Deposit Libraries Act 2003 s 10 (see the text to notes 4–23).

25 Legal Deposit Libraries Act 2003 s 10(10).

900. Regulations under the Legal Deposit Libraries Act 2003. Any power under the Legal Deposit Libraries Act 2003 to make regulations: (1) includes power to make different provision for different purposes, including in particular different media[1], descriptions of work, deposit libraries[2] or areas[3]; and (2) as well as being exercisable in relation to all cases to which it extends, may be exercised in relation to those cases subject to specified exceptions, or in relation to a particular case or class of cases[4].

Regulations under the Act may not be made unless the Secretary of State has consulted the deposit libraries[5], and the publishers appearing to the Secretary of State to be likely to be affected[6]. Regulations may not be made without the consent of the Welsh Ministers[7] if they would: (a) remove an entitlement conferred by or under the Act on the authority controlling the National Library of Wales[8]; or (b) confer an entitlement that is not conferred on that authority on any other deposit library[9]; but this does not apply where the entitlement is to delivery of copies of electronic publications[10] and that authority is provided with a means of accessing those publications electronically[11]. Where this provision[12] does not apply, regulations that would affect the authority controlling the National Library of Wales may not be made unless the Secretary of State has consulted the Welsh Ministers[13].

Regulations under the Act which confer an entitlement on the authority controlling the Library of Trinity College, Dublin may not be made unless the Secretary of State is satisfied as to certain matters[14].

1   As to the meaning of 'medium' see PARA 895 note 12.
2   As to the meaning of 'deposit library' see PARA 895 note 5.
3   Legal Deposit Libraries Act 2003 s 11(1)(a).
4   Legal Deposit Libraries Act 2003 s 11(1)(b). Regulations under s 1(4) (see PARA 895) or s 6 (see PARA 896) may not be made so as to apply to works published before the regulations are made: s 11(3). Regulations under s 1(4), s 2 (see PARA 895) or s 6 may not be made unless the Secretary of State considers that the costs likely to be incurred as a result of the regulations by persons who publish works to which the regulations relate are not disproportionate to the benefit to the public arising from the delivery of copies of such works: s 11(4). Regulations under ss 1(4), 2, 6, 7 (see PARA 896) or s 10(5) (see PARA 899) may not be made unless the Secretary of State considers that the regulations do not unreasonably prejudice the interests of persons who publish works to which the regulations relate: s 11(5). As to the regulations made see the Legal Deposit Libraries (Non-Print Works) Regulations 2013, SI 2013/777; and PARAS 895–896, 899. As to the meaning of 'publish' see PARA 895 note 2. As to the Secretary of State see PARA 802 note 2. As to the meaning of 'person' see PARA 803 note 17.
5   Legal Deposit Libraries Act 2003 s 11(2)(a). As to the exercise of the duty to consult see JUDICIAL REVIEW vol 61 (2010) PARA 627.
6   Legal Deposit Libraries Act 2003 s 11(2)(b).
7   The functions under the Legal Deposit Libraries Act 2003 s 12 originally vested in the National Assembly for Wales are now exercisable by the Welsh Ministers by virtue of the Government of Wales Act 2006 s 162(1), Sch 11 paras 30, 32. As to the Welsh Ministers see PARA 802. As to the circumstances in which the Secretary of State must either obtain the consent of, or consult with, the Scottish Ministers see the Legal Deposit Libraries Act 2003 s 12(1)–(3) (amended by the National Library of Scotland Act 2012 Sch 2 para 7(a)). As to the Scottish Ministers see CONSTITUTIONAL AND ADMINISTRATIVE LAW vol 20 (2014) PARA 67.
8   Legal Deposit Libraries Act 2003 s 12(4)(a). As to the National Library of Wales see PARA 902.
9   Legal Deposit Libraries Act 2003 s 12(4)(b).
10 As to the meaning of 'electronic publication' see PARA 896 note 25.
11 Legal Deposit Libraries Act 2003 s 12(4).
12 Ie the Legal Deposit Libraries Act 2003 s 12(4) (see the text to notes 7–11).
13 Legal Deposit Libraries Act 2003 s 12(5).
14 The Secretary of State must be satisfied, in relation to relevant material delivered pursuant to such an entitlement: (1) that as regards the restriction by the Legal Deposit Libraries Act 2003 s 7 (see PARA 896) (having regard to any regulations made under that section) of activities in relation to relevant material, the restriction of those activities under the laws of Ireland is not substantially less (s 13(1)(a)); (2) that as regards the protection under the laws of any part of the United Kingdom of copyright, publication right, database right and patents in relation to relevant material, the protection under the laws of Ireland of corresponding rights is not substantially less (s 13(1)(b)); and (3) that as regards the protection from liability under s 10(3) and (4) (see PARA 899) (or those subsections as applied by regulations under that section), the protection under the laws of Ireland in relation to corresponding liability is not substantially less (s 13(1)(c)). As to the meaning of 'relevant material' see PARA 896 note 18: definition applied by s 13(2).

(iii) Offences relating to Libraries

901. Offences relating to private libraries. Any person who, in one of certain libraries and reading rooms[1], to the annoyance or disturbance of any person using it (1) behaves in a disorderly manner[2]; (2) uses violent, abusive or obscene language[3]; or (3) after proper warning persists in remaining there beyond the hours fixed for closing[4], commits an offence[5].

1   These provisions apply to any library or reading room maintained by a society that is a registered society within the meaning of the Co-operative and Community Benefit Societies Act 2014 (see

FINANCIAL INSTITUTIONS vol 48 (2015) PARA 881), or is registered under the Friendly Societies Act 1974 (repealed with savings) (see FINANCIAL INSTITUTIONS vol 48 (2015) PARA 557): Libraries Offences Act 1898 s 3(b) (amended by the Co-operative and Community Benefit Societies Act 2014 Sch 4 para 20); Interpretation Act 1978 s 17(2)(a). They also apply to any library or reading room maintained by any registered trade union: Libraries Offences Act 1898 s 3(b) (as so amended). As to the meaning of 'trade union' see EMPLOYMENT vol 41 (2014) PARA 891.

2   Libraries Offences Act 1898 s 2(1).
3   Libraries Offences Act 1898 s 2(2).
4   Libraries Offences Act 1898 s 2(4).
5   See the Libraries Offences Act 1898 s 2 (amended by the Gambling Act 2005 Sch 16 Pt 1 para 2, Sch 17). The penalty for such an offence is, on summary conviction, a fine not exceeding level 1 on the standard scale: see the Libraries Offences Act 1898 s 2 (amended by virtue of the Criminal Justice Act 1982 s 46). As to the standard scale and magistrates' powers to levy unlimited fines see SENTENCING vol 92 (2015) PARA 176.

(iv) The British Library

A.   ESTABLISHMENT AND PURPOSE OF THE BRITISH LIBRARY

902.   The British Library. The British Library Act 1972, which came into force on receiving royal assent on 27 July 1972[1], established for the United Kingdom[2] a national library, known as the 'British Library' consisting of a comprehensive collection of books, manuscripts, periodicals, films and other recorded matter, whether printed or otherwise[3]. There is, however, also a National Library of Wales, which was established by royal charter in 1907[4].

The British Library is under the control and management of a public authority, known as the British Library Board, whose duty is to manage the library as a national centre for reference, study and bibliographical and other information services, in relation both to scientific and technological matters and to the humanities[5]. The board must make the services of the British Library available in particular to institutions of education and learning, other libraries and industry[6]. It is within the board's functions, so far as it thinks it expedient for achieving the objects of the 1972 Act and generally for contributing to the efficient management of other libraries and information services, to carry out and sponsor research[7]. The board may contribute to the expenses of library authorities[8], or of any other person[9] providing library facilities, whether for members of the public or otherwise[10]. Subject to such restrictions and conditions as it thinks necessary to safeguard its collections, the board may lend any item, and make any part of its collections, or of its premises, available in connection with events of an educational, literary or cultural nature[11]; but in deciding whether or not to lend any such item and in determining the time for which and the conditions subject to which any such item is to be lent, the board must have regard to the interests of students and other persons visiting the national library, to the physical condition and degree of rarity of the item in question and to any risks to which it is likely to be exposed[12].

1   Ie with the exception of the British Library Act 1972 s 3 (relating to the transfer of the British Museum Library: see PARA 903), which came into force on 1 July 1973: see s 3(1), (2); and the British Library (Appointed Day) Order 1973, SI 1973/1125.
2   As to the meaning of 'United Kingdom' see PARA 804 note 2.
3   British Library Act 1972 s 1(1). The establishment of a national library system with the British Library at its head was recommended by the *Report of the National Libraries Committee* (Chairman: Dr FS Dainton FRS) (Cmnd 4028) (1969) and proposed in the White Paper *The British Library* (Cmnd 4572) (1971). As to the deposit of publications with the British Library see PARA 895 et seq.
4   The National Library of Wales was established by a royal charter of 19 March 1907. Supplemental charters were given to the library in 1911 and 1978. On the 19 July 2006 a new supplemental

charter was granted dissolving the supplemental charter of 1978 and changing the constitution and the governance of the library. The library is now governed by a Board of Trustees. The library is an Assembly Government Sponsored Body and receives an annual grant in aid from the National Assembly for Wales which is the library's main source of income: see the National Library of Wales website which, at the date at which this volume states the law, can be found at www.llgc.org.uk. As to the Welsh Government see CONSTITUTIONAL AND ADMINISTRATIVE LAW vol 20 (2014) PARA 351 et seq. The Board of Trustees of the National Library of Wales is a specified transferee (but not transferor) for the purposes of the general powers of transfer between collections (see the Museums and Galleries Act 1992 s 6, Sch 5; and PARA 817) and a specified body for the purposes of the statutory provision for vesting of gifts to the nation where the donor has not specified a destination (see s 7; and PARA 818).

5   British Library Act 1972 s 1(2). As to the British Library Board see PARA 904.
6   British Library Act 1972 s 1(3).
7   British Library Act 1972 s 1(3)(a).
8   Ie within the meaning of the Public Libraries and Museums Act 1964 (see PARA 922).
9   As to the meaning of 'person' see PARA 803 note 17.
10 British Library Act 1972 s 1(3)(b).
11 British Library Act 1972 s 1(4).
12 British Library Act 1972 s 1(4) proviso. As to the government indemnity scheme for items on loan see PARA 1094.

903. Transfer of the British Museum Library. All articles which immediately before 1 July 1973[1] were the property of the trustees of the British Museum[2] and (1) formed part of the collections in the museum's Department of Printed Books, Department of Manuscripts and Department of Oriental Printed Books and Manuscripts[3]; or (2) were in normal use in those departments for the purposes of the collections, or of their storage or management, or of the administration of the department[4], ceased on that day to be property of the trustees and became property of the British Library Board[5]. This did not, however, apply to any article for which it had been agreed in writing[6] between the trustees and the board that it was not to become the board's property[7].

The trustees may transfer to the board any article from their collections as to which the board has indicated to the trustees that the article is required for the British Library[8]. This power is exercisable notwithstanding any trust or condition, whether express or implied, prohibiting or restricting the disposal of the article, and notwithstanding anything in the British Museum Act 1963[9]; but it does not apply to pictures[10]. There is, also, now a further general statutory power to transfer objects between certain specified bodies including the board and the trustees[11].

If any property was previously vested in the trustees subject to any trust or condition, on transfer to the board it remains subject to the same trust or condition in the board's hands[12]. The trustees may make any part of their premises available for the board's use, and may arrange for services to be rendered to the board by British Museum staff, on such terms, including terms as to payment, as may be agreed with the board[13].

1   Ie the date on which the British Library Act 1972 s 3 came into force: see s 3(1), (2); and the British Library (Appointed Day) Order 1973, SI 1973/1125.
2   As to the trustees of the British Museum see PARA 824.
3   British Library Act 1972 s 3(1)(a).
4   British Library Act 1972 s 3(1)(b).
5   British Library Act 1972 s 3(1), (2) (amended by SI 1992/1311). As to the British Library see PARA 902. As to the British Library Board see PARA 904.
6   As to the meaning of 'writing' see PARA 805 note 14.
7   British Library Act 1972 s 3(3).
8   British Library Act 1972 s 3(4).
9   British Library Act 1972 s 3(4). As to the British Museum Act 1963 see PARAS 822–831.
10 British Library Act 1972 s 3(4) (amended for this purpose by the National Heritage Act 1983 Sch 5 para 7).

11 See the Museums and Galleries Act 1992 s 6; and PARA 817.
12 British Library Act 1972 s 3(5).
13 British Library Act 1972 s 3(6).

B.   THE BRITISH LIBRARY BOARD

904. Constitution and proceedings of the British Library Board. The British Library Board consists of a chairman and not less than eight, nor more than 13, other members[1]. The board is a body corporate with perpetual succession and a common seal[2]. The board has power to regulate its own procedure[3]. The validity of any of its proceedings is not affected by any vacancy among its members or by any defect in the appointment of any member[4].

The application of the board's seal must be authenticated by the signature of the secretary or of some other person authorised by the board, either generally or specially, to act for that purpose[5]. Any document purporting to be a document duly executed under the board's seal, or to be signed on its behalf is receivable in evidence and must, unless the contrary is proved, be deemed to be so executed or, as the case may be, so signed[6].

Not later than such date in each year as the Secretary of State[7] may determine, the board must send him a report of its proceedings and activities during the previous 12 months[8], which report must include a report on the working of the Public Lending Right Scheme 1982[9] and the Secretary of State must lay copies of the report before each House of Parliament[10].

1   See the British Library Act 1972 s 2(1) (s 2(1) amended by SI 1992/1311). As to the appointment of the members of the board see further the British Library Act 1972 s 2(1)(a)–(c), (2), (2A) (s 2(1)(bb), (2A) added by SI 2000/1102; the British Library Act 1972 s 2(2) amended by SI 1992/1311). As to tenure of office of members see the British Library Act 1972 Schedule paras 2–4 (Schedule paras 3, 5 amended by SI 1992/1311). As to the payment of remuneration, allowances and pensions to members of the board see the British Library Act 1972 Schedule para 5 (as so amended). The chairman of the board is disqualified for membership of the House of Commons: see the House of Commons Disqualification Act 1975 s 1(1)(f), Sch 1 Pt III; and PARLIAMENT vol 78 (2010) PARA 908.
2   British Library Act 1972 Schedule para 1. As to bodies corporate see COMPANIES vol 14 (2009) PARA 2; CORPORATIONS vol 24 (2010) PARA 301 et seq. As to the corporate seal see CORPORATIONS vol 24 (2010) PARA 323 et seq. The board, so far as it is a charity, and any institution which is administered by or on its behalf and established for general or special purposes, is an exempt charity for the purposes of the Charities Act 2011: see s 22, Sch 3 para 25; and CHARITIES vol 8 (2015) PARA 318.
3   British Library Act 1972 Schedule para 7(2). As to quorum see Schedule para 7(1).
4   British Library Act 1972 Schedule para 8.
5   British Library Act 1972 Schedule para 9. As to the secretary see PARA 905.
6   British Library Act 1972 Schedule para 10.
7   As to the Secretary of State see PARA 802 note 2.
8   As to the meaning of 'month' see PARA 803 note 12.
9   As to the Public Lending Right Scheme 1982 see PARA 894.
10 British Library Act 1972 s 4(3) (amended by SI 1992/1311; and SI 2013/2352). As to laying documents before Parliament see STATUTES AND LEGISLATIVE PROCESS vol 96 (2012) PARA 1052.

905. Staff of the British Library Board. The British Library Board[1] must appoint a secretary and may appoint such other officers as it may determine, and may pay to them and other employees such remuneration and allowances as the Secretary of State[2] may determine with the approval of the Treasury[3]. In the case of such officers and other persons employed by the board (not being members of the board) as it may determine with the Treasury's approval, the board must pay such pensions, allowances or gratuities to or in respect of them as may be so determined, make such payments towards the provision of such pensions, allowances or gratuities as may be so determined or provide and maintain such schemes (whether contributory or not) for the payment of such pensions, allowances or gratuities as may be so determined[4].

The board must seek consultation with any organisation appearing to it to be appropriate with a view to the conclusion between the board and that organisation of such agreements as appear to the parties to be desirable with respect to the establishment and maintenance of machinery for:

(1)   the settlement by negotiation of terms and conditions of employment of the board's employees with provision for reference to arbitration in default of such settlement in such cases as may be determined by or under the agreement[5]; and

(2)   the promotion and encouragement of measures affecting the safety, health and welfare of the board's employees and the discussion of other matters of mutual interest to the board and such persons including efficiency in the operation of the board's services[6].

1   As to the British Library Board see PARA 904.
2   As to the Secretary of State see PARA 802 note 2.
3   British Library Act 1972 Schedule para 12(1) (amended by SI 1981/1670; SI 1992/1311). As to the meaning of 'Treasury' see PARA 809 note 4. As to the provision made in respect of the employment by the board of persons who before 1 July 1973 (ie the appointed day: see PARA 903 note 1) were employed either in the civil service or by the trustees of the British Museum see the British Library Act 1972 Schedule para 13 (amended by the Employment Protection (Consolidation) Act 1978 s 159(2), (3), Sch 16 para 15, Sch 17; and by the Employment Rights Act 1996 s 240, Sch 1 para 4).
4   British Library Act 1972 Schedule para 12(2) (amended by SI 1981/1670).
5   See the British Library Act 1972 s 6(1).
6   See the British Library Act 1972 s 6(2).

906. Incidental functions of the British Library Board. It is within the capacity of the British Library Board as a statutory corporation[1] to do all such things, and enter into all such transactions, as are incidental or conducive to the discharge of its functions; but the board does not have the power to borrow money[2]. The board may frame, and vary and revoke from time to time, rules relating to the exercise by it of any power or the manner of entering into any transaction, and, with the approval of the Secretary of State[3], the rules may provide for the imposition of charges for any services provided by the board or for the loan or use of any item from its collections[4].

The board may acquire or dispose of any property, whether or not for the purposes of its collections, subject to the following conditions[5]:

(1)   the board's power to dispose of an article transferred to it with the British Museum Library[6] is exercisable only if:
        (a)   it is a duplicate of another article in the board's collections, whether or not so transferred[7]; or
        (b)   it appears to the board to have been printed not earlier than 1850, and a copy of it made by photography or a process akin to photography is held by the board[8]; or
        (c)   in the board's opinion it is unfit to be retained in its collections and can be disposed of without detriment to the interests of students[9]; or
        (d)   the disposal is an exercise of the power conferred[10] by the Museums and Galleries Act 1992[11];

(2)   where any property in the board's hands, whether or not transferred to it from the British Museum Library[12], is subject to any trust or condition:

(a)　the board must not dispose of or deal with it in any manner inconsistent with the trust or condition, except as provided[13] by the Museums and Galleries Act 1992[14]; and

(b)　it must be subject to the same trust or condition in the hands of any person[15] acquiring it from the board[16].

The board is a specified transferor and transferee for the purposes of the general powers of transfer between collections[17], and a specified body for the purposes of the statutory provision for vesting of gifts to the nation where the donor has not specified a destination[18]. The Secretary of State may transfer land to the board[19].

In certain circumstances the board may transfer an object from its collections under the Holocaust (Return of Cultural Objects) Act 2009[20].

1　As to the British Library Board see PARA 904.
2　British Library Act 1972 Schedule para 11(1). As to the board's general functions see PARA 902.
3　As to the Secretary of State see PARA 802 note 2.
4　British Library Act 1972 Schedule para 11(2) (amended by SI 1992/1311).
5　See the British Library Act 1972 Schedule para 11(3).
6　Ie transferred to the board under the British Library Act 1972 s 3(1)(a) (see PARA 903).
7　British Library Act 1972 Schedule para 11(4)(a).
8　British Library Act 1972 Schedule para 11(4)(b).
9　British Library Act 1972 Schedule para 11(4)(c) (amended by the Museums and Galleries Act 1992 Sch 8 para 12(1)).
10　Ie by the Museums and Galleries Act 1992 s 6 (see PARA 817).
11　British Library Act 1972 Schedule para 11(4)(d) (added by the Museums and Galleries Act 1992 Sch 8 para 12(1)).
12　Ie under the British Library Act 1972 s 3(1)(a) (see PARA 903).
13　Ie by the Museums and Galleries Act 1992 s 6 (see PARA 817).
14　British Library Act 1972 Schedule para 11(5)(a) (amended by the Museums and Galleries Act 1992 Sch 8 para 12(2)).
15　As to the meaning of 'person' see PARA 803 note 17.
16　British Library Act 1972 Schedule para 11(5)(b).
17　See the Museums and Galleries Act 1992 s 6, Sch 5; and PARA 817.
18　See the Museums and Galleries Act 1992 s 7; and PARA 818.
19　See the Museums and Galleries Act 1992 s 8, Sch 6; and PARA 819. The British Library building at St Pancras and 3.4 hectares of land were transferred to the board on 1 July 1997: see 297 HC Official Report (6th series), 2 July 1997, written answers col *184*.
20　See PARA 1107.

907. Advisory councils constituted by the British Library Board. In accordance with directions of the Secretary of State[1], given after consultation with the British Library Board[2], the board must constitute advisory councils with responsibility for providing advice to the board, or to any department of the British Library[3], on such matters as the Secretary of State or the board may determine from time to time[4]. An advisory council constituted by the board must consist of a chairman and such number of other members as the Secretary of State may specify in his directions[5].

1　As to the Secretary of State see PARA 802 note 2.
2　As to the British Library Board see PARA 904.
3　As to the British Library see PARA 902.
4　British Library Act 1972 s 2(3) (amended by SI 1992/1311).
5　British Library Act 1972 Schedule para 14(1) (amended by SI 1992/1311). As to the payment of fees and allowances to the chairman and members of a council see the British Library Act 1972 Schedule para 14(2) (amended by SI 1981/1670; and SI 1992/1311).

908. Finance and accounts of the British Library Board. The Secretary of State[1] must, out of money provided by Parliament[2], make to the British Library Board[3] such payments as the Treasury[4] may approve towards expenditure incurred by the board, whether in respect of its management of the British Library (including the acquisition of new items for the board's collections), or of general administration, or otherwise; and so far as relates to the use and expenditure of sums so paid to the board, the board must act in accordance with such directions as may from time to time be given to it by the Secretary of State[5].

Money received by the board in any financial year[6], whether in respect of property disposed of, or services provided, or otherwise, must be applied by the board in such manner as the Secretary of State may, with Treasury approval, direct[7].

The board must keep proper accounts and other records and, in respect of each financial year, prepare statements of account in such form as the Secretary of State may, with Treasury approval, direct[8]. The statements must be submitted to the Secretary of State on or before 30 November next following the expiration of the financial year in question, and must be transferred by him to the Comptroller and Auditor General, who must examine and certify them and lay copies of them, together with his report on them, before each House of Parliament[9].

1   As to the Secretary of State see PARA 802 note 2.
2   As to the provision of money by Parliament see PARLIAMENT vol 78 (2010) PARA 804.
3   As to the British Library Board see PARA 904. As to the general functions of the board see PARA 902; and as to its incidental functions see PARA 906.
4   As to the meaning of 'Treasury' see PARA 809 note 4.
5   British Library Act 1972 s 5(1) (amended by SI 1992/1311).
6   'Financial year' means the 12 months ending 31 March: see the Interpretation Act 1978 s 5, Sch 1.
7   British Library Act 1972 s 5(2) (amended by SI 1992/1311). Any such direction may require the whole or any part of that money to be paid into the Consolidated Fund: British Library Act 1972 s 5(2). As to the Consolidated Fund see CONSTITUTIONAL AND ADMINISTRATIVE LAW vol 20 (2014) PARA 480.
8   British Library Act 1972 s 5(3) (amended by SI 1992/1311).
9   British Library Act 1972 s 5(3) (as amended: see note 8). As to the Comptroller and Auditor General see CONSTITUTIONAL AND ADMINISTRATIVE LAW vol 20 (2014) PARAS 494–496. As to the laying of documents before Parliament see STATUTES AND LEGISLATIVE PROCESS vol 96 (2012) PARA 1052.

(v) The Local Authority Library Service

A.   STATUTORY FRAMEWORK OF LOCAL AUTHORITY LIBRARY SERVICE

909.   The Public Libraries and Museums Act 1964. The local authority library service was put on a completely new basis by the Public Libraries and Museums Act 1964[1], which imposes a duty to provide an efficient and comprehensive library service for all persons desiring to make use of it on those local authorities which are library authorities[2]. The service in England is under the supervision of the Secretary of State, and in Wales of the Welsh Ministers[3].

The Act extends to the Isles of Scilly with modifications[4]. The Act has effect notwithstanding any inconsistent provision in a local Act, and any public library maintained by a library authority on 1 April 1965[5] under a power conferred by a local Act must after that date be treated as maintained under the Public Libraries and Museums Act 1964 and not under the power of the local Act[6]. Except for these provisions, nothing in the 1964 Act may be taken to derogate from the provisions of any local Act[7].

The Public Lending Right Act 1979 and the scheme made thereunder impose certain obligations on local library authorities[8].

1   See the Public Libraries and Museums Act 1964 ss 1–11, Sch 1; and PARA 910 et seq.

2 See the Public Libraries and Museums Act 1964 s 7(1); and PARA 925. As to library authorities see PARA 922.
3 See the Public Libraries and Museums Act 1964 ss 1, 2; and PARA 910. As to the Secretary of State and the Welsh Ministers see PARA 802.
4 See the Public Libraries and Museums Act 1964 s 24(1), (2) (s 24(1) amended by the Local Government Act 1972 s 208(3)(j)); and the Isles of Scilly (Public Libraries and Museums) Order 1965, SI 1965/511.
5 Ie the date on which the Public Libraries and Museums Act 1964 came into force: see ss 23, 26(7).
6 Public Libraries and Museums Act 1964 s 23. As to local Acts see STATUTES AND LEGISLATIVE PROCESS vol 96 (2012) PARA 626.
7 See the Public Libraries and Museums Act 1964 s 23.
8 See PARA 894.

B. ADMINISTRATION OF LOCAL AUTHORITY LIBRARY SERVICE

(A) General Duties and Powers regarding Library Authority

910. Supervision of libraries. The Secretary of State or, in relation to Wales, the Welsh Ministers[1] must superintend and promote the improvement of the public library service provided by local authorities, and secure the proper discharge by local authorities of the functions in relation to libraries conferred on them as library authorities under the Public Libraries and Museums Act 1964[2]. Every library authority must furnish such information, and provide such facilities for the inspection of library premises, stocks and records, as the Secretary of State or, as appropriate the Welsh Ministers may require for carrying out this duty[3]. In each year, the Secretary of State must lay before each House of Parliament, and the Welsh Ministers must lay before the National Assembly for Wales, a report on the exercise of his or their functions under the Public Libraries and Museums Act 1964[4].

As soon as might be after 1 April 1965[5], the Secretary of State was to designate by order as library regions areas together extending to the whole of England and Wales[6]. After consultation with the library authorities within the region, the Secretary of State or, in relation to Wales, the Welsh Ministers must make a scheme for each library region providing for:

(1) the constitution, incorporation and functioning of a library council for the region, consisting of persons[7] representing each of the authorities and such other persons as may be provided for by the scheme, and having a duty to make and supervise the working of arrangements for facilitating the co-operation of those authorities with one another and with other bodies within or outside the region having functions in relation to libraries[8]; and

(2) the observance by each of the authorities of any requirements made by the library council, including requirements as to the payment by the authority of contributions towards the expenses of the council[9],

and containing such other provisions directed to the promotion of inter-library co-operation within and outside the region as may appear to the Secretary of State or the Welsh Ministers to be expedient[10]. At least a majority of the library council for a region must consist of members of library authorities within the region, and an authority none of whose members is included in the library council must be represented on the council by such of the persons so included as may be determined in accordance with the scheme establishing the council[11].

With a view to improving the efficiency of the public library service or promoting its development, the Secretary of State or, in relation to Wales, the Welsh Ministers may require any library council established for a library region to enter into and carry into effect arrangements with another such council or with any other body having functions in relation to libraries[12].

1   The functions of the Secretary of State under the Public Libraries and Museums Act 1964 in so far as they relate to Wales were transferred to the National Assembly for Wales (see the National Assembly for Wales (Transfer of Functions) Order 1999, SI 1999/672, art 2, Sch 1) and are now exercisable by the Welsh Ministers (see the Government of Wales Act 2006 s 162(1), Sch 11 paras 30, 32). As to the Secretary of State and the Welsh Ministers see PARA 802. As to the meaning of 'Wales' see PARA 802 note 4.
2   Public Libraries and Museums Act 1964 s 1(1) (s 1 amended by SI 1992/1311). As to the meanings of 'local authority' and 'library authority' see PARA 922.
3   Public Libraries and Museums Act 1964 s 1(2) (as amended: see note 2).
4   See the Public Libraries and Museums Act 1964 s 17; National Assembly for Wales (Transfer of Functions) Order 1999, SI 1999/672, art 2, Sch 1; Government of Wales Act 2006 s 86, Sch 11 paras 30, 32. As to the laying of documents before Parliament see STATUTES AND LEGISLATIVE PROCESS vol 96 (2012) PARA 1052. As to the laying of documents by the Welsh Ministers before the National Assembly for Wales see CONSTITUTIONAL AND ADMINISTRATIVE LAW vol 20 (2014) PARA 384.
5   Ie the commencement date of the Public Libraries and Museums Act 1964: see ss 3(1), 26(7).
6   See the Public Libraries and Museums Act 1964 s 3(1) (s 3 amended by SI 1992/1311). In so far as this power remains to be exercised in relation to Wales it is now exercisable by the Welsh Ministers: see note 1. Any such order or scheme may be varied or revoked by a further order or scheme, provided that, before varying or revoking a scheme, the Secretary of State or the Welsh Ministers must consult the library council in question as well as the relevant library authorities: s 3(4) (as so amended). At the date at which this volume states the law no such order or scheme had been made.
7   As to the meaning of 'person' see PARA 803 note 17.
8   Public Libraries and Museums Act 1964 s 3(2)(a).
9   Public Libraries and Museums Act 1964 s 3(2)(b).
10   Public Libraries and Museums Act 1964 s 3(2) (as amended: see note 6). See also note 6.
11   Public Libraries and Museums Act 1964 s 3(3).
12   Public Libraries and Museums Act 1964 s 3(5) (as amended: see note 6).

911. Default powers of the Secretary of State and the Welsh Ministers. If:

(1)   a complaint is made to the Secretary of State or, in relation to Wales, the Welsh Ministers[1] that any library authority[2] has failed to carry out duties relating to the public library service imposed on it by or under the Public Libraries and Museums Act 1964[3]; or

(2)   the Secretary of State or the Welsh Ministers is or are of opinion that an investigation ought to be made as to whether any such failure by a library authority has occurred[4],

and, after causing a local inquiry[5] to be held into the matter, the Secretary of State or the Welsh Ministers is or are satisfied that there has been such a failure by the library authority, he or they may make an order declaring it to be in default and directing it for the purpose of removing the default to carry out such of its duties, in such manner and within such time, as may be specified in the order[6]. If the authority fails to comply with any requirement of the order, instead of enforcing it by mandatory order[7] or otherwise, the Secretary of State or the Welsh Ministers may:

(a)   if the authority is a joint board[8], make an order providing that on a specified date the board is dissolved[9] and that on its dissolution, the authorities constituting the board will again become library authorities[10] and the functions relating to the public library service of such of those authorities as may be specified in that behalf in the order are transferred to the Secretary of State or, as the case may be, the Welsh Ministers[11]; or

(b)   in any other case, make an order providing that the authority's functions relating to the public library service are transferred to the Secretary of State or, as the case may be, Welsh Ministers[12].

Where an authority's functions have been transferred to the Secretary of State or the Welsh Ministers by such an order, he or they may at any time by order transfer them back to the authority, and the order may contain such supplemental provisions as may appear to him or them to be expedient for that purpose[13].

1   The functions of the Secretary of State under the Public Libraries and Museums Act 1964 in so far as they relate to Wales were transferred to the National Assembly for Wales and are now exercisable by the Welsh Ministers: see the National Assembly for Wales (Transfer of Functions) Order 1999, SI 1999/672, art 2, Sch 1; Government of Wales Act 2006 s 162(1), Sch 11 paras 30, 32. As to the Secretary of State and the Welsh Ministers see PARA 802. As to the meaning of 'Wales' see PARA 802 note 4.
2   As to the meaning of 'library authority' see PARA 922.
3   Public Libraries and Museums Act 1964 s 10(1)(a) (s 10 amended by SI 1992/1311).
4   Public Libraries and Museums Act 1964 s 10(1)(b) (as amended: see note 3).
5   The Public Libraries (Inquiries Procedure) Rules 1992, SI 1992/1627, apply to any such inquiry: see r 3; and PARA 912 et seq.
6   Public Libraries and Museums Act 1964 s 10(1) (as amended: see note 3).
7   The Public Libraries and Museums Act 1964 s 10(2) refers to 'mandamus' which is now known as a mandatory order: see JUDICIAL REVIEW vol 61 (2010) PARA 703 et seq.
8   As to joint boards see PARA 923.
9   Public Libraries and Museums Act 1964 s 10(2)(b). As to the exercise of delegated powers see STATUTES AND LEGISLATIVE PROCESS vol 96 (2012) PARA 1045. As to the procedure in relation to subordinate legislation made by the Welsh Ministers see the Government of Wales Act 2006 Sch 11 paras 33–35; and STATUTES AND LEGISLATIVE PROCESS vol 96 (2012) PARA 1035.
10 Public Libraries and Museums Act 1964 s 10(2)(b)(i) (amended by the Local Government (Wales) Act 1994 s 66(6), (8), Sch 16 para 24(1)(d), Sch 18; Local Government Act 1972 ss 208(3), 272(1), Sch 30).
11 Public Libraries and Museums Act 1964 s 10(2)(b)(iii).
12 Public Libraries and Museums Act 1964 s 10(2)(c). Where the Secretary of State or the Welsh Ministers has or have by order transferred to himself or themselves any functions of a council or joint board, any expenses incurred by him or them in discharging its functions must be paid in the first instance out of money provided by Parliament; but the amount of those expenses as certified by him or them must on demand be paid to him or them by the body in default, and are recoverable by him or them from that body as a debt due to the Crown, and that body has the like power of raising the money required as it has of raising money for defraying expenses incurred directly by it: Public Health Act 1936 s 324(1) (s 324 amended by the Public Health (Control of Disease) Act 1984 s 78, Sch 3; and modified by the Public Libraries and Museums Act 1964 s 10(5)). The payment of any such expenses is, to such extent as may be sanctioned by the Secretary of State or the Welsh Ministers, a purpose for which a library authority or joint board may borrow money in accordance with the statutory provisions relating to borrowing by such an authority or board: Public Health Act 1936 s 324(2) (as so amended and modified).
13 Public Libraries and Museums Act 1964 s 10(4).

(B)   Public Inquiries regarding Library Authority

912. Power to hold public inquiry into matters relating to library authority functions. The Secretary of State or, in relation to Wales, the Welsh Ministers[1] may hold an inquiry into any matter relating to the functions of a library authority[2] under the Public Libraries and Museums Act 1964[3]. The procedure to be followed in any such inquiry is prescribed by rules made by the Lord Chancellor[4]. The Secretary of State or, as appropriate, the Welsh Ministers appoints the person to hold the inquiry (the 'appointed person')[5].

1   The functions of the Secretary of State under the Public Libraries (Inquiries Procedure) Rules 1992, SI 1992/1627, in so far as they relate to Wales were transferred to the National Assembly for Wales (see the National Assembly for Wales (Transfer of Functions) Order 1999, SI 1999/672, arts 2, 3, Sch 1) and are now exercisable by the Welsh Ministers (see the Government of Wales Act 2006

s 162(1), Sch 11 paras 30, 32). As to the Secretary of State and the Welsh Ministers see PARA 802.
As to the meaning of 'Wales' see PARA 802 note 4.

2   As to the meaning of 'library authority' see PARA 922.

3   Public Libraries and Museums Act 1964 s 16 (amended by the Local Government Act 1972
s 208(3)(h); and SI 1992/1311). There is also a specific power to hold a local inquiry under the
Public Libraries and Museums Act 1964 s 10(1) (see PARA 911).

4   See the Tribunals and Inquiries Act 1992 ss 9, 15; and JUDICIAL REVIEW vol 61 (2010) PARA
646. At the date at which this volume states the law, no such rules had been made but, by virtue
of the Interpretation Act 1978 s 17(2)(b), the Public Libraries (Inquiries Procedure) Rules 1992, SI
1992/1627 (see PARA 913 et seq) have effect as if so made: see note 5.

5   'Appointed person' means the person appointed by the Secretary of State or the Welsh Ministers
to hold the inquiry; and 'inquiry' means an inquiry to which the Public Libraries (Inquiries
Procedure) Rules 1992, SI 1992/1627, apply: r 2. The Rules apply in relation to any inquiry which
is caused by the Secretary of State or the Welsh Ministers to be held in respect of a library authority
pursuant to the Public Libraries and Museums Act 1964 s 10(1) (see PARA 911) or s 16 (see the
text to notes 1–3): Public Libraries (Inquiries Procedure) Rules 1992, SI 1992/1627, r 3. The
Secretary of State, the Welsh Ministers or the appointed person may at any time in any particular
case allow further time for the taking of any step which is to be taken by virtue of the Public
Libraries (Inquiries Procedure) Rules 1992, SI 1992/1627, and references therein to a day by
which, or a period within which, any step is to be taken must be construed accordingly: r 15.

913. Preliminary procedures for public inquiries. Where the Secretary of State
or, in relation to Wales, the Welsh Ministers[1] intend to cause an inquiry[2] to be
held, he or they must give written notice[3] to the library authority[4] and to such
other persons[5] or classes of persons as he or they may decide, and must as soon
as practicable thereafter publish in at least two newspapers circulating in the area
in respect of which the library authority is obliged to carry out its duties a notice
of the inquiry[6]. Not later than four weeks after the relevant date[7], he or they must
serve a statement of case[8] on the library authority and on each person on whom
the relevant notice was served and must send to the appointed person a copy of
the statement[9].

Not later than eight weeks after the relevant date, any person may serve a
statement of case on the Secretary of State or the Welsh Ministers and on the
library authority and also send it to the appointed person[10]. Not later than seven
days after receipt of the statement of case the Secretary of State or the Welsh
Ministers must send a copy of the statement to each other person on whom the
relevant notice was served[11].

The appointed person may require any person who has served a statement of
case in accordance with these provisions to provide such further information
about the matters concerned in the statement as he may specify[12]. The library
authority must afford to any person who so requests a reasonable opportunity to
inspect and, when practicable, take copies of any statement of case or other
document which, or a copy of which, has been served on the authority in
accordance with any of these provisions, and of its statement of case together with
a copy of any document, or of the relevant part of any document, referred to in
the list comprised in that statement or otherwise served by the authority pursuant
to these provisions; and must specify in its statement of case the time and place at
which the opportunity will be afforded[13].

1   The functions of the Secretary of State under the Public Libraries (Inquiries Procedure) Rules 1992,
SI 1992/1627, in so far as they relate to Wales were transferred to the National Assembly for Wales
(see the National Assembly for Wales (Transfer of Functions) Order 1999, SI 1999/672, arts 2, 3,
Sch 1) and are now exercisable by the Welsh Ministers (see the Government of Wales Act 2006
s 162(1), Sch 11 paras 30, 32). As to the Secretary of State and the Welsh Ministers see PARA 802.
As to the meaning of 'Wales' see PARA 802 note 4.

2   As to the meaning of 'inquiry' see PARA 912 note 5.

3   As to the meaning of 'written' see PARA 805 note 14. Notices or documents required to be served
or sent under any of the provisions of the Public Libraries (Inquiries Procedure) Rules 1992, SI
1992/1627, may be sent by post: r 16. Where an Act or subordinate legislation authorises or

requires any document to be served by post (whether the expression 'serve' or the expression 'give' or 'send' or any other expression is used) then, unless the contrary intention appears, the service is deemed to be effected by properly addressing, pre-paying and posting a letter containing the document and, unless the contrary is proved, to have been effected at the time at which the letter would be delivered in the ordinary course of post: see the Interpretation Act 1978 ss 7, 23(1); and STATUTES AND LEGISLATIVE PROCESS vol 96 (2012) PARA 1219. A requirement to send a document by post is not confined to sending it by the Post Office postal system: see the Postal Services Act 2000 Sch 8 Pt 1.

4   As to the meaning of 'library authority' see PARA 922.
5   As to the meaning of 'person' see PARA 803 note 17.
6   Public Libraries (Inquiries Procedure) Rules 1992, SI 1992/1627, r 4.
7   'Relevant date' means the date of the Secretary of State's or the Welsh Ministers' written notice to the library authority of the intention to cause an inquiry to be held; and 'relevant notice' means that notice: Public Libraries (Inquiries Procedure) Rules 1992, SI 1992/1627, r 2. As to the power to extend time limits under the rules see PARA 912 note 5.
8   'Statement of case' means a written statement which contains full particulars of the case which a person proposes to put forward at an inquiry, and a list of any documents which that person intends to refer to or put in evidence: Public Libraries (Inquiries Procedure) Rules 1992, SI 1992/1627, r 2. Any person serving a statement of case must serve with it a copy of any document, or of the relevant part of any document, referred to in the written statement: r 5(4).
9   Public Libraries (Inquiries Procedure) Rules 1992, SI 1992/1627, r 5(1). As to the meaning of 'appointed person' see PARA 912 note 5.
10 See the Public Libraries (Inquiries Procedure) Rules 1992, SI 1992/1627, r 5(2).
11 See the Public Libraries (Inquiries Procedure) Rules 1992, SI 1992/1627, r 5(2). Where the person serving the statement of case is not a person on whom the relevant notice was served, the Secretary of State or the Welsh Ministers must also send a copy of his statement of case to such person within seven days of receipt of that person's statement of case or, if he or they think fit, give notice in writing to that person within that period stating the times and places at which he may inspect the statement of case and, where practicable, take copies of it: r 5(2).
12 Public Libraries (Inquiries Procedure) Rules 1992, SI 1992/1627, r 5(3).
13 Public Libraries (Inquiries Procedure) Rules 1992, SI 1992/1627, r 5(5).

914. Pre-inquiry meetings. The appointed person[1] may hold a pre-inquiry meeting[2], or if appropriate more than one meeting, where he considers it desirable and must arrange for not less than 14 days' written notice[3] of any such meeting to be given to the Secretary of State or, as appropriate, the Welsh Ministers[4], the library authority[5], any person[6] on whom the relevant notice[7] was served and any other person whose presence at the meeting appears to him to be desirable[8].

The appointed person must preside at the pre-inquiry meeting and must determine the matters to be discussed and the procedure to be followed[9]. He may require any person present at the meeting who, in his opinion, is behaving in a disruptive manner to leave it and he may refuse to permit that person to return or to attend any further pre-inquiry meeting, or may permit him to return or to attend only on such conditions as he may specify[10].

1   As to the meaning of 'appointed person' see PARA 912 note 5.
2   'Pre-inquiry meeting' means a meeting held before an inquiry to consider what may be done with a view to securing that it is conducted efficiently and expeditiously: Public Libraries (Inquiries Procedure) Rules 1992, SI 1992/1627, r 2. As to the meaning of 'inquiry' see PARA 912 note 5.
3   As to the meaning of 'written' see PARA 805 note 14. As to the service of notices see PARA 913 note 3. As to the power to extend time limits under the rules see PARA 912 note 5.
4   The functions of the Secretary of State under the Public Libraries (Inquiries Procedure) Rules 1992, SI 1992/1627, in so far as they relate to Wales were transferred to the National Assembly for Wales (see the National Assembly for Wales (Transfer of Functions) Order 1999, SI 1999/672, arts 2, 3, Sch 1) and are now exercisable by the Welsh Ministers (see the Government of Wales Act 2006 s 162(1), Sch 11 paras 30, 32). As to the Secretary of State and the Welsh Ministers see PARA 802. As to the meaning of 'Wales' see PARA 802 note 4.
5   As to the meaning of 'library authority' see PARA 922.
6   As to the meaning of 'person' see PARA 803 note 17.
7   As to the meaning of 'relevant notice' see PARA 913 note 7.
8   Public Libraries (Inquiries Procedure) Rules 1992, SI 1992/1627, r 6(1).

9 Public Libraries (Inquiries Procedure) Rules 1992, SI 1992/1627, r 6(2). He may arrange the inquiry timetable at the pre-inquiry meeting (see PARA 915).
10 Public Libraries (Inquiries Procedure) Rules 1992, SI 1992/1627, r 6(2).

915. Inquiry timetable; date and notification of inquiry. The appointed person[1] may arrange a timetable for the proceedings at, or at part of, the inquiry[2] at any pre-inquiry meeting[3] or, where no such meeting is held, at any other time[4]. He must notify the timetable to the persons entitled to appear at the inquiry[5] and may at any time vary the timetable[6]. He may specify in such a timetable a date by which any proof of evidence and summary required[7] to be sent to him must be so sent[8].

The date fixed by the Secretary of State or, as the case may be, the Welsh Ministers[9] for the holding of the inquiry must be not later than 22 weeks after the relevant date[10] or, where the Secretary of State or Welsh Ministers is satisfied that in all the circumstances of the case it is impracticable to hold the inquiry within that period, the earliest practicable date after the end of that period[11]. Unless the Secretary of State or the Welsh Ministers agrees a lesser period of notice with the library authority[12], he or they must give not less than 28 days' written[13] notice of the date, time and place fixed for the holding of an inquiry to every person entitled to appear at the inquiry[14].

The Secretary of State or the Welsh Ministers may require the library authority to post a notice of the inquiry, within such period as he or they may specify, in a conspicuous place in all the public libraries in its area, and not less than 14 days before the date fixed for the holding of the inquiry he or they must publish in at least two of the newspapers circulating in the area in respect of which the library authority is obliged to carry out its duties a notice of the inquiry[15].

1 As to the meaning of 'appointed person' see PARA 912 note 5.
2 As to the meaning of 'inquiry' see PARA 912 note 5.
3 As to the meaning of 'pre-inquiry meeting' see PARA 914 note 2.
4 Public Libraries (Inquiries Procedure) Rules 1992, SI 1992/1627, r 7(1).
5 As to the persons entitled to appear see PARA 916. As to the service of notices see PARA 913 note 3. As to the meaning of 'person' see PARA 803 note 17.
6 Public Libraries (Inquiries Procedure) Rules 1992, SI 1992/1627, r 7(1).
7 Ie by the Public Libraries (Inquiries Procedure) Rules 1992, SI 1992/1627, r 10(1) (see PARA 917).
8 Public Libraries (Inquiries Procedure) Rules 1992, SI 1992/1627, r 7(2).
9 The functions of the Secretary of State under the Public Libraries (Inquiries Procedure) Rules 1992, SI 1992/1627, in so far as they relate to Wales were transferred to the National Assembly for Wales (see the National Assembly for Wales (Transfer of Functions) Order 1999, SI 1999/672, arts 2, 3, Sch 1) and are now exercisable by the Welsh Ministers (see the Government of Wales Act 2006 s 162(1), Sch 11 paras 30, 32). As to the Secretary of State and the Welsh Ministers see PARA 802. As to the meaning of 'Wales' see PARA 802 note 4.
10 Public Libraries (Inquiries Procedure) Rules 1992, SI 1992/1627, r 8(1)(a). As to the meaning of 'relevant date' see PARA 913 note 7. As to the power to extend time limits under the rules see PARA 912 note 5.
11 Public Libraries (Inquiries Procedure) Rules 1992, SI 1992/1627, r 8(1)(b).
12 As to the meaning of 'library authority' see PARA 922.
13 As to the meaning of 'written' see PARA 805 note 14.
14 Public Libraries (Inquiries Procedure) Rules 1992, SI 1992/1627, r 8(2). The Secretary of State or the Welsh Ministers may vary the date fixed for the holding of an inquiry, whether or not the date so varied is within the period mentioned in r 8(1) (see the text to notes 9–11), and r 8(2) applies to a date so varied as it applies to the date originally fixed: r 8(3). The Secretary of State or the Welsh Ministers may vary the time or place for the holding of an inquiry and must give such notice of any such variation as appears to him or them to be reasonable: r 8(4).
15 Public Libraries (Inquiries Procedure) Rules 1992, SI 1992/1627, r 8(5). Every notice of an inquiry so posted or published must contain a clear statement of the date, time and place of the inquiry, of the powers enabling the Secretary of State or the Welsh Ministers to cause the inquiry to be held and of the subject matter of the inquiry: r 8(6).

916. Appearances at inquiry. The persons[1] entitled to appear at an inquiry[2] are the Secretary of State or, as appropriate, the Welsh Ministers[3], the library authority[4], and any person on whom notice of the inquiry has been served[5] or who has served a statement of case[6] on the Secretary of State or the Welsh Ministers[7]. Nothing in these provisions, however, prevents the appointed person[8] from permitting any other person to appear at the inquiry, and such permission must not be unreasonably withheld[9].

Any person entitled or permitted to appear may do so on his own behalf or be represented by counsel, solicitor or any other person[10]. The appointed person may allow one or more persons to appear for the benefit of some or all of any persons having a similar interest in the matter under inquiry[11].

1 As to the meaning of 'person' see PARA 803 note 17.
2 As to the meaning of 'inquiry' see PARA 912 note 5.
3 The functions of the Secretary of State under the Public Libraries (Inquiries Procedure) Rules 1992, SI 1992/1627, in so far as they relate to Wales were transferred to the National Assembly for Wales (see the National Assembly for Wales (Transfer of Functions) Order 1999, SI 1999/672, arts 2, 3, Sch 1) and are now exercisable by the Welsh Ministers (see the Government of Wales Act 2006 s 162(1), Sch 11 paras 30, 32). As to the Secretary of State and the Welsh Ministers see PARA 802. As to the meaning of 'Wales' see PARA 802 note 4.
4 As to the meaning of 'library authority' see PARA 922.
5 Ie under the Public Libraries (Inquiries Procedure) Rules 1992, SI 1992/1627, r 4 (see PARA 913).
6 Ie under the Public Libraries (Inquiries Procedure) Rules 1992, SI 1992/1627, r 5(2) (see PARA 913). As to the meaning of 'statement of case' see PARA 913 note 8.
7 Public Libraries (Inquiries Procedure) Rules 1992, SI 1992/1627, r 9(1).
8 As to the meaning of 'appointed person' see PARA 912 note 5.
9 Public Libraries (Inquiries Procedure) Rules 1992, SI 1992/1627, r 9(2).
10 Public Libraries (Inquiries Procedure) Rules 1992, SI 1992/1627, r 9(3).
11 Public Libraries (Inquiries Procedure) Rules 1992, SI 1992/1627, r 9(4).

917. Service of proofs of evidence before inquiry. A person entitled to appear at the inquiry[1] who proposes to give, or to call another person to give, evidence at the inquiry by reading a proof of evidence must send a copy of the proof to the appointed person[2]. The Secretary of State or, as the case may be, the Welsh Ministers[3], the library authority[4], and any other person so directed by the appointed person must also supply a written summary of his, their or its proof[5]. The proof and any summary must be sent to the appointed person not later than three weeks before the date fixed for the holding of the inquiry[6], or, where a timetable has been arranged[7] which specifies a date by which the proof and any summary must be sent to the appointed person, that date[8].

Where the Secretary of State or the Welsh Ministers or the library authority sends or send a copy of a proof of evidence and a summary to the appointed person, they must at the same time send a copy to every other person entitled to appear at the inquiry; and where any other person so sends such a copy proof and any summary he must at the same time send a copy to the Secretary of State or the Welsh Ministers and the library authority[9]. The Secretary of State, the Welsh Ministers and the library authority must afford to any person who so requests a reasonable opportunity to inspect and, where practicable, to take copies of any document sent to or by them in accordance with any of these provisions[10].

Where the appointed person so directs, only the written summary of the proof of evidence may be read at the inquiry[11].

1 As to the persons entitled to appear see PARA 916. As to the meaning of 'person' see PARA 803 note 17. As to the meaning of 'inquiry' see PARA 912 note 5.
2 Public Libraries (Inquiries Procedure) Rules 1992, SI 1992/1627, r 10(1). Any person so required to send a copy of a proof of evidence to any other person must send with it a copy of the whole,

or the relevant part, of any document referred to in it and not previously supplied under r 5(4) (see PARA 913): r 10(5). As to the meaning of 'appointed person' see PARA 912 note 5.

3   The functions of the Secretary of State under the Public Libraries (Inquiries Procedure) Rules 1992, SI 1992/1627, in so far as they relate to Wales were transferred to the National Assembly for Wales (see the National Assembly for Wales (Transfer of Functions) Order 1999, SI 1999/672, arts 2, 3, Sch 1) and are now exercisable by the Welsh Ministers (see the Government of Wales Act 2006 s 162(1), Sch 11 paras 30, 32). As to the Secretary of State and the Welsh Ministers see PARA 802. As to the meaning of 'Wales' see PARA 802 note 4.

4   As to the meaning of 'library authority' see PARA 922.

5   Public Libraries (Inquiries Procedure) Rules 1992, SI 1992/1627, r 10(1).

6   As to the date fixed for the inquiry see PARA 915. As to the power to extend time limits under the rules see PARA 912 note 5.

7   Ie pursuant to the Public Libraries (Inquiries Procedure) Rules 1992, SI 1992/1627, r 7 (see PARA 915).

8   Public Libraries (Inquiries Procedure) Rules 1992, SI 1992/1627, r 10(2).

9   Public Libraries (Inquiries Procedure) Rules 1992, SI 1992/1627, r 10(3).

10 Public Libraries (Inquiries Procedure) Rules 1992, SI 1992/1627, r 10(6).

11 Public Libraries (Inquiries Procedure) Rules 1992, SI 1992/1627, r 10(4).

918. Procedure at inquiry. Except as otherwise provided by the statutory rules[1], the appointed person[2] determines the procedure at the inquiry[3]. He must conduct the inquiry in public unless for any reason he determines that the inquiry or any part of it must be in private[4].

Unless in any particular case the appointed person with the consent of the Secretary of State or, as the case may be, the Welsh Ministers[5] otherwise determines, the Secretary of State or the Welsh Ministers begin and have the right of final reply; and the other persons entitled or permitted to appear[6] are heard in such order as the appointed person may determine[7].

A person entitled to appear at an inquiry is entitled to call evidence and the Secretary of State or the Welsh Ministers and the library authority[8] are entitled to cross-examine any person giving evidence, but the calling of evidence and the cross-examination of persons giving evidence are otherwise[9] at the appointed person's discretion[10]. The appointed person may refuse to permit the giving or production of evidence[11], the cross-examination of persons giving evidence[12], or the presentation of any other matter[13], which he considers to be irrelevant or repetitious; but where he so refuses to permit the giving of oral evidence, the person wishing to give the evidence may submit to him any written evidence or other matter in writing[14] before the close of the inquiry[15].

Where a person gives evidence at an inquiry by reading a summary of his evidence[16], the proof of evidence[17] must, unless the person required to supply the summary notifies the appointed person that he now wishes to rely on the contents of that summary only, be treated as tendered in evidence, and the person whose evidence the proof contains is then subject to cross-examination on it to the same extent as if it were evidence he had given orally[18].

The appointed person may direct that facilities must be afforded to any person appearing at an inquiry to take or obtain copies of documentary evidence open to public inspection[19]. The appointed person may require any person appearing or present at an inquiry who, in his opinion, is behaving in a disruptive manner to leave and may refuse to permit that person to return, or may permit him to return only on such conditions as he may specify; but any such person may submit to him any evidence or other matter in writing before the close of the inquiry[20].

The appointed person may allow any person to alter or add to a statement of case previously served[21] so far as may be necessary for the purposes of the inquiry; but he must (if necessary by adjourning the inquiry) give any other person entitled to appear who is appearing at the inquiry an adequate opportunity of considering any fresh matter or document[22]. The appointed person may proceed with an inquiry in the absence of any person entitled to appear at it[23]. He may take into account any written representation or evidence or any other document received by him from any person before an inquiry opens or during the inquiry provided that he discloses it at the inquiry[24].

The appointed person may from time to time adjourn the inquiry and, if the date, time and place of the adjourned inquiry are announced at the inquiry before the adjournment, no further notice is required[25].

1   Ie by the Public Libraries (Inquiries Procedure) Rules 1992, SI 1992/1627.
2   As to the meaning of 'appointed person' see PARA 912 note 5.
3   Public Libraries (Inquiries Procedure) Rules 1992, SI 1992/1627, r 11(1). As to the meaning of 'inquiry' see PARA 912 note 5.
4   Public Libraries (Inquiries Procedure) Rules 1992, SI 1992/1627, r 11(2).
5   The functions of the Secretary of State under the Public Libraries (Inquiries Procedure) Rules 1992, SI 1992/1627, in so far as they relate to Wales were transferred to the National Assembly for Wales (see the National Assembly for Wales (Transfer of Functions) Order 1999, SI 1999/672, arts 2, 3, Sch 1) and are now exercisable by the Welsh Ministers (see the Government of Wales Act 2006 s 162(1), Sch 11 paras 30, 32). As to the Secretary of State and the Welsh Ministers see PARA 802. As to the meaning of 'Wales' see PARA 802 note 4.
6   As to the persons entitled or permitted to appear see PARA 916. As to the meaning of 'person' see PARA 803 note 17.
7   Public Libraries (Inquiries Procedure) Rules 1992, SI 1992/1627, r 11(3).
8   As to the meaning of 'library authority' see PARA 922.
9   Ie subject to the Public Libraries (Inquiries Procedure) Rules 1992, SI 1992/1627, r 11(3), (5), (6), (8): see the text to notes 6–7, 11–18, 20.
10 Public Libraries (Inquiries Procedure) Rules 1992, SI 1992/1627, r 11(4).
11 Public Libraries (Inquiries Procedure) Rules 1992, SI 1992/1627, r 11(5)(a).
12 Public Libraries (Inquiries Procedure) Rules 1992, SI 1992/1627, r 11(5)(b).
13 Public Libraries (Inquiries Procedure) Rules 1992, SI 1992/1627, r 11(5)(c).
14 As to the meanings of 'writing' and 'written' see PARA 805 note 14.
15 Public Libraries (Inquiries Procedure) Rules 1992, SI 1992/1627, r 11(5).
16 Ie in accordance with the Public Libraries (Inquiries Procedure) Rules 1992, SI 1992/1627, r 10(4) (see PARA 917).
17 Ie the proof of evidence referred to in the Public Libraries (Inquiries Procedure) Rules 1992, SI 1992/1627, r 10(1) (see PARA 917).
18 Public Libraries (Inquiries Procedure) Rules 1992, SI 1992/1627, r 11(6).
19 Public Libraries (Inquiries Procedure) Rules 1992, SI 1992/1627, r 11(7).
20 Public Libraries (Inquiries Procedure) Rules 1992, SI 1992/1627, r 11(8).
21 Ie under the Public Libraries (Inquiries Procedure) Rules 1992, SI 1992/1627, r 5 (see PARA 913). As to the meaning of 'statement of case' see PARA 913 note 8.
22 Public Libraries (Inquiries Procedure) Rules 1992, SI 1992/1627, r 11(9).
23 Public Libraries (Inquiries Procedure) Rules 1992, SI 1992/1627, r 11(10).
24 Public Libraries (Inquiries Procedure) Rules 1992, SI 1992/1627, r 11(11).
25 Public Libraries (Inquiries Procedure) Rules 1992, SI 1992/1627, r 11(12).

919. Site inspections of premises used as a public library. The appointed person[1] may make an unaccompanied inspection of any premises used or formerly used by the library authority[2] as a public library and referred to in any statement of case served[3] before or during an inquiry[4] without giving notice of his intention to the persons entitled to appear at the inquiry[5]. During an inquiry or after its close, he may inspect any such premises in the company of the Secretary of State or, as appropriate, the Welsh Ministers[6] and the library authority; and he must make such an inspection if so requested by the Secretary of State, the Welsh Ministers or the library authority before or during an inquiry[7].

In all cases where the appointed person intends to make an accompanied inspection he must announce during the inquiry the date and time at which he proposes to make it[8]. He is not, however, bound to defer such an inspection where any prescribed person[9] is not present at the time appointed[10].

1   As to the meaning of 'appointed person' see PARA 912 note 5.
2   As to the meaning of 'library authority' see PARA 922.
3   Ie under the Public Libraries (Inquiries Procedure) Rules 1992, SI 1992/1627, r 5 (see PARA 913). As to the meaning of 'statement of case' see PARA 913 note 8.
4   As to the meaning of 'inquiry' see PARA 912 note 5.
5   Public Libraries (Inquiries Procedure) Rules 1992, SI 1992/1627, r 12(1). As to the persons entitled to appear see PARA 916. As to the meaning of 'person' see PARA 803 note 17.
6   The functions of the Secretary of State under the Public Libraries (Inquiries Procedure) Rules 1992, SI 1992/1627, in so far as they relate to Wales were transferred to the National Assembly for Wales (see the National Assembly for Wales (Transfer of Functions) Order 1999, SI 1999/672, arts 2, 3, Sch 1) and are now exercisable by the Welsh Ministers (see the Government of Wales Act 2006 s 162(1), Sch 11 paras 30, 32). As to the Secretary of State and the Welsh Ministers see PARA 802. As to the meaning of 'Wales' see PARA 802 note 4.
7   Public Libraries (Inquiries Procedure) Rules 1992, SI 1992/1627, r 12(2).
8   Public Libraries (Inquiries Procedure) Rules 1992, SI 1992/1627, r 12(3).
9   Ie any person mentioned in the Public Libraries (Inquiries Procedure) Rules 1992, SI 1992/1627, r 12(2) (see the text to notes 6–7).
10   Public Libraries (Inquiries Procedure) Rules 1992, SI 1992/1627, r 12(4).

920. Procedure after inquiry. After the close of an inquiry[1], the appointed person[2] must make a report in writing[3] to the Secretary of State or, as the case may be, the Welsh Ministers[4] which must include his conclusions and his recommendations or his reasons for not making any recommendations[5].

If, after the close of an inquiry, the Secretary of State or the Welsh Ministers differ from the appointed person on any matter of fact mentioned in, or appearing to him or them to be material to, a conclusion reached by the appointed person, or take into consideration any new evidence or new matter of fact (not being a matter of government policy[6]), he or they must not come to a decision without first notifying the persons entitled to appear at the inquiry[7] who appeared at it of the difference and the reasons for it or the new evidence or matter of fact and affording to them an opportunity of making written representations within 21 days[8] of the date of the notification[9]. Where the Secretary of State or the Welsh Ministers have so taken into consideration any new evidence or new matter of fact and are for that reason disposed to disagree with a recommendation made by the appointed person, he or they must give the persons entitled to appear at the inquiry who appeared at it the opportunity of asking, within 21 days of the notification to them of the new evidence or matter of fact, for the reopening of the inquiry[10].

The Secretary of State or the Welsh Ministers may, as he or they think fit, cause an inquiry to be reopened to afford an opportunity for persons, including the Secretary of State or, as appropriate, the Welsh Ministers, to be heard on such matters relating to the subject-matter of the inquiry as he or they may specify, and he or they must do so if asked[11] by the library authority[12].

1   As to the meaning of 'inquiry' see PARA 912 note 5.
2   As to the meaning of 'appointed person' see PARA 912 note 5.
3   As to the meaning of 'writing' see PARA 805 note 14.
4   The functions of the Secretary of State under the Public Libraries (Inquiries Procedure) Rules 1992, SI 1992/1627, in so far as they relate to Wales were transferred to the National Assembly for Wales (see the National Assembly for Wales (Transfer of Functions) Order 1999, SI 1999/672, arts 2, 3, Sch 1) and are now exercisable by the Welsh Ministers (see the Government of Wales Act 2006 s 162(1), Sch 11 paras 30, 32). As to the Secretary of State and the Welsh Ministers see PARA 802. As to the meaning of 'Wales' see PARA 802 note 4.
5   Public Libraries (Inquiries Procedure) Rules 1992, SI 1992/1627, r 13(1).
6   In relation to Wales, any reference in the Public Libraries (Inquiries Procedure) Rules 1992, SI 1992/1627, to government policy has effect as if it included a reference to policy adopted or

formulated by the Welsh Ministers: see the Government of Wales Act 2006 Sch 11 para 30; the National Assembly for Wales (Transfer of Functions) Order 2000, SI 2000/253, art 6(1), (2), Sch 4.

7   As to the persons entitled to appear see PARA 916. As to the meaning of 'person' see PARA 803 note 17.

8   As to the power to extend time limits under the rules see PARA 912 note 5.

9   Public Libraries (Inquiries Procedure) Rules 1992, SI 1992/1627, r 13(2).

10 Public Libraries (Inquiries Procedure) Rules 1992, SI 1992/1627, r 13(3).

11 Ie pursuant to the Public Libraries (Inquiries Procedure) Rules 1992, SI 1992/1627, r 13(3) and in the circumstances and within the period mentioned in r 13(3) (see the text to note 10).

12 Public Libraries (Inquiries Procedure) Rules 1992, SI 1992/1627, r 13(4). As to the meaning of 'library authority' see PARA 922. Where an inquiry is reopened the Secretary of State or the Welsh Ministers must send to the persons entitled to appear at the inquiry who appeared at it a written statement of the specified matters (r 13(4)(a)) and r 8(2)–(6) (see PARA 915) applies as if references to an inquiry were references to a reopened inquiry (r 13(4)(b)).

921. Notification of decision of inquiry. The Secretary of State or, as the case may be, the Welsh Ministers[1] must notify his or their decision and the reasons for it in writing[2] to all persons entitled to appear at the inquiry[3] who did appear at it and to any other person who, having appeared at the inquiry, has asked to be notified of the decision[4]. Where a copy of the appointed person's report[5] is not sent with the notification of the decision, the notification must be accompanied by a copy of his conclusions and of any recommendations made by him; and if a person entitled to be notified of the decision has not received a copy of that report, he must be supplied with a copy of it on written application made to the Secretary of State or, as appropriate, the Welsh Ministers within four weeks of the decision[6].

1   The functions of the Secretary of State under the Public Libraries (Inquiries Procedure) Rules 1992, SI 1992/1627, in so far as they relate to Wales were transferred to the National Assembly for Wales (see the National Assembly for Wales (Transfer of Functions) Order 1999, SI 1999/672, arts 2, 3, Sch 1) and are now exercisable by the Welsh Ministers (see the Government of Wales Act 2006 s 162(1), Sch 11 paras 30, 32). As to the Secretary of State and the Welsh Ministers see PARA 802. As to the meaning of 'Wales' see PARA 802 note 4.

2   As to the meaning of 'writing' see PARA 805 note 14.

3   As to the persons entitled to appear see PARA 916. As to the meaning of 'person' see PARA 803 note 17. As to the meaning of 'inquiry' see PARA 912 note 5.

4   Public Libraries (Inquiries Procedure) Rules 1992, SI 1992/1627, r 14(1).

5   For these purposes, 'report' does not include any documents appended to the appointed person's report, but any person who has received a copy of the report may apply to the Secretary of State or, as appropriate, the Welsh Ministers in writing within six weeks of the date of receipt of the report for an opportunity of inspecting any such documents and the Secretary of State or the Welsh Ministers must afford him that opportunity: Public Libraries (Inquiries Procedure) Rules 1992, SI 1992/1627, r 14(3). As to the appointed person's report see PARA 920. As to the meaning of 'appointed person' see PARA 912 note 5. As to the power to extend time limits under the rules see PARA 912 note 5.

6   Public Libraries (Inquiries Procedure) Rules 1992, SI 1992/1627, r 14(2).

C.   LIBRARY AUTHORITIES

922. Meanings of 'local authority' and 'library authority'. The local authorities for the purposes of the Public Libraries and Museums Act 1964 in England[1] are county councils, London borough councils, district councils, the Common Council of the City of London and the Council of the Isles of Scilly[2]. Subject to the provisions relating to joint boards[3], 'library authority' means in England one of the following authorities:

(1)   the council of a non-metropolitan county[4];

(2)   the council of a London borough and the Common Council; and

(3)   the council of a metropolitan district[5].

The local authorities in Wales[6] for the purposes of the Act are county councils and county borough councils[7]; and, subject to the provisions relating to joint boards[8], library authorities in Wales are county councils and county borough councils[9].

1   As to the meaning of 'England' see PARA 804 note 2.
2   Local Government Act 1972 s 206 (amended by the Local Government Act 1985 s 102(2), Sch 17).
     As to local government areas and authorities in England and Wales see LOCAL GOVERNMENT vol 69 (2009) PARA 22 et seq. As to the application of the Public Libraries and Museums Act 1964 to the Isles of Scilly see PARA 909.
3   Ie the Public Libraries and Museums Act 1964 s 5 (see PARA 923.
4   'Non-metropolitan county' means any county other than a metropolitan county: Local Government Act 1972 s 270(2).
5   Public Libraries and Museums Act 1964 s 25; Local Government Act 1972 s 206 (as amended: see note 2).
6   As to the meaning of 'Wales' see PARA 802 note 4.
7   Public Libraries and Museums Act 1964 s 25 (definition added by the Local Government (Wales) Act 1994 s 66(6), Sch 16 para 24(3)).
8   See note 3.
9   Public Libraries and Museums Act 1964 s 4(3) (added by the Local Government (Wales) Act 1994 Sch 16 para 24(2)).

923. Library areas and joint boards. The functions of a library authority[1] as such are exercisable within an area (called a 'library area') consisting of the administrative area of the authority or, in the case of a joint board[2], consisting of the areas which, if the authorities constituting the board were library authorities, would form their library areas; and may also be exercised elsewhere than within its library area if the authority thinks fit[3].

With the agreement of two or more library authorities, the Secretary of State or, in relation to Wales, the Welsh Ministers[4] may by order provide for the formation of a joint board consisting of those authorities which, from the date on which it begins to exercise its functions, is a library authority in lieu of those authorities[5]. The order may[6] provide for the incorporation of the joint board, for its procedure (including quorum) and for the manner in which its expenses are to be defrayed[7]. On the date on which a joint board begins to exercise its functions:

(1)   the library officers[8] of the authorities constituting the board are, by the operation of this provision, transferred to and become officers of the board[9]; and

(2)   the library assets and liabilities[10] of those authorities are, save as may be provided by the order setting up the board, transferred to the board[11].

On the application of an authority comprised in a joint board, the Secretary of State or, as the case may be, the Welsh Ministers may by order provide for the dissolution of the board, and on its dissolution the authorities constituting the board again become library authorities[12]. On the dissolution of a joint board, each library officer of the board:

(a)   where at the board's formation he was a library officer of one of the authorities which on the dissolution of the board again become library authorities, is transferred to and again becomes an officer of that authority[13]; and

(b)   in any other case, is transferred to and becomes an officer of such one of the authorities which on the dissolution of the board again become library authorities as may be agreed between those authorities or, in default of agreement, determined by the Secretary of State or, as appropriate, the Welsh Ministers[14].

The library assets and liabilities of the board are divided among the authorities as provided by the order dissolving the board[15].

Where a joint board is dissolved, and:

(i)   at any time before its dissolution a gratuity by way of periodical payments or an annuity was granted to any person by the board on his ceasing to be employed by the board[16], or to the surviving spouse or surviving civil partner or any other dependant of a person who died while in the board's employment, or who died during the currency of such a gratuity so granted to him[17]; and

(ii)   if the board had not been dissolved at that time, one or more payments in respect of that gratuity would under the terms of the grant have fallen to be made by the board after that time, whether it would have been obliged to make those payments or not,

those payments must be made by such one of the authorities which on the dissolution of the board again become library authorities as the Secretary of State or, as appropriate, the Welsh Ministers may determine[18]. Without prejudice to these provisions, where for the purposes of any pensions provision[19] the board, if it had not been dissolved, would at any time after the date on which it is dissolved have been the employing authority or former employing authority in relation to a person who before that time died while in the board's employment or otherwise ceased to be employed by it, or in relation to the surviving spouse or surviving civil partner or any other dependant of such a person, such one of the authorities which on the dissolution of the board again become library authorities as the Secretary of State or the Welsh Ministers may determine must be treated as being at that time the employing authority or former employing authority for those purposes in relation to that person, or to that person's surviving spouse or surviving civil partner or other dependant, as the case may be[20].

1   As to the meaning of 'library authority' see PARA 922.
2   As to joint boards see the Public Libraries and Museums Act 1964 s 5; and the text to notes 4–15.
3   Public Libraries and Museums Act 1964 s 4(2) (amended by the Local Government (Wales) Act 1994 s 66(6), (8), Sch 16 para 24(1)(a), Sch 18).
4   The functions of the Secretary of State under the Public Libraries and Museums Act 1964 in so far as it relates to Wales were transferred to the National Assembly for Wales (see the National Assembly for Wales (Transfer of Functions) Order 1999, SI 1999/672, arts 2, 3, Sch 1) and are now exercisable by the Welsh Ministers (see the Government of Wales Act 2006 s 162(1), Sch 11 paras 30, 32). As to the Secretary of State and the Welsh Ministers see PARA 802. As to the meaning of 'Wales' see PARA 802 note 4.
5   Public Libraries and Museums Act 1964 s 5(1) (s 5 amended by SI 1992/1311). Such orders not being made by statutory instrument are not recorded in this work.
6   Ie without prejudice to the Local Government Act 1972 s 241: Public Libraries and Museums Act 1964 s 5(1); Interpretation Act 1978 s 17(2)(a). The Local Government Act 1972 s 241 applies to the formation under the Public Libraries and Museums Act 1964 s 5 of a joint board comprising the Common Council of the City of London as if the Common Council were a local authority within the meaning of the Local Government Act 1972 (see s 270(1); and LOCAL GOVERNMENT vol 69 (2009) PARA 22): Public Libraries and Museums Act 1964 s 5(1); Interpretation Act 1978 s 17(2)(a). Where any enactment, whether passed before or after 1 April 1974, authorises the formation by a provisional or other order of a joint board or joint committee, the constituent members of which are local authorities, for the discharge of any of the functions of those authorities, the provisional order or order may apply to the joint board or joint committee, subject to any necessary modifications, any of the provisions of the Local Government Act 1972: s 241. As to the Common Council of the City of London see LONDON GOVERNMENT vol 71 (2013) PARAS 34–38.
7   Public Libraries and Museums Act 1964 s 5(1).
8   'Library officer' means an officer of a local authority employed by the authority solely or mainly for the purposes of any functions exercisable by it in relation to the public library service; and 'officer' includes a servant: Public Libraries and Museums Act 1964 s 25. As to the meaning of 'local authority' see PARA 922.

9 Public Libraries and Museums Act 1964 s 5(2)(a). As to the transfer of library officers see further PARA 924.
10 'Library assets and liabilities' means property held by a local authority solely or mainly for the purposes of any functions exercisable by it in relation to the public library service and rights and liabilities to which the authority is entitled or subject by reason of the exercise of such functions: Public Libraries and Museums Act 1964 s 25.
11 Public Libraries and Museums Act 1964 s 5(2)(b).
12 Public Libraries and Museums Act 1964 s 5(3) (as amended (see note 5); further amended by the Local Government (Wales) Act 1994 s 66(6), (8), Sch 16 para 24(1)(b), Sch 18). Such orders not being made by statutory instrument are not recorded in this work.
13 Public Libraries and Museums Act 1964 s 5(4)(a)(i).
14 Public Libraries and Museums Act 1964 s 5(4)(a)(ii) (as amended: see note 5).
15 Public Libraries and Museums Act 1964 s 5(4)(b). Where any library assets and liabilities have been transferred by the operation of the Public Libraries and Museums Act 1964 from one local authority to another, those authorities may by agreement provide for the making of such adjustments in relation to their respective property, rights and liabilities as appear to them to be desirable having regard to the transfer, and any such agreements may in particular provide for the making of payments by either party: see s 11(3). Where it appears to the Secretary of State or, as the case may be, the Welsh Ministers that, having regard to any such transfer, it is desirable that any such adjustment, including any payment by either of the authorities concerned, should be made, then, subject to any agreement made by the authorities concerned and after consultation with them, the Secretary of State or, as the case may be, the Welsh Ministers may, by directions, make provision for that adjustment: see s 11(4) (s 11(4), (5) amended by SI 1992/1311). Where any question arises as to whether any library assets and liabilities have been so transferred from one local authority to another, the question must be determined by the Secretary of State or, as appropriate, the Welsh Ministers: see the Public Libraries and Museums Act 1964 s 11(5) (as so amended).
16 Public Libraries and Museums Act 1964 Sch 1 para 4(1)(a).
17 Public Libraries and Museums Act 1964 Sch 1 para 4(1)(b) (amended by SI 2014/3168).
18 Public Libraries and Museums Act 1964 Sch 1 para 4(1) (amended by SI 1992/1311).
19 For these purposes, 'pensions provision' means a provision relating to pensions contained in or made under a general or local Act: Public Libraries and Museums Act 1964 Sch 1 para 5.
20 Public Libraries and Museums Act 1964 Sch 1 para 4(2) (amended by SI 1992/1311; and SI 2014/3168).

924. Officers of library authorities. A person is not disqualified by reason of his being a teacher in, or being otherwise employed in, any school or other educational institution maintained or assisted by a local authority, for being a member of any committee of any local authority appointed for purposes connected with the execution of the Public Libraries and Museums Act 1964, or for being a representative of a local authority on a joint committee of the authority and another authority which has been appointed or established for any such purpose[1].

A library authority[2] to which a library officer[3] is transferred by the operation of any provision of the Public Libraries and Museums Act 1964 must secure that:

(1)   so long as he continues in the authority's employment by virtue of the transfer, and until he is served with a written[4] statement of new terms and conditions of employment, he enjoys terms and conditions of employment not less favourable than those he enjoyed immediately before the date of transfer[5]; and

(2)   the new terms and conditions are such that so long as he is engaged in duties reasonably comparable to those in which he was engaged immediately before the date of transfer, the scale of his salary or remuneration and the other terms and conditions of his employment are not less favourable than those he enjoyed immediately before the date of transfer[6].

These provisions operate separately from and without prejudice to provisions in employment legislation for the protection of employment rights on the transfer of an undertaking[7].

Where any library officers have been transferred by the operation of the Public Libraries and Museums Act 1964 from one local authority[8] to another, those authorities may by agreement provide for the making of such adjustments in relation to their respective rights and liabilities as appear to them to be desirable having regard to the transfer, and any such agreements may in particular provide for the making of payments by either party[9]. Where it appears to the Secretary of State or, in relation to Wales, the Welsh Ministers[10] that, having regard to any such transfer, it is desirable that any such adjustment, including any payment by either of the authorities concerned, should be made, then, subject to any agreement made by the authorities concerned and after consultation with them, the Secretary of State or, as the case may be, the Welsh Ministers may, by directions, make provision for that adjustment[11]. Where any question arises as to whether any library officers have been transferred from one authority to another, the question must be determined by the Secretary of State or, as appropriate, the Welsh Ministers[12].

1   See the Local Government Act 1972 s 104(2) (amended by the Education Reform Act 1988 s 237(2), Sch 13 Pt II; and SI 2010/1158); and LOCAL GOVERNMENT vol 69 (2009) PARA 372.
2   As to the meaning of 'library authority' see PARA 922.
3   As to the meaning of 'library officer' see PARA 923 note 8.
4   As to the meaning of 'written' see PARA 805 note 14.
5   Public Libraries and Museums Act 1964 s 11(1)(a).
6   Public Libraries and Museums Act 1964 s 11(1)(b). The Local Government Act 1972 s 255 (which requires provision to be made by regulations for the payment in certain cases of compensation for loss of employment or loss or diminution of emoluments: see LOCAL GOVERNMENT vol 69 (2009) PARA 7) applies as respects persons who suffer loss of employment or loss or diminution of emoluments in consequence of their transfer by the operation of any provision of the Public Libraries and Museums Act 1964 as it applies in the cases there provided: s 11(2) (amended by the Local Government (Wales) Act 1994 s 66(6), (8), Sch 16 para 24(1)(e), Sch 18); Interpretation Act 1978 s 17(2)(a).
7   As to transfers of undertakings see EMPLOYMENT vol 39 (2014) PARA 136 et seq.
8   As to the meaning of 'local authority' see PARA 922.
9   See the Public Libraries and Museums Act 1964 s 11(3).
10 The functions of the Secretary of State under the Public Libraries and Museums Act 1964 in so far as it relates to Wales were transferred to the National Assembly for Wales (see the National Assembly for Wales (Transfer of Functions) Order 1999, SI 1999/672, arts 2, 3, Sch 1) and are now exercisable by the Welsh Ministers (see the Government of Wales Act 2006 s 162(1), Sch 11 paras 30, 32). As to the Secretary of State and the Welsh Ministers see PARA 802. As to the meaning of 'Wales' see PARA 802 note 4.
11 See the Public Libraries and Museums Act 1964 s 11(4) (s 11(4), (5) amended by SI 1992/1311).
12 See the Public Libraries and Museums Act 1964 s 11(5) (as amended: see note 11).

D.   FUNCTIONS AND DUTIES OF LIBRARY AUTHORITIES

925. Duties of library authorities. It is the duty of every library authority[1] to provide a comprehensive and efficient library service for all persons[2] desiring to make use of it[3]. However, although a library authority has power to make facilities for the borrowing of books and other materials available to any person, it is not under a duty to make them available to persons other than those whose residence or place of work is within the authority's library area[4] or who are undergoing full-time education within that area[5].

In fulfilling its duty, a library authority must in particular have regard to the desirability of:

(1)   securing, by the keeping of adequate stocks, by arrangements with other
       library authorities, and by any other appropriate means, that facilities
       are available for the borrowing of, or reference to, books and other
       printed matter, and pictures, gramophone records, films and other
       materials, sufficient in number, range and quality to meet the general
       requirements and any special requirements of both adults and children[6];
       and

(2)   encouraging both adults and children to make full use of the library
       service, and providing advice as to its use and of making available such
       bibliographical and other information as may be required by persons
       using it[7]; and

(3)   in relation to any matter concerning the functions of both the library
       authority as such and any other authority whose functions are
       exercisable within the library area, securing that there is full
       co-operation between the persons engaged in carrying out those
       functions[8].

The duty to provide a comprehensive and efficient library service is qualified by
a requirement that performance of the duty should not interfere with the due
administration of justice; dissemination through a library authority service of
material the subject of an interlocutory injunction against publication would be
an interference with the due administration of justice[9]. A decision as to the library
stock taken on purely political grounds is a decision for an ulterior motive taking
into account an irrelevant consideration and is therefore susceptible to judicial
review[10].

Library authorities also have duties in relation to the public lending right
scheme[11].

1   As to the meaning of 'library authority' see PARA 922.
2   As to the meaning of 'person' see PARA 803 note 17.
3   Public Libraries and Museums Act 1964 s 7(1) (amended by the Local Government Act 1972
    s 272(1), Sch 30). See *R (on the application of Bailey) v Brent London Borough Council* [2011]
    EWCA Civ 1586, [2012] LGR 530 (local authority acted lawfully in decision to close public
    libraries); and *R (on the application of Green) v Gloucestershire County Council; R (on the
    application of Rowe) v Somerset County Council* [2011] EWHC 2687 (Admin), [2012] LGR 330
    (decisions of local authorities to make changes to their library services unlawful on account of
    failure to comply with public sector equality duties).
4   As to the meaning of 'library area' see PARA 923.
5   Public Libraries and Museums Act 1964 s 7(1) proviso.
6   Public Libraries and Museums Act 1964 s 7(2)(a).
7   Public Libraries and Museums Act 1964 s 7(2)(b).
8   Public Libraries and Museums Act 1964 s 7(2)(c).
9   *A-G v Observer Ltd, Re application by Derbyshire County Council* [1988] 1 All ER 385. However
    the omission to examine publications to ascertain whether they contained extracts from the book
    the subject of the interlocutory injunction in question did not constitute an interference with the
    administration of justice: see *A-G v Observer Ltd, Re application by Derbyshire County Council*
    at 399 per Knox J.
10 See *R v Ealing London Borough Council, ex p Times Newspapers Ltd, R v Hammersmith and
    Fulham London Borough Council, ex p Times Newspapers Ltd, R v Camden London
    Borough Council, ex p Times Newspapers Ltd* (1986) 85 LGR 316, [1987] IRLR 129, DC (library
    authorities decided, in support of print unions in an industrial dispute with management of
    publishers, to ban from public libraries newspapers and other publications which had previously
    been stocked; authorities held to have acted in a way amounting to an abuse of power for the
    reasons set out in the text).
11 As to the public lending right scheme see PARA 894.

926. Restriction on charges for library facilities. Except as set out below, no charge may be made by a library authority[1] (otherwise than to another library authority) for library facilities made available by the authority[2].

The Secretary of State or, in relation to Wales, the Welsh Ministers[3] may by regulations[4] authorise library authorities to make charges for such library facilities made available by them as may be specified in the regulations[5], and make such provision as regards charges by library authorities for library facilities, other than provision requiring the making of charges, as the Secretary of State or Welsh Ministers think fit[6]. Without prejudice to the generality of this power, the power to make regulations includes power:

(1)   to confer a discretion as to the amount of any charge made under the regulations[7];

(2)   to provide for such a discretion to be exercisable subject to such maximum amount or scale of maximum amounts as may be specified in or determined under the regulations[8];

(3)   to require library authorities to take steps as may be specified or described in the regulations for making the amounts of their charges for library facilities known to the public[9];

(4)   to make such other incidental provision and such supplemental, consequential and transitional provision as the Secretary of State or the Welsh Ministers think necessary or expedient[10]; and

(5)   to make different provision for different cases, including different provision in relation to different persons[11], circumstances or localities[12].

Nothing in any such regulations may, however, authorise any charges to be made by a library authority for lending any written material[13] to any person where:

(a)   it is the duty of the authority[14] to make borrowing facilities available to that person[15];

(b)   the material is lent in the course of providing such facilities to that person on any library premises[16];

(c)   the material is lent in a form which is readable without the use of any electronic or other apparatus[17]; and

(d)   that person is not a person who has required any such apparatus to be used, or made available to him, for putting the material into such a form in order that he may borrow it[18];

but heads (a) to (d) above do not prevent any such regulations from authorising the making of charges in respect of the use of any facility for the reservation of written materials or in respect of borrowed materials which are returned late or in a damaged condition[19].

Nothing in the regulations may authorise any charges to be made by a library authority for making facilities available to any person to do any of the following on any library premises, that is to say:

(i)   reading the whole or any part of the written materials for the time being held by the authority in a form in which they are readable without the use of any electronic or other apparatus or in microform[20];

(ii)   consulting, whether or not with the assistance of any such apparatus or of any person, such catalogues, indexes or similar articles as are maintained in any form whatever exclusively for the purposes of that authority's public library service[21].

1   As to the meaning of 'library authority' see PARA 922.
2   Public Libraries and Museums Act 1964 s 8(1).

3   The functions of the Secretary of State under the Public Libraries and Museums Act 1964 in so far
    as it relate to Wales were transferred to the National Assembly for Wales (see the National
    Assembly for Wales (Transfer of Functions) Order 1999, SI 1999/672, arts 2, 3, Sch 1) and are
    now exercisable by the Welsh Ministers (see the Government of Wales Act 2006 s 162(1), Sch 11
    paras 30, 32). As to the Secretary of State and the Welsh Ministers see PARA 802. As to the
    meaning of 'Wales' see PARA 802 note 4.
4   As to the exercise of delegated powers see STATUTES AND LEGISLATIVE PROCESS vol 96 (2012)
    PARA 1045. As to the procedure in relation to subordinate legislation made by the Welsh Ministers
    see the Government of Wales Act 2006 Sch 11 paras 33–35; and STATUTES AND LEGISLATIVE
    PROCESS vol 96 (2012) PARA 1035. As to the regulations made see the Library Charges (England
    and Wales) Regulations 1991, SI 1991/2712; and PARA 927.
5   Public Libraries and Museums Act 1964 s 8(2)(a) (s 8(2)–(5) substituted by the Local Government
    and Housing Act 1989 s 154(1); and Public Libraries and Museums Act 1964 s 8(2), (5) amended
    by SI 1992/1311).
6   Public Libraries and Museums Act 1964 s 8(2)(b) (as substituted and amended: see note 5).
7   Public Libraries and Museums Act 1964 s 8(5)(a) (as substituted: see note 5).
8   Public Libraries and Museums Act 1964 s 8(5)(b) (as substituted: see note 5).
9   Public Libraries and Museums Act 1964 s 8(5)(c) (as substituted: see note 5).
10 Public Libraries and Museums Act 1964 s 8(5)(d) (as substituted and amended: see note 5).
11 As to the meaning of 'person' see PARA 803 note 17.
12 Public Libraries and Museums Act 1964 s 8(5)(e) (as substituted: see note 5).
13 'Written material' means: (1) any book, journal, pamphlet or other similar article; or (2) any
    reprographic copy within the meaning of the Copyright, Designs and Patents Act 1988 of any such
    article or any other reproduction of such an article made by any means whatever: Public Libraries
    and Museums Act 1964 s 8(7) (added by the Local Government and Housing Act 1989 s 154(2)).
    'Reprographic process' means a process for making facsimile copies or involving the use of an
    appliance for making multiple copies, and includes, in relation to a work held in electronic form,
    any copying by electronic means, but does not include the making of a film or sound
    recording: Copyright, Designs and Patents Act 1988 s 178. The Copyright, Designs and Patents
    Act 1988 contains provisions permitting, in relation to prescribed libraries and archives, certain
    acts without infringing copyright: see ss 40A–44A; and COPYRIGHT vol 23 (2013) PARA 900 et
    seq.
14 Ie under the Public Libraries and Museums Act 1964 s 7(1) (see PARA 925).
15 Public Libraries and Museums Act 1964 s 8(3)(a) (as substituted: see note 5).
16 Public Libraries and Museums Act 1964 s 8(3)(b) (as substituted: see note 5). 'Library premises'
    means: (1) any premises which are occupied by a library authority where library facilities are made
    available by the authority, in the course of its provision of a public library service, to members of
    the public; (2) any vehicle which is used by a library authority for the purpose of providing such
    a service and is a vehicle in which facilities are so made available: s 8(7) (as added: see note 13).
17 Public Libraries and Museums Act 1964 s 8(3)(c) (as substituted: see note 5).
18 Public Libraries and Museums Act 1964 s 8(3)(d) (as substituted: see note 5).
19 Public Libraries and Museums Act 1964 s 8(3) (as substituted: see note 5).
20 Public Libraries and Museums Act 1964 s 8(4)(a) (as substituted: see note 5).
21 Public Libraries and Museums Act 1964 s 8(4)(b) (as substituted: see note 5).

927.   Charges which may be made by library authorities. A library authority[1]
whose library area[2] is in England or in Wales[3] (a 'relevant authority') may make
charges for the library facilities made available by it as follows[4]:

(1)   for lending library material or library apparatus[5];
(2)   for reserving for any person[6] library material or library apparatus,
         whether that material or apparatus is for the time being held by the
         relevant authority or needs to be obtained from elsewhere and whether
         for the purpose of lending the material or apparatus to that person or
         making it available for his use on library premises[7], and for notifying
         that person that that material or apparatus has become available or is
         not available for borrowing or use by him[8];
(3)   in respect of borrowed library material or library apparatus which is
         returned late[9];
(4)   for making library apparatus available for use on library premises[10];

(5)   in respect of library apparatus, library material and any other equipment or thing used in providing the library service which is lost, damaged or destroyed by, or whilst on loan to, the person paying the charge[11];

(6)   for assisting or instructing a person how to use a computer[12];

(7)   for researching and for collating information for and at the request of a person[13];

(8)   for supplying catalogues, indexes or similar articles where the articles become the property of the person to whom they are supplied[14];

(9)   for supplying library material which has been researched, collated, produced or copied[15] by the relevant authority where the material becomes the property of the person to whom it is supplied[16];

(10)   for supplying copies of library material obtained from another library not maintained by the relevant authority or from a holder of records[17] where the copies become the property of the person to whom they are supplied[18];

(11)   for providing, or procuring the provision of, library material to a person who does not wish to collect it or have it collected and for notifying a person who has requested provision other than by collection that the library material is not available[19];

(12)   for providing a room or cubicle on library premises for the purpose of working or studying to which only the person paying the charge is for the time being permitted access[20];

(13)   for making library facilities available other than on library premises, except that the relevant authority may not charge the individual users of facilities where the facilities are made available at a school, old people's home, hospital, prison, club or like institution, and the person who has arranged with the relevant authority for the facilities to be made available at that institution is charged[21];

(14)   for making available to any person library facilities which go beyond those ordinarily provided by the relevant authority as part of the library service[22].

Notwithstanding heads (1) and (14) above, no charge may be made for lending any written material[23] to any person where it is the authority's duty[24] to make facilities for borrowing available to that person and the statutory conditions[25] are fulfilled[26]. Notwithstanding head (4), head (6) and head (14) above, no charge may be made for making facilities available, or in respect of time spent by employees of the relevant authority in making facilities available, for any person, on library premises:

(a)   to read the whole or any part of any of the written materials for the time being held by the authority in a form in which they are readable without the use of any electronic or other apparatus, or in microform[27]; or

(b)   to consult such catalogues, indexes or similar articles as are maintained, in any form whatever, exclusively for the purposes of that authority's public library service[28].

The amount and the incidence of any charge made in accordance with the above provisions is at the discretion of the relevant authority[29] which may:

(i)   make different provision for different cases, including different provision in relation to different persons, circumstances and localities[30]; and

(ii)   make charges in respect of each use of the library facilities made available by it, or charge an annual subscription or a deposit in respect of all or some of those facilities[31].

A relevant authority which makes a charge in accordance with these provisions must display, in a conspicuous place within each library premises occupied by the relevant authority, a notice which is easily readable specifying the library facilities made available by the authority for which it makes a charge and, in the case of each such facility, the amount of the charge or the basis on which the charge will be calculated[32].

A local authority[33] maintaining premises under the Public Libraries and Museums Act 1964 may use the premises, or allow them to be used, whether in return for payment or not, for holding meetings and exhibitions, showing films and slides, giving musical performances and holding other events of an educational or cultural nature, and, notwithstanding anything in the statutory restriction on making charges[34], may make or authorise the making of a charge for admission in connection with those events[35].

1   As to the meaning of 'library authority' see PARA 922.
2   As to the meaning of 'library area' see PARA 923.
3   As to the meaning of 'England' see PARA 804 note 2. As to the meaning of 'Wales' see PARA 802 note 4.
4   See the Library Charges (England and Wales) Regulations 1991, SI 1991/2712, reg 3(1).
5   Library Charges (England and Wales) Regulations 1991, SI 1991/2712, reg 3(2)(a). This provision is expressed to be subject to reg 3(3) (see the text to notes 23–26). 'Library material' means: (1) words, figures, images, sounds or data recorded in or on any medium; (2) toys; and (3) educational artefacts: reg 2(1). 'Library apparatus' means electronic or other apparatus intended for use with library material: reg 2(1).
6   As to the meaning of 'person' see PARA 803 note 17.
7   As to the meaning of 'library premises' see PARA 926 note 16.
8   Library Charges (England and Wales) Regulations 1991, SI 1991/2712, reg 3(2)(b).
9   Library Charges (England and Wales) Regulations 1991, SI 1991/2712, reg 3(2)(c).
10 Library Charges (England and Wales) Regulations 1991, SI 1991/2712, reg 3(2)(d). This provision is expressed to be subject to reg 3(4) (see the text to notes 27–28).
11 Library Charges (England and Wales) Regulations 1991, SI 1991/2712, reg 3(2)(e).
12 Library Charges (England and Wales) Regulations 1991, SI 1991/2712, reg 3(2)(f). This provision is expressed to be subject to reg 3(4) (see the text to notes 27–28). 'Computer' means any device for storing and processing information: reg 2(1).
13 Library Charges (England and Wales) Regulations 1991, SI 1991/2712, reg 3(2)(g).
14 Library Charges (England and Wales) Regulations 1991, SI 1991/2712, reg 3(2)(h).
15 Any reference in the Library Charges (England and Wales) Regulations 1991, SI 1991/2712, to 'copying' and 'copies' must be construed in accordance with the Copyright, Designs and Patents Act 1988 s 17 (see COPYRIGHT vol 23 (2013) PARA 861): Library Charges (England and Wales) Regulations 1991, SI 1991/2712, reg 2(2).
16 Library Charges (England and Wales) Regulations 1991, SI 1991/2712, reg 3(2)(i).
17 'Records' means materials in written or other form setting out facts or events or otherwise recording information: see the Local Government (Records) Act 1962 s 8(1) (definition applied by the Library Charges (England and Wales) Regulations 1991, SI 1991/2712, reg 2(1)). As to the meaning of 'written' see PARA 805 note 14.
18 Library Charges (England and Wales) Regulations 1991, SI 1991/2712, reg 3(2)(j).
19 Library Charges (England and Wales) Regulations 1991, SI 1991/2712, reg 3(2)(k).
20 Library Charges (England and Wales) Regulations 1991, SI 1991/2712, reg 3(2)(l).
21 Library Charges (England and Wales) Regulations 1991, SI 1991/2712, reg 3(2)(m).
22 Library Charges (England and Wales) Regulations 1991, SI 1991/2712, reg 3(2)(n). This provision is expressed to be subject to reg 3(3), (4): see the text to notes 23–28.
23 As to the meaning of 'written material' see PARA 926 note 13.
24 Ie under the Public Libraries and Museums Act 1964 s 7(1) (see PARA 925).
25 Those conditions are that: (1) the material is lent in the course of providing such facilities to that person on any library premises (Library Charges (England and Wales) Regulations 1991, SI 1991/2712, reg 3(3)(b)); (2) it is lent in a form in which it is readable without the use of any

electronic or other apparatus (reg 3(3)(c)); and (3) that person is not a person who has required any such apparatus to be used, or made available to him, for putting the material into such a form in order that he may borrow it (reg 3(3)(d)).

26 See the Library Charges (England and Wales) Regulations 1991, SI 1991/2712, reg 3(3)(a).
27 Library Charges (England and Wales) Regulations 1991, SI 1991/2712, reg 3(4)(a).
28 Library Charges (England and Wales) Regulations 1991, SI 1991/2712, reg 3(4)(b).
29 Library Charges (England and Wales) Regulations 1991, SI 1991/2712, reg 4(1).
30 Library Charges (England and Wales) Regulations 1991, SI 1991/2712, reg 4(2)(a).
31 Library Charges (England and Wales) Regulations 1991, SI 1991/2712, reg 4(2)(b).
32 Library Charges (England and Wales) Regulations 1991, SI 1991/2712, reg 5.
33 As to the meaning of 'local authority' see PARA 922.
34 Ie anything in the Public Libraries and Museums Act 1964 s 8 (see PARA 926).
35 Public Libraries and Museums Act 1964 s 20.

928. Libraries in inner London. A London library authority[1] may lend or permit the use of any articles[2] provided by it in a library[3] in the same way as if the articles were provided in or for the purposes of a lending library[4].

Any person borrowing an article from a library is not entitled to retain it after the expiration of such period, not being in the case of a book less than 14 days, after the date of its being borrowed as may be prescribed in relation to that article by the authority by which the library is maintained[5]. Without prejudice to any other powers with respect to articles borrowed from a library, the authority by whom the library is maintained may recover from any person failing to return an article borrowed from the library within such period as may be so prescribed such reasonable sum as it may prescribe in respect of each day or each week or part of a week during which he fails to return the article, with any expenses incurred in sending to him notices in respect of the article[6]. Any such sum recoverable by two or more authorities may be recovered by any one of them[7].

Where an authority becomes entitled under these provisions to recover any sum from any person, that person does not have any right until that sum has been duly paid to borrow any other article from any library maintained by that authority, including any library maintained by it in combination with another authority or part of the cost of the maintenance of which is borne by the authority[8].

Nothing in these provisions is to be construed as authorising an infringement of copyright[9].

1 'Library authority' means the council of an inner London borough: London County Council (General Powers) Act 1955 s 37(1) (amended by SI 1965/540; and applied by the London County Council (General Powers) Act 1958 s 36(4)). See also note 3. As to the London boroughs and their councils see LONDON GOVERNMENT vol 71 (2013) PARA 20 et seq.
2 'Article' includes a book or gramophone record (London County Council (General Powers) Act 1955 s 37(1) (as applied: see note 1)) or other article provided in a library (London County Council (General Powers) Act 1958 s 36(3)). The articles which a library authority may provide in a library and may repair include statuary sculpture models and other articles of a similar nature: s 36(1)(d).
3 'Library' means any library maintained under the Public Libraries and Museums Act 1964 by a library authority (either alone or in combination with another authority) and any library maintained thereunder any part of the cost of the maintenance of which is borne by a library authority; and in relation to a library maintained by two or more authorities in combination or the cost of the maintenance of which is shared by two or more authorities, references to the authority by whom the library is maintained must be construed as references to those authorities: London County Council (General Powers) Act 1955 s 37(1) (as amended and applied: see note 1).
4 London County Council (General Powers) Act 1958 s 36(2).
5 London County Council (General Powers) Act 1955 s 37(2).
6 London County Council (General Powers) Act 1955 s 37(3).
7 London County Council (General Powers) Act 1955 s 37(4).
8 London County Council (General Powers) Act 1955 s 37(5).
9 London County Council (General Powers) Act 1958 s 36(5) (substituted by the Copyright, Designs and Patents Act 1988 s 303(1), Sch 7 para 7).

929. Manorial documents. Where any manorial documents[1] are transferred to any local authority, public library, museum or historical or antiquarian society in pursuance of a direction given by the Master of the Rolls[2], the local authority or the governing body of the public library, museum or historical or antiquarian society must cause to be furnished to the secretary of the Royal Commission on Historical Manuscripts an inventory of the documents in the prescribed form[3]; and must not, without the consent of the Master of the Rolls, permit any such documents to pass out of its custody[4]. The controlling authority of any such record repository[5] must cause all manorial documents to be kept and used under conditions suitable for their safe and proper preservation and must comply with any directions from time to time given by the Master of the Rolls[6] in that behalf[7]. Whenever requested by the lord of the manor[8] or the Master of the Rolls, the controlling authority of a record repository must produce manorial documents to him or in accordance with his directions[9].

Where the lord of the manor intends to remove manorial documents from any such record repository as is referred to above, he must, at least three months[10] before their removal, give to the secretary of the Royal Commission on Historical Manuscripts written[11] notice of his intention, containing particulars of the documents and stating the place to which he intends to remove them[12]. No manorial documents may be removed outside England and Wales without the consent of the Master of the Rolls[13].

The controlling authority of a record repository must on payment of the prescribed fees permit manorial documents to be inspected at all reasonable times by any person interested in land enfranchised by or under the Copyhold Act 1894, or the Law of Property Act 1922, and must permit the taking of copies of such documents; and must also, with the consent of the lord of the manor, permit the inspection of manorial documents, and the taking of copies thereof, for the purpose of historical research[14].

1 As to the meaning of 'manorial documents' see PARA 812 note 6.
2 Ie under the Law of Property Act 1922 s 144A(4) (see CUSTOM AND USAGE vol 32 (2012) PARA 101) or under that provision as applied by the Local Government (Records) Act 1962 s 7(1). The Master of the Rolls may appoint a judge of the Senior Courts to discharge this function: see the Courts and Legal Services Act 1990 s 73(1), (2), (5)(a), (b) (s 73(1), (2) amended by the Constitutional Reform Act 2005 s 59(5), Sch 11 para 4(1), (3)). In practice, the functions of the Master of the Rolls in relation to manorial documents are carried out by the Royal Commission on Historical Manuscripts (see PARA 812).
3 For the prescribed form see the Manorial Documents Rules 1959, SI 1959/1399, Schedule (amended by SI 1963/976).
4 See the Manorial Documents Rules 1959, SI 1959/1399 r 7 (amended by SI 1963/976). As to the preservation of manorial documents see further CUSTOM AND USAGE vol 32 (2012) PARA 99 et seq.
5 'Record repository' means the Public Record Office, any local authority, public library, museum, or historical or antiquarian society to which manorial documents are transferred in pursuance of such a direction as is mentioned in note 2 and any repository approved by the Master of the Rolls as a place of deposit for manorial documents under the Manorial Documents Rules 1959, SI 1959/1399, r 5 (see PARA 812): r 1(1) (definition amended by SI 1963/976). As to the Public Record Office see CONSTITUTIONAL AND ADMINISTRATIVE LAW vol 20 (2014) PARA 346.
6 Or by a judge of the Senior Courts (see note 2).
7 Manorial Documents Rules 1959, SI 1959/1399, r 8.
8 As to the meaning of 'lord of the manor' see PARA 812 note 6.
9 Manorial Documents Rules 1959, SI 1959/1399 r 9.
10 As to the meaning of 'month' see PARA 803 note 12.
11 As to the meaning of 'written' see PARA 805 note 14.
12 Manorial Documents Rules 1959, SI 1959/1399 r 5A (added by SI 1967/963).
13 Manorial Documents Rules 1959, SI 1959/1399, r 11.
14 Manorial Documents Rules 1959, SI 1959/1399 r 10. As to the enfranchisement of copyholds see REAL PROPERTY AND REGISTRATION vol 87 (2012) PARA 41 et seq.

930. Byelaws regulating the use of library facilities. A local authority[1] may make byelaws, to be confirmed by the Secretary of State or, in relation to Wales, the Welsh Ministers[2], regulating the use of facilities provided by it under the Public Libraries and Museums Act 1964 and the conduct of persons in premises where those facilities are provided[3]. Without prejudice to certain statutory provisions including those under which byelaws are allowed to include provision for imposing fines[4], byelaws may include provisions for enabling officers[5] of the local authority to exclude or remove from premises maintained by it under the Act any person who contravenes the byelaws[6].

As well as complying with certain statutory provisions including those requiring byelaws, when confirmed, to be made available to the public[7], a local authority must cause a copy of byelaws made by it and in force to be displayed in any premises maintained by it under the Public Libraries and Museums Act 1964 to which the public have access[8].

1   As to the meaning of 'local authority' see PARA 922.
2   The functions of the Secretary of State under the Public Libraries and Museums Act 1964 in so far as they relate to Wales were transferred to the National Assembly for Wales (see the National Assembly for Wales (Transfer of Functions) Order 1999, SI 1999/672, art 2, Sch 1) and are now exercisable by the Welsh Ministers (see the Government of Wales Act 2006 s 162(1), Sch 11 paras 30, 32). As to the Secretary of State and the Welsh Ministers see PARA 802. As to the meaning of 'Wales' see PARA 802 note 4.
3   See the Public Libraries and Museums Act 1964 s 19(1) (s 19 amended by the Local Government Byelaws (Wales) Act 2012 Sch 2 para 7; and the Public Libraries and Museums Act 1964 s 19(1) further amended by SI 1992/1311). Byelaws in force immediately before 1 April 1965 (ie the commencement date for the Public Libraries and Museums Act 1964: see s 26(7)) under the Museums and Gymnasiums Act 1891 s 7 (repealed) or the Public Libraries Act 1901 s 3 (repealed) were not invalidated by the repeal of those Acts but have effect as if they had been made, and confirmed by the Secretary of State or the Welsh Ministers, under the Public Libraries and Museums Act 1964 s 19: s 26(5).
4   Ie the Local Government Act 1972 s 237 (see LOCAL GOVERNMENT vol 69 (2009) PARA 571) and the Local Government Byelaws (Wales) Act 2012 s 10.
5   As to the meaning of 'officer' see PARA 923 note 8.
6   Public Libraries and Museums Act 1964 s 19(2) (as amended: see note 3); Interpretation Act 1978 s 17(2)(a).
7   Ie the Local Government Act 1972 s 236(8) (see LOCAL GOVERNMENT vol 69 (2009) PARA 557) and the Local Government Byelaws (Wales) Act 2012 s 8(5).
8   Public Libraries and Museums Act 1964 s 19(3) (as amended: see note 3); Interpretation Act 1978 s 17(2)(a).

E.   FINANCE AND EXPENSES OF LIBRARY AUTHORITIES

931. Contributions and grants for library facilities. A library authority[1] may make contributions towards the expenses of another library authority or of any other person[2] providing library facilities for members of the public[3]. The Secretary of State or, in relation to Wales, the Welsh Ministers[4] may make grants to any body which maintains book catalogues or indexes to which all library authorities are permitted to refer, or otherwise makes available to all library authorities facilities likely to assist them in the discharge of their duty[5] to provide a comprehensive and efficient library service[6].

The British Library Board may contribute to the expenses of library authorities or of any other person providing library facilities, whether for members of the public or otherwise[7] and must, by means of payments out of the central fund, reimburse local library authorities for expenditure incurred in giving effect to the public lending right scheme[8]. A library which is maintained by a library authority is one of the institutions falling within the government indemnity scheme for objects on loan[9].

Subject to the above provisions and those relating to charges for library authority services[10] and to grants or loans from the National Heritage Memorial Fund[11], the funding of local authority library services is determined by the general provisions as to local government finance[12].

1 As to the meaning of 'library authority' see PARA 922.
2 As to the meaning of 'person' see PARA 803 note 17.
3 Public Libraries and Museums Act 1964 s 9(1).
4 The functions of the Secretary of State under the Public Libraries and Museums Act 1964 in so far as they relate to Wales were transferred to the National Assembly for Wales (see the National Assembly for Wales (Transfer of Functions) Order 1999, SI 1999/672, art 2, Sch 1) and are now exercisable by the Welsh Ministers (see the Government of Wales Act 2006 s 162(1), Sch 11 paras 30, 32). As to the Secretary of State and the Welsh Ministers see PARA 802. As to the meaning of 'Wales' see PARA 802 note 4.
5 Ie under the Public Libraries and Museums Act 1964 s 7(1) (see PARA 925).
6 Public Libraries and Museums Act 1964 s 9(2) (amended by SI 1992/1311). As to local authorities' powers to incur expenditure on contributions to the funds of any body which provides any public service in the United Kingdom otherwise than for the purposes of gain see the Local Government Act 1972 s 137(3)(b); and LOCAL GOVERNMENT FINANCE vol 70 (2012) PARA 4. As to the meaning of 'United Kingdom' see PARA 804 note 2.
7 See the British Library Act 1972 s 1(3)(b); and PARA 902.
8 See the Public Lending Right Act 1979 s 3(6); and COPYRIGHT vol 23 (2013) PARA 1309.
9 See the National Heritage Act 1980 s 16; and PARA 1094.
10 See PARAS 926–927.
11 See PARA 815.
12 As to local government finance see generally LOCAL GOVERNMENT FINANCE,

(9) LITERARY AND SCIENTIFIC INSTITUTIONS

(i) Establishment of Literary and Scientific Institutions

932. Formation of literary and scientific institutions. Many of the learned societies in England and Wales are incorporated by royal charter[1]. The oldest of these, the Royal Society of London, was thus incorporated by Charles II in 1662[2]. Others have taken advantage of the provisions of the Companies Acts[3]. However, the majority of the literary and scientific institutions are not incorporated. Under the Friendly Societies Act 1992, incorporated friendly societies may include among their purposes the carrying on of social or benevolent activity, including fund-raising and other activities carried out for a charitable purpose[4]. A society established for the promotion of literature, science and the fine arts and registered as a friendly society under the Friendly Societies Act 1974 retains this status so long as the registration occurred prior to 1 February 1993[5].

1 As to incorporation by royal charter see CORPORATIONS vol 24 (2010) PARA 329 et seq.
2 As to the Royal Society of London, now known as the Royal Society, see the society's website which, at the date at which this volume states the law, can be found at www.royalsociety.org.
3 See the Companies Act 2006 ss 60–62; and COMPANIES vol 14 (2009) PARA 201. As to power conferred upon the Charity Commission to incorporate the trustees of any charity for religious, educational, literary, scientific or public charitable purposes see the Charities Act 2011 Pt 12 (ss 251–266); and CHARITIES vol 8 (2015) PARA 263 et seq.
4 See the Friendly Societies Act 1992 s 10(1), (2); and FINANCIAL INSTITUTIONS vol 48 (2015) PARA 571.
5 See the Friendly Societies Act 1992 s 93(1), (2); the Friendly Societies Act 1992 (Commencement No 3 and Transitional Provisions) Order 1993, SI 1993/16; and FINANCIAL INSTITUTIONS vol 48 (2015) PARA 622.

933. Technical and industrial institutions. The Technical and Industrial Institutions Act 1892 facilitates the acquisition of land by any institution established[1] for effecting all or any of the following purposes:

(1)   giving technical instruction;

(2)   providing the training, mental or physical, necessary for it;

(3)   in connection with those purposes, providing workshops, tools, scientific apparatus and plant of all kinds, libraries, reading rooms, halls for lectures, exhibitions and meetings, gymnasiums and swimming baths, general facilities for mental and physical training, recreation and amusement, and all necessary and proper accommodation for persons frequenting the institution[2].

The governing body of the institution may be any body corporate, council, public authority, local authority, commissioners, directors, committee, trustees or other body of persons, corporate or unincorporate, willing to undertake, or elected or appointed for the purpose of undertaking, or having, the government and management of the institution[3]. The governing body may:

(a)   make byelaws and rules for the management and conduct of the institution[4];

(b)   acquire land by agreement[5] whether by way of conveyance on sale, exchange or gift[6];

(c)   sell or exchange any land so acquired for other land[7];

(d)   invest money arising by the sale of land until its reinvestment in the purchase of land[8].

Every institution for which land has been acquired under an exercise of these powers must be open generally either to all persons or to all persons within specified limits as to age, qualification or otherwise, and either without payment or on specified terms as to times of attendance and payment of subscriptions or fees or otherwise, without preference being given to any person or class of persons within the specified limits[9].

These provisions are unaffected by the miscellaneous and financial powers of local authorities[10] under the Local Government Act 1972[11].

1   Ie whether before or after 27 June 1892 (see the Technical and Industrial Institutions Act 1892 s 2).
2   See the Technical and Industrial Institutions Act 1892 s 2.
3   Technical and Industrial Institutions Act 1892 s 3(1).
4   Technical and Industrial Institutions Act 1892 s 3(2).
5   See the Technical and Industrial Institutions Act 1892 ss 4, 5.
6   See the Technical and Industrial Institutions Act 1892 ss 6, 7.
7   See the Technical and Industrial Institutions Act 1892 s 9(1)–(3) (s 9(1) amended by the Charities Act 2006 s 75(1), Sch 8, para 8; and the Charities Act 2011 Sch 7 para 7). Land so purchased or taken in exchange must be devoted to the same purposes and is liable to the same incidents as originally were applicable to or affected the land sold or given in exchange: Technical and Industrial Institutions Act 1892 s 9(4).
8   See the Technical and Industrial Institutions Act 1892 s 9(5), (6) (s 9(5) substituted by, and s 9(6) added by, the Trustee Act 2000 s 40(1), Sch 2 Pt II para 4).
9   Technical and Industrial Institutions Act 1892 s 8.
10 Ie the provisions of the Local Government Act 1972 Pts VII (ss 111–146A), VIII (ss 148–178).
11 See the Local Government Act 1972 s 131(1)(b), (2)(a); and LOCAL GOVERNMENT vol 69 (2009) PARA 509. 'Local authority' for these purposes includes a parish meeting and the parish trustees of a parish: s 131(4).

934. Ascertainment of purposes of an institution. Where an institution has a written constitution or charter, this is generally the best evidence of the purposes for which it was instituted[1]. In considering whether the purposes for which an institution was originally instituted were or were not exclusively scientific, no assistance can be obtained by a consideration of byelaws made after the grant of its charter[2]. However, if it has no written constitution or charter or its written constitution or charter is not clear as to its purposes, regard may be had to the purposes which it has in fact pursued[3]. In the case of literary and scientific institutions it is important to determine the purposes for which a particular institution was instituted in order to ascertain whether it is a body governed by the Literary and Scientific Institutions Act 1854[4], and whether it may be entitled to enjoy any privileges and exemptions[5].

1 *Battersea Metropolitan Borough Council v British Iron and Steel Research Association* [1949] 1 KB 434 at 451, 453, CA, per Jenkins J and at 460 per Bucknill LJ; *British Launderers' Research Association v Hendon Borough Rating Authority* [1949] 1 KB 434 at 470, [1949] 1 All ER 21 at 25, CA, per Denning LJ; *Institution of Mechanical Engineers v Cane (Valuation Officer)* [1961] AC 696, [1960] 3 All ER 715, HL; see also *Institute of Fuel v Morley (Valuation Officer)* [1956] AC 245, [1955] 3 All ER 843, HL; *Berry v St Marylebone Borough Council* [1958] Ch 406 at 414, [1957] 3 All ER 677 at 680, CA, per Romer LJ. If a society's written constitution or charter specifies several objects, evidence of its activities may be relevant to show what its main objects are, but not to construe or limit the construction of the language of the society's constitution: *Berry v St Marylebone Borough Council* at 417 and at 682 per Romer LJ, explaining *Chartered Insurance Institute v London Corpn* [1957] 2 All ER 638 at 642, 643, [1957] 1 WLR 867 at 875, 876, DC, per Devlin J.

2 *Institute of Fuel v Morley (Valuation officer)* [1956] AC 245 at 252, [1955] 3 All ER 843 at 846, HL, per Lord Morton of Henryton.

3 *British Launderers' Research Association v Hendon Borough Rating Authority* [1949] 1 KB 434 at 470, 471, [1949] 1 All ER 21 at 25, CA, per Denning LJ.

4 See PARA 935.

5 As to tax exemptions and other privileges and exemptions see PARAS 1003, 1112–1114.

(ii) Institutions within the Literary and Scientific Institutions Act 1854

A. SCOPE OF THE ACT; GOVERNMENT OF THE INSTITUTIONS

935. Literary and Scientific Institutions Act 1854. The Literary and Scientific Institutions Act 1854 applies to all institutions, whether incorporated or not, for the time being[1] established for the promotion of science[2], literature, the fine arts, for adult instruction, the diffusion of useful knowledge, the foundation or maintenance of libraries[3] or reading rooms for general use among the members or open to the public, of public museums and galleries of paintings and other works of art, collections of natural history, mechanical and philosophical inventions, instruments or designs[4]. The Act is not confined to institutions of a public or charitable nature, but extends also to private institutions established for its purposes[5]. However, the Act does not apply to the Royal Institution[6]; nor does it authorise the establishment of institutions for recreation or enjoyment[7] as distinguished from instruction[8].

1 Ie existing at 11 August 1854 (the date of the passing of the Literary and Scientific Institutions Act 1854) or in the future: see *Re Russell Institution, Figgins v Baghino* [1898] 2 Ch 72.

2 'Science' is not confined to pure or speculative science, or science generally, but includes various branches of science: see *IRC v Forrest* (1890) 15 App Cas 334 at 353, HL, per Lord Macnaghten (decided under the Customs and Inland Revenue Act 1885 s 11(3) (repealed)); see also *Battersea Metropolitan Borough v British Iron and Steel Research Association* [1949] 1 KB 434 at 451, CA, per Jenkins J; *British Launderers' Research Association v Hendon Borough Rating Authority* [1949] 1 KB 434 at 468, [1949] 1 All ER 21 at 23, CA, per Denning LJ; *Central Council for Health Education v Hope (Valuation Officer)* (1958) 51 R & IT 634, Lands Tribunal (it is uncertain whether the promotion of healthy living is an art or a science).

3 As to libraries see the Public Libraries and Museums Act 1964; and PARA 910 et seq.

4 Literary and Scientific Institutions Act 1854 s 33.

5 *Re Russell Institution, Figgins v Baghino* [1898] 2 Ch 72.

6   Literary and Scientific Institutions Act 1854 s 33 proviso (amended by the Statute Law (Repeals)
    Act 1973). As to the Royal Institution of Great Britain see the institution's website which, at the
    date at which this volume states the law, can be found at www.rigb.org.
7   Eg the playing of cards, billiards etc: *Re Badger, Mansell v Viscount Cobham* [1905] 1 Ch 568.
8   *Re Badger, Mansell v Viscount Cobham* [1905] 1 Ch 568.

936. Governing body of any institution to which the Literary and Scientific Institutions Act 1854 applies. The governing body of any institution to which the Literary and Scientific Institutions Act 1854 applies[1] is the council, directors, committee or other body to whom, by Act of Parliament, charter or the rules and regulations of the institution, the management of its affairs is entrusted[2]. If on the establishment of the institution no such body was constituted, the members[3] may, upon due notice, create a governing body to act for the institution[4].

1   As to the institutions to which the Literary and Scientific Institutions Act 1854 applies see PARA
    935.
2   Literary and Scientific Institutions Act 1854 s 32.
3   As to the members see PARA 938.
4   See the Literary and Scientific Institutions Act 1854 s 32.

937. Byelaws for regulation of institutions. In any institution to which the Literary and Scientific Institutions Act 1854 applies[1] the governing body[2], if not otherwise legally empowered to do so, may at any meeting specially convened according to its regulations make byelaws[3] to regulate the institution, its members[4] and officers, and to further its purpose and objects, and may impose a reasonable pecuniary penalty for breach of any such byelaw[5].

Penalties for the breach of byelaws, when accrued, are recoverable at the option of the governing body in any local court of the district where the defendant resides or the institution is situated, but no pecuniary penalty imposed by any byelaws is recoverable unless the byelaw has been confirmed by the votes of three-fifths of the members present at a meeting specially convened for the purpose[6].

1   As to the institutions to which the Literary and Scientific Institutions Act 1854 applies see PARA
    935.
2   As to the governing body see PARA 936.
3   Byelaws made by a society cannot override the provisions of the Literary and Scientific Institutions
    Act 1854: *Re Bristol Athenaeum* (1889) 43 ChD 236.
4   As to the members see PARA 938.
5   Literary and Scientific Institutions Act 1854 s 24.
6   Literary and Scientific Institutions Act 1854 s 24.

B.   MEMBERSHIP OF INSTITUTION

938. Qualification for membership of institution. A member of an institution to which the Literary and Scientific Institutions Act 1854 applies[1] is a person who has been admitted according to the institution's rules and regulations and has paid a subscription, or has signed the roll or list of members[2].

No member is entitled to vote or to be counted a member in any proceedings if his current subscription is for the time being in arrear[3].

1   As to the institutions to which the Literary and Scientific Institutions Act 1854 applies see PARA
    935.
2   Literary and Scientific Institutions Act 1854 s 31.
3   Literary and Scientific Institutions Act 1854 s 31. He may be sued if his subscription is in arrear
    (see PARA 939).

939. Liability of members of institution. A member of an institution to which the Literary and Scientific Institutions Act 1854 applies[1] may be sued by an institution if his subscription is in arrear, or for possessing himself of and detaining any of the institution's property contrary to the rules, or for injuring or destroying any such property[2]. If the action against the member so sued fails, and he is adjudged his costs, he may elect to recover them from the officer in whose name the proceedings were taken or from the institution; and in the second case the member is entitled to have process against the property of the institution[3].

A society officer who wrongfully retains society funds may be restrained from collecting money payable to the society and from representing himself to be an officer of the society[4]. A member of an institution who wilfully and maliciously, or wilfully and unlawfully, destroys or injures the institution's property, so that the institution's funds may be exposed to loss, may be prosecuted and, if convicted, punished in the same manner as a non-member[5].

1   As to the institutions to which the Literary and Scientific Institutions Act 1854 applies see PARA 935. As to membership see PARA 938.
2   Literary and Scientific Institutions Act 1854 s 25. As to actions by and against such institutions see PARA 952. As to criminal damage to property see CRIMINAL LAW vol 25 (2010) PARA 326 et seq.
3   Literary and Scientific Institutions Act 1854 s 25.
4   Shaw v Hill (1845) 1 Holt Eq 99.
5   Literary and Scientific Institutions Act 1854 s 26 (amended by the Forgery Act 1913 s 20, Schedule; and the Larceny Act 1916 s 48(1), Schedule). As to theft by a member see CRIMINAL LAW vol 25 (2010) PARAS 278–288.

C.   PROPERTY AND FINANCE OF INSTITUTION

(A)   Personal Property and Gifts

940.   Personal property of institution. In the case of incorporated institutions to which the Literary and Scientific Institutions Act 1854 applies[1] having no provision applicable to the institution's personal property, and in all cases of unincorporated institutions to which the Act applies, the money, securities for money, goods, chattels and personal effects belonging to the institution, and not vested in trustees, are deemed to be vested for the time being in the institution's governing body[2].

1   As to the institutions to which the Literary and Scientific Institutions Act 1854 applies see PARA 935.
2   Literary and Scientific Institutions Act 1854 s 20. As to the governing body see PARA 936.

941.   Power of institution to receive gifts. A gift of real or personal property to an institution[1], not being a charity, or to the trustees of an institution is valid so long as there is nothing in the terms of the gift or in the rules of the institution to prevent the expenditure of the corpus of the property[2].

1   As to the institutions to which the Literary and Scientific Institutions Act 1854 applies see PARA 935.
2   Re Prevost, Lloyds Bank Ltd v Barclays Bank Ltd [1930] 2 Ch 383 (gift to the London Library). See also Carne v Long (1860) 2 De GF & J 75; Re Dutton, ex p Peake (1878) 4 Ex D 54; Re Clarke, Clarke v Clarke [1901] 2 Ch 110.

(B)   Acquisition of Land for Institution

942.   Power to acquire land for institution. Freehold land, not exceeding an acre, with or without buildings, may be granted or conveyed by way of gift, sale or exchange, in fee simple or for a term of years, by any person in England, Wales or Ireland having the present beneficial interest in the land, as a site for an institution governed by the Literary and Scientific Institutions Act 1854[1].

Any number of sites exceeding in the aggregate one acre in extent may be granted for distinct and separate institutions, so long as the site of each institution does not exceed that extent[2].

1   See the Literary and Scientific Institutions Act 1854 s 1 (amended by the Statute Law (Repeals) Act 1976; and the Commons Act 2006 ss 48(2)(c), 53, Sch 6 Pt 3). A grant by a tenant for life of such land will not be valid unless it is made with the written consent of the person (if any, and if legally competent) next entitled in remainder, in fee simple or fee tail: Literary and Scientific Institutions Act 1854 s 1 proviso (as so amended). As to the institutions to which the Literary and Scientific Institutions Act 1854 applies see PARA 935. Land forming part of the possessions of the Duchy of Lancaster or the Duchy of Cornwall may be granted to literary and scientific institutions: see the Literary and Scientific Institutions Act 1854 ss 2–4 (amended by the Statute Law Revision Act 1892 and the Statute Law (Repeals) Act 1976). As to the Duchy of Cornwall see CROWN AND CROWN PROCEEDINGS vol 29 (2014) PARA 232 et seq. As to the Duchy of Lancaster see CROWN AND CROWN PROCEEDINGS vol 29 (2014) PARA 214 et seq.
    For the development, improvement or general benefit of the settled land or any part of it, a tenant for life may make a grant in fee simple, or absolutely, or a lease for any term of years absolute, for a nominal price or rent, or for less than the best price paid or rent that can reasonably be obtained, or gratuitously, of any part of the settled land for the site or the extension of any existing site of a literary or scientific institution, not more than one acre being conveyed unless the full consideration is present or reserved in respect of the excess: see the Settled Land Act 1925 s 55(1); and SETTLEMENTS vol 91 (2012) PARA 765. As to the phasing out of strict settlements see the Trusts of Land and Appointment of Trustees Act 1996 s 2, Sch 1; and SETTLEMENTS vol 91 (2012) PARA 577.
2   See the Literary and Scientific Institutions Act 1854 s 10.

943. Conveyances to trustees for purposes of institution. Where an institution to which the Literary and Scientific Institutions Act 1854 applies[1] is not a corporation, the grant of any land, under the Act or otherwise, may be made to trustees for the purpose of the institution[2]. The trustees may be individuals or corporate bodies, sole or aggregate[3] and there may be any number of them[4]. The provisions of the Charities Act 2011 relating to the transfer of, and evidence of title to, property vested in trustees[5] apply in relation to any institution to which the Literary and Scientific Institutions Act 1854 applies as they apply in relation to a charity[6].

Grants, conveyances and assurances of sites under the Literary and Scientific Institutions Act 1854 may be made according to the statutory form, or as near to it as circumstances allow[7].

1   As to the institutions to which the Literary and Scientific Institutions Act 1854 applies see PARA 935.
2   Literary and Scientific Institutions Act 1854 s 11.
3   See the Literary and Scientific Institutions Act 1854 s 11.
4   See the Trustee Act 1925 s 34(3)(a); *Re Cleveland Literary and Philosophical Society's Land, Bolchow v Laughton* [1931] 2 Ch 247.
5   Ie the Charities Act 2011 s 334; see CHARITIES vol 8 (2015) PARAS 283–284.
6   Charities Act 2011 s 334(6).
7   See the Literary and Scientific Institutions Act 1854 s 13 (amended by the Statute Law (Repeals) Act 1976).

944. Conveyances by particular persons for purposes of institution. An equitable owner may not convey land for the purposes of the Literary and Scientific Institutions Act 1854 without the concurrence of the trustee or trustees in whom the legal estate is vested[1].

Any corporation, ecclesiastical or lay, sole or aggregate, and any officers, trustees or commissioners holding land for public, ecclesiastical, parochial, charitable or other purposes or objects may, subject to certain conditions, grant or convey, for the purpose of the Literary and Scientific Institutions Act 1854, sites not exceeding one acre each in extent[2]. The conditions are that (1) no ecclesiastical corporation sole, below the dignity of a bishop, may make such a grant without the written consent of the bishop of the diocese[3]; (2) a grant of parochial property requires the consent of the Secretary of State or, in relation to Wales, the Welsh Ministers[4]; and (3) a grant of property held on a charitable trust requires the consent of the Charity Commission or compliance with certain provisions[5] of the Charities Act 2011[6].

A grant by officers, trustees or commissioners, other than parochial trustees, is valid if a majority or quorum authorised to act, assembled at a meeting duly convened, assent to it and execute the deed of conveyance, although they may not constitute a majority of the actual body[7].

1   The Literary and Scientific Institutions Act 1854 s 5 (amended by the Statute Law (Repeals) Act 1976 s 1(1)) gave an equitable owner power to convey land without the concurrence of the trustees in whom the legal estate was vested, but the Law of Property Act 1925 s 1(7) provides that such a power operates only in equity. As to whether land is subject to a trust of land see PARAS 947–948.
2   Literary and Scientific Institutions Act 1854 ss 1, 6 (amended by the Local Government Act 1933 s 307(1)(b), Sch 11 Pt IV; and the Statute Law (Repeals) Act 1976).
3   See the Literary and Scientific Institutions Act 1854 s 6.
4   See the Literary and Scientific Institutions Act 1854 s 6 (amended by the Local Government Act 1929 s 137, Sch 12 Pt VII). The Literary and Scientific Institutions Act 1854 s 6 refers to the Poor Law Board the functions of which are now vested in the Secretary of State: see the Local Government Board Act 1871 s 2 (repealed); the Ministry of Health Act 1919 s 3(1)(a) (repealed); and various orders transferring functions including the Secretary of State for the Environment Order 1970, SI 1970/1681, the Secretary of State for the Environment, Transport and the Regions Order 1997, SI 1997/2971. The functions of the Secretary of State under the Literary and Scientific Institutions Act 1854 s 6 in so far as they relate to Wales were transferred to the National Assembly for Wales (see the National Assembly for Wales (Transfer of Functions) Order 1999, SI 1999/672, art 2, Sch 1) and are now exercisable by the Welsh Ministers (see the Government of Wales Act 2006 s 162(1), Sch 11 paras 30, 32). As to the Secretary of State and the Welsh Ministers see PARA 802. As to the meaning of 'Wales' see PARA 802 note 4.
5   Ie with such provisions of the Charities Act 2011 ss 117(2), 119–121 (see CHARITIES vol 8 (2015) PARA 401) as are applicable.
6   See the Literary and Scientific Institutions Act 1854 s 6 (amended by the Charities Act 2011 Sch 7 para 4). As to the Charity Commission see CHARITIES vol 8 (2015) PARA 543 et seq.
7   See the Literary and Scientific Institutions Act 1854 s 7 (amended by the Local Government Act 1933 Sch 11 Pt IV).

945.   Land conveyed for purposes of institution subject to lease or rent. Where a portion only of freehold land subject to a perpetual rent, or of leasehold land, is being conveyed for the purposes of the Literary and Scientific Institutions Act 1854, the rent and any renewal fines are apportionable as between the portion conveyed and the remainder of the land[1]. The apportionment may be settled by agreement between (1) the person for the time being entitled to the rent where the land is freehold, or the lessor or other owner subject to the lease of the lands comprised in the lease; (2) the person entitled to the fee subject to the rent, or the lessee or other person entitled to the land under the lease, or any assignment for the residue of the term; and (3) the person to whom the conveyance is being made[2]. An apportionment so made is binding on all underlessees and others, whether parties to the agreement or not[3].

Apportionment followed by execution of the conveyance renders the person entitled to the fee or other estate in the land subject to the rent, the lessee, and the persons entitled under him, liable as regards future accruing rents and renewal fines only in respect of the land not included in the conveyance[4]. Similarly, the persons entitled have the same rights and remedies for the recovery of their apportioned rents as they previously had for the entire rents[5]. Except as to the amount of rent and renewal fines, the covenants, conditions and agreements remain in force with respect to the land not included in the conveyance[6].

1 See the Literary and Scientific Institutions Act 1854 s 8. As to the conversion of perpetually renewable leases see LANDLORD AND TENANT vol 62 (2012) PARA 689.
2 See the Literary and Scientific Institutions Act 1854 s 8.
3 See the Literary and Scientific Institutions Act 1854 s 8.
4 See the Literary and Scientific Institutions Act 1854 s 9.
5 See the Literary and Scientific Institutions Act 1854 s 9. As to apportionment of rent generally see LANDLORD AND TENANT vol 62 (2012) PARA 279 et seq.
6 See the Literary and Scientific Institutions Act 1854 s 9.

946. Application of purchase money of land sold by ecclesiastical corporation sole. If the purchase money of land sold by an ecclesiastical corporation sole for the purposes of the Literary and Scientific Institutions Act 1854 does not exceed £20, the person conveying may retain the money for his own benefit, but, if it exceeds £20, the money must be applied for the benefit of the corporation sole as the bishop of the diocese directs, by writing registered in the diocesan registry[1]. The purchaser is not concerned with the proper application of the purchase money[2].

In consequence of the provisions of the real property legislation of 1925 there will normally be some persons who are empowered to convey the legal estate in land and to give a good receipt for purchase money, even where the beneficial owner is under disability[3]. Thus, although provision is made for the application of purchase money where land is acquired from incapacitated persons[4], it may only rarely be necessary to have recourse to it.

1 See the Literary and Scientific Institutions Act 1854 s 16. For the powers of sale of ecclesiastical property in general, and as to the application of purchase money, see ECCLESIASTICAL LAW vol 34 (2011) PARAS 929, 930.
2 See the Literary and Scientific Institutions Act 1854 s 16.
3 See eg PARA 948. See also the powers conferred by the Settled Land Act 1925 ss 38, 73, 75(1) (SETTLEMENTS vol 91 (2012) PARAS 705, 709, 728); the Trusts of Land and Appointment of Trustees Act 1996 s 10(3) (TRUSTS AND POWERS vol 98 (2013) PARA 477). As to the management of the property of persons under mental incapacity see MENTAL HEALTH AND CAPACITY vol 75 (2013) PARA 558.
4 See the Literary and Scientific Institutions Act 1854 s 17, applying the Lands Clauses Consolidation Act 1845 ss 69–74, 78, which provide for payment into court in certain cases (see COMPULSORY ACQUISITION OF LAND vol 18 (2009) PARAS 664, 669, 671, 682, 684, 685). The Literary and Scientific Institutions Act 1854 s 17 does not apply to purchases from the Chancellor and Council of the Duchy of Lancaster or the officers of the Duchy of Cornwall: s 17.

(C) *Powers of Disposition and Borrowing where Property held on Trust for Institution; Reverter*

947. Powers under Trusts of Land and Appointment of Trustees Act 1996. Where property consisting of or including land is held on charitable, ecclesiastical or public trusts after the commencement of the Trusts of Land and Appointment of Trustees Act 1996, it is subject to a 'trust of land'[1], and the trustees have in reference to such land all the powers which are conferred on the trustees of such a trust[2].

1 See the Trusts of Land and Appointment of Trustees Act 1996 ss 1, 2(5); and SETTLEMENTS vol 91 (2012) PARA 577.
2 See the Trusts of Land and Appointment of Trustees Act 1996 ss 6–13, 17; and SETTLEMENTS vol 91 (2012) PARA 566.

948. Power to deal with land held in trust for institution. Apart from the powers conferred by the Trusts of Land and Appointment of Trustees Act 1996[1], land or buildings, not previously part of the possessions of the Duchies of Lancaster or Cornwall[2], held in trust for a literary or scientific institution to which the Literary and Scientific Institutions Act 1854 applies[3] may, if a sale or exchange is deemed advisable, be sold by trustees having the legal estate, by the direction or with the consent of the governing body[4], if any, or exchanged for other land or buildings suitable to the purposes of the trust[5]. Money received to equalise an exchange or arising from a sale is applicable in the purchase of another site or in the improvement of other premises to be used for the purposes of the trust[6]. Similarly, trustees may let portions of the premises belonging to the institution, not required for its purposes, and apply the rents for the benefit of the institution[7].

1   See PARAS 947, 949.
2   As to the Duchy of Cornwall see CROWN AND CROWN PROCEEDINGS vol 29 (2014) PARA 232 et seq. As to the Duchy of Lancaster see CROWN AND CROWN PROCEEDINGS vol 29 (2014) PARA 214 et seq.
3   As to the institutions to which the Literary and Scientific Institutions Act 1854 applies see PARA 935.
4   As to the governing body see PARA 936.
5   See the Literary and Scientific Institutions Act 1854 s 18.
6   See the Literary and Scientific Institutions Act 1854 s 18.
7   See the Literary and Scientific Institutions Act 1854 s 18. The letting may be for such term and under such covenants or agreements as the governing body deems expedient: s 18.

949. Power to borrow for purposes of institution. A literary and scientific institution[1], unlike a commercial or trading undertaking[2], has no implied powers to borrow money for the purposes of its business; nor does the power of sale given to such institutions[3] include a power to borrow[4]; but under the Trusts of Land and Appointment of Trustees Act 1996 the trustees of land held on charitable, ecclesiastical or public trusts have all the powers of an absolute owner, including the power to borrow[5].

Moreover, in order to indemnify themselves against the payment of any rate, tax, charge, costs or expenses, to which as trustees and legal owners of the building or premises they have become liable[6], the trustees of such an institution may hold the building or other property vested in them as security for their repayment or mortgage or sell the property, or a part of it, free from the trusts of the institution, and apply the proceeds to their reimbursement, and any balance to the institution's benefit[7]. This power enables trustees to borrow in order to pay for necessary repairs to the institution's premises, but not for enlarging and improving them, at any rate where the improvement consists in providing such things as a billiard room[8].

1   As to such institutions see PARA 935.
2   See COMPANIES vol 15 (2009) PARA 1256.
3   As to the power of sale see PARA 948.
4   *Re Badger, Mansell v Viscount Cobham* [1905] 1 Ch 568.
5   See the Trusts of Land and Appointment of Trustees Act 1996 ss 1(1)(b), 2(5), 6(1); and TRUSTS AND POWERS vol 98 (2013) PARA 476.
6   It is the duty of the governing body to indemnify the trustees: see the Literary and Scientific Institutions Act 1854 s 19. As to the governing body see PARA 936.
7   See the Literary and Scientific Institutions Act 1854 s 19. The power is subject to the restrictions contained in the Act with regard to land given and land belonging to the Duchy of Lancaster or the Duchy of Cornwall (see s 4; and PARA 950): s 19.
8   *Re Badger, Mansell v Viscount Cobham* [1905] 1 Ch 568.

950. Cesser of use of site for institution. If an institution to which the Literary and Scientific Institutions Act 1854 applies[1] is removed to another site, the land previously occupied, unless it originally formed part of the possessions of the Duchies of Lancaster or Cornwall[2], may be exchanged or sold for the benefit of the institution, and money received for equality of exchange, or on a sale, may be applied towards the erection or establishment of the institution on the new site[3].

If land, or any part of land, given for the purposes of the institution otherwise ceases to be used for those purposes, the Literary and Scientific Institutions Act 1854 provided for its immediate reversion to the estate or manor out of which it was carved[4]; but instead of so reverting, the land now continues to be vested in the persons in whom it was vested before it ceased to be so used and is held on trust for the persons to whom it would otherwise have reverted[5]. The beneficiaries under the trust have no right to be consulted before the land is sold and no right to occupy the land, but the proceeds of any sale are held for their benefit[6].

1 As to the institutions to which the Literary and Scientific Institutions Act 1854 applies see PARA 935.
2 There is no exception from the reverter described in the text to note 4 in the case of duchy lands: see the Literary and Scientific Institutions Act 1854 s 4. Section 4 is, however, now subject to the Reverter of Sites Act 1987 s 1: see the text to notes 5–6. For the purposes of the Reverter of Sites Act 1987, 'land' includes any land an interest in which (including any future or contingent interest arising under the Literary and Scientific Institutions Act 1854) belongs to the Crown, the Duchy of Lancaster or the Duchy of Cornwall: see the Reverter of Sites Act 1987 s 7(2)(b). As to the Duchy of Cornwall see CROWN AND CROWN PROCEEDINGS vol 29 (2014) PARA 232 et seq. As to the Duchy of Lancaster see CROWN AND CROWN PROCEEDINGS vol 29 (2014) PARA 214 et seq.
3 See the Literary and Scientific Institutions Act 1854 s 4.
4 See the Literary and Scientific Institutions Act 1854 s 4.
5 See the Reverter of Sites Act 1987 ss 1(1), (2), 7(1)(b) (s 1(2) amended by the Trusts of Land and Appointment of Trustees Act 1996 s 5(1), Sch 2 para 6(1), (2)). This provision does not change the identity of the person to whom the land reverts, but transfers the rights of reverter from the site to the proceeds of sale: see *Marchant v Onslow* [1995] Ch 1, [1994] 2 All ER 707.
6 See the Reverter of Sites Act 1987 s 1(2) (as amended: see note 5). Section 1 does not confer any new rights on a beneficiary whose claim would have been statute-barred before 17 August 1987: see s 1(4) (amended by the Trusts of Land and Appointment of Trustees Act 1996 Sch 2 para 6(1), (3)). Where there is no identifiable beneficiary, the Charity Commission may make a scheme for the proceeds of sale to be held on charitable trusts: see the Reverter of Sites Act 1987 ss 1(5), 2–4; CHARITIES vol 8 (2015) PARAS 70–71; and EDUCATION vol 36 (2015) PARA 1297 (where these provisions are mentioned in relation to school sites).

D. LEGAL PROCEEDINGS

951. Description of property belonging to institution. In all legal proceedings the money, securities, goods, chattels and effects belonging to incorporated institutions to which the Literary and Scientific Institutions Act 1854 applies[1], and which have no provision for the vesting of their personal property, or belonging to unincorporated institutions, and not vested in trustees, may be described as belonging to the governing body, by its proper title[2].

1 As to the institutions to which the Literary and Scientific Institutions Act 1854 applies see PARA 935.
2 See the Literary and Scientific Institutions Act 1854 s 20. As to the governing body see PARA 936. As to the vesting of personalty see PARA 940.

952. Actions by and against institution. Incorporated institutions to which the Literary and Scientific Institutions Act 1854 applies[1] which are not entitled to sue and be sued by any corporate name, and unincorporated institutions, may sue or be sued in the name of the president, chairman, principal, secretary or clerk, as determined by the institution's rules, or, if the rules are silent, in the name of the person appointed for this purpose by the governing body[2]. Any person having a claim or demand against the institution may sue the president or chairman if, on application to the governing body, some other officer or person is not nominated to be the defendant[3].

Judgments recovered against the institution's nominees are enforceable against the institution's property and not the property of the nominees[4].

1 As to the institutions to which the Literary and Scientific Institutions Act 1854 applies see PARA 935.
2 See the Literary and Scientific Institutions Act 1854 s 21. As to the governing body see PARA 936. As to an action by an institution against a member see PARA 939.
3 See the Literary and Scientific Institutions Act 1854 s 21.
4 See the Literary and Scientific Institutions Act 1854 s 23 (amended by the Statute Law (Repeals) Act 1986). As to the enforcement of judgments see CIVIL PROCEDURE vol 12A (2015) PARA 1268 et seq.

E.   AMALGAMATION, TRANSFER AND DISSOLUTION

953. Alteration of purpose of institution and amalgamation. Where an institution to which the Literary and Scientific Institutions Act 1854 applies[1] (other than one with a royal charter[2] or established by or acting under a statute) has been established for some particular purpose, and the governing body[3] thinks that an alteration, extension or abridgment of that purpose, or an amalgamation with any other institution, is advisable, the proposed modification or amalgamation may be submitted by the governing body to the members[4] in a written or printed report and a special meeting may be convened to consider it[5]. However, no proposition may be carried into effect unless the report has been delivered or sent by post to every member ten days before the special meeting, and the proposition has been approved by the votes of three-fifths of the members present at the meeting and has been confirmed in the same way at a second special meeting held one month afterwards[6].

If not less than two-fifths of the members of an institution consider that a proposition so carried is calculated to injure the institution, then, within three months after the confirmation, they may apply in writing to the Secretary of State[7] who may, at his discretion, forbid the proposition being carried into effect; but the decision does not prevent the members from reconsidering the same proposition on a future occasion[8].

1 As to the institutions to which the Literary and Scientific Institutions Act 1854 applies see PARA 935.
2 As to incorporation by royal charter see CORPORATIONS vol 24 (2010) PARA 329 et seq.
3 As to the governing body see PARA 936.
4 As to membership see PARA 938.
5 See the Literary and Scientific Institutions Act 1854 s 27.
6 See the Literary and Scientific Institutions Act 1854 s 27.
7 The Literary and Scientific Institutions Act 1854 s 28 refers to 'the Lords of the Committee of Her Majesty's Privy Council for Trade and Foreign Plantations' which falls to be construed as a reference to the Board of Trade (in practice the Secretary of State for Business, Innovation and Skills who is President of the Board): see the Interpretation Act 1889 s 12(8) (repealed); and COMPETITION vol 18 (2009) PARA 5.
8 See the Literary and Scientific Institutions Act 1854 s 28.

954. Dissolution of institution. Three-fifths or any larger number of members may determine that an institution to which the Literary and Scientific Institutions Act 1854 applies[1] is to be dissolved, either immediately or at the time then agreed upon[2]. In this event all necessary steps must be taken for the disposal and settlement of the institution's property, its claims and liabilities, according to the rules of the institution, or, if the rules are inapplicable, at the discretion of the governing body[3]. In the event of a dispute among the governing body or members, the adjustment of the institution's affairs must be referred to the County Court[4]. The County Court may make the requisite orders, or, if it finds it necessary, may direct proceedings to be taken in the Chancery Division of the High Court[5]. The court will not order the dissolution of an institution which has not functioned for many years, although it will make an order for the disposition of its assets[6]. As an institution governed by the 1854 Act carries on no business[7], it probably cannot be wound up by the court as an unregistered company[8].

1 As to the institutions to which the Literary and Scientific Institutions Act 1854 applies see PARA 935. As to the members see PARA 938.
2 See the Literary and Scientific Institutions Act 1854 s 29.
3 See the Literary and Scientific Institutions Act 1854 s 29. As to the governing body see PARA 936.
4 See the Literary and Scientific Institutions Act 1854 s 29 proviso (amended by the Crime and Courts Act 2013 Sch 9 para 12). As to the County Court see COURTS AND TRIBUNALS vol 24 (2010) PARA 758 et seq.
5 See the Literary and Scientific Institutions Act 1854 s 29 proviso (as amended: see note 4). As to the Chancery Division of the High Court see COURTS AND TRIBUNALS vol 24 (2010) PARA 704.
6 *Re Harrow Literary Institution* [1953] 1 All ER 838, [1953] 1 WLR 551.
7 See the Literary and Scientific Institutions Act 1854 s 33; and PARA 935.
8 See *Re Bristol Athenaeum* (1889) 43 ChD 236; *Re Jones, Clegg v Ellison* [1898] 2 Ch 83; *Re Russell Institution, Figgins v Baghino* [1898] 2 Ch 72. As to winding up unregistered companies see the Insolvency Act 1986 ss 220–229; and COMPANY AND PARTNERSHIP INSOLVENCY vol 17 (2011) PARA 1109 et seq.

955. Application of surplus assets upon dissolution of institution. Upon the dissolution of an institution to which the Literary and Scientific Institutions Act 1854 applies[1], the property remaining, after all debts and liabilities have been satisfied, is not divisible among the members[2]. It must be given to some kindred institution, chosen by the members of the dissolving institution, or in default by the County Court[3], notwithstanding that the rules of the institution contain a provision for the division of the property of the society upon dissolution among the shareholders[4]. However, this restriction does not apply to an institution founded or established by the contributions of shareholders in the nature of a joint stock company[5].

1 As to the institutions to which the Literary and Scientific Institutions Act 1854 applies see PARA 935. As to the dissolution of institutions see PARA 954.
2 See the Literary and Scientific Institutions Act 1854 s 30. See also *Re Dutton, ex p Peake* (1878) 4 Ex D 54 at 59. As to the members see PARA 938.
3 See the Literary and Scientific Institutions Act 1854 s 30 (amended by the Crime and Courts Act 2013 Sch 9 para 141). As to county court proceedings on dissolution see PARA 954.
4 *Re Bristol Athenaeum* (1889) 43 ChD 236.
5 See the Literary and Scientific Institutions Act 1854 s 30 proviso. This provision would include eg a literary and scientific institution founded and established by the issue of transferable shares, entitling their holders to the property of the institution, but bearing no dividend (*Re Russell Institution, Figgins v Baghino* [1898] 2 Ch 72), or an institution having a common property arising out of the subscription of members, such property being held by numerous persons in transferable shares (*Re Jones, Clegg v Ellison* [1898] 2 Ch 83). In both these cases the dictum in *Re Bristol Athenaeum* (1889) 43 ChD 236 at 239 per Kay J that an institution which was not a joint stock company was not within the Literary and Scientific Institutions Act 1854 s 30 was commented on with disapproval. As to the meaning of 'joint stock company' see the Companies Act 2006 s 1041; and COMPANIES vol 14 (2009) PARA 33.

(10) ARTS COUNCILS

956. Establishment of arts councils. On 9 August 1946, the Arts Council of Great Britain was incorporated by royal charter[1]. That council was responsible for appointing committees, called the Scottish Arts Council and the Welsh Arts Council, to exercise, or advise the council on the exercise of, its functions in Scotland and Wales[2]. In 1994 all three bodies were replaced with three new bodies corporate, an independent Arts Council of England[3], the Scottish Arts Council[4] and an independent Arts Council of Wales[5].

The Arts Council of England had power to assume any rights, obligations and interests, including in land, of the former Arts Council of Great Britain[6].

The Arts Councils are distributing bodies for the purposes of the National Lottery Distribution Fund[7].

1 Charter of Incorporation of the Arts Council of Great Britain, 7 February 1967, preamble (revoked). As to incorporation by royal charter see CORPORATIONS vol 24 (2010) PARA 329 et seq. The provisions of the original charter, except in so far as they incorporated the council and conferred upon it perpetual succession, were revoked by the charter of 7 February 1967, but that revocation did not affect the legality or validity of anything lawfully done under the provisions of the original charter.
2 Charter of Incorporation of the Arts Council of Great Britain, 7 February 1967, art 8(1) (revoked).
3 The Arts Council of England was renamed 'Arts Council England' in 2003 (see PARA 957).
4 The Arts Council of Scotland is not discussed in this work.
5 As to the Arts Council of Wales see PARA 958.
6 Charter of Incorporation of the Arts Council of England, 30 March 1994, art 1(3) (revoked). Arts Council England owns the freeholds of the National Film Theatre, the Museum of the Moving Image, the Hayward Gallery, the Queen Elizabeth Hall, the Purcell Room, and the Royal Festival Hall, which are leased to the Southbank Centre; and the freehold of the Royal National Theatre, which is leased to and occupied by the Royal National Theatre Board Limited.
7 See the National Lottery etc Act 1993 s 23(1); and LICENSING AND GAMBLING vol 68 (2008) PARA 721.

957. Arts Council England. Arts Council England is a body corporate with perpetual succession and a common seal[1]. The council may sue and be sued in all courts and in all manner of actions and suits and has power to enter into contracts, to acquire, hold and dispose of property of any kind, to accept trusts and generally to do all matters and things incidental or appertaining to a body corporate[2].

The objects of the council are:

(1)   to develop and improve the knowledge, understanding and practice of the arts[3];

(2)   to increase accessibility of the arts to the public in England[4];

(3)   advance the education of the public and to further any other charitable purpose which relates to the establishment, maintenance and operation of museums and libraries (which are either public or from which the public may benefit) and to the protection of cultural property[5]; and

(4)   to advise and co-operate with government departments, local authorities, the Arts Councils for Scotland, Wales[6], and Northern Ireland (or their successors) and other bodies on any matter related to the objects in heads (1) and (3) above[7].

The money, property and income of the council must be applied solely towards these objects[8].

The council consists of a chair and the persons appointed[9] by the Secretary of State or the Mayor of London to be chairs of the area councils[10]. The terms of office and periods of appointment of the chair and the appointed members are determined by the Secretary of State[11]. The Secretary of State may appoint any person to be an observer to attend all or any meetings of the council or of any panel or committee established by the council[12]. The Council may act notwithstanding a vacancy in its number or any defect in the appointment of any member and, subject to the supplemental charter, may provide for its own procedure in regulations made by it[13]. The council must establish such area councils for the regions of England as may be approved by the Secretary of State and must delegate certain functions to those area councils[14].

Subject to the approval of the Secretary of State, the council may appoint a chief executive of the council[15], and may appoint other staff[16]. The council must keep proper accounts and records and must provide the Secretary of State with such financial and other annual reports in such form and at such times as he may require[17].

In October 2011 some of the functions of the Museums, Libraries and Archives Council were transferred to Arts Council England[18]. The Museums, Libraries and Archives Council was abolished in May 2012.

1 Supplemental Charter, 31 May 2013 (incorporating 2008, 2011 and 2013 amendments). The 1994 Charter, except in so far as it incorporates the council as a body corporate under the name of 'the Arts Council of England', with the powers and capacities specified in art 1(2) (see the text to note 2) is revoked: Supplemental Charter, 31 May 2013, art 1. The Council must provide for the safe custody of the seal of the council and the method of its use must be prescribed in regulations made by the council: art 13. The council has power, subject to the consent of Her Majesty the Queen, to change its name and to add to, amend or revoke any of the provisions of the Supplemental Charter or the remaining provisions of the 1994 Charter: see Supplemental Charter, 31 May 2013, arts 2, 14. In 2002 the Arts Council of England was merged with 10 regional arts boards and was re-named 'Arts Council England' in 2003. As to bodies corporate see COMPANIES vol 14 (2009) PARA 2; CORPORATIONS vol 24 (2010) PARA 301 et seq.
2 Charter of Incorporation of the Arts Council of England, 30 March 1994, art 1(2).
3 Supplemental Charter, 31 May 2013, art 4(1).
4 Supplemental Charter, 31 May 2013, art 4(2).
5 Supplemental Charter, 31 May 2013, art 4(3).
6 As to the Arts Councils for Scotland and Wales see PARAS 956, 958.
7 Supplemental Charter, 31 May 2013, art 4(4). The council is given various powers in furtherance of these objects: see art 5.
8 See the Supplemental Charter, 31 May 2013, art 6.
9 Ie in accordance with the Supplemental Charter, 31 May 2013, art 11.
10 See the Supplemental Charter, 31 May 2013, art 7(1). 'Secretary of State' means the Secretary of State for Culture, Media and Sport, or such other minister as for the time being is responsible for the arts, museums and libraries in England: art 3. As to the Secretary of State generally see PARA 802 note 2. As to the Mayor of London see LONDON GOVERNMENT vol 71 (2013) PARA 69.
11 Supplemental Charter, 31 May 2013, art 7(2). For the London based area council the Mayor of London acts in accordance with art 11: art 7(2)
12 Supplemental Charter, 31 May 2013, art 8.
13 Supplemental Charter, 31 May 2013, art 9.
14 See the Supplemental Charter, 31 May 2013, arts 5(1), 11.
15 Supplemental Charter, 31 May 2013, art 10.
16 See the Supplemental Charter, 31 May 2013, art 5(13).
17 See the Supplemental Charter, 31 May 2013, art 12.
18 See the Arts Council's Mission and Strategic Framework: *Great Art and Culture for Everyone, 10-year Strategic Framework 2010–2020* (2nd Edn, October 2013), a copy of which is available on the Arts Council England website which, at the date at which this volume states the law, can be found at www.artscouncil.org.uk. As to the Export Licensing Unit, whose functions were so transferred, see PARA 1096. Arts Council England also operates the government indemnity scheme, as to which see PARA 1094. The remaining functions of the Museums, Libraries and Archives Council were transferred to the National Archives (see PARA 812 note 5).

958. The Arts Council of Wales. The Arts Council of Wales (Cyngor Celfyddydau Cymru) is a body corporate with perpetual succession and a common seal[1]. The council may sue and be sued in all courts and in all manner of actions and suits and has power to enter into contracts, to acquire, hold and dispose of property of any kind, to accept trusts and generally to do all matters and things incidental or appertaining to a body corporate[2]. The objects for which the council is established and incorporated are:

(1)   to develop and improve the knowledge, understanding and practice of the arts;

(2)   to increase the accessibility of the arts to the public; and

(3)   to advise and co-operate with government departments, local authorities, the Arts Councils for England[3], Scotland and Northern Ireland and other bodies on any matters concerned, whether directly or indirectly, with those objects; and

(4)   to carry out the objects through the medium of both the Welsh and English languages[4].

The council consists of a chairman and not more than 17 other members, one of whom is the vice-chairman, and all of whom are appointed by the National Assembly for Wales[5]. The council may act notwithstanding a vacancy among the members and the validity of any of its proceedings is not affected by any defect in the appointment of a member[6].

The council may appoint a person or committees or panels to advise and assist it in the exercise of its functions[7]; and may regulate both its own procedure[8] and the procedure of any such committee or panel[9]. Any officer of the National Assembly for Wales who is appointed by the National Assembly for Wales to be an observer to the council or to any of its committees or panels is entitled to attend any meeting of the council or of the committee or panel to which they are so appointed[10].The council must, with the approval of the National Assembly for Wales, appoint a chief officer to be its principal executive officer, and it may appoint such other officers and employees as it may determine[11].

The council must keep proper accounts and other records, and prepare for each financial year statements of accounts in such form as the National Assembly for Wales, with the approval of the Treasury[12], may direct and must submit those statements of account to the National Assembly for Wales as directed[13]. The Council must also keep proper accounts and records of all monies and property received from all sources other than the National Lottery[14] in such form as the National Assembly for Wales may direct and submit those accounts to be audited by the Auditor General for Wales[15] who must examine, certify and report on such accounts, laying a copy of his report before the National Assembly for Wales[16]. The council must as soon as possible after the end of each financial year make report to the National Assembly for Wales on the exercise and performance of its functions during that year[17].

1   Charter of Incorporation of the Arts Council of Wales, 30 March 1994 (incorporating amendments of 24 November 1999 and 13 October 2004), art 1(1), (2). The application of the seal of the council must be authenticated by the signatures of the chairman or of some other members of the council authorised generally or especially by the council for that purpose, and of one of such officers of the council as may be authorised by the council so to act: art 13. The council has power to add to, amend, or revoke any of the provisions of the charter: see art 14. As to bodies corporate see COMPANIES vol 14 (2009) PARA 2; CORPORATIONS vol 24 (2010) PARA 301 et seq.
2   Charter of Incorporation of the Arts Council of Wales, 30 March 1994 (incorporating amendments of 24 November 1999 and 13 October 2004), art 1(2). The council also has specific power to assume any rights, obligations and interests, including in land, of the former Arts Council of Great Britain: see art 1(3).
3   As to the Arts Council England see PARA 957.
4   Charter of Incorporation of the Arts Council of Wales, 30 March 1994 (incorporating amendments of 24 November 1999 and 13 October 2004), art 2. All money and property received by the council, including any money voted by Parliament, must be applied solely towards the promotion of its objects: see art 3.
5   See the Charter of Incorporation of the Arts Council of Wales, 30 March 1994 (incorporating amendments of 24 November 1999 and 13 October 2004), art 4. As to the National Assembly for Wales see CONSTITUTIONAL AND ADMINISTRATIVE LAW vol 20 (2014) PARA 351 et seq.
6   Charter of Incorporation of the Arts Council of Wales, 30 March 1994 (incorporating amendments of 24 November 1999 and 13 October 2004), art 5(1).
7   See the Charter of Incorporation of the Arts Council of Wales, 30 March 1994 (incorporating amendments of 24 November 1999 and 13 October 2004), art 7.

8 See the Charter of Incorporation of the Arts Council of Wales, 30 March 1994 (incorporating amendments of 24 November 1999 and 13 October 2004), art 6.

9 See the Charter of Incorporation of the Arts Council of Wales, 30 March 1994 (incorporating amendments of 24 November 1999 and 13 October 2004), art 8.

10 See the Charter of Incorporation of the Arts Council of Wales, 30 March 1994 (incorporating amendments of 24 November 1999 and 13 October 2004), art 9.

11 See the Charter of Incorporation of the Arts Council of Wales, 30 March 1994 (incorporating amendments of 24 November 1999 and 13 October 2004), art 10.

12 As to the Treasury see CONSTITUTIONAL AND ADMINISTRATIVE LAW vol 20 (2014) PARAS 262–265.

13 See the Charter of Incorporation of the Arts Council of Wales, 30 March 1994 (incorporating amendments of 24 November 1999 and 13 October 2004), art 11(a).

14 As to the National Lottery see LICENSING AND GAMBLING vol 68 (2008) PARA 686 et seq.

15 As to the Auditor General for Wales see CONSTITUTIONAL AND ADMINISTRATIVE LAW vol 20 (2014) PARA 400.

16 See the Charter of Incorporation of the Arts Council of Wales, 30 March 1994 (incorporating amendments of 24 November 1999 and 13 October 2004), art 11(b).

17 See the Charter of Incorporation of the Arts Council of Wales, 30 March 1994 (incorporating amendments of 24 November 1999 and 13 October 2004) art 12.

(11) THE CRAFTS COUNCIL AND THE DESIGN COUNCIL

959. The Crafts Council. The Crafts Council is the national organisation promoting contemporary crafts in the United Kingdom[1]. The council is funded by Arts Council England and also receives grants from the Scottish Arts Council and Arts Council of Wales[2]. Formed in 1971 as the Crafts Advisory Committee, it became known as the Crafts Council in 1979 and was incorporated by royal charter in 1982[3].

1 As to the Crafts Council see the council's website which, at the date at which this volume states the law, can be found at www.craftscouncil.org.uk.

2 As to Arts Council England see PARA 957. As to the Arts Council of Wales see PARA 958. The Scottish Arts Council is not discussed in this work.

3 See the Charter of Incorporation of the Crafts Council, 20 July 1982.

960. The Design Council. The Design Council's role is to promote the use of design to improve people's lives by advancing design-led innovation, encouraging debate and informing government policy[1]. The Design Council was established in 1944 to elevate industrial design standards in goods manufacturing in the United Kingdom[2] to support Britain's economic recovery. The council was incorporated by royal charter in 1976 and is a registered charity[3]. It was formerly a non-departmental public body funded by an annual grant from the Department for Business, Innovation and Skills with co-sponsorship from the Department of Culture, Media and Sport but since April 1 2011 it has operated independently of the national government in the United Kingdom[4].

The Design Council is governed by a board of trustees consisting of a chairman and a maximum of 15 members[5].

1 See the Design Council Annual Report and Accounts 2014–2015. A copy can be found at the Design Council website which, at the date at which this volume states the law, can be found at www.designcouncil.org.uk.

2 As to the meaning of 'United Kingdom' see PARA 804 note 2.

3 The Design Council is registered as a charity under number 272099: see the Design Council Annual Report and Accounts 2014–2015. As to the registration of charities see CHARITIES vol 8 (2015) PARA 307 et seq.

4 In 2011 the design Council merged with the Commission for Architecture and the Built Environment ('Cabe'), the government's adviser on design in the built environment: see the Commission for Architecture and the Built Environment (Dissolution) Order 2012, SI 2012/147; and the Design Council website which, at the date at which this volume states the law,

can be found at www.designcouncil.org.uk. As to non-departmental public bodies see CONSTITUTIONAL AND ADMINISTRATIVE LAW vol 20 (2014) PARA 311 et seq.
5   See the Design Council Annual Report and Accounts 2014–2015.

(12) SPORTS COUNCILS

961. Establishment of sports councils. The Sports Council, the Sports Council for Wales (Cyngor Chwaraeon Cymru) and the Scottish Sports Council were established by royal charter in 1972 with the objects of fostering the knowledge and practice of sport and physical recreation among the public at large[1]. The Sports Council was replaced in 1996 by two new bodies corporate established by royal charter, the United Kingdom Sports Council and the English Sports Council, and in February 1997 consequential amendments were made to the charter of incorporation of the Sports Council for Wales[2].

The United Kingdom Sports Council is now known as UK Sport and works in partnership with the home country sports councils and other agencies to lead sport in the United Kingdom[3] to world-class success[4]. The English Sports Council is now known as Sport England and invests in organisations and projects to get more people playing sport and creating opportunities for people to excel at their chosen sport[5].

UK Sport, Sport England and the Sports Councils for Wales are all distributing bodies for the purposes of the National Lottery Distribution Fund[6]. UK Sport and Sport England are public bodies for the purposes of the Local Authorities (Goods and Services) Act 1970[7].

1   See the Civil Service Year Book 1997 col 781; the Charter of Incorporation of the Sports Council for Wales, 4 February 1972, preamble; and SPORTS LAW vol 96 (2012) PARA 20.
2   As to the objects of the Sports Council for Wales see SPORTS LAW vol 96 (2012) PARA 20.
3   As to the meaning of 'United Kingdom' see PARA 804 note 2.
4   See SPORTS LAW vol 96 (2012) PARA 20.
5   See SPORTS LAW vol 96 (2012) PARA 20.
6   See the National Lottery etc Act 1993 s 23(2); and LICENSING AND GAMBLING vol 68 (2008) PARA 721.
7   See the Local Authorities (Goods and Services) (Public Bodies) (Sports Councils) Order 1996, SI 1996/3092, art 2; and LOCAL GOVERNMENT vol 69 (2009) PARA 495.

(13) THE BRITISH COUNCIL

962. Constitution and powers of the British Council. The British Council was incorporated by royal charter of 7 October 1940[1] under the name of 'the British Council' with perpetual succession and a common seal[2]. The council may sue and be sued in all courts and in all manner of actions and suits and generally has power to do all matters and things incidental or appertaining to a body corporate[3]. The objects for which the council is established and incorporated are to advance any purpose which is exclusively charitable and which: (1) promotes cultural relationships and the understanding of different cultures between people and peoples of the United Kingdom and other countries[4]; (2) develops a wider knowledge of the English language; (3) encourages cultural, scientific, technological and other educational co-operation between the United Kingdom and other countries; or (4) otherwise promotes the advancement of education[5]. The income and property of the council wheresoever derived must be applied solely towards the promotion of the objects of the council[6].

All the powers of the council are vested in a board of trustees consisting of not less than ten and not more than 15 members[7]. The officers of the board are the chair and the deputy chair[8]. The board may delegate any of its powers[9] to a sub-committee, or sub-committees[10]. Subject to the provisions of the supplemental charter and the byelaws therein, the board has the power to regulate its meetings and the despatch of business thereat as it may from time to time decide[11]. The chair or deputy chair may, and at the request of three trustees must, at any time convene a meeting of the board[12].

The board may appoint a chief executive and such other employees on such terms as it thinks fit[13]. The accounts of the council must be made up for each financial year and must be audited[14].

1   The British Council was incorporated by royal charter in 1940 and a supplemental charter was granted on 26 November 1993. The charter was amended by Orders in Council dated 22 July 1976, 5 October 1983, 4 December 1984, 27 October 1993, 16 July 2002 and 8 June 2011. References to the charter in this paragraph are to the charter as so amended. As to incorporation by royal charter see CORPORATIONS vol 24 (2010) PARA 329 et seq.
2   Charter of Incorporation of the British Council, 7 October 1940, art 1. The provisions of the Charter of Incorporation of 1940, except in so far as they incorporate the council and confer upon it perpetual succession and a common seal, were revoked by the supplemental charter of 26 November 1993: see Supplemental Charter of the British Council, 26 November 1993, art 1. The board of the council may by special resolution alter, amend or add to any of the provisions of the supplemental charter (see art 18) and may likewise adopt byelaws or revoke, alter or add to such byelaws (art 19). The board may by special resolution surrender the supplemental charter subject to the sanction of Her Majesty the Queen: see art 24. The board may empower the chairman to appoint persons by name or by office to authorise the affixing of the common seal of the council to any instruments on its behalf and also to attest the same by signing the said instruments; provided that no fewer than two such persons must authorise the affixing of the common seal and sign each such instrument: Schedule, Byelaw 12. As to the corporate seal see CORPORATIONS vol 24 (2010) PARA 323 et seq.
3   Supplemental Charter of the British Council, 26 November 1993, art 2. As to bodies corporate see COMPANIES vol 14 (2009) PARA 2; CORPORATIONS vol 24 (2010) PARA 301 et seq.
4   As to the meaning of 'United Kingdom' see PARA 804 note 2.
5   Supplemental Charter of the British Council, 26 November 1993, art 3. For the purposes of these objects the council is given various powers: see art 4.
6   See the Supplemental Charter of the British Council, 26 November 1993, art 5.
7   See the Supplemental Charter of the British Council, 26 November 1993, arts 6–7, 9–12 Schedule Byelaws 2–8. As to honorary members see art 8. In execution of their powers under the charter, no trustee is liable for any loss to the property of the council arising by reason of any improper investment made in good faith (so long as where appropriate advice has been sought before making such investment) or for the negligence or fraud of any other trustee or by reason of any mistake or omission made in good faith by any board member or by reason of any other matter or thing whatsoever except wilful and individual fraud, wrong-doing or wrongful omission on the part of the trustee: art 11.
8   Supplemental Charter of the British Council, 26 November 1993, Schedule, Byelaw 4.1. The chair and deputy chair are elected by the board and must be previously approved by the Secretary of State for Foreign and Commonwealth Affairs and must hold office for such period and periods not exceeding three years as the Secretary of State approves: Schedule, Byelaw 4.2.
9   Ie other than its powers under the Supplemental Charter of the British Council, 26 November 1993, art 18 (see note 2) or art 19 (amendment of byelaws).
10 See the Supplemental Charter of the British Council, 26 November 1993, art 20.
11 Supplemental Charter of the British Council, 26 November 1993, Schedule, Byelaw 9.1.
12 See the Supplemental Charter of the British Council, 26 November 1993, Schedule, Byelaw 9.2.
13 Supplemental Charter of the British Council, 26 November 1993, Schedule, Byelaw 14. The appointment of the chief executive must be previously approved by the Secretary of State for Foreign and Commonwealth Affairs and he holds office for such period as the said Secretary of State may approve: Schedule, Byelaw 14.
14 Supplemental Charter of the British Council, 26 November 1993, Schedule, Byelaw 17.

(14) RESEARCH COUNCILS

963. Establishment of research councils. The following bodies established by royal charter are research councils[1]: (1) the Medical Research Council[2]; (2) the Engineering and Physical Sciences Research Council[3]; (3) the Natural Environment Research Council[4]; (4) any other body which is established for purposes connected with scientific research[5] and consists of persons appointed by a Minister of the Crown and which is declared by Order in Council to be established as a research council for purposes of the Science and Technology Act 1965[6]. In the exercise of these powers the following research councils have been established: (a) the Economic and Social Research Council[7]; (b) the Biotechnology and Biological Sciences Research Council[8]; (c) the Science and Technology Facilities Council[9]. The Technology Strategy Board was established by royal charter, and is a research council for the purposes of the Science and Technology Act 1965; it is now called 'Innovate UK' and is the United Kingdom's innovation agency, an executive non-departmental public body, sponsored by the Department for Business, Innovation and Skills[10].

Where any activities of a research council or government department in relation to scientific research are to be taken over from it by any research council or government department[11], then on the transfer accordingly of responsibility for those activities the Secretary of State[12] may by order made by statutory instrument transfer or provide for transferring property, rights, liabilities or obligations held, acquired or incurred in connection with the carrying on of the activities previously by any research council or government department; and a research council must comply with any directions of the Secretary of State requiring it to take over from, or transfer to, any research council or government department the responsibility for any activities in relation to scientific research[13]. On any such transfer of responsibility the Secretary of State may amend or repeal any provision in any enactment affecting a research council or government department concerned, so far as it appears to him necessary or expedient for giving full effect to the transfer[14].

The Arts and Humanities Research Council was also established by royal charter and is a research council[15].

1 Nothing in the Science and Technology Act 1965 prejudices or affects any power to amend or revoke the charters of any research council, or any power of Her Majesty to grant new charters or affect the operation of any amendment made or charter granted after 23 March 1965 (ie the date of the passing of the Act): s 6(2). As to incorporation by royal charter see CORPORATIONS vol 24 (2010) PARA 329 et seq.
2 Science and Technology Act 1965 s 1(1)(a) (amended by the Statute Law (Repeals) Act 1998). As to the Medical Research Council see PARA 965.
3 See the Science and Technology Act 1965 s 1(1)(b). Section 1(1)(b) refers to the Science Research Council which was subsequently renamed the Engineering and Physical Sciences Research Council: see the Engineering and Physical Sciences Research Council Order 1994, SI 1994/424; Research Councils (Transfer of Property etc) Order 1994, SI 1994/611; and PARA 969.
4 See the Science and Technology Act 1965 s 1(1)(b). As to the Natural Environment Research Council see PARA 966.
5 'Scientific research' means research and development in any of the sciences (including the social sciences) or in technology: Science and Technology Act 1965 s 6(1).
6 Science and Technology Act 1965 s 1(1)(c). No recommendation may be made to Her Majesty to make an Order in Council declaring a body to be a research council under s 1(1)(c) unless a draft of the order, specifying the objects or principal objects of that body, has been laid before Parliament and approved by a resolution of each House of Parliament: s 1(4). As to Orders in Council see CONSTITUTIONAL AND ADMINISTRATIVE LAW vol 20 (2014) PARA 581. As to the laying of documents before Parliament see STATUTES AND LEGISLATIVE PROCESS vol 96 (2012) PARA 1052.

7 See the Social Science Research Council Order 1965, SI 1965/2015; and PARA 967.
8 See the Biotechnology and Biological Sciences Research Council Order 1994, SI 1994/423; and PARA 968.
9 See the Science and Technology Facilities Council Order 2007, SI 2007/279; and PARA 970.
10 See the Technology Strategy Board Order 2007, SI 2007/280; and PARA 971.
11 Ie other than under the Science and Technology Act 1965 s 3 (see the text to notes 13–14).
12 As to the Secretary of State see PARA 802 note 2.
13 Science and Technology Act 1965 s 3(6) (s 3(6), Sch 3 amended by SI 1995/2985). The Science and Technology Act 1965 3(6), (7) (see the text to notes 14–15) has effect in relation to any activities carried on or to be carried on by the United Kingdom Atomic Energy Authority as if it were a government department: s 4(3). As to the United Kingdom Atomic Energy Authority see ENERGY AND CLIMATE CHANGE vol 44 (2011) PARA 787 et seq.
  In exercise of this power the following orders have been made: the Building Research Station (Transfer of Property etc) Order 1967, SI 1967/998 (which transferred certain property, rights, liabilities and obligations from the then Minister of Technology to the then Minister of Public Buildings and Works); the Research Councils (Transfer of Property etc) Order 1994, SI 1994/611 (see note 3); the Research Councils (Transfer of Property etc) Order 1995, SI 1995/630; the Research Councils (Transfer of Property etc) Order 2007, SI 2007/770 (see PARA 970); the Technology Strategy Board (Transfer of Property etc) Order 2007, SI 2007/1676 (see PARA 971); the Technology Strategy Board (Transfer of Property etc) Order 2008, SI 2008/1405; the United Kingdom Space Agency (Transfer of Property etc) Order 2011, SI 2011/822; and the Grant for Research and Development (Transfer of Contracts etc) Order 2011, SI 2011/1953.
  Under the Science and Technology Act 1965 s 3, the activities of the Council for Scientific and Industrial Research were to be taken over by such of the research councils as are concerned with the matters in question or by other government departments, and the Council for, and Department, of Scientific and Industrial Research were dissolved: see s 3(1). The former activities of the National Institute for Research in Nuclear Science were to be taken over by the then Science Research Council (see s 3(2)); and the Natural Environment Research Council was to carry on the former work of the National Oceanographic Council (see s 3(3) (substituted by the Nature Conservancy Council Act 1973 s 1(3), Sch 2 para 2)). For transitional provisions in relation to those transfers see the Science and Technology Act 1965 s 3(1)–(3), Sch 3 (as so amended).
14 Science and Technology Act 1965 s 3(7) (amended by SI 1995/2985). In connection with the amendment or repeal, the Secretary of State may make transitional, supplemental or incidental provision: Science and Technology Act 1965 s 3(7) (as so amended).
15 See the Higher Education Act 2004 s 1; and PARA 972.

964. Expenses and accounts of research councils. The Secretary of State[1] may pay out of money provided by Parliament to any research council[2] such sums in respect of its expenses as he may with Treasury[3] consent determine; and so far as relates to the use and expenditure of sums so paid the research council must act in accordance with such directions as may from time to time be given to it by the Secretary of State[4].

Each research council must furnish the Secretary of State with such returns, accounts and other information with respect to its property and activities as he may from time to time require, and must prepare programmes and estimates of expenditure in such form and at such times as he may require[5]. As soon as possible after the end of each financial year[6], each research council must make to the Secretary of State a report on the exercise and performance of its functions during that year[7]; and the Secretary of State must lay a copy of the report before each House of Parliament, together with such comments as he may think fit to make[8].

Each research council must keep proper accounts and other records, and must prepare for each financial year statements of account in such form as the Secretary of State, with Treasury approval, may direct and submit them to the Secretary of State at such time as he may direct[9]. On or before 30 November in any year, the Secretary of State must transmit to the Comptroller and Auditor General the statements of account of each research council for the financial year last ended[10].

The Comptroller and Auditor General must then examine and certify them and lay copies of them together with his report on them before each House of Parliament[11].

The obligations of the Medical Research Council[12] under these provisions in relation to the Secretary of State are in place of any corresponding obligations imposed on it by its charter or otherwise[13]. Subject to this, anything which under its charter is to be done by or to a committee of the Privy Council must be done instead by or to the Secretary of State[14].

Land occupied in the United Kingdom[15] by any research council is deemed, for the purposes of any rate on property, to be property occupied by or on behalf of the Crown for public purposes[16].

Nothing in the Science and Technology Act 1965 or in any of the enactments[17] relating to the general functions of any research council may be taken as restricting the activities of a research council to the United Kingdom, or any part of it, nor may the expenses to be paid by the Secretary of State[18] be restricted to those incurred in the United Kingdom[19]. It is lawful for a research council[20], and in specified circumstances, to adopt rules of eligibility for awards by confining eligibility to persons who are ordinarily resident in the United Kingdom or any part thereof, where those rules would otherwise be unlawful by reason of discrimination[21].

1   As to the Secretary of State see PARA 802 note 2.
2   As to the establishment of research councils see PARA 963.
3   As to the meaning of 'Treasury' see PARA 809 note 4.
4   Science and Technology Act 1965 s 2(1) (amended by SI 1995/2985). As to the provision of money by Parliament see PARLIAMENT vol 78 (2010) PARA 804.
5   Science and Technology Act 1965 Sch 1 para 1 (amended by SI 1995/2985).
6   As to the meaning of 'financial year' see PARA 908 note 6.
7   Science and Technology Act 1965 Sch 1 para 2(1) (amended by SI 1995/2985).
8   Science and Technology Act 1965 Sch 1 para 2(2) (amended by SI 1995/2985). As to the laying of documents before Parliament see STATUTES AND LEGISLATIVE PROCESS vol 96 (2012) PARA 1052.
9   Science and Technology Act 1965 Sch 1 para 3(1) (amended by SI 1995/2985).
10 Science and Technology Act 1965 Sch 1 para 3(2) (amended by SI 1995/2985). As to the Comptroller and Auditor General see CONSTITUTIONAL AND ADMINISTRATIVE LAW vol 20 (2014) PARAS 494–496.
11 Science and Technology Act 1965 Sch 1 para 3(3).
12 As to the Medical Research Council see PARA 965.
13 Science and Technology Act 1965 s 2(4) (amended by the Statute Law (Repeals) Act 1998; and SI 1995/2985).
14 Science and Technology Act 1965 s 2(4) (as amended: see note 13). As to the Privy Council see CONSTITUTIONAL AND ADMINISTRATIVE LAW vol 20 (2014) PARAS 268–272.
15 As to the meaning of 'United Kingdom' see PARA 804 note 2.
16 Science and Technology Act 1965 s 2(3).
17 As to the meaning of 'enactment' see PARA 805 note 5.
18 Ie under the Science and Technology Act 1965 s 2(1) (see the text to notes 1–4).
19 See the Science and Technology Act 1965 s 2(5). In the case of research councils other than the Medical Research Council, the research councils' expenses in respect of which payments may be so made do not include any expenses in so far as they may be incurred for objects falling outside the objects specified in relation to that council in s 1(2) (see PARA 969) or s 1(3) (see PARA 966) or in the Order in Council declaring it to be a research council: s 2(5) (amended by the Statute Law (Repeals) Act 1998).
20 Ie the Arts and Humanities Research Council (see PARA 972); the Biotechnology and Biological Sciences Research Council (see PARA 968); the Economic and Social Research Council (see PARA 967); the Engineering and Physical Sciences Research Council (see PARA 969); the Medical Research Council, the Natural Environment Research Council (see PARA 966); and the Science and Technology Facilities Council (see PARA 970): Education (Fees and Awards) (England) Regulations 2007, SI 2007/779, Sch 2 Pt 1. Schedule 2 Pt 1 refers to the Council for the Central Laboratory of the Research Councils, and the Particle Physics and Astronomy Research Council,

the rights, liabilities and obligations of both of which are now vested in the Science and Technology Facilities Council: see the Research Councils (Transfer of Property etc) Order 2007, SI 2007/770; and PARA 970.

21 See the Education (Fees and Awards) (England) Regulations 2007, SI 2007/779, reg 6; and EDUCATION vol 36 (2015) PARAS 1110–1111.

965. The Medical Research Council. The Medical Research Council was incorporated by royal charter on 1 April 1920[1]. Its principal function is the promotion of research on all aspects of health and disease[2].

1 See MEDICAL PROFESSIONS vol 74 (2011) PARA 178. As to the research councils in general see PARA 963. As to expenses and accounts see PARA 964.
2 See MEDICAL PROFESSIONS vol 74 (2011) PARA 178.

966. The Natural Environment Research Council. The Natural Environment Research Council is a body established wholly or mainly for objects consisting of or comprised in the following, namely, the carrying out of research in the earth sciences and ecology, the facilitating, encouragement and support of such research by other bodies or persons[1] or any description of bodies or persons and of instruction in subjects related to the council's activities, the dissemination of knowledge in the earth sciences and ecology, the provision of advice on matters related to the council's activities[2]. The council was established by royal charter in 1965 and is a non-departmental public body of the Department for Business, Innovation and Skills[3].

For the purpose of making and completing a geological survey of Great Britain[4] or any part of it, it is lawful for any surveyor or other person appointed by or acting under the orders of the Natural Environment Research Council, and for any person assisting or employed by any surveyor or other person so appointed or acting under such orders, to enter into and upon the land of any owner or person for the purpose of making and carrying on any geological survey authorised by that council, and to break up the surface of any part of the land for the purpose of ascertaining the rocks, strata or minerals within or under it[5]. Notice of the intention to enter must be given in writing[6]. Posts, stones, marks or objects to be used in the survey may be fixed, but the consent of the owner or occupier is required if they are to be fixed within any walled garden, orchard or pleasure ground[7]. If any person resists or wilfully obstructs or hinders any surveyor or other person employed or assisting in the execution of any such survey, or takes away or displaces, or wilfully defaces or destroys, any stone, post, mark or object set up and placed for the purposes of any such survey, he commits an offence[8].

1 As to the meaning of 'person' see PARA 803 note 17.
2 Science and Technology Act 1965 s 1(3) (amended by the Nature Conservancy Council Act 1973 ss 1(3), (7), 5(2), Sch 2 para 1, Sch 4). As to the research councils in general see PARA 963. As to expenses and accounts see PARA 964.
3 See the website of the Department for Business, Innovation and Skills which, at the date at which this volume states the law, can be found at www.bis.gov.uk. The Natural Environment Research Council is to close its pension scheme: see the Public Service Pensions Act 2013 s 31, Schs 7, 10: and PERSONAL AND OCCUPATIONAL PENSIONS vol 80 (2013) PARAS 320–322. As to non-departmental public bodies see CONSTITUTIONAL AND ADMINISTRATIVE LAW vol 20 (2014) PARA 311 et seq.
4 As to the meaning of 'Great Britain' see PARA 804 note 2.
5 Geological Survey Act 1845 s 1 (amended by the Statute Law Revision Act 1891; Science and Technology Act 1965 s 3(5), Sch 2). Power is also given to enter into or upon any land through which any such surveyor or other person so appointed or acting or employed finds it necessary to pass for the purposes of the survey, at any reasonable time in the day, until the survey is completed: see the Geological Survey Act 1845 s 1 (as so amended).
6 See the Geological Survey Act 1845 s 1 (as amended: see note 5).
7 See the Geological Survey Act 1845 s 1 (as amended: see note 5). The ground may be dug up for the purpose of fixing any such post, stone or mark: see s 1 (as so amended). As little damage must

be done as possible, and satisfaction must be made to the owner or occupier of the land, or the owner of any trees in any way injured, for any damage caused: see s 1 (as so amended). In case of dispute between the surveyor or other persons appointed or employed and the owner or occupier as to the amount of damage sustained, the same must be ascertained and determined by a magistrates' court: see s 1 (as so amended; and further amended by the Courts Act 2003 s 109(1), Sch 8 para 25). As to magistrates' courts see MAGISTRATES vol 71 (2013) PARA 470 et seq.

8   See the Geological Survey Act 1845 s 2 (amended by the Statute Law Revision Act 1891; Science and Technology Act 1965 s 3(5), Sch 2; and by virtue of the Criminal Justice Act 1982 ss 38, 46). The penalty for such an offence is, on summary conviction, a fine not exceeding level 1 on the standard scale: see the Geological Survey Act 1845 s 2 (as so amended). As to the standard scale and magistrates' powers to levy unlimited fines see SENTENCING vol 92 (2015) PARA 176.

967. The Economic and Social Research Council. The Economic and Social Research Council was established by royal charter under the name of the Social Science Research Council[1] and is a research council for purposes of the Science and Technology Act 1965[2]. Its objects are: (1) to encourage and support by any means research in the social sciences by any other person[3] or body[4]; (2) without prejudice to head (1), to provide and operate services for common use in carrying on such research[5]; (3) to carry out research in the social sciences[6]; (4) to make grants to students for postgraduate instruction in the social sciences[7]; and (5) to provide advice and disseminate knowledge concerning the social sciences[8]. The council is a non-departmental public body of the Department for Business, Innovation and Skills[9].

1   See the website of the Economic and Social Research Council which, at the date at which this volume states the law, can be found at www.esrcsocietytoday.ac.uk. The council was renamed with effect from 1 January 1984.

2   See the Social Science Research Council Order 1965, SI 1965/2015, art 1. As to the research councils in general see PARA 963. As to expenses and accounts see PARA 964. The Economic and Social Research Council is to close its pension scheme: see the Public Service Pensions Act 2013 s 31, Schs 7, 10: and PERSONAL AND OCCUPATIONAL PENSIONS vol 80 (2013) PARAS 320–322.

3   As to the meaning of 'person' see PARA 803 note 17.

4   Social Science Research Council Order 1965, SI 1965/2015, Schedule para (a).

5   Social Science Research Council Order 1965, SI 1965/2015, Schedule para (b).

6   Social Science Research Council Order 1965, SI 1965/2015, Schedule para (c).

7   Social Science Research Council Order 1965, SI 1965/2015, Schedule para (d).

8   Social Science Research Council Order 1965, SI 1965/2015, Schedule para (e).

9   See the website of the Department for Business, Innovation and Skills which, at the date at which this volume states the law, can be found at www.bis.gov.uk. As to non-departmental public bodies see CONSTITUTIONAL AND ADMINISTRATIVE LAW vol 20 (2014) PARA 311 et seq.

968. The Biotechnology and Biological Sciences Research Council. The Biotechnology and Biological Sciences Research Council was established by royal charter in 1994 by the incorporation of the former Agricultural and Food Research Council[1] with certain relevant research programmes of the former Science and Engineering Research Council[2]. The council is a research council for purposes of the Science and Technology Act 1965[3]. The objects of the council are:

(1)   to promote and support, by any means, high quality basic, strategic and applied research and related postgraduate training relating to the understanding and exploitation of biological systems[4];

(2)   to advance knowledge and technology, and provide trained scientists and engineers, which meet the needs of users and beneficiaries (including the agriculture, bioprocessing, chemical, food, health-care, pharmaceutical and other biotechnological-related industries), thereby contributing to the economic competitiveness of the United Kingdom[5] and the quality of life[6];

(3)   to provide advice, disseminate knowledge, and promote public understanding in the fields of biotechnology and the biological sciences[7].

The council is a non-departmental public body of the Department for Business, Innovation and Skills[8].

1 The former Agricultural and Food Research Council, incorporated under the name of the Agricultural Research Council by royal charters of 1931, 1933 and 1950 and renamed by royal charter in 1983, was charged with the organisation and development of agricultural research and had power, in particular, to establish institutions and make grants for investigation and research relating to the advancement of agriculture: see the Agricultural Research Act 1956 s 1(1) (repealed).

2 See the website of the Biotechnology and Biological Sciences Research Council which, at the date at which this volume states the law, can be found at www.bbsrc.ac.uk. See also the Research Councils (Transfer of Property etc) Order 1994, SI 1994/611.

3 Biotechnology and Biological Sciences Research Council Order 1994, SI 1994/423, art 1. As to the research councils in general see PARA 963. As to expenses and accounts see PARA 964. The Biotechnology and Biological Research Council is to close its pension scheme: see the Public Service Pensions Act 2013 s 31, Schs 7, 10: and PERSONAL AND OCCUPATIONAL PENSIONS vol 80 (2013) PARAS 320–322.

4 Biotechnology and Biological Sciences Research Council Order 1994, SI 1994/423, Schedule para (a).

5 As to the meaning of 'United Kingdom' see PARA 804 note 2.

6 Biotechnology and Biological Sciences Research Council Order 1994, SI 1994/423, Schedule para (b).

7 Biotechnology and Biological Sciences Research Council Order 1994, SI 1994/423, Schedule para (c).

8 See the website of the Department for Business, Innovation and Skills which, at the date at which this volume states the law, can be found at www.bis.gov.uk. As to non-departmental public bodies see CONSTITUTIONAL AND ADMINISTRATIVE LAW vol 20 (2014) PARA 311 et seq.

969. The Engineering and Physical Sciences Research Council. The Secretary of State[1] may defray out of money provided by Parliament[2] any expenses which, with Treasury consent, he may incur in carrying on or supporting scientific research or the dissemination of the results of scientific research[3], in furthering the practical application of the results of scientific research[4], and in making payments in respect of remuneration, allowances or pension benefits payable to or in respect of members of any advisory body established for the purposes of assisting him in matters connected with scientific research[5].

The Engineering and Physical Sciences Research Council was established by royal charter[6] and is a research council for purposes of the Science and Technology Act 1965[7]. The objects of the council are:

(1) to promote and support, by any means, high quality basic, strategic and applied research and related postgraduate training in engineering and the physical sciences[8];

(2) to advance knowledge and technology, and provide trained scientists and engineers, which meet the needs of users and beneficiaries (including the chemical, communications, construction, electrical, electronic, engineering, information technology, pharmaceutical, process and other industries), thereby contributing to the economic competitiveness of the United Kingdom[9] and the quality of life[10];

(3) to provide advice, disseminate knowledge, and promote public understanding in the fields of engineering and the physical sciences[11].

The Engineering and Physical Sciences Research council is a non-departmental public body of the Department for Business, Innovation and Skills[12].

1 The Science and Technology Act 1965 s 5(1) was amended so as to read 'the Secretary of State or the Minister of Agriculture, Fisheries and Food': see the Transfer of Functions (Scientific Research) Order 1999, SI 1999/2785, art 2(2). The Ministry of Agriculture, Fisheries and Food was dissolved and the functions of the minister transferred to the Secretary of State: see the Ministry of Agriculture, Fisheries and Food (Dissolution) Order 2002, SI 2002/794, art 2. The functions of a Minister of the Crown under the Science and Technology Act 1965 s 5, in so far as they relate to

Wales but except so far as relating to research councils, are exercisable by the Welsh Ministers concurrently with the Secretary of State; and are exercisable by the Welsh Ministers free from the requirement for Treasury consent: see the Government of Wales Act 2006 s 162(1), Sch 11 paras 30, 32; and the National Assembly for Wales (Transfer of Functions) Order 1999, SI 1999/672, art 2, Sch 1. As to the Secretary of State and the Welsh Ministers see PARA 802. As to the meaning of 'Wales' see PARA 802 note 4. As to the meaning of 'Treasury' see PARA 809 note 4.

2   As to the provision of money by Parliament see PARLIAMENT vol 78 (2010) PARA 804.

3   Science and Technology Act 1965 s 5(1)(a) (amended by SI 1971/719; and SI 1995/2985). As to the meaning of 'scientific research' see PARA 963 note 5. The functions of the United Kingdom Atomic Energy Authority include the undertaking of scientific research in such matters not connected with atomic energy as may, after consultation with the authority, be required by the Secretary of State: see the Science and Technology Act 1965 s 4(1) (amended by virtue of SI 1970/1537; SI 1974/692; SI 1992/1314). The Atomic Energy Authority Act 1954 s 2(2) applies as if the relevant research were research into matters connected with atomic energy: Science and Technology Act 1965 s 4(1). See further ENERGY AND CLIMATE CHANGE vol 44 (2011) PARA 793.

4   Science and Technology Act 1965 s 5(1)(b) (substituted by SI 1992/1296).

5   Science and Technology Act 1965 s 5(1)(c) (amended by SI 1995/2985). See note 1. The Engineering and Physical Sciences Research Council is to close its pension scheme: see the Public Service Pensions Act 2013 s 31, Schs 7, 10: and PERSONAL AND OCCUPATIONAL PENSIONS vol 80 (2013) PARAS 320–322.

6   See the Engineering and Physical Sciences Research Council website which, at the date at which this volume states the law, can be found at www.epsrc.ac.uk. The former Science and Engineering Research Council, established as the Science Research Council, was a body established wholly or mainly for objects consisting of or comprised in the carrying out of scientific research, the facilitating, encouragement and support of scientific research by other bodies or persons or any description of bodies or persons and of instruction in the sciences and technology, and the dissemination of knowledge in the sciences and technology: see the Science and Technology Act 1965 s 1(2). Its biotechnology and biological sciences programmes were incorporated into the Biotechnology and Biological Sciences Research Council in 1994 (see PARA 968) and most of its other property, rights, liabilities and obligations were transferred to the Engineering and Physical Sciences Research Council: see the Research Councils (Transfer of Property etc) Order 1994, SI 1994/611.

7   See the Engineering and Physical Sciences Research Council Order 1994, SI 1994/424, art 1. As to the research councils in general see PARA 963. As to expenses and accounts see PARA 964.

8   Engineering and Physical Sciences Research Council Order 1994, SI 1994/424, Schedule para (a).

9   As to the meaning of 'United Kingdom' see PARA 804 note 2.

10 Engineering and Physical Sciences Research Council Order 1994, SI 1994/424, Schedule para (b).

11 Engineering and Physical Sciences Research Council Order 1994, SI 1994/424, Schedule para (c). All rights, liabilities and obligations of the Engineering and Physical Sciences Research Council arising in connection with the award of the research grants and fellowships relating to nuclear physics were transferred to the Science and Technology Facilities Council: see the Research Councils (Transfer of Property etc) Order 2007, SI 2007/770, art 9, Sch 6; and PARA 970.

12 See the website of the Department for Business, Innovation and Skills which, at the date at which this volume states the law, can be found at www.bis.gov.uk. As to non-departmental public bodies see CONSTITUTIONAL AND ADMINISTRATIVE LAW vol 20 (2014) PARA 311 et seq.

970. The Science and Technology Facilities Council. The Science and Technology Facilities Council was established by royal charter[1] and is a research council for the purposes of the Science and Technology Act 1965[2]. The objects of the council are:

(1)   to promote and support high-quality scientific and engineering research by developing and providing, by any means, facilities and technical expertise in support of basic, strategic and applied research programmes funded by persons[3] established in the United Kingdom[4] and elsewhere[5];

(2)   to promote and support, by any means, high-quality basic, strategic and applied research and related postgraduate training in astronomy, particle physics, space science and nuclear physics and research in any

other field which makes use of scientific facilities where access is provided, arranged or otherwise made available by the council, having regard to the objects of the other research councils[6];

(3) to promote and support the advancement of knowledge and technology (including the promotion and support of the exploitation of research outcomes) and to provide trained scientists and engineers, and thereby to contribute to the economic competitiveness of the United Kingdom and the quality of life of its people, meeting the needs of users and beneficiaries[7];

(4) in relation to the activities as engaged in by the council above, and in such manner as the council may see fit, to generate public awareness, to communicate research outcomes, to encourage public engagement and dialogue, to disseminate knowledge, and to provide advice[8].

The council is a non-departmental public body of the Department for Business, Innovation and Skills[9].

1 See the website of the Department for Business, Innovation and Skills which, at the date at which this volume states the law, can be found at www.bis.gov.uk.
2 See the Science and Technology Facilities Council Order 2007, SI 2007/279, art 1. The council was formed through a merger of the former Council for the Central Laboratory of the Research Councils and the Particle Physics and Astronomy Research Council and the transfer of responsibility for nuclear physics from the Engineering and Physical Sciences Research Council (see PARA 969): see the Research Councils (Transfer of Property etc) Order 2007, SI 2007/770. As to the research councils in general see PARA 963. As to expenses and accounts see PARA 964.
3 As to the meaning of 'person' see PARA 803 note 17.
4 As to the meaning of 'United Kingdom' see PARA 804 note 2.
5 Science and Technology Facilities Council Order 2007, SI 2007/279, Schedule para (a).
6 Science and Technology Facilities Council Order 2007, SI 2007/279, Schedule para (b).
7 Science and Technology Facilities Council Order 2007, SI 2007/279, Schedule para (c).
8 Science and Technology Facilities Council Order 2007, SI 2007/279, Schedule para (d).
9 See the website of the Department for Business, Innovation and Skills which, at the date at which this volume states the law, can be found at www.bis.gov.uk. The Science and Technology Facilities Council is to close its pension scheme: see the Public Service Pensions Act 2013 s 31, Schs 7, 10: and PERSONAL AND OCCUPATIONAL PENSIONS vol 80 (2013) PARAS 320–322. As to non-departmental public bodies see CONSTITUTIONAL AND ADMINISTRATIVE LAW vol 20 (2014) PARA 311 et seq.

971. The Technology Strategy Board ('Innovate UK'). The Technology Strategy Board ('Innovate UK')[1], was established by royal charter[2] and is a research council for the purposes of the Science and Technology Act 1965[3]. The board is established and incorporated for purposes connected with research into, and the development and exploitation of, science, technology and new ideas, with the aim of increasing economic growth and improving quality of life in the United Kingdom[4]. In fulfilling these purposes the board is to have particular regard to the benefits to be gained by those engaging in business activities in the United Kingdom[5]. For these purposes, the board may, in particular:

(1) promote and support research into, and the development and exploitation of, science, technology and new ideas, by those engaged in business activities[6];

(2) promote and support the use of, and investment in, science, technology and new ideas, by those engaged in business activities[7];

(3) collect and disseminate knowledge about the use of, and investment in, science, technology and new ideas[8];

(4) contribute to building public confidence in, and understanding of, research into, and the development and exploitation of, science, technology and new ideas[9]; and

(5)   advise government on strategies for, and respond to questions posed by government about, the use of, and investment in, science, technology and new ideas, by those engaged in business activities[10].

The council is a non-departmental public body of the Department for Business, Innovation and Skills[11].

1   Innovate UK is the new name for the Technology Strategy Board: see the website of Innovate UK which, at the date at which this volume states the law, can be found at www.innovateuk.gov.uk.
2   See the *Technology Strategy Board (Innovate UK) Annual Report and Accounts 2014–2015*, a copy of which is available, at the date at which this volume states the law, at www.innovateuk.gov.uk.
3   See the Technology Strategy Board Order 2007, SI 2007/280, art 1. As to the research councils in general see PARA 963. As to expenses and accounts see PARA 964. All property, rights, liabilities and obligations of the Secretary of State in relation to certain contracts and grants have been transferred to the board: see the Technology Strategy Board (Transfer of Property etc) Order 2007, SI 2007/1676; the Technology Strategy Board (Transfer of Property etc) Order 2008, SI 2008/1405; and the Grant for Research and Development (Transfer of Contracts etc) Order 2011, SI 2011/1953. As to the Secretary of State see PARA 802 note 2.
4   Technology Strategy Board Order 2007, SI 2007/280, Schedule para 1(1). As to the meaning of 'United Kingdom' see PARA 804 note 2.
5   See the Technology Strategy Board Order 2007, SI 2007/280, Schedule para 1(1).
6   Technology Strategy Board Order 2007, SI 2007/280, Schedule para 1(2)(a).
7   Technology Strategy Board Order 2007, SI 2007/280, Schedule para 1(2)(b).
8   Technology Strategy Board Order 2007, SI 2007/280, Schedule para 1(2)(c).
9   Technology Strategy Board Order 2007, SI 2007/280, Schedule para 1(2)(d).
10 Technology Strategy Board Order 2007, SI 2007/280, Schedule para 1(2)(e).
11 See the website of Innovate UK which, at the date at which this volume states the law, can be found at www.innovateuk.gov.uk. The Technology Strategy Board is to close its pension scheme: see the Public Service Pensions Act 2013 s 31, Schs 7, 10: and PERSONAL AND OCCUPATIONAL PENSIONS vol 80 (2013) PARAS 320–322. As to non-departmental public bodies see CONSTITUTIONAL AND ADMINISTRATIVE LAW vol 20 (2014) PARA 311 et seq.

972.   The Arts and Humanities Research Council. The Arts and Humanities Research Council is a body established by royal charter wholly or mainly for objects consisting of, or comprised in, the following:
(1)   carrying out, facilitating, encouraging and supporting research in the arts and humanities, and instruction in the arts and humanities[1];
(2)   advancing and disseminating knowledge in, and promoting understanding of, the arts and humanities[2];
(3)   promoting awareness of its activities[3]; and
(4)   providing advice on matters relating to its activities[4].

The activities of the council are not restricted to the United Kingdom or any part of the United Kingdom[5].

The council must give the Secretary of State[6] such returns, accounts and other information relating to its property and activities as the Secretary of State requires[7]. As soon as possible after the end of each financial year[8], the council must give the Secretary of State a report on the performance of its functions during that year[9]; and the Secretary of State must lay a copy of any such report, including any comments which he has on the report[10], before each House of Parliament[11].

The Secretary of State may pay the council such sums as he determines in respect of the expenses that the council has incurred, or expects to incur, in carrying out its objects[12]. The council must comply with any direction of the Secretary of State as to the use or expenditure of such payments[13]; and must give the Secretary of State programmes and estimates of its expenses[14]. The council must keep proper accounts and other records[15], and must give the Secretary of State a statement of accounts in relation to each financial year[16]. The Secretary of State must transmit each statement of accounts to the Comptroller and Auditor General[17] on or before 30 November following the end of the financial year to which the statement relates[18]; and the Comptroller and Auditor General must examine and certify each such statement of accounts[19], and lay before each House of Parliament a copy of the accounts[20] and a report on the accounts[21].

The Secretary of State or, in relation to Wales, the Welsh Ministers[22] may: (a) carry out or support research in the arts and humanities[23]; (b) disseminate the results of research in the arts and humanities[24]; (c) further the practical application of the results of research in the arts and humanities[25]; (d) establish advisory bodies for the purpose of assisting the Secretary of State or, as the case may be, the Welsh Ministers in matters connected with research in the arts and humanities[26]; and (e) if such a body is established, appoint its members on terms which include the payment of remuneration, allowances or pension benefits to or in respect of them[27].

1 Higher Education Act 2004 s 1(a).
2 Higher Education Act 2004 s 1(b).
3 Higher Education Act 2004 s 1(c).
4 Higher Education Act 2004 s 1(d). All property, rights and liabilities to which the Arts and Humanities Research Board was entitled or subject immediately before 1 April 2005 were transferred to the council on that day: see s 2; Higher Education Act 2004 (Commencement No 3) Order 2005, SI 2005/767, art 2. Nothing in the Higher Education Act 2004 Pt 1 (ss 1–10) affects: (1) any power to amend or revoke the charter of the council (s 9(a)); or (2) the operation of any amendment made to the charter of the council (s 9(b)). Employment by the Arts and Humanities Research Council is included in the kinds of employment to which a scheme under the Superannuation Act 1972 s 1 (see PARA 893) can apply: Higher Education Act 2004 s 5. The Arts and Humanities Research Council is to close its pension scheme: see the Public Service Pensions Act 2013 s 31, Schs 7, 10: and PERSONAL AND OCCUPATIONAL PENSIONS vol 80 (2013) PARAS 320–322.
5 Higher Education Act 2004 s 8. As to the meaning of 'United Kingdom' see PARA 804 note 2.
6 As to the Secretary of State see PARA 802 note 2.
7 Higher Education Act 2004 s 4(1).
8 'Financial year' means a period of 12 months ending with 31 March: Higher Education Act 2004 ss 4(5), 6(6).
9 Higher Education Act 2004 s 4(2).
10 See the Higher Education Act 2004 s 4(4).
11 Higher Education Act 2004 s 4(3). As to the laying of documents before Parliament see STATUTES AND LEGISLATIVE PROCESS vol 96 (2012) PARA 1052.
12 Higher Education Act 2004 s 3(1). This provision applies whether the council has incurred, or expects to incur, the expenses in the United Kingdom or elsewhere: s 3(2).
13 Higher Education Act 2004 s 3(3).
14 Higher Education Act 2004 s 3(4). The programmes and estimates must be given in the form required by the Secretary of State (s 3(5)(a)), and at the times required by the Secretary of State (s 3(5)(b)).
15 Higher Education Act 2004 s 6(1).
16 Higher Education Act 2004 s 6(2). A statement of accounts must be given in the form required by the Secretary of State (s 6(3)(a)), and at the time required by the Secretary of State (s 6(3)(b)).
17 As to the Comptroller and Auditor General see CONSTITUTIONAL AND ADMINISTRATIVE LAW vol 20 (2014) PARAS 494–496.
18 Higher Education Act 2004 s 6(4).
19 Higher Education Act 2004 s 6(5)(a).
20 Higher Education Act 2004 s 6(5)(b)(i).
21 Higher Education Act 2004 s 6(5)(b)(ii).
22 The functions under the Higher Education Act 2004 s 10 were originally vested in the National Assembly for Wales and are now exercisable by the Welsh Ministers by virtue of the Government of Wales Act 2006 s 162(1), Sch 11 paras 30, 32. As to the Welsh Ministers see PARA 802. As to the meaning of 'Wales' see PARA 802 note 4.
23 Higher Education Act 2004 s 10(1)(a), (2)(a).
24 Higher Education Act 2004 s 10(1)(b), (2)(b).
25 Higher Education Act 2004 s 10(1)(c), (2)(c).

26 Higher Education Act 2004 s 10(1)(d), (2)(d).

27 See the Higher Education Act 2004 s 10(1)(e), (2)(e). Similar powers are given to the Scottish Ministers, in relation to Scotland, and the Northern Ireland Department having responsibility for higher education, in relation to Northern Ireland: see s 10(3), (4). See note 4. As to the Scottish Ministers, and devolved government in Northern Ireland, see CONSTITUTIONAL AND ADMINISTRATIVE LAW vol 20 (2014) PARAS 67, 83 et seq.

(15) THE NATIONAL TRUST

(i) Constitution of the National Trust

973. Unique position and incorporation of the National Trust. Many open spaces and recreation grounds have been provided by individuals[1] and by philanthropic bodies[2], and gifts for their provision constitute gifts for charitable purposes[3] provided they are capable of benefiting the whole community or a sufficiently large section of it[4]. However, few, if any, private persons have received statutory powers in respect of such matters, and the National Trust for Places of Historic Interest or Natural Beauty (commonly known as the National Trust)[5], is the only philanthropic body which, in recent years, has received statutory powers for such purposes exercisable beyond some particular district.

The trust was reincorporated in 1907 by private Act of Parliament[6] as a body corporate with perpetual succession and a common seal and with power to purchase, take, hold, deal with and dispose of land and other property[7]. The management of the affairs of the trust is currently governed by the National Trust Act 1971[8] but a scheme altering or affecting the management of the trust's affairs has been made to have effect from the appointed day[9].

1 Eg the museum and pleasure grounds (called the Larmer Grounds) provided by General Pitt Rivers at Rushmore on the borders of Dorset and Wiltshire. As to the terms of the trust relating to these grounds see *Re Pitt Rivers, Scott v Pitt Rivers* [1902] 1 Ch 403, CA.

2 Eg the Open Spaces Society (formerly the Commons, Open Spaces and Footpaths Preservation Society) and the Metropolitan Public Gardens Association.

3 See *Re Hadden, Public Trustee v More* [1932] 1 Ch 133; *IRC v City of London Corpn* [1953] 1 All ER 1075, [1953] 1 WLR 652, HL; *Re Morgan, Cecil-Williams v A-G* [1955] 2 All ER 632, [1955] 1 WLR 738; *Brisbane City Council and Myer Shopping Centres Pty Ltd v A-G for Queensland* [1979] AC 411, [1978] 3 All ER 30, PC; and CHARITIES vol 8 (2015) PARA 48. See also the Recreational Charities Act 1958; and CHARITIES vol 8 (2015) PARAS 52–55.

4 See *IRC v Baddeley* [1955] AC 572, [1955] 1 All ER 525, HL.

5 See the National Trust Act 1907 ss 1, 2; the National Trust Act 1937 ss 1, 2; the National Trust Act 1939 ss 1, 2; the National Trust Act 1953 ss 1, 2; and the National Trust Act 1971 ss 1, 3(1).

6 See the National Trust Act 1907 preamble, s 3. The National Trust Act 1907 has been subsequently amended and added to by the following Acts, all of which may be cited together as the National Trust Acts 1907 to 1971: the National Trust Charity Scheme Confirmation Act 1919, the National Trust Act 1937, the National Trust Act 1939, the National Trust Act 1953, and the National Trust Act 1971: see s 1(2). These Acts originally applied to the whole of the United Kingdom and the Isle of Man except that the National Trust Act 1937, the National Trust Act 1939 and the National Trust Act 1971 do not extend to Northern Ireland: see the National Trust Act 1939 s 16(2); National Trust Act 1971 s 33. The National Trust Act 1907, the National Trust Act 1937 and the National Trust Act 1939 are now repealed in relation to the Isle of Man: see the Statute Law (Repeals) Act 2004. As to the meaning of 'United Kingdom' see PARA 804 note 2.

7 See the National Trust Act 1907 s 3. Note that the reference to mortmain in s 3 is obsolete following the repeal of the law of mortmain by the Charities Act 1960 s 38: see CHARITIES vol 8 (2015) PARAS 83–84.

An association not for profit was registered in 1894 under the Companies Acts 1862 to 1890 (see COMPANIES vol 14 (2009) PARAS 10–11), having the same name and similar objects to those of the present trust. The property, rights and liabilities of this association were vested in the trust and its memorandum and articles made void but without prejudice to existing rights and liabilities:

see the National Trust Act 1907, preamble, ss 6–13 (s 10 repealed), 37. Provision was made for a copy of the National Trust Act 1907 to be delivered to the Registrar of Joint Stock Companies (see s 38 (repealed)) and for the costs of the passing of the Act to be paid by the National Trust (see s 39 (repealed)). Provision was made for the costs, charges and expenses of and incidental to the preparation of, the applying for and the obtaining and passing of the National Trust Acts or otherwise in relation to them to be paid by the National Trust, to be defrayed in whole or in part out of income: see the National Trust Act 1937 s 16 (repealed); the National Trust Act 1939 s 17 (repealed); the National Trust Act 1953 s 5 (repealed); and the National Trust Act 1971 s 34 (repealed).

8   See PARA 975.

9   From the appointed day until the new constitution date the National Trust must be administered in accordance with the provisions of the National Trust Acts 1907 to 1971 as modified by the transitional provisions set out in the scheme altering or affecting the trusts of the charity known as the National Trust for Places of Historic Interest or Natural Beauty under the Charities (National Trust) Order 2005, SI 2005/712, Appendix (the 'scheme'): see Appendix clause 2(1). As to the transitional provisions see the Schedule Pt 1. From the new constitution date the trust must be administered in accordance with the provisions of the National Trust Acts 1907 to 1971 as modified by the scheme: Appendix clause 2(2). The commissioners may decide any question put to them concerning the interpretation of the scheme, or the propriety or validity of anything done or intended to be done under it: Appendix clause 46. 'Appointed day' means the day on which the scheme is given effect by an order of the Secretary of State under the Charities Act 2011 s 73 (see CHARITIES vol 8 (2015) PARA 193); and 'new constitution date' means the later of 1 September 2005 and the date two months after that on which the scheme is given effect by such an order: see the Charities (National Trust) Order 2005, SI 2005/712, Appendix clause 1(1); and the Interpretation Act 1978 s 17(2)(a). At the date at which this volume states the law no such order had been made. As to the Secretary of State see PARA 802 note 2. As to the meaning of 'month' see PARA 803 note 12. 'Commissioners' means the Charity Commission for England and Wales: Charities (National Trust) Order 2005, SI 2005/712, Appendix clause 1(1) (definition amended by virtue of the Charities Act 2006 s 6(5)). As to the Charity Commission see CHARITIES vol 8 (2015) PARA 543 et seq.

974. Members of the National Trust. The members of the National Trust[1] are divided into the following classes: (1) ordinary subscribing members, being annual subscribers of such minimum annual subscription as from time to time may be determined by the Council of the National Trust[2]; (2) life members, being persons who have made a subscription of not less than such minimum amount as at the time when the subscription was made had been determined by resolution of the council[3]; (3) benefactors, being persons who have given to the trust such sum of money or other property as, in the council's opinion, is such as to entitle such persons to be distinguished as benefactors[4]; (4) corporate members, being such corporate or other bodies or associations as the council from time to time may by resolution determine who make annual subscriptions of such minimum amount as the council from time to time may by resolution determine[5]; (5) junior members, being annual subscribers of such minimum annual subscription and of such an age as the council from time to time may by resolution determine[6]; (6) family members, being persons who are members of the family of an ordinary subscribing member residing with that member and who make an annual subscription of such minimum amount as the council from time to time may by resolution determine[7]; and (7) such other classes as the council from time to time may by resolution determine[8].

No member is to be liable for, or to contribute towards, the payment of the debts and liabilities of the trust beyond the amount of his annual subscription or of any contribution agreed to be given and remaining unpaid[9]. No dividend, bonus or other profit may at any time be paid out of the income or property of the trust to any member[10].

As from a day to be appointed the powers and duties conferred on the council by the above provisions become powers and duties of the Board of Trustees[11].

1   As to the National Trust see PARA 973.

2 National Trust Act 1971 s 4(1)(a), (2). The minimum annual subscription is to be determined by resolution in accordance with the National Trust Act 1953 s 3: see the National Trust Act 1971 s 4(2). The council may by resolution from time to time determine the minimum amount of the annual subscription required for qualification as an ordinary subscribing member of the National Trust: see the National Trust Act 1953 s 3(1). As to the Council of the National Trust see PARA 975. As to the proceedings of the council see PARA 979.
3 National Trust Act 1971 s 4(1)(b), (3).
4 National Trust Act 1971 s 4(1)(c), (4).
5 National Trust Act 1971 s 4(1)(d), (5). Different minimum annual subscriptions may be determined for different classes of corporate members: see s 4(5).
6 National Trust Act 1971 s 4(1)(e), (6).
7 National Trust Act 1971 s 4(1)(f), (7).
8 National Trust Act 1971 s 4(1)(g).
9 National Trust Act 1907 s 16.
10 National Trust Act 1907 s 5. Notwithstanding this provision any member, not being a member of the council, may be permitted to occupy any trust property either at the best rent that could reasonably be obtained or, in the case of any property not acquired as an investment (under the National Trust Act 1937 s 4(a): see PARA 985), at a less rent or gratuitously and on such other terms and conditions as the council thinks fit to approve: National Trust Act 1971 s 26. However, a member of the executive committee, a regional committee, a local or other committee or a sub-committee of the council who resides in or occupies any of the trust property must declare the nature of his interest at any meeting of that committee at which any question in relation to that property is considered, and he may not take part in the consideration or discussion of, or vote on, the question: s 26 proviso. As from a day to be appointed s 26 is amended by the repeal of the words 'not being a member of council' and the repeal of s 26 proviso: see s 26 (prospectively amended by SI 2005/712). At the date at which this volume states the law no such day had been appointed. 'Trust property' includes all property from time to time vested for a legal estate in the National Trust: National Trust Act 1937 s 2; National Trust Act 1971 s 3(1).
11 See PARA 980.

975. The Council of the National Trust. Until a day to be appointed the following provisions have effect[1].

The affairs of the National Trust[2] are administered by a council[3] called the 'Council of the National Trust' consisting of 52 persons of whom 26 are elected members and 26 are appointed members[4]. The council is deemed fully constituted and all its acts and proceedings are deemed valid if and so long as 26 members have been elected to the council[5]. The council must elect from its number a chairman and a deputy chairman of the National Trust[6].

As from a day to be appointed the following provisions have effect[7].

As from the new constitution date[8] all powers and duties conferred on the council by any provision of the National Trust Acts 1907 to 1971 for the time being in force become powers and duties of the Board of Trustees[9].

The Council is to continue to have 52 members[10] and must meet at least once a year[11]. All members of the council hold office for three years from the date of their appointment or election, as the case may be[12]; and a member of the council may resign at any time by giving notice in writing[13] to the chairman[14]. The members of the council must appoint from their number a chairman (to be known as the 'chairman of the National Trust')[15], a deputy chairman (to be known as the 'deputy chairman of the National Trust')[16], and a person (the 'senior member of the council'), who must not be a member of the Board of Trustees, to exercise the functions conferred on him or her[17]. Provision is made for the payment of expenses and remuneration to the chairman, deputy chairman and members of the council[18].

1 As from a day to be appointed the National Trust Act 1971 ss 6–10, 16–19, Sch 1 are repealed by the Charities (National Trust) Order 2005, SI 2005/712, art 2, Appendix clause 2(3), Schedule Pt 2. At the date at which this volume states the law no such day had been appointed.
2 As to the National Trust see PARA 973.

3   In the National Trust Acts 1907 to 1971, the 'council' means the Council of the National Trust: National Trust Act 1907 s 2; National Trust Act 1937 s 2; National Trust Act 1939 s 2; National Trust Act 1953 s 2; National Trust Act 1971 s 3(1). As to the National Trust Acts 1907 to 1971 see PARA 973 note 6.

4   National Trust Act 1971 s 6(1). 'Elected member' means a member of the council elected pursuant to s 7; and 'appointed member' means a member of the council appointed pursuant to s 8: s 3(1) (definitions prospectively repealed by SI 2005/712). As to elected members see the National Trust Act 1971 s 7 (amended by the Statute Law (Repeals) Act 2004). As to appointed members see the National Trust Act 1971 s 8, Sch 1 (s 8 amended by the Statute Law (Repeals) Act 2004). No person is capable of being a member of the council if at the time of appointment he has attained the age of 75 (see the National Trust Act 1971 s 16(1), (4)(b)), and a member of the council must vacate his office at the conclusion of the annual general meeting next after he attains that age (see s 16(2)). If a member of the council, throughout a period of 12 consecutive months, fails to attend any meeting, then, unless the failure was due to some reason approved by resolution of the council, he ceases to be a member of the council: s 17(1). As to the meaning of 'month' see PARA 803 note 12. Members of the council may have their expenses incurred as members defrayed by the trust: see the National Trust Act 1971 s 19.

5   National Trust Act 1971 s 6(2). As to the filling of casual vacancies see s 10(1), (2).

6   National Trust Act 1971 s 9(1). The council may elect a person who is not a member of the council to be chairman and so long as that person holds office the membership of the council is increased to 53: s 9(1) proviso. A chairman or deputy chairman holds office for three years and must then retire but is eligible for re-election: s 9(2). The age limit for a chairman or deputy chairman is 70: see s 16(1), (4)(a). He must vacate his office at the conclusion of the annual general meeting commencing next after he attains that age: s 16(2). If the chairman or deputy chairman dies or resigns or becomes disqualified the council must appoint another person in his place: see s 10(3). As to the remuneration of the chairman see s 18(1).

7   As to the provisions in respect of the coming into force of the scheme altering or affecting the trusts of the National Trust under the Charities (National Trust) Order 2005, SI 2005/712, see PARA 973 note 9.

8   As to the meaning of 'new constitution date' see PARA 973 note 9.

9   Charities (National Trust) Order 2005, SI 2005/712, Appendix clause 2(4). As to the Board of Trustees see PARA 976.

10 See the Charities (National Trust) Order 2005, SI 2005/712, Appendix clause 14(1). 26 such members are to be persons elected by members of the trust ('elected members') (see Appendix clauses 1(1), 14(1)(a)) and 26 are to be appointed ('appointed members') (see Appendix clauses 1(1), 14(1)(b)). As to the election of members of the council see Appendix clause 16; and as to the appointment of members see Appendix clauses 17, 18, Sch Pts 3, 4 (Sch Pt 3 amended by SI 2013/755). 'Appointed member', in relation to the council, means a person appointed under the Charities (National Trust) Order 2005, SI 2005/712, Appendix clause 17; and 'elected member', in relation to the council, means a person elected under Appendix clause 16: Appendix clause 1(1). As to eligibility to serve as a member of council see Appendix clause 25. As to the filling of casual vacancies on the council see Appendix clause 21.

11 Charities (National Trust) Order 2005, SI 2005/712, Appendix clause 14(2). As to the functions of the council see PARA 979.

12 Charities (National Trust) Order 2005, SI 2005/712, Appendix clause 19(1). A person who has held office as an appointed member or as an elected member is eligible for appointment or re-appointment, or for election or re-election, as the case may be, to the council: Appendix clause 19(2).

13 As to the meaning of 'writing' see PARA 805 note 14.

14 Charities (National Trust) Order 2005, SI 2005/712, Appendix clause 20.

15 See the Charities (National Trust) Order 2005, SI 2005/712, Appendix clause 22(1)(a), (2), (3).

16 Charities (National Trust) Order 2005, SI 2005/712, Appendix clause 22(1)(b). The deputy chairman may exercise all the functions of the chairman at any meeting when the chairman is not present: Appendix clause 22(5).

17 Charities (National Trust) Order 2005, SI 2005/712, Appendix clause 22(1)(c). The functions referred to are those conferred by the scheme: see Appendix clause 22(1)(c). The chairman, deputy chairman and senior member of the council hold office for three years and must then retire from office, but are eligible for re-appointment: Appendix clause 22(4). A person who before being appointed as chairman or deputy chairman is not a member of the Board of Trustees becomes a member of the board upon appointment and remains a member for as long as he or she remains chairman or deputy chairman: Appendix clause 22(6). The council may by resolution remove the chairman, the deputy chairman or the senior member: Appendix clause 23. No person is eligible for appointment or election (as the case may be) as chairman or deputy chairman, or as a member

of the council, unless that person is a member of the trust: Appendix clause 26. As to when the senior member of the council must chair any part of any meeting of the council see Appendix clause 22(7)(c). As to the filling of casual vacancies in the office of chairman, deputy chairman or senior member of the council see Appendix clause 24. As to membership of the trust see PARA 974.

18 See the Charities (National Trust) Order 2005, SI 2005/712, Appendix clause 30.

976. Board of Trustees of the National Trust. As from a day to be appointed the following provisions have effect[1].

The Board of Trustees has a minimum of nine and a maximum of 15 members, unless a resolution is passed by the Council of the National Trust[2] and by the Board of Trustees to change the minimum or maximum numbers, or both numbers[3], and the commissioners[4] give their approval in writing[5] to such a change[6]. A majority of the members of the Board of Trustees must be members of the council[7]. All members of the Board of Trustees other than the chairman and the deputy chairman of the National Trust are appointed by the council in accordance with published procedures decided by the council[8]. Every member of the Board of Trustees is appointed for three years, and retiring members are eligible for re-appointment[9]. The chairman and deputy chairman of the National Trust act as chairman and deputy chairman of the Board of Trustees[10]. No person is eligible for appointment as a member of the Board of Trustees unless that person is a member of the National Trust[11]. Provision is made for the payment of expenses and remuneration to the members of the Board of Trustees[12].

1   As to the provisions in respect of the coming into force of the scheme altering or affecting the trusts of the National Trust under the Charities (National Trust) Order 2005, SI 2005/712, see PARA 973 note 9.
2   As to the Council of the National Trust see PARA 975. As to the National Trust see PARA 973.
3   Charities (National Trust) Order 2005, SI 2005/712, Appendix clause 3(4)(a).
4   As to the meaning of 'commissioners' see PARA 803 note 12.
5   As to the meaning of 'writing' see PARA 805 note 14.
6   Charities (National Trust) Order 2005, SI 2005/712, Appendix clause 3(4)(b).
7   Charities (National Trust) Order 2005, SI 2005/712, Appendix clause 3(5). The chairman and deputy chairman of the National Trust are automatically members of the Board of Trustees: Appendix clause 3(6). As to the chairman and deputy chairman of the trust see PARA 975.
8   Charities (National Trust) Order 2005, SI 2005/712, Appendix clause 3(7). As to the induction of new members of the board see Appendix clause 4. A record of new members of the Board of Trustees must be kept: see Appendix clause 5. As to the termination of membership of the board see Appendix clause 6. As to the filling of casual vacancies on the board see Appendix clause 7.
9   Charities (National Trust) Order 2005, SI 2005/712, Appendix clause 3(8). The council must exercise its powers with the object of ensuring that, so far as is practicable, the terms of office of approximately one third of the members of the Board of Trustees expire every year: Appendix clause 3(9). The Council may, exceptionally, appoint a member of the Board of Trustees for a term of less than three years where this is necessary to achieve the object referred to in clause 3(9): Appendix clause 3(10).
10 Charities (National Trust) Order 2005, SI 2005/712, Appendix clause 8.
11 See the Charities (National Trust) Order 2005, SI 2005/712, Appendix clause 26. As to membership of the trust see PARA 974.
12 See the Charities (National Trust) Order 2005, SI 2005/712, Appendix clause 30.

(ii) Purposes, Powers and Proceedings of the National Trust

977. General purposes of the National Trust. The National Trust[1] was established for the purposes of promoting the permanent preservation for the benefit of the nation of land and tenements, including buildings, of beauty or historic interest and, as regards land, for the preservation (so far as practicable) of its natural aspect, features and animal and plant life[2]. These purposes have since been extended so as to include the promotion of:

(1)   the preservation of buildings of national interest or architectural, historic or artistic interest and places of natural interest or beauty and the protection and augmentation of the amenities of such buildings, places and their surroundings[3];

(2)   the preservation of furniture and pictures and chattels of any description having national or historic or artistic interest[4]; and

(3)   the access to and enjoyment of such buildings, places and chattels by the public[5].

The purposes of the trust have been held to be charitable[6].

1   As to the National Trust see PARA 973.
2   National Trust Act 1907 s 4(1). As to the general powers of the National Trust over its property see s 4(2); and PARA 978.
3   National Trust Act 1937 s 3(a).
4   National Trust Act 1937 s 3(b).
5   National Trust Act 1937 s 3(c).
6   See *Re Verrall, National Trust for Places of Historic Interest or Natural Beauty v A-G* [1916] 1 Ch 100; and CHARITIES vol 8 (2015) PARA 36.

978.   General powers of the National Trust. The National Trust[1] may maintain and manage, either alone or jointly with other bodies or persons[2], open spaces or places of public resort and buildings for public recreation, resort or instruction, for the convenience of persons using them or resorting to them, and may, for the comfort and convenience of persons using or resorting to them, improve any property which belongs to it, or in which it has any interest, and may exercise full powers of ownership over such property[3].

For the carrying into effect of its objects the trust may act in concert with and make arrangements and agreements with any local authority, or any residents or committee of residents in the neighbourhood of any property of the trust or with any other persons[4]. The trust may purchase any land or buildings or investments of the nature which it is authorised to hold[5] for the purpose of providing by the resulting rents and profits or income a fund for the maintenance of any other specific property or for its general purposes[6].

1   As to the National Trust see PARA 973.
2   See the National Trust Act 1907 s 31; and the text to note 4. As to the meaning of 'person' see PARA 803 note 17.
3   See National Trust Act 1907 s 4(2). The National Trust may be liable for failure to take reasonable care to prevent unnecessary danger to users of its property: see *Quinn v Scott* [1965] 2 All ER 588, [1965] 1 WLR 1004. See also the National Trust Act 1971 s 24(1); and PARA 982. As to the extension of the power of the National Trust to act as trustee see the National Trust Act 1939 s 13; and PARA 987.
4   National Trust Act 1907 s 31. As to the power of local authorities to contribute to the expenses of the trust see the National Trust Act 1937 s 7(2); and PARA 993.
5   Ie by the National Trust Act 1953 s 4 (see PARA 990): National Trust Act 1937 s 4(b) (amended by the National Trust Act 1953 s 4(4)).
6   See the National Trust Act 1937 s 4(a), (b) (as amended: see note 5).

979.   Powers and proceedings of the Council of the National Trust. Until a day to be appointed the following provisions have effect[1].

The entire business of the National Trust[2] must be arranged and managed by its council[3]. The council may exercise all the powers of the trust except those which are exercisable only by a general meeting[4]. The council may appoint from its own number any committee for any special purpose and may add to any such committee for such length of time and with such powers of voting or otherwise as the council may think fit any member or other person whose aid it judges useful to forward the objects of the trust[5].

There is an executive committee of the trust consisting of the chairman of each of the regional committees and other persons appointed by the council[6]. The executive committee may exercise all the powers conferred on the council except in regard to certain specified matters[7] and any other power which the council expressly withholds[8]. The executive committee may appoint sub-committees for special purposes[9], and may make regulations as to its own procedure[10]. With the approval of the council the executive committee may delegate to regional committees such powers and duties as it thinks fit, and a regional committee may appoint local committees for special purposes[11].

The council must meet at least four times a year[12] and may make regulations as to its own procedure[13], appoint officers and servants[14], and exercise the powers of borrowing on mortgage conferred on the trust[15]. Vacancies in the council or committees, and defects in the qualification or election of members, do not invalidate acts or proceedings of the council, executive committee or any regional, local or other committee or sub-committee[16]. Any instrument which if made by a private person would be required to be under seal must be under the seal of the trust[17].

As from a day to be appointed the following provisions have effect[18].

As from the new constitution date[19] all powers and duties conferred on the council by any provision of the National Trust Acts 1907 to 1971 for the time being in force become powers and duties of the Board of Trustees[20].

The council must appoint the members of the Board of Trustees and hold them to account[21]. The council's responsibilities include:

(1)   monitoring the fulfilment by the National Trust of its statutory purposes[22];
(2)   appointing the chairman and deputy chairman of the trust[23];
(3)   appointing and, if necessary, removing members of the Board of Trustees in accordance with the 2005 scheme[24];
(4)   monitoring the performance of, and calling to account, the Board of Trustees in its control and management of the administration of the trust[25];
(5)   arranging the procedures for election of members of the council[26];
(6)   reviewing every six years the list of appointing bodies[27];
(7)   making available annually to the members of the trust a report on the activities of the council[28];
(8)   commenting on proposals from the Board of Trustees for the alteration of the National Trust Acts 1907 to 1971 or byelaws or of the 2005 scheme or any other scheme of the Charity Commission relating to the trust[29].

The council must whenever the involvement of a nominations committee is provided for[30] in relation to the election of members to it[31], and whenever the council is to make an appointment to the Board of Trustees or is to appoint the chairman or deputy chairman of the trust[32], appoint a nominations committee to assist the council (and, in the case of elections to the council, the members of the trust)[33]. The council by resolution[34] may establish a committee of inquiry to investigate any aspect of the affairs of the trust[35]. The committee of inquiry must report back to the council and the council must then decide what action, if any, to take[36].

The Board of Trustees may from time to time make regulations for the conduct of the business of the council and any committee[37]. The acts and proceedings of the council or of any committee are not invalidated by any vacancy in its number or any defect or irregularity its constitution[38].

1   As from a day to be appointed the National Trust Act 1971 ss 11–19, Sch 3 are repealed by the Charities (National Trust) Order 2005, SI 2005/712, art 2, Appendix clause 2(3), Schedule Pt 2. At the date at which this volume states the law no such day had been appointed.
2   As to the National Trust see PARA 973.
3   National Trust Act 1971 s 11(1). No regulation made or resolution passed by the trust in general meeting invalidates any prior act of the council which would have been valid if that regulation or resolution had not been made or passed: s 11(1). As to the Council of the National Trust see PARA 975. As to general meetings see PARA 983.
4   National Trust Act 1971 s 11(1).
5   National Trust Act 1971 s 11(5).
6   See the National Trust Act 1971 s 12(1). A to the membership of the executive committee and tenure of office see further ss 12(1), (2), 16. As to vacation of office due to failure to attend meetings see s 17. Members of committees and sub-committees may have their expenses as members defrayed by the trust: see s 19.
7   As to the matters in respect of which the executive committee is not to exercise powers conferred on the council see the National Trust Act 1971 Sch 3 paras 1–13.
8   National Trust Act 1971 s 12(4). The council may impose such conditions and limitations as it thinks fit as to the exercise of any powers conferred on the committee under these provisions: s 12(4) proviso. The chairman and deputy chairman of the trust are ex officio chairman and deputy chairman of the executive committee unless the council otherwise determines, in which case the committee must elect its own chairman and deputy chairman from its own members: s 12(3). As to the remuneration of the chairman of the executive committee see s 18(1). As to the chairman and deputy chairman of the trust see PARA 975.
9   See the National Trust Act 1971 s 12(5). This power is similar in all respects to the power conferred on the council by s 11(5) (see the text to note 5): s 12(5). As to the remuneration of the chairman of a sub-committee see s 18(2), (3).
10 See the National Trust Act 1971 s 12(6). However, no regulations may contravene the provisions of the Act: s 12(6) proviso.
11 See the National Trust Act 1971 s 13. As to the remuneration of the chairman of a regional committee see s 18(1).
12 National Trust Act 1971 s 11(6). As to the keeping of minutes of any meeting of the council or committees and of the general meetings of the trust, and the keeping of a register of members see s 14(3), (4).
13 See the National Trust Act 1971 s 11(2). However, the regulations must not contravene the provisions of the National Trust Acts 1907 to 1971: National Trust Act 1971 s 11(2) proviso. As to the National Trust Acts 1907 to 1971 see PARA 973 note 6.
14 See the National Trust Act 1971 s 11(3).
15 See the National Trust Act 1971 s 11(4). As to such powers see PARA 991.
16 See the National Trust Act 1971 s 14(1), (2).
17 National Trust Act 1971 s 15(1). Subject to this, any notice, consent, approval or other document issued by or on behalf of the trust is deemed to be duly executed if signed by the chairman, deputy chairman or secretary; but any appointment, contract, order or other document made by or proceeding from the trust is deemed to be duly executed either if sealed with the seal of the trust or signed by two or more members of the council authorised to sign by a resolution of the council or the executive committee but it is not necessary in any legal proceedings to prove that the members signing any such contract, order or other document were authorised to sign and such authority is to be presumed until the contrary is proved: s 15(2). As to documents required to be under seal see DEEDS AND OTHER INSTRUMENTS vol 32 (2012) PARA 232.
18 As to the provisions in respect of the coming into force of the scheme altering or affecting the trusts of the National Trust under the Charities (National Trust) Order 2005, SI 2005/712, see PARA 973 note 9.
19 As to the meaning of 'new constitution date' see PARA 973 note 9.
20 Charities (National Trust) Order 2005, SI 2005/712, Appendix clause 2(4). As to the Board of Trustees see PARA 976. As to the powers of the board see PARA 980.
21 Charities (National Trust) Order 2005, SI 2005/712, Appendix clause 15(1).
22 Charities (National Trust) Order 2005, SI 2005/712, Appendix clause 15(2)(a).
23 Charities (National Trust) Order 2005, SI 2005/712, Appendix clause 15(2)(b).
24 Charities (National Trust) Order 2005, SI 2005/712, Appendix clause 15(2)(c). The 2005 scheme is the scheme altering or affecting the trusts of the National Trust under the Charities (National Trust) Order 2005, SI 2005/712 (see PARA 973).

25 Charities (National Trust) Order 2005, SI 2005/712, Appendix clause 15(2)(d).
26 Charities (National Trust) Order 2005, SI 2005/712, Appendix clause 15(2)(e). As to the election of members of the council see PARA 975.
27 Charities (National Trust) Order 2005, SI 2005/712, Appendix clause 15(2)(f). As to the appointing bodies see PARA 975.
28 Charities (National Trust) Order 2005, SI 2005/712, Appendix clause 15(2)(g). As to membership of the trust see PARA 974.
29 Charities (National Trust) Order 2005, SI 2005/712, Appendix clause 15(2)(h). As to byelaws see PARA 982. As to the power of the Charity Commission to make schemes see the Charities Act 2011 s 73; and CHARITIES vol 8 (2015) PARA 193.
30 Ie under the Charities (National Trust) Order 2005, SI 2005/712, Appendix clauses 16 or 18 (see PARA 975).
31 Charities (National Trust) Order 2005, SI 2005/712, Appendix clause 27(1)(a).
32 Charities (National Trust) Order 2005, SI 2005/712, Appendix clause 27(1)(b).
33 Charities (National Trust) Order 2005, SI 2005/712, Appendix clause 27(1). The size and criteria for membership of each nominations committee must be determined by resolution of the council provided that at least one member of each nominations committee must be a person who is external to the trust: Appendix clause 27(2). A person is external to the trust if that person: (1) is not a member of the Board of Trustees, the council, any country or regional committee, or any advisory panel; (2) has not been a member of any such body within the previous three years; (3) is not, and has not been within the previous three years, an employee of the trust; and (4) is not the spouse, parent or child of a person falling within any of heads (1), (2) or (3) above: Appendix clause 1(2). For these purposes (a) 'child' includes a stepchild and an illegitimate child; (b) a person living with another as that person's husband, wife or long term partner is treated as that person's spouse; and (c) the fact that a person is a member of the trust does not preclude that person from being external to the trust: Appendix clause 1(3). As to country and regional committees and advisory panels see PARA 981.
34 A resolution to establish a committee of inquiry is not valid unless supported by at least two-thirds of the members of the council present at the meeting at which the resolution is considered: Charities (National Trust) Order 2005, SI 2005/712, Appendix clause 28(5).
35 Charities (National Trust) Order 2005, SI 2005/712, Appendix clause 28(1). The composition, procedures and terms of reference of a committee of inquiry so established must be specified in the resolution by which the committee is established: Appendix clause 28(2). A committee of inquiry has all necessary powers of calling for documents, assistance and evidence from the Board of Trustees and from the staff of the trust: Appendix clause 28(3).
36 Charities (National Trust) Order 2005, SI 2005/712, Appendix clause 28(4).
37 See the Charities (National Trust) Order 2005, SI 2005/712, Appendix clause 43; and PARA 984.
38 See the Charities (National Trust) Order 2005, SI 2005/712, Appendix clause 29; and PARA 984.

980. Powers of Board of Trustees of the National Trust. As from a day to be appointed the following provisions have effect[1].

As from the new constitution date[2] all powers and duties conferred on the Council of the National Trust[3] by any provision of the National Trust Acts 1907 to 1971[4] for the time being in force become powers and duties of the Board of Trustees[5].

The members of the Board of Trustees are the trustees of the National Trust[6]. The Board of Trustees must exercise all powers conferred on the trust by the National Trust Acts 1907 to 1971 and the 2005 scheme[7], except those, which in accordance with any provision of the scheme, are exercisable only by the trust in general meetings[8] or are exercisable only by the council[9].

Except as otherwise provided[10], the members of the Board of Trustees must exercise their powers jointly, at meetings convened in accordance with the 2005 scheme[11].

The Board of Trustees may from time to time amend the 2005 scheme if it is satisfied that it is expedient in the interests of the National Trust to do so[12], but must consult the council before making any such amendment[13]. The Board of Trustees must not make any amendment which would have the effect directly or indirectly of:

(1) altering or extending the purposes of the trust[14];

(2)   authorising the Board of Trustees to do anything which is expressly
         prohibited by the trusts of the trust[15];

(3)   causing the trust to cease to be a charity at law[16]; or

(4)   altering or extending this power of amendment[17].

The Board of Trustees must obtain the prior written[18] approval of the
commissioners[19] before making any amendment which would have the effect
directly or indirectly of:

(a)   enabling them to spend permanent endowment or capitalise income of
         the trust[20];

(b)   conferring a benefit of any kind on all or any of the current members of
         the Board of Trustees or their successors[21];

(c)   restricting (without the consent of that person[22]) the existing right of any
         person to appoint or remove a member of the Board of Trustees, or to
         intervene in the administration of the trust[23];

(d)   changing provisions in the 2005 scheme as to the size of the council or
         the minimum or maximum size of the Board of Trustees, or changing the
         method by which members of those bodies are elected or appointed[24]; or

(e)   varying the name of the trust[25].

An amendment may be made only by a resolution passed at a meeting of the
Board of Trustees of which not less than 21 days' notice has been given[26]. The
Board of Trustees must: (i) prepare a written memorandum of each amendment
that it makes, which must be signed at the meeting at which the amendment is
made by the person chairing the meeting[27]; (ii) send to the commissioners a copy
of the memorandum certified by a person authorised by the board to do so within
three months[28] of the date of the meeting[29]; and (iii) retain the memorandum as
part of the governing documents[30].

The Board of Trustees may appoint employees of the trust and fix their
remuneration and conditions of employment[31], and may delegate any of its
functions to any such employee[32]. Employees must report to the Board of Trustees
in accordance with any instructions given by the board[33].

1   As to the provisions in respect of the coming into force of the scheme altering or affecting the trusts
     of the National Trust under the Charities (National Trust) Order 2005, SI 2005/712, see PARA 973
     note 9.
2   As to the meaning of 'new constitution date' see PARA 973 note 9.
3   As to the Council of the National Trust see PARA 975. As to the powers and proceedings of the
     council see PARA 979.
4   As to the National Trust Acts 1907 to 1971 see PARA 973 note 6.
5   Charities (National Trust) Order 2005, SI 2005/712, Appendix clause 2(4). As to the Board of
     Trustees see PARA 976.
6   Charities (National Trust) Order 2005, SI 2005/712, Appendix clause 3(1). As to the National
     Trust see PARA 973.
7   Ie the scheme altering or affecting the trusts of the National Trust under the Charities (National
     Trust) Order 2005, SI 2005/712.
8   Charities (National Trust) Order 2005, SI 2005/712, Appendix clause 3(2)(a). As to general
     meetings see PARA 983.
9   Charities (National Trust) Order 2005, SI 2005/712, Appendix clause 3(2)(b).
10   Ie except as otherwise provided by the Charities (National Trust) Order 2005, SI 2005/712,
     Appendix clauses 10(3), 12(3) (see PARA 981) and 13(2) (see the text to note 32).
11   Charities (National Trust) Order 2005, SI 2005/712, Appendix clause 3(3).
12   Charities (National Trust) Order 2005, SI 2005/712, Appendix clause 45(1).
13   Charities (National Trust) Order 2005, SI 2005/712, Appendix clause 45(2). As to the exercise of
     the duty to consult see JUDICIAL REVIEW vol 61 (2010) PARA 627.
14   Charities (National Trust) Order 2005, SI 2005/712, Appendix clause 45(3)(a).
15   Charities (National Trust) Order 2005, SI 2005/712, Appendix clause 45(3)(b).
16   Charities (National Trust) Order 2005, SI 2005/712, Appendix clause 45(3)(c). As to the holding
     of the purposes of the trust to be charitable see PARA 977.

17 Charities (National Trust) Order 2005, SI 2005/712, Appendix clause 45(3)(d). The power of amendment is that conferred by Appendix clause 45: Appendix clause 45(3)(d).
18 As to the meaning of 'written' see PARA 805 note 14.
19 As to the meaning of 'commissioners' see PARA 973 note 9. As to the power of the commissioners to decide any question put to them concerning the interpretation of the 2005 scheme, or the propriety or validity of anything done or intended to be done under it, see PARA 973 note 9.
20 Charities (National Trust) Order 2005, SI 2005/712, Appendix clause 45(4)(a).
21 Charities (National Trust) Order 2005, SI 2005/712, Appendix clause 45(4)(b).
22 As to the meaning of 'person' see PARA 803 note 17.
23 Charities (National Trust) Order 2005, SI 2005/712, Appendix clause 45(4)(c).
24 Charities (National Trust) Order 2005, SI 2005/712, Appendix clause 45(4)(d).
25 Charities (National Trust) Order 2005, SI 2005/712, Appendix clause 45(4)(e).
26 Charities (National Trust) Order 2005, SI 2005/712, Appendix clause 45(5). The notice must set out the terms of the proposed amendment: Appendix clause 45(5).
27 Charities (National Trust) Order 2005, SI 2005/712, Appendix clause 45(6)(a).
28 As to the meaning of 'month' see PARA 803 note 12.
29 Charities (National Trust) Order 2005, SI 2005/712, Appendix clause 45(6)(b).
30 Charities (National Trust) Order 2005, SI 2005/712, Appendix clause 45(6)(c).
31 Charities (National Trust) Order 2005, SI 2005/712, Appendix clause 13(1).
32 See the Charities (National Trust) Order 2005, SI 2005/712, Appendix clause 13(2).
33 Charities (National Trust) Order 2005, SI 2005/712, Appendix clause 13(3).

981. Proceedings of Board of Trustees of the National Trust. As from a day to be appointed the following provisions have effect[1].

The Board of Trustees[2] must make provision for its meetings[3]. Unless otherwise expressly provided in the 2005 scheme[4], every matter must, in case of difference, be decided by a majority of the members of the Board of Trustees present and voting at a duly convened meeting of the Board of Trustees[5]. However, a decision supported by all members of the Board of Trustees and taken otherwise than at a meeting is as valid as if it had been made at a meeting of the Board of Trustees[6], provided that it is recorded in writing[7] in a single document signed by all members of the Board of Trustees, or else in two or more similar documents which together bear the signatures of all members of the Board of Trustees[8]. The Board of Trustees must keep a proper record of its meetings[9].

The Board of Trustees may from time to time establish and dissolve committees including country and regional committees and advisory panels[10], and may delegate any of its functions to any committee so established[11]. A committee established under these provisions must report to the Board of Trustees in accordance with any instructions given[12] by the Board of Trustees[13] and must keep a proper record of its proceedings[14].

The acts and proceedings of the Board of Trustees or of any committee, sub-committee or advisory panel are not invalidated by any vacancy in its number or any defect or irregularity in its appointment[15].

1 As to the provisions in respect of the coming into force of the scheme altering or affecting the trusts of the National Trust under the Charities (National Trust) Order 2005, SI 2005/712, see PARA 973 note 9.
2 As to the Board of Trustees see PARA 976.
3 See the Charities (National Trust) Order 2005, SI 2005/712, Appendix clause 9(1). Such arrangements are to be made in accordance with Appendix clause 43 (see PARA 984): see Appendix clause 9(1). The quorum for meetings of the Board of Trustees must be half of the members for the time being of the Board of Trustees, rounded up when there is an odd number of members of the Board of Trustees, or six members of the Board of Trustees, whichever is the greater: Appendix clause 9(2).
4 Ie the scheme altering or affecting the trusts of the National Trust under the Charities (National Trust) Order 2005, SI 2005/712 (see PARA 973).
5 Charities (National Trust) Order 2005, SI 2005/712, Appendix clause 10(1). The chairman of the meeting may cast a second or casting vote only if there is a tied vote: Appendix clause 10(2).
6 Charities (National Trust) Order 2005, SI 2005/712, Appendix clause 10(3).
7 As to the meaning of 'writing' see PARA 805 note 14.

8 See the Charities (National Trust) Order 2005, SI 2005/712, Appendix clause 10(4).

9 Charities (National Trust) Order 2005, SI 2005/712, Appendix clause 11.

10 Charities (National Trust) Order 2005, SI 2005/712, Appendix clause 12(1). Except for country and regional committees and advisory panels, a committee established must include at least one person who is a member of the Board of Trustees and may include persons who are not members of the Board of Trustees: Appendix clause 12(2).

11 Charities (National Trust) Order 2005, SI 2005/712, Appendix clause 12(3).

12 Ie under the Charities (National Trust) Order 2005, SI 2005/712, Appendix clause 43 (see PARA 984).

13 Charities (National Trust) Order 2005, SI 2005/712, Appendix clause 12(4).

14 Charities (National Trust) Order 2005, SI 2005/712, Appendix clause 12(5).

15 See the Charities (National Trust) Order 2005, SI 2005/712, Appendix clause 29; and PARA 984.

982. Byelaws for purposes of National Trust property. The National Trust[1] may make byelaws for the regulation and protection of, and for the prevention and suppression of nuisances and the preservation of order upon, and regulation of the conduct and securing the safety of any person[2] resorting to, any land or property held by it for the benefit of the nation[3]. In particular, and without prejudice to the generality of those purposes, the trust may make byelaws for certain specified purposes[4]. As regards buildings open to the public, whether on payment[5] or not, or whether generally or at specified times or for specified periods only, the trust may make byelaws for certain purposes[6] as if it were a library authority[7]. The provisions of the Local Government Act 1972 as to the procedure for making and confirming, and the enforcement and evidence of, byelaws[8] apply to such byelaws made by the trust as if it were a local authority and its secretary were the clerk to that local authority[9]. Copies of byelaws must be exhibited by the trust on its property in such way as the trust thinks best calculated to give information to persons resorting to it[10].

1 As to the National Trust see PARA 973.

2 As to the meaning of 'person' see PARA 803 note 17.

3 National Trust Act 1971 s 24(1). For these purposes, any property in which the trust is entitled to a leasehold interest in possession is deemed to be property of the trust held for the benefit of the nation: s 24(5).

4 National Trust Act 1971 s 24(1). The specified purposes are:

   (1) prohibiting any person without lawful authority from digging, cutting or taking turves, sods, gravel, stone, clay or other substance on or from such lands or property and from cutting, felling or injuring any gorse, heather, timber or other tree, shrub, brushwood or other plant growing there (s 24(1)(a));

   (2) prohibiting or regulating the lighting of fires (s 24(1)(b));

   (3) prohibiting or regulating the firing or discharge of firearms or the throwing or discharge of missiles on such lands or property without lawful authority (s 24(1)(c));

   (4) prohibiting the deposit on such lands or property or in any pond on such lands or property of road-sand, materials for repair of roads or wood or any dung, rubbish or other offensive matter (s 24(1)(d));

   (5) prohibiting the injury, defacement or removal of any building, structure or other thing on such lands or property or of seats, fences, notice boards or other things put up or maintained by the trust (s 24(1)(e));

   (6) prohibiting or regulating the posting or painting of bills, placards, advertisements or notices on trees or fences or notice boards on such lands or property (s 24(1)(f));

   (7) prohibiting any person without lawful authority from bird catching, setting traps or nets or liming trees or laying snares for birds or other animals, taking birds' eggs or nests and shooting, driving or chasing game or other animals on such lands or property (s 24(1)(g));

   (8) prohibiting or regulating the use without lawful authority of vehicles, and the erection without the consent of the trust of any buildings or other structure, and authorising an officer of the trust to remove any vehicle or structure in contravention of the byelaws and prescribing any roads other than public roads on which motor cars and cycles may be used (s 24(1)(h));

(9) prohibiting or regulating the placing on such lands or property of any show, exhibition, swing, roundabout or other like thing and authorising an officer of the trust to remove any thing placed on such lands or property in contravention of the byelaws (s 24(1)(i));

(10) regulating games and recreations and assemblages of persons on such lands or property (s 24(1)(j));

(11) regulating the use of any land or property temporarily closed or set apart for any purpose (s 24(1)(k));

(12) prohibiting or regulating the exercise or breaking in of horses on such lands without lawful authority (s 24(1)(l));

(13) prohibiting any person without lawful authority from turning out or permitting to remain on such lands any cattle, sheep or other animals and authorising an officer of the trust to remove such animals in contravention of the byelaws or suffering from disease (s 24(1)(m));

(14) generally prohibiting any act or thing tending to injure or disfigure such trust lands or property or to interfere with public enjoyment and use of it (s 24(1)(n));

(15) authorising an officer of the trust after due warning to remove or exclude from such lands or property any person who in his view commits an offence against the byelaws (s 24(1)(o));

(16) prohibiting the hindrance or obstruction of an officer of the National Trust in the exercise of his powers or duties under the National Trust Act 1971 or any byelaws made under it (s 24(1)(p));

(17) permitting the public or specified persons to view and make copies or reproductions of or extracts from any chattel vested in the trust on terms prescribed by the Council of the National Trust (s 24(1)(q));

(18) regulating the speed of vehicles on any road on such lands or property other than a road within the meaning of the Road Traffic Act 1960 s 257(1) (see ROAD TRAFFIC vol 89 (2011) PARA 6) (National Trust Act 1971 s 24(1)(r));

(19) prohibiting or regulating sailing, boating, bathing, fishing and other forms of recreation on any waterway forming part of such lands or property (s 24(1)(s)).

'Officer of the trust' includes a voluntary worker as well as a paid officer; and 'waterway' means any lake, river, canal or other waters: see s 24(2). As to the council see PARA 975. As from a day to be appointed the powers and duties conferred on the council by any provision of the National Trust Acts 1907 to 1971 become powers and duties of the Board of Trustees (see PARA 980).

All byelaws made by the trust under the National Trust Act 1907 s 32 (repealed), and in force immediately prior to the passing of the National Trust Act 1971 (ie 17 February 1971), continue to have effect until revoked by the trust: s 24(3). Byelaws made under these provisions do not affect the powers of certain water authorities (see s 24(6)) nor do they empower the trust to make any byelaw prohibiting or interfering with rights of navigation in any tidal waters or in any waterway which is not tidal water (s 24(7)). As to rights of navigation see WATER AND WATERWAYS vol 101 (2009) PARA 688 et seq.

5 As to the power to charge for admission see PARA 985.
6 Ie for the purposes specified in the Public Libraries Act 1901 s 3 (repealed) (see the Public Libraries and Museums Act 1964 s 26(5); and PARA 930): National Trust Act 1907 s 33.
7 National Trust Act 1907 s 33; National Trust Act 1937 s 11(2). The provisions of the Libraries Offences Act 1898 s 2 (see PARA 901) apply to any such building: National Trust Act 1907 s 33. As to the meaning of 'library authority' see PARA 922.
8 Ie the Local Government Act 1972 ss 236–238 (see LOCAL GOVERNMENT vol 69 (2009) PARA 556 et seq): see the National Trust Act 1937 s 12(1) (amended by the National Trust Act 1971 s 24(4)); and the Local Government Act 1972 s 272. The confirming authority for this purpose is the Secretary of State or, in relation to Wales, the Welsh Ministers: see the National Trust Act 1937 s 12(1); the Government of Wales Act 2006 Sch 11 para 30; and the National Assembly for Wales (Transfer of Functions) Order 1999, SI 1999/672, art 2, Sch 1. As to the Secretary of State and the transfer of functions to the Welsh Ministers see PARA 802.
9 National Trust Act 1937 s 12(1).
10 National Trust Act 1907 s 34.

983. General meetings of the National Trust. Until a day to be appointed the following provisions have effect[1].

General meetings of the National Trust[2] must be held at least once in every year and must be called and held in accordance with the statutory regulations[3]. Such regulations may be altered or added to by a resolution of the council[4], passed by a majority of not less than two-thirds of the members of the council present[5] and approved at the next annual general meeting[6].

As from a day to be appointed the following provisions have effect[7].

There are two types of general meeting of the trust, annual general meetings[8] and extraordinary general meetings[9]. Notice of every general meeting, and the agenda, must be sent to the members not less than 21 days before the meeting[10]. Provision is made as to the quorum of general meetings[11], the chairman of meetings[12], and the adjournment[13] of and voting[14] at meetings.

At each annual general meeting the Board of Trustees must present to the meeting a report of the activities of the trust in the preceding financial year and the accounts of the trust for that year[15].

The Board of Trustees may convene an extraordinary general meeting whenever it thinks fit[16]. The Board of Trustees must within 28 days of receiving a valid requisition to do so send out a notice to convene an extraordinary general meeting[17]; and if the Board of Trustees does not, within 28 days of receiving a valid requisition, send out a notice to convene an extraordinary general meeting, the requisitionists may convene an extraordinary general meeting[18]. The only business which may be dealt with at an extraordinary general meeting is business of which notice has been given in the notice convening the meeting[19].

Except where otherwise provided[20] any direction or decision by the chairman of a general meeting as to the conduct of the meeting, or on any question of procedure or point of order, is final[21]. The Board of Trustees by resolution and the members of the trust by resolution in general meeting may from time to time agree to replace these provisions[22] relating to general meetings with new or amended provisions[23].

1 As from a day to be appointed the National Trust Act 1971 s 5 is repealed by the Charities (National Trust) Order 2005, SI 2005/712, art 2, Appendix clause 2(3), Schedule Pt 2. At the date at which this volume states the law no such day had been appointed.
2 As to the National Trust see PARA 973. As to membership of the trust see PARA 974.
3 National Trust Act 1971 s 5(1). The statutory regulations are those contained in Sch 2: see s 5(1), Sch 2. The annual general meeting is called the ordinary meeting and all other general meetings are called extraordinary meetings: Sch 2 para 1. At ordinary meetings the council must lay before the meeting a report and accounts relating to the year: see Sch 2 para 2 (substituted by the National Trust at its annual general meeting in 1985). As to the convening of extraordinary meetings see Sch 2 para 3; and as to the date when ordinary meetings are to be held see Sch 2 para 4. As to notice of general meetings and of business and resolutions see Sch 2 paras 5–10 (para 7 amended by the National Trust at its annual general meeting of 1976). As to quorum see Sch 2 para 11. As to business which may be transacted without a quorum see Sch 2 para 12. As to voting see Sch 2 paras 13–16 (para 15 amended in 1983). As to chairmanship of the meeting and the adjournment of business see Sch 2 para 17.
4 National Trust Act 1971 s 5(2). The resolution must be passed at a meeting of the council of which not less than 21 days' notice has been given setting out the resolution to be proposed: s 5(3)(a). As to the Council of the National Trust see PARA 975.
5 National Trust Act 1971 s 5(3)(b).
6 National Trust Act 1971 s 5(3)(c).
7 As to the provisions in respect of the coming into force of the scheme altering or affecting the trusts of the National Trust under the Charities (National Trust) Order 2005, SI 2005/712, see PARA 973 note 9.
8 Charities (National Trust) Order 2005, SI 2005/712, Appendix clause 31(a). The annual general meeting must be held on such date between 1 September and 31 December each year, at such time and in such place as the Board of Trustees decides: Appendix clause 33(1). The only business which may be dealt with at an annual general meeting is: (1) business which in accordance with the National Trust Acts 1907 to 1971 and the 2005 scheme is required or authorised to be dealt with at annual general meetings (Charities (National Trust) Order 2005, SI 2005/712, Appendix clause 33(2)(a)); (2) a resolution proposed by members (a 'members' resolution'), and notice of which is given in the notice of the meeting (see Appendix clause 33(2)(b)); and (3) a resolution proposed by the Board of Trustees, and notice of which is given in the notice of the meeting

(Appendix clause 33(2)(c)). As to the National Trust Acts 1907 to 1971 see PARA 973 note 6. The '2005 scheme' is the scheme altering or affecting the trusts of the National Trust under the Charities (National Trust) Order 2005, SI 2005/712 (see PARA 973). As to the Board of Trustees see PARA 976. As to members' resolutions see Appendix clause 35.

9   Charities (National Trust) Order 2005, SI 2005/712, Appendix clause 31(b).
10 Charities (National Trust) Order 2005, SI 2005/712, Appendix clause 32(1). The notice must be in such form and must be sent in such manner as the Board of Trustees from time to time decides: Appendix clause 32(2). As to the service of documents generally see PARA 984.
11 See the Charities (National Trust) Order 2005, SI 2005/712, Appendix clause 37.
12 See the Charities (National Trust) Order 2005, SI 2005/712, Appendix clause 38.
13 See the Charities (National Trust) Order 2005, SI 2005/712, Appendix clause 39.
14 See the Charities (National Trust) Order 2005, SI 2005/712, Appendix clause 40.
15 Charities (National Trust) Order 2005, SI 2005/712, Appendix clause 34(1). Copies of the report and accounts must be available at each annual general meeting and on written application to the secretary of the trust: Appendix clause 34(2). As to the meaning of 'written' see PARA 805 note 14. As to the keeping of accounts see PARA 992.
16 Charities (National Trust) Order 2005, SI 2005/712, Appendix clause 36(1).
17 Charities (National Trust) Order 2005, SI 2005/712, Appendix clause 36(2). As to the validity of requisitions see Appendix clause 36(3), (4).
18 Charities (National Trust) Order 2005, SI 2005/712, Appendix clause 36(5).
19 Charities (National Trust) Order 2005, SI 2005/712, Appendix clause 36(6).
20 Ie except where the Charities (National Trust) Order 2005, SI 2005/712, provides otherwise.
21 Charities (National Trust) Order 2005, SI 2005/712, Appendix clause 41.
22 Ie the provisions set out in the Charities (National Trust) Order 2005, SI 2005/712.
23 Charities (National Trust) Order 2005, SI 2005/712, Appendix clause 42.

984.   Validity and regulation of procedures of Board of Trustees of the National Trust; documents and notices. As from a day to be appointed the following provisions have effect[1].

The acts and proceedings of the Board of Trustees[2], the council[3], or of any committee, sub-committee or advisory panel are not invalidated by:

(1)   any vacancy in their number[4];

(2)   any defect or irregularity in the appointment, or in the qualification for appointment, of any person as a member, chairman, or deputy chairman of any of those bodies, or as chairman or deputy chairman of the National Trust or as senior member of the council[5]; or

(3)   (in the case of elected members[6]) any defect or irregularity in the election, or in the qualification for election, of the member[7].

The Board of Trustees may from time to time make regulations[8] for the management and administration of the National Trust, the holding of meetings and the conduct of the business of the trust and of the Board of Trustees, the council and any committee, sub-committee or advisory panel[9]. Subject to the National Trust Acts 1907 to 1971[10] and the 2005 scheme[11], and to any such regulations, the Board of Trustees, the council and any committee, sub-committee or advisory panel each has power to regulate its own procedures[12].

Regulations made under the above provisions[13] may lay down procedures for the sealing, signature or execution on behalf of the trust of documents of any kind[14]. It is not necessary in legal proceedings to prove that the person or persons who sealed, signed or executed any such document was or were duly authorised to do so, and such document must be presumed to be duly signed, sealed or executed unless the contrary is proved[15].

In relation to any notice or document which the trust is required by the National Trust Acts 1907 to 1971 or the 2005 scheme to send to any person[16]:

(a)   where the trust sends a notice or document to one member of a joint, group, or family membership of the trust[17], the trust is not required to send separate notices or documents to the other members of that joint, group or family membership[18];

(b)   the trust is not required to send notices or documents to members of the
        trust who enjoy a concessionary membership rate by reason of their
        living at the same address as another member of the trust[19];

(c)   the fact that a notice or document is not sent to or received by any
        person entitled to receive it does not invalidate any meeting held or
        action taken in accordance with the 2005 scheme[20].

1   As to the provisions in respect of the coming into force of the scheme altering or affecting the trusts
    of the National Trust under the Charities (National Trust) Order 2005, SI 2005/712, see PARA 973
    note 9.
2   As to the Board of Trustees see PARA 976. As to the powers of the board see PARA 980; and as
    to the proceedings of the board see PARA 981.
3   As to the Council of the National Trust see PARA 975. As to the powers and proceedings of the
    council see PARA 979.
4   Charities (National Trust) Order 2005, SI 2005/712, Appendix clause 29(a).
5   Charities (National Trust) Order 2005, SI 2005/712, Appendix clause 29(b). As to the chairman
    and deputy chairman of the National Trust and the senior member of the council see PARA 975.
    As to the National Trust see PARA 973.
6   As to the meaning of 'elected member' see PARA 975 note 4.
7   Charities (National Trust) Order 2005, SI 2005/712, Appendix clause 29(c).
8   'Regulations' includes rules, standing orders and instructions: Charities (National Trust) Order
    2005, SI 2005/712, Appendix clause 43(4).
9   Charities (National Trust) Order 2005, SI 2005/712, Appendix clause 43(1). Without prejudice to
    the generality of clause 43(1) regulations made under that clause may specify the quorum for the
    council or for any committee, sub-committee or advisory panel: Appendix clause 43(2).
10 As to the National Trust Acts 1907 to 1971 see PARA 973 note 6.
11 The '2005 scheme' is the scheme altering or affecting the trusts of the National Trust under the
    Charities (National Trust) Order 2005, SI 2005/712 (see PARA 973).
12 Charities (National Trust) Order 2005, SI 2005/712, Appendix clause 43(3).
13 Ie regulations made under the Charities (National Trust) Order 2005, SI 2005/712, Appendix
    clause 43 (see the text to notes 8–12).
14 Charities (National Trust) Order 2005, SI 2005/712, Appendix clause 44(1). Such regulations may
    lay down different procedures for different kinds of documents, and may specify the person or
    persons, being members of the Board of Trustees or staff of the trust, who may seal, sign or execute
    documents of the kinds specified in the regulations: Appendix clause 44(2).
15 Charities (National Trust) Order 2005, SI 2005/712, Appendix clause 44(3).
16 Charities (National Trust) Order 2005, SI 2005/712, Appendix clause 47(1). As to the meaning of
    'person' see PARA 803 note 17.
17 As to membership of the trust see PARA 974.
18 Charities (National Trust) Order 2005, SI 2005/712, Appendix clause 47(2).
19 Charities (National Trust) Order 2005, SI 2005/712, Appendix clause 47(3).
20 Charities (National Trust) Order 2005, SI 2005/712, Appendix clause 47(4).

(iii) Property of the National Trust

985. Powers of ownership. The National Trust[1], either alone or jointly with
other bodies or persons[2], may acquire by purchase (other than compulsorily), gift
or otherwise, land, buildings and hereditaments and any interests in them and any
other property of whatsoever nature and may act as a trustee of any property
devoted to public purposes[3]. It may also acquire and retain any land, buildings
and hereditaments which in the council's[4] opinion it is desirable to hold as
investments[5]. Certain property vested in the trust[6] is not chargeable with any debts
and liabilities and is inalienable[7]. The council may also by resolution determine
that any other land and tenements, including buildings, which may at any time
become vested in the trust are proper to be held for the benefit of the nation and
such land and buildings then become inalienable[8]. Certain statutory powers,
including that of compulsory acquisition, are not exercisable in respect of land
held by the trust inalienably[9].

The trust may make such reasonable charges for the admission of the public to any of its property or for the use by the public of such property as it may from time to time determine[10]. However, the trust must not make any admission charges to any common or commonable land or any other property of the trust to which the public had right of access at the date when such property was acquired by the trust, except such parts of common or commonable land as may be from time to time set apart[11] for games, meetings or athletic sports[12]. The trust may also make such reasonable charges as it may from time to time determine in respect of recreation on any of its land or property or waterways[13].

With the consent of the Secretary of State[14] or, in relation to Wales, the Welsh Ministers[15], and any other government department or authority whose consent would be required if the intended transaction were a sale by deed, a local authority may assure to the trust any land or building vested in it which the trust has power to acquire and hold[16].

As from a day to be appointed the powers and duties conferred on the council by the above provisions become powers and duties of the Board of Trustees[17].

1   As to the National Trust see PARA 973.
2   See the National Trust Act 1907 s 31; and PARA 978. As to the meaning of 'person' see PARA 803 note 17.
3   See the National Trust Act 1907 s 4(2). Section 4(2) also made special provision concerning the law of mortmain, which is repealed: see CHARITIES vol 8 (2015) PARAS 82–83. Special powers of management are given to the trust in relation to the Wey Navigation and Godalming Navigation: see the National Trust Act 1971 Pt IV (ss 29–31).
4   As to the Council of the National Trust see PARA 975. As to the powers and proceedings of the council see PARA 979.
5   See the National Trust Act 1937 s 4(a).
6   Ie the properties specified in the National Trust Act 1907 Sch 1 Pt I.
7   See the National Trust Act 1907 s 21(1).
8   National Trust Act 1907 s 21(2). In addition to properties made inalienable by s 21, any mansion house or amenity land assured to the trust under the National Trust Act 1939 (see PARA 987) is inalienable: s 8. 'Assurance' includes a gift, conveyance, appointment, lease, transfer, settlement, mortgage, charge, incumbrance, devise, bequest and every other assurance by deed, will or other instrument; and 'assure' and 'assuror' have corresponding meanings: Mortmain and Charitable Uses Act 1888 s 10 (repealed); applied by the National Trust Act 1937 s 2. The trust may nevertheless grant leases of its inalienable property with the sanction of the Charity Commission: see the National Trust Charity Scheme Confirmation Act 1919 s 1, Schedule (s 1 amended by the Charities Act 2006 s 75(1), Sch 8 paras 16, 17; National Trust Charity Scheme Confirmation Act 1919 Schedule amended by the National Trust Act 1937 s 13; and the Charities Act 2006 s 75(1), Sch 8 paras 16, 18). As to leases of charity land generally see CHARITIES vol 8 (2015) PARA 401 et seq. The trust may also grant an easement or right (not including a right to the exclusive possession of the surface) over or in respect of its inalienable property, and if such grant is by way of lease, the sanction of the Charity Commission is not required: National Trust Act 1939 s 12 (amended by virtue of the Charities Act 2006 s 6(5)). As to the Charity Commission see CHARITIES vol 8 (2015) PARA 543 et seq.
9   As to compulsory acquisition see PARA 989. The Law of Property Act 1925 s 84 (which gives power to modify or discharge restrictive covenants: see REAL PROPERTY AND REGISTRATION vol 87 (2012) PARA 1093 et seq) does not apply to restrictions imposed for the purpose of preserving, or protecting or augmenting the amenities of, or securing the access to and enjoyment by the public of any property which is or becomes inalienable under the National Trust Act 1907 s 21 (see the text to notes 7–8), or the National Trust Act 1939 s 8 (see note 8): National Trust Act 1971 s 27. The right of tenants of certain properties to acquire the freehold which is given by the Leasehold Reform Act 1967 (see LANDLORD AND TENANT vol 64 (2012) PARA 1505 et seq) does not extend to property if an interest in the property is vested inalienably in the trust: see s 32.
10 National Trust Act 1907 s 30(1).
11 Ie under the National Trust Act 1907 s 29(1)(F) (see PARA 986).
12 National Trust Act 1907 s 30(2).
13 National Trust Act 1907 s 30(3) (s 30(3)–(5) added by the National Trust Act 1971 s 25). The recreation referred to in the text is in respect of the playing of games, sailing, boating, bathing, fishing and other forms of recreation on any land or property or waterway of the trust: see the National Trust Act 1907 s 30 (as so added). However, this provision does not empower the trust to make any charge in respect of navigation in tidal waters: National Trust Act 1907 s 30(5) (as

so added). 'Waterway' means any lake, river, canal or other waters: s 30(4) (as so added). As to rights of navigation see WATER AND WATERWAYS vol 101 (2009) PARA 688 et seq.

14 The National Trust Act 1937 s 7(1) refers to the Minister of Health, whose functions have been transferred to the Secretary of State (see PARA 802 note 2).

15 As to the transfer of functions to the Welsh Ministers see PARA 802. As to the meaning of 'Wales' see PARA 802 note 4.

16 See the National Trust Act 1937 s 7(1). As to contributions to the trust by local authorities see PARA 993.

17 See PARA 980.

986. Commons vested in the National Trust. The National Trust[1] must keep any land registered as common land[2], and certain other land[3], vested in it uninclosed and unbuilt on as open spaces for the recreation and enjoyment of the public[4]; and must prevent, resist and abate, by all lawful means, all inclosures and encroachments on the property or attempts to do so or to appropriate the soil, timber or roads for any purpose inconsistent with the National Trust Act 1907[5]. The trust also has the following powers in relation to such lands:

(1) to plant, drain, level and otherwise improve and alter any part of the property so far as it deems necessary or desirable and it may make temporary inclosures for this purpose and for protecting or renovating turf and for protecting trees and plantations[6];

(2) to make and maintain roads, footpaths and ways over the property and make and maintain ornamental ponds and waters on it[7];

(3) to erect sheds for tools and materials and maintain and repair them[8];

(4) to set apart from time to time parts of the property for persons to play games, or hold meetings or gatherings for athletic sports[9].

In addition to these powers, the trust has the power to do anything appearing to it to be desirable for the purpose of providing or improving opportunities for the enjoyment of the commons or commonable land by the public, and in the interest of persons resorting to them; in particular to provide or arrange for the provision of facilities and services for the enjoyment or convenience of the public, including meals and refreshments, parking places for vehicles, shelters and lavatory accommodation and to erect buildings and carry out works[10]. Notwithstanding the prohibition on charging admission to any common or commonable land[11], the trust may make reasonable charges for the use by the public of any facilities, services, parking places or other accommodation provided with respect to such land for public enjoyment or convenience[12].

Before any highway authority[13] may enter any common or commonable land the soil of which is vested in the trust for the purpose of obtaining highway materials, the consent of the trust is required, and if this consent is withheld the highway authority may apply for an order of the justices of the peace, who may prescribe such conditions as to the mode of working and restitution of the surface as they consider expedient[14].

All existing rights of common and commonable or other similar rights, rights of way and all existing private rights are preserved[15] unless otherwise expressly provided[16].

1 As to the National Trust see PARA 973.

2 National Trust Act 1907 s 29(2)(a) (s 29(1) renumbered as such by, and s 29(2) added by, the Commons Act 2006 s 44(1), Sch 4 para 3(1), (2), (4)). As to the registration of land as common land see COMMONS vol 13 (2009) PARA 506 et seq.

3 Ie:

(1) land not registered as common land which is:

(a) regulated by an Act made under the Commons Act 1876 confirming a provisional order of the Inclosure Commissioners, or

    (b)   subject to a scheme under the Metropolitan Commons Act 1866 or the Commons
             Act 1899 (National Trust Act 1907 s 29(2)(b) (as added: see note 2)); and
  (2)   land not registered as common land or falling within head (1) above which is in the New
       Forest and is subject to rights of common (s 29(2)(c) (as so added)).
See further COMMONS vol 13 (2009) PARA 475.

4 See the National Trust Act 1907 s 29(1)(A) (as so numbered: see note 2). However,
notwithstanding this duty to keep commons or commonable land uninclosed, the trust may erect
fences on such land by exercising its power under the National Trust Act 1971 s 23 (see the text
to notes 10–12) to do anything appearing to it to be desirable for the purpose of providing or
improving opportunities for the enjoyment of the commons by the public, and in the interest of the
persons resorting to them: *National Trust for Places of Historic Interest or Natural Beauty v
Ashbrook* [1997] 4 All ER 76, [1997] 30 LS Gaz R 29, 141 Sol Jo LB 148, (1997) Times, 3 July.

5 See the National Trust Act 1907 s 29(1)(E) (as so numbered: see note 2).
6 National Trust Act 1907 s 29(1)(B) (as so numbered: see note 2).
7 National Trust Act 1907 s 29(1)(C) (as so numbered: see note 2).
8 National Trust Act 1907 s 29(1)(D) (as so numbered: see note 2).
9 National Trust Act 1907 s 29(1)(F) (as so numbered: see note 2).
10 National Trust Act 1971 s 23(1). The erection of any building (other than a shed for tools and
materials), or the construction of any other work, whereby access by the public to any such trust
property (see PARA 974 note 10) is prevented or impeded is not lawful unless the consent of the
Secretary of State or, in relation to Wales, the Welsh Ministers is obtained: s 23(2) (amended by
the Commons Act 2006 ss 44(1), 53, Sch 4 para 4(1), (2), Sch 6 Pt 2). The Commons Act 2006
ss 39 and 40 (see COMMONS vol 13 (2009) PARAS 613–614) apply in relation to an application
for consent as they apply in relation to an application for consent under s 38(1): National Trust
Act 1971 s 23(2A) (s 23(2A)–(2C) added by the Commons Act 2006 s 44(1), Sch 4 para 4(1), (3)).
The Commons Act 2006 s 41 (see COMMONS vol 13 (2009) PARA 615) applies in relation to the
carrying out of works in contravention of the National Trust Act 1971 s 23(2) as it applies to
works carried out in contravention of the Commons Act 2006 s 38(1) (and as if references to
consent under that provision were to consent under the National Trust Act 1971 s 23(2)): s 23(2B)
(as so added). Nothing in the Commons Act 2006 s 38 (see COMMONS vol 13 (2009) PARA 612)
applies in relation to land to which the National Trust Act 1907 s 29 (see the text to notes 2–3)
applies: National Trust Act 1971 s 23(2C) (as so added). As to the erection of fences in the exercise
of the power under s 23 see *National Trust for Places of Historic Interest or Natural Beauty v
Ashbrook* [1997] 4 All ER 76, [1997] 30 LS Gaz R 29, 141 Sol Jo LB 148, (1997) Times, 3 July;
and note 4. As to the Secretary of State, and as to the transfer of functions to the Welsh Ministers
see PARA 802. As to the meaning of 'Wales' see PARA 802 note 4.
11 Ie the prohibition in the National Trust Act 1907 s 30(2) (see PARA 985).
12 National Trust Act 1971 s 23(3).
13 As to highway authorities see HIGHWAYS, STREETS AND BRIDGES vol 55 (2012) PARA 52 et seq.
14 See the National Trust Act 1907 s 36; applying the Commons Act 1876 s 20 (amended by
the Statute Law Revision Act 1894 s 1, Sch 1; Statute Law Revision Act 1898, s 1, Schedule
Pt I; Courts Act 2003 s 109(1), Sch 8 para 54): see COMMONS vol 13 (2009) PARA 587.
15 Ie those rights existing before the passing of the National Trust Act 1907 (ie 21 August 1907): s 37.
16 See the National Trust Act 1907 s 37.

987. National Trust property subject to settlements. For the purposes of the
statutory power of tenants for life to grant land for public and charitable
purposes[1], any grant or lease to the National Trust[2] of settled land is deemed to
be made for the general benefit of the settled land and for charitable purposes in
connection with it and, in the application of that power to grants or leases to the
National Trust, five acres are substituted for one acre[3].

If a settlement[4] comprises a principal mansion house[5], then, subject to certain
conditions[6], the National Trust may accept and retain, and the tenant for life[7] may
grant gratuitously or otherwise to the National Trust in fee simple or absolutely
or for the whole or any less estate[8] comprised in the settlement (1) the principal
mansion house and the pleasure grounds and park and land, if any, usually
occupied with them[9]; (2) any land occupied or enjoyed for the purposes of
agriculture, sport or afforestation which, in the opinion of the Council of the
National Trust, it is desirable to acquire for preserving the amenities of the
principal mansion house[10]; and (3) an endowment consisting of (a) an annual sum
charged upon any other land or buildings comprised in the settlement[11], or (b) the

settled interest in any such land or buildings[12], or (c) capital money or investments[13] subject to the settlement[14] which, in the opinion of the council, it may be desirable to hold for the purpose of providing for the maintenance and preservation of the mansion house and amenity land[15].

Any such disposition which is not otherwise authorised is void unless (i) either the written consent of the trustees of the settlement or a court order authorising the disposition to be carried into effect has been obtained[16]; (ii) the Secretary of State[17] certifies that the principal mansion house concerned is or comprises a building of national interest or architectural, historic or artistic interest[18]; (iii) upon or within three months of the disposition, the National Trust executes a lease of the property transferred or such part of it as is agreed between it and the tenant for life[19]; and (iv) the National Trust is subject to an obligation to maintain and preserve the mansion house and amenity lands included in the disposition so far as there are funds available from the endowment but not further[20].

The lease must be for such term at such nominal or other yearly rent and subject to such covenants and conditions as are approved by the trustees of the settlement or the court[21], but must contain a covenant by the lessee to admit the public to view such part or parts of the property at such times and on such terms as may be agreed upon by the National Trust[22], and also restrictive covenants by the lessee for ensuring that the principal mansion house is used only as a private dwelling house and for preserving its amenities[23].

If an application is made to the court[24] for an order authorising the disposition, the court must have regard to: (A) the interest of all persons, born or unborn, who have or may be expected to have beneficial interests under the settlement[25]; (B) any benefit which may be expected to accrue to the property not proposed to be assured to the National Trust either from the preservation of its amenities or otherwise[26]; (C) the amount of the funds which will be available for the preservation and maintenance of the property by the National Trust[27]; (D) the relation between the endowment provided[28] and the sum previously expended on the maintenance of the property[29]; (E) the desirability in the public interest of the preservation of the property[30]; and (F) such other considerations as in the circumstances of each case the court may consider to be relevant[31].

Before giving their consent, the trustees of the settlement must give notice in writing[32] to all beneficiaries of full age, other than those interested after an estate tail[33] and must have regard to the same considerations as are applicable to the court if it is requested by any such beneficiary not to consent[34] and to such other considerations as in the circumstances of the case they may consider to be relevant[35].

The powers given to a tenant for life are also exercisable by statutory owners, but only with a court order[36].

These special powers conferred on the National Trust or on tenants for life are in addition to and not in derogation of any other powers conferred on them by Act of Parliament, deed or will[37].

As from a day to be appointed the powers and duties conferred on the council by the above provisions become powers and duties of the Board of Trustees[38].

1   Ie for the purposes of the Settled Land Act 1925 s 55 (see SETTLEMENTS vol 91 (2012) PARA 765).
2   As to the National Trust see PARA 973.
3   National Trust Act 1937 s 6(2). If the council declares by resolution that in furtherance of the general purposes of the National Trust it is desirable that the public should have access to any land, building, furniture, picture or chattel of any description the National Trust may act in any trusts for or as trustee of such property as if the same were devoted to public purposes within the

meaning of the National Trust Act 1907 s 4(2) (see PARA 978): National Trust Act 1939 s 13. As to the Council of the National Trust see PARA 975. As to the powers and proceedings of the council see PARA 979.

4 'Settlement' includes an instrument or instruments which under the Settled Land Act 1925 is or are deemed to be or which together constitute a settlement; and a settlement which is deemed to have been made by any person or to be subsisting for the purposes of the Act: s 117(1)(xxiv) (definition applied by the National Trust Act 1939 s 2). As to the phasing out of strict settlements under the 1925 Act see the Trusts of Land and Appointment of Trustees Act 1996 s 2, Sch 1; LIMITATION PERIODS vol 68 (2008) PARA 1022; REAL PROPERTY AND REGISTRATION vol 87 (2012) PARA 104; SETTLEMENTS vol 91 (2012) PARA 506.

5 'Principal mansion house' means a principal mansion house on settled land within the meaning of the Settled Land Act 1925 s 65: National Trust Act 1939 s 2. The Settled Land Act 1925 s 65 does not expressly define 'principal mansion house', but where a house is usually occupied as a farmhouse or where the site of any house and the pleasure grounds and park and land, if any, usually occupied with it do not together exceed 25 acres, the house is not deemed a principal mansion house: see s 65(2); and SETTLEMENTS vol 91 (2012) PARA 690. 'Settled land' includes land which is deemed to be settled land: s 117(1)(xxiv) (definition applied by the National Trust Act 1939 s 2). See also note 4.

6 See the National Trust Act 1939 s 4; and heads (i)–(iv) in the text.

7 'Tenant for life' includes a person (not being a statutory owner) who has the powers of a tenant for life under the Settled Land Act 1925 and includes one or more persons together constituting the tenant for life: s 117(1)(xxviii) (definition applied by the National Trust Act 1939 s 2). 'Statutory owner' means the trustees of the settlement or other persons who during a minority, or at any other time when there is no tenant for life, have the powers of a tenant for life under the Settled Land Act 1925; but it does not include the trustees where under a court order or otherwise they have power to convey the settled land in the name of the tenant for life: s 117(1)(xxvi) (definition applied by the National Trust Act 1939 s 2). See also note 4.

8 Ie not being a leasehold interest created under the National Trust Act 1939 s 4: see the text to (notes 16–20).

9 National Trust Act 1939 s 3(1)(a).

10 National Trust Act 1939 s 3(1)(b). These lands are referred to as 'amenity lands': see s 3(1)(b).

11 National Trust Act 1939 s 3(1)(c)(i).

12 Ie including any rights, easements or interest in or over them: National Trust Act 1939 s 3(1)(c)(ii).

13 Any such transfer of capital money or investments must be executed by the trustees of the settlement by the direction of the tenant for life: National Trust Act 1939 s 3(3). As to the meaning of 'trustees of the settlement' see the Settled Land Act 1925 s 30 (see SETTLEMENTS vol 91 (2012) PARA 651): definition applied by the National Trust Act 1939 s 2.

14 National Trust Act 1939 s 3(1)(c)(iii).

15 National Trust Act 1939 s 3(1). Any such disposition is deemed to be a transaction authorised by the Settled Land Act 1925, and that Act applies accordingly: National Trust Act 1939 s 3(2).

16 National Trust Act 1939 s 4(a).

17 The National Trust Act 1939 s 4(b) refers to the Commissioner of Works, whose functions have now been transferred to the Secretary of State (see PARA 802 note 2).

18 National Trust Act 1939 s 4(b).

19 National Trust Act 1939 s 4(c). As to the lease see further s 4(c). See also s 5; and the text to notes 21–23.

20 National Trust Act 1939 s 4(d).

21 National Trust Act 1939 s 5(1).

22 National Trust Act 1939 s 5(2)(a).

23 National Trust Act 1939 s 5(2)(b). The lease may contain a covenant, condition or agreement by the lessee against assignment, underletting, charging or parting with possession without the licence or consent of the National Trust; such licence or consent not to be unreasonably withheld: s 5(2)(c). The statutory power to discharge or modify restrictive covenants affecting land (ie the Law of Property Act 1925 s 84: see REAL PROPERTY AND REGISTRATION vol 87 (2012) PARA 1093 et seq) does not apply to restrictions imposed by the lease: National Trust Act 1939 s 5(3).

24 Ie under the National Trust Act 1939 s 4(a) (see the text to note 16). On such an application, the settlement trustees, all persons (whether of full age or not) having beneficial interests under the settlement not limited to take effect subsequent to an estate tail to which a person already in existence is or may become entitled in possession and such other persons, if any, as the court directs must be made respondents: s 7. The Settled Land Act 1925 s 113 (see SETTLEMENTS vol 91 (2012) PARA 693) governs the jurisdiction and procedure of the court: National Trust Act 1939 s 11.

25 National Trust Act 1939 s 7(i). This includes the benefit, whether financial or of any other character, to be derived by such persons from the lease and from any future lease or tenancy that may be granted: s 7(i).

26 National Trust Act 1939 s 7(ii).

27 National Trust Act 1939 s 7(iii).

28 Ie under the National Trust Act 1939 s 3(1)(c) (see head (3) in the text).

29 National Trust Act 1939 s 7(iv).

30 National Trust Act 1939 s 7(v).

31 National Trust Act 1939 s 7(vi).

32 The regulations respecting notices in the Law of Property Act 1925 s 196 (see LANDLORD AND TENANT vol 63 (2012) PARA 769; MORTGAGE PARA 457) extend to such a notice: National Trust Act 1939 s 10.

33 erson to whom such notice is given within three months after service requests the trustees in writing not to consent or if any person having such a beneficial interest is under 21 or of unsound mind: s 6(1).

34 Ie those considerations set out in the National Trust Act 1939 s 7(i)–(v): see the text to notes 25–30.

35 National Trust Act 1939 s 6(2). The trustees are not liable for giving any such consent: see the Settled Land Act 1925 s 97(a) (applied by the National Trust Act 1939 s 6(3)); and SETTLEMENTS vol 91 (2012) PARA 792.

36 See the National Trust Act 1939 s 9(2), (3).

37 See the National Trust Act 1939 s 15. The National Trust or tenant for life as the case may be may exercise all such other powers as if the National Trust Act 1939 had not been passed: s 15. Section 15 also refers to trustees for sale on whom powers were conferred by the Law of Property Act 1925 s 28(1) (repealed) and by virtue of the National Trust Act 1939 s 9(1) (not repealed, but in practice no longer relevant). As to the replacement of the former system of trusts for sale of land with a new system of trusts of land see the Trusts of Land and Appointment of Trustees Act 1996 s 1; and LIMITATION PERIODS vol 68 (2008) PARA 1023; and REAL PROPERTY AND REGISTRATION vol 87 (2012) PARA 104.

38 See PARA 980.

988. Agreements restrictive of the use of land. In addition to the power of the National Trust[1] to enforce restrictive agreements and covenants benefiting its land in the same manner as any other landowner[2], it may enter into an agreement with, or take a covenant from, any person[3] who is able to bind land to the effect that the land is to be subject, permanently or for a specified period, to conditions restricting its planning, development[4] or use in any manner, and the agreement or covenant is enforceable by the trust against the persons deriving title under the other party to such agreement or covenant to the same extent as if the trust were possessed of or entitled to or interested in adjacent land and as if the agreement or covenant had been, and had been expressed to be, entered into for the benefit of such adjacent land[5].

1 As to the National Trust see PARA 973.

2 See eg *National Trust for Places of Historic Interest or Natural Beauty v Midlands Electricity Board* [1952] Ch 380, [1952] 1 All ER 298. For the general law as to the enforcement of restrictive covenants see REAL PROPERTY AND REGISTRATION vol 87 (2012) PARA 1079 et seq.

3 As to the meaning of 'person' see PARA 803 note 17.

4 For the statutory control of development generally see PLANNING vol 81 (2010) PARA 292 et seq.

5 See the National Trust Act 1937 s 8; and *Gee v National Trust for Places of Historic Interest or Natural Beauty* [1966] 1 All ER 954, [1966] 1 WLR 170, CA. Registration either under the Land Charges Act 1972 as a Class D(ii) land charge (see REAL PROPERTY AND REGISTRATION vol 87 (2012) PARAS 725, 727), or in the case of registered land under the Land Registration Act 2002 (see REAL PROPERTY AND REGISTRATION vol 87 (2012) PARA 235 et seq) is necessary to enable such an agreement or covenant to be enforced against a purchaser for value from the original party to the agreement or covenantor, and the effect of this statutory provision is merely to enable the National Trust to enforce such an agreement or covenant, which would otherwise not be enforceable, without the necessity of showing that it possessed adjacent land capable of being benefited.

989. Exemptions for National Trust property. The property of the National Trust[1] is entitled to special treatment in the following circumstances:

(1)   if a compulsory purchase order is served under the provisions of the Acquisition of Land Act 1981 in respect of any land held inalienably by the trust and is not withdrawn after objection, the acquisition becomes subject to special parliamentary procedure[2];

(2)   land forming part of the property of the trust cannot be acquired for the purposes of allotments or cottage holdings[3];

(3)   certain powers of compulsory acquisition conferred by the National Parks and Access to the Countryside Act 1949[4] and the power of compulsory acquisition under the Forestry Act 1967[5] are not exercisable in respect of land held inalienably by the trust;

(4)   where the interest of the landlord or any superior landlord in the property comprised in any tenancy belongs to the trust, the Secretary of State or the Welsh Ministers[6] may certify that it is requisite, for the purpose of securing that the property will be used or occupied in a manner better suited to its nature, that the use or occupation of the property should be changed[7].

1   As to the National Trust see PARA 973.
2   See the Acquisition of Land Act 1981 s 18; and COMPULSORY ACQUISITION OF LAND vol 18 (2009) PARA 603 et seq. As to special parliamentary procedure see STATUTES AND LEGISLATIVE PROCESS vol 96 (2012) PARA 958 et seq.
3   See the Land Settlement (Facilities) Act 1919 s 28(4); and AGRICULTURAL LAND vol 1 (2008) PARA 546. As to the application to cottage holdings see the Small Holdings and Allotments Act 1926 s 12 (repealed); the Agricultural Land (Utilisation) Act 1931 s 12(1); and AGRICULTURAL LAND vol 1 (2008) PARA 597 et seq.
4   National Parks and Access to the Countryside Act 1949 s 113. The powers referred to are those conferred by Pt V (ss 59–83), Pt VI (ss 85–115): see eg ss 76, 77; and OPEN SPACES AND COUNTRYSIDE vol 78 (2010) PARAS 633–634.
5   See the Forestry Act 1967 s 40(4) (substituted by the Forestry Act 1981 s 2); and FORESTRY vol 52 (2014) PARA 46.
6   The Landlord and Tenant Act 1954 s 57(7) refers to the Minister of Works, whose functions have been transferred to the Secretary of State: see PARA 802 note 2. In relation to Wales the certification function is exercisable by the Welsh Ministers (Government of Wales Act 2006 Sch 11 para 30) concurrently with any Minister of the Crown by whom it is exercisable: see the National Assembly for Wales (Transfer of Functions) Order 1999, SI 1999/672, art 2, Sch 1. As to the transfer of functions to the Welsh Ministers see PARA 802. As to the meaning of 'Wales' see PARA 802 note 4.
7   See the Landlord and Tenant Act 1954 s 57(7); and LANDLORD AND TENANT vol 63 (2012) PARA 886.

(iv) Finance of the National Trust

990. Application of revenue of the National Trust. The revenue of the National Trust[1] must be applied, first in payment of the expenses incurred in connection with the trust and its property, then in payment of interest on and instalments of money borrowed by it, and the balance, if any, must be applied in furtherance of the objects of the trust[2] or invested in investments in which the trustees are by law entitled to invest trust funds[3]. However, the Council of the National Trust[4] may resolve that the expenses of any particular purpose must be defrayed out of a specified fund[5]. The capital of the trust must be applied, subject to any conditions attached to any particular gifts and to the trust's powers of investment[6], in the repayment of loans or otherwise in furthering the objects of the trust[7].

Subject to any special trusts or directions affecting any particular property, the council[8] may invest the balance of its annual revenue and any money received by it on capital account in (1) investments for the time being authorised by law for the investment of trust funds[9]; (2) the public funds of any of Her

Majesty's dominions or territories under her protection or the United States of America[10]; and (3) deposit receipts, bonds, debentures, debenture stock, mortgages, preference, ordinary, deferred or common stock or shares or other securities in any municipal, railway, public utility, commercial or industrial corporation, company or body registered or incorporated in the United Kingdom[11] or any of Her Majesty's dominions or territories under her protection or the United States of America[12]. The trust may retain and hold any investments transferred to it otherwise than by way of purchase notwithstanding that they are not otherwise authorised[13].

As from a day to be appointed the powers and duties conferred on the council by these provisions become powers and duties of the Board of Trustees[14].

1 As to the National Trust see PARA 973.
2 For the objects of the trust see PARA 977.
3 See the National Trust Act 1907 s 27 (amended by the National Trust Act 1937 s 14). For the investments authorised see the text to notes 8–13.
4 As to the Council of the National Trust see PARA 975. As to the powers and proceedings of the council see PARA 979.
5 See the National Trust Act 1937 s 10.
6 See the text to notes 8–13.
7 National Trust Act 1907 s 28.
8 Until a day to be appointed, all investments made by the council must be made with the advice and under the direction of a finance committee: see the National Trust Act 1953 s 4(3) (prospectively repealed by SI 2005/712). At the date at which this volume states the law no such day had been appointed. As to the appointment of committees by the council see PARA 979.
9 National Trust Act 1953 s 4(1)(i). As to the investment of trust funds see TRUSTS AND POWERS vol 98 (2013) PARA 446 et seq.
10 National Trust Act 1953 s 4(1)(ii). As to Her Majesty's dominions and protected territories see COMMONWEALTH vol 13 (2009) PARAS 707, 708.
11 As to the meaning of 'United Kingdom' see PARA 804 note 2.
12 See the National Trust Act 1953 s 4(1)(iii).
13 National Trust Act 1953 s 4(2).
14 See PARA 980.

991. Borrowing powers of the National Trust. The National Trust[1] may raise money by borrowing on the security of certain of its property[2] by way of specific mortgage and by charging or appropriating as security for money borrowed the rents, profits and income derived from any of its land, including that which it holds for the benefit of the nation[3].

1 As to the National Trust see PARA 973.
2 Ie property other than that specified in the National Trust Act 1907 Sch 1, or which is otherwise inalienable (see PARA 985).
3 National Trust Act 1907 s 22. The provisions of the Companies Clauses Consolidation Act 1845 ss 45, 47–55 (see COMPANIES vol 15 (2009) PARA 1744 et seq) are applicable to the raising of money by the trust: see the National Trust Act 1907 s 23. Mortgagees, other than those of specific property with a power of foreclosure and sale, may appoint a receiver where the principal in arrears is not less than £1,000: see s 24. As to the power of foreclosure see MORTGAGE PARA 571 et seq; and as to receivers see MORTGAGE PARAS 478 et seq, 565 et seq; RECEIVERS vol 88 (2012) PARA 1 et seq.

992. Accounts of the National Trust. The National Trust[1] must cause to be kept proper books of accounts with respect to: (1) all sums of money received and expended by the trust and the matters in respect of which the receipt and expenditure takes place[2]; (2) all purchases and sales of the trust's property[3]; and (3) the trust's assets and liabilities[4]. Proper books of account are not deemed to be kept with respect to these matters if there are not kept such books as are necessary to give a true and fair view of the state of the affairs of the trust and to explain its transactions[5]. Separate accounts must be kept of sums received or expended by the trust and not applicable at the discretion of the Council of the National Trust[6] to its general purposes[7]. Certain information must be included in the accounts laid before an ordinary meeting[8] and the accounts must comply with certain requirements[9]. Once at least in every year the accounts of the trust must be examined and audited by an auditor or auditors to be elected annually[10] at the annual general meeting[11].

1   As to the National Trust see PARA 973.
2   National Trust Act 1971 s 20(1)(a).
3   National Trust Act 1971 s 20(1)(b).
4   National Trust Act 1971 s 20(1)(c).
5   National Trust Act 1971 s 20(2).
6   As to the Council of the National Trust see PARA 975. As to the powers and proceedings of the council see PARA 979.
7   National Trust Act 1937 s 9. As to the general purposes of the trust see PARA 977.
8   As to ordinary meetings see PARA 983.
9   The accounts to be laid before an ordinary meeting must include: (1) statements dealing with income and expenditure and with all other movements on funds of the trust and, so far as practicable, of trusts administered by the trust for the preceding year (see the National Trust Act 1971 s 21(1)(a)); and (2) statements of funds, assets and liabilities (see s 21(1)(b)). The accounts must give a true and fair view of the trust's state of affairs and transactions for the year; but it is not necessary to place any value on inalienable property or on other property or personal chattels held in trust, or acquired by the trust for preservation and it is not necessary to take account of any obligation for the future maintenance of property held by the trust for preservation: s 21(2). 'Year' means a period of 12 months ending on 31 December: s 3(1). For the particulars to be shown in the accounts see s 21(3), (6); and, as from a day to be appointed, the Charities (National Trust) Order 2005, SI 2005/712, Appendix clause 30(3). At the date at which this volume states the law no such day had been appointed. The accounts must be approved by the Council of the National Trust and signed by two of its members (s 21(4)) and an auditors' report must be annexed to them (see s 21(5)).
10 A person is not eligible for appointment as auditor unless eligible for appointment as a statutory auditor under the Companies Act 2006 Pt 42 (ss 1209–1264) (see COMPANIES vol 15 (2009) PARA 957 et seq): National Trust Act 1971 s 22 proviso (amended by SI 2008/948).
11 National Trust Act 1971 s 22. Any previously elected auditor or auditors is be eligible for re-election: s 22. As to general meetings see PARA 983.

993. Contributions, grants and loans to the National Trust. Certain members of the National Trust subscribe to its funds[1].

A local authority may, with the consent of the Secretary of State[2] or, in relation to Wales, the Welsh Ministers[3], contribute to the expenses of the acquisition by the trust of any land or building wholly or partly within, or in the neighbourhood of, its district or towards the expenses of maintaining and preserving any such land or building[4].

In relation to buildings in Wales, the Welsh Ministers[5] have power to make grants to the trust to defray any expenses incurred in the acquisition of buildings which appear to them to be of outstanding historic or architectural interest[6]; or to make grants to defray the expense of repairing or maintaining such a building or of keeping up any adjacent land or of repairing or maintaining any objects kept in such a building, or of keeping up a garden or other land which appears to them to be of outstanding historic interest but which is not adjacent to such a building[7]. In relation to buildings situated in England, equivalent powers belong to the Historic Buildings and Monuments Commission for England ('the Commission')[8].

Grants and loans may be made by the trustees of the National Heritage Memorial Fund[9].

1   See PARA 974. As to the National Trust see PARA 973.
2   In relation to the Greater London Council such consent is not required: see the National Trust Act 1937 s 7(2) (amended by SI 1966/1305). The Greater London Council ceased to exist on 1 April 1986 and its functions were transferred mainly to the London borough councils and the Common Council of the City of London (see the Local Government Act 1985 s 1(1)(a), (2),

Pt II (ss 2–17); and LOCAL GOVERNMENT vol 69 (2009) PARA 17. The National Trust Act 1937 s 7 refers to the Minister of Health, whose functions have been transferred to the Secretary of State (see PARA 802 note 2).

3   As to the transfer of functions to the Welsh Ministers see PARA 802. As to the meaning of 'Wales' see PARA 802 note 4.

4   See the National Trust Act 1937 s 7(2). As to grants of land to the trust by local authorities see PARA 985.

5   The Historic Buildings and Ancient Monuments Act 1953 refers to the Minister of Works, whose functions were transferred to the Secretary of State: see PARA 802 note 2. The Historic Buildings and Ancient Monuments Act 1953 ss 4, 6 apply only where the property or buildings are not situated in England: see s 4(1) (amended by the Town and Countries Amenities Act 1974 s 12; and the National Heritage Act 1983 Sch 4), and the Historic Buildings and Ancient Monuments Act 1953 s 6(4) (added by the National Heritage Act 1983 s 33, Sch 4). The powers of the Secretary of State under the Historic Buildings and Ancient Monuments Act 1953 in relation to Wales are transferred to the Welsh Ministers (Government of Wales Act 2006 Sch 11 para 30): see the National Assembly for Wales (Transfer of Functions) Order 1999, SI 1999/672, art 2, Sch 1. The Historic Buildings and Ancient Monuments Act 1953 does not extend to Northern Ireland (see s 22(5)) and thus the Secretary of State's powers under ss 4, 6 extend to Scotland only. As to the Welsh Ministers see PARA 802. As to the meaning of 'England' see PARA 804 note 2.

6   See the Historic Buildings and Ancient Monuments Act 1953 s 6(2); and PARA 1079.

7   See the Historic Buildings and Ancient Monuments Act 1953 s 4; and PARA 1074.

8   See the Historic Buildings and Ancient Monuments Act 1953 ss 3A, 5B; and PARAS 1073, 1078. As to the Historic Buildings and Monuments Commission for England ('the Commission') see PARA 803.

9   See the National Heritage Act 1980 s 3; and PARA 815.

(16) THE ORDNANCE SURVEY

994. Function of Ordnance Survey. Ordnance Survey is Great Britain's national mapping agency. Formerly a non-ministerial government department and executive agency, it has since April 2015 operated as a limited company incorporated in England and Wales ('Ordnance Survey Ltd'), the entire share capital of which is held by the Secretary of State[1] on behalf of the government[2]. Ordnance Survey collects, maintains and distributes the most accurate and up-to-date geographic information for Great Britain in accordance with its public task and this data is used and relied upon by government, business and individuals[3].

Ordnance Survey was created in 1791 with the aim of producing accurate maps for military purposes but is no longer a military operation. The Ordnance Survey Act 1841 was passed to authorise and facilitate the completion of a survey of Great Britain[4].

The Ordnance Survey Board remains accountable to the Secretary of State[5].The Director General of Ordnance Survey is the chief executive and is appointed by the shareholder[6]. The Director General acts as an assessor to the Boundary Commission for England and the Boundary Commission for Wales[7].

1   Ie the Secretary of State for Business, Innovation and Skills. As to the Secretary of State see PARA 802 note 2.

2   See the *Ordnance Survey Annual Report and Accounts 2014-2015* Strategic Report. A copy of the report is available on the government website which, at the date at which this volume states the law, can be found at www.gov.uk. As to the trading fund status of the Ordnance Survey see the Ordnance Survey Trading Fund Order 1999, SI 1999/965 (amended by SI 2006/2835; and SI 2010/1096).

3   See the *Ordnance Survey Annual Report and Accounts 2014-2015* Strategic Report.

4   See the Ordnance Survey Act 1841 long title. The Act no longer applies to the Isle of Man: Ordnance Survey Act 1841 long title (amended by the Statute Law (Repeals) Act 1993). See further PARAS 996-1001. As to the completion of the geological survey of Great Britain and Ireland see the Geological Survey Act 1845; and PARA 966.

5   See note 1.

6   See note 1; and see the *Ordnance Survey Shareholder Framework Document* (31 March 2015).

7   See the Parliamentary Constituencies Act 1986 Sch 1 para 5 (see ELECTIONS AND REFERENDUMS vol 37 (2013) PARA 69); and the *Ordnance Survey Shareholder Framework Document* (31 March 2015).

995. Ordnance survey maps as evidence. Ordnance survey[1] maps are not evidence as to the boundaries of parishes[2], or as to boundaries between private owners[3]. Such maps may, however, be used to show the position of features at the time the survey was taken[4].

1   As to the Ordnance Survey see PARA 994.
2   *Bidder v Bridges* (1885) 54 LT 529. See also PARA 1001.
3   *Coleman v Kirkaldy* [1882] WN 103. See also PARA 1001.
4   See *A-G and Croydon RDC v Moorsom-Roberts* (1908) 72 JP 123 (position of fence); *Caton v Hamilton* (1889) 53 JP 504 (position of fence line); *A-G v Antrobus* [1905] 2 Ch 188 (position of visible track); *Great Torrington Commons Conservators v Moore Stevens* [1904] 1 Ch 347 (position of the medium filum of a river). As to the presumption of ownership of non-tidal waters to the centre line of the stream (ie usque ad medium filum aquae) see WATER AND WATERWAYS vol 100 (2009) PARA 74.

996. Appointment of persons to assist in ascertaining boundaries. A local authority[1] may, for the purpose of enabling the Ordnance Survey[2] to make and complete surveys and maps of England, on the application in writing of any officer appointed by the Ordnance Survey, nominate and appoint one or more persons to aid and assist, when required, any so appointed officer in examining, ascertaining, and marking out the reputed boundaries of each area[3]. Such person must from time to time act under and obey the directions he receives from the officer or other person appointed by the Ordnance Survey to make such surveys and maps[4].

1   This power was originally exercisable by the justices assembled at quarter sessions. These were abolished by the Courts Act 1971 s 3 (repealed). Any function of courts of quarter sessions, or of committees of quarter sessions which relates to any matter which is not of a judicial nature is transferred to the local authorities for the areas to which those matters relate: s 3 (repealed), Sch 8 para 1(1)(c). As to local government areas and authorities in England and Wales see LOCAL GOVERNMENT vol 69 (2009) PARA 22 et seq.
2   As to the Ordnance Survey see PARA 994.
3   Ordnance Survey Act 1841 s 1 (amended by the Statute Law Revision (No 2) Act 1890; and the Statute Law (Repeals) Act 1993). The Ordnance Survey Act 1841 s 1 specifies such areas as any county, city, borough, town, parish, burghs royal, parliamentary burghs, burghs of regality and barony, extra-parochial and other places, districts, and divisions in England.
4   Ordnance Survey Act 1841 s 1 (amended by the Statute Law (Repeals) Act 1993).

997. Entry to lands to carry on survey. Any person appointed by the local authority[1], and any other person acting under the orders of such a person, and any officer or person appointed by or acting under the orders of the Ordnance Survey[2] (the 'appointed person'), is authorised (written notice of intention to enter having been given to the owner or occupier) to enter any estate or property of any county, or any body politic or corporate, ecclesiastical or civil, or into and upon any land, ground, or heritages of any person or persons for the purpose of making and carrying on any survey authorised by the Ordnance Survey Act 1841, or by the order of the Ordnance Survey[3]. He is also authorised to enter to fix any mark or object[4] to be used in the survey, and to fix any such object in any such estate or property, land or ground, or heritages, and to dig up any ground, for the purpose of fixing any such object for such purpose, and also to enter such estates, through which any such appointed person, deems it necessary and proper to carry any boundary line for the purposes of the Act at any reasonable time in the day, until the surveying, ascertaining, and marking out of any reputed boundary line is completed[5]. However, in every case in which it is necessary for any appointed person, or his assistant or assistants, to fix any such object within any walled garden, orchard, or pleasure ground, he must give three days' notice to the occupier of his intention to do so[6]. The occupier may employ any person whom he thinks fit to fix the object within the garden, orchard, or pleasure ground, at such time, in such place or places, and in such manner, as the appointed person or his assistant or assistants so direct[7]. However, the appointed person or his assistant or assistants and workmen must do as little damage as may be in the execution of the powers granted by the Ordnance Survey Act 1841, and must make satisfaction to the owners or occupiers of such lands, grounds, and heritages, or owners of trees, which are any way hurt, damaged, or injured, for all damage sustained[8]. Disputes between the appointed person and the owner or occupier (as the case may be) as to the amount of damage sustained, must be ascertained and determined by a magistrates' court; and any owner or occupier who is aggrieved by the decision of the magistrates' court may appeal against it to the Crown Court[9].

1   As to such appointments see PARA 996.
2   As to the Ordnance Survey see PARA 994.
3   Ordnance Survey Act 1841 s 2 (amended by the Statute Law (Revision) (No 2) Act 1888).
4   This includes any post, stone, or boundary mark: see the Ordnance Survey Act 1841 s 2.
5   Ordnance Survey Act 1841 s 2.
6   Ordnance Survey Act 1841 s 2.
7   Ordnance Survey Act 1841 s 2.
8   Ordnance Survey Act 1841 s 2.
9   Ordnance Survey Act 1841 s 2 (amended by the Courts Act 1971 s 56(2), (4), Sch 9 Pt I, Sch 11 Pt IV; and the Courts Act 2003 s 109(1), Sch 8 para 11). As to magistrates' courts see MAGISTRATES vol 71 (2013) PARA 470 et seq. As to the Crown Court see COURTS AND TRIBUNALS vol 24 (2010) PARA 716 et seq.

998. Local authority clerk to attend surveyor on 21 days' notice. For the purpose of surveying, ascertaining, and marking out the reputed boundaries of any county, any appointed person[1] may require the attendance of any and every such clerk of the local authority[2] in or for any and every such county or adjoining county, either in the same or any adjoining county, at such time (not being less than 21 days after the notice) and at such place as specified in the notice, and to produce to the appointed person any books, maps, papers, or other documents, in his custody or possession as clerk of the local authority[3]. Every such clerk of the local authority must attend and assist the appointed person, but is not obliged to attend at such time or at such place or in such manner as interferes with the proper discharge of his ordinary duties as clerk of the local authority, nor may he be called upon to produce any books, maps, papers, or other documents, the production of which can in any way injuriously affect the interests of each such county[4].

1   As to the appointed person see PARA 996.
2   Ie by notice in writing signed with the appointed person's name, and directed and delivered to any such clerk of the local authority: Ordnance Survey Act 1841 s 5 (amended by the Statute Law Revision (No 2) Act 1888). The Ordnance Survey Act 1841 s 5 refers to the clerk of the peace, whose office was abolished by the Courts Act 1971 s 44(1)(a). Any function of the clerks of the peace or deputy clerks of the peace relating to: (1) the deposit of plans or documents, other than those relating to judicial business; (2) the keeping of records other than those relating to judicial business; or (3) any other matter which is not of a judicial nature, are transferred to the clerks of the local authorities for the areas to which those matters relate: Sch 8 para 1(1), (2). As to the Ordnance Survey see PARA 994. As to local government areas and authorities in England and Wales see LOCAL GOVERNMENT vol 69 (2009) PARA 22 et seq.
3   Ordnance Survey Act 1841 s 5.
4   Ordnance Survey Act 1841 s 5 (amended by the Courts Act 1971 s 56(4), Sch 11 Pt IV).

999. Removing or defacing boundary stones. If any person not duly authorised takes away, removes, displaces, or alters the situation of any boundary stone, post, block, bolt, or mark, which is set up and placed for the purposes of the Ordnance Survey Act 1841[1] he is guilty of an offence[2].

1 As to the marking of boundaries etc see PARA 997. As to the Ordnance Survey see PARA 994.
2 Ordnance Survey Act 1841 s 7 (amended by the Statute Law Revision (No 2) Act 1888; the Statute Law Revision Act 1892; and the Criminal Damage Act 1971 s 11(8), Schedule Pt II). The penalty for such an offence is, on summary conviction, a fine not exceeding level 1 on the standard scale: Ordnance Survey Act 1841 s 7 (amended by the Statute Law (Repeals) Act 1993). As to the standard scale and magistrates' powers to levy unlimited fines see SENTENCING vol 92 (2015) PARA 176.

1000. Obstruction of the survey. If any person wilfully obstructs or hinders any person in the execution of the Ordnance Survey Act 1841[1] he is guilty of an offence[2].

1 As to powers under the Ordnance Survey see PARAS 996–998. As to the Ordnance Survey see PARA 994.
2 Ordnance Survey Act 1841 s 8 (amended by the Summary Jurisdiction Act 1884 s 4, Schedule; the Statute Law Revision (No 2) Act 1888; and the Statute Law Revision Act 1892). The penalty for such an offence is, on summary conviction, a fine not exceeding level 1 on the standard scale: Ordnance Survey Act 1841 s 8 (amended by the Statute Law (Repeals) Act 1993). As to the standard scale and magistrates' powers to levy unlimited fines see SENTENCING vol 92 (2015) PARA 176.

1001. Boundaries and rights of property. The Ordnance Survey Act 1841[1] does not extend to ascertain, define, alter, enlarge, increase or decrease, or affect in any way, any boundary or boundaries of any area[2], or the boundary or boundaries of any land or property, with relation to any owner or owners, or claimant or claimants of any such land respectively, or affect the title of any such owner or owners, or claimant or claimants respectively, to any such lands or property[3].

1 As to the Ordnance Survey see PARA 994.
2 Ie of any county, city, borough, town, parish, burghs royal, parliamentary burghs, burghs of regality and barony, extra-parochial and other places, districts, and divisions: see the Ordnance Survey Act 1841 s 12.
3 Ordnance Survey Act 1841 s 12 (amended by the Statute Law Revision (No 2) Act 1888; and the Statute Law (Repeals) Act 1993).

(17) CHARITABLE INSTITUTIONS GENERALLY

1002. Charitable institutions. Institutions founded for such purposes as the advancement of education[1], arts, culture, heritage or science[2] may be charitable, if the necessary element of public benefit is present[3]. An institution may have been founded for a single purpose which, at the time of the institution's foundation, was considered charitable, but which may not be considered to be charitable by a later generation; in such a case, in the absence of a general charitable intention, a gift in perpetuity to the institution would fail[4].

1 See CHARITIES vol 8 (2015) PARAS 20–26.
2 See CHARITIES vol 8 (2015) PARA 36.
3 See CHARITIES vol 8 (2015) PARA 2 et seq; and see eg *Beaumont v Oliveira* (1869) 4 Ch App 309 (society for the improvement and diffusion of geographical knowledge); *Royal Society of London and Thompson* (1881) 17 ChD 407 (societies for improving natural knowledge); *Re Lopes, Bence-Jones v Zoological Society of London* [1931] 2 Ch 130 (society for the advancement of zoology and animal physiology etc); and *Institution of Civil Engineers v IRC* [1932] 1 KB 149, CA (society for the general advancement of mechanical science); cf *Geologists' Association v IRC* (1928) 14 TC 271, CA; *Midland Counties Institution of Engineers v IRC* (1928) 14 TC 285, CA; *Anglo-Swedish Society v IRC* (1931) 47 TLR 295; *IRC v National Book League* [1957] Ch 488, [1957] 2 All ER 644, CA (all bodies primarily of benefit to members, rather than of general public

utility). As to the jurisdiction of the Charity Commission in respect of institutions of a charitable nature and the property of such institutions see CHARITIES vol 8 (2015) PARA 543 et seq; and as to the jurisdiction of the Secretary of State in that respect see CHARITIES vol 8 (2015) PARA 585.

4   *National Anti-Vivisection Society v IRC* [1948] AC 31 at 74, [1947] 2 All ER 217 at 238, HL, per Simonds LJ. A trust with a political purpose is not, however, charitable: *McGovern v A-G* [1982] Ch 321, [1981] 3 All ER 493.

1003. Privileges and exemptions in relation to charitable institutions. Societies whose purposes entitle them to be regarded as charitable institutions are only liable to pay one fifth of the non-domestic rates which would otherwise be chargeable in respect of property which they occupy, where such property is wholly or mainly used for charitable purposes, and are not liable to pay non-domestic rates in respect of unoccupied properties[1]. Further reduction or remission of the chargeable amount is permissible, where the billing authority so decides, for such societies and for premises owned or occupied by societies which are not established or conducted for profit and whose main objects are charitable or otherwise philanthropic or religious or concerned with education, social welfare, science, literature or the fine arts[2].

Fair and accurate reports of findings or decisions of associations for the purpose of promoting or encouraging the exercise of or interest in art, science, religion or learning may enjoy qualified privilege in proceedings for defamation[3].

A lottery promoted wholly on behalf of a non-commercial society[4] is exempt from the requirement for an operating licence[5].

Certain literary, scientific and cultural institutions are exempt, in so far as they are charities, from the requirement of registration under the Charities Act 2011[6].

Charitable and other institutions enjoy certain exemptions from tax[7].

1   See the Local Government Finance Act 1988 ss 43(5), (6), 45A; and LOCAL GOVERNMENT FINANCE vol 70 (2012) PARAS 122, 127.
2   See the Local Government Finance Act 1988 s 47(2)(b), (3), (4); and LOCAL GOVERNMENT FINANCE vol 70 (2012) PARAS 129–130.
3   See the Defamation Act 1996 s 15, Sch 1 Pt II para 14(a); and DEFAMATION vol 32 (2012) PARAS 633, 635.
4   A society is non-commercial if it is established and conducted (1) for charitable purposes; (2) for the purpose of enabling participation in, or of supporting, sport, athletics or a cultural activity; or (3) for any other non-commercial purpose other than that of private gain: see the Gambling Act 2005 ss 19(1), 353(1); and LICENSING AND GAMBLING vol 67 (2008) PARA 377.
5   See the Gambling Act 2005 Sch 11 para 30; and LICENSING AND GAMBLING vol 68 (2008) PARA 662.
6   See the Charities Act 2011 ss 22(1), 30(2)(a); and CHARITIES vol 8 (2015) PARAS 308, 318. The relevant institutions are: (1) the Board of Trustees of the Victoria and Albert Museum (see PARA 861); (2) the Board of Trustees of the Science Museum (see PARA 867); (3) the Board of Trustees of the Armouries (see PARA 873); (4) the Board of Trustees of the Royal Botanic Gardens, Kew (see PARA 880); (5) the Board of Trustees of the National Museums and Galleries on Merseyside; (6) the trustees of the British Museum (see PARA 824) and of the Natural History Museum (see PARA 823); (7) the Board of Trustees of the National Gallery (see PARA 833); (8) the Board of Trustees of the Tate Gallery (see PARA 833); (9) the Board of Trustees of the National Portrait Gallery (see PARA 833); (10) the Board of Trustees of the Wallace Collection (see PARA 833); (11) the trustees of the Imperial War Museum (see PARA 841); (12) the trustees of the National Maritime Museum (see PARA 847); (13) any institution which is administered by or on behalf of an institution included in heads (1)–(12) and established for the general purposes of, or for any special purpose of or in connection with, that institution; and (14) the British Library Board (see PARA 904): see the Charities Act 2011 Sch 3 (amended by the Co-operative and Community Benefit Societies Act 2014 Sch 4 paras 181, 183).
7   See PARAS 1113, 1114.

3. IMMOVEABLE CULTURAL HERITAGE

(1) WORLD HERITAGE SITES

1004. World Heritage Sites. The purpose of the UNESCO Convention concerning the Protection of the World Cultural and Natural Heritage[1] is to establish an effective system of collective protection of the cultural and natural heritage of outstanding universal value, organised on a permanent basis and in accordance with modern scientific methods[2].

For the purposes of the convention, the following are considered as 'cultural heritage':

(1) monuments: architectural works, works of monumental sculpture and painting, elements or structures of an archaeological nature, inscriptions, cave dwellings and combinations of features, which are of outstanding universal value from the point of view of history, art or science;

(2) groups of buildings: groups of separate or connected buildings which, because of their architecture, their homogeneity or their place in the landscape, are of outstanding universal value from the point of view of history, art or science;

(3) sites: works of man or the combined works of nature and man, and areas including archaeological sites which are of outstanding universal value from the historical, aesthetic, ethnological or anthropological point of view[3];

and the following are considered as 'natural heritage':

(a) natural features consisting of physical and biological formations or groups of such formations, which are of outstanding universal value from the aesthetic or scientific point of view;

(b) geological and physiographical formations and precisely delineated areas which constitute the habitat of threatened species of animals and plants of outstanding universal value from the point of view of science or conservation;

(c) natural sites or precisely delineated natural areas of outstanding universal value from the point of view of science, conservation or natural beauty[4].

Each state which is a party to the convention[5] must identify and delineate the different cultural heritage and natural heritage situated on its territory[6]. Each state undertakes to take measures for ensuring the identification, protection, conservation, presentation and transmission to future generations of its cultural and natural heritage[7].

An intergovernmental committee for the protection of the cultural and natural heritage of outstanding universal value, called the 'World Heritage Committee', is established within UNESCO[8]. The committee must establish, keep up to date and publish, a list (the 'World Heritage List') of properties forming part of the cultural heritage and natural heritage which it considers as having outstanding universal value in terms of such criteria as it establishes[9]. The committee must also establish, keep up to date and publish, whenever circumstances so require, a list (the 'list of World Heritage in Danger') of the property appearing in the World Heritage List for the conservation of which major operations are necessary and for which assistance has been requested under the convention[10]. The committee must consider requests for international assistance from states party to the convention with respect to property forming part of their cultural or natural heritage and included or potentially suitable for inclusion in these lists[11]. The purpose of such requests may be to secure the protection, conservation, presentation or rehabilitation of such property, or to help identify such property[12]. The committee must determine an order of priorities for its operations and draw up, keep up to date and publicise a list of property for which international assistance has been granted[13].

A fund for the protection of the world cultural and natural heritage of outstanding universal value, called the 'World Heritage Fund', is established under the convention, and this is administered by the committee[14]. The states party to the convention must endeavour by all appropriate means, and in particular by educational and information programmes, to strengthen appreciation and respect by people of their cultural and natural heritage, and keep the public broadly informed of the dangers threatening this heritage and of the activities carried on in pursuance of the convention[15].

There are currently 28 world heritage sites in the United Kingdom[16]. Conserving and enhancing the historic environment is an important component of the National Planning Policy Framework's[17] drive to achieve sustainable development in England[18] and the government has issued planning practice guidance on conserving and enhancing the historic environment[19], including guidance on the level of protection and management required for world heritage sites[20].

1 Ie UNESCO Convention concerning the Protection of the World Cultural and Natural Heritage (Paris, 1972).
2 See the UNESCO Convention concerning the Protection of the World Cultural and Natural Heritage (Paris, 1972) preamble.
3 UNESCO Convention concerning the Protection of the World Cultural and Natural Heritage (Paris, 1972) art 1.
4 UNESCO Convention concerning the Protection of the World Cultural and Natural Heritage (Paris, 1972) art 2.
5 The convention was ratified by the United Kingdom on 29 May 1984.
6 See the UNESCO Convention concerning the Protection of the World Cultural and Natural Heritage (Paris, 1972) art 3.
7 See the UNESCO Convention concerning the Protection of the World Cultural and Natural Heritage (Paris, 1972) arts 4–7.
8 See the UNESCO Convention concerning the Protection of the World Cultural and Natural Heritage (Paris, 1972) arts 8–10.
9 See the UNESCO Convention concerning the Protection of the World Cultural and Natural Heritage (Paris, 1972) arts 11, 12.
10 See the UNESCO Convention concerning the Protection of the World Cultural and Natural Heritage (Paris, 1972) arts 11, 12.
11 See the UNESCO Convention concerning the Protection of the World Cultural and Natural Heritage (Paris, 1972) art 13. As to the conditions and arrangements for international assistance see arts 19–26.
12 See the UNESCO Convention concerning the Protection of the World Cultural and Natural Heritage (Paris, 1972) art 13.
13 See the UNESCO Convention concerning the Protection of the World Cultural and Natural Heritage (Paris, 1972) art 13.
14 See the UNESCO Convention concerning the Protection of the World Cultural and Natural Heritage (Paris, 1972) arts 15–18.
15 See the UNESCO Convention concerning the Protection of the World Cultural and Natural Heritage (Paris, 1972) art 27.
16 A list of all the sites is available on the UNESCO website which, at the date at which this volume states the law, can be found at whc.unesco.org. As to the meaning of 'United Kingdom' see PARA 804 note 2.
17 The National Planning Policy Framework (March 2012) sets out the Government's planning policies for England and how they are expected to be applied. A copy of the National Planning

Policy Framework (March 2012) can be found, at the date at which this volume states the law, at www.communities.gov.uk. See also PLANNING vol 81 (2010) PARA 17. As to the position in Wales see PLANNING vol 81 (2010) PARAS 17–18.
18 See the *National Planning Policy Framework* (March 2012) chapter 12.
19 See *Planning Practice Guidance: Conserving and enhancing the historic environment* (March 2014) which is available on the Department for Communities and Local Government website which, at the date at which this volume states the law, can be found at www.communities.gov.uk.
20 See *Further Guidance on World Heritage Sites* (March 2014) which is available on the Department for Communities and Local Government website which, at the date at which this volume states the law, can be found at www.communities.gov.uk. As to sentencing guidelines for offences of theft involving historic objects or loss of the nation's heritage see PARA 1046 note 5.

(2) ARCHAEOLOGICAL SITES AND MONUMENTS

(i) European Convention

1005. European Convention on the Protection of the Archaeological Heritage. The aim of the European Convention on the Protection of the Archaeological Heritage[1] is to protect the archaeological heritage as a source of the European collective memory and as an instrument for historical and scientific study[2]. To this end, all remains and objects and any other traces of mankind from past epochs are considered to be elements of the archaeological heritage:

(1)   the preservation and study of which help to retrace the history of mankind and its relation with the natural environment;

(2)   for which excavations or discoveries and other methods of research into mankind and the related environment are the main sources of information; and

(3)   which are located in any area within the jurisdiction of the states party to the convention[3].

'Archaeological heritage' includes structures, constructions, groups of buildings, developed sites, moveable objects, monuments of other kinds as well as their context, whether situated on land or under water[4].

The states party to the convention[5] each undertake:

(a)   to institute a legal system for the protection of archaeological heritage[6];

(b)   to preserve archaeological heritage and guarantee the scientific significance of archaeological research work[7];

(c)   to implement measures for the physical protection of archaeological heritage[8];

(d)   to seek to reconcile and combine the respective requirements of archaeology and development plans by ensuring that archaeologists participate in planning policies designed to ensure well-balanced strategies for the protection, conservation and enhancement of sites of archaeological interest[9];

(e)   to arrange for public financial support for archaeological research and conservation[10];

(f)   to take steps to facilitate the collection and dissemination of scientific information concerning archaeological matters[11];

(g)   to promote public awareness of the value of the archaeological heritage and to promote public access to important elements of its archaeological heritage[12];

(h)   to take steps for the prevention of the illicit circulation of elements of the archaeological heritage[13].

The main legislation relating to the protection of ancient monuments and archaeological areas in England and Wales is the Ancient Monuments and Archaeological Areas Act 1979[14].

1　Ie the European Convention on the Protection of the Archaeological Heritage (revised) (Council of Europe ETS No 143: Valetta 1992).

2　European Convention on the Protection of the Archaeological Heritage (revised) (Council of Europe ETS No 143: Valetta 1992) art 1.1.

3　European Convention on the Protection of the Archaeological Heritage (revised) (Council of Europe ETS No 143: Valetta 1992) art 1.2.

4　European Convention on the Protection of the Archaeological Heritage (revised) (Council of Europe ETS No 143: Valetta 1992) art 1.3.

5　The convention was ratified by the United Kingdom on 19 September 2000.

6　See the European Convention on the Protection of the Archaeological Heritage (revised) (Council of Europe ETS No 143: Valetta 1992) art 2. As to the protection of ancient monuments and archaeological areas see PARA 1006 et seq.

7　See the European Convention on the Protection of the Archaeological Heritage (revised) (Council of Europe ETS No 143: Valetta 1992) art 3.

8　See the European Convention on the Protection of the Archaeological Heritage (revised) (Council of Europe ETS No 143: Valetta 1992) art 4.

9　See the European Convention on the Protection of the Archaeological Heritage (revised) (Council of Europe ETS No 143: Valetta 1992) art 5. For planning practice guidance in this respect see *Planning Practice Guidance: Conserving and enhancing the historic environment* (March 2014) which is available on the Department for Communities and Local Government website which, at the date at which this volume states the law, can be found at www.communities.gov.uk. See also PARA 1004.

10　See the European Convention on the Protection of the Archaeological Heritage (revised) (Council of Europe ETS No 143: Valetta 1992) art 6.

11　See the European Convention on the Protection of the Archaeological Heritage (revised) (Council of Europe ETS No 143: Valetta 1992) arts 7, 8.

12　See the European Convention on the Protection of the Archaeological Heritage (revised) (Council of Europe ETS No 143: Valetta 1992) art 9.

13　See the European Convention on the Protection of the Archaeological Heritage (revised) (Council of Europe ETS No 143: Valetta 1992) art 10. As to export and import control see PARA 1096 et seq.

14　See PARA 1006 et seq.

(ii)　Ancient Monuments and Archaeological Areas

A.　INTRODUCTION TO THE ANCIENT MONUMENTS AND ARCHAEOLOGICAL AREAS ACT 1979

1006.　Application of the Ancient Monuments and Archaeological Areas Act 1979. The Ancient Monuments and Archaeological Areas Act 1979 was passed to consolidate and amend the law relating to ancient monuments[1] and make provision for the investigation, preservation and recording of matters of archaeological or historical interest and for the regulation of operations affecting such matters[2]. The Act applies to England, Wales and Scotland[3]; and may be applied by order, subject to consultation with the Council of the Isles of Scilly, to those Isles[4]. The provisions are applied to Crown land[5], ecclesiastical property[6] and monuments[7] in territorial waters[8]; and specific provision is made as to the application of the Act to the Broads[9].

1　As to the meaning of 'ancient monument' see PARA 1029.

2　See PARA 1007 et seq.

3　See the Ancient Monuments and Archaeological Areas Act 1979 s 65(3). In relation to Scotland see also the Historic Environment Scotland Act 2014. As to the meaning of 'England' see PARA 804 note 2. As to the meaning of 'Wales' see PARA 802 note 4.

4　See the Ancient Monuments and Archaeological Areas Act 1979 s 52. The Act applies as if that council were a district council (s 52(a)), and subject to any modifications specified in the order (s 52(b)). At the date at which this volume states the law no such order had been made. As to the making of orders see PARA 1009. As to the Council of the Isles of Scilly see LOCAL GOVERNMENT vol 69 (2009) PARA 36. As to the exercise of the duty to consult see JUDICIAL REVIEW vol 61 (2010) PARA 627.

5   See the Ancient Monuments and Archaeological Areas Act 1979 s 50; and PARA 1007.
6   See the Ancient Monuments and Archaeological Areas Act 1979 s 51; and PARAS 1010, 1024 note 5, 1025 note 5. 'Ecclesiastical property' means land belonging to an ecclesiastical benefice of the Church of England, or being or forming part of a church subject to the jurisdiction of a bishop of any diocese of the Church of England or the site of such a church, or being or forming part of a burial ground subject to such jurisdiction: s 51(5). Where any ecclesiastical property is vested in the incumbent of a benefice which is vacant, for the purposes of the Ancient Monuments and Archaeological Areas Act 1979 it is treated as being vested in the Diocesan Board of Finance for the diocese in which the land is situated: s 51(2) (amended by the Church of England (Miscellaneous Provisions) Measure 2006 s 14, Sch 5 para 20). 'Land' means, in England and Wales, any corporeal hereditament, including a building or a monument and, in relation to any acquisition of land, includes any interest in or right over land: Ancient Monuments and Archaeological Areas Act 1979 s 61(1). As to the Church of England see ECCLESIASTICAL LAW vol 34 (2011) PARA 50 et seq. As to corporeal hereditaments see REAL PROPERTY AND REGISTRATION vol 87 (2012) PARA 11.
7   As to the meaning of 'monument' see PARA 1013.
8   See the Ancient Monuments and Archaeological Areas Act 1979 s 53; and PARA 1008.
9   The Ancient Monuments and Archaeological Areas Act 1979 Pt I (ss 1–32) (see PARAS 1013–1046) and Pt II (ss 33–41) (see PARAS 1047–1059) and s 45(2), (3) (see PARA 1065) apply, in relation to the Broads (as defined by the Norfolk and Suffolk Broads Act 1988: see WATER AND WATERWAYS vol 101 (2009) PARA 735), as if the Broads Authority were a local authority: Ancient Monuments and Archaeological Areas Act 1979 s 52A (added by the Norfolk and Suffolk Broads Act 1988 s 2(5), (6), Sch 3 Pt I). The Ancient Monuments and Archaeological Areas Act 1979 Pt I (ss 1–32) and Pt II (ss 33–41) have effect as if in relation to any monument in a National Park for which a National Park authority is the local planning authority, or to any area the whole or any part of which is comprised in such a park, the references in those Parts to a local authority included references to that National Park authority: Environment Act 1995 Sch 9 para 10(1). The Ancient Monuments and Archaeological Areas Act 1979 s 45(2), (3) (see PARA 1065) has effect as if a National Park authority were a local authority for the purposes of the Act and as if the relevant park were the authority's area: Environment Act 1995 Sch 9 para 10(3). 'Local authority' means: in England, the council of a county or district, the council of a London borough, and the Common Council of the City of London; and in Wales, the council of a county or county borough: Ancient Monuments and Archaeological Areas Act 1979 s 61(1) (definition amended by the Local Government Act 1985 s 102, Sch 17; Local Government (Wales) Act 1994 s 66(6), (8), Sch 16 para 56(3), Sch 18). As to the Broads Authority see WATER AND WATERWAYS vol 101 (2009) PARA 734. As to National Park authorities see OPEN SPACES AND COUNTRYSIDE vol 78 (2010) PARA 526. As to local government areas and authorities in England and Wales see LOCAL GOVERNMENT vol 69 (2009) PARA 22 et seq. As to the London boroughs and their councils see LONDON GOVERNMENT vol 71 (2013) PARA 20 et seq.

1007. Monuments which are Crown land. Notwithstanding any interest of the Crown in Crown land[1], but subject as follows below[2], (1) a monument[3] which for the time being is Crown land may be included in the schedule of monuments[4]; and (2) any restrictions or powers imposed or conferred by any of the provisions of the Ancient Monuments and Archaeological Areas Act 1979 apply and are exercisable in relation to Crown land and in relation to anything done on Crown land otherwise than by or on behalf of the Crown, but not so as to affect any interest of the Crown therein[5].

Except with the consent of the appropriate authority[6], no power under the Act to enter, or to do anything, on any land is exercisable in relation to land which for the time being is Crown land[7]; and no interest in land which for the time being is Crown land may be acquired compulsorily[8] under the Act[9].

1   'Crown land' means land in which there is a Crown interest or a Duchy interest; 'Crown interest' means an interest belonging to Her Majesty in right of the Crown, or belonging to a government department, or held in trust for Her Majesty for the purposes of a government department, and includes any estate or interest held in right of the Prince and Steward of Scotland; 'Duchy interest' means an interest belonging to Her Majesty in right of the Duchy of Lancaster, or belonging to the Duchy of Cornwall; and 'government department' includes any Minister of the Crown: Ancient Monuments and Archaeological Areas Act 1979 s 50(4). For the purposes of s 50, the Welsh Assembly Commission is treated as a government department (and references to the Crown in that

section must be construed accordingly): see the National Assembly for Wales Commission (Crown Status) (No 2) Order 2007, SI 2007/1353, art 3. As to the meaning of 'land' see PARA 1006 note 6. As to the Crown see CONSTITUTIONAL AND ADMINISTRATIVE LAW vol 20 (2014) PARA 150; CROWN AND CROWN PROCEEDINGS vol 29 (2014) PARA 1 et seq. As to the Duchy of Lancaster see CROWN AND CROWN PROCEEDINGS vol 29 (2014) PARA 214 et seq. As to the Duchy of Cornwall see CROWN AND CROWN PROCEEDINGS vol 29 (2014) PARA 232 et seq. As to the Welsh Assembly Commission see CONSTITUTIONAL AND ADMINISTRATIVE LAW vol 20 (2014) PARA 366.

　　For the purposes of the Ancient Monuments and Archaeological Areas Act 1979: (1) the interest of a corporate officer or the corporate officers in any land must be regarded as a Crown interest within the meaning of s 50; (2) any operations carried out by or on behalf of a corporate officer or the corporate officers must be regarded as carried out by or on behalf of the Crown; and (3) the use of the land for the purposes of the House of Lords, the House of Commons or both those Houses must be regarded as use by or on behalf of the Crown: Parliamentary Corporate Bodies (Crown Immunities etc) Order 1992, SI 1992/1732, art 3(1)(a)–(c). In relation to land which is Crown land, within the meaning of the Ancient Monuments and Archaeological Areas Act 1979 s 50, by virtue only of head (1) above, the 'appropriate authority' for the purposes of that section (see note 6) is the corporate officer or, as the case may be, the corporate officers in whom is vested the interest in the land: Parliamentary Corporate Bodies (Crown Immunities etc) Order 1992, SI 1992/1732, art 3(1). To the extent that a corporate officer or the corporate officers has or have responsibility for the management of any land in which he or they has or have no interest but which forms part of the Palace of Westminster, the corporate officer or corporate officers must be regarded as having the status of a government department for the purposes of the Ancient Monuments and Archaeological Areas Act 1979 s 50(4)(a) (see note 6): Parliamentary Corporate Bodies (Crown Immunities etc) Order 1992, SI 1992/1732, art 3(2). In art 3 'land' has the same meaning as in the Ancient Monuments and Archaeological Areas Act 1979 but a licence is not regarded as an interest in land: see arts 1(3), 3(3). 'Corporate officer' means either the corporate officer of the House of Lords or the corporate officer of the House of Commons and 'corporate officers' means those two corporate officers acting jointly: art 1(2). As to the corporate officers of the House of Lords and the House of Commons see PARLIAMENT vol 78 (2010) PARA 990.

2　Ie subject to the Ancient Monuments and Archaeological Areas Act 1979 s 50 (see the text and notes 1, 3–9).
3　As to the meaning of 'monument' see PARA 1013.
4　Ancient Monuments and Archaeological Areas Act 1979 s 50(1)(a). As to the schedule of monuments see PARA 1014.
5　Ancient Monuments and Archaeological Areas Act 1979 s 50(1)(b).
6　In relation to any land, 'appropriate authority' means: (1) in the case of land belonging to Her Majesty in right of the Crown and forming part of the Crown Estate, the Crown Estate Commissioners, and, in relation to any other land belonging to Her Majesty in right of the Crown, the government department having the management of that land (Ancient Monuments and Archaeological Areas Act 1979 s 50(4)(a)); (2) in relation to land belonging to Her Majesty in right of the Duchy of Lancaster, the Chancellor of the Duchy (s 50(4)(b)); (3) in relation to land belonging to the Duchy of Cornwall, such person as the Duke of Cornwall, or the possessor for the time being of the Duchy of Cornwall, appoints (s 50(4)(c)); and (4) in the case of land belonging to a government department or held in trust for Her Majesty for the purposes of a government department, that department (s 50(4)(d)). If any question arises as to what authority is the appropriate authority in relation to any land, the question must be referred to the Treasury, whose decision is final: s 50(4). As to the application of s 50(4) to the corporate officers of the House of Lords and the House of Commons see note 1. The function of the Treasury under s 50, in so far as it is exercisable in relation to Wales, is not transferred to the Welsh Ministers: see the National Assembly for Wales (Transfer of Functions) Order 1999, SI 1999/672, art 2, Sch 1; Government of Wales Act 2006 Sch 11 para 30. As to the meaning of 'Treasury' see PARA 809 note 4. As to the Welsh Ministers see PARA 802. As to the meaning of 'Wales' see PARA 802 note 4. As to the Crown Estate Commissioners see CROWN AND CROWN PROCEEDINGS vol 29 (2014) PARA 192 et seq.
7　Ancient Monuments and Archaeological Areas Act 1979 s 50(2)(a). As to powers of entry see PARAS 1061–1064.
8　Ie under the Ancient Monuments and Archaeological Areas Act 1979 Pt I (ss 1–32).
9　Ancient Monuments and Archaeological Areas Act 1979 s 50(2)(b). As to the compulsory acquisition of ancient monuments see PARA 1030.

1008. Monuments in territorial waters. A monument[1] situated in, on or under the sea bed[2] within the seaward limits of United Kingdom territorial waters[3] adjacent to the coast of Great Britain (a 'monument in territorial waters') may be included[4] in the schedule of monuments[5]. The entry in the schedule relating to any monument in territorial waters must describe the monument as lying off the coast of England, or of Scotland, or of Wales[6]; and any such monument is treated for the purposes of the Ancient Monuments and Archaeological Areas Act 1979 as situated in the country specified for this purpose in the entry relating to the monument in the schedule[7].

Without prejudice to any jurisdiction exercisable apart from this provision, proceedings for any offence under the Ancient Monuments and Archaeological Areas Act 1979 committed in United Kingdom territorial waters adjacent to the coast of Great Britain may be taken, and the offence may for all incidental purposes be treated as having been committed, in any place in Great Britain[8].

Notwithstanding that by virtue of these provisions[9] the Ancient Monuments and Archaeological Areas Act 1979 may affect individuals or bodies corporate outside the United Kingdom, it applies to any individual whether or not he is a British subject[10], and to any body corporate whether or not incorporated under the law of any part of the United Kingdom[11].

1   As to the meaning of 'monument' see PARA 1013.
2   References in the Ancient Monuments and Archaeological Areas Act 1979 s 53 to the 'sea bed' do not include the seashore or any other land which, although covered (intermittently or permanently) by the sea, is within Great Britain: s 53(7). As to the meaning of 'land' see PARA 1006 note 6. As to the meaning of 'Great Britain' see PARA 804 note 2.
3   As to the United Kingdom's territorial waters see WATER AND WATERWAYS vol 100 (2009) PARA 31. As to the meaning of 'United Kingdom' see PARA 804 note 2.
4   Ie under the Ancient Monuments and Archaeological Areas Act 1979 s 1(3) (see PARA 1014).
5   Ancient Monuments and Archaeological Areas Act 1979 s 53(1). Sections 54–65 extend accordingly to any such monument which is a scheduled monument, but not otherwise: s 53(1). As to the meaning of 'scheduled monument' see PARA 1014.
6   As to the meaning of 'England' see PARA 804 note 2. As to the meaning of 'Wales' see PARA 802 note 4.
7   Ancient Monuments and Archaeological Areas Act 1979 s 53(2). A constable on any monument in territorial waters has all the powers, protection and privileges which he has in the area for which he acts as constable: s 53(6). As to the office of constable see POLICE AND INVESTIGATORY POWERS vol 84 (2013) PARA 1 et seq.
8   Ancient Monuments and Archaeological Areas Act 1979 s 53(4).
9   Ie the Ancient Monuments and Archaeological Areas Act 1979 s 53.
10 For the purpose of enactments passed before 1983, the expression 'British subject' is defined by the British Nationality Act 1981 s 51(1): see BRITISH NATIONALITY vol 4 (2011) PARA 469 et seq.
11 Ancient Monuments and Archaeological Areas Act 1979 s 53(5).

1009. Regulations and orders under the Ancient Monuments and Archaeological Areas Act 1979.

Any power of the Secretary of State or, in relation to Wales, the Welsh Ministers[1] to make regulations and certain orders[2] under the Ancient Monuments and Archaeological Areas Act 1979 is exercisable by statutory instrument[3].

Any regulations or order made under the Act may make different provision for different cases to which the regulations or order apply[4].

1   The functions of the Secretary of State under the Ancient Monuments and Archaeological Areas Act 1979, in so far as they relate to Wales, were transferred to the National Assembly for Wales (see the National Assembly for Wales (Transfer of Functions) Order 1999, SI 1999/672, art 2, Sch 1) and are now exercisable by the Welsh Ministers (see the Government of Wales Act 2006 s 162(1), Sch 11 paras 30, 32). As to the Secretary of State and the Welsh Ministers see PARA 802. As to the meaning of 'Wales' see PARA 802 note 4.
2   Ie orders under the Ancient Monuments and Archaeological Areas Act 1979 s 3 (scheduled monument consent: see PARA 1017); s 37 (exemption from restrictions as to operations in archaeological areas: see PARA 1056); s 52 (Isles of Scilly: see PARA 1006); s 61 (specification of statutory undertakers: see PARA 1055 note 6); and s 65 (commencement).

3 See the Ancient Monuments and Archaeological Areas Act 1979 s 60(2). As to the exercise of delegated powers see STATUTES AND LEGISLATIVE PROCESS vol 96 (2012) PARA 1045 et seq. As to the procedure in relation to subordinate legislation made by the Welsh Ministers see the Government of Wales Act 2006 Sch 11 paras 33–35; and CONSTITUTIONAL AND ADMINISTRATIVE LAW vol 20 (2014) PARA 380; STATUTES AND LEGISLATIVE PROCESS vol 96 (2012) PARA 1035.
4 Ancient Monuments and Archaeological Areas Act 1979 s 60(1).

1010. Service of documents under the Ancient Monuments and Archaeological Areas Act 1979. Any notice or other document required or authorised to be served under the Ancient Monuments and Archaeological Areas Act 1979 may be served either:

(1)   by delivering it to the person[1] on whom it is to be served[2]; or

(2)   by leaving it at his usual or last known place of abode or, where he has given an address for service, at that address[3]; or

(3)   by sending it in a pre-paid registered letter, or by the recorded delivery service, addressed to him at his usual or last known place of abode or, where he has given an address for service, at that address[4]; or

(4)   in the case of an incorporated company or body, by delivering it to its secretary or clerk at its registered or principal office, or sending it in a pre-paid registered letter, or by the recorded delivery service, addressed to the secretary or clerk at that office[5].

Where any such notice or document is required or authorised to be served on any person as being the owner[6] or occupier of any monument[7] or other land, it may be addressed to the 'owner' or, as the case may require, to the 'occupier' of that monument or land (describing it) without further name or description[8]; and if his usual or last known place of abode cannot be found, it may be served by being affixed conspicuously to the monument or to some object on the site of the monument[9] or, as the case may be, on the land[10]. Where any notice is required to be served on an owner of land, and the land is ecclesiastical property[11], a like notice must be served on the Diocesan Board of Finance for the diocese in which the land is situated[12].

1 As to the meaning of 'person' see PARA 803 note 17.
2 Ancient Monuments and Archaeological Areas Act 1979 s 56(1)(a).
3 Ancient Monuments and Archaeological Areas Act 1979 s 56(1)(b).
4 Ancient Monuments and Archaeological Areas Act 1979 s 56(1)(c). A requirement to send a document by post is not confined to sending it by the Post Office postal system: see the Postal Services Act 2000 Sch 8 Pt 1. As to the service of documents by post generally see the Interpretation Act 1978 s 7; and PARA 913 note 3.
5 Ancient Monuments and Archaeological Areas Act 1979 s 56(1)(d). As to the registered office of a company see COMPANIES vol 14 (2009) PARA 129.
6 Except in connection with applications for scheduled monument consent under the Ancient Monuments and Archaeological Areas Act 1979 Sch 1 para 2(1), or regulations made for the purpose (see PARA 1018), 'owner', in relation to any land in England and Wales, means a person, other than a mortgagee not in possession, who, whether in his own right or as trustee for any other person, is entitled to receive the rack rent of the land, or, where the land is not let at a rack rent, would be so entitled if it were so let: s 61(1). 'Possession' includes receipt of rents and profits or the right to receive any rents and profits (if any): s 61(1). As to the meaning of 'land' see PARA 1006 note 6. As to the meaning of 'England' see PARA 804 note 2. As to the meaning of 'Wales' see PARA 802 note 4.
7 As to the meaning of 'monument' see PARA 1013. As to the meaning of 'ancient monument' see PARA 1029.
8 Ancient Monuments and Archaeological Areas Act 1979 s 56(2)(a).
9 As to the meaning of 'site of a monument' see PARA 1013.
10 Ancient Monuments and Archaeological Areas Act 1979 s 56(2)(b).
11 As to the meaning of 'ecclesiastical property' see PARA 1006 note 6.
12 See the Ancient Monuments and Archaeological Areas Act 1979 s 51(1) (amended by the Church of England (Miscellaneous Provisions) Measure 2006 s 14, Sch 5 para 20(a)). This provision is

expressed to be without prejudice to the provisions of the Acquisition of Land Act 1981 with respect to notices served under that Act: see the Ancient Monuments and Archaeological Areas Act 1979 s 51(1); Interpretation Act 1978 s 17(2)(a). As to Diocesan Boards of Finance see ECCLESIASTICAL LAW vol 34 (2011) PARAS 241–242.

1011. Information as to interests in land comprising ancient monument or archaeological area. For the purpose of enabling the Secretary of State or, in relation to Wales, the Welsh Ministers[1], or the Historic Buildings and Monuments Commission for England ('the Commission')[2] or a local authority[3] to exercise any function[4] under the Ancient Monuments and Archaeological Areas Act 1979, the Secretary of State, the Welsh Ministers, the Commission or the local authority may require the occupier of any land[5] and any person[6] who, either directly or indirectly, receives rent in respect of any land to state in writing[7] the nature of his interest in it, and the name and address of any other person known to him as having an interest in it, whether as a freeholder, owner[8], mortgagee, lessee or otherwise[9].

A person is guilty of an offence[10] if:

(1)   having been required under these provisions to give any information, he fails without reasonable excuse to give it[11];

(2)   having been so required to give any information, he knowingly makes any misstatement in respect of it[12].

1   The functions of the Secretary of State under the Ancient Monuments and Archaeological Areas Act 1979, in so far as they relate to Wales, were transferred to the National Assembly for Wales (see the National Assembly for Wales (Transfer of Functions) Order 1999, SI 1999/672, art 2, Sch 1) and are now exercisable by the Welsh Ministers (see the Government of Wales Act 2006 s 162(1), Sch 11 paras 30, 32). As to the Secretary of State and the Welsh Ministers see PARA 802. As to the meaning of 'Wales' see PARA 802 note 4.

2   As to the Historic Buildings and Monuments Commission for England ('the Commission') see PARA 803.

3   As to the meaning of 'local authority' see PARA 1006 note 9.

4   'Functions' includes powers and duties: Ancient Monuments and Archaeological Areas Act 1979 s 61(1).

5   As to the meaning of 'land' see PARA 1006 note 6.

6   As to the meaning of 'person' see PARA 803 note 17.

7   As to the meaning of 'writing' see PARA 805 note 14.

8   As to the meaning of 'owner' see PARA 1010 note 6.

9   Ancient Monuments and Archaeological Areas Act 1979 s 57(1) (amended by the National Heritage Act 1983 Sch 4 para 66).

10 A person who has an enforcement function in relation to an offence under the Ancient Monuments and Archaeological Areas Act 1979 is a regulator for the purposes of the Regulatory Enforcement and Sanctions Act 2008: see CONSTITUTIONAL AND ADMINISTRATIVE LAW vol 20 (2014) PARAS 331–339.

11 See the Ancient Monuments and Archaeological Areas Act 1979 s 57(2). The penalty for such an offence is, on summary conviction, a fine not exceeding level 3 on the standard scale: s 57(2) (amended by virtue of the Criminal Justice Act 1982 s 46). As to the standard scale and magistrates' powers to levy unlimited fines see SENTENCING vol 92 (2015) PARA 176. As to offences by bodies corporate see PARA 1012.

12 See the Ancient Monuments and Archaeological Areas Act 1979 s 57(3). The penalty for such an offence is (1) on summary conviction, a fine not exceeding the statutory maximum (s 57(3)(a)); or (2) on conviction on indictment, a fine (s 57(3)(b)). As to the statutory maximum and magistrates' powers to levy unlimited fines see SENTENCING vol 92 (2015) PARA 176.

1012. Offences under the Ancient Monuments and Archaeological Areas Act 1979 by corporations. Where an offence under the Ancient Monuments and Archaeological Areas Act 1979 which has been committed by a body corporate is proved to have been committed with the consent or connivance of or to be attributable to any neglect on the part of, a director[1], manager, secretary or other similar officer of the body corporate, or any person who was purporting to act in any such capacity, he, as well as the body corporate, is guilty of that offence and is liable to be proceeded against accordingly[2].

1   In relation to any body corporate established by or under an enactment for the purpose of carrying on under national ownership an industry or part of an industry or undertaking, being a body corporate whose affairs are managed by its members, 'director' means a member of that body corporate: Ancient Monuments and Archaeological Areas Act 1979 s 58(2). 'Enactment' includes an enactment in any local or private Act, and an order, rule, regulation, byelaw or scheme made under an Act: s 61(1). As to the meaning of 'enactment' generally see PARA 805 note 5. As to sentencing guidelines for offences of theft involving historic objects or loss of the nation's heritage see PARA 1046 note 5. As to bodies corporate see COMPANIES vol 14 (2009) PARA 2; CORPORATIONS vol 24 (2010) PARA 301 et seq.
2   Ancient Monuments and Archaeological Areas Act 1979 s 58(1).

B.   ANCIENT MONUMENTS

(A)   Protection of Ancient Monuments

1013.   Meaning of 'monument'. In the Ancient Monuments and Archaeological Areas Act 1979, 'monument' means: (1) any building, structure or work, whether above or below the surface of the land[1], and any cave or excavation[2]; (2) any site comprising the remains of any such building, structure or work or of any cave or excavation[3]; and (3) any site comprising, or comprising the remains[4] of, any vehicle, vessel, aircraft or other moveable structure or part of it which neither constitutes nor forms part of any work which is a monument within head (1) above[5]. Any machinery attached to a monument is regarded as part of the monument if it could not be detached without being dismantled[6].

References in the Act to a monument include references to the site of the monument in question[7], and to a group of monuments or any part of a monument or group of monuments[8]. The site of a monument includes not only the land in or on which it is situated but also any land comprising or adjoining it which appears to the Secretary of State or, in relation to Wales, the Welsh Ministers[9], or the Historic Buildings and Monuments Commission for England ('the Commission')[10] or a local authority[11], in the exercise in relation to that monument of any of their functions[12] under the Act, to be essential for the monument's support and preservation[13]. References in the Act to the site of a monument are references to the monument itself where it consists of a site[14], and in any other case include references to the monument itself[15].

1   As to the meaning of 'land' see PARA 1006 note 6.
2   Ancient Monuments and Archaeological Areas Act 1979 s 61(1), (7)(a). Head (1) in the text does not apply to any ecclesiastical building for the time being used for ecclesiastical purposes: s 61(8).
3   Ancient Monuments and Archaeological Areas Act 1979 s 61(1), (7)(b).
4   'Remains' includes any trace or sign of the previous existence of the thing in question: Ancient Monuments and Archaeological Areas Act 1979 s 61(13).
5   Ancient Monuments and Archaeological Areas Act 1979 s 61(1), (7)(c). Head (3) in the text does not apply to a site comprising any object or its remains unless the situation of that object or its remains in that particular site is a matter of public interest (s 61(8)(a)), or to a site comprising, or comprising the remains of, any vessel which is protected by an order under the Protection of Wrecks Act 1973 s 1 (see PARA 1068), designating an area round the site as a restricted area (Ancient Monuments and Archaeological Areas Act 1979 s 61(8)(b)).
6   Ancient Monuments and Archaeological Areas Act 1979 s 61(7).
7   Ancient Monuments and Archaeological Areas Act 1979 s 61(10)(a).
8   Ancient Monuments and Archaeological Areas Act 1979 s 61(10)(b).
9   The functions of the Secretary of State under the Ancient Monuments and Archaeological Areas Act 1979, in so far as they relate to Wales, were transferred to the National Assembly for Wales (see the National Assembly for Wales (Transfer of Functions) Order 1999, SI 1999/672, art 2, Sch 1) and are now exercisable by the Welsh Ministers (see the Government of Wales Act 2006

s 162(1), Sch 11 paras 30, 32). As to the Secretary of State and the Welsh Ministers see PARA 802. As to the meaning of 'Wales' see PARA 802 note 4.
10 As to the Historic Buildings and Monuments Commission for England ('the Commission') see PARA 803.
11 As to the meaning of 'local authority' see PARA 1006 note 9.
12 As to the meaning of 'functions' see PARA 1011 note 4.
13 Ancient Monuments and Archaeological Areas Act 1979 s 61(9) (amended by the National Heritage Act 1983 Sch 4 para 67).
14 Ancient Monuments and Archaeological Areas Act 1979 s 61(11)(a).
15 Ancient Monuments and Archaeological Areas Act 1979 s 61(11)(b).

1014. Schedule of monuments. The Secretary of State or, in relation to Wales, the Welsh Ministers[1] must compile and maintain a schedule of monuments[2] in such form as he or they think fit[3]. Any monument for the time being included in the schedule is known as a 'scheduled monument'[4].

On first compiling the schedule, or at any time thereafter, the Secretary of State or, as the case may be, the Welsh Ministers may include any monument which appears to him or them to be of national importance[5]. However, this power does not apply to any structure which is occupied as a dwelling house by any person other than a person employed as its caretaker or his family[6].

The Secretary of State[7] or the Welsh Ministers may exclude any monument from the schedule[8], or may amend the entry in the schedule relating to any monument[9]. The Secretary of State or the Welsh Ministers must inform the owner of the inclusion of a monument in the schedule[10], and must publish a list of monuments included[11].

An entry in the schedule recording the inclusion of a monument situated in England and Wales is a local land charge[12].

1 The functions of the Secretary of State under the Ancient Monuments and Archaeological Areas Act 1979, in so far as they relate to Wales, were transferred to the National Assembly for Wales (see the National Assembly for Wales (Transfer of Functions) Order 1999, SI 1999/672, art 2, Sch 1) and are now exercisable by the Welsh Ministers (see the Government of Wales Act 2006 s 162(1), Sch 11 paras 30, 32). As to the Secretary of State and the Welsh Ministers see PARA 802. As to the meaning of 'Wales' see PARA 802 note 4.
2 The schedule of monuments is referred to in the Ancient Monuments and Archaeological Areas Act 1979 as 'the schedule': ss 1(1), 61(1). As to the meaning of 'monument' see PARA 1013. As to the inclusion in the schedule of monuments in territorial waters see PARA 1008.
3 Ancient Monuments and Archaeological Areas Act 1979 s 1(1). On first compiling the schedule the Secretary of State had to include therein: (1) any monument included in the list last published before the commencement of the Ancient Monuments and Archaeological Areas Act 1979 under the Ancient Monuments Consolidation and Amendment Act 1913 s 12 (repealed) (Ancient Monuments and Archaeological Areas Act 1979 s 1(2)(a)); and (2) any monument in respect of which the Secretary of State had before the commencement of the Ancient Monuments and Archaeological Areas Act 1979 served notice on any person in accordance with the Ancient Monuments Act 1931 s 6(1) (repealed) of his intention to include it in a list to be published under s 12 (Ancient Monuments and Archaeological Areas Act 1979 s 1(2)(b)). As to the meaning of 'person' see PARA 803 note 17.
4 See the Ancient Monuments and Archaeological Areas Act 1979 ss 1(11), 61(1).
5 Ancient Monuments and Archaeological Areas Act 1979 s 1(3). The Secretary of State must consult the Historic Buildings and Monuments Commission for England ('the Commission') before he includes in the schedule a monument situated in England: s 1(3) (amended by the National Heritage Act 1983 s 33(3), Sch 4 para 25). As to the Commission see PARA 803. As to the meaning of 'England' see PARA 804 note 2. The Secretary of State has a broad discretion under the Ancient Monuments and Archaeological Areas Act 1979 s 1(3) and is under no duty to include a monument even though he accepts it is of national importance: *R v Secretary of State for the Environment, ex p Rose Theatre Trust Co* [1990] 1 QB 504, [1990] 1 All ER 754 (remains of Elizabethan theatre).
6 Ancient Monuments and Archaeological Areas Act 1979 s 1(4).

7   In the case of a monument situated in England, the Secretary of State must consult with the Commission before he makes an exclusion from or amendment to the schedule: see the Ancient Monuments and Archaeological Areas Act 1979 s 1(5) (amended by the National Heritage Act 1983 Sch 4 para 25).
8   Ancient Monuments and Archaeological Areas Act 1979 s 1(5)(a).
9   Ancient Monuments and Archaeological Areas Act 1979 s 1(5)(b).
10 See the Ancient Monuments and Archaeological Areas Act 1979 ss 1(6), (6A), 1A; and PARA 1015.
11 See the Ancient Monuments and Archaeological Areas Act 1979 ss 1(7), (7A), 1A; and PARA 1015.
12 Ancient Monuments and Archaeological Areas Act 1979 s 1(9). As to local land charges see REAL PROPERTY AND REGISTRATION vol 87 (2012) PARA 763 et seq.

1015. Notification of entry in the schedule of monuments. As soon as may be after:

(1)   including[1] any monument[2] in the schedule of monuments[3];
(2)   amending the entry in the schedule relating to any monument[4]; or
(3)   excluding any monument from the schedule[5],

the Secretary of State[6], as regards a monument situated in England[7], must inform the Historic Buildings and Monuments Commission for England ('the Commission')[8] of the action taken, and in a case falling within head (1) or (2) above must also send to the Commission a copy of the entry or, as the case may be, of the amended entry in the schedule relating to that monument[9]. The Secretary of State must from time to time supply the Commission with a list of the monuments situated in England and which are for the time being included in the schedule, whether as a single list or in sections containing the monuments situated in particular areas[10]. The Secretary of State must from time to time supply the Commission with amendments of any such list[11].

As soon as may be after the Commission has been informed[12] as mentioned above[13], and in a case falling within head (1) or (2) above has received a copy of the entry or (as the case may be) of the amended entry from the Secretary of State[14], the Commission must inform the owner[15] and (if the owner is not the occupier) the occupier of the monument, and any local authority[16] in whose area the monument is situated, of the inclusion, amendment or exclusion and, in a case falling within head (1) or (2) above, must also send to him or them a copy of the entry or (as the case may be) of the amended entry in the schedule relating to that monument[17]. As soon as may be after the Commission receive a list or a section of a list[18] it must publish the list or section (as the case may be)[19].

In relation to a monument in Wales, the Welsh Ministers[20] must, as soon as may be after taking any of the steps in heads (1) to (3) above, inform the owner and, if the owner is not the occupier, the occupier of the monument, and any local authority in whose area the monument is situated, of the action taken and, in a case falling within head (1) or (2) above, must also send to him or it a copy of the entry or, as the case may be, of the amended entry in the schedule relating to that monument[21]. The Welsh Ministers must from time to time publish a list of all the monuments in Wales which are for the time being included in the schedule, whether as a single list or in sections containing the monuments situated in particular areas[22]. The Welsh Ministers may from time to time publish amendments of any such list[23].

1   Ie under the Ancient Monuments and Archaeological Areas Act 1979 s 1(3) (see PARA 1014).
2   As to the meaning of 'monument' see PARA 1013.
3   Ancient Monuments and Archaeological Areas Act 1979 s 1(6)(a). As to the schedule of monuments see PARA 1014.
4   Ancient Monuments and Archaeological Areas Act 1979 s 1(6)(b).
5   Ancient Monuments and Archaeological Areas Act 1979 s 1(6)(c).
6   As to the Secretary of State see PARA 802 note 2.
7   As to the meaning of 'England' see PARA 804 note 2.

8   As to the Historic Buildings and Monuments Commission for England ('the Commission') see PARA 803. As to the service of documents see PARA 1010.

9   See the Ancient Monuments and Archaeological Areas Act 1979 s 1(6A) (added by the National Heritage Act 1983 Sch 4 para 25(5)).

10 Ancient Monuments and Archaeological Areas Act 1979 s 1(7A) (added by the National Heritage Act 1983 Sch 4 para 25(7)). In the case of a list supplied in sections, all sections of the list need not be supplied simultaneously: Ancient Monuments and Archaeological Areas Act 1979 s 1(7A) (as so added).

11 Ancient Monuments and Archaeological Areas Act 1979 s 1(8A) (added by the National Heritage Act 1983 Sch 4 para 25(8)).

12 Ie as mentioned in the Ancient Monuments and Archaeological Areas Act 1979 s 1(6A) (see the text to notes 6–9).

13 Ancient Monuments and Archaeological Areas Act 1979 s 1A(1)(a) (s 1A added by the National Heritage Act 1983 Sch 4 para 26).

14 Ancient Monuments and Archaeological Areas Act 1979 s 1A(1)(b) (as added: see note 13).

15 As to the meaning of 'owner' see PARA 1010 note 6.

16 As to the meaning of 'local authority' see PARA 1006 note 9.

17 Ancient Monuments and Archaeological Areas Act 1979 s 1A(1) (as added: see note 13).

18 Ie in pursuance of the Ancient Monuments and Archaeological Areas Act 1979 s 1(7A) (see the text to note 10).

19 Ancient Monuments and Archaeological Areas Act 1979 s 1A(2) (as added: see note 13). The Commission must from time to time publish amendments of any list published under s 1A(2), and any such list as amended is evidence of the inclusion in the schedule for the time being (1) of the monuments listed (s 1A(3)(a) (as so added)); and (2) of any matters purporting to be reproduced in the list from the entries in the schedule relating to monuments listed (s 1A(3)(b) (as so added)).

20 The functions of the Secretary of State under the Ancient Monuments and Archaeological Areas Act 1979, in so far as they relate to Wales, were transferred to the National Assembly for Wales (see the National Assembly for Wales (Transfer of Functions) Order 1999, SI 1999/672, art 2, Sch 1) and are now exercisable by the Welsh Ministers (see the Government of Wales Act 2006 s 162(1), Sch 11 paras 30, 32). As to the Welsh Ministers see PARA 802. As to the meaning of 'Wales' see PARA 802 note 4.

21 See the Ancient Monuments and Archaeological Areas Act 1979 s 1(6) (amended by the National Heritage Act 1983 s 33(3), Sch 4 para 25).

22 Ancient Monuments and Archaeological Areas Act 1979 s 1(7) (amended by the National Heritage Act 1983 Sch 4 para 25(6)). In the case of a list published in sections, all sections of the list need not be published simultaneously: Ancient Monuments and Archaeological Areas Act 1979 s 1(7) (as so amended).

23 See the Ancient Monuments and Archaeological Areas Act 1979 s 1(8). Any such list, as amended, is evidence of the inclusion in the schedule for the time being (1) of the monuments listed (s 1(8)(a)); and (2) of any matters purporting to be produced in the list from the entries in the schedule relating to the monuments listed (s 1(8)(b)).

1016. Control of works affecting ancient monuments. It is an offence for any person[1] to execute or cause or permit to be executed any of the following works[2] unless the works are authorised[3] under a scheduled monument consent[4]. The works are:

(1)   any works resulting in the demolition or destruction of or any damage to a scheduled monument[5];

(2)   any works for the purpose of removing or repairing a scheduled monument or any part of it or of making any alterations or additions to it[6];

(3)   any flooding or tipping operations on land in, on or under which there is a scheduled monument[7].

If a person executing or causing or permitting to be executed any works to which a scheduled monument consent relates fails to comply with any condition attached to the consent he is guilty of an offence unless he proves that he took all reasonable precautions and exercised all due diligence to avoid contravening the condition[8].

In any proceedings for an offence under these provisions it is a defence to prove that the works were urgently necessary in the interests of safety or health and that notice in writing of the need for the works was given to the Secretary of State or, as appropriate, the Welsh Ministers as soon as reasonably practicable[9].

1 As to the meaning of 'person' see PARA 803 note 16.
2 'Works' includes operations of any description and, in particular (but without prejudice to the generality of the following definitions), flooding or tipping operations and any operations undertaken for purposes of agriculture (within the meaning of the Town and Country Planning Act 1990 (see s 336(1); and PLANNING vol 81 (2010) PARA 23)), or forestry (including afforestation): Ancient Monuments and Archaeological Areas Act 1979 s 61(1) (definition amended by the Planning (Consequential Provisions) Act 1990 s 4, Sch 2 para 43(2)). 'Flooding operations' means covering land with water or any other liquid or partially liquid substance; and 'tipping operations' means tipping soil or spoil or depositing building or other materials or matter (including waste materials or refuse) on any land: Ancient Monuments and Archaeological Areas Act 1979 s 61(1). As to the meaning of 'land' see PARA 804 note 30.
3 Ie under the Ancient Monuments and Archaeological Areas Act 1979 Pt I (ss 1–32) or by development consent: see the Ancient Monuments and Archaeological Areas Act 1979 s 2(1) (amended by the Planning Act 2008 Sch 2 paras 16, 17). 'Development consent' means development consent under the Planning Act 2008 (see PLANNING): Ancient Monuments and Archaeological Areas Act 1979 s 61(1) (definition added by the Planning Act 2008 s 36, Sch 2 paras 16, 20).
    Without prejudice to any other authority to execute works conferred under the Ancient Monuments and Archaeological Areas Act 1979 Pt 1, works are authorised under that Part if: (1) the Secretary of State or, in relation to Wales, the Welsh Ministers have granted scheduled monument consent for the execution of the works (see s 2(3)(a); and PARA 1017); and (2) the works are executed in accordance with the terms of the consent and of any conditions attached to the consent (s 2(3)(b)). As to the meaning of 'scheduled monument' see PARA 1014. As to the meaning of 'monument' see PARA 1013.
    The functions of the Secretary of State under the Ancient Monuments and Archaeological Areas Act 1979, in so far as they relate to Wales, were transferred to the National Assembly for Wales (see the National Assembly for Wales (Transfer of Functions) Order 1999, SI 1999/672, art 2, Sch 1) and are now exercisable by the Welsh Ministers (see the Government of Wales Act 2006 s 162(1), Sch 11 paras 30, 32). As to the Secretary of State and the Welsh Ministers see PARA 802. As to the meaning of 'Wales' see PARA 802 note 4.
4 Ancient Monuments and Archaeological Areas Act 1979 s 2(1) (as amended: see note 3). The penalty for an offence under the Ancient Monuments and Archaeological Areas Act 1979 s 2 is, on summary conviction, a fine not exceeding the statutory maximum (s 2(10)(a)); or (2) on conviction on indictment, a fine (s 2(10)(b)). As to the statutory maximum and magistrates' powers to levy unlimited fines see SENTENCING vol 92 (2015) PARA 176. As to offences by bodies corporate see PARA 1012. A person who has an enforcement function in relation to an offence under the Ancient Monuments and Archaeological Areas Act 1979 is a regulator for the purposes of the Regulatory Enforcement and Sanctions Act 2008: see CONSTITUTIONAL AND ADMINISTRATIVE LAW vol 20 (2014) PARAS 331–339.
5 Ancient Monuments and Archaeological Areas Act 1979 s 2(2)(a). In any proceedings for an offence under s 2 in relation to works within s 2(2)(a) it is a defence for the accused to prove that he took all reasonable precautions and exercised all due diligence to avoid or prevent damage to the monument (s 2(7)) or that he did not know and had no reason to believe that the monument was within the area affected by the works or, as the case may be, that it was a scheduled monument (see s 2(8)). As to the standard of proof on the accused see CRIMINAL PROCEDURE vol 28 (2015) PARAS 449–451.
6 Ancient Monuments and Archaeological Areas Act 1979 s 2(2)(b).
7 Ancient Monuments and Archaeological Areas Act 1979 s 2(2)(c). In any proceedings for an offence under s 2 in relation to works within s 2(2)(c) it is a defence for the accused to prove that he did not know and had no reason to believe that the monument was within the area affected by the works or, as the case may be, that it was a scheduled monument: see s 2(8).
8 Ancient Monuments and Archaeological Areas Act 1979 s 2(6). As to the penalty for such offence see note 4.
9 Ancient Monuments and Archaeological Areas Act 1979 s 2(9).

1017. Scheduled monument consent.
'Scheduled monument consent' means consent to carry out works[1] on a scheduled monument[2] granted in writing[3] upon application to the Secretary of State or, in relation to Wales, the Welsh Ministers[4].

Such consent may be granted either unconditionally or subject to conditions, whether with respect to the manner in which or the persons[5] by whom the works or any of the works are to be executed or otherwise[6]. The consent may subsequently be modified or revoked[7]. A condition attached to a scheduled monument consent may, in particular, require that a person authorised by the Historic Buildings and Monuments Commission of England[8] in a case where the monument in question is situated in England[9], or the Welsh Ministers or a person authorised by them in the case where the monument is situated in Wales[10], be afforded the opportunity, before any works to which the consent relates are begun, to examine the monument and its site[11] and carry out such excavations there as appear to them to be desirable for the purposes of archaeological investigation[12].

The Secretary of State or, in relation to Wales, the Welsh Ministers may by order[13] grant consent[14] for the execution of works of any class or description specified in the order, and any such consent may apply to scheduled monuments of any class or description so specified[15]. The Secretary of State or the Welsh Ministers may direct[16] that scheduled monument consent granted by such an order is not to apply to any scheduled monument specified in the direction, and may withdraw any such direction[17].

Any scheduled monument consent (including scheduled monument consent granted by order[18]), except so far as it otherwise provides, enures for the benefit of the monument and of all persons for the time being interested therein[19].

1 As to the meaning of 'works' see PARA 1016 note 2. As to the control of works see PARA 1016.
2 As to the meaning of 'scheduled monument' see PARA 1014. As to the meaning of 'monument' see PARA 1013.
3 As to the meaning of 'writing' see PARA 805 note 14.
4 See the Ancient Monuments and Archaeological Areas Act 1979 s 2(3)(a). References to a scheduled monument consent do not include references to a scheduled monument consent granted by an order under s 3 (see the text to notes 13–17) unless the contrary intention is expressed: s 3(5). The functions of the Secretary of State under the Ancient Monuments and Archaeological Areas Act 1979, in so far as they relate to Wales, were transferred to the National Assembly for Wales (see the National Assembly for Wales (Transfer of Functions) Order 1999, SI 1999/672, art 2, Sch 1) and are now exercisable by the Welsh Ministers (see the Government of Wales Act 2006 s 162(1), Sch 11 paras 30, 32). As to the Secretary of State and the Welsh Ministers see PARA 802. As to the meaning of 'Wales' see PARA 802 note 4.
5 As to the meaning of 'person' see PARA 803 note 17.
6 Ancient Monuments and Archaeological Areas Act 1979 s 2(4).
7 See PARA 1020.
8 As to the Historic Buildings and Monuments Commission for England ('the Commission') see PARA 803.
9 Ancient Monuments and Archaeological Areas Act 1979 s 2(5)(a) (s 2(5)(a), (b) substituted by the National Heritage Act 1983 s 33, Sch 4 para 27). As to the meaning of 'England' see PARA 804 note 2.
10 See the Ancient Monuments and Archaeological Areas Act 1979 s 2(5)(b) (as substituted: see note 9).
11 As to the meaning of 'site of a monument' see PARA 1013.
12 See the Ancient Monuments and Archaeological Areas Act 1979 s 2(5). 'Archaeological investigation' means any investigation of any land, objects or other material for the purpose of obtaining and recording any information of archaeological or historical interest and (without prejudice to the generality of the preceding provision) includes in the case of an archaeological investigation of any land: (1) any investigation for the purpose of discovering and revealing and (where appropriate) recovering and removing any objects or other material of archaeological or historical interest situated in, on or under the land (s 61(4)(a)); and (2) examining, testing, treating, recording and preserving any such objects or material discovered during the course of any excavations or inspections carried out for the purposes of any such investigation (s 61(4)(b)). As to the meaning of 'land' see PARA 1006 note 6. As to powers of entry see ss 5, 6 (PARAS 1027–1028); s 26 (PARA 1045); ss 43, 44 (PARAS 1061–1063); and s 50(2) (PARA 1007).

13 As to the making of orders see PARA 1009. As to the order made see the Ancient Monuments (Class Consents) Order 1994, SI 1994/1381.

14 Before granting consent in relation to monuments of a class or description which includes monuments situated in England, the Secretary of State must consult with the Commission in relation to the monuments so situated: Ancient Monuments and Archaeological Areas Act 1979 s 3(1) (amended by the National Heritage Act 1983 Sch 4 para 28). As to the Commission see PARA 803. As to the meaning of 'England' see PARA 804 note 2. As to the exercise of the duty to consult see JUDICIAL REVIEW vol 61 (2010) PARA 627.

15 Ancient Monuments and Archaeological Areas Act 1979 s 3(1). Any conditions attached by virtue of the Ancient Monuments and Archaeological Areas Act 1979 s 2 (see the text to notes 1–12) to a scheduled monument consent granted by an order under s 3 apply in such class or description of cases as may be specified in the order: s 3(2).

16 Such a direction does not take effect until notice of it has been served on the occupier or (if there is no occupier) on the owner of the monument in question: Ancient Monuments and Archaeological Areas Act 1979 s 3(4). As to the meaning of 'owner' see PARA 1010 note 6. As to the service of notices see PARA 1010.

17 Ancient Monuments and Archaeological Areas Act 1979 s 3(3). Before making a direction in relation to a monument situated in England, or withdrawing such a direction, the Secretary of State must consult with the Commission: s 3(3) (amended by the National Heritage Act 1983 Sch 4 para 28).

18 Ie an order under the Ancient Monuments and Archaeological Areas Act 1979 s 3 (see the text to notes 13–17).

19 Ancient Monuments and Archaeological Areas Act 1979 Sch 1 para 1(2). As to the duration of consent see PARA 1019.

1018. Applications for scheduled monument consent. Regulations[1] may be made as to the form and manner in which applications for scheduled monument consent[2] are to be made, the particulars to be included and the information to be provided by applicants or the Secretary of State or, as the case may be, the Welsh Ministers[3]. The Secretary of State or the Welsh Ministers may refuse to entertain an application if it is not accompanied by one or more of the following certificates signed by or on behalf of the applicant[4]:

(1)   a certificate stating that, at the beginning of the period of 21 days ending with the application, no person other than the applicant was the owner[5] of the monument[6];

(2)   a certificate stating that the applicant has given the requisite notice of the application to all the persons other than the applicant who, at the beginning of that period, were owners of the monument[7];

(3)   a certificate stating that the applicant is unable to issue a certificate in accordance with either head (1) or head (2) above, that he has given the requisite notice of the application to such one or more of the persons mentioned in head (2) above as are specified in the certificate, that he has taken such steps as are reasonably open to him to ascertain the names and addresses of the remainder of those persons and that he has been unable to do so[8];

(4)   a certificate stating that the applicant is unable to issue a certificate in accordance with head (1) above, that he has taken such steps as are reasonably open to him to ascertain the names and addresses of the persons mentioned in head (2) above and that he has been unable to do so[9].

The Secretary of State or the Welsh Ministers may grant scheduled monument consent in respect of all or any part of the works[10] to which an application for such consent relates[11], but before determining whether or not to grant consent on any application, he or they must either cause a public local inquiry to be held[12], or afford to the applicant, and to any other person to whom it appears to the Secretary of State or the Welsh Ministers expedient to afford it, an opportunity of appearing before and being heard by a person appointed for the purpose[13]. The Secretary of State or the Welsh Ministers must: (a) in every case consider any representations made by any person with respect to the application before the time when he or they consider the decision on it, whether in consequence of any notice given to that person in accordance with any requirements of regulations[14] or of any publicity given to the application by the Secretary of State or the Welsh Ministers, or otherwise[15]; (b) if any inquiry or hearing has been held, consider the report of the person who held it[16]. If the monument in question is situated in England, the Secretary of State must also consult with the Historic Buildings and Monuments Commission for England ('the Commission')[17].

The Secretary of State or the Welsh Ministers must serve notice of his or their decision with respect to the application on the applicant and on every person who has made representations to him or them with respect to it[18]. Any person aggrieved by the decision may appeal to the High Court[19].

1 As to the making of regulations see PARA 1009. As to the regulations made see the Ancient Monuments (Applications for Scheduled Monument Consent) Regulations 1981, SI 1981/1301; and the Ancient Monuments (Applications for Scheduled Monument Consent) (Welsh Forms and Particulars) Regulations 2001, SI 2001/1438.

2 As to the meaning of 'scheduled monument consent' and as to applications for consent see PARA 1017. As to the meaning of 'scheduled monument' see PARA 1014. As to the meaning of 'monument' see PARA 1013.

3 Ancient Monuments and Archaeological Areas Act 1979 Sch 1 para 1(1). As soon as practicable after receiving an application for scheduled monument consent in relation to a monument situated in England, the Secretary of State must send a copy of the application to the Historic Buildings and Monuments Commission for England ('the Commission'): Sch 1 para 2A (added by the National Heritage Act 1983 s 33(3), Sch 4 para 68(2)). As to the Commission see PARA 803. As to the meaning of 'England' see PARA 804 note 2.

The functions of the Secretary of State under the Ancient Monuments and Archaeological Areas Act 1979, in so far as they relate to Wales, were transferred to the National Assembly for Wales (see the National Assembly for Wales (Transfer of Functions) Order 1999, SI 1999/672, art 2, Sch 1) and are now exercisable by the Welsh Ministers (see the Government of Wales Act 2006 s 162(1), Sch 11 paras 30, 32). As to the Secretary of State and the Welsh Ministers see PARA 802. As to the meaning of 'Wales' see PARA 802 note 4.

4 Ancient Monuments and Archaeological Areas Act 1979 Sch 1 para 2(1). Any certificate issued for this purpose must contain such further particulars of the matters to which the certificate relates as may be prescribed by regulations and be in the form prescribed by regulations: Sch 1 para 2(2). See also note 1.

If any person issues a certificate which purports to comply with the requirements of Sch 1 para 2, and which contains a statement which he knows to be false or misleading in a material particular, or recklessly issues a certificate which purports to comply with those requirements and which contains a statement which is false or misleading in a material particular, he is guilty of an offence and liable on summary conviction to a fine not exceeding level 3 on the standard scale: Sch 1 para 2(4) (amended by virtue of the Criminal Justice Act 1982 s 46). As to the meaning of 'person' see PARA 803 note 17. As to offences by bodies corporate see PARA 1012. As to the standard scale and magistrates' powers to levy unlimited fines see SENTENCING vol 92 (2015) PARA 176. A person who has an enforcement function in relation to an offence under the Ancient Monuments and Archaeological Areas Act 1979 is a regulator for the purposes of the Regulatory Enforcement and Sanctions Act 2008: see CONSTITUTIONAL AND ADMINISTRATIVE LAW vol 20 (2014) PARAS 331–339.

5 Regulations made for the purposes of the Ancient Monuments and Archaeological Areas Act 1979 Sch 1 para 2 may make provision as to who, in the case of any monument, is to be treated as the owner for those purposes: Ancient Monuments and Archaeological Areas Act 1979 Sch 1 para 2(3). As to the meaning of 'owner' see PARA 1010 note 6.

6 Ancient Monuments and Archaeological Areas Act 1979 Sch 1 para 2(1)(a).

7 Ancient Monuments and Archaeological Areas Act 1979 Sch 1 para 2(1)(b). 'Requisite notice' means notice in the form prescribed by regulations made for this purpose: Sch 1 para 2(2). See also note 1. As to the service of notices see PARA 1010.

8 Ancient Monuments and Archaeological Areas Act 1979 Sch 1 para 2(1)(c).

9 Ancient Monuments and Archaeological Areas Act 1979 Sch 1 para 2(1)(d).

10 As to the meaning of 'works' see PARA 1016 note 2. As to the control of works see PARA 1016.
11 Ancient Monuments and Archaeological Areas Act 1979 Sch 1 para 3(1).
12 Ancient Monuments and Archaeological Areas Act 1979 Sch 1 para 3(2)(a). The provisions of the Local Government Act 1972 s 250(2)–(5) (see LOCAL GOVERNMENT vol 69 (2009) PARA 105) apply to a public local inquiry held in relation to a monument situated in England or Wales as they apply where a minister or Secretary of State causes an inquiry to be held under s 250(1): Ancient Monuments and Archaeological Areas Act 1979 Sch 1 para 4(1).
13 Ancient Monuments and Archaeological Areas Act 1979 Sch 1 para 3(2)(b).
14 Ie regulations made by virtue of the Ancient Monuments and Archaeological Areas Act 1979 Sch 1 para 2 (see note 5).
15 Ancient Monuments and Archaeological Areas Act 1979 Sch 1 para 3(3)(a).
16 Ancient Monuments and Archaeological Areas Act 1979 Sch 1 para 3(3)(b).
17 Ancient Monuments and Archaeological Areas Act 1979 Sch 1 para 3(3)(c) (added by the National Heritage Act 1983 Sch 4 para 68). As to the exercise of the duty to consult see JUDICIAL REVIEW vol 61 (2010) PARA 627.
18 Ancient Monuments and Archaeological Areas Act 1979 Sch 1 para 3(4).
19 See the Ancient Monuments and Archaeological Areas Act 1979 s 55; and PARA 1023.

1019. Duration of scheduled monument consent. If no works[1] to which a scheduled monument consent[2] relates are executed or started within the period of five years beginning with the date on which the consent was granted, or such longer or shorter period as may be specified for the purposes of this provision in the consent, the consent ceases to have effect at the end of that period unless previously revoked[3].

1 As to the meaning of 'works' see PARA 1016 note 2. As to the control of works see PARA 1016.
2 As to the meaning of 'scheduled monument consent' see PARA 1017. As to the meaning of 'scheduled monument' see PARA 1014. As to the meaning of 'monument' see PARA 1013. As to applications for consent see PARA 1018.
3 Ancient Monuments and Archaeological Areas Act 1979 s 4(1). This provision does not apply to a scheduled monument consent which provides that it will cease to have effect at the end of a specified period: s 4(2). As to the revocation of consents see PARA 1020.

1020. Modification or revocation of scheduled monument consent. If it appears to the Secretary of State or, in relation to Wales, the Welsh Ministers[1] expedient to do so, he or they may by a direction[2] modify or revoke a scheduled monument consent[3] to any extent he or they consider expedient[4]. Before giving such a direction the Secretary of State or, as the case may be, the Welsh Ministers must serve a notice[5] of proposed modification or revocation on the owner[6] of the monument and, if the owner is not the occupier, the occupier of the monument[7], and on any other person[8] who in the opinion of the Secretary of State or the Welsh Ministers would be affected by the proposal[9].

A person served with such a notice may object to the proposal[10]. If no objection is made, or if all objections are withdrawn, the Secretary of State or, as appropriate, the Welsh Ministers may give a direction modifying or revoking the scheduled monument consent in accordance with the notice[11].

1 The functions of the Secretary of State under the Ancient Monuments and Archaeological Areas Act 1979, in so far as they relate to Wales, were transferred to the National Assembly for Wales (see the National Assembly for Wales (Transfer of Functions) Order 1999, SI 1999/672, art 2, Sch 1) and are now exercisable by the Welsh Ministers (see the Government of Wales Act 2006 s 162(1), Sch 11 paras 30, 32). As to the Secretary of State and the Welsh Ministers see PARA 802. As to the meaning of 'Wales' see PARA 802 note 4.
2 Where a direction would (if given) affect a monument situated in England, the Secretary of State must consult with the Historic Buildings and Monuments Commission for England ('the Commission') before he gives such a direction: Ancient Monuments and Archaeological Areas Act 1979 s 4(3) (amended by the National Heritage Act 1983 Sch 4 para 29). As to the meaning of 'monument' see PARA 1013. As to the meaning of 'England' see PARA 804 note 2. As to the Commission see PARA 803. As to the exercise of the duty to consult see JUDICIAL REVIEW vol 61 (2010) PARA 627.

3   As to the meaning of 'scheduled monument consent' see PARA 1017. As to the meaning of
    'scheduled monument' see PARA 1014.
4   Ancient Monuments and Archaeological Areas Act 1979 s 4(3). This provision extends without
    prejudice to its generality, to specifying a period for the duration of a scheduled monument
    consent, or altering any period specified, for the purposes of s 4(1) (see PARA 1019), and to
    including or altering a provision that a consent will cease to have effect at the end of a specified
    period: s 4(4).
5   Such notice must: (1) contain a draft of the proposed modification or revocation and a brief
    statement of the reasons for it (Ancient Monuments and Archaeological Areas Act 1979 Sch 1
    para 5(2)(a)); and (2) specify the time allowed by Sch 1 para 5(5) (see PARA 1021) for making
    objections to the proposed modification or revocation and the manner in which any such
    objections can be made (Sch 1 para 5(2)(b)). Where the effect of a proposed modification or any
    part of it would be to exclude any works from the scope of the consent in question or in any
    manner to affect the execution of any of the works to which it relates, the notice must indicate that
    the works affected must not be executed after the receipt of the notice or, as the case may require,
    must not be so executed in a manner specified in the notice: Sch 1 para 5(3). A notice of proposed
    revocation must indicate that the works to which the consent relates must not be executed after
    receipt of the notice: Sch 1 para 5(4). As to the service of notices see PARA 1010. As to the meaning
    of 'works' see PARA 1016 note 2. As to the control of works see PARA 1016.
6   As to the meaning of 'owner' see PARA 1010 note 6.
7   Ancient Monuments and Archaeological Areas Act 1979 Sch 1 para 5(1)(a).
8   As to the meaning of 'person' see PARA 803 note 17.
9   Ancient Monuments and Archaeological Areas Act 1979 Sch 1 para 5(1)(b). Where the monument
    in question is situated in England, the Secretary of State must consult with the Commission before
    serving a notice, and on serving such a notice he must send a copy of it to the Commission: Sch
    1 para 5(1A) (added by the National Heritage Act 1983 Sch 4 para 68(4)).
10 See the Ancient Monuments and Archaeological Areas Act 1979 Sch 1 para 5(5); and PARA 1021.
11 Ancient Monuments and Archaeological Areas Act 1979 Sch 1 para 6(1).

1021.   Objection to modification or revocation of scheduled monument consent.

A person[1] who has been served with a notice[2] that the Secretary of State or, in
relation to Wales, the Welsh Ministers[3] propose to give a direction modifying or
revoking a scheduled monument consent[4] may make an objection to the proposed
modification or revocation at any time before the end of the period of 28 days
beginning with the date on which the notice was served[5]. If any such objection is
not withdrawn, then, before giving a direction, the Secretary of State or, as the
case may be, the Welsh Ministers must either cause a public local inquiry to be
held[6], or afford to the objector an opportunity of appearing before and being
heard by a person appointed by the Secretary of State or the Welsh Ministers for
the purpose[7]. The Secretary of State or the Welsh Ministers must consider any
objections duly made and not withdrawn, and consider the report of the person
who held any inquiry or hearing[8]. After such consideration the Secretary of State
or the Welsh Ministers may give the direction either in accordance with the notice
or with any variation appearing to him or them to be appropriate[9].

1   As to the meaning of 'person' see PARA 803 note 17.
2   Ie a notice served under the Ancient Monuments and Archaeological Areas Act 1979 Sch 1
    para 5(1) (see PARA 1020).
3   The functions of the Secretary of State under the Ancient Monuments and Archaeological Areas
    Act 1979, in so far as they relate to Wales, were transferred to the National Assembly for Wales
    (see the National Assembly for Wales (Transfer of Functions) Order 1999, SI 1999/672, art 2, Sch
    1) and are now exercisable by the Welsh Ministers (see the Government of Wales Act 2006
    s 162(1), Sch 11 paras 30, 32). As to the Secretary of State and the Welsh Ministers see PARA 802.
    As to the meaning of 'Wales' see PARA 802 note 4.
4   Ie a direction under the Ancient Monuments and Archaeological Areas Act 1979 s 4(3) (see PARA
    1020). As to the meaning of 'scheduled monument consent' see PARA 1017. As to the meaning of
    'scheduled monument' see PARA 1014.
5   Ancient Monuments and Archaeological Areas Act 1979 Sch 1 para 5(5). As to the service of
    notices see PARA 1010.
6   Ancient Monuments and Archaeological Areas Act 1979 Sch 1 para 6(2)(a). The provisions of the
    Local Government Act 1972 s 250(2)–(5) (see LOCAL GOVERNMENT vol 69 (2009) PARA 105)
    apply to a public local inquiry held under the Ancient Monuments and Archaeological Areas Act

1979 Sch 1 para 6(2)(a) as they apply where an inquiry is to be held under the Local Government Act 1972 s 250(1): see the Ancient Monuments and Archaeological Areas Act 1979 Sch 1 para 9(1). The provisions of the Local Government Act 1972 s 250(4) as to costs do not apply except in so far as the Secretary of State or the Welsh Ministers are of the opinion, having regard to the object and result of the inquiry, that his or their costs should be defrayed by any party to it: see the Ancient Monuments and Archaeological Areas Act 1979 Sch 1 para 9(2).

7 Ancient Monuments and Archaeological Areas Act 1979 Sch 1 para 6(2)(b). If any person by whom an objection has been made avails himself of the opportunity of being heard, the Secretary of State or the Welsh Ministers must afford to each other person served with notice of the proposed modification or revocation, and to any other person to whom it appears to the Secretary of State or the Welsh Ministers expedient to afford it, an opportunity of being heard on the same occasion: Sch 1 para 6(3).

8 See the Ancient Monuments and Archaeological Areas Act 1979 Sch 1 para 6(4).

9 See the Ancient Monuments and Archaeological Areas Act 1979 Sch 1 para 6(5). As to the effect of a direction see PARA 1022.

1022. Effect of direction modifying or revoking a scheduled monument consent.

As soon as may be after giving a direction modifying or revoking a scheduled monument consent[1], the Secretary of State or, in relation to Wales, the Welsh Ministers[2] must send[3] a copy of the direction to each person[4] served with notice of its proposed effect[5] and to any other person afforded an opportunity of being heard[6] in respect of the proposed direction[7].

Where[8] a notice of the proposed direction indicates that any works[9] specified in the notice must not be executed after receipt of the notice[10], or that any works specified in the notice must not be executed after receipt of the notice in a manner so specified[11], the works so specified must not be regarded as authorised[12] if executed or, as the case may be, executed in that manner at any time after the relevant service date[13]. However, these provisions cease to apply: (1) if within the period of 21 months[14] beginning with the relevant service date the Secretary of State or the Welsh Ministers give a direction[15] with respect to the modification or revocation proposed by that notice, on the date when he or they give that direction[16]; (2) if within that period the Secretary of State or the Welsh Ministers serve notice on the occupier or, if there is no occupier, on the owner of the monument that he or they have determined not to give such a direction, on the date when that notice is served[17]; and (3) in any other case, at the end of that period[18].

1 Ie a direction under the Ancient Monuments and Archaeological Areas Act 1979 s 4 (see PARA 1020). As to the meaning of 'scheduled monument consent' see PARA 1017. As to the meaning of 'scheduled monument' see PARA 1014.

2 The functions of the Secretary of State under the Ancient Monuments and Archaeological Areas Act 1979, in so far as they relate to Wales, were transferred to the National Assembly for Wales (see the National Assembly for Wales (Transfer of Functions) Order 1999, SI 1999/672, art 2, Sch 1) and are now exercisable by the Welsh Ministers (see the Government of Wales Act 2006 s 162(1), Sch 11 paras 30, 32). As to the Secretary of State and the Welsh Ministers see PARA 802. As to the meaning of 'Wales' see PARA 802 note 4.

3 As to the service of notices and documents see PARA 1010.

4 As to the meaning of 'person' see PARA 803 note 17.

5 Ie in accordance with the Ancient Monuments and Archaeological Areas Act 1979 Sch 1 para 5 (see PARA 1020).

6 Ie in accordance with the Ancient Monuments and Archaeological Areas Act 1979 Sch 1 para 6(3) (see PARA 1021).

7 Ancient Monuments and Archaeological Areas Act 1979 Sch 1 para 7.

8 Ie in accordance with the Ancient Monuments and Archaeological Areas Act 1979 Sch 1 para 5(3), (4) (see PARA 1020).

9 As to the meaning of 'works' see PARA 1016 note 2. As to the control of works see PARA 1016.

10 See the Ancient Monuments and Archaeological Areas Act 1979 Sch 1 para 8(1), (3).

11 See the Ancient Monuments and Archaeological Areas Act 1979 Sch 1 para 8(2).

12 Ie under the Ancient Monuments and Archaeological Areas Act 1979 Pt 1 (ss 1–32) (see PARA 1016).

13 See the Ancient Monuments and Archaeological Areas Act 1979 Sch 1 para 8(1)–(3). 'Relevant
   service date' means, in relation to a notice under Sch 1 para 5 (see PARA 1020) with respect to
   works affecting any monument, the date on which that notice was served on the occupier or (if
   there is no occupier) on the owner of the monument: Sch 1 para 8(5). As to the meaning of
   'monument' see PARA 1013. As to the meaning of 'owner' see PARA 1010 note 6.
14 As to the meaning of 'month' see PARA 803 note 12.
15 Ie in accordance with the Ancient Monuments and Archaeological Areas Act 1979 Sch 1 para 6
   (see PARA 1021).
16 Ancient Monuments and Archaeological Areas Act 1979 Sch 1 para 8(4)(a).
17 See the Ancient Monuments and Archaeological Areas Act 1979 Sch 1 para 8(4)(b).
18 Ancient Monuments and Archaeological Areas Act 1979 Sch 1 para 8(4)(c).

1023. Questioning the validity of action by the Secretary of State or the Welsh Ministers regarding scheduled monument consent.

If any person is aggrieved[1]:

(1)   by any decision of the Secretary of State or, in relation to Wales, the
        Welsh Ministers[2] on an application for scheduled monument consent[3],
        or

(2)   the giving by him or them of any direction[4] modifying or revoking such
        consent[5],

and desires to question the validity of that action on specified grounds then,
within six weeks from the relevant date[6], he may apply to the High Court[7]. The
specified grounds are: (a) that the action is not within the powers of the Ancient
Monuments and Archaeological Areas Act 1979; or (b) that any of the relevant
requirements[8] have not been complied with in relation to the action[9].

On the application the court may by interim order suspend the operation of the
action questioned until the final determination of the proceedings[10]; and, if
satisfied that the action is not within the powers of the Act or that the
applicant's interests have been substantially prejudiced by a failure to comply with
any of the relevant requirements in relation to it, may quash the action in whole
or in part[11].

The validity of any such action may not otherwise be questioned in any legal
proceedings whatsoever, although this does not affect the exercise of any
jurisdiction of any court in respect of any refusal or failure on the part of the
Secretary of State or the Welsh Ministers to take a decision on an application for
scheduled monument consent[12].

1 As to the meaning of 'person' see PARA 803 note 17. As to the meaning of 'person aggrieved' see
  JUDICIAL REVIEW vol 61 (2010) PARA 656.
2 The functions of the Secretary of State under the Ancient Monuments and Archaeological Areas
  Act 1979, in so far as they relate to Wales, were transferred to the National Assembly for Wales
  (see the National Assembly for Wales (Transfer of Functions) Order 1999, SI 1999/672, art 2, Sch
  1) and are now exercisable by the Welsh Ministers (see the Government of Wales Act 2006
  s 162(1), Sch 11 paras 30, 32). As to the Secretary of State and the Welsh Ministers see PARA 802.
  As to the meaning of 'Wales' see PARA 802 note 4.
3 See the Ancient Monuments and Archaeological Areas Act 1979 s 55(3)(a). As to applications for
  scheduled monument consent see PARA 1018. As to the meaning of 'scheduled monument consent'
  see PARA 1017. As to the meaning of 'scheduled monument' see PARA 1014.
4 Ie under the Ancient Monuments and Archaeological Areas Act 1979 s 4 (see PARA 1020).
5 See the Ancient Monuments and Archaeological Areas Act 1979 s 55(3)(b).
6 'Relevant date' means the date on which the action was taken: see the Ancient Monuments and
  Archaeological Areas Act 1979 s 55(4)(b).
7 See the Ancient Monuments and Archaeological Areas Act 1979 s 55(1)(b). As to the High Court
  of Justice in England and Wales see COURTS AND TRIBUNALS vol 24 (2010) PARA 695 et seq.
8 'Relevant requirements' means any requirements of the Ancient Monuments and Archaeological
  Areas Act 1979 or of the Tribunals and Inquiries Act 1992, or of any regulations or rules made
  under either of those Acts which are applicable to the action: see the Ancient Monuments and
  Archaeological Areas Act 1979 s 55(6)(b) (amended by the Tribunals and Inquiries Act 1992
  s 18(1), Sch 3 para 12).
9 See the Ancient Monuments and Archaeological Areas Act 1979 s 55(1)(b).

10 See the Ancient Monuments and Archaeological Areas Act 1979 s 55(5)(a).
11 See the Ancient Monuments and Archaeological Areas Act 1979 s 55(5)(b).
12 Ancient Monuments and Archaeological Areas Act 1979 s 55(7). As to judicial review of decisions expressed to be final see JUDICIAL REVIEW vol 61 (2010) PARA 655.

1024. Compensation for refusal of scheduled monument consent. The Historic Buildings and Monuments Commission for England ('the Commission')[1], where the monument[2] in question is situated in England[3], or the Welsh Ministers, where the monument is situated in Wales[4], must pay compensation[5] to any person who has an interest in the whole or any part of a monument and who incurs expenditure or otherwise sustains any loss or damage in consequence of the refusal, or the granting subject to conditions, of a scheduled monument consent[6] in relation to any of the following[7]:

(1) works[8] which are reasonably necessary for carrying out any development[9] for which planning permission[10] had been granted (otherwise than by a general development order[11]) before the time when the monument in question became a scheduled monument and was still effective at the date of the application for scheduled monument consent[12];

(2) works which do not constitute development, or constitute development such that planning permission is granted for it by a general development order[13]; and

(3) works which are reasonably necessary for the continuation of any use[14] of the monument for any purpose for which it was in use immediately before the date of the application for scheduled monument consent[15].

In calculating, for the purposes of these provisions, the amount of any loss or damage consisting of depreciation of the value of an interest in land, it must be assumed that any subsequent application for scheduled monument consent in relation to works of a like description would be determined in the same way[16]; but if in the case of a refusal of scheduled monument consent, the Secretary of State or the Welsh Ministers, on refusing that consent, undertook to grant such consent for some other works affecting the monument in the event of an application being made in that behalf, regard must be had to that undertaking[17].

1 As to the Historic Buildings and Monuments Commission for England ('the Commission') see PARA 803.
2 As to the meaning of 'monument' see PARA 1013.
3 As to the meaning of 'England' see PARA 804 note 2.
4 The functions of the Secretary of State under the Ancient Monuments and Archaeological Areas Act 1979, in so far as they relate to Wales, were transferred to the National Assembly for Wales (see the National Assembly for Wales (Transfer of Functions) Order 1999, SI 1999/672, art 2, Sch 1) and are now exercisable by the Welsh Ministers (see the Government of Wales Act 2006 s 162(1), Sch 11 paras 30, 32). As to the Secretary of State and the Welsh Ministers see PARA 802. As to the meaning of 'Wales' see PARA 802 note 4.
5 References in the Ancient Monuments and Archaeological Areas Act 1979 ss 7, 8 (see PARA 1025) to compensation being paid in respect of any works are references to compensation being paid in respect of any expenditure incurred or other loss or damage sustained in consequence of the refusal, or the granting subject to conditions, of a scheduled monument consent in relation to those works: s 7(1). Any claim for compensation under the Ancient Monuments and Archaeological Areas Act 1979 must be made within the time and in the manner prescribed: s 47(1). 'Prescribed' means prescribed by regulations made by the Secretary of State or the Welsh Ministers: see s 61(1). The Ancient Monuments (Claims for Compensation) (England) Regulations 1991, SI 1991/2512, and the Ancient Monuments (Claims for Compensation) (Wales) Regulations 1991, SI 1991/2647, prescribe the forms for claiming compensation and provide for the time within which a claim is to be made under the Ancient Monuments and Archaeological Areas Act 1979 s 7. Any question of disputed compensation under the Act must be referred to and determined by the Upper Tribunal: s 47(2) (amended by SI 2009/1307). As to the Upper Tribunal see COMPULSORY ACQUISITION OF LAND vol 18 (2009) PARA 720. The Land Compensation Act 1961 s 4 (see COMPULSORY ACQUISITION OF LAND vol 18 (2009) PARAS 716–717) applies in relation to the determination

of any such question, but the references in s 4 to the acquiring authority are to be construed as references to the authority by which the compensation claimed is payable under the Ancient Monuments and Archaeological Areas Act 1979: see s 47(3) (amended by SI 2009/1307).

For the purpose of assessing any compensation under the Ancient Monuments and Archaeological Areas Act 1979 s 7 or s 9 (see PARA 1026) in respect of loss or damage consisting of depreciation of the value of an interest in land (s 27(2)), the rules set out in the Land Compensation Act 1961 s 5 (see COMPULSORY ACQUISITION OF LAND vol 18 (2009) PARA 754) have effect, so far as applicable and subject to any necessary modifications, as they have effect for the purpose of assessing compensation for the compulsory acquisition of an interest in land: Ancient Monuments and Archaeological Areas Act 1979 s 27(1). Where an interest in land is subject to a mortgage (1) any compensation to which s 27 applies, which is payable in respect of depreciation of the value of that interest, is assessed as if the interest were not subject to the mortgage (s 27(3)(a)); (2) a claim for any such compensation may be made by any mortgagee of the interest, but without prejudice to the making of a claim by the person entitled to the interest (s 27(3)(b)); (3) no compensation to which s 27 applies is payable in respect of the interest of the mortgagee (as distinct from the interest which is subject to the mortgage) (s 27(3)(c)); and (4) any compensation to which s 27 applies which is payable in respect of the interest which is subject to the mortgage must be paid to the mortgagee, or, if there is more than one mortgagee, to the first mortgagee, and must in either case be applied by him as if it were proceeds of sale (s 27(3)(d)). Any sum which under s 7, s 9, or s 46 (see PARA 1066) is payable in relation to land which is ecclesiastical property, and apart from s 51(3) would be payable to an incumbent, must be paid to Diocesan Board of Finance for the diocese in which the land is situated, to be applied for the purposes for which the proceeds of a sale by agreement of the land would be applicable under any enactment or Measure authorising or disposing of the proceeds of such a sale: s 51(3) (amended by the Church of England (Miscellaneous Provisions) Measure 2006 s 14, Sch 5 para 20(a)). As to the meaning of 'land' see PARA 1006 note 6. 'Compulsory acquisition' does not include the vesting in a person by an Act of Parliament of property previously vested in some other person; and 'mortgage' includes any charge or lien on any property for securing money or money's worth: Town and Country Planning Act 1990 s 336(1) (definitions applied by the Ancient Monuments and Archaeological Areas Act 1979 s 32(1)). As to the meaning of 'person' see PARA 803 note 17. As to the meaning of 'ecclesiastical property' see PARA 1006 note 6. As to Diocesan Boards of Finance see ECCLESIASTICAL LAW vol 34 (2011) PARA 241 et seq. As to the meaning of 'enactment' see PARA 1012 note 1. As to legislation by Measure see ECCLESIASTICAL LAW vol 34 (2011) PARA 111.

6   As to the meaning of 'scheduled monument consent' see PARA 1017. As to the meaning of 'scheduled monument' see PARA 1014.

7   Ancient Monuments and Archaeological Areas Act 1979 s 7(1) (amended by the National Heritage Act 1983 Sch 4 para 33). Compensation payable under the Ancient Monuments and Archaeological Areas Act 1979 s 7 carries interest at the rate for the time being prescribed under the Land Compensation Act 1961 s 32 (see COMPULSORY ACQUISITION OF LAND vol 18 (2009) PARA 641) from the date of the refusal, or grant subject to conditions, of scheduled monument consent until payment: see the Planning and Compensation Act 1991 s 80(1), Sch 18 Pt I. One or more payments on account of such compensation or interest may be made: see s 80(2). As to the recovery of compensation on subsequent grant of scheduled monument consent see the Ancient Monuments and Archaeological Areas Act 1979 s 8; and PARA 1025.

8   As to the meaning of 'works' see PARA 1016 note 2. As to the control of works see PARA 1016.

9   'Development' has the meaning given in the Town and Country Planning Act 1990 s 55, and 'develop' must be construed accordingly: see s 336(1) (definition applied by the Ancient Monuments and Archaeological Areas Act 1979 s 32(1)); and PLANNING vol 81 (2010) PARA 292.

10 'Planning permission' means permission under the Town and Country Planning Act 1990 Pt III (ss 55–106C): see s 336(1) (definition applied by the Ancient Monuments and Archaeological Areas Act 1979 s 32(1)); and PLANNING vol 81 (2010) PARA 288 et seq.

11 References in the Ancient Monuments and Archaeological Areas Act 1979 s 7 to a general development order are references to a development order made as a general order applicable (subject to such exceptions as may be specified in it) to all land: s 7(7). 'Development order' has the meaning given in the Town and Country Planning Act 1990 s 59: see s 336(1) (definition applied by the Ancient Monuments and Archaeological Areas Act 1979 s 32(1)); and PLANNING vol 81 (2010) PARA 387.

12 Ancient Monuments and Archaeological Areas Act 1979 s 7(2)(a). Compensation payable in respect of any works within s 7(2)(a) is limited to compensation in respect of any expenditure incurred or other loss or damage sustained by virtue of the fact that, in consequence of the decision of the Secretary of State or, as the case may be, the Welsh Ministers, any development for which the planning permission in question was granted could not be carried out without contravening s 2(1) (see PARA 1016): s 7(3). As to applications for scheduled monument consent see PARA 1018.

13 Ancient Monuments and Archaeological Areas Act 1979 s 7(2)(b). A person is not entitled to compensation by virtue of s 7(2)(b) if the works in question or any of them would or might result in the total or partial demolition or destruction of the monument, unless those works consist solely of operations involved in or incidental to the use of the site of the monument for the purposes of agriculture or forestry (including afforestation): s 7(4). As to the meaning of 'agriculture' see the Town and Country Planning Act 1990 s 336(1) (definition applied by the Ancient Monuments and Archaeological Areas Act 1979 s 32(1)); and PLANNING vol 81 (2010) PARA 23.

14 'Use', in relation to land, does not include the use of land for the carrying out of any building or other operations on it: Town and Country Planning Act 1990 s 336(1) (definition applied by the Ancient Monuments and Archaeological Areas Act 1979 s 32(1)). 'Building operations' has the meaning given by the Town and Country Planning Act 1990 s 55: s 336(1) (definition substituted by the Planning and Compensation Act 1991 s 32, Sch 7 para 52(1), (2)(c); and applied by the Ancient Monuments and Archaeological Areas Act 1979 s 32(1)). As to building and other operations in the context of the Town and Country Planning Act 1990 see PLANNING vol 81 (2010) PARAS 292–293.

15 Ancient Monuments and Archaeological Areas Act 1979 s 7(2)(c). For this purpose any use in contravention of any legal restrictions for the time being applying to the use of the monument must be disregarded: s 7(2). Where scheduled monument consent is granted subject to conditions, a person is not entitled to compensation by virtue of s 7(2)(c) unless compliance with those conditions would in effect make it impossible to use the monument for the purpose mentioned: s 7(5).

16 Ancient Monuments and Archaeological Areas Act 1979 s 7(6)(a).

17 Ancient Monuments and Archaeological Areas Act 1979 s 7(6)(b).

1025. Recovery of compensation on subsequent grant of scheduled monument consent. In granting or modifying a scheduled monument consent[1] in the cases listed below, the Secretary of State or, in relation to Wales, the Welsh Ministers[2] may do so on terms that no works[3] in respect of which compensation was paid[4] are to be executed in pursuance of the consent until the recoverable amount[5] has been repaid to or secured to the Historic Buildings and Monuments Commission for England ('the Commission')[6] or secured to its satisfaction[7] or, as the case may be, repaid to the Welsh Ministers or secured to their satisfaction[8].

The cases are as follows:

(1)   in a case where compensation was paid in consequence of the refusal of a scheduled monument consent, if the Secretary of State or the Welsh Ministers subsequently grant scheduled monument consent for the execution of all or any of the works in respect of which the compensation was paid[9]; and

(2)   in a case where compensation was paid in consequence of the granting of a scheduled monument consent subject to conditions, if the Secretary of State or the Welsh Ministers subsequently so modify that consent that those conditions, or any of them, cease to apply to the execution of all or any of the works in respect of which the compensation was paid or grant a new consent in respect of all or any of those works free from conditions, or any of them[10].

However, these provisions do not apply unless the compensation paid exceeded £20[11] and the following requirement is fulfilled[12]. The requirement is that: (a) where the monument in question is situated in England[13], the Commission has caused notice of the payment of compensation to be deposited[14] with the council of each district or London borough in which the monument is situated or (where it is situated in the City of London, the Inner Temple or the Middle Temple) with the Common Council of the City of London[15]; and (b) where the monument in question is situated in Wales, the Welsh Ministers have caused such notice to be deposited with the council of each county or county borough in which the monument is situated[16].

1   As to the meaning of 'scheduled monument consent' see PARA 1017. As to the meaning of 'scheduled monument' see PARA 1014. As to the modification of scheduled monument consent see PARA 1020.
2   The functions of the Secretary of State under the Ancient Monuments and Archaeological Areas Act 1979, in so far as they relate to Wales, were transferred to the National Assembly for Wales (see the National Assembly for Wales (Transfer of Functions) Order 1999, SI 1999/672, art 2, Sch 1) and are now exercisable by the Welsh Ministers (see the Government of Wales Act 2006 s 162(1), Sch 11 paras 30, 32). As to the Secretary of State and the Welsh Ministers see PARA 802. As to the meaning of 'Wales' see PARA 802 note 4.
3   As to the meaning of 'works' see PARA 1016 note 2. As to the control of works see PARA 1016.
4   Ie under the Ancient Monuments and Archaeological Areas Act 1979 s 7 (see PARA 1024). As to the meaning of references to compensation being paid in respect of any works see PARA 1024 note 5.
5   'Recoverable amount' means such amount (being an amount representing the whole of the compensation previously paid or such part of it as the Secretary of State or the Welsh Ministers think fit) as the Secretary of State or the Welsh Ministers may specify in giving notice of his or their decision on the application for scheduled monument consent or, as the case may be, in the direction modifying the consent: Ancient Monuments and Archaeological Areas Act 1979 s 8(3). Where a person who has an interest in the whole or any part of a monument is aggrieved by the amount specified by the Secretary of State or the Welsh Ministers as the recoverable amount, that person may require the determination of that amount to be referred to the Upper Tribunal, in which case the recoverable amount is such amount (being an amount representing the whole or any part of the compensation previously paid) as that tribunal may determine to be just in the circumstances of the case: s 8(4) (amended by SI 2009/1307). As to the meaning of 'monument' see PARA 1013. As to the meaning of 'person' see PARA 803 note 17. As to the meaning of 'person aggrieved' see JUDICIAL REVIEW vol 61 (2010) PARA 656. As to the Upper Tribunal see COMPULSORY ACQUISITION OF LAND vol 18 (2009) PARA 720.
    Where any sum is recoverable under the Ancient Monuments and Archaeological Areas Act 1979 s 8 in respect of land which is ecclesiastical property the Diocesan Board of Finance for the diocese in which the land is situated may apply any money or securities held by them in the payment of that sum: s 51(4) (amended by the Church of England (Miscellaneous Provisions) Measure 2006 s 14, Sch 5 para 20(a)). As to the meanings of 'land' and 'ecclesiastical property' see PARA 1006 note 6. As to Diocesan Boards of Finance see ECCLESIASTICAL LAW vol 34 (2011) PARA 241 et seq.
6   As to the Historic Buildings and Monuments Commission for England ('the Commission') see PARA 803.
7   See the Ancient Monuments and Archaeological Areas Act 1979 s 8(3) (amended by the National Heritage Act 1983 Sch 4 para 34).
8   See the Ancient Monuments and Archaeological Areas Act 1979 s 8(3).
9   Ancient Monuments and Archaeological Areas Act 1979 s 8(1)(a).
10 Ancient Monuments and Archaeological Areas Act 1979 s 8(1)(b).
11 Ancient Monuments and Archaeological Areas Act 1979 s 8(2)(a).
12 Ancient Monuments and Archaeological Areas Act 1979 s 8(2)(b) (substituted by the National Heritage Act 1983 Sch 4 para 34).
13 As to the meaning of 'England' see PARA 804 note 2.
14 A notice deposited under the Ancient Monuments and Archaeological Areas Act 1979 s 8(2A) must specify the decision which gave rise to the right to compensation, the monument affected by the decision, and the amount of the compensation: s 8(5). A notice so deposited is a local land charge; and for the purposes of the Local Land Charges Act 1975 the council with which any such notice is deposited is treated as the originating authority as respects the charge thereby constituted: Ancient Monuments and Archaeological Areas Act 1979 s 8(6). As to local land charges see REAL PROPERTY AND REGISTRATION vol 87 (2012) PARA 763 et seq.
15 Ancient Monuments and Archaeological Areas Act 1979 s 8(2A)(a) (s 8(2A) added by the National Heritage Act 1983 Sch 4 para 34). As to local government areas and authorities in England and Wales see LOCAL GOVERNMENT vol 69 (2009) PARA 22 et seq.
16 Ancient Monuments and Archaeological Areas Act 1979 s 8(2A)(c) (as added (see note 15); and amended by the Local Government (Wales) Act 1994 s 66(6), Sch 16 para 56(1)).

1026.   Compensation where works affecting a scheduled monument cease to be authorised. Where any works[1] affecting a scheduled monument[2] which were previously authorised[3] cease to be so, then, if any person[4] who has an interest in the whole or any part of the monument has incurred expenditure in carrying out works[5] which are rendered abortive by the fact that any further works have ceased to be so authorised[6], or has otherwise sustained loss or damage which is directly attributable to that fact[7], the Historic Buildings and Monuments Commission for England ('the Commission')[8], where the monument in question is situated in England, or the Welsh Ministers[9], where the monument in question is situated in Wales, must pay to him compensation[10] in respect of that expenditure, loss or damage[11]. However, these provisions only apply where the works cease to be authorised by virtue of: (1) the fact that a scheduled monument consent granted by order[12] ceases to apply to any scheduled monument[13]; or (2) the modification or revocation of a scheduled monument consent by a direction[14]; or (3) the service of a notice[15] of proposed modification or revocation of a scheduled monument consent[16].

1 As to the meaning of 'works' see PARA 1016 note 2. As to the control of works see PARA 1016.
2 As to the meaning of 'scheduled monument' see PARA 1014.
3 Ie authorised under the Ancient Monuments and Archaeological Areas Act 1979 Pt I (ss 1–32) (see PARA 1017).
4 As to the meaning of 'person' see PARA 803 note 17.
5 For this purpose any expenditure incurred in the preparation of plans for the purposes of any works, or on other similar preparatory matters, is taken to be included in the expenditure incurred in carrying out those works: Ancient Monuments and Archaeological Areas Act 1979 s 9(4). Subject to this provision, no compensation may be paid in respect of any works carried out before the grant of the scheduled monument consent in question, or in respect of any other loss or damage (not being loss or damage consisting of depreciation of the value of an interest in land) arising out of anything done or omitted to be done before the grant of that consent: s 9(5). As to the meaning of 'scheduled monument consent' see PARA 1017. As to the meaning of 'land' see PARA 1006 note 6.
6 Ancient Monuments and Archaeological Areas Act 1979 s 9(1)(a).
7 Ancient Monuments and Archaeological Areas Act 1979 s 9(1)(b).
8 As to the Historic Buildings and Monuments Commission for England ('the Commission') see PARA 803. As to the meaning of 'England' see PARA 804 note 2.
9 The functions of the Secretary of State under the Ancient Monuments and Archaeological Areas Act 1979, in so far as they relate to Wales, were transferred to the National Assembly for Wales (see the National Assembly for Wales (Transfer of Functions) Order 1999, SI 1999/672, art 2, Sch 1) and are now exercisable by the Welsh Ministers (see the Government of Wales Act 2006 s 162(1), Sch 11 paras 30, 32). As to the Secretary of State and the Welsh Ministers see PARA 802. As to the meaning of 'Wales' see PARA 802 note 4.
10 As to compensation see PARA 1024. The Ancient Monuments (Claims for Compensation) (England) Regulations 1991, SI 1991/2512 (amended by SI 1997/2971; and SI 2009/1307), and the Ancient Monuments (Claims for Compensation) (Wales) Regulations 1991, SI 1991/2647, prescribe the forms for claiming compensation and provide for the time within which a claim is to be made under the Ancient Monuments and Archaeological Areas Act 1979 s 9.
11 Ancient Monuments and Archaeological Areas Act 1979 s 9(1) (amended by the National Heritage Act 1983 Sch 4 para 35). Compensation payable under the Ancient Monuments and Archaeological Areas Act 1979 s 9 carries interest at the rate for the time being prescribed under the Land Compensation Act 1961 s 32 (see COMPULSORY ACQUISITION OF LAND vol 18 (2009) PARA 641) from the date the works ceased to be authorised until payment: see the Planning and Compensation Act 1991 s 80(1), Sch 18 Pt I. One or more payments on account of such compensation or interest may be made: see s 80(2).
12 Ie by order under the Ancient Monuments and Archaeological Areas Act 1979 s 3 (see PARA 1017).
13 Ancient Monuments and Archaeological Areas Act 1979 s 9(2)(a). This applies whether the consent ceases to apply by virtue of variation or revocation of the order or by virtue of a direction under s 3(3) (see PARA 1017): s 9(2)(a). A person is not entitled to compensation under s 9 in a case falling within s 9(2)(a) unless, on an application for scheduled monument consent for the works in question, consent is refused, or is granted subject to conditions other than those which previously applied under the order: s 9(3).
14 Ancient Monuments and Archaeological Areas Act 1979 s 9(2)(b). The direction referred to is one under s 4 (see PARA 1020).

15 Ie in accordance with the Ancient Monuments and Archaeological Areas Act 1979 Sch 1 para 8, a notice under Sch 1 para 5 (see PARA 1022).

16 Ancient Monuments and Archaeological Areas Act 1979 s 9(2)(c).

1027. Execution of works by the Secretary of State or the Welsh Ministers for preservation of a scheduled monument. If it appears to the Secretary of State or, in relation to Wales, the Welsh Ministers[1] that any works[2] are urgently necessary for the preservation of a scheduled monument[3], he or they may enter[4] the site of the monument[5] and execute those works, after giving the owner[6] and, if the owner is not the occupier, the occupier of the monument not less than seven days' written notice[7] of his or their intention to do so[8]. Where the Secretary of State or the Welsh Ministers execute works under this provision for repairing any damage to a scheduled monument, any compensation order previously made against a convicted person[9] in respect of that damage in favour of any other person is enforceable, so far as not already complied with, as if it had been made in favour of the Secretary of State or the Welsh Ministers[10], and any such order subsequently made in respect of that damage must be made in favour of the Secretary of State or the Welsh Ministers[11].

If it appears to the Secretary of State that any works are urgently necessary for the preservation of a scheduled monument situated in England[12], he may instead[13] authorise the Historic Buildings and Monuments Commission for England ('the Commission')[14] to enter the site of the monument and execute such works as are specified in the authorisation[15]. In that case, the Commission may enter the site and execute the works after giving the owner and, if the owner is not the occupier, the occupier of the monument not less than seven days' written notice of its intention to do so[16].

1 The functions of the Secretary of State under the Ancient Monuments and Archaeological Areas Act 1979, in so far as they relate to Wales, were transferred to the National Assembly for Wales (see the National Assembly for Wales (Transfer of Functions) Order 1999, SI 1999/672, art 2, Sch 1) and are now exercisable by the Welsh Ministers (see the Government of Wales Act 2006 s 162(1), Sch 11 paras 30, 32). As to the Secretary of State and the Welsh Ministers see PARA 802. As to the meaning of 'Wales' see PARA 802 note 4.

2 As to the meaning of 'works' see PARA 1016 note 2. As to the control of works see PARA 1016.

3 As to the meaning of 'scheduled monument' see PARA 1014.

4 As to powers of entry generally see PARAS 1062–1063.

5 As to the meaning of 'site of a monument' see PARA 1013.

6 As to the meaning of 'owner' see PARA 1010 note 6.

7 As to the meaning of 'written' see PARA 805 note 14. As to the service of notices and documents see PARA 1010.

8 Ancient Monuments and Archaeological Areas Act 1979 s 5(1).

9 Ie any order made under the Powers of Criminal Courts (Sentencing) Act 2000 s 130: see SENTENCING vol 92 (2015) PARA 281 et seq. As to the meaning of 'person' see PARA 803 note 17.

10 Ancient Monuments and Archaeological Areas Act 1979 s 5(2)(a) (amended by the Powers of Criminal Courts (Sentencing) Act 2000 s 165(1), Sch 9 para 58).

11 Ancient Monuments and Archaeological Areas Act 1979 s 5(2)(b).

12 As to the meaning of 'England' see PARA 804 note 2.

13 Ie instead of acting as provided in the Ancient Monuments and Archaeological Areas Act 1979 s 5(1) (see the text to notes 1–8).

14 As to the Historic Buildings and Monuments Commission for England ('the Commission') see PARA 803.

15 Ancient Monuments and Archaeological Areas Act 1979 s 5(3) (s 5(3), (5) added by the National Heritage Act 1983 Sch 4 para 30). Where the Secretary of State gives such an authorisation, the Ancient Monuments and Archaeological Areas Act 1979 s 5(2) (see the text to notes 9–11) has effect with the substitution of 'Commission' for 'Secretary of State': s 5(5) (as so added).

16 Ancient Monuments and Archaeological Areas Act 1979 s 5(4) (added by the National Heritage Act 1983 Sch 4 para 30).

1028. Entry for inspection etc of scheduled monuments. Any person[1] duly authorised in writing[2] by the Secretary of State or, in relation to Wales, the Welsh Ministers[3] may at any reasonable time enter[4] any land[5] for any of the following purposes:

(1)   inspecting any scheduled monument[6] in, on or under the land with a view to ascertaining its condition and whether any works[7] affecting the monument are being carried out in contravention of the legislation[8], or whether it has been or is likely to be damaged by any such works or otherwise[9];

(2)   inspecting any scheduled monument in, on or under the land in connection with any application for scheduled monument consent[10] for works affecting that monument[11], or any proposal by the Secretary of State or the Welsh Ministers to modify or revoke a scheduled monument consent for any such works[12];

(3)   observing the execution on the land of any works to which a scheduled monument consent relates[13], and inspecting the condition of the land and the scheduled monument in question after the completion of any such works[14], so as to ensure that the works in question are or have been executed in accordance with the terms of the consent and of any conditions attached to the consent[15];

(4)   in the case of land on which any works to which a scheduled monument consent relates are being carried out: inspecting the land, including any buildings[16] or other structures on it, with a view to recording any matters of archaeological or historical interest[17]; and observing the execution of those works with a view to examining and recording any objects or other material of such interest, and recording any matters of such interest, discovered during the course of those works[18].

Any person duly authorised in writing by the Welsh Ministers may enter any land in Wales[19] in, on or under which a scheduled monument is situated, with the consent of the owner[20] and (if the owner is not the occupier) of the occupier of the land, for the purpose of erecting and maintaining on or near the site of the monument[21] such notice boards and marker posts as appear to the Welsh Ministers to be desirable with a view to preserving the monument from accidental or deliberate damage[22].

Any person duly authorised in writing by the Historic Buildings and Monuments Commission for England ('the Commission')[23] may at any reasonable time enter any land in England for any of the following purposes:

(a)   inspecting any scheduled monument in, on or under the land with a view to ascertaining whether any works affecting the monument have been or are being carried out in contravention of the legislation[24] and so enabling the Commission to decide whether to institute proceedings in England for an offence[25] under the legislation[26];

(b)   observing the execution on the land of any works to which a scheduled monument consent relates[27], and inspecting the condition of the land and the scheduled monument in question after the completion of any such works[28], with a view to ascertaining whether the works in question are or have been executed in accordance with the terms of the consent and of any conditions attached to the consent, and so enabling the Commission to decide whether to institute proceedings in England for an offence[29] under the legislation[30];

(c)   inspecting any scheduled monument in, on or under the land in connection with any consultation made[31] in respect of the monument[32];

(d)   in the case of any land in, on or under which a scheduled monument is situated, with the consent of the owner and (if the owner is not the occupier) of the occupier of the land, for the purpose of erecting and maintaining on or near the site of the monument such notice boards and marker posts as appear to the Commission to be desirable with a view to preserving the monument from accidental or deliberate damage[33].

1   As to the meaning of 'person' see PARA 803 note 17.
2   As to the meaning of 'writing' see PARA 805 note 14.
3   The functions of the Secretary of State under the Ancient Monuments and Archaeological Areas Act 1979, in so far as they relate to Wales, were transferred to the National Assembly for Wales (see the National Assembly for Wales (Transfer of Functions) Order 1999, SI 1999/672, art 2, Sch 1) and are now exercisable by the Welsh Ministers (see the Government of Wales Act 2006 s 162(1), Sch 11 paras 30, 32). As to the Secretary of State and the Welsh Ministers see PARA 802. As to the meaning of 'Wales' see PARA 802 note 4.
4   As to powers of entry see further PARAS 1062–1063.
5   As to the meaning of 'land' see PARA 1006 note 6.
6   As to the meaning of 'scheduled monument' see PARA 1014.
7   As to the meaning of 'works' see PARA 1016 note 2. As to the control of works see PARA 1016.
8   Ancient Monuments and Archaeological Areas Act 1979 s 6(1)(a). The contravention referred to is contravention of s 2(1): see PARA 1016.
9   Ancient Monuments and Archaeological Areas Act 1979 s 6(1)(b).
10 As to the meaning of 'scheduled monument consent' see PARA 1017. In the Ancient Monuments and Archaeological Areas Act 1979 s 6 scheduled monument consent includes consent granted by order under s 3 (see PARA 1017): s 6(6).
11 Ancient Monuments and Archaeological Areas Act 1979 s 6(2)(a).
12 Ancient Monuments and Archaeological Areas Act 1979 s 6(2)(b). As to modification or revocation of consent see PARAS 1020–1022.
13 Ancient Monuments and Archaeological Areas Act 1979 s 6(3)(a).
14 Ancient Monuments and Archaeological Areas Act 1979 s 6(3)(b).
15 Ancient Monuments and Archaeological Areas Act 1979 s 6(3).
16 'Building' includes any structure or erection, and any part of a building, as so defined, but does not include plant or machinery comprised in a building: Town and Country Planning Act 1990 s 336(1) (definition applied by the Ancient Monuments and Archaeological Areas Act 1979 s 32(1)).
17 Ancient Monuments and Archaeological Areas Act 1979 s 6(4)(a). As to the treatment and preservation of finds see s 54; and PARA 1064.
18 Ancient Monuments and Archaeological Areas Act 1979 s 6(4)(b).
19 The Ancient Monuments and Archaeological Areas Act 1979 s 6(5) does not apply to land in England: see s 6(5) (amended by the National Heritage Act 1983 s 33(3), Sch 4 para 31)). As to the meaning of 'England' see PARA 804 note 2.
20 As to the meaning of 'owner' see PARA 1010 note 6.
21 As to the meaning of 'site of a monument' see PARA 1013.
22 Ancient Monuments and Archaeological Areas Act 1979 s 6(5).
23 As to the Historic Buildings and Monuments Commission for England ('the Commission') see PARA 803.
24 Ie in contravention of the Ancient Monuments and Archaeological Areas Act 1979 s 2(1) (see PARA 1016).
25 Ie an offence under the Ancient Monuments and Archaeological Areas Act 1979 s 2(1) (see PARA 1016).
26 Ancient Monuments and Archaeological Areas Act 1979 s 6A(1) (s 6A added by the National Heritage Act 1983 s 33, Sch 4 para 32).
27 Ancient Monuments and Archaeological Areas Act 1979 s 6A(2)(a) (as added: see note 26). References to scheduled monument consent in s 6A include references to consent granted by order under s 3: s 6A(5) (as so added).
28 Ancient Monuments and Archaeological Areas Act 1979 s 6A(2)(b) (as added: see note 26).
29 Ie an offence under the Ancient Monuments and Archaeological Areas Act 1979 s 2(1) (see PARA 1016).
30 Ancient Monuments and Archaeological Areas Act 1979 s 6A(2) (as added: see note 26).

31 Ie made under the Ancient Monuments and Archaeological Areas Act 1979 s 4(3) (see PARA 1020) or Sch 1 para 3(3)(c) (see PARA 1018).
32 Ancient Monuments and Archaeological Areas Act 1979 s 6A(3) (as added: see note 26).
33 Ancient Monuments and Archaeological Areas Act 1979 s 6A(4) (as added: see note 26).

(B) Acquisition and Guardianship of Ancient Monuments

1029. Meaning of 'ancient monument'. 'Ancient monument' means:

(1) any scheduled monument[1]; and

(2) any other monument[2] which in the opinion of the Secretary of State or, in relation to Wales, the Welsh Ministers[3] is of public interest by reason of the historic, architectural, traditional, artistic or archaeological interest attaching to it[4].

In addition, references to an 'ancient monument' in the provisions relating to the acquisition[5] and guardianship[6] of ancient monuments include references to any land[7] adjoining or in the vicinity of an ancient monument which appears to the Secretary of State or the Historic Buildings and Monuments Commission for England ('the Commission')[8] in relation to land in England, the Welsh Ministers in relation to land in Wales, or a local authority[9] to be reasonably required for any of the following purposes[10]:

(a) the maintenance of the monument or its amenities[11];

(b) providing or facilitating access to it[12];

(c) the exercise of proper control or management with respect to it[13];

(d) the storage of equipment or materials for the purpose mentioned in head (1) above[14];

(e) the provision of facilities and services for the public for, or in connection with, affording public access to the monument[15].

1 Ancient Monuments and Archaeological Areas Act 1979 s 61(1), (12)(a). As to the meaning of 'scheduled monument' see PARA 1014.
2 As to the meaning of 'monument' see PARA 1013.
3 The functions of the Secretary of State under the Ancient Monuments and Archaeological Areas Act 1979, in so far as they relate to Wales, were transferred to the National Assembly for Wales (see the National Assembly for Wales (Transfer of Functions) Order 1999, SI 1999/672, art 2, Sch 1) and are now exercisable by the Welsh Ministers (see the Government of Wales Act 2006 s 162(1), Sch 11 paras 30, 32). As to the Secretary of State and the Welsh Ministers see PARA 802. As to the meaning of 'Wales' see PARA 802 note 4.
4 Ancient Monuments and Archaeological Areas Act 1979 s 61(1), (12)(b).
5 Ie references in the Ancient Monuments and Archaeological Areas Act 1979 ss 10, 11 (see PARAS 1030–1031).
6 Ie references in the Ancient Monuments and Archaeological Areas Act 1979 s 12 (see PARA 1032).
7 As to the meaning of 'land' see PARA 1006 note 6.
8 As to the Historic Buildings and Monuments Commission for England ('the Commission') see PARA 803. As to the meaning of 'England' see PARA 804 note 2.
9 As to the meaning of 'local authority' see PARA 1006 note 9.
10 See the Ancient Monuments and Archaeological Areas Act 1979 s 15(1) (amended by the National Heritage Act 1983 Sch 4 para 41). One of the purposes in heads (1)–(5) in the text is sufficient to support the compulsory acquisition of any such land under the Ancient Monuments and Archaeological Areas Act 1979 s 10(1) (see PARA 1030) instead of the purpose there mentioned: see s 15(1). As to the meaning of 'compulsory acquisition' see PARA 1024 note 5.
11 Ancient Monuments and Archaeological Areas Act 1979 s 15(1)(a). 'Maintenance' includes fencing, repairing, and covering in, of a monument and the doing of any other act or thing which may be required for the purpose of repairing the monument or protecting it from decay or injury; and 'maintain' must be construed accordingly: s 13(7).
12 Ancient Monuments and Archaeological Areas Act 1979 s 15(1)(b).
13 Ancient Monuments and Archaeological Areas Act 1979 s 15(1)(c).
14 Ancient Monuments and Archaeological Areas Act 1979 s 15(1)(d).
15 Ancient Monuments and Archaeological Areas Act 1979 s 15(1)(e).

1030. Compulsory acquisition of ancient monuments. The Secretary of State or, in relation to Wales, the Welsh Ministers[1] may acquire compulsorily[2] any ancient monument[3] for the purpose of securing its preservation[4]. For the purpose of assessing compensation in respect of any compulsory acquisition under this provision of a monument which, immediately before the date of the compulsory purchase order, was scheduled[5], it must be assumed that scheduled monument consent[6] would not be granted for any works[7] which would or might result in the demolition, destruction or removal of the monument or any part of it[8].

1   The functions of the Secretary of State under the Ancient Monuments and Archaeological Areas Act 1979, in so far as they relate to Wales, were transferred to the National Assembly for Wales (see the National Assembly for Wales (Transfer of Functions) Order 1999, SI 1999/672, art 2, Sch 1) and are now exercisable by the Welsh Ministers (see the Government of Wales Act 2006 s 162(1), Sch 11 paras 30, 32). As to the Secretary of State and the Welsh Ministers see PARA 802. As to the meaning of 'Wales' see PARA 802 note 4.
2   As to the meaning of 'compulsory acquisition' see PARA 1024 note 5.
3   As to the meaning of 'ancient monument' see PARA 1029. References to a monument in relation to the acquisition or transfer of any monument include references to any interest in or right over the monument: Ancient Monuments and Archaeological Areas Act 1979 s 32(2). The Acquisition of Land Act 1981 (see COMPULSORY ACQUISITION OF LAND vol 18 (2009) PARA 556) applies to any compulsory acquisition by the Secretary of State or the Welsh Ministers under this provision of an ancient monument: Ancient Monuments and Archaeological Areas Act 1979 s 10(2) (amended by the Acquisition of Land Act 1981 s 34, Sch 4 para 1, Sch 6 Pt I).
4   Ancient Monuments and Archaeological Areas Act 1979 s 10(1). However, the Secretary of State must consult with the Historic Buildings and Monuments Commission for England ('the Commission') before making a compulsory purchase order: see s 10(1) (amended by the National Heritage Act 1983 s 33(3), Sch 4 para 36). As to the Commission see PARA 803. As to the exercise of the duty to consult see JUDICIAL REVIEW vol 61 (2010) PARA 627.
5   As to the meaning of 'scheduled monument' see PARA 1014.
6   As to the meaning of 'scheduled monument consent' see PARA 1017.
7   As to the meaning of 'works' see PARA 1016 note 2. As to the control of works see PARA 1016.
8   Ancient Monuments and Archaeological Areas Act 1979 s 10(4).

1031. Acquisition of ancient monuments by agreement or gift. The Secretary of State (after consulting the Historic Buildings and Monuments Commission for England ('the Commission')[1]) or, in relation to Wales, the Welsh Ministers[2] may acquire by agreement any ancient monument[3], as may any local authority[4] in respect of any ancient monument situated in or in the vicinity of its area[5]. Similarly, the Secretary of State (after consulting the Commission) or, in relation to Wales, the Welsh Ministers, or any local authority may accept a gift, whether by deed or will, of any ancient monument[6].

With the consent of the Secretary of State, the Commission may acquire by agreement[7] or accept a gift, whether by deed or will[8], of any ancient monument situated in England[9].

Financial assistance for the acquisition of an ancient monument may be available from the National Heritage Memorial Fund[10].

1   See the Ancient Monuments and Archaeological Areas Act 1979 s 11(1) (amended by the National Heritage Act 1983 Sch 4 para 37). As to the Historic Buildings and Monuments Commission for England ('the Commission') see PARA 803.
2   The functions of the Secretary of State under the Ancient Monuments and Archaeological Areas Act 1979, in so far as they relate to Wales, were transferred to the National Assembly for Wales (see the National Assembly for Wales (Transfer of Functions) Order 1999, SI 1999/672, art 2, Sch 1) and are now exercisable by the Welsh Ministers (see the Government of Wales Act 2006 s 162(1), Sch 11 paras 30, 32). As to the Secretary of State and the Welsh Ministers see PARA 802. As to the meaning of 'Wales' see PARA 802 note 4.
3   Ancient Monuments and Archaeological Areas Act 1979 s 11(1). The Compulsory Purchase Act 1965 Pt I (ss 1–32) (so far as applicable), other than ss 4–8, 10, 31, applies in relation to any acquisition of an ancient monument under the Ancient Monuments and Archaeological Areas Act 1979 s 11(1) or s 11(2) (see the text to notes 4–5): see s 11(4); and see COMPULSORY

ACQUISITION OF LAND vol 18 (2009) PARA 550 et seq. As to the meaning of 'ancient monument' see PARA 1029. As to the meaning of references to the acquisition of a monument see PARA 1030 note 3.

4   As to the meaning of 'local authority' see PARA 1006 note 9.

5   See the Ancient Monuments and Archaeological Areas Act 1979 s 11(2). See also note 3.

6   See the Ancient Monuments and Archaeological Areas Act 1979 s 11(3) (amended by the National Heritage Act 1983 Sch 4 para 37).

7   See the Ancient Monuments and Archaeological Areas Act 1979 s 11(1A) (added by the National Heritage Act 1983 Sch 4 para 37).

8   See the Ancient Monuments and Archaeological Areas Act 1979 s 11(3A) (added by the National Heritage Act 1983 Sch 4 para 37).

9   See the Ancient Monuments and Archaeological Areas Act 1979 s 11(1A), (3A) (as added: see notes 7, 8). As to the meaning of 'England' see PARA 804 note 2.

10 See the National Heritage Act 1980 s 3; and PARA 815.

1032. Power to place ancient monument under guardianship. A person[1] who has a sufficient interest[2] in an ancient monument situated in England may, with the consent of the Secretary of State[3] constitute the Secretary of State, or with the consent of the Historic Buildings and Monuments Commission for England ('the Commission')[4] constitute the Commission, by deed guardian of the monument[5]. Likewise, a person who has a sufficient interest in an ancient monument situated in Wales may, with the consent of the Welsh Ministers[6], constitute the Welsh Ministers by deed guardian of the monument[7]; and a person who has any such interest in an ancient monument situated in either England or Wales may, with the consent of any local authority[8] in or in the vicinity of whose area the monument is situated, constitute that authority by deed guardian of the monument[9]. The Secretary of State, the Commission, the Welsh Ministers or a local authority must not consent to become guardians of any structure which is occupied as a dwelling house by any person other than a person employed as the caretaker thereof or his family[10].

A person who is not the occupier of an ancient monument may not establish guardianship of the monument under these provisions unless the occupier is also a party to the deed executed for these purposes[11]; and any person who has an interest in an ancient monument may be a party to any such deed in addition to the person establishing the guardianship of the monument and (where the latter is not the occupier) the occupier[12].

A guardianship deed[13] relating to any ancient monument situated in England and Wales is a local land charge[14]. Every person deriving title to any ancient monument from, through or under any person who has executed a guardianship deed is bound by the guardianship deed unless he derives title by virtue of any disposition made by the person who executed the deed before the date of the deed[15].

Except as provided by the Ancient Monuments and Archaeological Areas Act 1979, any person who has any estate or interest in a monument under guardianship has the same right and title to, and estate or interest in, the monument in all respects as if the Secretary of State, the Commission, the Welsh Ministers or the local authority in question (as the case may be) had not become guardians of the monument[16].

1   As to the meaning of 'person' see PARA 803 note 17.

2   Ie an interest of any description mentioned in the Ancient Monuments and Archaeological Areas Act 1979 s 12(3): see s 12(1)(a). The interests in an ancient monument situated in England and Wales which qualify a person to establish guardianship of the monument under s 12(1), (1A) or (2) (see the text to notes 3–9) are the following (s 12(3) (amended by the National Heritage Act 1983 s 33, Sch 4 para 38(4))): (1) an estate in fee simple absolute in possession (Ancient Monuments and Archaeological Areas Act 1979 s 12(3)(a)); (2) a leasehold estate or interest in possession, being an estate or interest for a term of years of which not less than 45 are unexpired

or (as the case may be) renewable for a term of not less than 45 years (s 12(3)(b)); and (3) an interest in possession for his own life or the life of another, or for lives (whether or not including his own), under any existing or future trust of land under which the estate or interest for the time being subject to the trust falls within head (1) or head (2) above (s 12(3)(c) (amended by the Trusts of Land and Appointment of Trustees Act 1996 s 25(1), Sch 3 para 17(a))). As to the meaning of 'ancient monument' see PARA 1029. As to the meaning of 'England' see PARA 804 note 2. As to the meaning of 'Wales' see PARA 802 note 4. 'Trust of land' and 'trustees of land' have the same meanings as in the Trusts of Land and Appointment of Trustees Act 1996 (see TRUSTS AND POWERS vol 98 (2013) PARAS 6, 151): Interpretation Act 1978 s 5, Sch 1 (definition added by the Trusts of Land and Appointment of Trustees Act 1996 s 25(4), Sch 3 para 16).

3 The Secretary of State must consult with the Historic Buildings and Monuments Commission for England ('the Commission') before he so consents: see the Ancient Monuments and Archaeological Areas Act 1979 s 12(1) (amended by the National Heritage Act 1983 s 33, Sch 4 para 38(2)). As to the Secretary of State see PARA 802 note 2. As to the Commission see PARA 803. As to the exercise of the duty to consult see JUDICIAL REVIEW vol 61 (2010) PARA 627.

4 Such consent may only be given after obtaining the consent of the Secretary of State: see the Ancient Monuments and Archaeological Areas Act 1979 s 12(1A) (added by the National Heritage Act 1983 s 33, Sch 4 para 38(3)).

5 See the Ancient Monuments and Archaeological Areas Act 1979 s 12(1), (1A) (as added: see note 4). As to the powers of limited owners for the purposes of s 12 see PARA 1038. Objects which are or have been kept in a building of which the Secretary of State or the Welsh Ministers (see the text and notes 6–7) are guardians under the Ancient Monuments and Archaeological Areas Act 1979 may be accepted in satisfaction of inheritance tax: see PARA 1112.

6 The functions of the Secretary of State under the Ancient Monuments and Archaeological Areas Act 1979, in so far as they relate to Wales, were transferred to the National Assembly for Wales (see the National Assembly for Wales (Transfer of Functions) Order 1999, SI 1999/672, art 2, Sch 1) and are now exercisable by the Welsh Ministers (see the Government of Wales Act 2006 s 162(1), Sch 11 paras 30, 32). As to the Welsh Ministers see PARA 802.

7 See the Ancient Monuments and Archaeological Areas Act 1979 s 12(1).

8 As to the meaning of 'local authority' see PARA 1006 note 9.

9 See the Ancient Monuments and Archaeological Areas Act 1979 s 12(2).

10 Ancient Monuments and Archaeological Areas Act 1979 s 12(10) (amended by the National Heritage Act 1983 s 33, Sch 4 para 38(4), (6)).

11 Ancient Monuments and Archaeological Areas Act 1979 s 12(4) (amended by the National Heritage Act 1983 s 33, Sch 4 para 38(4), (6)).

12 Ancient Monuments and Archaeological Areas Act 1979 s 12(5).

13 In relation to any monument of which the Secretary of State, the Commission, the Welsh Ministers or any local authority has been constituted guardian under the Ancient Monuments and Archaeological Areas Act 1979, references in ss 13–65 to the 'guardianship deed' are references to the deed executed for the purposes of s 12(1), (1A) or (2) (see the text to notes 1-9) (as the case may be): s 12(6) (amended by the National Heritage Act 1983 s 33, Sch 4 para 38(5)).

14 Ancient Monuments and Archaeological Areas Act 1979 s 12(7). As to local land charges see REAL PROPERTY AND REGISTRATION vol 87 (2012) PARA 763 et seq.

15 See the Ancient Monuments and Archaeological Areas Act 1979 s 12(9)(a).

16 Ancient Monuments and Archaeological Areas Act 1979 s 12(11) (amended by the National Heritage Act 1983 s 33, Sch 4 para 38(7)). As to the effect of guardianship generally see PARA 1033. As to the termination of guardianship see PARA 1034.

1033. Effect of guardianship of monuments. The Secretary of State[1], the Welsh Ministers[2], the Historic Buildings and Monuments Commission for England ('the Commission')[3] and any local authority[4] are under a duty to maintain[5] any monument[6] which is under their guardianship by virtue of the Ancient Monuments and Archaeological Areas Act 1979[7]; and, subject to any provision to the contrary in the guardianship deed[8], have full control and management of any such monument[9]. With a view to fulfilling their duty to maintain a monument of which they are the guardians, the Secretary of State, the Welsh Ministers, the Commission and any local authority have power, subject to the guardianship deed[10], to do all such things as may be necessary for the maintenance of the monument and for the exercise by them of proper control and management with respect to the monument[11].

Without prejudice to the generality of the preceding provisions, the Secretary of State, the Welsh Ministers, the Commission or any local authority has power, subject to the guardianship deed[12], to: (1) make any examination of a monument which is under their guardianship[13]; (2) open up any such monument or make excavations in it for the purpose of examination or otherwise[14]; and (3) remove the whole or any part of any such monument to another place for the purpose of preserving it[15]. The Secretary of State, the Welsh Ministers, the Commission or local authority may at any reasonable time enter the site of a monument[16] which is under their guardianship for the purpose of exercising any of the powers under these provisions in relation to the monument, and may authorise any other person[17] to exercise any of those powers on their behalf[18].

1   As to the Secretary of State see PARA 802 note 2.
2   The functions of the Secretary of State under the Ancient Monuments and Archaeological Areas Act 1979, in so far as they relate to Wales, were transferred to the National Assembly for Wales (see the National Assembly for Wales (Transfer of Functions) Order 1999, SI 1999/672, art 2, Sch 1) and are now exercisable by the Welsh Ministers (see the Government of Wales Act 2006 s 162(1), Sch 11 paras 30, 32). As to the Welsh Ministers see PARA 802. As to the meaning of 'Wales' see PARA 802 note 4.
3   As to the Historic Buildings and Monuments Commission for England ('the Commission') see PARA 803.
4   As to the meaning of 'local authority' see PARA 1006 note 9.
5   As to the meaning of 'maintain' see PARA 1029 note 11.
6   A monument under guardianship will be an ancient monument: see the Ancient Monuments and Archaeological Areas Act 1979 s 12; and PARA 1032. As to the meaning of 'ancient monument' see PARA 1029.
7   Ancient Monuments and Archaeological Areas Act 1979 s 13(1) (amended by the National Heritage Act 1983 Sch 4 para 39). As to guardianship see PARA 1032.
8   See the Ancient Monuments and Archaeological Areas Act 1979 s 13(6). As to the meaning of 'guardianship deed' see PARA 1032 note 13.
9   Ancient Monuments and Archaeological Areas Act 1979 s 13(2) (amended by the National Heritage Act 1983 Sch 4 para 39).
10 See the Ancient Monuments and Archaeological Areas Act 1979 s 13(6).
11 Ancient Monuments and Archaeological Areas Act 1979 s 13(3) (amended by the National Heritage Act 1983 Sch 4 para 39).
12 See the Ancient Monuments and Archaeological Areas Act 1979 s 13(4), (6) (s 13(4) amended by the National Heritage Act 1983 Sch 4 para 39).
13 Ancient Monuments and Archaeological Areas Act 1979 s 13(4)(a). As to the preservation of finds see PARA 1064.
14 Ancient Monuments and Archaeological Areas Act 1979 s 13(4)(b).
15 Ancient Monuments and Archaeological Areas Act 1979 s 13(4)(c).
16 As to the meaning of 'site of a monument' see PARA 1013.
17 As to the meaning of 'person' see PARA 803 note 17.
18 Ancient Monuments and Archaeological Areas Act 1979 s 13(5) (amended by the National Heritage Act 1983 Sch 4 para 39). As to powers of entry see further PARAS 1062–1063.

1034. Termination of guardianship of monuments. Where the Secretary of State[1], the Welsh Ministers[2], the Historic Buildings and Monuments Commission for England ('the Commission')[3] or a local authority[4] has become guardian of any monument[5], they may by agreement[6] made with the persons who are for the time being immediately affected by the operation of the guardianship deed[7], exclude any part of the monument from guardianship[8] or renounce guardianship of the monument[9]; but except as provided above, the monument remains under guardianship, unless it is acquired by its guardians, until an occupier of the monument who is entitled to terminate the guardianship[10] gives notice in writing[11] to that effect to the guardians of the monument[12].

Neither the Secretary of State, the Welsh Ministers, the Commission nor a local authority may enter into any such agreement unless satisfied with respect to the part of the monument or, as the case may be, with respect to the whole of the monument in question[13] that satisfactory arrangements have been made for ensuring its preservation after termination of the guardianship[14], or that it is no longer practicable to preserve it, whether because of the cost of preserving it or otherwise[15].

1   As to the Secretary of State see PARA 802 note 2.
2   The functions of the Secretary of State under the Ancient Monuments and Archaeological Areas Act 1979, in so far as they relate to Wales, were transferred to the National Assembly for Wales (see the National Assembly for Wales (Transfer of Functions) Order 1999, SI 1999/672, art 2, Sch 1) and are now exercisable by the Welsh Ministers (see the Government of Wales Act 2006 s 162(1), Sch 11 paras 30, 32). As to the Welsh Ministers see PARA 802. As to the meaning of 'Wales' see PARA 802 note 4.
3   As to the Historic Buildings and Monuments Commission for England ('the Commission') see PARA 803.
4   As to the meaning of 'local authority' see PARA 1006 note 9.
5   A monument in guardianship will be an ancient monument: see the Ancient Monuments and Archaeological Areas Act 1979 s 12; and PARA 1032. As to the meaning of 'ancient monument' see PARA 1029.
6   A local authority must consult with the Secretary of State or, as appropriate, the Welsh Ministers before entering into any such agreement; the Secretary of State must consult with the Commission before entering into any such agreement; and the Commission must consult with the Secretary of State before entering into any such agreement: see the Ancient Monuments and Archaeological Areas Act 1979 s 14(2) (amended by the National Heritage Act 1983 Sch 4 para 40). Any agreement under the Ancient Monuments and Archaeological Areas Act 1979 s 14 relating to a monument in England and Wales must be made under seal: s 14(4). As to the meaning of 'England' see PARA 804 note 2. As to deeds under seal see DEEDS AND OTHER INSTRUMENTS vol 32 (2012) PARA 227 et seq.
7   For these purposes a person is to be taken to be immediately affected by the operation of a guardianship deed relating to any land if he is bound by the deed and is in possession or occupation of the land: see the Ancient Monuments and Archaeological Areas Act 1979 s 61(3). As to the meaning of 'person' see PARA 803 note 17. As to the meaning of 'guardianship deed' see PARA 1032 note 13. As to the meaning of 'land' see PARA 1006 note 6. As to the meaning of 'possession' see PARA 1010 note 6.
8   Ancient Monuments and Archaeological Areas Act 1979 s 14(1)(a).
9   Ancient Monuments and Archaeological Areas Act 1979 s 14(1)(b).
10 An occupier of a monument is entitled to terminate the guardianship of the monument if: (1) he has any interest in the monument which would qualify him to establish guardianship of the monument under the Ancient Monuments and Archaeological Areas Act 1979 s 12 (see PARA 1032) (s 14(1)(a)); and (2) he is not bound by the guardianship deed (s 14(1)(b)).
11 As to the meaning of 'writing' see PARA 805 note 14. As to the service of notices and documents see PARA 1010.
12 Ancient Monuments and Archaeological Areas Act 1979 s 14(1) (amended by the National Heritage Act 1983 Sch 4 para 40).
13 Ancient Monuments and Archaeological Areas Act 1979 s 14(3) (amended by the National Heritage Act 1983 Sch 4 para 40).
14 Ancient Monuments and Archaeological Areas Act 1979 s 14(3)(a).
15 Ancient Monuments and Archaeological Areas Act 1979 s 14(3)(b).

1035. Acquisition and guardianship of land in the vicinity of an ancient monument. Where it appears to the Secretary of State[1], the Welsh Ministers[2], the Historic Buildings and Monuments Commission for England ('the Commission')[3] or a local authority[4] that land adjoining or in the vicinity of an ancient monument[5] is reasonably required for any of certain ancillary purposes[6], that land may be acquired[7] or taken into guardianship[8] either at the same time as the monument or subsequently[9].

The Secretary of State, the Welsh Ministers, the Commission and any local authority have full control and management of any land which is under their guardianship[10] after being taken into guardianship by virtue of these provisions for a purpose relating to an ancient monument, and have power to do all such things as may be necessary[11] for: (1) the exercise by them of proper control and management with respect to the land[12]; and (2) the use of the land for any of the ancillary purposes[13]. For the purpose of exercising such powers, the Secretary of State, Welsh Ministers, Commission or any local authority may at any reasonable time enter any land under their guardianship and may authorise any other person[14] to do so and exercise that power on their behalf[15].

The provisions as to the termination of guardianship[16] apply in relation to any land taken into guardianship by virtue of these provisions for any purpose relating to an ancient monument as they apply in relation to a monument, but, apart from any termination of guardianship by virtue of those provisions, any such land also ceases to be under guardianship if the monument in question ceases to be under guardianship otherwise than by virtue of being acquired by its guardian or ceases to exist[17].

1   As to the Secretary of State see PARA 802 note 2.
2   The functions of the Secretary of State under the Ancient Monuments and Archaeological Areas Act 1979, in so far as they relate to Wales, were transferred to the National Assembly for Wales (see the National Assembly for Wales (Transfer of Functions) Order 1999, SI 1999/672, art 2, Sch 1) and are now exercisable by the Welsh Ministers (see the Government of Wales Act 2006 s 162(1), Sch 11 paras 30, 32). As to the Welsh Ministers see PARA 802. As to the meaning of 'Wales' see PARA 802 note 4.
3   Land may be acquired, or taken into guardianship, by the Commission by virtue of the Ancient Monuments and Archaeological Areas Act 1979 s 15 only if the land is situated in England: see s 15(1) (amended by the National Heritage Act 1983 s 33, Sch 4 para 42). As to the Historic Buildings and Monuments Commission for England ('the Commission') see PARA 803. As to the meaning of 'England' see PARA 804 note 2. As to the meaning of 'land' see PARA 1006 note 6.
4   As to the meaning of 'local authority' see PARA 1006 note 9.
5   As to the meaning of 'ancient monument' see PARA 1029.
6   Ie the purposes specified in the Ancient Monuments and Archaeological Areas Act 1979 s 15(1)(a)–(e) (see PARA 1029).
7   As to the acquisition of ancient monuments see PARAS 1030–1031.
8   As to guardianship of ancient monuments see PARA 1032.
9   See the Ancient Monuments and Archaeological Areas Act 1979 s 15(1), (2) (s 15(1), (6) amended by the National Heritage Act 1983 s 33, Sch 4 para 41). References in the Ancient Monuments and Archaeological Areas Act 1979, in relation to any monument of which the Secretary of State, the Welsh Ministers, the Commission or a local authority is the owner or guardian by virtue of the Act, to land associated with that monument (or to associated land) are references to any land acquired or taken into guardianship by virtue of s 15 for a purpose relating to that monument, or appropriated for any such purpose under a power conferred by any other enactment: ss 15(6) (as so amended), 61(6). In relation to any monument in territorial waters which is under the ownership or guardianship of the Secretary of State, the Welsh Ministers, the Commission or any local authority by virtue of the Ancient Monuments and Archaeological Areas Act 1979, references in the Act to land associated with the monument (or to associated land) include references to any part of the sea bed occupied by the Secretary of State, the Welsh Ministers, the Commission or a local authority for any such purpose relating to the monument as is mentioned in s 15(1): s 53(3) (amended by the National Heritage Act 1983 s 33, Sch 4 para 64). For the purposes of the Ancient Monuments and Archaeological Areas Act 1979 Pt I (ss 1–32) the Secretary of State, the Welsh Ministers, the Commission or a local authority is the owner of a monument by virtue of the Act if the Secretary of State, Welsh Ministers, Commission or local authority (as the case may be) has acquired it under s 10 (see PARA 1030), s 11 (see PARA 1031) or s 21 (see PARA 1039): s 32(3) (amended by the National Heritage Act 1983 s 33, Sch 4 para 53). As to the meaning of 'enactment' see PARA 1012 note 1. As to monuments in territorial waters see PARA 1008.
10 Ie by virtue of the Ancient Monuments and Archaeological Areas Act 1979.
11 Ancient Monuments and Archaeological Areas Act 1979 s 15(3) (amended by the National Heritage Act 1983 s 33, Sch 4 para 41).
12 Ancient Monuments and Archaeological Areas Act 1979 s 15(3)(a).
13 Ancient Monuments and Archaeological Areas Act 1979 s 15(3)(b). The ancillary purposes are those mentioned in s 15(1)(a)–(e) (see PARA 1029).
14 As to the meaning of 'person' see PARA 803 note 17.
15 Ancient Monuments and Archaeological Areas Act 1979 s 15(4) (amended by the National Heritage Act 1983 Sch 4 para 41). As to powers of entry see PARAS 1062–1063.

16 Ie the Ancient Monuments and Archaeological Areas Act 1979 s 14(1), (2) (see PARA 1034).
17 Ancient Monuments and Archaeological Areas Act 1979 s 15(5).

1036. Acquisition of easements and other rights in relation to ancient monuments. The Secretary of State[1] or, in relation to Wales, the Welsh Ministers[2] may acquire, by agreement[3] or compulsorily[4], over land adjoining or in the vicinity of any monument[5] which is under his or their ownership[6] any easement[7] which appears to him or them to be necessary:

(1)   for any of the purposes[8] relating to the monument for which such land may be acquired or taken into guardianship[9]; or

(2)   for the use[10] of any land associated with that monument[11] for any of those purposes[12].

Similarly, the Historic Buildings and Monuments Commission for England ('the Commission'), in respect of land which is situated in England, and a local authority[13] may by agreement acquire over land which adjoins or is in the vicinity of any monument under its ownership[14] any such easement as the Secretary of State or the Welsh Ministers may acquire under the above provisions[15].

The Secretary of State, the Welsh Ministers, the Commission or any local authority may acquire, for the benefit of any monument or land under their guardianship[16], a right of any description which they would be authorised to acquire under any of the above provisions if the monument or land was under their ownership by virtue of the Ancient Monuments and Archaeological Areas Act 1979, and those provisions apply accordingly in any such case[17]. Any such right which is acquired by agreement under these provisions for a purpose relating to any monument under guardianship, or for the use of any land associated with any such monument for any purpose relating to that monument:

(a)   subject to any provision to the contrary in the agreement under which it was acquired, may be revoked by the grantor[18]; and

(b)   may be revoked by any successor in title of the grantor as respects any of the land over which it is exercisable in which he has an interest[19],

if the monument ceases to be under guardianship otherwise than by virtue of being acquired by its guardians or ceases to exist[20].

1   Where the land in question is situated in England, the Secretary of State must consult with the Historic Buildings and Monuments Commission for England ('the Commission') before entering into the agreement or making the compulsory purchase order (as the case may be): see the Ancient Monuments and Archaeological Areas Act 1979 s 16(1) (amended by the National Heritage Act 1983 s 33, Sch 4 para 42). As to the meaning of 'land' see PARA 1006 note 6. As to the meaning of 'England' see PARA 804 note 2. As to the Secretary of State see PARA 802 note 2. As to Commission see PARA 803. As to the exercise of the duty to consult see JUDICIAL REVIEW vol 61 (2010) PARA 627.

2   The functions of the Secretary of State under the Ancient Monuments and Archaeological Areas Act 1979, in so far as they relate to Wales, were transferred to the National Assembly for Wales (see the National Assembly for Wales (Transfer of Functions) Order 1999, SI 1999/672, art 2, Sch 1) and are now exercisable by the Welsh Ministers (see the Government of Wales Act 2006 s 162(1), Sch 11 paras 30, 32). As to the Welsh Ministers see PARA 802. As to the meaning of 'Wales' see PARA 802 note 4.

3   The Compulsory Purchase Act 1965 Pt I (ss 1–32) (so far as applicable), other than ss 4–8, 10, 31, applies in relation to any acquisition by agreement under the Ancient Monuments and Archaeological Areas Act 1979 s 16 of any easement over land in England and Wales: s 16(11). See further COMPULSORY ACQUISITION OF LAND vol 18 (2009) PARA 550. As to the powers of limited owners for the purposes of s 16 see PARA 1038.

4   As to the meaning of 'compulsory acquisition' see PARA 1024 note 5. The Acquisition of Land Act 1981 applies to any compulsory acquisition by the Secretary of State or the Welsh Ministers under the Ancient Monuments and Archaeological Areas Act 1979 s 16 of any easement over land in England and Wales: s 16(9) (amended by the Acquisition of Land Act 1981 s 34, Sch 4 para 1, Sch 6 Pt I). See generally COMPULSORY ACQUISITION OF LAND vol 18 (2009) PARA 501 et seq.

5 Any such monument will be an ancient monument: see the Ancient Monuments and Archaeological Areas Act 1979 ss 10, 11; and PARAS 1030–1031. As to the meaning of 'ancient monument' see PARA 1029.

6 Ie by virtue of the Ancient Monuments and Archaeological Areas Act 1979. As to the meaning of 'owner' in this context see PARA 1035 note 9.

7 The power of acquiring an easement under the Ancient Monuments and Archaeological Areas Act 1979 s 16(1), (1A) or (2) (see the text to notes 13–15) includes power to acquire any such easement by the grant of a new right: s 16(3) (amended by the National Heritage Act 1983 Sch 4 para 42).

8 Ie any of the purposes mentioned in the Ancient Monuments and Archaeological Areas Act 1979 s 15(1) (see PARA 1029).

9 See the Ancient Monuments and Archaeological Areas Act 1979 s 16(1)(a).

10 As to the meaning of 'use' see PARA 1024 note 14.

11 As to the meaning of 'land associated with the monument' see PARA 1035 note 9.

12 Ancient Monuments and Archaeological Areas Act 1979 s 16(1)(b).

13 As to the meaning of 'local authority' see PARA 1006 note 9.

14 Ie by virtue of the Ancient Monuments and Archaeological Areas Act 1979. See also note 7.

15 See the Ancient Monuments and Archaeological Areas Act 1979 s 16(1A), (2) (s 16(1A) added by the National Heritage Act 1983 Sch 4 para 42).

16 Ie by virtue of the Ancient Monuments and Archaeological Areas Act 1979. As to guardianship see PARA 1032.

17 Ancient Monuments and Archaeological Areas Act 1979 s 16(4) (amended by the National Heritage Act 1983 Sch 4 para 42). Any such right is treated for the purposes of its acquisition under the Ancient Monuments and Archaeological Areas Act 1979 s 16 and in all other respects as if it were a legal easement (s 16(5)(a)), and may be enforced by the guardians for the time being of the monument or land for whose benefit it was acquired as if they were the absolute owner in possession of that monument or land (s 16(5)(b)). Any such right is a local land charge: see s 16(8)(a). As to local land charges see REAL PROPERTY AND REGISTRATION vol 87 (2012) PARA 763 et seq.

18 Ancient Monuments and Archaeological Areas Act 1979 s 16(6)(a).

19 Ancient Monuments and Archaeological Areas Act 1979 s 16(6)(b).

20 Ancient Monuments and Archaeological Areas Act 1979 s 16(6). As to the termination of guardianship see PARA 1034.

1037. Agreements concerning ancient monuments and land in their vicinity. The Secretary of State[1] or the Historic Buildings and Monuments Commission for England ('the Commission')[2] in the case of an ancient monument[3] situated in England[4], and the Welsh Ministers in the case of an ancient monument situated in Wales[5], may enter into an agreement with the occupier[6] of an ancient monument or any land adjoining or in the vicinity of an ancient monument[7], and a local authority[8] may enter into an agreement with the occupier of any ancient monument situated in or in the vicinity of its area or with the occupier of any land adjoining or in the vicinity of any such ancient monument[9], for all or any of the following purposes with respect to the monument or land in question:

(1) the maintenance[10] and preservation of the monument and its amenities[11];

(2) the carrying out of any such work, or the doing of any such other thing, in relation to the monument or land as may be specified in the agreement[12];

(3) public access to the monument or land and the provision of facilities and information or other services for the use of the public in that connection[13];

(4) restricting the use[14] of the monument or land[15];

(5) prohibiting in relation to the monument or land the doing of any such thing as may be so specified[16]; and

(6) the making by the Secretary of State, the Welsh Ministers, the Commission or the local authority, as the case may be, of payments in such manner, of such amounts and on such terms as may be so

specified, and whether for or towards the cost of any work provided for under the agreement or in consideration of any restriction, prohibition or obligation accepted by any other party to it[17].

The agreement may also contain such incidental and consequential provisions as appear to the Secretary of State, the Welsh Ministers, the Commission or the local authority, as the case may be, to be necessary or expedient[18].

1   As to the Secretary of State see PARA 802 note 2.
2   As to the Historic Buildings and Monuments Commission for England ('the Commission') see PARA 803.
3   As to the meaning of 'ancient monument' see PARA 1029. References to an ancient monument in the Ancient Monuments and Archaeological Areas Act 1979 s 17(1A), (3) (see note 6) so far as it applies for the purposes of s 17(1A), is to be construed as if the reference in s 61(12)(b) (see PARA 1029) to the Secretary of State were to the Commission: s 17(9) (added by the National Heritage Act 1983 s 33, Sch 4 para 43).
4   References in the Ancient Monuments and Archaeological Areas Act 1979 s 17 to an ancient monument situated in England include any such monument situated in, on or under the seabed within the seaward limits of the United Kingdom territorial waters adjacent to England; and an order under the National Heritage Act 1983 s 33(10) (orders determining limits of waters adjacent to England: see PARA 804 note 2) applies for these purposes as it applies for the purposes of s 33(9): Ancient Monuments and Archaeological Areas Act 1979 s 17(10) (added by the National Heritage Act 2002 s 2(2)). As to the meanings of 'England' and 'United Kingdom' see PARA 804 note 2. As to United Kingdom territorial waters see WATER AND WATERWAYS vol 100 (2009) PARA 31.
5   The functions of the Secretary of State under the Ancient Monuments and Archaeological Areas Act 1979, in so far as they relate to Wales, were transferred to the National Assembly for Wales (see the National Assembly for Wales (Transfer of Functions) Order 1999, SI 1999/672, art 2, Sch 1) and are now exercisable by the Welsh Ministers (see the Government of Wales Act 2006 s 162(1), Sch 11 paras 30, 32). As to the Welsh Ministers see PARA 802. As to the meaning of 'Wales' see PARA 802 note 4.
6   In addition to the occupier, any person who has an interest in an ancient monument or in any land adjoining or in the vicinity of an ancient monument may be a party to an agreement under the Ancient Monuments and Archaeological Areas Act 1979 s 17: s 17(3). See also note 3. As to the meaning of 'person' see PARA 803 note 17. As to the meaning of 'land' see PARA 1006 note 6. As to the power of a limited owner to enter into an agreement see PARA 1038.
7   Ancient Monuments and Archaeological Areas Act 1979 s 17(1), (1A) (s 17(1A) added by the National Heritage Act 1983 Sch 4 para 43). Nothing in any agreement to which the Secretary of State or the Welsh Ministers are a party is to be construed as operating as a scheduled monument consent: Ancient Monuments and Archaeological Areas Act 1979 s 17(8). As to the meaning of 'scheduled monument consent' see PARA 1017.
8   As to the meaning of 'local authority' see PARA 1006 note 9.
9   Ancient Monuments and Archaeological Areas Act 1979 s 17(2). See also note 6.
10 As to the meaning of 'maintenance' see PARA 1029 note 11.
11 Ancient Monuments and Archaeological Areas Act 1979 s 17(4)(a).
12 Ancient Monuments and Archaeological Areas Act 1979 s 17(4)(b).
13 Ancient Monuments and Archaeological Areas Act 1979 s 17(4)(c). As to public access to monuments under public control see s 19; and PARA 1041.
14 As to the meaning of 'use' see PARA 1024 note 14.
15 Ancient Monuments and Archaeological Areas Act 1979 s 17(4)(d). The Law of Property Act 1925 s 84 (power to discharge or modify restrictive covenants: see REAL PROPERTY AND REGISTRATION vol 87 (2012) PARA 1093 et seq) does not apply to an agreement under the Ancient Monuments and Archaeological Areas Act 1979 s 17: s 17(7) (substituted by the Title Conditions (Scotland) Act 2003 s 128(1), Sch 14 para 8; and amended by SI 2009/1307).
16 Ancient Monuments and Archaeological Areas Act 1979 s 17(4)(e).
17 Ancient Monuments and Archaeological Areas Act 1979 s 17(4)(f) (amended by the National Heritage Act 1983 Sch 4 para 43).
18 Ancient Monuments and Archaeological Areas Act 1979 s 17(4) (amended by the National Heritage Act 1983 Sch 4 para 43). Where an agreement expressly provides that the agreement as a whole or any restriction, prohibition or obligation arising under it is to be binding on the successors of any party to the agreement (but not otherwise), then, as respects any monument or land in England and Wales, every person deriving title to the monument or land in question from, through or under that party is bound by the agreement, or, as the case may be, by that restriction,

prohibition or obligation, unless he derives title by virtue of any disposition made by that party before the date of the agreement: Ancient Monuments and Archaeological Areas Act 1979 s 17(5).

1038. Powers of limited owners to establish guardianship of land.

Notwithstanding that he is a limited owner[1] of the land, a person[2] may establish guardianship of any land[3] or join in executing a guardianship deed[4]. A person who is a limited owner of the land may also: (1) grant any easement, servitude or other right over land which the Secretary of State[5], the Welsh Ministers[6], the Historic Buildings and Monuments Commission for England ('the Commission')[7] or any local authority[8] is authorised[9] to acquire[10]; or (2) enter into an agreement[11] with respect to any land[12].

1 For this purpose: (1) a body corporate or corporation sole is a limited owner of any land in which it has an interest (Ancient Monuments and Archaeological Areas Act 1979 s 18(3)(a)); and (2) any other person is a limited owner of land in which he has an interest only if he holds that interest (a) as tenant for life or statutory owner within the meaning of the Settled Land Act 1925 (see SETTLEMENTS vol 91 (2012) PARAS 572, 667) (Ancient Monuments and Archaeological Areas Act 1979 s 18(3)(b), (4)(a)); (b) as trustee of land (s 18(3)(b), (4)(b) (substituted by the Trusts of Land and Appointment of Trustees Act 1996 s 25(1), Sch 3 para 17(b))); (c) as trustee for a charity or as commissioner or trustee for ecclesiastical, collegiate or other public purposes (Ancient Monuments and Archaeological Areas Act 1979 s 18(3)(b), (4)(d)). As to the meaning of 'owner' see PARA 1010 note 6. As to the meaning of 'land' see PARA 1006 note 6. As to the meaning of 'trustee of land' see PARA 1032 note 2. As to bodies corporate see COMPANIES vol 14 (2009) PARA 2; CORPORATIONS vol 24 (2010) PARA 301 et seq. As to corporations sole see CORPORATIONS vol 24 (2010) PARAS 314–315.

2 As to the meaning of 'person' see PARA 803 note 17.

3 Ie under the Ancient Monuments and Archaeological Areas Act 1979 s 12(1), (1A) or (2) (see PARA 1032).

4 Ancient Monuments and Archaeological Areas Act 1979 s 18(1) (amended by the National Heritage Act 1983 s 33(3), Sch 4 para 44). As to the meaning of 'guardianship deed' see PARA 1032 note 13.

Where a person, who is a limited owner of any land by virtue of holding an interest in the land in any of the capacities mentioned in the Ancient Monuments and Archaeological Areas Act 1979 s 18(4) (see heads (2)(a)–(2)(c) in note 1), executes a guardianship deed in relation to the land, the guardianship deed binds every successive owner of any estate or interest in the land: s 18(6). However, where the land to which a guardianship deed relates is at the date of the deed subject to any incumbrance not capable of being overreached by the limited owner in exercise of any powers of sale or management conferred on him by law or under any settlement or other instrument, the deed does not bind the incumbrancer: s 18(7).

5 As to the Secretary of State see PARA 802 note 2.

6 The functions of the Secretary of State under the Ancient Monuments and Archaeological Areas Act 1979, in so far as they relate to Wales, were transferred to the National Assembly for Wales (see the National Assembly for Wales (Transfer of Functions) Order 1999, SI 1999/672, art 2, Sch 1) and are now exercisable by the Welsh Ministers (see the Government of Wales Act 2006 s 162(1), Sch 11 paras 30, 32). As to the Welsh Ministers see PARA 802. As to the meaning of 'Wales' see PARA 802 note 4.

7 As to the Historic Buildings and Monuments Commission for England ('the Commission') see PARA 803.

8 As to the meaning of 'local authority' see PARA 1006 note 9.

9 Ie under the Ancient Monuments and Archaeological Areas Act 1979 s 16 (see PARA 1036).

10 Ancient Monuments and Archaeological Areas Act 1979 s 18(2)(a) (amended by the National Heritage Act 1983 Sch 4 para 44).

11 Ie an agreement under the Ancient Monuments and Archaeological Areas Act 1979 s 17 (see PARA 1037).

12 Ancient Monuments and Archaeological Areas Act 1979 s 18(2)(b). Where an agreement under s 17 to which a limited owner is a party expressly provides that the agreement as a whole or any restriction, prohibition or obligation arising thereunder is to be binding on his successors (but not otherwise), s 18(6), (7) (see note 4) applies to the agreement or, as the case may be, to the restriction, prohibition or obligation in question as it applies to a guardianship deed: s 18(8).

1039. Transfer of ancient monuments.

In respect of any monument[1] of which the Secretary of State[2], the Welsh Ministers[3], the Historic Buildings and Monuments Commission for England ('the Commission')[4] or a local authority[5] is the owner or guardian[6], or any land associated with any such monument[7], the Secretary of State, Welsh Ministers, Commission or local authority may enter into and carry into effect any agreement for the transfer of the monument or land or the guardianship of that monument or land[8] from:

(1)   the Secretary of State or the Welsh Ministers to the local authority[9];
(2)   the local authority to the Secretary of State or the Welsh Ministers[10];
(3)   the local authority to another local authority[11];
(4)   the Secretary of State to the Commission[12];
(5)   the Commission to the Secretary of State[13];
(6)   the Commission to the local authority[14]; or
(7)   the local authority to the Commission[15].

Where the Secretary of State, the Welsh Ministers, the Commission or the local authority in question is guardian of a monument or associated land, he, they or it may not enter into such an agreement with respect to that monument or land without the consent of the persons[16] who are for the time being immediately affected by the operation of the guardianship deed[17].

1   Any such monument will be an ancient monument: see the Ancient Monuments and Archaeological Areas Act 1979 ss 10–12; and PARAS 1030–1032. As to the meaning of 'ancient monument' see PARA 1029.
2   As to the Secretary of State see PARA 802 note 2.
3   The functions of the Secretary of State under the Ancient Monuments and Archaeological Areas Act 1979, in so far as they relate to Wales, were transferred to the National Assembly for Wales (see the National Assembly for Wales (Transfer of Functions) Order 1999, SI 1999/672, art 2, Sch 1) and are now exercisable by the Welsh Ministers (see the Government of Wales Act 2006 s 162(1), Sch 11 paras 30, 32). As to the meaning of 'Wales' see PARA 802 note 4.
4   The Commission may not enter into an agreement under the Ancient Monuments and Archaeological Areas Act 1979 21(1) in respect of a monument or land not situated in England: s 21(3) (s 21(3)–(6) added by the National Heritage Act 1983 s 33, Sch 4 para 47). As to the Historic Buildings and Monuments Commission for England ('the Commission') see PARA 803. As to the meaning of 'England' see PARA 804 note 2.
5   As to the meaning of 'local authority' see PARA 1006 note 9.
6   Ie by virtue of the Ancient Monuments and Archaeological Areas Act 1979. As to the meaning of 'owner' in this context see PARA 1035 note 9. As to guardianship see PARA 1032.
7   As to the meaning of 'land associated with any monument' see PARA 1035 note 9.
8   Ancient Monuments and Archaeological Areas Act 1979 s 21(1) (amended by the National Heritage Act 1983 s 33, Sch 4 para 47).
9   Ancient Monuments and Archaeological Areas Act 1979 s 21(1)(a). The Secretary of State may not enter into an agreement mentioned in s 21(1)(a) or s 21(1)(b) (see the text to note 10) in respect of a monument or land situated in England without consulting the Commission: s 21(4) (as added: see note 4). As to the exercise of the duty to consult see JUDICIAL REVIEW vol 61 (2010) PARA 627.
10 Ancient Monuments and Archaeological Areas Act 1979 s 21(1)(b). See also note 9.
11 Ancient Monuments and Archaeological Areas Act 1979 s 21(1)(c).
12 Ancient Monuments and Archaeological Areas Act 1979 s 21(1)(d) (s 21(1)(d)–(g) added by the National Heritage Act 1983 Sch 4 para 47).
13 Ancient Monuments and Archaeological Areas Act 1979 s 21(1)(e) (as added: see note 12).
14 Ancient Monuments and Archaeological Areas Act 1979 s 21(1)(f) (as added: see note 12). The Commission may not enter into an agreement mentioned in s 21(1)(f) without consulting the Secretary of State: s 21(5) (as added: see note 4).
15 Ancient Monuments and Archaeological Areas Act 1979 s 21(1)(g) (as added: see note 12). The Commission may not enter into an agreement mentioned in s 21(1)(g) without the consent of the Secretary of State: s 21(6) (as added: see note 4).
16 As to the meaning of 'person' see PARA 803 note 17.
17 Ancient Monuments and Archaeological Areas Act 1979 s 21(2) (amended by the National Heritage Act 1983 Sch 4 para 47). For these purposes a person is to be taken to be immediately affected by the operation of a guardianship deed relating to any land if he is bound by the deed and is in possession or occupation of the land: see the Ancient Monuments and Archaeological Areas Act 1979 s 61(3).

1040. Disposal of land acquired or placed under guardianship. The Secretary of State[1], the Welsh Ministers[2], the Historic Buildings and Monuments Commission for England ('the Commission')[3] or any local authority[4] may dispose of any land acquired by them under the statutory provisions[5] relating to the acquisition or transfer of ancient monuments[6]. Where the land in question is or includes a monument, the Secretary of State, the Welsh Ministers, the Commission or the local authority (as the case may be) may only dispose of it on such terms as will in their opinion ensure the preservation of the monument[7]; but this does not apply in any case where he, they or it is or are satisfied that it is no longer practicable to preserve the monument (whether because of the cost of preserving it or otherwise)[8].

1 The Secretary of State must consult with the Historic Buildings and Monuments Commission for England ('the Commission') before disposing of any land situated in England under these provisions: Ancient Monuments and Archaeological Areas Act 1979 s 30(1A) (added by the National Heritage Act 1983 s 33, Sch 4 para 52). 'Disposal' means disposal by way of sale, exchange or lease, or by way of the creation of any easement, right or privilege, or in any other manner, except by way of appropriation, gift or mortgage, and 'dispose of' must be construed accordingly: Town and Country Planning Act 1990 s 336(1) (definition applied by the Ancient Monuments and Archaeological Areas Act 1979 s 32(1)). As to the Secretary of State see PARA 802 note 2. As to the Commission see PARA 803. As to the meaning of 'land' see PARA 1006 note 6. As to the meaning of 'England' see PARA 804 note 2. As to the exercise of the duty to consult see JUDICIAL REVIEW vol 61 (2010) PARA 627.
2 The functions of the Secretary of State under the Ancient Monuments and Archaeological Areas Act 1979, in so far as they relate to Wales, were transferred to the National Assembly for Wales (see the National Assembly for Wales (Transfer of Functions) Order 1999, SI 1999/672, art 2, Sch 1) and are now exercisable by the Welsh Ministers (see the Government of Wales Act 2006 s 162(1), Sch 11 paras 30, 32). As to the Welsh Ministers see PARA 802. As to the meaning of 'Wales' see PARA 802 note 4.
3 The Commission must consult with the Secretary of State before disposing of any land under these provisions: Ancient Monuments and Archaeological Areas Act 1979 s 30(1B) (added by the National Heritage Act 1983 s 33, Sch 4 para 52).
4 A local authority must consult with the Secretary of State or, as appropriate, the Welsh Ministers before disposing of any land under these provisions: Ancient Monuments and Archaeological Areas Act 1979 s 30(2). As to the meaning of 'local authority' see PARA 1006 note 9.
5 Ie under the Ancient Monuments and Archaeological Areas Act 1979 s 10 (see PARA 1030), s 11 (see PARA 1031) or s 21 (see PARA 1039).
6 Ancient Monuments and Archaeological Areas Act 1979 s 30(1) (amended by the National Heritage Act 1983 s 33, Sch 4 para 52). As to the meaning of 'ancient monument' see PARA 1029.
7 Ancient Monuments and Archaeological Areas Act 1979 s 30(3) (amended by the National Heritage Act 1983 Sch 4 para 52).
8 Ancient Monuments and Archaeological Areas Act 1979 s 30(4) (amended by the National Heritage Act 1983 Sch 4 para 52).

(C) Public Access to Monuments and Facilities

1041. Public access to monuments. Subject to the following provisions, the public have a right of access to any monument[1] under the ownership[2] or guardianship of the Secretary of State[3], the Welsh Ministers[4], the Historic Buildings and Monuments Commission for England ('the Commission')[5] or any local authority[6] by virtue of the Ancient Monuments and Archaeological Areas Act 1979[7]. The Secretary of State, the Welsh Ministers, the Commission and any local authority[8] may nevertheless control the times of normal public access to any such monument under their ownership or guardianship and may also, if they consider it necessary or expedient to do so in the interests of safety or for the maintenance[9] or preservation of the monument, entirely exclude the public from access to any such monument or to any part of it, for such period as they think fit[10]. Notwithstanding the general right of public access[11], any person[12] authorised in that behalf by the Secretary of State, the Welsh Ministers, the Commission or a local authority may refuse admission:

(1)   to any monument under the ownership or guardianship of the Secretary of State, Welsh Ministers, the Commission or that local authority, as the case may be, by virtue of the Ancient Monuments and Archaeological Areas Act 1979[13]; or

(2)   in the case of the Secretary of State or the Welsh Ministers, to any monument[14] otherwise under his or their control or management[15],

to any person he has reasonable cause to believe is likely to do anything which would tend to injure or disfigure the monument or its amenities or to disturb the public in their enjoyment of it[16].

The Secretary of State, the Welsh Ministers and any local authority may, by regulations[17], regulate public access to any monument, or to all or any of the monuments under their ownership or guardianship by virtue of the Ancient Monuments and Archaeological Areas Act 1979 and any such regulations made by the Secretary of State or the Welsh Ministers may also apply to any monument, or to all or any of the monuments, under his or their control or management for any other reason[18]. The Secretary of State may also by regulations make such provision as appears to him necessary for prohibiting or regulating any act or thing which would tend to injure or disfigure any monument under the ownership or guardianship of the Commission, or the monument's amenities, or to disturb the public in their enjoyment of it[19]. If any person contravenes or fails to comply with any provision of any regulations made under the above provisions he commits an offence[20].

1   Any such monument under ownership or guardianship will be an ancient monument: see the Ancient Monuments and Archaeological Areas Act 1979 ss 10–12, 21; and PARAS 1030–1032, 1039. As to the meaning of 'ancient monument' see PARA 1029.
2   As to the meaning of 'ownership' in this context see PARA 1035 note 9.
3   As to the Secretary of State see PARA 802 note 2.
4   The functions of the Secretary of State under the Ancient Monuments and Archaeological Areas Act 1979, in so far as they relate to Wales, were transferred to the National Assembly for Wales (see the National Assembly for Wales (Transfer of Functions) Order 1999, SI 1999/672, art 2, Sch 1) and are now exercisable by the Welsh Ministers (see the Government of Wales Act 2006 s 162(1), Sch 11 paras 30, 32). As to the Welsh Ministers see PARA 802. As to the meaning of 'Wales' see PARA 802 note 4.
5   As to the Historic Buildings and Monuments Commission for England ('the Commission') see PARA 803.
6   As to the meaning of 'local authority' see PARA 1006 note 9.
7   Ancient Monuments and Archaeological Areas Act 1979 s 19(1) (amended by the National Heritage Act 1983 Sch 4 para 45). In relation to any monument under guardianship, the Ancient Monuments and Archaeological Areas Act 1979 s 19(1) is subject to any provision to the contrary in the guardianship deed: s 19(9). As to the meaning of 'guardianship deed' see PARA 1032 note 13. As to guardianship see PARA 1032. As to the provision of facilities for the public see PARA 1042.
8   This power of a local authority to control the times of normal public access to any monument is only exercisable by regulations made under the Ancient Monuments and Archaeological Areas Act 1979 s 19 (s 19(2)(a)); and the power under this provision of a local authority entirely to exclude the public from access to any monument with a view to its preservation is only exercisable with the consent of the Secretary of State or, as appropriate, the Welsh Ministers (s 19(2)(b)). Regulations made by a local authority under s 19 do not take effect unless they are submitted to and confirmed by the Secretary of State or, as the case may be, the Welsh Ministers, and the Secretary of State or the Welsh Ministers may confirm any such regulations either with or without modifications: s 19(8). Such regulations, not being made by statutory instrument, are not recorded in this work.
9   As to the meaning of 'maintenance' see PARA 1029 note 11.
10 Ancient Monuments and Archaeological Areas Act 1979 s 19(2) (amended by the National Heritage Act 1983 Sch 4 para 45).

11 Ie notwithstanding the Ancient Monuments and Archaeological Areas Act 1979 s 19(1) (see the text to notes 1–7).

12 As to the meaning of 'person' see PARA 803 note 17.

13 Ancient Monuments and Archaeological Areas Act 1979 s 19(6)(a) (s 19(6) amended by the National Heritage Act 1983 Sch 4 para 45).

14 This provision extends to monuments other than ancient monuments. As to the meaning of 'monument' see PARA 1013.

15 Ancient Monuments and Archaeological Areas Act 1979 s 19(6)(b).

16 Ancient Monuments and Archaeological Areas Act 1979 s 19(6) (as amended: see note 13).

17 The Secretary of State must consult with the Commission before he makes any such regulations in relation only to monuments situated in England: Ancient Monuments and Archaeological Areas Act 1979 s 19(3) (amended by the National Heritage Act 1983 s 33, Sch 4 para 45). As to the making of regulations see PARA 1009. See also note 8. At the date at which this volume states the law no such regulations had been made.

18 Ancient Monuments and Archaeological Areas Act 1979 s 19(3) (as amended: see note 17). Without prejudice to the generality of the Ancient Monuments and Archaeological Areas Act 1979 s 19(3), regulations made by the Secretary of State, the Welsh Ministers or a local authority thereunder may prescribe the times when the public are to have access to monuments to which the regulations apply and may make such provision as appears to them to be necessary for (1) the preservation of any such monument and its amenities or of any property of the Secretary of State, Welsh Ministers or local authority (s 19(4)(a)); and (2) prohibiting or regulating any act or thing which would tend to injure or disfigure any such monument or its amenities or to disturb the public in their enjoyment of it (s 19(4)(b)), and may prescribe charges for the admission of the public to any such monument or to any class or description of monuments to which the regulations apply (s 19(4) (amended by the National Heritage Act 1983 Sch 4 para 45)). Without prejudice to the Ancient Monuments and Archaeological Areas Act 1979 s 19(3), (4), the Secretary of State, the Welsh Ministers, the Commission and any local authority have power to make such charges as they may from time to time determine for the admission of the public to any monument under their ownership or guardianship by virtue of the Ancient Monuments and Archaeological Areas Act 1979 or, in the case of the Secretary of State or the Welsh Ministers, to any monument otherwise under his or their control or management: s 19(5) (amended by the National Heritage Act 1983 Sch 4 para 45).

19 Ancient Monuments and Archaeological Areas Act 1979 s 19(4A) (s 19(4A), (4B) added by the National Heritage Act 1983 Sch 4 para 45). The Secretary of State must consult with the Commission before making any such regulations: Ancient Monuments and Archaeological Areas Act 1979 s 19(4B) (as so added). At the date at which this volume states the law no such regulations had been made. As to damage to monuments see PARA 1046.

20 See the Ancient Monuments and Archaeological Areas Act 1979 s 19(7). The penalty for such an offence is, on summary conviction, a fine not exceeding level 3 on the standard scale: s 19(7) (amended by the Criminal Justice Act 1982 ss 38, 46). As to the standard scale and magistrates' powers to levy unlimited fines see SENTENCING vol 92 (2015) PARA 176. As to offences by bodies corporate see PARA 1012. A person who has an enforcement function in relation to an offence under the Ancient Monuments and Archaeological Areas Act 1979 is a regulator for the purposes of the Regulatory Enforcement and Sanctions Act 2008: see CONSTITUTIONAL AND ADMINISTRATIVE LAW vol 20 (2014) PARAS 331–339. As to sentencing guidelines for offences of theft involving historic objects or loss of the nation's heritage see PARA 1046 note 5.

1042. Provision of facilities for public access to monuments. The Secretary of State[1], the Welsh Ministers[2], the Historic Buildings and Monuments Commission for England ('the Commission')[3] and any local authority[4] may provide such facilities and information or other services for the public as appear to them to be necessary or desirable for or in connection with affording public access[5] to: (1) any monument under their ownership or guardianship by virtue of the Ancient Monuments and Archaeological Areas Act 1979[6]; or (2) in the case of the Secretary of State or the Welsh Ministers, any monument[7] otherwise under his or their control or management[8]. The Secretary of State, the Welsh Ministers, the Commission and any local authority may make such charges as they from time to time determine for the use of any facility or service so provided[9].

The Commission, as respects a monument situated in England[10], or the Welsh Ministers, as respects a monument situated in Wales, may contribute towards the cost of the provision of facilities or services for the public by a local authority under the above provisions[11].

1   As to the Secretary of State see PARA 802 note 2.
2   The functions of the Secretary of State under the Ancient Monuments and Archaeological Areas Act 1979, in so far as they relate to Wales, were transferred to the National Assembly for Wales (see the National Assembly for Wales (Transfer of Functions) Order 1999, SI 1999/672, art 2, Sch 1) and are now exercisable by the Welsh Ministers (see the Government of Wales Act 2006 s 162(1), Sch 11 paras 30, 32). As to the Welsh Ministers see PARA 802. As to the meaning of 'Wales' see PARA 802 note 4.
3   As to the Historic Buildings and Monuments Commission for England ('the Commission') see PARA 803.
4   As to the meaning of 'local authority' see PARA 1006 note 9.
5   Ancient Monuments and Archaeological Areas Act 1979 s 20(1) (amended by the National Heritage Act 1983 Sch 4 para 46). Facilities and information or other public services may be provided under the Ancient Monuments and Archaeological Areas Act 1979 s 20 in or on the monument itself or on any land associated with it: s 20(2). As to public access see PARA 1041. As to the meaning of 'land associated with a monument' see PARA 1035 note 9.
6   Ancient Monuments and Archaeological Areas Act 1979 s 20(1)(a). A monument in this case will be an ancient monument. As to the meaning of 'ancient monument' see PARA 1029. As to the meaning of 'owner' in this context see PARA 1035 note 9. As to guardianship see PARA 1032.
7   Such a monument will not necessarily be an ancient monument. As to the meaning of 'monument' see PARA 1013.
8   Ancient Monuments and Archaeological Areas Act 1979 s 20(1)(b).
9   Ancient Monuments and Archaeological Areas Act 1979 s 20(3) (amended by the National Heritage Act 1983 Sch 4 para 46).
10 This reference to a monument situated in England includes any monument situated in, on or under the seabed within the seaward limits of the United Kingdom territorial waters adjacent to England; and an order under the National Heritage Act 1983 s 33(10) (orders determining limits of waters adjacent to England: see PARA 804 note 2) applies for these purposes as it applies for the purposes of s 33(9) (see PARA 804): Ancient Monuments and Archaeological Areas Act 1979 s 24(3AA) (added by the National Heritage Act 2002 s 2(3)). As to the meanings of 'England' and 'United Kingdom' see PARA 804 note 2. As to United Kingdom territorial waters see WATER AND WATERWAYS vol 100 (2009) PARA 31.
11 See the Ancient Monuments and Archaeological Areas Act 1979 s 24(3), (3A) (s 24(3) amended by, s 24(3A) added by, the National Heritage Act 1983 Sch 4 para 48). As to expenditure in respect of ancient monuments generally see PARA 1043.

(D)   *Expenditure and Assistance in respect of Ancient Monuments*

1043. Expenditure on acquisition or preservation of ancient monuments. The Historic Buildings and Monuments Commission for England ('the Commission')[1], as respects an ancient monument[2] situated in England[3], and the Welsh Ministers[4], as respects an ancient monument situated in Wales:

(1)   may defray or contribute towards the cost of the acquisition by any person[5] of any ancient monument[6];

(2)   may undertake, or assist in, or defray or contribute towards the cost of the removal of any ancient monument or of any part of any such monument to another place for the purpose of preserving it, and may at the request of the owner[7] undertake, or assist in, or defray or contribute towards the cost of the preservation, maintenance[8] and management of any ancient monument[9].

At the request of the owner, any local authority[10] may undertake, or assist in, or defray or contribute towards the cost of the preservation, maintenance and management of any ancient monument situated in or in the vicinity of its area[11].

No expenses may be incurred by the Commission, the Welsh Ministers or any local authority under these provisions in connection with any monument which is occupied as a dwelling house by any person other than a person employed as its caretaker or his family[12].

The Secretary of State, the Welsh Ministers or any local authority may receive voluntary contributions for or towards the cost of any expenditure incurred by them under the Ancient Monuments and Archaeological Areas Act 1979[13], whether in relation to any particular monument[14] or land[15] or otherwise[16].

1 As to the Historic Buildings and Monuments Commission for England ('the Commission') see PARA 803.
2 As to the meaning of 'ancient monument' see PARA 1029.
3 See the Ancient Monuments and Archaeological Areas Act 1979 s 24(3A), (3B) (both added by the National Heritage Act 1983 Sch 4 para 48). This reference to a monument situated in England includes any monument situated in, on or under the seabed within the seaward limits of the United Kingdom territorial waters adjacent to England; and an order under the National Heritage Act 1983 s 33(10) (orders determining limits of waters adjacent to England: see PARA 804 note 2) applies for these purposes as it applies for the purposes of s 33(9) (see PARA 804 note 2): Ancient Monuments and Archaeological Areas Act 1979 s 24(3AA) (added by the National Heritage Act 2002 s 2(3)). As to the meanings of 'England' and 'United Kingdom' see PARA 804 note 2. As to United Kingdom territorial waters see WATER AND WATERWAYS vol 100 (2009) PARA 31.
4 The functions of the Secretary of State under the Ancient Monuments and Archaeological Areas Act 1979, in so far as they relate to Wales, were transferred to the National Assembly for Wales (see the National Assembly for Wales (Transfer of Functions) Order 1999, SI 1999/672, art 2, Sch 1) and are now exercisable by the Welsh Ministers (see the Government of Wales Act 2006 s 162(1), Sch 11 paras 30, 32). As to the Secretary of State and the Welsh Ministers see PARA 802. As to the meaning of 'Wales' see PARA 802 note 4.
5 As to the meaning of 'person' see PARA 803 note 17.
6 Ancient Monuments and Archaeological Areas Act 1979 s 24(1) (amended by the National Heritage Act 1983 Sch 4 para 48).
7 As to the meaning of 'owner' see PARA 1010 note 6.
8 As to the meaning of 'maintenance' see PARA 1029 note 11.
9 Ancient Monuments and Archaeological Areas Act 1979 s 24(2) (amended by the National Heritage Act 1983 Sch 4 para 48).
10 As to the meaning of 'local authority' see PARA 1006 note 9.
11 Ancient Monuments and Archaeological Areas Act 1979 s 24(4).
12 Ancient Monuments and Archaeological Areas Act 1979 s 24(5) (amended by the National Heritage Act 1983 Sch 4 para 48).
13 Ie under the Ancient Monuments and Archaeological Areas Act 1979 Pt I (ss 1–32) (see PARA 1014 et seq).
14 As to the meaning of 'monument' see PARA 1013.
15 As to the meaning of 'land' see PARA 1006 note 6.
16 Ancient Monuments and Archaeological Areas Act 1979 s 31.

1044. Advice and superintendence as respects ancient monuments. The Historic Buildings and Monuments Commission for England ('the Commission')[1], as respects an ancient monument[2] situated in England[3], or the Welsh Ministers[4], as respects an ancient monument situated in Wales, may give advice with reference to the treatment of any such monument[5]. The Commission and the Welsh Ministers may also, if in their opinion it is advisable, superintend any work in connection with any ancient monument if invited to do so by the owner[6], and must superintend any such work, whether required to do so by the owner or not, in connection with any scheduled monument[7], if in their opinion it is advisable[8].

1 As to the Historic Buildings and Monuments Commission for England ('the Commission') see PARA 803.
2 As to the meaning of 'ancient monument' see PARA 1029.
3 See the Ancient Monuments and Archaeological Areas Act 1979 s 25(3A), (3B) (both added by the National Heritage Act 1983 Sch 4 para 49). As to the meaning of 'England' see PARA 804 note 2.
4 The functions of the Secretary of State under the Ancient Monuments and Archaeological Areas Act 1979, in so far as they relate to Wales, were transferred to the National Assembly for Wales

(see the National Assembly for Wales (Transfer of Functions) Order 1999, SI 1999/672, art 2, Sch 1) and are now exercisable by the Welsh Ministers (see the Government of Wales Act 2006 s 162(1), Sch 11 paras 30, 32). As to the Secretary of State and the Welsh Ministers see PARA 802. As to the meaning of 'Wales' see PARA 802 note 4.

5   See the Ancient Monuments and Archaeological Areas Act 1979 s 25(1) (amended by the National Heritage Act 1983 s 33, Sch 4 para 49).

6   As to the meaning of 'owner' see PARA 1010 note 6.

7   As to the meaning of 'scheduled monument' see PARA 1014.

8   Ancient Monuments and Archaeological Areas Act 1979 s 25(2) (s 25(2), (3) amended by the National Heritage Act 1983 Sch 4 para 49). The Commission and the Welsh Ministers may make a charge for giving advice and superintendence under this provision or may give it free of charge, as they think fit: Ancient Monuments and Archaeological Areas Act 1979 s 25(3) (as so amended).

1045.   Entry on land believed to contain an ancient monument. A person[1] duly authorised in writing[2] by the Secretary of State or, in relation to Wales, the Welsh Ministers[3] may at any reasonable time enter any land[4] in, on or under which the Secretary of State knows or has reason to believe or the Welsh Ministers know or have reason to believe there is an ancient monument[5] for the purpose of inspecting the land, including any building[6] or other structure on the land, with a view to recording any matters of archaeological or historical interest[7]. A person entering any land in exercise of this power may carry out excavations[8] in the land for the purpose of archaeological investigation[9].

1   As to the meaning of 'person' see PARA 803 note 17.

2   As to the meaning of 'writing' see PARA 805 note 14.

3   The functions of the Secretary of State under the Ancient Monuments and Archaeological Areas Act 1979, in so far as they relate to Wales, were transferred to the National Assembly for Wales (see the National Assembly for Wales (Transfer of Functions) Order 1999, SI 1999/672, art 2, Sch 1) and are now exercisable by the Welsh Ministers (see the Government of Wales Act 2006 s 162(1), Sch 11 paras 30, 32). As to the Secretary of State and the Welsh Ministers see PARA 802. As to the meaning of 'Wales' see PARA 802 note 4.

4   As to the meaning of 'land' see PARA 1006 note 6. As to powers of entry see further PARAS 1062–1063.

5   As to the meaning of 'ancient monument' see PARA 1029.

6   As to the meaning of 'building' see PARA 1028 note 16.

7   Ancient Monuments and Archaeological Areas Act 1979 s 26(1). As to the treatment and preservation of finds see PARA 1064.

8   No excavations may be made in exercise of this power except with the consent of every person whose consent to the making of the excavation would otherwise be required: Ancient Monuments and Archaeological Areas Act 1979 s 26(3).

9   Ancient Monuments and Archaeological Areas Act 1979 s 26(2). As to the meaning of 'archaeological investigation' see PARA 1017 note 12.

(E)   Offence of Damaging Monuments

1046.   Damage to monuments. A person[1] who without lawful excuse destroys or damages any protected monument[2] knowing that it is a protected monument[3] and intending to destroy or damage the monument, or being reckless as to whether the monument would be destroyed or damaged[4], is guilty of an offence[5]. This applies to anything done by or under the authority of the owner[6] of the monument, other than an act for the execution of excepted works[7], as it applies to anything done by any other person[8].

Where the owner or any other person is convicted of an offence involving damage to a monument situated in England[9] and Wales which was at the time of the offence under the guardianship of the Secretary of State, the Welsh Ministers, the Historic Buildings and Monuments Commission for England ('the Commission') or any local authority under the Ancient Monuments and Archaeological Areas Act 1979, any compensation order[10] made in respect of that damage must be made in favour of the Secretary of State, the Welsh Ministers, the Commission or the local authority in question, as the case may require[11].

1 As to the meaning of 'person' see PARA 803 note 17. As to offences by bodies corporate see PARA 1012.
2 'Protected monument' means any scheduled monument and any monument under the ownership or guardianship of the Secretary of State, the Welsh Ministers, the Historic Buildings and Monuments Commission for England ('the Commission') or a local authority by virtue of the Ancient Monuments and Archaeological Areas Act 1979: s 28(3) (amended by the National Heritage Act 1983 s 33(3), Sch 4 para 50). As to the meaning of 'scheduled monument' see PARA 1014. A monument under the ownership or guardianship of the Secretary of State, the Welsh Ministers, the Commission or a local authority will be an ancient monument. As to the meaning of 'ancient monument' see PARA 1029. As to the meaning of 'owner' in this context see PARA 1035 note 9. As to guardianship see PARA 1032. As to the Commission see PARA 803. As to the meaning of 'local authority' see PARA 1006 note 9.
   The functions of the Secretary of State under the Ancient Monuments and Archaeological Areas Act 1979, in so far as they relate to Wales, were transferred to the National Assembly for Wales (see the National Assembly for Wales (Transfer of Functions) Order 1999, SI 1999/672, art 2, Sch 1) and are now exercisable by the Welsh Ministers (see the Government of Wales Act 2006 s 162(1), Sch 11 paras 30, 32). As to the Secretary of State and the Welsh Ministers see PARA 802. As to the meaning of 'Wales' see PARA 802 note 4.
3 Ancient Monuments and Archaeological Areas Act 1979 s 28(1)(a).
4 Ancient Monuments and Archaeological Areas Act 1979 s 28(1)(b).
5 Ancient Monuments and Archaeological Areas Act 1979 s 28(1). A person guilty of such an offence is liable, on summary conviction, to a fine not exceeding the statutory maximum, or to imprisonment for a term not exceeding six months or both (s 28(4)(a)), or, on conviction on indictment, to a fine or to imprisonment for a term not exceeding two years or both (s 28(4)(b)).
   As to the statutory maximum and magistrates' powers to levy unlimited fines see SENTENCING vol 92 (2015) PARA 176. A person who has an enforcement function in relation to an offence under the Ancient Monuments and Archaeological Areas Act 1979 is a regulator for the purposes of the Regulatory Enforcement and Sanctions Act 2008: see CONSTITUTIONAL AND ADMINISTRATIVE LAW vol 20 (2014) PARAS 331–339.
   See also Sentencing Council Definitive Guideline *Theft Offences* (published 6 October 2015) (in which the Sentencing Council has issued definitive guidelines on theft which specify that if an offence involves theft of historic objects or the loss of the nation's heritage this can make the offence more serious): and SENTENCING vol 92 (2015) PARA 562.
6 As to the meaning of 'owner' see PARA 1010 note 6.
7 'Excepted works' means works for which scheduled monument consent has been given under the Ancient Monuments and Archaeological Areas Act 1979, including any consent granted by order under s 3 (see PARA 1017): s 28(2). As to the meaning of 'works' see PARA 1016 note 2. As to the control of works see PARA 1016. As to the meaning of 'scheduled monument consent' see PARA 1017.
8 Ancient Monuments and Archaeological Areas Act 1979 s 28(2).
9 As to the meaning of 'England' see PARA 804 note 2.
10 Ie under the Powers of Criminal Courts (Sentencing) Act 2000 s 130 (compensation orders against convicted persons): see SENTENCING vol 92 (2015) PARA 281.
11 Ancient Monuments and Archaeological Areas Act 1979 s 29 (amended by the National Heritage Act 1983 Sch 4 para 51; and the Powers of Criminal Courts (Sentencing) Act 2000 s 165(1), Sch 9 para 59).

C. ARCHAEOLOGICAL AREAS

(A) Designation Orders for Archaeological Areas

1047. Designation by the Secretary of State or the Welsh Ministers of archaeological areas. The Secretary of State or, in relation to Wales, the Welsh Ministers[1] may from time to time by order[2] designate as an area of archaeological importance[3] any area which appears to him or them to merit treatment as such for the purposes of the Ancient Monuments and Archaeological Areas Act 1979[4]. Before making such a designation order the Secretary of State or the Welsh Ministers must: (1) consult[5] each of the local authorities concerned[6] (and the Secretary of State must also consult with the Historic Buildings and

Monuments Commission for England ('the Commission'))[7]; and (2) publish notice of the proposal to make the order[8].

The order must be in such form as the Secretary of State considers or the Welsh Ministers consider appropriate[9] and must describe by reference to a map the area affected[10]. The Secretary of State or the Welsh Ministers may make the order, either without modifications or with such modification only as consists in reducing the area affected, at any time after the end of a period of six weeks beginning with the date on which notice of the proposal to make the order is first published[11]. On making the order the Secretary of State or the Welsh Ministers must publish notice of the making of the order[12] and deposit a copy of the order and map with each local authority concerned[13]. The order does not come into operation until the end of the period of six months[14] beginning with the date on which it is made[15].

1　The functions of the Secretary of State under the Ancient Monuments and Archaeological Areas Act 1979, in so far as they relate to Wales, were transferred to the National Assembly for Wales (see the National Assembly for Wales (Transfer of Functions) Order 1999, SI 1999/672, art 2, Sch 1) and are now exercisable by the Welsh Ministers (see the Government of Wales Act 2006 s 162(1), Sch 11 paras 30, 32). As to the Secretary of State and the Welsh Ministers see PARA 802. As to the meaning of 'Wales' see PARA 802 note 4.

2　An order under the Ancient Monuments and Archaeological Areas Act 1979 s 33 designating an area as an area of archaeological importance, whether by the Secretary of State, the Welsh Ministers, a local authority or the Historic Buildings and Monuments Commission for England ('the Commission'), is known as a 'designation order': see ss 33(3), 61(1) (s 33(3) amended by the Local Government Act 1985 s 6, Sch 2 para 2(2)). As to the meaning of 'local authority' see PARA 1006 note 9. As to orders by a local authority see PARA 1048. As to the Commission see PARA 803. As to orders by the Commission see PARA 1049. A designation order relating to an area in England and Wales is a local land charge: Ancient Monuments and Archaeological Areas Act 1979 s 33(5). As to the meaning of 'England' see PARA 804 note 2. As to local land charges see REAL PROPERTY AND REGISTRATION vol 87 (2012) PARA 763 et seq.

3　'Area of archaeological importance' means an area designated as such under the Ancient Monuments and Archaeological Areas Act 1979 s 33 (see the text and notes 1–2, 4–15; and PARAS 1048, 1049): s 61(1).

4　Ancient Monuments and Archaeological Areas Act 1979 s 33(1). As to challenges to the validity of a designation order see PARA 1051.

5　The consultations required by the Ancient Monuments and Archaeological Areas Act 1979 Sch 2 para 2(a), (aa) (see the text to notes 6, 7) must precede the publication of the notice required by Sch 2 para 2(b) (see the text to note 8): Sch 2 para 3(1) (amended by the National Heritage Act 1983 Sch 4 para 69). As to the exercise of the duty to consult see JUDICIAL REVIEW vol 61 (2010) PARA 627.

6　Ancient Monuments and Archaeological Areas Act 1979 Sch 2 para 2(a). A local authority is a local authority concerned in relation to a designation order or an order varying or revoking such an order if the area affected by the designation order, or any part of that area, is within the area of the local authority: Sch 2 para 20(2). As to the variation and revocation of orders see PARA 1050.

7　See the Ancient Monuments and Archaeological Areas Act 1979 s 33(1), Sch 2 para 2(aa) (s 33(1) amended by the National Heritage Act 1983 Sch 4 para 54; Ancient Monuments and Archaeological Areas Act 1979 Sch 2 para 2(aa) added by the National Heritage Act 1983 Sch 4 para 69).

8　Ancient Monuments and Archaeological Areas Act 1979 Sch 2 para 2(b). The notice must be published in two successive weeks in the London Gazette and in one or more local newspapers circulating in the locality in which the area affected is situated: Sch 2 para 3(2)(a). The notice must state that the Secretary of State or, as the case may be, the Welsh Ministers propose to make the order, describe the area affected and the effect of the order (Sch 2 para 3(2)(b)), and indicate where a copy of the draft order and the map to which it refers may be inspected (Sch 2 para 3(2)(c)). 'Area affected' in relation to a designation order means the area to which the order for the time being relates: Sch 2 para 20(1).

　　Copies of the draft order and of the map to which it refers must be deposited with each of the local authorities concerned on or before the date on which notice of the proposal to make the order is first published (Sch 2 para 4(a)); and must be sent to the Commission (if the area which would be designated by the order is situated in England) (Sch 2 para 4(aa) (added by the National

Heritage Act 1983 s 33, Sch 4 para 69)); and must be kept available for public inspection by each of those authorities, free of charge, at reasonable hours and at a convenient place, until the Secretary of State or the Welsh Ministers make the order or notify the local authority in question that he or they have determined not to make it (Ancient Monuments and Archaeological Areas Act 1979 Sch 2 para 4(b)). Copies of the draft order and of the map to which it refers must similarly be kept available by the Secretary of State or the Welsh Ministers, until he or they make the order or determine not to make it: Sch 2 para 5.

9 See the Ancient Monuments and Archaeological Areas Act 1979 Sch 2 para 1(2).

10 See the Ancient Monuments and Archaeological Areas Act 1979 Sch 2 para 1(1). The map must be to such a scale as the Secretary of State or the Welsh Ministers consider appropriate: see Sch 2 para 1(2).

11 Ancient Monuments and Archaeological Areas Act 1979 Sch 2 para 6.

12 A notice must be published in two successive weeks in the London Gazette and in one or more local newspapers circulating in the locality in which the area affected is situated, stating that the order has been made and describing the area affected and the effect of the order: see the Ancient Monuments and Archaeological Areas Act 1979 Sch 2 para 7(a).

13 Ancient Monuments and Archaeological Areas Act 1979 Sch 2 para 7(b). In a case where the area designated is situated in England, the Secretary of State must also send to the Commission a copy of the order and of the map to which it refers: Sch 2 para 7(c) (added by the National Heritage Act 1983 Sch 4 para 69).

14 As to the meaning of 'month' see PARA 803 note 12.

15 See the Ancient Monuments and Archaeological Areas Act 1979 Sch 2 para 16(1).

1048. Designation by local authority of archaeological areas. A local authority[1] may from time to time by a designation order[2] designate as an area of archaeological importance[3] any area within the area of that local authority which appears to it to merit treatment as such for the purposes of the Ancient Monuments and Archaeological Areas Act 1979[4]. Before making a designation order the authority must consult[5] any other local authority concerned[6] and publish notice of its proposal to make the order[7].

A designation order made by a local authority must be in such form as may be prescribed[8] and must describe by reference to a map the area affected[9]. The authority may make the order, either without modifications or with such modification only as consists in reducing the area affected, and submit it to the Secretary of State or, in relation to Wales, the Welsh Ministers for confirmation[10], at any time after the end of the period of six weeks beginning with the date on which notice of its proposal to make the order was first published[11]. A designation order made by a local authority does not take effect unless it is confirmed by the Secretary of State or, as appropriate, the Welsh Ministers, and the Secretary of State or Welsh Ministers may confirm any such order either without modifications or with such modification only as consists in reducing the area affected[12]. A designation order made by a local authority and confirmed by the Secretary of State or, as the case may be, the Welsh Ministers does not come into operation until the end of the period of six months[13] beginning with the date on which it is confirmed[14].

1 As to the meaning of 'local authority' see PARA 1006 note 9.

2 As to the meaning of 'designation order' see PARA 1047 note 2.

3 As to the meaning of 'area of archaeological importance' see PARA 1047 note 3.

4 Ancient Monuments and Archaeological Areas Act 1979 s 33(2). Where the area in question is situated in England the local authority must first notify the Historic Buildings and Monuments Commission for England ('the Commission') of its intention to make the order: see s 33(2), Sch 2 para 9A (s 33(2) amended by and Sch 2 para 9A added by, the National Heritage Act 1983 Sch 4 paras 54, 69). As to the Historic Buildings and Monuments Commission for England ('the Commission') see PARA 803. As to the meaning of 'England' see PARA 804 note 2. As to challenges to the validity of a designation order see PARA 1051.

5 The consultation must precede the publication of the notice required by the Ancient Monuments and Archaeological Areas Act 1979 Sch 2 para 9(b) (see the text to note 7): Sch 2 para 10(1).

6   Ancient Monuments and Archaeological Areas Act 1979 Sch 2 para 9(a). As to the meaning of
    'local authority concerned' see PARA 1047 note 6.
7   Ancient Monuments and Archaeological Areas Act 1979 Sch 2 para 9(b). The notice must be in the
    prescribed form and must otherwise comply with Sch 2 para 3(2) (see PARA 1047 note 8) (with the
    necessary modifications): Sch 2 para 10(2). Copies of the draft order and of the map to which it
    refers (1) must be deposited with each of the local authorities concerned (other than the local
    authority proposing to make the order) on or before the date on which notice of the proposal to
    make the order is first published in accordance with Sch 2 para 3(2)(a) as applied by Sch 2 para 10
    (Sch 2 para 11(a)); and (2) must be kept available for public inspection by each of the local
    authorities concerned, free of charge at reasonable hours and at a convenient place, until the local
    authority proposing to make the order either make it or determine not to make it and, in the case
    of any other local authority concerned, notifies that local authority of its determination (Sch 2
    para 11(b)). 'Prescribed' means prescribed by regulations made by the Secretary of State or the
    Welsh Ministers: see s 61(1). As to the making of regulations see PARA 1009. At the date at which
    this volume states the law no such regulations had been made.
        The functions of the Secretary of State under the Ancient Monuments and Archaeological
    Areas Act 1979, in so far as they relate to Wales, were transferred to the National Assembly for
    Wales (see the National Assembly for Wales (Transfer of Functions) Order 1999, SI 1999/672,
    art 2, Sch 1) and are now exercisable by the Welsh Ministers (see the Government of Wales Act
    2006 s 162(1), Sch 11 paras 30, 32). As to the Secretary of State and the Welsh Ministers see PARA
    802. As to the meaning of 'Wales' see PARA 802 note 4.
8   See the Ancient Monuments and Archaeological Areas Act 1979 Sch 2 para 8(2). At the date at
    which this volume states the law no regulations had been made for this purpose.
9   See the Ancient Monuments and Archaeological Areas Act 1979 Sch 2 para 8(1). The map must
    be to such a scale as may be prescribed: see Sch 2 para 8(2). At the date at which this volume states
    the law no regulations had been made for this purpose. As to the meaning of 'area affected' see
    PARA 1047 note 8.
10 The Secretary of State or the Welsh Ministers may by regulations prescribe the procedure for
    submitting orders for confirmation: Ancient Monuments and Archaeological Areas Act 1979 Sch
    2 para 15. At the date at which this volume states the law no such regulations had been made.
11 Ancient Monuments and Archaeological Areas Act 1979 Sch 2 para 12.
12 Ancient Monuments and Archaeological Areas Act 1979 Sch 2 para 13. If the Secretary of State
    confirms or the Welsh Ministers confirm the order the local authority must on being notified that
    the order has been confirmed: (1) publish notice of the making of the order in the manner and form
    prescribed (Sch 2 para 14(a)); and (2) deposit a copy of the order and of the map to which it refers
    with any other local authority concerned (Sch 2 para 14(b)); and (3) send to the Commission a
    copy of the order and of the map to which it refers, if the area designated by the order is situated
    in England (Sch 2 para 14(c) (added by the National Heritage Act 1983 s 33, Sch 4 para 69)). At
    the date at which this volume states the law no regulations had been made for the purposes of head
    (1) above.
13 As to the meaning of 'month' see PARA 803 note 12.
14 Ancient Monuments and Archaeological Areas Act 1979 Sch 2 para 16(2).

1049. Designation by the Historic Buildings and Monuments Commission for England of archaeological areas.

The Historic Buildings and Monuments Commission for England ('the Commission')[1] may from time to time by a designation order[2] designate as an area of archaeological importance[3] any area in Greater London[4] which appears to it to merit treatment as such for the purposes of the Ancient Monuments and Archaeological Areas Act 1979[5]. Before making a designation order the Commission must consult[6] any local authority concerned[7], and publish notice of its proposal to make the order[8].

A designation order made by the Commission must be in such form as may be prescribed[9] and describe by reference to a map the area affected[10]. The Commission may make the order, either without modifications or with such modification only as consists in reducing the area affected, and submit it to the Secretary of State for confirmation[11], at any time after the end of the period of six weeks beginning with the date on which notice of its proposal to make the order is first published[12]. A designation order made by the Commission does not take effect unless it is confirmed by the Secretary of State, and the Secretary of State may confirm any such order either without modifications or with such modification only as consists in reducing the area affected[13].

1 As to the Historic Buildings and Monuments Commission for England ('the Commission') see PARA 803.
2 As to the meaning of 'designation order' see PARA 1047 note 2.
3 As to the meaning of 'area of archaeological importance' see PARA 1047 note 3.
4 As to the meaning of 'Greater London' see PARA 856 note 4.
5 Ancient Monuments and Archaeological Areas Act 1979 s 33(2A) (added by the Local Government Act 1985 s 6, Sch 2 para 2(2)). As to challenges to the validity of a designation order see PARA 1051.
6 The consultation must precede the publication of the notice under the Ancient Monuments and Archaeological Areas Act 1979 Sch 2 paras 9(b), 15A(b) (see the text to note 8): Sch 2 paras 10(1), 15A (added by the Local Government Act 1985 Sch 2 para 2(4)).
7 See the Ancient Monuments and Archaeological Areas Act 1979 Sch 2 paras 9(a), 15A(b) (as added: see note 6). As to the meaning of 'local authority concerned' see PARA 1047 note 6.
8 See the Ancient Monuments and Archaeological Areas Act 1979 Sch 2 paras 9(b), 15A(b) (as added: see note 6). The notice must be in the prescribed form and must otherwise comply with Sch 2 para 3(2) (see PARA 1047 note 8), with the necessary modifications: see Sch 2 paras 10(2), 15A (as so added). Copies of the draft order and of the map to which it refers (1) must be deposited with each of the local authorities concerned on or before the date on which notice of the proposal to make the order is first published in accordance with Sch 2 para 3(2)(a) as applied by Sch 2 para 10 (see Sch 2 paras 11(a), 15A(c) (as so added)); and (2) must be kept available for public inspection by each of the local authorities concerned, free of charge at reasonable hours and at a convenient place, until the Commission either makes it or determines not to make it and, in the case of any local authority concerned, notifies that local authority of its determination (see Sch 2 paras 11(b), 15A(c) (as so added)). 'Prescribed' means prescribed by regulations made by the Secretary of State: see s 61(1). As to the making of regulations see PARA 1009. As to the Secretary of State see PARA 802 note 2. At the date at which this volume states the law no such regulations had been made.
9 See the Ancient Monuments and Archaeological Areas Act 1979 Sch 2 paras 8(2), 15A(a) (as added: see note 6). At the date at which this volume states the law no regulations had been made for this purpose.
10 See the Ancient Monuments and Archaeological Areas Act 1979 Sch 2 paras 8(1), 15A (as added: see note 6). The map must be to such scale as may be prescribed: see Sch 2 paras 8(2), 15A (as so added). At the date at which this volume states the law no regulations had been made for this purpose. As to the meaning of 'area affected' see PARA 1047 note 8.
11 The Secretary of State may by regulations prescribe the procedure to be followed by the Commission in submitting orders for confirmation: see the Ancient Monuments and Archaeological Areas Act 1979 Sch 2 paras 15, 15A(a) (as added: see note 6). At the date at which this volume states the law no such regulations had been made.
12 See the Ancient Monuments and Archaeological Areas Act 1979 Sch 2 paras 12, 15A(a) (as added: see note 6).
13 See the Ancient Monuments and Archaeological Areas Act 1979 Sch 2 paras 13, 15A(a) (as added: see note 6). If the Secretary of State confirms the order the Commission must on being notified that the order has been confirmed: (1) publish notice of the making of the order in the manner and form prescribed (see Sch 2 paras 14(a), 15A(b) (as so added)); and (2) deposit a copy of the order and of the map to which it refers with any local authority concerned (Sch 2 paras 14(b), 15A(b) (as so added)). At the date at which this volume states the law no regulations had been made for the purposes of head (1) above.

1050. Variation or revocation of designation order for archaeological area. The Secretary of State or, in relation to Wales, the Welsh Ministers[1] may at any time by order[2] vary or revoke a designation order[3], but the power to vary such an order is confined to reducing the area designated by the order[4]. Before and on making an order varying or revoking a designation order the Secretary of State or the Welsh Ministers must follow the procedure laid down for the making by them of a designation order[5].

An order varying or revoking a designation order must describe by reference to a map the area affected by the designation order and (in the case of an order varying a designation order) the reduction of that area made by the order[6].

The map must be to such a scale, and the order in such form, as the Secretary of State or the Welsh Ministers consider appropriate[7].

1   The functions of the Secretary of State under the Ancient Monuments and Archaeological Areas Act 1979, in so far as they relate to Wales, were transferred to the National Assembly for Wales (see the National Assembly for Wales (Transfer of Functions) Order 1999, SI 1999/672, art 2, Sch 1) and are now exercisable by the Welsh Ministers (see the Government of Wales Act 2006 s 162(1), Sch 11 paras 30, 32). As to the Secretary of State and the Welsh Ministers see PARA 802. As to the meaning of 'Wales' see PARA 802 note 4.

2   As to the making of orders see PARA 1009.

3   As to the meaning of 'designation order' see PARA 1047 note 2.

4   Ancient Monuments and Archaeological Areas Act 1979 s 33(4). The Secretary of State must consult with the Historic Buildings and Monuments Commission for England ('the Commission') before varying or revoking an order relating to an area situated in England: s 33(4) (amended by the National Heritage Act 1983 Sch 4 para 54). As to the Commission see PARA 803. As to the meaning of 'England' see PARA 804 note 2. As to the exercise of the duty to consult see JUDICIAL REVIEW vol 61 (2010) PARA 627. As to challenges to the validity of an order varying or revoking a designation order see PARA 1051.

5   Ancient Monuments and Archaeological Areas Act 1979 Sch 2 para 18. Accordingly Sch 2 paras 2–7 (see PARA 1047) apply, taking references to the area as references to the area affected by the designation order: see Sch 2 para 18.

6   Ancient Monuments and Archaeological Areas Act 1979 Sch 2 para 17(1).

7   Ancient Monuments and Archaeological Areas Act 1979 Sch 2 para 17(2).

1051. Questioning the validity of a designation order for archaeological area or an order varying or revoking it.

If any person is aggrieved[1] by a designation order[2] or an order[3] varying or revoking a designation order[4] and desires to question its validity on the grounds that it is not within the powers of the Ancient Monuments and Archaeological Areas Act 1979 or that any of the relevant requirements[5] have not been complied with in relation to it, then, within six weeks from the relevant date[6], he may make an application to the High Court[7]. On such application the court may by interim order suspend the operation of the order until the final determination of the proceedings[8], and, if satisfied that the order is not within the powers of the Act or that the applicant's interests have been substantially prejudiced by a failure to comply with any of the relevant requirements, may quash the order in whole or in part[9].

Except as provided above, the validity of any designation order or order varying or revoking a designation order may not be questioned in any legal proceedings whatsoever[10].

1   As to the meaning of 'person aggrieved' see JUDICIAL REVIEW vol 61 (2010) PARA 656. As to the meaning of 'person' see PARA 803 note 17.

2   As to the meaning of 'designation order' see PARA 1047 note 2.

3   Ie an order under the Ancient Monuments and Archaeological Areas Act 1979 s 33(4) (see PARA 1050).

4   See the Ancient Monuments and Archaeological Areas Act 1979 s 55(1)(a), (2).

5   'Relevant requirements' means any requirements of the Ancient Monuments and Archaeological Areas Act 1979 or of any regulations made under it which are applicable to the order: s 55(6)(a).

6   'Relevant date' means the date on which notice of the making of the order is published or first published in accordance with the Ancient Monuments and Archaeological Areas Act 1979 Sch 2 (see Sch 2 paras 7, 14, 18; and PARAS 1047–1050): s 55(4)(a).

7   See the Ancient Monuments and Archaeological Areas Act 1979 s 55(1). As to the High Court of Justice in England and Wales see COURTS AND TRIBUNALS vol 24 (2010) PARA 695 et seq.

8   See the Ancient Monuments and Archaeological Areas Act 1979 s 55(5)(a).

9   Ancient Monuments and Archaeological Areas Act 1979 s 55(5)(b).

10   See the Ancient Monuments and Archaeological Areas Act 1979 s 55(7). As to judicial review of decisions expressed in this way to be immune from challenge see JUDICIAL REVIEW vol 61 (2010) PARA 655.

(B)   Operations in Areas of Archaeological Importance

1052. Investigating authorities for areas of archaeological importance. The Secretary of State or, in relation to Wales, the Welsh Ministers[1] may at any time appoint any person[2], whom he or they consider to be competent to undertake archaeological investigations[3], to exercise in relation to any area of archaeological importance[4] the functions conferred[5] on the investigating authority[6] for such an area[7]. A person's appointment as investigating authority may be cancelled at any time by the Secretary of State or, as appropriate, the Welsh Ministers[8]. On appointing or cancelling the appointment of any person as investigating authority for an area of archaeological importance, the Secretary of State or the Welsh Ministers must notify each local authority[9] in whose area the area of archaeological importance in question is wholly or partly situated[10].

Where there is for the time being no investigating authority for an area of archaeological importance, the functions of the investigating authority for that area are exercisable in the case of an area situated in England by the Historic Buildings and Monuments Commission for England ('the Commission') or in the case of an area situated in Wales by the Welsh Ministers[11].

A person duly authorised in writing[12] by any person by whom the functions of an investigating authority are for the time being exercisable may act on his behalf in the exercise of those functions[13].

1   The functions of the Secretary of State under the Ancient Monuments and Archaeological Areas Act 1979, in so far as they relate to Wales, were transferred to the National Assembly for Wales (see the National Assembly for Wales (Transfer of Functions) Order 1999, SI 1999/672, art 2, Sch 1) and are now exercisable by the Welsh Ministers (see the Government of Wales Act 2006 s 162(1), Sch 11 paras 30, 32). As to the Secretary of State and the Welsh Ministers see PARA 802. As to the meaning of 'Wales' see PARA 802 note 4.
2   The appointment is on such terms and for such period as the Secretary of State or, as the case may be, the Welsh Ministers think fit: see the Ancient Monuments and Archaeological Areas Act 1979 s 34(1). As to the meaning of 'person' see PARA 803 note 17. The Secretary of State must consult with the Historic Buildings and Monuments Commission for England ('the Commission') before making an appointment in relation to an area situated in England: s 34(1) (amended by the National Heritage Act 1983 s 33(3), Sch 4 para 55). As to the Commission see PARA 803. As to the meaning of 'England' see PARA 804 note 2. As to the exercise of the duty to consult see JUDICIAL REVIEW vol 61 (2010) PARA 627.
3   As to the meaning of 'archaeological investigation' see PARA 1017 note 12.
4   As to the meaning of 'area of archaeological importance' see PARA 1047 note 3.
5   Ie by the Ancient Monuments and Archaeological Areas Act 1979 Pt II (ss 33–41) (see PARA 1053 et seq). As to the meaning of 'functions' see PARA 1011 note 4.
6   The 'investigating authority' for an area of archaeological importance is the person for the time being holding appointment as such under the Ancient Monuments and Archaeological Areas Act 1979 s 34 or (if there is no such person) the Commission in a case where the area is situated in England, or the Welsh Ministers in a case where the area is situated in Wales: see s 41(2) (amended by the National Heritage Act 1983 Sch 4 para 59).
7   Ancient Monuments and Archaeological Areas Act 1979 s 34(1).
8   Ancient Monuments and Archaeological Areas Act 1979 s 34(2). Before cancelling an appointment the Secretary of State must consult with the Commission: see s 34(2) (amended by the National Heritage Act 1983 Sch 4 para 55).
9   As to the meaning of 'local authority' see PARA 1006 note 9.
10 See the Ancient Monuments and Archaeological Areas Act 1979 s 34(3). If the area is wholly or partly situated in Greater London the Secretary of State must also notify the Commission: see s 34(3) (amended by the Local Government Act 1985 s 6, Sch 2 para 2(3)). As to the meaning of 'Greater London' see PARA 856 note 4.
11 See the Ancient Monuments and Archaeological Areas Act 1979 s 34(4) (amended by the National Heritage Act 1983 Sch 4 para 55).
12 As to the meaning of 'writing' see PARA 805 note 14.
13 Ancient Monuments and Archaeological Areas Act 1979 s 34(5).

1053.   Operations in archaeological areas. If any person[1] carries out, or causes or permits to be carried out, any operations on land[2] in an area of archaeological importance[3] (being operations which disturb the ground[4], flooding operations[5] or tipping operations[6]) without first having served an operations notice[7] relating to those operations[8], or within six weeks of serving such a notice[9], he is guilty of an offence[10].

Where an operations notice is served with respect to operations which are to be carried out after clearance of any site[11], the developer[12] must notify the investigating authority[13] for the area of archaeological importance in question of the clearance of the site immediately on completion of the clearance operations[14].

A district council, London borough council or the Common Council of the City of London[15] in whose area the site of the operations is wholly or partly situated may institute proceedings for an offence under these provisions in respect of operations on any site situated partly in its area notwithstanding that the operations are confined to a part of the site outside its area[16]. Any such council may take High Court proceedings for an injunction prohibiting those operations from being carried out in contravention of these provisions[17] if it appears to it that: (1) any operations are being, or are about to be, carried out in contravention of these provisions on any site situated wholly or partly in its area[18]; and (2) the site contains, or is likely to contain, anything of archaeological or historical interest which will be disturbed, damaged, destroyed or removed without proper archaeological investigation[19] if operations are carried out on the site without regard for the statutory provisions[20] relating to archaeological areas[21].

In any proceedings for an offence under the above provisions it is a defence for the accused to prove either: (a) that he did not know and had no reason to believe that the site of the operations was within an area of archaeological importance[22]; or (b) that the operations were urgently necessary in the interests of safety or health and that written[23] notice of the need for the operations was given to the Secretary of State or, in relation to Wales, the Welsh Ministers[24] as soon as reasonably practicable[25].

1   As to the meaning of 'person' see PARA 803 note 17.
2   References to operations on any land include references to operations in, under or over the land: Ancient Monuments and Archaeological Areas Act 1979 s 41(1)(c). As to the meaning of 'land' see PARA 1006 note 6.
3   As to the meaning of 'area of archaeological importance' see PARA 1047 note 3.
4   See the Ancient Monuments and Archaeological Areas Act 1979 s 35(2)(a). In any proceedings for an offence under s 35 consisting in carrying out, or causing or permitting to be carried out, any operations which disturb the ground, it is a defence for the accused to prove that he took all reasonable precautions and exercised all due diligence to avoid or prevent such disturbance of the ground: s 37(5). As to defences generally see the text to notes 22–25. As to the standard of proof on the accused see CRIMINAL PROCEDURE vol 28 (2015) PARAS 449–451.
5   See the Ancient Monuments and Archaeological Areas Act 1979 s 35(2)(b). As to the meaning of 'flooding operations' see PARA 1016 note 2.
6   See the Ancient Monuments and Archaeological Areas Act 1979 s 35(2)(c). As to the meaning of 'tipping operations' see PARA 1016 note 2.
7   'Operations notice' means a notice complying with the Ancient Monuments and Archaeological Areas Act 1979 s 35(4), (5) (see PARA 1054): see ss 35(3), 41(1)(a). For exemptions from the requirement to serve such a notice see PARA 1056. As to the service of notices and documents see PARA 1010.
8   Ancient Monuments and Archaeological Areas Act 1979 s 35(1)(a).
9   Ancient Monuments and Archaeological Areas Act 1979 s 35(1)(b).
10 Ancient Monuments and Archaeological Areas Act 1979 s 35(1). The penalty for such an offence is, on summary conviction, a fine not exceeding the statutory maximum (s 35(9)(a)) or, on conviction on indictment, a fine (s 35(9)(b)). As to the statutory maximum and magistrates' powers to levy unlimited fines see SENTENCING vol 92 (2015) PARA 176. A person who has an enforcement function in relation to an offence under the Ancient Monuments and Archaeological

Areas Act 1979 is a regulator for the purposes of the Regulatory Enforcement and Sanctions Act 2008: see CONSTITUTIONAL AND ADMINISTRATIVE LAW vol 20 (2014) PARAS 331–339.

11 References to the clearance of any site are references to the demolition and removal of any existing building or other structure on the site and the removal of any other materials on it so as to clear the surface of the land, but do not include the levelling of the surface or the removal of materials from below the surface: Ancient Monuments and Archaeological Areas Act 1979 s 41(1)(d).

12 'Developer' means the person carrying out or proposing to carry out the operations in question: see the Ancient Monuments and Archaeological Areas Act 1979 ss 35(3), 41(1)(a).

13 As to the meaning of 'investigating authority' see PARA 1052 note 6.

14 Ancient Monuments and Archaeological Areas Act 1979 s 35(7). 'Clearance operations' means operations undertaken for the purpose of or in connection with the clearance of any site: see s 41(1)(e). If, in a case falling within s 35(7), the developer carries out, or causes or permits to be carried out, any of the operations to which the operations notice relates without having first notified the investigating authority of the clearance of the site, s 35 has effect in relation to those operations as if the operations notice had not been served: s 35(8). Section 35 has effect in relation to land in a National Park as if any notice required under it to be served on a local authority were required instead to be served on the National Park authority: Environment Act 1995 Sch 9 para 10(2)(a). As to National Park authorities see OPEN SPACES AND COUNTRYSIDE vol 78 (2010) PARA 526.

15 As to local government areas and authorities see LOCAL GOVERNMENT vol 69 (2009) PARA 22 et seq. As to the London boroughs and their councils see LONDON GOVERNMENT vol 71 (2013) PARA 20 et seq. The Ancient Monuments and Archaeological Areas Act 1979 s 35 has effect, in relation to any land within the Broads (as defined by the Norfolk and Suffolk Broads Act 1988: see WATER AND WATERWAYS vol 101 (2009) PARA 735), as if the Broads Authority were the district council (to the exclusion of the authority which is otherwise the district council for the area in question) and the Broads were its local authority area: Ancient Monuments and Archaeological Areas Act 1979 s 35(11) (added by the Norfolk and Suffolk Broads Act 1988 s 2(5), Sch 3 para 30(2)). As to the Broads Authority see WATER AND WATERWAYS vol 101 (2009) PARA 734. The Ancient Monuments and Archaeological Areas Act 1979 s 35 has effect in relation to land in a National Park as if the functions conferred on a local authority by virtue of s 35 had been conferred instead on the National Park authority: Environment Act 1995 Sch 9 para 10(2)(b).

16 Ancient Monuments and Archaeological Areas Act 1979 ss 35(10), 41(1)(b). Section 35(10) is expressed to be without prejudice to the Local Government Act 1972 s 222 (see LOCAL GOVERNMENT vol 69 (2009) PARA 573).

17 Ie in contravention of the Ancient Monuments and Archaeological Areas Act 1979 s 35. As to the High Court of Justice in England and Wales see COURTS AND TRIBUNALS vol 24 (2010) PARA 695 et seq.

18 Ancient Monuments and Archaeological Areas Act 1979 s 35(10)(a). See also note 16.

19 As to the meaning of 'archaeological investigation' see PARA 1017 note 12.

20 Ie the Ancient Monuments and Archaeological Areas Act 1979 Pt II (ss 33–41) (see PARA 1047 et seq).

21 Ancient Monuments and Archaeological Areas Act 1979 s 35(10)(b). See also note 16.

22 Ancient Monuments and Archaeological Areas Act 1979 s 37(6)(a). See also note 4. As to orders designating areas of archaeological importance as local land charges see PARA 1047 note 2.

23 As to the meaning of 'written' see PARA 805 note 14.

24 The functions of the Secretary of State under the Ancient Monuments and Archaeological Areas Act 1979, in so far as they relate to Wales, were transferred to the National Assembly for Wales (see the National Assembly for Wales (Transfer of Functions) Order 1999, SI 1999/672, art 2, Sch 1) and are now exercisable by the Welsh Ministers (see the Government of Wales Act 2006 s 162(1), Sch 11 paras 30, 32). As to the Secretary of State and the Welsh Ministers see PARA 802. As to the meaning of 'Wales' see PARA 802 note 4.

25 Ancient Monuments and Archaeological Areas Act 1979 s 37(6)(b). See also note 4.

1054. Operations notice for archaeological areas. An operations notice[1] must be in the prescribed form[2] and must specify:

(1)   the operations to which it relates;

(2)   the site on which they are to be carried out;

(3)   the date on which it is proposed to begin them; and

(4)   where they are to be carried out after clearance of the site[3], the developer's[4] estimated date for completion of the clearance operations[5].

The notice must be accompanied by a certificate in the prescribed form[6].

The operations notice must be served[7] by the developer: (a) in the case of land in England[8], on the district council, London borough council or the Common Council of the City of London or, as the case may be, on each such council in whose area the site is wholly or partly situated[9]; (b) in the case of land in Wales, on the council of each county or county borough in which the site of the operations is wholly or partly situated[10]; or (c) where the developer is any such council, on the Secretary of State or, in relation to Wales, the Welsh Ministers[11]. Regulations made by the Secretary of State or the Welsh Ministers may prescribe the steps to be taken by any council on whom an operations notice is so served[12].

1 As to the meaning of 'operations notice' see PARA 1053 note 7.
2 Ancient Monuments and Archaeological Areas Act 1979 s 35(4)(c). 'Prescribed' means prescribed by regulations made by the Secretary of State or, in relation to Wales, the Welsh Ministers: see s 61(1). As to the making of regulations see PARA 1009. For the prescribed form see the Operations in Areas of Archaeological Importance (Forms of Notice etc) Regulations 1984, SI 1984/1285, reg 2, Sch 1 Pt I (modified in relation to areas of archaeological importance within a National Park by SI 1995/2803; SI 1996/1243; and SI 2015/770). As to the meaning of 'area of archaeological importance' see PARA 1047 note 3.
    The functions of the Secretary of State under the Ancient Monuments and Archaeological Areas Act 1979, in so far as they relate to Wales, were transferred to the National Assembly for Wales (see the National Assembly for Wales (Transfer of Functions) Order 1999, SI 1999/672, art 2, Sch 1) and are now exercisable by the Welsh Ministers (see the Government of Wales Act 2006 s 162(1), Sch 11 paras 30, 32). As to the Secretary of State and the Welsh Ministers see PARA 802. As to the meaning of 'Wales' see PARA 802 note 4.
3 As to the meaning of 'clearance of the site' see PARA 1053 note 11.
4 As to the meaning of 'developer' see PARA 1053 note 12.
5 Ancient Monuments and Archaeological Areas Act 1979 s 35(4)(a). As to the meaning of 'clearance operations' see PARA 1053 note 14.
6 Ancient Monuments and Archaeological Areas Act 1979 s 35(4)(b). As to such certificates see s 36; and PARA 1055. As to the prescribed form of certificate see the Operations in Areas of Archaeological Importance (Forms of Notice etc) Regulations 1984, SI 1984/1285, reg 3, Sch 1 Pt II (modified in relation to areas of archaeological importance within a National Park by SI 2015/770). In relation to any operations proposed to be carried out on Crown land otherwise than by or on behalf of the Crown, an operations notice served under the Ancient Monuments and Archaeological Areas Act 1979 s 35 is not effective for the purposes of that section unless it is accompanied by a certificate from the appropriate authority in the prescribed form consenting to the exercise in relation to that land in connection with those operations of the powers conferred by s 38 (see PARA 1057) and s 40 (see PARA 1059): s 50(3). As to the meaning of 'Crown land' see PARA 1007 note 1. As to the meaning of 'appropriate authority' see PARA 1007 note 6.
7 As to the service of notices and documents see PARA 1010.
8 As to the meaning of 'England' see PARA 804 note 2.
9 Ancient Monuments and Archaeological Areas Act 1979 ss 35(5)(a), 41(1)(b) (s 35(a) amended by the Local Government (Wales) Act 1994 s 66(6), Sch 16 para 56(2)). As to local government areas and authorities in England and Wales see LOCAL GOVERNMENT vol 69 (2009) PARA 22 et seq. As to the London boroughs and their councils see LONDON GOVERNMENT vol 71 (2013) PARA 20 et seq. The Ancient Monuments and Archaeological Areas Act 1979 s 35 has effect in relation to land in a National Park as if any notice required under it to be served on a local authority were required instead to be served on the National Park authority, and the functions conferred on a local authority by virtue of that section had been conferred instead on the National Park authority: Environment Act 1995 Sch 9 para 10(2)(a). As to National Park authorities see OPEN SPACES AND COUNTRYSIDE vol 78 (2010) PARA 526. The Ancient Monuments and Archaeological Areas Act 1979 s 35 has effect, in relation to any land within the Broads (as defined by the Norfolk and Suffolk Broads Act 1988: see WATER AND WATERWAYS vol 101 (2009) PARA 735), as if the Broads Authority were the district council (to the exclusion of the authority which is otherwise the district council for the area in question) and the Broads were its local authority area: Ancient Monuments and Archaeological Areas Act 1979 s 35(11) (added by the Norfolk and Suffolk Broads Act 1988 s 2(5), Sch 3 para 30(2)). As to the Broads Authority see WATER AND WATERWAYS vol 101 (2009) PARA 734.
10 Ancient Monuments and Archaeological Areas Act 1979 s 35(5)(aa) (added by the Local Government (Wales) Act 1994 s 66(6), Sch 16 para 56(2)).
11 Ancient Monuments and Archaeological Areas Act 1979 s 35(5)(c).
12 Ancient Monuments and Archaeological Areas Act 1979 s 35(6). A district council, London borough council or the Common Council of the City of London on whom an operations notice is

served must: (1) within seven days of receipt of the notice serve a copy of it (together with the certificate and any other documents accompanying the notice) on the investigating authority appointed for the relevant area of archaeological importance, or where no particular authority is so appointed, on the Historic Buildings and Monuments Commission for England ('the Commission') (Operations in Areas of Archaeological Importance (Forms of a Notice etc) Regulations 1984, SI 1984/1285, reg 4(a); Ancient Monuments and Archaeological Areas Act 1979 s 41(1)(b)); and (2) if the operations described in the notice are to be carried out after clearance of the site, advise the developer in writing within 14 days of receipt of the notice of the name and address of the relevant investigating authority and of his duty under the Ancient Monuments and Archaeological Areas Act 1979 s 35(7) (see PARA 1053) to notify the investigating authority of the clearance of the site immediately on completion of the clearance operations (Operations in Areas of Archaeological Importance (Forms of Notice etc) Regulations 1984, SI 1984/1285, reg 4(b)). These provisions are modified in relation to any area of archaeological importance within a National Park: see reg 4 (modified by SI 1995/2803; SI 1996/1243; 2005/421; and SI 2015/770). As to the meaning of 'investigating authority' see PARA 1052 note 6. As to the Commission see PARA 803. As to the meaning of 'writing' see PARA 805 note 14.

1055. Certificate to accompany operations notice. A person[1] is qualified to issue a certificate to accompany an operations notice[2] if he either: (1) has an interest in the site of the operations which, apart from any restrictions imposed by law, entitles him to carry out the operations in question[3]; or (2) has a right to enter on and take possession of that site under the statutory powers[4] of entry on land subject to compulsory purchase[5]. Statutory undertakers[6] are qualified to issue a certificate if they are entitled by or under any enactment to carry out the operations in question[7].

Any such certificate must: (a) be signed by or on behalf of a person or persons qualified[8] to issue it[9]; (b) state that the person issuing the certificate has an interest within head (1) or, as the case may be, a right within head (2) above or, in the case of a certificate issued by statutory undertakers, state that it is so issued and specify the enactment by or under which they are entitled to carry out the operations in question[10]; and (c) if the person issuing the certificate is not the developer[11], state that he has authorised the developer to carry out the operations[12].

If any person issues a certificate which purports to comply with these requirements and which contains a statement which he knows to be false or misleading in a material particular, or recklessly issues a certificate which purports to comply with these requirements and which contains a statement which is false or misleading in a material particular, he is guilty of an offence[13].

1 As to the meaning of 'person' see PARA 803 note 17.
2 Ie a certificate for the purposes of the Ancient Monuments and Archaeological Areas Act 1979 s 35(4)(b) (see PARA 1054). As to the meaning of 'operations notice' see PARA 1053 note 7.
3 Ancient Monuments and Archaeological Areas Act 1979 s 36(1)(a). As to the meaning of 'operations on any land' see PARA 1053 note 2.
4 Ie under the Compulsory Purchase Act 1965 s 11(1) or s 11(2) (see COMPULSORY ACQUISITION OF LAND vol 18 (2009) PARAS 639, 645).
5 Ancient Monuments and Archaeological Areas Act 1979 s 36(1)(b).
6 'Statutory undertakers' means: (1) persons authorised by any enactment to carry on any railway, light railway, tramway, road transport, water transport, canal, inland navigation, dock, harbour, pier or lighthouse undertaking, or any undertaking for the supply of hydraulic power (see ROAD TRAFFIC vol 90 (2011) PARA 891 et seq; RAILWAYS AND TRAMWAYS vol 86 (2013) PARAS 331, 504; WATER AND WATERWAYS vol 100 (2009) PARA 134 et seq); (2) the Civil Aviation Authority, a universal postal service provider in connection with the provision of a universal postal service and any other authority, body or undertakers which by virtue of any enactment are to be treated as statutory undertakers for any of the purposes of the Town and Country Planning Act 1990 (see PLANNING vol 83 (2010) PARA 1186); and (3) any other authority, body or undertakers specified in an order made by the Secretary of State or, in relation to Wales, the Welsh Ministers under this provision: Ancient Monuments and Archaeological Areas Act 1979 s 61(2) (amended by the Gas Act 1986 s 67(4), Sch 9 Pt I; the Airports Act 1986 s 83(5), Sch 6 Pt I; the Water Act 1989 s 190(1), Sch 25 para 58; the Electricity Act 1989 s 112(4), Sch 18; the Planning (Consequential Provisions) Act 1990 s 4, Sch 2 para 43(2); and the Coal Industry Act 1994 s 67(1),

(8), Sch 9 para 22, Sch 11 Pt II; SI 2001/1149). The undertaking of a universal postal service provider so far as relating to the provision of a universal postal service must be taken to be his statutory undertaking for the purposes of the Ancient Monuments and Archaeological Areas Act 1979; and references in the Act to his undertaking must be construed accordingly: s 61(2A) (added by SI 2001/1149). As to the meaning of 'enactment' see PARA 1012 note 1. As to the Civil Aviation Authority see AIR LAW vol 2 (2008) PARA 50. As to the provision of a universal postal service see POSTAL SERVICES vol 85 (2012) PARA 252 et seq.

　　The functions of the Secretary of State under the Ancient Monuments and Archaeological Areas Act 1979, in so far as they relate to Wales, were transferred to the National Assembly for Wales (see the National Assembly for Wales (Transfer of Functions) Order 1999, SI 1999/672, art 2, Sch 1) and are now exercisable by the Welsh Ministers (see the Government of Wales Act 2006 s 162(1), Sch 11 paras 30, 32). As to the Secretary of State and the Welsh Ministers see PARA 802. As to the meaning of 'Wales' see PARA 802 note 4. At the date at which this volume states the law no order had been made under the Ancient Monuments and Archaeological Areas Act 1979 s 61(2). As to the making of orders see PARA 1009.

7　Ancient Monuments and Archaeological Areas Act 1979 s 36(2).
8　Ie qualified in accordance with the Ancient Monuments and Archaeological Areas Act 1979 s 36(1) or s 36(2) (see the text to notes 1–7).
9　Ancient Monuments and Archaeological Areas Act 1979 s 36(3)(a).
10　Ancient Monuments and Archaeological Areas Act 1979 s 36(3)(b).
11　As to the meaning of 'developer' see PARA 1053 note 12.
12　Ancient Monuments and Archaeological Areas Act 1979 s 36(3)(c).
13　Ancient Monuments and Archaeological Areas Act 1979 s 36(4). The penalty for such an offence is, on summary conviction, a fine not exceeding level 3 on the standard scale: s 36(4) (amended by the Criminal Justice Act 1982 s 46). As to the standard scale and magistrates' powers to levy unlimited fines see SENTENCING vol 92 (2015) PARA 176. A person who has an enforcement function in relation to an offence under the Ancient Monuments and Archaeological Areas Act 1979 is a regulator for the purposes of the Regulatory Enforcement and Sanctions Act 2008: see CONSTITUTIONAL AND ADMINISTRATIVE LAW vol 20 (2014) PARAS 331–339.

1056.　Exemptions from requirement to give operations notice. The requirement to give an operations notice[1] does not apply to any operations[2] carried out with the consent of the investigating authority[3] for the area of archaeological importance[4] in question[5]; nor to the carrying out of any operations for which development consent has been granted[6].

　　The Secretary of State or, in relation to Wales, the Welsh Ministers[7] may by order[8] direct that the requirements are not to apply to the carrying out, or to the carrying out by any class or description of persons[9] specified in the order, of operations of any class or description so specified[10]. The Secretary of State or the Welsh Ministers may direct[11] that any exemption conferred by such an order is not to apply to the carrying out on any land specified in the direction, or to the carrying out on any land so specified by any class or description of persons so specified, of operations of any class or description so specified, and may withdraw any such direction[12].

1　Ie the requirement under the Ancient Monuments and Archaeological Areas Act 1979 s 35 (see PARA 1053). As to the meaning of 'operations notice' see PARA 1053 note 7.
2　As to the meaning of 'operations on any land' see PARA 1053 note 2.
3　As to the meaning of 'investigating authority' see PARA 1052 note 6.
4　As to the meaning of 'area of archaeological importance' see PARA 1047 note 3.
5　Ancient Monuments and Archaeological Areas Act 1979 s 37(1).
6　Ancient Monuments and Archaeological Areas Act 1979 s 37(1A) (added by the Planning Act 2008 s 36, Sch 2 paras 16, 19). As to development consent see PLANNING vol 81 (2010) PARA 158 et seq.
7　The functions of the Secretary of State under the Ancient Monuments and Archaeological Areas Act 1979, in so far as they relate to Wales, were transferred to the National Assembly for Wales (see the National Assembly for Wales (Transfer of Functions) Order 1999, SI 1999/672, art 2, Sch 1) and are now exercisable by the Welsh Ministers (see the Government of Wales Act 2006 s 162(1), Sch 11 paras 30, 32). As to the Secretary of State and the Welsh Ministers see PARA 802. As to the meaning of 'Wales' see PARA 802 note 4.
8　As to the making of orders see PARA 1009.
9　As to the meaning of 'person' see PARA 803 note 17.

10 Ancient Monuments and Archaeological Areas Act 1979 s 37(2). Any such exemption may be either unconditional or subject to any conditions specified in the order: s 37(2). Section 35 does not apply to the carrying out of operations of the following descriptions, subject to any particular conditions mentioned in the heads below: see the Areas of Archaeological Importance (Notification of Operations) (Exemption) Order 1984, SI 1984/1286, art 2. The operations are:

   (1)   operations in connection with the use of land of agriculture, horticulture or forestry; provided that such operations do not disturb the ground below a depth of 600 millimetres (Schedule para 1);

   (2)   operations in connection with the landscaping (including screening by the erection of fences or walls), layout, planting, or maintenance of public or private gardens, grounds or parks; provided that such operations do not disturb the ground below a depth of 600 millimetres (Schedule para 2);

   (3)   tunnelling or other operations affecting the ground in the area only at a depth of 10 metres or more (Schedule para 3);

   (4)   mining operations, provided that the operations are carried out in accordance with the Code of Practice for Minerals Operators dated April 1982 (Schedule para 4);

   (5)   works of repair, renewal or maintenance or emergency works carried out by a drainage body or a navigation authority (Schedule para 5);

   (6)   operations for the repair, maintenance, relaying or resurfacing of a highway within the meaning of the Highways Act 1980 (see HIGHWAYS, STREETS AND BRIDGES vol 55 (2012) PARA 7) or of a footpath as defined in that Act (see HIGHWAYS, STREETS AND BRIDGES vol 55 (2012) PARA 68), or of a railway; provided that such operations do not disturb the ground below a depth of 600 millimetres or below the existing foundations, if deeper (Schedule para 6);

   (7)   operations for the repair, maintenance or renewal of mains, pipes, cables or other apparatus connected with the supply of electricity, gas, water, drainage services, sewerage services, highway or transport authority services or telecommunication services (Schedule para 7);

   (8)   operations for the installation or laying of new mains, pipes, cables or other apparatus connected with the supply of electricity, gas, water, drainage services, sewerage services or telecommunication services where there is a duty by or under any enactment to undertake those operations and to do so within six months of the duty first arising (Schedule para 8);

   (9)   operations for the erection or repositioning of street lighting columns not involving excavations to a depth exceeding 1.5 metres (Schedule para 9);

   (10)   further operations on a site, wholly specified as the site of other operations in an operations notice already served, provided the further operations are begun at least six weeks after, but not more than five years after, the giving of that notice (Schedule para 10);

   (11)   operations for which scheduled monument consent is granted (Schedule para 11).

'Drainage body' (WATER AND WATERWAYS vol 101 (2009) PARA 573) and 'navigation authority' (see WATER AND WATERWAYS vol 100 (2009) PARA 189) have the same meanings as in the Land Drainage Act 1991; and 'mining operations' means the winning and working of minerals in, on or under land, whether by surface or underground working: Areas of Archaeological Importance (Notification of Operations) (Exemption) Order 1984, SI 1984/1286, art 1(3); Interpretation Act 1978 s 17(2)(a). The order applies only to operations in areas of archaeological importance in England and Wales: Areas of Archaeological Importance (Notification of Operations) (Exemption) Order 1984, SI 1984/1286, art 1(2). As to the meaning of 'England' see PARA 804 note 2. As to the meaning of 'land' see PARA 1006 note 6. As to the meaning of 'enactment' see PARA 1012 note 1. As to the meaning of 'month' see PARA 803 note 12. As to the meaning of 'scheduled monument consent' see PARA 1017.

11 Any such direction does not take effect until notice of it has been served on the occupier or, if there is no occupier, on the owner of the land in question: Ancient Monuments and Archaeological Areas Act 1979 s 37(4). As to the service of notices and documents see PARA 1010. As to the meaning of 'owner' see PARA 1010 note 6.

12 Ancient Monuments and Archaeological Areas Act 1979 s 37(3). The Secretary of State must consult with the Historic Buildings and Monuments Commission for England ('the Commission') before giving or withdrawing any such direction in relation to land situated in England: s 37(3) (amended by the National Heritage Act 1983 Sch 4 para 56). As to the Commission see PARA 803. As to the exercise of the duty to consult see JUDICIAL REVIEW vol 61 (2010) PARA 627.

1057. Power to enter and excavate.

Where an operations notice[1] is served with respect to any operations[2], the investigating authority[3] for the area of archaeological importance[4] in which the site of operations is situated, has a right to enter, at any reasonable time, the site and any land[5] giving access to the site, for either or both of the following purposes:

(1)   inspecting the site, including any buildings or other structures on it, with a view to recording any matters of archaeological or historical interest and determining whether it would be desirable to carry out any excavations in the site[6]; and

(2)   observing any operations carried out on the site with a view to examining and recording any objects or other material of archaeological or historical interest, and recording any matters of archaeological or historical interest, discovered during the course of those operations[7].

Where an operations notice is served with respect to any operations[8], and the investigating authority serves notice[9] of its intention to excavate the site[10], the investigating authority has a right to carry out excavations in the site for the purpose of archaeological investigation[11] at any time during the period allowed for excavation[12]. Where the investigating authority has served notice[13] of its intention to excavate the site[14], and the six-week period beginning with the date of service of the operations notice has expired[15], that authority has a right to carry out excavations in the site for the purpose of archaeological investigation notwithstanding that the period allowed for excavation[16] has not yet begun, but only if the authority does not thereby obstruct the execution on the site by the developer of clearance operations[17] or any other operations to which the requirements as to operations notices[18] do not apply[19]. The investigating authority may at any reasonable time enter the site and any land giving access to the site for the purpose of exercising a right[20] to excavate the site[21].

If operations to which the operations notice relates are carried out on the site at a time when the investigating authority has a right to excavate the site[22], the requirements as to operations notices[23] have effect in relation to those operations as if the operations notice had not been served, subject, however, to any exemption or defence[24] relating thereto[25].

At any time, the Secretary of State[26] or, in relation to Wales, the Welsh Ministers may direct[27] that: (a) an investigating authority must comply with any conditions specified in the direction in exercising any of its powers under the above provisions in relation to any site[28]; or (b) any such power is to cease to be exercisable by an investigating authority in relation to the whole or any part of any site[29].

1   As to the meaning of 'operations notice' see PARA 1053 note 7.
2   As to the meaning of 'operations on any land' see PARA 1053 note 2.
3   As to the meaning of 'investigating authority' see PARA 1052 note 6.
4   As to the meaning of 'area of archaeological importance' see PARA 1047 note 3.
5   As to the meaning of 'land' see PARA 1006 note 6.
6   Ancient Monuments and Archaeological Areas Act 1979 s 38(1)(a). As to the treatment and preservation of finds see s 54; and PARA 1064. For supplementary provisions as to powers of entry see s 44; and PARAS 1062–1063.
7   Ancient Monuments and Archaeological Areas Act 1979 s 38(1)(b).
8   Ancient Monuments and Archaeological Areas Act 1979 s 38(2)(a).
9   The investigating authority only has a right to excavate the site of any operations in accordance with the Ancient Monuments and Archaeological Areas Act 1979 s 38(2) if before the end of the period of four weeks beginning with the date of service of the operations notice the authority:
    (1)   serves notice in the prescribed form of its intention to excavate on the developer (s 38(3)(a)); and
    (2)   serves a copy of that notice on any council served with the operations notice and also (unless the functions of the investigating authority are for the time being exercisable by the Secretary of State or the Welsh Ministers) on the Secretary of State or the Welsh Ministers (s 38(3)(b)); and

(3)   where the site in question is situated in England, serves a copy of that notice on the
Historic Buildings and Monuments Commission for England ('the Commission') (unless
the investigating authority is for the time being the Commission) (s 38(3)(c) (added by
the National Heritage Act 1983 s 33(3), Sch 4 para 57)).

As to the service of notices and documents see PARA 1010. As to the meaning of 'developer' see
PARA 1053 note 12. 'Prescribed' means prescribed by regulations made by the Secretary of State
or, in relation to Wales, the Welsh Ministers: see the Ancient Monuments and Archaeological
Areas Act 1979 s 61(1). As to the making of regulations see PARA 1009. For the prescribed form
of notice see the Operations in Areas of Archaeological Importance (Forms of Notice etc)
Regulations 1984, SI 1984/1285, reg 5, Sch 2 (modified in relation to areas of archaeological
importance wholly or partly within a National Park by SI 2015/770). As to the meaning of
'functions' see PARA 1011 note 4. As to the Commission see PARA 803. As to the meaning of
'England' see PARA 804 note 2.
    The functions of the Secretary of State under the Ancient Monuments and Archaeological
Areas Act 1979, in so far as they relate to Wales, were transferred to the National Assembly for
Wales (see the National Assembly for Wales (Transfer of Functions) Order 1999, SI 1999/672,
art 2, Sch 1) and are now exercisable by the Welsh Ministers (see the Government of Wales Act
2006 s 162(1), Sch 11 paras 30, 32). As to the Secretary of State and the Welsh Ministers see PARA
802. As to the meaning of 'Wales' see PARA 802 note 4.
10 Ancient Monuments and Archaeological Areas Act 1979 s 38(2)(b).
11 As to the meaning of 'archaeological investigation' see PARA 1017 note 12.
12 Ancient Monuments and Archaeological Areas Act 1979 s 38(2). The period allowed for
excavation is the period of four months and two weeks beginning: (1) with the date immediately
following the end of the period of six weeks beginning with the date of service of the operations
notice (s 38(4)(a)); or (2) where the operations specified in the operations notice are to be carried
out after clearance of the site, with the date of receipt of the notification of clearance of the site
required under s 35(7) (see PARA 1053) or with the date first mentioned in head (1) above
(whichever last occurs) (s 38(4)(b)); or (3) with any earlier date agreed between the investigating
authority and the developer (s 38(4)(c)). As to the meaning of 'month' see PARA 803 note 12. As
to the meaning of 'clearance of any site' see PARA 1053 note 11.
13 Ie in accordance with the Ancient Monuments and Archaeological Areas Act 1979 s 38(3) (see note
9).
14 Ancient Monuments and Archaeological Areas Act 1979 s 38(5)(a).
15 Ancient Monuments and Archaeological Areas Act 1979 s 38(5)(b).
16 Ie in accordance with the Ancient Monuments and Archaeological Areas Act 1979 s 38(4) (see note
12).
17 As to the meaning of 'clearance operations' see PARA 1053 note 14.
18 Ie the Ancient Monuments and Archaeological Areas Act 1979 s 35 (see PARA 1053).
19 Ancient Monuments and Archaeological Areas Act 1979 s 38(5).
20 Ie in accordance with the Ancient Monuments and Archaeological Areas Act 1979 s 38(2) or (5)
(see the text to notes 8–19).
21 Ancient Monuments and Archaeological Areas Act 1979 s 38(6).
22 See note 20.
23 Ie the Ancient Monuments and Archaeological Areas Act 1979 s 35 (see PARA 1053).
24 Ie any exemption or defence conferred by or under the Ancient Monuments and Archaeological
Areas Act 1979 s 37 (see PARAS 1053, 1056).
25 Ancient Monuments and Archaeological Areas Act 1979 s 38(7).
26 The Secretary of State must consult with the Commission before giving, varying or revoking a
direction under the Ancient Monuments and Archaeological Areas Act 1979 s 38(8) in relation to
a site situated in England: s 38(8) (amended by the National Heritage Act 1983 Sch 4 para 57). As
to the exercise of the duty to consult see JUDICIAL REVIEW vol 61 (2010) PARA 627.
27 On giving such a direction the Secretary of State or the Welsh Ministers must serve a copy of it on
the investigating authority (Ancient Monuments and Archaeological Areas Act 1979 s 38(9)(a)),
any council served with the operations notice in question (s 38(9)(b)), the developer (s 38(9)(c)),
and any person other than the developer by whom the certificate accompanying the operations
notice in accordance with s 35(4)(b) (see PARA 1054) was issued (s 38(9)(d)); and on varying or
revoking any such direction the Secretary of State or the Welsh Ministers must notify the same
persons, giving particulars of the effect of any variation (s 38(9)). On giving such a direction in
relation to a site situated in England, the Secretary of State must send a copy of the direction to
the Commission, if the investigating authority is not the Commission (s 38(10) (s 38(10), (11)
added by the National Heritage Act 1983 Sch 4 para 57)); and on varying or revoking such a
direction in relation to a site situated in England, the Secretary of State must notify

the Commission, giving particulars of the effect of any variation, if the investigating authority is not the Commission (Ancient Monuments and Archaeological Areas Act 1979 s 38(11) (as so added)).

28 Ancient Monuments and Archaeological Areas Act 1979 s 38(8)(a). The Secretary of State or the Welsh Ministers may vary or revoke any direction given under this provision: s 38(8). See also note 27.

29 Ancient Monuments and Archaeological Areas Act 1979 s 38(8)(b).

1058. Power to enter and investigate in advance of operations notice. If an authority possessing compulsory purchase powers[1] notifies the investigating authority[2] for any area of archaeological importance[3] that it proposes to carry out, or to authorise someone else to carry out, on any site in the area, any operations in respect of which an operations notice must be served[4], other than exempt operations[5], the investigating authority has a right to enter, at any reasonable time, the site and any land giving access to it, for the purpose of inspecting the site, including any buildings or other structures on it, with a view to recording any matters of archaeological or historical interest and determining whether it would be desirable to carry out any excavations in the site[6]. This right of entry ceases at the end of one month[7] beginning with the day on which it is first exercised[8]. The Secretary of State or, in relation to Wales, the Welsh Ministers[9] may give directions as to the exercise of this power[10].

1 'Authority possessing compulsory purchase powers' means any person or body of persons who could be or have been authorised to acquire an interest in land compulsorily: Ancient Monuments and Archaeological Areas Act 1979 s 39(5). As to the meaning of 'person' see PARA 803 note 17. As to the meaning of 'land' see PARA 1006 note 6.

2 As to the meaning of 'investigating authority' see PARA 1052 note 6.

3 As to the meaning of 'area of archaeological importance' see PARA 1047 note 3.

4 Ie operations of a description mentioned in the Ancient Monuments and Archaeological Areas Act 1979 s 35(2) (see PARA 1053).

5 'Exempt operations' means operations excluded from the application of the Ancient Monuments and Archaeological Areas Act 1979 s 35 by an order under s 37 (see PARA 1056): s 39(1).

6 See the Ancient Monuments and Archaeological Areas Act 1979 s 39(1). As to supplementary provisions as to powers of entry see s 44; and PARAS 1062–1063.

7 As to the meaning of 'month' see PARA 803 note 12.

8 Ancient Monuments and Archaeological Areas Act 1979 s 39(2).

9 The functions of the Secretary of State under the Ancient Monuments and Archaeological Areas Act 1979, in so far as they relate to Wales, were transferred to the National Assembly for Wales (see the National Assembly for Wales (Transfer of Functions) Order 1999, SI 1999/672, art 2, Sch 1) and are now exercisable by the Welsh Ministers (see the Government of Wales Act 2006 s 162(1), Sch 11 paras 30, 32). As to the Secretary of State and the Welsh Ministers see PARA 802. As to the meaning of 'Wales' see PARA 802 note 4.

10 The Ancient Monuments and Archaeological Areas Act 1979 s 38(8) (see PARA 1057) applies in relation to the power of entry under s 39 as it applies in relation to the powers of an investigating authority under that section: s 39(3). Section 38(9) (see PARA 1057) does not apply in relation to a direction under s 38(8) with respect to the exercise of the power of entry under s 39, but on giving any such direction the Secretary of State or the Welsh Ministers must serve a copy of the direction on each of the following persons, that is to say: (1) the investigating authority (s 39(4)(a)); (2) the authority possessing compulsory purchase powers (s 39(4)(b)); (3) the owner and (if the owner is not the occupier) the occupier of the site in question (s 39(4)(c)); and, in the case of the Secretary of State, on the Historic Buildings and Monuments Commission for England ('the Commission') (if the investigating authority is not the Commission) (see s 39(4)(d) (added by the National Heritage Act 1983 s 33, Sch 4 para 58)). On varying or revoking any such direction the Secretary of State or the Welsh Ministers must notify the same persons (giving particulars of the effect of any variation): Ancient Monuments and Archaeological Areas Act 1979 s 39(4). As to the meaning of 'owner' see PARA 1010 note 6. As to the Commission see PARA 803. As to the service of notices and documents see PARA 1010.

1059. Other powers of entry to enable recording of matters of archaeological or historical interest. Where an operations notice[1] is served with respect to any operations:

(1)   any person[2] duly authorised in writing[3] by the Secretary of State or, in relation to Wales, the Welsh Ministers[4] may at any reasonable time enter the site of the operations for the purpose of inspecting the site, including any building or other structure on it, and recording any matters of archaeological or historical interest observed in the course of that inspection[5]; and

(2)   any person duly authorised in writing by the Historic Buildings and Monuments Commission for England ('the Commission')[6] may at any reasonable time enter the site for the purpose of inspecting any building or other structure on the site and recording any matters of archaeological or historical interest observed in the course of that inspection[7].

1   As to the meaning of 'operations notice' see PARA 1053 note 7.
2   As to the meaning of 'person' see PARA 803 note 17.
3   As to the meaning of 'writing' see PARA 805 note 14.
4   The functions of the Secretary of State under the Ancient Monuments and Archaeological Areas Act 1979, in so far as they relate to Wales, were transferred to the National Assembly for Wales (see the National Assembly for Wales (Transfer of Functions) Order 1999, SI 1999/672, art 2, Sch 1) and are now exercisable by the Welsh Ministers (see the Government of Wales Act 2006 s 162(1), Sch 11 paras 30, 32). As to the Secretary of State and the Welsh Ministers see PARA 802. As to the meaning of 'Wales' see PARA 802 note 4.
5   Ancient Monuments and Archaeological Areas Act 1979 s 40(a).
6   The Ancient Monuments and Archaeological Areas Act 1979 s 40(b) refers to the Royal Commission on Historical Monuments which has now been merged with the Historic Buildings and Monuments Commission for England ('the Commission') (see PARA 803).
7   Ancient Monuments and Archaeological Areas Act 1979 s 40(b).

D.   RESTRICTIONS ON THE USE OF METAL DETECTORS

1060.   Restrictions on the use of metal detectors in a protected place. A person[1] commits an offence if, without the written[2] consent of the Historic Buildings and Monuments Commission for England ('the Commission')[3], in the case of a place situated in England, or of the Welsh Ministers[4], in the case of a place situated in Wales[5], he:

(1)   uses a metal detector[6] in a protected place[7]; or

(2)   removes any object of archaeological or historical interest which he has discovered by the use of a metal detector in a protected place[8].

A consent granted by the Commission or the Welsh Ministers may be granted either unconditionally or subject to conditions[9]. If any person (a) in using a metal detector in a protected place in accordance with any such consent[10]; or (b) in removing or otherwise dealing with any object which he has discovered by the use of a metal detector in a protected place in accordance with any such consent[11], fails to comply with any condition attached to the consent, he is guilty of an offence[12].

In any proceedings for an offence under head (1) above, it is a defence for the accused to prove that he used the metal detector for a purpose other than detecting or locating objects of archaeological or historical interest[13]; and in any proceedings for an offence under head (1) or (2) above, it is a defence for the accused to prove that he had taken all reasonable precautions to find out whether the place where he used the metal detector was a protected place and did not believe that it was[14].

A metal detector ranks as apparatus for wireless telegraphy and its use may also require the authority of a licence issued by the Office of Communications ('OFCOM')[15].

1 As to the meaning of 'person' see PARA 803 note 17. As to offences by bodies corporate see PARA 1012.

2 As to the meaning of 'written' see PARA 805 note 14.

3 As to the Historic Buildings and Monuments Commission for England ('the Commission') see PARA 803. As to the meaning of 'England' see PARA 804 note 2.

4 The functions of the Secretary of State under the Ancient Monuments and Archaeological Areas Act 1979, in so far as they relate to Wales, were transferred to the National Assembly for Wales (see the National Assembly for Wales (Transfer of Functions) Order 1999, SI 1999/672, art 2, Sch 1) and are now exercisable by the Welsh Ministers (see the Government of Wales Act 2006 s 162(1), Sch 11 paras 30, 32). As to the Secretary of State and the Welsh Ministers see PARA 802. As to the meaning of 'Wales' see PARA 802 note 4.

5 See the Ancient Monuments and Archaeological Areas Act 1979 s 42(1), (3) (both amended by the National Heritage Act 1983 s 33, Sch 4 para 60).

6 'Metal detector' means any device designed or adapted for detecting or locating any metal or mineral in the ground: Ancient Monuments and Archaeological Areas Act 1979 s 42(2).

7 See the Ancient Monuments and Archaeological Areas Act 1979 s 42(1) (as amended: see note 5). The penalty for such an offence is, on summary conviction, a fine not exceeding level 3 on the standard scale: Ancient Monuments and Archaeological Areas Act 1979 s 42(1) (amended by virtue of the Criminal Justice Act 1982 s 46). As to the standard scale and magistrates' powers to levy unlimited fines see SENTENCING vol 92 (2015) PARA 176.
   'Protected place' means any place which is either: (1) the site of a scheduled monument or of any monument under the ownership or guardianship of the Secretary of State, the Welsh Ministers, the Commission or a local authority by virtue of the Ancient Monuments and Archaeological Areas Act 1979 (s 42(2)(a) (amended by the National Heritage Act 1983 s 33, Sch 4 para 60)); or (2) situated in an area of archaeological importance (Ancient Monuments and Archaeological Areas Act 1979 s 42(2)(b)). As to the meaning of 'scheduled monument' see PARA 1014. As to the meaning of 'monument' see PARA 1013. As to monuments under the ownership or guardianship of the persons listed see the Ancient Monuments and Archaeological Areas Act 1979 ss 10–12, 21; and PARA 1030 et seq. As to the meaning of 'local authority' see PARA 1006 note 9. As to the meaning of 'area of archaeological importance' see PARA 1047 note 3.

8 See the Ancient Monuments and Archaeological Areas Act 1979 s 42(3) (as amended: see note 5). The penalty for such an offence is, on summary conviction, a fine not exceeding the statutory maximum, or, on conviction on indictment, a fine: see s 42(3). As to the statutory maximum and magistrates' powers to levy unlimited fines see SENTENCING vol 92 (2015) PARA 176. As to sentencing guidelines for offences of theft involving historic objects or loss of the nation's heritage see PARA 1046 note 5.

9 Ancient Monuments and Archaeological Areas Act 1979 s 42(4) (amended by the National Heritage Act 1983 s 33, Sch 4 para 60).

10 See the Ancient Monuments and Archaeological Areas Act 1979 s 42(5)(a) (amended by the National Heritage Act 1983 s 33, Sch 4 para 60).

11 Ancient Monuments and Archaeological Areas Act 1979 s 42(5)(b).

12 Ancient Monuments and Archaeological Areas Act 1979 s 42(5). The penalty for such an offence is, in a case falling within head (a) in the text, on summary conviction, a fine not exceeding level 3 on the standard scale; and in a case falling within head (b) in the text, on summary conviction, a fine not exceeding the statutory maximum, or, on conviction on indictment, a fine: see s 42(5). As to the standard scale, the statutory maximum and magistrates' powers to levy unlimited fines see SENTENCING vol 92 (2015) PARA 176.

13 Ancient Monuments and Archaeological Areas Act 1979 s 42(6). As to the standard of proof on the accused see CRIMINAL PROCEDURE vol 28 (2015) PARAS 449–451.

14 Ancient Monuments and Archaeological Areas Act 1979 s 42(7). As to the listing of a scheduled monument, a guardianship deed, or a designation order in respect of an area of archaeological importance, as a local land charge see PARAS 1014, 1032, 1047.

15 See the Wireless Telegraphy Act 2006 s 8; the Wireless Telegraphy (Exemption) Regulations 2003, SI 2003/74; and BROADCASTING vol 4 (2011) PARA 514. As to OFCOM see TELECOMMUNICATIONS vol 97 (2015) PARA 2 et seq.

E.   POWERS OF ENTRY AND TREATMENT OF FINDS

1061. Power of entry for survey and valuation. At any reasonable time, any authorised person[1] may enter any land[2] for the purpose of surveying it[3], or estimating its value, in connection with any proposal to acquire that or any other land under the Ancient Monuments and Archaeological Areas Act 1979[4], or in connection with any claim for compensation under the Act in respect of any such acquisition or for any damage to that or any other land[5].

Where under this power a person proposes to carry out works[6] authorised for the purposes mentioned above, he may not carry out those works unless the prior notice of intended entry[7] included notice of his intention to carry out those works[8], and if the land in question is held by statutory undertakers[9] who object to the proposed works on the grounds that the carrying out of the works would be seriously detrimental to the carrying on of their undertaking, the works must not be carried out except with the authority of the Secretary of State or, in relation to Wales, the Welsh Ministers[10].

1   A person is authorised under this provision if he is an officer of the Valuation Office of Her Majesty's Revenue and Customs or a person duly authorised in writing by the Secretary of State or, in relation to Wales, the Welsh Ministers, or other authority proposing to make the acquisition which is the occasion of the survey or valuation or, as the case may be, from whom, in accordance with the Ancient Monuments and Archaeological Areas Act 1979, compensation in respect of the damage is recoverable: s 43(2) (amended by virtue of the Commissioners for Revenue and Customs Act 2005 s 50). As to the Valuation Office see BUILDING CONTRACTS vol 6 (2011) PARA 493. As to the meaning of 'person' see PARA 803 note 17. As to the meaning of 'writing' see PARA 805 note 14. As to compensation for damage see the Ancient Monuments and Archaeological Areas Act 1979 s 46; and PARA 1066).

    The functions of the Secretary of State under the Ancient Monuments and Archaeological Areas Act 1979, in so far as they relate to Wales, were transferred to the National Assembly for Wales (see the National Assembly for Wales (Transfer of Functions) Order 1999, SI 1999/672, art 2, Sch 1) and are now exercisable by the Welsh Ministers (see the Government of Wales Act 2006 s 162(1), Sch 11 paras 30, 32). As to the Secretary of State and the Welsh Ministers see PARA 802. As to the meaning of 'Wales' see PARA 802 note 4.

2   As to the meaning of 'land' see PARA 1006 note 6.

3   Subject to the Ancient Monuments and Archaeological Areas Act 1979 s 44(9) (see the text to notes 6–10), the power to survey land conferred by s 43 is to be construed as including power to search and bore for the purposes of ascertaining the nature of the subsoil or the presence of minerals in it: s 43(3).

4   As to acquisition of land under the Ancient Monuments and Archaeological Areas Act 1979 see PARAS 1030–1031, 1035–1036.

5   Ancient Monuments and Archaeological Areas Act 1979 s 43(1). As to the exercise of the power of entry see PARAS 1062–1063.

6   Ie any works authorised by virtue of the Ancient Monuments and Archaeological Areas Act 1979 s 43(3) (see note 3).

7   Ie the notice under the Ancient Monuments and Archaeological Areas Act 1979 s 44(2)(a) (see PARA 1062).

8   See the Ancient Monuments and Archaeological Areas Act 1979 s 44(9)(a).

9   As to the meaning of 'statutory undertakers' see PARA 1055 note 6.

10   Ancient Monuments and Archaeological Areas Act 1979 s 44(9)(b).

1062. Prerequisites to entry. In the exercise of any power of entry under the Ancient Monuments and Archaeological Areas Act 1979[1], other than the power conferred for the purposes of survey and valuation[2], no person[3] may enter any building or part of a building occupied as a dwelling house without the occupier's consent[4].

In the exercise of any power of entry under the Act, other than the power to enter to execute works urgently necessary[5], no person may demand admission as of right to any land[6] which is occupied unless prior notice of the intended entry has been given[7] to the occupier: (1) where the purpose of the entry is to carry out any works[8] on the land, not less than 14 days before the day on which admission is demanded[9]; or (2) in any other case, not less than 24 hours before admission is demanded[10].

If so required by or on behalf of the owner[11] or occupier of the land, a person seeking to enter it in exercise of any power of entry under the Act must produce evidence of his authority before entering[12].

1   Powers of entry arise under the Ancient Monuments and Archaeological Areas Act 1979 s 5(1) (entry to execute works urgently necessary: see PARA 1027); s 6 (entry to inspect scheduled monument: see PARA 1028); s 13(5) (entry on site of monument under guardianship: see PARA 1033); s 15(1) (entry on land under guardianship: see PARA 1035); s 26(1) (entry on land believed to contain ancient monuments: see PARA 1045); s 38(6) (entry to excavate after operations notice: see PARA 1057); s 39(1) (entry to investigate in advance of operations notice: see PARA 1058); s 40 (entry to inspect and record: see PARA 1059); and s 43(1) (entry to survey and value: see PARA 1061). As to the exercise of powers of entry see PARA 1063.

2   Ie the power conferred by the Ancient Monuments and Archaeological Areas Act 1979 s 43(1) (see PARA 1061).

3   As to the meaning of 'person' see PARA 803 note 17.

4   Ancient Monuments and Archaeological Areas Act 1979 s 44(1).

5   Ie the power of entry under the Ancient Monuments and Archaeological Areas Act 1979 s 5 (see PARA 1027).

6   As to the meaning of 'land' see PARA 1006 note 6.

7   As to the service of notices and documents see PARA 1010.

8   This does not apply to excavations in exercise of the power under the Ancient Monuments and Archaeological Areas Act 1979 s 26 (see PARA 1045) or s 38 (see PARA 1057): see s 44(2)(a). As to the meaning of 'works' see PARA 1016 note 2.

9   Ancient Monuments and Archaeological Areas Act 1979 s 44(2)(a). Where the entry is under s 43 for the purpose of survey and valuation and it is intended to carry out works authorised by s 43(3), the notice must also give notice of that intention: see s 44(9)(a); and PARA 1061.

10 Ancient Monuments and Archaeological Areas Act 1979 s 44(2)(b).

11 As to the meaning of 'owner' see PARA 1010 note 6.

12 Ancient Monuments and Archaeological Areas Act 1979 s 44(3).

1063. Exercise of power of entry. Any power of entry under the Ancient Monuments and Archaeological Areas Act 1979[1] is to be construed as including power for any person[2] entering any land[3] in exercise of the power to take with him any assistance or equipment reasonably required for the purpose to which his entry relates and to do there anything reasonably necessary for carrying out that purpose[4]. Where a person enters any land in exercise of any power of entry under the Act for the purpose of carrying out any archaeological investigation[5] or examination of the land[6], he may[7] take and remove such samples of any description as appear to him to be reasonably required for the purpose of archaeological analysis[8].

Where any works[9] are being carried out on any land in relation to which any power of entry under the Act is exercisable, a person acting in the exercise of that power must comply with any reasonable[10] requirements or conditions imposed by the person by whom the works are being carried out for the purpose of preventing interference with, or delay to, the works[11].

Any person who intentionally obstructs a person acting in the exercise of any power of entry under the Act is guilty of an offence[12].

1   As to powers of entry under the Ancient Monuments and Archaeological Areas Act 1979 see PARA 1062 note 1.

2   As to the meaning of 'person' see PARA 803 note 17.

3   As to the meaning of 'land' see PARA 1006 note 6.

4   Ancient Monuments and Archaeological Areas Act 1979 s 44(4).

5   As to the meaning of 'archaeological investigation' see PARA 1017 note 12.

6   'Archaeological examination of any land' means any examination or inspection of the land, including any buildings or other structures on it, for the purpose of obtaining and recording any information of archaeological or historical interest: Ancient Monuments and Archaeological Areas Act 1979 s 61(5).

7   Ie without prejudice to the Ancient Monuments and Archaeological Areas Act 1979 s 44(4): see the text to notes 1–4.

8   Ancient Monuments and Archaeological Areas Act 1979 s 44(5).

9   The Ancient Monuments and Archaeological Areas Act 1979 s 44(6) does not apply where the works in question are being carried out in contravention of s 2(1) or s 2(6) (see PARA 1039) or s 35 (see PARA 1053): see s 44(7). As to the meaning of 'works' see PARA 1016 note 2.

10 Any requirements or conditions so imposed are not to be regarded as reasonable for this purpose if compliance with them would in effect frustrate the exercise of the power of entry or the purpose of the entry: Ancient Monuments and Archaeological Areas Act 1979 s 44(7).

11 Ancient Monuments and Archaeological Areas Act 1979 s 44(6).

12 Ancient Monuments and Archaeological Areas Act 1979 s 44(8). The penalty for such an offence is, on summary conviction, a fine not exceeding level 3 on the standard scale: see s 44(8) (amended by the Criminal Justice Act 1982 s 46). As to the standard scale and magistrates' powers to levy unlimited fines see SENTENCING vol 92 (2015) PARA 176. As to offences by bodies corporate see PARA 1012.

1064.   Treatment and preservation of finds. Where a person[1] enters any land[2] in exercise of any power of entry under the Ancient Monuments and Archaeological Areas Act 1979[3]:

(1)   to carry out any excavations in the land or any operations affecting any ancient monument[4] situated in, on or under the land[5];

(2)   to observe any operations on the land in exercise of any of certain statutory powers[6]; or

(3)   to carry out any archaeological examination of the land[7],

he may take temporary custody of any object of archaeological or historical interest discovered during the course of those excavations or operations or, as the case may be, during the course of that examination, and remove it from its site for the purpose of examining, testing, treating, recording or preserving it[8].

The Secretary of State or, in relation to Wales, the Welsh Ministers[9], or other authority by or on whose behalf the power of entry was exercised may not retain the object without the owner's[10] consent beyond the period reasonably required for examining and recording it and carrying out any test or treatment which appears desirable for the purpose of archaeological investigation[11] or analysis or with a view to restoring or preserving the object[12].

Nothing in these provisions affects any right of the Crown under the Treasure Act 1996[13].

1   As to the meaning of 'person' see PARA 803 note 17.

2   As to the meaning of 'land' see PARA 1006 note 6.

3   As to powers of entry under the Ancient Monuments and Archaeological Areas Act 1979 see PARA 1062 note 1.

4   As to the meaning of 'ancient monument' see PARA 1029.

5   Ancient Monuments and Archaeological Areas Act 1979 s 54(1)(a).

6   Ancient Monuments and Archaeological Areas Act 1979 s 54(1)(b). The powers concerned are those conferred by s 6(3)(a) or s 6(4)(b) or s 6A(2)(a) (see PARA 1028): see s 54(1)(b) (amended by the National Heritage Act 1983 s 33(3), Sch 4 para 65).

7   Ancient Monuments and Archaeological Areas Act 1979 s 54(1)(c). As to the meaning of 'archaeological examination of the land' see PARA 1063 note 6.

8   Ancient Monuments and Archaeological Areas Act 1979 s 54(1).

9   The functions of the Secretary of State under the Ancient Monuments and Archaeological Areas Act 1979, in so far as they relate to Wales, were transferred to the National Assembly for Wales (see the National Assembly for Wales (Transfer of Functions) Order 1999, SI 1999/672, art 2, Sch 1) and are now exercisable by the Welsh Ministers (see the Government of Wales Act 2006 s 162(1), Sch 11 paras 30, 32). As to the Secretary of State and the Welsh Ministers see PARA 802. As to the meaning of 'Wales' see PARA 802 note 4.

10 As to the meaning of 'owner' see PARA 1010 note 6.

11 As to the meaning of 'archaeological investigation' see PARA 1017 note 12.
12 Ancient Monuments and Archaeological Areas Act 1979 s 54(2).
13 Ancient Monuments and Archaeological Areas Act 1979 s 54(3) (amended by the Treasure Act 1996 s 14(2)). As to the law relating to treasure see PARA 1088 et seq. As to the application of the Ancient Monuments and Archaeological Areas Act 1979 to Crown land see PARA 1007.

F. FINANCIAL PROVISION UNDER THE ANCIENT MONUMENTS AND ARCHAEOLOGICAL AREAS ACT 1979

1065. Expenditure on archaeological investigation. The Historic Buildings and Monuments Commission for England ('the Commission')[1], in relation to any land[2] in England, or the Welsh Ministers[3], in relation to any land in Wales, may undertake, or assist in, or defray or contribute towards the cost of, an archaeological investigation[4] of any land which it or they consider may contain an ancient monument[5] or anything else of archaeological or historical interest[6]. Any local authority[7] may undertake, or assist in, or defray or contribute towards the cost of an archaeological investigation of any land in or in the vicinity of its area, being land which it considers may contain an ancient monument or anything else of archaeological or historical interest[8].

The Commission, Welsh Ministers or any local authority may publish the results of any archaeological investigation undertaken, assisted, or wholly or partly financed by them under these provisions in such manner and form as they think fit[9].

1 As to the Historic Buildings and Monuments Commission for England ('the Commission') see PARA 803. As to the meaning of 'England' see PARA 804 note 2.
2 As to the meaning of 'land' see PARA 1006 note 6.
3 The functions of the Secretary of State under the Ancient Monuments and Archaeological Areas Act 1979, in so far as they relate to Wales, were transferred to the National Assembly for Wales and are now exercisable by the Welsh Ministers: see the National Assembly for Wales (Transfer of Functions) Order 1999, SI 1999/672, art 2, Sch 1; Government of Wales Act 2006 s 162(1), Sch 11 paras 30, 32. As to the Secretary of State and the Welsh Ministers see PARA 802. As to the meaning of 'Wales' see PARA 802 note 4.
4 As to the meaning of 'archaeological investigation' see PARA 1017 note 12.
5 As to the meaning of 'ancient monument' see PARA 1029. The reference to an ancient monument in relation to the Commission is to construed as if the reference in the Ancient Monuments and Archaeological Areas Act 1979 s 61(12)(b) (definition of 'ancient monument': see PARA 1029) to the Secretary of State were to the Commission: s 45(1A) (s 45(1), (4) amended by, s 45(1A) added by, the National Heritage Act 1983 s 33(3), Sch 4 para 61).
6 See the Ancient Monuments and Archaeological Areas Act 1979 s 45(1), (1A) (s 45(1) as amended, s 45(1A) as added: see note 5). Without prejudice to the application, by virtue of the Ancient Monuments and Archaeological Areas Act 1979 s 53 (see PARAS 1006, 1008, 1035), of any other provisions of the Act to land which is not within Great Britain, the powers conferred by s 45 are exercisable in relation to any land which is not within England or Wales and which forms part of the sea bed within the seaward limits of United Kingdom territorial waters adjacent to the coast of England or, as the case may be, Wales: see s 45(4) (as amended: see note 5). As to the meanings of 'Great Britain' and 'United Kingdom' see PARA 804 note 2. As to territorial waters see WATER AND WATERWAYS vol 100 (2009) PARA 31.
7 As to the meaning of 'local authority' see PARA 1006 note 9. The provisions of the Ancient Monuments and Archaeological Areas Act 1979 s 45(2), (3) apply, in relation to the Broads as if the Broads Authority were a local authority: see s 52A; and PARA 1006. The provisions of the Ancient Monuments and Archaeological Areas Act 1979 s 45(2), (3) have effect as if a National Park authority were a local authority for the purposes of the Act and as if the relevant park were the authority's area: see the Environment Act 1995 Sch 9 para 10. As to National Park authorities see OPEN SPACES AND COUNTRYSIDE vol 78 (2010) PARA 526.
8 Ancient Monuments and Archaeological Areas Act 1979 s 45(2).
9 Ancient Monuments and Archaeological Areas Act 1979 s 45(3) (amended by the National Heritage Act 1983 Sch 4 para 61).

1066. Compensation for damage. Where, in the exercise in relation to any land[1] of any power to enter, or to do anything, on any land under the Ancient Monuments and Archaeological Areas Act 1979[2], any damage has been caused to that land or to any chattels on that land, any person[3] interested in that land or those chattels may recover compensation[4] in respect of that damage from the Secretary of State, the Welsh Ministers, the Historic Buildings and Monuments Commission for England ('the Commission')[5] or other authority by or on whose behalf the power was exercised[6].

Where any such damage is caused in the exercise of any such power by or on behalf of any person for the time being holding appointment as the investigating authority[7] for an area of archaeological importance[8], compensation is recoverable in accordance with these provisions from the Commission if the area in question is situated in England[9], or from the Welsh Ministers if the area in question is situated in Wales[10].

1   As to the meaning of 'land' see PARA 1006 note 6.
2   Ie any power to enter, or to do anything, on any land under the Ancient Monuments and Archaeological Areas Act 1979 ss 6, 6A (see PARA 1028); s 26 (see PARA 1045); s 38 (see PARA 1057); s 39 (see PARA 1058); s 40 (see PARA 1059); or s 43 (see PARA 1061): s 46(3) (amended by the National Heritage Act 1983 s 33(3), Sch 4 para 62).
3   As to the meaning of 'person' see PARA 803 note 17.
4   Any claim for compensation under the Ancient Monuments and Archaeological Areas Act 1979 must be made within the time and in the manner prescribed: s 47(1). 'Prescribed' means prescribed by regulations made by the Secretary of State or the Welsh Ministers: see s 61(1). As to the prescribed time and manner see the Ancient Monuments (Claims for Compensation) (England) Regulations 1991, SI 1991/2512, reg 2, Schedule Pt 1 (amended by SI 1997/2971; and SI 2009/1307); and the Ancient Monuments (Claims for Compensation) (Wales) Regulations 1991, SI 1991/2647, reg 2, Schedule Pt 1. Any question of disputed compensation under the Ancient Monuments and Archaeological Areas Act 1979 must be referred to and determined by the Upper Tribunal: s 47(2) (amended by SI 2009/1307). As to the Upper Tribunal see COMPULSORY ACQUISITION OF LAND vol 18 (2009) PARA 720. The Land Compensation Act 1961 s 4 (see COMPULSORY ACQUISITION OF LAND vol 18 (2009) PARAS 716–717) applies in relation to the determination of any such question, but the references in s 4 to the acquiring authority are to be construed as references to the authority by which the compensation claimed is payable under the Ancient Monuments and Archaeological Areas Act 1979: see s 47(3) (amended by SI 2009/1307).
    The functions of the Secretary of State under the Ancient Monuments and Archaeological Areas Act 1979, in so far as they relate to Wales, were transferred to the National Assembly for Wales (see the National Assembly for Wales (Transfer of Functions) Order 1999, SI 1999/672, art 2, Sch 1) and are now exercisable by the Welsh Ministers (see the Government of Wales Act 2006 s 162(1), Sch 11 paras 30, 32). As to the Secretary of State and the Welsh Ministers see PARA 802. As to the meaning of 'Wales' see PARA 802 note 4.
5   As to the Historic Buildings and Monuments Commission for England ('the Commission') see PARA 803.
6   Ancient Monuments and Archaeological Areas Act 1979 s 46(1) (amended by the National Heritage Act 1983 Sch 4 para 62). Compensation payable under the Ancient Monuments and Archaeological Areas Act 1979 s 46 carries interest at the rate for the time being prescribed under the Land Compensation Act 1961 s 32 (see COMPULSORY ACQUISITION OF LAND vol 18 (2009) PARA 641) from the date of entry on the land until payment: see the Planning and Compensation Act 1991 s 80(1), Sch 18 Pt I. Payments on account of interest may be made: see s 80(2).
7   As to the meaning of 'investigating authority' see PARA 1052 note 6.
8   As to the meaning of 'area of archaeological importance' see PARA 1047 note 3.
9   As to the meaning of 'England' see PARA 804 note 2.
10 Ancient Monuments and Archaeological Areas Act 1979 s 46(2) (amended by the National Heritage Act 1983 Sch 4 para 62).

1067. Grants to the Architectural Heritage Fund. The Secretary of State or, in relation to Wales, the Welsh Ministers[1] may make grants to the Architectural Heritage Fund[2]. The Historic Buildings and Monuments Commission for England ('the Commission')[3] may make grants to the fund for the purpose of enabling it to perform its functions[4] in, or in relation to, England[5].

A grant under these provisions may be made subject to such conditions as the Secretary of State, the Welsh Ministers or the Commission (as the case may be) may think fit to impose[6].

1   The functions of the Secretary of State under the Ancient Monuments and Archaeological Areas Act 1979, in so far as they relate to Wales, were transferred to the National Assembly for Wales (see the National Assembly for Wales (Transfer of Functions) Order 1999, SI 1999/672, art 2, Sch 1) and are now exercisable by the Welsh Ministers (see the Government of Wales Act 2006 s 162(1), Sch 11 paras 30, 32). As to the Secretary of State and the Welsh Ministers see PARA 802. As to the meaning of 'Wales' see PARA 802 note 4.
2   Ancient Monuments and Archaeological Areas Act 1979 s 49(1) (amended by the National Heritage Act 1983 s 33(3), Sch 4 para 63). 'Architectural Heritage Fund' means the institution registered under that name under the Charities Act 2011: Ancient Monuments and Archaeological Areas Act 1979 s 49(3) (added by the National Heritage Act 1983 Sch 4 para 63; and amended by the Charities Act 2011 Sch 7 para 36). As to the registration of charities see CHARITIES vol 8 (2015) PARA 307 et seq. Information on the Architectural Heritage Fund is available on the fund's website which, at the date at which this volume states the law, can be found at www.ahfund.org.uk.
3   As to the Historic Buildings and Monuments Commission for England ('the Commission') see PARA 803.
4   As to the meaning of 'functions' see PARA 1011 note 4.
5   Ancient Monuments and Archaeological Areas Act 1979 s 49(1A) (added by the National Heritage Act 1983 Sch 4 para 63). As to the meaning of 'England' see PARA 804 note 2.
6   Ancient Monuments and Archaeological Areas Act 1979 s 49(2) (amended by the National Heritage Act 1983 Sch 4 para 63).

(3) HISTORIC SHIPWRECKS AND MILITARY REMAINS

(i) Historic Shipwrecks

1068. Protection of sites of historic wrecks. If the Secretary of State or, in relation to Wales, the Welsh Ministers[1], as the case may be, are satisfied with respect to any site in United Kingdom waters[2] that:

(1)   it is, or may prove to be, the site of a vessel lying wrecked on or in the sea bed[3]; and

(2)   on account of the historical, archaeological or artistic importance of the vessel, or of any objects contained or formerly contained in it which may be lying on the sea bed in or near the wreck, the site ought to be protected from unauthorised interference[4],

he or they may by order[5] designate an area round the site as a 'restricted area'[6].

Such an order must identify the site where the vessel lies or formerly lay, or is supposed to lie or have lain[7], and: (a) the restricted area must be all within such distance of the site (so identified) as is specified in the order, but excluding any area above high water mark of ordinary spring tides[8]; and (b) the distance specified for the purposes of head (a) above must be whatever the Secretary of State or the Welsh Ministers think appropriate to ensure protection for the wreck[9].

A person who interferes with a restricted area commits an offence[10].

1   The functions of the Secretary of State under the Protection of Wrecks Act 1973 ss 1, 3 in so far as they relate to Wales, were transferred to the National Assembly for Wales (see the National Assembly for Wales (Transfer of Functions) Order 1999, SI 1999/672, art 2, Sch 1) and are now exercisable by the Welsh Ministers (see the Government of Wales Act 2006 s 162(1), Sch 11 paras 30, 32). As to the Secretary of State and the Welsh Ministers see PARA 802. As to the meaning of 'Wales' see PARA 802 note 4.
2   'United Kingdom waters' means any part of the sea within the seaward limits of United Kingdom territorial waters and includes any part of a river within the ebb and flow of ordinary spring tides;

and 'sea' includes any estuary or arm of the sea: see the Protection of Wrecks Act 1973 s 3(1). As to the meaning of 'United Kingdom' see PARA 804 note 2. As to the United Kingdom's territorial waters see WATER AND WATERWAYS vol 100 (2009) PARA 31.

3   Protection of Wrecks Act 1973 s 1(1)(a). References to the 'sea bed' include any area submerged at high water of ordinary spring tides: s 3(1).

4   Protection of Wrecks Act 1973 s 1(1)(b).

5   Before making such an order, the Secretary of State or the Welsh Ministers must consult with such persons as he or they consider appropriate having regard to the purposes of the order, although this consultation may be dispensed with if he or they are satisfied that the order should be made as a matter of immediate urgency: see the Protection of Wrecks Act 1973 s 1(4). An order may be varied or revoked by a subsequent order, and the Secretary of State or the Welsh Ministers must revoke any such order if he or they are of opinion that there is not, or is no longer, any wreck in the area which requires protection under the Protection of Wrecks Act 1973: see s 3(2)(a). Numerous orders have been made; see eg the Protection of Wrecks (Designation) (England) Order 2007, SI 2007/61; Protection of Wrecks (Designation) (England) (No 2) Order 2007, SI 2007/721; Protection of Wrecks (Designation) (England) Order 2009, SI 2009/2394; Protection of Wrecks (Designation) (England) Order 2012, SI 2012/1773; Protection of Wrecks (Designation) (England) (No 2) Order 2012, SI 2012/1807; Protection of Wrecks (Designation) (England) Order 2013, SI 2013/1636; Protection of Wrecks (Designation) (England) Order 2014, SI 2014/753. As to the meaning of 'person' see PARA 803 note 17. As to the exercise of the duty to consult see JUDICIAL REVIEW vol 61 (2010) PARA 627. As to the exercise of delegated powers see STATUTES AND LEGISLATIVE PROCESS vol 96 (2012) PARA 1045 et seq. As to the procedure in relation to subordinate legislation made by the Welsh Ministers see the Government of Wales Act 2006 Sch 11 paras 33–35; and CONSTITUTIONAL AND ADMINISTRATIVE LAW vol 20 (2014) PARA 380; STATUTES AND LEGISLATIVE PROCESS vol 96 (2012) PARA 1035.

6   Protection of Wrecks Act 1973 s 1(1).

7   Protection of Wrecks Act 1973 s 1(2).

8   Protection of Wrecks Act 1973 s 1(2)(a).

9   Protection of Wrecks Act 1973 s 1(2)(b).

10 See PARA 1069.

1069. Interfering with sites of historic shipwrecks. A person[1] commits an offence[2] if, in a restricted area[3], he does any of the following things otherwise than under the authority of a licence granted by the Secretary of State or, in relation to Wales, the Welsh Ministers[4]:

(1)   he tampers with, damages or removes any part of a vessel lying wrecked on or in the sea bed[5], or any object formerly contained in such a vessel[6]; or

(2)   he carries out diving or salvage operations directed to the exploration of any wreck or to removing objects from it or from the sea bed, or uses equipment constructed or adapted for any purpose of diving or salvage operations[7]; or

(3)   he deposits, so as to fall and lie abandoned on the sea bed, anything which, if it were to fall on the site of a wreck (whether it so falls or not), would wholly or partly obliterate the site or obstruct access to it or damage any part of the wreck[8];

(4)   he causes or permits any of those things to be done by others in a restricted area, otherwise than under the authority of such a licence[9].

Where a person is authorised by a licence granted by the Secretary of State or the Welsh Ministers to carry out diving or salvage operations, it is an offence for any other person to obstruct him, or cause or permit him to be obstructed, in doing anything which is authorised by the licence[10].

However, nothing is to be regarded as constituting an offence where it is done by a person:

(a)   in the course of any action taken by him for the sole purpose of dealing with an emergency of any description[11]; or

(b)   in exercising, or seeing to the exercise of, functions conferred by or under an enactment[12], local or other, on him or a body for which he acts[13]; or

(c)   out of necessity due to stress of weather or navigational hazards[14].

1   As to the meaning of 'person' see PARA 803 note 17.
2   A person guilty of an offence under the Protection of Wrecks Act 1973 s 1 is liable, on summary conviction, to a fine of not more than the prescribed sum, or, on conviction on indictment, to a fine; and proceedings for such an offence may be taken, and the offence may for all incidental purposes be treated as having been committed, at any place in the United Kingdom where he is for the time being: s 3(4) (amended by the Magistrates' Courts Act 1980 s 32). As to the prescribed sum and magistrates' powers to levy unlimited fines see SENTENCING vol 92 (2015) PARA 176. As to the meaning of 'United Kingdom' see PARA 804 note 2. As to sentencing guidelines for offences of theft involving historic objects or loss of the nation's heritage see PARA 1046 note 5.
3   As to the designation of restricted areas see PARA 1068.
4   A licence granted by the Secretary of State or the Welsh Ministers for these purposes must be in writing: Protection of Wrecks Act 1973 s 1(5). As to the meaning of 'writing' see PARA 805 note 14. The Secretary of State or the Welsh Ministers must, in respect of a restricted area, grant licences only to persons who appear to him or them either: (1) to be competent and properly equipped to carry out salvage operations in a manner appropriate to the historical, archaeological or artistic importance of any wreck which may be lying in the area and of any objects contained or formerly contained in a wreck (s 1(5)(a)(i)); or (2) to have any other legitimate reason for doing in the area that which can only be done under the authority of a licence (s 1(5)(a)(ii)). A licence may be granted subject to conditions or restrictions, and may be varied or revoked by the Secretary of State or the Welsh Ministers at any time after giving not less than one week's notice to the licensee: s 1(5)(b). Anything done contrary to any condition or restriction is to be treated for the purposes of s 1(3) as done otherwise than under the authority of the licence: s 1(5)(c).
    The functions of the Secretary of State under the Protection of Wrecks Act 1973 ss 1, 3 in so far as they relate to Wales, were transferred to the National Assembly for Wales (see the National Assembly for Wales (Transfer of Functions) Order 1999, SI 1999/672, art 2, Sch 1) and are now exercisable by the Welsh Ministers (see the Government of Wales Act 2006 s 162(1), Sch 11 paras 30, 32). As to the Secretary of State and the Welsh Ministers see PARA 802. As to the meaning of 'Wales' see PARA 802 note 4.
5   As to the meaning of 'sea bed' see PARA 1068 note 3.
6   Protection of Wrecks Act 1973 s 1(3)(a).
7   Protection of Wrecks Act 1973 s 1(3)(b).
8   Protection of Wrecks Act 1973 s 1(3)(c).
9   Protection of Wrecks Act 1973 s 1(3).
10 Protection of Wrecks Act 1973 s 1(6). As to the penalty for such offence see note 2.
11 Protection of Wrecks Act 1973 s 3(3)(a).
12 As to the meaning of 'enactment' see PARA 805 note 5.
13 Protection of Wrecks Act 1973 s 3(3)(b).
14 Protection of Wrecks Act 1973 s 3(3)(c).

1070. Wrecks to which the Protection of Wrecks Act 1973 do not apply. The Merchant Shipping Act 1995 contains provision as to wreck[1] including provision as to vessels in distress, dealing with wreck, unclaimed wreck, offences, and removal of wrecks. These provisions are covered in detail elsewhere in this work[2].

1   See the Merchant Shipping Act 1995 Pt IX (ss 224–255).
2   See CROWN AND CROWN PROCEEDINGS vol 29 (2014) PARA 184 et seq; SHIPPING AND MARITIME LAW vol 94 (2008) PARA 987 et seq.

(ii) Military Remains

1071. Protection of military remains. The Protection of Military Remains Act 1986 secures the protection from unauthorised interference of the remains of military aircraft and vessels that have crashed, sunk or been stranded and of associated human remains[1]. Provision is made as to offences relating to such interference[2] and for the grant of licences to carry out certain works or operations[3]. These provisions are covered in detail elsewhere in this work[4].

1   See the Protection of Military Remains Act 1986 s 1.
2   See the Protection of Military Remains Act 1986 ss 2, 6, 7 (amended by the Powers of Criminal Courts Sentencing Act 2000 Sch 9 para 100; and SI 1994/2795). As to sentencing guidelines for offences of theft involving historic objects or loss of the nation's heritage see PARA 1046 note 5.
3   See the Protection of Military Remains Act 1986 ss 4, 5.
4   See ARMED FORCES vol 3 (2011) PARA 393 et seq.

(4) HISTORIC BUILDINGS

(i) European Convention for the Protection of the Architectural Heritage of Europe

1072. European architectural heritage. The Convention for the Protection of the Architectural Heritage of Europe[1] aims to set out the framework for a common policy for the conservation and enhancement of the architectural heritage[2]. 'Architectural heritage' comprises the following permanent properties:

(1)   monuments: all buildings and structures of conspicuous historical, archaeological, artistic, scientific, social or technical interest, including their fixtures and fittings;

(2)   groups of buildings: homogeneous groups of urban or rural buildings conspicuous for their historical, archaeological, artistic, scientific, social or technical interest which are sufficiently coherent to form topographically definable units;

(3)   sites: the combined works of man and nature, being areas which are partially built upon and sufficiently distinctive and homogeneous to be topographically definable and are of conspicuous historical, archaeological, artistic, scientific, social or technical interest[3].

The states party to the convention[4] undertake to:

(a)   maintain inventories of the monuments, groups of buildings and sites to be protected[5], and to take statutory measures to protect the architectural heritage[6];

(b)   to implement appropriate supervision and authorisation procedures for the legal protection of the properties in question and to prevent the disfigurement, dilapidation or demolition of protected properties[7];

(c)   to prohibit the removal, in whole or in part, of any protected monument, except where the material safeguarding of such monuments makes removal imperative[8];

(d)   to provide financial support for the maintenance and restoration of the architectural heritage and to encourage the conservation of this heritage[9];

(e)   to promote measures for the general enhancement of the environment in the surroundings of monuments, within groups of buildings and within sites[10];

(f)   to ensure that infringements of the law protecting the architectural heritage are met with a relevant and adequate response by the competent authority[11];

(g) to adopt integrated conservation policies which include the protection of the architectural heritage as an essential town and country planning objective and ensure that this requirement is taken into account at all stages both in the drawing up of development plans and in the procedures for authorising work[12];

(h) to foster, taking account of the architectural and historical character of the heritage, the use of protected properties in the light of the needs of contemporary life and the adaptation, when appropriate, of old buildings for new uses[13];

(i) while recognising the value of permitting public access to protected properties, to take such action as may be necessary to ensure that the consequences of permitting this access, especially any structural development, do not adversely affect the architectural and historical character of such properties and their surroundings[14];

(j) to develop public awareness of the value of conserving the architectural heritage, both as an element of cultural identity and as a source of inspiration and creativity for present and future generations[15];

(k) to promote training in the various occupations and craft trades involved in the conservation of the architectural heritage[16];

(l) to exchange information on their conservation policies and to provide mutual assistance and training[17].

As regards the protection of architectural heritage in England and Wales provision is made for grants and loans for the preservation of historic buildings, related land and objects[18], for the acquisition of such buildings, land and objects[19], for the acceptance of endowments[20], for the listing of buildings and the creation of conservation areas[21], and for the protection of historic gardens[22]. There is also a non-statutory register of historic battlefields[23].

1 Ie the Convention for the Protection of the Architectural Heritage of Europe (Council of Europe ETS No 121: Granada 1985).
2 See the Convention for the Protection of the Architectural Heritage of Europe (Council of Europe ETS No 121: Granada 1985) preamble.
3 Convention for the Protection of the Architectural Heritage of Europe (Council of Europe ETS No 121: Granada 1985) art 1.
4 The convention was ratified by the United Kingdom on 13 November 1987.
5 See the Convention for the Protection of the Architectural Heritage of Europe (Council of Europe ETS No 121: Granada 1985) art 2.
6 See the Convention for the Protection of the Architectural Heritage of Europe (Council of Europe ETS No 121: Granada 1985) art 3.
7 See the Convention for the Protection of the Architectural Heritage of Europe (Council of Europe ETS No 121: Granada 1985) art 4.
8 See the Convention for the Protection of the Architectural Heritage of Europe (Council of Europe ETS No 121: Granada 1985) art 5.
9 See the Convention for the Protection of the Architectural Heritage of Europe (Council of Europe ETS No 121: Granada 1985) arts 6, 8.
10 See the Convention for the Protection of the Architectural Heritage of Europe (Council of Europe ETS No 121: Granada 1985) art 7.
11 See the Convention for the Protection of the Architectural Heritage of Europe (Council of Europe ETS No 121: Granada 1985) art 9.
12 See the Convention for the Protection of the Architectural Heritage of Europe (Council of Europe ETS No 121: Granada 1985) art 10.
13 See the Convention for the Protection of the Architectural Heritage of Europe (Council of Europe ETS No 121: Granada 1985) art 11.
14 See the Convention for the Protection of the Architectural Heritage of Europe (Council of Europe ETS No 121: Granada 1985) art 12.
15 See the Convention for the Protection of the Architectural Heritage of Europe (Council of Europe ETS No 121: Granada 1985) art 15.

16 See the Convention for the Protection of the Architectural Heritage of Europe (Council of Europe ETS No 121: Granada 1985) art 16.
17 See the Convention for the Protection of the Architectural Heritage of Europe (Council of Europe ETS No 121: Granada 1985) arts 17–20.
18 See PARA 1073 et seq.
19 See PARA 1076 et seq.
20 See PARAS 1080–1081.
21 See PARAS 1082–1083.
22 See PARAS 1084–1086.
23 See PARA 1087.

(ii) Grants and Loans for Preservation of Historic Buildings etc

1073. Grants and loans for preservation of historic buildings etc in England.
The Historic Buildings and Monuments Commission for England ('the Commission')[1] may make grants or loans[2] for the purpose of defraying, in whole or in part, any expenditure incurred or to be incurred in the repair or maintenance of:

(1) a building which is situated in England and which appears to the Commission to be of outstanding historic or architectural interest; or

(2) in the upkeep of any land which is situated in England and which comprises, or is contiguous or adjacent to, any such building; or

(3) in the repair or maintenance of any objects ordinarily kept in any such building, or

(4) in the upkeep of a garden or other land which is situated in England and which appears to the Commission to be of outstanding historic interest but which is not contiguous or adjacent to a building which appears to the Commission to be of outstanding historical or architectural interest[3].

Where a grant is so made to the National Trust for Places of Historic Interest or Natural Beauty (the 'National Trust)[4], the grant may, if the Commission thinks fit, be made by way of endowment, subject to such provisions, by way of trust, contract or otherwise, as may appear to the Commission to be requisite for securing that, so long as it is reasonably practicable to give effect to the purposes of the endowment, the sum granted will be retained and invested by the National Trust as a source of income for defraying the expenditure in respect of which the grant is made[5].

Any grant or loan made under these provisions may be made subject to conditions imposed by the Commission for the purpose of securing public access to the whole or part of the property[6] to which the grant or loan relates, or for other purposes, as the Commission may think fit[7]; and any such loan must be made on such terms as to repayment, payment of interest and otherwise as the Commission may determine[8].

1 As to the Historic Buildings and Monuments Commission for England ('the Commission') see PARA 803. As to the meaning of 'England' see PARA 804 note 2. As to grants for the preservation of the historic buildings, their contents and land in Wales see PARA 1074.
2 See the Historic Buildings and Ancient Monuments Act 1953 s 3A(2) (s 3A added by the National Heritage Act 1983 s 33, Sch 4 para 3).
3 Historic Buildings and Ancient Monuments Act 1953 s 3A(1) (as added: see note 2). In the exercise, with respect to any buildings or other land in a conservation area, of any functions under or by virtue of the Historic Buildings and Ancient Monuments Act 1953 Pt I (ss 1–9) special attention must be paid to the desirability of preserving or enhancing the character or appearance of that area: see the Planning (Listed Buildings and Conservation Areas) Act 1990 s 72(1), (2); and PLANNING vol 83 (2010) PARA 1320.

4   As to the National Trust see PARA 973.
5   Historic Buildings and Ancient Monuments Act 1953 s 3A(3) (as added: see note 2).
6   'Property' means real or personal property of any description: see the Historic Buildings and
    Ancient Monuments Act 1953 s 9(2).
7   Historic Buildings and Ancient Monuments Act 1953 s 3A(4) (as added: see note 2). As to the
    recovery of grants see PARA 1075.
8   Historic Buildings and Ancient Monuments Act 1953 s 3A(5) (as added: see note 2).

1074. Grants and loans for preservation of historic buildings etc in Wales. The
Welsh Ministers[1] may make grants or loans[2] for the purpose of defraying, in whole
or in part, any expenditure incurred or to be incurred:

(1)   in the repair or maintenance of a building which is situated in Wales and
       which appears to them to be of outstanding historic or architectural
       interest; or

(2)   in the upkeep of any land comprising, or contiguous or adjacent to, any
       such building; or

(3)   in the repair or maintenance of any objects ordinarily kept in any such
       building, or

(4)   in the upkeep of a garden or other land which is situated in Wales and
       appears to them to be of outstanding historic interest but which is not
       contiguous or adjacent to a building which appears to them to be of
       outstanding historic or architectural interest[3].

Where a grant is so made to the National Trust for Places of Historic Interest
or Natural Beauty (the National Trust)[4], the grant may, if the Welsh Ministers
think fit, be made by way of endowment, subject to such provisions, by way of
trust, contract or otherwise, as may appear to the Welsh Ministers to be requisite
for securing that, so long as it is reasonably practicable to give effect to the
purposes of the endowment, the sum granted will be retained and invested by the
National Trust and used as a source of income for defraying the expenditure in
respect of which the grant is made[5].

A grant or loan[6] made under these provisions may be made subject to
conditions imposed by the Welsh Ministers for the purposes of securing public
access to the whole or part of the property[7] to which the grant relates, or for other
purposes, as they may think fit[8]; and any such loan must be made on such terms
as to repayment, payment of interest and otherwise as the Welsh Ministers may
determine[9].

1   The functions of the Secretary of State under the Historic Buildings and Ancient Monuments Act
    1953 and the Civic Amenities Act 1967, in so far as they relate to Wales, were transferred to the
    National Assembly for Wales (see the National Assembly for Wales (Transfer of Functions) Order
    1999, SI 1999/672, art 2, Sch 1) and are now exercisable by the Welsh Ministers (see the
    Government of Wales Act 2006 s 162(1), Sch 11 paras 30, 32). As to the Secretary of State and
    the Welsh Ministers see PARA 802. As to the meaning of 'Wales' see PARA 802 note 4. As to the
    protection of the historic environment in Wales see further PARA 810.
2   The power conferred by the Historic Buildings and Ancient Monuments Act 1953 s 4(1) to make
    grants for the purposes mentioned therein includes power to make loans for those purposes, and
    references to grants in s 4(3) (see the text to notes 6–8) must be construed accordingly: Civic
    Amenities Act 1967 s 4(1).
3   See the Historic Buildings and Ancient Monuments Act 1953 s 4(1) (amended by the Town
    and Country Amenities Act 1974 s 12; and by the National Heritage Act 1983 s 33, Sch 4 para 4).
    In the exercise, with respect to any buildings or other land in a conservation area, of any functions
    under or by virtue of the Historic Buildings and Ancient Monuments Act 1953 Pt I (ss 1–9) special
    attention must be paid to the desirability of preserving or enhancing the character or appearance
    of that area: see the Planning (Listed Buildings and Conservation Areas) Act 1990 s 72(1), (2); and
    PLANNING vol 83 (2010) PARA 1320.
4   As to the National Trust see PARA 973.
5   Historic Buildings and Ancient Monuments Act 1953 s 4(2).
6   See note 2.

7   As to the meaning of 'property' see PARA 1073 note 6.
8   Historic Buildings and Ancient Monuments Act 1953 s 4(3). As to the recovery of grants see PARA 1075.
9   See the Civic Amenities Act 1967 s 4(2).

1075. Recovery of grants made for the preservation of historic buildings etc. The following provisions apply to any grant[1] made for the preservation of historic buildings, their contents and adjoining land on terms that it is to be recoverable under these provisions, but any such grant is only to be regarded for these purposes as so made if, before or on making the grant, the Historic Buildings and Monuments Commission for England ('the Commission')[2] or, as the case may be, the Welsh Ministers[3] give to the grantee notice in writing[4]: (1) summarising the effect of these provisions[5]; and (2) specifying the period[6] during which the grant is to be recoverable[7] in the case of a grant made for certain specified purposes[8]. If any condition subject to which such a grant was made is contravened or not complied with, the Commission or the Welsh Ministers may recover the amount of the grant or such part of it as they think fit from the grantee[9].

If, during the period specified under head (2) above in the case of such a grant made to any person[10] for the purpose of defraying, in whole or in part, any expenditure on the repair, maintenance or upkeep of any property, the grantee disposes[11] of the relevant interest held by him in the property[12], the Commission or the Welsh Ministers may recover the amount of the grant or such part of it as they think fit from the grantee[13].

1   Ie any grant under the Historic Buildings and Ancient Monuments Act 1953 s 3A (see PARA 1073) or s 4 (see PARA 1074).
2   As to the Historic Buildings and Monuments Commission for England ('the Commission') see PARA 803.
3   The functions of the Secretary of State under the Historic Buildings and Ancient Monuments Act 1953, in so far as they relate to Wales, were transferred to the National Assembly for Wales (see the National Assembly for Wales (Transfer of Functions) Order 1999, SI 1999/672, art 2, Sch 1) and are now exercisable by the Welsh Ministers (see the Government of Wales Act 2006 s 162(1), Sch 11 paras 30, 32). As to the Secretary of State and the Welsh Ministers see PARA 802. As to the meaning of 'Wales' see PARA 802 note 4.
4   Historic Buildings and Ancient Monuments Act 1953 s 4A(1) (s 4A added by the Ancient Monuments and Archaeological Areas Act 1979 s 48(2); Historic Buildings and Ancient Monuments Act 1953 s 4A(1), (3), (4), (8) amended by the National Heritage Act 1983 s 33, Sch 4 para 5). As to the meaning of 'writing' see PARA 805 note 14.
5   Historic Buildings and Ancient Monuments Act 1953 s 4A(1)(a) (as added: see note 4).
6   The period so specified in the case of any grant must be a period beginning with the day on which the grant is made and ending not more than ten years after that day: Historic Buildings and Ancient Monuments Act 1953 s 4A(2) (as added: see note 4).
7   Ie in accordance with the Historic Buildings and Ancient Monuments Act 1953 s 4A(4) (see the text to notes 10–13).
8   Historic Buildings and Ancient Monuments Act 1953 s 4A(1)(b) (as added: see note 4). The specified purposes are those mentioned in s 4A(4): see the text to notes 10–13. In the exercise, with respect to any buildings or other land in a conservation area, of any functions under or by virtue of the Historic Buildings and Ancient Monuments Act 1953 Pt I (ss 1–9) special attention must be paid to the desirability of preserving or enhancing the character or appearance of that area: see the Planning (Listed Buildings and Conservation Areas) Act 1990 s 72(1), (2); and PLANNING vol 83 (2010) PARA 1320.
9   Historic Buildings and Ancient Monument Act 1953 s 4A(3) (as added and amended: see note 4). Nothing in the Historic Buildings and Ancient Monuments Act 1953 s 4A(3), (4) (see the text to notes 10–13) is to be taken as conferring on the Commission or the Welsh Ministers a right to recover, by virtue of a breach of more than one condition or disposals of several parts of an interest in property, amounts in the aggregate exceeding the amount of the grant: s 4A(8) (as so added and amended). As to the meaning of 'property' see PARA 1073 note 6.
10 As to the meaning of 'person' see PARA 803 note 17.

11 The Historic Buildings and Ancient Monuments Act 1953 s 4A(4) only applies where the grantee disposes of the relevant interest or any part of it by way of sale or exchange or lease for a term of not less than 21 years: s 4A(5) (as added: see note 4).

12 'Relevant interest' means the interest, or any part thereof, held by the grantee in the property on the day on which the grant is made: see the Historic Buildings and Ancient Monuments Act 1953 s 4A(4) (as added: see note 4).

13 Historic Buildings and Ancient Monuments Act 1953 s 4A(4) (as added and amended: see note 4). See also s 4A(8); and note 9. If a person becomes entitled by way of gift from the grantee, whether directly or indirectly, but otherwise than by way of will, to a part of the relevant interest, a disposal by the donee in any manner mentioned in s 4A(5) (see note 11) of the interest so acquired by him in the property, or any part of that interest, is treated for the purposes of s 4A(4) as a disposal by the grantee of a part of the relevant interest: s 4A(6) (as so added). If a person becomes entitled by way of any such gift to the whole of the relevant interest, s 4A(4) has effect, except for the purpose of determining the relevant interest, as if the donee were the grantee: s 4A(7) (as so added). 'Gift' includes devise, bequest, appointment, conveyance, assignment, transfer and any other assurance of property: s 9(2).

(iii) Acquisition of Historic Buildings etc

1076. Acquisition by the Secretary of State or the Welsh Ministers of historic buildings etc. Subject as provided below[1], the Secretary of State[2] has or, in relation to Wales, the Welsh Ministers[3] have power[4]:

(1)   to acquire by agreement, whether by purchase, lease or otherwise, or to accept a gift[5] of:

    (a)   any building appearing to the Secretary of State or the Welsh Ministers to be one of outstanding historic or architectural interest[6];

    (b)   any land comprising, or contiguous or adjacent to, any such building[7];

(2)   to purchase by agreement, or to accept a gift of, any objects which are or have been ordinarily kept in:

    (a)   a building which, or any interest in which, is vested in the Secretary of State or the Welsh Ministers, or a building which is under his or their control or management, being in either case a building appearing to the Secretary of State or the Welsh Ministers to be of outstanding historic or architectural interest[8]; or

    (b)   a building of which the Secretary of State or the Welsh Ministers are guardian under the Ancient Monuments and Archaeological Areas Act 1979[9]; or

    (c)   a building which, or any interest in which, is vested in the National Trust[10];

(3)   to make such arrangements[11] as the Secretary of State or the Welsh Ministers may think fit as to the management or custody of any property[12] so acquired or accepted by him or them, and as to the use of any such property, and to dispose of or otherwise deal with any such property as he or they may from time to time determine[13].

The Secretary of State must consult with the Historic Buildings and Monuments Commission for England ('the Commission') before acquiring or accepting any property under these provisions, and before taking any step by way of disposing of or otherwise dealing with any such property so acquired or accepted, other than any step taken by him in the course of managing or keeping the property and making arrangements as to its use; but this does not prevent the

Secretary of State from acquiring or accepting any property without such consultation in a case where the acquisition or acceptance thereof appears to him to be a matter of immediate urgency[14].

1　Ie subject to the Historic Buildings and Ancient Monuments Act 1953 s 5(4) (see the text to note 14).
2　As to the Secretary of State see PARA 802 note 2.
3　The functions of the Secretary of State under the Historic Buildings and Ancient Monuments Act 1953, in so far as they relate to Wales, were transferred to the National Assembly for Wales (see the National Assembly for Wales (Transfer of Functions) Order 1999, SI 1999/672, art 2, Sch 1) and are now exercisable by the Welsh Ministers (see the Government of Wales Act 2006 s 162(1), Sch 11 paras 30, 32). As to the Welsh Ministers see PARA 802. As to the meaning of 'Wales' see PARA 802 note 4.
4　In the exercise, with respect to any buildings or other land in a conservation area, of any functions under or by virtue of the Historic Buildings and Ancient Monuments Act 1953 Pt I (ss 1–9) special attention must be paid to the desirability of preserving or enhancing the character or appearance of that area: see the Planning (Listed Buildings and Conservation Areas) Act 1990 s 72(1), (2); and PLANNING vol 83 (2010) PARA 1320.
5　As to the meaning of 'gift' see PARA 1075 note 13.
6　Historic Buildings and Ancient Monuments Act 1953 s 5(1)(a). As to the acceptance of endowments in respect of such buildings see s 8; and PARA 1080. Certain redundant places of worship may be acquired by the Secretary of State under s 5: see the Redundant Churches and Other Religious Buildings Act 1969 ss 4, 5; and ECCLESIASTICAL LAW vol 34 (2011) PARA 907.
7　Historic Buildings and Ancient Monuments Act 1953 s 5(1)(b).
8　Historic Buildings and Ancient Monuments Act 1953 s 5(2)(a).
9　Historic Buildings and Ancient Monuments Act 1953 s 5(2)(b) (amended by the Ancient Monuments and Archaeological Areas Act 1979 s 64(2), Sch 4 para 3(1)). As to guardianship under the Ancient Monuments and Archaeological Areas Act 1979 see PARA 1032.
10　Historic Buildings and Ancient Monuments Act 1953 s 5(2)(c). As to the National Trust see PARA 973.
11　The Historic Buildings and Monuments Commission for England ('the Commission') may be a party to such arrangements if the arrangements relate to property situated in England: Historic Buildings and Ancient Monuments Act 1953 s 5(3A) (added by the National Heritage Act 1983 s 33, Sch 4 para 6). As to the Commission see PARA 803. As to the meaning of 'England' see PARA 804 note 2.
12　As to the meaning of 'property' see PARA 1073 note 6.
13　See the Historic Buildings and Ancient Monuments Act 1953 s 5(3).
14　Historic Buildings and Ancient Monuments Act 1953 s 5(4) (amended by SI 2006/63). As to the exercise of the duty to consult see JUDICIAL REVIEW vol 61 (2010) PARA 627.

1077. Acquisition by the Historic Buildings and Monuments Commission for England of historic buildings etc. The Historic Buildings and Monuments Commission for England ('the Commission')[1] has power[2], subject to the consent of the Secretary of State[3], to acquire by agreement, whether by purchase, lease or otherwise, or to accept a gift[4] of:

(1)　any building which is situated in England[5] and which appears to the Commission to be one of outstanding historic or architectural interest[6];

(2)　any building which is situated in England and in an area designated as a conservation area[7] and which appears to the Commission to be of special historic or architectural interest[8];

(3)　any land which is situated in England and which comprises, or is contiguous or adjacent to, any building mentioned in head (1) or head (2) above[9];

(4)　any garden or other land which is situated in England and which appears to the Commission to be of outstanding historic interest but which is not contiguous or adjacent to a building which appears to the Commission to be of outstanding historic or architectural interest[10].

The Commission also has power to purchase by agreement, or to accept a gift of, any objects which it would be historically appropriate to keep[11] in:

(a)   a building which, or any interest in which, is vested in the Commission, or a building which is under its management or in its custody, being in either case a building appearing to the Commission to be of outstanding historic or architectural interest[12]; or

(b)   a building of which the Commission is guardian under the Ancient Monuments and Archaeological Areas Act 1979[13]; or

(c)   a building situated in England which, or any interest in which, is vested in the National Trust for Places of Historic Interest or Natural Beauty (the 'National Trust')[14].

The Commission may make such arrangements as it may think fit as to the management or custody of any property acquired or accepted by it under these provisions, and as to the use of any such property, and may dispose of, or otherwise deal with, any such property as it may from time to time determine[15].

1   As to the Historic Buildings and Monuments Commission for England ('the Commission') see PARA 803.

2   As to the power of the Commission to accept endowments see the Historic Buildings and Ancient Monuments Act 1953 ss 8A, 8B; and PARAS 1081, 1084. Certain redundant places of worship may be acquired by the Commission under s 5A: see the Redundant Churches and Other Religious Buildings Act 1969 ss 4, 5; and ECCLESIASTICAL LAW vol 34 (2011) PARA 907. In the exercise, with respect to any buildings or other land in a conservation area, of any functions under or by virtue of the Historic Buildings and Ancient Monuments Act 1953 Pt I (ss 1–9) special attention must be paid to the desirability of preserving or enhancing the character or appearance of that area: see the Planning (Listed Buildings and Conservation Areas) Act 1990 s 72(1), (2); and PLANNING vol 83 (2010) PARA 1320.

3   The Commission must not acquire or accept any property under the Historic Buildings and Ancient Monuments Act 1953 s 5A(1) without the consent of the Secretary of State, which may be given subject to such conditions as he thinks fit: s 5A(4) (s 5A added by the National Heritage Act 1983 s 33, Sch 4 para 7). As to the Secretary of State see PARA 802 note 2. As to the meaning of 'property' see PARA 1073 note 6.

4   As to the meaning of 'gift' see PARA 1075 note 13.

5   As to the meaning of 'England' see PARA 804 note 2.

6   Historic Buildings and Ancient Monuments Act 1953 s 5A(1)(a) (as added: see note 3).

7   Ie under the Planning (Listed Buildings and Conservation Areas) Act 1990 s 69 (see PLANNING vol 83 (2010) PARA 1318).

8   Historic Buildings and Ancient Monuments Act 1953 s 5A(1)(b) (as added (see note 3); and amended by the Planning (Consequential Provisions) Act 1990 s 4, Sch 2 para 4(1)).

9   Historic Buildings and Ancient Monuments Act 1953 s 5A(1)(c) (as added: see note 3).

10   Historic Buildings and Ancient Monuments Act 1953 s 5A(1)(d) (as added: see note 3).

11   For these purposes, an object is one which it would be historically appropriate to keep in a building if: (1) it is or has been ordinarily kept in the building (Historic Buildings and Ancient Monuments Act 1953 s 5A(5)(a) (as added: see note 3)); or (2) it is historically associated with the building or connected with a person or event historically associated with the building (s 5A(5)(b) (as so added)); or (3) objects of its kind were produced or used in a period falling within the lifetime of the building (s 5A(5)(c) (as so added)); or (4) the Commission is of opinion that it would for some other reason be historically appropriate to keep it in the building (s 5A(5)(d) (as so added)). As to the meaning of 'person' see PARA 803 note 17.

12   Historic Buildings and Ancient Monuments Act 1953 s 5A(2)(a) (as added: see note 3).

13   Historic Buildings and Ancient Monuments Act 1953 s 5A(2)(b) (as added: see note 3). As to guardianship under the Ancient Monuments and Archaeological Areas Act 1979 see PARA 1032.

14   Historic Buildings and Ancient Monuments Act 1953 s 5A(2)(c) (as added: see note 3). As to the National Trust see PARA 973.

15   Historic Buildings and Ancient Monuments Act 1953 s 5A(3) (as added: see note 3).

1078. Grants by the Historic Buildings and Monuments Commission for England for acquisition of historic buildings in England.

The Historic Buildings and Monuments Commission for England ('the Commission')[1] may make grants for the purpose of defraying in whole or in part any expenses incurred by a local authority or National Park authority[2] in England[3] in the acquisition of property[4] situated in England under its statutory powers[5] to acquire listed buildings compulsorily or by agreement[6].

The Commission may also make grants to the National Trust for Places of Historic Interest or Natural Beauty (the 'National Trust')[7] for the purposes of defraying, in whole or in part, any expenses incurred by it in the acquisition of:

(1) any building which is situated in England and which appears to the Commission to be of outstanding historic or architectural interest[8];

(2) any land which is situated in England and which comprises, or is contiguous or adjacent to, any such building[9]; or

(3) any garden or other land which is situated in England and which appears to the Commission to be of outstanding historic interest but which is not contiguous or adjacent to a building which appears to the Commission to be of outstanding historic or architectural interest[10].

1 As to the Historic Buildings and Monuments Commission for England ('the Commission') see PARA 803.

2 In relation to any building or land in any National Park, the powers conferred on a local authority are exercisable by the National Park authority: see the Environment Act 1995 s 70, Sch 9 para 13(1), (2). As to National Park authorities see OPEN SPACES AND COUNTRYSIDE vol 78 (2010) PARA 526.

3 As to the meaning of 'England' see PARA 804 note 2.

4 As to the meaning of 'property' see PARA 1073 note 6.

5 Ie under the Planning (Listed Buildings and Conservation Areas) Act 1990 s 47 (see PLANNING vol 83 (2010) PARAS 1304, 1306) or s 52 (see PLANNING vol 83 (2010) PARA 1310).

6 See the Historic Buildings and Ancient Monuments Act 1953 s 5B(1) (s 5B added by the National Heritage Act 1983 s 33, Sch 4 para 7; Historic Buildings and Ancient Monuments Act 1953 s 5B(1) amended by the Planning (Consequential Provisions) Act 1990 s 4, Sch 2 para 4(2)). In the exercise, with respect to any buildings or other land in a conservation area, of any functions under or by virtue of the Historic Buildings and Ancient Monuments Act 1953 Pt I (ss 1–9) special attention must be paid to the desirability of preserving or enhancing the character or appearance of that area: see the Planning (Listed Buildings and Conservation Areas) Act 1990 s 72(1), (2); and PLANNING vol 83 (2010) PARA 1320.

7 As to the National Trust see PARA 973.

8 Historic Buildings and Ancient Monuments Act 1953 s 5B(2)(a) (as added: see note 6).

9 Historic Buildings and Ancient Monuments Act 1953 s 5B(2)(b) (as added: see note 6).

10 Historic Buildings and Ancient Monuments Act 1953 s 5B(2)(c) (as added: see note 6).

1079. Grants by the Welsh Ministers for acquisition of historic buildings in Wales. The Welsh Ministers[1] may make grants for the purpose of defraying, in whole or in part, any expenses incurred by a local authority or a National Park authority[2] in the acquisition of property[3] situated in Wales under its statutory powers[4] to acquire listed buildings compulsorily or by agreement[5].

The Welsh Ministers may also makes grants to the National Trust[6] for the purpose of defraying, in whole or in part, any expenses incurred by it in the acquisition of buildings in Wales which appear to the Welsh Ministers to be of outstanding historic or architectural interest[7].

1 The functions of the Secretary of State under the Ancient Monuments and Archaeological Areas Act 1979, in so far as they relate to Wales, were transferred to the National Assembly for Wales (see the National Assembly for Wales (Transfer of Functions) Order 1999, SI 1999/672, art 2, Sch 1) and are now exercisable by the Welsh Ministers (see the Government of Wales Act 2006 s 162(1), Sch 11 paras 30, 32). As to the Secretary of State and the Welsh Ministers see PARA 802. As to the meaning of 'Wales' see PARA 802 note 4.

2 In relation to any building in any National Park, the powers conferred on a local authority are exercisable by the National Park authority: see the Environment Act 1995 s 70, Sch 9 para 13(1), (2). As to National Park authorities see OPEN SPACES AND COUNTRYSIDE vol 78 (2010) PARA 526.

3 As to the meaning of 'property' see PARA 1073 note 6.

4   Ie under the Town and Country Planning Act 1947 s 41 (repealed): see now the Planning (Listed
    Buildings and Conservation Areas) Act 1990 s 47 (see PLANNING vol 83 (2010) PARAS 1304,
    1306) or s 52 (see PLANNING vol 83 (2010) PARA 1310).
5   See the Historic Buildings and Ancient Monuments Act 1953 s 6(1), (4) (added by the National
    Heritage Act 1983 s 33, Sch 4); Interpretation Act 1978 s 17(2)(a). In the exercise, with respect to
    any buildings or other land in a conservation area, of any functions under or by virtue of the
    Historic Buildings and Ancient Monuments Act 1953 Pt I (ss 1–9) special attention must be paid
    to the desirability of preserving or enhancing the character or appearance of that area: see the
    Planning (Listed Buildings and Conservation Areas) Act 1990 s 72(1), (2); and PLANNING vol 83
    (2010) PARA 1320. As to the preservation of the historic environment in Wales see further PARA
    810.
6   As to the National Trust see PARA 973.
7   See the Historic Buildings and Ancient Monuments Act 1953 s 6(2), (4) (as added: see note 5).

(iv) Endowments for the Upkeep of Historic Buildings

1080. Powers of Secretary of State or the Welsh Ministers to accept endowments. Where any instrument coming into operation after 31 July 1953[1] contains a provision purporting to be a gift[2] of property[3] to the Secretary of State or, in relation to Wales, the Welsh Ministers[4] upon trust to use the income of it, either for a limited time or in perpetuity, for or towards the upkeep of:

(1)   a building acquired or accepted by the Secretary of State or the Welsh
       Ministers under their statutory powers[5] or a building which the
       Secretary of State or the Welsh Ministers propose so to acquire or
       accept[6]; or

(2)   a building which at the coming into operation of the trust instrument is
       or will shortly be vested in or under the control or management of the
       Secretary of State or the Welsh Ministers, being a building which
       appears to him or them to be one of outstanding historic or architectural
       interest[7]; or

(3)   a building of which at that time the Secretary of State is or will shortly
       be, or the Welsh Ministers are or will shortly be, guardian under the
       Ancient Monuments and Archaeological Areas Act 1979[8],

or for or towards the upkeep of any such buildings together with other property, the Secretary of State or the Welsh Ministers may accept the gift and, if he or they do so, and the provision does not constitute a charitable trust, the following provisions have effect[9].

The validity of the gift and of the trust to use the income as above (the 'endowment trust') is deemed not to be, or to ever have been, affected by any rule of law or equity which would not have affected their validity if the trust had been charitable[10].

In relation to the property, of whatsoever nature, comprised in the gift and any property for the time being representing that property (the 'trust fund') the Secretary of State or the Welsh Ministers have, during the continuance of the endowment trust and without prejudice to any additional or larger powers conferred on the Secretary of State or on the Welsh Ministers by the trust instrument, the like powers of management, disposition and investment as, in the case of land subject to a trust of land[11], are conferred by law on the trustees of land in relation to the land and to the proceeds of its sale[12].

If, while the endowment trust continues, an event happens such that immediately thereafter the Secretary of State is, or the Welsh Ministers are, neither entitled to any interest in the building to which the trust relates, nor have the building under his or their control or management, nor is or are guardian of the building under the Ancient Monuments and Archaeological Areas Act 1979, and the endowment trust would otherwise not then be determined or be deemed to have failed, then, on the happening of that event, the endowment trust ceases and the trust fund devolves accordingly as on a failure of the trust[13].

If the trust instrument contains a provision whereby on the failure or determination of the endowment trust the trust fund purports to be given, or to be directed to be held, on charitable trusts, the validity of that gift or direction is deemed not to be, or to ever have been, affected by any rule of law or equity relating to perpetuities[14].

1   Ie the date on which the Historic Buildings and Ancient Monuments Act 1953 was passed.
2   As to the meaning of 'gift' see PARA 1075 note 13.
3   As to the meaning of 'property' see PARA 1073 note 6.
4   The functions of the Secretary of State under the Historic Buildings and Ancient Monuments Act 1953, in so far as they relate to Wales, were transferred to the National Assembly for Wales (see the National Assembly for Wales (Transfer of Functions) Order 1999, SI 1999/672, art 2, Sch 1) and are now exercisable by the Welsh Ministers (see the Government of Wales Act 2006 s 162(1), Sch 11 paras 30, 32). As to the Secretary of State and the Welsh Ministers see PARA 802. As to the meaning of 'Wales' see PARA 802 note 4.
5   Ie under the Historic Buildings and Ancient Monuments Act 1953 s 5 (see PARA 1076).
6   Historic Buildings and Ancient Monuments Act 1953 s 8(1)(a).
7   Historic Buildings and Ancient Monuments Act 1953 s 8(1)(b).
8   Historic Buildings and Ancient Monuments Act 1953 s 8(1)(c) (amended by the Ancient Monuments and Archaeological Areas Act 1979 s 64(2), Sch 4 para 3). As to guardianship under the Ancient Monuments and Archaeological Areas Act 1979 see PARA 1032.
9   Historic Buildings and Ancient Monuments Act 1953 s 8(1). As to charitable trusts see CHARITIES vol 8 (2015) PARA 68 et seq. In the exercise, with respect to any buildings or other land in a conservation area, of any functions under or by virtue of the Historic Buildings and Ancient Monuments Act 1953 Pt I (ss 1–9) special attention must be paid to the desirability of preserving or enhancing the character or appearance of that area: see the Planning (Listed Buildings and Conservation Areas) Act 1990 s 72(1), (2); and PLANNING vol 83 (2010) PARA 1320.
10 See the Historic Buildings and Ancient Monuments Act 1953 s 8(2).
11 As to the meanings of 'trust of land' and 'trustees of land' see PARA 1032 note 2.
12 Historic Buildings and Ancient Monuments Act 1953 s 8(3) (amended by the Trusts of Land and Appointment of Trustees Act 1996 s 25(1), Sch 3 para 9). Where the Historic Buildings and Monuments Commission for England ('the Commission') is requested in pursuance of the Historic Buildings and Ancient Monuments Act 1953 s 8(3) to manage any property the income from which is applicable for or towards the upkeep of property situated in England, the Commission may undertake the management: s 8(7) (added by the National Heritage Act 1983 s 33, Sch 4 para 9). As to the Commission see PARA 803.
13 Historic Buildings and Ancient Monuments Act 1953 s 8(4) (amended by the Ancient Monuments and Archaeological Areas Act 1979 Sch 4 para 3).
14 See the Historic Buildings and Ancient Monuments Act 1953 s 8(5). As to the rule against perpetuities see PERPETUITIES AND ACCUMULATIONS vol 80 (2013) PARA 9.

1081. Power of the Historic Buildings and Monuments Commission for England to accept endowments. Where any instrument coming into operation after 1 October 1983[1] contains a provision purporting to be a gift[2] of property[3] to the Historic Buildings and Monuments Commission for England ('the Commission') upon trust to use the income of it, either for a limited time or in perpetuity, for or towards the upkeep of:

(1)   a building acquired or accepted by the Commission[4], or a building which the Commission proposes so to acquire or accept[5]; or

(2)   a building which at the coming into operation of the trust instrument is or will shortly be vested in or under the management or in the custody of the Commission, being a building which is situated in England[6] and which appears to the Commission to be one of outstanding historic or architectural interest[7]; or

(3)　　a building of which at that time the Commission is or will shortly be guardian under the Ancient Monuments and Archaeological Areas Act 1979[8], or for or towards the upkeep of any such building together with other property situated in England[9],

the Commission may accept the gift and, if it does so, and the provision does not constitute a charitable trust[10], the following provisions have effect[11].

The validity of the gift and of the trust so to use the income (the 'endowment trust') is deemed not to be, or ever to have been, affected by any rule of law or equity which would not have affected their validity if the trust had been charitable[12].

In relation to the property, of whatsoever nature, comprised in the gift and any property for the time being representing that property (the 'trust fund') the Commission during the continuance of the endowment trust has, without prejudice to any additional or larger powers conferred on it by the trust instrument, the like powers of management, disposition and investment as, in the case of land subject to a trust of land[13], are conferred by law on the trustees of land in relation to the land and to the proceeds of its sale[14].

If, while the endowment trust continues, an event happens such that immediately thereafter the Commission is neither entitled to any interest in the building to which the trust relates, nor has the building under its management or in its custody, nor is guardian of the building under the Ancient Monuments and Archaeological Areas Act 1979, and the endowment trust would otherwise not then be determined or be deemed to have failed, then, on the happening of that event, the endowment trust ceases and the trust fund devolves accordingly as on a failure of the trust[15].

If the trust instrument contains a provision whereby on the failure or determination of the endowment trust the trust fund purports to be given, or to be directed to be held, on charitable trusts, the validity of that gift or direction is deemed not to be, or ever to have been, affected by any rule of law or equity relating to perpetuities[16].

1　Ie the date of the establishment of the Historic Buildings and Monuments Commission for England ('the Commission'): see the National Heritage Act 1983 s 32; and the National Heritage Act 1983 (Commencement No 3) Order 1983, SI 1983/1437, art 2(a). As to the Commission see PARA 803.
2　As to the meaning of 'gift' see PARA 1075 note 13.
3　As to the meaning of 'property' see PARA 1073 note 6.
4　Ie under the Historic Buildings and Ancient Monuments Act 1953 s 5A (see PARA 1077).
5　Historic Buildings and Ancient Monuments Act 1953 s 8A(1)(a) (s 8A added by the National Heritage Act 1983 s 33, Sch 4 para 10).
6　As to the meaning of 'England' see PARA 804 note 2.
7　Historic Buildings and Ancient Monuments Act 1953 s 8A(1)(b) (as added: see note 5).
8　As to guardianship under the Ancient Monuments and Archaeological Areas Act 1979 see PARA 1032.
9　Historic Buildings and Ancient Monuments Act 1953 s 8A(1)(c) (as added: see note 5).
10　As to charitable trusts see CHARITIES vol 8 (2015) PARA 68 et seq.
11　Historic Buildings and Ancient Monuments Act 1953 s 8A(1) (as added: see note 5). In the exercise, with respect to any buildings or other land in a conservation area, of any functions under or by virtue of the Historic Buildings and Ancient Monuments Act 1953 Pt I (ss 1–9) special attention must be paid to the desirability of preserving or enhancing the character or appearance of that area: see the Planning (Listed Buildings and Conservation Areas) Act 1990 s 72(1), (2); and PLANNING vol 83 (2010) PARA 1320.
12　Historic Buildings and Ancient Monuments Act 1953 s 8A(2) (as added: see note 5).
13　As to the meanings of 'trust of land' and 'trustees of land' see PARA 1032 note 2.
14　See the Historic Buildings and Ancient Monuments Act 1953 s 8A(3) (as added (see note 5); and amended by the Trusts of Land and Appointment of Trustees Act 1996 s 25(1), Sch 3 para 9).
15　Historic Buildings and Ancient Monuments Act 1953 s 8A(4) (as added: see note 5).

16 Historic Buildings and Ancient Monuments Act 1953 s 8A(5) (as added: see note 5). As to the rule against perpetuities see PERPETUITIES AND ACCUMULATIONS vol 80 (2013) PARA 9.

(v) Listed Buildings

1082. Listed buildings. The Planning (Listed Buildings and Conservation Areas) Act 1990 provides for the compilation of lists of buildings of special architectural or historic interest[1] and institutes a regime for the control of works affecting listed buildings[2] and for the enforcement of the statutory provisions[3]. Provision is also made for the prevention of damage or deterioration to listed buildings[4]. The Act is covered in detail elsewhere in this work[5].

Conserving and enhancing the historic environment is an important component of the National Planning Policy Framework's[6] drive to achieve sustainable development in England[7] and the government has issued planning practice guidance on conserving and enhancing the historic environment, including listed buildings[8]. The designation of historic sites enables the planning system to protect them, through the complementary systems of listed building consent and conservation area control, coupled with controls over scheduled monument consent[9].

1 See the Planning (Listed Buildings and Conservation Areas) Act 1990 Pt I Ch I (ss 1–6).
2 See the Planning (Listed Buildings and Conservation Areas) Act 1990 Pt I Ch II (ss 7–26K).
3 See the Planning (Listed Buildings and Conservation Areas) Act 1990 Pt I Ch IV (ss 38–46).
4 See the Planning (Listed Buildings and Conservation Areas) Act 1990 Pt I Ch V (ss 47–59).
5 See PLANNING vol 83 (2010) PARA 1233 et seq.
6 The National Planning Policy Framework (March 2012) sets out the Government's planning policies for England and how they are expected to be applied. A copy of the National Planning Policy Framework (March 2012) is available on the Department for Communities and Local Government website which, at the date at which this volume states the law, can be found at www.communities.gov.uk. See also PLANNING vol 81 (2010) PARA 17. As to the position in Wales see PLANNING vol 81 (2010) PARAS 17–18.
7 See the *National Planning Policy Framework* (March 2012) ch 12. See also note 6.
8 See *Planning Practice Guidance: Conserving and enhancing the historic environment* (March 2014) which is available on the Department for Communities and Local Government website which, at the date at which this volume states the law, can be found at www.communities.gov.uk.
9 See *Principles of Selection for Listing Buildings* (March 2010), which sets out the general principles applied by the Secretary of State when deciding whether a building is of special architectural or historic interest and should be added to the list of buildings compiled under the Planning (Listed Buildings and Conservation Areas) Act 1990. A copy of *Principles of Selection for Listing Buildings* (March 2010) is available on the Department for Culture, Media and Sport website which, at the date at which this volume states the law, can be found at www.culture.gov.uk. As to the Secretary of State see PARA 802 note 2. As to conservation areas see PARA 1083. As to scheduled monument consent see PARA 1017.

(5) CONSERVATION AREAS

1083. Conservation areas. The Planning (Listed Buildings and Conservation Areas) Act 1990 places a duty on local planning authorities, including in relation to Greater London the Historic Buildings and Monuments Commission for England ('the Commission')[1], to designate as conservation areas those parts of their area which they determine are of special architectural or historic interest the character or appearance of which it is desirable to preserve or enhance[2]. Local planning authorities must formulate and publish proposals for the preservation and enhancement of their conservation areas[3], and various powers are given to them for the control of demolition in conservation areas[4] and the making of grants and loans for their preservation or enhancement[5]. The Act is covered in detail elsewhere in this work[6].

Conserving and enhancing the historic environment is an important component of the National Planning Policy Framework's[7] drive to achieve sustainable development in England[8] and the government has issued planning practice guidance on conserving and enhancing the historic environment, including conservation areas[9].

1   As to the Historic Buildings and Monuments Commission for England ('the Commission') see PARA 803.
2   See the Planning (Listed Buildings and Conservation Areas) Act 1990 ss 69–70.
3   See the Planning (Listed Buildings and Conservation Areas) Act 1990 s 71.
4   See the Planning (Listed Buildings and Conservation Areas) Act 1990 ss 74–76 (amended by the Planning Act 2008 Sch 2 paras 38, 41, Sch 10 paras 15, 21 ; the Enterprise and Regulatory Reform Act 2013 Sch 17 paras 7, 12, 13(a), (b); SI 2006/1281; and SI 2014/2773).
5   See the Planning (Listed Buildings and Conservation Areas) Act 1990 ss 77–80 (amended by the Local Government (Wales) Act 1994 Sch 6 para 25(9); the Environment Act 1995 Sch 10 para 33(3); and SI 2006/63).
6   See PLANNING vol 83 (2010) PARA 1318 et seq.
7   The National Planning Policy Framework (March 2012) sets out the Government's planning policies for England and how they are expected to be applied. A copy of the National Planning Policy Framework (March 2012) is available on the Department for Communities and Local Government website which, at the date at which this volume states the law, can be found at www.communities.gov.uk. See also PLANNING vol 81 (2010) PARA 17. As to the position in Wales see PLANNING vol 81 (2010) PARAS 17–18.
8   See the *National Planning Policy Framework* (March 2012) ch 12. See also note 7.
9   See also *Planning Practice Guidance: Conserving and enhancing the historic environment* (March 2014) which is available on the Department for Communities and Local Government website which, at the date at which this volume states the law, can be found at www.communities.gov.uk.

(6) HISTORIC GARDENS

1084. Endowment of gardens in England. Where any instrument coming into operation after 1 October 1983[1] contains a provision purporting to be a gift[2] of property[3] to the Historic Buildings and Monuments Commission for England ('the Commission') upon trust to use the income of it, either for a limited time or in perpetuity, for or towards the upkeep of a garden or other land acquired or accepted by the Commission under its statutory power[4], or a garden or other land which the Commission proposes so to acquire or accept, or for or towards the upkeep of any such garden or other land together with other property situated in England[5], the Commission may accept the gift and, if it does so, and the provision does not constitute a charitable trust[6], the following provisions have effect[7].

The validity of the gift and of the trust so to use the income (the 'endowment trust') is deemed not to be, or ever to have been, affected by any rule of law or equity which would not have affected their validity if the trust had been charitable[8].

In relation to the property, of whatsoever nature, comprised in the gift and any property for the time being representing that property (the 'trust fund') the Commission during the continuance of the endowment trust has, without prejudice to any additional or larger powers conferred on it by the trust instrument, the like powers of management, disposition and investment as, in the case of land subject to a trust of land[9], are conferred by law on the trustees of land in relation to the land and to the proceeds of its sale[10].

If, while the endowment trust continues, an event happens such that immediately thereafter the Commission is not entitled to any interest in the garden or other land to which the trust relates, and the endowment trust would not otherwise then be determined or be deemed to have failed, then, on the happening of that event, the endowment trust ceases and the trust fund devolves accordingly as on a failure of the trust[11].

If the trust instrument contains a provision whereby on the failure or determination of the endowment trust the trust fund purports to be given, or to be directed to be held, on charitable trusts, the validity of that gift or direction is deemed not to be, or ever to have been, affected by any rule of law or equity relating to perpetuities[12].

1   Ie the date of the establishment of the Historic Buildings and Monuments Commission for England ('the Commission'): see the National Heritage Act 1983 s 32; National Heritage Act 1983 (Commencement No 3) Order 1983, SI 1983/1437, art 2(a). As to the Commission see PARA 803.
2   As to the meaning of 'gift' see PARA 1075 note 13.
3   As to the meaning of 'property' see PARA 1073 note 6.
4   Ie under the Historic Buildings and Ancient Monuments Act 1953 s 5A(1)(d) (see PARA 1077).
5   As to the meaning of 'England' see PARA 804 note 2.
6   As to charitable trusts see CHARITIES vol 8 (2015) PARA 68 et seq.
7   Historic Buildings and Ancient Monuments Act 1953 s 8B(1) (s 8B added by the National Heritage Act 1983 s 33, Sch 4 para 10). In the exercise, with respect to any buildings or other land in a conservation area, of any functions under or by virtue of the Historic Buildings and Ancient Monuments Act 1953 Pt I (ss 1–9) special attention must be paid to the desirability of preserving or enhancing the character or appearance of that area: see the Planning (Listed Buildings and Conservation Areas) Act 1990 s 72(1), (2); and PLANNING vol 83 (2010) PARA 1320.
8   Historic Buildings and Ancient Monuments Act 1953 s 8B(2) (as added: see note 7).
9   As to the meanings of 'trust of land' and 'trustees of land' see PARA 1032 note 2.
10 Historic Buildings and Ancient Monuments Act 1953 s 8B(3) (as added (see note 7); and amended by the Trusts of Land and Appointment of Trustees Act 1996 s 25(1), Sch 3, para 9).
11 Historic Buildings and Ancient Monuments Act 1953 s 8B(4) (as added: see note 7).
12 Historic Buildings and Ancient Monuments Act 1953 s 8B(5) (as added: see note 7). As to the rule against perpetuities see PERPETUITIES AND ACCUMULATIONS vol 80 (2013) PARA 9.

1085. Register of gardens in England. Where the Historic Buildings and Monuments Commission for England[1] compiles a register of gardens and other land situated in England[2] and appearing to the Commission to be of special historic interest[3], it must, as soon as practicable after including in the register an entry relating to any garden or land, notify the following persons[4] of the inclusion and send to them a copy of the entry[5]:

(1)   the owner and, if the owner is not the occupier, the occupier of the garden or land[6];

(2)   any county planning authority[7], and any district planning authority, in whose area the garden or land, or any part of the garden or land, is situated[8]; and

(3)   the Secretary of State[9].

Conserving and enhancing the historic environment is an important component of the National Planning Policy Framework's[10] drive to achieve sustainable development in England[11] and the government has issued planning practice guidance on conserving and enhancing the historic environment, including parks and gardens[12].

1   As to the Historic Buildings and Monuments Commission for England ('the Commission') see PARA 803.
2   As to the meaning of 'England' see PARA 804 note 2.
3   Historic Buildings and Ancient Monuments Act 1953 s 8C(1) (s 8C added by the National Heritage Act 1983 s 33, Sch 4 para 10). In the exercise, with respect to any buildings or other land in a conservation area, of any functions under or by virtue of the Historic Buildings and Ancient

Monuments Act 1953 Pt I (ss 1–9) special attention must be paid to the desirability of preserving or enhancing the character or appearance of that area: see the Planning (Listed Buildings and Conservation Areas) Act 1990 s 72(1), (2); and PLANNING vol 83 (2010) PARA 1320. As to a register of gardens in Wales see PARA 1086.

4   As to the meaning of 'person' see PARA 803 note 17.
5   Historic Buildings and Ancient Monuments Act 1953 s 8C(2) (as added: see note 3).
6   Historic Buildings and Ancient Monuments Act 1953 s 8C(3)(a) (as added: see note 3).
7   As to planning authorities see PLANNING vol 81 (2010) PARA 43 et seq.
8   Historic Buildings and Ancient Monuments Act 1953 s 8C(3)(b) (as added: see note 3).
9   Historic Buildings and Ancient Monuments Act 1953 s 8C(3)(c) (as added: see note 3). As to the Secretary of State see PARA 802 note 2.
10 The National Planning Policy Framework (March 2012) sets out the Government's planning policies for England and how they are expected to be applied. A copy of the National Planning Policy Framework (March 2012) is available on the Department for Communities and Local Government website which, at the date at which this volume states the law, can be found at www.communities.gov.uk. See also PLANNING vol 81 (2010) PARA 17. As to the position in Wales see PLANNING vol 81 (2010) PARAS 17–18.
11 See the *National Planning Policy Framework* (March 2012) ch 12. See also note 10.
12 See *Planning Practice Guidance: Conserving and enhancing the historic environment* (March 2014) which is available on the Department for Communities and Local Government website which, at the date at which this volume states the law, can be found at www.communities.gov.uk.

1086. Non-statutory register of gardens etc in Wales. A non-statutory register of landscapes, parks and gardens of special historic interest in Wales has been prepared by Cadw[1]. The register includes parks and gardens which are considered to be of national importance and has been compiled in order to aid the informed conservation of historic parks and gardens by owners, local planning authorities, developers, statutory bodies and all concerned with them[2].

Planning policy issued by the Welsh Government indicates that local planning authorities are to take the register into account in preparing their development policies[3].

1   As to Cadw see PARA 810.
2   See the Cadw website which, at the date at which this volume states the law, can be found at www.cadw.wales.gov.uk.
3   See *Planning Policy Wales* (March 2002) Ch 6.4.10. As to the Welsh Government see CONSTITUTIONAL AND ADMINISTRATIVE LAW vol 20 (2014) PARA 373 et seq. As to local development policies see PLANNING vol 81 (2010) PARA 87.

(7) HISTORIC BATTLEFIELDS

1087. Register of Historic Battlefields. The Register of Historic Battlefields was established by the Historic Buildings and Monuments Commission for England ('the Commission')[1] to encourage local authorities, owners and others to understand the importance of these sites. Designation on the register introduces no additional statutory controls, but its purpose is to offer protection through the planning system. Another aim is to promote a better understanding of the significance of such battlefields and public enjoyment of them[2].

Conserving and enhancing the historic environment is an important component of the National Planning Policy Framework's[3] drive to achieve sustainable development in England[4] and the government has issued planning practice guidance on conserving and enhancing the historic environment, including battlefields[5].

1   As to the Historic Buildings and Monuments Commission for England ('the Commission') see PARA 803.
2   See the Historic England website which, at the date at which this volume states the law, can be found at www.historicengland.org.uk.

3 The National Planning Policy Framework (March 2012) sets out the Government's planning policies for England and how they are expected to be applied. A copy of the National Planning Policy Framework (March 2012) is available on the Department for Communities and Local Government website which, at the date at which this volume states the law, can be found at www.communities.gov.uk. See also PLANNING vol 81 (2010) PARA 17. As to the position in Wales see PLANNING vol 81 (2010) PARAS 17–18.

4 See the *National Planning Policy Framework* (March 2012) ch 12. See also note 3.

5 See *Planning Practice Guidance: Conserving and enhancing the historic environment* (March 2014) which is available on the Department for Communities and Local Government website which, at the date at which this volume states the law, can be found at www.communities.gov.uk.

4. MOVEABLE CULTURAL HERITAGE

(1) TREASURE

1088. Application of the Treasure Act 1996. The common law doctrine of treasure trove, which provided that any gold or silver in coin, plate or bullion found deliberately concealed in a house, or in the earth or other private place, with the intention of recovery, the owner thereof being unknown, belonged to Her Majesty or a grantee having the franchise of treasure trove[1], has been replaced by a new regime under the Treasure Act 1996[2].

Any treasure[3] found on and after 24 September 1997[4], whatever the nature of the place where the treasure was found[5] and whatever the circumstances in which it was left, including being lost or being left with no intention of recovery[6], vests, subject to prior interests[7] and rights, in the franchisee[8], if there is one[9], or otherwise in the Crown[10]. Treasure so vesting in the Crown is to be treated[11] as part of the hereditary revenues of the Crown[12]. Any such treasure may be transferred, or otherwise disposed of, in accordance with directions given by the Secretary of State[13]; and the Crown's title to any such treasure may be disclaimed at any time by the Secretary of State[14].

At the date at which this volume states the law, the coroner retains jurisdiction to hold inquests into treasure[15]. As from a day to be appointed[16], jurisdiction to conduct investigations concerning items of treasure and to hold inquests in respect thereof is vested in the Coroner for Treasure[17].

If treasure has vested in the Crown[18] and is to be transferred to a museum[19], the Secretary of State must determine whether a reward is to be paid by the museum before the transfer[20]. If he determines that a reward is to be paid, he must also determine, in whatever way he thinks fit, the treasure's market value[21], the amount of the reward[22], to whom the reward is to be payable[23] and, if it is to be payable to more than one person, how much each is to receive[24].

Cases of treasure and potential treasure should be dealt with as expeditiously as possible[25].

1   See Chitty's Law of the Prerogatives of the Crown 152, cited with approval in *A-G v Moore* [1893] 1 Ch 676 at 683 per Stirling J and in *A-G v Trustees of British Museum* [1903] 2 Ch 598 at 608 per Farwell J; 3 Co Inst 132; *A-G of the Duchy of Lancaster v GE Overton (Farms) Ltd* [1982] Ch 277, [1982] 1 All ER 524, CA.

2   For the purposes of the Coroners and Justice Act 2009, 'treasure trove' does not include anything found on or after 24 September 1997: s 48(1). See also note 4.

3   As to the meaning of 'treasure' see PARA 1090. As to treasure generally see CROWN AND CROWN PROCEEDINGS vol 29 (2014) PARA 287.

4   24 September 1997 is the date on which the Treasure Act 1996, other than s 11, came into force: see the Treasure Act 1996 (Commencement No 2) Order 1997, SI 1997/1977, art 2. The Treasure Act 1996 s 11 (see PARA 1089) came into force on 13 March 1997: see the Treasure Act 1996 (Commencement No 1) Order 1997, SI 1997/760, art 2.

5   See the Treasure Act 1996 s 4(4)(a).

6   See the Treasure Act 1996 s 4(4)(b).

7   Prior interests and rights are any which, or which derive from any which, were held when the treasure was left where it was found (Treasure Act 1996 s 4(2)(a)) or, if the treasure had been moved before being found, were held when it was left where it was before being moved: (s 4(2)(b)).

8   The 'franchisee' for any treasure is the person who (1) was, immediately before 24 September 1997; or (2) apart from the Treasure Act 1996, as successor in title, would have been, the franchisee of the Crown in right of treasure trove for the place where the treasure was found: s 5(1). It is as franchisees in right of treasure trove that Her Majesty and the Duke of Cornwall are to be treated as having enjoyed the rights to treasure trove which belonged respectively to the Duchy of Lancaster and the Duchy of Cornwall immediately before 24 September 1997: s 5(2). As to franchisees see the *Treasure Act 1996 Code of Practice (2nd Revision) (England and Wales)*

Pt D (paras 19–22). As to the Code of Practice generally and its status see PARA 1089. As to the meaning of 'person' see PARA 803 note 17. As to the Duchy of Cornwall see CROWN AND CROWN PROCEEDINGS vol 29 (2014) PARA 232 et seq. As to the Duchy of Lancaster see CROWN AND CROWN PROCEEDINGS vol 29 (2014) PARA 214 et seq.

9　Treasure Act 1996 s 4(1)(a). If the treasure would have been treasure trove if found before 24 September 1997, neither the Crown nor any franchisee has any interest in it or right over it except in accordance with the Treasure Act 1996: s 4(3).

10　Treasure Act 1996 s 4(1)(b). See also note 9.

11　Ie in accordance with the Civil List Act 1952 s 1 (surrender of hereditary revenues to the Exchequer): see CONSTITUTIONAL AND ADMINISTRATIVE LAW vol 20 (2014) PARA 477; CROWN AND CROWN PROCEEDINGS vol 29 (2014) PARA 120.

12　Treasure Act 1996 s 6(1).

13　Treasure Act 1996 s 6(2). As to the Secretary of State see PARA 802 note 2.

14　Treasure Act 1996 s 6(3). If the Crown's title is disclaimed, the treasure is deemed not to have vested in the Crown under the Treasure Act 1996 (s 6(4)(a)) and, without prejudice to the interests or rights of others, may be delivered to any person in accordance with the Code of Practice published under s 11 (see PARA 1089) (s 6(4)(b)). As to the Secretary of State's power to disclaim objects see further the *Treasure Act 1996 Code of Practice (2nd Revision) (England and Wales)* Pt F (paras 48–52). As to disclaimer see also the Coroners and Justice Act 2009 s 29; and PARA 1092.

15　See PARAS 1091–1093.

16　The Coroners and Justice Act 2009 ss 25–29, Sch 4, come into force on a day or days to be appointed: see s 182(4)(a), (5). At the date at which this volume states the law no such day or days had been appointed.

17　See the Coroners and Justice Act 2009 ss 26–29; and PARA 1092. As from a day to be appointed the following provisions have effect. The Lord Chancellor may appoint a person as the Coroner for Treasure: s 25, Sch 4 para 1 (not yet in force). As to qualification for such appointment and the terms thereof see Sch 4 paras 2–6 (not yet in force). The Chief Coroner may designate one or more assistant coroners to act as Assistant Coroners for Treasure (see Sch 4 paras 7–10 (not yet in force)) who may perform any functions of the Coroner for Treasure during a period when the Coroner for Treasure is absent or unavailable, during a vacancy in the office of Coroner for Treasure, or at any other time with the consent of the Coroner for Treasure (Sch 4 para 11(1) (not yet in force)). Accordingly a reference to the Coroner for Treasure is to be read, where appropriate, as including an Assistant Coroner for Treasure: Sch 4 para 11(2) (not yet in force). The Lord Chancellor may appoint staff to assist the Coroner for Treasure and any Assistant Coroners for Treasure in the performance of their functions: see Sch 4 para 12 (not yet in force). At the date at which this volume states the law no such day or days had been appointed for the coming into force of Sch 4 paras 1–12. The Chief Coroner may, with the agreement of the Lord Chancellor, make regulations about the training of the Coroner for Treasure and Assistant Coroners for Treasure: see s 37; and CORONERS vol 24 (2010) PARA 33. The Coroner for Treasure is disqualified for membership of the House of Commons: see the House of Commons Disqualification Act 1975 s 1(1)(f), Sch 1 Pt III (amended by the Coroners and Justice Act 2009 Sch 21 para 26); and PARLIAMENT vol 78 (2010) PARA 908. As to the Lord Chancellor see CONSTITUTIONAL AND ADMINISTRATIVE LAW vol 20 (2014) PARA 256 et seq. As to the Chief Coroner and the regulation of coroners generally see CORONERS vol 24 (2010) PARAS 8, 58 et seq.

18　Treasure Act 1996 s 10(1)(a). The vesting referred to is that under s 4 (see the text to notes 3–10).

19　Treasure Act 1996 s 10(1)(b).

20　Treasure Act 1996 s 10(2).

21　Treasure Act 1996 s 10(3)(a).

22　Treasure Act 1996 s 10(3)(b).

23　Treasure Act 1996 s 10(3)(c).

24　Treasure Act 1996 s 10(3)(d). The total reward must not exceed the treasure's market value: s 10(4). The reward may be payable to (1) the finder or any other person involved in the find (s 10(5)(a)); (2) the occupier of the land at the time of the find (s 10(5)(b)); or (3) any person who had an interest in the land at that time or has had such an interest at any time since then (s 10(5)(c)); or (4) as from a day to be appointed, any person who gave notice under s 8A (see PARA 1091) in respect of the treasure (s 10(5)(d) (prospectively added by the Coroners and Justice Act 2009 s 30(2))). At the date at which this volume states the law no day had been appointed for the coming into force of the Treasure Act 1996 s 10(5)(d). As to valuation of treasure see the *Treasure Act 1996 Code of Practice (2nd Revision) (England and Wales)* Pt I (paras 65–70); and as to rewards see Pt J (paras 71–85).

25　See the *Treasure Act 1996 Code of Practice (2nd Revision) (England and Wales)* Pt L (paras 87–88).

1089. Code of practice relating to treasure. The Secretary of State[1] must prepare a code of practice relating to treasure[2], keep the code under review[3], and revise it when appropriate[4]. If the Secretary of State considers that different provision should be made for England and Wales and Northern Ireland, or that different provision should otherwise be made for treasure found in different areas, he may prepare two or more separate codes[5].

The code must in particular set out the principles and practice to be followed by the Secretary of State when considering to whom treasure should be offered[6], when making a determination as to the payment of rewards[7], and where the Crown's title to treasure is disclaimed[8]. The code may include guidance for those who search for or find treasure[9], and for museums and others who exercise functions in relation to treasure[10]. Before preparing the code or revising it, the Secretary of State must consult such persons[11] appearing to him to be interested as he thinks appropriate[12]. A copy of the code and of any proposed revision of the code must be laid before Parliament[13]; and neither the code nor any revision comes into force until approved by a resolution of each House of Parliament[14].

The Secretary of State must publish the code in whatever way he considers appropriate for bringing it to the attention of those interested[15]. The code is intended to provide guidance for all those concerned with treasure[16].

As from a day to be appointed the following provisions also have effect[17]. The code of practice may make provision to do with objects in respect of which notice of disclaimer[18] is given[19]. No civil liability on the part of the Coroner for Treasure[20] arises where he or she delivers an object, or takes any other action, in accordance with the code of practice[21].

1   As to the Secretary of State see PARA 802 note 2.
2   Treasure Act 1996 s 11(1)(a). As to the meaning of 'treasure' see PARA 1090.
3   Treasure Act 1996 s 11(1)(b).
4   Treasure Act 1996 s 11(1)(c). In pursuance of this requirement the Secretary of State prepared and published the Treasure Act 1996: Code of Practice (England and Wales) in July 1997. This was revised in 2002 and 2007 and is now known as the *Treasure Act 1996 Code of Practice (2nd Revision) (England and Wales)*. Further reviews of the code may take place, at the discretion of the Secretary of State, five years after the publication of the revised code of practice: see the *Treasure Act 1996 Code of Practice (2nd Revision) (England and Wales)* para 89. A separate code of practice has been prepared for Northern Ireland.
      The code contains the following parts and appendices: (A) Summary (paras 1–3); (B) Commencement of the Act and Treasure (Designation) Order 2002 (para 4); (C) Definition of treasure (paras 5–18); (D) The ownership of treasure; franchisees (paras 19–22); (E) Guidance for finders and others concerned with treasure (paras 23–47); (F) Secretary of State's power to disclaim objects (paras 48–52); (G) Procedure when a find has been reported to the coroner; treasure inquests (paras 53–62); (H) Acquisition of treasure (paras 63–64); (I) Valuation of treasure (paras 65–70); (J) Rewards (paras 71–85); (K) Annual Report (para 86); (L) Speed of handling cases (paras 87–88); (M) Codes of Practice (para 89); Appendix 1: The Treasure Act 1996; The Treasure (Designation) Order 2002; Appendix 2: Sources of further advice; Appendix 3: Coins commonly found in England and Wales that contain less than 10% of gold or silver; Appendix 4: The care of finds; Appendix 5: Treasure Receipt Form; Appendix 6: National Council for Metal Detecting Code of Conduct; Appendix 7: Treasure Act Flow Chart. As to restrictions on the use of metal detectors see PARA 1060.
5   See the Treasure Act 1996 s 11(8). As to the meaning of 'England' see PARA 804 note 2. As to the meaning of 'Wales' see PARA 802 note 4.
6   Treasure Act 1996 s 11(2)(a).
7   Treasure Act 1996 s 11(2)(b). Such a determination is one made under s 10 (see PARA 1088).
8   Treasure Act 1996 s 11(2)(c). As to disclaimer of the Crown's title see PARA 1088.
9   Treasure Act 1996 s 11(3)(a).
10 Treasure Act 1996 s 11(3)(b).
11 As to the meaning of 'person' see PARA 803 note 17.
12 Treasure Act 1996 s 11(4).

13 Treasure Act 1996 s 11(5). As to the laying of documents before Parliament see STATUTES AND LEGISLATIVE PROCESS vol 96 (2012) PARA 1052.

14 Treasure Act 1996 s 11(6).

15 Treasure Act 1996 s 11(7). A copy of the code is available on the Department for Culture, Media and Sport website which, at the date at which this volume states the law, can be found at www.culture.gov.uk.

16 See the *Treasure Act 1996 Code of Practice (2nd Revision) (England and Wales)* Introduction. However, questions of whether or not any object constitutes treasure and how a coroner should conduct an inquiry into treasure are for the coroner to decide on the facts and circumstances of each case; and nothing in the code obviates the need for a finder to give independent consideration as to whether something he has found might constitute treasure: see the *Treasure Act 1996 Code of Practice (2nd Revision) (England and Wales)* Introduction. As to the jurisdiction of coroners see PARA 1092.

17 The Coroners and Justice Act 2009 s 31 comes into force on a day to be appointed: see s 182(4)(a). At the date at which this volume states the law no such day had been appointed.

18 Ie notice under the Coroners and Justice Act 2009 s 29(1) or (2) (see PARA 1092).

19 See the Coroners and Justice Act 2009 s 31(1) (not yet in force).

20 As to the Coroner for Treasure see PARA 1088 note 17.

21 See the Coroners and Justice Act 2009 s 31(2) (not yet in force).

1090. Meaning of 'treasure'. 'Treasure' is[1]:

(1) any object at least 300 years old[2] when found which:

    (a) is not a coin[3] but has metallic content of which at least 10 per cent by weight[4] is precious metal[5];

    (b) when found, is one of at least two coins in the same find[6] which are at least 300 years old at that time and have that percentage of precious metal[7]; or

    (c) when found, is one of at least ten coins in the same find which are at least 300 years old at that time[8];

(2) any object at least 200 years old when found which belongs to a designated class[9];

(3) any object which would have been treasure trove if found before 24 September 1997[10];

(4) any object which, when found, is part of the same find as:

    (a) an object within head (1), (2) or (3) above found at the same time or earlier[11]; or

    (b) an object found earlier which would be within head (1) or (2) above if it had been found at the same time[12].

Treasure does not include objects which: (i) are unworked natural objects[13]; or (ii) are minerals as extracted from a natural deposit[14]; or (iii) belong to a designated class[15]. Nor is an object treasure if it is wreck[16].

For the purposes of the Coroners and Justice Act 2009, 'treasure' means anything that is treasure for the purposes of the above definition (and accordingly does not include anything found before 24 September 1997)[17].

1 As to the meaning of 'treasure' see further the *Treasure Act 1996 Code of Practice (2nd Revision) (England and Wales)* Pt C (paras 5–18). See also Pt H (paras 63–64) as to the acquisition of treasure. As to the code of practice see PARA 1089.

2 An object which can reasonably be taken to be at least a particular age is to be presumed to have been at least that age, unless shown not to be: Treasure Act 1996 s 3(1), (6).

3 'Coin' includes any metal token which was, or can reasonably be assumed to have been, used or intended for use as or instead of money: Treasure Act 1996 s 3(1), (2).

4 The figure of 10% was not chosen arbitrarily but was chosen because, if an alloy has more than 10% gold or silver, the gold or silver's presence is not accidental; where objects have a lesser precious metal content, it is possible that the gold or silver was not deliberately added to the alloy. The requirement of 10% also excludes from the operation of the Treasure Act 1996 objects which are plated with gold or silver: see HC Official Report SC F (Treasure Bill), 17 April 1996, cols 10,

11. As to the coins commonly found in England and Wales which contain less than 10% of gold or silver see the *Treasure Act 1996 Code of Practice (2nd Revision) (England and Wales)* Appendix 3.

5 Treasure Act 1996 s 1(1)(a)(i). 'Precious metal' means gold or silver: s 3(1), (3).

6 When an object is found, it is part of the same find as another object if: (1) they are found together; (2) the other object was found earlier in the same place where they had been left together; (3) the other object was found earlier in a different place, but they had been left together and had become separated before being found: Treasure Act 1996 s 3(1), (4). If the circumstances in which objects are found can reasonably be taken to indicate that they were together at some time before being found, the objects are to be presumed to have been left together, unless shown not to have been: s 3(1), (5).

7 Treasure Act 1996 s 1(1)(a)(ii).

8 Treasure Act 1996 s 1(1)(a)(iii).

9 Treasure Act 1996 s 1(1)(b). A designated class is one designated under s 2(1): see s 1(1)(b). The Secretary of State may by order, for this purpose, designate any class of object which he considers to be of outstanding historical, archaeological or cultural importance: s 2(1). As to the Secretary of State see PARA 802 note 2. The following classes of objects are designated pursuant to s 2(1): (1) any object, other than a coin, any part of which is base metal, which, when found is one of at least two base metal objects in the same find which are of prehistoric date (Treasure (Designation) Order 2002, SI 2002/2666, art 3(a)); (2) any object, other than a coin, which is of prehistoric date, and any part of which is gold or silver (art 3(b)). 'Base metal' means any metal other than gold or silver; and 'of prehistoric date' means dating from the Iron Age or any earlier period: art 2.

The Treasure Act 1996 s 2 supplements s 1, which sets out the categories of object which can qualify as treasure for the purposes of the Treasure Act 1996, empowering the Secretary of State by order to designate additional classes of object as treasure, and to remove classes of object from the definition of treasure. Section 2 is intended to introduce an element of flexibility in the new regime relating to finds of treasure. The definition of treasure contained in s 1 operates to exclude objects such as hoards of Bronze Age tools, weapons etc, not because such objects are not of archaeological importance, but because of the difficulty of drafting a definition of treasure which would include them but that would exclude everyday finds such as iron nails, pottery shards and buttons which are of limited archaeological interest. Accordingly s 2 allows adjustments to be made to the definition following a review of the operation of the new system, without having to introduce primary legislation: see HC Official Report SC F (Treasure Bill), 17 April 1996, cols 14, 15.

10 Treasure Act 1996 s 1(1)(c). 24 September 1997 was the date on which the Treasure Act 1996 s 4 (ownership of treasure which is found: see PARA 1088) came into force: see s 1(1)(c); and the Treasure Act 1996 (Commencement No 2) Order 1997, SI 1997/1977, art 2. As to the common law doctrine of treasure trove see PARA 1088.

11 Treasure Act 1996 s 1(1)(d)(i).

12 Treasure Act 1996 s 1(1)(d)(ii).

13 Treasure Act 1996 s 1(2)(a).

14 Treasure Act 1996 s 1(2)(b).

15 Treasure Act 1996 s 1(2). A designated class is one designated under s 2(2): see s 1(2). The Secretary of State may by order, for this purpose, designate any class of object which, apart from the order, would be treasure: s 2(2). At the date at which this volume states the law, no such order had been made. The Government has, however, given a commitment to the Church of England that it will bring forward an order under s 2 exempting objects found in association with human burials in a consecrated place and objects (except for treasure trove) covered by the Church of England's own legal systems of controls: see the *Treasure Act 1996 Code of Practice (2nd Revision) (England and Wales)* para 18. As to the Church of England see ECCLESIASTICAL LAW vol 34 (2011) PARA 50 et seq.

16 Treasure Act 1996 s 3(1), (7). 'Wreck' includes jetsam, flotsam, lagan and derelict found in or on the shores of the sea or any tidal water: see the Merchant Shipping Act 1995 Pt IX s 255(1) (definition applied by the Treasure Act 1996 s 3(1), (7)); and SHIPPING AND MARITIME LAW vol 94 (2008) PARA 987. As to objects found on the foreshore see the *Treasure Act 1996 Code of Practice (2nd Revision) (England and Wales)* para 17.

17 See the Coroners and Justice Act 2009 s 48(1). 24 September 1997 is the day on which the Treasure Act 1996 came into force: see PARA 1088 note 4.

1091. Duty of finder to notify coroner. A person[1] who finds an object which he believes or has reasonable grounds for believing is treasure[2] must notify the coroner for the district[3] in which the object was found before the end of the notice period[4], that period being 14 days beginning with the day after the find[5] or, if later, the day on which the finder first believes or has reason to believe the object is treasure[6]. Any person who fails to comply with this provision is guilty of an offence[7]. In proceedings for such an offence it is a defence for the accused to show that he had, and has continued to have, a reasonable excuse[8] for failing to notify the coroner[9].

As from a day to be appointed the following provisions have effect[10].

A person who acquires property in an object[11], and believes or has reasonable grounds for believing that the object is treasure[12] and that notification[13] in respect of the object has not been given[14], must notify the Coroner for Treasure[15] before the end of the notice period[16]. Any person who fails to comply with this provision is guilty of an offence if notification[17] in respect of the object has not been given[18], and there has been no investigation[19] in relation to the object[20]. In proceedings for such an offence, it is a defence for the defendant to show that he had, and has continued to have, a reasonable excuse for failing to notify the Coroner for Treasure[21].

Proceedings for an offence under the provisions set out above[22] may be brought within the period of six months[23] from the date on which evidence sufficient in the opinion of the prosecutor to warrant the proceedings came to the prosecutor's knowledge; but no such proceedings may be brought by virtue of this provision more than three years after the commission of the offence[24].

1   As to the meaning of 'person' see PARA 803 note 17.
2   As to the meaning of 'treasure' see PARA 1090.
3   As from a day to be appointed, the notification must be given to the Coroner for Treasure instead of to the coroner for the district in which the object was found: see the Treasure Act 1996 s 8(1) (prospectively amended by the Coroners and Justice Act 2009 Sch 21 paras 37, 39(1), (2)). At the date at which this volume states the law no such day had been appointed.
     If the office of coroner for a district is vacant, the person acting as coroner for that district is the coroner for these purposes: Treasure Act 1996 s 8(5). As from a day to be appointed, if the office of Coroner for Treasure is vacant, notification under s 8(1) must be given to an Assistant Coroner for Treasure: s 8(5) (prospectively substituted by the Coroners and Justice Act 2009 Sch 21 paras 37, 39(1), (4)). At the date at which this volume states the law no such day had been appointed. As to the Coroner for Treasure and Assistant Coroners for Treasure see PARA 1088 note 17.
4   Treasure Act 1996 s 8(1). As from a day to be appointed s 8 has effect subject to s 8B: s 8(6) (prospectively added by the Coroners and Justice Act 2009 Sch 21 paras 37, 39(1), (4)). As from a day to be appointed, the Treasure Act 1996 s 8B provides as follows. A requirement under the Treasure Act 1996 s 8 or 8A (see the text to notes 10–21) to give a notification to the Coroner for Treasure (or an Assistant Coroner for Treasure) may, if the relevant place falls within an area for which there is a designated officer, be complied with by giving the notification to that officer: s 8B(1) (s 8B added by the Coroners and Justice Act 2009 Sch 21 paras 37, 40). A designated officer must notify the Coroner for Treasure of all such notifications (see the Treasure Act 1996 s 8B(2) (as so added)), or if the office of Coroner for Treasure is vacant, notify an Assistant Coroner for Treasure (see s 8B(3) (as so added)). 'Designated officer' means an officer designated by an order made by statutory instrument by the Secretary of State: s 8B(4) (as so added). 'Relevant place' means: (1) in relation to a requirement under s 8, the place where the object in question was found; or (2) in relation to a requirement under s 8A, the place where the treasure in question is located: s 8B(4) (as so added). At the date at which this volume states the law no day had been appointed for the coming into force of s 8B and at the date at which this volume states the law no orders have been made under s 8B(4). As to the Secretary of State see PARA 802 note 2.
5   Treasure Act 1996 s 8(2)(a).
6   Treasure Act 1996 s 8(2)(b). For guidance for finders and others concerned with treasure see the *Treasure Act 1996 Code of Practice (2nd Revision) (England and Wales)* Pt E (paras 23–47). As to the code of practice see PARA 1089. The common law offence of concealment of treasure trove (see eg *R v Toole* (1867) 11 Cox CC 75; *R v Thomas and Willett* (1863) 12 WR 108) was abolished by the Theft Act 1968 s 32(1)(a). As to sentencing guidelines for offences of theft involving historic objects or loss of the nation's heritage see PARA 1046 note 5.

7 See the Treasure Act 1996 s 8(3). A person guilty of such an offence is liable on summary conviction to (1) imprisonment for a term not exceeding three months (s 8(3)(a)); or (2) to a fine not exceeding level 5 on the standard scale (s 8(3)(b)); or (3) to both (s 8(3)(c)). As from a day to be appointed, s 8(3)(a) is amended so as to replace the duration of the term of imprisonment under head (1) above with one not exceeding 51 weeks: see s 8(3)(a) (prospectively amended by the Criminal Justice Act 2003 s 280(2), (3), Sch 26 para 48). At the date at which this volume states the law, no such day had been appointed. As to the standard scale and magistrates' powers to levy unlimited fines see SENTENCING vol 92 (2015) PARA 176.

8 For example, in considering a case, the court may take into account whether the finder could have been expected to know that his find was treasure: see 277 HC Official Report (6th series) cols 579, 587–588. As to the standard of proof on the accused see CRIMINAL PROCEDURE vol 28 (2015) PARAS 449–451.

9 Treasure Act 1996 s 8(4). As from a day to be appointed, s 8(4) is amended so as to substitute for the word 'coroner' the words 'Coroner for Treasure': see s 8(4) (prospectively amended by the Coroners and Justice Act 2009 Sch 21 paras 37, 39(1), (3)). At the date at which this volume states the law no such day had been appointed.

10 On a day or days to be appointed, the Treasure Act 1996 ss 8A, 8C (both added by the Coroners and Justice Act 2009 s 30(1), Sch 21 paras 37, 40) and the Coroners and Justice Act 2009 s 30, Sch 21 para 40 come into force: see s 182(4)(a), (e). At the date at which this volume states the law no such day or days had been appointed.

11 Treasure Act 1996 s 8A(1)(a) (not yet in force). In determining for these purposes whether a person has acquired property in an object, the Treasure Act 1996 s 4 (see PARA 1088) is to be disregarded: s 8A(7) (not yet in force).

12 Treasure Act 1996 s 8A(1)(b)(i) (not yet in force).

13 Ie under the Treasure Act 1996 s 8(1) (see the text to notes 1–4) or s 8A(1).

14 Treasure Act 1996 s 8A(1)(b)(ii) (not yet in force).

15 If the office of Coroner for Treasure is vacant, notification must be given to an Assistant Coroner for Treasure: s 8A(6) (not yet in force).

16 Treasure Act 1996 s 8A(1) (not yet in force). The notice period is 14 days beginning with (1) the day after the person acquires property in the object (s 8A(2)(a) (not yet in force)); or (2) if later, the day on which the person first believes or has reason to believe that the object is treasure, and that notification in respect of the object has not been given under s 8(1) (see the text to notes 1–4) or s 8A(1) (s 8A(2)(b) (not yet in force)). For the purposes of an investigation in relation to an object in respect of which notification has been given under s 8A(1), the object is to be presumed, in the absence of evidence to the contrary, to have been found in England and Wales after 24 September 1997 (ie the commencement of s 4 (see PARA 1088)): see s 8A(8) (not yet in force). Section 8A has effect subject to s 8B (see note 4): s 8A(9) (not yet in force). As to the meaning of 'England' see PARA 804 note 2. As to the meaning of 'Wales' see PARA 802 note 4.

17 Ie under the Treasure Act 1996 s 8(1) (see the text to notes 1–4) or s 8A(1) (see the text to notes 11–16).

18 Treasure Act 1996 s 8A(3)(a) (not yet in force).

19 'Investigation' means an investigation under the Coroners and Justice Act 2009 s 26 (see PARA 1092): Treasure Act 1996 s 8A(10) (not yet in force).

20 Treasure Act 1996 s 8A(3)(b) (not yet in force). Any person guilty of such an offence is liable, on summary conviction, to (1) imprisonment for a term not exceeding 51 weeks (s 8A(4)(a) (not yet in force)); (2) a fine of an amount not exceeding level 5 on the standard scale (s 8A(4)(b) (not yet in force)); or (3) both (s 8A(4)(c) (not yet in force)). In relation to such an offence committed before the commencement of the Criminal Justice Act 2003 s 280(2) (see note 7), the reference in head (1) above to 51 weeks is to be read as a reference to three months: Coroners and Justice Act 2009 s 30(3) (not yet in force). At the date at which this volume states the law the Criminal Justice Act 2003 s 280(2) is not in force.

21 Treasure Act 1996 s 8A(5) (not yet in force).

22 Ie an offence under the Treasure Act 1996 s 8 or 8A (see the text to notes 7–9, 17–21).

23 As to the meaning of 'month' see PARA 803 note 12.

24 Treasure Act 1996 s 8C(1) (not yet in force). For these purposes:
    (1) a certificate signed by or on behalf of the prosecutor and stating the date on which the evidence came to the prosecutor's knowledge is conclusive evidence to that effect (s 8C(2)(a) (not yet in force)); and
    (2) a certificate to that effect and purporting to be so signed is deemed to be so signed unless the contrary is proved (s 8C(2)(b) (not yet in force)).

1092. Jurisdiction of coroners in respect of treasure. Until a day to be appointed the following provisions have effect[1].

A coroner has jurisdiction to inquire into any treasure which is found in his district[2] and to inquire who were, or are suspected of being, the finders[3], such jurisdiction being exercisable in relation to anything which is treasure[4] for the purposes of the Treasure Act 1996[5]. The jurisdiction is not exercisable for the purposes of the law relating to treasure trove in relation to anything found after 24 September 1997[6]. An inquest held by virtue of these provisions is to be held without a jury unless the coroner orders otherwise[7].

As from a day to be appointed the following provisions have effect[8].

The Coroner for Treasure[9] must conduct an investigation concerning an object in respect of which notification[10] is given[11]; and may conduct an investigation concerning an object in respect of which notification has not been given[12] if he or she has reason to suspect that the object is treasure[13]. The Coroner for Treasure may also conduct an investigation concerning an object if he or she has reason to suspect that the object is treasure trove[14]. The purpose of an investigation is to ascertain:

(1)   whether or not the object in question is treasure or treasure trove[15];
(2)   if it is treasure or treasure trove, who found it, where it was found and when it was found[16].

The Lord Chancellor may make regulations ('treasure regulations') for regulating the practice and procedure at or in connection with investigations concerning objects that are or may be treasure or treasure trove (other than the practice and procedure at or in connection with inquests concerning such objects)[17].

The Coroner for Treasure may, as part of an investigation, hold an inquest (known as a 'treasure inquest') concerning the object in question[18]. A treasure inquest must be held without a jury, unless the Coroner for Treasure thinks there is sufficient reason for it to be held with a jury[19].

Where the Coroner for Treasure is conducting, or proposes to conduct, an investigation concerning:

(a)   an object that would vest in the Crown[20] or in the franchisee[21] under the Treasure Act 1996 if the object was in fact treasure and there were no prior interests or rights[22]; or
(b)   an object that would belong to the Crown or the franchisee under the law relating to treasure trove if the object was in fact treasure trove[23],

the Secretary of State[24] may give notice[25] to the Coroner for Treasure disclaiming, on behalf of the Crown, any title that the Crown may have to the object[26], or (as the case may be) the franchisee may give notice to the Coroner for Treasure disclaiming any title that the franchisee may have to the object[27]. Any such notice may be given only before the making of a determination[28] by the Coroner for Treasure[29]. Where such a notice is given:

(i)   the object is to be treated as not vesting in or belonging to the Crown, or (as the case may be) the franchisee, under the Treasure Act 1996, or the law relating to treasure trove[30];
(ii)   the Coroner for Treasure may not conduct an investigation concerning the object or, if an investigation has already begun, may not continue with it[31];
(iii)   without prejudice to the interests or rights of others, the object may be delivered to a person in accordance with a code of practice published under the Treasure Act 1996[32].

Where the Coroner for Treasure has conducted an investigation, a determination as to the question mentioned in head (1) above, and (where applicable) the questions mentioned in head (2) above, must be made: (A) by the Coroner for Treasure after considering the evidence (where an inquest is not held)[33]; (B) by the Coroner for Treasure after hearing the evidence (where an inquest is held without a jury)[34]; or (C) by the jury after hearing the evidence (where an inquest is held with a jury)[35].

1   The Coroners Act 1988 s 30 is repealed by the Coroners and Justice Act 2009 s 182(4)(g)(i), Sch 23 Pt 1. However, transitory provision has been made for the Coroners Act 1988 s 30 to be treated as not repealed until such time as the Coroners and Justice Act 2009 ss 25–31, Sch 4 come into force: see the Coroners and Justice Act 2009 (Commencement No 15, Consequential and Transitory Provisions) Order 2013, SI 2013/1869, art 3(a). At the date at which this volume states the law no order had been made for the coming into force of the Coroners and Justice Act 2009 ss 25–31, Sch 4. As from a day to be appointed, the provisions of the Treasure Act 1996 s 7 are substituted by the Coroners and Justice Act 2009 s 182(4)(e), Sch 21 paras 37, 38. At the date at which this volume states the law no such day had been appointed.
2   Coroners Act 1988 s 30(a) (repealed: see note 1). Any reference to a coroner in the Coroners Act 1988 is to be treated as a reference to a coroner appointed under the Coroners and Justice Act 2009 s 23, Sch 3 (Coroners and Justice Act 2009 (Commencement No 15, Consequential and Transitory Provisions) Order 2013, SI 2013/1869, art 3(b)); and any reference to a coroner district in the Coroners Act 1988 is to be treated as a reference to a coroner area constituted under the Coroners and Justice Act 2009 s 22, Sch 2 (Coroners and Justice Act 2009 (Commencement No 15, Consequential and Transitory Provisions) Order 2013, SI 2013/1869, art 3(c)). See CORONERS vol 24 (2010) PARA 28 et seq.
3   Coroners Act 1988 s 30(b) (repealed: see note 1). As to the finder's duty to notify the coroner of finds see PARA 1091.
4   As to the meaning of 'treasure' see PARA 1090.
5   See the Treasure Act 1996 s 7(1) (prospectively repealed). The provisions of the Coroners Act 1988, so far as applicable, apply to every such inquest (see s 30); but the Coroners Act 1988, and anything saved by virtue of s 36(5) (saving for existing law and practice etc), has effect subject to the Treasure Act 1996 s 7 (see s 7(3) (prospectively repealed)). In practice it will only be necessary for a coroner to hold inquests on finds which a museum wishes to acquire: see the *Treasure Act 1996 Code of Practice (2nd Revision) (England and Wales)* para 54. As to the code of practice see PARA 1089. As to the procedure on inquests see PARA 1093.
6   Treasure Act 1996 s 7(2) (prospectively repealed). 24 September 1997 is the date that when s 4 (ownership of treasure which is found: see PARA 1088) came into force: see s 7(2) (prospectively repealed); and the Treasure Act 1996 (Commencement No 2) Order 1997, SI 1997/1977, art 2. As to the common law doctrine of treasure trove see PARA 1088.
7   Treasure Act 1996 s 7(4) (prospectively repealed).
8   The provisions of the Coroners and Justice Act 2009 ss 26–29, 44 are to be brought into force on such day as the Lord Chancellor may by order appoint (see the Coroners and Justice Act 2009 s 182(4)(a)); and the provisions of the Treasure Act 1996 s 7 are to be substituted as from a day to be appointed (see note 1). At the date at which this volume states the law no such day or days had been appointed. As to the Lord Chancellor see CONSTITUTIONAL AND ADMINISTRATIVE LAW vol 20 (2014) PARA 256 et seq.
9   As regards England and Wales, the Coroners and Justice Act 2009 Pt 1 Ch 4 (ss 25–31) confers jurisdiction on the Coroner for Treasure in relation to an object that is or may be treasure, or treasure trove found before 24 September 1997 (ie the date of the commencement of the Treasure Act 1996 s 4 (see PARA 1088)) (see s 7(5) (not yet in force)). Senior coroners, area coroners and assistant coroners have no functions in relation to objects that are or may be treasure or treasure trove: Coroners and Justice Act 2009 s 26(6) (not yet in force). This is subject to Sch 4 para 11 (see PARA 1088 note 17) (which enables an assistant coroner acting as an Assistant Coroner for Treasure to perform functions of the Coroner for Treasure): s 26(6) (not yet in force). As to the Coroner for Treasure see PARA 1088 note 17. As to the meaning of 'England' see PARA 804 note 2. As to the meaning of 'Wales' see PARA 802 note 4. As to the meaning of 'treasure' for the purposes of the Coroners and Justice Act 2009 see PARA 1090. As to the meaning of 'treasure trove' see PARA 1088 note 2. As to senior coroners, area coroners and assistant coroners see CORONERS vol 24 (2010) PARA 27 et seq.
10   Ie under the Treasure Act 1996 s 8(1) (see PARA 1091).
11   Coroners and Justice Act 2009 s 26(1) (not yet in force). Section 26(1)–(3) is subject to s 29 (see the text to notes 21–32: see s 26(4) (not yet in force).
12   Ie under the Treasure Act 1996 s 8 (see PARA 1091).
13   See the Coroners and Justice Act 2009 s 26(2) (not yet in force). See note 11.
14   See the Coroners and Justice Act 2009 s 26(3) (not yet in force). See note 11.
15   Coroners and Justice Act 2009 s 26(5)(a) (not yet in force).

16 Coroners and Justice Act 2009 s 26(5)(b) (not yet in force).

17 Coroners and Justice Act 2009 s 44(1) (not yet in force). Treasure regulations may be made only if the Lord Chief Justice, or a judicial office holder (as defined in the Constitutional Reform Act 2005 s 109(4): see COURTS AND TRIBUNALS vol 24 (2010) PARA 961) nominated for these purposes by the Lord Chief Justice, agrees to the making of the regulations: Coroners and Justice Act 2009 s 44(2) (not yet in force). Treasure regulations may make (but not so as to be read as limiting the power in s 44(1) (s 44(3) (not yet in force)):

    (1)   provision for the discharge of an investigation (including provision as to fresh investigations following discharge) (s 44(3)(a) (not yet in force));

    (2)   provision for or in connection with the suspension or resumption of investigations (s 44(3)(b) (not yet in force));

    (3)   provision for the delegation by the Coroner for Treasure (or an Assistant Coroner for Treasure) of any of his or her functions (s 44(3)(c) (not yet in force));

    (4)   provision allowing information to be disclosed or requiring information to be given (s 44(3)(d) (not yet in force));

    (5)   provision giving to the Lord Chancellor or the Chief Coroner power to require information from the Coroner for Treasure (s 44(3)(e) (not yet in force));

    (6)   provision requiring a summary of specified information given to the Chief Coroner by virtue of head (5) to be included in reports under s 36 (see CORONERS vol 24 (2010) PARA 59) (s 44(3)(f) (not yet in force));

    (7)   provision of the kind mentioned in s 43(3)(h) or (i) (see CORONERS vol 24 (2010) PARA 40) (s 44(3)(g) (not yet in force)).

Treasure regulations may apply any provisions of coroners rules: s 44(4) (not yet in force). Where Treasure regulations apply any provisions of coroners rules, those provisions may be applied to any extent, with or without modifications and as amended from time to time (s 44(5)(a)–(c) (not yet in force)). As to the Lord Chief Justice see COURTS AND TRIBUNALS vol 24 (2010) PARA 604. As to the Chief Coroner and the coroners rules see CORONERS vol 24 (2010) PARAS 8, 41.

The following provisions are already in force (see the Coroners and Justice Act 2009 (Commencement No 14) Order 2013, SI 2013/1628): Coroners rules may make (a) provision for the delegation by the Coroner for Treasure (or an Assistant Coroner for Treasure), of any of his or her functions, except for functions that involve making judicial decisions or exercising any judicial discretion; (b) provision as to the matters to be taken into account by the Coroner for Treasure in deciding whether to hold an inquest concerning an object that is or may be treasure or treasure trove: Coroners and Justice Act 2009 s 45(2)(f)(ii), (2)(i). Coroners rules may make provision conferring power on a senior coroner or the Coroner for Treasure (i) to give a direction excluding specified persons from an inquest, or part of an inquest, if the coroner is of the opinion that the interests of national security so require; (ii) to give a direction excluding specified persons from an inquest during the giving of evidence by a witness under the age of 18, if the coroner is of the opinion that doing so would be likely to improve the quality of the witness' evidence: s 45(3). In s 45(3) 'specified persons' means persons of a description specified in the direction, or all persons except those of a description specified in the direction: s 45(3). Coroners rules may apply any provisions of Treasure regulations: s 45(5)(b). Where any provisions or rules are so applied, they may be applied to any extent, with or without modifications and as amended from time to time: s 45(6). See further CORONERS vol 24 (2010) PARA 41.

18 Coroners and Justice Act 2009 s 27(1) (not yet in force).

19 Coroners and Justice Act 2009 s 27(2) (not yet in force). In relation to a treasure inquest held with a jury, ss 8 and 9 (see CORONERS vol 24 (2010) PARAS 138, 141, 150, 188) apply with modifications: see s 27(3) (not yet in force).

20 As to the vesting of treasure in the Crown see PARA 1088.

21 For these purposes the 'franchisee', in relation to an object, is the person who (1) was, immediately before the commencement of the Treasure Act 1996 s 4 (see PARA 1088); or (2) apart from that Act, as successor in title, would have been, the franchisee of the Crown in right of treasure trove for the place where the object was found: Coroners and Justice Act 2009 s 29(5) (not yet in force). As to the meaning of 'franchisee' under the Treasure Act 1996 see PARA 1088 note 8.

22 See the Coroners and Justice Act 2009 s 29(1)(a) (not yet in force), (2)(a) (not yet in force). The code of practice under the Treasure Act 1996 s 11 (see PARA 1089) may make provision to do with objects in respect of which notice is given under s 29(1) or (2): see s 31(1); and PARA 1089.

23 See the Coroners and Justice Act 2009 s 29(1)(b), (2)(b). See also note 23.

24 As to the Secretary of State see PARA 802 note 2.

25 The code of practice under the Treasure Act 1996 s 11 (see PARA 1089) may make provision to do with objects in respect of which notice is given under s 29(1) or (2): see s 31(1); and PARA 1089.

26 Coroners and Justice Act 2009 s 29(1) (not yet in force).

27 Coroners and Justice Act 2009 s 29(2) (not yet in force).

28 Ie under the Coroners and Justice Act 2009 s 28 (see the text to notes 33–35).

29 See the Coroners and Justice Act 2009 s 29(3) (not yet in force).
30 Coroners and Justice Act 2009 s 29(4)(a) (not yet in force).
31 Coroners and Justice Act 2009 s 29(4)(b) (not yet in force).
32 Coroners and Justice Act 2009 s 29(4)(c) (not yet in force). As to the code of practice see the
    Treasure Act 1996 s 11; and PARA 1089.
33 Coroners and Justice Act 2009 s 28(a) (not yet in force).
34 Coroners and Justice Act 2009 s 28(b) (not yet in force).
35 Coroners and Justice Act 2009 s 28(c) (not yet in force).

1093. Procedure for inquests and investigations in respect of treasure. Until a
day to be appointed the following provisions have effect[1].
   A coroner proposing to conduct an inquest[2] must notify the Museum, if his
district is in England[3], or the National Museum of Wales, if it is in Wales[4]. Before
conducting the inquest, the coroner must take reasonable steps to notify any
person[5] who it appears to him may have found the treasure[6], and any person who,
at the time the treasure was found, occupied land[7] which it appears to him may
be where it was found[8]. During the inquest the coroner must take reasonable steps
to notify any such person not already notified[9]. Before or during the inquest the
coroner must take reasonable steps to obtain from any person so notified[10] the
names and addresses of interested persons[11] and to notify any interested person
whose name and address he obtains[12]. The coroner must take reasonable steps to
give any interested person notified under these provisions[13] an opportunity to
examine witnesses at the inquest[14]. A coroner has no power to make any legal
determination as to title between the occupier, the landowner and the finder; and
this question will, if necessary, need to be resolved by the courts[15]. A
coroner's decisions in relation to treasure may be subject to review by the courts[16].
   As from a day to be appointed the following provisions have effect[17].
   In England and Wales[18], before conducting an investigation[19] concerning an
object, the Coroner for Treasure[20] must: (1) notify the appropriate national
museum[21]; (2) take reasonable steps to notify any person who the coroner thinks
may have found the object[22], and any person who, at the time the object was
found, occupied land that the coroner thinks may be where it was found[23]. During
an investigation the Coroner for Treasure must take reasonable steps to notify any
person within head (2) who has not already been notified[24]; and before or during
an investigation, the Coroner for Treasure must take reasonable steps to obtain
the names and addresses of any other interested persons[25], and to notify any
interested person whose name and address he obtains[26]. The Coroner for Treasure
must take reasonable steps to give any interested person an opportunity to
examine witnesses at any inquest held as part of an investigation[27].

1 As from a day to be appointed, the Treasure Act 1996 s 9 is substituted by the Coroners and Justice
   Act 2009 s 182(4)(e), Sch 21 paras 37, 41. At the date at which this volume states the law no such
   day had been appointed.
2 'Inquest' means an inquest held under the Treasure Act 1996 s 7 (see PARA 1092): s 9(1)
   (prospectively repealed). As to the procedure where a find has been reported to the coroner, and
   as to treasure inquests see the *Treasure Act 1996 Code of Practice (2nd Revision) (England and
   Wales)* Pt G (paras 53–62). As to the code of practice see PARA 1089. Detailed guidelines on the
   procedure to be followed by coroners in treasure inquests are set out in *Home Office Circular
   44/1997*.
3 Treasure Act 1996 s 9(2)(a) (prospectively repealed). As to coroners' districts in England see
   CORONERS vol 24 (2010) PARA 10. As to the Museum see PARA 822. As to the meaning of
   'England' see PARA 804 note 2.
4 Treasure Act 1996 s 9(2)(b) (prospectively repealed). As to coroners' districts in Wales see
   CORONERS vol 24 (2010) PARA 11. As to the National Museum of Wales see PARA 889. As to
   the meaning of 'Wales' see PARA 802 note 4.
5 As to the meaning of 'person' see PARA 803 note 17.
6 Treasure Act 1996 s 9(3)(a) (prospectively repealed). As to the meaning of 'treasure' see PARA
   1090.

7   As to the meaning of 'land' see PARA 804 note 30.

8   Treasure Act 1996 s 9(3)(b) (prospectively repealed).

9   Treasure Act 1996 s 9(4) (prospectively repealed).

10 Ie under the Treasure Act 1996 s 9(3) or (4) (see the text to notes 5–9).

11 Treasure Act 1996 s 9(5)(a) (prospectively repealed). 'Interested person' means a person who appears to the coroner to be likely to be concerned with the inquest: (1) as the finder of the treasure or having been otherwise involved in the find (s 9(7)(a) (prospectively repealed)); (2) as the occupier, at the time the treasure was found, of the land where it was found (s 9(7)(b) (prospectively repealed)); or (3) as having had an interest in that land at that time or since (s 9(7)(c) (prospectively repealed)).

12 Treasure Act 1996 s 9(5)(b) (prospectively repealed).

13 Ie under the Treasure Act 1996 s 9(3), (4) or s 9(5) (see the text to notes 5–12).

14 Treasure Act 1996 s 9(6) (prospectively repealed).

15 *A-G v Moore* [1893] 1 Ch 676; *A-G v Trustees of the Museum* [1903] 2 Ch 598; *A-G of the Duchy of Lancaster v GE Overton (Farms) Ltd* [1982] Ch 277, [1982] 1 All ER 524, CA; *Waverley Borough Council v Fletcher* [1996] QB 334, [1995] 4 All ER 756, CA.

16 Ie under the Coroners Act 1988 s 13 (see CORONERS vol 24 (2010) PARA 235) or by way of judicial review: see the *Treasure Act 1996 Code of Practice (2nd Revision) (England and Wales)* para 61. The Coroners Act 1988 s 13 applies to inquests into treasure as well as into deaths; but, where an application is made both with the Attorney General's consent under s 13 and for judicial review, it is appropriate to consider the matter under s 13 only: *R v HM Coroner for Wiltshire, ex p Chaddock* (1992) 157 JP 209, DC. As to judicial review see CORONERS vol 24 (2010) PARAS 236–237; and JUDICIAL REVIEW vol 61 (2010) PARA 601 et seq.

17 The provisions of the Treasure Act 1996 s 9 are to be substituted as from a day to be appointed (see note 1). At the date at which this volume states the law no such day or days had been appointed.

18 See the Treasure Act 1996 s 9(6) (not yet in force).

19 'Investigation' means an investigation under the Coroners and Justice Act 2009 s 26 (see PARA 1092): Treasure Act 1996 s 9(5) (not yet in force).

20 As to the Coroner for Treasure see PARA 1088 note 17.

21 Treasure Act 1996 s 9(1)(a) (not yet in force). 'Appropriate national museum' means the British Museum, if the object in question was found or is believed to have been found in England; and the National Museum of Wales, if it was found or is believed to have been found in Wales: s 9(5) (not yet in force).

22 Treasure Act 1996 s 9(1)(b)(i) (not yet in force). As to the duty to notify the Coroner for Treasure of finds see PARA 1091.

23 Treasure Act 1996 s 9(1)(b)(ii) (not yet in force).

24 Treasure Act 1996 s 9(2) (not yet in force).

25 Treasure Act 1996 s 9(3)(a) (not yet in force). 'Interested person', in relation to an object that is or may be treasure or treasure trove, or an investigation or inquest under the Coroners and Justice Act 2009 Pt 1 Ch 4 (ss 25–31) (see PARA 1092) concerning such an object, means: (1) the British Museum, if the object was found or is believed to have been found in England; (2) the National Museum of Wales, if the object was found or is believed to have been found in Wales; (3) the finder of the object or any person otherwise involved in the find; (4) the occupier, at the time the object was found, of the land where it was found or is believed to have been found; (5) a person who had an interest in that land at that time or who has had such an interest since; (6) any other person who the Coroner for Treasure thinks has a sufficient interest: s 47(6) (definition applied by the Treasure Act 1996 s 9(5) (not yet in force)).

26 Treasure Act 1996 s 9(3)(b) (not yet in force).

27 Treasure Act 1996 s 9(4) (not yet in force).

(2) OBJECTS ON LOAN

1094.   The government indemnity scheme. The Secretary of State[1] or, in relation to Wales, the Welsh Ministers[2] may undertake to indemnify certain institutions, bodies or persons[3] for the loss of, or damage to[4], any object belonging to it while on loan to any other such institution, body or person, in such cases and to such extent as he or they may determine[5]. However, the Secretary of State or, as the case may be, the Welsh Ministers must not give such an undertaking unless:

(1)   he or they consider the loan will facilitate public access to the object in question or contribute materially to public understanding or appreciation of it[6];

(2)   the loan is made in accordance with conditions approved by the Secretary of State and the Treasury or by the Welsh Ministers, and the Secretary of State or the Welsh Ministers are satisfied that appropriate arrangements have been made for the safety of the object while it is on loan[7].

For each of the successive periods of six months[8] ending with 31 March and 30 September in each year, the Secretary of State or, as appropriate, the Welsh Ministers must prepare a report specifying[9]: (a) the number of undertakings given by him or them during that period[10]; and (b) the amount or value, expressed in sterling, of any contingent liabilities as at the end of that period in respect of such of the undertakings given by him or them at any time as remain outstanding at the end of that period[11].

1   The functions of the Secretary of State under the National Heritage Act 1980 ss 16, 16A may be exercised by, or by employees of, such person (if any) as may be authorised in that behalf by the Secretary of State:
    (1)   either wholly or to such extent as may be specified in the authorisation (see the Contracting Out (Functions in Relation to Cultural Objects) Order 2005, SI 2005/1103, arts 2(b), 3(a));
    (2)   either generally or in such cases or areas as may be so specified (see arts 2(b), 3(b)); and
    (3)   either unconditionally or subject to the fulfilment of such conditions as may be so specified (see arts 2(b), 3(c)).
    As to the Secretary of State see PARA 802 note 2. As to the meaning of 'person' see PARA 803 note 17.
2   The functions of the Secretary of State under the National Heritage Act 1980 ss 16, 16A, in so far as they relate to Wales, were transferred to the National Assembly for Wales (see the National Assembly for Wales (Transfer of Functions) Order 1999, SI 1999/672, art 2, Sch 1) and are now exercisable by the Welsh Ministers (see the Government of Wales Act 2006 s 162(1), Sch 11 paras 30, 32). As to the Welsh Ministers see PARA 802. As to the meaning of 'Wales' see PARA 802 note 4.
3   The institutions, bodies and persons are: (1) a museum, art gallery or similar institution in the United Kingdom for the preservation for the public benefit of a collection of historic, artistic or scientific interest and which is maintained (a) wholly or mainly out of money provided by Parliament or money appropriated by Measure; or (b) by a local authority or university in the United Kingdom; (2) a library maintained (a) as in head (1)(a) above, or (b) by a library authority, or the main function of which is to serve the needs of teaching or research at a United Kingdom university; (3) the National Trust; (4) the National Trust for Scotland; or (5) any other body or person approved by the Secretary of State with Treasury consent or, in relation to Wales, by the Welsh Ministers: National Heritage Act 1980 s 16(2)(a)–(e) (s 16(2) amended by the Museums and Galleries Act 1992 s 10(1); National Heritage Act 1980 s 16(2)(e) further amended by SI 1992/1311). 'Library authority' means a library authority within the meaning of the Public Libraries and Museums Act 1964 (see PARA 922), a statutory library authority within the meaning of the Public Libraries (Scotland) Act 1955 or an Education and Library Board within the meaning of the Education and Libraries (Northern Ireland) Order 1972, SI 1972/1263; and 'university' includes a university college and a college, school or hall of a university: National Heritage Act 1980 s 16(6). As to the meaning of 'United Kingdom' see PARA 804 note 2. As to the National Trust see PARA 973. As to the meaning of 'Treasury' see PARA 809 note 4.
4   References to the loss of or damage to, or the safety of, an object while on loan include references to the loss of or damage to, or the safety of, the object while being taken to or returned from the place where it is to be or has been kept while on loan: National Heritage Act 1980 s 16(7).
5   National Heritage Act 1980 s 16(1) (amended by the Museums and Galleries Act 1992 ss 10(1), 11(3), Sch 9; and SI 1992/1311). As to such indemnities see further the *Government Indemnity Scheme Guidelines for National Institutions* (Arts Council England, for and on behalf of the Secretary of State for Culture, Media and Sport: July 2012) a copy of which is available on the Arts Council website which, at the date at which this volume states the law, can be found at www.artscouncil.org.uk. In relation to Wales, Museums Archives and Libraries Wales ('CyMAL'), a division of the Welsh Government, advises the Deputy Minister for Culture, Sport and Tourism

on the Government Indemnity Scheme; for further information see the CyMAL website which, at the date at which this volume states the law, can be found at www.cymal.wales.gov.uk.

6 See the National Heritage Act 1980 s 16(3) (s 16(3)–(5) amended by SI 1992/1311).

7 See the National Heritage Act 1980 s 16(4) (as amended: see note 6). See also note 4. The provisions of the National Heritage Act 1980 s 16(1)–(4) apply in relation to the loan of an object belonging to an institution, body or person in Northern Ireland with the substitution for references to the Secretary of State and the Treasury of references to the Department of Education for Northern Ireland and the Department of Finance for Northern Ireland: National Heritage Act 1980 s 16(5) (as amended: see note 6).

8 As to the meaning of 'month' see PARA 803 note 12.

9 National Heritage Act 1980 s 16A(1) (s 16A added by the Museums and Galleries Act 1992 s 10(2); National Heritage Act 1980 s 16A(1), (3) amended by SI 1992/1311). A report by the Secretary of State must be laid before Parliament not later than two months after the end of the period to which it relates: see the National Heritage Act 1980 s 16A(2) (as so added). As to the laying of documents before Parliament see STATUTES AND LEGISLATIVE PROCESS vol 96 (2012) PARA 1052. As to the laying of documents by the Welsh Ministers before the National Assembly for Wales see the Government of Wales Act 2006 s 86; and CONSTITUTIONAL AND ADMINISTRATIVE LAW vol 20 (2014) PARA 384.

　　The National Heritage Act 1980 s 16A(1), (2) applies in relation to undertakings given by the Department for Education for Northern Ireland with the substitution for references to the Secretary of State of references to that department and with the substitution for the reference to Parliament of a reference to the Northern Ireland Assembly: s 16A(3) (as so added and amended). As to the Northern Ireland Assembly see CONSTITUTIONAL AND ADMINISTRATIVE LAW vol 20 (2014) PARA 85.

10 National Heritage Act 1980 s 16A(1)(a) (as added: see note 9).

11 National Heritage Act 1980 s 16A(1)(b) (as added: see note 9).

1095. Protection of cultural objects on loan from outside the United Kingdom.

An object is a protected object[1] if the following conditions are met when it enters the United Kingdom[2]. The conditions are:

(1)　　the object is usually kept outside the United Kingdom[3];

(2)　　it is not owned by a person[4] resident in the United Kingdom[5];

(3)　　its import does not contravene a prohibition or restriction on the import of goods, imposed by or under any enactment[6], that applies to the object, a part of it or anything it conceals[7];

(4)　　it is brought to the United Kingdom for public display[8] in a temporary exhibition[9] at a museum or gallery[10]; and

(5)　　the museum or gallery has complied with any requirements prescribed by regulations made by the Secretary of State about the publication of specified information about the object[11].

The protection continues only so long as the object is in the United Kingdom for any of the specified purposes[12], and for not more than 12 months beginning with the day when the object enters the United Kingdom[13]. A new period of protection begins each time an object enters the United Kingdom and the conditions in heads (1) to (5) above are met[14].

While an object is protected it may not be seized or forfeited[15] under any enactment or rule of law, unless it is seized or forfeited under or by virtue of an order made by a court in the United Kingdom[16], and the court is required to make the order under, or under provision giving effect to, a EU obligation[17] or any international treaty[18]. Protection does not affect liability for an offence of importing, exporting or otherwise dealing with the object, but[19] any power of arrest or otherwise to prevent such an offence is not exercisable so as to prevent the object leaving the United Kingdom[20].

The above provisions bind the Crown[21].

Objects loaned by United Kingdom institutions to borrowers outside the United Kingdom may be covered by similar government indemnity schemes operating in the relevant overseas jurisdictions, and may also be protected from judicial seizure or other involvement in judicial proceedings by means of local immunity statutes[22].

Objects temporarily loaned abroad may require an export licence[23].

1 Ie an object protected under the Tribunals, Courts and Enforcement Act 2007 s 135 (see the text to notes 15–20).

2 Tribunals, Courts and Enforcement Act 2007 s 134(1). 'United Kingdom' includes the territorial sea adjacent to the United Kingdom (within the meaning given by the Territorial Sea Act 1987 s 1: see WATER AND WATERWAYS vol 100 (2009) PARA 31): Tribunals, Courts and Enforcement Act 2007 s 137(1), (10). As to the meaning of 'United Kingdom' generally see PARA 804 note 2.

3 Tribunals, Courts and Enforcement Act 2007 s 134(2)(a).

4 A person owns an object for these purposes whether he owns it beneficially or not and whether alone or with others: Tribunals, Courts and Enforcement Act 2007 s 134(3). As to the meaning of 'person' see PARA 803 note 17.

5 Tribunals, Courts and Enforcement Act 2007 s 134(2)(b). An individual is resident in the United Kingdom if he is ordinarily resident in the United Kingdom for the purposes of income tax, or would be if he were receiving income on which tax is payable: s 137(1), (6). The trustees of a settlement are resident in the United Kingdom if they are resident and ordinarily resident in the United Kingdom for the purposes of income tax, or would be if they were receiving income on which tax is payable: s 137(1), (7). A partnership (including a limited partnership) or unincorporated association is resident in the United Kingdom if it is established under the law of any part of the United Kingdom: s 137(1), (8). A body corporate is resident in the United Kingdom if it is incorporated under the law of any part of the United Kingdom: s 137(1), (9).

6 'Enactment' includes an enactment comprised in, or in an instrument made under, an Act of the Scottish Parliament: Tribunals, Courts and Enforcement Act 2007 s 137(1), (2). As to the Scottish Parliament see CONSTITUTIONAL AND ADMINISTRATIVE LAW vol 20 (2014) PARA 66.

7 Tribunals, Courts and Enforcement Act 2007 s 134(2)(c).

8 'Public display' means display to which the public are admitted, on payment or not, but does not include display with a view to sale: Tribunals, Courts and Enforcement Act 2007 s 137(3).

9 'Temporary exhibition' means an exhibition of one or more objects which is open to the public for a period of less than 12 months, whether at a single location or at a succession of locations: Tribunals, Courts and Enforcement Act 2007 s 137(4). As to the meaning of 'month' see PARA 803 note 12.

10 Tribunals, Courts and Enforcement Act 2007 s 134(2)(d). A temporary exhibition is at a museum or gallery if it is held at or under the direction of the museum or gallery: s 137(5). 'Museum or gallery' means an institution in the United Kingdom approved by the appropriate authority: s 136(1). The matters that the appropriate authority must have regard to when deciding whether to approve an institution include: (1) the institution's procedures for establishing the provenance and ownership of objects (s 136(2)(a)); and (2) in particular, compliance by the institution with guidance about such procedures published by the Secretary of State from time to time (s 136(2)(b)). The appropriate authority may withdraw approval from an institution if it thinks fit, and, in particular, if: (a) it thinks that the institution's procedures for establishing the provenance or ownership of objects are inadequate (because of the institution's failure to comply with guidance published by the Secretary of State or for some other reason) (s 136(3)(a)); or (b) the institution has failed to comply with a requirement of regulations under s 134(9) (see note 11) (s 136(3)(b)). The withdrawal of approval from an institution does not affect the application of ss 134, 135 to any object which is a protected object immediately before the withdrawal: s 136(4). 'Appropriate authority' means: (i) the Secretary of State, in relation to an institution in England (s 136(5)(a)); and (ii) the Welsh Ministers, in relation to an institution in Wales (s 136(5)(b)). As to the Secretary of State and the Welsh Ministers see PARA 802. As to the meaning of 'England' see PARA 804 note 2. As to the meaning of 'Wales' see PARA 802 note 4. As to the approval of museums and galleries in England see further the *Note on the approval of museums and galleries under Section 136 of the Tribunals, Courts and Enforcement Act 2007* (Department for Culture, Media and Sport April 2008). A copy of the Note and a list of approved institutions are available on the Department for Culture, Media and Sport website which, at the date at which this volume states the law, can be found at www.culture.gov.uk.

11 Tribunals, Courts and Enforcement Act 2007 s 134(2)(e). The Secretary of State may make regulations requiring a museum or gallery to provide persons with specified information about an object in specified circumstances (which may include in particular compliance with conditions imposed by or under the regulations): s 134(9). Such regulations may not be made without the consent of the Scottish Ministers, the Welsh Ministers and the Department for Culture, Art and Leisure in Northern Ireland (s 134(10)(a)), and must be made by statutory instrument

(s 134(10)(b)). As to the regulations made see the Protection of Cultural Objects on Loan (Publication and Provision of Information) Regulations 2008, SI 2008/1159.

12 Tribunals, Courts and Enforcement Act 2007 s 134(4)(a). The specified purposes are: (1) public display in a temporary exhibition at a museum or gallery (s 134(7)(a)); (2) going to or returning from public display in a temporary exhibition at a museum or gallery (s 134(7)(b)); (3) related repair, conservation or restoration (s 134(7)(c)); (4) going to or returning from related repair, conservation or restoration (s 134(7)(d)); (5) leaving the United Kingdom (s 134(7)(e)). Repair, conservation or restoration is related if it is carried out in the United Kingdom and is done (a) to prepare the object for public display in a temporary exhibition at a museum or gallery (s 134(8)(a)); or (b) because of damage suffered in the course of something within s 134(7) (s 134(8)(b)).

13 Tribunals, Courts and Enforcement Act 2007 s 134(4)(b). However, the protection continues after the end of this period if the object has suffered damage while protected, and (1) it is undergoing repair, conservation or restoration in the United Kingdom because of the damage (s 134(5)(a)); or (2) it is leaving the United Kingdom following repair, conservation or restoration because of the damage (s 134(5)(b)).

14 Tribunals, Courts and Enforcement Act 2007 s 134(6).

15 In the Tribunals, Courts and Enforcement Act 2007 s 135 references to seizure or forfeiture in relation to an object include references to: (1) taking control of the object under Sch 12 (in England and Wales) (see CIVIL PROCEDURE vol 12A (2015) PARA 1334 et seq) (s 135(3)(a)); (2) execution or distress (in England and Wales or Northern Ireland) (s 135(3)(b)); (3) diligence or sequestration (in Scotland) (s 135(3)(c)); (4) seizure, confiscation or forfeiture, or any other measure relating to the custody or control of the object, in the course of a criminal investigation or criminal proceedings (against the owner, the museum or gallery or any other person) (s 135(3)(d)); (5) the making or enforcement of an order relating to the custody or control of the object in civil proceedings (against the owner, the museum or gallery or any other person) (s 135(3)(e)). As to execution generally see CIVIL PROCEDURE vol 12A (2015) PARA 1371 et seq. As to distress generally see LANDLORD AND TENANT vol 62 (2012) PARA 288 et seq.

16 Tribunals, Courts and Enforcement Act 2007 s 135(1)(a).

17 As to the meaning of 'EU obligation' see the European Communities Act 1972 s 1, Sch 1 Pt II (definition amended by the European Union (Amendment) Act 2008 s 3, Schedule Pt 1).

18 Tribunals, Courts and Enforcement Act 2007 s 135(1)(b).

19 Ie subject to the Tribunals, Courts and Enforcement Act 2007 s 135(1) (see the text to notes 15–18).

20 Tribunals, Courts and Enforcement Act 2007 s 135(2).

21 Tribunals, Courts and Enforcement Act 2007 s 138.

22 As to the UNESCO Convention on the Means of Prohibiting and Preventing the Illicit Import, Export and Transfer of Ownership of Cultural Property see PARA 1098. As to the return of cultural objects unlawfully removed from member states see PARA 1099 et seq. As to dealing in tainted cultural objects see PARA 1104. As to Nazi spoliation see PARAS 1106–1107.

23 See PARA 1096.

(3) EXPORT AND IMPORT CONTROL OF CULTURAL OBJECTS

1096. Export control of cultural objects. The export of antiques and other cultural objects is subject to control under both United Kingdom and European Union ('EU') law[1].

The export of cultural goods[2] outside the customs territory of the EU is subject to the presentation of an export licence[3]. The export licence is valid throughout the EU[4]. The direct export from the customs territory of the EU of national treasures having artistic, historic or archaeological value which are not cultural goods is subject to the national law of the member state of export[5].

The Secretary of State[6] may by order make provision for or in connection with the imposition of export controls in relation to goods of any description; and for this purpose 'export controls', in relation to any goods, means the prohibition or regulation of their exportation from the United Kingdom[7] or their shipment as stores[8]. Any objects of cultural interest[9] manufactured or produced more than 50 years before the date of exportation[10] except:

(1)   postage stamps and other articles of philatelic interest;

(2)   birth, marriage or death certificates or other documents relating to the personal affairs of the exporter or the spouse of the exporter;

(3)   letters or other writings[11] written by or to the exporter or the spouse of the exporter; and

(4)   goods exported by, and being the personal property of, the manufacturer or producer thereof, or the spouse, widow or widower of that person,

are prohibited to be exported to any destination except under the authority of a licence in writing granted by the Secretary of State, and in accordance with all the conditions attached to the licence[12].

The export control regime for cultural goods is operated by the Export Licensing Unit at Arts Council England[13]. An application for an export licence may be referred to an expert adviser for scrutiny as to national importance[14]. There is a Reviewing Committee on the Export of Works of Art and Objects of Cultural Interest which is a non-statutory independent body set up to advise the Secretary of State whether a cultural object for which an application for an export licence has been made is a national treasure[15]. Objects are assessed against the following criteria, known as the 'Waverley criteria'[16], namely, if the object's departure from the United Kingdom would be a misfortune on one or more of the following grounds:

(a)   it is closely connected with the history and national life of the United Kingdom;

(b)   it is of outstanding aesthetic importance;

(c)   it is of outstanding significance for the study of some particular branch of art, learning or history[17].

If the reviewing committee decides that an object satisfies any of the Waverley criteria, the committee recommends to the Secretary of State that a decision on the licence application should be deferred for a specified period to enable an offer to purchase to be made at or above the fair market price, with a view to keeping the object in the United Kingdom[18]. If the object does not satisfy one or more of the Waverley criteria, the committee recommends that the export licence should be granted[19].

Where a decision has been deferred and an offer to purchase is received from a public source such as a museum or gallery, the owner of the object is under no compulsion to accept the offer but the existence of the offer is taken into account in deciding on the licence application and a licence will normally be refused[20]. Where an offer to purchase is received from a private source, the existence of the offer is only taken into account where it is combined with a signed undertaking to guarantee reasonable public access to the object, to provide satisfactory conservation conditions and not to sell it for a specified period[21].

The Reviewing Committee is guided in its policy advice by the membership of the Advisory Council on the Export of Works of Art which was established to provide a forum for the discussion of the principles and operation of the export control system[22]. The Reviewing Committee publishes an annual report which is presented to Parliament and outlines the committee's policy discussions and gives detailed accounts of the cases considered[23].

The export control regime for cultural goods applies to museums and galleries which must apply for export licences where appropriate, even when arranging a temporary loan of an object for an exhibition abroad[24]. A temporary licence application by a national museum or gallery is not, however, normally referred to an expert adviser[25].

1   See the text to notes 2–24.
2   'Cultural goods' means:
    (1)   archaeological objects more than 100 years old which are the products of excavations and finds on land or under water, archaeological sites, archaeological collection;
    (2)   elements forming an integral part of artistic, historical or religious monuments which have been dismembered, of an age exceeding 100 years;
    (3)   pictures and paintings, other than those included in head (4) or (5) below, executed entirely by hand in any medium and on any material, of a value of £125,011 or more;
    (4)   water-colours, gouaches and pastels executed entirely by hand on any material, of a value of £25,002 or more;
    (5)   mosaics in any material executed entirely by hand, other than those falling in head (1) or (2) above, and drawings in any medium executed entirely by hand on any material, of a value of £12,501 or more;
    (6)   original engravings, prints, serigraphs and lithographs with their respective plates and original posters, of a value of £12,501 or more;
    (7)   original sculptures or statuary and copies produced by the same process as the original, other than those in head (1) above, of a value of £41,670 or more;
    (8)   photographs, films and negatives thereof, of a value of £12,501 or more;
    (9)   incunabula and manuscripts, including maps and musical scores, singly or in collections;
    (10) books more than 100 years old, singly or in collections, of a value of £41,670 or more;
    (11) printed maps more than 200 years old, of a value of £12,501 or more;
    (12) archives, and any elements thereof, of any kind or any medium which are more than 50 years old;
    (13) collections and specimens from zoological, botanical, mineralogical or anatomical collections; and collections of historical, palaeontological, ethnographic or numismatic interest, in each case of a value of £41,670 or more;
    (14) means of transport more than 75 years old, of a value of £41,670 or more;
    (15) any other antique items not included in heads (1)–(14) above more than 50 years old, and of a value of £41,670 or more: Council Regulation (EC) 116/2009 (OJ L39, 10.2.2009, p 1) on the export of cultural goods Annex 1; *UK Export Licensing for Cultural Goods: Procedures and Guidance for Exporters of Works of Art and other Cultural Goods* (An Arts Council England Notice: 2015 Issue 2) Table 2. A copy of the guidance is available on the Arts Council England website which, at the date at which this volume states the law, can be found at www.artscouncil.org.uk.
3   See Council Regulation (EC) 116/2009 (OJ L39, 10.2.2009, p 1) on the export of cultural goods, art 2(1), (2). As to the form of export licences see Commission Implementing Regulation (EU) 1081/2012 for the purposes of Council Regulation (EC) 116/2009 on the export of cultural goods (OJ L324, 22.11.2012, p 1) (corrected in OL L93, 20.3.2014, p 86). As to the direct effect of EU regulations see EUROPEAN UNION vol 47A (2014) PARA 110. As to the return of cultural objects unlawfully removed from member states see PARA 1099 et seq.
4   Council Regulation (EC) 116/2009 (OJ L39, 10.2.2009, p 1) art 2(3).
5   See Council Regulation (EC) 116/2009 (OJ L39, 10.2.2009, p 1) art 2(4).
6   As to the Secretary of State see PARA 802 note 2.
7   As to the meaning of 'United Kingdom' see PARA 804 note 2.
8   See the Export Control Act 2002 s 1(1), (2), 11(1); and TRADE AND INDUSTRY vol 97 (2015) PARA 911 et seq.
9   'Objects of cultural interest' includes objects of historical or scientific interest: Export Control Act 2002 s 11(1).
10 'Exportation' includes shipment as stores and, unless the context otherwise requires, means exportation from the United Kingdom to any destination except for the Isle of Man: Export of Objects of Cultural Interest (Control) Order 2003, SI 2003/2759, art 1(2).
11 As to the meaning of 'writing' see PARA 805 note 14.
12 See the Export of Objects of Cultural Interest (Control) Order 2003, SI 2003/2759, arts 1(2), 2, Schedule. An EU licence or a licence granted by the Secretary of State under art 2 may be:
    (1)   general or specific (art 3(1)(a) (art 3(1) amended by SI 2011/1043));
    (2)   unlimited or limited so as to expire on a specified date unless renewed (Export of Objects of Cultural Interest (Control) Order 2003, SI 2003/2759, art 3(1)(b) (as so amended)); and

(3)   subject to or without conditions, and any such condition may require any act or omission before or after the exportation of objects under the licence (art 3(1)(c) (as so amended)).

Any such licence may be varied, suspended or revoked by the Secretary of State at any time and in such circumstances and on such terms as the Secretary of State thinks fit, by serving a notice to that effect on the holder of the licence: Export of Objects of Cultural Interest (Control) Order 2003, SI 2003/2759, art 3(2). Pursuant to these powers the Secretary of State has issued the Open General Export Licence (Objects of Cultural Interest) dated 1 May 2004, a copy of which is available on the Arts Council England website which, at the date at which this volume states the law, can be found at www.artscouncil.org.uk. The provisions of this licence only apply for the purposes of the Export of Objects of Cultural Interest (Control) Order 2003, SI 2003/2759, and do not remove the need for other consents which may be required by Council Regulation (EC) 116/2009 (OJ L39, 10.2.2009, p 1) (see the text and notes 1–5). See further TRADE AND INDUSTRY vol 97 (2015) PARA 916.

The functions of the Secretary of State in relation to such licences may be exercised by, or by employees of, such person (if any) as may be authorised in that behalf by the Secretary of State: see the Contracting Out (Functions in Relation to Cultural Objects) Order 2005, SI 2005/1103, arts 2(c), 3. As to the meaning of 'person' see PARA 803 note 17.

13 As to Arts Council England see PARA 957.
14 See *UK Export Licensing for Cultural Goods: Procedures and Guidance for Exporters of Works of Art and other Cultural Goods* (An Arts Council England Notice: 2015 Issue 2) Part I paras 22–23. Special considerations apply to manuscripts (see *UK Export Licensing for Cultural Goods: Procedures and Guidance for Exporters of Works of Art and other Cultural Goods* (An Arts Council England Notice: 2015 Issue 2) Part I paras 17–19, Appendix G) and the export of manorial documents require the permission of the Master of the Rolls (see *UK Export Licensing for Cultural Goods: Procedures and Guidance for Exporters of Works of Art and other Cultural Goods* (An Arts Council England Notice: 2015 Issue 2) Part I paras 20). As to the Royal Commission on Historical Manuscripts and as to manorial documents see PARA 812.
15 See *UK Export Licensing for Cultural Goods: Procedures and Guidance for Exporters of Works of Art and other Cultural Goods* (An Arts Council England Notice: 2015 Issue 2) Part II para 38, Appendix E.
16 See *UK Export Licensing for Cultural Goods: Procedures and Guidance for Exporters of Works of Art and other Cultural Goods* (An Arts Council England Notice: 2015 Issue 2) Part II para 40.
17 See *UK Export Licensing for Cultural Goods: Procedures and Guidance for Exporters of Works of Art and other Cultural Goods* (An Arts Council England Notice: 2015 Issue 2) Part II paras 39, 41.
18 See *UK Export Licensing for Cultural Goods: Procedures and Guidance for Exporters of Works of Art and other Cultural Goods* (An Arts Council England Notice: 2015 Issue 2) Part II paras 44–52. See also *R v Secretary of State for National Heritage, ex p J Paul Getty Trust* (27 October 1994, unreported), CA (an application for judicial review of the decision of the Secretary of State to extend the period for which an application for an export licence was to be deferred).
19 See *UK Export Licensing for Cultural Goods: Procedures and Guidance for Exporters of Works of Art and other Cultural Goods* (An Arts Council England Notice: 2015 Issue 2) Part I para 24.
20 See *UK Export Licensing for Cultural Goods: Procedures and Guidance for Exporters of Works of Art and other Cultural Goods* (An Arts Council England Notice: 2015 Issue 2) Part II paras 61–63.
21 See *UK Export Licensing for Cultural Goods: Procedures and Guidance for Exporters of Works of Art and other Cultural Goods* (An Arts Council England Notice: 2015 Issue 2) Part II paras 64–66.
22 See *UK Export Licensing for Cultural Goods: Procedures and Guidance for Exporters of Works of Art and other Cultural Goods* (An Arts Council England Notice: 2015 Issue 2) Part II para 83, Appendix F.
23 See *UK Export Licensing for Cultural Goods: Procedures and Guidance for Exporters of Works of Art and other Cultural Goods* (An Arts Council England Notice: 2015 Issue 2) Part II para 85.
24 See *UK Export Licensing for Cultural Goods: Procedures and Guidance for Exporters of Works of Art and other Cultural Goods* (An Arts Council England Notice: 2015 Issue 2) Part I para 25.
25 See *UK Export Licensing for Cultural Goods: Procedures and Guidance for Exporters of Works of Art and other Cultural Goods* (An Arts Council England Notice: 2015 Issue 2) Part I para 25.

1097. Iraqi cultural property. Under European Union (EU) law there is prohibited the import of or the introduction into the territory of the EU of, the export of or removal from the territory of the EU of, and the dealing in, Iraqi cultural property and other items of archaeological, historical, cultural, rare scientific and religious importance, if they have been illegally removed from locations in Iraq[1].

The importation or exportation[2] of any item of illegally removed Iraqi cultural property[3] is prohibited[4]. Any person[5] who holds or controls any item of illegally removed Iraqi cultural property must cause the transfer of that item to a constable[6]; and any person who fails to do so is guilty of an offence, unless he proves[7] that he did not know and had no reason to suppose that the item in question was illegally removed Iraqi cultural property[8]. Similarly, any person who deals in any item[9] of illegally removed Iraqi cultural property is guilty of an offence, unless he proves[10] that he did not know and had no reason to suppose that the item in question was illegally removed Iraqi cultural property[11].

1 See Council Regulation (EC) 1210/2003 (OJ L169, 8.7.2003, p 6) concerning certain specific restrictions on economic and financial relations with Iraq, art 3. As to the direct effect of EU regulations see EUROPEAN UNION vol 47A (2014) PARA 110.
2 'Export' includes shipment as stores: Iraq (United Nations Sanctions) Order 2003, SI 2003/1519, art 4. 'Shipment' includes loading into an aircraft, and 'shipped' and cognate expressions must be construed accordingly; and 'stores' means, subject to the Customs and Excise Management Act 1979 s 1(4), goods for use in a ship or aircraft and includes fuel and spare parts and other articles of equipment, whether or not for immediate fitting: s 1(1) (definition applied by the Iraq (United Nations Sanctions) Order 2003, SI 2003/1519, art 4).
3 'Illegally removed Iraqi cultural property' means Iraqi cultural property and any other item of archaeological, historical, cultural, rare scientific or religious importance illegally removed from any location in Iraq since 6 August 1990; and it is immaterial whether the removal was illegal under the law of a part of the United Kingdom or of any other country or territory: Iraq (United Nations Sanctions) Order 2003, SI 2003/1519, art 8(4). As to the meaning of 'United Kingdom' see PARA 804 note 2.
4 Iraq (United Nations Sanctions) Order 2003, SI 2003/1519, art 8(1).
5 As to the meaning of 'person' see PARA 803 note 17.
6 As to the office of constable see POLICE AND INVESTIGATORY POWERS vol 84 (2013) PARA 1 et seq.
7 As to the standard of proof on the accused see CRIMINAL PROCEDURE vol 28 (2015) PARAS 449–451.
8 Iraq (United Nations Sanctions) Order 2003, SI 2003/1519, art 8(2). Any person guilty of an offence under art 8(2) or 8(3) (see the text to notes 9–11) is liable:
   (1) on conviction on indictment to imprisonment for a term not exceeding seven years or to a fine or to both (art 20(1)(a)); or
   (2) on summary conviction to imprisonment for a term not exceeding six months or to a fine not exceeding the statutory maximum or to both (art 20(1)(b)).
As to the statutory maximum and magistrates' powers to levy unlimited fines see SENTENCING vol 92 (2015) PARA 176. Where any body corporate is guilty of such an offence, and that offence is proved to have been committed with the consent or connivance of, or to be attributable to any neglect on the part of, any director, manager, secretary or other similar officer of the body corporate or any person who was purporting to act in any such capacity, he, as well as the body corporate, is guilty of that offence and is liable to be proceeded against and punished accordingly: art 20(6). Notwithstanding anything in the Magistrates' Courts Act 1980 s 127(1) (see MAGISTRATES vol 71 (2013) PARA 526), a summary offence may be tried by a magistrates' court in England and Wales if an information is laid at any time within three years after the commission of the offence and within 12 months after the date on which evidence sufficient in the opinion of the prosecutor to justify the proceedings comes to his knowledge: Iraq (United Nations Sanctions) Order 2003, SI 2003/1519, art 20(7). As to the meaning of 'month' see PARA 803 note 12. A certificate signed by or on behalf of the prosecutor as to the date on which such evidence came to his knowledge is conclusive evidence of that fact (art 20(10)(a)); and a certificate purporting to be so signed must be presumed to be so signed unless the contrary is proved (art 20(10)(b)). Proceedings against any person for an offence may be taken before the appropriate court in the United Kingdom having jurisdiction in the place where that person is for the time being: art 20(11). No proceedings for an offence, other than for a summary offence, may be instituted except by the Secretary of State or with the consent of the Attorney General: provided that this provision does not prevent the arrest, or the issue or execution of a warrant for the arrest, of any person in respect of such an offence, or the remand in custody or on bail of any person charged with such an offence, notwithstanding that the necessary consent to the institution of proceedings for the offence has not been obtained: see art 20(15). As to the Secretary of State see PARA 802 note 2. As to the Attorney

       General see CONSTITUTIONAL AND ADMINISTRATIVE LAW vol 20 (2014) PARA 273. As to powers of arrest see POLICE AND INVESTIGATORY POWERS vol 84A (2013) PARA 483 et seq.

9   A person deals in an item if (and only if) he: (1) acquires, disposes of, imports or exports it (Iraq (United Nations Sanctions) Order 2003, SI 2003/1519, art 8(5)(a)); (2) agrees with another to do an act mentioned in head (1) (art 8(5)(b)); or (3) makes arrangements under which another person does such an act or under which another person agrees with a third person to do such an act (art 8(5)(c)). 'Acquires' means buys, hires, borrows or accepts (art 8(6)(a)); 'disposes of' means sells, lets on hire, lends or gives (art 8(6)(b)); and in relation to agreeing or arranging to do an act, it is immaterial whether the act is agreed or arranged to take place in the United Kingdom or elsewhere (art 8(6)(c)).

10   See note 7.

11   Iraq (United Nations Sanctions) Order 2003, SI 2003/1519, art 8(3). As to the penalty for such an offence see note 8.

(4) ILLICIT TRADE IN CULTURAL OBJECTS

(i) UNESCO Convention

1098. Prevention of illicit trade in cultural objects: the UNESCO Convention. The UNESCO Convention on the Means of Prohibiting and Preventing the Illicit Import, Export and Transfer of Ownership of Cultural Property[1] provides that the import, export or transfer of ownership of cultural property[2] effected contrary to the provisions adopted under the convention by the states party to it, is illicit[3]. The states party to the convention[4] undertake:

(1)   to oppose the illicit import, export and transfer of ownership of cultural property and to help to make the necessary reparations[5];

(2)   to set up within their territories one or more national services for the protection of the cultural heritage[6];

(3)   to introduce a system of export certificates authorising the export of cultural property[7] with sanctions for the infringement thereof[8];

(4)   to prevent museums and similar institutions within their territories from acquiring cultural property originating in another party state which has been illegally exported; to prohibit the import of cultural property stolen from a museum or a religious or secular public monument or similar institution in another such state, and to take appropriate steps to recover and return any such imported property[9];

(5)   to prevent transfers of ownership of cultural property likely to promote the illicit import or export of such property[10];

(6)   to restrict movement of cultural property illegally removed from any state party to the convention and to oblige antique dealers, subject to penal or administrative sanctions, to maintain a register of each item of cultural property sold and to inform the purchaser of the cultural property of the export prohibition to which such property may be subject[11];

(7)   to endeavour by educational means to create and develop in the public mind a realisation of the value of cultural property and the threat to the cultural heritage created by theft, clandestine excavations and illicit exports[12].

Any state party to the convention whose cultural patrimony is in jeopardy from pillage of archaeological or ethnological materials may call upon other state parties who are affected; and, in these circumstances, the state parties undertake to participate in a concerted international effort to determine and to carry out the necessary concrete measures, including the control of exports and imports and international commerce in the specific materials concerned[13].

The export and transfer of ownership of cultural property under compulsion arising directly or indirectly from the occupation of a country by a foreign power is regarded as illicit[14]. States party to the convention must respect the cultural heritage within the territories for the international relations of which they are responsible, and must take all appropriate measures to prohibit and prevent the illicit import, export and transfer of ownership of cultural property in such territories[15]. In order to prevent illicit export and to meet the obligations arising from the convention, each state party to the convention should, as far as it is able, provide the national services responsible for the protection of its cultural heritage with an adequate budget and, if necessary, should set up a fund for this purpose[16].

1   Ie the UNESCO Convention on the Means of Prohibiting and Preventing the Illicit Import, Export and Transfer of Ownership of Cultural Property 1970 (Paris, 14 November 1970).

2   'Cultural property' means property which, on religious or secular grounds, is specifically designated by each state party to the UNESCO Convention on the Means of Prohibiting and Preventing the Illicit Import, Export and Transfer of Ownership of Cultural Property 1970 (Paris, 14 November 1970) as being of importance for archaeology, prehistory, history, literature, art or science and which belongs to the following categories:

(1)   rare collections and specimens of fauna, flora, minerals and anatomy, and objects of palaeontological interest;

(2)   property relating to history, including the history of science and technology and military and social history, to the life of national leaders, thinkers, scientists and artists and to events of national importance;

(3)   products of archaeological excavations (including regular and clandestine) or of archaeological discoveries;

(4)   elements of artistic or historical monuments or archaeological sites which have been dismembered;

(5)   antiquities more than 100 years old, such as inscriptions, coins and engraved seals;

(6)   objects of ethnological interest;

(7)   property of artistic interest, such as:

(a)   pictures, paintings and drawings produced entirely by hand on any support and in any material (excluding industrial designs and manufactured articles decorated by hand);

(b)   original works of statuary art and sculpture in any material; (c) original engravings, prints and lithographs; (d) original artistic assemblages and montages in any material;

(8)   rare manuscripts and incunabula, old books, documents and publications of special interest (historical, artistic, scientific, literary, etc) singly or in collections;

(9)   postage, revenue and similar stamps, singly or in collections;

(10)   archives, including sound, photographic and cinematographic archives;

(11)   articles of furniture more than 100 years old and old musical instruments: art 1.

For the purposes of the Convention property which belongs to the following categories forms part of the cultural heritage of each state:

(i)   cultural property created by the individual or collective genius of nationals of the state concerned, and cultural property of importance to the state concerned created within the territory of that state by foreign nationals or stateless persons resident within such territory (art 4(a));

(ii)   cultural property found within the national territory (art 4(b));

(iii)   cultural property acquired by archaeological, ethnological or natural science missions, with the consent of the competent authorities of the country of origin of such property (art 4(c));

(iv)   cultural property which has been the subject of a freely agreed exchange (art 4(d));

(v)   cultural property received as a gift or purchased legally with the consent of the competent authorities of the country of origin of such property (art 4(e)).

3   See the UNESCO Convention on the Means of Prohibiting and Preventing the Illicit Import, Export and Transfer of Ownership of Cultural Property 1970 (Paris, 14 November 1970) art 3.

4   The United Kingdom deposited an instrument of acceptance in respect of the convention on 1 August 2002. This followed a recommendation by the Ministerial Advisory Panel on the Illicit Trade in Cultural Objects (ITAP) established by the Secretary of State for Culture, Media and

Sport. ITAP considered that the current state of UK law and practice would enable the UK to implement the convention without new legislation, a position with which the government agreed. As to the first case which openly applied the convention see *Government of the Islamic Republic of Iran v Barakat Galleries Ltd* [2007] EWCA Civ 1374 (where Iran sought to assert ownership of antiquities originating from Iran as against Barakat Galleries which had the antiquities in its possession in London). The government also agreed to a recommendation by ITAP that there be created a new criminal offence of trading in illegally removed cultural objects, accepting that this offence would complement its treaty obligations and reinforce its implementation in the UK: see the Dealing in Cultural Objects (Offences) Act 2003 Explanatory Notes paras 3–6. As to the Dealing in Cultural Objects (Offences) Act 2003 see PARA 1104.

5 See the UNESCO Convention on the Means of Prohibiting and Preventing the Illicit Import, Export and Transfer of Ownership of Cultural Property 1970 (Paris, 14 November 1970) art 2.

6 See the UNESCO Convention on the Means of Prohibiting and Preventing the Illicit Import, Export and Transfer of Ownership of Cultural Property 1970 (Paris, 14 November 1970) art 5.

7 See the UNESCO Convention on the Means of Prohibiting and Preventing the Illicit Import, Export and Transfer of Ownership of Cultural Property 1970 (Paris, 14 November 1970) art 6.

8 See the UNESCO Convention on the Means of Prohibiting and Preventing the Illicit Import, Export and Transfer of Ownership of Cultural Property 1970 (Paris, 14 November 1970) art 8.

9 See the UNESCO Convention on the Means of Prohibiting and Preventing the Illicit Import, Export and Transfer of Ownership of Cultural Property 1970 (Paris, 14 November 1970) arts 7, 8.

10 See the UNESCO Convention on the Means of Prohibiting and Preventing the Illicit Import, Export and Transfer of Ownership of Cultural Property 1970 (Paris, 14 November 1970) art 13.

11 See the UNESCO Convention on the Means of Prohibiting and Preventing the Illicit Import, Export and Transfer of Ownership of Cultural Property 1970 (Paris, 14 November 1970) art 10(a).

12 See the UNESCO Convention on the Means of Prohibiting and Preventing the Illicit Import, Export and Transfer of Ownership of Cultural Property 1970 (Paris, 14 November 1970) art 10(b).

13 See the UNESCO Convention on the Means of Prohibiting and Preventing the Illicit Import, Export and Transfer of Ownership of Cultural Property 1970 (Paris, 14 November 1970) art 9.

14 See the UNESCO Convention on the Means of Prohibiting and Preventing the Illicit Import, Export and Transfer of Ownership of Cultural Property 1970 (Paris, 14 November 1970) art 11.

15 See the UNESCO Convention on the Means of Prohibiting and Preventing the Illicit Import, Export and Transfer of Ownership of Cultural Property 1970 (Paris, 14 November 1970) art 12.

16 See the UNESCO Convention on the Means of Prohibiting and Preventing the Illicit Import, Export and Transfer of Ownership of Cultural Property 1970 (Paris, 14 November 1970) art 14.

(ii) Return of Cultural Objects Unlawfully Removed from Member States

1099. Cultural objects unlawfully removed from the territory of a member state. Arrangements have been introduced enabling member states of the European Union (EU) to secure the return[1] to their territory of cultural objects which are, or may be, classified as national treasures and which have been unlawfully removed[2]. For these purposes, 'cultural object' means an object which is classified[3], before or after its unlawful removal from the territory of a member state, among the national treasures possessing artistic, historic or archaeological value[4].

Cultural objects which have been unlawfully removed on or after 1 January 1993 must be returned in the prescribed circumstances in accordance with the prescribed procedure[5]. Each member state may apply the arrangements provided for by the Directive to requests for the return of cultural objects unlawfully removed from the territory of other member states prior to that date[6].

Ownership of a cultural object after return is governed by the law of the member state which has requested its return[7]. The provisions of the Directive are without prejudice to any civil or criminal proceedings that may be brought, under the national laws of the member states, by the requesting member state and/or the owner of a cultural object that has been stolen[8].

1 'Return' means the physical return of the cultural object to the territory of the requesting member state; and 'requesting member state' means the member state from whose territory the cultural object has been unlawfully removed: European Parliament and Council Directive (EU) 2014/60 (OJ L159, 28.5.2014, p 1) on the return of cultural objects unlawfully removed from the territory of a member state, arts 2(3), (5), 20; Return of Cultural Objects Regulations 1994, SI 1994/501, reg 2(1), (2) (reg 2(1) substituted, and reg 2(2) amended, by SI 2015/1926). 'Unlawfully removed from the territory of a member state' means removed from its territory in breach of its rules on the protection of national treasures or in breach of Council Regulation (EC) 116/2009 (OJ L39, 10.2.2009, p 1) (see PARA 1096) or not returned at the end of a period of lawful temporary removal or any breach of another condition governing such temporary removal: European Parliament and Council Directive (EU) 2014/60 (OJ L159, 28.5.2014, p 1) arts 2(2), 20; Return of Cultural Objects Regulations 1994, SI 1994/501, reg 2(1), (2) (as so substituted and amended).
2 See European Parliament and Council Directive (EU) 2014/60 (OJ L159, 28.5.2014, p 1). The Return of Cultural Objects Regulations 1994, SI 1994/501, have been made for the purpose of implementing the Directive: see PARA 1100 et seq.
3 Ie under national legislation or administrative procedures within the meaning of the Treaty on the Functioning of the European Union (Rome, 25 March 1957; TS 1 (1973); Cmnd 5179) art 36. As to the Treaty (commonly abbreviated to 'TFEU') see EUROPEAN UNION vol 47A (2014) PARA 6.
4 European Parliament and Council Directive (EU) 2014/60 (OJ L159, 28.5.2014, p 1) arts 2(1), 20; Return of Cultural Objects Regulations 1994, SI 1994/501, reg 2(1), (2) (as amended: see note 1).
5 See European Parliament and Council Directive (EU) 2014/60 (OJ L159, 28.5.2014, p 1) arts 3, 14; the Return of Cultural Objects Regulations 1994, SI 1994/501; and PARA 1100 et seq.
6 European Parliament and Council Directive (EU) 2014/60 (OJ L159, 28.5.2014, p 1) art 15(2).
7 European Parliament and Council Directive (EU) 2014/60 (OJ L159, 28.5.2014, p 1) art 13.
8 European Parliament and Council Directive (EU) 2014/60 (OJ L159, 28.5.2014, p 1) art 16. As to the offence of dealing in tainted cultural objects see PARA 1104.

1100. Investigation by the Secretary of State of unlawfully removed cultural objects. Upon application by a member state[1], the Secretary of State[2] must seek a specified cultural object[3] which has been unlawfully removed from its territory[4], and must take steps to identify any possessor or holder[5]. The Secretary of State is not, however, under any duty by virtue of this obligation unless the application includes all information needed to facilitate the search and, in particular, information with reference to the actual or presumed location of the object[6].

The Secretary of State must notify the member state concerned, where a cultural object is found in the United Kingdom[7] (whether or not as the result of such a search) and there are reasonable grounds for believing that it has been unlawfully removed from the territory of that state[8]. The Secretary of State must:

(1)   take steps to enable the competent authorities of the member state concerned to check that the object in question is a cultural object[9];

(2)   take any necessary measures, in co-operation with the member state concerned, for the physical preservation of an object which appears as a result of such a check to be a cultural object[10];

(3)   prevent, by the necessary interim measures, any action to evade the return procedure[11].

The High Court[12] has power, on an application made by the Secretary of State[13] for the purpose of performing his functions under these provisions, to make such order as it considers appropriate[14]:

(a)   to enable a check to be made under head (1) above[15];

(b)   for the physical preservation of an object which appears as a result of such a check to be a cultural object[16];

(c)   to prevent any action to avoid the return procedure[17].

1 As to the meaning of 'member state' see the Interpretation Act 1978 s 5, Sch 1; and the European Communities Act 1972 s 1(2), Sch 1 Pt II.
2 As to the Secretary of State see PARA 802 note 2.

3 The Return of Cultural Objects Regulations 1994, SI 1994/501, apply only to cultural objects
   unlawfully removed from the territory of a member state on or after 1 January 1993: Return of
   Cultural Objects Regulations 1994, SI 1994/501, reg 1(3). As to the meaning of 'cultural object'
   see PARA 1099. As to the meaning of 'unlawfully removed from the territory of a member state'
   see PARA 1099 note 1. As to the lawful export of cultural objects see PARA 1096.
4 Return of Cultural Objects Regulations 1994, SI 1994/501, reg 3(1)(a).
5 Return of Cultural Objects Regulations 1994, SI 1994/501, reg 3(1)(b). 'Possessor' means the
   person physically holding the cultural object on his own account; and 'holder' means the person
   physically holding it for third parties: European Parliament and Council Directive (EU) 2014/60
   (OJ L159, 28.5.2014, p 1) art 2(6), (7); Return of Cultural Objects Regulations 1994, SI 1994/501,
   reg 2(1), (2) (reg 2(1) substituted, and reg 2(2) amended, by SI 2015/1926).
6 Return of Cultural Objects Regulations 1994, SI 1994/501, reg 3(2).
7 As to the meaning of 'United Kingdom' see PARA 804 note 2.
8 Return of Cultural Objects Regulations 1994, SI 1994/501, reg 3(3).
9 Return of Cultural Objects Regulations 1994, SI 1994/501, reg 3(4)(a). If the check for which
   reg 3(4)(a) provides is not made within six months of the notification under reg 3(3) (see the text
   to notes 7–8), the Secretary of State ceases to be under any duty by virtue of reg 3(4): reg 3(5)
   (amended by SI 2015/1926). As to the meaning of 'month' see PARA 803 note 12.
10 Return of Cultural Objects Regulations 1994, SI 1994/501, reg 3(4)(b). Expenses incurred in
   taking necessary measures for the preservation of a cultural object must be borne by the member
   state which made the application as respects the object or (where no such application is made)
   which, having been notified under reg 3(3) (see the text to notes 7–8) as respects the object, seeks
   its return (whether by proceedings under reg 6 (see PARA 1102) or otherwise): reg 3(6).
11 Return of Cultural Objects Regulations 1994, SI 1994/501, reg 3(4)(c). The return procedure is
   that under the Return of Cultural Objects Regulations 1994, SI 1994/501: see PARAS 1099–1102.
12 As to the High Court of Justice in England and Wales see COURTS AND TRIBUNALS vol 24 (2010)
   PARA 695 et seq.
13 An application for an order may be made ex parte (Return of Cultural Objects Regulations 1994,
   SI 1994/501, reg 4(2)(a)) and must be supported by an affidavit (reg 4(2)(b)).
14 Return of Cultural Objects Regulations 1994, SI 1994/501, regs 2(4)(a), 4(1). Without prejudice
   to the generality of reg 4(1), the power to make such an order includes power to authorise the
   Secretary of State's officer to take possession of the object (reg 4(3)(a)) and to hand the object over
   to the custody of a person or institution specified in the order (reg 4(3)(b)). As to the meaning of
   'person' see PARA 803 note 17.
15 Return of Cultural Objects Regulations 1994, SI 1994/501, reg 4(1)(a).
16 Return of Cultural Objects Regulations 1994, SI 1994/501, reg 4(1)(b).
17 Return of Cultural Objects Regulations 1994, SI 1994/501, reg 4(1)(c).

1101. Powers of entry and search in relation to unlawfully removed cultural objects. If on an application made by the Secretary of State[1] for the purpose of performing his functions in relation to the return of cultural objects[2] the High Court[3] is satisfied:

(1)   that there are reasonable grounds for believing that a cultural object has been unlawfully removed from the territory of a member state[4], and that it is on premises specified in the application[5]; and

(2)   that that admission to the premises has been refused, or that the case is one of urgency, or that an application for admission to the premises would defeat the object of the entry[6],

the court may make an order authorising an officer of the Secretary of State to enter and search the premises and such an order may authorise other persons to accompany that officer[7].

An order so made must authorise an entry on one occasion only and must identify, so far as practicable, the cultural object to be sought[8] and must specify: (a) the name of the officer and of any other person authorised to accompany him[9]; (b) the date on which it is made[10]; (c) that it is made under these provisions[11]; and (d) the premises to be searched[12]. Entry and search under an order must be within one month[13] from the date of the order and must be at a reasonable hour unless it appears to the officer executing it that the object of the entry may be defeated on an entry at a reasonable hour[14]. A search under such an order may only be a search to the extent required for the purpose for which the order was made[15].

1   An application may be made ex parte (Return of Cultural Objects Regulations 1994, SI 1994/501, reg 5(3)(a)), must be supported by an affidavit (reg 5(3)(b)), and must specify the premises which it is desired to enter and search, and identify, so far as practicable, the cultural object to be sought (reg 5(3)(c)). As to the Secretary of State see PARA 802 note 2. As to the meaning of 'cultural object' see PARA 1099.
2   Ie the functions of the Secretary of State under the Return of Cultural Objects Regulations 1994, SI 1994/501, reg 3 (see PARA 1100). As to the meaning of 'return' see PARA 1099 note 1.
3   See the Return of Cultural Objects Regulations 1994, SI 1994/501, reg 2(4)(a). As to the High Court of Justice in England and Wales see COURTS AND TRIBUNALS vol 24 (2010) PARA 695 et seq.
4   Return of Cultural Objects Regulations 1994, SI 1994/501, reg 5(1)(a)(i). As to the meaning of 'unlawfully removed from the territory of a member state' see PARA 1099 note 1.
5   Return of Cultural Objects Regulations 1994, SI 1994/501, reg 5(1)(a)(ii).
6   See the Return of Cultural Objects Regulations 1994, SI 1994/501, reg 5(1)(b), (2).
7   Return of Cultural Objects Regulations 1994, SI 1994/501, reg 5(1). As to the meaning of 'person' see PARA 803 note 17.
8   Return of Cultural Objects Regulations 1994, SI 1994/501, reg 5(4)(b).
9   Return of Cultural Objects Regulations 1994, SI 1994/501, reg 5(4)(a)(i).
10 Return of Cultural Objects Regulations 1994, SI 1994/501, reg 5(4)(a)(ii).
11 Return of Cultural Objects Regulations 1994, SI 1994/501, reg 5(4)(a)(iii).
12 Return of Cultural Objects Regulations 1994, SI 1994/501, reg 5(4)(a)(iv).
13 As to the meaning of 'month' see PARA 803 note 12.
14 Return of Cultural Objects Regulations 1994, SI 1994/501, reg 5(5). Where the officer seeks to execute such an order he must, if requested by the occupier or other person appearing to him to be in charge of the premises, identify himself and produce the order to that person: reg 5(6).
15 Return of Cultural Objects Regulations 1994, SI 1994/501, reg 5(7).

1102. Member state's right to take proceedings for return of cultural object. A member state[1] has a right of action against the possessor[2] or, failing him, the holder[3], for the return[4] of a cultural object[5] which has been unlawfully removed from its territory[6]. Proceedings under these provisions may not, however, be brought if removal from the national territory of the member state is no longer unlawful at the time when they are to be initiated[7].

Proceedings must be brought in the High Court[8]. The document initiating the proceedings must be accompanied by a document describing the object covered by the request and stating that it is a cultural object[9], and a declaration by the competent authorities of the member state that the object has been unlawfully removed from its territory[10]. The court must order the return of the object where it finds it to be the cultural object covered by the request[11] and to have been removed unlawfully from the national territory of the member state[12]. However, the court must not make an order for the return of the object if it is satisfied that: (1) the proceedings were brought more than three years after the competent central authority of the requesting member state became aware of the location of the cultural object and of the identity of its possessor or holder[13]; or (2) they were brought after the expiry of the special limitation period[14].

Expenses incurred in implementing an order for the return of a cultural object must be borne by the requesting member state[15].

1   As to the meaning of 'member state' see the Interpretation Act 1978 s 5, Sch 1; and the European Communities Act 1972 s 1(2), Sch 1 Pt II.
2   As to the meaning of 'possessor' see PARA 1100 note 5.
3   As to the meaning of 'holder' see PARA 1100 note 5.
4   As to the meaning of 'return' see PARA 1099 note 1.
5   As to the meaning of 'cultural object' see PARA 1099.
6   Return of Cultural Objects Regulations 1994, SI 1994/501, reg 6(1). As to the meaning of 'unlawfully removed from the territory of a member state' see PARA 1099 note 1.
7   Return of Cultural Objects Regulations 1994, SI 1994/501, reg 6(2).

8 See the Return of Cultural Objects Regulations 1994, SI 1994/501, regs 2(4)(a), 6(3).
9 Return of Cultural Objects Regulations 1994, SI 1994/501, reg 6(4)(a).
10 Return of Cultural Objects Regulations 1994, SI 1994/501, reg 6(4)(b).
11 Return of Cultural Objects Regulations 1994, SI 1994/501, reg 6(5)(a).
12 Return of Cultural Objects Regulations 1994, SI 1994/501, reg 6(5)(b). As to orders for compensation see PARA 1103.
13 Return of Cultural Objects Regulations 1994, SI 1994/501, reg 6(6)(a) (amended by SI 2015/1926).
14 Return of Cultural Objects Regulations 1994, SI 1994/501, reg 6(6)(b). The special limitation period in the case of objects forming part of public collections, referred to in European Parliament and Council Directive (EU) 2014/60 (OJ L159, 28.5.2014, p 1) (see art 2(8); and PARA 1099), and of objects belonging to inventories of ecclesiastical or other religious institutions subject to special protection arrangements under the national law of the member state, is the period of 75 years commencing with the date on which the object was unlawfully removed from the territory of the requesting member state: Return of Cultural Objects Regulations 1994, SI 1994/501, reg 6(7) (amended by SI 2015/1926). In any other case the special limitation period is the period of 30 years commencing with that date: Return of Cultural Objects Regulations 1994, SI 1994/501, reg 6(8). These rules have effect in place of any other rule as to the limitation of actions: reg 6(9). As to the meaning of 'requesting member state' see PARA 1099 note 1. As to limitation of actions generally see LIMITATION PERIODS vol 68 (2008) PARA 901 et seq.
15 Return of Cultural Objects Regulations 1994, SI 1994/501, reg 8.

1103. Order for compensation when return of cultural object is ordered. Where return[1] of a cultural object[2] is ordered[3], the High Court[4] must order the requesting member state[5] to pay the possessor[6] fair compensation[7]. However, the court must not order the payment of compensation unless the possessor demonstrates that he exercised due care and attention in acquiring the object[8]. In determining whether the possessor exercised due care and attention, the competent court must consider all the circumstances of the acquisition, in particular: (1) the documentation on the object's provenance[9]; (2) the authorisations for removal required under the law of the requesting member state[10]; (3) the character of the parties[11]; (4) the price paid[12]; and (5) whether the possessor consulted any accessible register of stolen cultural objects and any relevant information which he could reasonably have obtained, or took any other step which a reasonable person would have taken in the circumstances[13].

1 As to the meaning of 'return' see PARA 1099 note 1.
2 As to the meaning of 'cultural object' see PARA 1099.
3 As to orders for the return of cultural objects see PARA 1102.
4 See the Return of Cultural Objects Regulations 1994, SI 1994/501, reg 2(4)(a). As to the High Court of Justice in England and Wales see COURTS AND TRIBUNALS vol 24 (2010) PARA 695 et seq.
5 As to the meaning of 'requesting member state' see PARA 1099 note 1.
6 As to the meaning of 'possessor' see PARA 1100 note 5.
7 Return of Cultural Objects Regulations 1994, SI 1994/501, reg 7(1) (amended by SI 2015/1926).
8 Return of Cultural Objects Regulations 1994, SI 1994/501, reg 7(2) (amended by SI 2015/1926). In the application of the Return of Cultural Objects Regulations 1994, SI 1994/501, reg 7(2) where there has been a donation or succession, the possessor must not be in a more favourable position than the person from whom he acquired the object upon the donation or succession: reg 7(3). As to the meaning of 'person' see PARA 803 note 17.
9 Return of Cultural Objects Regulations 1994, SI 1994/501, reg 7(2A)(a) (reg 7(2A) added by SI 2015/1926).
10 Return of Cultural Objects Regulations 1994, SI 1994/501, reg 7(2A)(b) (as added: see note 9).
11 Return of Cultural Objects Regulations 1994, SI 1994/501, reg 7(2A)(c) (as added: see note 9).
12 Return of Cultural Objects Regulations 1994, SI 1994/501, reg 7(2A)(d) (as added: see note 9).
13 Return of Cultural Objects Regulations 1994, SI 1994/501, reg 7(2A)(e) (as added: see note 9).

(iii) Dealing in Tainted Cultural Objects

1104. Offence of dealing in tainted cultural objects. A person[1] is guilty of an offence if he dishonestly deals in[2] a cultural object[3] that is tainted, knowing or believing that the object is tainted[4]; and for these purposes, it is immaterial whether he knows or believes that the object is a cultural object[5].

A cultural object is tainted if, after 30 December 2003[6], a person:

(1) removes the object:

    (a) from a building or structure of historical, architectural or archaeological interest where the object has at any time formed part of the building or structure[7], or

    (b) from a monument[8] of such interest[9]; or

(2) excavates the object[10], and

the removal or excavation constitutes an offence[11]. For these purposes, it is immaterial whether:

(i) the removal or excavation was done in the United Kingdom or elsewhere[12];

(ii) the offence is committed under the law of a part of the United Kingdom or under the law of any other country or territory[13];

(iii) a building, structure or work is above or below the surface of the land[14];

(iv) a site is above or below water[15].

If an offence of dealing in tainted cultural objects[16] committed by a body corporate is proved to have been committed with the consent or connivance of an officer[17], or to be attributable to any neglect on his part[18], he (as well as the body corporate) is guilty of the offence and liable to be proceeded against and punished accordingly[19].

Proceedings for an offence relating to the dealing in a tainted cultural object[20] may be instituted by the Director of Public Prosecutions or by order of the Commissioners for Her Majesty's Revenue and Customs[21] if it appears to the director or to the commissioners that the offence has involved the importation or exportation of such an object[22]. Where the Commissioners investigate, or propose to investigate, any matter with a view to determining:

(A) whether there are grounds for believing that a person has committed an offence which relates to the dealing in a tainted cultural object and which involves the importation or exportation of such an object[23], or

(B) whether a person should be prosecuted for such an offence[24],

the matter is to be treated as an assigned matter within the meaning of the Customs and Excise Management Act 1979[25].

1   As to the meaning of 'person' see PARA 803 note 17.

2   For these purposes (see the Dealing in Cultural Objects (Offences) Act 2003 s 3(5)), a person deals in an object if (and only if) he: (1) acquires, disposes of, imports or exports it (s 3(1)(a)); (2) agrees with another to do an act mentioned in head (1) (s 3(1)(b)); or (3) makes arrangements under which another person does such an act or under which another person agrees with a third person to do such an act (s 3(1)(c)). 'Acquires' means buys, hires, borrows or accepts: s 3(2). 'Disposes of' means sells, lets on hire, lends or gives: s 3(3). In relation to agreeing or arranging to do an act, it is immaterial whether the act is agreed or arranged to take place in the United Kingdom or elsewhere: s 3(4). See also PARA 1105. As to the meaning of 'United Kingdom' see PARA 804 note 2.

3   'Cultural object' means an object of historical, architectural or archaeological interest: Dealing in Cultural Objects (Offences) Act 2003 s 2(1).

4   Dealing in Cultural Objects (Offences) Act 2003 s 1(1). A person guilty of the offence is liable:

    (1) on conviction on indictment, to imprisonment for a term not exceeding seven years or a fine (or both) (s 1(3)(a));

    (2) on summary conviction, to imprisonment for a term not exceeding six months or a fine not exceeding the statutory maximum (or both) (s 1(3)(b)).

As to the statutory maximum and magistrates' powers to levy unlimited fines see SENTENCING vol 92 (2015) PARA 176. The Department for Culture, Media and Sport has produced guidance on this offence: see *Dealing in Tainted Cultural Objects: Guidance on the Dealing in Cultural*

Objects (Offences) Act 2003 (Department for Culture, Media and Sport; January 2004). A copy of the guidance is available at www.old.culture.gov.uk.

5 Dealing in Cultural Objects (Offences) Act 2003 s 1(2).

6 Ie the date of the commencement of the Dealing in Cultural Objects (Offences) Act 2003: see ss 2(2), 6(2).

7 See the Dealing in Cultural Objects (Offences) Act 2003 s 2(2)(a), (4)(a).

8 For these purposes, 'monument' means: (1) any work, cave or excavation; (2) any site comprising the remains of any building or structure or of any work, cave or excavation; (3) any site comprising, or comprising the remains of, any vehicle, vessel, aircraft or other moveable structure, or part of any such thing: Dealing in Cultural Objects (Offences) Act 2003 s 2(5)(a)–(c), (8). 'Remains' includes any trace or sign of the previous existence of the thing in question: s 2(6), (8).

9 See the Dealing in Cultural Objects (Offences) Act 2003 s 2(2)(a), (4)(b).

10 See the Dealing in Cultural Objects (Offences) Act 2003 s 2(2)(a).

11 Dealing in Cultural Objects (Offences) Act 2003 s 2(2)(b). As to sentencing guidelines for offences of theft involving historic objects or loss of the nation's heritage see PARA 1046 note 5.

12 Dealing in Cultural Objects (Offences) Act 2003 s 2(3)(a).

13 Dealing in Cultural Objects (Offences) Act 2003 s 2(3)(b).

14 Dealing in Cultural Objects (Offences) Act 2003 s 2(7)(a). As to the meaning of 'land' see PARA 804 note 30.

15 Dealing in Cultural Objects (Offences) Act 2003 s 2(7)(b).

16 Ie an offence under the Dealing in Cultural Objects (Offences) Act 2003 s 1 (see the text to notes 1–5).

17 Dealing in Cultural Objects (Offences) Act 2003 s 5(1)(a). 'Officer', in relation to a body corporate, means (1) a director, manager, secretary or other similar officer of the body (s 5(2)(a)); (2) a person purporting to act in any such capacity (s 5(2)(b)). If the affairs of a body corporate are managed by its members, s 5(1) applies in relation to the acts and defaults of a member in connection with his functions of management as if he were a director of the body: s 5(3).

18 Dealing in Cultural Objects (Offences) Act 2003 s 5(1)(b).

19 Dealing in Cultural Objects (Offences) Act 2003 s 5(1).

20 An offence relates to the dealing in a tainted cultural object if it is (1) an offence under the Dealing in Cultural Objects (Offences) Act 2003 s 1 (see the text to notes 1–5) (s 4(2)(a)); or (2) an offence of inciting the commission of, or attempting or conspiring to commit, such an offence (s 4(2)(b)). The reference in head (2) above to (or to conduct amounting to) the common law offence of inciting the commission of another offence, has effect as a reference to (or to conduct amounting to) the offences under the Serious Crime Act 2007 Pt 2 (ss 44–67) (encouraging or assisting crime: see CRIMINAL LAW vol 25 (2010) PARA 64 et seq): see s 63(1), Sch 6 Pt 1 para 45.

21 As to the Director of Public Prosecutions see CRIMINAL PROCEDURE vol 27 (2015) PARA 25. As to the Commissioners for Her Majesty's Revenue and Customs see INCOME TAXATION vol 58 (2014) PARAS 33–34.

22 Dealing in Cultural Objects (Offences) Act 2003 s 4(1) (amended by the Commissioners for Revenue and Customs Act 2005, s 50(6), Sch 4, para 128(a); and SI 2014/834). Proceedings for an offence which are instituted by order of the commissioners are to be commenced in the name of an officer of Revenue and Customs, but may be continued by another officer: Dealing in Cultural Objects (Offences) Act 2003 s 4(3) (amended by the Commissioners for Revenue and Customs Act 2005, s 50(6), Sch 4, para 128(b)). 'Officer of Revenue and Customs' has the meaning given by the Commissioners for Revenue and Customs Act 2005 s 2(1) (see INCOME TAXATION vol 58 (2014) PARA 33: Interpretation Act 1978 s 5, Sch 1 (definition added by the Commissioners for Revenue and Customs Act 2005 s 2(7)). Nothing in the Dealing in Cultural Objects (Offences) Act 2003 s 4 affects any powers of any person (including any officer) apart from that section: s 4(5).

23 Dealing in Cultural Objects (Offences) Act 2003 s 4(4)(a).

24 Dealing in Cultural Objects (Offences) Act 2003 s 4(4)(b).

25 Dealing in Cultural Objects (Offences) Act 2003 s 4(4) (amended by the Commissioners for Revenue and Customs Act 2005 s 50(6), Sch 4, para 128(c)). 'Assigned matter' means any matter in relation to which the Commissioners, or officers of Revenue and Customs, have a power or duty: see the Customs and Excise Management Act 1979 s 1(1) (definition substituted by the Commissioners for Revenue and Customs Act 2005 s 50(6), Sch 4 paras 20, 22(a)); and CUSTOMS AND EXCISE vol 31 (2012) PARA 1164.

1105. Handling stolen cultural objects. A person may commit an offence under the Theft Act 1968 of handling stolen goods[1] if he handles cultural objects which have been stolen from a foreign country in breach of the laws of that country[2].

1 Ie an offence under the Theft Act 1968 s 22 (see CRIMINAL LAW vol 25 (2010) PARA 298).
2 See *R v Tokeley-Parry* [1999] Crim LR 578.

(iv) Nazi Spoliation

1106. Nazi spoliation and the Spoliation Advisory Panel. The term 'spoliation' refers to the systematic programme for the forced transfer of works of art and other cultural objects instigated by the Nazis between 1933, when they came to power, and the end of World War II in 1945[1].

In 1943 the United Kingdom and 16 other governments, in recognition of this situation, issued a declaration reserving the rights of governments to declare invalid any transfers of, or dealings in property subject to such spoliation[2]. In 1998 the Washington Conference on Holocaust-Era Assets endorsed certain principles for dealing with Nazi spoliated art[3], and in 1999 the Parliamentary Assembly of the Council of Europe passed a resolution calling for the restitution of looted Jewish cultural property in Europe[4]. Following on from the Washington conference, the Vilnius International Forum on Holocaust Era Looted Cultural Assets agreed in 2000 to a declaration asking all governments to undertake every reasonable effort to achieve the restitution of spoliated cultural assets to the original owners or their heirs[5]; and subsequently a further such declaration was issued in 2009 at the Holocaust Era Assets Conference in the Czech Republic[6].

The Spoliation Advisory Panel was first appointed in 2000[7]. The task of the Panel is to consider claims from anyone (or from any one or more of their heirs), who lost possession of a cultural object during the Nazi era (1933–1945), where such object is now in the possession of a United Kingdom[8] national collection or in the possession of another UK museum or gallery established for the public benefit[9]. The Panel must advise the claimant and the institution on what would be appropriate action to take in response to such a claim; and is also available to advise about any claim for an item in a private collection at the joint request of the claimant and the owner[10]. In any case where the Panel considers it appropriate, it may also advise the Secretary of State on what action should be taken in relation to general issues raised by the claim, and/or where it considers that the circumstances of the particular claim warrant it, on what action should be taken in relation to that claim[11]. In performing these functions, the Panel's paramount purpose is to achieve a solution which is fair and just both to the claimant and to the institution[12].

The Panel performs its functions and conducts its proceedings in strictest confidence[13]. It is not the function of the Panel to determine legal rights[14]; the Panel's proceedings are an alternative to litigation[15]. Any recommendation made by the Panel is not intended to be legally binding on the claimant, the institution or the Secretary of State[16], but if the claimant accepts the recommendation of the Panel and that recommendation is implemented, the claimant is expected to accept the implementation in full and final settlement of his claim[17]. If the Panel upholds the claim in principle, it may recommend either:

(1)   the return of the object to the claimant; or

(2)   the payment of compensation to the claimant, the amount being in the discretion of the Panel having regard to all relevant circumstances including the current market value, but not tied to that current market value; or

(3)   an ex gratia payment to the claimant; or

(4)   the display alongside the object of an account of its history and provenance during and since the Nazi era, with special reference to the claimant's interest therein; and

(5)   that negotiations should be conducted with the successful claimant in order to implement such a recommendation as expeditiously as possible[18].

The panel publishes reports in respect of the claims considered by it[19].

1 For a discussion of international action relating to Nazi spoliation see *Restitution of Objects Spoliated in the Nazi-Era: A Consultation Document* (Department for Culture, Media and Sport, July 2006). A copy of the document is available on the Department for Culture, Media and Sport website which, at the date at which this volume states the law, can be found at www.culture.gov.uk.

2 See the Inter-Allied Declaration Against Acts of Dispossession Committed in Territories Under Enemy Occupation or Control (London, January 5 1943).

3 See the Statement of Principles of the Washington Conference on Holocaust-Era Assets (Washington DC, December 3 1998).

4 See Council of Europe Resolution 1205 on Looted Jewish Cultural Property (1999).

5 See the Declaration of the Vilnius International Forum on Holocaust Era Looted Cultural Assets (Vilnius, 5 October 2000).

6 See the Declaration of the Holocaust Era Assets Conference (Terezin, 30 June 2009).

7 The members of the Spoliation Advisory Panel are appointed by the Secretary of State on such terms and conditions as he thinks fit; and the Secretary of State must appoint one member as chairman of the Panel: *Spoliation Advisory Panel Constitution and Terms of Reference* (Department for Culture, Media and Sport) para 1. As to the Secretary of State see PARA 802 note 2.

8 As to the meaning of 'United Kingdom' see PARA 804 note 2.

9 *Spoliation Advisory Panel Constitution and Terms of Reference* (Department for Culture, Media and Sport) para 3. As to the procedure of the Panel see the *Spoliation Advisory Panel Rules of Procedure* (Department for Culture, Media and Sport). See also *Spoliation Advisory Panel: Functions and Procedures of the Secretariat & Legal Advisers.*

10 *Spoliation Advisory Panel Constitution and Terms of Reference* (Department for Culture, Media and Sport) para 3.

11 *Spoliation Advisory Panel Constitution and Terms of Reference* (Department for Culture, Media and Sport) para 4. When so advising the Secretary of State, the Panel is free to recommend any action which it considers appropriate, and in particular may direct the attention of the Secretary of State to the need for legislation to alter the powers and duties of any institution: see para 14.

12 *Spoliation Advisory Panel Constitution and Terms of Reference* (Department for Culture, Media and Sport) para 11.

13 See the *Spoliation Advisory Panel Constitution and Terms of Reference* (Department for Culture, Media and Sport) para 9.

14 See the *Spoliation Advisory Panel Constitution and Terms of Reference* (Department for Culture, Media and Sport) para 5.

15 See the *Spoliation Advisory Panel Constitution and Terms of Reference* (Department for Culture, Media and Sport) para 6.

16 *Spoliation Advisory Panel Constitution and Terms of Reference* (Department for Culture, Media and Sport) para 7.

17 *Spoliation Advisory Panel Constitution and Terms of Reference* (Department for Culture, Media and Sport) para 8.

18 *Spoliation Advisory Panel Constitution and Terms of Reference* (Department for Culture, Media and Sport) para 13.

19 See eg the *Report of the Spoliation Advisory Panel in respect of 8 drawings now in the possession of the Samuel Courtauld Trust.* Copies of the reports are available on the Department of Culture Media and Sport website which, at the date at which this volume states the law, can be found at www.culture.gov.uk.

1107. Holocaust (Return of Cultural Objects) Act 2009. The Holocaust (Return of Cultural Objects) Act 2009 confers power to return certain cultural objects on grounds relating to events occurring during the Nazi era[1].

A body to which the Act applies[2] may transfer an object from its collections if the following conditions are met[3]. The conditions are (1) that the Advisory Panel has recommended the transfer[4]; and (2) that the Secretary of State has approved the Advisory Panel's recommendation[5]. This power is an additional power[6], and does not affect any trust or condition subject to which any object is held[7].

The Advisory Panel is a panel for the time being designated by the Secretary of State for these purposes[8]. The Secretary of State may designate a panel only if the panel's functions consist of the consideration of claims which (a) are made in respect of objects[9]; and (b) relate to events occurring during the Nazi era[10].

The Holocaust (Return of Cultural Objects) Act 2009 expires at the end of the period of ten years beginning with 12 November 2009[11].

1 See the Holocaust (Return of Cultural Objects) Act 2009, Preliminaries. The Act extends to England and Wales, and to Scotland: s 4(2). The Act came into force on 13 January 2010: see the Holocaust (Return of Cultural Objects) Act 2009 (Commencement) Order 2010, SI 2010/50, art 2. The Act is subject to a sunset clause: see the text to note 11.

2 The Act applies to the following bodies: the board of trustees of the Armouries (see PARA 873); the British Library board (see PARA 904); the trustees of the British Museum (see PARA 824); the trustees of the Imperial War Museum (see PARA 841); the board of trustees for the National Galleries of Scotland; the board of trustees of the National Gallery (see PARA 833); the National Library of Scotland; the trustees of the National Maritime Museum (see PARA 847); the board of trustees of the National Museums and Galleries on Merseyside; the board of trustees of the National Museums of Scotland; the board of trustees of the National Portrait Gallery (see PARA 833); the trustees of the Natural History Museum (see PARA 823); the board of trustees of the Royal Botanic Gardens, Kew (see PARA 880); the board of trustees of the Science Museum (see PARA 867); the board of trustees of the Tate Gallery (see PARA 833); the board of trustees of the Victoria and Albert Museum (see PARA 861); the board of trustees of the Wallace Collection (see PARA 833): Holocaust (Return of Cultural Objects) Act 2009 s 1 (amended by the National Library of Scotland Act 2012 Sch 2 para 8(a)).

3 Holocaust (Return of Cultural Objects) Act 2009 s 2(1).

4 Holocaust (Return of Cultural Objects) Act 2009 s 2(2).

5 Holocaust (Return of Cultural Objects) Act 2009 s 2(3). The Secretary of State may approve a recommendation for the transfer of an object from the collections of a Scottish body only with the consent of the Scottish Ministers: s 2(4). 'Scottish body' means the Board of Trustees for the National Galleries of Scotland, the Trustees of the National Library of Scotland, and the Board of Trustees of the National Museums of Scotland: s 2(5) (amended by the National Library of Scotland Act 2012 Sch 2 para 8(b)). As to the Secretary of State see PARA 802 note 2. As to the Scottish Ministers see CONSTITUTIONAL AND ADMINISTRATIVE LAW vol 20 (2014) PARA 67.

6 Holocaust (Return of Cultural Objects) Act 2009 s 2(7).

7 Holocaust (Return of Cultural Objects) Act 2009 s 2(6).

8 Holocaust (Return of Cultural Objects) Act 2009 s 3(1). The Spoliation Advisory Panel has been so designated: see PARA 1106.

9 Holocaust (Return of Cultural Objects) Act 2009 s 3(2)(a).

10 Holocaust (Return of Cultural Objects) Act 2009 s 3(2)(b). 'Nazi era' means the period beginning with 1 January 1933 and ending with 31 December 1945: s 3(3).

11 See the Holocaust (Return of Cultural Objects) Act 2009 s 4(7). 12 November 2009 is the date on which the Act received royal assent.

5. CULTURAL HERITAGE AND ARMED CONFLICT

1108. Destruction of cultural heritage as a war crime. The International Criminal Court (the 'ICC')[1] has jurisdiction, inter alia, in respect of war crimes[2] and this is the case in particular when these are committed as part of a plan or policy or as part of a large-scale commission of such crimes[3]. For the purpose of the Statute establishing the court, 'war crimes' includes other serious violations of the laws and customs applicable in international armed conflict, within the established framework of international law, including intentionally directing attacks against buildings dedicated to religion, education, art, science or charitable purposes, and historic monuments, provided they are not military objectives[4].

The International Criminal Court Act 2001 incorporates the offences in the Statute establishing the ICC[5] into the law of the United Kingdom[6] so that United Kingdom authorities will be in a position to investigate and prosecute any ICC crimes committed in the UK, or committed overseas by a UK national, a UK resident or a person subject to UK service jurisdiction, and to make provision, where necessary, to enable the UK to meet its obligations under the ICC Statute[7]. It is an offence against the law of England and Wales[8] for a person[9] to commit a war crime[10]. It is also an offence against the law of England and Wales for a person to engage in conduct ancillary to a war crime but which, being committed (or intended to be committed) outside England and Wales, does not constitute such an offence[11].

1   The International Criminal Court is the first permanent, treaty based, international criminal court established to deal with the most serious humanitarian crimes. At the end of World War II international tribunals were established at Nuremberg and Tokyo to try humanitarian crimes arising from that war. Subsequently ad hoc tribunals have been established by the United Nations to try crimes committed during particular conflicts, for example the International Criminal Tribunal for the former Yugoslavia (ICTY) (see www.icty.org) and the International Criminal Tribunal for Rwanda (ICTR) (see www.ictr.org). The International Criminal Court was created under the Statute of the International Criminal Court (Rome 17 July 1998; Cm 4555). The Rome Statute entered into force on 1 July 2002. The ICC is a court of last resort. It will not act if a case is investigated or prosecuted by a national judicial system unless the national proceedings are not genuine, and it only tries those accused of the gravest crimes. For further information about the court and for a copy of the Rome Statute see the court's website which, at the date at which this volume states the law, can be found at www.icc-cpi.int. See also ARMED CONFLICT AND EMERGENCY vol 3 (2011) PARA 110 et seq.

2   See the Statute of the International Criminal Court (Rome 17 July 1998; Cm 4555) art 5(1)(c).

3   See the Statute of the International Criminal Court (Rome 17 July 1998; Cm 4555) art 8(1).

4   See the Statute of the International Criminal Court (Rome 17 July 1998; Cm 4555) art 8(2)(b)(ix). For an example of a case involving allegations of the destruction or wilful damage of cultural buildings and objects see case IT-01-42 *The Prosecutor of the International Criminal Tribunal for the former Yugoslavia v Strugar*. Copies of the indictment and other papers relating to the case can be found on the tribunal's website which, at the date at which this volume states the law, can be found at www.icty.org.

5   Ie the Statute of the International Criminal Court (Rome 17 July 1998; Cm 4555): see the text to notes 1–4.

6   As to the meaning of 'United Kingdom' see PARA 804 note 2.

7   See the International Criminal Court Act 2001 Explanatory Notes. As to the International Criminal Court Act 2001 see further INTERNATIONAL RELATIONS LAW vol 61 (2010) PARA 438 et seq.

8   As to the meaning of 'England' see PARA 804 note 2. As to the meaning of 'Wales' see PARA 802 note 4.

9   As to the meaning of 'person' see PARA 803 note 17.

10   See the International Criminal Court Act 2001 s 51(1); and INTERNATIONAL RELATIONS LAW vol 61 (2010) PARA 454. This provision applies to acts committed in England or Wales, or outside the United Kingdom by a United Kingdom national, a United Kingdom resident or a person subject

to UK service jurisdiction: s 51(2). 'War crime' means a war crime as defined in the Statute of the International Criminal Court (Rome 17 July 1998; Cm 4555) art 8.2 (see the text to note 4): International Criminal Court Act 2001 s 50(1).

11 See the International Criminal Court Act 2001 s 52(1), (2); and INTERNATIONAL RELATIONS LAW vol 61 (2010) PARA 455.

1109. The Convention for the Protection of Cultural Property in the Event of Armed Conflict. The Convention for the Protection of Cultural Property in the Event of Armed Conflict[1] is the principal international instrument devoted specifically to the protection of cultural property in armed conflict. For the purposes of the Convention, 'cultural property' means, irrespective of origin or ownership:

(1)   moveable or immoveable property of great importance to the cultural heritage of every people, such as monuments of architecture, art or history, whether religious or secular; archaeological sites; groups of buildings which, as a whole, are of historical or artistic interest; works of art; manuscripts, books and other objects of artistic, historical or archaeological interest; as well as scientific collections and important collections of books or archives or of reproductions of the property defined above;

(2)   buildings whose main and effective purpose is to preserve or exhibit the moveable cultural property defined in head (1) such as museums, large libraries and depositories of archives, and refuges intended to shelter, in the event of armed conflict, the moveable cultural property defined in head (1)[2];

and the protection of cultural property comprises the safeguarding of and respect for such property[3].

The state parties to the Convention undertake to prepare in time of peace for the safeguarding of cultural property situated within their own territory against the foreseeable effects of an armed conflict[4]; to respect cultural property situated within their own territory and that of other state parties[5]; when in occupation of the whole or part of the territory of another state party, to support the competent national authorities of the occupied country in safeguarding and preserving its cultural property[6]; and to introduce into their military regulations or instructions such provisions as may ensure observance of the Convention, and to foster in the members of their armed forces a spirit of respect for the culture and cultural property of all peoples[7]. The Convention is supported by two protocols: the purpose of the First Protocol is to prevent state parties from exporting cultural property from territories occupied by them during armed conflict, and to provide for the return of cultural property deposited with a third state for safekeeping during a conflict[8]; and the purpose of the Second Protocol is to improve the application and effectiveness of the Convention[9].

The United Kingdom government did not ratify the Convention, but announced in May 2004 its intention to do so and to accede to both its protocols. The government subsequently issued a consultation paper as to the most suitable way to achieve this[10].

1   Ie the Convention for the Protection of Cultural Property in the Event of Armed Conflict (The Hague, 14 May 1954). A copy of the Convention and its two protocols is available on the UNESCO website which, at the date at which this volume states the law, can be found at www.unesco.org.
2   Convention for the Protection of Cultural Property in the Event of Armed Conflict art 1.
3   Convention for the Protection of Cultural Property in the Event of Armed Conflict art 2.
4   See the Convention for the Protection of Cultural Property in the Event of Armed Conflict art 3.
5   See the Convention for the Protection of Cultural Property in the Event of Armed Conflict art 4.

6　See the Convention for the Protection of Cultural Property in the Event of Armed Conflict art 5.
7　See the Convention for the Protection of Cultural Property in the Event of Armed Conflict art 7.
8　See the Protocol to the Convention for the Protection of Cultural Property in the Event of Armed Conflict 1954 (The Hague, 14 May 1954).
9　See the Second Protocol to the Hague Convention of 1954 for the Protection of Cultural Property in the Event of Armed Conflict 1999 (The Hague, 26 March 1999).
10　See *Consultation Paper on the 1954 Hague Convention on the Protection of Cultural Property in the Event of Armed Conflict and its two Protocols of 1954 and 1999* (Department for Culture, Media and Sport, September 2005); and the draft Cultural Property (Armed Conflicts) Bill (January 2008).

6. EUROPEAN CULTURAL CONVENTION ETC

1110. The European Cultural Convention. The European Cultural Convention[1] is designed to foster among the nationals of all member states of the Council of Europe[2], and of such other European states as may accede thereto, the study of the languages, history and civilisation of the others and of the civilisation which is common to them all[3]. Each state party to the convention[4] undertakes to:

   (1)   take appropriate measures to safeguard and to encourage the development of its national contribution to the common cultural heritage of Europe[5];

   (2)   in so far as may be possible, to encourage the study by its nationals of the languages, history and civilisation of the other contracting states and grant facilities to those states to promote such studies in its territory; and endeavour to promote the study of its language or languages, history and civilisation in the territory of the other contracting states and grant facilities to the nationals of those states to pursue such studies in its territory[6];

   (3)   consult with other contracting states within the framework of the Council of Europe with a view to concerted action in promoting cultural activities of European interest[7];

   (4)   in so far as may be possible, facilitate the movement and exchange of persons as well as of objects of cultural value so heads (2) and (3) above may be implemented[8];

   (5)   regard the objects of European cultural value placed under its control as integral parts of the common cultural heritage of Europe, and take appropriate measures to safeguard them and to ensure reasonable access thereto[9].

1   Ie the European Cultural Convention (Paris, 19 December 1954).
2   As to the Council of Europe see INTERNATIONAL RELATIONS LAW vol 61 (2010) PARA 534.
3   European Cultural Convention (Paris, 19 December 1954) preamble.
4   The convention was ratified by the United Kingdom on 5 May 1955.
5   European Cultural Convention (Paris, 19 December 1954) art 1.
6   European Cultural Convention (Paris, 19 December 1954) art 2.
7   European Cultural Convention (Paris, 19 December 1954) art 3.
8   European Cultural Convention (Paris, 19 December 1954) art 4.
9   European Cultural Convention (Paris, 19 December 1954) art 5.

1111. The European Heritage Label. A European Union ('EU') action entitled 'European Heritage Label' has been established[1]. The action is open to the participation, on a voluntary basis, of the member states[2]. Sites[3] are eligible for the attribution of the label based on the following criteria:

   (1)   candidate sites for the label must have a symbolic European value and must have played a significant role in the history and culture of Europe and/or the building of the EU[4];

   (2)   candidate sites for the label must submit a project, the implementation of which is to begin by the end of the designation year at the latest[5];

   (3)   candidate sites for the label must submit a work plan[6].

A European panel of independent experts is established to carry out the selection and monitoring at EU level[7], and the European Commission[8] designates the sites to be awarded the label[9]. The label is awarded on a permanent basis[10], subject to certain monitoring conditions[11] and to the continuation of the action[12].

The Commission and the member states must ensure the added value and complementarity of the action with regard to other initiatives in the field of cultural heritage such as the UNESCO World Heritage List[13], the UNESCO

Representative List of the Intangible Cultural Heritage of Humanity[14] and the Council of Europe's European Cultural Routes[15].

At the date at which this volume states the law the United Kingdom is not participating in the scheme but may join by notifying the European Commission in a letter[16].

1 See European Parliament and Council Decision (EU) 1194/2011 (OJ L303, 22.11.2011, p 1) establishing a European Union action for the European Heritage Label, art 1. As to the objectives see art 3.

2 European Parliament and Council Decision (EU) 1194/2011 (OJ L303, 22.11.2011, p 1) art 4. As to the application procedure see arts 9–11. As to member states see EUROPEAN UNION vol 47A (2014) PARA 8.

3 'Sites' means monuments, natural, underwater, archaeological, industrial or urban sites, cultural landscapes, places of remembrance, cultural goods and objects and intangible heritage associated with a place, including contemporary heritage: European Parliament and Council Decision (EU) 1194/2011 (OJ L303, 22.11.2011, p 1) art 2(1). Sites within the meaning of art 2 are eligible for the attribution of the label: art 6. Special provision is made for transnational sites (see art 12) and national thematic sites (see art 13). 'Transnational sites' means several sites, located in different member states, which focus on one specific theme in order to submit a joint application or one site located on the territory of at least two member states (art 2(2)); and 'national thematic sites' means several sites, located in the same member state, which focus on one specific theme in order to submit a joint application (art 2(3)).

4 See the European Parliament and Council Decision (EU) 1194/2011 (OJ L303, 22.11.2011, p 1) art 7(1)(a).

5 See the European Parliament and Council Decision (EU) 1194/2011 (OJ L303, 22.11.2011, p 1) art 7(1)(b).

6 See the European Parliament and Council Decision (EU) 1194/2011 (OJ L303, 22.11.2011, p 1) art 7(1)(c).

7 See the European Parliament and Council Decision (EU) 1194/2011 (OJ L303, 22.11.2011, p 1) art 7(1). As to the constitution and duties of the panel see art 8(2)–(6).

8 As to the European Commission see EUROPEAN UNION vol 47A (2014) PARA 48.

9 See the European Parliament and Council Decision (EU) 1194/2011 (OJ L303, 22.11.2011, p 1) art 14(1).

10 Ie without prejudice to European Parliament and Council Decision (EU) 1194/2011 (OJ L303, 22.11.2011, p 1) art 16 (withdrawal or renunciation of the label).

11 Ie laid down in European Parliament and Council Decision (EU) 1194/2011 (OJ L303, 22.11.2011, p 1) art 15 (monitoring).

12 European Parliament and Council Decision (EU) 1194/2011 (OJ L303, 22.11.2011, p 1) art 14(2). As to practical arrangements and evaluation of the action see arts 17–18. As to financial provision see art 20.

13 See PARA 1004.

14 See PARA 1004.

15 European Parliament and Council Decision (EU) 1194/2011 (OJ L303, 22.11.2011, p 1) art 5.

16 See the *Guide for the Implementation of the European Heritage Label* (guidelines for member states), available at the date at which this volume states the law at www.ec.europa.eu/programmes/creative-europe/actions/heritage-label/index_en.htm.

7. TAXATION OF NATIONAL CULTURAL PROPERTY AND BODIES

(1) INHERITANCE TAX

1112. Acceptance of property in satisfaction of inheritance tax. On the application of any person[1] liable to pay inheritance tax or interest thereon, the Commissioners for Her Majesty's Revenue and Customs[2] may, if they think fit and the Secretary of State or, in relation to Wales, the Welsh Ministers[3] agree, accept in satisfaction of the whole or any part of it any such land[4] as may be agreed upon between the Commissioners and the person liable to pay tax[5]. These provisions also apply to any objects which are or have been kept in any building:

(1)   if the Commissioners have determined to accept or have accepted that building in satisfaction or part satisfaction of tax or of estate duty; or

(2)   if the building or any interest in it belongs to Her Majesty in right of the Crown or of the Duchy of Lancaster, or belongs to the Duchy of Cornwall or belongs to a Government department or is held for the purposes of a Government department; or

(3)   if the building is one of which the Secretary of State is guardian under the Ancient Monuments and Archaeological Areas Act 1979[6]; or

(4)   if the building belongs to any specified body[7],

in any case where it appears to the Secretary of State desirable for the objects to remain associated with the building[8]. The provisions also apply to:

(a)   any picture, print, book, manuscript, work of art, scientific object or other thing which the Secretary of State is satisfied is pre-eminent for its national, scientific, historic or artistic interest; and

(b)   any collection or group of pictures, prints, books, manuscripts, works of art, scientific objects or other things if the Secretary of State is satisfied that the collection or group, taken as a whole, is pre-eminent for its national, scientific, historic or artistic interest[9].

Any property accepted in satisfaction of tax[10] must be disposed of as the Secretary of State or, in relation to Wales, the Welsh Ministers[11] may direct; and he or they may direct that it must be transferred (either directly or indirectly) to any of certain institutions or bodies willing to accept it, including the National Art Collections Fund, any museum, art gallery, library or other similar institution having as its purpose or one of its purposes the preservation for the public benefit of a collection of historic, artistic or scientific interest and any body having as its purpose, or one of its purposes, the provision, improvement or preservation of amenities enjoyed or to be enjoyed by the public or the acquisition of land to be used by the public[12].

1   As to the meaning of 'person' see PARA 803 note 17.

2   As to the Commissioners for Her Majesty's Revenue and Customs see INCOME TAXATION vol 58 (2014) PARAS 33–34.

3   As to the Secretary of State see PARA 802 note 2. Functions of the Secretary of State under the Inheritance Tax Act 1984 s 230, so far as exercisable in relation to Wales, are transferred to the National Assembly for Wales and are now exercisable by the Welsh Ministers (see the Government of Wales Act 2006 s 162(1), Sch 11 paras 30, 32), except that, where there is both a Welsh interest and another interest in the property to which the Inheritance Tax Act 1984 s 230 applies, the functions of the Secretary of State are exercisable by the Welsh Minsters concurrently with the Secretary of State: see the National Assembly for Wales (Transfer of Functions) Order 2004, SI 2004/3044, arts 2,3, Sch 1; and INHERITANCE TAXATION vol 59A (2014) PARA 300.

4   See the Inheritance Tax Act 1984 s 230(1) (amended by virtue of the Commissioners for Revenue and Customs Act 2005 s 50; and amended by SI 1992/1311); and INHERITANCE TAXATION vol 59A (2014) PARA 300. As to exemptions from inheritance tax see PARA 1113.

5   See the Inheritance Tax Act 1984 s 230(2) (amended by virtue of the Commissioners for Revenue and Customs Act 2005 s 50); and INHERITANCE TAXATION vol 59A (2014) PARA 300.

6   As to guardianship under the Ancient Monuments and Archaeological Areas Act 1979 see PARA 1032.

7   Ie any body within the Inheritance Tax Act 1984 Sch 3. The relevant bodies for the purpose of this title are: the National Gallery (see PARA 832 et seq); the British Museum (see PARA 822 et seq); the National Museums of Scotland; the National Museum of Wales (see PARA 889); the Ulster Museum; any other similar national institution which exists wholly or mainly for the purpose of preserving for the public benefit a collection of scientific, historic or artistic interest and which is approved for these purposes by the Treasury; any museum or art gallery in the United Kingdom which exists wholly or mainly for that purpose and is maintained by a local authority or university in the United Kingdom; any library the main function of which is to serve the needs of teaching and research at a university in the United Kingdom; the Historic Buildings and Monuments Commission for England (see PARA 803 et seq); the National Trust for Places of Historic Interest or Natural Beauty (see PARAS 973–993); the National Trust for Scotland for Places of Historic Interest or Natural Beauty; the National Art Collections Fund (see PARA 813); the Trustees of the National Heritage Memorial Fund (see PARAS 814–816); the Friends of the National Libraries; and the Historic Churches Preservation Trust: see Sch 3 (amended for these purposes by the National Heritage (Scotland) Act 1985 Sch 2 para 4). As to the meaning of 'United Kingdom' see PARA 804 note 2.

8   See the Inheritance Tax Act 1984 s 230(3) (amended by SI 1992/1311; SI 1995/1625); and INHERITANCE TAXATION vol 59A (2014) PARA 300.

9   See the Inheritance Tax Act 1984 s 230(4) (amended by SI 1992/1311); and INHERITANCE TAXATION vol 59A (2014) PARA 300. 'National interest' includes interest within any part of the United Kingdom; and in determining whether an object or collection or group of objects is pre-eminent, regard must be had to any significant association of the object, collection or group with a particular place: Inheritance Tax Act 1984 s 230(5).

10 As to the acceptance of property in satisfaction of tax under the National Heritage Act 1980 ss 8–13 see further INHERITANCE TAXATION vol 59A (2014) PARA 302.

11 The functions of the Secretary of State under the National Heritage Act 1980 s 9, in so far as they relate to Wales, were transferred to the National Assembly for Wales (see the National Assembly for Wales (Transfer of Functions) Order 1999, SI 1999/672, art 2, Sch 1) and are now exercisable by the Welsh Ministers (see the Government of Wales Act 2006 s 162(1), Sch 11 paras 30, 32).

12 See the National Heritage Act 1980 s 9 (amended by the National Heritage Act 1997 s 3, Schedule para 2; SI 1992/1311; and SI 1999/1756); and INHERITANCE TAXATION vol 59A (2014) PARA 302.

1113. Exemptions from inheritance tax for property bequeathed to the nation or to which the public to have reasonable access. For the purposes of inheritance tax, a transfer of value is an exempt transfer to the extent that the value transferred by it is attributable to property which is given to charities[1] or which becomes the property of certain specified bodies[2].

The Commissioners for Her Majesty's Revenue and Customs may designate[3] as being eligible for conditional exemption from inheritance tax[4], the following:

(1)   any relevant object which appears to the Commissioners to be pre-eminent for its national, scientific, historic or artistic interest;

(2)   any collection or group of relevant objects which, taken as a whole, appears to the Commissioners to be pre-eminent for its national, scientific, historic or artistic interest;

(3)   any land which in the opinion of the Commissioners is of outstanding scenic or historic or scientific interest;

(4)   any building for the preservation of which special steps should in the opinion of the Commissioners be taken by reason of its outstanding historic or architectural interest; and any area of land which in their opinion is essential for the protection of the character and amenities of such a building;

(5)   any object which in the opinion of the Commissioners is historically associated with such a building as is mentioned in head (4) above[5].

The exemption is conditional upon the giving of certain undertakings regarding preservation of the property and reasonable access to the public[6].

1   See the Inheritance Tax Act 1984 s 23; and INHERITANCE TAXATION vol 59A (2014) PARA 134.
2   See the Inheritance Tax Act 1984 s 25; and INHERITANCE TAXATION vol 59A (2014) PARA 137.
    The specified bodies are those within Sch 3 (see PARA 1112 note 7).
3   See the Inheritance Tax Act 1984 s 31(1) (amended by virtue of the Commissioners for Revenue
    and Customs Act 2005 s 50). This was previously a Treasury function: see INHERITANCE
    TAXATION vol 59A (2014) PARAS 6, 148. As to the Commissioners for Her Majesty's Revenue
    and Customs see INCOME TAXATION vol 58 (2014) PARAS 33–34.
4   See the Inheritance Tax Act 1984 s 30(1)(a), (2); and INHERITANCE TAXATION vol 59A (2014)
    PARA 148.
5   See the Inheritance Tax Act 1984 s 31(1)(a)–(e) (amended by the Finance Act 1998 s 142, Sch 25
    para 4).
6   See the Inheritance Tax Act 1984 s 30(1)(b) (amended by the Finance Act 1985 Sch 26 para 1); the
    Inheritance Tax Act 1984 s 31; and INHERITANCE TAXATION vol 59A (2014) PARAS 148–149.

(2) TAX ON INCOME, CAPITAL AND SUPPLIES; STAMP DUTY

1114. Exemptions from tax applying to charitable, heritage and scientific research bodies. If a charitable company[1] receives a gift of a sum of money from a company which is not a charity[2], the gift is treated as an amount in respect of which the charitable company is chargeable to corporation tax, under the charge to corporation tax on income[3] but the gift is not taken into account in calculating total profits so far as it is applied to charitable purposes only[4]. If a body receives a gift of a sum of money from a company, the gift is not taken into account in calculating total profits if the body receiving the gift qualifies as a relevant scientific research association for the relevant accounting period[5]. A body qualifies as a scientific research association for an accounting period if:
(1)   it is an association[6];
(2)   it has as its object the undertaking of research and development[7] which may lead to or facilitate an extension of any class or classes of trade[8];
(3)   the memorandum of association or other similar instrument regulating the body's functions[9] precludes the direct or indirect payment or transfer to members of any of its income or property by way of dividend, gift, division, bonus or otherwise by way of profit[10].

Charities and certain heritage bodies are exempt from tax in respect of chargeable gains[11] and inheritance tax[12].

Whilst there is no general exemption of value added tax for charities and heritage bodies, certain supplies and exports by charities are zero-rated[13], and educational[14] and health supplies are exempt[15]. Certain supplies of works of art are also exempt[16], as are fund raising events by charities and other qualifying bodies[17]. The supply by certain bodies of a right of admission to a museum, art gallery, art exhibition or zoo, or to a theatrical, musical or choreographic performance of a cultural nature is also an exempt supply[18].

Conveyances, transfers or leases to a charitable company or trustees of a charitable trust, or to the Trustees of the National Heritage Memorial Fund, are exempt from stamp duty[19]; and for the purpose of stamp duty relief[20], the Historic Buildings and Monuments Commission for England is treated as a charitable company[21].

1   As to the meaning of 'charitable company' see INCOME TAXATION vol 58A (2014) PARA 1622.
    As to gifts of money made to charitable trusts see INCOME TAXATION vol 58A (2014) PARA 1635.

2 As to the meaning of 'charity' for these purposes see INCOME TAXATION vol 58A (2014) PARA 1622.
3 See the Corporation Tax Act 2010 s 473(1); and INCOME TAXATION vol 58A (2014) PARA 1635.
4 See the Corporation Tax Act 2010 s 473(2); and INCOME TAXATION vol 58A (2014) PARA 1635. A claim must be made (see the Corporation Tax Act 2010 s 473(3); and INCOME TAXATION vol 58A (2014) PARA 1635 to the Commissioners for Her Majesty's Revenue and Customs (see INCOME TAXATION vol 58 (2014) PARAS 33–34). Exemptions also apply to charitable companies in relation to: profits of a charitable trade (see the Corporation Tax Act 2010 ss 478–482), profits arising from a VAT-exempt event (see s 483), profits from lotteries (see s 484), property income (see s 485), investment income and non-trading profits from loan relationships (see s 486), public revenue dividends (see s 487), gains and income from intangible fixed assets etc (see s 488) and income from estates in administration (see s 489); and see INCOME TAXATION vol 58A (2014) PARA 1637 et seq. Such provisions which confer exemptions apply: (1) in relation to a body which qualifies as a scientific research association for the relevant accounting period; and (2) in relation to an eligible body, as they apply in relation to a charitable company but in relation to such bodies those provisions have effect as if the whole income of the body were applied to charitable purposes: see the ss 490, 491; and INCOME TAXATION vol 58 (2014) PARA 205. The eligible bodies for these purposes are: (a) the trustees of the National Heritage Memorial Fund (s 468(a)); (b) the Historic Buildings and Monuments Commission for England (s 468(b)); (c) the trustees of the British Museum (s 468(c) (amended by SI 2012/964); and (d) the trustees of the Natural History Museum (See the Corporation Tax Act 2010 s 468(d) (amended by SI 2012/964). See INCOME TAXATION vol 58A (2014) PARA 1661. As to the National Heritage Memorial Fund see PARAS 814–816. As to the Historic Buildings and Monuments Commission for England (the Commission') see PARAS 803–809. As to the trustees of the British Museum see PARA 824. As to the trustees of the Natural History Museum see PARA 823.
5 See the Corporation Tax Act 2010 s 477(1). A claim must be made: see s 477(2). The 'relevant accounting period' means the accounting period for which the exemption is to be claimed: s 477(3). In the case of a body which qualifies as a scientific research association and is also a charitable company s 477 applies instead of s 473 (as to which see the text and notes 1–4): s 477(4).
6 See the Corporation Tax Act 2010 s 469(1)(a). The Treasury may by regulations make provision specifying what is to be treated as being, or as not being, an association for the purposes of s 469(1)(a), or prescribe circumstances in which a body is to be treated as not meeting condition A (see s 469(2): and the text and note 8) or condition B (see s 469(3): and the text and note 10) with respect to an accounting period: s 469(5)(a). At the date at which this volume states the law no such regulations had been made. As to scientific research councils see PARAS 963–971.
7 'Research and development' means (subject to the Corporation Tax Act 2010 s 1138(3), (4)) activities that fall to be treated as research and development in accordance with generally accepted accounting practice. (ss 470, 1138(1), (2)) and unless otherwise expressly provided does not include oil and gas exploration and appraisal (s 1138(5)).
8 See the Corporation Tax Act 2010 s 469(1)(b), (2). The Treasury may by regulations prescribe circumstances in which a body is to be treated as not meeting condition A (see s 469(2)) or condition B (see s 469(3); and the text and note 10) with respect to an accounting period: Corporation Tax Act 2010 s 469(5)(b). At the date at which this volume states the law no such regulations had been made. As to the Treasury see CONSTITUTIONAL AND ADMINISTRATIVE LAW vol 20 (2014) PARA 263.
9 For these purposes it is not necessary that the memorandum of association or other similar instrument regulating the body's functions should prevent the payment to its members of:
    (1) reasonable remuneration for goods, labour or power supplied, or for services provided (Corporation Tax Act 2010 s 469(4)(a));
    (2) reasonable interest for money lent (s 469(4)(b)); or
    (3) reasonable rent for premises (s 469(4)(c)).
As to company membership see COMPANIES vol 14 (2009) PARA 321 et seq.
10 See the Corporation Tax Act 2010 s 469(1)(b), (3). See note 8.
11 See the Taxation of Chargeable Gains Act 1992 s 271(6), (7); and CAPITAL GAINS TAXATION vol 6 (2011) PARA 884. See also ss 256–257A; and CAPITAL GAINS TAXATION vol 6 (2011) PARAS 878, 879.
12 See PARA 1113. As to the acceptance of property in satisfaction of inheritance tax and the designation of conditionally exempt property see PARA 1112.
13 See the Value Added Tax Act 1994 s 30(2), Sch 8 Pt II Group 15; and VALUE ADDED TAX vol 99 (2012) PARA 240. Books etc are also zero-rated: see Sch 8 Pt II Group 3; and VALUE ADDED TAX vol 99 (2012) PARA 223.
14 See the Value Added Tax Act 1994 s 31(1), Sch 9 Pt II Group 6; and VALUE ADDED TAX vol 99 (2012) PARA 211.

15 See the Value Added Tax Act 1994 Sch 9 Pt II Group 7; and VALUE ADDED TAX vol 99 (2012) PARA 212.
16 See the Value Added Tax Act 1994 Sch 9 Pt II Group 11; and VALUE ADDED TAX vol 99 (2012) PARA 216.
17 See the Value Added Tax Act 1994 Sch 9 Pt II Group 12; and VALUE ADDED TAX vol 99 (2012) PARA 217.
18 See the Value Added Tax Act 1994 Sch 9 Pt II Group 13; and VALUE ADDED TAX vol 99 (2012) PARA 218.
19 See the Finance Act 1982 s 129; and STAMP TAXES vol 96 (2012) PARA 363.
20 Ie for the purposes of the Finance Act 1982 s 129: see STAMP TAXES vol 96 (2012) PARA 363.
21 See the Finance Act 1983 s 46(3)(c) (amended by the Finance Act 1985 s 98(6), Sch 27; the Income and Corporation Taxes Act 1988 s 844(1), Sch 29 para 32; and the Finance Act 2010 Sch 6 para 9); and STAMP TAXES vol 96 (2012) PARA 363.

INDEX

Mistake

References are to paragraph numbers; superior figures refer to notes

References are to paragraph numbers; superior figures refer to notes

Mortgage

References are to paragraph numbers; superior figures refer to notes

References are to paragraph numbers; superior figures refer to notes

FORECLOSURE—*continued*
  order nisi—*continued*
    one period of redemption fixed, where 606
    second mortgagee and mortgagor, against 602
    successive redemptions 603
    unnecessary expense, directions for avoiding 600
  procedure 595
  proceedings—
    account of rents and profits, asking for 591
    adjournment etc, powers of 596
    declaration of title 594
    delivery of possession, claim for 592
    form of 589
    parties to—
      equity of redemption, persons interested in 585
      persons having direct charge on property 587
      several properties in one mortgage, where 588
      subsequent incumbrancers 586
    payment under covenant, claim for 593
    person instigating—
      co-mortgagees 584
      mortgagee or assignee 582
      personal representatives 583
      trustees 583
    sale, with claim for 590
  rate of interest recoverable in 736
  registered land, in respect of 613
  right to claim under covenant for payment, loss of 545
  right, where arising—
    equitable mortgage or charge, as to 581
    payment of interim interest, loan for term conditional on 580
    proviso for redemption—
      depending on 578
      payment of interest, conditional on 579
  sale appropriate remedy, where—
    direction for 576,577
    generally 574
    statutory jurisdiction to order 575
  sale, order for
    See ORDER FOR SALE

FORFEITURE
  mortgagee's right to relief from 403
FRAUD
  mortgage—
    avoidance 114
FREEHOLD
  legal mortgage of 161
FREIGHT
  mortgage of 213
FRIENDLY SOCIETY
  party to mortgage, as 131
GOODWILL
  mortgagee, entitlement of 172
HARDSHIP
  mitigation of—
    regulated mortgages 533
HIGH COURT OF JUSTICE
  covenant for payment, claim on 547
  mortgage claim—
    allocation 535
    commencement in 537
    covenant—
      claims, procedure for payment of 547
    jurisdiction 534
HIRE-PURCHASE AGREEMENT
  equitable mortgagee, no priority of 249
HOVERCRAFT
  mortgage of—
    generally 214
    statutory, transfer of 376
  registered mortgagee, power of sale 453
INCORPOREAL HEREDITAMENT
  mortgage of 178
INSOLVENCY
  mortgagee's remedies, effect on—
    companies and partnerships, of—
      administration, mortgagor in 521
      disclaimer by liquidator 525
      liquidation, mortgagor in 524
      moratorium, effect of 523
      preferences, order as to 526
      transaction at undervalue, order as to 526
      voluntary arrangement 522
    individual mortgagors, of—
      deceased mortgagor, right against insolvent estate of 531
      individual voluntary arrangement 527

References are to paragraph numbers; superior figures refer to notes

References are to paragraph numbers; superior figures refer to notes

MORTGAGE—*continued*
  hovercraft, of 214
  illegal consideration 114
  interest—
    accounts of
      See MORTGAGE ACCOUNTS
          (principal and interest, of)
    legal mortgage
      See LEGAL MORTGAGE (principal
          and interest, provisions as to)
  land, of—
    equitable mortgage
      See EQUITABLE MORTGAGE
    legal mortgage
      See LEGAL MORTGAGE
  lease—
    mortgagor's powers
      See MORTGAGOR
    priority between mortgagee and
        tenants
      See PRIORITY OF MORTGAGE
  leasehold enfranchisement
    See LEASEHOLD
        ENFRANCHISEMENT (mortgage
        on landlord's estate)
  legal mortgage
    See LEGAL MORTGAGE
  legal proceedings
    See MORTGAGE CLAIM
  limitation of actions, foreclosure
    See FORECLOSURE
  local authority—
    transfer of 374
  mental capacity, persons lacking—
    capacity to mortgage 141
    right of redemption, exercise on
        behalf of 141
  merger
    See MERGER
  mortgage claim
    See MORTGAGE CLAIM
  mortgagee
    See MORTGAGEE
  mortgagor
    See MORTGAGOR
  parties
    See PARTIES TO MORTGAGE
  pawn distinguished 112
  payment
    See DISCHARGE OF MORTGAGE
  personal representative by—
    all personal representatives joining
        in 152
    power of 151

MORTGAGE—*continued*
  personalty of
    See EQUITABLE MORTGAGE;
        LEGAL MORTGAGE
  pledge distinguished 112
  possession—
    mortgagee in
      See MORTGAGEE IN POSSESSION
    proceedings for
      See MORTGAGE CLAIM
  priority
    See PRIORITY OF MORTGAGE
  receiver
    See RECEIVER OF MORTGAGED
        PROPERTY
  recovery of possession
    See MORTGAGE CLAIM (possession
        proceedings)
  redemption proceedings
    See REDEMPTION OF MORTGAGE
  regulated
    See REGULATED MORTGAGE
        CONTRACT
  remedies
    See MORTGAGEE'S REMEDIES
  repossession
    See MORTGAGE CLAIM (possession
        proceedings)
  sale distinguished 109
  securitisation 388
  share in partnership, of 138
  statutory charge distinguished 111
  sub-mortgage
    See SUB-MORTGAGE
  suretyship
    See SURETY (mortgage, and);
        SURETYSHIP
  title deeds
    See TITLE DEEDS
  transfer of—
    aircraft 378
    amount originally advanced, receipt
        for 383
    arrears of rent or interest, effect on
        381
    assignment under hand 368
    building society mortgage 373
    collateral securities, conveyance of
        372
    deed, by 369
    equitable, by deposit 369
    form of 367
    hovercraft 378
    indorsed receipt, by 371
    less than mortgage debt, for 380
    local authority mortgage 374

MORTGAGE—*continued*
  transfer of—*continued*
    manner of 368
    mortgage debt—
      dealings debt prior to transfer
        384
      payment without notice of
        transfer 385
      person paying off, subrogated
        rights of 386
    mortgagee's right of 366
    nature of 367
    outstanding equities, subject to 382
    securitisation 388
    ship 378
    statutory 376
    trustees, mortgage to 375
    variations in form 370
  waiver—
    additional security, taking 704
    debt, of 701
    express 702
    implied 703
    nature of 701
    substituted security, taking 705
MORTGAGE ACCOUNTS
  mortgagee in possession, by—
    adverse title, mortgagee setting up
      723
    arrears of interest, effect of
      subsequent payment of 724
    continuous 718
    deficiency in receipts, effect of 719
    fresh, where necessary 726
    rests, with—
      order for 722
      satisfaction of debt, effect after
        721
      taking 720
    sale of part of property, application
      of proceeds of sale 725
    surplus receipts, effect of 719
  mortgagor and mortgagee, between—
    application of money, general
      principle 712
    claim to be distinctly alleged and
      proved 714
    direction for 709
    errors, correcting 715
    form of 710
    general, nature of 709
    persons bound by 716
    persons not bound by 717
    second mortgagee, taken by 711
    setting off 715

MORTGAGE ACCOUNTS—*continued*
  mortgagor and mortgagee,
    between—*continued*
    settled accounts, reopening 713
  principal and interest, of—
    amount secured, proof as to 731
    bonus or commission, stipulation
      for 729
    commissions 737
    current account—
      appropriation of payments in 732
      security covering 730
    default of repayment by instalments,
      fines on 737
    further advances 730
    interest—
      agreement to pay 733
      capitalisation on transfer or
        redemption by late
        mortgagee 742
      covenant merging in judgment,
        on 735
      damages for delay, as 734
      foreclosure or redemption, rate
        recoverable in 736
      mortgage of settled property, on
        740
      overpayments and
        underpayments 741
      tender, ceasing to run after 738
    limitation 739
    principal debt, proof of 728
    special matters pleaded or set out
      727
  right of mortgagor to 339
MORTGAGE ACTION
  See MORTGAGE CLAIM
MORTGAGE CLAIM
  allocation of proceedings 535
  commencement—
    High Court, in 537
  County Court, in—
    allocation 535
    jurisdiction 534
  covenant for payment, claim on
    See COVENANT
  equity of redemption
    See EQUITY OF REDEMPTION
  foreclosure
    See FORECLOSURE
  High Court, in—
    allocation 535
    commencement in 537
    jurisdiction 534

MORTGAGE CLAIM—*continued*
possession proceedings—
acknowledgement of service 552
case management directions 554
claim form 551
commencement 551
defence 552
evidence in 554
hearing 554
hearing date 552
judgment in default, no power of 552
jurisdiction 549
occupiers, notice to 553
particulars of claim 551
parties to 550
payment deferred with provision for earlier payment—
extension of powers 559
reasonable period, likelihood of payment within 560
possession order—
dwelling house, suspension or adjournment in case of 557
form of 563
restrictions on mortgagee's ability to obtain 556
suspension of order for money judgment, and 562
suspension to allow mortgagor to effect sale 561
power to adjourn 555
procedure 549
summary judgment, no power of 549
procedure 536
receiver's appointment
See RECEIVER OF MORTGAGED PROPERTY
redemption proceedings
See REDEMPTION OF MORTGAGE
sale, order for
See ORDER FOR SALE
MORTGAGE INDEMNITY POLICY
sums under, entitlement to 174
MORTGAGE MONEY
meaning 104n[1]
MORTGAGED PROPERTY
maintenance and repair, expenses of 749
order for sale
See ORDER FOR SALE
possession proceedings
See MORTGAGE CLAIM

MORTGAGED PROPERTY—*continued*
possession, mortgagee's right to—
actual possession 415
forcible entry 413
part, entry on 412
person treated as being in possession 414
receiver, appointment of 418
right of entry, exercise of—
means of 410
notice, without 411
prior possession by receiver, effect of 411
tenancy created by mortgage deed, effect of 417
tenant, notice to,—
cross-claim by mortgagor, effect of 407
default of payment, rights of entry arising on 408
equitable incumbrancer, position of 405
legal mortgagee or chargee 404
rents and profits, right of equitable mortgagee to 406
sale out of court—
breach of duty by mortgagor, mortgagee proving 462
conditions of sale 464
easements and covenants, of 468
effect of 474
equity of redemption, destruction of 474
exercise of power—
different securities held by one mortgagee, where 463
mortgagee, duty of 461
mortgagor seeking relief 461
time for 459
express power of—
exercise of 455
paramount effect 444
terms of 443
fixtures, sale of 466
implied power of—
chattels, of 445
choses in action, of 445
minerals, of 467
mode of 462
mortgagee restrained from, where 460
notice requiring payment—
form of 458
service of 457

References are to paragraph numbers; superior figures refer to notes

References are to paragraph numbers; superior figures refer to notes

References are to paragraph numbers; superior figures refer to notes

References are to paragraph numbers; superior figures refer to notes

References are to paragraph numbers; superior figures refer to notes

References are to paragraph numbers; superior figures refer to notes

National Cultural Heritage

References are to paragraph numbers; superior figures refer to notes

References are to paragraph numbers; superior figures refer to notes

References are to paragraph numbers; superior figures refer to notes

HISTORIC BUILDING—*continued*
　acquisition—*continued*
　　Secretary of State, by 1076
　　Welsh Ministers, by 1076
　Commission
　　See HISTORIC BUILDINGS AND
　　　MONUMENTS COMMISSION
　　　FOR ENGLAND
　endowment for upkeep of—
　　Historic Buildings and
　　　Monuments Commission for
　　　England, power to accept 1081
　　Secretary of State, power to accept
　　　1080
　　Welsh Ministers, power to accept
　　　1080
　European architectural heritage 1072
　grants and loans for preservation of
　　buildings etc in Wales 1074
　Historic Buildings and
　　Monuments Commission for
　　England, grant by 1078
　Welsh Ministers, grant by 1079
HISTORIC BUILDINGS AND
　MONUMENTS COMMISSION
　FOR ENGLAND
　accounts and records 803
　ancient monument: meaning 804n[2]
　battlefields, register of historic 1087
　company, power to form 806
　constitution 803
　contracts and agreements by 804
　contribution towards—
　　excavation 804
　　survey 804
　directions from the Secretary of State
　　for Culture, Media and Sport 805
　enactment: meaning 805
　English Heritage, formerly known as
　　803n[1]
　expenditure 809
　functions 804
　functions in relation to monuments in
　　England 808
　garden, historic—
　　endowment of 1084
　　non-statutory register, Wales 1086
　　register of 1085
　grants and loans for protection of
　　historic buildings—
　　generally 1073
　　recovery of 1075
　historic building: meaning 804n[3]
　Historic England, now known as
　　803n[1]

HISTORIC BUILDINGS AND
　MONUMENTS COMMISSION
　FOR ENGLAND—*continued*
　inspection of land 803
　intellectual property—
　　meaning 804n[23]
　　exploitation of 804
　land—
　　meaning 804n[30]
　　power of entry to inspect 807
　ministerial functions 805
　person: meaning 803n[17]
　property, acquisition and disposal of
　　804
　protected wreck: meaning 804n[25]
　Treasury: meaning 809n[4]
　writing: meaning 805n[14]
HISTORIC ENGLAND
　See HISTORIC BUILDINGS AND
　　MONUMENTS COMMISSION
HISTORIC GARDEN
　See under HISTORIC BUILDINGS AND
　　MONUMENTS COMMISSION FOR
　　ENGLAND
HUMAN REMAINS
　museums, in—
　　care of 820
　public display of 821
IMPERIAL WAR MUSEUM
　meaning 841n[1]
　board of trustees—
　　companies, power to form 844
　　establishment 841
　　land, power to hold 845
　　powers and duties 843
　　vesting, lending and disposal of
　　　objects 846
　director general 842
　staff 842
INHERITANCE TAX
　See TAX
INTELLECTUAL PROPERTY
　meaning 806n[6]
　Historic Buildings and
　　Monuments Commission,
　　exploitation by 804
LIBRARY
　British Library
　　See BRITISH LIBRARY
　delivery of books to—
　　delivery of non-print publications to
　　　libraries 896
　　deposit of publications with
　　　libraries 895

References are to paragraph numbers; superior figures refer to notes

NATIONAL PORTRAIT
  GALLERY—*continued*
  board of trustees—*continued*
    general functions 835
    powers in relation to pictures etc—
      acquisition and disposal 839
      lending and borrowing 840
    Secretary of State, report to 836
  establishment of 832
  land transferred to 838
  new board: meaning 833n[6]
  pictures and other objects—
    acquisition and disposal of 839
    lending and borrowing of 840
  predecessor trustees: meaning 833n[8]
NATIONAL TRUST
  accounts 992
  appointed member 975
  assurance: meaning 985n[8]
  board of trustees—
    committees 984
    documents and notices 984
    members 974
    powers and duties to be conferred
      on 980
    powers of 980
    proceedings 981
    validity and regulation of
      procedures 984
  borrowing powers 991
  byelaws 982
  commons vested in 986
  contributions to 993
  council—
    administration by 979
    committees 979
    documents and notices 984
    members 974
    powers and proceedings 979
    validity and regulation of
      procedures 984
  documents and notices 984
  elected member: meaning 975n[4]
  general meetings 978
  general powers 978
  general purposes 977
  grants and loans to 973
  management 974
  members 974
  property—
    admission charges 985
    agreements restrictive of use 988
    commons 986
    inalienable 985
    ownership, power of 985

NATIONAL TRUST—*continued*
  property—*continued*
    settlements, subject to 987
    special treatment, circumstances
      for 973
    reincorporation 973
    revenue, application of 990
    settlement: meaning 987n[4]
    statutory powers 973
    tenant for life: meaning 987n[7]
NATURAL ENVIRONMENT
  RESEARCH COUNCIL
  establishment 966
  geological survey 966
NATURAL HISTORY MUSEUM
  authorised repository 828
  British Museum, separation from 823
  director of 825
  disposal of objects, trustees by 830
  keeping of the collections 827
  lending of objects from 829
  Natural History trustees: meaning 823
  staff of 825
  trustees—
    keeping of the collections 827
    powers of 826
NAZI SPOLIATION
  meaning 1106
  cultural objects, return of 1107
  spoliation advisory panel 1106
ORDNANCE SURVEY
  boundary stones, offences as to 999
  creation of 994
  Director General 994
  evidence, maps as 995
  mapping agency, as 994
  survey by—
    boundaries, not affecting 1001
    entry on lands to carry out 997
    local authority clerk, attendance of
      998
    obstruction of 1000
    persons to assist in ascertaining
      boundaries, appointment of
      996
    rights of property, not affecting
      1001
PROTECTION OF CULTURAL
  HERITAGE
  cultural heritage and armed conflict—
    destruction of cultural heritage as a
      war crime 1108
    protection of cultural property in
      the event of armed conflict
      1109

References are to paragraph numbers; superior figures refer to notes

References are to paragraph numbers; superior figures refer to notes

TRANSFER OF LAND
  specified museums or galleries,
    occupied by 819
TRANSFER OF OBJECTS
  transfers between museums and
    galleries 817
TREASURE
  meaning 1090
  code of practice 1089
  coin: meaning $1090n^3$
  coroner—
    inquest by 1088, 1092–1093
  Coroner for Treasure—
    investigation by 1088, 1092–1093
    treasure inquest 1092
  finder of, duty to notify coroner
    or Coroner for Treasure 1088
  franchisee: meaning $1088n^8$
  inquest into 1093
  investigation into 1092
  regulations, power to make 1092
  statutory regime 1088
  treasure trove 1088
UNITED KINGDOM
  meaning $804n^2$
VICTORIA AND ALBERT MUSEUM
  board of trustees—
    general functions 863
    procedure 861
  director 862
  staff 862
WALES
  meaning $802n^4$
  Cadw 810
  historic environment 810
  Royal Commission on the Ancient and
    Historical Monuments of Wales
    811

WALES—*continued*
  Welsh Ministers, powers relating to
    historic environment 810
WALLACE COLLECTION
  board of trustees—
    appointment of director 834
    appointment of staff 834
    companies, power to form 837
    establishment of 833
    general functions 835
    powers in relation to pictures etc—
      acquisition and disposal 839
      lending and borrowing 840
    Secretary of State, report to 836
  establishment of 832
  land transferred to 838
  pictures and other objects—
    acquisition and disposal of 839
    lending and borrowing of 840
WELLINGTON MUSEUM
  Apsley house—
    maintenance of 853
    use as museum 852
  establishment of 851
WORK OF ART
  gift to the nation 818
  transfer of objects or related
    documents between museums and
    galleries 817
  See also CULTURAL OBJECTS
WORLD HERITAGE FUND
  establishment of 1004
WORLD HERITAGE SITE
  UNESCO convention, provisions
    of 1004

References are to paragraph numbers; superior figures refer to notes

Words and Phrases

Words in parentheses indicate the context in which the word or phrase is used

administrative receiver 484n[8]

ancient monument—
  (Ancient Monuments and
    Archaeological Areas Act 1979)
    1029
  (National Heritage Act 1983) 804n[2]

archaeological investigation 1017n[12]

archive 815n[19]

assurance 985n[8]

authorised lease 355n[1]

building lease 351n[4]

building purposes 351n[4]

Cadw 810

charge 127n[5]

cinematograph film 826n[12]

coin 1090n[3]

commonhold unit 177n[1]

conservation area 804n[5]

consolidation 502

conveyance 168n[1]

cultural goods 1096n[2]

cultural object 1099

disposition 197n[2]

dwelling house 557n[2]

elected member 975n[4]

enactment 805

England 804n[2]

equitable charge 106

equitable interests 105n[2]

equitable mortgage 105

equity of redemption 107

financial year 803n[12]

franchisee 1088n[8]

gift 816n[7]

hereditament 104n[2]

historic building 804n[3]

incumbrance 197n[4]

incumbrancer 197n[4]

instrument 197n[1]

intellectual property (National Heritage
    Act 1983) 804n[23], 806n[6]

land—
  (Law of Property Act 1925) 104n[2]
  (National Heritage Act 1983) 804n[30]
  (Reverter of Sites Act 1987) 950n[2]

landlord covenant 425n[7]

lease 349n[5]

legal mortgage—
  (generally) 104n[1]
  (land registration) 160
  (Rent Act 1977) 532n[2]

legal mortgagee 104n[1]

legal sub-mortgage 127n[8]

lessee 352n[5]

lessor 353n[3]

library authority 922

local authority—
  (Local Government Act 1986) 374n[1]
  (Public Libraries and Museums Act
    1964) 922

London 856n[4]

lord of the manor 812n[6]

manor 104n[2]

mortgage—
  (Administration of Justice Act 1970)
    557n[1]
  (Civil Procedure Rules) 535n[4]
  (Law of Property Act 1925) 101n[4]

mortgage money 104n[1]

mortgaged property 621n[6]

mortgagee—
  (Administration of Justice Act 1970)
    557n[1]
  (Civil Procedure Rules) 535n[4]
  (Law of Property Act 1925) 104n[1]
  (Rent Act 1977) 532n[4]

mortgagee in possession 104n[1]

mortgagor—
  (Administration of Justice Act 1970)
    557n[1]
  (Law of Property Act 1925) 104n[1]
  (Rent Act 1977) 532n[4]

natural history trustees 823

Nazi spoliation 1106

References are to paragraph numbers; superior figures refer to notes